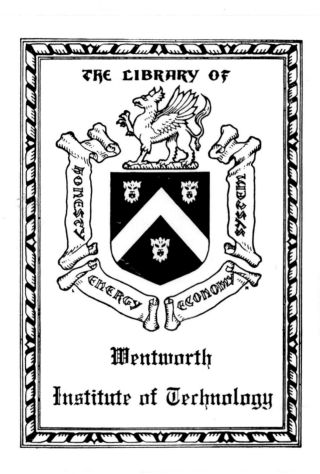

THE McGRAW-HILL RECYCLING HANDBOOK

Herbert F. Lund Editor in Chief

McGraw-Hill, Inc.

New York   St. Louis   San Francisco   Auckland   Bogotá
Caracas   Lisbon   London   Madrid   Mexico   Milan
Montreal   New Delhi   Paris   San Juan   São Paulo
Singapore   Sydney   Tokyo   Toronto

To all of our grandchildren
for their future education

Library of Congress Cataloging-in-Publication Data

Lund, Herbert F.
    The McGraw-Hill recycling handbook / Herbert F. Lund.
        p.   cm.
    Includes index.
    ISBN 0-07-039096-7
    1. Recycling (Waste, etc.) 2. Recycling (Waste, etc.)—United
States. I. Title.
    TD794.5.L84 1993
    363.72'82—dc20   92-18267
                                       CIP

ISBN   0-07-039096-7

*The sponsoring editor for this book was Harold B. Crawford, the editing
supervisor was Dennis Gleason, and the production supervisor was
Donald F. Schmidt. This book was set in Times Roman. It was
composed by McGraw-Hill's Professional Book Group composition unit.*

Printed and bound by R. R. Donnelley & Sons Company.

*This book is printed on recycled acid-free paper containing a
minimum of 50% total recycled fiber with 10%
postconsumer de-inked fiber.*

CONTENTS

Chapter 5. Separation and Collection Systems Performance Monitoring   5.1

Chapter 6. Processing Facilities for Recyclable Materials   6.1

Chapter 7. Marketing Development Problems and Solutions   7.1

Chapter 8. Financial Planning and Management of Recycling Programs and Facilities   8.1

Chapter 9. Need for Aggressive Public Awareness Programs   9.1

Chapter 28. Processing Equipment   28.1

Chapter 29. Recycling Program Planning and Implementation   29.1

Chapter 30. Public Awareness Programs   30.1

Chapter 31. Training Personnel and Managers   31.1

Chapter 32. Recycling Program Factors and Decisions   32.1

Chapter 33. Data Collection and Cost Control   33.1

ABOUT THE EDITOR IN CHIEF

Herbert F. Lund is the former recycling manager for the city of Hollywood, Florida, a professional engineer, and an independent recycling consultant. He is a major contributor to professional magazines, the recipient of the Jesse H. Neal Editorial Achievement Award for best single article in a trade magazine, a fellow of the American Society of Mechanical Engineers, and editor in chief of *The Industrial Pollution Control Handbook*. Mr. Lund resides in Pompano Beach, Florida.

CONTRIBUTORS

Ann Adams   *Roy F. Weston, Inc., Detroit, Mich.* (CHAP. 19)

Ron Albrecht   *Ron Albrecht Associates, Annapolis, Md.* (CHAP. 16)

Mary Aldridge   *The Solid Waste Association of North America, Silver Spring, Md.* (APP. A)

C. Kenna Amos   *ENSR Consulting and Engineering, Fort Collins, Colo.* (CHAP. 19)

Michael H. Blumenthal   *Scrap Tire Management Council, Washington, D.C.,* (CHAP. 18)

Durene Buckholz   *Malcolm Pirnie, Inc., White Plains, N.Y.* (CHAP. 12)

R. Chris Brockway   *Black & Veatch, Kansas City, Mo.* (CHAP. 23)

David Bullock   *Gershman, Brickner, & Straton, Inc., Falls Church, Va.* (CHAP. 4)

David S. Cerrato   *Malcolm Pirnie, Inc., White Plains, N.Y.* (CHAP. 3)

Keith R. Connor   *Black & Veatch, Kansas City, Mo.* (CHAP. 24)

Gregory L. Crawford   *Steel Can Recycling Institute, Pittsburgh, Pa.* (CHAP. 15)

David A. Dorau   *Black & Veatch, Kansas City, Mo.* (CHAP. 24)

Kenneth Ely   *Ely Enterprises, Inc., Cleveland, Ohio* (CHAP. 28)

Byron Friar   *Recycling Consultant, Lake Worth, Fla.* (CHAP. 11)

Frank G. Gerlock   *Camp Dresser and McKee, Inc., Melbourne, Fla.* (CHAP. 33)

Michael W. Gilmore   *Camp Dresser and McKee, Inc., Tampa, Fla.* (CHAP. 13)

John C. Glaub   *EMCON Associates, San Jose, Calif.* (CHAPS. 21, 25)

R. G. Graham   *Resource Integration Systems, Ltd., Toronto, Ont., Canada* (CHAP. 27)

Peter L. Grogan   *R. W. Beck and Associates, Seattle, Wash.* (CHAP. 2)

Lisa Wagner Haley   *Haley Environmental, Kirkland, Wash.* (CHAP. 35)

Robert Hauser, Jr.   *Camp Dresser and McKee, Inc., Tampa, Fla.* (CHAP. 8)

Tammy L. Hayes   *Camp Dresser and McKee, Inc., Tampa, Fla.* (CHAP. 13)

Richard L. Hlauka   *SCS Engineers, Bellevue, Wash.* (CHAP. 26)

Teresa Ilan   *TIA Solid Waste Management Consultants, Inc., Tampa, Fla.* (CHAP. 31)

Thomas A. Jones   *R. W. Beck and Associates, Waltham, Mass.* (CHAP. 29)

Richard R. Jordan   *The David J. Joseph Company, Cincinnati, Ohio* (CHAPS. 15, 17)

Thomas M. Kaczmarski   *Waste Management of North American, Oakbrook, Ill.* (CHAP. 6)

Steven A. Katz *New England CRINC, Chelmsford, Mass.* (CHAP. 34)

Liane R. Levetan *Chief Executive Officer, De Kalb (Atlanta) County, Ga.* (CHAP. 22)

Linda Long *Recycle America, Fort Lauderdale, Fla.* (CHAP. 9)

Belle Lund *Pompano Beach, Fla.* (APP. B)

Herbert F. Lund *Recycling Consultant, Pompano Beach, Fla.* (APPS. A, B)

Kevin McCarthy *CH₂M Hill, Bellevue, Wash.* (CHAP. 35)

Penny McCornack *Environmentalist, Portland, Oreg.* (CHAP. 10)

Abbie Page McMillan *McMillan Environmental, Inc., Harborside, Maine* (CHAP. 5)

Lisa Max *Betterworld, Inc., Fort Lauderdale, Fla.* (CHAP. 11)

Betty Muse *Resource Integration Systems Ltd., Toronto, Ont., Canada* (CHAP. 31)

Wayne Pearson *Plastice Recycling Foundations, Kennett Square, Pa.* (CHAP. 14)

Reuter Recycling of Florida *Pembroke Pines, Fla.* (CHAP. 35)

Joseph A. Ruiz *Attwoods, Inc., Coconut Grove, Fla.* (CHAP. 1)

Abdul Mulia Saleh *Camp Dresser and McKee, Inc., Tampa, Fla.* (CHAP. 8)

Rosario Salvador *Gershman, Brickner, & Stratton, Inc., Falls Church, Va.* (CHAP. 4)

L. T. Schaper *Black & Veatch, Kansas City, Mo.* (CHAP. 23)

Scott Spring *New England CRINC, Chelmsford, Mass.* (CHAP. 34)

Barbara Stevens *ECODATA, Westport, Conn.* (CHAP. 32)

Daniel E. Strobridge *Camp Dresser and McKee, Inc., Tampa, Fla.* (CHAP. 33)

David C. Sturtevant *CH₂M Hill, Bellevue, Wash.* (CHAP. 35)

Gregg Sutherland *Resource Integration Systems, Ltd., Granby, Conn.* (CHAP. 7)

Lori Swain *The Solid Waste Association of North America, Silver Spring, Md.* (APP. A)

Edward L. von Stein *CalRecovery Systems, New Haven, Conn.* (CHAP. 20)

Peter L. Wolfe *Malcolm Pirnie, Inc., White Plains, N.Y.* (CHAP. 10)

Kim Zarillo *Scientific Environmental Applications, Inc., Melbourne Village, Fla.* (CHAP. 9)

FOREWORD

Recycling is happening almost everywhere you turn. It is roaring through the halls of government and business like a freight train and there is no stopping it.

Cities and states across the country are passing recycling laws as fast as they can. As this is written, virtually every state in the country has some kind of recycling requirement on its books. Homeowners and businesses alike are now incorporating recycling into their day-to-day activities at an increasing rate.

Recycling is destined to become a permanent part of how we manage waste in this country, but it will take some patience on our part to get there. We will not turn around decades of past practices overnight; nor will we as a society embrace without qualification a practice that, in the end, does not deliver what we wanted.

Laws are now on the books, programs are being put in place, industry is making major investments in plants and equipment to process and reuse the materials collected for recycling. Markets are being developed and habits are slowly being changed. This is all for the good—but it will take some time and the expenditure of precious resources. But the basic system is coming together, and if we give it time, recycling will assume a permanent and major role in our lives.

Of course, this all presumes that we do it well, that the programs we put in place do what they are supposed to do. The recycling landscape has evolved so rapidly in the past few years, that keeping up with the changes is a major challenge. That is where this valuable new book comes in. In *The McGraw-Hill Recycling Handbook*, Herbert Lund has put together a collection of information from experts that covers all aspects of recycling in this country. While primarily aimed at all professionals responsible for planning and operating recycling programs, this book can be of enormous help to local government officials and to the business community as well.

From yard waste to refrigerators, from setting realistic recycling goals to setting up reporting systems, this volume provides a comprehensive look at the state of recycling today and where it is likely to be tomorrow.

As a nation, we are moving to make recycling a permanent part of our lives. This Handbook can help make that transition as efficient as possible.

William D. Ruckelshaus

PREFACE

New words have entered our vocabulary: curbside, precycling, commingled, windrow, material recovery facility, tipping fee, PET, MSW, refuse-derived fuel, cost avoidance, flow control, etc. Recycling is not only here, but it is growing fast.

It seems that history is repeating itself. Twenty years ago McGraw-Hill published the *Industrial Pollution Control Handbook* with Herbert F. Lund as the volume's editor in chief. Then, as now, a new phenomenon was upon us: pollution control. Everybody was racing to conferences and seminars to grab bits of information. It was so new that the EPA wasn't born yet. And there was no practical reference to guide managers, city officials, and professionals.

Because of this need, we devised a strong contents format for a new handbook and searched for the best available experts as contributing authors. Early in 1971, McGraw-Hill published the reference, now a classic, *Industrial Pollution Control Handbook*.

Two decades and a year later, we have the same set of circumstances. A new field, recycling, sweeps across the country. It had been a sleeping giant for many years, but then the landfills filled up and closures began. There was no room for disposing of our solid wastes except up the stack or down into the ground. Hazardous wastes, toxics from old dumping grounds showed up in groundwater.

Then the scurrying to conferences and seminars began. They came at us from all directions. So many organizations put on conferences that there was no room on our calendars, or in our budgets, to attend them all. In fact, during the third week in August, 1990, two major associations scheduled full recycling conferences on the west coast; one at San Diego and the other in Vancouver.

History did repeat, and, for the infant recycling field, there was no single practical reference to offer guidance to public works directors, city officials, and professionals. McGraw-Hill's editor Hal Crawford and I got together in 1989 to start again. The result is *The McGraw-Hill Recycling Handbook*, which we feel is your best information source.

As in the previous volume, we pulled together a practical, all-encompassing topic outline and searched the country for the best, most knowledgeable contributing authors to fit each chapter topic. All the major professional recycling consulting firms have donated their expertise. Many individual specialized consultants were also recruited. We have polled these firms to determine approximately how much in consulting fees they have contributed to this project. With seventeen consulting firms, the agglommeration of consulting fees reached $370,000. That's only part of the value in this Handbook on recycling.

We also enlisted the aid of experts from professional associations in the recycling and solid waste fields. You will note significant sections have been prepared by the Plastics Recycling Foundation, Solid Waste Association of North America (formerly GRCDA), National Solid Waste Management Association, Scrap Tire Management Council, and the Steel Can Recycling Institute.

As with the *Industrial Pollution Control Handbook*, the *Recycling Handbook* will serve as a practical communications bridge between the recycling experts and those now responsible for planning and implementing recycling programs. Not only have we obtained talent from professional consultants and associations, but we have found recycling expertise within the major solid waste collection and processing firms. In alphabetical order, they are: Attwoods, Inc.; Browning-Ferris Industries, Inc.; and Waste Management of North America, Inc.

Our formula for presenting recycling information follows classic editorial style: start with the general material and then dig into the details. Thus, following the inspiring Foreword by William D. Ruckelshaus, Chairman and CEO of Browning-Ferris Industries, Inc., we open with the Evolution of Recycling. Joseph Ruiz, Jr., Vice President of Attwoods, Inc., treats us with a historical review, an overview, and growth predictions. This opening section includes a legislative evaluation, characterization of solid wastes, setting goals and priorities, separation and collection systems, processing facilities, marketing problems and solutions, financial planning and management, and concludes with the psychology of recycling, why one person recycles and another will not.

Then we proceed into the recycling details with a whole section devoted to each important recyclable material: different papers, aluminum cans, glass beverage containers, plastics, metal and steel cans, yard waste, white goods, tires, batteries, construction and demolition materials, and household hazardous wastes. For each, the author discusses collection, separation, marketing, reuse potential, costs, and problems and solutions.

Further details of facilities design and recycling equipment are covered in chapters on drop-off and buy-back centers, transfer stations, and MRFs (material recovery facilities), processing yard waste, collection and processing equipment, and the all-important incorporation of recycling into landfills and incinerators.

None of this would have any meaning or point if a manager or municipality couldn't implement and control a recycling program. For this reason, we have pulled together a nuts-and-bolts section covering: (1) program planning and implementation, (2) putting together a public awareness program, (3) recycling training for managers and personnel, (4) practical recycling factors including contractor negotiations and selection, and (5) data collection and cost control. Because recyclables quality is extremely important for revenues, we have added a chapter on monitoring materials. And the final chapter in this how-to section presents successful case histories from across the country; small, medium, and large municipalities as well as rural communities.

One of the secrets of a strong practical reference is the quality of the back-of-the-book material. We feel the over 20-page glossary and abbreviations section is the best available. From the computer bank of SWANA (Solid Waste Association of North America) we are grateful for a valuable appendix section. Both my wife Belle and I spent considerable time preparing the index. This is a key Handbook element. A comprehensive index is vital to make sure the reader can find what he or she is looking for. As we did 20 years ago for the *Industrial Pollution Control Handbook*, we cross-referenced subjects to make sure this *Recycling Handbook* becomes your indispensable desktop reference.

Herb Lund

CHAPTER 1
RECYCLING OVERVIEW AND GROWTH

Joseph A. Ruiz, Jr.,
Vice President, Attwoods, Inc.
Coconut Grove, Florida

RECYCLING DEFINED

The Recycling Perplexity

Recycling? This is a seductive word to the environmentally aware among us. But what is it? What does it mean? What is it all about? Who does it? Why should I? These questions seem almost endless. Some have simple answers. Many answers are a part of a much more complex issue. Many more are yet unresolved and others are only now evolving. Just addressing the question of definition becomes an evermore complex issue as almost every governmental entity, industrial and commercial trade organizations, professional associations, academics, and practitioners attempt to define what it is. Because each has a different perspective and goal, each has a slightly different definition. Even a dispassionate search for a bias-free definition is difficult perhaps because of the circular nature or the subject.

When does the cycle begin or end? Does it ever? Does paper recycled for use as a raw material in making boxboard constitute a virgin material? What about the boxboard trimmings that were made from recycled materials? Are they waste again? If so, were they ever recycled? Perhaps a better understanding of how and why we got here can make any current definition more meaningful.

What It Is Today

Recycling today is, and must be understood as, a solid waste management strategy. A method of solid waste management equally useful as landfilling or incineration and environmentally more desirable. Today it is clearly the environmentally preferred method of solid waste management.

The Beginning

Early humans did not have a solid waste management strategy per se simply because the hunter-gatherer existence did not require one. Never staying in one place long enough to accumulate any significant amount of solid waste, as well as a need to utilize scarce resources to their highest degree, probably did not create any concern or action. However, as humans began to settle in permanent communities with higher concentrations of waste-producing individuals and activities, the need for waste management became evident. Although this occurred around 10,000 B.C. in some places, it occurred much later in others and remains much less a concern in the less populated and more rural areas of the planet even today.

By 500 B.C. Athens organized the first municipal dump in the western world, and scavengers were required to dispose of waste at least 1 mile from city walls. This imperative continued from place to place, going forward and backward relative to the desires and ability of governments. During the middle ages waste disposal continued to be an individual responsibility commensurate with the lack of enlightened authority by government.

In 1388 the English Parliament banned waste disposal in public waterways and ditches. A few short years later in 1400 garbage was piled so high outside the Paris gates that it interfered with the defense of the city. These examples are cited because they indicated a desire on the part of government to assume responsibility for this element of the health and safety of the community primarily when other responsibilities such as drainage and defense were involved. This growth in governmental concern for health and safety with regard to waste disposal lead to additional regulations and operations. By the 1840s the western world began to enter the "Age of Sanitation" as filthy conditions began to be seen as a nuisance that the public demanded government to resolve. Sanitarians employed by government primarily to deal with sewage disposal increasingly turned their attention to solid wastes.

Government's increasing assumption of solid waste management soon led to systematic approaches including the "destructor," an incineration system in Nottingham, England, in 1874. America's first municipal incinerator on Governor's Island in New York was built in 1885.

Government response continued to include a wide variety of innovative programs designed to address both specific elements of the solid waste stream as well as the broad brush approach of dumps and incinerators. Municipalities cleaned streets and sanitary engineers invented new technologies to reduce costs and volume. Fats and oils were recovered for reuse in manufacturing soap and candles. Incinerators generated steam for power and heat. Rags were increasingly recycled for use in making paper, and the inherent value of metals was always enhanced during war times to a sufficient level to promote public recycling programs. But environmental concerns were generally limited beyond the next hill, out at sea and out of sight. Ocean dumping and open space outside of the urban areas continued to be both environmentally acceptable and economical.

Recycling in Modern Times—Awakening to Solid Waste Responsibilities

Only after World War II did fast-growing populations, greatly enhanced scientific understanding of the environment, and later the concept of finite resources combine to truly afford an opportunity for a conscious examination of the detrimental nature of land or ocean disposal practices. A rapid expansion in understanding the long-term impacts of groundwater and air pollution began to demand even greater regulation of disposal practices. In many areas of the nation both open

FIGURE 1.1 Horse-drawn garbage collection carts at the turn of the century.

FIGURE 1.2 Horsepower replaces horses in this 1915 version of high-technology garbage pickup truck.

burning of solid waste at dumps and ocean disposal remained an acceptable practice well into the 1970s.

The inability of local governments to deal with these larger problems quickly led to a federal interest and assumption of responsibilities. The first federal solid waste management law was the Solid Waste Disposal Act (SWDA) of 1965, which authorized research and provided state grants. Three years later in 1968 President Johnson commissioned the National Survey of Community Solid Waste Practices. It provided the first comprehensive data on solid waste on a national basis. Two years later the Solid Waste Disposal Act was amended by the Resource Recovery Act, and the federal government was required to issue waste disposal guidelines.

The year 1970 also saw passage of the Clean Air Act, which established federal authority to combat smog and air pollution leading to the shutdown of many solid waste incinerators and the elimination of open burning of solid waste. Significantly the first Earth Day was celebrated that same year on April 22, 1970, indicating a worldwide heightened environmental awareness including that of the solid waste disposal dilemma. Within a year Oregon became the first state to pass a bottle bill, thereby creating a procedure for government regulation covering the reuse and recycling of designated portions of the waste stream during peacetime without the imperative of wartime economics. Although all 50 states had some kind of solid waste regulation by the mid-1970s, it was the Resource Conservation and Recovery Act of 1976 (RCRA) that created the first truly significant role for the federal government in solid waste management. The act emphasized conservation of resources, particularly energy conservation, and recycling as preferred solid waste management alternatives. It also provided for the national hazardous waste management program, recognizing the detrimental effect of hazardous waste on solid waste management alternatives as well as the environment in general.

The stimulus of the Arab oil embargo, the Public Utilities Regulatory Policies Act of 1978, which guarantees markets for small energy producers, and RCRA combined to encourage an explosive growth for waste-to-energy plants and to some extent the recovery of methane for fuel from landfills. The banning of open dumping of solid waste by the EPA in 1979 increased the attractiveness of waste-to-energy plants because of their volume reduction capabilities. In addition, waste-to-energy plants are generally perceived to be a form of recycling solid waste, as its use as a fuel to create energy does return a significant part of the waste stream to a useful product. This view was, and still is, enhanced by the continuing demand for electrical energy derived from nonfossil fuel sources. However, others, including the State of Florida, do not consider the burning of and recovery of energy from solid waste as recycling. Even today the debate continues with positions taken on both sides as to whether or not waste to energy is legitimately considered recycling.

Although previously preferred to landfills, waste-to-energy plants have now become almost as unpopular with communities unwilling to exchange potential groundwater pollution for potential air pollution. The disposal crisis created by the ever-diminishing lack of acceptable disposal capacity is exemplified by EPA's estimate that over 10,000 landfills (70 percent of the total) closed between 1978 and 1988.

All of those considerations have led to both a public and a legislated demand for recycling as the preferred solid waste management strategy today and in the future. The willingness of government to require and subsidize recycling when necessary has grown to enormous proportions. Significantly the dominant theme of Earth Day 1990 was recycling.

Defining Recycling

Recycling remains, however, one of those elusive concepts about which everyone thinks they have a clear understanding until they begin to practice it. Although most people understand the relatively simple tasks required by individuals in order for them to participate, the subtleties necessary for the interplay of both the public and private sectors needed to return those materials to industry as raw materials and the methods employed to do so require definitions other than common language and as a matter of law. In addition, the concept gives rise to other terms required to fully implement the concept. The terms recyclable materials, recovered materials, and recycled materials all are needed to define the concept of recycling and usually require definition in various state regulations. Therefore, only a dictionary definition of recycling can convey a general concept of a term that has been, and will continue to be, defined through committee discussions, contractual negotiations, and legislation designed to meet specific needs.

Public Perceptions

Although rapidly changing in response to local public awareness campaigns, the general public's perception of what recycling is remains largely limited to those visible elements including curbside programs, recycling centers, and so on, and a vague understanding that this is good for the environment because these materials do not go to a landfill or incinerator. This view also usually incorporates a demand for recycling a greater variety of materials than is practical or economically feasible at this time or a misunderstanding about what can or cannot be recycled.

Legislative definitions at this time in the evolution of legislation promoting and requiring recycling generally center on those materials in the waste stream that are selectively easy to separate and for which known and relatively stable markets exist. In addition, these definitions ignore previously established industrial recycling efforts based on purely economic needs of avoided cost of disposal and intrinsic value of industrial raw material–derived waste. This kind of legislative definition is directed at promoting additional recycling activities rather than accounting for existing economic considerations.

Current legislation focuses on providing for the promotion of recycling those materials that have not been recycled because the economic reasons to do so do not exist or at least are not readily apparent to the private sector of the economy.

THE WHY'S OF RECYCLING

Recycling occurs for three basic reasons: altruistic reasons, economic imperatives, and legal considerations. In the first instance, protecting the environment and conserving resources have become self-evident as being in everyone's gen-

FIGURE 1.3

eral interest. Second, the avoided cost of environmentally acceptable disposal of waste has risen to a level where when combined with the other costs associated with recycling, it now makes economic sense to recycle many materials. Finally, in responding to both public demand and a growing lack of alternative waste disposal methods, government is requiring recycling and providing for a wide variety of economic and civil penalties and incentives in order to encourage recycling.

GROWTH

The support for recycling on both a state and federal basis continues to be explosive and generally responsive to widespread public support and demand. This is a demand that has in many instances outstripped both the public and private sectors of the economy's ability to meet the requirements and/or intent of legislation. In the rush to require recycling, the market for those materials has often been ignored or misunderstood. The entry of the public sector into a traditional and well-established private sector activity has created severe stresses and difficulties in the commodities marketplace for recycled materials. The commodities market is commerce and industry's source of raw materials. It is a traditionally volatile element of the economy that is very sensitive to the relationship between supply and demand for materials. The sudden growth in legislation promoting recycling created an external stimulus that increased the supply of newspaper in the northeastern United States to the point where a glut occurred. In 1989 the price fell not only to zero but was further depressed when communities that were prevented from landfilling recovered newspaper began paying to have it taken away. The phenomenon of negative prices for this commodity severely impacted public programs that were dependent in the past on revenues from this material and those portions of the private sector that were engaged in the recycling of these materials.

However, these kinds of lessons have been helpful and will contribute to better planned and thereby more effective programs in the future. Governments at all levels appear to be directing more and more of their legislation to ensuring markets by creating demand for recycled products through preferential procurement practices. In addition the concept of tax incentives to encourage both recycling and the use of products containing recycled materials continues to gain favor.

PROGRAM OPTIONS

Whether anyone wants to recycle for altruistic reasons or because "the law makes us do it," a wide variety of options for recycling are available. Although each option is discussed in detail in other chapters, a central issue that must be considered is that no single option yet available provides all the answers. It is most likely that there is no single option that is best for everyone. There is, however, a best option or combination of options for everyone when a careful evaluation is made to determine what is available to meet specific needs and circumstances.

Recycling debate has evolved into several broad configurations for which examples can be rapidly found in operation today. Innovation, creativity, and practicality provide many variations.

Both residential and commercial establishments can participate in recycling by separating materials before they are mixed with wastes. In these programs recyclable materials are kept separate in a variety of containers whether in the home or in the workplace. At appropriate intervals, they are placed for collection or transported to centralized collection and/or processing facilities.

Curbside Collection

Single-family residential units are often served by curbside programs. These programs may require residents to use one or more containers to separate and store recyclable materials that are diverted from the normal waste stream. The type and number of containers can vary dependent on the variety of materials collected and the degree of separation desired. The design, capacity, and construction of the containers can also vary. Some programs provide containers and others do not. Containers may be rigid, specialized plastics, paper or plastic bags, or even bundled or contained at the participant's discretion.

Commercial Collection

Similar programs are also used for multidwelling residential units and commercial applications. However, of necessity these programs do not include curbside collection. These programs require recyclable materials to be placed in specialized containers of the type traditionally used in those applications. Therefore, if a multidwelling unit residence is normally served as a single-family unit for waste, then it can be served as a single family for recycling service. Similarly, if it is served as a commercial establishment for waste collection, then it will probably require recycling service in a similar manner.

Commingled or Source-Separated?

In both residential and commercial applications, the degree of separation may vary significantly. A great deal of commingling can be allowed or required in all instances if a centralized processing facility where commingled materials can be separated after collection is used. Even if a centralized processing facility is not available, single-family residential units can always be allowed to commingle materials by using a truckside sort collection method (Fig. 1.4). This method requires the collector to manually separate the material in the containers and keep them separate in the collection vehicles until delivered to markets or intermediate processing facilities.

Material Recovery Facilities

The use of material recovery facilities (MRFs) serving commingled residential programs is rapidly gaining popularity (Fig. 1.5). Commingled programs used in a multidwelling unit or commercial application can allow efficient collection methods where space available for placement of collection containers is limited.

FIGURE 1.4 Specialized curbside recycling materials: collection truck with compartments, dual sides, and hydraulic top loading.

FIGURE 1.5 Materials recovery facility (MFR) infeed conveyors for commingled materials at Community Recycling, an Attwoods Company in Dade County, Florida, that serves over 265,000 homes.

Drop-off/Buy-Back Centers

Voluntary participation in recycling programs is often related to the ease with which an individual can participate. Therefore drop-off centers that depend on altruistic motivations add a degree of inconvenience that can reduce participation. These centralized locations where recyclable materials are collected are easier and less expensive to implement than curbside programs. They are especially effective in areas where regular waste collection is not required or available.

Buy-back centers offer all of the benefits of drop-off centers and the increased incentives of monetary benefits to participants. They are, however, more expensive to operate because they must be staffed, secured, and handle cash.

Waste may also be segregated and collected by broader categories such as wet and dry, putrescible and nonputrescible, household waste or yard waste, etc., prior to recycling. It can still be recycled to greater or lesser extent even if it is mixed.

Recycling at Waste-to-Energy Facilities

Waste-to-energy facilities increasingly employ separation systems to recover nonorganic recyclable materials. The degree and type of material recovery depends largely on whether the materials are recovered prior to or after incineration. Recovery of materials after incineration, known as *back-end systems,* are frequently used with mass burn waste-to-energy facilities. They can recover high percentages of ferrous and nonferrous metals through the use of simple technology. Although the quality and quantity of the recovered materials may be diminished, back-end systems can offer a relatively inexpensive retrofit for existing facilities.

Front-end separation systems that remove recyclable materials prior to incineration are used in facilities that prepare a refuse-derived fuel by removing the inorganic fraction of the waste prior to incineration. These materials are then recycled or, when no markets exist, landfilled with other nonprocessible materials. Although many front-end designs and technologies are available, they are all more complex and therefore more expensive to construct and operate than back-end systems. However, they offer a greater opportunity to recover a wider variety and higher quality of recovered materials.

Composting

The methodologies and technologies used in separating materials from mixed waste can also be used in the preparation of compost. Long championed as the solution to the solid waste dilemma, the composting of mixed waste has met with limited success. Although easy to do on a small scale, its success has been hindered by a lack of markets and other applications in large quantities. Compost from mixed waste has recently fallen into disfavor with some environmental groups on the basis that it discourages other kinds of recycling. Its use is even being prohibited by several states because of the potential negative consequences of contaminants such as heavy metals that may be present in compost made from mixed waste.

Higher degrees of separation of metals and other contaminants will be necessary for successful composting of mixed waste in the future. Programs for composting clean yard waste and other homogeneous materials offer greater promise. Although still limited by a lack of markets, they are enjoying a much higher degree of success.

SUMMARY

All collection and processing methods are technologies that have their merits and limitations. There is no single answer or solution. Recycling, in whatever manner, is and must be part of integrated solid waste management strategies. When compared to the environmental risks associated with landfilling or incineration, recycling is the preferred solid waste management strategy.

CHAPTER 2
LEGISLATIVE EVALUATIONS

Peter L. Grogan
Director of Materials Recovery
R. W. Beck and Associates
Seattle, Washington

INTRODUCTION

From Maine to Hawaii, legislative printing presses have been producing reams of new solid waste recycling and reduction legislation. Comprehensive recycling laws are now on the books in 41 states and the District of Columbia. The conservative target for states setting waste reduction goals is 25 percent. Some states, including Washington, New York, Maine, Iowa, Indiana, and California, have set 50 percent waste reduction goals.

Solid waste recycling legislation is inducing a new infrastructure for the delivery of services. To date, 4000 cities have implemented residential curbside collection programs, including 6 of the nation's 10 largest cities. By early 1992, over 200 material recovery facilities were on line in the United States. These services will be provided by local governments and by the private sector.

Some local governments have developed their own legislation to reduce waste and, in some cases, to mandate service provision or citizen participation. The federal government has begun to develop waste reduction legislation as part of the Resource Conservation and Recovery Act reauthorization, which is likely to set a waste reduction goal for states without goals.

The following summaries provide an overview of federal laws, legislation for 16 states, and the regulatory approaches of several cities and municipalities.

FEDERAL LEGISLATION

Recycling legislation has been national law since 1970's National Environmental Policy Act (NEPA), which focuses on government's responsibility to maintain harmony between people and the environment. Section 4331(a) declares that

It is the continuing policy of the Federal Government, in cooperation with State and local governments, and other concerned public and private organizations, to use all practicable means and measures, including financial and technical assistance, in a manner calculated to foster and promote the general welfare, to create and maintain conditions under which man and nature can exist in productive harmony, and fulfill the social, economic and other requirements of present and future generations of Americans.

Since 1970, maintaining the delicate balance within our environment has been one of Congress's broad mandates.

Section 4331(b) states that it is also the responsibility of the federal government to "(6) enhance the quality of renewable resources and approach the maximum attainable recycling of depletable resources." Section 4331 also addresses the government's continuing responsibility to act as the "trustee of the environment" using all "practical means."

Reacting to both public outrage and the realities of the solid waste disposal problem, Congress has begun to focus renewed attention upon waste reduction and recycling. A plethora of waste reduction and recycling legislation has been sponsored in the last 2 years. Proposed legislation follows directly from responsibilities dictated in the 1970 NEPA act. As of January 1990, 50 bills pertaining to recycling issues have been introduced in the House and Senate. Outlines of some of the most important bills follow.

In 1976, Congress passed the Resource Conservation and Recovery Act (RCRA). RCRA further emphasized the preservation of the environment through the following priorities: waste reduction, recycling, resource recovery, and landfilling. Although RCRA was passed as comprehensive solid waste management legislation, its main focus has been on the management of hazardous waste. RCRA is presently up for reauthorization and numerous bills have been introduced which place more of an emphasis on waste reduction and recycling.

In the House, Representative Thomas A. Luken proposed H.R. 3735, the Waste Materials Management Act of 1989. Senator Baucus proposed Senate Bill 1113 to the Senate. Both bills focus on nonhazardous solid waste management issues and are similar in their proposals concerning waste reduction and recycling. Both are offered as bills to amend the Solid Waste Disposal Act (SWDA), more frequently called the Resource Conservation and Recovery Act (RCRA). Nearly 70 bills were introduced in the 101st Congress addressing solid waste issues; it is likely that both the Luken and Baucus bills will serve as the basis for Senate and House reauthorization legislation.

If adopted, states will be required to submit comprehensive solid waste management plans outlining waste management and waste reduction strategies for the next two decades. Both pieces of legislation call for interim goals of 25 percent. A 50 percent recycling rate would be required within approximately 10 years.

Both bills would compel the EPA to establish a national clearinghouse to collect and disseminate information on waste reduction and recycling. A products and packaging board would also be established to study waste reduction with respect to consumer products and packaging. The recycling of lead-acid batteries and motor oil would also be required. Both bills are presently under review. Other bills deal with the possibilities of imposing usage taxes on virgin materials or requiring plastic container labeling. Several address the percentage of recycled content in newsprint, lubricating oil, plastics, and tires.

One of the EPA's publications, "The Solid Waste Dilemma: An Agenda for Action," addresses the EPA's goal of managing 25 percent of the United States' municipal solid waste through source reduction and recycling. While the 25 percent goal is not federal law, the EPA provides recommendations through which the goal can be reached. The EPA has published numerous reports regarding waste reduction and recycling.

In regulations proposed under the federal Clean Air Act, the EPA proposed that waste-to-energy incinerators be required to reduce the amount of garbage they burn by 25 percent through recycling and composting. The EPA sees this plan as a way to cut toxic substance emissions, reduce the amount of landfilled ash, and promote its goal of 25 percent national waste reduction. Also, these facilities could not burn lead-acid batteries. The President's Council on Competitiveness, chaired by Vice President Quayle, rejected the proposed legislation.

National waste reduction and recycling legislation is on the move. There are many reasons for this, including the need for federal action to induce recyclable commodity market development. Grass-roots organizational opposition to land disposal of solid waste has played a factor in potential federal legislation. The interstate transportation issue of solid waste disposal has also created a concern at the state level that will require federal action. The federal government is also likely to provide the legislative authority for waste reduction to some rural states that have not yet developed aggressive waste reduction legislation.

STATE LEGISLATION

Many states have been actively studying the solid waste problem and developing solutions that include recycling, composting, and waste reduction strategies. These states have been moving aggressively to develop and fund programs to reduce the solid waste stream. These laws are designed to change the individual solid waste management behavior of every citizen in the perspective state (Tables 2.1 through 2.4).

The impetus for the legislation in many cases was the lack of available landfill capacity, the not-in-my-backyard (NIMBY) syndrome, the escalating expense of waste disposal, and the environmental consequences of disposal. Some states have replicated portions of laws from other states that have developed viable solutions. A summary of 16 state laws follows.

California

In 1989 the state of California passed 17 bills relating to waste management and reduction through reuse, recycling, and composting. One bill—Assembly Bill 939—created the Integrated Waste Management Board, whose six members will supervise the development and implementation of countywide integrated waste management plans. The general provisions of the new law promote the following waste management practices in order of priority:

1. Source reduction
2. Recycling and composting
3. Environmentally sound transformation and environmentally safe land disposal

"Transformation" as defined in the California legislation means incineration, pyrolysis, distillation, gasification, or biological conversion other than composting. Before July 1991, each city was to have prepared a solid waste plan

TABLE 2.1 State Solid Waste Legislation

Date passed	WR/R goal	Comp. date	Product and disposal bans	Funding	Other unique characteristics
				California	
1989	25% 50%	1995 2000	None	Statewide disposal surcharge. Advance disposal fee on tires.	Bottle bill deposit increase to $.05 per two beverage containers. Tax credit on purchasing of recycling equipment. Newspaper publishers to use news with 25% recycled content by 1991 and 50% by 2000. Commission to study market opportunities. Plastics coding.
				Connecticut	
1987	25%	1991	Disposal ban on designated recyclables.	Oil overcharge monies. Recycling Trust Fund. Grants provided to agencies and groups.	IPC in each of 15 regions. Municipal recycling programs required. State procurement of recycled products. Market development study. Newsprint publishers required to use more recycled newsprint.
				Florida	
1988	30%	1994	Product ban on detachable pull-rings, some nonbiodegradable plastic packaging. Disposal ban on tires, oil, and lead-acid batteries.	Advance disposal fees, sales tax, business registration. Oil overcharge monies. Solid waste management trust fund.	Additional advance disposal fees if recycling targets not met. Plastic coding. State agencies to use compost and recovered construction materials.
				Indiana	
1990	35% 50%	1996 2001	Disposal ban on designated recyclables will be implemented if deemed necessary.	Statewide disposal surcharge.	Counties required to form solid waste management districts. Low-interest loans for recycling organizations. Educational programs are being developed for students, consumers and businesses.

State						
Louisiana						
1989	25%	1992	Product ban on non-biodegradable 6-pack yokes. Disposal ban on oil, tires, white goods, lead-acid batteries.	Surcharge on disposal, recycling, & processing. Oil overcharge monies.	State agency procurement of recycled products. Coding of plastic bottles. Parish solid waste management plans required.	
Maine						
1989	25% 50%	1992 1994	Product ban on multi-layer juice containers, plastic cans, 6-pack yokes.	Disposal surcharge. Advance disposal fee on special wastes.	Plastics coding. 30% tax credit on recycling equipment purchases. Bottle Bill extended to all beverage containers. Creates Waste Management Agency. State agencies to purchase recycled paper. Commercial sector to recycle.	
Michigan						
1988	None	None	Product ban on non-biodegradable 6-pack yokes.	Plastics recycling development fund.	Plastics coding. Creates Recycling Target Enterprise Council. Creates oil recycling system. State offices to recycle paper.	
Minnesota						
			Disposal ban on lead-acid batteries and white goods.	Extension of 6% sales tax to municipal solid waste collection and disposal services.	Goals vary according to population density. Metropolitan counties have goals of 35%, while all other counties have a goal of 25%. State agencies have set a goal of 40%. Schools, state and local governments are encouraged to act as model waste-reduction and recycling programs.	
New Mexico						
1990	25% 50%	1995 2000	To be established by the environmental improvement board by July 1991.	Solid Waste Facility Grant Fund derived from a disposal fee on waste disposed outside the district in which it was generated.	State agencies and postsecondary educational institutions to implement programs including education, source reduction and separation. Composting required in educational institution programs.	

TABLE 2.1 State Solid Waste Legislation (*Continued*)

Date passed	WR/R goal	Comp. date	Product and disposal bans	Funding	Other unique characteristics
New York					
1988	50%	1997	None	Oil overcharge monies, DEC recycling grants.	Mandatory recycling. Municipalities to pass and enforce recycling ordinances. Funding for public education, school curricula, and market investigation. Voluntary guidelines to increase the use of recycled newsprint.
North Carolina					
1989	25%	1993	Product ban on detachable pull-ring, packaging with CFC, nonrecyclable polystyrene and plastic bags, uncoded plastics. Disposal ban on lead-acid batteries, oil, yard waste, and white goods.	State trust fund and grants. Advance disposal fee on tires.	County and municipal recycling required by July 1991. State agencies to purchase recycled products and compost. Development of WR/R curriculum and student awareness programs.
Oregon					
1986	None	None	None	Municipal funding through garbage collection fees. State funding for regulation.	Requires "Opportunity to Recycle." Local governments with populations over 4000 must provide residential recycling collection service. Businesses, industries, apartment owners and garbage haulers required to inform people of recycling. By 1991 governments with populations over 5000 must ban tires, vehicles, appliances, and oil from landfills.
Pennsylvania					
1988	25%	1997	None	Disposal surcharge.	Municipal recycling programs required. Businesses, government offices, hospitals and schools required to source separate. Funding for market research and development. Low interest loans available to recycling companies. Development of recycling curriculum.

			Rhode Island		
1986	15%	1990	Product ban on detachable pull-rings, and mixed resin food or beverage containers. Disposal ban on lead-acid batteries.	Subsidized tipping fee for source separated waste.	Government agencies required to recycle. Municipalities to deposit source separated materials free of charge at MRF. Municipalities to enforce public participation in recycling.
			Washington		
1989	50%	1995	Disposal ban on lead-acid batteries.	Advanced disposal fee on tires. Solid waste collection tax. County disposal surcharge.	County solid waste management plans to include WR/R education programs and market strategies. Market development committee established.
			Wisconsin		
1990	N/A	N/A	Disposal ban on lead-acid batteries, major appliances, waste oil by 1991; scrap tires, old corrugated containers, newspaper, magazines, office paper, glass containers, foam polystyrene scrap, metal containers by 1995.	Fee on businesses, a newspaper recycling fee for publishers not meeting recycled content requirement and appropriations from the State's General Fund.	State is divided into "responsible units" for management of local recycling activities. Mandatory 45% recycled content for newsprint by 2001 and mandatory 10% recycled plastic containers by 1995. Requirement to use recycled materials in highway construction.

Source: R. W. Beck and Associates.

TABLE 2.2 State Recycling Goals

State	Recycling goals, %	Year	State	Recycling goals, %	Year
Alabama	25	1995	Nebraska	25, 50	1994, 2000
Arkansas	30, 40	1995, 2000	Nevada	25	1994
California	25, 50	1995, 2000	New Hampshire	40	2000
Connecticut	37	2010	New Jersey	60	1995
District of Columbia	20	1991	New Mexico	25	1995
Florida	30	1994	New York	50	1997
Georgia	25	1996	North Carolina	25, 40	1993, 2001
Hawaii	25, 50	1995, 2000	Ohio	25	1994
Illinois	25, 25	1997*, 2000†	Oregon	50	2000
Indiana	35, 50	1995, 2000	Pennsylvania	25	1997
Iowa	25, 50	1994, 2000	Rhode Island	15	(No year)
Kentucky	25, 50	1994, 2000	South Carolina	25	1997
Louisiana	25	1992	South Dakota	25, 50	1996, 2000
Maine	25, 50	1992, 1994	Tennessee	25	1995
Maryland	15, 20	1992, 1994	Texas	40	1994
Massachusetts	23, 46	1992, 2000	Vermont	40	2000
Michigan	30	2005	Virginia	10, 25	1991, 1995
Minnesota	35	1993	Washington	50	1995
Mississippi	25	1996	West Virginia	20, 50	1993, 2000
Missouri	40	1998	Wyoming	10, 30	1991, 1993
Montana	25	1996			

*Greater than 100,000 population.
†Less than 100,000 population.
Source: National Solid Wastes Management Association.

consistent with the above hierarchy. The state program emphasizes implementation and will include the following:

1. A waste characterization component
2. A source education component
3. A recycling component
4. A composting component
5. A solid waste facility capacity component
6. An education and public information component
7. A funding component
8. A special waste component
9. A household hazardous waste component

The law requires the city or county to divert 50 percent of its waste stream by January 2000 through source reduction, recycling, and composting activities. The interim goal is 25 percent by 1995.

Senate Bill 1221 increased the redemption fee of the existing Assembly Bill 2020 program for beverage containers to improve redemption percentages. Assembly Bill 4 will stimulate the market for recycled products by setting procurement preferences for recycled materials for all state agencies. To increase the demand for recycled goods, Assembly Bill 1305 requires newsprint consumers—publishers—to increase their recycled paper content usage to 25 percent by 1991. A series of increases will raise the requirement to 50 percent by January 2000.

TABLE 2.3 State Disposal Bans

State	Lead-acid batteries	Yard waste	Unprocessed tires	Used oil	Large appliances	Other
California	•					
Connecticut	•	•[a]		○		b
Florida	•	○	•	•	•	c
Louisiana	○		•	•	•	
Maine	○					
Michigan	•					
Minnesota	•	•	○	○	•	d
North Carolina	•	•	•	•	•	
New York	•	•				
Oregon	•		•			e
Pennsylvania	•	•[a]	•			
Rhode Island			•		•	
Washington	•					
Wisconsin	•	•	•	•	•	f

[a]Yard waste disposal bans only apply to leaves.
[b]Nickel-cadmium batteries.
[c]Construction and demolition debris.
[d]Dry cell batteries that contain mercuric oxide or silver oxide electrodes, nickel-cadmium or sealed lead-acid. Mixed unprocessed waste in metro area.
[e]Recyclable material that has already been separated.
[f]Aluminum, plastic, steel and glass containers, corrugated paper and paper board, foam polystyrene packaging, magazines, newspaper and officer paper are banned from disposal unless municipalities are certified as having an "effective" source separation program.
Source: National Solid Wastes Management Association.

The state also enacted a fine of $1000 for each violation as an enforcement measure. This action is dependent upon recycled stock meeting specific quality standards, as well as being competitively priced.

Senate Bill 432–Assembly Bill 1308 created tax credits as incentives for investment within the private sector. Tax credits up to 40 percent encourage buyers of machinery or equipment used to manufacture products made of recycled materials. Credit is capped at $250,000 for each piece of equipment and expires after November 1994. Additional legislation creates a 25 cent tire disposal fee to support tire recovery, while another bill mandates the coding of all rigid plastic containers by 1992.

Connecticut

Connecticut took a new approach to developing recycling markets in House Bill 6641, effective October 1, 1990. Connecticut newspaper publishers, including those with an average daily in-state circulation of more than 40,000, are required to use de-inked newsprint. The new law defines "de-inked" newsprint as newsprint that contains at least 40 percent postconsumer recycled paper. Newspapers must use 20 percent de-inked newsprint by 1993 and 90 percent by 1998. Publishers have 2 years to comply. After that, the state Department of Environmental Protection (DEP) can exempt publishers from the mandate if they prove there are

TABLE 2.4 State Procurement Guidelines for Recyclables

State legislation	Characteristics	Status
Alaska—HBN 481	Relates to state procurement of recycled paper and other products and to the state's use of paper. Establishes a waste reduction and recycling task force.	06/21/90 Public Law 90-175
Illinois—HBN 1562	Directs the central management services department to study the possible expansion of its procurement program to include products made from recycled plastics, glass, etc., for various things that might include, but not limited to, traffic control products.	06/19/90 Passed House
Kansas—HBN 2805	An act concerning state procurement practices; relating to products made from recycled materials and recyclable materials.	03/13/90 To Senate; referred to Energy Committee
Oklahoma—HBN 1903	Changing the name of the state paper recycling act to the Oklahoma State Recycling and Recycled Materials Procurement Act; modifying definitions and providing for products manufactured with recycled materials; modifying legislative intent; expanding authority of Office of Public Affairs to allow contracts utilizing the services of inmates of county jails and the state penitentiary.	05/01/90 Effective 07-01-90
Utah—HBN 330	Regarding procurement; requiring the purchase of recycled paper and paper products by public procurement units; and requiring recycling under certain circumstances.	03/13/90 Approved by House
Virginia—HJR 158	Requesting the Department of Waste Management to study how to most effectively promote the procurement and use of recycled products by state agencies.	03/07/90 Adopted by House
Washington—HBN 2570	Requiring the Department of Ecology to develop a waste reduction, recycling and procurement plan for state agencies and local governments.	02/22/90 Passed House reported to Senate with amendment

Source: Courtesy of *Municipal Solid Waste News,* January 1991. See Appendix C for model procurement policy ordinance.

insufficient quantities of de-inked newsprint at prices comparable to virgin newsprint. The bill also creates a task force of government and industry representatives to assist newspapers with compliance.

Connecticut's packaging law contains a number of provisions in addition to recycled content requirements. It sets a goal of maintaining the state's per capita waste generation rate and requires the DEP to develop a source reduction plan to meet this goal. The DEP will regulate packaging to increase its recyclability and recycled content, and reduce the volume, weight, and toxicity of packaging material.

Beginning in July 1993, consumer products containing nonremovable nickel-cadmium (rechargeable) batteries have been banned and municipalities are required to recycle them. Retail stores that use plastic bags will be required to also offer paper bags to their customers and inform customers of the choice they have between paper and plastic. The Department of Administrative Services will develop and implement a plan to reduce the use of disposable products. The DEP will develop a public waste-reduction education program, paid for by a $1 million allocation from the state's Recycling Trust Fund.

Connecticut's packaging legislation creates more funding for the state's Recycling Trust Fund by imposing a $1 per ton waste disposal fee. The fund will cover administrative costs, as well as the costs of studies and grants. In July 1987, well before House Bill 6641, Connecticut enacted mandatory recycling legislation. House Bill 5686 set Connecticut's statewide recycling goal of 25 percent by 1991. The DEP divided the state into 15 regions, each to be served by a materials recovery facility (MRF).

Municipalities were required to pass ordinances mandating recycling by 1991 and take their source-separated waste to their regional MRF. Residents will recycle old corrugated containers, newspaper, office paper, scrap metal, vehicle batteries, used motor oil, and yard waste. Connecticut's mandatory recycling law also created the $13 million Municipal Solid Waste Recycling Trust Fund, which is financed by oil overcharge monies and allocations from the legislature. Presently, nine regions have developed or are developing plans for MRFs. One MRF is already operating in Groton, Connecticut. Two rural regions have opted for an alternative approach to MRFs; they will sort materials at the collection vehicles.

Florida

The state of Florida's June 1988 Solid Waste Management Bill—Senate Bill 1192—is one of the boldest pieces of mandatory state recycling legislation to date. In addition to establishing a 30 percent waste reduction-recycling goal by 1994, the bill bans the use of certain nonbiodegradable packaging materials and prohibits the disposal of certain special wastes in landfills and waste-to-energy facilities.

Senate Bill 1192 sets guidelines for local governments and encourages the creation of regional solid waste authorities. Counties are responsible for developing and enforcing their own recycling programs, either through centralized processing or curbside collection.

Newspaper, glass, plastic bottles, metal cans, lead-acid batteries, tires, used oil, and yard waste must be separated from the waste stream. Whole tires, used oil, and lead-acid batteries are prohibited from landfills. White goods, and construction and demolition debris must be separated and recycled when possible, but must be disposed of only at specially permitted sites and together with tires and yard waste can account for no more than half the waste that must be separated out to meet the 30 percent reduction goal.

The law bans beverage containers with detachable metal rings and containers connected by a separate plastic ring or other device, unless the connectors are biodegradable within 120 days. Over the next few years, materials containing fully halogenated chlorofluorocarbons will be prohibited as will plastic bags for consumer products, unless they are made of material that degrades within 120 days and are so labeled. Polystyrene foam or coated-paper food packaging will be prohibited unless it biodegrades within 12 months. Coding plastic containers by resin type will also be required.

These mandates require local governments to significantly change their solid waste management practices in a relatively short time. To assist counties with program implementation, Florida created a new Solid Waste Management Trust Fund within the Department of Environmental Regulation. The fund comprises unallocated sales tax collection monies and business registration fees, transfers from oil overcharge settlement funds, and advanced disposal fees on items deemed significant contributors to the solid waste problem. Funds are expected to total approximately $25 million annually.

The waste newsprint disposal fee imposes a charge of 10 cents/ton on newsprint consumed. A credit of 10 cents/ton against the fee is granted for the use of recycled newsprint in publication or overruns.

Advanced disposal fees for containers made from plastic, glass, aluminum, and plastic-coated paper have been scheduled for implementation in July 1992, if it appears that these materials are not being recycled at a rate of 50 percent. A fee of 1 cent per container may be placed upon containers that are not continually recycled at this rate.

State agencies will begin recycling programs and use composted materials when feasible. The Department of Education will develop guidelines within the state education system and the Department of Transportation is to expand the use of recovered materials in construction programs and find new ways to use these materials in paving projects. Numerous counties have completed their waste reduction-recycling plans and many have begun implementation. The state legislature was in the process of updating this law in mid-1992.

Indiana

With House Bill 1240 signed by the governor in March 1990, the state of Indiana set goals to reduce the amount of solid waste landfilled or incinerated by 35 percent before 1996, and 50 percent by 2001. Source reduction, recycling, and other solid waste management alternatives are preferred to landfilling and incineration.

Beginning January 1, 1991, a fee of 50 cents/ton will be charged on waste disposed of or incinerated in the state. Solid waste generated outside Indiana will be charged a variable fee, which will equate tipping charges with the disposal facility nearest the area where the waste was generated. This approach has been challenged and will be decided in the courts. The minimum fee for out-of-state solid waste will be 50 cents/ton. Revenue generated from the fees will be deposited in the state solid waste management fund.

The bill requires counties to form solid waste management districts. Counties may form their own districts or join with others. Districts are responsible for developing and implementing solid waste management plans that provide for an integrated approach to solid waste management. Funding for the plan's administration and development may be generated through fees upon final disposal facilities within the district.

The Indiana Recycling and Energy Development Board was created through this legislation. The board consists of 13 members who will work to create markets for products made from recycled materials. The Solid Waste Management Board is charged with adapting rules that will prohibit the disposal of recyclable materials in a final disposal facility. They will also determine a date after which the disposal of recyclables will be prohibited or restricted as much as possible.

The Indiana Recycling and Promotion and Assistance fund is established and funded through appropriations from the solid waste management fund and other sources. The board may use the money to make loans to assist in the establishment and expansion of recycling businesses, as well as assisting manufacturers in the retrofitting of equipment which will be used to recycle or reuse secondary materials. The board is authorized to make grants for research and development projects involving recycling.

The Department of Environmental Management is charged with developing programs to educate students, consumers, and businesses about the benefits of recycling.

Louisiana

The state of Louisiana's House Bill 1199 was enacted in September 1989. The solid waste and recycling bill set a goal of reducing the state's solid waste stream by 25 percent before the end of 1992. Each county, in conjunction with the major municipalities, will submit a solid waste management plan that meets the state's goal. State agencies will procure recycled goods to the extent possible. Solid waste management facilities will provide drop-off locations for recyclable materials, if they become necessary to meet state goals.

House Bill 1199 charges the Department of Environmental Quality (DEQ) with establishing permits and regulations that will encourage recycling. The DEQ will create a list of recyclable materials and will annually review recycling technologies, markets, and materials costs. They will also develop and implement public education programs and act as a source of information on state recycling businesses for the purpose of matching recovered materials with markets.

Initial funding for House Bill 1199 programs and activities will come from $2.5 million in oil overcharge settlements. Solid waste management facilities may impose a surcharge on the disposal, recycling, processing, or storing of solid waste. Half the funds will be dedicated to local governmental recycling programs directly, and half will provide state support for local activities and statewide recycling education.

The DEQ has determined guidelines for the uses and application rates of compost products and established product requirements for various applications of compost. It also began a permitting system for used-oil collection sites and developed incentive programs for the reuse, recycling, and marketing of used oil. The disposal of used oil, waste tires, white goods, and lead-acid batteries were scheduled for prohibition in 1991. House Bill 1199 also requires the coding of plastic bottles. The sale of nonrecyclable or nondegradable plastic six-pack yokes have been designated as prohibited after January 1991.

Maine

The state of Maine passed several solid waste management and recycling bills in July 1989. The most comprehensive—Legislative Document 1431—set a goal of recycling 25 percent of the waste stream by 1992, increasing to 50 percent by 1994. Legislative Document 1431 also created the Maine Waste Management Agency, which controls waste disposal in the state and which is developing a state waste management and recycling plan.

The agency and its programs are funded by the Solid Waste Management Fund derived from new disposal fees of $4/ton for municipal solid waste and $6/ton for special wastes. Towns that do not implement recycling programs will pay additional disposal fees and can be prohibited from using state-owned facilities. An advance disposal fee is charged on hard-to-dispose-of items such as tires, appliances, electronic goods, and lead-acid batteries.

Legislative Document 1431 will help funding in a number of areas including local government recycling grants, tax credits on purchases of recycling equipment, and loans for local business recycling projects. State agencies, including universities and prisons, are required to purchase recycled paper and implement recycling programs. The state is developing recycling education programs for public schools, grades kindergarten through high school. The Transportation Agency will evaluate the use of recyclable materials in construction.

Multilayer juice containers, plastic cans, and plastic yoke connectors are banned in Maine. All plastic containers must be labeled by resin type, and the state's "Bottle Bill" was expanded to include all beverage containers of 1 gallon or less, with the exception of dairy products.

Businesses with more than 14 employees must implement office paper and cardboard recycling programs by July 1993. Retailers are required to provide paper bags, unless customers request plastic. Other Maine legislation establishes a $10 deposit on lead-acid batteries and allocates $5 million in capital grants to local and regional governments for recycling equipment and facilities.

Michigan

Since 1988, a dozen bills have been signed into law in the state of Michigan that deal either directly or indirectly with recycling in the state. Eight passed in 1988 alone. The first of those eight bills—number 414 of the Public Acts of 1988—requires the labeling of all plastic products with a resin-content code by January 1992. Violators will be subject to fines.

Bill number 415 of the Public Acts of 1988 creates a plastics recycling development fund and a consortium to administer the fund. It also establishes a plastics recycling development grant and loan program. The fund will be a Department of Treasury account administered and expended by the consortium for the purpose of making grants and loans for market development and research. The fund will not exceed $5 million and will be funded from the proceeds of a state bond sale and appropriations by the Legislature.

Under bill number 416 of the Public Acts of 1988, a "recycling target enterprise development council" was created to identify the needs of recycling enterprises and to advise the DNR, the Department of Commerce, the Legislature, and the governor on recycling issues and the development of recycling enterprises. The council must also create a development plan to improve the state's business climate for recycling, encourage existing and new public and private recycling enterprises, and promote the use of recycled products. The recycling target enterprise development council has yet to be established and its source of funding is still unclear.

Three of the bills target either recycling in state offices or state procurement of recycled products. Number 411 of the Public Acts of 1988 requires all state offices to recycle office paper. There had been a voluntary recycling program for state offices in operation for about 12 years; however, the passage of Public Act number 411 increased the participation rate to 97 percent.

Money collected under the program is used to offset program costs. Under bill number 412 of the Public Acts of 1988, the Department of Management and budget must purchase—to the extent available—paper products made from recycled paper, if the cost is not greater than 110 percent of the cost of paper without recycled fibers. The amount bought must increase each year so that, by 1991, 50 percent of the paper the department buys should have been recycled paper.

Bill number 413 of the Public Acts of 1988 requires the state to buy—to the extent available—all supplies, materials, and equipment made from recycled materials, if the cost does not exceed 110 percent of the cost of supplies, materials, and equipment not containing recycled materials. The bill specified that the amount purchased increase each year until, by 1991, 20 percent of the supplies, materials, and equipment the state buys contained recycled materials. Bill number 428 of the Public Acts of 1988 promotes the reduction of materials entering the waste stream by encouraging source and site separation, and requiring recycling in solid waste management plan updates. The final "recycling" bill passed in 1988, number 430 of the Public Acts of 1988, requires certain state facilities to collect used oil. Collection-station siting is underway.

In 1989, the following recycling-related bills were adopted. Bill number 138 of the Public Acts of 1989 provides for a county surcharge on households for waste reduction and recycling programs, and bill number 52 provides for the regulation and management of solid waste incinerator ash, requiring county solid waste management plan updates to contain an analysis or evaluation of recycling.

Bill number 63 of the Public Acts of 1989 standardizes the labeling for resins used in plastic containers. Finally, bill number 186 provides for the establishment of a department of solid waste management in certain counties.

The year 1990 saw only one bill pass that affected recycling. Bill number 20 of the Publics Acts of 1990 prohibits the disposal of lead-acid, mercury, and nickel-cadmium batteries in solid waste collection systems, and requires retailers to post a written notice notifying consumers.

By the following year, at least another 10 pieces of legislation encouraging recycling were pending in committee. Pending legislation ran the gamut from regulating the collection, storage, and disposal of scrap tires to ordering the DNR to promulgate rules requiring persons to recycle paper, plastic, glass, and metals.

Minnesota

The state of Minnesota's Select Committee on Recycling and the Environment (SCORE) proposed waste reduction and recycling legislation that was enacted on October 3, 1989. The legislation requires all metropolitan counties in the state to recycle at least 35 percent of their solid waste by the end of 1993. All other counties must recycle at least 25 percent of their solid waste by the end of 1993. State agencies within metropolitan areas must recycle at least 40 percent within the same time frame.

Funding for the programs required to reach these goals will come from an extension of Minnesota's 6 percent sales tax. The state tax now applies to municipal solid waste collection and disposal services, but recycling collection and management are exempt. Minnesota estimates that extending the sales tax will provide $30 million in increased revenue annually.

The office of waste management will distribute approximately 75 percent of that revenue directly to county governments in one of two ways, whichever is larger. Counties have the choice of receiving a set minimal level of funding from the state; an amount that has not yet been determined. The other option is to receive an amount equal to 50 percent of the new taxes collected from waste collection and disposal facilities within the county. The funds must be used to underwrite local waste reduction, recycling, and problem-materials management programs. The remaining 25 percent is appropriated to state agencies for the study and management of statewide issues. Market development, waste education, and problem-material management are some of the programs that will be funded through state grants.

Schools and state and local governments are encouraged to act as model waste-reduction and recycling programs. Procurement of recycled paper is encouraged through a 10 percent price preference. State and local agencies were required to recycle at least three materials by January 1, 1991, for the metropolitan area and January 1, 1993, for the nonmetropolitan areas.

Additional legislation of note placed a $5 refundable surcharge on lead-acid batteries; required the licensing of solid waste haulers; and banned major appliances from disposal in mixed municipal solid waste or in processing-disposal facilities after July 1, 1990.

New Mexico

The state of New Mexico's Solid Waste Act, signed on February 28, 1990, sets a 25 percent diversion goal for the state by July 1, 1995, increasing to 50 percent by July 1, 2000. The Health and Environment Department (HED) is responsible for preparing and submitting a state solid waste management plan. The plan must include the following elements: waste characterization, source reduction, recycling, composting, education and public information, funding mechanisms, special waste, and household hazardous waste. The HED must implement programs consistent with the plan by July 1, 1993.

Senate Bill 2 creates the Solid Waste Facility Grant Fund. Commercial haulers pay a solid waste assessment fee when they dispose of waste at a facility outside the solid waste district in which the waste was generated. In association with the General Services Department, the HED will manage source reduction and recycling program grants. The HED will provide technical assistance on household hazardous waste management to counties, municipalities, and other government entities as well.

The Solid Waste Act includes provisions for the development of recyclable materials markets. The Economic Development and Tourism Department will encourage and support businesses that produce minimal wastes, engage in source reduction and recycling activities, promote markets for recyclable commodities, and develop products made of recycled materials. In association with other state agencies, the HED will research markets and market development, develop a recycling businesses directory, and serve as a coordinator in matching recycled materials with markets.

Senate Bill 2 requires state procurement of recycled materials and implementation of recycling programs in state agencies as well. State purchasing agents will establish specifications, policies, and practices for buying recycled supplies and materials. Recycled materials will be purchased at a price preference of up to 5 percent. State agencies and postsecondary educational institutions are required to implement in-house source reduction and source separation programs that include collection of high grade paper, corrugated paper, and glass. These agencies and institutions must also appoint recycling coordinators and implement education programs for the employees and/or students. In addition to source reduction and separation, postsecondary education institutions are required to include composting in their programs.

New York

The state of New York's Chapter 70 Bill, passed in May 1988, appropriated $61 million for solid waste management throughout the state. By September 1992, all municipalities in the state are required to pass a mandatory source separation ordinance with a diversion goal of 50 percent by 1997. Each municipality is responsible for enforcing recycling ordinances. The state will regulate all municipal and solid waste facilities, issuing permits only after recycling plans have been approved and implemented.

As of 1990, the state's Department of Environmental Conservation granted nearly $8 million to 88 county and local governments for recycling programs. Funds are appropriated in five sections. A total of $6 million was set aside for small-scale, low-technology resource recovery programs. Plans called for another $6 million to be added to $2 million in oil overcharges and designated for the Local Resource, Reuse and Recovery Program.

Counties and municipalities will be reimbursed up to 75 percent of their start-up administration costs for recycling programs. Additional funds will cover public education programs such as school curricula, educational videos, and advertisements as well as investigations of market strategies.

The state is instructed to provide $7.5 million to counties or multiple townships for assistance in the development of their solid-waste management plans. The Department of Economic Development is directed to use $3.5 million to establish secondary markets for recyclable materials. Any remaining funds must cover the DEC's administrative costs.

Governor Cuomo and major newspaper publishers in the state of New York have established a voluntary agreement whereby publishers will use a total of 11 percent recycled content paper in 1992, 23 percent by 1995, and 40 percent by the year 2000. If newspaper publishers are unable to meet the voluntary goals, it is likely that mandatory legislation will follow.

North Carolina

Senate Bill 111 set a goal of reducing and recycling 25 percent of the state of North Carolina's waste stream by January 1993. Counties and municipalities were directed to start recycling programs by July 1991. In addition to recycling, state agencies must buy products with recycled content and use compost whenever possible. The school board will develop student awareness programs and the Department of Public Instruction will develop a waste reduction and recycling curriculum.

Senate Bill 111 bans detachable metal rings on beverage containers, packaging materials containing fully halogenated chlorofluorocarbons, nonrecyclable poly-styrene, uncoded plastics, and nonrecyclable plastic bags. If less than 25 percent of the plastic bags used in the state are being recycled in 1993, all plastic bags will be banned. The act also prohibits landfilling lead-acid batteries, used oil, yard waste, and white goods.

The bill bestowed new responsibilities on counties and municipalities, and the state Department of the Environment, Health, and Natural Resources (DEHNR). Every county and municipality will develop comprehensive solid-waste management plans, which will be updated biennially. The DEHNR will develop a similar plan for the state, to be updated every 3 years, that includes provisions for technical assistance and public education programs.

The DEHNR, counties, and municipalities will report annually on the status of their waste reduction and recycling programs. In addition to relating recycling activities, their reports will cover the percentages of public participation and waste stream reduction each year. The DEHNR will also report yearly on market development efforts for recyclable commodities.

Oregon

In 1991 the Oregon State Legislature updated its solid waste legislation with Senate Bill No. 66, which was passed ino law. Senate Bill No. 66 sets a goal of 50 percent waste stream reduction by the year 2000. It requires each city over 4000 in population to either:

1. Provide recycling containers to residential service customers by January 1, 1993; weekly curbside collection of source-separated materials on the same day as garbage collection; and expanded educational waste reduction promotional programs, or
2. Provide three of the following eight service elements:
    a. Recycling containers
    b. Weekly same-day residential curbside collection
    c. Expanded education and promotion
    d. Collection of at least four principal recyclable materials from each multi-family housing complex of five or more units
    e. An effective residential yard trimmings collection and composting program
    f. Commercial and institutional recycling of source-separated material at firms employing 10 or more individuals and occupying 1000 ft^2 in a single location
    g. Expanded recycling drop-off facilities
    h. Solid waste residential collection rates that encourage waste reduction, reuse, and recycling through reduced rates for smaller containers, and a rate which does not decrease on a per-pound basis for larger containers, or
3. Provide an alternative method that complies with the rules of the EQC.

Cities over 10,000 in population must either:

1. Provide recycling containers to residential source customers by January 1, 1993; weekly curbside collection of source-separated materials on the same day as garbage service; and an expanded waste reduction education and

promotion program, and implement one other element from (a) through (h), or

2. Implement five elements of (a) through (h), or
3. Implement an alternative method that complies with EQC rules

Senate Bill No. 66 also requires the state highway department to conduct pilot research projects to test feasibility of using scrap tires and recyclable plastics in construction and maintenance projects. The new law also sets up a recycling markets development council which is appointed by the governor. The duties of the council include developing market strategies for each secondary commodity, encouraging uniform recycling definitions, expanding business opportunities, and promoting the purchase of products composed of recovered commodities. The new law also implements landfill bans for vehicles, appliances, used oil, and tires.

Implementation of the market development portion of the bill is funded through the commodity commission assessments described earlier. The collection portion of the bill is funded through a 35 cent per ton increase in the solid waste disposal fee, a 10 cent increase in the solid landfill permit fees, and $144,500 from the general fund.

Pennsylvania

The Recycling and Solid-Waste Management Bill, State Bill 528, was signed in July 1988, making the state of Pennsylvania the fourth state in the United States to adopt mandatory recycling legislation. The state's new recycling act stipulates a recovery goal of 25 percent by 1997.

Municipalities with populations of more than 10,000 must start recycling programs within 3 years, and those with populations from 5000 to 10,000 must start programs within 2 years. At least three materials, as well as leaves, must be separated from household waste for recycling. Municipalities must provide curbside containers, and recyclables must be collected at least monthly. Businesses, municipal offices, hospitals, and schools must separate office paper, aluminum, corrugated paper, and leaf waste.

Some funding will be provided by a disposal surcharge of $2 for each ton of waste taken to municipal landfills and resource recovery facilities. Communities with a landfill or resource recovery facility may additionally charge up to $1 for each ton deposited. Seventy percent of the recycling fund will be allocated to municipalities for developing and starting recycling programs, which covers 90 percent of program startup costs. Up to 10 percent will be spent on feasibility studies for municipal waste processing and disposal facilities. The Department of Environmental Resources will use nearly 30 percent for public education and assistance programs.

The governor has authorized a state program to market recycled goods in connection with the recyclables generated by Senate Bill 528 for mandatory recycling. The state Department of Commerce will administer $5 million in low-interest loans to assist companies involved in recycling. Another $1 million will be available for research and development of recycled products.

The Pennsylvania Energy Office will administer a demonstration grant program to encourage the use of recycled newsprint. Also the Department of Agriculture was assigned the task to examine the use of shredded paper as livestock bedding or in soil-erosion prevention projects. Major daily newspapers within the state have made a voluntary commitment to use at least 50 percent recycled content newsprint on an annual basis by 1995. Laws requiring mandatory recycled content have been put on hold, with the hope that the publishers will reach and surpass their voluntary goal.

The Department of Education will develop a curriculum focusing on recycling and waste reduction. Pennsylvania's marketing program started in September 1990 in the 408 municipalities with populations of 10,000 or more. Communities with populations of 5000 to 10,000 followed with the program 1 year later.

Rhode Island

The state of Rhode Island passed mandatory recycling legislation in 1986 that requires both residential and commercial recycling across the state and a 15 percent reduction of the state's waste stream by January 1991. All 39 municipalities are required to implement recycling collection programs by the end of 1990.

Both the Department of Environmental Management (DEM) and the quasi-governmental Solid Waste Management Corporation (SWMC) have legislative responsibilities for solid waste management in Rhode Island. The DEM is required to provide technical assistance, improve public education programs, and help administer the state's financial aid for municipal recycling.

The SWMC owns the Johnston landfill and MRF, and provides funds to municipalities during the first 3 years of their recycling programs. To raise these funds and to allow for free deposit of residential recyclables at the MRF, the SWMC charges a tipping fee at the landfill of $59/ton for commercial waste and $13/ton for residential waste. Rhode Island legislation mandates the operation of MRFs for the processing of recyclables. The Johnston MRF is operating, and the SWMC has designated operation of the second MRF.

Municipalities are required to dispose of solid waste at SWMC facilities unless they have their own landfills or prior contracts for disposal at other facilities. To enforce recycling, the state randomly inspects loads of waste delivered to the Johnston landfill. Loads containing recyclables above an acceptable percentage are rejected. Fourteen municipalities have mandatory recycling programs, and the recycling rate has already surpassed the state's 15 percent goal.

Rhode Island's most recent solid waste legislation imposes fees on lubricating oil, antifreeze, organic solvents, and tires. In addition, $3 per vehicle will be paid on all new cars. Funds generated from the fees will pay for at least three, and perhaps five, permanent hazardous waste collection sites, to be managed by the DEM. In July 1989, Rhode Island residents began paying a $5 deposit on new lead-acid batteries, refundable when the batteries are returned for recycling. Metal beverage containers with pull tabs are banned, as are plastic food or beverage containers made with more than one resin.

Washington

House Bill 1671, Washington state's recycling legislation passed in May 1989, set a recycling and waste-reduction goal of 50 percent by 1995. The state currently reports a recovery rate of 24 percent. The bill also outlined a preferred waste-management hierarchy that begins with waste reduction and recycling. The second choice is the energy recovery, incineration, or landfilling of separated wastes, and the similar disposal of mixed wastes is last. The goal is source separation of all materials with resource value or environmental hazards.

In their comprehensive solid waste management plans, Washington counties will feature curbside collection in urban areas, drop boxes and buy-back centers in rural areas, and yard-waste collection groups where feasible. Their plans will also cover waste reduction and recycling education programs and market strategies. Counties can add a disposal surcharge to pay the administration and planning costs for compliance with state requirements. Additional funding comes from a 1 percent statewide tax on solid waste collection services.

A $1 fee will be imposed on new tire retail sales for 5 years. The seller keeps 10 percent of the fee to pay for the proper management of waste tires. Ninety percent will go to the state treasury's Vehicle Tire Recycling Account, administered by the Department of Ecology, that grants funding to local governments for certain pilot tire-recycling projects. Legislation also mandated the formation of a recycling markets committee responsible for making new market development recommendations.

The legislation of Washington and other states illustrates how the plans necessitate action and planning by county and municipal governments. An analysis of legislation would not be complete without a look at the ways local governments have chosen to respond.

Wisconsin

The state of Wisconsin's recycling law, Act 335, was signed by Governor Tommy Thomson on April 27, 1990. The act designates "responsible units," a municipality or in some cases a county that has responsibility for local recycling activities. Responsible units are eligible to receive grants from the state and are given the authority and funding to develop, implement, and enforce recycling programs. Responsible units must submit implementation plans by January 1, 1995, and must meet a list of criteria in order to continue to receive state funding. The following illustrates some of the criteria for continued funding: a public education program; recycling services for single-family residences; a requirement that all dwelling units, commercial, industrial, and governmental facilities separate their recyclables or deliver mixed waste to a facility that will recover these materials; a system of volume-based fees to provide revenue and an enforcement program.

An $18.5 million fund, administered by the Department of Natural Resources, provides grants to help with the costs of planning, implementing, and operating recycling programs. The recycling fund consists of revenues from a newspaper recycling fee, imposed on publishers not meeting the recycled content requirement for newsprint, a fee charged to businesses, and appropriations from the general fund.

The first one-third was automatically provided to all municipalities on July 1, 1990. The second and third payments were to go to all responsible units in January and June of 1991. Funds will also be provided for long-term activities, for innovative waste reduction and recycling projects, and for the closure of "nonapproved" landfills.

Market development is addressed through financial assistance to businesses as well as procurement specifications. A total of $8.25 million is provided for grants, startup and expansion loans, loan guarantees, and rebates for businesses, funded from a fee imposed on businesses. An alternative funding mechanism will be introduced after fiscal year 1992–1993. The creation of long-term markets for recyclable materials will be emphasized. The law also requires state and local government agencies to encourage the purchase of recyclable products and to use paper made of at least 40 percent recyclable material by 1995.

Out-of-state waste will be allowed only if the generating community has an effective recycling program. A higher fee will also be charged for out-of-state waste disposed of in Wisconsin after January 1, 1995.

Other requirements include mandatory recycled content legislation for newsprint, mandating a 45 percent recycled content percentage by 2001, a requirement that plastic containers be made of at least 10 percent recycled resin by January 1, 1995, and a requirement that recycled materials be used for highway construction to the maximum amount possible. Also, numerous wastes are banned from disposal: by 1991, lead-acid batteries, appliances, and waste oil; by 1993, yard waste (except Christmas trees); and by 1995, scrap tires, old corrugated containers, newspaper, magazines, office paper, glass containers, foam polystyrene scrap, and metal containers (aluminum, steel, and bimetal). The state of Wisconsin legislation includes the largest list of materials banned from landfilling.

CITIES AND MUNICIPALITIES

Unlike federal and state governments, the local municipality or county has direct responsibility for the garbage generated in its region. Landfill closures, high transportation costs, and NIMBY attitudes affect the locality directly.

Many cities and counties have found that state legislation—and most certainly federal legislation—falls short of the waste reduction and recycling goals that they consider necessary for their areas. Motivated by high disposal costs and grassroots demands, local governments have enacted waste reduction and recycling legislation that often surpasses state goals. The following cities and municipalities are prime examples of local governments taking control of the waste reduction for waste generated by their constituents.

Seattle, Washington

The city of Seattle is committed to recycling 60 percent of its waste stream by 1998. The city's solid waste management plan—titled *On the Road to Recovery*—features an ambitious strategy for reducing and recycling Seattle's solid waste stream.

Seattle's aggressive waste reduction and recycling program evolved in response to the closure of its two landfills and skyrocketing tipping fees. As a result, recycling and waste reduction were quickly thrust into the limelight.

The Seattle Solid Waste Utility contracted two collectors to provide curbside collection to all single- through four-unit residences within the city limits. A total of 153,000 households are eligible for the citywide voluntary curbside collection.

The northern half of Seattle is serviced by Recycle America, which provides weekly service to residences. Three colorful bins are used to source-separate materials. Newspaper, mixed paper, and commingled steel, aluminum, and select plastics are dumped into Recycle America's collection truck compartments. As of June 1990, Recycle America was experiencing an 89 percent participation rate from 65,000 eligible households. In the southern half of the city, residents place recyclable material in a 90-gal toter cart. Rabanco, the Recycle Seattle operator, was able to use its fleet of rear-compactor trucks with minimal modification. Recyclables are collected monthly, and Recycle Seattle was experiencing a 66 percent participation rate as of June 1990.

Seattle's Solid Waste Utility credits the 76 percent citywide participation rate to several factors. Extensive education, preexisting recycling programs, and public enthusiasm accompany a variable garbage can rate. Citizens who recycle their waste benefit from lower garbage collection fees, and the financial incentive reduces garbage generation.

Ordinance 114205 states that yard waste must be separated from garbage. To handle the yard waste, the city has focused on backyard composting, curbside yard waste collection, and a clean green program at transfer stations.

Philadelphia, Pennsylvania

The city of Philadelphia, the second largest city on the eastern seaboard, is struggling to dispose of its waste. Lack of space for landfills and soaring landfill tipping fees provided the incentive to adopt ambitious pieces of recycling legislation.

The city passed Bill 1251-A, mandating a 50 percent recycling level by the end of 1991. The bill calls for the development and establishment of six intermediate processing centers and market development in addition to the development of procurement specifications that give preference to products containing recycled materials. The bill allows for waste composition studies to adjust or verify the goal.

Philadelphia is presently implementing its citywide curbside recycling program, which will serve 1.6 million residents. Participants are asked to separate newspapers, metal containers, PET and HDPE plastics, and glass. Carrying out the ambitious task was delegated to the Philadelphia Recycling Office (PRO). They will be responsible for reeducating 1.6 million people in their daily solid waste handling practices, as well as planning and developing the collection and marketing strategies for the city. Philadelphia's block leader program encourages selected neighborhood blocks to place recyclables at a designated corner. The program encourages participation through friendly peer group pressure and also serves to make the collection process more efficient.

Jersey City, New Jersey

The city of Jersey City is the second largest city in New Jersey with 230,000 residents. Their experience illustrates the difficulty of enforcing mandatory recycling in a diverse urban community.

In 1987, New Jersey passed the Mandatory Source Separation and Recycling Act. This comprehensive legislation mandates residential source separation of leaves and at least three marketable materials such as newspaper, glass, and cans. Jersey City responded to this law by providing a recycling collection system as well as passing ordinance 2241A, which provides police officers, sanitation inspectors, and other authorized personnel with enforcement powers.

The city hired three full-time recycling inspectors to enforce mandatory recycling. Serving as both educators and enforcers, the inspectors are issuing from 200 to 400 warnings a month. They dispense an additional 60 to 100 citations, many of which are in the $500 to $1000 range. Before issuing tickets, the city advertised heavily and sent notices to all residents and businesses. Next, they posted day-glow warning stickers on garbage containers and provided verbal warnings. After several violations, they issue $100 fines. After the third $100 fine, future violations require a court appearance and can carry an additional fine of up to $1000 as well as community service work.

Jersey City chose recycling inspectors as a means to reach New Jersey's 25 percent recycling goal but emphasizes the necessity of public education. Their present participation rate is approximately at the 30 percent level and they predict that it will continue to grow as people become increasingly educated about the program and the potential fines that accompany noncompliance.

Groton, Connecticut

State recycling legislation has resulted in more funding for Groton, Connecticut's recycling program and intermediate processing center. One of the first intermediate processing centers (IPC) in the country and the basis for the state of Connecticut's regional approach to recycling legislation, Groton's IPC has recently received state funding to upgrade its facility. Initiated in 1982, Groton's recycling program serves as an example for other communities in the state of Connecticut. The program is achieving a participation rate of 85 percent and a diversion rate of approximately 10 to 12 percent of the town's waste stream. Currently, newspaper, beverage container, and magazine separation is mandated and collected on a weekly basis by either private or municipal waste haulers, depending on a neighborhood's location. Leaves, cardboard, white office paper, tin cans, scrap metal, used motor oil, lead-acid batteries, and tires are now collected on a regular basis as well. Tires, currently stored, will be used in rubberized asphalt and pyrolysis. Household collection containers were to be distributed to all residents by the spring of 1991.

The majority of program funding for Groton comes from the state's Municipal Solid Waste Recycling Trust Fund of $13 million, a direct benefit of Connecticut's recycling mandate enacted in July 1987. The town was recently awarded a state "demonstration grant" of $18,003 for the purposes of increasing tonnages of recovered materials. Local funds are collected from a $70 disposal charge on nonseparated waste.

Enforcement of Groton's program is handled by the town's recycling inspector. The inspector works with the commercial waste haulers, checks the contents of both what enters the landfill and materials that residents set out at the curb. No tickets have been issued, but dumping privileges have been denied to noncomplying citizens and businesses.

Islip, New York

Ninety-five percent of Islip's 300,000 residents participate in the town's mandatory curbside collection program, diverting 38 percent of municipal solid waste from the landfill. Household collection containers are provided to residents, and recyclables are collected on a weekly basis. Newspaper, cardboard, glass, steel cans, aluminum, mixed paper, HDPE, and PET are commingled in a 32-gal container and separated at Islip's material recovery facility. The program serves 85,000 residences, of both single- and double-family occupancy. Multifamily housing will soon be incorporated into the collection program.

Curbside yard waste collection was begun in the fall of 1989. From then and during 1990, over 55,000 tons have been composted and used by landscapers and residents in the area. Mandatory source-separation legislation was passed in 1980 and has strict enforcement. Inspection officers inspect recyclables from randomly selected households on collection day. In addition, a program of warnings and fines is applied to households not in compliance with the source-separation ordinance, and prizes are awarded to those households that do cooperate. Funding for Islip's program is appropriated from the town's general fund, and the revenue from the sale of recyclable materials.

West Linn, Oregon

Curbside collection of recyclables began in West Linn, Oregon, in August 1983, 3 years before the enactment of the state Recycling Opportunity Act. In an effort to stop the building of a regional waste incinerator in 1983, a citizen task force initiated the recycling program with a goal of recovering 50 percent of the city's waste stream. In 1989, 84 percent of West Linn's population placed recyclables on the curbside weekly, including newspaper, glass, tin cans, aluminum, used motor oil, scrap metal, and cardboard. A yard waste collection program began 1 year later, leading to a 50 percent reduction of yard waste in the waste stream. West Linn recycled about 40 percent of its total waste stream in 1988.

West Linn's program was off to a good start by the time the state legislation took effect in 1986. However, the Recycling Opportunity Act did prompt more promotional activities from the city as it more clearly defined the roles the city and the hauler would take in future recycling activities. The city of West Linn serves as an example for its innovative education and promotion programs in schools, businesses, and residences. School education programs, including classroom presentations and assemblies, have reached every kindergarten through middle school student, and half the high school students in West Linn. Public surveys conducted immediately following a series of school programs showed an additional 12 percent increase in public participation in the city's recycling program. In addition to school programs, informational and "thank you" fliers are distributed to the public at least twice a year, recycling programs appear on cable television, and the city's recycling program is featured in local newspapers regularly.

Enforcement of West Linn's program is minimal. One hauler collects recyclables for the entire population, leaving promotion and administrative responsibilities to the city. Funding for promotional programs and administrative costs is derived from a number of sources. For example, the public is charged $3 to deposit the first cubic yard, and $2 for each additional cubic yard at the city's composting facility of yard waste. The compost material, named "OSCAR" (organic soil conditioning amendment recycled), is sold to the public for $5 a cubic yard. Each household is charged 95¢ per can per month in addition to the regular garbage can rate of $12 per can. Grants have also been provided by the state.

SUMMARY

There are likely to be hundreds of 55-gal drums of ink emptied to produce waste reduction legislation at the federal, state, and local levels in the next few years.

The laws that are currently in place and working effectively will be used as models for the legislation yet to be drafted.

Common to most of the legislation will be regulations requiring state and local participation in waste-paper recycling programs and procurement of recycled paper. Also, because most of the legislation requires education of school children regarding waste reduction, recycling, and composting, most states will eventually have educational programs similar to Michigan's WISE, Rhode Island's OSCAR, and Washington's Waste-Not.

Funding for all this progressive legislation will be critical for program success. Citizens will pay the cost of delivery of services, but the method of payment will vary widely in different states. Advanced disposal fees (product charge) are in vogue, and this strategy can certainly achieve a cradle-to-grave, environmentally sound recovery program, where the user pays the bill. User's fees and surcharges on collection and disposal, or both, will also continue to be a viable option for funding waste reduction services. Traditional municipal bonding methods will be used to fund infrastructure facilities such as material recovery facilities. Some communities will pass the cost along to citizens through normal property taxes by increasing the mil levy. An important component of the economics will be the ability of the municipality to pass back financial savings to taxpayers or ratepayers.

Many states are banning specific materials from landfilling. The prime targets are yard waste, tires, lead-acid batteries, white goods, and demolition wastes. It is likely that through a combination of state and federal legislation these materials and other materials will be banned from landfilling on a national basis.

Some states and cities are attempting to ban unrecoverable materials from the waste stream. This attempt to create a more recoverable "designer" waste stream is being tested in the courts. Regardless of the outcome, one thing is certain: state government will play an active role in creating a more recoverable waste stream.

New recycled fiber content legislation such as that of California and Connecticut, ordering publishers to use recycled newsprint, is inducing voluntary agreements whereby the industry is agreeing to increase its use of recycled fiber. This form of legislation will be replicated in many states and will also be under consideration for other products from glass to napkins to appliances and phonebooks. Wisconsin has passed recycled minimum content standards for plastic, and California has pending legislation for recycled standards for glass.

Design for recycling legislation is likely to appear on a national basis. California is considering legislation that would ban plastic-window envelopes and rubberized labels on advertising mailings, making the product more recyclable. Market development legislation will be of prime importance for the next 10 years to support the feedstock of waste materials diverted from the waste stream to the stream of commerce. State legislators have been reviewing an average of 2000 solid waste bills each year over the past few years. This trend will continue as legislators develop effective waste reduction programs.

Without question, solid waste recycling is becoming the law of the land whereby every citizen will be expected to sort recyclable materials and send them to local processing facilities. State governments, through recent progressive legislation, have demonstrated that solid waste recycling will be a primary strategy for reducing the amount of solid waste disposed. This legislation is producing positive actions at the industry level as waste haulers and end users of recyclable materials develop new strategic plans to collect and process the new volumes of materials that are becoming available as a result of legislative implementation. While market development will be a primary concern throughout the 1990s, state governments have begun to seriously address how to effectively induce markets for recyclable commodities.

As the United States continues to address its solid waste disposal problem, it is likely that legislation at all levels of the government will continue to change the way that Americans view waste disposal. At all levels of society, garbage will be increasingly seen as a resource that the United States can no longer afford to waste.

A summary highlighting specifics of state legislation and sources of legislative information follows.

SUMMARY OF STATE LEGISLATION

California

State of California, Assembly Bill Nos. 4, 1305, 1308, and 939; Senate Bill Nos. 432 and 1221.

Connecticut

Cinnochowski, John, Office of Recycling, Connecticut Department of Environmental Protection, personal communication.

State of Connecticut, Substitute House Bill 5686, Public Act No. 87-544.

State of Connecticut, Substitute House Bill No. 6641, Public Act No. 89-385.

Stoddard, Lynn, Senior Environmental Analyst, Recycling Specialist, Connecticut Department of Environmental Protection, personal communication.

White, Jackie, Recycling Coordinator, Connecticut Department of Environmental Protection, personal communication.

Florida

State of Florida, Conference Committee Report, CS/CS/SB 1192, June 3, 1988.

Indiana

State of Indiana, House Enrolled Act No. 1240.

Louisiana

State of Louisiana, House Bill 1199, Act 185.

Maine

Harris, Jody, Maine Waste Management Agency, personal communication.

State of Maine, HP 1025–LD 1431, Chapter 585, "An Act to Promote Reduction, Recycling and Integrated Management of Solid Waste and Sound Environmental Regulation," July 12, 1989.

Michigan

Clinton, Fred, former Chief of Resource Recovery, Michigan Department of Natural Resources, personal communication.
State of Michigan, Public Acts of 1988 Nos. 411–416, 430.
State of Michigan, Public Acts of 1989 Nos. 63, 138.
State of Michigan, Public Acts of 1990 No. 20.

Minnesota

Waste Reduction and Recycling Legislation, Articles 18–24 of the Special Session Tax Bill.

New Jersey

City of Jersey City, Recycling Master Plan.
Killeen, Thomas, Jersey City Incinerator Authority, personal communication.
Ordinance of Jersey City, N.J., C-652.

New Mexico

State of New Mexico, Senate Bill No. 2, February 1990.

New York

Bedinotti, Del, New York State Department of Environmental Conservation, personal communication.
Domizio, Linda, Public Information Officer, New York State Department of Environmental Quality and Engineering, personal communication.
Howard, Sheri, New York State Department of Environmental Conservation, personal communication.
State of New York, Chapter 70.

North Carolina

State of North Carolina, Senate Bill 111.

Oregon

Department of Environmental Quality Waste Reduction Section, *State of Oregon Recycling Opportunity Act, 1987 Data Report.* March 1989.
Rossel, Dave, Department of Environmental Quality, personal communication.

Spendelow, Peter, Recycling Specialist, Department of Environmental Quality, personal communication.

Pennsylvania

City of Philadelphia, Bill No. 1251-A.

Hursh, Carl, Pennsylvania Department of Environmental Resources, personal communication.

Klein, Tom, Philadelphia Recycling Office, personal communication.

Nolan, Richard, Pennsylvania Department of Environmental Resources, personal communication.

State of Pennsylvania, Senate Bill 528, Act No. 1988-101.

Rhode Island

Boghossian, Tanya, Rhode Island Solid Waste Management Corporation, personal communication.

Brennan, Mary, Division of Recycling, Rhode Island Solid Waste Management Corporation, personal communication.

Marks, Adam, *Overview of Rhode Island Municipal and Commercial Solid Waste Recycling Programs,* Rhode Island Solid Waste Management Corporation, June 22, 1988.

Washington

Seattle Solid Waste Utility, *On the Road to Recovery,* August 1989.

Skumatz, Lisa, Seattle Solid Waste Utility, personal communication.

State of Washington, House Bill No. 1671.

Wisconsin

State of Wisconsin, 1989 Act 335, April 27, 1990.

Federal

CRS Report for Congress, *Solid Waste Disposal Act: Comparison of Reauthorization Bills,* January 1990.

Environmental Protection Agency, "The Solid Waste Dilemma: An Agenda for Action," February 1989.

H.R. 3735 introduced by Rep. Luken.

National Environmental Policy Act, 1970.

Resource Conservation and Recovery Act, 1976.

S.B. 1113 introduced by Sen. Baucus.

APPENDIX A.   MODEL ORDINANCE ESTABLISHING A RECYCLED PRODUCT PROCUREMENT POLICY

Whereas, the volume of material disposed of at the (city/county) landfill(s) has been increasing annually, and

Whereas, sanitary landfill space is at a premium and it is becoming increasingly difficult to site new landfills, and

Whereas, much of the material that enters the waste stream can be recycled, reused or incorporated in the manufacture of new products, and

Whereas, (city/county) participation in and promotion of recycling programs can significantly reduce the volume of material entering the waste stream thereby extending (city/county) landfill life expectancy and reducing expenses, and

Whereas, for recycling programs to be effective, markets must be developed for products that incorporate postconsumer materials in their manufacture, are reusable, or are designed to be recycled, and

Whereas, California State Law requires that local agencies buy recycled products if fitness, quality and price are equal to nonrecycled products and allows local agencies to adopt purchasing preferences for recycled products.

Now therefore be it resolved by the (Council/Board of Supervisors) of the (City/County) of _____ as follows:

That _____ is hereby amended by adding Section _____ to read as follows:

1. Within twelve months subsequent to the effective date of this section, all (city/county) departments, agencies, offices, boards and commissions must conduct a review of existing product and service specifications to determine whether existing specifications either require the use of products manufactured from virgin materials or exclude the use of recycled products, reusable products, or products designed to be recycled.

2. In the event that such specifications do exclude the use of recycled products or require the use of virgin materials, then such exclusions or requirements must be eliminated unless the pertinent department or entity can demonstrate to the satisfaction of the (city manager/chief executive office/etc.) that these recycled products would not achieve a necessary performance standard.

3. Within the same 12 month period, all (city/county) departments and agencies must recommend changes to the (city manager/chief administrative officer/etc.) to ensure that performance standards for particular products can be met and that specifications are not overly stringent, and to recommend changes to ensure that specifications will incorporate a requirement for the use of recycled materials, reusable products, and products designed to be recycled to the maximum extent practicable, subject to an alternative showing that either the performance of the product will be jeopardized or that the product will negatively impact health, safety or operational efficiency.

4. Outside contractors bidding to provide products or services to the (city/county), including printing services, must demonstrate that they will comply with the specifications described in paragraph 3 to the greatest extent feasible.

5. (City/county) staff will work to encourage the copier industry to develop high-speed copiers that will accept recycled paper. In addition, recycled paper shall be purchased and used in all copy machines that will accept it.

6. When recycled products are used, reasonable efforts shall be undertaken to label the products to indicate that they contain recycled materials. (City/county) departments and agencies shall use for their mast-head stationery and envelopes recycled paper that includes postconsumer recycled content and indicate on the paper and envelopes that they contain recycled material. Other recycled products used by the (city/county) shall also indicate that they contain recycled material to the extent practicable.

7. A (10% or greater) price preference may be given to recycled products, reusable products offered as alternatives to disposable products, and products designed to be recycled where they are offered as alternatives to non-recyclable products. The preference percentage shall be based on the lowest bid or price quoted by the supplier or suppliers offering non-recycled products.

8. The (city/county) will cooperate to the greatest extent feasible with neighboring city and county governments in an effort to develop a comprehensive, consistent and effective procurement effort intended to stimulate the market for recycled products, reusable products, and products designed to be recycled.

9. All related (city/county) departments and agencies shall work cooperatively to further the purposes of the ordinance. The (city/county)'s economic development process shall incorporate the goal of stimulating the market for recycled material.

APPENDIX B. INTER-LOCAL AGREEMENT AND GRANT EVALUATION, BROWARD COUNTY, FLORIDA

Inter-Local Agreement between Broward County and the City of for Solid Waste Recycling Coordination

This Inter-local Agreement is being entered into this _____ day of, 1991, by and between Broward County (hereinafter referred to as County) and the City of _____ (hereinafter referred to as Contract Community) for the purpose of regional planning and coordination of solid waste recycling efforts in compliance with the Florida Solid Waste Management Act of 1988 (F.S. Section 403) and application, distribution, and control of state recycling-education grant funds.

Whereas, the State of Florida has passed the Solid Waste Management Act of 1988 requiring County Governments and their Partner Cities to reduce their solid waste stream by 30% by the end of 1994; and,

Whereas, recycling program costs can best be controlled by realizing economies of scale resulting from coordinated planning of programs including public education and recoverable materials marketing; and,

Whereas, it is recognized that it is in the best interest of all communities to have a regional processing facility in place to sort and process co-mingled recyclables that are collected from residential units and the commercial sector; and

Whereas, each community must maintain control of the flow of materials in order to direct recyclables to the best markets; and,

Whereas, a Solid Waste Disposal District headed by the Resource Recovery Board and Technical Advisory Committee has been created to oversee solid waste issues in Broward; and,

Whereas, State grant funding will be made available to the Partner Cities for fiscal years 1992, and 1993 without requirement of matching funds as long as 75% of Broward's municipal population are represented by this agreement; and,

Whereas, any contract community which drops out of this agreement will be required to return all grant funds received from Fiscal Year 1992, and 1993 grant funds thereafter; and

Whereas, it is the expressed commitment of each contract community to make a joint application to DER for grant funds through 1993.

Now therefore, the County and Contract Communities hereto mutually agree as follows:

Section 1. Effective Date and Expiration:

This Agreement shall be effective on July 1, 1991. The agreement shall extend through September 30, 1993 to coincide with the planned expiration date of the Department of Environmental Regulation Recycling and Education Grant Program. This Agreement shall be extended automatically if the Department of Environmental Regulation Grant Program is extended; and may be extended voluntarily upon mutual consent of County and each Contract Community.

Section 2. County Obligations:

County shall be responsible for the grant administrative coordination and support of all recycling programs within its jurisdiction. This responsibility shall include, but not be limited to, the following activities.

1. The County Solid Waste Management Division's Recycling Section will prepare a long range recycling plan which will bring the County and the contract communities into compliance with the State law. This plan will include both residential and commercial recycling programs, new facility construction needs, market development strategies, projected recovered material tonnages, community education activities, and probable funding needs. This plan will be presented to the Technical Advisory Committee for review, comment, and final modification prior to submission to the Resource Recovery Board and subsequent adoption by the County Commission.

2. Continuation of planning and implementation of county-wide public education activities including the BREEZ Campaign, general media advertising, bimonthly Municipal Information Exchange meetings, periodic workshops and recycling events, preparation of public school education activities and events, graphic arts support of Municipal publications, and other related activities.

3. Continuation of Market Development activities including the planning and design of one or more Materials Recovery Facilities capable of accepting comingled recyclables; support of a county-wide Market Development. Subcommittee to advise the Technical Advisory Committee on short term and long term Market-related issues; and continuous monitoring of foreign and domestic markets to assure Broward and its contract communities of the highest paying and most dependable markets.

4. Continuation of grants management activities required to assure that

Broward and its Contract Communities receive their full entitlement of grant funds including: preparation of annual Department of Environmental Regulation Recycling Grant application, preparation of quarterly cost reimbursement requests, preparation of annual Municipal contracts, administrative support of the Grants Review Committee, preparation of Annual Report for Department of Environmental Regulation (and other reports the Department of Environmental Regulation requests), compilation of material recovery reports for both private sector and Municipally controlled recycling programs, and other related activities.

5. Continuation of program development support services for each Contract Community and unincorporated districts to complete implementation of curbside collection programs, to plan and implement multi-family, commercial and industrial recycling programs, to supply information to Municipal leaders on recycling issues, and to perform the necessary administrative actions to advocate on behalf of the Contract Communities within the Broward County Recycling Program Office.

Section 3. Contract Community Obligations:

Contract Community shall be responsible for planning, implementing, and monitoring recycling programs within its community for the purpose of meeting the State Mandated 30% waste reduction goal. These responsibilities will include:

1. Appointing a Contract Community representative and alternate to the Technical Advisory Committee and assuring this representative's active participation in meetings, workshops, Subcommittees, and special projects. The Contract Community representative or alternate shall attend at least 75% of the Technical Advisory Committee and Municipal Information Exchange meetings.

2. Submitting annual Recycling Grant Application to the Grants Review Subcommittee by July 15th of each year. Contract Community agrees to accept the allocation of grant funds as approved annually by the Resource Recovery Board and Broward County Board of Commissioners.

3. Submitting complete and accurate monthly reports on recycling materials collected within the Contract Community's jurisdiction on a standard form provided by the County.

4. Assuring control of the flow of recyclable materials for curbside, multi-family, and commercial collections within the Contract Community's jurisdiction to the fullest extent allowed by ordinance or contract.

5. Promulgating procurement guidelines or policies for municipally purchased products made with recycled content.

6. Reviewing Municipal ordinances or building codes that prohibit or restrict recycling containers or which adversely affect implementation of recycling activities.

7. Reviewing appropriate municipal building codes or specifications for new construction (or major renovations) to specifically require provision of space and containers for recycling and recovered materials collection.

Section 4. Grant Distribution Formula:

County will be allocated approximately 20% of the Recycling and Education Grant funds each year to carry out County obligations described in Section 2; however, the use of the amount allocated to County shall be subject to the approval of the Grant Review Committee, Technical Advisory Committee and Resource Recovery Board. Additionally, County shall supplement grant funds with an amount necessary to provide the personnel, operations, and overhead costs required to carry out the activities specified in Section 2 required to reach the State recycling goals.

The distribution of the remaining approximately 80% of Grant funds will be allocated upon recommendation of the Grant Review Committee.

The Grant Review Committee will be a five (5) person group made up of two representatives from small Contract Communities (less than 50,000 population), two representatives from large Contract Communities (over 50,000 population), and one County representative. The Technical Advisory Committee shall select the representatives to make up the Grant Review Committee.

Each Contract Community will be informed of its share of the grant funds as recommended by the Grant Review Committee. The Contract Community shall have the right of appeal to the Technical Advisory Committee and then to the Resource Recovery Board. Contract Community agrees to accept the recommendation of the Resource Recovery Board when approved by the Broward County Board of County Commissioners for the final allocation of grant funds.

Section 5. Penalty for Default and Termination:

The failure of any party to comply with the provisions of this agreement shall place that party in default. Prior to terminating this agreement, the non defaulting party shall notify the defaulting party in writing. Notification shall make specific reference to the provision giving rise to the default and shall specify a reasonable period of time not less than 30 days for the defaulting party to come into compliance.

If the defaulting party is a Contract Community and, in the event that the defaulting party elects not to cure the default, this agreement shall be terminated and all Recycling and Education Grant funds received by the defaulting party beginning Fiscal Year 1992 and continuing through the period of time of the default shall be returned to County. All such funds returned by the defaulting Contract Community shall by re-allocated by the Technical Advisory Committee (via the Grants Review Committee) to the remaining Contract Communities.

Section 6. Modification:

This agreement may be modified at any time by mutual written consent of the County and the Contract Communities.

Section 7. Indemnification:

Subject to the provisions of Section 768.28, F.S. and to the extent permitted by law, the County and each of the Contract Communities agree to indemnify, save and hold harmless all other party members from any and all liabilities, claims or damages of any kind which are or may be imposed for any of its negligent acts or omissions or the negligent acts or omissions of its officers, employees or agents arising out of or pursuant to this agreement and/or the recycling programs for which these grant funds are sought.

Section 8. Recording:

The County, upon execution of this agreement by all the parties, will record a copy of this agreement in the public records of Broward County Florida.

In witness thereof, the parties hereto have caused this inter-local agreement to be executed for the uses and purposes therein expressed on the day and year first above-written.

COUNTY

ATTEST:

BROWARD COUNTY, through its BOARD OF COUNTY COMMISSIONERS

_____

County Administrator and Ex-Officio Clerk of the Board of County Commissioners of Broward County, Florida County

By_____
               Chair

Approved as to form by Office of the County Attorney for Broward County, Florida JOHN J. COPELAN, JR, County Attorney for Broward County, Governmental Center, Suite 423 115 South Andrews Avenue Ft. Lauderdale, Florida 33301 Telephone: (305) 357-7600

By_____
     Assistant County Attorney

CONTRACT COMMUNITY:

_____
Name of Contract Community

ATTEST:

_____
Clerk

_____
Mayor or Manager

_____ day of _____ , 1991

(Corporate Seal)

Approved as to form:

_____
Attorney

Tentative/Revised Memorandum

TO: Resource Recovery TAC Members

FROM: William "Bill" Duffy, Chairman, Grants Review Committee

DATE: June 11, 1991

SUBJECT: Grant Evaluation for Years 3-4-5

The Grants Review Committee met on June 4, 1991, to review the Grant Evaluation criteria approved by the Technical Advisory Committee (TAC) on February 16, 1990, and proposed the following revisions which provide a more equitable distribution of grant funds:

Priority #1 = 15% of Grant Funds

Priority #2 = 65% of Grant Funds

Priority #3 = 20% of Grant Funds

An explanation of each priority is as follows:

Priority #1—Market Development—Broward County

A. MRF/IPC—Construction of a countywide recycling facility, owned and operated by the County, or a contract vendor, but open for use by all contract communities. This facility would process and market all materials brought in from Interlocal Agreement Contract Community collection programs. An Intermediate Processing Center could be integrated with a front end system at the resource recovery facility.

Priority #2—Collection Programs

A. Unfunded Municipal/and Residential Multi-Material Expansion—All program requests that have *not* been previously funded will be given first priority in this category. Expansion to 100% of all residential multimaterial curbside programs will be given priority.

B. Multifamily—Programs designed to address condominiums with associations greater than 50 units and high rises should be targeted.

C. Commercial—Funding for bars, restaurants, retail stores, malls, schools, and offices (i.e., medical, dental, law, banks, etc.). Funds for this category will be based on quantity of institutions serviced.

D. Yard Waste—Funding will be considered for programs that will provide a large service area (i.e., a program designed to cover 50% of the City is more likely to be funded than a program covering only 10% of the City).

E. Local Education Programs

Distribution of Priority #2 Funds

I. Basic grants will be passed through to eligible large cities and County:

II. The remaining grant dollars for Priority #2 will be divided as follows:

Priority 2a. One Half of the Priority #2 dollars remaining after the distribution of *basic grant pass through funds* will be allocated on a per capita basis (per DER) to municipalities that submit applications meeting all of the following criteria:

Any funds not allocated under this section as a result of the per capita limitation will be added to the amount in Incentive Distribution.

1. Did not receive Basic Grant pass-through funds;

2. Application filed with Recycling Office prior to the stated deadline;

3. Application form complete;

4. No request for operating expenses;

5. Representative attended Recycling Office Grant Workshop;

6. Application meets an element of Priority #2 A through E; and

7. Agreement of governing body of municipality accompanies application supporting the proposed recycling program and acknowledging grant funding will be provided on a reimbursable basis, i.e., no advanced funding.

Incentive Distribution System

Priority 2b. The remaining one half of the Priority #2 dollars will go to municipal or county programs that are *NOT FULLY FUNDED* in Priority #2A and will be allocated on a per capita basis.

To be eligible for Priority #2B funds municipalities and county shall submit applications meeting the following criteria:

1. Application filed with Recycling Office prior to the stated deadline;
2. Application form complete;
3. No request for operating expenses;
4. Representative attended Recycling Grant Workshop;
5. Application meets an element of Priority #2 A through E; and
6. Interlocal Agreement of governing body of municipality accompanies application supporting the proposed recycling program and acknowledging grant funding will be provided on a reimbursable basis, i.e., no advanced funding.

Priority #3—Education—Countywide by Broward County

A. *Mass Media:* Continued development of radio, TV, newspaper, bus, benches, etc., advertising, promotions and similar programs.
B. *School Programs:* Development of lecture series, new character development, skits, and awareness programs.

CHAPTER 3

CHARACTERIZATION OF WASTE STREAMS

David S. Cerrato
Senior Project Manager, Malcolm Pirnie, Inc.
White Plains, New York

OVERVIEW

Why Identify Garbage Contents?

Every man, woman, and child generates garbage. Our businesses, factories, and institutional establishments generate garbage. The question is not whether we will or will not generate garbage, but how much, what kinds, and whether there is any secondary use for solid waste before we decide to bury or burn it.

Figure 3.1 illustrates the steady increase in the solid waste stream in the United States over the past 30 years. As can be seen, annual solid waste generation in the United States has steadily increased from an estimated 82 million tons in 1960 to an estimated 155 million tons in 1990. This averages out to an increase of approximately 2 percent per year over the last 30 years. Our propensity to produce and discard more has put an ever-increasing burden on our society to effectively manage our solid waste stream.

In order to face up to this challenge we need to know what constitutes our solid waste stream. This is the only way we can plan environmentally sound disposal and, more importantly, efficient and effective resource management and recycling programs.

Impact of Characterization Results

Over the past, say, 20 years, a considerable amount of attention has been given to planning for the disposal of the municipal solid waste stream. Our efforts have

Anthony J. DeBenedetto, a research scientist at Malcolm Pirnie, assisted with the compilation and analysis of data contained in this chapter.

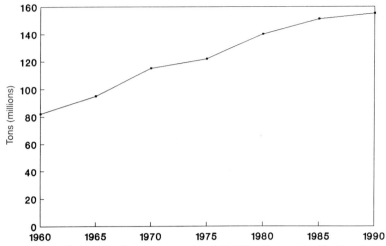

FIGURE 3.1   Estimated solid waste generation 1960–1990. (*Source: Franklin Associates, Ltd.*)

focused primarily on the quantity of solid waste generated and to a lesser extent the compositional breakdown of the solid waste stream.

In the past, solid waste characterization was typically one component of a solid waste quantification study. The major concern focused on quantity and not quality. Through the years, however, an increasing awareness as to the composition of the solid waste has been found to be essential for effective long-term solid waste management. As a result, solid waste characterization continues to be an essential element to adequately assess the feasibility of various disposal technologies.

The quantity and composition of the solid waste stream has a direct impact on the technologies selected for management and disposal. For example, the evaluation of waste-to-energy technologies requires a thorough understanding of the solid waste stream, including its value as a fuel source. The composition of the solid waste stream will ultimately determine its higher heating value as a fuel for generating power. The higher heating value (which is the measurement of the amount of energy released from a fuel, in this case solid waste, when burned) will have a direct effect on, first, the feasibility of a waste-to-energy technology: whether the solid waste will burn; and, second, on the sizing of the waste-to-energy facility: as solid waste burns hotter, its processing rate decreases. As a result, the rate of throughput at a waste-to-energy facility is adjusted based upon the higher heating value of the solid waste stream being processed.

The composition of the solid waste stream is also used to assess the potential environmental impacts associated with its disposal. The old adage is true: *You get out what you put in.* Again, using our waste-to-energy example, knowing the constituents of the solid waste stream to be processed in a waste-to-energy facility allows scientists to determine what chemical compounds and gases are likely to be formed during and after the combustion process. This knowledge then enables engineers to design state-of-the-art air pollution control systems capable of mitigating potential adverse environmental impacts.

have gat
ticular c
and brin
Wher
ample, a
await to
that had
from the
tem, it is
a previo
system
wrote, '
valuable
of the la
their hea
business
kets cap
ernment
The f
agement
be unde
Underst
knowled
require (
waste cl
informat
pable of
sound di

METH(

Develop

Underst
veloping
study ar
study mu
disaggre
ous pacl
Anotl
effective
this case
the amou
disposal
characte
waste g(
analysis
can be s
across w

In the instance of landfill disposal, the composition of the solid waste to be buried has an impact on the assumed in-place density, which in turn affects landfill capacity or landfill life expectancy. The solid waste characterization data are also used to determine what potential chemical compounds are likely to be released in the form of leachate as rain percolates through the landfill. This again enables scientists and engineers to design appropriate leachate collection and treatment systems to mitigate potential adverse environmental impacts.

In the past, solid waste characterization studies tended to be structured to address a limited number of solid waste management issues. The studies typically addressed an overall strategy for waste disposal. Let us call this the *macroapproach*. When conducting a solid waste quantity and characterization study, the macroapproach would typically identify the following solid waste constituents:

Paper and paperboard	Glass
Metals	Plastic
Rubber and leather	Textiles
Wood	Food wastes
Yard wastes	Other wastes
Miscellaneous inorganic wastes	

Although a solid waste composition study must characterize these solid waste constituents at a minimum, it has become essential that a *microapproach* be adopted to analyze each waste constituent by subcomponent. The microapproach identifies solid waste constituents by subcomponent. The microapproach provides information that enables the assessment of various recycling and materials marketing strategies as well as detailed information necessary to plan comprehensive waste management systems. The following is what the breakdown of solid waste subcomponents might look like:

- Paper: newsprint, corrugated, books, magazines, tissue-towels, commercial printed, office paper, packaging
- Glass: container glass (clear, green, amber), other glass
- Metals: aluminum cans, aluminum foil, ferrous, tin
- Plastics: polyethylene tetraphthalate (PET), polystyrene, clear high-density polyethylene (HDPE), colored high density polyethylene (HDPE), polyvinyl chloride (PVC)
- Food wastes
- Rubber
- Leather
- Textiles: fabrics, clothing
- Wood: stumps, pallets, furniture
- Yard wastes: leaves, grass, limbs
- Ceramics
- Construction and demolition debris
- Tires
- Waste oil

- Otl
- Mi:

Relia

Alth(
the r
a lev
of th
plain
    W
and (
subc(
plan
of so
ation
char
desig
timat
nomi

Char

The
ful ir
solid
ysis,
how(
that
prefe
creas
dispc
pure
    Tl
clabl
hom(
true.
mate
held
al's f
deve
and f
    In
wast(
what
ket v
befoi
used
crew

As can be seen by just these few variations, the microapproach must be modified for different scenarios to gather information beyond basic solid waste stream characterization. However, prior to designing the various modifications to the microapproach, there must be a fundamental consistency to the basic approach. Consistency in the solid waste characterization study methods and procedures is an essential element if we are ever to have the capability of comparing and extrapolating solid waste characterization data between various regions and populations across the United States and abroad.

Industry Standards

As discussed earlier, the macroapproach to solid waste characterization is first modified to provide a more detailed understanding of solid waste composition. Understanding that the solid waste stream, once separated by component and subcomponent to the maximum extent possible, allows for more efficient and effective solid waste planning. Making the solid waste characterization study parameters consistent allows the solid waste planner to analyze data obtained from other studies to develop comparisons of regional solid waste characteristics.

The American Society for Testing and Materials (ASTM) considered procedures and methods submitted to them to allow solid waste characterization studies to be undertaken by standard protocol. From these submittals, one protocol in particular has attained some level of industry recognition. The particular protocol is known as ASTM Standards, Draft Number 2, October 21, 1988, "Method for Determination of the Composition of Unprocessed Municipal Solid Waste" (the "Standards"). This method provides proposed procedures for measuring the composition of unprocessed municipal solid waste by employing manual sorting. The proposed procedure allows the user to estimate the mean composition of solid waste based on the collection and manual sorting of solid waste samples over a period of time, usually 1 or 2 weeks. The 1- or 2-week procedures can then be repeated during various periods within a year to obtain seasonal solid waste characterization variations.

Summary of Methods.   The number of samples to be taken and sorted to estimate solid waste composition is calculated based upon statistical criteria discussed later in this chapter. Vehicle loads of waste are designated for sampling or randomly selected, and sorting samples are collected from the various discharged vehicle loads. Each sorting sample is then manually separated into its individual waste components. Consequently, a weight fraction is calculated for each component, and the mean waste composition is determined using the results of the composition analyses from each of the sorting samples.

Described below are a group of terms used within the prepared Standards that will be used throughout this chapter. These definitions have been included in order to provide a better understanding of the language used when describing the methods involved with undertaking a waste characterization analysis.

The proposed Standards define *unprocessed municipal solid waste* as solid waste in its discarded form, or waste that has not undergone size-reduction or processing. Unprocessed municipal solid waste can be divided into *waste components,* consisting of materials of similar physical properties and chemical composition. These categories include ferrous metals, glass, newsprint, yard waste, aluminum, and so forth.

During the waste stream characterization, *sorting samples,* which are approximately 200- to 300-lb portions of a solid waste disposal vehicle load determined to be representative of the entire vehicle load, are taken and manually sorted into the various waste components. In addition, the waste characterization study may also include laboratory analyses of the waste stream. In this case, a sample such as a *composite item,* which could consist of multiple waste constituents contained in the original sorting sample would be analyzed in a laboratory to determine the higher heating value of the waste and chemical makeup of the waste stream.

Once all waste characterization activities are completed, all the data obtained during the course of the study are compiled and analyzed. The data regarding *solid waste composition* are then typically presented in terms of mass fraction or weight percentage.

Calculations. The Standards provide the formulas and calculations necessary to the number of sorting samples needed during a sampling session. The number of sorting samples required to achieve the level of confidence desired so that the samples taken are representative of the entire solid waste stream under consideration is a function of the solid waste constituency. The proposed ASTM equation for determining the number of samples n is

$$n = \left(\frac{t^*s}{e\bar{x}}\right)^2$$

where t^* is the Student t characteristic that corresponds to the desired level of confidence (see Table 3.1), s is the estimated standard deviation, and x is the estimated mean (see Table 3.2). When utilizing this formula, all values should be represented in decimal notation. For example, a precision value e of 20 percent is presented as 0.2. Table 3.2 provides the suggested values of s and x for waste components. Values of t^* are provided in Table 3.1 for 90 and 95 percent levels of confidence. Then, based upon the desired level of precision and confidence, estimate the number of samples n and components using the proposed ASTM equation provided.

Since the required number of samples varies by component, the sample size, that is, the number of samples to be sorted, is controlled by the component from which the total number of samples to be taken was derived. After determining the number of samples n to be taken, return to Table 3.1 and select the Student t statistic t^* that corresponds to n. Then recalculate using the same formula in order to determine the total number of samples to be taken during the solid waste characterization study.

IMPLEMENTING THE STUDY

Introduction

Waste characterization studies are typically undertaken during the first phase of planning for a comprehensive solid waste management plan that may include re-

TABLE 3.1 Values of t Statistics (t^*) as a Function of Number of Samples and Confidence Interval

Number of samples, n	90%	95%
2	6.314	12.706
3	2.920	4.303
4	2.353	3.182
5	2.132	2.776
6	2.015	2.571
7	1.943	2.447
8	1.895	2.365
9	1.860	2.306
10	1.833	2.262
11	1.812	2.228
12	1.796	2.201
13	1.782	2.179
14	1.771	2.160
15	1.761	2.145
16	1.753	2.131
17	1.746	2.120
18	1.740	2.110
19	1.734	2.101
20	1.729	2.093
21	1.725	2.086
22	1.721	2.080
23	1.717	2.074
24	1.714	2.069
25	1.711	2.064
26	1.708	2.060
27	1.706	2.056
28	1.703	2.052
29	1.701	2.048
30	1.699	2.045
31	1.697	2.042
36	1.690	2.030
41	1.684	2.021
46	1.697	2.014
51	1.676	2.009
61	1.671	2.000
71	1.667	1.994
81	1.664	1.990
91	1.662	1.987
101	1.660	1.984
121	1.658	1.980
141	1.656	1.977
161	1.654	1.976
189	1.653	1.973
201	1.653	1.972

Source: Proposed ASTM Standards, Draft Number 2, October 21, 1988.

TABLE 3.2 Values of Mean x and of Standard Deviation s for Within Week Sampling to Determine MSW Component Composition*

Component	Standard deviation, s	Mean, x
Mixed paper	0.05	0.22
Newsprint	0.07	0.10
Corrugated	0.06	0.14
Plastic	0.03	0.09
Yard waste	0.14	0.04
Food waste	0.03	0.10
Wood	0.06	0.06
Other organics	0.06	0.05
Ferrous	0.03	0.05
Aluminum	0.004	0.01
Glass	0.05	0.08
Other inorganics	0.03	0.06
		1.00

*The tabulated mean values and standard deviations are estimates based on field test data reported for municipal solid waste sampled during weekly sampling periods at several locations around the United States.

Source: Proposed ASTM Standards, Draft Number 2, October 21, 1988.

source recovery, various recycling, and other processing and disposal systems. Before the actual field studies are undertaken, background information is required in order to adequately design the program methodology. To achieve a complete understanding of the waste stream, the implementing agency must determine how much waste is being generated, where it is coming from, and what it is made up of in general terms.

The solid waste characterization study must subdivide the solid waste stream into microcomponents, for example, plastics should be further separated into PET, HDPE, PVC, and mixed other plastics, if it is going to provide the information necessary for effective solid waste planning. In order to evaluate the potential for source reduction, the waste stream is broken down into specific and indirect waste products. As a means of reducing waste generation, particular attention is given to the waste stream, that is, packaging, advertisements, labels, and so on. Sampling programs must also provide for both seasonal and geographical fluctuations in the quantity and composition of waste types.

Additionally, waste composition programs must provide information on waste flow by specific generator types, enabling the agency undertaking the solid waste characterization study to target specific generators for recycling programs to increase the agency's potential for success. Developing the solid waste characterization study specific to program needs will save a significant amount of time and money and can help to assure an accurate accounting of the entire solid waste stream.

Presampling Activities

The importance of planning prior to initiating a solid waste characterization study cannot be overstressed. No matter how much time is spent planning from an office, without a full understanding of study objectives and knowledge of facility operations at the site where the field work is going to take place prior to initiating the solid waste characterization study, there is the potential risk of incorrectly designing the program methodology.

As previously discussed, understanding the full range of informational needs to meet study objectives is essential to developing the solid waste characterization study methodology. A solid waste characterization study that includes, for example, 4 weeks of sampling, one in each season of the year to capture seasonal variations, and complete laboratory testing is an expensive undertaking for any municipality. Such studies can range in cost from $300,000 to $700,000, depending on the level of detail required, number of sites for sampling, and so on. Since the majority of the study costs relate directly to the field work, it is critical that all informational needs be identified prior to initiating the solid waste characterization study. All study objectives must be clearly defined. Every effort must be made during the field sampling activities to acquire all essential data. Any data needs not adequately addressed could result in repeating field efforts. Repetition of any portion of the field effort will ultimately have a considerable impact on study costs.

To help eliminate the possibility of not addressing the full complement of study needs, the project team should at a minimum:

- Define the study area
- Review socioeconomic data within the study area
- Develop a list of all private and public waste haulers operating in the study area
- Contact all of the haulers identified and discuss the solid waste characterization study
- Visit each disposal location whether sampling is to take place there or not
- Review previous solid waste plans and recycling programs
- Analyze quantities and composition of recyclables removed from the waste stream prior to disposal
- Schedule the sampling periods to address possible seasonal and cyclical variations that may impact waste generation

Once the project team has clearly defined the study parameters, the solid waste characterization study, including these presampling activities, can begin.

Waste Categories. The next step following the presampling activities discussed in Section 3.2 is to define the waste categories to be sampled. A sample list of waste components for sorting is shown in Table 3.3. A description of some of the waste component categories provided in Table 3.1 is given in Table 3.4. Other waste components can also be defined and sorted as needed. Table 3.3 includes those components most commonly used to define and report the composition of solid waste. For consistency, it is recommended that, at least, the left-justified categories in Table 3.3 be sorted. Similar breakdowns of solid waste composition would thus be available for comparison, if desired.

Inspecting the Site. To make sure that the solid waste characterization study will generate the information required and present a statistically reliable

TABLE 3.3 List of Waste Component Categories

Mixed paper	Other organics
High-grade paper:	Ferrous:
Computer printout	Cans
Other office paper	Other ferrous
Newsprint	Aluminum:
Corrugated	Cans
Plastic:	Foil
PET bottles*	Other aluminum
HDPE bottles†	Glass:
Film	Clear
Other plastic	Brown
Yard waste	Green
Food waste	Other inorganics
Wood	

*PET = polyethylene tetroputhalate.
†HDPE = high-density polyethylene.

TABLE 3.4 Description of Some Waste Component Categories

Category	Description
Mixed paper	Office paper, computer paper, magazines, glossy paper, waxed paper, other paper not fitting categories of "newsprint" and "corrugated."
Newsprint	Newspaper.
Corrugated	Corrugated medium, corrugated boxes or cartons, brown paper (i.e., corrugated) bags.
Plastic	All plastics.
Yard waste	Branches, twigs, leaves, grass, other plant material.
Food waste	All food waste except bones.
Wood	Lumber, wood products.
Other organics and combustibles	Textiles, rubber, leather, other primarily burnable materials not included in the above component categories.
Ferrous	Iron, steel, tin cans, bimetal cans.
Aluminum	Aluminum, aluminum cans, aluminum foil.
Glass	All Glass.
Other inorganics and noncombustibles	Rock, sand, dirt, ceramics, plaster, nonferrous nonaluminum metals (copper, brass, etc.), bones.

breakdown of the solid waste stream, those persons who will actually be involved with the field work should visit and tour each of the sites with the operators of the involved facilities. It should take no longer than 3 to 5 days to acquire the information necessary prior to starting the actual solid waste sampling program. During these site visits, staff should also examine the physical aspects of the study area and obtain information regarding the following:

- Identification and quantification of incoming waste
- Identification and quantification of all types of incoming waste routes, schedules and delivery information
- Private hauler information
- Facility operating procedure
- Utilities accessibility, e.g., electricity, water
- Identification of primary and secondary sampling areas

The information obtained will be used to refine and finalize the sampling procedures. It will enable easy access to vehicles to be sampled and allow for operations to take place as safely and efficiently as possible. This extra planning effort minimizes potential problems in the field, facilitates vehicle identification, familiarizes field staff with vehicle schedules, and involves facility operators and inspectors. The information obtained will be extremely valuable to field staff during the actual study.

The cooperation of the owner and operator of the solid waste management facility where the solid waste sampling will take place is critical to the success of the solid waste characterization study. All parties involved both directly and indirectly must understand the objectives, the procedure to be used, and data needs. In addition, private haulers utilizing the disposal location where the solid waste sampling is to take place must be contacted to obtain cooperation. It is recommended that private haulers and site operators be sent written confirmation of these discussions to ensure cooperation prior to initiating the field work. This information should include

- Waste sampling schedules
- Proposed methods and procedures that may affect operations
- Draft questionnaire to be used to obtain data from operators and facility users
- Weighing procedures
- Location of weighing and sorting areas
- Overall management of sorted solid waste

Crew Size.   The size of the field sampling crew is governed by the scope of the solid waste characterization study, the amount of total incoming waste at the sampling location, and the recommended number of samples to be sorted. A composition study that involves only a waste characterization by component analysis usually will require approximately four to six sorters as well as one supervisor who functions as the scale operator and data recorder. If the solid waste characterization study includes visual inspections of incoming waste loads, commercial and industrial waste assessments, and hauler interviews, additional staff will be required. Each added activity may require up to an additional two staff persons. Actual staffing, however, is usually suggested by the agency proposing the study prior to actually staffing. The estimated staffing requirements presented here are provided as a guide to allow that sufficient personnel are available on site. It is recommended, however, that the study sponsor discuss personnel and staffing with the study performer prior to the commencement of the field work. This will enable the sponsor to modify or supplement staffing in a manner that may reduce the solid waste characterization study costs.

Field Safety Plan.   The field safety plan is an important part of the field sampling program. Sorters manually picking through mixed municipal solid waste may encounter potentially hazardous conditions. In order to minimize the risks associated with waste sorting, a field sorter safety plan should be developed. This safety plan should include, at a minimum, the following:

- Standard operating procedures and precautions
- Identification of required protective equipment
- General first aid procedures
- Procedures in the event hazardous waste is encountered
- Emergency procedures

Prior to the initiation of site activities, the precautions and procedures for the study should be reviewed with operating and sorting personnel. It should be remembered that solid waste is likely to contain sharp objects such as nails, razor blades, and pieces of glass. It may also include hypodermic needles, poisonous sprays, punctured aerosol cans, and so forth. Personnel should be reminded of this danger and instructed to brush waste particles aside while sorting, as opposed to forcefully projecting their hands into the mixture. Personnel handling and sorting solid waste should wear appropriate protection, including heavy leather or rubber (puncture-proof) gloves, hardhats, safety glasses, and heavy duty footgear with steel toes.

During the process of collecting samples for sorting, large machinery will be involved. This may include refuse collection vehicles, payloaders, dumptrucks, and so forth. The dumping process can scatter refuse, create dust, and throw waste products into the air. Such projectiles can include flying glass particles from breaking glass containers and metal lids from plastic and metal containers that burst under pressure when run over by heavy equipment. The problem is particularly acute when the waste handling surface is of high compressive strength, e.g., concrete. Field personnel should be made aware of the danger and wear eye and head protection. Additionally, personnel should be instructed to refrain from looking in the direction of unloading vehicles or of heavy equipment that is in the process of moving or placing solid waste. Field personnel must also be dressed appropriately in heavy-duty clothing and vests with iridescent markings. Safety lights should also be used around the sorting area.

Apparatus. Sufficient metal, plastic, or fiber containers for sorting and weighing each waste component, labeled accordingly, should be acquired for use throughout the solid waste sampling study. For components that will have a substantial moisture content (e.g., food waste), metal or plastic containers should be used to avoid absorption of moisture by the containers, and thus preclude numerous weighings to maintain an accurate tare weight for the container. Storage containers should be weighed at the beginning of each day, or more frequently if necessary, in order to maintain accurate tare weights. An electronic scale with a capacity of at least 200 lb, and a precision of at least 0.1 lb, should be used. These scales should be calibrated daily according to manufacturer's specifications. Table-top scales should be positioned on a clean, flat, and level surface. Portable truck scales may also be employed when the sampling site is not equipped with a truck scale to determine arriving quantities of waste as well as a method to calculate waste density.

Sorting personnel should be equipped with heavy-duty tarps, shovels, rakes, push brooms, dust pans, hand brooms, magnets, a sorting table, first aid kit, miscellaneous small hand tools, traffic cones, traffic safety vests, puncture-proof gloves, hardhats, safety glasses, and heavy-duty steel-toed boots.

The area and location selected for performing designated manual sorting activities and weighing operations should be flat, level, and distinctly set away from the normal waste handling and processing areas at the study site. The surface should be swept clean or covered with a clean, durable tarp prior to discharge of the load. A sample layout of a typical sorting area is presented as Fig. 3.2.

Solid Waste Samples for Manual Sorting. As previously discussed, the number of samples to be sorted is calculated based upon a statistical formula. The methods and procedures described here summarize the ASTM proposed procedures.

Sorting samples are collected from normal refuse collection vehicles. A refuse collection vehicle could be carrying an 8- to 10-ton load. Therefore, a solid waste sample must be drawn from that load which is representative of the entire load. The sorting sample is then manually sorted into its waste components and weight fractions calculated for each component. The mean waste composition can be calculated later using the results of the composition of each of the sorting samples.

Vehicles for sampling can be selected at random during each day of the sampling period or can be preselected to provide a solid waste mix from varying socioeconomic strata within a regional jurisdiction. This decision is made during the presampling activities. For a weekly sampling period of x days, the number of vehicles sampled each day shall be approximately n/x, where n is the total number of vehicle loads to be selected for estimating waste composition. A weekly period can vary from 5 to 7 days.

Vehicles designated for sampling are directed to the area set aside for discharge of the load and collection of the sorting sample. The vehicle operator is instructed to discharge the load onto the clean surface in one continuous pile, that is, to avoid gaps in the discharged load. Information from the vehicle operator regarding the waste load is also collected at this time, prior to the vehicle leaving the discharge area. Once the vehicle has discharged its waste at the designated area, it is necessary to remove a manageable portion of the load that is

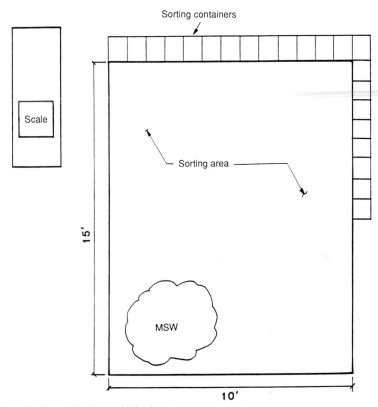

FIGURE 3.2 Sorting activities layout.

representative of the entire vehicle load. There are basically two procedures that can be employed to accomplish this.

The first method requires using a payloader. The operator of the payloader uses the bucket of the payloader to thoroughly mix the entire vehicle waste load and levels it off into one continuous pile. Then the operator, once again using the bucket of the payloader, removes approximately one-fourth of the vehicle's load and places it away from the remainder of the discharged waste load. Again, the removed portion is mixed and one-quarter is separated. This procedure is repeated until the remaining quarter is approximately 200 to 300 lb. This final waste sample is then hand-sorted into its waste constituents.

The second method also requires a payloader and operator. In this instance, however, rather than mixing the entire vehicle's discharged waste load before removing a sample, the sample is removed longitudinally along one entire side of the discharged load. The sample should form a mass weighing approximately 1000 lb. The sample is then thoroughly mixed and one-quarter of it is selected to be manually sorted. This method is less time consuming and the results are consistent with those of the first method described.

Only one sorting sample can be selected from each designated collection vehicle load. All handling and manipulation should be conducted on clean surfaces.

If necessary, the sorting sample should be removed to a secured manual sorting area. Waste material not selected for manual sorting should be removed from the area as soon as possible and disposed of.

Manual Sorting Procedures

To prepare a sort area, a tarp or a sheet of plastic is placed on a level area near the discharge location. The tarp or plastic sheet is surrounded (and held down) by the containers used to hold the sorted materials. The number of containers should be in approximate proportion to the expected waste composition. Corrugated cardboard may be too bulky to place in the containers, so a separate area should be identified for corrugated storage. The containers should be located around the sorting area so that, where possible, containers for the same component are located on opposite sides of the sample pile to provide easy access for the sorting crew. A sorting table can be used for the manual sorting process. A table makes the sorting process easier for the field crew members and enables the identification of fine materials that may be lost if sorting were to take place on the floor. Tables can also be designed to include cut-outs where screens of various sizes can be used to allow fine materials to fall through into containers for later evaluation.

The sort containers are weighed empty to obtain tare weights. The containers are labeled or numbered and the tare weights clearly marked on each container. The tare weight corresponding to each container label or number is recorded for future reference. The containers should be cleaned periodically to ensure a consistent and accurate tare weight.

To begin the sorting operation, the first portion of a sample is brought to the sorting area and dumped onto the main sorting table. The crew members begin sorting the sample by hand. The crew supervisor oversees the operation, checking each container for separation quality and assists in classifying questionable items. When about 90 percent of the first portion of the sample has been sorted, another portion of the same sample is dumped on top of the first portion and the sorting continues.

All components are sorted manually. After the entire sample has been sorted, the fines on the sort table are dumped into a container. The table is removed and the sheet is picked up at the corners and the contents are examined and placed into the appropriate containers.

The plastic sheet is then cleaned and placed back on the ground. The filled containers are weighed, and the gross weights recorded. The containers are emptied and placed in their appropriate locations for the next round of sorting.

Sample selection and sorting in this manner can be performed in approximately one hour. Time reductions can be achieved when

- The next sample to be sorted is being selected while the previous sample is being sorted.
- Multiple sorting areas are provided adjacent to one another and additional staff are provided.

When the sorting of one sample is completed and all data compiled, additional comments on the characteristics of the material may need to be recorded following visual analysis. For example, the approximate percentage of sheet stock and castings might be noted for the aluminum fraction. Similarly, a higher than normal moisture content in the newsprint or aluminum categories should be noted as well as weather conditions. The results of the survey, however, should be recorded with no adjustments for moisture characteristics, and so on.

Laboratory Analyses

If the solid waste characterization study includes an analytical assessment of the compounds found in the solid waste during sorting activities represented by the samples taken, the assistance of a certified laboratory will be required. The laboratory selected to perform the tests should be qualified to do so and should submit a full protocol prior to beginning any testing. Typically, the following tests are required:

- *Heating value:* Heating value is usually expressed in British thermal units per pound (Btu/lb) of waste and is a measure of the waste's energy content available through burning it.
- *Proximate analysis:* the determination of total moisture content, volatile matter, fixed carbon, and ash content.
- *Ultimate analysis:* includes the determination of ash, carbon, hydrogen, sulfur, oxygen, nitrogen, and chlorine in the waste.
- *Elemental analysis:* a broad category including the determination of parameters such as acidity, herbicides, asbestos, and dioxin.

The laboratory will be required to handle samples weighing between 10 and 20 lb, be able to grind and thoroughly mix the samples without contamination, and to conduct the analytical testing.

Samples are selected for laboratory analysis by either reconstructing those samples taken in the field in proportion (percent weight) to the original sample weight or by repeating a similar exercise to that of the quartering method where the 200- to 300-lb sample is placed in a conical pile and shaved until a 20- to 25-lb sample remains. Grab sampling is inappropriate because of the statistical unreliability of the data. Each sample taken in the field or a daily composite sample of all samples taken on a particular day for each generator segment (residential, commercial, etc.) is sent to the laboratory for testing. Proximate and ultimate analyses of the samples are conducted in accordance with ASME, ASTM Committee E-38 Standards and Procedures.

- *Proximate analysis:* total moisture, ash (including percent by volume), volatiles, fixed carbon, heating value (Btu/lb on an as-received and moisture-free basis)
- *Ultimate analysis:* ash, carbon, hydrogen, nitrogen, oxygen, sulfur

Incoming Solid Waste Survey

As part of the solid waste characterization study, it is important to quantify all incoming solid waste to the facility from which the sampling is taking place. Data should be collected related to all incoming waste quantities. Sufficient personnel should be made available to staff the solid waste facility scalehouse to collect information on waste quantity. Every incoming truck (to the extent possible) will be studied, weighed, and the driver surveyed. The drivers are queried as to the type of waste carried (commercial, residential, mixed, etc.), the area where the waste was collected, the type of establishment where the waste was generated, and percentage of the vehicle full. In addition, drivers of mixed loads are asked to estimate the percentage breakdown of the load by waste type.

The amount of waste entering the solid waste disposal facility is quantified according to its point of origin and generator segment (e.g., residential, commercial, or industrial). Additionally, every vehicle will be quantified as to its weight or volume and density. The quantity data for solid waste generated within the study area shall be defined within the following framework:

• Quantity of waste types by geographic points (origin).

• Specific route information, if available.

• Weight or volume and corresponding density characteristics expressed in terms of daily, average, peak, and minimum flow to the solid waste facility for the seasonal sampling in question and for the year as a whole.

• The total quantity of waste for the region, by type, shall be clearly depicted in the results. Weight, volume, and corresponding density characteristics expressed in terms of regional daily, average, peak, and minimum flow for seasonal periods and for the year as a whole.

Visual Inspection

Although not as reliable as the solid waste sorting process, a visual inspection of incoming solid waste is a recommended addition to any solid waste characterization study. The purpose of the visual inspection is to visually characterize by component all incoming solid waste. This effort allows for a complete understanding of the general characteristics of all solid waste being disposed of in the study area.

Sufficient personnel should be available to visually inspect all incoming waste loads. The waste inspectors are responsible for analyzing the waste to estimate its composition. This information will ultimately be cross-referenced with information obtained by the scalehouse data collectors to enhance overall data reliability.

During a visual waste inspection, two phases of study are undertaken. The first phase is a hauler interview and the second is a waste characterization. A hauler interview consists of a series of short-answer questions which are used to develop a "history" or background information on a particular delivery of waste. Some of the questions include inquiries as to where the waste was collected, from what types of establishments, the types of waste composing the load, and the capacity of the vehicle utilized. The waste characterization consists of disaggregating the waste by component. Following the hauler interview, the vehicle is observed during its normal discharging cycle. Once the vehicle discharges its load, staff estimates the composition of the waste. The compositional analysis here is not as detailed as the sorting analysis, but it can provide valuable information as to its general characteristics. The solid waste can be characterized by percent as residential, commercial, industrial, and so forth, and can provide insight as to the general character of the solid waste stream as a whole. The two phases serve to complement each other where each is used to justify or qualify the other.

Samples of the types of survey forms used during a visual waste inspection for both a hauler/scalehouse interview and waste assessment are included as Figs. 3.3 through 3.7.

Seasonal Variations

Quantities of waste delivered to a disposal site can vary by the hour, day of the week, week of the month, month of the year, seasonally, and annually. As a result, fluctuations in the solid waste stream may occur over a period of time. Typically the solid waste characterization study analyzes variations on a seasonal basis. Seasonal estimates usually require four separate week-long programs (winter, spring, summer, fall) at each site. The week-long programs are considered a minimum and also provide estimates of variations with the day of the week.

Although a 4-week program (one sampling in each of the four seasons of the year) is the most preferred approach, it is usually possible to assess significant seasonal variations by conducting the solid waste characterization study in two of the four seasons, for example, winter and summer. Notwithstanding, it is essential that when scheduling the weeks of sampling that specific regional characteristics are considered. For example, certain industries may manufacture specific goods and services during certain times of the year. Their processes may have a considerable impact on the overall solid waste stream being generated during certain times of the year. Therefore, it is necessary that the solid waste characterization study coincide with their production schedules. Additionally, certain regions experience increased tourism during one or more seasons of the year that effect solid waste generation from both a quantity and quality standpoint. The solid waste characterization study must assess these associated impacts to solid waste generation.

With respect to solid waste quantities, seasonal variations in waste quantity are estimated from site records and waste stream assessment data. In order to better understand how seasonal variation has an effect on the waste stream, Table 3.5 has been provided and presents a summary of seasonal variation data obtained during several waste composition studies. As can be seen in Table 3.5, subtle changes can be noticed between seasons for certain materials; that is, newsprint, corrugated, plastics, and other wastes show greater variation than other paper, ferrous metals, aluminum, and glass between the seasons.

Geographical Variations

The composition of solid waste varies dramatically with respect to geography. Waste composition can vary from city to city, county to county, state to state, country to country, and even continent to continent. These differences could be due in whole or in part to any of the following factors: economics, population, proximity to collection, or political and social factors.

Table 3.6 provides a summary of seasonal variation data compiled from waste composition studies conducted in four regions of the United States.

INTERVIEW SURVEY FORM

Date:

MPI Personnel:

Vehicle I.D. (permit sticker):

Carter:

Vehicle Type (Circle One):   PACKER   ROLL-OFF   TRANSFER   TRAILER   OTHER (Specify)

Vehicle Capacity (Cubic Yards):

Vehicle Capacity Utilized (%):

Net Weight (Pounds/Tons):

Waste Type (Circle Applicable):   RESIDENTIAL   COMMERCIAL/LIGHT   INDUSTRIAL   OTHER (Specify)

Percent of Total Load: RESIDENTIAL _____   COMMERCIAL/LIGHT INDUSTRIAL _____   OTHER _____

Waste Origin:	Municipality	Percent of Total Load	Percent Residential	Percent Commercial/Light Industrial
1.				_____
2.				
3.				
		100%	100%	100%

How much waste originates from apartment complexes?

Vehicle Destination (Circle One):   LANDFILL   SHREDDER

FIGURE 3.3   Survey form—equipment visual inspection.

SHREDDER/LANDFILL SURVEY FORM

Date:

MPI Personnel:

Vehicle I.D. (permit sticker):

Carter:

Vehicle Type (Circle One): PACKER ROLL-OFF TRANSFER TRAILER OTHER (specify)

Vehicle Capacity (Cubic Yards):

Percent of Total Load
_____

Waste Characterization: RESIDENTIAL

COMMERCIAL/LIGHT INDUSTRIAL

OTHER (Specify)
_____
100%

Processable vs. Unprocessable: Percent of Total Load
_____

PROCESSABLE

UNPROCESSABLE
_____
100%

FIGURE 3.4 Survey form—equipment visual inspection.

Residential waste analysis

MPI Personnel:

Hauler Name:

Vehicle Type (Circle One): Packer Roll-Off Transfer Trailer Other (Specify)

Waste Stream Analysis:

Component	Quantity, % (Circle One)																			
Paper	5	10	15	20	25	30	35	40	45	50	55	60	65	70	75	80	85	90	95	100
Bagged Household	5	10	15	20	25	30	35	40	45	50	55	60	65	70	75	80	85	90	95	100
Corrugated	5	10	15	20	25	30	35	40	45	50	55	60	65	70	75	80	85	90	95	100
Metals	5	10	15	20	25	30	35	40	45	50	55	60	65	70	75	80	85	90	95	100
Glass	5	10	15	20	25	30	35	40	45	50	55	60	65	70	75	80	85	90	95	100
Plastic	5	10	15	20	25	30	35	40	45	50	55	60	65	70	75	80	85	90	95	100
Wood	5	10	15	20	25	30	35	40	45	50	55	60	65	70	75	80	85	90	95	100
Yard waste	5	10	15	20	25	30	35	40	45	50	55	60	65	70	75	80	85	90	95	100
Tires/rubber	5	10	15	20	25	30	35	40	45	50	55	60	65	70	75	80	85	90	95	100
Brick/concrete	5	10	15	20	25	30	35	40	45	50	55	60	65	70	75	80	85	90	95	100
Dirt/fines	5	10	15	20	25	30	35	40	45	50	55	60	65	70	75	80	85	90	95	100
Textiles	5	10	15	20	25	30	35	40	45	50	55	60	65	70	75	80	85	90	95	100

FIGURE 3.5 Form—data collection, residential waste.

Landfill Survey Form

Date: _____ Hauler Name: _____ Vehicle I.D.: _____

Vehicle Type (Circle One): PACKER   ROLL-OFF   TRANSFER TRAILER   OTHER (Specify): _____

Vehicle Capacity: _____ Vehicle Capacity Utilized (%): _____

Waste type (Circle Applicable): RESIDENTIAL   COMMERCIAL   INDUSTRIAL   OTHER (Specify): _____

Percent of Total Load: RESIDENTIAL _____ COMMERCIAL _____ INDUSTRIAL _____ OTHER _____

Waste Origin:

Municipality		% of Total Load				Residential (%)			Commercial (%)		Industrial (%)		Other (%)

1.
2.
3.
4.
5.

Waste Stream Analysis:

Component	Quantity, % (Circle One)																			
Paper	5	10	15	20	25	30	35	40	45	50	55	60	65	70	75	80	85	90	95	100
Bagged household	5	10	15	20	25	30	35	40	45	50	55	60	65	70	75	80	85	90	95	100
Corrugated	5	10	15	20	25	30	35	40	45	50	55	60	65	70	75	80	85	90	95	100
Metals	5	10	15	20	25	30	35	40	45	50	55	60	65	70	75	80	85	90	95	100
Glass	5	10	15	20	25	30	35	40	45	50	55	60	65	70	75	80	85	90	95	100
Plastic	5	10	15	20	25	30	35	40	45	50	55	60	65	70	75	80	85	90	95	100
Wood	5	10	15	20	25	30	35	40	45	50	55	60	65	70	75	80	85	90	95	100
Yard waste	5	10	15	20	25	30	35	40	45	50	55	60	65	70	75	80	85	90	95	100
Tires/rubber	5	10	15	20	25	30	35	40	45	50	55	60	65	70	75	80	85	90	95	100
Brick/concrete	5	10	15	20	25	30	35	40	45	50	55	60	65	70	75	80	85	90	95	100
Textiles	5	10	15	20	25	30	35	40	45	50	55	60	65	70	75	80	85	90	95	100
Carcasses	5	10	15	20	25	30	35	40	45	50	55	60	65	70	75	80	85	90	95	100
Coal mine waste	5	10	15	20	25	30	35	40	45	50	55	60	65	70	75	80	85	90	95	100
Sludge	5	10	15	20	25	30	35	40	45	50	55	60	65	70	75	80	85	90	95	100

FIGURE 3.6 Form—date collection, landfill survey.

Field Waste Study

MPI Personnel:

Name of Business:

Type of Business:

Waste Stream Analysis:

Component	Quantity, % (Circle One)																			
Paper	5	10	15	20	25	30	35	40	45	50	55	60	65	70	75	80	85	90	95	100
Corrugated	5	10	15	20	25	30	35	40	45	50	55	60	65	70	75	80	85	90	95	100
Metals	5	10	15	20	25	30	35	40	45	50	55	60	65	70	75	80	85	90	95	100
Glass	5	10	15	20	25	30	35	40	45	50	55	60	65	70	75	80	85	90	95	100
Plastic	5	10	15	20	25	30	35	40	45	50	55	60	65	70	75	80	85	90	95	100
Wood	5	10	15	20	25	30	35	40	45	50	55	60	65	70	75	80	85	90	95	100
Textiles	5	10	15	20	25	30	35	40	45	50	55	60	65	70	75	80	85	90	95	100
Others	5	10	15	20	25	30	35	40	45	50	55	60	65	70	75	80	85	90	95	100

FIGURE 3.7 Form—data collection, field waste study.

TABLE 3.5 Seasonal Variation and Waste Composition

	Winter, %	Summer, %
Newsprint	5–10	8–12
Corrugated	5–10	8–12
Other paper	35–40	32–36
Plastics	8–12	10–15
Ferrous metals	3–6	2–6
Aluminum	<1	<1
Glass	5–10	8–12
Other wastes	25–30	18–30

TABLE 3.6 Geography and Waste Composition in the United States

	Northeast, %	Southeast, %	Midwest, %	West, %
Newsprint	8–10	8–12	5–8	2–12
Corrugated	9–12	8–12	5–12	5–15
Other paper	22–32	30–35	20–25	15–25
Plastics	7–10	5–10	5–10	6–10
Yard waste	10–17	3–7	9–13	2–12
Ferrous metals	2–6	1–5	3–6	5–8
Aluminum	1–3	1–5	<1	<1
Glass	6–12	5–8	2–6	2–8
Other wastes	18–23	20–25	5–15	5–10

Commercial vs. Residential

In order to develop a comprehensive understanding of the total waste stream, the waste is often segmented according to residential and commercial-industrial generators. Therefore, it is necessary to sample a representative number of each of these waste generators. Since solid waste is delivered in open as well as closed refuse vehicles, a sampling, either physical or visual, of a representative number of both types of vehicles should be undertaken.

It should be understood that the composition of the residential and commercial waste streams can vary dramatically. In Table 3.7, a comparison between the commercial and residential waste streams of a typical suburban population is presented. As can be seen in Table 3.7, the amount of some waste constituents (e.g., corrugated) can differ significantly in composition between the residential and commercial waste streams.

In addition, the subcomponents of each of the waste types tend to differ between the residential and commercial sectors. For instance, the paper category in the residential sector consists of newsprint, tissue, paper towels, and other types of paper which are discarded with everyday household trash. But in the commercial sector, the paper category is mainly composed of office paper discards in-

TABLE 3.7 Residential vs. Commercial Waste Composition

	Residential, %	Commercial, %
Paper	20–40	25–50
Corrugated	8–12	20–30
Plastics	6–8	10–15
Metals	4–8	2–5
Other wastes*,†	40–50	18–24

*Residentially generated "other wastes" are typically composed of the following and estimated at the following percentages by weight: yard wastes, 17%; aluminum, 1%; glass, 6%; textiles, 4%; food waste, 9%; wood, 5%; rubber, 2%; miscellaneous wastes, 3%. Total = 47%.

†Commercially generated "other wastes" are typically composed of the following and estimated at the following percentages by weight: glass, 3%; food waste, 9%; wood, 4%; miscellaneous wastes, 4%. Total = 20%.

cluding computer paper. This is a prime example of what makes each of these generator sectors so unique. Often when solid waste characterization studies are in the planning phases, special and unique approaches need to be developed and tailored to the specific needs of each individual study. An example of one such unique procedure is discussed later in this chapter.

Waste Sampling and Composition

The sampling methodology represents the procedures for measuring the composition of solid waste generated within the study area. The procedure considers the mean composition of solid waste based on the collection and manual sorting of a number of samples of waste over the study period. This procedure is then duplicated for each additional sampling session. The procedure should identify

- A representative number of sorting samples to be representative of the total waste stream
- Manual sorting of the waste into individual components
- Data reduction
- Reporting of the results

Selected trucks are unloaded and at the sorting area. Samples of approximately 200 to 300 lb are to be selected from each load at random. Random identification can be performed either conceptually or physically but cannot be left to the discretion of the sort crew. A waste composition worksheet (Table 3.8) is needed to collect data of waste stream components.

ANALYZING THE RESULTS

Solid Waste Quantity and Composition

It is important to determine the level of detail required from the waste assessment program. The basic measures of solid waste quantity are tons per hour, tons per

TABLE 3.8 Waste Composition Worksheet
Sheet No. ____ of ____

Date:
Researcher:
Vehicle ID:
Sample Number:

Waste type: Residential Commercial Industrial Other (specify):

Waste stream components	Sample weight, lb.										
	A	B	C	D	E	F	G	H	I	J	Total
Newspaper											
Corrugated paper											
Mixed Paper											
Other paper											
Plastic beverage containers											
Plastic milk bottles											
Other plastics											
Plastic film											
Aluminum cans											
Other aluminum											
Ferrous scrap											
Tin cans											
Textiles/fabric											
Food waste											
Container glass											
Other glass											
Wood											
Dirt and debris											
Ceramics and fines											
Yard waste											
Rubber											
Leather											
										New weight:	

day, tons per week, and tons per year. These basic measures may be divided into components such as

- Tons per day of residential, commercial, industrial, and demolition wastes
- Tons per day collected by individual hauler or from specific routes in the study area
- Pounds per capita per day generated or collected based on various socioeconomic characteristics

Quantity measurements may also include waste volumes expressed in cubic yards, but volume measurements must also be associated with weight information since variations in waste density can occur. These variations occur primarily because of differences in waste composition and compaction equipment.

The units most often used when referring to solid waste quantity are tons per day and pounds per capita per day. Tons per day is typically used in reference to the quantity of waste received at a facility, while pounds per capita per day refers to waste generation as a function of population.

Following the field survey, the quantity data for each day and week for each site should be analyzed. Load-density measurements should be computed by dividing net load weights by truck capacity (in cubic yards). It may be helpful to include a column on the data collection forms for this computation, as well as the computation of net weight.

Local seasonality of waste generation is best estimated using quantity data kept by the site operator. Data on daily truck and/or vehicle arrivals, load weights if a scale is employed at the site, volume estimates, or billings records are useful for estimating seasonality of waste generation.

Solid waste composition data are typically compiled and analyzed for each of the individual samples taken. All samples are then combined to determine mean averages for each waste component. The means are then presented as representative of the solid waste as a whole for the study area.

Laboratory Results

The laboratory should be required to submit a separate report that presents the results of the tests undertaken. The test data should be correlated by sample number to each of the samples sorted in the field. This is extremely important if the laboratory tests the combustibility of only the combustible fraction of each of these samples taken. If this is done, the higher heating value of the solid waste stream is based upon only the combustible fraction. To determine the actual higher heating value of the solid waste on an as-received basis, the noncombustible fraction (metals, inerts, etc.) removed from each sample must be analyzed to reflect heat and energy loss. A new series of higher heating values is then developed for each of the samples. The series of values are reviewed and any clear outlines are removed and a range of higher heating values is presented. Typical ranges experienced in the United States are between 4200 and 5500 Btu/lb.

The chemical analyses conducted can estimate what chemical compounds are likely to be released during the disposal process in the form of gases from a waste-to-energy facility and leachate from a landfill. These estimates can be compared to parameters for emissions and leachate to determine whether the environmental discharges associated with the disposal alternative chosen will be within regulatory standards.

PRESENTING THE RESULTS

Once all of the data have been compiled and organized, they should be presented in an orderly and concise manner. Tables and graphics are valuable tools to illustrate solid waste characterization study results.

Pie charts, bar graphs, or other forms of visual representation all serve the purpose of creating a picture and personality for the solid waste stream. Some

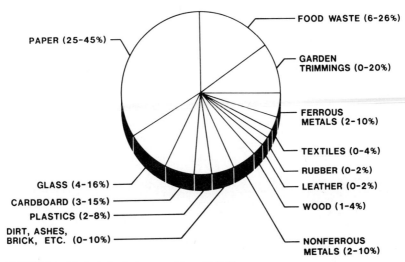

FIGURE 3.8 Typical physical composition of MSW.

samples of graphics that could be used in presenting the results from a solid waste characterization study are provided in Figs. 3.8 through 3.12. Figure 3.9 describes the solid waste composition by component for a residential sector. Figure 3.10 describes the composition of an entire solid waste stream. Figure 3.11 presents residential tonnage deliveries to various waste destinations in a study area. Figure 3.12 depicts commercial and residential recycling estimates and projections.

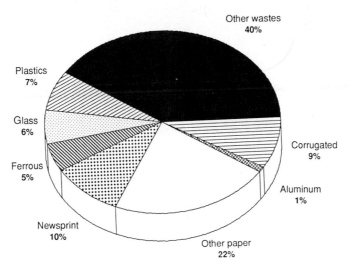

FIGURE 3.9 Residential sector waste stream composition, Westchester County, New York.

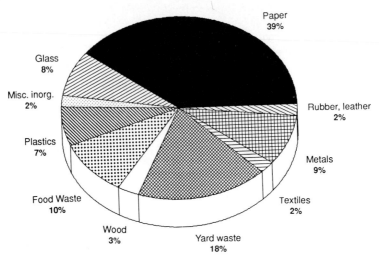

FIGURE 3.10 Composition of an entire solid waste stream, Westchester County, New York.

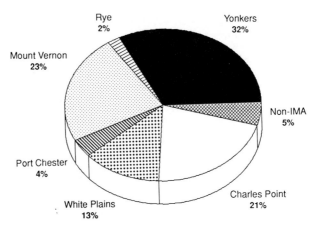

FIGURE 3.11 Residential tonnage deliveries, 1989, Westchester County, New York, by transfer station.

The final report format and the level of detail desired may be specified by the uses of the survey data. If not, the results should be reported in summary form with a brief review of the procedure used (assumptions, data sources, etc.). Two important items which shall be addressed are:

- Reporting the quantity and composition data by generator and region.
- Reporting the results of the survey in such a manner that others may use the data later and understand its limitations.

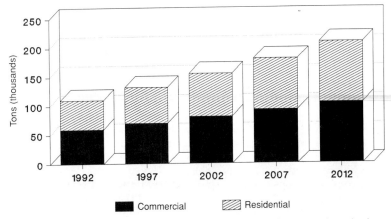

FIGURE 3.12 Commercial and residential recycling estimates and projections, Westchester County, New York.

RECYCLING AND SOLID WASTE CHARACTERIZATION

There are two major considerations when assessing the impact of recycling on solid waste characterization. The first consideration is, what effect do existing recycling programs have on the data obtained during the solid waste characterization study and the second consideration deals with the long-term effects of recycling on the data obtained relative to the planning of solid waste disposal systems.

Effect on Study Results

If the study area where the solid waste characterization study takes place already has a recycling program in place, the solid waste characterization study will not provide a true picture of the generator patterns within the study area. Since all of the sampling takes place at the disposal or processing location, materials previously removed from the waste stream through recycling are not accounted for. Since it is the preferred approach to report solid waste from a generation perspective, it will be necessary to account for all recyclables removed from the waste stream prior to disposal.

Therefore, the solid waste characterization study must quantify recyclables in terms of overall quantity removed and its composition. This can be accomplished by reviewing available records that report on the quantities and types of recyclables removed from the waste stream prior to disposal. Such reports should be available from municipal sources, local recycling brokers, and other recycling markets. Once the quantity and types of materials recycled are known, they can be added to the sampling data as appropriate to formulate solid waste quantity and composition data from a generation perspective. This is beneficial to the solid waste planning agency when it desires to assess ultimate disposal needs should there be a market failure for recyclables. Also, it provides an update of overall recycling program success and can identify potential markets for materials found in the solid waste stream that are not currently being recycled.

Study Result Effects

Both the quantity and quality of the waste stream will have a direct impact on the various technologies and systems implemented within each component. Sizing of solid waste management facilities is dependent upon projections of future waste stream quantities and characteristics, and upon recycling capture rates that may not be readily defined before the recycling program is implemented. Undoubtedly, recycling will affect waste availability.

The amount and types of waste removed from the waste stream through recycling will have a direct effect on the energy content (higher heating value) of the waste stream and its in-place density at a landfill. Both of these effects will impact disposal capacity requirements. Typically, during the initiation phase of recycling programs, newspaper and other paper goods, including corrugated material, are removed from the waste at a far greater rate than cans, bottles, and other noncombustibles. When this is the case, there is a marginal decrease in the higher heating value of the overall waste stream. As a recycling program becomes more effective, larger quantities of recyclable materials are removed from the waste stream. These materials are typically noncombustible and cause the higher heating value of the waste stream to increase. At a 25 to 30 percent recycling level, there can be an increase in the higher heating value of up to 10 percent. This could reduce the waste-to-energy processing capacity by a like amount.

Combined with expected growth in commercial activity, potential and expected increases in materials such as packaging wastes will have a significant effect on the quantity as well as the processable composition of the refuse. As paper, plastics, and packaging increase, the higher heating value continues to increase. Similarly, as inert or low heating value materials such as glass and ferrous and noncombustible found in yard wastes are removed, the higher heating value of the remaining refuse also increases. Such increases have to be taken into consideration when planning for disposal capacity.

SPECIAL AND CREATIVE APPROACHES

In certain instances, a full solid waste characterization with waste sorting may not be warranted and unique and creative approaches may be acceptable.

A unique and creative approach was undertaken for Westchester County, New York, in an attempt to estimate the amount of recyclables in the commercial segment of its waste stream. In order to plan for commercial recycling, a comprehensive analysis of the quantity and composition of the commercial waste stream was required.

There are considerable advantages to having the commercial industry participate in municipal and private recycling programs. The advantages of initiating recycling programs in the commercial sector include

- The commercial waste stream typically consists of a large fraction of recyclable materials, such as paper, corrugated cardboard, and wood.

- Commercial recyclables are both readily identifiable and easily separated from the commercial waste stream.
- A significant amount of commercial recycling is usually already going on, and these efforts can be enhanced or used as examples for other programs.
- Due to increasing disposal and collection costs, commercial recycling becomes an economically attractive business decision.
- Commercial recycling activity will help municipalities reach mandated state recycling goals by increasing recycling rates and therefore reducing the overall commercial waste stream requiring disposal.

If presented clearly to the commercial community, such advantages can stimulate local business leaders to initiate recycling programs. This can be accomplished by advertising in local business journals, presenting the benefits of recycling at local business organizational meetings, and establishing a task force or committee of business leaders and public officials to develop the necessary incentives in the private sector to promote recycling.

Prior to initiating recycling programs in the commercial sector, the commercial solid waste stream should be assessed to determine its compositional breakdown. It is important to determine the components of the commercial waste stream so that the types and quantities of materials available for recycling can be identified. Waste quantification and characterization require the joint efforts of the municipality, commercial establishments, and private waste carting industry.

Usually to develop waste quantity and composition data to this level of detail, waste deliveries from commercial establishments are weighed, the weights recorded, and representative samples drawn for composition analyses as described earlier in this chapter. This method requires a minimum of several weeks of field samplings, is labor intensive and costly, and its results are affected by many variables, such as seasonality, daily disposal patterns, and business cycles.

However, there are other methods available to determine the type and quantity of waste generated by the commercial sector. For example, this can be done by analyzing scalehouse data and/or by conducting municipal surveys. A much more challenging task, however, is disaggregating the commercial waste stream by municipality and generator and assessing its content and quantity. This method allows for targeting specific commercial generators for recycling based upon their actual waste generation patterns.

During the development of Westchester County's Solid Waste Management Plan, an innovative method was proposed to determine the quantity and composition of the county's commercial generator types. The method proposed consisted of reviewing available information from waste composition studies conducted within other regions of the United States, conducting surveys of the commercial business community, disaggregating the commercial business sector based upon county planning data, meeting with and interviewing key members of the private carting industry within the county, and conducting limited waste sampling programs at specific generator locations (Fig. 3.13).

The first step in the study required the development of commercial waste generator segments. Based on information available through the county's planning department, the commercial sector was broken down into the six major business types or generator segments listed here:

- Office
- Industrial

FIGURE 3.13   Conducting field sampling.

- Transportation, communication, and utilities
- Retail
- Wholesale, warehouse, and distribution
- Public and institutional

Generation rates per square foot of occupied floor space were chosen as the variable to estimate waste production since commercial waste production is a function of the type of business activity and not necessarily of the number of employees working at a particular business location (Fig. 3.14). Once the generator segments had been identified, various surveys and studies were conducted to develop estimates of the quantity and composition of the commercial waste stream.

> Pounds per person per day
>
> versus
>
> Pounds per occupied square foot of floor space

FIGURE 3.14   Generation determination (slide).

The basic survey and study premise proceeded using the following guidelines: question, compile data, assess and analyze the results, and test. For example, large business complexes were contacted and *asked* to provide information relating to the size of their office space (square footage), number of employees, business type (office, retail, etc.), amount of waste generated, and waste storage capacity (number and size of containers). All of the information was *compiled* and *assessed* to determine specific generator patterns (pounds of waste generated per square foot of office space per week). These estimates were then *tested* for accuracy by field weighing and composition studies conducted at specific commercial waste generator locations. The following is a listing of the surveys and studies conducted:

- Municipal phone survey
- Commercial business survey
- Private hauler survey
- Specific generator studies
- Assessor's survey
- Field survey
- Major business survey

As previously mentioned, various sources of information and methods were utilized in an effort to develop an acceptable confidence level for determining the amount of waste currently being generated by the commercial sector. However, each method of investigation presented a varied degree of confidence with respect to each of the commercial waste generator segments studied (i.e., office; industrial; transportation, communications, and utilities; retail; wholesale, warehouse, and distribution; and public and institutional).

As a result, it was necessary to review the results from each method of analysis to estimate waste generation for each of the respective generator segments and to make an assumption as to which method presented the most reasonable results. The criteria used to establish reasonableness in the ultimate waste quantity determination was the selection of an estimate which could be supported by at least two of the other estimating methods conducted. Methods which resulted in generation rates clearly outside the range of the expected true mean for a specific generator segment were eliminated from further consideration.

Following the determination of the estimated commercial waste quantities, available commercial waste composition data was used together with the information obtained from the additional surveys and studies undertaken to provide a breakdown of the commercial waste stream into principal components. Each of the individual surveys was reviewed in terms of the generator's knowledge of the compositional breakdown of its waste stream. A matrix was then developed illustrating for each of the surveys undertaken the reported waste composition. The reported estimates were then analyzed during the field waste composition studies at each of the generator segment locations and revised according to actual field data. A graphic representation of this data is provided as Fig. 3.15. Table 3.9 provides the estimated compositional breakdown of the commercial waste sector in Westchester County by generator segment.

The information gleaned on waste quantity and composition was then presented to the private haulers, who are responsible for collecting 90 percent of the commercial waste generated in the county. The private haulers found the waste quantity information to be accurate based upon their records and the waste com-

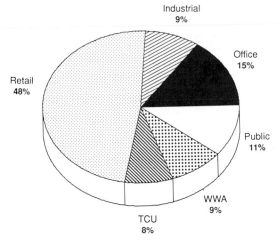

FIGURE 3.15 Classes of commercial waste generation, 1992, Westchester County, New York.

TABLE 3.9   Commercial Waste Quantity and Composition

Generator segment	Waste composition					Total tons
	Paper, %	Corrugated, %	Plastic, %	Metals, %	Others, %	
Office	65	15	6	2	12	54,290
Industrial	35	20	25	6	14	33,060
Retail	35	40	8	1	16	178,390
TCU*	20	15	15	5	45	31,500
WWA†	25	32	25	7	11	31,860
Pulic	45	10	5	6	34	42,000
Total tons	142,000	105,200	40,600	11,200	71,600	371,100

*TCU = Transportation, communications, and utilities.
†WWA = Wholesale, warehouse, and distribution.

position data to be a reasonable estimate based upon their knowledge of waste composition throughout the county.

Based upon the results of this study, the county began to target large commercial generators of recyclable materials as participants in its recycling program. In summary, the design and implementation of a solid waste characterization study can include various methods and techniques other than those traditionally used such as manual sorting to achieve reliable results.

STUDY COSTS

As mentioned at the beginning of this chapter, the cost to conduct a comprehensive solid waste characterization study as set forth in this chapter could range from $200,000 to $600,000. There are many variables, however, that affect cost. They are

- The scope of the study
- Labor requirements
- The number of sites to be analyzed
- The number of weekly programs
- Sampling scheduling
- The amount of incoming solid waste
- The amount of samples to be taken to reach the desired level of precision and confidence
- Equipment requirements
- Analyses undertaken
- Laboratory testing

The majority of costs are found in the labor requirements of the study. For example, if a four-person sampling crew is needed for waste sorting, two additional persons for visual inspection and hauler interviews of the scale house, a total of 10 persons, including supervision, will be on the site. For the field effort alone, 10 persons working 40 h per week for 4 weeks equals 1,600 h of labor. Adding laboratory costs, data compilation and review of data analyses, and program planning and reporting, it is easy to see how the labor costs alone reach the $200,000 range including administrative costs, overhead, and profit. Adding to this, expenses and special equipment needs and, in some instances, simultaneous study at several sites, one begins to realize that a comprehensive solid waste characterization study is an expensive undertaking.

Costs can be reduced, however, by lowering, for example, labor requirements and the number of seasonal samplings that take place. It is recommended, therefore, that planners review potential alternatives to labor and scheduling that could reduce study costs prior to initiating the solid waste characterization study. Additionally, alternative and creative approaches should be explored to potentially reduce cost. The creative approach developed for Westchester County, New York, resulted in savings in excess of $100,000 from manual sorting techniques and produced reliable and accurate data for planning purposes.

For planning purposes, however, the agency sponsoring a comprehensive solid waste characterization study should estimate that for each week of sampling, the costs will range from approximately $50,000 to $150,000 depending on the level of effort required to meet the study's objectives and producing the information desired. Therefore, as discussed throughout this chapter, know your study objectives and informational needs, and discuss viable options.

REFERENCES

1. Franklin Associates, Ltd., *Characterization of Municipal Solid Waste in the United States, 1960 to 2000,* United States Environmental Protection Agency, July 11, 1986.

2. Franklin Associates, Ltd., *Characterization of Municipal Solid Waste in the United States, 1960 to 2000 (Update 1988),* United States Environmental Protection Agency, March 30, 1988.

3. United States Environmental Protection Agency, *Characterization of Municipal Solid Waste in the United States: 1990 Update,* United States Environmental Protection Agency, June 1990.

4. Cal Recovery Systems Incorporated, *Broward County Resource Recovery Project Waste Characterization Study,* Broward County, Florida Resource Recovery Office, February 1988.

5. William F. Cosulich Associates, P.C., *Quantitative and Qualitative Analysis of Broward County Solid Waste—Phase I,* Broward County, Florida, September 28, 1983.

6. William F. Cosulich Associates, P.C., *Quantitative and Qualitative Analysis of Broward County Solid Waste—Phase II,* Broward County, Florida, November 14, 1983.

7. SCS Engineers, *Solid Waste Assessment Guidebook,* Michigan Department of Natural Resources, Community Assistance Division, Resource Recovery Section, June 1986.

8. G. Savage, *Proposed ASTM Standards, Draft Number 2, Method for Determination of the Composition of Unprocessed Municipal Solid Waste,* ASTM Committee, October 21, 1988.

9. D. S. Cerrato, "Estimating Recyclables in the Commercial Waste Stream," *Resource Recovery Magazine,* August 1989.

10. D. S. Cerrato, "Is There Gold in Garbage?" *National Development Magazine,* November/December 1989.

11. D. S. Cerrato, *Recycling and Resource Recovery Facility Sizing,* Fifth Annual Winter Conference of the Resource Recovery Institute, Miami, Florida, February 22, 1990.

12. N. Starobin and J. Kornberg, "A Cleaner Bangkok," *National Development Magazine,* March 1989.

13. Malcolm Pirnie, Inc., *Solid Waste Management Plan—Phase II,* Westchester County Department of Public Works Solid Waste Management Division, May 1988.

14. Malcolm Pirnie, Inc., *ANSWERS Wasteshed Recycling Plan,* City of Albany, New York, July 1988.

15. Malcolm Pirnie, Inc., *Solid Waste Quantification and Characterization Phase I Sampling Program,* Ulster County Resource Recovery Agency, Ulster County, New York, March 30, 1988.

16. Franklin Associates, Ltd., Environmental Consulting and Technology, Inc., and Resource Integration Systems Ltd., *Dakota County Solid Waste Generation and Characterization Study,* Dakota County, Minnesota, February 1991.

CHAPTER 4
SETTING RECYCLING GOALS AND PRIORITIES

David R. Bullock
Vice President, Gershman, Brickner & Bratton, Inc.
Falls Church, Virginia

Rosario Salvador
Recycling Consultant, Gershman, Brickner & Bratton, Inc.
Falls Church, Virginia

INTRODUCTION

Strategic planning is critical to the success of recycling programs. Numerous technical and institutional components need to be coordinated and managed to ensure smooth program start-up and eventual expansion. The central issue facing planners will be how to incorporate recycling into an existing solid waste management system. As with any new venture, short- and long-term goals need to be developed so that the process can be guided and monitored along the way.

In general, short-term goals for a recycling program will be oriented toward planning and implementation. These will include developing a recycling plan; determining which recyclables will initially be targeted and how the residential, commercial, and institutional sectors of the community will be served; and securing market agreements and processing capacity. Long-term goals will usually pertain to program expansion and the attainment of a mandated or self-imposed waste reduction-recycling goal. Typical short- and long-term goals are presented in Table 4.1.

The development of recycling programs across the United States has borne out one enduring principle—there is no one program that works for every community. Each community has its own geographic and demographic identity, a particular waste collection and disposal network, a unique set of legal and financial constraints, and specific market requirements. The most successful recycling programs, then, are planned with each of these local variables in mind. Priorities or goals are established according to the particular needs of a given community.

TABLE 4.1   Typical Short- and Long-Term Recycling Program Goals

Short-term goals	Long-term goals
Draft and complete recycling plan	Achieve and surpass diversion goals
Determine target recyclables to be collected	Secure long-term processing and marketing capacity
Secure marketing arrangements	Continue to explore methods to reduce costs
Secure processing capacity	Expand list of targeted recyclables
Design and initiate public education/promotional campaign	Identify additional markets
Plan and implement first phase of community drop-off program	Monitor program effectiveness
Plan and implement first phase of residential curbside program	Review need for mandatory legislation and implement if necessary
Initiate outreach–technical assistance plan for commercial sector	
Select communities for expanded curbside program	
Determine need for and hire recycling staff	
Develop and institute record keeping system	

REVIEWING EXISTING PRACTICES

Recycling program planning for any community begins with a careful examination of the existing solid waste management picture. This includes understanding the types and amounts of solid waste generated. A waste stream analysis should serve as the basis for determining the sources, quantities, and characteristics of a community's solid waste. This type of detailed assessment yields valuable information on available recyclables and serves as a tool for planning the most appropriate collection, marketing, and processing options for these materials.

The current waste stream may be analyzed in one of two ways. The more accurate, yet costly and time-consuming, way is to physically sort composite samples of municipal solid waste into designated sort categories. Representative seasonal samples of waste may be taken at the landfill or transfer station, at another disposal or processing facility, or at curbside. Examples of sort categories are shown in Table 4.2. Alternately, when faced with cost or time constraints, a community may decide to use existing data (i.e., information from communities with similar demographics and waste sources, existing state or county planning data) combined with local knowledge (local haulers and facility operators) to develop a snapshot of the types and amounts of waste generated in the area.

Existing collection practices determine, to a large extent, how a recycling program is instituted. Since collection is frequently the most costly component of a local waste management system, recyclables collection needs to be incorporated in as cost-effective a manner as possible. Program planners need to know the following:

TABLE 4.2 Category Description List

Component	Description
Newsprint	Newspapers
Corrugated	Corrugated cardboard boxes
Office paper	Computer printout, white and colored ledger paper
Kraft	Brown paper bags and other kraft items
Magazines and glossy inserts	All magazines and glossy inserts from newspapers
Other paper	Envelopes, paper towels, shoe boxes, wax-coated paper, milk and juice containers, tissues, books, food packaging, paper bags other than kraft
Plastic, PET, nonsoda*	Nonsoda PET
Plastic, colored HDPE†	Colored HDPE containers with symbol 2, detergent containers, shampoo, and cleaner bottles (non-milk and juice containers)
Other plastics	Clear food wrap, flexible food containers (trash bags, baggies, zip-lock, etc.), toothpaste containers, food containers such as margarine, plastic toys, formed parts (from appliances), disposable eating utensils, etc. Containers with symbol 3, 4, 5, 6, 7
Leaves	Leaves
Grass	Grass
Brush	Tree branches, shrubbery, etc.
Wood waste	Lumber, furniture, tool handles, wooden toys, wooden kitchen implements, etc. (not yard waste)
Food waste	Kitchen scraps or any other sortable and identifiable food items
Textiles	Clothing, shoes, rags, carpets, etc.
Tires	Tires
Ferrous cans—nonsoda	Food and beverage cans that are magnetic, nonsoda and beer
Other ferrous	All other magnetic metal items

- Is collection accomplished by the public sector, the private sector, or a combination of both?
- What are personnel needs for collection? Is union labor being used?
- What types of vehicles are currently being used to collect solid waste (i.e., rear, side or front loaders; roll-offs and tilt frames; transfer trailers) and what is their availability for recycling?
- What types of containers are used for collection (i.e., containers for mechanized collection; metal or plastic cans; paper or plastic bags; 55-gal drums)?
- What are the residential and commercial points of collection (curbside/alley; backyard/on-property; drop-off centers)?

These and other elements of the local disposal system need to be well understood. In some rural communities, for example, residents take their garbage di-

TABLE 4.2 Category Description List (*Continued*)

Component	Description
Household hazardous waste	Cleaners, solvents, paints, etc.
Miscellaneous organics	Sweepings and other items remaining after sorting; other items not fitting above
Miscellaneous inorganics	Rock, brick, stones, sheet rock, ceramics, flower pots, sand, and related items
Diapers	Diapers
Glass bottles—soft drink	Soft drink bottles
Glass bottles—beer	Beer bottles
Other noncontainer glass	Broken glass, other glass non-containers, and plate glass (light bulbs, etc.)
Aluminum cans—soft drink	Aluminum soda cans
Aluminum cans—beer	Aluminum beer cans
Other aluminum	Small food and juice containers, foil, siding, cast aluminum products, other aluminum objects
Other nonferrous	All nonmagnetic metals other than aluminum
Other glass containers	All glass containers not soft drink or beer
Fines	Sweepings less than ¼ in in diameter
Bimetal soft drink cans	Soft drink cans with magnetic sides
Bimetal cans—beer	Beer cans with magnetic sides
Plastic soda bottles	Plastic PET soda bottles
HDPE, milk, juice, water	Clear HDPE, milk, juice, water bottles

*PET = polyethylene tetraphthalate.
†HDPE = high-density polyethylene.

rectly to a transfer station or landfill. In this case, recycling opportunities can be provided directly at the point of disposal. On the other hand, residents accustomed to receiving municipal or private collection at the curb may desire a more convenient curbside program. Another issue that needs to be addressed is the presence of any municipal contracts with disposal facilities, such as incinerators or waste-to-energy plants. "Put or pay" agreements, which obligate communities to delivery a specified amount of waste to a disposal facility, can hinder the development of comprehensive recycling programs.

The last component of the current solid waste management system that needs to be identified and quantified are any existing recycling programs or activities. Municipally sponsored recycling programs (pilot or full-scale curbside programs; drop-off or buy-back centers; government office paper recycling efforts, etc.) should already be well documented. The identification of other types of activities, however, requires further investigation. For example, in many communities, metal recycling efforts, including segregation of white goods delivered to the landfill and ferrous scrap recovery through scrap dealers, are common. Aluminum beverage can recycling programs for charitable purposes are also widespread. Large amounts of commercially generated corrugated cardboard may already be recovered through "dump and pick" operations at transfer stations or landfills or through contractual arrangements between the business or industry and private waste haulers. Commercial or hauler surveys can help to quantify these activities. The surge of interest in the environment has led to a rise in school or college-based recycling programs. These programs commonly target paper (newspaper, high-grade and mixed papers) and aluminum. Finally, planners need to be aware of any special programs, such as those for used oil, antifreeze, batteries, or tires. In general, program planners should learn how a particular solid waste system works, who the players are, where the waste goes, and who controls the system.

IDENTIFY AND EVALUATE INCENTIVES TO PARTICIPATE

The ultimate success of recycling programs depends, in large part, on public participation. If sufficient quantities of high-quality recyclables are to be recovered and diverted from the landfill, every resident, employee, and business owner needs to incorporate recycling into his or her daily life. Incentives to participation must be created and maintained. For some citizens, participation will spring from a desire to "help the environment." For most, legal or economic incentives will be deciding factors.

The recent dramatic increase in state waste reduction legislation, designed to encourage communities to recycle, has served as a powerful impetus for the development of recycling programs. A growing number of states have set mandatory recycling goals ranging between 20 and 50 percent to be met by the year 2000. These legislative initiatives differ in their approach. Some mandate that local governments (municipalities) pass ordinances requiring citizens and businesses within their jurisdictions to source-separate and recycle a specified number of materials. Others require local governments to provide citizens with recycling services but do not mandate that they adopt ordinances. Oregon's 1983 Opportunity to Recycle Act was an early example of this type of legislation. A third variety of legislation mandates only that local governments reach a certain waste reduction-recycling goal.

Several states have also enacted bans on the disposal of certain materials— usually yard waste, tires, used oil, white goods, and batteries. Wisconsin has focused and expanded on this approach to encourage recycling by banning the disposal of most recyclables from landfills and incinerators. Furthermore, the law requires municipalities to meet certain recycling program criteria by 1995 in order to have access to these disposal facilities.

Comprehensive state waste reduction laws frequently contain provisions that stimulate the development of markets for recyclables. For example, state agencies may be required to purchase products made from recyclable materials or to use compost whenever possible. Companies making products from recyclable materials or seeking to purchase recycling equipment may receive tax credits or become eligible for grants or low-interest loans. Many state recycling laws also make grants or loans available to local governments for the development of recycling programs. Another financial incentive that some states offer is funding for market research and development.

Whereas some financial incentives stimulate recycling by encouraging the procurement of recycled products or the investment in recycling technologies, a few states have chosen to adopt mandatory deposit legislation aimed at containers and vehicle batteries. The intent of this type of legislation is to reduce litter and divert these materials from disposal by encouraging their redemption.

Another approach is to impose product fees or taxes on certain consumer goods, for example, tires. Such fees represent an attempt to incorporate the cost of disposal into the cost of production. Ultimately, manufacturers pass this cost on to the consumer. Florida's Solid Waste Management Act mandates that an advanced disposal fee (ADF) of 1¢ per container will be assessed on all containers made from glass, plastic, plastic-coated paper, aluminum, and other metals if these containers are not recycled at a sustained rate of 50 percent by October 1992. The ADF is increased to 2¢ per container if the 50 percent recycling rate is not achieved by October 1994.

Clearly, the passage of state legislation requiring local governments either to meet mandatory goals, provide recycling services, or pass mandatory recycling ordinances has boosted recycling efforts in many communities. Planners need to be fully aware of all legal and financial incentives at their disposal. Some communities, however, may choose to institute regulatory measures of their own.

In communities with an open collection system, where residents contract with a private hauler of their choice for garbage collection, the municipality may not have a strong economic incentive to recycle. In this case, the local government may pass an ordinance detailing the level of recycling services that each hauler must provide to its customers and require that hauler licensure be contingent on the provision of these services. The local government, in turn, can provide financial assistance by providing curbside collection containers, funding some or all of the promotional costs, or developing a materials recovery facility (MRF) for the processing and marketing of the recovered recyclables.

Increasingly, communities are beginning to consider volume-based waste disposal fees as a way to encourage recycling and source reduction. Under these pay-per-container systems, residential waste generators pay according to the amount of garbage they generate. Residents can presumably be expected to attempt to minimize their bills, in this case by generating less garbage and availing themselves of recycling opportunities which are offered at reduced or no charge. Several options are available for implementing variable-rate collection systems, including charging customers based on the number of containers set out, the frequency of collection, or the weight collected.

CONDUCT RESEARCH ON COMMUNITY WILLINGNESS TO PARTICIPATE

Community participation is critical to the success of a recycling program. The efficient recovery of large volumes of high-quality recyclables depends on citizen involvement. Whereas public perception of the validity of recycling as a waste management strategy is growing, program planners need to anticipate some resistance to change. Not all residents and businesses can be expected to embrace recycling wholeheartedly at the outset. If community attitudes and/or objections to recycling behaviors can be identified and characterized, however, planners can design programs that achieve a maximum level of recovery with a minimum level of inconvenience.

It has been suggested that a portion of the public will participate in recycling programs no matter how well promoted or convenient the opportunities are. These individuals are probably motivated by a sincere environmental ethic. Therefore, there is no need to try to convince these people to participate (i.e., don't "preach to the choir"). On the other hand, another small segment of the population will be unlikely to participate regardless of the level or types of publicity. It is probably not worthwhile, therefore, to spend a significant amount of money or time trying to move the immovable. The majority of the populace, however, can be affected by responsible information and promotional programs, and it is this larger segment of the population that it is important to know more about and understand.

One way to gauge public interest in and support for recycling is to survey residents and businesses about their attitudes toward waste disposal and recycling issues. Written and phone surveys can be administered to a wide audience in the jurisdiction. Responses received are then tabulated, analyzed, and used to guide program design and public education efforts. Figure 4.1 presents a sample attitudinal survey form.

Another way to assess local attitudes toward recycling is to conduct one or several focus groups. Focus groups are a recognized, small group survey technique in which a moderator asks a series of open-ended questions to a small sample of individuals (generally 10 to 25 people), who are either chosen at random or demographically representative of a target population. This survey approach enables moderators to gather qualitative data that are not easily gathered through more traditional phone or mail survey techniques. Though the results are rarely statistically valid because the sample population is so small, focus groups do provide more detailed information about a wide range of issues than multiple choice or true-false questions. In addition, moderators can structure questions to assess knowledge levels at the start of the session and monitor how quickly the group's knowledge levels rise during the course of the meeting.

During the course of planning and implementing a recycling program, a municipality or a county may decide to develop a recycling facility. Siting solid waste processing facilities is typically met with opposition from some local citizens. This public outcry has come to be known as the not-in-my-back-yard (NIMBY) syndrome. Dealing with NIMBY opposition has generated much discussion among waste management professionals and public education experts. To what extent do you involve the public? How much technical information do you try to condense for a lay audience—often an audience armed with misinformation? Do public meetings present media opportunities for nay-sayers or promote consensus building? Does risk communication improve a community's understanding of solid waste projects or increase public anxiety that can lead to public opposition? Does an open communication policy lead to politically motivated solid waste management decision making at the expense of technical considerations? These questions are not easily answered, nor is one answer going to be appropriate for all communities. Ultimately, each jurisdiction will have to develop a communication strategy that is most effective for its particular citizenry.

An important component of a community outreach plan is the development of a citizen's advisory committee or task force. Such citizen groups can include local civic and business leaders (and others who have local influence) as well as local technical experts. Advisory committees or task forces can serve as valuable

1. Which of the following best describes your home?

   (a) ( ) Single-family detached
   (b) ( ) Duplex or townhouse
   (c) ( ) Multifamily unit (up to 4 stories)
   (d) ( ) Multifamily unit (5 to 8 stories)
   (e) ( ) Highrise (9 or more stories)

2. How many people live in your house? _____

3. Would you say you listen to/read about environmental issues?

   (a) ( ) Very closely
   (b) ( ) Somewhat closely
   (c) ( ) Not closely
   (d) ( ) Not at all

4. Have you heard or read anything in the news or in conversations among friends and associates about recycling in [*name of municipality or community*]?

   (1) ( ) Yes   (2) ( ) No

   If yes, how have you heard or read about recycling (check as many as apply)?

   (a) ( ) Newspaper
   (b) ( ) Television
   (c) ( ) AM radio
   (d) ( ) FM radio
   (e) ( ) Magazines or newsletters
   (f) ( ) Billboards
   (g) ( ) Buses, subway stations
   (h) ( ) Other:_____

5. Do you currently recycle any of the following materials?

   (a) ( ) Newspapers
   (b) ( ) Other paper or cardboard
   (c) ( ) Glass
   (d) ( ) Cans (aluminum or tin)
   (e) ( ) Plastic
   (f) ( ) Leaf/yard waste
   (g) ( ) Other
   (h) ( ) Don't recycle now

6. If you do recycle, what is the *principal* reason?

   (a) ( ) Concern for the environment
   (b) ( ) Concern about availability of landfill space
   (c) ( ) My children encourage me to recycle
   (d) ( ) I get paid for my recyclables
   (e) ( ) Other:_____

7. If you do not recycle, what would you say is the *principal* reason you don't?

   (a) ( ) Inconvenience
   (b) ( ) Believe there are better ways to handle my garbage
   (c) ( ) Other:_____

FIGURE 4.1 Sample attitudinal survey form.

8. How long have you been recycling?

    (a) ( ) Less than 1 year
    (b) ( ) 1–2 years
    (c) ( ) 3–5 years
    (d) ( ) More than 5 years

NOTE: Questions 9 through 14 can be used in communities that plan to expand or modify a drop-off program or assess the effectiveness of a drop-off program.

9. [*Name of municipality/community*] has placed bins or containers in several areas where residents may deposit [*list materials*]. Have you ever *seen* these recycling centers?

    (a) ( ) Yes
    (b) ( ) No
    (c) ( ) Don't know

10. Have you ever brought materials to one of these centers?

    (a) ( ) Yes
    (b) ( ) No
    Which one?_____

11. [*Name of community*] is likely to increase the number of places you can take recyclable materials soon. What can [*name of community*] do to make it more likely that you will take your recyclables to these recycling centers?

    (a) ( ) Pay for recyclable materials
    (b) ( ) Locate centers closer to my home
    (c) ( ) Make recycling mandatory
    (d) ( ) Provide more information
    (e) ( ) Not likely to go to recycling center

12. How much time would you be willing to spend [or do you now spend] driving *one way* to a recycling center?

    (a) ( ) Less than 10 min
    (b) ( ) 10 min
    (c) ( ) 11–15 min
    (d) ( ) 16–20 min
    (e) ( ) More than 20 min
    (f) ( ) Not likely to go to recycling center

13. What day of the week is more convenient for you to go to a recycling center?
    _____

14. What locations for recycling drop-off centers would be most convenient for you?

    (a) ( ) Fire or police station
    (b) ( ) Shopping area or grocery store
    (c) ( ) Park or recreation area
    (d) ( ) Centrally located special area dedicated to recycling
    (e) ( ) Other_____

FIGURE 4.1 (*Continued*) Sample attitudinal survey form.

15. If [*name municipality or private haulers*] picked up cans, glass, plastic and other recyclable materials at your curb, would you be more likely to recycle than under the current system?

    (a) ( ) Yes, more likely
    (b) ( ) No, not more likely
    (c) ( ) No difference, I'd recycle anyway
    (d) ( ) No difference, I wouldn't recycle

16. If you answered "yes" to question 15, would you say you would:

    (a) ( ) Definitely recycle
    (b) ( ) Be very likely to recycle
    (c) ( ) Be somewhat likely to recycle
    (d) ( ) Would recycle reluctantly

17. How much extra would you be willing to pay on your monthly trash collection bill for curbside recycling?

    (a) ( ) \$.50 or less
    (b) ( ) \$.50–\$1
    (c) ( ) \$1–\$2
    (d) ( ) \$2–\$5
    (e) ( ) Would not be willing to pay for curbside recycling

18. Do you think [*name of community*] residents should be required by law to recycle, or should it be voluntary?

    (a) ( ) By law
    (b) ( ) Voluntary
    (c) ( ) Unsure

19. Do you have any specific comments you'd like to make about [*name of municipality or community*] recycling program?

    _____
    _____
    _____

20. Age of respondent_____

21. Yearly salary of household (all residents combined).

    (a) ( ) Less than \$9,000
    (b) ( ) \$9000–\$15,000
    (c) ( ) \$15,001–\$25,000
    (d) ( ) \$25,001–\$35,000
    (e) ( ) \$35,001–\$45,000
    (f) ( ) \$45,001–\$55,000
    (g) ( ) Over \$55,000

FIGURE 4.1 (*Continued*) Sample attitudinal survey form.

allies during the program planning process by building consensus, involving stakeholders in the decision-making process, soliciting public input, harnessing local resources, educating possible opponents about the importance and value of the project, and shaping public opinion through involving local opinion leaders.

MARKET RESEARCH AND IDENTIFICATION

In order for any community to achieve its recycling goals, it must ensure that markets are available to absorb recovered recyclables. Over the years, many communities have experienced setbacks in their recycling programs due to the faltering of one or more markets. In some cases, separated materials were stored in anticipation of a short-term changing of market conditions and landfilled when markets did not improve. For some materials, markets will naturally grow as new supplies become available. For others, the public and private sectors must work together to promote growth in industries that can rely on secondary materials in their production processes. Planners should keep in mind that many markets (especially for lower grade materials) have had a cyclical history with fluctuating prices.

The community must concern itself with both existing and future markets for recyclable materials. The first step is to refer to any market research studies already completed. In states that have enacted comprehensive waste reduction and recycling legislation, it is likely that the state's environmental agency or department of commerce has conducted a recyclables market analysis. Additionally, regional studies performed for a group of counties can be consulted.

In the absence of existing studies, a local government may need to conduct its own research in order to identify and secure recyclable materials markets. Two types of markets should be investigated: intermediate and final. Intermediate markets include both processors and brokers of materials. In general, intermediate markets handle a variety of materials which they purchase from industrial and private sources as well as municipal recycling programs. They accumulate, process, store, and transport the recyclables to final markets. Final markets, generally manufacturing facilities, convert recyclables into new products. These markets usually handle only one material to produce one type of product (i.e., glass bottles, metal cans, newsprint, etc.).

Market identification can be systematically accomplished with the help of a variety of resources. The yellow pages in the local phone book contain a wealth of information. Following is a listing of some of the headings that can be referred to:

Recycling centers	Nurseries
Waste paper	Lawn maintenance
Rubbish and garbage removal	Garden centers
Thrift shops	Mulches
Junk dealers	Sod and sodding services
Scrap metals	Automobile wrecking
Landscapers	

Trade associations can also be contacted for information on local markets. Following is a partial listing of some of these material-specific organizations:

The Steel Can Recycling Institute

Glass Packaging Institute

The Aluminum Association

American Paper Institute

Council for Solid Waste Solutions

National Association for Plastic Container Recovery (NAPCOR)

National Soft Drink Association

American Retreaders Association

Institute of Scrap Recycling Industries

In addition, recycling journals such as *American Recycling Market, American Metals Market, Fibre Market News,* and *Recycling Times* frequently publish useful market information.

Specialized local markets for certain recyclables should also be investigated. For example, some communities may be able to shred collected newspaper for use as animal bedding by local farmers, cooperative extensions, agricultural organizations, and agricultural service companies. Newspaper and mixed paper grades can also be used in hydromulch applications by seeding contractors, land improvement contractors, or soil conservation services. Glass may be used by fiberglass manufacturers or as aggregate or glassphalt.

Once a list of potential markets has been compiled, these markets should be surveyed to determine the type and quantity of materials that they can accept. The survey should also establish price, material specifications, assistance that is available from the market for processing, transportation or storage of materials, and any other available information on market conditions (i.e., availability of short-term or long-term contracts). Figure 4.2 presents a sample survey form that can be used for interviewing prospective markets. In addition to serving as a useful tool for compiling necessary information, it can also be used either for mail or phone surveys.

Finally, program planners should be aware of any local waste exchange systems that match industrial waste generators with potential users of these wastes. Waste exchanges typically deal with both hazardous and nonhazardous materials, such as acids, alkalis, and inorganic chemicals; solvents and other organic chemicals; oils and waxes; plastics and rubber; textiles and leather; wood and paper; and metals and metal sludges.

If it becomes apparent that existing markets for recyclables are not sufficient to handle the materials collected in the region, a market development program can be initiated. The fluctuating nature of recyclables markets requires that program planners accept a certain level of uncertainty and design programs with flexibility in mind. Market analysis and development, then, will be an ongoing process, since recycling programs will need to continually respond to market oscillations. One of the most important roles that program officials can play in market development is to ensure that recyclable materials that enter the market meet industry specifications. They should also let potential markets know about the timing and availability of new supplies.

Company name: _____ Date: _____
Contact name: _____ Title:_____
Telephone number:_____
County in which facility is located:_____
Address:_____
City: _____ State: _____ Zip: _____
Please complete the following chart, indicating what materials you accept, prices paid, and purchase requirements.

	Materials specifications (Baled-loose-crushed-shredded)					Will you pick up [P] or must it be delivered [D]	Price/ton*	Minimum quantity, tons
	B	L	C	S	Comments			
Paper								
Newsprint (please specify grade #)								
Corrugated								
Computer printout								
White ledger								
Colored ledger								
Mixed Paper								
Glass								
Mixed cullet								
Green								
Clear								
Amber								
Metal								
Aluminum								
Tin cans								
Bimetal cans								
Heavy ferrous								
White goods								
Batteries (car)								
Plastic								
PET bottles								
HDPE bottles								
Other plastics								
Tires								
Other materials								

*We are aware that prices fluctuate frequently and do not expect you to be committed to these prices.

FIGURE 4.2 Sample marketing interview survey form.

---

1. Is your firm a Broker _____
                   Dealer/processor _____
                   Manufacturer _____

2. If you are a manufacturer, what products do you make from the recycled materials?

3. To enable us to gauge the current amount of recycling in your area, please provide an estimate of the amount of materials you purchase annually (please give a separate quantity for each material).

4. What kind of additional capacity do you feel you have available?

5. What is your firm's preferred method of transportation to receive materials?
   Rail _____
   Truck _____

6. Would you be willing to pick up trailer-load quantities of any material?
   Yes _____
   No _____

7. Would you be willing to provide with a contract for the purchase of material?
   Yes _____ No _____

   If yes, for what duration? _____ Years

8. Would you be willing to provide storage and/or processing equipment or capability (Gaylord boxes, trailers, compactors, etc.)?
   Yes _____ No _____

   If yes, what type of equipment/capabilities?

9. Estimated cost to provide such equipment:
   $ _____ per ton $ _____ per load $ _____ flat rate

10. Any additional requirements or comments:
    Return forms to:

FIGURE 4.2 (*Continued*) Sample marketing interview survey form.

There are a variety of market development tools available to public and private agencies to increase the markets for recyclables. Generally, these involve offering financial incentives and technical assistance to businesses and industries that use recycled materials. State, city, and county economic development agencies can attract and retain these businesses by providing assistance with siting, zoning, financing, labor, real estate development, and environmental issues. The institution of preferential procurement policies also helps develop markets by signaling local commitment to purchase products with recycled content.

Some smaller or more rural communities may not generate sufficient quantities of recyclables to interest local markets. In this case, several counties or municipalities can consolidate and process their recyclables to provide final market buyers with the quantities and quality of materials they consistently require. This consolidation has been termed regional or cooperative marketing and represents an effective market development initiative available to certain groups of communities. One of the earliest and best-known examples of such a cooperative is the New Hampshire Resource Recovery Association (NHRRA), created in 1981 to provide technical, educational, and marketing services to its members. NHRRA staff identifies market options and, in conjunction with a marketing committee, recommends buyers to municipal representatives on the board of directors. The board will then enter into a contractual agreement with a buyer for each specific recyclable material.

Export Markets

Recyclable materials separated from the waste stream become commodities, similar to virgin materials. Program planners, then, should understand the many factors affecting the commodities' markets and, thus, the prices paid for these materials. Domestic production capacity, imports, consumption, energy and transportation costs, changing technology, new product opportunities, availability of substitute material, and other factors affect the markets for recyclable materials. Factors affecting international markets include these same forces plus foreign trade tariffs, currency exchange rates, trade policy and programs, and other political forces.

Export markets for recyclable materials have been developing in the United States at increasing rates. Paper is a prime example. Greatly expanded recycling programs on the East Coast have generated more paper than regional mills could absorb. At the same time, the growing economies of the Pacific Rim countries demanded fiber that could not be produced locally, causing them to import recycled paper from the United States and Europe. Paper is now the largest single export (in annual tons) from the port of New York City.

The greater quantity of factors involved in the export markets serve to increase the volatility of prices paid for recycled materials. It is important to understand that domestic users (markets) of recyclable materials must compete with export markets for the same materials. All of these factors combined with the geographic location of the generating community should be considered when investigating export markets for recyclable materials.

INSTITUTIONAL ARRANGEMENTS

There are roles to be played by both the public and private sectors in solid waste management. The optimum balance of responsibilities for carrying out recycling programs depends on the specific program elements and on the objectives and philosophies of the local jurisdiction.

Municipal solid waste collection is usually accomplished through a combination of public and private sector efforts. Generally, the private sector collects from commercial and industrial establishments, and local governments often collect or arrange for collection from the residential sector.

One of the most important decisions that needs to be made is how to incorporate recycling into the existing system. Planners are cautioned against prematurely restructuring current collection services. In communities with open collection systems, for example, residents may be very loyal to their particular hauler and may not respond well to a change in service (i.e., a switch to municipal collection of recyclables). Planners should consult local haulers and citizen advisory groups on their interest in providing recycling services and involve them in the planning process. Successful recycling programs often depend on the solid support of haulers.

If a community decides to allow existing haulers to provide recycling services, they must still monitor the program and retain some control (especially in states with strict diversion mandates). Reporting, verification, and inspection requirements are key components in a system that relies heavily on private-sector initiatives, and these components place burdens on the local government to see that claims and reports are accurate. In these situations, the local government may wish to include recycling services and reporting in licensing requirements.

IDENTIFY POTENTIAL FOR WASTE REDUCTION AT THE SOURCE

Source reduction activities focus on preventing the generation of solid waste in the first place, generally by decreasing the volume and toxicity of materials produced and consumed. Methods of reducing waste include reducing the use of nonrecyclable materials; replacing disposable materials with durable-reusable materials; reducing packaging; minimizing yard waste generation; establishing volume-based garbage rate structures; and increasing efficient use of materials (including paper products, glass, metals, plastics, and other materials).

Some states have established reduction goals as part of recycling legislation. These goals generally range from 5 to 10 percent of the Municipal Solid Waste (MSW) stream. Legislation also exists to require or encourage waste reduction addressing the methods mentioned above.

Planners need to be aware of any incentives that are already in place as well as to identify existing consumer awareness campaigns and local reuse or salvage industries. These types of activities can have positive effects on a planned recycling program.

IDENTIFY MATERIALS TO BE RECYCLED

A common goal of recycling programs is to divert substantial quantities of material from the waste stream; an accompanying goal is to offset recycling system costs with material revenues to the maximum extent possible. Therefore, the materials a community selects for recycling depend, in part, on available markets. Most larger communities have well-developed markets for paper, metal, and glass recyclables. Yard waste, which usually represents a significant portion of the municipal waste stream and is increasingly being prohibited from disposal, can contribute significantly to the achievement of recycling goals; however, a community must commit to the development of yard waste processing facilities to handle projected amounts of these materials as well as markets and uses for the finished products. Plastic containers [high-density polyethylene (HDPE) and polyethylene tetraphthalate (PET)] are an easily targeted portion of the waste stream, but their high volume to weight ratio makes cost-effective collection difficult. With the advent of on-board compaction equipment and specialized recycling vehicles, however, plastics are being included in a growing number of recycling programs. Other types of plastics [i.e., polyvinyl chloride (PVC), mixed polymer containers, and film plastics] are experiencing increased market demand and are increasingly being included in residential and commercial recycling programs.

There are many other materials that may be collected in recycling programs, including textiles, batteries, food waste, household ferrous scrap, and reusable items. A recent survey investigated the materials most commonly included in municipal recycling programs. The results are tabulated in Table 4.3.

TABLE 4.3 Most Popular Materials Included in Municipal Recycling Programs by Percent

Material	%	Material	%
Newspaper	96.2	Waste oil	46.2
Glass	93.9	High-grade paper	41.3
Aluminum	88.3	Mixed paper	32.2
Plastic bottles	67.0	Other (batteries, tin)	15.2
Cardboard	60.6	Rigid plastics	11.0
Scrap metal	52.3	Chip board	6.4
Yard waste	47.3		

Source: *Public Administration Review,* May–June 1991, based on 264 recycling coordinators' responses to a survey conducted by David H. Folz, University of Tennessee, Knoxville.

Program planners should keep in mind that collecting a material without having secured a market can result in unexpected storage or disposal costs. In addition, public opposition may arise if recyclables are dropped from the program due to lack of markets. Established habits and practices are difficult to change.

EVALUATE COLLECTION METHODS

Many alternatives are available for collecting recyclable materials from the municipal solid waste stream. The collection system is usually the most expensive component of a recycling program. Therefore, careful consideration must be given to providing reliable and convenient collection services in a cost-effective manner.

Factors affecting the collection of recyclable materials from the generator are often quite similar—and in some cases the same—as those affecting collection of regular refuse. General factors affecting both recyclables and waste collection include crew size, vehicle size, and maintenance issues. Community-specific factors affecting residential collection of both recyclables and refuse include community size and housing density; quantities of waste and recyclables to be collected; present collection system and available equipment; traffic patterns; weather; and institutional issues such as wages to be paid to collectors, frequency of collection, and point of set-out (curbside, back door, etc.). In most cases, the collection of recyclable materials in a community will be superimposed upon an existing waste collection approach, either municipally or privately operated. The most economical approach is to integrate the two collection approaches, maximizing the benefits associated with regular refuse amounts decreasing as recyclables set-outs increase.

RESIDENTIAL CURBSIDE COLLECTION

Curbside collection of recyclables has become a standard approach to the recovery of recyclable materials from the residential waste stream. Like regular curbside refuse collection, this method of collection provides participating residents with a convenient and consistent method of recovering recyclables for processing and marketing. Furthermore, properly operated and publicized curbside programs that provide residents with regularly scheduled pickup of recyclables (often on the same day as regular trash collection) have been demonstrated to be effective in capturing large amounts of recyclables.

The way in which recyclables are set out at the curb, and the containers used for home storage and placement at the curb, vary from program to program. In general, there are three main approaches to set-out and collection; commingled set-out with commingled collection; commingled set-out with curbside sorting of materials; and source-separated set-out with separated collection. The amount of sorting—either at the curb or at a centralized processing facility—will be determined at least in part by the conditions under which locally available markets will agree to purchase recovered materials. If, for example, no local market is available for mixed-color glass, color separation will need to take place in the home, at the curb, or at a processing facility.

The type of home storage container used will vary with the set-out approach chosen. Containers for commingled set-outs need to be sized appropriately to store expected quantities of target materials. These containers typically cost less than multiple bin systems; however, costs associated with sorting at the curb or at materials processing facilities may offset the savings. Commingled collection is considered by some to maximize participant convenience and minimize the presence of bulky containers in the household, thereby increasing the likelihood of participation.

Multiple bin systems, used for source-separated set-outs and collection, range from eight-can systems on a wheeled cart to 90-gal cans with removable baskets for collecting the separated waste streams. The most popular approach to multiple bin collection is the use of a stacked, three-bin system. The cost of these containers is greater than single bins, but their use may result in lower processing costs due to decreased sorting requirements. Other factors to consider when evaluating bin specifications include ease of storage in the home and cost of replacement. Bins wear out, are stolen, are appropriated for unintended purposes, and are treated less than gently by collectors. These issues need to be considered when determining the type of collection and set-out approach and the style of home storage containers employed.

In addition to reusable home storage container bins, some communities have opted to collect recyclables in plastic bags. Participating residents put their recyclables in some type of a "recycling bag" (usually polyethylene or woven polypropylene) and place it at the curb. In some programs that have used bags, recyclables and trash bags are picked up by the hauler at the same time in the same truck, and the recyclables are pulled from the regular waste stream at a processing facility (landfill, transfer station, materials recovery facility, or waste-to-energy facility). Once separated, the bags are opened, and recyclables are processed and marketed. Issues to keep in mind when considering bag co-collection with trash are breakage (especially glass), material contamination, material loss, and, sometimes, poor public perception.

The decision to use bags in some communities has been based on several factors. Bags are usually purchased by the system users (residents and businesses), whereas bins are often provided by the municipality. Residents might leave bins at the curb after collection, resulting in a higher incidence of theft and damage. Whether a community chooses to use plastic bags or bins affects other components of the recycling system such as type of collection vehicle used, the amount of material separation required, and the types of processing equipment or capacity needed. There is no hard-and-fast rule for a community to apply when considering bags versus bins. Careful analysis and discussions with other communities that have faced similar decisions will be useful.

Frequency of collection is also a major consideration when designing a residential recycling program. Weekly collection has become the standard for curbside, although some communities institute every-other-week collection as a cost-saving measure. Twice monthly collections can reduce operational costs, but require more extensive promotional efforts to remind residents of their collection day. Participation may suffer with once-a-month collection since residents may not want "trash"—even recyclable trash—accumulating in their homes. Furthermore, if residents miss a collection day, they may decide to dispose of recyclables that may have overflowed in the storage container(s) in order to avoid the nuisance.

MULTIFAMILY COLLECTION

The principle behind collecting recyclables from multifamily residential dwellings is no different from curbside collection from single-family residences—maximize ease of participation for the resident. Planning for the collection of recyclables from multifamily units must take into account the existing procedures for refuse disposal (residents may take their garbage to a trash room, may access trash chutes, or may be required to take their waste to an outside dumpster).

Home storage of the recyclable materials needs to be considered. Apartments typically have small kitchens and limited storage space. Commingled collection is generally advisable under such settings—one storage container takes up less space than three. Residents would then deliver the commingled recyclables up to the set-out point, where they may be required to sort the materials into appropriate bins or place them in a single large container. Each multifamily situation will present unique challenges. Creative, flexible approaches to collection may be more appropriate than a strictly prescriptive approach.

RESIDENTIAL DROP-OFF COLLECTION

Drop-off recycling programs are the most common recycling collection systems currently in operation in the United States. Drop-off centers may be publicly or privately operated or run by nonprofit community groups, and may offer a buy-back component for some or all materials. Systems rarely are capital intensive or require high operation costs; they present a relatively low cost and flexible way for recycling programs to be designed to fit the specific needs of the community.

In communities where the majority of residents take their refuse to the landfill or a transfer station, the placement of drop-off centers at these sites may be the most appropriate way to recover recyclables. In other communities, however, planners need to weigh the benefits of a drop-off system (reduced capital expenditures and lower operating and maintenance costs) against potential drawbacks. Drop-off systems generally achieve lower diversion rates than more convenient curbside programs since they require that residents not only keep recyclables separate from other refuse but also deliver these materials to the drop-off facility during its hours of operation.

COMMERCIAL WASTE STREAM COLLECTION

When designing recyclables collection systems for the commercial sector, it is critical to understand what can be efficiently recovered from the commercial waste stream. Industry typically recovers and recycles a large amount of preconsumer scrap. Many other postconsumer commercial recycling activities exist; however, the most prevalent programs recover paper products, mostly corrugated cardboard. Office paper and commercially generated glass and cans also present a commercial sector recycling opportunity.

Designing a system for the collection of recyclables from a commercial establishment must take into consideration how the waste stream is generated and how it leaves the generator. Incentives for separation can encourage recovery rates. For example, in a corrugated recovery program, tipping fees could be reduced for corrugated-rich loads and/or the generator could be paid for the materials. Private paper dealers and/or haulers may put baling or storage equipment on site to encourage separation, collection, and storage of the target material.

The collection mechanism for recyclables in the commercial sector will probably vary little from the collection of garbage. Typically collection is mechanized. Sometimes adding a separate container for cardboard is all that is necessary. If cardboard makes up the largest component of the waste stream, a smaller container for noncardboard materials may be the only adjustment needed. Buyers of recovered office paper, on the other hand, may provide for separate collection from centrally located set-out points. Obviously, local markets, processing capabilities, and many other factors must be considered in starting a commercial collection system.

INSTITUTIONAL-GOVERNMENTAL COLLECTION SYSTEMS

Institutions can be major solid waste producers, and significant quantities of recyclables can be removed from institutional and governmental waste. To successfully implement recycling programs in institutions, three issues must be addressed, either collectively or on an individual basis: (1) obtaining reliable markets and transportation for recyclables collected; (2) developing a well-organized and convenient internal recyclables' collection program accessible to employees and those being served by the institution; and (3) providing adequate educational and promotional support for the program. Many of the same principles involved in commercial recycling programs apply to institutional systems.

audi(
prom
dio a
natu
with
effec
reacl
secto
oppc
sour
dio s
ties.
  N
tain
shou
riety
radic
exce
slots
  V
prog
telev
Othe

• Pa
• Pr
• Di
• Pr
• Bu

MC

Rur:

  F
  S
  1
  t

Legi
a pl
duc
The

Cur

• T
  y

COLLECTION EQUIPMENT

A properly designed collection system with the most suitable collection vehicles forms the backbone of a successful recycling program. Selecting the most appropriate collection vehicles for a recycling program requires careful consideration and analysis of the entire program structure. The collection vehicle is vital to obtaining the best collection efficiency available, given the particulars of home storage systems, market requirements, transportation routes, and processing capabilities. In some communities, existing equipment can be used or modified, resulting in substantial cost savings. Other communities, however, may need to invest in the purchase of dedicated recycling collection vehicles. When selecting appropriate equipment, program planners should keep the following considerations in mind:

• Total system cost can be minimized if programs are designed with interchangeable equipment.
• Curbside collection vehicles for separate collection should be designed with a low materials loading height, sufficient capacity for full collection routes, readily accessible cabs, and quick off-loading of materials.
• Commercial collection vehicles should be able to maneuver well in tight areas near participating businesses.

PROCESSING ALTERNATIVES

A system (including one or more facilities) to receive and process recyclables generated by residential and commercial-institutional sectors is a critical element in an efficient, comprehensive recycling program. To ensure that the recycled materials are marketable, the system must have the capability to upgrade materials to a variety of specifications. It must also have the flexibility to adapt to new specifications should new markets be engaged. Meeting market specifications can be ensured to the greatest extent possible by processing the materials in a materials recovery facility (MRF). The MRF receives collected recyclables, removes prohibited contaminated materials, and provides for storage and loadout of large quantities so that economies of transportation to markets are achieved. As neighboring communities begin to recycle, it will become increasingly important to process and upgrade a large flow of material to meet a range of current and future market specifications. Another strong argument for developing a MRF is that it allows haulers flexibility in the type of equipment they can use for collection. Large haulers with specialized recycling vehicles can be accommodated as easily as smaller haulers with trailers, stake-body trucks, or compactors.

Yard waste composting facilities may also be required to process increasing supplies of grass, brush, and/or leaves. Developing a yard waste processing system is attractive for several reasons. First, the market for the end product (wood chips or compost) is generally available at the local level (municipal or landscaping operations). Second, yard waste represents a significant portion of the waste stream in many communities and is easily identified and separated. Significant reductions in landfill disposal of waste can be achieved through yard waste recovery operations.

- Seventy percent of the residential MSW is delivered directly to a county disposal facility (one of six staffed compactor sites or the county landfill) by residents. Approximately 50 percent of county waste is collected by private haulers.

- Most of the MSW generated in the county (from all sectors) is disposed of at the landfill. A smaller, unknown quantity is burned or buried on-site or illegally dumped.

- White goods are accepted at the compactor sites, but residents are encouraged to bring them to the landfill.

- The tip fee at the landfill for private haulers has recently been raised from $15 to $40 per ton. Residents may deliver garbage for free.

- Revenues for the waste management system are raised through tip fees and a special assessment on each improved lot in the county.

Existing Recycling

- White goods and scrap metal segregation at the landfill.
- Roll-off boxes placed at local military installation for scrap metal recovery.
- Old corrugated containers (OCC) separation at several local supermarkets.
- Office paper recycling programs in several county offices.
- Newspaper recycling through The Optimist Club (when markets are favorable).
- Local markets identified for newspaper, high grade office paper, white goods, and scrap metal.
- Regional markets identified for glass, OCC, metal cans, and plastic containers (HDPE and PET).

Setting Goals

Short-Term

- Analyze the county's waste stream and determine the potential quantities of recyclable materials available for recovery from residential, commercial, and institutional-governmental sources.

- Review existing recycling activities in the county and quantify amounts of materials currently recovered through these efforts.

- Identify markets available to the county for the targeted recyclable materials.

- Evaluate collection alternatives, including the legal basis for county involvement in recyclables collection activities.

- Analyze existing in-county processing options for handling targeted recyclables.

- Review regional processing alternatives, including the feasibility of establishing a regional materials recovery facility and/or sharing processing equipment with neighboring counties.

- Review possible ownership and operation structures for any needed facilities.

- Develop reporting requirements and data collection mechanisms necessary to accurately document the county's progress toward its goals.

- Review financing mechanisms available to the county to pay for the planned systems and programs.

- Take advantage of residential self-haul practices and pursue an aggressive residential drop-off system using existing compactor sites.
- Develop public education and promotion campaign.
- Document existing commercial recycling that can be credited toward goal.

Medium-Term

- Monitor progress of residential drop-off program. Modify existing sites as needed to accommodate increasing amounts of targeted recyclables or additional materials. Determine if curbside system is indicated in order to attain recycling goal.
- Take action to increase commercial sector recycling through a combination of technical assistance and financial incentives such as:

Requiring or offering a recyclables collection service to commercial establishments.

Facilitating cooperative marketing of commercial recyclables.

Providing businesses with balers or separate dumpsters for OCC collection.

Waiving tip fee or offering a reduced tip fee for loads of commercial recyclables.

Prohibiting disposal of loads containing designated recyclables.

Long-Term

- Meet and maintain state-mandated recycling goal within the county's budget constraints.

Implementation Schedule

Short-Term

Residential Program

- Determine what materials will be collected and what types of containers will be used.
- Determine the role of the public and private sectors in operating the drop-off sites.
- Develop bid specifications for and procure drop-off equipment.
- Modify existing compactor sites to accommodate roll-off containers for recycling.
- Procure appropriate signage.
- Train compactor site attendants.
- Begin accepting targeted recyclables from county residents.
- Monitor collection and assess public attitudes toward the program.

Commercial-Institutional Recycling Program

- Conduct survey of selected commercial establishments to determine current level of recycling and to guide the development of a technical assistance–outreach program.
- Meet with local haulers and processors to encourage private sector collection of commercial and institutional recyclables.

- Expand in-house recycling programs for county offices.
- Develop and institute reporting mechanism to quantify and document commercial and institutional recycling activities.

Marketing

- Work with state to identify and develop markets for targeted recyclables.
- Negotiate and secure sales agreements with preferred markets.

Processing

- Determine if private sector processing capacity will be utilized. If so, develop and issue procurement documents and draft contracts.
- If county-owned and -operated processing facility is chosen:

Select and prepare site(s).

Secure necessary permits.

Develop and issue bid documents for building and equipment.

Select preferred contractor(s), execute agreements, and monitor facility construction and testing.

- Evaluate feasibility of private or regional yard waste processing facility.
- If county-operated composting facility is chosen, secure necessary permits; select and prepare site; procure necessary equipment; and begin receiving yard waste.

Public Education

- Develop and institute aggressive promotional campaign aimed at both residential and commercial sectors.

Administration

- Hire appropriate staff.
- Determine reporting procedures and documentation needs for commercial and institutional generators and/or local haulers and processors.
- Develop and implement enforcement strategy.
- Develop procurement policy for recycled products.

Medium-Term

Residential Program

- Evaluate drop-off program and make changes as needed (i.e., need for additional sites).
- Evaluate potential sites for additional drop-off capacity at other county locations.
- Evaluate need for more aggressive residential collection measures (i.e., curbside collection of recyclables from those residents who use private haulers).

Commercial-Institutional Program

- Evaluate the contribution of commercial recycling activities toward recycling goal through reporting and documentation systems.

- Continue outreach–technical assistance program for this sector.
- Consider appropriate incentives and disincentives to encourage increased recycling.
- Expand recycling programs to include all county facilities; consider including multiple materials (scrap metal, yard waste, batteries, used oil, tires, etc.).

Marketing

- Monitor market conditions and existing market arrangements.
- Renegotiate market agreements as needed.

Processing

- Monitor process flow, receiving procedures, storage and handling methods, and adjust as needed.
- Procure additional equipment or services as needed.

Public Education

- Continue educational and promotional campaign for general recycling programs.
- Implement waste reduction campaign.

Administration

- Evaluate staffing and budget allocations and request adjustments as needed.
- Provide ongoing management of the recycling program.
- Document recycling recovery rates and contribution that each sector is making toward recycling goal; report to the state as needed.
- Assess progress toward goal and consider program adjustments if shortfall is encountered.
- Prepare timetable to enact or amend necessary legislation, ordinances, codes, and other governmental tools to achieve recycling goals.
- Monitor evolving federal and state legislative proposals and keep abreast of potential impacts on county program.
- Implement and expand procurement policy for recycled products.

Long-Term

Residential

- Monitor all existing collection systems and adjust as necessary.
- Implement curbside collection in indicated areas.

Commercial-Institutional Collection

- Monitor effectiveness of commercial-institutional collection programs and make adjustments as needed.

Marketing

- Monitor market conditions and existing market arrangements; renegotiate as needed.

Processing

- Monitor processing of recyclables and yard waste; adjust operating procedures as needed.
- Procure additional equipment as needed.

Public Education

- Continue ongoing educational and promotional campaigns.
- If mandatory ordinance is implemented, develop appropriate media relations strategy and public outreach efforts.

Administration

- Document recycling recovery rates and report to state.
- Implement mandatory recycling ordinance if necessary.
- Monitor legislative needs and initiatives.
- Evaluate staffing and budget allocations and request adjustments as needed.
- Provide ongoing management of the recycling program.

Large Municipality

Population: 3,500,000

Demographics: 1,000,000 households (single and multifamily)

Total MSW: 4,000,000 tons per year (55 percent commercial; 35 percent residential; 10 percent institutional)

Legislative Background and Recycling Goals.   The state's comprehensive Waste Management Act requires that every county in the state reduce its waste streams by 50 percent by the year 2000. An interim goal of 25 percent reduction-recycling must be achieved by 1995. The act provides for the disbursement of grants and loans to help jurisdictions implement recycling programs. Recycling plans are required from each of the counties; however, municipalities with populations over 500,000 may choose to submit their own plans.

Current Solid Waste Management System

- Twice-per-week municipal collection from residential sector (single-family and multifamily up to four units) with city crews and vehicles.
- Currently, three-person collection crews manually empty garbage into compactor trucks. Under this system, over 700 city trucks are necessary to accomplish collection. City is considering switch to semiautomated collection of wheeled carts in some residential areas and reducing collection frequency so that existing trucks can be diverted for recycling collection.
- Front-end loader collection trucks used to collect waste from dumpsters from city institutional buildings, housing projects, and a smaller number of condominiums.
- Schools use their own vehicles to collect their own waste.
- Commercial establishments receive private waste collection.

- All of the city's waste is delivered either to a privately owned and operated waste-to-energy facility or the city-owned and -operated landfill.
- Tip fee is $65/ton at the landfill and at the waste-to-energy facility.
- A tip fee surcharge imposed at the waste-to-energy facility and the landfill is credited toward a recycling fund, which can be used for program development and implementation.
- The city has retained the services of a consulting firm to conduct a waste stream analysis and to prepare its recycling plan in accordance with state regulations.

Existing Recycling

- White goods are segregated at the landfill.
- Ferrous metal is magnetically recovered from ash at the waste-to-energy facility.
- The city has recently launched a 2000 household pilot curbside program. City crews collect mixed paper, plastic containers (HDPE and PET), metal cans, glass containers, and leaves from these residents on a weekly basis.
- There are 10 city-sponsored community drop-offs and 2 private buy-back centers.
- The city provides vacuum collection of leaves from city parks, recreation areas, and two upper-income suburban neighborhoods within the city. These leaves are taken to one of two composting facilities.
- Several city offices have instituted office paper recycling programs.
- Local markets have been identified for newspaper, old corrugated containers (OCC), office and mixed paper, plastic containers (HDPE and PET), and steel cans and scrap.
- The city is currently diverting 8 percent of its generated waste stream through existing recycling programs from residential and commercial-institutional sources.

Major Policy Considerations

- Achievement of a 50 percent reduction-recycling goal necessitates a full-scale recycling program serving all sectors of the population. Adequate financial, administrative, and legal resources must be committed if the program is to satisfy state requirements.
- Consultants have recommended that, in order to meet its recycling implementation deadlines, the city should couple its recycling program with a switch to a semiautomated collection system for refuse. As semiautomated collection of refuse is introduced in residential areas, manual collection vehicles will be diverted to provide recycling collection. The consultants have determined that the increased efficiency realized with semiautomated collection will offset the costs of implementing citywide residential recycling.
- The aggressive nature of the recycling program necessary to achieve the state-mandated recycling goal will require the commitment of adequate staff. At a minimum, the city needs to hire qualified personnel to include division heads for recycling and waste reduction; coordinators or specialists to handle several distinct program areas (i.e., public education, marketing, commercial recycling

initiatives, and residential recycling activities); and clerical or support personnel.

- Traffic congestion issues need to be considered when incorporating recycling into the current refuse collection system.

Setting Goals

Short-Term

- Apply for state funding for program implementation, facility development, and/ or equipment purchase through grant or loan program.
- Distribute wheeled carts for once-per-week refuse collection and implement once-per-week recycling collection in selected communities.
- Test yard waste collection alternatives and select most appropriate option(s).
- Allocate available collection resources (personnel and vehicles) to accommodate both refuse and recyclables collection.
- Continue expanding once-per-week refuse collection and once-per-week recycling collection to all city-collected households.
- By working with private haulers, businesses, and property management firms, implement a commercial collection program.
- As curbside recycling programs are initiated in neighborhoods, develop program of education, warnings, and enforcement to encourage participation and compliance.
- Develop a record-keeping system that will be used to monitor all recycling activities (including drop-off and buy-back centers) and assess progress toward the recycling goal.
- Target recyclable materials that will be included in the city's program, based on the results of the waste stream analysis, potential contribution toward achievement of the recycling goal, and the presence of local or regional markets.
- Identify and secure markets for recovered materials.
- Identify and secure adequate processing capacity. If necessary, apply for funding to finance the development of a materials recovery facility and/or a yard waste composting facility.
- Develop an aggressive public education–promotional campaign for residential, institutional, and commercial sectors.
- Hire appropriate staff to manage comprehensive recycling program.
- Consider imposing landfill bans on designated materials.
- Ensure that all new public convenience centers or other waste-receiving facilities are designed with recyclables handling capabilities.

Medium-Term

- Monitor progress of programs and adjust as needed to assure attainment of 25 percent recycling goal.
- Expand program to include other materials that can contribute toward the 50 percent reduction goal.
- Consider mixed waste processing or composting to achieve 50 percent goal.
- Provide ongoing outreach and technical assistance to commercial and institutional sectors.

- Consider passing ordinances requiring private haulers to offer recycling services to their clients and making hauler licensure contingent upon the provision of these services.

Long-Term

- Achieve and maintain 50 percent reduction goal.

Implementation Schedule

Short-Term

Residential Program

- Expand pilot curbside program.
- Begin shift to semiautomated collection of refuse with once-per-week refuse and once-per-week recycling collection; begin training existing personnel in recyclables collection methods.
- Procure and distribute wheeled refuse collection carts and home storage recycling bins for household recyclables and yard wastes (as appropriate).
- Pass ordinance requiring homeowners in areas receiving curbside collection to keep recyclables separate from trash. Allow residents choice of participating in curbside program or taking recyclables to drop-off or buy-back center.
- Institute pilot multifamily collection programs.
- Monitor collection and assess public attitudes toward the programs.

Commercial-Institutional Recycling Program

- Identify selected commercial and institutional waste generators and issue survey to identify recycling potential and existing recycling practices.
- Implement technical assistance–outreach program to commercial sector.
- Develop and institute reporting mechanism to quantify and document commercial-institutional recycling activities.
- Establish a voluntary program whereby local haulers are encouraged to offer the collection of recyclables to their commercial-institutional accounts. If a good response is not received, pass ordinances requiring private haulers to provide their customers with recycling collection.
- Place special emphasis on programs to recover materials from schools to help foster the development of a recycling ethic in school-aged children.
- Expand in-house recycling programs for city offices.

Marketing

- Investigate feasibility of collective marketing agreement with county.
- Work with state to identify and develop markets for targeted recyclables.
- Negotiate and secure sales agreements with preferred markets.

Processing

- Begin procurement of processing capacity through a Request for Proposals (RFP).
- Develop yard waste processing capacity through public or private sources.

Public Education

- Develop and institute an aggressive, general promotional campaign aimed at both residential and commercial-institutional sectors.
- Develop specific media relations and a public outreach strategy to offset potentially a negative response to mandatory recycling ordinances.
- Promote and initiate block leader programs in areas receiving curbside collection as a way of encouraging participation and generating community pride in and "ownership" of the program.

Administration

- Institute landfill disposal ban on lead-acid batteries and tires, concurrent with the development of recycling programs to handle these materials.
- Hire appropriate staff.
- Develop procurement policy for recycled products.
- Determine reporting procedures and documentation needs for commercial-institutional generators and/or local haulers and processors.
- Develop and implement enforcement strategy.

Medium-Term

Residential Program

- Evaluate ongoing curbside and drop-off programs, identify problems regarding participation, equipment, collection, and markets, and make changes as needed to ensure achievement of interim 25 percent recycling goal.
- Evaluate potential sites for additional drop-off centers.
- Continue expansion of curbside program.
- Expand multifamily programs working with building owners and managers and private haulers.

Commercial-Institutional Program

- Evaluate the contribution of commercial-institutional recycling activities toward the recycling goal through reporting and documentation systems.
- Continue outreach–technical assistance program for this sector.
- Consider appropriate incentives and disincentives to encourage increased recycling.
- Expand recycling programs to include all city facilities; begin including additional materials, concurrent with identification of available markets.

Marketing

- Evaluate market conditions and existing market arrangements.
- Renegotiate market agreements as needed to accommodate increased quantities and additional materials in program.

Processing

- Evaluate process flow, receiving procedures, and storage and handling methods and adjust as needed for public or private MRFs.

- Procure additional equipment and/or capacity as needed.
- Begin project development work for mixed waste processing or composting if appropriate.

Public Education

- Continue general educational and promotional campaign for all sectors.
- Implement waste reduction campaign.

Administration

- Consider landfill ban on yard waste and other designated recyclables.
- Evaluate staffing and budget allocations and request adjustments as needed.
- Provide ongoing management of the recycling program.
- Document recycling recovery rates and contribution that each sector is making toward recycling goal; report to the state as needed.
- Assess progress toward goal and consider program adjustments if shortfall is encountered.
- Implement and expand procurement policy for recycled products.

Long-Term

Residential

- Monitor all existing collection systems and adjust as necessary.
- Expand curbside collection to include all city-collected residences.

Commercial-Institutional Collection

- Monitor effectiveness of commercial-institutional collection programs and make adjustments as needed.

Marketing

- Evaluate market conditions and existing market arrangements; renegotiate as needed.

Processing

- Monitor processing of recyclables and yard waste; adjust operating procedures as needed.
- Procure additional equipment and/or capacity (including mixed waste processing or composting) as needed.

Public Education

- Continue ongoing educational and promotional campaigns.

Administration

- Document recycling recovery rates and report to state.
- Monitor legislative needs and initiatives.
- Evaluate staffing and budget allocations and request adjustments as needed.

• Provide ongoing management of the recycling program.

Small Town

Population: Year round 36,000.

Demographics: Major state university is located in the town. Forty thousand students attend the university.

Total MSW: 44,000 tons per year (including 8000 tons per year generated by the university).

Legislative Background and Recycling Goals. The state's comprehensive recycling law sets a mandatory recycling goal of 30 percent to be achieved by 1997. The law states that each municipality must pass an ordinance mandating source separation and collection of recyclables from each resident, business, or institutional establishment within its borders. This provision requires all primary and secondary schools, colleges, and universities to implement recycling programs.

Current Solid Waste Management System

• The county in which the town is located is a member of a regional solid waste authority (the authority), which is the lead agency for the recycling program.

• The town's waste is taken to the authority's transfer station, where it is subsequently transported to a neighboring county's landfill.

• The authority has implemented a surcharge on each ton of waste disposed at its transfer station to fund the local portion of the capital costs of the recycling program.

• The authority's transfer station is being modified to accommodate an intermediate processing center (IPC) for recyclables and a scale house.

Existing Recycling

• Through a grant, the state environmental regulatory agency has provided funding to the authority for program planning, contract development, and equipment and facilities for the service area.

• The authority has prepared a recycling plan for its member municipalities describing markets for the sale of recyclables; an initial curbside recycling service area; locations for drop-off centers; volumes of materials that can be anticipated; and details on the proposed IPC.

• The proposed recycling program will be multimaterial, mandatory, regional, authority-sponsored, and will provide the weekly collection of recyclables from residences.

• The authority has hired a full-time recycling program manager to help implement the program and work closely with member municipalities.

• The town, as a member municipality, has entered into a recycling agreement with the authority. Under the terms of the agreement, the authority accepts responsibility for all program planning, financing, implementation, and administration; application for funding; adoption of regulations; and provision of public education. The municipality is obligated to adopt a mandatory recycling ordinance and to cooperate and assist the authority with the development of the recycling program.

- The state university located in the town has also entered into a recycling agreement with the authority. Under the terms of this agreement, the university purchases all equipment needed to collect recyclable materials and provides transport of the materials to the authority's IPC at the transfer station. In turn, the authority pursues state funding to cover part of the start-up costs for the recycling program.
- The town is reviewing a draft recycling ordinance developed by the authority.
- The authority is sponsoring recycling demonstration programs, including limited curbside collection, establishment of drop-offs, pilot commercial programs, and yard waste processing and tire recycling projects. It plans to expand these programs.

Setting Goals.   By choosing to become a member municipality of a regional authority, the town has simplified its role in the development of a comprehensive recycling program for its residents. Essentially, the town's short-, medium-, and long-term goals can be combined as follows:

- Achieve the state's recycling mandate in the most economical manner by working through the authority and other municipalities.
- Adopt the mandatory source separation and collection ordinance.
- Through the town representative on the authority's board, monitor the recycling agreement with the authority to assure that the town stays in compliance with state law.
- Approve, through town council, any funds required or loans that need to be guaranteed in connection with the recycling program.
- Adopt any legislative measures necessary to comply with the state law or the achievement of the reduction goal.

CHAPTER 5

SEPARATION AND COLLECTION SYSTEMS PERFORMANCE MONITORING

Abbie (Page) McMillen*

President, McMillen Environmental Inc.
Harborside, Maine

INTRODUCTION

Since the mid-1980s, recycling has blossomed as an entrepreneurial activity within both government and the private sector. The public desire to recycle has created a demand for many new products and services. *Products* include specialized recycling containers, collection vehicles, and processing equipment/facilities; *services* include collection, separation, processing, transportation, marketing, and public information. Business and government have both been eager to fill these needs for products and services, in many cases competing for the opportunity to provide them.

This chapter will discuss the products and services at the "front end" of the recycling cycle. Once the decision has been made to recycle, there are literally hundreds of decisions that need to be made concerning how to go about it. Perhaps the first decisions that are faced (and certainly the decisions with the greatest public visibility) are how to separate the recyclables from the rest of the refuse stream and, once separated, how to collect them for processing and marketing. These decisions are crucial to the success of the recycling effort. They must be made with full consideration of the fact that postconsumer recycling is essentially a remanufacturing process which usually depends upon thousands of volunteers as the source of the raw materials. If these thousands of sources of raw material are reluctant or unreliable, the remanufacturing process will be expensive at best, or even unfeasible.

This chapter addresses both the selection process and the available options for a separation and collection system, as well as measuring the performance of the selected separation and collection system. A critical objective is "to move the material from the point of generation to the market in the least costly and most efficient fashion."[83]

---

*During the initial preparation of this chapter, the author was project director for Roy F. Weston, Inc. of Burlington, Massachusetts.

Separation

The most fundamental question concerning separation is whether and to what degree to rely on separation at the point of generation. *Mixed-refuse collection and processing* systems ask the least of the generator. They also require the least change in the established collection system. However, far more effort is required in processing, since the recyclable materials must be separated from the balance of the refuse by human and mechanical means. This is expensive. *Source separation* places far more reliance on the generator, and in addition requires that modifications be made in the established collection practice. This can also be expensive.

Collection

Completely interrelated with the question about whether and how much source separation to rely upon is the question about whether to institute a special collection of recyclables (commonly called *curbside collection* when applied to residential refuse), or whether to rely instead upon the generator to transport the recyclables to a *drop-off* or *buy-back* location. Curbside collections generally yield much more material per capita but are also much more expensive than drop-off or buy-back collection. Quantity and marketability of the collected recyclables are of paramount concern. If it can be shown that the collected recyclables are much greater in quantity or much more marketable if collected in an expensive way rather than in cheaper, alternative way, then the extra cost of the more expensive collection system might be justifiable.

Measuring Performance

As a practical matter, the total quantity of recyclables in the refuse stream cannot all be recovered for recycling. For example, newspaper which is used for wrapping putrescible refuse, and glass containers which are broken into pieces too small to sort, will not be available for recycling. The term *capture rate* is used to denote the weight percent of an eligible material in the total refuse stream which is actually separated out for recycling.[15] This performance measure is of the greatest importance in measuring the success of a separation and collection program. Note that the capture rate is a term that usually applies to an individual recyclable material. For example, the capture rate of aluminum may be very different from the capture rate for newspaper.

For residential refuse, the individual unit of refuse generation is the household. For commercial and industrial sources of refuse, the individual unit is the business. *Participation rate* is the term used to denote the percent of households or businesses which regularly separate out recyclables; i.e., that separate some eligible items at least once during a given period of time.[29] Although usually applied to participation in curbside collection, participation rate has also been applied as a measure of the effectiveness of drop-off or buy-back centers. In fact, participation in a curbside collection program could be lower than expected if there is an effective network of drop-off or buy-back centers, but the overall capture rate might be high. On a monthly basis, it is estimated that 80 percent of households will participate at least to some degree in a well-designed and properly publicized curbside collection program, but a high participation rate does not necessarily mean that the capture rate will meet expectations. Participation rate is a very loosely defined term with the potential to mislead people into believing that a recycling program is more effective in capturing recyclables than it actually is.[32]

Other performance measures have been developed for specific program design purposes. For example, *set-out rate* indicates the participation on any given collection day. In a community with weekly curbside collection experiencing an 80 percent residential participation rate, the set-out rate may be in the range of 50 to 60 percent. This factor is important in determining collection vehicle requirements.

Recycling rate is sometimes used to denote the pounds of total recyclables that are collected per household per month.[27] It has been expressed as per household served by the program, per household in the community, or per household participating. In other cases, it is used to denote the weight percent of total refuse that is recycled instead of being landfilled or incinerated. This term can be misleading unless the specific materials being recycled and the characteristics of the refuse stream are both specified.[32] For example, if a town generates 20 tons per day (TPD) of total refuse (residential plus commercial) and sends to the remanufacturing industries a total of 2 TPD (net of processing residue and rejects), the recycling rate is 10 percent of total waste but probably about 20 percent of residential waste (assuming residential and commercial tonnages are roughly equivalent, as they are in many communities).

Another performance measure is the *net diversion rate,* which represents the weight percent of total refuse that is not landfilled (or, in some cases, not incinerated either). Thus, if the objective of the program is to minimize the weight of refuse (including processing residues and incinerator ash) sent to a landfill through a combination of strategies (such as source reduction, recycling, and incineration), the ultimate performance measure is the net diversion rate. It is also possible to estimate a *volumetric* net diversion rate by knowing the compacted densities and weights of the materials diverted. Although not commonly computed, this measure would be a useful one, since landfills do not become full because they have become too *heavy,* but rather because their available *volume* has been consumed. Thus, high-volume, low-weight materials (such as some plastics) can contribute to a more rapid depletion of landfill space than their refuse weight percentage might imply.

SEPARATION

As in other aspects of recycling, there is confusion concerning the definition of terms relating to separation, for example, *commingled, source-separated,* and *curbside-separated.* The confusion is enhanced with additional qualifiers such as "fully commingled." In this chapter, we shall adhere to the following guidelines for use of these terms:

> *Commingling* is an attribute which can only be fully understood if the materials which are commingled are also listed (for example, "commingled food and beverage containers" or "all fiber and nonfiber recyclables commingled"). There does not seem to be an easy way out of this more lengthy description, if clarity of meaning is to be preserved.

Source-separated should be a term reserved to mean separated into any number of categories of refuse by the generator of the refuse. Thus, the act of separating all recyclables from all other refuse is an act of source separation, even though only two categories result (refuse, and all recyclables commingled). Refuse can also be source-separated into multiple categories of recyclables, plus a remainder which is still refuse.

Curbside-separated refers to the process by which the collector receives commingled recyclables and separates them into categories during the act of putting them into a compartmentalized collection vehicle. (For example, "residents source-separate newspapers and containers from the refuse, placing the newspapers and commingled containers at the curbside, where the collectors curbside-separate the commingled containers into four categories: three colors of glass, and all other.")

The "generator" of waste is considered to be the person discarding it. Ranking separation concepts from those that make the least demands on the generator to those that make the most demands on the generator results in a hierarchy somewhat like the one shown in Fig. 5.1.

In general, participation rates can be expected to be greatest for the separation concepts that place the least demand on the generator, although motivational factors are complex and it has been possible to achieve high participation with methods that place relatively large demands on the generator. This section describes separation concepts and their effectiveness in detail.

No Source Separation: Mixed-Refuse Collection/Processing

In addition to being the easiest for the refuse generator, mixed refuse is also the easiest for the collector. Participation in a no-sort system is by definition 100 per-

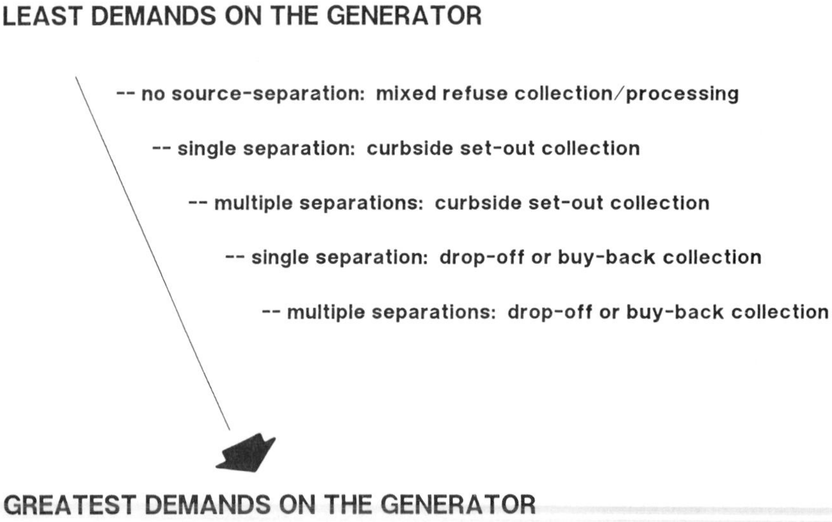

LEAST DEMANDS ON THE GENERATOR

-- no source-separation: mixed refuse collection/processing

-- single separation: curbside set-out collection

-- multiple separations: curbside set-out collection

-- single separation: drop-off or buy-back collection

-- multiple separations: drop-off or buy-back collection

GREATEST DEMANDS ON THE GENERATOR

FIGURE 5.1 Hierarchy of effort in source separation.

cent. However, the challenges to the processor should not be underestimated. All refuse is discarded in a single container and it is up to a processor to separate out the usable components, then upgrade these components to meet marketing specifications.

Availability.   There are few examples of unsorted residential refuse being processed to remove recyclables. "Although a few mixed refuse recycling facilities are operating in the United States and Europe, common wisdom in residential recycling has always been that the process starts at the home. The responsibility for keeping recyclables out of the refuse bin and storing the materials rests with the resident."[29] This assumption may be about to undergo a change, however, due to the increasing availability of innovative sorting and processing techniques, the generally higher cost of refuse disposal which makes such techniques cost-effective, and the inability of source-separation schemes to keep pace with refuse diversion goals set by policy makers.

In recent years, attempts have been made to engage the residents of inner-city areas in curbside collection. Where adequate data have been collected, it has been shown that participation and capture rates have been lower than experienced by curbside collection programs in the more affluent suburbs and in areas where the population is less transient.[10,53,87] The reasons for this phenomenon are perhaps intuitively obvious, including the fact that economically stressed individuals may have more pressing priorities than source-separating their refuse, and transients are not in one place long enough to receive instructions. Communities are therefore taking an interest in mixed-refuse collection (followed by mixed-refuse processing) to recover recyclables. If the efficiency of the mixed-refuse processing system is high enough to recover a sufficient quantity of recyclables to meet program goals and mandates at an affordable price, the mixed-refuse processing might be a good solution for some cities.

In addition to the potential for recovering recyclables without effort on the part of the generator, there is the consideration of collection equipment cost. It is expensive to replace or supplement an existing fleet of refuse-collection vehicles with those designed to collect recyclables. Some cities' fiscal management policies require that they allocate the entire cost of publicly purchased recycling vehicles and in-home source-separation containers to the budget year in which they are purchased, rather than amortizing the cost over time. This results in the appearance of a large, immediate impact on the budget. To reduce this impact, a service contract with a mixed-waste processor could achieve diversion goals while spreading the cost out over time. (Another way, of course, is to phase-in the new vehicles over a period of years.)

Mixed-waste processing of the "dump and pick" variety is popular for reclaiming materials from the commercial waste stream. Mixed commercial loads tend to be more homogeneous and less noxious than residential refuse, so they are good candidates for mixed-refuse processing and in fact can be included to improve the economics of a mixed residential refuse collection and processing operation. For example, in Marin County, California, mixed loads of commercial refuse are hand-sorted, and cardboard, glass bottles, aluminum cans, scrap metal, paper, and wood are recovered. The nonrecoverable components (mostly nonrecyclable cardboard, food refuse, paper, and various plastics) go to a transfer station. It was found that plastics are so lightweight that they are difficult to pull out of the refuse, and their market prices were not high enough to cover the cost of recovering them.[49]

Mixed-waste processing system designs differ substantially in the ratio of hand separation to mechanical separation. While it is not the purpose of this section to describe in detail the processing steps that take place in these facilities, in general they are quite similar to those used in the production of refuse-derived fuel. The mixed refuse is unloaded onto conveyors where workers hand-pick some easy-to-remove items (e.g., corrugated cardboard, newspapers, large pieces of brush, items that might damage the machinery). Bags are then broken open, and the refuse is separated into components using various combinations of shredding, screening, magnetic separation, eddy-current separation, air classification, and hand-sorting. New technology may soon be available that will distinguish among plastic resins.[90]

TABLE 5.1 Mixed-Waste Processing System Suppliers

Firm	Location	Telephone
American Recovery Corporation	Washington, D.C.	(202) 775-5150
Ashbrook-Simon-Hartley	Birmingham, Alabama	(205) 823-5231
Bedminster Bioconversion Co.	Cherry Hill, New Jersey	(609) 795-5767
Catrel	Edison, New Jersey	(201) 225-4849
Enviro-Gro Technologies	Baltimore, Maryland	(301) 644-9600
Environmental Recovery Systems	Denver, Colorado	(303) 623-1011
Ebara International Corporation	Greenburg, Pennsylvania	(412) 832-1200
Fairfield Service Co.	Marion, Ohio	(614) 387-3335
Harbert Triga	Birmingham, Alabama	(205) 987-5500
K/R Biochem	Tulsa, Oklahoma	(918) 492-9060
Lundell Mfg. Co.	Cherokee, Iowa	(712) 722-3709
National Recovery Technology, Inc.	Nashville, Tennessee	(615) 329-9088
ORFA	Cherry Hill, New Jersey	(609) 662-6600
Omni Technical Services	Uniondale, New York	(516) 222-0709
Raytheon Service Company	Burlington, Massachusetts	(617) 272-9300
RECOMP	Denver, Colorado	(303) 753-0945
Refuse Resource Recovery Systems	Omaha, Nebraska	(402) 342-8446
Reuter, Inc.	Hopkins, Minnesota	(612) 935-6921
Riedel Environmental, Inc. (Dano)	Portland, Oregon	(503) 286-4656
Taulman Composting Systems	Atlanta, Georgia	(404) 261-2535
Trash Reduction Systems, Inc.	Overland Park, Kansas	(913) 661-9494
U.S. Waste Recovery Systems	Fort Worth, Texas	(817) 877-0147
Waste Management of North America Inc.	Oak Brook, Illinois	(708) 572-8800
Waste Processing Corp. (Dano)	Bloomington, Minnesota	(612) 854-8666
Waste Reduction Services, Inc.	Scottsdale, Arizona	(602) 483-8586
Wheelabrator/Buhler-Maig	Danvers, Massachusetts	(508) 777-2207
XL Disposal Corporation	Crestwood, Illinois	(703) 389-6312

Sources: Roy F. Weston, Inc., vendor files.
Note: Some of these systems may require some presorting of the refuse. Not all vendors have systems operating in the United States.

A list of mixed-waste processing system suppliers is shown in Table 5.1, and these may be contacted for the details of their processes. A process flow diagram for one type of mixed waste processing system is shown in Fig. 5.2.

Effectiveness and Cost.   The products most likely to be recovered by manual or mechanical separation from mixed municipal (primarily residential) refuse include aluminum cans, aluminum scrap, steel cans, glass containers, plastic containers, newspaper, corrugated cardboard, mixed paper, refuse-derived fuel, and compost substrate. The kind and amount of recyclables recovered depend on:

- The processing steps that are employed in the particular facility design
- The ability of those processing steps to remove the materials from the particular refuse stream presented to them as feedstock
- The existence of markets for the quality of processed recyclables that can be produced, given the facility design and the refuse feedstock

Contamination of various degrees is bound to occur in a mixed-refuse collection. As market revenue rises, it becomes more worthwhile to employ ever more sophisticated and costly recovery and cleanup processes, whether manual or mechanical. It will be noted that one highly recyclable commodity, glass, is often not recovered in mixed-refuse collection and processing systems due to breakage both during collection and in the early stages of mixed-refuse processing, where refuse bags are being mechanically broken open and the waste tumbled around.

It is possible for mixed-waste processing systems to recover many recyclables (for example, steel cans) at capture rates that rival curbside collection. In addition, mixed-waste processing may have a very high landfill diversion rate through the production of fuel and/or compost. Some claim diversion rates in the neigh-

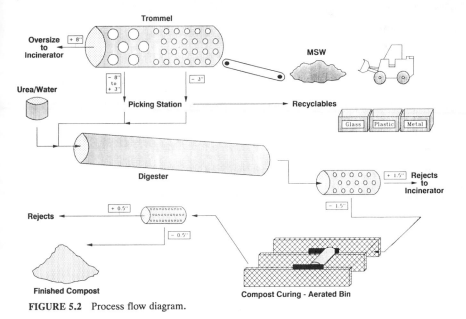

FIGURE 5.2   Process flow diagram.

borhood of 75 percent (not counting ash from combustion of the fuel fraction). Achieving this high a rate depends on being able to market the fuel and/or compost produced by the facility.

The cost of mixed-waste processing varies so widely that it would be misleading to generalize. However, it should be noted that all waste would typically be processed, so the facility would tend to be large and to have a relatively high capital cost (although much lower than a waste-to-energy incinerator of the same capacity). For example, if a curbside collection program were projected to capture enough recyclables to warrant construction of a 100-TPD intermediate processing center (IPC) or material recovery facility (MRF), then (assuming a typical curbside recycling rate of about 12 percent) a mixed-waste processing facility of about 830 TPD might be an alternative to the curbside-collection-plus-MRF scenario (since a total waste quantity of about 830 TPD would generate 12 percent—about 100 TPD—of recyclables). Whereas a 100-TPD MRF might be constructed for about $3 million, an 830-TPD mixed-waste processing facility might have a construction cost over $15 million, making it attractive for project financing. Associated with the curbside collection alternative would also be the capital and operating cost of collection vehicles and operating cost of the MRF: associated with the mixed-waste processing facility would be its operating cost.

Single Source Separation

Availability. In a single-sort system, generators segregate their refuse into just two categories: recyclable, and not recyclable. Next to no separation at all, this is the easiest method for the waste generator. Clearly, there have to be some limitations on what should be mixed together in the "recyclable" category. It would make little sense, for example, to mix leaves and yard waste with cans and bottles. The materials usually included in the recyclables category are newspaper, other fibers, and food and beverage containers of all types.

Usually, one-sort systems employ curbside collection. While it is theoretically possible to operate a drop-off or a buy-back program that accepts *all* recyclables (fiber and nonfiber) mixed together, there do not appear to be any examples of this approach. Some generators may choose to mix all fiber and nonfiber recyclables together in one container as a convenience in the home and separate them when they arrive at the drop-off or buy-back center. However, there are no data to support the supposition that this occurs. As a practical matter, it would seem to be neater, more convenient, and more efficient to separate newspapers and other fiber from cans, bottles, and other containers in the home if the resident is going to transport them to a drop-off or buy-back center.

There are, of course, limited drop-off centers, drop boxes, and reverse vending machines that accept only one material such as newspapers, plastic grocery bags, or aluminum beverage cans.[67] If these represent the only recycling opportunity available in a town, then they constitute in a sense a single-separation "system." However, such a limited system will not be discussed further in this section. Drop boxes and reverse vending machines can be a useful part of a more comprehensive recycling system, however.

A "new" one-separation concept (which has actually been undergoing development in Europe for some time) involves separating refuse into "wet" and "dry" fractions. The dry (paper, plastic, metal, etc.) fraction is further separated at a processing facility into marketable recyclables and fuel, while the wet (organic putrescible) fraction is processed into compost. In parts of Germany, residents who separate out their wet garbage for recycling pay a lower refuse collection bill.[17] In one town in the Netherlands, a two-sort, yellow and blue bag system was tried. The participation rate was 67 percent. The contents of the blue bags were composted with other organic waste. The contents of the yellow bags were further separated in a processing facility, but this proved to be technologically unfeasible. In another town, the dry fraction was more restrictively specified (cardboard and paper, tin cans, rags, and plastics). However, in this case, the separation of the dry fraction still proved unfeasible due to labor costs. The paper/plastic separation was found to be particularly difficult.[8] Canada has also been experimenting with wet/dry systems, using green bags or covered buckets for food waste. However, most of the Canadian experiments also involve multiple source separations.[78]

The most prominent example in the United States of a one-sort system is in Seattle, Washington. This city began a residential curbside collection experiment in 1988. In the southern half of the city, residents received a 60- or 90-gal container for the commingling of all recyclables. Recyclables in these containers were collected monthly. (For the northern half of the city, residents received three stackable bins for newspaper, mixed containers, and mixed paper. These containers were emptied weekly.)[59] A single source separation has also been used in a pilot project serving apartments in Tukwila, Washington. The recycling dumpster is located outside of the building and accepts all paper, cardboard, glass, metals, and plastics. Detailed instructions are printed on the dumpster, which is emptied by the same contractor serving the Seattle collection. In this case, dumpsters were the preferred container because of their greater volume capacity to accept cardboard, mechanical unloading ability, and lower tendency to be stolen.[6]

An alternative approach to providing separate collections for the two waste fractions (recyclables and nonrecyclables) is the provision of special bags in which residents place their recyclables. The bags are placed in the same container as the balance of the refuse and are collected in the same manner. At the processing facility, the bags are manually removed, opened, and the contents are processed. This method of collecting recyclables is termed *co-collection*.[33] The chief advantage of co-collection is that high capture rates are theoretically possible without the cost of a special recyclables collection. There are several problems which remain to be fully resolved, however. To be durable enough to withstand the collection process without breaking, the special bags are relatively expensive (on the order of 30 to 50 cents apiece). People do not always put the right materials in them. Breakage of glass is a problem, especially if paper is not included in the bag to cushion the glass. And retrieval of the bags from the mixed refuse and opening them for processing is labor-intensive.

Effectiveness and Cost.   A prominent recycling consulting firm, Resource Integration Systems Ltd. (RIS) concludes that "commingling of all materials (i.e., paper fiber materials with glass, metal, and plastic food and beverage containers) is not recommended. In programs where this is done, the recovery of all materials, especially paper, suffers. The amount of paper lost in processing is significant, and the quality of the processed paper is lowered by glass shards and other contaminants, limiting marketability. The trash residue of recycling processing plants

FIGURE 5.3 Plastic insert for keeping glass containers out of the otherwise commingled recyclables. (*Photograph by A. McMillen, Mercer Island, Washington.*)

that receive this material is significantly greater than for facilities which receive paper fibers separate from food and beverage containers."[15]

Glass particles in the paper pose problems for recycled paper mills. Because of the glass breakage problem, the firm in Seattle, Washington, that has been collecting materials in the single-separation system is distributing plastic inserts that will fit into the 90-gal carts to hold glass containers, which will be separated by the collector. (See Fig. 5.3.) In addition, pickup will be more frequent than monthly in the future, since a cart of 90-gal capacity may not hold all the recyclables that a household generates in one month.[4]

Multiple Source Separations

What Is the Optimal Degree of Source Separation?   By far the greatest number of recycling programs employ more than one separation on the part of the refuse generator. Theoretically dozens of categories of waste could be separated, leading to popular cartoons, such as the one shown in Fig. 5.4, which drives home the point that extra effort is required of the participants. The level of source separation required can be expected to have a direct impact on participation and capture rates. "As a general rule, the less residents have to do to participate in a recycling program, the more likely they are to participate. This convenience factor points out the need for multiple separations to be conducted somewhere other than at the household."[13]

One thing seems to be clear: the responsibility of sorting into categories will not be the *overriding* consideration of residents in their decision to participate. For example, a survey conducted by the National Solid Waste Management Association (NSWMA) in 1986 showed a higher participation in Santa Rosa, Cali-

FIGURE 5.4   Recycling cartoon. (*Source: Don Addis in The St. Petersburg Times, August 1988.*)

fornia (70 percent), where residents were asked to sort into three categories (news, glass, and metals) than in Islip, New York (30 percent), where all containers could be commingled.[59] (For factors leading to individual participation decisions, see Chap. 10 of this Handbook.)

The Center for the Biology of Natural Systems (CBNS) at Queens College in New York undertook an extensive recycling experiment in East Hampton, Long Island, New York. The researchers determined that four household containers would be needed for effective separation of about 70 percent of household refuse. As shown in Fig. 5.5, the four containers would receive:

- Food waste (plus other organics such as disposable diapers and yard waste, to be mixed with sewage sludge and brush at a compost plant). This category functions like the "wet" category described earlier
- All clean paper (to be separated at a paper separation plant and sold)
- All bottles and cans (to be separated at a separation plant and sold)
- All other refuse (to be landfilled with the rejects from the other three plants).

Hazardous waste and bulky waste would require separate collection and disposal systems.[54] However, this sorting scheme has not yet been widely implemented in its entirety, due to cost and current unavailability of mixed-paper separating facilities and mixed-organics composting facilities.

Three levels of multiple source separations (i.e., three degrees of commingling) have been attempted at various times in various municipalities (though variations of these are possible). These are shown schematically in Fig. 5.6:

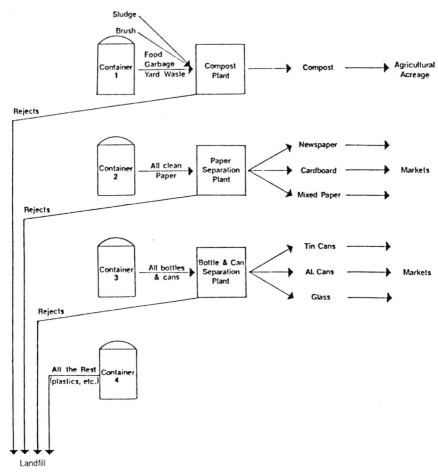

FIGURE 5.5 Basic separation scheme. (*From "Non-Burn System for Total Waste Stream, BioCycle, pp. 30–31, April 1987.*)

2 separations, plus refuse

REFUSE	FIBER	CONTAINERS
	newspaper old corrugated containers	food /beverage containers (glass, metal, plastic)

4 separations, plus refuse

REFUSE	FIBER	GLASS	METAL	PLASTIC
	newspaper OCC	bottles jars	cans	PET HDPE

8 separations, plus refuse

REFUSE	BROWN GLASS	GREEN GLASS	CLEAR GLASS	NEWS	FERROUS	ALUMINUM	PLASTIC	OCC
	bottles, jars	bottles, jars	bottles, jars		tin cans bimetals	cans	PET HDPE	

FIGURE 5.6 Multiple recyclables sorting schemes.

1. Two separations plus refuse
2. Four separations plus refuse
3. Higher degrees of source separation plus refuse (for example, newspaper, glass containers, tin and bimetal cans, aluminum cans, plastic containers (PET/HDPE), and corrugated cardboard).

There are many successful municipal programs with commingled food and beverage container collection (i.e., two separations plus refuse). Commingling of cans and bottles facilitates participation because just one in-home recycling container is required. The alternative of having a series of containers in the home suffers from higher cost of in-home containers, containers taking up too much space in the home, and requirements for too much participant effort—both in sorting and in physically setting out the containers. The collector's efficiency is improved because only one separation is necessary at the curb; i.e., news and paper fibers in one compartment, and commingled food and beverage containers in the other.[15] The major nationwide recycling collection firms seem to be trending toward two source separations.[4]

However, materials (especially glass) collected in a commingled state tend to have a lower market value, and research in New Jersey shows that smaller communities (especially those under 10,000 population) may find participation and capture to be entirely satisfactory in systems that require higher orders of source separation.[4] In a pilot project, Fitchburg, Wisconsin's, 3,000 households are separating numerous recyclables into three bins plus an HDPE sack full of polystyrene. Participation in the polystyrene experiment has been 83 percent (but the weekly set-out rate for the sacks has been only about 11 percent, because it takes a long time for most homes to fill them).[37]

Curbside Separation versus Source Separation.   Many communities rely on two source separations plus further curbside separation by the collector. For example, Anne Arundel Country, Maryland, asks the collector to separate recyclables into five truck compartments: three for the different colors of glass, one for mixed cans, and one for newspaper plus corrugated cardboard. In Palm Beach County, Florida, the collector sorts recyclables into four categories: glass (all three colors commingled), aluminum cans, plastics, and newspaper.[13] Fitchburg, Wisconsin, which has three source separations, further separates at the collection truck into 10 bins.[37]

Those who favor curbside sorting believe it "enables the community to sell quality separated materials to markets without installing an extensive processing system" with its attendant capital and operating costs.[13] Curbside sorted material is delivered directly to a storage/aggregation facility rather than to an IPC or MRF. Less glass is wasted, since most of the breakage occurs after the glass is color-separated.[69] Curbside sorting may be one answer for municipalities "whose operating budgets are more easily increased than their access to capital monies," and for smaller communities of about 10,000 or fewer stops.[13]

In addition to the advantage of avoiding some of the costs of a processing facility, proponents of curbside sorting point out the educational advantage of curbside sorting: nonrecyclables are left in the container. Sorting at the curb allows the collector to correct a householder by leaving a "contamination note" attached to the reject in the bin.[73] "Over time, the level of contamination in a commingled program actually gets worse...Our homeowner learns *the first time* he or she puts the wrong item in the box...so we get fewer and fewer contaminants."[69]

Another advantage of curbside sorting is said to be its ability to accommodate change. "One of the advantages of initially beginning a curbside program with curbside sorting is the fact that the capabilities of the processing method can change as the program grows without changing the separation behavior of the residents."[13]

On the other hand, curbside sorting does slow down the collection process. "In timing studies conducted in three communities comparing commingling with curbside sorting, the advantages of commingled collection are apparent. Two communities averaged slightly more than 30 seconds per stop with 5 separations at the curb. These same communities reduced time per stop between 7 and 10 seconds with commingled collection (one compartment for paper and another for mixed containers). This time savings resulted in extending route sizes substantially."[13] (Note that other estimates for curbside separation have shown that it takes 50 to 60 seconds to serve one stop,[69] and that 450 to 500 stops can be made in 9 hours of collection time.[4]

Another problem with curbside sorting is that "When a collection truck is divided into four or five compartments it is difficult to size each compartment so that they all fill up at the same rate....This improper ratio of compartment space results in the truck being forced off route with one or more compartments full (usually paper and/or plastic compartments)...Better utilization of truck capacity results in fewer trips to the processing/storage facility, therefore less nonproductive time and more efficient collection."[13] For example, data from San Diego, California, shows that when six materials were collected, the two glass compartments (flint and colored) were only 35 percent full when the newspaper, mixed paper, mixed cans, and mixed plastic container compartments were 90 to 100 percent full.[4]

Two of the major nationwide waste collection firms, Browning-Ferris Industries (BFI) and Waste Management, Inc. (WMI), are reported to hold opposing views on the value and cost of curbside sorting. BFI has taken the position that the improvement in material quality and reduced processing cost are worth the increased collection cost of curbside sorting, and WMI has taken the position that curbside sorting keeps the collectors on their routes too long.[73]

In summary, commingled materials collection is cheaper than curbside separation, encourages participation, and less glass breakage occurs due to cushioning effects.[73] But, contamination levels are probably higher. Separating at the curb may improve participation over requiring multiple source separations, but it slows down collection. Separation of recyclables that arrive at a processing facility in a commingled state requires relatively more extensive and expensive processing, but, in any source-separation system, some materials upgrading still must ordinarily be done by the collector or processor since "residents cannot be relied on to make perfect sorts every time."[13]

The availability of favorable markets should dictate choice of separation to a large degree; e.g., a high-paying market with a low tolerance for contamination may imply a need for either greater degrees of source separation or curbside separation, or a heavier investment in processing and cleaning.[15]

Mandatory versus Voluntary Source Separation

Effect on Participation and Capture.   The NSWMA survey conducted in the mid-1980s found that participation in mandatory programs averaged about 55 percent

TABLE 5.2   Recycling Rate for Mandatory and Voluntary Programs

Municipality	Type of separation	Pounds per capita per year collected
Essex County, New Jersey	Mandatory	600
Madison, Wisconsin	Mandatory	50
Monclair, New Jersey	Mandatory	250
Portland, Oregon	Mandatory	75
Prairie du Sac, Wisconsin	Mandatory	250
Wilton, New Hampshire	Mandatory	600
Ann Arbor, Michigan	Voluntary	95
Austin, Texas	Voluntary	550
Champaign, Illinois	Voluntary	130
Kitchener, Ontario	Voluntary	100
Marin County, California	Voluntary	190
Mecklenburg County, North Carolina	Voluntary	115
Minneapolis, Minnesota	Voluntary	55
San Jose, California	Voluntary	115
Santa Monica, California	Voluntary	45
Urbana, Illinois	Voluntary	110

Source: Peters, Anne, and Pete Grogan, "Community Recycling," *BioCycle,* pp. 37–38, May–June 1988.

compared with 34 percent for voluntary programs.[54] But the existence or nonexistence of mandates will not be the overriding consideration of residents in their decision to participate. Other factors are of equal if not greater importance, such as whether collection is curbside or through drop-off centers, whether in-home containers are provided, and the extensiveness of the public education effort. The survey showed a higher participation in Santa Rosa, California (70 percent), where participation was not mandatory than in Islip, New York (30 percent), where participation was mandatory.[59]

The data in Tables 5.2 and 5.3 show that mandatory programs may generally achieve somewhat greater recovery and participation than voluntary programs.

Enforcement of Mandatory Source Separation.   It would be very difficult to enforce source separation in programs where collection occurs by means of drop-off centers. In cases where residents must bring all refuse to a central drop-off point, it is conceivable that bags might be opened and violators of source-separation regulations could be fined. This confrontational approach is rarely used with residents, although Groton, Connecticut, uses indirect enforcement at the landfill. The tipping fee goes from $30 per ton to $100 per ton if recyclables are discovered in a collector's load. The private collectors therefore do not pick up refuse containing recyclables.[87]

Enforcement is much more common where recyclables are curbside-collected. In Woodbury, New Jersey, and East Lyme, Connecticut, the inspector precedes the collection vehicles to see if the regular refuse cans and bags have recyclables in them. The State of Rhode Island suggests that a local recycling coordinator

TABLE 5.3 Curbside Collection Participation and Recycling Rates (1990 Survey)

	Weekly programs	Biweekly or monthly programs	All programs
	Participation rates, %		
Mandatory programs			
High			90
Average	84		75
Low			49
Voluntary programs			
High			92
Average	72		70
Low			55
All programs			
High			92
Average	75	60	
Low			49
	Recycling rates (lb/household/month)		
All programs			
High	65.4	64.2	
Average	44.3	37	
Low	18.7	22.7	

Source: Glenn, Jim, "Curbside Recycling Reaches 40 Million," *BioCycle,* pp. 30–37, July 1990.

might ride on the recycling truck as it makes its pickups. The driver would point out nonparticipating households, and the recycling coordinator would write them a letter. In Woonsocket, Rhode Island (population 50,000), the recycling coordinator reports that neighbors, landlords, and "busybodies" call to inform him that others are not recycling, and he calls the person being reported.[87]

For apartments the problem is more complex. "When tenants are accused of failure to participate in recycling, they often say the landlord never told them about the law, or never provided recycling containers. When landlords are accused, they usually blame tenants for the lack of recycling."[87]

Containers for Source Separation

Source separation requires home storage containers. The type and capacity of container (or multiple containers), and who provides them, depends to a large extent on the collection system.

Who Should Supply the Containers? Containers are usually provided by the municipality (through a contract with a container supplier). If a private company is doing the collecting, that company may provide the containers. Sometimes, containers are supplied by the participants, particularly if collection is through drop-off centers.

The main argument for the public provision of containers (as opposed to having the private collector provide them) is that since a very large number of containers will be required (at least one per household), government procurement may be cheaper. There are several arguments for having containers provided by one entity (whether it be the municipality, a single collection company, or other supplier under contract to the municipality), as opposed to having the containers provided by the participants:[15]

- Having one entity responsible for containers assures uniformity of appearance, capacity, design, and recognizability.
- Collection methods and equipment can be standardized if only one type of container is used.
- Uniform containers can be an excellent vehicle for publicizing the collection program at the point of startup. The distribution of a free permanent household collection container to program participants has a significant positive impact on participation rates and recovery levels; it provides an ongoing promotional reminder to residents about the program both in the home and at the curb.

Having containers provided to the potential participants seems unequivocally to increase participation. For example, Urbana, Illinois, supplied containers to three of four test routes. These routes had participation rates of 50, 75, and 85 percent. The route without containers had 25 percent participation. In Brampton, Ontario, the routes with containers had 50 to 60 percent participation and the routes without containers had 30 to 40 percent participation. In San Jose, California, providing containers resulted in 57 percent participation, while in routes without containers participation was 26 percent. Springfield Township, Pennsylvania, jumped from 40 to 60 percent participation when containers were provided. Kitchener, Ontario, went from 39 to 83 percent.[26] Minneapolis, Minnesota, reported 54 to 97 percent increases.[72]

Containers make it easy to collect materials in the home, remind people to do so, and when set out at curbside form a "not-so-subtle bit of peer pressure."[26,83] For the collector, the uniform-appearing container is easy to spot, eliminates confusion about recyclables versus refuse, makes it easier to load the collection vehicle, and reduces litter, especially over having random boxes and bags set out.

Types of Containers. Four kinds of containers are employed for aggregating recyclables:

1. Single containers
2. Stackable multicontainer systems
3. Wheeled carts
4. Recyclables collection bags

Capacity, cost, uses, collection method, and other features of these containers are shown in Table 5.4.

What type of container is best? Clearly, if the collection program is of the one-sort, all-recyclables-commingled type, then a single container is the most efficient option. The choice between a wheeled cart, as used in Seattle, Washington, or a bag depends on the collection method (separate collection or cocollection). The alternative, a series of smaller containers, would have to be stored in the home until collection day, taking up valuable space.

For two or more source-separated recyclables, the following guidance is offered:[15]

TABLE 5.4 Containers and Their Characteristics

	Capacity, ft^3	Cost, 1988 $	Uses	Collection method	Other features
Single containers	0.7 to 3	$1 to $8	Source-separated food and beverage containers	Curbside Drop-off	Round bucket Rectangular box
Stackable multi-container systems	1.5 to 1.6 each	$15 to $20 per set of three	Source-separated newspapers, cans and bottles/jars	Curbside Drop-off	
Wheeled carts	32 to 96	$35 to $80	All recyclables commingled Yard waste, possibly all organic waste	Curbside Back-door	Most have lids Some have inner compartments for further separations Mechanical unloading possible All-weather, outdoor storage possible
Bags	Various	Less than $1 each	Source-separated food and beverage containers All recyclables commingled	Curbside Drop-off Co-collection	Higher replacement rates and handling costs when used in curbside collection

Sources: Glenn, Jim, "Containers at Curbside," *BioCycle*, pp. 26–29, March 1988; and Schmerling, Elaine, "Recycling Container Choices," *BioCycle*, pp. 36–37, March 1990.

- Rectangular boxes are preferred over round buckets by both participants and collection crews; in addition to ease of collection, they are less susceptible to being blown away by high winds. They are somewhat more expensive, however.
- Containers should have holes in the bottom to release liquids.
- For a weekly collection schedule with all food and beverage containers commingled, recycling collection containers should have a capacity of 14 gal per household.
- Containers should not have lids (for ease of collection and cost).
- The municipality's recycling logo should be imprinted on each container.
- A flyer should be distributed along with each container, including basic information about acceptable materials, method of preparation and set-out, and collection schedule.
- A recycling "hot-line" telephone number can be printed on the container and on the promotional material.

There are circumstances which would result in exceptions to the above advice, of course. For example, in Marin County, California, a bank provided round buckets free of charge. From the bank's standpoint, the advertising printed on the recycling container was viewed as more valuable than advertising in the newspaper.[44] Philadelphia, Pennsylvania, also favors buckets for their low cost, ease of carrying, small space requirements in the home, and lack of appeal for other uses such as storing laundry or records.[72] La Porte, Indiana, also uses donated 5-gal pails that would otherwise have been sent to the landfill as refuse. It costs about 5 cents to stencil a logo onto each pail. This city claims to have diverted 20 percent of its refuse, including 7,500 pails.[55] Palo Alto, California, supplies residents with two burlap sacks: one for aluminum and tin cans, the other for glass.[70] In Albuquerque, New Mexico, residents commingle in one plastic bag or orange bag the following materials: aluminum cans, papers, cardboard boxes, and plastics. Glass containers are set out separately in a box.[52] Some communities use clear plastic bags, so that recyclables can be easily distinguished from refuse.[83] In the pilot program to collect polystyrene, Fitchburg, Wisconsin, uses plastic bags to contain the lightweight material and keep it from blowing around the neighborhood.[37] East Lyme, Connecticut, began its program by passing out stickers to be affixed to the resident's own containers. In Newark, New Jersey, residents are supposed to provide their own sturdy reusable container for bottles and cans, and newspapers should be bundled and tied with string.[11] Lexington, Kentucky, uses a 45-gal wheeled cart with three inner compartments (but this was found to take more time unloading than desired). Plastic bags containing plastic containers are tied onto the outside.[47]

In communities which have tested a variety of containers, the open-top box of approximately 14-gal capacity seems to be favored. Mecklenburg County, North Carolina, tested three different container designs (two kinds of rectangular box and one type of cylindrical pail) to determine which the householders and collectors preferred, and whether the estimated 1.5-ft³ volume was sufficient. It was found that although residents had initially expressed concern that 1.5 ft³ would be too small, it proved to be adequate. The householders requested boxes rather than pails. Drivers preferred a box shape rather than a pail, because the pail made it more difficult for them to sort recyclables and to identify nonrecyclable items. One problem was that the containers tended to fade in the sunlight, a problem

FIGURE 5.7   Different kinds of curbside containers tested in Montgomery County, Maryland. (*Photograph courtesy Resource Recycling Magazine.*)

that could be remedied by a warranty.[20] Montgomery Country, Maryland, tested five kinds of container: the 14-gal open-top box, a 13-gal container with attached lid, a 16-gal container with detachable lid, an 18-gal container with attached lid, and a 24-gal wheeled cart with attached lid (see Fig. 5.7). Contrary to expectations, the largest container was set out the most frequently, but it was only 50 percent full on the average. The 14-gal lidless box, in addition to being the cheapest, was also the most full when set out (83 percent full), perhaps because it was not stored outside. The attractive 16-gal containers were not only stolen more often, but were not liked by the collectors because they had to remove and replace the lids. The collectors preferred the 14-gal open boxes.[9]

Sources of Containers.   Table 5.5 displays a list of home storage container suppliers. Location and telephone numbers are provided so that convenient suppliers may be contacted for the latest information on product specifications, prices, availability, lead times for ordering, and shipping information.

Container Volume Required.   To calculate the volume of recyclables likely to be set out in containers and therefore the volume of the containers needed, one must have an idea of the weight of each material likely to be set out and the density of that material. To find the needed volume of the container, determine the weight of each recyclable that will be set out by the average household in the container each week (if the recyclables are to be collected weekly), and divide by the density of that recyclable, then add up the resulting volumes:

$$\text{Total volume required} = \Sigma_i \frac{\text{weight of recyclable } i}{\text{density of recyclable } i}$$

TABLE 5.5 Home Storage Container Suppliers

Firm	Location	Telephone
A-1 Products	Etobicoke, Ontario, Canada	(416) 626-6446
Advanced Recycling Systems	Washington, Iowa	(800) 255-5571
American Container	Plainwell, Michigan	(800) 525-1686
Ameri-Kart Corp.	Goddard, Kansas	(316) 794-2213
The Bag Connection	Newberg, Oregon	(800) 228-2247
		(503) 538-8180
Bonar Inc.	Montreal, Quebec, Canada	(514) 481-7987
Buckhorn Inc.	Milford, Ohio	(800) 543-4453
Busch-Coskery of Canada	Mississauga, Ontario, Canada	(416) 828-9898
		(416) 897-8618
Champion Plastic Container	Ajax, Ontario, Canada	(416) 427-9756
Dover Parkersburg	Fall River, Massachusetts	(800) 225-8140
Grief Brothers Corp.	Hebron, Ohio	(614) 928-0070
Heil Co.	Chattanooga, Tennessee	(615) 899-9100
Household Recycling Products	Andover, Massachusetts	(508) 475-1776
IPL Products Ltd.	North Andover, Massachusetts	(508) 683-7668
Kirk Manufacturing	Houma, Louisiana	(800) 447-1687
Letica Corp.	Rochester, Michigan	(313) 652-0557
LewiSystems	Watertown, Wisconsin	(800) 558-9563
Management Sciences Applications	Upland, California	(714) 981-0894
Master Cart	Fresno, California	(209) 233-3270
Microphor, Inc.	Willits, California	(707) 459-5563
North American Rotomolding	Vancouver, Washington	(206) 693-6074

The weight of each recyclable that might be set out by the average household can be estimated by dividing the total weight of refuse generated in the community by the number of households, and multiplying the result by the weight percent of each component in the refuse as determined by composition studies:

Per household weight of recyclable i

$$= \% \text{ of recyclable } i \text{ in the total waste stream} \times \frac{\text{weight of total waste stream}}{\text{number of households}}$$

Table 5.6 gives approximate densities of common recyclables and a sample calculation of weekly volume. It will be noted that despite their light weight, plastics contribute a great deal to the volume requirements of in-home recycling containers (and collection vehicles, as well).[3] Because households differ substantially in the number and size of plastic bottles used, a much larger container might be required for some households.

How Many Containers Should Be Provided?   The correct number of containers equals the number of categories into which participants are expected to source-

TABLE 5.5 Home Storage Container Suppliers (*Continued*)

Firm	Location	Telephone
Otto Industries	Charlotte, North Carolina	(704) 588-9191
Plastican	Leominster, Massachusetts	(508) 537-4911
Philadelphia Can Co.	Philadelphia, Pennsylvania	(215) 223-3500
Piper Casepro	Dallas, Texas	(800) 238-3202
Refuse Removal Systems	Fair Oaks, California	(800) 231-2212
Rehrig Pacific Co.	Los Angeles, California	(231) 262-5154 (800) 421-6244
Reuter, Inc.	Hopkins, Minnesota	(612) 935-6921
RMI-C Division of Rotonics Molding Inc.	Itasca, Illinois	(708) 773-9510
Ropak Atlantic	Dayton, New Jersey	(201) 329-3020
Rotational Molding	Gardena, California	(213) 327-5401
Shamrock Industries Inc.	Minneapolis, Minnesota	(800) 822-2342 (612) 332-2100
Snyder Industries	Lincoln, Nebraska	(402) 467-5221
Spectrum International Inc.	Shrewsbury, New Jersey	(201) 747-1313
SSI Schaefer Systems	Charlotte, North Carolina	(704) 588-2150
	Northbrook, Illinois	(312) 498-4004
Toter Inc.	Statesville, North Carolina	(704) 872-8171 (800) 288-6837
Windsor Barrel Works	Kempton, Pennsylvania	(215) 756-4344
Zarn, Inc.	Riedsville, North Carolina	(919) 349-3323

Sources: "Directory, Home Storage Container Suppliers and Recycling Vehicle Manufacturers," *BioCycle*, pp. 38–39, July 1990; and "Recycling Container Guide," *Waste Alternatives*, pp. 30–33, June 1989.

separate their recyclables (with the possible exception of corrugated cardboard, which can be stacked alongside or placed under other containers, and newspapers, which can be tied or placed in paper bags). There are a number of arguments for the provision of just one container:[15]

- A single container is more convenient than multiple containers for participants; it takes up less space in the home and is easier to move to the curb for collection.
- A single container can save collection crew labor if the nonfiber recyclables are placed into the collection truck in a commingled state. (On the other hand, if the collector has to sort the commingled containers at the curbside, collection labor is increased.
- A single container is obviously less expensive to provide than multiple containers.
- Placing food and beverage containers in a single collection container accommodates changes in the mixture of recyclables which may occur over time, especially if the program is expanded to include additional materials.

TABLE 5.6   Calculation of Container Volume Required for 100 percent Capture of Selected Recyclables (Milwaukee Example)

Recyclables	Density, lb/ft^3 (1)	Weight, % of refuse (2)	Weight per household per week, lb (3)	Volume per household per week, ft^3 (4)
Newspaper	18	12.2	6.5	0.36
Glass bottles	15	8.1	4.3	0.29
Tin cans	8	2.5	1.3	0.16
Aluminum cans	2	0.6	0.3	0.15
PET bottles	0.9	0.5	0.3	0.33
Milk bottles (HDPE)	0.7	0.5	0.3	0.43
Total (excluding newspapers, which are set on top of container)				1.36
				(allow 1.5 ft^3 or 12 gal)

Sources: (1) Glenn, Jim, "Containers at Curbside," *BioCycle,* pp. 26–29, March 1988. (2) *City of Milwaukee Residential Waste Characterization 1989–1990,* Department of Public Works, City of Milwaukee, Wisconsin, 1990. (3) Milwaukee's 241,000 households generate about 333,000 TPY or 33 lbs per household per week. The weight of each material per household per week is thus 53 lbs times the weight percent of refuse. (4) Weight divided by density. (Gallon = 231 cubic inches.)

Container Replacement.   A small percentage of containers will need to be replaced annually. Considering the demographic composition of the municipality, the replacement rate can be expected to be between approximately 2 and 10 percent per year.[15] In some areas, losses as high as 5 percent per month have been experienced due to theft. One replacement bin is often given for free and after that they must be purchased.[53]

Containers for Apartments and Condominiums.   Collection of recyclables from apartments and condominiums presents special challenges, including transient populations, space constraints, lack of interest in recycling by building managers, and high cost of collection. Many experiments are being conducted to determine what works best.

Containers are not usually provided to the individual household, but larger containers are provided for the building, and they function much like drop-off centers. (Drop-off centers are discussed later in this section.) The types of containers that have been used include:[15]

- Roll-out carts
- Sheds to hold paper materials and to conceal roll-out carts
- Roll-off boxes for large quantities of materials
- Sectionalized roll-off boxes or dumpsters
- "Igloos" or other containers for glass, aluminum, metal, and plastic

Collection vehicles are available which hydraulically unload many of these containers. Sheds containing 90-gal carts for mixed recyclables and a designated area for newspaper can be strategically placed in parking lots or areas adjacent to the building. The shed can be an attractive reminder of the recycling program and can encourage regular participation.[15]

Marin Country, California, has a population of 90,000, of which 83 percent live in multifamily dwellings. There are 57 drop-off sites in the county.[57] Each site has three differently colored, 2-yd^3 bins: green for mixed glass, brown for mixed cans, and blue for newspaper.[49] These bins are replaced when half full. There were some scavenging problems, so the lids were modified so that materials could only be deposited into them and not retrieved from them without special equipment.[57] (Scavenging is discussed later in this section.)

In York, Pennsylvania (population 45,000), where 45 percent of the total housing is rental, four types of containers are provided depending on the type of building.[12]

1. For high-rise buildings (75 or more units), containers in "trash rooms" are located on each floor of the building. These are emptied into larger containers outdoors by building staff.

2. For smaller (15- to 75-unit) buildings, dumpsters or wheeled carts are provided outside which residents fill directly from in-home 6.5-gal buckets.

3. For 5- to 15-unit buildings, curbside collection buckets (6.5-gal capacity) are provided to each rental unit. Residents are responsible for labeling their own containers and placing them at the curb.

4. For buildings with less than 5 units, 14-gal rectangular curbside collection containers are provided to each rental unit.

Prince George's County, Maryland, is testing six different models, involving various combinations of 11-gal stackable bins, 90-gal wheeled carts, and recycling bags on racks. These are located in trash chute rooms, basement trash rooms, outdoor trash corrals, laundry rooms, or elsewhere, depending on the building architecture and space available. Preliminary results indicate that it is difficult to expect the collector to replace recycling bags on the racks, and that collectors as well as maintenance staff, residents, and building managers should definitely be involved in the design of the system from the start.[40]

In St. Paul, Minnesota, 11,000 households in 309 buildings use 90-gal wheelable bins placed throughout the apartment complex, rather than in a few out-of-the-way areas. The most cost-effective pickups were found to occur when containers were within 25 ft of the truck. To improve participation, residents are given reminder flyers every 10 to 12 months; posters are hung every 3 months; and information flyers for new tenants are given to building managers. Contamination is the most important problem. "Unless residents feel well treated at their building, they feel they are doing the building owner a favor by recycling."[82]

One experiment involving 896 units in Fitchburgh, Wisconsin, showed that providing apartment residents with plastic bags for recyclables without a strong educational program was not very effective (less than 5 percent diversion rate and 40 percent contamination by nonrecyclable items).[36]

A firm in Miami Beach, Florida, is marketing a system in which a typical garbage chute in a high-rise apartment complex is "retrofitted" with a rotating turntable in the basement. Push-button controls on each floor allow residents to rotate the appropriate container to a position under the chute where it can accept one source-separated recyclable commodity at a time. Glass, plastic, aluminum, and newspapers have been collected from high-rise apartments using this device.[95]

Containers for Source Separation at the Workplace.   Recycling at offices and other workplaces is just beginning, even though in many cities the commercial sector accounts for at least 50 percent of total refuse generated. For example, in Palo Alto, California, the city's estimated population of 56,000 is doubled on normal work days by commuters. These workers and the companies that employ them discard a great deal of material. It is estimated that 20 percent of the total material landfilled is corrugated cardboard, with 75 percent of that coming from commerce and industry.[70] Other materials that can be collected in addition to corrugated cardboard include aluminum cans, white office paper, computer paper, glass, and PET soft drink bottles, newspapers, and telephone directories.

Often, the recycler who picks up the material will provide some containers (such as large, wheeled hampers for paper). In general, it is easy in an office to separate high-grade paper (such as computer paper) from other paper if receiving containers are placed where the paper is normally discarded. Employees can also easily source-separate white paper in their offices, if supplied with a brightly colored bin. The bin should be large enough so that paper does not have to be stacked neatly in order to be inserted.

One of the pioneering companies in workplace recycling is Coca-Cola in Atlanta, Georgia, where 3000 employees generate over 1,000,000 aluminum cans each year.[31] These are collected in large cardboard boxes lined with plastic bags. Recyclable paper is collected in small containers in each office and removed nightly by custodial staff members, who put the paper into 95-gal wheeled carts. Corrugated cardboard is compacted separately from other trash. In these respects, Coca-Cola's program resembles that of many other forward-looking companies, but Coca-Cola takes recycling a step further. Telephone books and glass containers from the laboratory are also collected. The company has also set up an area where employees can bring recyclables from home and place them in wheeled carts. The eight elements that make the program a success are considered to be:[31]

1. Securing top management support
2. Appointing a coordinator
3. Knowing what wastes are generated by the company, and what it costs to dispose of them
4. Securing building managers' and custodial support
5. Using reliable recyclers to pick up the material
6. Providing employees with convenient drop-off locations
7. Communicating regularly with employees
8. Educating new employees.

It is also very important to most companies that sites devoted to recycling, both inside and outside the building, present a neat appearance at all times. Collection containers must be attractively designed and large enough so that there are no overflows.

Keys to Successful Source Separation

Publicity.   If source separation is necessary, as it is for all but the mixed-waste collection/processing schemes, public willingness is essential. Publicity and education are the primary keys to successful source separation. Techniques are covered elsewhere in this Handbook, and include hiring of public relations firms, direct mail, news media events, a consistent graphic theme, billboards, brochures, public service announcements, public school information, adult education, and so on. "Public education and information is a key to all successful recycling programs, and this is especially true with efforts aimed at apartment residents."[12] Mailings must be addressed to the occupant and not just to the owner, even though apartment recycling typically involves a great deal of individual attention to building owners and managers.[39] Once a few buildings are doing a great job of recycling, they can be used as examples when other landlords claim that recycling will not work in their buildings.[87]

Convenience.   Feelings toward recycling may be more important than convenience in encouraging a citizen to participate initially. Therefore, administrators should plan public information literature that stresses positive benefits of recycling, rather than convenience.[5] However, continued participation depends on the quality of recycling service offered.

Containers.   Another key factor in successful separation seems to be the provision of containers. A 1988 survey of over 20 different programs of various sizes and types concluded that providing containers and having citizens put them out on the same day as regular trash collection increases participation.[57]

Lower Apparent Cost.   A third incentive to participate in source separation is to make it more economical to the participant through refuse collection charges which reward source separation. From its inception, recyclables collection was subsidized by Seattle, Washington. In 1979, the variable-can rate was tested. Residents who set out less regular refuse paid less: recyclables were collected for free. The recycling rate was higher in the variable-can rate routes than in the others.[53] Perkasie, Pennsylvania, has a pay-by-the-bag-system. When it was instituted, the town experienced a 40 percent decline in tonnage of residential refuse, with two-thirds of that attributable to recycling through curbside and drop-off programs.[66] The economic incentive to participate will only occur if recycling services are offered to the public at a cheaper rate than regular refuse service. On a strictly computed cost-of-service basis, recycling is sometimes more expensive. "...no one, including the project directors, expects home sorting and collection of recyclables to break even or make money."[53]

Deposit Legislation.   Another incentive to source-separate is the "bottle bill." Although legislation has been enacted in nine states (some with many years of experience) and is being proposed for an additional half-dozen or so, container deposit laws remain controversial. Seven of the states with deposit legislation report high capture rates: 75 to 95 percent for aluminum, 88 to 95 percent for glass, and 70 to 90 percent for plastics.[91] Container deposit legislation causes redemption centers (whether grocery stores or specialized centers) to function essentially as buy-back centers. If deposit legislation were extended beyond beverage containers, would the capture rates equal those experienced for beverage containers without the expense of curbside collection?

Lottery.   In a 1982 study of 615 homes, Tallahassee, Florida, tried four approaches to increase participation:

1. "Prompting" (i.e., distributing leaflets about a week in advance of each scheduled pickup)
2. Payment for material (1 cent per pound of newspaper: news was fetching $40 per ton at the time)
3. A lottery prize of $5 drawn at random from the collection day's participants
4. Shifting the frequency of collection from biweekly to weekly.

The lottery demonstrated greatest improvement in participation (about 16 percent); the other methods increased participation about half as much. None of the methods was cost-effective, but long-term or residual effects of the methods were not analyzed.[42]

Program Consistency. After separation habits have been established, it is very important that the program continue unchanged, except for the addition of new recyclables to the collection. "Once this habit of separation is interrupted, tremendous efforts will be necessary to re-educate and re-interest the citizens."[46]

COLLECTION SYSTEMS

Curbside Collection versus Drop-off and Buy-Back Centers

Most communities have found that the way to ensure high participation is to provide a convenient method of participating. Drop-off and buy-back centers are not as convenient as curbside collection, and will typically result in much lower participation and capture rates.[57,83] Curbside collection can divert up to 20 to 25 percent of the refuse coming from the homes provided the collection service.[29] However, there are examples of drop-off programs capturing as much material as curbside programs operating in the same community (for example, Bloomsburg, Pennsylvania; and Everett, Washington).[30] Communities such as Wilton, New Hampshire, and Wellesley, Massachusetts, where residents have traditionally brought *all* residential refuse and recyclables to a central point, experience very high participation in drop-off programs.[57] Drop-off centers may be the only practical choice in areas where waste disposal is cheap and in rural areas where there is a long driving distance between residences.[30]

Curbside collection may be more effective in recovering materials, but it is more expensive to establish and maintain.[61] Drop-off centers offer the advantage that equipment, personnel, and maintenance needs are minimal. Another advantage of some drop-off centers is that a consistently clean supply of marketable materials is generated. Especially with centers that are staffed, greater control can be exercised over the quality of the material accepted. In this respect, staffed drop-off centers function somewhat like curbside separation, producing a product that does not have to be upgraded in an expensive processing facility.

Still another advantage of drop-off centers is that they can accept a greater variety of recyclables than are practical to collect at curbside. For example, used motor oil, automobile batteries, yard waste, construction debris, tires, furniture, white goods, latex paint, and pieces of scrap metal are all candidate recyclables for the "super self-help" stations being established in Milwaukee, Wisconsin.[7] In Palo Alto, California, and other communities, yard debris is not collected; but gardeners and residents can bring it to a composting location at the landfill.[70]

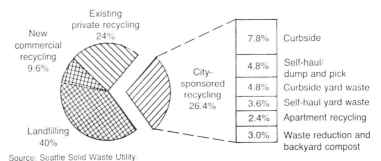

Source: Seattle Solid Waste Utility.

FIGURE 5.8 Contribution of programs to 60 percent waste reduction/recycling program. (*Source: Tom Watson, "Seattle blazes new ground with diverse approach," Resource Recycling, pp. 28–31, 73–74, November 1989.*)

As in Milwaukee, Wisconsin, many locations offer both curbside collection and drop-off locations. As shown in Fig. 5.8, Seattle, Washington, expects that both will contribute significantly to material recovery in the future.[86] A private collector with subsidiary companies operating in the San Francisco, California, area uses five methods for collecting recyclables: stationary buy-back centers, mobile buy-back centers, apartment house roll-out carts (originally for newspaper only, now for newspaper and glass), three-container curbside collection, and single-container curbside collection.[68] Mecklenburg County, North Carolina (population 460,000), has curbside collection plus staffed and unstaffed drop-off centers. One of the staffed drop-off centers accepts household refuse and recyclables three days per week, taking household refuse only if the user brings in recyclables.[20] In Palo Alto, California, half of what is recycled comes from curbside collection and half from the drop-off center. Some of the material dropped off comes from citizens of nearby cities where there is no curbside pickup.[70]

Everett, Washington, decided to test whether curbside collection or drop-off centers would better serve its needs. Table 5.7 shows that weekly curbside collection would cost the most but also would probably recover the most material. The low recovery from buy-back centers in this instance could be due in part to their less convenient locations.[63]

Sometimes the quantity of material delivered to drop-off centers may actually rise upon the institution of curbside collection, as experienced in Durham, North Carolina, and Bloomsburg, Pennsylvania.[30] However, typically, one would expect that capture at drop-off centers would decline when curbside collection is instituted. For example, quantities of materials have declined by 40 to 65 percent at Seattle, Washington, drop-off sites since the city began curbside collection in the spring of 1988. Charity newspaper collection drop boxes received about 33 percent less material after the first year of curbside collection, and 47 percent less after 18 months of curbside collection; noncharity drop boxes lost 47 percent after a year and 64 percent after 18 months. (Quantities delivered to buy-back centers also declined, but not as dramatically).[86] This phenomenon may help to explain the opposition of some established recycling industries to curbside collection, especially if there is a risk that the municipality may institute a competitive bid for the right to process its curbside collected material rather than simply giving it to the businesses which are currently getting the material at zero cost through a network of drop-off boxes.

TABLE 5.7 Cost and Recovery Estimates for Various Collection Alternatives Everett, Washington

	Recovery achieved in 6-month pilot, lb/households participating	Estimated costs for full program implementation (60,000 population), 1988 $
Curbside (weekly), 2 bins provided (newspaper/aluminum + glass)	131	599,000
Curbside (monthly), 2 bins provided (newspaper/aluminum + glass)	86	289,000
Drop-off igloos (in-home bags provided)	67	208,000
Buy-back	49	37,000

Source: Poremba, Gregory A. and Katherine M. Vick, "Best Yield for Recycling Investment," *BioCycle,* pp. 66–67, February 1990.

Drop-off Centers

Location of Drop-off Centers. The ideal environment for an effective drop-off center seems to be in a community without collection services, where residents are accustomed to transporting all of their refuse to a central place, such as a transfer station or a landfill. It is very little extra effort to transport recyclables separately, and the presence of the drop-off center at the refuse aggregation point provides a weekly reminder to do so. In Peterborough, New Hampshire, incoming cars make stops at two open-air drop-off stations before proceeding to unload their mixed refuse. The first station is for glass, which residents separate into clear, brown, and green; the second is for plastics, aluminum, and paper.[35]

Wellesley, Massachusetts, has never provided collection services, so people are accustomed to using the recycling and disposal facility. Located at a closed dump, the facility has a "parklike setting and layout" and is staffed with one full-time and six part-time employees. Refuse and recyclables are brought by residents along with materials to exchange, such as books and firewood. Of the town's 27,000 citizens, 75.2 percent participate voluntarily. High participation is attributed in part to demographics: the citizens are highly educated and in the upper economic strata. Since Massachusetts is a "bottle bill state," contributors are given receipts if they want to take a tax deduction for donating returnable bottles and cans. In 1985, when the town experienced a dramatic (over 42 percent) increase in refuse tonnage due to the return of privately collected refuse that formerly was taken to other disposal sites, the tipping fee for nonsegregated refuse was raised, but no tipping fee was charged for separated recyclables.[34] This provided economic incentive to recycle.

In communities where refuse is collected, drop-off centers need to be in convenient locations, within 3 to 5 miles of the home.[30] Candidate sites are shopping centers, grocery stores, schools, churches, and fire stations. For example, Woodridge, Illinois' drop-off center is between the library, the post office, the police station, and a soccer field.[51] The drop-off center should be in a visible place, which helps to make patrons feel more secure and helps to control litter and illegal dumping. One rule of thumb for planning is to establish one drop-off center per 5,000 to 10,000 people, but it is more important to put the centers in frequently used locations and make them larger if necessary. Santa Monica, California, has 66 sites serving 70,000 residents, one within one-half mile of every resident. Participation is reported to be about 35 percent.[30] In parts of Germany, there are drop-off centers for paper and glass with a density of 1 per 1,000 residents.[17] Recycling at apartment complexes essentially involves the establishment of a "mini" drop-off center for residents of the complex.

The owner of the site must be fully cooperative. In Cobb County, Georgia, local businesses "adopt a site," providing space and controlling litter.[15]

Larger-scale drop-off centers have been established at landfills. For example, in Deschutes County, Oregon, a recycling center was set up at one of the existing landfills through the cooperation of a refuse collection company, the county which owned the landfills, and a nonprofit corporation. One acre of land at the landfill is leased to the collector for $1 per year. The collector constructed a facility to reclaim materials such as cardboard, which is dumped and picked. The collector's investment is paid back by avoiding the landfill fees it would otherwise pay. The site is operated by the nonprofit corporation.[74]

Drop boxes are widely used for specialized collections of single materials. For example, drop boxes for newspaper are used in the southeast, sponsored by recycled paper mills. Plastic grocery sacks are now widely collected in grocery stores, promoted by the makers of the sacks. The cost of the collection is largely borne by the grocery stores. Store customers' response has been "overwhelming," with returns at 15 to 20 percent of the weight of sacks purchased by the store.[2]

Equipment for Drop-off Centers. The most noticeable pieces of equipment at drop-off centers are containers, which are increasingly evolving and becoming more specialized. Whatever containers are provided for recyclables, it is also important to provide a container for ordinary refuse to help control litter and the dumping of refuse in the same containers as the recyclables.

Three basic types of containers are found at drop-off centers:[21]

1. Two- or three-cubic-yard bins, some compartmentalized. These cost $300 to $500 each.
2. Fifteen- to forty-cubic-yard roll-off containers, which are hauled to the processing facility as trailers. If uncompartmentalized, these containers cost $2,300 to $4,000 (in 1989). Compartmentalization can cost up to $2,500 more per container. Hoists to load the roll-offs cost from $10,000 to $23,000, depending on the size of the roll off.
3. Specialized containers which are emptied on site by special equipment; for example, a truck-mounted crane which costs from $18,000 to $30,000. These specialized containers can be:

   - Compartmentalized (for example, a box-shaped container with two 2.1-yd^3 compartments)
   - Separate for each recyclable (for example, the popular dome-shaped igloos which cost from $350 for 1.1 yd^3 to $650 for 4 yd^3

See the section on "Containers for Source Separation" for a description of containers for separation of recyclables at apartment and condominium com-

TABLE 5.8 Suppliers of Drop-off Center Equipment

Firm	Location	Telephone
Specialized Containers:		
Environmental Container Corp.	Hemet, California	(714) 652-4339
Fibrex Plastics, Inc.	Hayward, California	(415) 887-0779
Igloo Recycling Systems	New York, New York	(212) 265-6426
SSI Schaefer	Northbrook, Illinois	(312) 498-4004
Specialized Container Cranes:		
Hiab Cranes and Loaders	New Castle, Delaware	(302) 328-5100
Omark Industries	Zebulon, North Carolina	(919) 269-7421
IMT Cranes	Gainer, Iowa	(800) 247-5959
Roll-off Containers:		
J. V. Manufacturing	Springdale, Arizona	(800) 858-8563
Parker IMP	Winamac, Indiana	(219) 946-6614
Quality Products/McClain Ind.	Kalamazoo, Michigan	(616) 381-2620
Rudco Products	Vineland, New Jersey	(609) 691-0800
Roll-off Hoists:		
Converto Mfg.	Cambridge City, Indiana	(317) 478-3201
Galbreath, Inc.	Winamac, Indiana	(219) 946-6631
G & H MFG	Mansfield, Texas	(817) 467-9883
Quality Products/McClain Ind.	Kalamazoo, Michigan	(616) 381-2620
Small Containers:		
Ameri-Kan	North Warsaw, Indiana	(219) 269-3035
Perkins Manufacturing	Chicago, Illinois	(312) 927-0200
Riblet Products	Elkhart, Indiana	(219) 264-9565
Small Container Collection Units:		
Mobile Equipment Company	Bakersfield, California	(805) 327-8476
Perkins Manufacturing	Chicago, Illinois	(312) 927-0200
Multipurpose Equipment:		
Hiab Cranes and Loaders	New Castle, Delaware	(302) 328-5100
Marrel Corporation	Hendersonville, Tennessee	(615) 822-3536
Multitek, Inc.	Prentice, Wisconsin	(715) 428-2000

Source: "Dropoff Collection Equipment," *BioCycle,* pp. 46–47, February 1989.

plexes. Table 5.8 gives a list of drop-off equipment makers. Locations and telephone numbers are provided so that convenient suppliers may be contacted for the latest information on product specifications, prices, availability, lead-times for ordering, and shipping information.

Figure 5.9 shows one type of drop-off center designed for Hollywood, Florida. A state grant provided funds for 128 centers to be located throughout the city. The containers are emptied and maintained by a volunteer charitable organization at no cost to the city. Revenues go to the charity.

Improving Participation and Capture at Drop-Off Centers. Given their advantages (low cost and the fact that it is practical to accept many different kinds of recyclables at drop-off centers), it would be desirable to increase participation and capture at drop-off centers so that a level of refuse diversion acceptable to the community could occur without the expense of curbside collection and elaborate MRFs. It is possible that participation in drop-off centers could be im-

FIGURE 5.9   A convenient corner drop-off center in Hollywood, Florida, accepts aluminum cans and three colors of glass. (*Photograph courtesy of Haul-All Equipment Systems Ltd., Lethbridge, Canada.*)

proved if the municipality operating them would concentrate on two factors: (1) convenience to participants, and (2) public education.[30] For example, home storage containers provided by the municipality would help a drop-off program in a similar manner as they do a curbside program. Direct purchase by the municipality of the recyclables collected would provide incentives to both volunteer and private drop-off centers. For example, Delaware County, Pennsylvania, gives each group sponsoring a glass collection site $20 for each ton of glass collected. A similar approach is used in Dallas, Texas, and Snohomish County, Washington.[30] The quantities of recyclables received per resident and per drop-off center are shown for several municipalities in Table 5.9, and the figures show order-of-magnitude differences from one program to another.

Block-Corner Drop-Off.   A variation on the drop-off center for densely populated areas is block-corner collection. Periodically (once every other week) residents carry recyclables to a designated location at the end of their blocks. This method is in use in Philadelphia, Pennsylvania, and is actually a hybrid drop-off/curbside program.

A municipal truck with three municipal employees collects the recyclables from each corner and takes them to a private purchaser of recyclables. Because the truck stops only once for the recyclables from 30 to 150 homes and because all three workers assist with the loading, collection efficiency is said to be high, with the crew handling 670 lb of recyclables per labor-hour (including travel time to the buyer), compared with 180 lb in the city's curbside pilot.[61] A three-person crew takes about 40 min to pick up 1 ton of recyclables, and up to an hour to off-load 3.5 tons. Using these figures and estimates of driving time, the time to

TABLE 5.9 Quantity of Recyclables Received at Selected Drop-off Centers

Location	Population	No. of sites	Tons/year received	Lb/year (per person)	Tons/year (per site)
Champaign County, Illinois	171,000	15	1000	12	67
Columbia County, Pennsylvania	50,000	17	469	19	28
Cook & Lake County, Illinois	270,000	18	7140	53	397
Delaware Co., Pennsylvania	500,000	50	1800	7	36
Durham County, North Carolina	120,000	10	1200	20	120
Fairfax County, Virginia	75,000	8	1000	27	125
Kent/Ottawa County, Michigan	650,000	30	3200	10	107
Santa Monica, California	70,000	66	1398	40	21

Source: Glenn, Jim, "New Age Dropoff Programs," *BioCycle*, pp. 42–45, February 1989.

TABLE 5.10   Eight Steps to Establishing Block-Corner Collection

---

Step 1. Form a well-organized and responsible neighborhood recycling committee, preferably an offshoot of a recognized neighborhood organization. Duties of the committee include:

- Coordinate with the city recycling officials
- Determine the geographic area to be served
- Estimate how much material can realistically be recovered, using the population of the area to be served
- Establish and clearly articulate the purposes of the project
- Make up a good publicity logo to be used on all promotional materials
- Serve as, and recruit other, block coordinators
- Estimate program expenses and revenues
- Determine where startup and ongoing funds will come from
- Determine how revenues (if any) will be distributed
- Open a bank account for the receipt of revenues
- Determine how the materials are to be prepared by residents: degree of separation required, etc.

Step 2. Find a buyer, using the estimate of the amount that will be collected:

- Look for buyers who are close to the neighborhood, (to minimize transportation costs) and visit the buyer
- Find out what the potential buyer's requirements and flexibility is concerning matters such as:

  What materials are purchased and for what price
  What the materials preparation specifications are
  How the weight of the materials is determined
  How payments are made
  Days and hours open to receive materials
  Availability of unloading machinery or labor assistance
  Whether the buyer also would be willing to pick up the materials

- Select a buyer who is reliable, preferably one who has dealt with other recycling groups that can be contacted as a reference.

---

complete a route, and time to off-load could be estimated (it may take more than one trip to the buyer).

In Philadelphia, revenues from the sale of recyclables are returned to the volunteer neighborhood organization which organizes the collection and provides staff for the corners on drop-off day, rather than to the city which subsidizes the collection and transportation cost of about $140 per ton.[60] Success of a block-corner collection program depends on a strong neighborhood organizational structure and good cooperation between city officials and the neighborhood groups.[61]

Table 5.10 lists and describes the eight steps to establishing a block corner collection program in urban areas.

To determine the amount of material that can realistically be recovered through a block-corner collection program, organizers can obtain (from local, state, or federal officials) the refuse generation rate per person of the materials to be solicited, then multiply by the number of people in the service area. The result should be discounted substantially, recognizing that not all residents in the area

TABLE 5.10   Eight Steps to Establishing Block-Corner Collection (*Continued*)

Step 3. Arrange a collection and transportation method. This is the most expensive part of the operation.

- Find a truck to service the route. The options are:

  The city provides the service

  A private hauler provides the service (disadvantages: private hauler might want the revenue from the sale of recyclables and, if the revenues dropped, the private hauler might abandon the route)

  The neighborhood recycling committee operates a rented truck (disadvantages: might result in legal liabilities, reliance on volunteer labor which probably cannot be a permanent arrangement, and is expensive)

- Formalize the arrangement with the trucker in a written contract covering route, schedule, delivery to buyer, revenues, payments, etc.
- Map the exact route (include all pickup locations and the route to the buyer)
- Set a collection schedule (semimonthly pickup, not on a regular refuse day to avoid confusion: establish set-out time to minimize vandalism and scavenging)
- Equip trucks with compartments (e.g., pallets and barrels)
- Train truckers to recognize what materials are acceptable to the buyer and what materials must be left behind (but not as piles of litter).

Step 4. Publicize the refuse crisis and the benefits of recycling, using the neighborhood association's newsletter or a weekly newspaper.

Step 5. Find block coordinators. Duties:

- Help select a corner
- Monitor the corner on pickup day
- Pass out leaflets and reminders
- Answer residents' questions

Step 6. Select a program startup date, taking into account the need for advance publicity.

Step 7. Several weeks before program startup, publicize the details of participation using all media means available (posters, flyers, articles, newsletters).

Step 8. Begin the program and measure progress:

- Continue sending reminder flyers for first several months
- Follow the trucks initially to ensure cleanup of broken glass and litter
- Assure that all goes smoothly with the buyer
- Measure program's success against its original goals
- Expand into materials, restaurant glass, office paper, and school projects

Source: Pierson, Robert W., Jr., "Eight Steps To Block Corner Success," *Waste Age,* pp. 147–149, 152, 154, 156, 158.

will participate and those that do will not contribute all their recyclables. A discount factor of 75 percent might not be unreasonable.[60]

In deciding how materials should be prepared for block-corner collection, early experiments in Philadelphia, Pennsylvania, determined that newspapers are best tied or placed in large paper bags; aluminum cans can be handled in paper bags; glass should be separated at the corner into color; and, on rainy days, paper bags should not be used for glass.[60]

Cost of Drop-Off Centers.   In estimating the cost of drop-off centers (whether one center or a network), all of the factors listed in Table 5.11 must be taken into

TABLE 5.11 Factors Influencing the Cost of Collecting Recyclables at Drop-off Centers

Center design:
    Site work required (roads, paving, grading, fencing, utilities, landscaping)
    Type of structures (e.g., shed for workers, scales)

Receiving containers:
    Number of categories of recyclables accepted
    Density of materials being accepted
    Number of containers needed
    Capacity/type of containers
    Frequency of replacement
    Ease of unloading/trailering

Density of centers:
    Number of centers serving geographic area
    Driving distance/time between centers
    Number of centers that can be serviced by transport vehicles

Workers:
    Number of workers staffing each center
    Number of staffed hours (including security, cleanup and maintenance)
    Wages and fringes
    Length of work day
    Performance (attitude, efficiency, speed)

Transport vehicles:
    Initial cost
    Maintenance cost
    Mileage efficiency
    Cycle time for automatic lifting equipment
    Unloading efficiency
    Whether used for other uses (e.g., leaf pickup)

Weather
Distance/time to processing center from drop-off center
Amount of publicity required to achieve desired capture rates

account. Drop-off centers vary as much in their costs as they do in their effectiveness: there is no such thing as a "typical" drop-off center.

Buy-Back Centers

Stationary Buy-Back Centers. Buy-back centers offer the advantage that collectors are paid for the recyclables they bring in. Popular in urban areas, these centers frequently grew up as an adjunct to long-established scrap metal and paper dealerships. Prices paid for recyclables brought in depend on the market, which for some recyclables is notoriously volatile, dropping to zero with little warning. Traditional buy-back centers have not proven to be a reliable means of capturing the desired amount of recyclable material from the refuse stream. If they were, there would have been little need to develop drop-off centers or curbside collection. However, particularly in inner-city urban areas, buy-back centers offer an incentive to the economically disadvantaged.

Several buy-back centers have attempted to increase interest among patrons by adopting a theme, such as a circus, with attendant storybook parklike atmosphere that appeals to small children. Originally, many of these theme centers were funded in part by beverage container interests to help thwart bottle bill initiatives. With the rise of curbside collection as an alternative, that support has diminished. However, some theme buy-back centers run by not-for-profit organizations are thriving, in part because they are less sensitive to market price fluctuations (especially the decline in paper prices) and in part because they receive several kinds of public subsidy such as free land, volunteer labor, and donations.[88] Information on establishing a theme buy-back center is available from the Glass Packaging Institute in Washington, D.C.

A buy-back center was recently established in a rural area of North Carolina. Transporting and marketing the collected recyclables would have been a challenge, but an existing buy-back center in a nearby city agreed to pick up the recyclables for a small fee. Participation is clearly highest among residents who live closest to the center. The county landfill diversion rate is estimated to be about 0.5 percent due to the buy-back center, although this figure is uncertain as waste is not weighed at the landfill.[16]

Mobile Buy-Back Centers. If not carefully tended, stationary drop-off and buy-back centers can look like eyesores and collect debris. The use of a mobile buy-back center avoids this problem. It also costs less to equip and operate than an attended stationary center. Vallejo, California (population 100,000), a San Francisco suburb, has had a mobile buy-back service, making about 10 scheduled stops each weekday at convenient locations like schools and churches. The driver stays at each location for 15 to 45 min. Materials are weighed and paid for on the spot. The truck used is a flatbed truck and trailer with 1- and 2-yd bins and a scale mounted on it.[43]

Difficulties experienced by a mobile buy-back center include finding the right locations to park, considering the need for acceptable access and safety.[43] Scheduling also probably presents a problem: if the vehicle is delayed in its scheduled route, people are unlikely to wait very long for it. In areas with severe winters, this collection method is likely to be impractical.

Reverse Vending Machines. A reverse vending machine functions as a mini-buy-back center for used beverage containers. There are some 7000 machines operating in the United States. The most successful are located in bottle-bill states. Depending on their design, the machines can be sited outdoors or indoors. They give cash or in-store credit. Some models dispense lottery tickets or operate as a slot machine. Costs range from $500 for small, hand-crank indoor units to $35,000 for giant outdoor versions. Many units accept aluminum cans; some accept steel cans, plastic bottles, and/or glass bottles. Some color-sort and shred or crush PET and glass bottles. Like any vending machine, they are subject to significant wear and tear.[85] The leading suppliers operating in the United States are

- Aries Aluminum Corp. (Hilliard, Ohio)
- CoinBak (New Rochelle, New York)
- Egapro Management AG (Zurich, Switzerland)
- Envipco (Fairfax, Virginia)
- Gadar Industries (Forest Lake, Minnesota)
- Kansmacker, Inc. (Lansing, Michigan)

- Tomra Systems Inc. (London, Ontario, Canada)

Curbside Collection

Diversity of Curbside Collection Programs. There are about 1,600 curbside recyclables collection programs in the United States in 1990 and the number is expected to increase, mostly east of the Mississippi.[18,27] Table 5.12 shows the great diversity of curbside collection systems with respect to such program factors as

- Who does the collection
- Size of crew
- Average route size
- Average stops per route
- Frequency of collection
- Degree of source separation

Planning for Curbside Collection. Many factors must be considered in planning for curbside collection of recyclables, among them the population density of the area to be served (possible stops per mile of route), degree of source separation the residents will be willing to tolerate and still participate, the desired capture levels, the amount of money available to pay for the program, and the source of funds. Planning for collection cannot be divorced from planning for processing and marketing. For example, Mecklenburg County, North Carolina, began planning for curbside collections in the fall of 1986. The pilot collection program began in February 1987. Countywide collections were originally scheduled to start in 1988, but were postponed to 1989 because of delays in the construction of the central processing facility.[20]

Once a policy decision has been made to collect recyclables at curbside, adequate time must be allowed for municipal staff and collectors to undertake detailed program design and promotion. It takes 6 to 12 months after the decision to collect curbside to get trucks on the road. Some specific program design issues for curbside collection of residential recyclables include:

- Who will perform recyclables collection, the public sector or the private sector?
- If collection is to be performed by the private sector, will the municipality be divided into districts, or will multiple collectors be allowed to overlap their service territories (open collection)?
- Should recyclables collection be the same day as refuse collection? How many days per month? Will back-door collection service be permitted?
- Who will be responsible for education and promotion? For enforcement?
- How will collection be handled for apartments and condominium units?
- What will the program cost?

The issues concerning source separation and the provision of containers were previously discussed. In addition, there are questions concerning whether the municipality wishes to undertake additional collections for different kinds of

TABLE 5.12 Examples of Diversity of Curbside Collection Programs
(22 Communities Surveyed)

Program characteristics	Number of programs with this characteristic
Household separation	
Required?	
Voluntary	14
Mandatory	8
Containers provided?	
Yes	20
No	2
Source separation	
None	1
One	1
Two	6
Three	11
Four	1
Five	1
Materials separated from refuse	
Newspaper	22
Glass	22
Aluminum	22
Tin Cans	20
HDPE	11
PET	10
Mixed Paper	5
Cardboard	4
Number of materials collected	
Three	1
Four	6
Five	4
Six	8
Seven	2
Eight	1
Number of households served	
Less than 5,000	4
5,000 to 20,000	8
20,000 to 40,000	6
Over 40,000	4
Pounds collected per household served per year	
100 to 200	5
200 to 300	2
300 to 400	5
400 to 500	7
500 to 600	1
600 to 700	1

TABLE 5.12 Examples of Diversity of Curbside Collection Programs (22 Communities Surveyed) (*Continued*)

Program characteristics	Number of programs with this characteristic
Collection	
Day	
Same day as refuse	13
Different day	6
Some of each	3
Frequency	
Weekly	19
Bimonthly	1
Monthly	2
Private or municipal?	
Private	13
Municipal	9
Crew size	
One	11
One to Two	1
Two	4
Three	3
Three to Four	1
Route size range	
350 to 1,000	9
1,000 to 1,500	8
1,501 to 2,000	3
Unreported	2
Stops per route	
240 to 400	5
401 to 500	2
501 to 600	5
1,000	1
Unreported	9

Source: Glenn, Jim, "Curbside Recycling Reaches 40 Million," *BioCycle,* pp. 30–37, July 1990.

recyclables, particularly yard wastes, which are readily compostable and make up a large fraction (up to around 20 percent) of some municipal refuse streams. For example, in 1989, Seattle, Washington (population 500,000), mandated the source separation of yard waste. For $2 per month, residents of Seattle can set out as many as 20 cans, bags, or bundles of yard debris (branches up to 4 in. diameter) to be collected at curbside (see Fig. 5.10). The collector composts the material at a site outside the city. Since yard waste is accepted in plastic bags, a challenge is to remove the bags from the compost. Self-haul of yard waste to the city's two transfer stations is another option for residents.[86] Collection of yard waste cost the city $48 per ton in 1989.[25] Seattle also picks up white goods for $15 per item.

FIGURE 5.10   An overflowing container of yard debris awaiting pickup. (*Photograph by A. McMillen, Mercer Island, Washington.*)

Public or Private Collection?   Four alternative approaches to the question of who should collect recyclables have been employed. Which of these approaches offers the best service and the lowest-cost service depends on local circumstances, and is typically a very "hot" political issue. The first three are private sector approaches while the fourth is the public sector approach.

1. Competitive-bid *contract collection,* with one or more private collectors providing services under contract to the municipality, which pays the contractor directly for the service.
2. *Franchise collection,* wherein the collector is granted a specific territory in which to collect recyclables, and the collection cost is billed directly to the collector's customers.
3. Unrestricted private *open collection,* with multiple collectors contracting directly with individual residents and businesses for recycling services.
4. *Municipal collection* performed by municipal employees.

In the short term, the collection crews who are most familiar with the service area could be expected to perform the most effectively, and there seems to be a trend to favor the same arrangement as is used for collection of regular refuse.[59] Table 5.13 indicates what might be expected to be the relative cost of these four options, whether the collection is of refuse or recyclables.

Collection workers are on the "front lines" of the recycling effort. They are the ones who create the public impression about the municipality's recycling program. They are frequently also charged with the responsibility of enforcement of

TABLE 5.13   Relative Costs of Collection

Type of collection	Who collects?	Relative cost
Municipal	Employees of the local government	1.27 to 1.37
Contract	A private firm hired by the community provides service in a specific territory	1.00
Franchise	Same as contract, except the private firm bills the customers rather than being paid by the municipality	1.15
Open	Multiple private firms compete: no service territories specified by the municipality	1.27 to 1.37

Source: Stevens, Barbara J., "How to Finance Curbside Recycling," *BioCycle,* pp. 31–33, February 1989.

a city mandatory ordinance, or at least are expected to notify the enforcement officer of violations. They are the ones who put the reminder notices in the recycling containers. Intelligence, diligence, and good public relations ability are required for this job if a recycling program is to make a good impression.

Municipal Collection.   In some municipalities with public refuse collection, the collection workers face an ongoing challenge from advocates of "privatization" who are eager to see the service taken over by the private sector. Data from a 22-community survey seems to support the contention that private collection is generally more efficient (528 stops per day) than municipal collection (415 stops per day);[27] however, without knowing the terrain of the route, this hypothesis cannot be conclusively proven. If for some reason the public sector employees cannot compete with the private sector to provide efficient, low-cost recycling collection services (for example, due to union rules which require two, three, or four persons on a collection truck), then a municipality may need to consider the private collection of recyclables. With refuse quantities potentially decreasing significantly due to source reduction (for example, backyard composting and mulch mowing), one way for public collection workers to preserve their jobs would be to undertake efficient recycling collections. This was the approach of the sanitation workers' union in Milwaukee, Wisconsin, which agreed to having only one worker on a recycling truck (special recycling trucks were purchased).

If the municipality is already served by private refuse collection (whether contract, franchise, or open), the option to establish an entire "department" to carry out recycling collections would result in considerable debate and a relatively long startup period. A decision for public collection in this instance could also be portrayed as ignoring private business interests and not using collection resources that might be already available in the private sector.[15]

However, early in the decision process over who is to do the collection, it is useful to identify services and quantify the associated costs *as if* the collection were to be done with public forces (employees and equipment). There are three reasons for this exercise:[15]

1. It provides a benchmark to evaluate private sector bids. If the level of service and cost are not equivalent to, or better than, what the municipality would provide with its own forces, the argument for using private collection is considerably weakened.

2. Since private collectors' true costs are difficult to determine (most collectors consider the information confidential and privileged), the estimated cost of the collection program can be based on a public-sector model. Numbers of households to be included, expected capture rates, vehicle types, and other logistical aspects of collection can be used to develop and evaluate the cost of alternative program designs until the most desirable program is decided upon, and then put out for private sector bid.

3. If unsatisfactory bids are received for collection services, the municipalities could implement an already planned and costed public collection. This would be especially useful if a decision had been made to divide the municipality into districts and some of the districts were unsuccessfully bid.

Open Collection.   This approach allows households to contract directly with collectors of their choice to provide trash and recycling collection service. This approach permits the greatest freedom to the private sector, particularly the very small collection firms. For example, citizens' intense loyalty to their trash haulers influenced the decision of Manheim Township, Pennsylvania, to revise its plans to have a bid system. Instead, it was decided that each hauler would be responsible for collecting both recyclables and trash.[28] However, higher costs are often associated with this alternative because of inefficiency of service delivery. In addition, the multihauler approach is difficult and cumbersome for the municipality to monitor. Some collectors may simply dump the collected recyclables in the landfill.[28] Recycling program promotion, and scheduling of the commencement of service, are more difficult under this alternative. Collections might begin sporadically in different parts of the municipality at different times and may never reach the entire municipality. Residents and businesses may be subject to payment for overlapping services. The ability to rely on recycling as a significant component of a comprehensive refuse management plan could be limited.[15] For example, Portland, Oregon, has over 100 private collectors. But the recycling rate is only about 2 percent in Portland, compared with 10 percent and above for other curbside collection programs.[28]

What would be the rationale for open collection of recyclables, besides customer loyalty? For one thing, the existing collectors are familiar with the territory, and they may exert considerable political leverage. To make open collection work, a municipality has to be willing to spend the time and money to put the program in place and monitor its progress, and take some responsibility for controlling the collectors' actions. Also, the collectors must support the program.[28]

To remedy some of the problems with open collection of recyclables, the municipality could undertake some or all of the following responsibilities:[15]

- Identify the specific services to be offered (collection frequency, day of collection, materials collected, etc.).
- Develop uniform education and publicity to support the program.
- Provide household set-out containers to all households.
- Provide technical assistance to collectors, including:

  Collection strategies for specific needs (e.g., single family, apartments, condominiums, etc.)

  Information regarding available equipment and latest collection techniques;

- Provide a MRF or other processing facility for collected materials.

Division of the municipality into districts: are the divisions logical?

Should the lines be drawn elsewhere?

Services requested: can the collectors perform them with existing equipment? Are the requests reasonable?

Compliance: What are the enforcement responsibilities of the collectors and of the municipality?

Where will the collectors bring collected recyclables, and how far away is it?

- Release bid specifications for collection services
- Evaluate bid responses and award contracts according to:

Ability to perform services with available equipment and personnel,

Price bid for services,

Other municipal procurement requirements (bid bond, legal certification, collection permits in place, etc.).

Franchise Collection.   An arrangement wherein a municipality grants collectors an exclusive right to collect in a specific geographic area without a competitively bid contract is problematic. In some states, such arrangements have been viewed as unconstitutionally anticompetitive. In essence, the municipality is creating a monopoly. Unless a regulatory authority is established to oversee the collector's rate structure, residents are offered little protection from unnecessarily high costs. The problem is compounded when the collector is allowed to bill the customers in advance of the service being provided.

If, however, the collector has to compete for the collection district and the municipality regulates the rates charged, then the only real difference between franchise and contract collection is in who sends the bill to the customer.

In summary, "recycling collection should be as compatible as possible with existing refuse disposal practices and the needs of each area. For areas with private hauler infrastructure, we recommend that the municipality use the existing hauler infrastructure to collect recyclables, but in a manner whereby the municipality's needs are identified and met through contracted services."[15]

Frequency and Timing of Collection.   Recycling collections typically occur on a weekly, biweekly, or monthly basis. The more frequent the collection service the higher the operating costs. However, weekly collection offers two important advantages:[15]

1. Participation levels are increased because residents do not have to remember which week is recycling week.
2. Capture rates are increased because residents do not have to store large quantities of materials in their homes between collections.

The timing of recycling collection is also a factor. Some programs collect recyclables on the same day as refuse, while others collect on a separate day. Same-day collection (i.e., same day as regular refuse service) does seem to improve participation. Among 13 required-participation programs, the average participation rate was 76.5 percent for same-day schedule and 41 percent for different-day schedule.[59] But whether the recyclables collection occurs on the same day or on a different day, a regular schedule is essential. "As long as public

Division of the municipality into districts: are the divisions logical? Should the lines be drawn elsewhere?

Services requested: can the collectors perform them with existing equipment? Are the requests reasonable?

Compliance: What are the enforcement responsibilities of the collectors and of the municipality?

Where will the collectors bring collected recyclables, and how far away is it?

- Release bid specifications for collection services
- Evaluate bid responses and award contracts according to:

Ability to perform services with available equipment and personnel,

Price bid for services,

Other municipal procurement requirements (bid bond, legal certification, collection permits in place, etc.).

Franchise Collection.   An arrangement wherein a municipality grants collectors an exclusive right to collect in a specific geographic area without a competitively bid contract is problematic. In some states, such arrangements have been viewed as unconstitutionally anticompetitive. In essence, the municipality is creating a monopoly. Unless a regulatory authority is established to oversee the collector's rate structure, residents are offered little protection from unnecessarily high costs. The problem is compounded when the collector is allowed to bill the customers in advance of the service being provided.

If, however, the collector has to compete for the collection district and the municipality regulates the rates charged, then the only real difference between franchise and contract collection is in who sends the bill to the customer.

In summary, "recycling collection should be as compatible as possible with existing refuse disposal practices and the needs of each area. For areas with private hauler infrastructure, we recommend that the municipality use the existing hauler infrastructure to collect recyclables, but in a manner whereby the municipality's needs are identified and met through contracted services."[15]

Frequency and Timing of Collection.   Recycling collections typically occur on a weekly, biweekly, or monthly basis. The more frequent the collection service the higher the operating costs. However, weekly collection offers two important advantages:[15]

1. Participation levels are increased because residents do not have to remember which week is recycling week.

2. Capture rates are increased because residents do not have to store large quantities of materials in their homes between collections.

The timing of recycling collection is also a factor. Some programs collect recyclables on the same day as refuse, while others collect on a separate day. Same-day collection (i.e., same day as regular refuse service) does seem to improve participation. Among 13 required-participation programs, the average participation rate was 76.5 percent for same-day schedule and 41 percent for different-day schedule.[59] But whether the recyclables collection occurs on the same day or on a different day, a regular schedule is essential. "As long as public

nization as an outside contractor. Districting also facilitates phasing in of the program.

Some companies offer processing and marketing services, in addition to collection of recyclables. Contracting for the recycling collection component separately would make sense under the following conditions:

- When the community has access to a preexisting public processing center (e.g., a regional or state-provided processing center such as in Connecticut or Rhode Island)
- When the community wants to encourage an existing private processing center (e.g., the municipality may want to retain and encourage existing scrap processors who may feel that their business would be threatened)[89]
- If there is little competition in the area among full-service national firms (the larger firms are not typically interested if the population is under 50,000)[79]
- If the community is procuring general refuse collection services and wants to add recycling collection into the same contract(s), perhaps at a community-specified percentage of the refuse collection bid price.[79]

A procurement document for recycling collection services should include the following elements:[79]

- A list of what materials are to be collected, or at least the number of separate materials
- Provision for future change in the list of items
- The number of sorts that residents will set out and for which the collector must provide separate compartments in the collection vehicle
- Which households are to receive recycling collection service
- The correct number of households in each category to be served (e.g., single family, two-family, etc.)
- When and how often recyclables will be picked up
- Where recyclables are to be picked up (curbside or otherwise)
- What kind of educational responsibilities the collector will have, (e.g., whether the municipality will retain approval rights over flyers, what kind of "reminder" notices are to be issued, etc.)
- Where the recyclables are to be taken for processing, and what the unloading configuration/limitations will be at the processing facility

To develop and issue the procurement document, the following tasks need to be accomplished:[15]

- Assess municipal demographics and divide the municipality into recycling collection districts
- Develop education/publicity program and determine collector's role
- Secure markets for materials as-collected, and secure processing capabilities for collected materials not proceeding directly to markets
- Develop bid specification document describing all services requested and subject this procurement document to legal review
- Hold prebid conferences with collectors; potential topics:

• Assume market responsibility, either directly, or indirectly through MRF services (For example in Dakota County, Minnesota, the county's MRF pays the collectors for the recyclables delivered.[28]).

• Regulate the rates that the collectors charge their customers for recycling collections (for example, in Lenexa, Kansas, collectors were allowed a $1.50 per household per month additional charge as of November 1989[28]).

To assure that services are performed in conformance with the minimal standards acceptable to the municipality, collectors will need to do some or all of the following:[15]

• Procure the necessary equipment and designate necessary personnel.

• Coordinate enforcement procedures between the municipality and households (materials, inappropriate set-out units, any participation requirements, etc.).

• Maintain a telephone service line for household inquiries and complaints.

• Set appropriate standards for the physical appearance of crew and vehicles.

• Conform to local safety regulations.

• Apply the uniform municipal logo on set-out containers and recycling vehicles.

• Use publicity and information that is consistent with the municipality's recycling program.

• Deliver reports to the municipality on pickup routes, tonnages delivered to the MRF, participation rates, and other documentation needed by the municipality.

Contract Collection.   One way to help defray the costs of a recycling collection program may be to switch from open or municipal collection of refuse to contract collection for both refuse and recyclables.[81] Advantages of the contract collection approach include the following:[15]

• Offers the most control to the municipality of the private sector recycling collection options.

• Uses the existing refuse collection infrastructure to perform recycling services

• Ensures service to each household

• Allows rapid startup of the curbside collection program

• Ensures qualified collectors would be performing the service

• Promotes efficiency by controlling the number of collectors of recyclables operating within a service area

• Promotes orderly and routine collection

• Facilitates coordination of program promotion and the scheduling of pickups

The municipality may determine that some areas may not be appropriate for contracted collection; i.e., the competitive selection process might not identify collectors willing to perform collections at a price the municipality can afford. Alternative options for limited areas may involve municipal collection, or a decision to allow open collection.[15] The jurisdiction can be divided into districts, and different services procured for the different districts (provided residents of a district do not subsidize a service that they do not receive). Newark, New Jersey (population 300,000; land area 24 mi²), was divided into nine collection zones. In Newark, collection is divided between city forces and a local handicapped orga-

2. Since private collectors' true costs are difficult to determine (most collectors consider the information confidential and privileged), the estimated cost of the collection program can be based on a public-sector model. Numbers of households to be included, expected capture rates, vehicle types, and other logistical aspects of collection can be used to develop and evaluate the cost of alternative program designs until the most desirable program is decided upon, and then put out for private sector bid.

3. If unsatisfactory bids are received for collection services, the municipalities could implement an already planned and costed public collection. This would be especially useful if a decision had been made to divide the municipality into districts and some of the districts were unsuccessfully bid.

Open Collection. This approach allows households to contract directly with collectors of their choice to provide trash and recycling collection service. This approach permits the greatest freedom to the private sector, particularly the very small collection firms. For example, citizens' intense loyalty to their trash haulers influenced the decision of Manheim Township, Pennsylvania, to revise its plans to have a bid system. Instead, it was decided that each hauler would be responsible for collecting both recyclables and trash.[28] However, higher costs are often associated with this alternative because of inefficiency of service delivery. In addition, the multihauler approach is difficult and cumbersome for the municipality to monitor. Some collectors may simply dump the collected recyclables in the landfill.[28] Recycling program promotion, and scheduling of the commencement of service, are more difficult under this alternative. Collections might begin sporadically in different parts of the municipality at different times and may never reach the entire municipality. Residents and businesses may be subject to payment for overlapping services. The ability to rely on recycling as a significant component of a comprehensive refuse management plan could be limited.[15] For example, Portland, Oregon, has over 100 private collectors. But the recycling rate is only about 2 percent in Portland, compared with 10 percent and above for other curbside collection programs.[28]

What would be the rationale for open collection of recyclables, besides customer loyalty? For one thing, the existing collectors are familiar with the territory, and they may exert considerable political leverage. To make open collection work, a municipality has to be willing to spend the time and money to put the program in place and monitor its progress, and take some responsibility for controlling the collectors' actions. Also, the collectors must support the program.[28]

To remedy some of the problems with open collection of recyclables, the municipality could undertake some or all of the following responsibilities:[15]

- Identify the specific services to be offered (collection frequency, day of collection, materials collected, etc.).
- Develop uniform education and publicity to support the program.
- Provide household set-out containers to all households.
- Provide technical assistance to collectors, including:

  Collection strategies for specific needs (e.g., single family, apartments, condominiums, etc.)

  Information regarding available equipment and latest collection techniques;

- Provide a MRF or other processing facility for collected materials.

education is continuous, and the pick-up schedule is highly reliable, the public seems willing to follow whatever schedule is established for collecting recyclables."[83]

One way to compensate for the extra cost of collecting recyclables is to reduce the number of regular refuse collections per household per month. Reducing from twice per week collection to once per week typically reduces costs by 20 percent: [81] the money saved can be applied toward the increased cost of a weekly or biweekly recyclables collection.

Curbside Versus Back-Door Collection.   Back-door (or backyard) collection of recyclables is not practical. "Not every residence will have recyclables out for collection every collection day because residents are asked to put their containers out only when they are full. Although participation rates may reach 85 to 90 percent or better on a monthly basis...it may be in the range of 50 to 60 percent on a weekly basis. Collection crews will therefore take up valuable time going to the rear of each residence to determine if recyclables have been set-out."[15]

Actually, eliminating back-door collection of refuse is another way to help pay for the additional cost of collecting recyclables. Going strictly to curbside collection results in savings in the 25 percent range; i.e., curbside collection costs about 75 percent of backyard collection.[80,81] The savings from elimination of back-door collection in Seattle, Washington, more than paid for the cost of a special yard waste collection. In Seattle, back-door collection of refuse is still available but at a much higher cost.[86] Milwaukee, Wisconsin (population 620,000), estimated that eliminating back-door collection from the residents that still receive this service would save the city on the order of $2 million annually.[10]

Vehicle Types, Capabilities, and Costs.   It is expensive to replace or supplement an existing fleet of refuse collection vehicles with new vehicles specifically designed to collect recyclables. Therefore, many communities have tried at least initially to retrofit existing refuse collection equipment. In 1971, Madison, Wisconsin, designed a newspaper rack welded to the frame of the refuse truck to collect bundled newspaper.[83] But such retrofits usually are not well suited to the collection of many different source-separated recyclables.

Some communities use pickup trucks that follow the refuse truck. The recyclables are set out in clear plastic bags to make them easily distinguished from the refuse.[83] A different approach involves using existing refuse compaction vehicles ("packer trucks") to collect newspaper or mixed fiber, with a separate vehicle (such as a pickup truck) for commingled containers. This approach would reduce capital expense at the startup of the program.

Packer trucks are used in some recycling programs to collect commingled containers, but more breakage of glass items occurs. In this case, more residue can be expected at the point of processing, especially from glass items. This reduces recovery levels and increases total net program cost.[15]

Many municipalities have found it necessary to make the investment in a fleet of specialized recycling vehicles. There are three categories of specialized recycling collection vehicles: closed-body trucks, open-top trucks, and trailers. Although a step van is in the same cost range, it is less efficient because of its inability to off-load by lifting hydraulically, and the subsequent need to unload the vehicle manually. Factors to be weighed in the selection of a vehicle type include:[15,20]

- Considerations to minimize worker fatigue, including:

Ease of entering and exiting the truck

Loading height

Street-side driving/vehicle entry-exit

Other drivers' safety and comfort features

- Overall net tonnage capacity (capacity should be large enough to allow the truck to be on the collection route for the entire day without having to make an intermediate stop at the processing facility, especially if it is far away)
- Ability to adjust material compartment sizes to allow for changes in collection quantities and to permit addition of new materials
- Material loading efficiency (e.g., ability to serve 90-gal carts from apartment buildings)
- Fuel efficiency
- Operating costs
- Flexibility of vehicle for other uses (e.g., in Milwaukee, Wisconsin, vehicles capable of carrying a snowplow were selected because the city's packer trucks have traditionally been used to plow snow)
- Safety and maneuvering considerations (e.g., attaching a trailer to a dump truck results in a very lengthy apparatus[1])
- Chassis and power requirements compatible with the terrain (more engine power for hilly rural areas; more maneuverability for more heavily populated areas)
- Design of the receiving area of the processing facility (or vice versa, if the truck fleet already exists, the processing facility receiving design should accommodate it)

In Palo Alto, California, a three-bin trailer system is used (glass, newspaper, and cans). Flattened cardboard and lightweight scrap metal are placed in the bed of the van. Used motor oil, packaged in unbreakable containers with tight-fitting lids, is placed in the space between the wheels of the trailer. The intent of this collection design is to recover both high-volume items such as glass and newspaper, and low-volume items with high pollution potential, such as batteries and oil. Three trailers are sent out each day, and each returns with full bins three times, unloading into roll-off containers.[70]

Some collectors have designed their own trucks. For example, a collector operating in the Windsor Locks, Connecticut, area, has designed the SAC I and SAC II (for "*s*eparation *a*t *c*urbside") (see Fig. 5.11). SAC I holds 17 yd³; SAC II holds 34 yd³. Collectors sort recyclables at the truck into five categories: three colors of glass, newspapers, and cans. The company has also designed an on-board plastics densification machine.[69] In another instance, a collector worked with a manufacturer and city officials to design a two-compartment collection truck (20 yd³ for mixed paper, 11 yd³ for commingled containers). The container side began filling up too quickly when residents began putting out mixed plastic containers.[68]

It has been estimated that an 80-TPD container recycling plant will save landfill space equivalent to a building 20 ft high, 100 ft wide, and a quarter-mile long.[77] This is also approximately the total volume of containers that will have to be hauled in a year by the collection vehicles serving the facility: 98,000 yd³ or 3,900 truck load equivalents for a 25-yd³ recycling collection vehicle (calculation

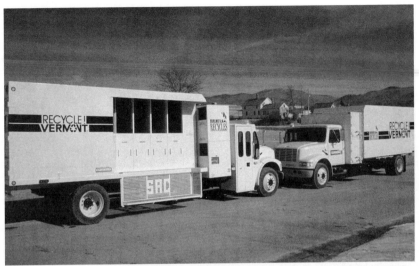

FIGURE 5.11   SAC trucks in Vermont. Note the two on-board plastic densification receiving ports just behind the cab on the passenger side. (*Photograph courtesy of John Casella.*)

ignores landfill cover material). Additional truck load equivalents would be required for any papers collected.

Table 5.14 gives a list of collection vehicles suppliers. As with the previous supplier lists, location and telephone numbers are provided so that convenient suppliers may be contacted for the latest information on product specifications, prices, availability, lead times for ordering, and shipping information.

Optimal Crew Size.   For regular refuse collection, a two-person crew may be more efficient than a one-person crew, if households are quite close together and where low traffic permits service to both sides of the street simultaneously. The same would apply to the collection of recyclables, except that the effective distance between households is much longer because of set-out and participation rates, so one-person crews are more efficient in most cases.[80] For example, in Mecklenburg County, North Carolina, trucks stopped at an average of about 32 of the 105 households passed per hour.[20] "The personnel required for separate collection of recyclables is the largest operating cost component of residential recycling programs. It is therefore not surprising that the most cost-efficient programs use one-person collection crews servicing one side of the street at a time. The addition of extra crew members has been found to have a negligible impact on collection productivity, at considerable increased expense."[15]

Collection Productivity.   Typically, curbside recycling routes are comprised of about 1,000 households passed by in one day.[20] However, there can be considerable variation between municipalities and between routes within an municipality. For example, in Mecklenburg County, North Carolina, passbys averaged about 105 households per hour, with 5.47 productive collection hours per day.[20] East Lyme, Connecticut's, single truck and crew of two serves 4,100 to 4,200 homes each week, picking up newspaper, cardboard, and mixed containers.

TABLE 5.14 Suppliers of Recycling Collection Vehicles

Firm	Location	Telephone
Able Body Co.	Newark, California	(415) 796-5611
Accurate Industries, Inc.	Williamstown, New Jersey	(609) 629-2800
All Seasons Recycling	Stroudsburg, Pennsylvania	(717) 424-1818
Amertek, Inc.	Woodstock, Ontario, Canada	(519) 539-7461
Amthor's, Inc.	Walden, New York	(914) 778-5576
Automated Waste Equipment Co., Inc.	Trenton, New Jersey	(609) 588-5400
Brothers Industries, Inc.	Morris, Minnesota	(800) 950-6045
Consolidated Truck & Equipment	Rehoboth, Massachusetts	(508) 252-3339
Dempster Systems	Toccoa, Georgia	(404) 886-6556
Eager Beaver Recycling Equip.	Thorofare, New Jersey	(800) 257-8163
Fitzgerald Truck Equip.	Cattaraugus, New York	(716) 257-3494
Frink America	Clayton, New York	(315) 686-5531
Full Circle	Paris, Illinois	(217) 465-6414
Galbreath, Inc.	Winamac, Indiana	(219) 946-6631
General Engines, inc.	Thorofare, New Jersey	(800) 257-8163
Haul-All Equipment Systems	Lethbridge, Alberta, Canada	(403) 328-7719
The Heil Co.	Chattanooga, Tennessee	(615) 899-9100
Hiab Cranes & Loaders	New Castle, Delaware	(302) 328-5100
Holden Trailer Sales, Inc.	Southwest City, Missouri	(417) 762-3218
Impact Products	New Lenox, Illinois	(815) 485-1808
Jaeger Industries, Inc.	St. Thomas, Ontario	(519) 631-5100
Kann Manufacturing	Guttenberg, Iowa	(319) 252-2035
Labrie Equipment Ltd.	Beaumont, Quebec, Canada	(800) 463-6638
Leach Co.	Oshkosh, Wisconsin	(414) 231-2770

The productivity of collection vehicles (the number of stops per day per vehicle) is affected by four major factors:[15]

1. Demographic and geographic characteristics of the area including density of housing, flatness of the terrain, parked cars, and street configuration
2. The design and capacity of the vehicle used
3. The total nonproductive time per day (travel time to and from the processing facility; lunch and coffee breaks)
4. Materials collected, their densities and their capture rates, and whether they are source-separated or curbside-separated

The number of stops that can be attained in a day can be estimated by knowing the set-out rate, the average distance between the households that set out recyclables, the driving time between stops, the average time it takes to unload a household's set-out containers into the truck, and the daily hours spent in actual driving and collecting.

TABLE 5.14 Suppliers of Recycling Collection Vehicles (*Continued*)

Firm	Location	Telephone
Lodal, Inc.	Kingsford, Michigan	(800) 435-3500
Maxi-Product Co., Inc.	Jamesville, Wisconsin	(608) 755-1199
May Manufacturing	Arvada, Colorado	(303) 423-6200
Midwest Body Corp.	Paris, Illinois	(217) 465-6414
Mobile Equipment Co.	Bakersfield, California	(805) 327-8476
Multitek, Inc.	Prentice, Wisconsin	(800) 243-LIFT
National Recycling Equipment Co.	Warwick, Rhode Island	(401) 732-2525
Norcia Corp.	North Brunswick, New Jersey	(201) 297-1101
P-M/Rudco	Vineland, New Jersey	(609) 696-4323
Parker Industries	Silver Lake, Indiana	(800) 526-8997
Peerless Corp.	Tualatin, Oregon	(503) 639-6131
Perkins Mfg. Co.	Chicago, Illinois	(312) 927-0200
Rand Systems	Raleigh, North Carolina	(800) 543-7263
Refuse Truck, Inc.	Chino, California	(714) 590-0200
Reliable Recycling Systems	South Windsor, Connecticut	(203) 569-6246
SAC Recycling	South Windsor, Connecticut	(203) 282-8282
Scranton Mfg. Co.	Scranton, Iowa	(800) 831-1858
Summit Trailer Sales	Summit Station, Pennsylvania	(717) 754-3511
Sunnyvale Truck Equipment	Sunnyvale, California	(408) 739-5475
Walinga, Inc.	Guelph, Ontario, Canada	(519) 824-8520
Wayne Engineering Corp.	Cedar Falls, Iowa	(319) 266-1721

Sources: "Guide to Vehicles for Recyclables Collection," *Waste Age,* pp. 157–164, February 1990; and "Directory, Home Storage Container Suppliers and Recycling Vehicle Manufacturers," *BioCycle,* pp. 38–39, July 1990.

Number of Vehicles Required. The size of the recycling collection vehicle can be estimated by knowing the volume, in cubic yards, of the recyclables likely to be set out by the average household each collection day and the number of set-outs that a single vehicle can serve in a day, including the time it takes to drive to the route in the morning, to the processing facility, and back to the vehicle's overnight parking area. For example, if each household generates 0.0375 yd^3 of recyclables each week and the recycling vehicle can drive by 800 households stopping at 480 of them, then the vehicle should have a capacity of at least 480 times 0.0375 or 18 yd^3, assuming that the vehicles' compartments are the ideal volume for the materials collected and that the compartments can be completely filled. (In practice, conditions are not ideal, so a somewhat larger truck should be selected.)

The total number of such vehicles required is estimated by the number of collection days per week that collection is to occur, the total number of set-outs expected on each day, and the number that each truck can serve. In the above example, 10 vehicles would be required if collection occurred 5 days per week, each truck could serve 480 set-outs per collection day, and 24,000 households set out materials once each week.

Costs of Curbside Collection.   Curbside collection is one of the most costly aspects of postconsumer recycling. In estimating the cost of curbside collection, all of the factors listed in Table 5.15 must be taken into account. There are numerous examples in the literature of attempts to justify recyclables collection cost on the basis of the "avoided cost of landfilling," but this approach can be very misleading.[32]

Costs can sometimes be justified when set against the full costs of the system without recycling, including the costs of funds that will have to be used to close and monitor landfills.[45] The cost for curbside collection of recyclables ranges from $1.00 to $2.80 per household served per month in 1990.[27] In Tallahassee, Florida, the collector is paid $1.32 per month per household for recyclables collection.[71] The City of Rockford, Illinois, is paying the collector $1.78 per month per household for weekly collection of newspapers, magazines, glass, plastic bottles, tin, steel, and aluminum cans. These are curbside-separated into eight categories.[41]

In any given municipality, recyclables collection is likely to have a cost similar to regular refuse collection because many of the cost elements are similar: labor

TABLE 5.15   Factors Influencing the Cost of Collecting Recyclables at Curbside

Set-out containers:
  Number per household or business
  Capacity of containers
  Frequency of replacement
  Ease of unloading

Density of set-out locations and set-out rates
  Driving distance/time between stops
  Number of pickups per stop

Compartmentalization
  Materials to be collected and their densities
  Number of categories of recyclables set out
  Number of compartments in collection truck
  Volume of each compartment
  Whether collectors sort at curbside or not

Drivers and workers:
  Number on each collection vehicle
  Wages and fringes
  Length of work day
  Performance (attitude, efficiency, speed)

Vehicles:
  Initial cost
  Maintenance cost
  Mileage efficiency
  Suitability for terrain (e.g., tight turns)
  Cycle time for automatic lifting equipment
  Unloading efficiency
  Whether used for other uses (e.g., snowplowing)

Weather

Distance/time to processing center from end of collection route

Amount of publicity required to achieve desired participation, set-out, and capture rates

earns about the same wages, recycling collection vehicles plus associated in-home containers cost about as much as garbage trucks, and vehicle operating costs are similar. The key to controlling costs is to establish an efficient collection and processing system. "It is extremely unlikely that inefficient collection and expensive recycling systems will be self-financing [*i.e., operate at zero net cost*] unless market prices for recycled goods are at historic highs and disposal fees near $200 per ton. Even the efficient collection and processing system will be self-financing only in areas of the country where the prevailing disposal fees are in the $25 per ton range" (parenthetical added).[81]

To reduce the overall net cost of the entire solid waste management system, the whole picture needs to be examined to see if there are possible cost-savings measures. For example, considering the cost of collection, savings could be realized by eliminating back-door collection, switching to contract collection for refuse if municipal collection costs have gotten out of hand, or reducing the number of regular refuse collections from two per week to one per week. For example, a private firm operating in the middle-class suburbs of San Francisco, California, estimated the cost savings due to recycling 48 TPD [12,500 tons per year (TPY)] were the following:[49]

- Savings through five fewer daily refuse collection routes (labor, capital, and operating expenses)—$787,000
- Savings through avoided transfer and disposal costs—$262,000

A comparison of the almost-twin towns of Longmeadow and East Longmeadow, Massachusetts, on a system-cost basis shows that the town with a recycling collection had lower net per-household cost in 1989. In this simple example, both towns employ the same collection firm and the same equipment (a 17-yd^3 right-hand drive, one-person, side-loading packer). The results of the analysis are shown in Table 5.16.

The reasons that East Longmeadow's system cost is less with recycling include the following:[64]

- Participation rate of 90 percent
- An inexpensive collection system: a cleaned-out packer truck is sent out one week to pick up old newspapers and the following week for corrugated cardboard and paperboard
- Adequate revenue from material sales (corrugated cardboard and paperboard received $30 per ton and newspaper revenue was $10 per ton when the costs were analyzed)

In addition to paying for the additional cost of recycling collections through surcharges and cost-savings measures adopted in other parts of the refuse management system, municipalities can sometimes obtain grants. For example, Coca-Cola donated $99,000 to Mecklenburg County for PET recycling support.[57] It is also sometimes possible to rely to some extent, at least on a limited or temporary basis, on donated collection services by public-spirited organizations.

Collecting plastics for recycling presents a particularly difficult economic challenge. Because of the materials' low density, collection trucks carrying uncompacted plastic are carrying around a lot of dead airspace. In Rhode Island, it was estimated that adding plastics to a curbside collection program would result in an incremental cost of $54 to $108 per ton of plastic collected, while Milwaukee,

TABLE 5.16 Comparison of System Costs with and without Recycling in Two Communities in Massachusetts

	Longmeadow	East Longmeadow
Demography:		
Population	16,380	12,910
Housing units	5,450	4,400
Road miles	94	83
Houses per road mile	58	53
Annual per capita income	$20,306	$12,693
Topography	Flat	Flat
Area, mi^2	9.0	13.2
Refuse tonnage:		
Frequency of refuse collection	Weekly	Biweekly
Annual refuse generation	6,605 tons	5,060 tons
Annual recycling:		
Newspaper	1,298	
Corrugated/paperboard	237	
Glass containers	70	
Aluminum	10	
Annual disposal	4,990	5,060
Percent waste reduction	24%	0%
Costs		
Cost of refuse collection	$181,000	$160,000
Recycling collection	68,000	0
Disposal @$34 per ton	169,660	172,040
Revenue, sale of recyclables	(30,460)	0
Total solid waste cost	$388,200	$322,040
Annual cost per residence	$71.23	$75.50

Source: Powell, Jerry, "Recycling is cheaper: the Massachusetts experience," *Resource Recycling*, pp. 37, 61, October 1989.

Wisconsin, estimated that collection and processing of one ton of postconsumer plastic in its pilot program cost $975 compared with $115 for paper.[48] Even with a maximum theoretical revenue on the order of $800 per ton, the curbside collection of undensified plastic may not be economical. (Actual average revenues for plastics are more in the range of $120 to $160 per ton, depending on resin type, and can be as low as $40 per ton for mixed plastics).[94]

A common way to raise revenues to support recycling is to increase the tipping fees at the landfill, as is done in Mecklenburg Country, North Carolina.[57] However, unless there is strict flow control in some form so that refuse cannot escape paying the increased fees, a positive feedback loop is created: the more recycling that takes place, the fewer tons arrive at the landfill to pay the increased tipping fees which must rise even further on a per-ton basis to pay for the increased system costs.[15]

MONITORING PERFORMANCE

The first step in monitoring performance of a separation and collection system is to have a clear idea of what the goals of the overall program are. Is the recycling program being undertaken to involve as many citizens as possible in recycling? Or to divert the maximum amount of material from the landfill? Or to minimize the cost of the solid waste management system in the long run? To employ as many people as possible? To foster the growth and development of local recycling industries? Or all of the above? The performance measurements chosen should reflect the goals of the program. For example, Mecklenburg County, North Carolina, collected data during its initial program phase that would allow it to compute and evaluate a number of performance measures including:[20]

- Household participation and material set-out rates
- Material recovery rates
- Adequacy of the volume and design of the in-home container
- Impact of variables on collection production rates
- Collection vehicle design parameters, efficiencies, and costs
- Optimum size of collection routes
- Processing efficiencies and costs

Whatever measurements are taken, for all but the smallest of communities a computerized data base will be necessary. For example, the city of Philadelphia developed a dBASE III + program which incorporates census data so that participation can be predicted. Data on participation, set-out of unacceptable materials, and other parameters are recorded by block and entered daily, as are cost data.[75]

Measuring Participation

The most common measurement taken of curbside collection programs is the participation rate. Participation is measured in various ways from pure guessing to actual sampling.[27] Participation is commonly measured on a monthly basis since not all households set out recyclables each week.

Use of Bar Code Scanners to Record Participation.   Bar coding of set-out containers is gaining in popularity. Advocates think that widespread use of bar coding might create some consistency in the current "hodgepodge" of methods for tabulation and estimation of participation rate.[84] Bar coding offers the additional advantage that worker productivity is automatically registered, allowing program managers to adjust route sizes. In addition, nonparticipating households can be automatically identified, so that individualized attention and education can be given to them. In addition, if there are differential rates charged to participating households, the households that actually participate can be accurately rewarded for their efforts.

The technical challenge to successful bar code recording is to provide a suitable label that sticks to the bins despite their ultraviolet light–resistant coatings,

FIGURE 5.12   A worker scans a set-out container's bar code. (*Photograph courtesy of the City of St. Louis Park.*)

and that does not become unreadable over time. Hand-held scanners seem to function without major problems (even in cold weather), and the procedures do not seem to slow the workers down inordinately. Different collection firms hold different views on the utility and difficulty of bar coding, however.

A pioneer in the use of bar coding is St. Louis Park, Minnesota (population 43,000) (Fig. 5.12.). This community uses a stackable, triple 10-gal bin system, and collection is bimonthly. The 2,500 TPY collected is said to be 16 percent of residential waste. It is important that participation be measured accurately, because a quarterly $6.60 recycling credit (from a basic garbage service charge of $11 per month) is granted to residents who set out recyclables at least three times within a 3-month period. (A credit is also given to citizens using buy-back and drop-off centers.) When the bar coding and credit system went into effect, participation rose from 75 to 87 percent.[84] Bar code scanners, computers, documentation, and training costs were $25,000 for the 12,000 households covered in the collection.[92] Each household was sent a set of bar code stickers that included the household's utility billing account number. Data from the hand-held scanners are transferred electronically to the utility's billing office. Bar coding is also used in Tonka Bay, Minnesota; Rolling Hills Estates, California; Munster, Indiana; Clinton County, Pennsylvania; and is soon to be used in Charlotte, North Carolina.[84] Munster, Indiana, also uses a reduced-rate incentive to participate, and Rolling Hills Estates uses a lottery.

Measuring Participation by Sign-Up.   In communities where residents must subscribe in order to receive recycling collection, participation is measured by the percent of residences that have signed up. In Seattle, Washington, sign-up for the three-bin collection on the northern side is 85.8 percent; sign-up for the one-cart system serving the south side is 62.4 percent, for a 72.7 percent sign-up rate overall.[86] The difference in sign-up rate between the north and south side has been attributed to weekly pickup (therefore a weekly reminder) in the north, more brightly colored bins in the north, and cultural influences (the south has more low-income residents and a wider range of ethnic backgrounds).[86]

Other Methods of Estimating Participation. The traditional way of determining participation rate is to have the collection worker keep records. However, this slows down collection, places an additional burden on the collector, and results in a large data recording and analysis job for someone in an office.

Estimating participation rate from weekly set-out rates can be unreliable, unless sampling is done to calibrate the set-out rate. In Santa Cruz, California, 35 to 45 percent of residents with stackable recycling containers put them at the curb in any one week. A study route was chosen. Out of 640 residences, 417 distinct addresses set out materials during a 7-week period, for a participation rate of 65.2 percent.[76] (Note that the rate would be expected to be smaller if the study period were the more typical 1-month duration.)

Estimating participation rate for apartment complexes is very difficult unless each apartment has its own containers set out at the curb.

Lexington, Kentucky, asked participants in its 6-month pilot project to volunteer to keep weekly diaries of the number of containers (aluminum, glass, and plastic) and the number of newspapers they set out each week. Over 100 participants volunteered and completed at least one of the 6 one-page diary sheets mailed to them.[47] This method is unlikely to be very useful over a long period of time, as it depends on self-reporting.

Measuring Capture

The quantity of refuse that could theoretically be recycled has been variously estimated. In one composition study, it was found to be as high as 50.3 percent on a weight basis and 63.3 percent on a volume basis. (Recyclables in this study included clean wood, leaves and twigs, textiles, and boxes.) There was a significant difference depending on the day of the week that the sample was taken, with refuse sampled early in the week being richer in recyclables.[56] How much of this theoretically recyclable material is actually captured depends on what materials are accepted for collection, and how faithfully participants set out all that they can.

Not all participants set out for collection all the materials that are accepted for collection. For example, in Minneapolis, Minnesota, about half of all participants set out all materials, 25 percent set out only two items, and 25 percent set out only paper. Plymouth, Minnesota, claimed that 30 percent set out only paper. In Austin, Texas, less than 50 percent set out containers.[29] In Santa Cruz, California, three-quarters of participants put out newspapers, two-thirds included glass, and one-half included cans. Many HDPE milk and water bottles were set out, even though they were not eligible in this program (although PET bottles were).[76] In general, newspaper is the most frequent material set out. It usually makes up about 75 percent of the weight of material collected, with glass contributing 15 to 25 percent, and metal 5 to 10 percent.[29]

Measuring capture rate requires two measurements: the amount of the recyclable correctly source-separated, and the amount that was not source-separated but instead placed in the refuse. The accurate way to do this is through periodic waste composition analysis from a statistically valid sample of randomly selected recycling routes, analyzing the composition of both the recyclables stream and the regular refuse stream. This is the approach used in Milwaukee, Wisconsin, and in several other cities. In Milwaukee, the waste composition analysis is conducted at the city's three transfer stations, and 50 separate materials are classified, including all materials currently thought to be recyclable by any means (even those that the city does not currently accept in its curbside and drop-off programs).[7] In Mecklenburg County, North Carolina, capture rates were measured with a refuse sampling study. In 1987, the curbside collection program was estimated to recover about 8.75 percent of the residential refuse stream. This recycling rate is consistent with other similar curbside recycling programs.[20]

Fitchburg, Wisconsin, has analyzed the capture rate for polystyrene in its experimental curbside collection of this material. The weight of polystyrene collected from a sample of residences was obtained from the collector. The weight of polystyrene left over in the refuse stream was determined by sorting over 9 tons of refuse from the same homes. Approximately 83 percent of the polystyrene was captured. Of the material captured, 8.5 percent was not polystyrene and another 8.5 percent was contaminated.[37]

More information on waste composition analysis is found in Chap. 3 of this Handbook.

Measuring Costs of Separation and Collection

Measuring costs of the separation and collection program should be a straightforward matter. Why, then, does the literature on this subject tend to be somewhat obscure? Perhaps the answer lies in the fact that collection of recyclables is expensive. Looking only at the short-term economics, many recycling programs have a net positive cost to a community, and collection is largely responsible.

Recyclables collection cost is normally added onto the regular refuse collection cost. The factors determining the costs of recyclables collection are almost exactly the same as the factors determining the cost of regular refuse collection, and include crew wages, distance between houses, frequency of collection, point of collection (curbside or backyard), quantity of material to collect, terrain, weather, crew size, and vehicle efficiency (i.e., whether all compartments are sized so that they fill up at the same time). Without a serious community effort at source reduction, the total amount of refuse collected will not change appreciably whether it is picked up in a recyclables truck or a refuse collection truck.

It is possible that cost savings can occur in regular refuse collection as a result of diverting material to a recyclables collection. However, it takes several years to determine how much larger the regular collection routes can be as a result of the diversion of material into the recycling collection, and even longer to make the necessary cost-saving changes in the regular collection routes. In addition, lengthening the regular refuse collection routes does not result in a dollar-for-dollar cost saving...adding a recycling collection at the same frequency as regular refuse collection will cost about as much as would adding an extra weekly pickup to the regular refuse collection schedule."[80] Increasing collection frequency from once per week to twice per week increases collection costs about 26 percent, and increasing frequency from twice a week to three times in a week increases total collection cost by about 18 percent.[80] But, this assumes the same vehicles and crew can be used. The costs may actually be higher if specialized vehicles are needed.

If recyclables collection should happen to be cheaper than regular refuse collection for some reason (such as a different contractor collecting the material, cheaper collection trucks, shorter haul distance to unloading location, low degree of source separation, and no curbside separation required), then there should be a point at which the entire collection system cost is lower as a result of the recyclables collection. For example, Tukwila, Washington, found that since contract refuse collection service for apartments was more expensive per ton than contract recyclables collection service for the same apartments, there would be a point at which the public provision of dumpsters for recyclables would break even economically. For that program, the break-even point was estimated to occur when about 30 percent of the waste was recovered in the recycling collection.[6] (In this instance, the recyclables were separated in a single source separation with all recyclables commingled.)

The concept of avoided disposal cost is frequently misused in discussing the cost of recyclables sorting and collection.[32] The only accurate and rational basis to compare costs is on a system cost basis, where the full cost of refuse management is added up for the system with recycling and compared to the system without recycling (or with a different kind of recycling). Full system cost should include any quantifiable costs of landfill development and closure, as well as any cost savings in regular refuse collection and disposal. The subject of full system cost is exceedingly important, but it is beyond the scope of this section to provide a detailed method. Table 5.17 provides a list of many of the myriad cost and revenue elements that go into a full system cost calculation.

Public Support/Satisfaction

Public satisfaction with the separation and collection system is the engine that will drive successful recycling. Business and political support are also essential: political support translates into program dollars; private sector support results in donated expertise and other resources.

There are two ways to "measure" public support and satisfaction. One way is to wait until voters have let their elected officials know what they think of the program, which may result in some unplanned program changes. Another way is by public attitude surveys.

Mecklenburg County did a series of surveys before and after commencing its pilot curbside collection program. After the program began, 96 percent of respondents said they were recycling, whereas before the program (when only drop-off centers were available) 31 percent said they were recycling.[20] Lexington, Kentucky, also developed a method of evaluating a 6-month pilot curbside collection program at the outset.

Attitude surveys were conducted before and after the pilot. The survey response rates were 47 percent before and 68 percent after the pilot, indicating a heightened interest. After the pilot, 94 percent favored expanding the program. Only 6 percent still thought it would be hard to change people's habits. Fewer people in the "after" survey thought source separation would be time consuming or difficult.[47]

Public attitudes can be shaped by public relations efforts, in addition to being shaped by actual experience with the program. For example, Mecklenburg County, North Carolina, found that extensive public education and promotion resulted in numerous telephone calls from citizens wondering when their households would be added to the program,[20] a good sign of public support. A similar experience was reported in Milwaukee, Wisconsin.

TABLE 15.17 Elements of Total Solid Waste System Costs

System planning costs and source reduction costs
  Education and outreach
  Administration costs for volume-based rates
  Enforcement costs

Costs for collection from point of generation and delivery to initial drop-off location
  Equipment
    Regular collection and special recycling collection vehicles, purchase cost of special
    bins or roll-off carts, if provided for either regular waste or recyclables, and re-
    placement of same

  Labor
    Salaries and wages for all collection workers and supervisors, regular waste and
    other special collection (e.g., recyclables, yard waste, white goods)
    Fringe benefits for collectors
    Other labor-related costs (e.g., overtime)

  Operating and maintenance costs of all vehicles, including:
    Fuel usage
    Tires
    Truck maintenance
    Insurance and licenses
    Other
  [Alternatively, the cost of collection may be the cost of contracts for collection.]

Costs for transfer and processing facilities:
  Drop-off centers for recyclables, regular waste, yard waste
  Transfer stations
  Transfer stations for special materials (e.g., household hazardous waste)
  Intermediate processing facilities (IPFs)
  Material recovery facilities (MRFs)
  Composting facilities
  Special processing facilities (e.g., construction debris)
  Waste-to-energy facilities
  Mixed-waste processing facilities

  Site and equipment
    Site investigation/selection/purchase costs
    Permitting costs
    Costs for construction labor
    Site preparation costs (earthwork, utilities, fencing, etc.)
    Costs for buildings, structures
    Costs for on-site mobile equipment
    Material processing equipment costs
    Costs for controls, all other auxiliary equipment
    Performance testing costs
    Startup operations may also be included

  Operating labor
    Salaries and wages for site workers and supervisors
    Fringe benefits
    Other labor-related costs

TABLE 15.17   Elements of Total Solid Waste System Costs (*Continued*)

Operating and maintenance costs for site and equipment
    Fuel
    Vehicle maintenance
    Equipment maintenance
    Site maintenance
    Equipment repair and replacement (including deposits to sinking funds)
Environmental and other permit compliance monitoring and testing costs
[*Alternatively, the cost of furnishing and equipping and/or operating, any of these facilities could be on a contract basis. In this case, the cost would be the contractually specified costs.*]
Costs for haul from transfer/processing facility to disposal sites and/or markets
    Equipment
        Cost of mobile equipment used for hauling (tractors, trailers, spares, etc.)
    Labor
        Salaries and wages for hauling workers and supervisors
        Fringe benefits for haulers
        Other labor-related costs (e.g., overtime)
    Operating and maintenance cost of all vehicle, including:
        Fuel usage
        Tires
        Truck maintenance
        Insurance and licenses
        Other
[*Alternatively, the cost of hauling may be the cost of contracts for hauling. In some cases, markets may pick up the material for a somewhat lower revenue than if it were delivered.*]
Costs for disposal
    Landfill development costs
        site investigation/selection/purchase costs
        Permitting costs
        Costs for construction labor
        Site preparation costs (earthwork, utilities, fencing, etc.)
        Costs for buildings, structures, liners, leachate controls, methane controls
        Costs for on-site mobile equipment
        Costs for all other auxiliary equipment
    Operating labor
        Salaries and wages for site workers and supervisors
        Fringe benefits
        Other labor-related costs
    Operating and maintenance costs
        Fuel
        Vehicle maintenance
        Equipment maintenance
        Site maintenance
        Equipment repair and replacement (including deposits to sinking funds)
        Additional liners, cover material, etc., as cells are developed
        Landfill closure costs and post-closure monitoring costs (escrow fund deposits)

TABLE 15.17   Elements of Total Solid Waste System Costs (*Continued*)

Environmental and other permit compliance monitoring and testing costs
[*Alternatively, the cost of furnishing and equipping, and/or operating, a landfill could be on a contract basis. In this case, the cost would be the contractually specified costs.*]

General administrative costs
  Administrative labor and fringe benefits
  Education and public relations cost
  Costs associated with advisory committees
  Memberships, travel, and other professional costs
  Legal, accounting, and other professional services

Revenues
  Tipping fee revenues
  Contract revenues
  Franchise fee revenues
  General fund revenues
  Special assessment revenues
  User charges
  Revenues from the sale of recyclables and compost
  Revenues from the sale of energy (steam, electricity, and fuel products)
  Landfill reserve capacity fees
  Grants-in-aid (federal or state) and other subsidiaries
  Fines (where specifically dedicated)

Notes: All costs are likely to be financed by some mixture of debt and equity. The costs of financing, including letters of credit or other security, and underwriter's costs, would need to be added to the total construction and equipment cost to derive the capital cost for facilities and equipment.

Costs borne by individuals hauling material to drop-off or disposal or in "backyard composting" or other individual waste management activities are not commonly included in analysis of system costs.

In trying to determine or predict public support and satisfaction with a program, all waste generators must be listened to if the program is to be truly successful. One cannot rely on "experts" to indicate what public reaction to a particular program feature will be. "It is argued that people will not cooperate on a voluntary basis. This argument is often stated by speakers who then indicate their own situation. In other cases, these people are influenced by objective arguments and calculations, but for sorting at the source they make decisions on the basis of their personal prejudices."[46]

Additional information on public attitudes can be found in Chap. 30 of this Handbook.

Scavenging

No discussion of separation and collection would be complete without an acknowledgement that scavenging occurs. Scavenging was noted as a problem even in the early experiments with curbside collection.[53]

In societies where reliance on highly mechanized refuse collection and disposal is not widespread, scavenging is the primary means of recovering valuable resources. For example, in Egypt, 15,000 people live in a refuse ghetto, paying for the privilege of collecting refuse in the city using donkey carts for collection vehicles. These people support themselves entirely by the hand-picking and sale of salvagable goods. Sorting is done in their front yards. Marketing involves a daily negotiated price with intermediaries, who sell the separated materials to conversion plants.[62]

Although China has an extensive state-controlled waste recovery administration extending down to the neighborhood level[24,58], widespread informal scavenging takes place on the streets and at the dumps of other Asian cities like Cairo, Calcutta, Bali, Manila, and Bangkok. Intermediaries control the scavengers, and sometimes these operations function at the edge of legality. "Municipalities are now asserting their rights over wastes that formerly they were only too glad to have others deal with, and ownership issues are becoming contentious...public authorities see street picking as risky and degrading for the whole community; welfare groups wish to protect scavengers' traditional rights and access...health considerations raise some of the most difficult issues. Should groups be permitted to continue in unhealthy occupations if they so wish?"[23]

Mexico City has a recycling infrastructure somewhat similar to Cairo's. In this city an estimated 5,000 to 20,000 scavengers make their living off the dump. These people have an average life expectancy of about 35 years and their infant mortality rate is almost 50 percent. Phasing out scavenging has been difficult for the government because scavenging is important to the fragile economy of the city and because of pressure from influential people who profit from it. There are many purchasers of reclaimed material, and the city's sanitation workers can almost double their income by sorting through the trash for salable items like cardboard. For the Mexico City metropolitan area, a study using linear programming analysis showed that the most cost-effective recycling would occur when businesses recycled their own waste, residents and street sweepers recycled residential waste, and recycling centers were sited at a density of one per 2 km^2.[50]

In the United States, scavenging is a problem for some urban areas that undertake curbside collection. One solution is to adopt a strictly enforced antiscavenging ordinance. Some communities have chosen to overlook scavenging, as long as it does not create a public nuisance. In Milwaukee, Wisconsin, some citizens had been setting out their aluminum cans separately for years before the city had a curbside collection program, specifically so that scavengers could have easier access to them. (However, in December 1990, a recorded message on the Milwaukee recycling "hot-line" asks callers for their views on whether scavenging should remain legal.) A unique solution to a scavenging problem was adopted in Hollywood, Florida, where a scavenger (who would otherwise have been in violation of an antiscavenging law) was officially assigned the areas of the city that could not be served by city crews.[93] In areas with many buy-back centers, there tends to be more scavenging.[68] Buy-back centers have also had to deal with suspected thieves who have stolen valuable commodities like aluminum siding and copper wire from construction sites, guard rails, and, in some cases, from dwellings. If extensive, scavenging can undermine the economics of a curbside collection program since the scavengers typically take the most valuable materials (especially aluminum), the revenues from which are important for helping to offset recycling program costs.

Will scavenging become a greater problem for organized recycling in the United States as world resources become more scarce and costly? The answer to this question is currently unclear.

CONCLUSIONS

Recycling is a manufacturing industry which depends on donated raw materials from millions of individuals making trillions of trivial daily decisions, such as whether to place a particular can, bottle, or paper in a recycling bin or in the trash. The industry has grown from the grass roots by popular demand. There is a strong undercurrent of willingness to participate.

Recycling separation and collection programs are as varied as the communities they serve, and this is appropriate. "Programs that have been custom-developed to suit the particular needs of the locale which they serve are showing the best results."[57] Still, there are some generalizations that have proven useful in most cases.

For maximum capture, participation must be made convenient. Convenience can be enhanced by provision of in-home storage containers and regular weekly or biweekly curbside collection. Drop-off and buy-back opportunities should be provided to supplement regular collection.

For any community, a carefully designed implementation plan is needed, with data collection procedures built in at the beginning so that the municipality can proceed with program expansion using separation and collection equipment and procedures that have proven to be the most effective.[20]

There may be new mixed-waste processing facilities on the horizon that will relieve the waste generator of the responsibility to source-separate. This development is heralded by some, and viewed with skepticism by those who believe that people *should* become more involved with the refuse they generate, so that they will generate less of it and preserve the earth's resources.

Finally, as world resources inevitably deplete due to growth in world population, more recycling is also inevitable; therefore, "people must stop regarding garbage as something they have just finished with and start thinking of it as something someone else is just starting with."[23]

REFERENCES

1. Abramowitz, Richard, "Source Separation in Austin," *BioCycle,* The J. G. Press, Inc., Emmaus, Pa., pp. 36–37, September 1987.

2. Amidon, Arthur, "Plastic Grocery Sack Recycling," *Resource Recycling,* Resource Recycling, Inc., Portland, Oreg., pp. 24–31, November 1990.

3. Anderson, Peter, and Steven Brachman, "Making Plastics Recycling Practical: New Roles for Cities and Industry," *Environmental Decisions,* National League of Cities, Institute, Washington, D.C., pp. 14–24, October 1990.

4. Apotheker, Steve, "Curbside Collection: Complete Separation versus Commingled Collection," *Resource Recycling,* pp. 58–63, 105–109, October 1990.

5. Bennett, Linda, "Behavior Study on Recycling Participation," *BioCycle,* p. 37, November 1990.

6. Benton, Craig H., and Rebecca Fox, "Commingled Recycling Tested in Apartments," *Resource Recycling,* pp. 48–50, 87, June 1990.

7. Bid Specifications and Request for Proposals, prepared for the City of Milwaukee by Roy F. Weston, Inc., Burlington, Mass., October 1990.

8. Boesmans, B., "Production of Source-Separated Domestic Waste Fractions," *Conser-*

vation & Recycling, Vol. 9, No. 1, Pergamon Press Ltd., Great Britain, pp. 29–34, 1986.

9. Bowing, Esther R., "A Comparison of Commingled Collection Containers," *Resource Recycling,* pp. 36–40, 104, April 1990.

10. Brachman, Steve, Department of Public Works, City of Milwaukee, Wis., personal communication, 1990.

11. Bryant, Gloria, "Newark Claims East Coasts' Largest Recycling Program," *World Wastes,* Publication Management Communication Channels Inc., Atlanta, Ga., pp. 47–49, December 1988.

12. Bucher, Ginger L., "York's Approach to Apartment Recycling," *Environmental Decisions,* pp. 16–19, April 1990.

13. Bullock, Dave, and Debbie Burk, "Commingled vs. Curbside Sort," *BioCycle,* pp. 35–36, June 1989.

14. *City of Milwaukee Residential Waste Characterization 1989–1990,* Department of Public Works, City of Milwaukee, Wis., 1990.

15. *Cobb County Solid Waste Management Plan: Volume 2, Draft for Public Review and Comment.* Roy F. Weston, Inc. and Resource Integration Systems Ltd., Norcross, Ga., August 1990.

16. Cole, Timothy J., "Buy-Back Recycling in Rural North Carolina," *Resource Recycling,* pp. 64–67, June 1990.

17. Cunningham, Sarah Lynn, "From Blue Angels to Variable Can Rates," *BioCycle,* pp. 44–45, June 1990.

18. "Curbside Collection Capturing Attention," *Recycling Today,* GIE Inc., Publishers, Cleveland, Ohio, p. 85, March 1990.

19. "Directory, Home Storage Container Suppliers and Recycling Vehicle Manufacturers," *BioCycle,* pp. 38–39, July 1990.

20. Dorn, Betsy, "County Launches Recycling Program," *Public Works,* pp. 63–66, August 1988.

21. "Dropoff Collection Equipment," *BioCycle,* pp. 46–47, February 1989.

22. "European Models for Organic Waste Composting," *BioCycle,* p. 31, June 1990.

23. Furedy, Christine, "Socio-Political Aspects of the Recovery and Recycling of Urban Wastes in Asia," *Conservation & Recycling,* Vol. 7, No. 2–4, pp. 167–173, 1984.

24. Furedy, Christine, "Waste Recovery in China," *BioCycle,* pp. 80–84, June 1990.

25. Gale, Diana, and Timothy Croll, "Coping with Seattle's Solid Waste Crisis," *Waste Alternatives,* Washington, D.C., pp. 10–16, June 1989.

26. Glenn, Jim, "Containers at Curbside," *BioCycle,* pp. 26–29, March 1988.

27. Glenn, Jim, "Curbside Recycling Reaches 40 Million," *BioCycle,* pp. 30–37, July 1990.

28. Glenn, Jim, "How Many Haulers Should Collect Recyclables," *BioCycle,* October 1990.

29. Glenn, Jim, "Junior, Take Out the Recyclables," *BioCycle,* pp. 26–31, May–June 1988.

30. Glenn, Jim, "New Age Dropoff Programs," *BioCycle,* pp. 42–45, February 1989.

31. Glenn, Jim, "Recycling Hits the Workplace," *BioCycle,* pp. 34–36, February 1990.

32. Goldman, Matthew, "What Do Those Recycling Numbers Mean?," Roy F. Weston, Inc., Burlington, Mass., February 1990.

33. Goldstein, J. G., "New Approach to Collecting Recyclables," *BioCycle,* pp. 54–55, November 1989.

34. Grady, Julie C., "Recyclers—In Saabs and Volvos," *Waste Age,* Washington, D.C., pp. 71–72, 74, February 1987.

35. Grady, Julie C., "Thrifty Yankees Recycle & Save," *Waste Age,* pp. 39–40, 42, December 1987.

36. Gruder-Adams, Sherrie, "Recycling in Multifamily Units," *BioCycle,* pp. 36–37, August 1990.

37. Gruder-Adams, Sherrie, "Residential Polystyrene Recycling," *Resource Recycling,* pp. 72–79, October 1990.

38. "Guide to Vehicles for Recyclables Collection," *Waste Age,* pp. 157–164, February 1990.

39. Hurd, David J., Stephen Gallagher, and Kevin Taylor, "Recycling at Apartments Can Work," *Waste Alternatives,* Washington, D.C., pp. 31–32, June 1988.

40. Hyde, Jennifer, "An Experimental Apartment Recycling Program," *Resource Recycling,* pp. 30–32, June 1990.

41. *Integrated Waste Management,* McGraw-Hill, New York, December 26, 1990.

42. Jacobs, Harvey E., and Jon S. Bailey, "Evaluating Participation in a Residential Recycling Program," *J. Environmental Systems* Vol. 12 (2), pp. 141–152, 1982–1983.

43. Jantzef, Monica F., "A Buyback Center," *Waste Age,* pp. 122–123, November 1988.

44. Johnson, Bruce, "Curbside Recycling Program Successful in California," *World Wastes,* pp. 56, 58, 60, 69, July 1986.

45. Johnson, Bruce, "Seattle Calculates Recycling Savings," *World Wastes,* pp. 22–23, November 1986.

46. Joosten, J. M., "Sorting at the Source," *Resource Recovery and Conservation,* 5, Nos. 2–4, Elsevier Scientific Publishing Company, Amsterdam, pp. 15–19, 1980.

47. Kilner, Suzanne M., Steven B. Feese, and Robert D. Wiseman, "The Future Looks Rosie," report on a cart-based recycling program, *Resource Recycling,* pp. 82–88, October 1990.

48. Lamb, Jennifer, and Marion Chertow (editors), "Plastics Collection," *BioCycle,* pp. 62–63, April 1990.

49. Mattheis, Ann H., "Going Back to Get to the Future," *Waste Age,* pp. 50–52, 54, 56, 58, July 1988.

50. Milke, M. W., and F. J. Aceves, "Systems Analysis of Recycling in the Distrito Federal of Mexico," *Resources, Conservation and Recycling 2,* Elsevier Science Publishers, B.V./Pergamon Press, The Netherlands, pp. 171–197, 1989.

51. Misner, Michael, "Prime Location Is Key to Drop-off Success," *Waste Age,* pp. 94–95, October 1990.

52. Mullen, Tom, "Recycling in New Mexico: Challenging and Growing," *Resource Recycling,* pp. 36–37, July 1989.

53. Mulligan, Kevin, "Project SORT—Source Separation in Seattle," *Compost Science/ Land Utilization,* pp. 26–27, January–February 1979.

54. "Non-Burn System for Total Waste Stream," *BioCycle,* pp. 30–31, April 1987.

55. Nudd, Rick, "Reuse Begins Recycling Program," *Waste Age,* pp. 74–76, November 1990.

56. "Over 50 Percent of Refuse Can be Recycled, Phoenix Study Reports," *Public Works,* pp. 73, 108, 110, October 1988.

57. Peters, Anne, and Pete Grogan, "Community Recycling," *BioCycle,* pp. 37–38, May–June 1988.

58. Peterson, Charles, "China's Dilemma," *Waste Alternatives,* pp. 59–61, June 1988.

59. Pettit, C. L., "Trends in Collecting Recyclables," *Waste Age,* pp. 49, 52–55, July 1986.

60. Pierson, Robert W., Jr., "Eight Steps To Block Corner Success," *Waste Age,* pp. 147–149, 152, 154, 156, 158, November 1988.

61. Pierson, Robert W., Jr., "Low-Cost Recycling: Block Corner Pickup," *Waste Age*, pp. 126, 128, October 1988.
62. Pollock, Eugene, "Recycling System in Cairo, Egypt, Follows Ancient Custom, but Does the Job," *Solid Wastes Management*, p. 52D, January 1978.
63. Poremba, Gregory A., and Katherine M. Vick, "Best Yield for Recycling Investment," *BioCycle*, pp. 66–67, February 1990.
64. Powell, Jerry, "Recycling is Cheaper: the Massachusetts Experience," *Resource Recycling*, pp. 37, 61, October 1989.
65. "Recycling Container Guide," *Waste Alternatives*, pp. 30–33, June 1989.
66. Riggle, David, "Only Pay for What You Throw Away," *BioCycle*, pp. 39–41, February 1989.
67. Riggle, David, "Recycling Plastic Grocery Bags," *BioCycle*, pp. 40–41, June 1990.
68. Salimando, Joe, "Adjusting Residential Collection to Fit," *Waste Age*, pp. 35–40, February 1990.
69. Salimando, Joe, "Call Him Separatin' Sam," *Waste Age*, pp. 44–48, February 1990.
70. Salimando, Joe, "Recycling's Future Is Now," *Waste Age*, pp. 75, 77–78, 80, October 1987.
71. Schaefer, Susan, *Costs for Tallahassee Recycling*, Roy F. Weston, Inc., internal memorandum, July 1990.
72. Schmerling, Elaine, "Recycling Container Choices," *BioCycle*, pp. 36–37, March 1990.
73. Sedlock, Joseph T., "Curbside Sorting or Source Separation?," *Waste Age*, pp. 143–144, October 1990.
74. Shotwell, Robert E., "Three-Way Partnership Recycles in Bend," *Waste Age*, pp. 38–40, July 1987.
75. Siderer, Jack P., and Mark Bersalona, "A Computer Evaluation of the Philadelphia Curbside Recycling Program," City of Philadelphia.
76. Smedberg, Jeffrey, "Calculating Participation: A Look at that Tricky Multiplier," *Resource Recycling*, pp. 26ff., October 1989.
77. Spaulding, Mark, "Recycling Saves Camden $500,000 a Year," *Packaging*, Cahners Publishing, Des Plaines, Ill., pp. 12, 14, July 1987.
78. Spencer, Robert, "Food Waste Composting in Canada," *BioCycle*, pp. 30–32, June 1990.
79. Stevens, Barbara J., "Contracting for Recycling Services," *BioCycle*, pp. 40–41, June 1989.
80. Stevens, Barbara J., "Cost Analysis of Curbside Programs," *BioCycle*, pp. 37–38, May–June 1988.
81. Stevens, Barbara J., "How to Finance Curbside Recycling," *BioCycle*, pp. 31–33, February 1989.
82. T'Kach, Mary, and Patricia Schoenecker, "Practical Approaches to Multifamily Recycling," *BioCycle*, October 1990.
83. Walsh, Patrick, and Phil O'Leary, "Collecting and Processing Reclaimed Materials," *Waste Age*, pp. 106–108, 110, 112, February 1988.
84. Watson, Tom, "Curbside Goes High-Tech," *Resource Recycling*, pp. 32–36, October 1990.
85. Watson, Tom, "Reverse Vending Revisited: Great Losses and High Hopes," *Resource Recycling*, pp. 26–29, 74–77, March 1990.
86. Watson, Tom, "Seattle Blazes New Ground with Diverse Approach," *Resource Recycling*, pp. 28–31, 73–74, November 1989.
87. Watson, Tom, "The Garbage Police," *Resource Recycling*, pp. 32ff, July 1989.

88. Watson, Tom, "Theme Buy-Back Centers Endure Despite Problems," *Resource Recycling,* pp. 36–37, 67–71, March 1990.

89. Weissman, Nancy, "Recycling Means Business for Cities," *BioCycle,* August 1989.

90. Wolfe, Paris, "From Sortation to Marketing the Vinyl Loop Gets Stronger," *Recycling Today,* pp. 55–57, March 1990.

91. Wolfe, Paris, "The Troops Are Organized for the Bottle Bill Battle," *Recycling Today,* pp. 78–82, March 1990.

92. Wysopal, Wally, "Economic Incentives Improve Voluntary Efforts," *BioCycle,* pp. 32–33, June 1989.

93. Lund, Herbert F., personal communication, January 26, 1991.

94. Englebart, Mike, Department of Public Works, City of Milwaukee, Wis., personal communication, February 1991.

95. *The Miami Herald,* February 17, 1991, p. 3.

CHAPTER 6
PROCESSING FACILITIES FOR RECYCLABLE MATERIALS

Thomas M. Kaczmarski
Manager, Recycling*
Waste Management of North America, Inc.
Oakbrook, Illinois

William P. Moore
Vice President, Paper Recycling International, Inc.
Norcross, Georgia

INTRODUCTION—DIFFERENT PROCESSING ALTERNATIVES

Processing material from the municipal solid waste (MSW) stream is becoming more an art than an exact science. Factors such as demographics, collection practices, disposal costs, end-market uses, and most importantly, the desires of the residential or commercial customers being serviced, will determine the type of processing facility used to most effectively process the material. For example, at one end of the spectrum, there are small 10 ton per day (TPD) facilities accepting residential "source-separated" materials. These facilities may have nothing more than a hand sort conveyer, an aluminum can flattener, and a portable scale. At the other end are large-scale, mixed MSW facilities that can accept and process up to 2000 TPD of residential and commercial trash. This material typically has not been separated at its source.

The definition of source separation processing includes a collection system where residential and commercial customers are required to do some degree of "front-end" separation of the materials. This can range from implementing collection programs where homeowners are asked to place their recyclables [i.e., old newspaper (ONP), aluminum cans, ferrous metals, three colors of glass, plastic soda bottles (PET), and milk jugs (HDPE), etc.] into separate containers. This

*Coauthors from Waste Management include Tom Kaczmarski, Marty Felker, Russ Filtz, Dan Kemna, and Bill Moore.

technique is currently being practiced in many west coast communities. Another technique used is to have the homeowner do as little as separate "wet" material (i.e., organic food waste, yard waste, pet droppings, etc.) from the "dry" stream (i.e., all other noncompostable material) using two bins. This approach is used quite effectively in Europe and the provinces of Canada. These two techniques can also be applied to the commercial/industrial waste stream as well. A more detailed explanation of each program description is covered in the section on source-separated processes.

Mixed MSW processing, on the other hand, deals with processing the entire waste stream. Typically, the residential or residential and commercial/light industrial material is processed without any separation occurring by the generators. Although not as prominent as the source-separated approach, this processing technique is receiving more and more attention due to the simplification of the collection system. Various forms of mixed MSW processing will be discussed in more detail in the following section.

There are considerable differences both in terms of material balance, economics, and recovery rates between the three different systems described above. Table 6.1 presents a typical material balance of the various processing options. Table 6.2 presents a matrix of these options, including relative cost comparisons, appropriate materials recovered and projected diversion rates. *It is important to note that the information contained in these tables represents estimates only. They are not to be used as a baseline for establishing local program costs or budgets. A separate analysis factoring in local site conditions must be performed.*

MIXED MUNICIPAL SOLID WASTES PROCESSING APPROACHES

Introduction

As described above, this form of operation is generally used on large-scale waste streams running anywhere from 200 to 2,000 TPD. Four general approaches for MSW processing are typically used. They are refuse-derived fuel (RDF), composting, hybrid composting/RDF, and anaerobic digestion for methane recovery. Mixed MSW processing generally needs outlets for lower-quality recyclables than the source-separated approach. The outlet market must be able to accommodate large amounts of RDF or a low- to medium-quality compost. See Fig. 6.1 for a sample process flow diagram of a typical mixed MSW-RDF processing facility.

Europe vs. the United States

Beginning in the early 1970s, the United States was experimenting quite extensively on mixed MSW processing technology. During the latter half of the 1970s, a group of about a dozen MSW processing plants were built in the United States, many of which have since been shut down. The reasons that these facilities were closed vary. In some cases the processing technologies which were employed were borrowed from other industries and were ill equipped to handle a feedstock as variable as MSW. While the overall concept of processing was sound, problems such as shredder explosions and difficulties in material handling surfaced. In

TABLE 6.1 Residential Recycling Options: Material Balance Percent Recovered by Weight of RMSW*

	ONP	RMWP	Aluminum	Tin cans	HDPE/PET	MRC	Glass	RDF	To compost	Residue % of material processed	RMSW % diverted from disposal
Curbside† recycling (TSS)	4	10	1	2	3	2	2	N/A	N/A	N/A	15 30 w/options
Curbside recycling (CSS)	4	10	1	2	3	2	2	N/A	N/A	N/A	15 30 w/options
Curbside recycling (MR)	4	10	1	2	3	2	2	N/A	N/A	N/A	15 30 w/options
Curbside recycling (FCM)	4	10	1	2	3	2	2	N/A	N/A	N/A	15 30 w/options
Yard waste source-separated	N/A	N/A	N/A	N/A	N/A	N/A	N/A	N/A	10	5	10
Wet/dry‡	4	30	1	3	3	4	2	N/A	25	35	65
RMSW processing RDF	0	0	1	3	1	0	0	60	20	15	75
RMSW processing compost	0	0	1	3	1	0	0	0	60	30	60

*RMSW—residential municipal solid waste; OCC—old corrugated cardboard; RMWP—residential mixed waste paper; MRC—mixed rigid containers; ONP—old newsprint; TSS—truckside sort; CSS—Curbside sort; MR—mixed recyclables; FCM—Fully commingled; RDF—refuse-derived fuels.
†Curbside recycling capture rates based on 70 percent participation.
‡Wet/dry, RMSW processing—RDF and compost, capture rates based on 100 percent participation.

6.3

TABLE 6.2 Residential Recycling Options

	House-hold container	Collection vehicle type	Collection cost	Processing methods	Processing capital cost	Processing operating cost	Material recovered	Recovered material quality	% of RMSW diverted from disposal	Significant issues
Curbside recycling, truckside sort (TSS)	Single, 18 gal	3-bin recycling truck	High	Conventional MRF	Med	Low–Med	ONP Aluminum HDPE/PET Tin cans Glass RMWP, OCC (opt.) MRC (opt.)	High High High High High Med–high Med–high	15 10 5	RMWP markets, PRA ability to take MRC
Curbside recycling, curbside sort (CSS)	3–11 gal	3-bin recycling truck	Med–high	Conventional MRF	Med	Med	ONP Aluminum HDPE/PET Tin cans Glass RMWP, OCC (opt.) MRC (opt.)	High High High High High Med–high Med–high	15 10 5	RMWP markets, PRA ability to take MRC
Curbside recycling, mixed recyclables (MR)	Single, 18 gal	2-bin recycling truck	Med	Conventional MRF	Med	Med	ONP Aluminum HDPE/PET Tin cans Glass RMWP, OCC (opt.) MRC (opt.)	High High High High Med–high Med–high Med–high	15 10 5	RMWP markets, PRA ability to take MRC

Curbside recycling, fully commingled (FCM)	Single, 18 gal	Residential packer	Low	BRINI MRF	Med	Med-high	ONP / Aluminum / HDPE/PET / Tin cans / Glass / RMWP, OCC (opt.) / MRC (opt.)	High / High / High / High / Med-high / Med-high / Med-high	15 / 10 / 5	Glass breakage
Yard waste, source-separated	Bags or cart	Residential packer	Low	Windrow composting	Low	Med	Compost	High	10	
Wet/dry	2-bin, 63 gal	2 residential packers or split packer	Low	Advanced BRINI MRF	Med-high	Med	ONP / Aluminum / HDPE/PET / Tin cans / Glass / RMWP, OCC (opt.) / Compost	Med-high / Med-high / High / Med / Med / High	50 / 15	Glass breakage, RMWP markets
Mixed MSW processing—RDF	Bags or 95-gal cart	Residential packer	Low	BRINI RDF processing	High	Med	OCC / Aluminum / HDPE/PET / Tin cans / RDF	Med / High / Med / Med / High	20 / 55	RDF markets
Mixed MSW processing—compost	Bags or 95-gal cart	Residential packer	Low	Buhler-type compost processing	High	Med	OCC / Aluminum / HDPE/PET / Tin cans / Compost	Med / High / Med / Med / Low–Med	5 / 55	MSW compost markets

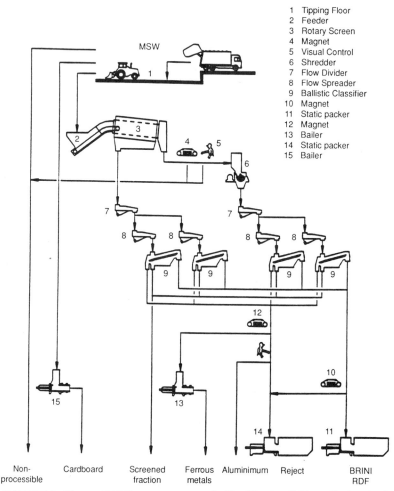

FIGURE 6.1 Diagram BRINI resource recovery facility. (*Courtesy Sellbergs Engineering.*)

other instances, markets for the materials which were recovered or produced at these facilities were unstable. These factors combined to raise the overall cost of processing to levels which could not be justified in a time of relatively low landfill disposal costs.

In Europe, throughout the later seventies and eighties, there had been a fair amount of activity in mixed MSW processing facilities. This is due to some of the basic differences in the waste stream that existed in Europe (i.e., a higher vegetative content and lower packaging content). All of the industrialized nations saw a compositional difference which can be attributed to more convenience in terms of life-style. For example, frozen and packaged foods gained in popularity with consumers. In addition, the high cost of petroleum-based fuels led to more mixed MSW plants surfacing in Europe. RDFs were used to produce steam and hot water in numerous district heating systems.

Front-End Processing for Waste-to-Energy (WTE) Plants

There has been a small amount of front-end processing of mixed MSW prior to mass burn plants in Europe. We have yet to see any significant efforts in this area in the United States. The Environmental Protection Agency (EPA) is expected to promulgate regulations requiring a 25 percent recycling rate on the waste stream entering WTE plants. Once this legislation is in place, this could spark a renewed interest in the United States in front-end processing. The processing techniques used would be similar to those used in a mixed MSW plant. The goal of this front-end system, however, would be to pull out as much of the heavy metals and inert materials as possible. The fibrous material could conceivably be separated, however, but doing do would impede the Btu characteristics needed to fuel the burners.

RDF/Alternative Fuels

Several different types of technologies exist for making RDF from mixed MSW. Proprietary systems such as the BRINI, Buhler, Lundell, and several others are available in the marketplace. All of these approaches use various screening techniques, either trommels, disk screens, or other types of classifiers to perform the separation required. Exhibits 6.1 to 6.4 are photos of a typical RDF facility including incoming waste stream, ballistic separation equipment, and finished product. Many different grades of RDF can be produced from MSW. Generally speaking, the higher the fuel quality, the lower the fuel yield. For example, an RDF plant in Albany, New York, simply shreds the incoming waste and then passes the shredded material across a magnetic separator to remove the ferrous compo-

EXHIBIT 6.1   Typical mixed MSW waste stream at refuse-derived-fuel (RFD) facility.

EXHIBIT 6.2 Ballistic separator used to produce high-quality RFD material.

EXHIBIT 6.3 Shredded mixed MSW inside ballistic separator.

EXHIBIT 6.4   Pelletized RDF—finished product.

nent. The fuel yield is roughly 95 percent, while the average Btu value of this fuel would be similar to raw MSW. Conversely, in order to produce a pelletized fuel, much preprocessing must be done. Fuel yields in the neighborhood of 50 percent, when based on the total incoming waste, can be achieved, which would have a heating value which approximates 6,500 to 7,000 Btu/lb. The type of fuel that must be prepared in a mixed-waste processing facility must be dictated by the combustion equipment. Early RDF plants after shredding the waste stream, did a minimum amount of screening and separation and produced a rather inferior-quality fuel material.

Today's state-of-the-art facility shreds the MSW, screens it, and allows for the recovery of both an organic (yard and food waste) fraction for composting and also material recovery in the form of corrugated boxes, aluminum, plastic bottles, and steel. After the compost fraction is removed and the material recovered, secondary grinding forms the fuel fraction, which can either be delivered in a fluff form or a densified pellet or cube. Table 6.1 gives an estimated material balance for this type of facility.

In the United States today a handful of these types of plants are operating. One of the earlier generation plants still operating is the Ames, Iowa, facility. Buhler technology is in use today at the Eden Prairie, Minnesota, plant. Early large and very complex processing facilities in Milwaukee and Rochester have now been shut down. The success of the active operating facilities can be directly tied to the availability of combustion facilities for the fuels which are produced.

An example of a large-scale, complex processing facility (using Raytheon technology) is the northern Delaware facility. This facility is equipped to produce an RDF from the organic fraction while recovering such materials as aluminum and glass. Recently, an incinerator was added in order to burn the RDF on the site and produce electricity.

Composting—Windrow and In-Vessel

Three types of separation approaches are used for making compost from mixed MSW. Generally the greater the degree of front-end separation, the higher the cost of processing. Naturally this means that more equipment and/or sorters will be used in order to isolate the organic fraction of the MSW. After separation, there are two general approaches for making the compost. The first approach was described above in the RDF type plant, with an organic fraction coming off of the MSW/RDF processing.

The second approach is to shred the entire waste stream and then compost it with minimal screening and material recovery while attempting to clean the material up after the composting process is complete. This system produces a product which tends to contain small pieces of glass and plastic and other inert contaminants. The end use for this material may be limited because of these physical contaminants, but market applications are currently being sought. One facility that employs this technology in Dade County, Florida, is Agripost. Several other operations in the United States employ similar technology.

The third approach to the separation focuses on a fair amount of front-end screening and material picking before finally grinding what's left of the waste stream for composting. This differs from the first approach by not making an RDF fraction. After the separation of the organics is complete, two general approaches are used for composting: windrow and in-vessel processing.

Windrow processing can be accomplished either out-of-doors or in an enclosed or semienclosed building. Buildings are used mainly to effect some control over the amount of moisture present in the compost heap and also to aid in odor control since the air which is captured in the building can be discharged through a biofilter or similar containment equipment. In either case, the windrows, which are triangular piles roughly 8 ft by 8 ft by 8 ft, are formed for the natural composting process to take place. Turning for aeration and some homogenization is accomplished by mechanical means as the material decomposes.

In the in-vessel approach, structures are used that contain either trenches or circular reactor type vessels which are filled with the organic feedstock. The organic feedstock is turned and mixed periodically to provide the proper environment to convert the material to compost. Many factors come into play when choosing a composting method. One must keep in mind, however, that the process of decomposition which takes place in either a windrow or a vessel is the same. How a technology is applied must be based on the local conditions. For instance, if ample space is available at a remote location, a windrow-type composting system may offer the best solution. However, where space is at a premium and odor control is critical, a system which would offer the greatest degree of process and odor control, such as a composting vessel, may be needed. The end-product market needs will also play a role in determining the type of processing to be employed. If it is desirable to produce a landfill cover, little up-front processing would be called for. However, if horticultural markets are targeted for the finished product, great care should be taken with the up-front collection and processing to ensure the highest quality of material possible.

Methane Recovery—Anaerobic Digestion

There have been some attempts to subject a full MSW waste stream to anaerobic digestion to produce methane. One of the most well-known in the United States was the RefCom project in Pompano, Florida. In this approach, the MSW was shredded and water added to a cylindrical reactor vessel, which is maintained in a mixed anaerobic state to produce methane.

Some systems attempt to remove contaminants and screen out undesirable materials. Many difficulties were encountered with handling and mixing the anaerobic reactors. The methane from the reactors is either upgraded for use in pipeline gas or used to fire turbines directly. At present, we know of no active U.S. methane recovery operations for MSW. In Europe, the Valorga technology is in use in several locations. This technology is similar to what was described in the above paragraph.

Many factors are responsible for impeding the development of anaerobic digestion facilities in the United States. These factors include:

- Heterogenic nature of the mixed-waste stream makes material handling particularly troublesome.
- Lack of available equipment specifically designed for methane recovery systems.
- Relative abundance of cheap fuels.

When compared with the European market, the economics of an anaerobic digestion process makes it difficult to justify. As fuels costs and tipping fees continue to rise, the economic viability of an anaerobic process is enhanced.

SOURCE-SEPARATED PROCESSING APPROACHES

Introduction

Recycling, a form of waste reduction, offers a variety of cost-competitive and environmentally safe alternatives to waste disposal by converting source-separated MSW into valuable resources. Source-separated processing as the name implies is characterized by producing very high quality materials for distribution to the end market. The processing techniques used are typically less complicated than those needed for a mixed MSW stream and therefore less costly to operate and maintain. Residential source-separated systems and techniques highlighted in this section include the following:

- Commingled approach
- Multiple-bin approach
- Truckside sort approach
- Fully commingled approach
- Wet/dry approach

Due to the similarities in handling techniques, a less detailed analysis of commercial/industrial source-separation programs will also be discussed.

Commingled Approach

Residential source-separation facilities are generally built to handle recyclable waste streams ranging from 10 to 250 TPD. In a commingled material recycling program only one container is provided to the homeowner. A commingled MRF's main objective is to receive, process, and ship to market, residential curbside-collected recyclables. These recyclables typically consist of glass, high-density polyethylene (HDPE) and polyethylene terephthalate (PET) plastics, and aluminum and ferrous metal containers mixed together (often referred to as "hard recyclables") and old newspapers (ONP). The ONP is always kept separate in this approach. The facility has a tipping floor designed to handle these two streams while keeping them separated (i.e., hard recyclables and ONP). A main processing line for the hard recyclables is necessary for sorting these materials by grade. The paper-processing line may or may not have a distinct sorting station, but the material should have at least a quality control inspection station before baling or loose filling into an open-top trailer. Since commercial loads accepting old corrugated containers (OCC) and high-grade paper are not much different to handle than ONP, most commingled MRFs should have adequate space to accept these materials and process them on the paper line.

At present, the commingled approach is a more cost-effective alternative than a multiple-bin program primarily due to the productivity gains achieved in the collection of the material. In other words, when looking at the total cost of providing the service, it is typically less expensive to collect and process commingled material than material collected in several containers. The rest of this section will present a typical design for an average 100-TPD commingled MRF. Process flow description and a diagram are included along with a plant layout. This design is not fixed and should be viewed as a general guideline to be incorporated into a specific project. Most MRFs will be unique designs, but there are still many common elements that can be used from this example.

Process Flow Description.   A general arrangement for a typical 100-TPD commingled facility is presented on Fig. 6.2. The process flow diagram is shown on Fig. 6.3. Recyclable materials are delivered to this facility by specially designed two-compartment collection vehicles. The design of this facility is flexible enough to handle materials collected in the form of separated glass, plastics, and cans. This is often necessary when there is one facility servicing both residential and multifamily collection programs.

When designing an MRF, careful consideration must be given to a flexible equipment layout to allow for future expansion capability. The characteristics of the recyclable materials which are processed generally dictate two separate process lines. One line is configured to process the "light-fraction" recyclables including newspaper, cardboard, mixed paper, and plastic film. The second line is designed to handle various types and sizes of "heavy-fraction" materials (i.e., glass, aluminum, steel, wood, rubber, plastics, etc.)

For this facility the equipment has been selected with the capability to process additional materials as they are added to the collection program. Eventually this type of facility could also be converted to facilitate processing of the dry fraction of the municipal solid waste stream.

Newspaper is tipped directly onto the receiving floor adjacent to the in-floor

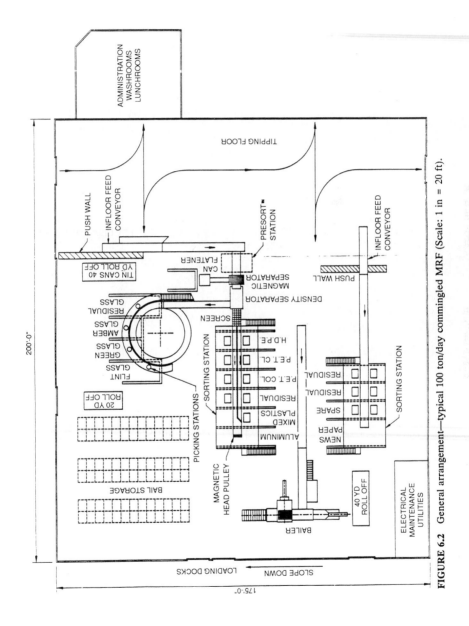

FIGURE 6.2 General arrangement—typical 100 ton/day commingled MRF (Scale: 1 in = 20 ft).

6.13

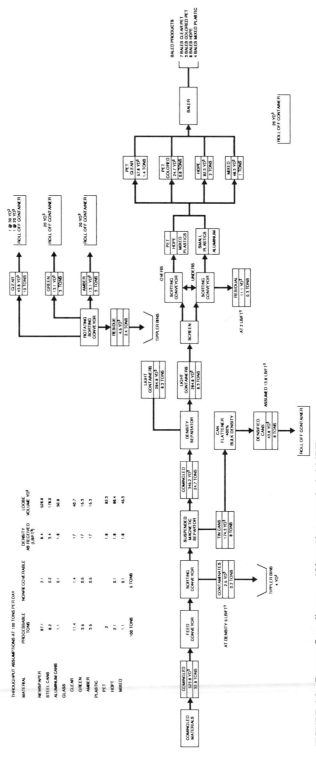

FIGURE 6.3 Process flow diagram—100 ton/day commingled MRF.

EXHIBIT 6.5 Tipping floor and infeed newspaper conveyor.

feed conveyor and push wall (see Exhibit 6.5). The material is then pushed by a front-end loader onto the in-feed conveyor where it is conveyed up to the elevated sorting platform and picking stations. Manual sorting pulls out contaminants and drops them down into storage bunkers beneath sorting stations. It is critical that these material's storage bunkers be sized with adequate capacity to store enough material to make at least three bales. The concept of separating sorting from baling operations maximizes the availability and efficiency of the baler. The best approach is to follow a negative sort (i.e., remove contaminants and smaller-quantity recoverable materials and let the ONP accumulate in the last bunker of the sorting line). If less material is physically handled, it reduces labor costs and increases throughput capability of the processing line.

Commingled containers are tipped into a continuous-feed floor conveyor which is typically fitted with a rubber-lined skirt onto the receiving edge (see Exhibit 6.6). This skirt acts as a buffer to minimize the breakage of glass. Materials are conveyed up to the presort station by a slider belt conveyor. *Note:* The necessity to include a presort station depends on the level of contamination in the incoming feed stream. This would allow for the removal of contaminants such as steel paint cans, film plastics, and batteries typically not included in commingled recycling programs.

Ferrous materials (e.g., steel can) are the first items to be separated from the commingled stream. This is accomplished through the use of a suspended magnetic separator. The separator will remove 90 to 95 percent of the steel present in the commingled stream. The separated cans are then passed through a can flattener to decrease volume, or alternatively, can be conveyed to a concrete bunker and flattened by front-end loader.

The remaining commingled materials are passed on to a density separator which splits the materials into a light and a heavy fraction (see Exhibit 6.7). Sep-

EXHIBIT 6.6   Commingled plastics and cans infeed conveyor.

arators in place today could be one of several devices (i.e., vibrating gravity table, air separation, density brush, etc.). A cost/benefit analysis to justify the addition of these components needs to be performed. Factors to be considered
include labor rates, utility costs, equipment life-cycle cost, and projected volume.

The heavy fraction as it leaves the density separator is primarily glass containers. This glass may be conveyed either onto a straight sorting belt or collected
onto a rotating sorting conveyor for subsequent manual color separation. The advantage of using a sorting ring conveyor is that temporary storage is provided. It
also allows sorters to be allocated more effectively since they are not required on
the sorting ring until it is at capacity.

The light fraction is passed through a trommel-type screen which separates according to size (see Exhibit 6.8). The resultant materials on the divided sorting
conveyor are large plastic containers on one side and aluminum and small plastics
on the other. The divided conveyor allows for negative sorting of the aluminum
cans and the ability to transfer any aluminum cans which pass through to the
large or oversize side of the sorting belt. Manual separation is required for all of
the materials except for the aluminum, which is left on the sorting conveyor. The
aluminum undergoes a second ferrous magnetic sort to assure product purity.

All material are stored in the bunkers located beneath the picking stations on
the elevated sorting platforms. When sufficient quantities of material have been
accumulated, the bunker is emptied by front-end loader and the material pushed
onto the baler feed conveyor. Glass containers are sorted into bunkers beneath
the sorting ring, or alternatively, then can be dropped directly into roll-off containers for shipping or fed into crushers to increase density prior to shipping.

EXHIBIT 6.7 Density "air classification" system separates aluminum and plastic from glass. (*The Forge Recycling and Transfer Station, Philadelphia, Pennsylvania.*)

EXHIBIT 6.8   Size separation using Trommel screen. (*Note:* Aluminum and plastic separation.) (*The Forge, Philadelphia, Pennsylvania.*)

The 100-TPD MRF represents the state of the art with respect to available technology and cost effectiveness. This facility primarily consists of two sorting systems; however, this general layout also allows flexibility for the future implementation of a ballistic separator capable of separating recyclables mixed together. With this information, classified materials can be delivered to the facility "fully commingled" (i.e., newspaper, mixed paper, cardboard and containers can be mixed together during collection). Even greater collection productivity can be achieved with this approach.

Multiple-Bin Approach

The concept behind a multiple-bin MRF is to let the homeowner help out by doing most of the sorting. Any sort beyond the commingled approach of hard recyclables separated from paper is considered multiple-bin. The most familiar program is the three-bin system with glass/plastic, aluminum and ferrous cans, and ONP sorted separately by the homeowner. Plastics are a problem because the options are to mix and lose space, bundle ONP on the side, or add a fourth bin. All not very good choices, and what about truck design? The natural inclination is to believe that since the material is already at least partially sorted, that there will be savings in running a processing facility. Possibly, but there are other factors which outweigh the savings in sorting costs. These factors include:

- Increased collection costs
- Longer time at each stop to empty bins
- Possibility of one truck bin filling up first increases
- Longer to dump, once at the MRF
- Redundant processing lines to handle each partial stream

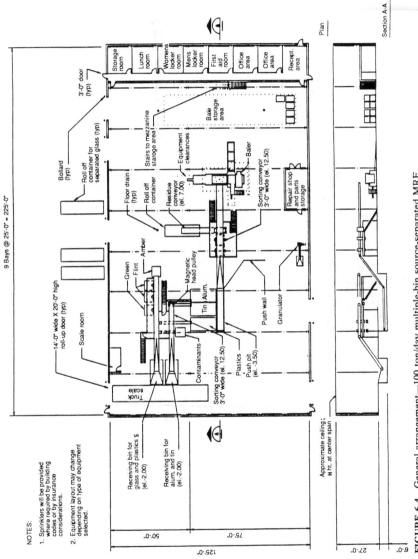

FIGURE 6.4 General arrangement—100 ton/day multiple-bin source-separated MRF.

NOTES:

1. Sprinklers will be provided where required by building codes or by insurance considerations.

2. Equipment layout may change depending on type of equipment selected.

6.19

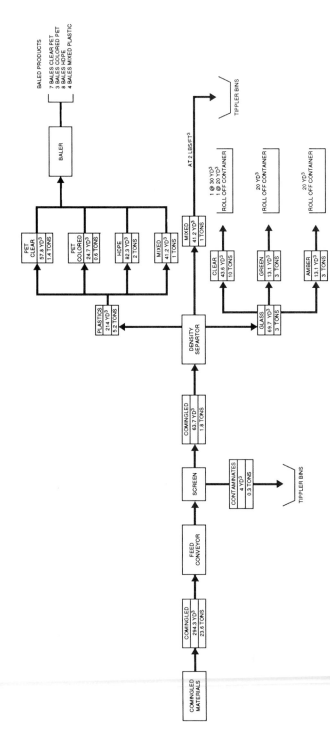

FIGURE 6.5 (*a*) Process flow diagram—source-separated glass and plastic containers.

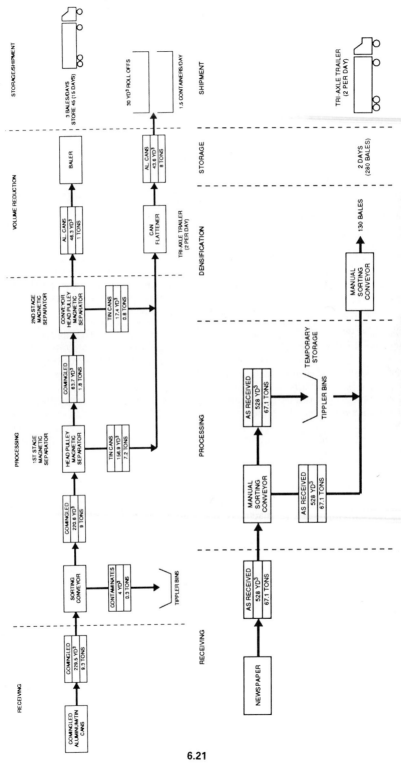

FIGURE 6.5 (*Continued*) (*b*) Process flow diagram—source-separated cans. (*c*) Process flow diagram—source-separated newspapers.

Given the above reasons it is reasonable to assume that in most instances the multiple-bin system should be avoided. However, successful programs still exist, especially in areas with small populations where constructing a large typical processing operation is described below.

Process Flow Description. A general arrangement for a typical 100-TPD multiple-bin facility is presented in Fig. 6.4. The process flow diagram is shown in Fig. 6.5a to c. Recyclable materials are delivered to this facility by specially designed multicompartment collection vehicles.

Receiving bins are typically set below the floor grade next to the truck scales, which allow for weighed loading of material in the following mixes:

1. Glass and plastics.
2. Aluminum and tin cans.
3. ONP.

The trucks tip the newspaper on the tipping floor designed to hold typically 1 day's worth of material. Conveyors from the in-floor loading pits convey recyclables up to elevated sorting lines. These conveyors are typically slider-belt types with high-sided troughs. The conveyors run horizontally for the full length of the pit, inclining to their respective sorting conveyors.

Glass and Plastics. Glass and plastics sorting conveyor is also a slider belt type. Manual sorting pulls out contaminants and drops them down a chute onto a conveyor leading to a tippler bin. Manual sorting separates all plastics out of the material stream and drops down a chute to the plastic conveyor below.

Glass is color-sorted manually and dropped through chutes onto separate slider-belt conveyors that transport the material to exterior receptacles. A slider-belt conveyor brings in sorted plastics from the glass and plastics sorting line and elevates material up into the intermediate self-emptying storage bin. The slider belt at ground level is horizontal, and inclines to feed the plastics storage bin.

Aluminum and Tin Cans. An aluminum and tin sorting conveyor at the elevated platform is horizontal and is a slider-belt conveyor on which manual sorting will pick out contaminants, (e.g., bimetal cans) and through a chute, direct them to the same contaminant conveyor described above. The aluminum and tin continue on the conveyor. At the discharge point a magnetic head pulley and chute network allow aluminum to be discharged to one conveyor, while tin is discharged to another conveyor, both of which are inclined to feed their respective storage bins.

The sorted tin conveyor is a slider-belt conveyor in a high-sided trough, inclined to feed the tin storage bin. The sorted aluminum conveyor is a slider belt conveyor in a high-sided trough inclined to feed the aluminum storage bin. A front-end loader is used to spread the ONP over the tipping floor. Major contaminants are sorted and the clean newspaper is stored for baling.

Tin and aluminum cans and newspaper are individually conveyed onto a sorting conveyor and onto an elevated conveyor leading to the baler inlet hopper opening. The material is baled to meet marketing specifications.

Plastics are processed in the same way as described above, except at the sorting station, HDPE milk jugs and mixed plastics are manually sorted from the PET soda bottles and directed through a metal chute into a tippler bin. The plastics are baled according to marketing specifications.

All bales are taken by a fork-lift truck to either a transfer truck or storage area. The glass deposited into tippler bins is taken to larger roll-off containers (30 to 40 yd^3) located outside the facility.

Truckside Sort Approach

As in a multiple-bin program, materials are delivered to the processing facility already sorted to some degree. However, for the homeowner, the materials are placed in one bin, just as in a commingled program. Sorting is done at curbside by the recycling truck driver. This method works well for pilot programs or smaller communities (i.e., 10,000 to 20,000 range) that have no or limited processing facilities. Once the material is presorted by the driver, the material flow and process description is similar in nature to the multiple-bin approach.

Wet/Dry Approach

As discussed in the previous section, MRFs are typically designed to process a selected number of recyclable materials which have been source-separated in a variety of ways. The recyclable materials generally arrive as one or more discrete materials or in commingled streams. At the processing facility the commingled stream and/or the source-separated materials are sorted to remove any contamination or nonrecyclable products collected with the recyclable products. This type of recycling system recovers a portion of the recyclable materials, the amount recovered ranging from 10 to 20 percent of the domestic waste stream. Many factors affect the recovery rate, such as public participation, collection frequency and convenience, collection system including type of household container, and collection vehicles.

There has been a trend to increase the number of materials being collected in such systems as markets for recovered materials are developed. This results in significant problems to the collection system and also at the MRF.

There are generally two existing methods for collecting residential separated recyclable materials. Both of these present systems separate into at least two categories: newspaper and containers. The options for collection after this level of separation can include curbside and subsequent vehicle separation into separate glass, plastics, and tin/aluminum can components. As a rule, a higher level of separation at the curbside translates to higher overall collection and processing costs. This is a factor of the increased time to sort materials at the curbside and the reduced capacity of the recycling collection vehicle.

In Europe over the past decade recycling programs have developed in many municipalities to recover significantly greater quantities of recyclable materials, in the order of 50 to 60 percent of the waste stream. This has been achieved by designing collection systems and MRF facilities which process the *total* dry fraction of the waste stream (see Exhibit 6.9). Rather than having a portion of the recyclable materials being available at the MRF, all these materials are delivered to the facility together with many other dry materials which may not be recyclable. The dry fraction has been defined as all the domestic waste except for food wastes, yard wastes, and wet or contaminated dry wastes. While this type of system has a significant effect on the residents' waste management practices, it has been found to be as convenient to the public as the system which involves a small recyclable materials container. These containers in themselves can limit the extent of recycling through their size. Public attitude surveys which have been car-

EXHIBIT 6.9   Dry fraction processing—wet/dry facility, Skara, Sweden.

ried out in Canada have indicated a strong support for the collection of the dry part of the waste stream. A number of such programs are being implemented in Ontario to meet a 50 percent reduction of the waste stream since this is a goal of municipalities, the provincial government, and the federal government. In Europe it has also been found that the remaining wet wastes can be processed readily and cost effectively into a contaminant-free high-quality compost since the potentially toxic components in the waste stream are collected with the dry fraction and removed at the MRF (see Exhibit 6.10).

EXHIBIT 6.10   Wet fraction processing—wet/dry facility, Skara, Sweden.

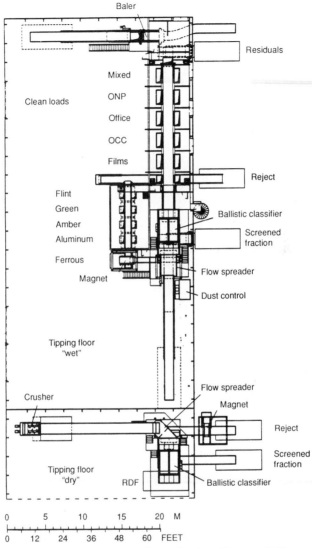

FIGURE 6.6 Wet/dry plant, Skara, Sweden. (*Courtesy Sellbergs Engineering.*)

A general arrangement for a typical 200-TPD wet/dry facility is presented in Fig. 6.6. The process flow diagram is shown on Fig. 6.7.

*Wet/Dry Program Profile.** As a result of the lack of landfill capacity in the County of Neunkirchen, Austria, during 1984, the county's waste management association considered many waste management options including: refuse-derived fuel, mass incineration, materials recovery processes, and export of

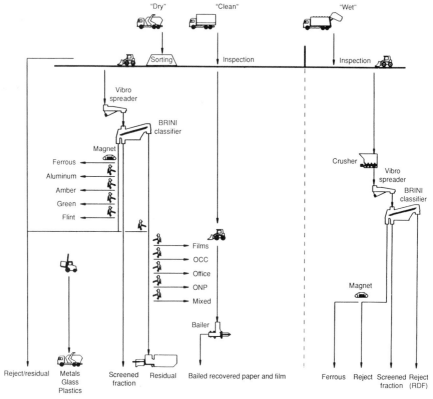

FIGURE 6.7 Process flow diagram—wet/dry, Skara, Sweden. (*Courtesy Sellbergs Engineering.*)

wastes to Hungary. The materials recovery system was selected because it resulted in the greatest reduction in waste requiring disposal in a landfill, minimal environmental effects, and the lowest cost. Authority was given to commence the design of the facility in August 1985, with startup targeted for January 1986.

The project involved the separate collection of dry and wet wastes from approximately 100,000 residents and businesses in 43 municipalities within the County of Neunkirchen in Austria. The dry waste is processed to remove recyclable materials, the wet waste being composted. The technology presently of interest with respect to MRF design is the dry processing facility; however, the Neunkirchen plant is an integrated facility consisting of dry waste processing and composting.

In 1985 an operating company was formed as a joint venture between the County's Waste Management Association and the Hamburger Paper Mill company. Construction of the facility began in September and was completed by January 1986. The dry mixed waste is delivered to the facility, located on 3 acres, in collection vehicles serving the various municipalities and weighed on a truck scale. Records of the weights of materials from each municipality are recorded by

---

*Extracted from technical paper written by Engineer Reinhard Goechl, Managing Director.

computer for invoicing purposes. Waste is deposited on the tipping floor (10,000 ft²) and pushed by small front-end loader onto a feed conveyor which discharges the material into a specially modified ballistic separator (BRINI classifier). This separator, which has a capacity of 7.5 tons per hour, divides the mixed dry waste into light and heavy fractions and screens out particles less than 2 in.

The light fraction is discharged onto a sorting conveyor elevated 12 ft above the floor. Newspaper, cardboard, film plastic, and textiles are removed by five operators and deposited in live-bottom bunkers beneath the conveyor. The residuals, which consist of mixed paper, are also stored in a bunker. Materials in the bunkers are conveyed periodically to an in-floor conveyor which feeds the baler. All materials separated from the light fraction are baled and stored inside the building prior to shipping to markets.

The heavy fraction, separated by the ballistic separator, is conveyed to a magnetic separator for ferrous metal removal. Waste is then conveyed to a density separator which diverts glass and other heavy materials to a ring conveyor for storage and manual sorting into three glass fractions and aluminum. Plastic containers and other light materials are conveyed to the sorting room for the manual separation of plastic containers. Once the materials are separated from the ring conveyor, hazardous materials are removed and the remaining is conveyed to storage bins for landfill disposal.

The facility is operated for two 8-h shifts, 5 days per week, 52 weeks per year. In the first 2 years of operation the plant was only closed as a result of equipment maintenance for 1 day. Overall energy consumption of the process equipment in the facility is 175 kW (27 kW/ton) of which heating requirements are 30 kW.

Materials which are sold from this facility include newspaper, cardboard, mixed paper, plastic film, glass, ferrous metals, aluminum cans, and mixed nonferrous metals. The hazardous materials and wood recovered are disposed of separately from the plant residues. The materials meet specifications of markets in Austria and Germany consistently. In 1986 there were markets for textiles; however, currently no market exists.

The Hamburger Paper Mill purchases all the cardboard and mixed paper; newspaper is purchased by Lekykam, glass is purchased by Vetropack, and metals are purchased by a local scrap iron dealer.

The facility is operated by a staff of nine, which includes a clerk to operate the weigh scale, a plant manager, five sorters, one baler operator, and one mobile equipment operator.

The most significant aspects of this facility are that the facility averages 58 percent recovery of the dry wastes delivered, it is the first facility to utilize the ballistic separator on mixed dry waste, and that this facility was the first two-container wet/dry facility ever constructed.

Commercial/Industrial Approach

Commercial/industrial (C/I) MRFs are similar to many of the operations run by paper stock companies today. Most facilities are designed to bale clean loads of old corrugated containers (OCC), ONP, computer printout (CPO), and mixed paper. From a design basis, the plants can be compared to the paper portion of a typical residential MRF (see Exhibits 6.11 and 6.12). A similar system that handles strictly ONP can be adapted easily to sort other paper products.

Another type of C/I facility combines MRF activities with a transfer station operation. Many transfer stations today are recovering material, even if it's only

EXHIBIT 6.11 Typical commercial industrial dry fraction waste system.

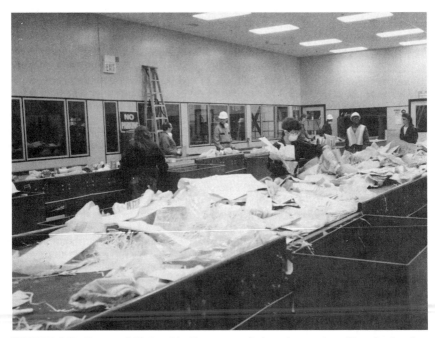

EXHIBIT 6.12 Commercial-industrial climate-controlled sorting section. (*Recycle America, Etobicoke, Canada.*)

6.28

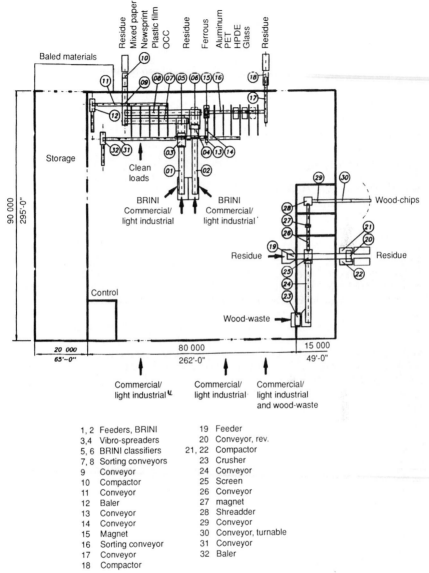

FIGURE 6.8 Typical 300-ton/day commercial-industrial MRF with 600 TPD transfer operator.

1, 2 Feeders, BRINI	19 Feeder
3,4 Vibro-spreaders	20 Conveyor, rev.
5, 6 BRINI classifiers	21, 22 Compactor
7, 8 Sorting conveyors	23 Crusher
9 Conveyor	24 Conveyor
10 Compactor	25 Screen
11 Conveyor	26 Conveyor
12 Baler	27 magnet
13 Conveyor	28 Shreadder
14 Conveyor	29 Conveyor
15 Magnet	30 Conveyor, turnable
16 Sorting conveyor	31 Conveyor
17 Conveyor	32 Baler
18 Compactor	

select OCC loads. The setup is convenient since residue or contaminants don't have to be hauled twice. Having a transfer station integral to the C/I MRF will make it much easier to go after marginally clean loads. These loads normally wouldn't be handled by a standalone MRF and are destined for disposal. With a combined facility, the dirty loads can be sorted to attain maximum diversion and the residue is easily handled by the transfer portion. Siting considerations are easier since there's only one site instead of two. Zoning and permitting may be a little more complicated than with just one type of facility, but may be worth the effort. Figure 6.8 depicts a sample facility layout of a 300-TPD C/I MRF coupled with a 600-TPD transfer operation.

The typical method of separation used in these facilities is to dump the material onto a tipping floor and sort out contaminants by hand. If, however, an operation is bringing 50 percent corrugated loads to be separated, a cost/benefit analysis comparing the revenue potential vs. the costs of processing the material is required. If the volumes of "dirty" commercial loads are great enough (more than 50 TPD), then the application of some sort of mechanical separation system should be investigated.

CONSTRUCTION AND DEMOLITION WASTE PROCESSING

Introduction

In addition to regular municipal solid waste and household garbage, a significant volume of mixed construction and demolition (C&D) waste is being hauled to landfills. This type of waste, which is bulky and often not suitable for regular compaction, has a high index of recoverable and recyclable materials such as wood, aggregates, and metals.

The main objective for C&D processing facilities is *diversion* of the material from the landfill. The viability of any system depends on end uses for the materials. Local markets will determine the degree of "contamination" allowed for each type of product. For a system to be financially successful, it is essential to produce a *usable product* and have adequate outlets for the recovered materials.

The processing technology exists and is available. Construction and demolition waste is generated from construction, renovation, demolition of

* Buildings
* Roads and bridges
* Docks and piers
* Site conversion, etc.

  Amounts of C&D waste generated is dependent upon

* Population level
* General construction and demolition activity
* Extraordinary projects such as urban renewal, road and bridge repair, and disaster cleanup

In recent studies, it has been estimated that *23 percent of municipal solid waste* can be classified as construction/demolition waste (1989 Franklin Associates study). This corresponds to 262 pcy (pounds per capita per year).

C&D waste represents a significant fraction of the solid waste stream. Implementing C&D waste processing, recycling, and diversion programs will aid municipalities, counties, and states in meeting mandatory recycling goals.

A suggested methodology for estimating volumes of C&D waste in any particular area includes analyzing

- Population trends
- Construction and demolition permits
- Types of construction and demolition projects
- Disposal estimates (be aware these sometimes *underestimate* generation)
- Past, present, *and* future trends
- Planning for "baseload" and "peakload" generation

Contents of C&D Waste

Typical contents of C&D waste are presented in Table 6.3. As discussed in the section that follows, the major components of a C&D waste stream will vary depending on its "type."

Types of C&D Waste

For the purposes of this discussion to introduce processing strategies for C&D waste, it is appropriate to categorize C&D waste into two main types.

Type I—Roadway and Site Conversion C&D Waste. C&D waste is typically classified as Type I if a large percentage of the waste stream (80 to 90 percent) consists of a small number of fairly "clean" fractions of material (i.e., rubble, wood).

TABLE 6.3   Contents of C&D Waste

Waste type	Contents
Rubble	Soil, rock, concrete, asphalt, bricks
Tar-based materials	Shingles, tar paper
Ferrous metal	Steel rebar, pipes, roofing, flashing, structural members, ductwork
Nonferrous metal	Aluminum, copper, brass
Harvested wood	Stumps, brush, treetops and limbs
Untreated wood	Framing, scrap lumber, pallets
Treated wood	Plywood, pressure-treated, creosote-treated, laminates
Plaster	Drywall, sheetrock
Glass	Windows, doors
Plastic	Vinyl siding, doors, windows, blinds, material packaging
White goods/bulky items	Appliances, furniture, carpeting
Corrugated	Material packaging, cartons, paper
Contaminants	Lead paint, lead piping, asbestos, fiberglass, fuel tanks

The rubble in Type I waste is typified by virgin soil/rock and concrete/asphalt bridges and pavements. The wood fraction often consists of stumps, brush, pallets, lumber, etc., and is typically generated by land clearing, landscaper activity, and residential home builders. Type I waste can be considered "clean" if large volumes are delivered for processing in a form that is easily separable into single waste types (material is dumped in separate pile or can be presorted with front-end loader, bobcat, etc.). Of course, Type I material is sometimes collected and hauled in mixed forms which make it difficult to separate.

A typical approximate composition of Type I C&D waste by *weight* might be:

Rubble

Concrete, asphalt	40%
Soil, rock	20%
Wood	30%
Metals, plastic	10%

Type II—Construction and Interior Demolition Waste.   C&D waste classified as Type II is generated from the construction and demolition of urban structures (office buildings, stores, etc.). Type II waste differs from Type I waste in that the material, as it exists in a building and in the way it is collected, is in "mixed" form (thoroughly mixed fractions of concrete, drywall, framing, ductwork, roofing, windows, corrugated, packaging, etc.) and thus difficult to separate. This material is typically collected and hauled in open-top trailers, roll-offs, etc.

A typical approximate composition of Type II C&D waste by *volume* might be:

Rubble	25%
Wood	33%
Metals	20%
Corrugated	12%
Other (carpet, residue, etc.)	10%

It should be realized that the *density* of C&D waste can vary dramatically. Material composed mainly of rubble can approach densities of 2000 lb/yd^3. Conversely, material containing large amounts of brush, insulation, or drywall can have densities as low as 250 lb/yd^3. If a single number is needed for an "approximate" density for *mixed* C&D waste, either Type I or Type II, 1000 lb/yd^3 is often a good estimate.

The throughput of a C&D processing facility will depend on the equipment used and more importantly on the type (rubble and wood vs. building demolition) and nature ("clean" or mixed) of the material.

Primary reduction equipment used with Type I rubble and wood have large throughput capacities. Impactors and jaw crushers used to crush rubble can process anywhere from 50 to 400 tons/h depending on machine size and characteristics of the rubble. The throughput of hammermills and stump grinders used to shred wood typically range between 10 to 50 tons/h. Conversely, Type II C&D waste requires more hand sorting, which can lower system throughput dramatically. Facilities that receive urban building demolition waste and process 500 TPD or more would be considered a fairly large system.

C&D Waste-Processing Strategies

The waste stream composition and the end uses for the recovered materials determine the processing strategy and thus the equipment required for sorting and reduction. Table 6.4 presents end-use markets for recycled C&D waste.

In many cases, the rubble and wood received at facilities are bulky and vary in size. End-use markets typically require this material to be crushed or reduced into a smaller, consistent size. The primary reduction equipment that is characteristic to C&D facilities includes impactors or jaw crushers for rubble material and hammermills or stump grinders for wood waste. It should be noted that many of the processing system components are *modular* and can be added as necessary to address a certain fraction of the waste stream. For example, some C&D processors receive only rubble and therefore need only an impactor and operator, a front-end loader and operator, and possibly some screening equipment.

TABLE 6.4 End-Use Markets for Recycled C&D

Waste type	End use
Dirt	Soil, soil conditioner, landscaping, landfill daily cover
Bricks	Masonry, landscaping, ornamental stone
Concrete, cinder blocks, rocks	Fill, roadbed, landfill haul roads
Asphalt	Road/bridge resurfacing, landfill haul roads
Tar-based materials	Mixed with used asphalt for resurfacing
Ferrous pipes, roofing, flashing	To scrap metal buyers
Aluminum	"The gold of C&D," remelted
Copper	"The other gold of C&D," reused
Steel, brass	To scrap metal buyers
Stumps, treetops, and limbs	Chipped for fuel, landscaping, compost bulking, animal bedding, manufactured building products, landfill haul roads
Framing, scraps	Chipped for fuel, landscaping, compost bulking, animal bedding, manufactured building products, landfill haul roads
Plywood, pressure-treated	May or may not be chipped for fuel, landscaping, compost bulking, animal bedding, manufactured building products
Creosote-treated, laminates	End use depends on local regulations concerning chemicals in material. If use is approved, uses are similar to those for other wood materials (listed above)
Used cardboard	Fuel pellets
Plaster, sheetrock	In place of sand in concrete/aggregate fill
Glass	In place of sand in concrete/aggregate
White goods/appliances	Scrap recyclers for crushing
Lead paint, asbestos, fiberglass, fuel tanks	None known

An expensive processing system is not needed for clean, separated material as the primary reduction equipment alone can provide quality end products. The sorting components of the system give access to the *mixed* material fraction of the waste stream. The type and nature of the mixed material determines the basic processing strategy:

1. Sort and separate, crush and reduce
2. Crush and reduce, sort and separate

It is important to note that with all mixed loads, the cost of separation versus disposal of the mixed fraction mush be weighed. Certain loads may be so contaminated or mixed that separation may not be viable, with disposal being the only economic alternative.

Regardless of whether the material is Type I or Type II, all mixed material should be *presorted* as much as possible via judicious "tipping" and "picking" with bobcats, front-end loaders, etc. Generally, bulky items that are often presorted include major pieces of metal, large pieces of rubble or wood, white goods, furniture, and other undesirable materials such as carpet and tires.

Type I C&D Waste Processing Strategy. With Type I C&D material, the decision to sort first or crush first depends on the nature of the mixed material. Clean rubble and wood can be fed directly to an impactor and hammermill for reduction. In cases where mixed material contains any significant amount of plastics, paper, rags, or other contaminants (paint, lead pipe, etc.), it makes sense to sort and separate, then crush and reduce. The combination of a disk screen and trommel can remove the fine soil and small rocks. Any contaminants, ferrous, nonferrous, and oversize rubble can be removed via magnets and picking, leaving "medium"-size rock and wood for reduction.

When the remaining wood is mixed with rock, a flotation tank is sometimes used to separate the wood (which floats) from the rock (which sinks). With large amounts of rubble material the water tends to clean the product, which is beneficial. It should be noted that an air classifier could also be used to separate the lighter wood from the heavier rock. The air system costs more to operate because of the 50- to 75-hp blower that is required. However, depending on the type of material and the local environmental regulations, the wash water from a flotation tank may require treatment before discharge to a sewer or septic system. This could be costly and make the air system more attractive. It should be noted that a flotation tank *is not effective* for separating Type II material, which typically contains more fibrous contaminants which may become "soggy."

In cases where the Type I material is fairly clean with a large portion (80 to 90 percent) consisting of rubble (soil, rock, concrete, asphalt, etc.) and wood, and minimal contamination in the mixed fractions, it may be acceptable to crush and reduce, then sort and separate. This type of processing strategy is often used with roadway demolition projects and/or site conversion projects where there may be significant amounts of harvested and treated/untreated wood waste. A flotation tank is often effective with this Type I waste for separating the mixed wood from the rock, but environmental and wastewater treatment concerns must be addressed to determine if air classification is a better alternative.

The processing layout (Fig. 6.9) for this variety of Type I material displays a fundamental processing scheme that is being successfully implemented in various parts of the country. Note that this system is available in stationary or essentially self-contained, portable modes. The portable system can be desirable for maximum flexibility and reduction of hauling costs by processing "on site."

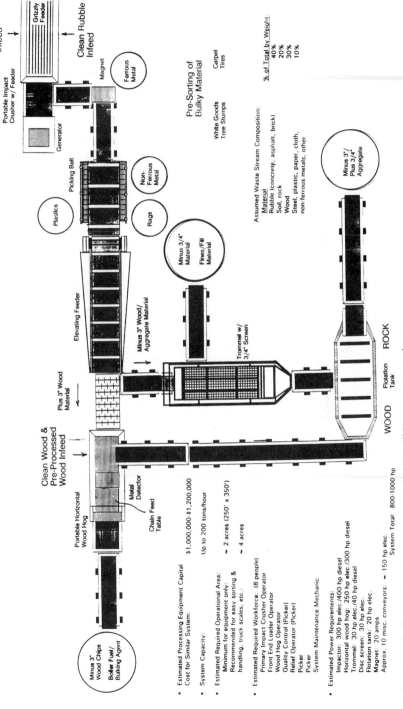

FIGURE 6.9 Process flow diagram—construction/demolition waste processing.

Mixed Material Infeed

Grizzly Feeder

Portable Impact Crusher w/ Feeder

Clean Rubble Infeed

Generator

Magnet

Ferrous Metal

Picking Belt

Plastics

Non-Ferrous Metal

Rags

Elevating Feeder

Minus 3/4" Material / Fines/Fill Material

Minus 3" Wood/ Aggregate Material

Plus 3" Wood Material

Clean Wood & Pre-Processed Wood Infeed

Portable Horizontal Wood Hog

Metal Detector

Chain Feed Table

Minus 3" Wood Chips

Boiler Fuel/ Bulking Agent

Trommel w/ 3/4" Screen

WOOD   Flotation Tank   ROCK

Minus 3"/ Plus 3/4" Aggregate

Pre-Sorting of Bulky Material

White Goods   Carpet
Tree Stumps   Tires

Assumed Waste Stream Composition:

Material	% of Total by Weight
Rubble (concr'e/p, asphalt, brick)	40%
Soil, rock	20%
Wood	30%
Steel, plastic, paper, cloth, non-ferrous metals, other	10%

- Estimated Processing Equipment Capital
  Cost for Similar System: $1,000,000-$1,200,000

- System Capacity: Up to 200 tons/hour

- Estimated Required Operational Area:
  Minimum for equipment only: ~ 2 acres (250' x 350')
  Recommended for easy sorting &
  handling, truck scales, etc.:   ~ 4 acres

- Estimated Required Workforce: (8 people)
  Primary Impact Crusher Operator
  Front End Loader Operator
  Wood Hog Operator
  Quality Control (Picker)
  Relief Operator (Picker)
  Picker
  Picker
  System Maintenance Mechanic

- Estimated Power Requirements:
  Impactor: 300 hp elec./400 hp diesel
  Horizontal wood hog: 250 hp elec./300 hp diesel
  Trommel: 30 hp elec./40 hp diesel
  Disc screen: 30 hp diesel
  Flotation tank: 20 hp elec.
  Magnet: 20 amps
  Approx. 10 misc. conveyors: ~ 150 hp elec.
                    System Total: 800-1000 hp

6.35

Type II C&D Waste Processing Strategy.   In almost all cases, it is important that Type II building demolition waste be sorted and separated *before* being crushed. This waste stream may contain asbestos, paint, lead pipe, etc., that could become fragmentized if crushed, thus contaminating large amounts of material or causing environmental concerns.

After the bulky material has been removed via presorting, the mixed material is introduced to the system for separation and sorting. Building demolition processors have found that an effective first step for mixed material is to separate the soil and rocks *prior to hand picking* of the cleaned and uncrushed recyclables (sort and separate, then crush and reduce). This can be achieved by the combination of a specially designed trommel or disk screen system to separate two fractions of soil and rocks. Additional screening and air classification can be performed if needed. Hand pickers recover the various recyclables on a sorting platform that follows. This type of process has been shown, in some instances, to increase the efficiency of hand pickers and improve the recovery rate of recyclable materials such as wood, metals, and corrugated. In addition, the soil and rock fractions tend to be free of pieces of plastic, cardboard, paper, and other materials that are undesirable to fill or aggregate material. The recovered wood fraction can be shredded into a marketable form. Crushing, screening, and further classification of the cleaned rocks can be performed if required by local markets.

C&D Processing Equipment.   In the area of C&D waste processing, equipment can essentially be grouped into three types:

• Conveying
• Crushing and reduction
• Screening and separation

Conveying Equipment.   The majority of conveying equipment used is rubber-belted conveyors. Troughed idler conveyors are attractive for many systems as opposed to pan-type conveyors because of the grit associated with this waste stream. In certain ares of the system such as the main infeed point, heavy-duty steel-apron-type converters from the aggregate industry, for example, are used. Conveyors can be made portable rather easily for use in the portable systems that are available.

Crushing and Reduction Equipment.   The actual types of equipment used will depend on what components of the C&D waste stream are to be reduced. For example, on rubble material, an impactor (rock crusher) or jaw crusher is used. For wood demolition, some type of hammermill (vertical or horizontal) is typically used at some point in the process because of the consistent-sized product it can provide. For bulky wood waste (large stumps, etc.), a stump-grinding machine can be used as a primary shredder with a secondary hammermill further reducing the material. For bulky waste such as furniture, white goods, etc., low-speed shredders can be used if it is more economical to reduce the material than to haul or dispose of the material whole.

Screening and Separation Equipment.   Screening and separation equipment is used in C&D processing to split similar materials into various-size fractions and to segregate different materials from one another. Vibratory equipment such as grizzly feeders or shaker screens are common. Disk screens and trommels are other conventional types of mechanical screening and separation equipment.

Various types of magnets are used to remove steel items from the waste stream. Flotation tanks are sometimes used to exploit the specific gravity difference between wood (floats) and rock (sinks). Separation of material by air (light from heavy) will be used more often as C&D processing evolves.

SPECIAL MATERIALS PROCESSING—
VARIOUS APPROACHES

Tire Processing

On an annual basis in the United States, we discard about 250 million tires per year. At the present time, it is estimated that approximately 2 billion tires exist in a variety of illegal stockpiles around the country.

Illegal tire piles form a major safety and environmental hazard. Not only do tires make excellent breeding grounds for mosquitoes, but they are also very vulnerable to fires which create dangerous air pollution as well as groundwater pollution from potential oil runoff during a fire. Approximately 20 states now have restrictions on disposal of whole tires, with an emphasis toward beneficial use. The landfilling of whole tires has been discouraged for years because of the space they take up and the tendency for the tires to float to the top of the landfill.

Two varied approaches are used for the processing of scrap tires. The whole-tire-burning approach is being practiced at a single plant operated by Oxford Energy in Modesto, California. There are present plans to increase the number of plants burning whole tires in the United States.

The predominant form of processing scrap tires is shredding and disposal or beneficial use of the shreds that are produced. The output of these machines are tire chips that range anywhere in size from 1 in square to 6 in square. The larger chips are only suitable for disposal, but the reduction in size eliminates some of the difficult issues with landfilling tires, and does save valuable disposal space. The smaller-sized chips have value as either gravel substitutes in landfills or as fuels. As a gravel substitute, small tire chips can be used in constructing drainage layers in sanitary landfills. (See Chap. 18, "Tires," for details.)

As a fuel, tires contain almost 15,000 Btu/lb and make an excellent alternative energy source for either cement kilns, paper boilers, other industrial boilers, or utility operations.

As a future potential use, further processing of tire shreds (i.e., the use of granulators) to produce crumb materials is being investigated. The crumb rubber produced via the granulation process can then be used in a variety of molded rubber products and also rubberized asphalt.

Batteries

Lead-Acid Automobile Batteries. The largest amount of batteries by weight in the United States are discarded automobile batteries. The traditional lead-acid battery can pose an environmental threat due to its lead content when disposed with municipal solid waste. Many efforts are made to keep lead-acid batteries out of the waste stream.

The prime recycling method is for automotive shops, when replacing the batteries, to stockpile them for bulk shipment to battery recyclers. The battery recycling stream as listed in the drawing below is called "battery breaking." This process, practiced by a handful of vendors around the country, involves the physical breaking of the case and removal of the lead components. In addition, the polypropylene plastic case is also recovered.

Household Batteries. Household batteries range from the traditional dry cell based on manganese and zinc, to mercury-containing button batteries, nickel-cadmium rechargeable cells, and alkaline cells. Some effort is being expended in an attempt to recycle household batteries. Various toxic materials such as mercury, cadmium, and zinc are found in individual batteries. The problem that exists today is that there are no good collection networks in the United States for the recovery of these materials. Dry cells and alkaline batteries have virtually no recycling processing capacity and are disposed of as hazardous waste. The so-called button batteries that are based on silver oxide and used in various small appliances, hearing aids, etc., and the nickel-cadmium batteries do have some recycling processing capability in the country. These processes, which shred and extract the valuable metals, hold some economic promise so that we may continue to recover more of these products from the waste stream. However, until a sufficient, steady quantity of these button batteries is available so that a facility can be developed which could take advantage of the economies of scale, there will be little incentive to achieve an economically feasible recovery system. (See Chap. 19, "Batteries," for details.)

Waste Oil

As with batteries described above, waste oil is a problem in disposal facilities. In the category of materials known as household hazardous waste, waste oil is the largest single identifiable material in this stream. As with batteries, the collection infrastructure for household-produced waste oil is not good. Because of the toxic nature and classification of waste oils, more and more oil companies are beginning to collect and treat the waste oils. The processing of these oils consists of either direct reuse as a fuel or the dissolution and treatment of the waste oil to upgrade it for use again as a lubricant. These types of reprocessing facilities will continue to become more common so that this material can be reused rather than disposed of at a higher and higher cost. Like lead-acid batteries, the automotive and quick-change oil center collection infrastructure is in place.

Various companies perform the service of collecting commercially generated waste oils. Their processing consists of either direct reuse as a fuel, or the distillation and treatment of the waste oil to upgrade it for use again as a lubricating fluid.

ACKNOWLEDGMENTS

The authors gratefully acknowledge the following for their valuable assistance in the preparation of this chapter: Russ Filtz, Senior Engineer, and Marty Felker, Staff Engineer, Facilities Support Group; and Dana Kemna, Recycling Compost Manager, Waste Management of North America, Inc., Oakbrook, Illinois.

CHAPTER 7
MARKET DEVELOPMENT: PROBLEMS AND SOLUTIONS

Gregg D. Sutherland
Eastern Regional Director
Resource Integration Systems Ltd.
Granby, Connecticut

INTRODUCTION

Typical economic behavior tells us that price and quantity are directly related. As price increases, quantity supplied should increase to take advantage of the new price. This traditional behavior is supposed to work in the other direction as well, so that when prices fall, quantity supplied should decrease due to reduced price incentive.

However, recent recycling markets have not followed these traditional economic precepts, at least on the surface. In fact, for many grades of recyclable materials, the volume supplied has increased to record levels while prices have fallen to historic lows. How can such contrary behavior occur? The answer lies in the fact that the supply of recyclables has been artificially stimulated by government mandate, while the demand for recyclables has been largely unaffected. The result is growing supplies along with declining prices.

The development of end markets for recyclable materials is now advancing to the forefront of vital recycling issues. Without effective development of these markets, recycling cannot grow. Accordingly, market development is now receiving the attention from government policy makers, from recyclers, and from industry that it requires in order to "close the loop" on recycling.

This chapter will

* Define market development within the broader context of the overall recycling system.

* Delineate the appropriate goals of market development.

* Examine why market development is typically overlooked in the early stages of expanding recycling systems.

* Identify the major barriers to market development. This section will also explore actions and policies that can overcome each barrier in order to effectively promote market development.

- Discuss alternative markets as a way to help recycling programs cope with disruptions of traditional markets.

DEFINITION OF TERMS

When discussing market development, it is important to start with a clear understanding of the terminology. This is because the term *market* depends largely on perspective. For a generator of waste material, the "market" is the recycler who collects the material. That recycler then sorts, grades, and processes the material for shipment to his "market," a manufacturer who is an end user of that material as a raw feedstock for his product. The end user then sells the product to her "market," a consumer who purchases the finished product with recycled material content. Figure 7.1 illustrates this loop, showing the definitions as they are used in this chapter.

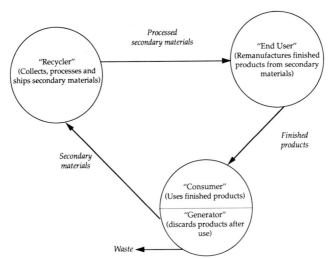

FIGURE 7.1   Definition of key recycling entities.

While recognizing that generally accepted terminology for many recycling terms is still widely debated, for the purposes of this chapter the following definitions will be used:

- A *consumer* is a person or other entity who purchases a finished product that may or may not include recycled content. After consuming the product, the consumer becomes a *generator* of any remaining waste material. Consumers and generators can be individuals, businesses, or government units. Examples include homeowners who produce old newspapers and scrap packaging or businesses that produce used corrugated boxes.
- A *recycler* is a person or other entity who collects scrap materials for sorting, processing, and shipping to a manufacturer. Manufacturers often make the point that, technically, the term "recycler" does not apply fully to the business

that serves in this intermediate role, since these businesses usually do not complete the loop by turning the material into a finished product. Nonetheless, because they take the first step toward diverting material from the waste stream and they are widely dispersed and visible to generators, these businesses are commonly called recyclers anyway. In this chapter, that common definition will be used. Examples include scrap metal dealers, municipally mandated recycling facilities for residential recyclables, and paper stock dealers.

- An *end user* is a person or other entity who remanufactures a finished product from secondary, scrap material that has been diverted from the waste stream. This use of the term end user is based on the concept of secondary material as a raw material. Thus, the end user is the manufacturer who uses that raw material, as opposed to the consumer who then buys the finished product with recycled content. Examples include steel mills, paper mills, glass plants, and plastic bottle plants that use scrap as a feedstock. End users often combine secondary materials with virgin materials.

Given these definitions, *market development* means development of end users of secondary materials. This chapter addresses ways to promote the development of end users as the final market for recyclable materials. Because generators and recyclers must produce and separate these raw materials and because consumers must purchase the finished products with recycled content, these groups will be addressed as well, but only as they affect market development, the development of end users of secondary materials.

THE GOALS OF MARKET DEVELOPMENT

Before discussing ways to promote market development, it is important to understand the goals of this activity. There are several appropriate goals, summarized in Table 7.1, for market development.

TABLE 7.1 Goals of Market Development

- Prevent imbalances
- Promote economically sustainable recycling
- Minimize need for government intervention
- Promote economic development
- Conserve ancillary resources

Prevent Imbalances

The most obvious goal of market development is to match end-use infrastructure growth with collection infrastructure growth. Imbalances, where collection grows rapidly compared to end-use markets, have resulted in severe material gluts that threaten the operational and financial viability of many recycling programs.

Figure 7.2 shows graphically that collection programs and infrastructure can grow rapidly without a corresponding increase in diversion of materials from the waste stream. Recycling is like a pipeline, where the smallest-volume section de-

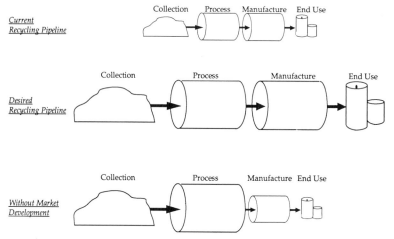

FIGURE 7.2   Consequences of ignoring market development.

termines the maximum flow through the entire system. When end markets do not grow with collection, end markets constrain the entire recycling system. Thus, the first goal of market development is to create a system balance between collection and end use.

Promote Economically Sustainable Recycling

While creating a balance between collection and end use is the most obvious goal of market development, it is not the only goal. In fact, from a long-term perspective, there may be an even more important goal of market development: to promote economically sustainable recycling.

Much of the growth of recycling is shifting away from programs initiated and operated strictly for the sake of private sector profitability and toward government-mandated systems. Accordingly, the economics of government-mandated systems are coming under scrutiny. In many cases, the value of recyclable materials recovered from a municipal recycling program does not cover collection, processing, and shipping costs. Adding the avoided costs of disposal to that equation may or may not show a recycling program to be economically justified, depending largely on local disposal fees and the means by which those disposal fees are calculated.

Most government-mandated systems are not initiated strictly on the basis of economics, however. Municipal recycling is rapidly becoming a standard municipal service, just like sewage treatment, water supply, street maintenance, police and fire protection, and trash removal.

Nonetheless, as local governments assume more responsibility with less federal funding, they are encountering unprecedented budget problems. This means that expansion even of government-mandated systems is threatened by economics. For example, one large state had originally planned to build an entire network of materials recovery facilities (MRFs) to process recyclables from residential recycling programs. However, after funding the first MRF, the state discovered that it had inadequate funding for additional MRFs and, as of this writing, none have been built since. A key element of the problem is that the glut of household recyclable materials has driven revenue from these programs so low that they often require substantial government subsidies to operate. A particularly significant factor in the glut is old newspapers, which comprise the majority of household recycling collections.

The same economic problem occurs as governments attempt to promote recycling by commercial waste generators. Almost by definition, commercial waste generators already recycle most of the materials that are economically viable to recover. Government programs typically put the burden on commercial generators to recycle more by requiring recycling plans or by banning certain materials from disposal.

In some cases, this prompts businesses who were missing out on savings to realize their mistake and implement a recycling program. However, this approach often becomes a hidden tax to subsidize recycling, since mandatory recycling can force commercial generators to pay more than they normally would for recycling. This is because they no longer recycle only for economic reasons; they now recycle because it is illegal not to. As a result, many commercial generators are told to recycle beyond any directly measurable economic incentive to do so.

While some economic improvement can result from improved collection and operating technology, the variable with greatest impact on the viability of most recycling programs is the market value of materials collected. This is where market development becomes critical, whether for residential or commercial recycling programs.

Because market development promotes the demand for recyclable materials, the price of those materials increases. Figure 7.3 illustrates a classic economic supply and demand curve, showing that price (as well as quantity) increases from point 1 to point 2 if market development can shift the demand curve out by causing a structural increase in demand.

Market development improves the economics of recycling. An improvement in the economic motives to recycle makes all varieties of recycling programs more viable and sustainable.

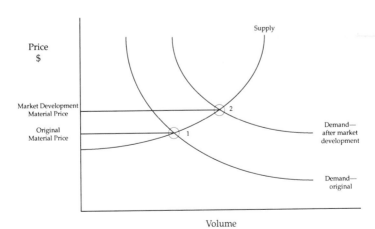

FIGURE 7.3 Graph: Market development effect on price.

Minimize Need for Government Intervention

Another goal of market development is to minimize the need for governmental involvement in recycling programs. Currently, most public sector policy toward recycling is based on overcoming economic barriers to recycling by funding new collection and processing systems (in the case of residential recycling) or by mandating generators to bear the incremental costs of increased recycling that may or may not be directly economical (in the case of commercial recycling). To implement and enforce these policies can be expensive, intrusive, and bureaucratic.

Some public sector decisions are made without the realization that, before the advent of municipal involvement in recycling, millions of tons of scrap materials were already recycled each year by private industry for economic gain. While there is little dispute that increased government involvement is needed to achieve recycling targets, it is imperative to remember that the private sector can play an effective role in achieving those goals. The best way to harness the private sector is through economic incentives. Market development is the most effective way to provide those economic incentives.

To the degree that government can rely on private industry to achieve recycling goals, government can commit less of its own scarce resources. Government can also take a less intrusive and bureaucratic role in the process.

Promote Economic Development

Another goal for market development is that of general economic development. Most jurisdictions have committed resources toward economic development. As a matter of local public policy, these actions usually focus on providing information to prospective new businesses and on making special arrangements to attract specific, large-scale new businesses. Recycling end users are excellent targets for such market development efforts, because

- End users are often large-scale businesses that can be significant employers.
- End users engage in an activity, recycling, that holds widespread public appeal.
- Recycling is a sustainable use of resources and usually has significant energy savings over virgin material use.
- Recycling is perceived as a long-term growth industry that can lend economic stability to a jurisdiction.

Market development promotes recycling, which is often a legitimate economic development objective.

Conserve Ancillary Resources

One other goal for market development is that jurisdictions are eager to take advantage of the ancillary resource conservation that recycling can cause. Manufacturing that uses secondary materials generally takes less energy and water and produces less waste than that which uses virgin materials. Increasingly, proactive jurisdictions are eager to take advantage of this resource conservation. For example, some utilities have granted millions of dollars to paper mills that undergo retooling to install equipment that would utilize secondary paper rather than virgin pulp. Utilities have justified these grants on the grounds that using secondary paper is significantly less energy intensive than producing and using virgin pulp.

From a utility's perspective, grants are a cost-effective investment in energy conservation. From a market development perspective, grants are an effective way to initiate investment in remanufacturing capacity.

THE NEGLECT OF MARKET DEVELOPMENT

Because end markets are a downstream activity from the generation of waste, there has been a natural tendency for most people to pay less attention to market development than to collection. However, the reasons for market development neglect are often much more subtle than this.

Traditional steps in developing recycling systems have consistently led to market debacles. First, collection-based programs are launched, and a local collection and intermediate processing infrastructure is built. As a glut of materials builds, the jurisdiction implements procurement programs, only to discover that recycled-content products are in short supply. This history has been repeated in jurisdiction after jurisdiction for both residential and commercial recycling programs. The result of this approach, until the final step of market development is implemented, is to create both a glut of recovered materials for which there is an inadequate end market and procurement programs for which there are few suppliers.

The reasons for the neglect of market development are illustrated in Table 7.2 and described below:

- Whether targeted at the individual, collector, or processor, collection and procurement programs are generally inexpensive, especially on a unit-cost basis. For end users, investing in remanufacturing equipment for secondary materials is often, by contrast, expensive. For example, adding a deinking system to an existing moderately sized newsprint mill could cost over $50 million.

- The time frame for the expansion of collection and procurement programs is quite short, especially as measured in lead time for the key element of equip-

TABLE 7.2 Reasons Market Development Is Neglected

Who recycles	How to increase	Unit cost	Lead time	Government level
Individual	Promote, provide collection container	$ 5	30 days	Local
Recycler/collector	Buy trucks	$ 90,000	60 days	Local
Recycler/processor	Buy balers	$ 200,000	90 days	Local
End User	Build cleaning systems	$50,000,000	3 to 5 years	State/regional
Consumer	Buy recycled content	$ 0	Immediate	Local

ment. The time frame for market development is much longer, because typically it takes years to obtain an internal capital budget; apply for and receive zoning, land, water, air, waste, and operating permits for facility construction; and order, install, and debug the necessary equipment.

- Collection and procurement programs are typically implemented at the local, municipal level. Compared to federal or state levels, these jurisdictions can move relatively quickly to implement collection programs, especially in areas that enjoy widespread public support for recycling. However, promoting large-scale capacity expansion among end users is frequently beyond the limited scope of local government. It usually takes the authority and resources of a state, regional, or federal government to create the incentives and minimize the obstacles to develop significant markets. Gaining consensus and initiating action at these governmental levels is inherently more difficult and time-consuming than at a local level.

There are also perceptual reasons why market development is neglected. Collection is a highly visible activity that requires the participation of the individuals in the jurisdiction. As such, collection is an obvious magnet for activity by community, political, industry, and advocacy groups. The visibility and participation of collection programs are important to each of these groups.

By contrast, market development often involves complex negotiation with small corporate committees far outside the associated jurisdictions. This lack of visibility and grass-roots participation make it easy for many types of groups to overlook market development.

However, for all the reasons why ignoring market development is easy, there is one compelling reason why it cannot be ignored for long: *without market development, the overall recycling system cannot grow.* Without growth of the overall system, the visible and participatory collection and procurement programs start to fail in a highly visible way. As a result, well-deserved attention is now being focused on market development, particularly by state- and provincial-level governments and by industry.

BARRIERS AND OPPORTUNITIES

Market development is a complex process that calls for the careful integration of government, the public, and private industry across a well-developed set of policies and programs. This section will identify barriers to market development and opportunities to overcome those barriers.

There are several key areas for effective market development strategies:

- *Supply:* Market development depends upon a reliable, high-volume, high-quality stream of secondary raw materials.

- *Consumer demand:* Market development can only succeed if consumers purchase the finished goods that have recycled content.

- *Technology:* Effective market development will require investment in new technologies as industry moves away from using virgin raw materials.

- *Government role:* Government action can have a large impact—positive or negative—on market development.

- *Economics:* Market development is primarily economically driven.
- *Alternative end markets:* Developing nontraditional end uses can take the pressure off oversupplied markets.

Supply

Some government recycling authorities quietly endorse the concept of intentionally creating collection policies that produce a glut of secondary materials to "force" industry into expanding end markets. Others insist that collection programs should only be initiated after end markets are well established and the overall economics are favorable.

In fact, these opposing positions are a false dilemma. The expansion of markets and of collection should proceed in step with each other. Imbalances resulting from uncoordinated development only frustrate the overall system. In other words, collecting a supply and creating a demand are both necessary conditions, but neither alone is a sufficient condition.

In order to convince potential end users to expand their capacity, there must be an assurance of a reliable supply channel. End users typically invest millions of dollars in their manufacturing systems and must look to a long-term return on their investment. This has traditionally caused many manufacturers to integrate backward into enterprises that allow them to control their virgin raw material feedstocks. For example, paper mills often own large tracts of forest land. Plastics producers are often petrochemical producers, or they have established long-term agreements with such producers. The attitude of "controlling the raw material supply channel" is well entrenched in most large manufacturers.

There has long been concern among manufacturers about relying on a scrap collection network that is highly fragmented among thousands of small, regional recyclers whose programs are dependent on widely fluctuating and virtually unpredictable scrap material prices. Add to this a public and government that have had a checkered history of implementing sustainable recycling, and the result is that many large manufacturers (with some notable exceptions) have traditionally minimized the use of scrap as a significant raw material.

However, several factors (see Table 7.3) are changing to improve the quality and reliability of supply channels:

TABLE 7.3 Supply Opportunities

- Backward integration of manufacturers
- Government-mandated supply reliability
- Quality improvement of recyclable materials
- Development of robust cleaning systems
- Attention to market specifications
- Restrict contaminants

- Manufacturing firms are integrating backward into ownership of or joint ventures with large recycling companies. This technique, long practiced by traditional scrap end users, is now becoming common among new end users in order to secure their supply channels. In fact, one emerging model is that large trash hauling firms acquire traditional recyclers. These increasingly concentrated recyclers then form alliances with large end users. As long as they do not interfere with a competitive industry structure, such ventures can help to create markets through the development of secure, integrated supply lines that are integrated with end users.

• The collection of recyclable materials was once almost completely driven by spot markets and by mostly small, entrepreneurial recyclers. Such a system did achieve excellent economies for a given amount of recycling but produced sometimes wide fluctuations in price and quantity. Now that recycling is becoming a public policy goal and a public service expectation, collecting recyclables is an increasingly formalized, predictable process. This evolution serves to assure manufacturers that their investment in new systems will continue to have raw materials available to them, because the collection programs are government-mandated.

• One drawback associated with the growth of government-mandated recycling is that the quality of the secondary raw material has, in many cases, been reduced. This is partly because the growth in recycling programs has sometimes put inexperienced municipal or private operators in control of operations, and that lack of experience has resulted in lower quality material. Also, the focus of recycling is now shifting toward maximizing diversion from disposal. This focus places a lower emphasis upon quality of material. For example, some office recycling programs that used to collect only white and computer paper have expanded into all office paper (often as a result of government mandates). This lowers the overall grade of paper collected. Solutions to this barrier include

The development of more robust cleaning systems by end users. Some tissue mills, for example, have achieved a significant competitive advantage by developing cleaning processes that allow them to use lower grade materials at lower prices.

More careful attention to market specifications by recyclers and by government-mandated collection programs. One large city added a wide diversity of plastic to its ongoing curbside recycling program, only to discover that the overseas end user could not actually use such a broad range of resin types. The city reverted to a limited range of plastic bottles for which secure markets were available. Another municipal program, located in an area infamous for disruptive gluts of low-grade paper, launched its collection program to include all household paper, not just newspaper. As a result, markets for this mixture of low-grade paper are often unavailable, prices are always low, and stockpiling the baled paper is common. While private and government recycling programs should challenge end users to take a broader range of materials, they do not promote market development by dumping scrap of unacceptable quality onto end users.

Materials that pose significant contamination hazards to end users are being restricted or banned. Manufacturing finished goods from recycled raw materials is a demanding process. Contaminants can disrupt an entire processing run, which works against market development. Increasingly, governments in the United States and abroad are restricting or banning materials that could cause such contamination problems at end users' facilities. Examples of some potentially problematic contaminants include polyvinyl chloride (PVC) bottles or components in polyethylene tetraphthalate (PET) bottle reclamation streams (some European countries have banned PVC bottles for this reason), hot melt glues in paper (some jurisdictions are considering prohibiting newspapers from printing advertising specialties that include such glues), and ceramics in glass bottle reclamation streams (some jurisdictions now prohibit specialty ceramic bottles or bottle components). Industry must ensure that its packages and products are compatible with the recycling infrastructure, with the assurance that governments will act to restrict them if they do not restrict themselves.

Effective market development tools relating to supply include developing secure supply channels and working to improve the quality of materials for recycling end use.

Consumer Demand

End users have traditionally shied away from recycled materials because of perceptions that these materials do not meet the quality standards of virgin materials. Even end users who do use secondary materials typically kept that fact quiet in order to avoid creating an impression that their product was second-rate. Without consumers willing to buy products with recycled content, market development will fail. Fortunately, consumers are convincing end users that they often actually prefer products with recycled content. At the same time, end-user technology is maturing, which improves the quality of recycled-content products. Consumer demand methods for market development are listed in Table 7.4.

TABLE 7.4 Consumer Demand Opportunities

- Purchasing preference
- Recycled content mandates
- Labeling standards

Purchasing Preference. An increasingly aware public is more interested than ever in buying products and packages with recycled content. This is true on an individual consumer level, as numerous market preference studies indicate. Some tissue mills have always had a very high percentage of recycled content, which was used initially to gain a cost advantage over their competitors. In marketing tests, some of these mills started labeling certain products to promote the recycled content. As a result of the labeling, products labeled with recycled content sell faster in certain markets than similar but unlabeled products with the same recycled content. Several large consumer products companies have also started promoting the recycled content of their plastic bottles and paperboard boxes, tapping into the consumer preference for such items.

Consumer demand is also growing among businesses and governments. Increasingly, these organizations demand recycled content in their packaging, paper, and other products. In fact, some organizations now demand similar procurement standards from their suppliers and vendors. This trend could expand the scope of procurement standards dramatically.

Recycled-Content Mandates. In addition to internally initiated procurement standards, there is an emerging trend toward externally imposed procurement standards. Newsprint is perhaps the best example, since the majority of the U.S. population now lives in states that have some form of recycled-content standards for newsprint. Several states and provinces are implementing similar recycled-content standards for a variety of products and packages. Plastic bottles and bags are favorite targets, but jurisdictions may set recycled-content rates for a wide variety of other materials as well. Some proposed legislation would set recycled-content targets for all packaging.

Labeling Standards.   Ironically, the promotion of recycled content, which should facilitate market development, has created a need for standards for product labeling. If these labeling standards are addressed incorrectly, they could actually work against market development. In the absence of a uniform, national approach to labeling regarding recycled content, local jurisdictions will develop their own standards. With thousands of jurisdictions in the United States, the proliferation of such inconsistent and even contradictory labeling standards has already driven many manufacturers to eliminate labeling claims on their products and packages. Thus, whereas the label should give a competitive edge to the company that has made the investment and commitment to use secondary materials, that company may be forced to drop the recycled-content label entirely. This is because, as a national manufacturer, it cannot afford to set up differently labeled products to meet each individual jurisdiction's standards.

There are currently several competing approaches to labeling. Some labeling programs indicate a "seal of approval" approach. Examples include Germany's Blue Angel program, Canada's Environmental Choice program, and private initiatives in the United States. A seal of approval is consistent with many state-level rules, which allow the word "recycled" only if the product meets certain levels of recycled content (which may be different from other materials and from other jurisdictions).

Others are advocating a full disclosure type labeling that would describe a wider range of recycled content. With this approach, manufacturers who used recycled content can use the word recycled but must indicate the specifics about composition. One recycled paper dealer has even developed a sliding scale of recycled ratings, depending on the proportions of preconsumer, postconsumer, and virgin materials.

The subject of labeling issues and guidelines is currently being addressed by a wide variety of groups, including the Environmental Protection Agency, the Recycling Advisory Council of the National Recycling Coalition, the American Society for Testing and Materials, the National Association of State Purchasing Officials, several industry associations such as the Paper Recycling Coalition, state and local governments, and many others. While the resolution of labeling issues is beyond the scope of this chapter, it is valuable to establish market development goals for labeling:

- Labeling policies should reward those manufacturers which make a commitment to using recycling content. This reward should be proportional to the level of end-user recycled content. This means that variable, incremental labeling with full disclosure of the amount and type of recycled content is preferable to labeling that does not disclose those factors.
- Labeling should be nationally consistent. The expenses of small production runs, increased safety stocks, and distribution logistics can prohibit end users from labeling products rather than attempt to meet a variety of standards.

Technology Development

To some degree, all end use of recycled materials is dependent upon effective technology. Technology for end users to utilize secondary materials is improving. Flotation systems for newsprint production can now utilize coated ground-wood paper; depolymerizing PET plastic allows that resin to be recycled back into soft drink bottles; detinners now routinely use old steel, tin-coated cans as part of their feedstock. However, other technologies are still struggling. Laser-printed paper is a problem for many paper and tissue mills; ceramics are an easily concealed contaminant for glass; and boxboard, although having a high recycled content, is not readily recycled.

Improving the technology of end users is an important market development tool. In addition, technology development is an area where government and industry have historically enjoyed a mutually productive partnership. Expanding technology development programs, through government research laboratories, universities, and technology transfer programs, can help promote market development.

Government Level

Collection of recyclables is usually a local government role. With residential programs, local governments typically establish curbside collection and drop-off programs. With commercial programs, local governments typically mandate that businesses separate specified materials and ban those materials from disposal. These types of activity are within the charter and authority of most local governments.

However, a local government is often severely limited in its potential impact on market development. This is because the local government usually does not have the authority or resources to significantly affect market development decisions. To significantly affect such decisions, large-scale procurement programs, product labeling standards, economic incentives, and technology support must be implemented. That level of authority and resources is usually placed at the state or federal level.

Unfortunately, obtaining a consensus and charting a course of action is often more difficult at these higher levels of government. On their own initiative as well as at the prompting of local government and industry, state governments are increasingly addressing market development issues in a meaningful way. Currently, most U.S. states have some type of market development program underway. In the absence of clear, definitive federal leadership, several states are banding together, formally or informally, to establish regional recycling initiatives, including market development programs. Such state-level and regional approaches can be very effective in implementing market development programs.

Economics

In the end, market development is driven by economics. In fact, as discussed under "Goals," one of the key goals of market development is to improve the economics of the entire recycling system. There are a variety of ways to improve the economics of end use of recyclable materials (see Table 7.5), but broadly, they fit into one of two categories:

TABLE 7.5 Economics

---

* Economic intervention
  Loans
  Grants
  Subsidies
  Tax incentives
  Recycled content credits
* Free market promotion
  Removal of virgin material subsidies
  Disposal pricing
  External cost accounting

---

* *Economic intervention:* One way to improve end-use economics is to intervene in the marketplace with direct economic intervention, typically with government funds. Examples include loans, grants, subsidies, tax incentives, and recycling credits.
* *Free market promotion:* In some ways, end markets are constrained due to restrictions on a free market that would normally favor recycling more than is currently the case. By promoting a free market, these variables would improve the economics of recycling markets compared to virgin materials. Examples include accurate disposal pricing and removal of virgin material subsidies.

Economic Intervention. Economic intervention can be a very effective market development tool, but it must be approached with caution. Inappropriate use of economic intervention can easily allocate scarce recycling resources into end uses that are ineffective and not sustainable. In general, policies that help to cover start-up or capital costs are preferable to policies that subsidize ongoing losses. End markets that require ongoing subsidies are not, by definition, sustainable. In addition, committing public funds to ongoing losses subjects end markets to the uncertainty of the public sector budgeting process.

Loans and Loan-Guarantee Programs. Already, several state and federal programs facilitate loans or loan guarantees to new ventures in the name of business development. When applied to market development, such programs can be effective. This is because market development often requires a manufacturer in a capital-intensive industry to retool. Such a requirement can be a significant burden on the end user's balance sheet. A below-market or guaranteed loan can make the necessary funding available to the end user.

Grants. The same logic applies to grants. Grants often depend upon specific criteria established by the granting agency. Typically, such grants focus on feasibility studies and research projects. However, grants are also being used to fund capital and start-up costs as well. Some grants are targeted toward promotion of ancillary resource conservation, particularly energy conservation.

Subsidies. Subsidies usually address some ongoing portion of the end user's costs. Subsidies may be structured as a tax credit for the consumption of recycled materials. Some subsidies are structured to phase out over a set period of time. This minimizes the potential of funding an end user that is not sustainable.

Tax Incentives. Tax incentives can take many forms. However, many tax incentives are not effective because they have a relatively small financial impact.

For example, some local jurisdictions offer credits on property, sales, income, and other taxes for specific market development investments and expenses. However, the tax burden imposed by these local jurisdictions is sometimes so small that it has little impact on investment decision making.

States may use tax incentives to better advantage, since their tax effect is usually larger. Several states now exempt property taxes and sales taxes for purchases of new recycling equipment. In the case of large manufacturing systems, these tax exemptions can be significant incentives to the economic decision to invest in market development.

In addition to tax exemptions, some states are implementing investment tax credits (ITCs). These credits can be very effective because they may be targeted to offset taxes that will significantly affect end-user decision making. For example, in several states, corporate income tax is a much larger dollar item than many other taxes. An ITC can be specifically structured to offset that significant tax. By focusing on a specific tax, the ITC can result in a significant dollar impact.

Recycled-Content Credits. One interesting approach toward using a market-based economic intervention tool is to create a market in recycled-content credits. This approach is patterned after federal air emission regulations, where power plants that emit air pollutants are each granted a limited number of "pollution credits." These credits could be bought and sold, which enables plants that cannot economically retrofit with pollution-control equipment to buy credits from other plants. Overall, air pollution is reduced, an economic incentive is created to install pollution-control equipment, and specific plants are spared the problems of trying to apply blanket regulations to a variety of cases.

This same approach could apply to recycled content for certain materials in specific applications. The federal government could issue a limited number of credits for the use of virgin materials. The amount of these credits would be limited and would decrease over time. Manufacturers who wish to continue using virgin materials would have to buy credits from manufacturers who use recycled, rather than virgin, materials. Bills along these lines have been introduced in the U.S. Congress for the use of recycled content in a variety of materials.

The benefits of such an approach are the same as for pollution control. The credits provide a direct economic incentive to utilize recycled materials, while specific manufacturers are not "forced" to switch technologies. The drawback is that a complex reporting and auditing mechanism would be required to implement and enforce this system of credits.

Free Market Promotion. Free market promotions often do not produce the quick, dramatic impacts of economic intervention steps, but their role can be much more significant over the long run. In our economy, there are several government-imposed market dislocation mechanisms that work against recycling. These mechanisms were established when national policy favored increased exploitation of natural resources for national security and economic development reasons. However, today those reasons are vague at best. The real impediment to removing these dislocations is the fact that many large industries have grown accustomed to taking advantage of them.

Recycling markets would be promoted if several specific market dislocations were removed:

- *Federal depletion allowances:* Federal depletion allowances give tax credits to the petroleum and mining industries based on the depletion of the resource in the mine or well. The effect is to subsidize the expense of the operation with tax dollars and promote the use of virgin ores and plastics over their recycled alternatives. This also keeps the cost of energy artificially low, which minimizes the energy savings that recycled materials usually have over virgin materials.

- *Forest Service policies:* Federal Forest Service policies promote logging by funding site preparation and reclamation without full compensation for these activities from the timber companies that harvest the timber. In effect these policies subsidize the expense of logging on federal lands with tax dollars. This also promotes the use of virgin pulp over recycled paper stock.

- *Timing of deductions:* The timing of deductions for exploration, development, and reforestation is accelerated for extractive and forestry activity. The effect of these deductions is to subsidize the investment of extraction and logging with tax dollars. This subsidy also promotes the use of virgin materials over recycled materials, which do not generally enjoy such accelerated deductions.

Calculating the impact of these subsidies for virgin materials is difficult. However, a recent Office of Technology Assessment estimate exceeds $1 billion per year in subsidies. On the other hand, other federal studies would indicate that the actual impact of these subsidies on recycling is slight.

In order to create a level playing field for recycled materials, there are three possible approaches:

- *Eliminate virgin materials subsidies:* While this is perhaps the most direct way to deal with the problem, it is not likely to happen quickly. Most of the subsidies are written into complex federal tax law, and it would require significant revisions to remove them. More significantly, large and powerful virgin-materials-based industries are not likely to let these subsidies go away without a battle.

- *Create subsidies for recycled materials equal to those that apply to virgin materials:* This is a complex task, since the subsidy structures are not directly transferable from virgin materials to recycled materials. Furthermore, economists point out that adding one market dislocation upon another is not the most efficient way to resolve a problem. However, this may turn out to be the most politically acceptable compromise. This approach retains the existing subsidies for virgin materials, yet it has the potential to offset the financial advantages of those virgin material subsidies by creating comparable subsidies for recycled materials.

- *Create a tax for virgin materials roughly equal to the subsidies:* Known as a "virgin materials tax," this approach has already been introduced to the state and federal policy debate. It has the advantage of potentially offsetting the virgin material subsidies while adding a new source of revenue to the treasury. However, as a new tax, it is subject to attack from many sources and has not yet gained a solid constituency.

Disposal Costs.   There is another type of subsidy that works against the development of recycling markets: artificially low disposal costs. While disposal costs are rising rapidly in many parts of the country, they are still free or nominal in many parts of the United States. In fact, even in areas with relatively high disposal costs, economists point out that a finite resource like disposal capacity should be priced on its replacement value, not just on its current operating costs.

In other words, added into disposal costs should be the expenses of closure of the disposal facility, long-term monitoring and remediation of the facility, and development of new (and increasingly expensive) disposal facilities. Very few jurisdictions consciously include those long-term costs in their disposal fees.

By keeping the cost of disposal artificially low, more materials are diverted into the waste stream rather than into the recycling stream. This is because, economically, the effect of an increase in disposal costs is the same as an increase in market value of the material. Both improve the economics of recycling over disposal, which promotes market development.

The effect of artificially low disposal costs is that, since end markets must compete with disposal facilities, disposal facilities have a subsidized advantage over end markets.

External Costs. Many environmentalists and economists argue that the environmental impacts of virgin material extraction and use are not fully accounted for. Examples include loss of wildlife habitat, loss of recreational opportunity, process pollution, spills, and consumption of ancillary resources, such as power and water. By not internalizing those costs into the price of virgin materials, those materials enjoy an apparent economic advantage over recycled materials, which typically use fewer ancillary resources.

This topic is controversial because it raises all the difficult issues of external costs, such as how to account for them, how to measure them, how to weigh them against each other, and how to build those costs into the economic system.

ALTERNATIVE END MARKETS

Municipal recycling programs tend to collect steady streams of materials. However, the end markets for those materials are increasingly undependable. The result is that market fluctuations often threaten the viability of a collection program. Some recycling programs are able to protect themselves by developing long-term agreements with reliable end markets. Other programs are diversifying their end markets to include emerging, local, or revived end uses. For example, some programs that collect newspapers are shredding that paper into animal bedding rather than selling the paper to traditional end users like newsprint mills.

On the surface, developing alternative markets can be economically unattractive. Almost by definition, the reason the market is an "alternative" to traditional markets is that the end value of the reclaimed product is lower or the processing costs are higher. However, such a limited analysis does not account for the political, disposal, environmental and community costs of disrupting a collection program during market downturns.

A more significant limitation of many alternative markets is that they tend to be small-scale. However, even if the size of an alternative market does not completely replace the traditional market, it can ease the pressure caused by market disruptions.

Table 7.6 shows a matrix of alternative end markets for a variety of commonly collected materials. Often, these markets can be developed locally, at least on a small-scale basis.

TABLE 7.6 Alternative Markets

Material collected	Traditional markets	Alternative products and markets
Newspapers	Newsprint mills Paperboard mills	Shredded animal bedding; farmers Grocery bags and corrugating medium; kraft paper mills Compost; farmers, nurseries, public works
Corrugated boxes	Kraft paper mills Paperboard mills	Shredded animal bedding; farmers Compost; farmers, nurseries, public works
Glass bottles	Glass bottle plants	Asphalt additive ("glassphalt"); paving contractors, public works Drain bedding; public works "Sand" blasting and abrasive medium; industrial users, contractors, public works
Plastics	Multipurpose resin reclaimers Virgin resin replacement in products such as strapping and pipe	Plastic "lumber," concrete, and wood substitutes; public works, commercial and government establishments
Office paper	Tissue mills Writing and printing paper mills Paperboard mills	White linerboard; premium product packagers (fruit, office supplies, etc.)

CONCLUSION

The current state of recycling is that a glut of many materials grows daily while prices for those same materials fall. This apparently noneconomic behavior is caused primarily by government-mandated collection programs that are out of sync with end markets. The solution to this problem is to promote the development of end markets.

Developing end markets has several goals:

- Prevent imbalances
- Promote economically sustainable recycling
- Minimize need for government intervention
- Promote economic development
- Conserve ancillary resources

Market development is not as visible as development of collection programs. Market development requires a comparatively high level of investment, a long lead time, and a high level of government involvement. Accordingly, it is all too easy to overlook market development, until that lack of markets begins to threaten the collection programs themselves.

Market development can be promoted in a variety of ways. Market development strategies fall into one of these categories:

- Supply
- Consumer demand
- Technology
- Government role
- Economics
- Alternative markets

Market development is a challenging process necessitating careful policy implementation at high governmental levels, but it is a challenge that must be met in order to advance recycling. Without market development for recyclable materials, there can be no growth in recycling.

CHAPTER 8

FINANCIAL PLANNING AND MANAGEMENT OF RECYCLING PROGRAMS AND FACILITIES

Robert Hauser, Jr.
Vice President, Camp Dresser & McKee, Inc.
Tampa, Florida

INTRODUCTION

Today, many communities are looking at recycling as an integral element of their solid waste management strategies. All of the benefits associated with recycling must be considered when evaluating a particular recycling program, or combination of programs, as a component of a total solid waste management system. However, implementing a recycling program in many communities often introduces a number of new issues not directly addressed by current solid waste systems. Of particular importance are issues associated with the financing or funding of the program and its management.

Recycling goals adopted by communities or mandated by legislation impose new responsibilities on a community and require the development of programs which the existing solid waste management structure may not be equipped to address. Therefore, it may be necessary to change or evolve a new management structure to address the new responsibilities.

The individual components of an overall recycling program, such as curbside collection, drop-off centers, processing facilities, and public education, all introduce new costs to a community. Depending upon the specific components, they may have high or low capital funding requirements and high or low operating and maintenance costs. Financial commitments may be short-term or long-term. Revenues from the sale of materials, state or other program grants, and/or avoided costs will offset the costs of the recycling program. However, these revenue sources are also highly erratic and introduce a high level of uncertainty in their realization. Finally, experience and financial planning show that recycling programs, particularly very aggressive programs, do not generate sufficient revenues to cover their costs. Thus, it becomes apparent that funding to support recycling programs is required.

The additional funding required should not be viewed as an unnecessary cost. All solid waste systems, including elements of collection, transportation, processing, and disposal, cost money. Recycling is part of an overall integrated program and it is as reasonable to expend funds for this purpose as it is to expend funds for other parts of the solid waste system. Moreover, recycling produces benefits not attained by other solid waste disposal systems.

This chapter addresses the financing and funding and management alternatives available to implement recycling programs. These alternatives are basically the same ones available to implement any solid waste management system. However, the new responsibilities and opportunities available through recycling programs require some communities to look at these alternatives for the first time, while for others it requires a whole new look at their existing solid waste programs. No two communities are the same, and the selection of a funding and management program must be made considering that community's own unique set of goals and objectives as well as constraints.

RECYCLING PROGRAM IMPLEMENTATION RISKS

In any recycling program development, many decisions regarding financial planning and management of the program involve risks that must be recognized and properly allocated to the program participants. The risk of most concern to communities and private firms in recycling programs is monetary loss. Thus, the allocation of risk is the assignment of monetary loss, if it occurs, to a specific party prior to the actual occurrence of the loss. It is important to note that monetary loss does not refer to a net program loss but rather a loss exceeding that budgeted and funded using responsible assumptions.

The factors which lead to risk exposure for recycling programs can be grouped into five categories:

- Technology
- Waste stream
- Markets
- Legal and regulatory
- *Force majeure* (unforeseen circumstances)

The following paragraphs briefly review these five categories. It is important to note that these risk factors apply to all recycling programs, as well as individually to each element of the program whether it is a curbside collection program, drop-off centers, or a major processing facility such as a compost operation. The relative importance of the risks, however, may shift depending upon the specific element of the program.

Technology

Risks associated with technology include completing the construction of recycling and processing facilities on time and within a specified cost. This category also includes technical problems that might affect the ability to complete the facility as designed and unanticipated construction cost increases.

The procurement or bid documents for recycling and recovery facilities should require guarantees that the facility will be completed by a certain date, for a certain cost, and in compliance with specified performance and/or design criteria. These guarantees would be supported by a construction bond and/or insurance.

Technological causes of risk also include those associated with actual program operation—that the facility or operational program such as curbside collection will operate as planned and guaranteed, and that program requirements such as material quantity and quality are met. Most of those performance guarantees will be as specified in the bid documents or negotiated in the procurement process. Under a turnkey or full-service procurement, the contractor will be responsible for meeting the prescribed performance criteria, correcting any reasons for not meeting those criteria, or paying financial penalties for noncompliance.

It is advantageous if the risks associated with technological causes can be negotiated and allocated to the various project participants in an equitable and precise manner. These risks also demonstrate the critical nature of proper technology and specific program selection to meet the individual needs of a community.

Waste Stream

Another cause of risk to any recycling or materials recovery program is the assurance of an adequate and reliable supply of recovered materials and/or waste of the proper composition and quality. Waste stream control is a major cause of risk allocated to a city, county, or authority, whether or not that entity owns the facility. Waste stream control is particularly important in programs using tipping fees, surcharges, or other quantity-related revenue sources as the bases of support to program funding.

The degree of waste stream control is directly tied to the recycling program selected by a community and must be considered in the selection of that system. It further must be considered in terms of its applicability to residential wastes and commercial or industrial wastes and the various programs to recover materials from each of these waste streams.

A final consideration is the nature of any publicly mandated goals to achieve minimum levels of recycling or recovery. Many states have legislatively mandated recycling and recovery goals. In most cases, attaining these goals has been assigned as the responsibility of a city, county, or other "responsible" agency. The ability to achieve and exceed these goals must be met through a proper program which may require waste stream control at a level not initially envisioned.

Methods of waste stream control include:

- *Economics:* Program and/or facility tipping fees could be set or subsidized to be the least costly disposal option within the area, or economic incentives to recycle materials could otherwise be provided.

- *Legislation:* Responsible public agencies could submit special legislation to provide exemptions from regulatory antitrust statutes, empower the public entity to control the collection and disposal of recycled materials within a specified geographic area, and grant the entity waste flow control. This is particularly important in recycling programs where recycled materials are often excluded from the definitions of solid waste under regulatory programs. Waste generators within the area could also be required to deliver recycled materials to the location specified by the municipal jurisdiction. The implementation of this legislation, with appropriate enforcement and combined with one or more of the other methods of control, significantly reduces the risk of providing a reliable supply of waste and/or recovered materials.

- *Contract agreement:* The city, county, and perhaps an authority may designate the programs to be implemented and the facility to be used through agreements with contract collectors. Franchising of collectors for residential, commercial, and recyclable routes can be done.

- *Municipal collection:* The city, county, or authority could assure that the waste is delivered to the facility simply because its forces and equipment perform the operation of the program.

In addition, any of the above could be implemented in combination with the others.

Other causes of risk exist which are related to the quality of the waste stream rather than controlling waste delivery. For example, a central materials recovery system's guarantee may be contingent upon a specified quality of waste, including minimum percentages of paper, glass, and aluminum. Waste quality could change for numerous reasons (for example, enactment of beverage container deposit legislation). Public entities must often assume the responsibilities and costs of this risk.

Markets

In recycling and materials recovery programs, securing markets to purchase (or even to receive) recovered materials is critical. Historically, secondary material markets are very volatile with constantly changing price structures and quality requirements. For some materials, markets or outlets are still developing. It is difficult to secure long-term contracts to receive materials. Some legislatively mandated programs require recycling of materials irrespective of market conditions.

These factors affect not only program selection but, importantly, the ability to budget, fund, and operate the program. The risk associated with markets can be mitigated primarily by maintaining program flexibility with respect to the materials recovered and their quality, and sound budgeting that recognizes market factors. Establishing a good relationship with markets can help assure outlets for materials through market ups and downs. The budgeting process should allow, where necessary, the payment of a tipping fee to markets to accept the material, recognizing that this may still provide benefits and can be economical as compared to the cost of disposal associated with other methods.

Legal and Regulatory

This set of risk causes are not possible to anticipate. Changes do occur in state or federal legislation and associated rules and regulations which may affect recycling programs. In addition, it is difficult to anticipate how courts will, in the future, interpret present laws and regulations.

Significant legal and regulatory issues that could affect the project include

- *Tax laws:* Federal income taxation legislation has undergone major changes. Such changes may impact upon the financing options and revenues generated. Also, tax laws affecting the use of virgin materials as compared to recycled materials impact the markets.

- *Environmental protection regulations:* Environmental protection laws and regulations could change. For example, federal or state air or water (including groundwater) quality regulations could be altered and could result in significant constraints on the operational practices of an existing recovery facility. Changes in administrative practices could affect governmental procedures associated with various facilities (such as environmental renewals). Finally, regulatory changes may affect the goals of recycling programs, thus requiring additional program elements to meet goals or resulting in changes to the composition of the waste stream.

- *Antitrust challenges:* The program could be faced with federal antitrust challenges as a result of the need to direct material flow. Special state legislation can substantially reduce this risk.

- *Other regulatory issues:* Laws related to packaging legislation, bottle bills, government procurement policies, etc., can all affect recycling and materials recovery programs. Many can be positive.

Force Majeure

This category of risk causes is the term for all of the unanticipated occurrences that might affect the operation of the program. These causes include war, sabotage, and other occurrences beyond control, including acts of God, such as earthquakes and other natural disasters. Proper risk allocation for the *force majeure* causes requires a comprehensive listing of the potential causes and a program to allocate responsibility for such risks, particularly costs.

Summary

In determining a risk posture, consideration must be given to each of the above risk categories both in terms of each individual program element as well as the entirety of the recycling program. This will assist in fully defining the financial requirements of the program to assure proper funding of all capital, operating, and maintenance costs.

FINANCING AND OWNERSHIP ALTERNATIVES

A key element in the success of a recycling program is the development of a plan and structure for capital financing and ownership of any facilities required for the program. Decisions related to these issues extend into the selection of a procurement approach. These decisions must be made by each community on an individual basis, considering its overall program and its goals and objectives. The following describes the general framework of alternatives available to communities.

Financing Alternatives

A key element in the success of a solid waste management project is the development of a plan and structure for capital financing. The financing program must be structured to meet the overall objectives of the governmental sponsor. At the same time, it must also meet the needs of the financial community in order to attract adequate funds for project implementation, including the equitable allocation of risks among the project participants.

Public Ownership Financing Options. The major sources of capital funds for a publicly owned recycling facility include general obligation bonds, revenue bonds, and bonds and grants issued by state and private agencies.

1. *General obligation (G.O. bonds):* In order to finance many non-revenue-producing capital projects, local governments have typically issued long-term general obligation debt. While such debt could be repaid from project revenues, the bonds are secured by a pledge of the full faith and credit and taxing powers of the governmental sponsor. If project revenues fail to materialize, the debt service must be covered by tax revenues.

G.O. bonds and other tax-exempt debt instruments can be issued with lower interest rates than taxable bonds because the holders of G.O. bonds are not required to pay income taxes on the interest income they receive. Consequently, the public entity that issues G.O. debt pays less interest over the term of the bonds, which usually results in considerable savings. The spread between G.O. bonds and private financing alternatives depends upon the credit rating of the governmental sponsor and the specifics of the project.

2. *Project revenue bonds:* Typically, project revenue bonds are the preferred form of financing when a project is capable of producing revenues sufficient to support the project and entirely repay the bonded debt. Revenues include not only revenues from the sale of materials but also revenues from other pledged funding sources such as tipping fees. However, the rate of interest charged on such a bond issue will generally be higher than for G.O. bonds. It depends upon potential investors' perception of the overall economic viability of the project (the "coverage" of expenses and debt service by project revenues); the contractual requirements, if any, of the arrangements (including the financial strengths of the contracting parties); and the perceived value of any backup pledge revenues to further guarantee the project's fiscal integrity.

3. *Other bond and grant programs:* Many states provide opportunities for communities to finance recycling projects from state bond or loan programs. These have many of the characteristics associated with those previously financing methods described above. However, they represent an opportunity for a community to obtain an outside funding source.

Also, some states, federal agencies, and private companies or foundations offer specific grants which may be utilized by a community. The availability of such programs is generally limited, and further they are often restricted as to what purposes they may be applied. However, they can represent a significant source for financing projects or to defer their associated costs. These need to be investigated on a project-by-project basis.

Private Ownership Financing Options. The major source of capital funds for a privately owned solid waste facility would be private equity and industrial development bonds (IDBs). In addition, some private grant programs may be available to privately finance recycling facilities.

If the proposed facility is to be owned by a private party, then the capital financing would be obtained through either a combination of an equity capital contribution by a private party and the issuance of tax-exempt private activity bonds, or total private equity for less capital-intensive facilities. With a combination of private capital equity and private activity bonds, the equity capital contribution must be structured in order for the private party to be recognized by the U.S. Internal Revenue Service (IRS) as the facility owner, and thus be eligible for the tax benefits associated with facility ownership.

IDBs are tax-exempt bonds issued by a public agency on behalf of a private party proposing a project with a public benefit, such as economic revitalization or increased employment opportunities. Actions by the United States Congress in revising federal tax laws have put a cap on the annual issuance of IDBs in each state as well as other restrictions. The availability of funds and the methodology for allocating funds to projects varies in each state but represents a significant potential source of funding for recycling facilities.

Ownership Alternatives

In most cases, the financing and ownership choices must be made in tandem. Thus, with municipal G.O. bonds or municipal revenue bonds, the governmental sponsor will own the facility, and with the use of private equity capital and IDBs, a private entity will own the facility. This does not mean that the selection of the source of capital funds should precede the decision as to whether a public- or private-sector party should own the desired facility. In fact, both of these basic issues should be discussed separately but decided upon simultaneously.

Public Ownership. Public ownership of the facilities gives the governmental sponsor maximum control over providing solid waste disposal for its citizens. However, the governmental sponsor must also assume certain additional risks associated with ownership. Capital financing would be accomplished through either the sale of G.O. bonds or revenue bonds.

Advantages of Public Ownership

- Public-ownership financing may be less complex, less time consuming, and more assured of implementation than private-ownership financing because there are fewer parties involved.
- Ownership of the facility site will be retained at the end of the bond term. Even if the facility (for example, a materials processing facility) must be totally reconstructed at the end of the bond term, the facility site is a valuable resource.
- The governmental sponsor will benefit from the economic usefulness (residual value) of the facility at the end of the bond term.
- The governmental sponsor will enjoy more control over the operation of the facility and ongoing flexibility in implementing its recycling program.

Disadvantages of Public Ownership

- Certain additional financial risks accrue to the governmental sponsor, including equipment serviceability at the end of the bond term.

- Any potential cost savings associated with private-owner equity capital contributions cannot be realized.
- The public sector usually must assume a greater risk position.

Private Ownership. If the private ownership option is selected, the governmental sponsor will negotiate with a private party to obtain the services and facilities desired. The governmental sponsor will derive some financial benefit from the equity capital contribution associated with private ownership. In some instances, the private sector may provide all of the capital funding; in others, financing would consist of an equity capital contribution by the private party and the sale of IDBs issued by the governmental sponsor on behalf of the private party.

Under this approach, the governmental sponsor would negotiate with one or more private parties to finance, design, construct, own, and operate the facility. The allocation of risks and responsibilities would be documented in the service contracts governing construction, operation, and ownership. Disposition of the revenues of sales of materials must be included in the contract. The private participant is the owner of the facility and will always own that facility even if IDBs are used to finance it. The facility could be sold after the debt is retired at fair market value.

Advantages of Private Ownership

- The equity capital contributed by the owner will reduce the amount of borrowed capital, which should result in cost savings to the overall recycling program. (This assumes that the equity capital is less costly to rate payers than debt capital.)
- More of the financial and operating risks associated with the facility must be assumed by the private owner.
- There is a greater sense of security where the operator has at risk a sizable investment of its own equity capital (assuming the equity capital is contributed by the contractor).
- Property taxes (or payments in lieu of taxes) will accrue to the local governmental unit.

Disadvantages of Private Ownership

- If IDBs are used to finance the facility, rate payers have, in effect, retired the project debt in part through the tipping fees or other payments; however, unlike a publicly owned project, the rate payers do not own the facility when all debt is retired. To the extent the facility has remaining economic usefulness (residual value), that value may be lost to the community.
- Financing of a facility which is to be privately owned may be more complex, costly, and time consuming than financing a publicly owned facility.
- The financial rewards (net revenues after expenses and debt service) associated with the facility accrue to the private owner.

Procurement Alternatives

Procurement approaches indicate with whom responsibility for design, construction, and operation of the facility will rest. Three procurement approaches are available for publicly owned recycling and materials recovery facilities. These include

- *Classical architect and engineer (A&E) approach:* The public owner hires an engineer to design the facility. The facility is then bid for construction. Operations may be the responsibility of the public owner or another contractor.
- *Turnkey approach:* The public owner hires one firm to take responsibility for both the design and construction of the facility. That firm must meet performance specifications identified by the public owner. Upon meeting those specifications, the owner will take physical control of the facility. The owner or another contractor may operate the facility.
- *Full-service approach:* The public owner selects one firm to design, construct, and operate the facility. That firm must meet performance specifications upon completion of the project and during operation of the project.

In the case of privately owned facilities, the full-service approach is typically used, as all of the project functions will be under the control of the private owner of the facility.

Under the turnkey and full-service approaches, two procurement methodologies may be used. The first is sole-source. Under this approach, the governmental sponsor would simply select a firm to be the developer of the project.

The second approach is the RFQ/RFP approach. Under this approach, firms are invited to submit qualifications to finance, construct, and operate the desired facilities. Following an evaluation, firms deemed qualified are invited to submit technical and business proposals. One firm is then selected on the basis of predetermined qualitative and quantitative criteria.

Sole-source procurement is usually restricted to cases where time constraints are extremely critical and/or those projects which have such special circumstances that only one firm has the ability to meet the project's needs.

The RFQ/RFP approach offers several advantages over sole-source procurement. First, it allows an opportunity to structure the request for proposals to meet the specific project needs and to fully reflect local decisions. Second, through an open, competitive proposal process, the community has the best opportunity to receive proposals which meet its needs and which are priced competitively.

The A&E approach is often used for recycling and materials recovery facilities. This approach allows the public owner to actively participate in the design process, ensuring that community needs and standards are incorporated in the facility. It also provides for price competition, through the bid process, for construction of the facility.

A summary of the responsibility of assignments under each procurement approach is provided in Table 8.1.

INSTITUTIONAL FRAMEWORK AND MANAGEMENT ALTERNATIVES

It is important that a recycling and materials recovery program adopted by a community be acceptable to its citizens, provide for efficient operation, and be established within the framework of legal constraints. The program should be

TABLE 8.1 Design, Construction, and Operation Responsibilities for Various Procurement Approaches

Function	Procurement Approach		
	A&E	Turnkey	Full-service
Design	Consulting engineer or government staff	Vendor	System vendor
Construction	Best-bid contractor or government	Vendor	System vendor
Operation	Public or contractor	Public	System vendor
Ownership	Public	Public	System vendor or third party

backed by sufficient authority to provide adequate funding, site acquisition, and effective operation. It should have the adaptability and flexibility to meet changing conditions, and be structured so that it will have access to state and federal funds. The advantages of local control should be balanced against the economy of large-scale operation to reduce duplicated effort.

The following sections discuss these and other associated issues. It is important to recognize that the institutional and management issues discussed below relate to the program implementation responsibilities of public entities. Communities may, and often do, assign these responsibilities to the private sector. However, the ultimate responsibility for program implementation rests with a governmental entity.

Assignment of Responsibilities

As recycling programs have developed, they have often been undertaken apart from the remainder of a solid waste management system. Also, solid waste system planners have often neglected or underestimated the impacts of the system upon recycling programs. These problems have strongly demonstrated the need for an integrated approach to improving the total solid waste management system. The best approach to the problem is to establish clear and definite assignment of responsibility among involved governmental entities to meet particular local needs and preferences. It is then incumbent upon these governmental entities to assume the assigned responsibilities and to arrange the details of administration, financing, and operation.

The assignment of responsibility includes a determination of the various functions which need to be performed and the jurisdictional levels available.

A solid waste system includes several functional components, including:

• Collection
• Transfer and haul
• Source separation and recycling
• Processing
• Disposal

Solid waste management can be considered as a single function in all its aspects and dealt with accordingly; however, since each of the functional components has its own distinct activities with its own characteristics, it may be more suitable to treat these activities as separate management or jurisdictional functions.

Recycling programs, however, complicate this picture. Depending upon the type of recycling program, it may include elements crossing two or more of the functional components listed above. For example, curbside collection is, in effect, part of the collection system. Composting may be considered solid waste processing. Recycling programs will affect disposal programs and vice versa. Therefore, while each of the functional solid waste components may be managed and implemented by different jurisdictions, there must be coordination between the programs and common goals and objectives. This introduces a sixth component to the system, which is program management.

Another dimension to the problem of assignment of responsibilities is related to the geographic scope of existing governmental jurisdictions, which range from cities and counties at the most local level to multicounty jurisdictions. There are five potential geographic or jurisdictional configurations to which various functional responsibilities may be assigned:

- Cities
- Counties
- Service areas
- Multicounty areas
- Regional planning groups

Cities and counties require no explanation. They are the most local units of government, and citizen access to them is generally easiest. These entities also represent the configuration under which most solid waste responsibilities are currently assigned.

Service areas are defined by an existing solid waste system sharing facilities or other functions. They may comprise groups of counties (and associated cities) when they are sending waste to the same landfill sites.

Regional planning groups refer to existing regional agencies with planning responsibilities over a large regional area. The possibilities for assignment of primary functional responsibilities can be displayed in matrix form as shown in Table 8.2.

In theory, at least, each of the six solid waste management functions can be assigned as the primary responsibility of any of the five geographic levels, thus giving 30 alternative sets for evaluation. However, it is usually possible to reduce the number of alternatives to a handful by making a few straightforward assumptions based upon the existing system and other political considerations.

At this point, two additional matters require comment. While the assignment of functional responsibilities is a major component of the management system, it is not the only one. It helps assure multijurisdictional solutions by arranging the most desirable pattern of intergovernmental responsibility and coordination, but other more detailed management components must be assessed. These other matters include financing, administration, and private versus public operation. The assignments made at this stage, however, determine what level of government bears responsibility for arranging these detailed matters.

Secondly, for each of the five jurisdictional frameworks outlined above, there is a distinct set of legal mechanisms that can be used to carry out the assigned responsibilities. Some legal mechanisms cannot be used at certain geographic lev-

TABLE 8.2 Matrix for Assignment of Primary Functional Responsibilities

Functional area					
Program management					
Collection					
Transfer and haul					
Source separation and recycling					
Processing					
Disposal					
	Cities	Counties	Service areas	Multicounty area	Regional planning group

els or for certain functions. Since the availability of these mechanisms is a defining characteristic of each geographic level, they are presented in this section. The ease with which they may be employed is a factor in the selection of an assignment of responsibilities and is discussed in the next section.

Institutional Mechanisms

There are several kinds of institutional mechanisms which may be considered to manage recycling programs as well as solid waste management systems. The specific powers and legal parameters associated with these vary among the states. However, in general they may be grouped as follows:

- General governmental powers
- Interlocal service agreements
- Agreements for joint activities
- Special-purpose districts
- Public authorities

These mechanisms represent a continuum and, depending upon the specific arrangements associated with each mechanism, they may significantly overlap one another.

General Governmental Power. Each city and county has the authority to undertake solid waste handling and recycling activities as a municipal function within its borders. In some cases, specific charter provisions may place special conditions or limitations on these powers. In all cases, the authority extends to acquisition of property and financing with either general tax revenues or service charges. This mechanism is obviously available where primary functional responsibility is assigned at either the local level or at the county level.

Interlocal Service Agreements. Most states allow any governmental entity to enter into an agreement whereby it undertakes to supply solid waste management services to another unit. An interlocal agreement must be approved by each participating governmental unit. Interlocal service agreements are commonly used between counties and cities for the provision of services. They are flexible and allow a wide range of latitude between governmental units in negotiating them and assigning responsibilities. They can range from relatively simple arrangements to cooperate to detailed "contractual arrangements" between the governmental units.

Usually one governmental unit is designated as the lead agency and assigned primary administrative and control activities. They also may be negotiated to include oversight committees and requirements for review and approvals from all participating units before any action can be taken by the lead agency. Interlocal service agreements provide a good mechanism where it is necessary to administer and manage activities at a level higher than each individual county. However, the total powers under such an agreement cannot exceed the powers of any governmental unit participating in the project. Moreover, the assignment of such powers by an entity only extends as far as included in the agreement.

Agreements for Joint Activities. These agreements are similar to interlocal service assignments. The major difference is that activities are carried out jointly and a joint governing body may be created comprising designated elected officials of participating governmental entities or their appointees or others as specified. Agreements for joint activities may also be used to carry out responsibilities at a service-area level or multicounty level or wherever appropriate. These agreements include the same considerations as described for interlocal service agreements.

Special-Purpose Districts. Counties and cities may create special solid waste collection and disposal districts. Such district operations may be financed through special benefit assessments or *ad valorem* assessments against the properties in the district. The special service district may be an appropriate legal mechanism for carrying out functional responsibilities at a service-area level. Districts would probably have a small role to play unless countywide operation of a solid waste function was impossible to organize for political reasons. The primary benefits of this option are related to funding mechanisms.

Public Authorities. A public authority (sometimes called a public corporation) is generally a corporate instrument of the state, usually created by the state legislature or referendum for the furtherance of self-liquidating public improvements. As creations of the state, such authorities can be formed for a multiplicity of purposes and with a wide range of powers. The ultimate structure of an authority will be determined by the cities and counties and the state legislature. The powers invested in the authority may range only from those necessary to coordinate activities to very strong powers overruling those of individual counties and cities (including the power to tax and to acquire facility sites).

Evaluation Considerations

A number of factors are relevant to selecting a jurisdictional arrangement to handle recycling program functions. Some of these factors are derived from economic and technological characteristics of the physical system. Others have their origin in legal or political aspects of available organizational mechanisms. All of the factors are pertinent to each recycling program function, but they are not of equal importance. Nine factors which must be considered are discussed below.

Economy of Scale.   One of the most important considerations in organizing the management system is the realization of any efficiencies of scale that may be inherent in various techniques of recycling program management. Here, where investigation, dissemination of information, organization of markets, and influencing procurement practices are the major activities, a single entity can be more efficient than parallel activity by several smaller entities. Also, curbside collection and the construction of materials recovery facilities may also be more cost efficient at larger scales.

Duplication of Technical and Administrative Services.   Certain technical and administrative services are always required but, once available, can easily be applied to many activities. Thus, this factor represents a special case of economies of scale.

Local Control.   It is important that the parties who obtain the benefits and incur the costs of various recycling functions be able to influence the decision-making process. Generally speaking, people have more influence in a smaller group, which suggests that more local control can be achieved when functions are assigned at the local level. The need for local control, however, is not the same for all functions. Curbside collection or drop-off centers are highly visible and of keen local concern, whereas remote activities such as a composting operation are more removed and of lesser local concern for most people.

Financing Considerations.   There are two ways in which matters related to financing can affect assignment of functional responsibilities. First, certain financing techniques are not available under some legal mechanisms. These must be evaluated very carefully under any strategy. The second financing consideration relates to constitutional limits on local debt and taxing powers and to municipal credit ratings. Counties and cities are subject to constitutional real estate tax limits. This limits the financial ability of any entity to undertake expensive projects on a regional basis.

Ease of Establishing Appropriate Mechanisms.   One of the most significant factors to consider is whether it will be necessary to create new legal mechanisms in order to implement a given arrangement. Other things being equal, it is more desirable to employ existing governmental units rather than add layers of local jurisdiction to solve the solid waste management problem. By this reasoning, there is an advantage to assigning functions at the county or city level.

In order to place primary responsibility at the service-area level or multi-county level, it is necessary to create new legal mechanisms—either interlocal agreements or an authority.

Management Flexibility.   This factor concerns the extent to which the jurisdictional framework constrains responsible agencies to focus on a narrow range of alternatives. The greater the opportunity to analyze and implement a wide range of choices in operating the system, the greater the management flexibility.

Access to Federal and State Programs.   It is important that any jurisdictional arrangement have access to all potential forms of funding and program assistance.

Given the very limited availability of such programs and funding from such sources, any mechanism which can provide access to these services would be favorable. In fact, given the need to maximize the effectiveness of funding to provide real solutions, the regional programs and organizations have a much better opportunity to obtain funding and program assistance.

Power to Obtain Necessary Facility Sites.   Any jurisdictional organization must be able to obtain sites, including the power to condemn sites. On a local basis, cities and counties have such powers. However, their political ability to exercise such powers for a regional solution is questionable. Therefore, this power should be performed by the highest level of governmental power.

Ability to Adapt.   This factor is closely related to management flexibility and becomes particularly important where consideration is given to assigning functions to a service-area mechanism. If, at some point in the future, developments indicate a change in service areas is appropriate, it is easier for a regionwide agency to adapt to these changes than for a service area or county to make the adjustment.

FUNDING

As a community proceeds with the implementation of a recycling program, a number of important issues must be addressed. One significant issue is the development of a funding mechanism to pay the costs of the program. The financing alternatives discussed previously only address capital financing. Communities will be responsible for paying all system costs, including any debt service charges and annual operating and maintenance (O&M) costs net of revenues from the sale of materials. Even with a private system, this cost will be paid by the community through a service fee.

The method of funding recycling programs directly impacts the recycling program selected for implementation. Program elements such as drop-off centers have much lower costs than elements such as curbside collection or various processing facilities. However, the lower-cost programs generally result in lower recycling rates of a limited number of materials. As program goals to achieve higher recycling and reuse rates increase either by local decision or legislative mandates, the program must become more extensive and the associated costs rise. This in turn requires more funding and greater flexibility in the use of funds.

The remainder of this section discusses the issues associated with funding and the alternative funding mechanisms.

Key Issues

Any community evaluating alternative funding mechanisms must consider a number of issues. For the most part, these issues are interrelated. A decision with respect to one will affect the direction of the decisions on the others. The final selection of a funding alternative, or alternatives, will involve elements of these key issues and compromises which must be made. The key issues which must be considered in the evaluation are as follows:

1. *Funding of existing solid waste systems:* An important consideration is the funding system currently used by a community for collection, disposal, etc. Minimizing changes to a funding system is always easier than changing the system. Conversely, some communities may use the recycling program as a vehicle to change the entire solid waste funding mechanism. Many of the alternative funding mechanisms will affect the existing solid waste system, including the mix of private and public activities. The impacts will include the manner in which private haulers operate, and the rates and level of service to both residential and commercial users. Finally, the community's position with respect to encouraging, promoting, and funding commercial and industrial recycling activities must be considered as these mechanisms may be quite different from those used to fund residential programs.

2. *Avoided costs:* Costs savings to the overall solid waste system are likely to occur as avoided costs of collection, processing, and disposal because of the wastes are diverted by a recycling program. The ability of a management system to accurately measure these costs and credit them to the recycling program can be an important mechanism to provide funding to a recycling program from funding services used to support the solid waste system.

3. *Waste flow control:* The degree to which waste flow control and the level of enforcement associated with it is exercised can be directly impacted by the funding method used. This issue affects the sizing of any recycling facilities, the degree of risk that must be accepted in procurement, operation, and the financing strategy for the overall program.

4. *Flow of funds:* For almost all of the various financing and ownership options available, as well as for many of the operating contract strategies, there will be a requirement to assume the payment of funds on a regular basis. The degree to which the flow of funds to the program can be controlled to assure the availability of funds on a regular, reliable basis will impact the financability and cost structure of the project and the level of risk.

5. Ad valorem *taxes versus user fees:* Each community's position with respect to user fees, *ad valorem* taxes, other taxing mechanisms, or a mix of these must be considered.

6. *Availability of infrastructure:* Several of the funding alternatives available require development of an extensive data base and the commitment of resources to compute and issue bills, receive and account for funds, and provide for enforcement. The extent to which such services can be performed within the existing organizational structures and the cost of implementing such a system must be considered when evaluating funding mechanisms.

Evaluation of Funding Mechanisms

The preceding discussion presented a number of key issues which a community should consider in identifying alternative funding mechanisms. These may limit the number and feasibility of the alternative funding mechanisms available to that community and impact the selection of its recycling program. For a community to further evaluate alternative funding mechanisms, several evaluation criteria are presented as the basis that a community may use for evaluation within the context of its own specific goals and objectives. These criteria are discussed below.

Equity. Equity is a concept basic to all rate making, whether it be for recycling programs or other types of utilities. Perfect equity means that each user of a system pays exactly the full cost of the service provided to that user. Because every customer is somewhat different in terms of participation and contribution to the system, the rate structure should ideally be able to reflect the differences of each customer to provide perfect equity. Perfect equity is never achieved in practice. However, to be considered acceptable, a funding mechanism and rate structure must be generally perceived as equitable by rate makers, the decision-making body, and users.

Effectiveness. An effective funding mechanism or rate structure is one that encourages generators to recycle and/or dispose of their wastes in the manner directed by the governing body. For example, one measure of effectiveness is the extent to which participation in the recycling program is encouraged. The funding mechanism must encourage the use of recycling facilities and not provide incentives for users to bypass the system.

Adequacy. Another criterion is the ability of a given funding mechanism or rate structure to generate adequate revenues to meet all of the financial requirements of the recycling program.

Legality. The extent to which an alternative complies with statutory and case law is an important consideration. Legality is intended to indicate an alternative's ability to successfully withstand legal review and possible challenges.

Administrative Simplicity. This criterion relates to the time, cost, and effort required to implement, collect, and update the rates based upon the selected funding mechanism.

Alternative Funding Mechanisms

Tipping Fees. Tipping fees or gate fees are charges collected from each vehicle passing through the gate of the disposal facility. These fees are revenues collected at the time service is provided based upon the amount of service required in terms of tonnage disposal.

Where tipping fees are currently in use to fund part or all of a solid waste system, many communities and some states have imposed surcharges on the tipping fees or receive a percentage of the receipts with the money specifically earmarked to support recycling programs. This may be done in most areas, whether the facility is privately or publicly owned and operated. The use of differential tipping fees may be used to encourage and promote recycling. An example would be the imposition of a higher tipping fee on waste loads at a landfill containing recyclable materials which have not been recovered.

Tipping fees are usually equitable in funding solid waste system costs as each user pays according to use of the disposal system. As a funding method for recycling programs, however, waste generators are paying for the program although they may not be directly involved. The use of tipping fees is generally easy to implement, but if fees rise too high or if enforcement is low, illegal dumping could result.

User Charges. User charges differ from tipping fees in that they are charged by sending a bill directly to the service customers or to those receiving the benefits from the program. Customers are required to pay for the service in direct proportion to their actual or potential system use.

User charges may be collected in several different ways. A line item for solid waste service may be included on another utility bill or the user charge may be billed separately to each customer. A user charge could also be imposed by a separate line item on the annual tax bill identified specifically as a solid waste fee. Finally, user charges could be collected through private haulers who could directly bill their customers, then remit the receipts to the community. This system would, of course, require all customers to receive such service.

User charges can be a good funding mechanism. The major potential problem with user charges is that rates are based upon averages for a class of generators. Acceptable rates can be readily established for residential customers, but opposition by commercial customers can be a problem. Thus, the process used to establish commercial rates must be perceived as fair and equitable, and effective commercial recycling programs must be in place and/or not interfere with existing commercial recycling.

User charges can also encourage recycling in that the fee will have already been paid and there is little incentive not to participate. However, tipping fees must still be used to some extent in order to regulate disposal and to identify system users. If properly developed, user charges should provide adequate revenues.

User charges are becoming more widespread for all types of utilities including recycling programs due to the desirability of matching costs with benefits received. However, user charges can be difficult to administer, particularly during implementation. Constant supervision and enforcement are required.

Ad Valorem *Taxes*. Recovery of recycling program costs can be accomplished through *ad valorem* taxes. This mechanism is currently used by many communities around the country. A rate could be calculated annually and levied upon properties as part of a community's general revenues or as a separate line item on the tax bill. A significant restriction to their use are the legal limits on *ad valorem* rates.

This method of solid waste system cost recovery is often considered poor on an equity basis. This assertion is made because property values or other bases upon which the taxes may be calculated bear no relationship to the level of recycling activity. *Ad valorem* taxes can be an effective mechanism for solid waste cost recovery. The reason, similar to that for user charges, is that no financial incentive exists to avoid participation in the program.

Special Assessment Districts. Properties receiving a special benefit from some particular improvement or service may be levied a special assessment. Generally such a fee for a recycling program would be a user fee or *ad valorem* tax. The implementation of such a district and its exact form varies greatly from state to state, and there may be very restrictive legal constraints. However, in some areas it provides a mechanism to provide funding and to avoid other restrictions associated with the use of general *ad valorem* taxes. It also allows the fees or taxes to be applied to a limited area rather than, for example, an entire county.

Other Funding Mechanisms

State and Federal Funding Alternatives. A number of states provide funding to local communities for the implementation of recycling programs, including grants for the construction of facilities and/or funds to defray operating costs. Also, as discussed earlier, loan or state bond programs may be available. The state funds used are generated from a number of sources, including general tax funds, sales taxes, special trust accounts, tipping fee surcharges, fees or taxes on specific products and/or materials, and occasionally federal funds. State funds may have significant restrictions that limit their use to specific purposes.

Communities should be monitoring and locating sources of state funding. Such programs are always being developed and modified. Moreover, the level of funding can significantly change from year to year depending upon revenues generated and the general fiscal condition of the state. States providing such funding usually have a lead agency and contact person who can assist communities in identifying the availability of such funds. Local state legislators also can assist.

With respect to federal funding, there are essentially no programs currently being funded to provide monies for recycling program implementation. Occasionally, grants from the United States Environmental Protection Agency (EPA) and the Department of Energy (DOE) are available, usually to demonstrate new technologies. However, as in the past, the federal government may consider instituting a grant program for funding recycling programs in the future.

Private Grants.   In the past and currently, some private companies and industry associations representing manufacturers in glass, paper, plastics, steel, and various consumer products make grants available to communities to assist in implementing recycling programs. These funds are generally used to demonstrate a specific program or technology. Many of them also provide assistance to communities in setting up recycling programs.

Product Taxes and Fees.   Some states have implemented programs to tax or levy fees on the production, use, and sale of various products such as batteries, newsprint, and certain container packaging. The funds generated are used to pay for programs related to these materials and/or become available to communities through state programs. Generally, such funding mechanisms are only available at a state level and extremely rarely as a local community source of funding. Similar programs may, in the future, be imposed by the federal government as a funding source.

Avoided Costs.   As discussed earlier, avoided costs of collection, processing, and disposal are likely to be realized as a result of a recycling program. Often the problem is quantifying these savings. Recycling programs funded and managed apart from the overall solid waste management program may be able to receive reimbursement from the overall management program through its funding sources for documentable savings.

Other Fees or Charges.   Some communities have utilized creative variations on the user charge concept. One category that has been successfully used by a number of communities to fund recycling programs as well as to encourage recycling is based upon the collection system. A community or company will sell special bags to users in which to place their recyclable materials. These bags are then collected as recyclables and the charges for the bags are used to fund the program. They have been particularly successful for the collection of commingled materials and yard waste. Other programs have used differential fees for the collection of recyclable materials versus nonrecycled materials. However, many of these programs are used more for enforcement than as a source of funds.

Impact fees have been used by some localities to recover the cost of providing capacity in utility systems for new customers. They potentially could be used to assist in funding capital facilities. There are many legal restrictions associated with the use of impact fees and they are difficult to implement.

Summary

As discussed above, many methods are available to a community to fund its recycling program. Each method has its own advantages and disadvantages. The correct funding method in any particular community is dependent upon the specific goals and objectives of that community, its recycling program, and its political environment. Recycling is part of an integrated waste management program. Therefore, the existing solid waste system and funding mechanisms will significantly impact the evaluation of funding mechanisms for recycling. However, each community has a number of options to choose from, one or more of which will meet that community's needs.

PROGRAM DEVELOPMENT

The development of a recycling program demands that a number of issues be identified, evaluated, and resolved. One of the major reasons for projects failing to achieve significant recycling rates has been that the community is often unable to identify or resolve critical issues. While any issue may not have seemed critical earlier in the program, it later became of sufficient importance to stop or substantially delay the project.

The selection of an organizational strategy to implement the recycling program and the evaluation of financing and funding options are an integral part of the program development. In fact, these issues may directly impact the feasibility of various recycling components in a specific community. The discussion below contains an outline for the development of a recycling program. The specific requirements will vary in each community. However, an important consideration is to retain as much flexibility as possible throughout the implementation program. Changes in goals and objectives and the experience gained as a result of initial programs will impact the direction at later stages.

Design of the Program

The first step in any recycling program is the design of the program. This step includes the planning, evaluation, and decision making necessary to develop a detailed implementation program. The elements of this step include the following:

- *Governmental requirements:* Determine local and/or state requirements for recycling program that the community must meet.
- *Existing solid waste system:* The existing system, residential and commercial, will impact the direction of any recycling programs and the feasibility and ease of implementation of various programs.
- *Solid waste quantities:* The total solid waste quantities, existing and projected, as well as the composition must be determined leading to a determination of the quantity of various potentially recyclable materials.

- *Materials markets:* A detailed evaluation of material markets must be performed, including local markets such as end users and brokers as well as available national markets. Material quantity and quality constraints should be determined. The price structure for various materials, including past changes and projected future costs, must be evaluated. This should consider transportation costs and other requirements, as necessary. The willingness of a buyer to enter into a contract should be established. This evaluation should look beyond existing markets and consider the potential development of new markets, locally and nationally, for materials such as compost.

- *Alternative recycling methods and programs:* A detailed evaluation of alternative recycling methods and programs must be made specific to a community's needs. The evaluation should include likely recovery rates, material quality and program costs, including all costs and revenues. This analysis should consider commercial programs as well as residential programs.

- *Organization:* Appropriate organizational and management alternatives should be evaluated to identify and assign responsibility for implementing the entire program as well as each element of the program. At this time, the potential for developing regional or multijurisdictional programs should be considered.

- *Financing and funding:* The financing requirements for each alternative should be identified, both short- and long-term, and funding needs determined. Alternative financing and funding programs should be evaluated.

In performing the above evaluations, total programs should be evaluated, considering the following factors:

Level of service

Impact upon existing solid waste system

Siting considerations

Environmental considerations

Flexibility

Comparative costs

Funding

Ability to achieve goals and objectives

Implementability

Goals and Objectives

As the evaluation of alternative recycling programs proceeds, a community must establish a detailed set of goals and objectives. These become the key factors affecting system implementation. Goals and objectives should meet a community's specific needs such as minimizing landfill requirements and being economically efficient. They must also include any local, state, or federal legislative requirements. Both short-term and long-term goals need to be established.

The goals and objectives should specifically identify materials to be recovered, recovery rates, funding, pilot programs, and so on, tied in with specific schedules. It is important that the goals and objectives be measurable so that a community can assess its progress and identify when changes may be necessary.

Once goals and objectives have been established and the design of the program completed, a detailed implementation plan should be prepared. An implementation plan must identify all activities which must be accomplished in order for the program to be successfully implemented. The implementation plan can help assure that these decisions are well-informed and made on a timely basis. The implementation plan must also provide project continuity as personnel, laws and regulations, and other factors change over the time frames required during program development.

The implementation plan must also depict the proper work task sequence so that decision making can occur at the proper times. Also, through inclusion of all the work tasks and properly timed activities, the funding and resource requirements for the implementation activities can be determined and adequate provision made for their availability at the proper time.

Operations Plan Development

A detailed operations plan should be developed prior to recycling program startup. This plan should detail personnel, schedule, pricing, daily operating procedures for each program component, transportation, administration, and public education program.

Steps which should be included are

- *Public education and information:* The public education program should start well before the actual recycling program. Public education is the most important means of ensuring public acceptance and the participation necessary to generate high recovery rates. Public education programs should continue throughout the recycling program operation. A substantial portion of the overall project budget may need to be earmarked for this program element. During this stage, a public education program strategy should be developed
- *Economic analysis:* The financing analysis and funding requirements conducted previously must be developed in detail to reflect the overall program. The financing and funding program must be implemented.
- *Personnel and equipment:* Based upon the organizational structure selected and facilities required and the procurement/operational strategy (i.e., public or private), the appropriate personnel should be hired and put in place. At a minimum, a day-to-day operations program coordinator and appropriate support staff should be hired. At this time, procurement or purchase of necessary equipment should be undertaken.
- *Site selection:* Sites required for any and all facilities required by the plan must be undertaken. Specific criteria that need to be considered include convenience to population centers, accessibility for residential and truck traffic, security, available space, zoning requirements, suitable access roads, and building permits.
- *Evaluate:* It is very important that an ongoing evaluation of the recycling program be included as part of the operations. This should include review not only by staff but by public officials and the general public. As required, changes to the plan should be made based upon this input.
- *Recordkeeping and reporting system:* In order to justify any recycling program from the point of view of solid waste reduction and materials reuse, it is essential to establish a practical, accurate recordkeeping and reporting system of total generated solid wastes and tonnages of various recyclables collected, pro-

cessed, and reused. In many states where mandatory percentages of reduction are legally established, reporting percent recycled compared to total solid waste generated has become the responsibility of municipalities and county governments.

CHAPTER 9

NEED FOR AGGRESSIVE PUBLIC AWARENESS PROGRAMS

Kim Zarillo
President, Scientific Environmental Applications, Inc.
Melbourne Village, Florida

Lynda Long
Director, Corporate and Public Affairs
Waste Management of North America, Inc.,
Southeast Region
Fort Lauderdale, Florida

BACKGROUND

Until recently, industry leaders were unaware of the seriousness of consumer's demand for recycling and recyclable packaging. Slowly they are responding to consumer demand and to the government intervention brought on by the need for alternatives to expensive waste disposal practices.

"Awareness," according to *Webster's New Collegiate Dictionary,* means "having or showing realization, perception, or knowledge." In this chapter we assume there is a need to increase public awareness about recycling. In doing so we discover that to achieve the result, which is participation within recycling programs, we must increase awareness about other interrelated aspects of solid waste management. Furthermore, we perceive awareness as the first and necessary step leading to adoption or rejection of a product or recycling service. If we are to follow through on the steps in between, a need for awareness and achieving participation, we must plan strategy as the marketing professional does.

Well-known innovators Boone and Kurtz[1] fractionate the "consumer adoption process" into five stages:

1. Awareness
2. Interest
3. Evaluation

4. Trial

5. Adoption or rejection

A recycling program's success or failure overwhelmingly depends on the adoption by the entire community.

Naturally, there are other reasons for developing the public's awareness. Encouraging the public to make informed solid waste management decisions helps solid waste managers overcome barriers to program implementation, to mobilize communication networks within the community, to persuade government officials to commit funds for programs, and to emphasize the long-term benefits of improving environmental and public health. Making industry and manufacturing representatives aware of the community's need to recycle and how consumer spending is affected by factors associated with the ability to recycle is extremely important.

If materials are going to be recycled, private-sector firms need to participate in the recycling process. Industry leaders are just beginning to react to consumers' demands for recyclable containers and the need for new channels of distribution. "Backward channels" allow consumers to return recyclable materials to the firm for reuse.

Public-sector managers responsible for the disposal of municipal solid waste (MSW) realize that management expenses in terms of dollars and external pollution control costs will continue to skyrocket. Managers who have entered the public limelight due to the solid waste crisis can choose to see community awareness as an asset in managing solid waste. Without community support, managers are faced with the responsibility for making decisions regarding disposal processes that can lead to increased spending due to lengthy and involved permitting processes.

There is a need for public awareness programs that are capable of uniting constituencies in support of safe and effective MSW management practices. This chapter provides the fundamental elements and reasons why they are required in a recycling awareness program.

PUBLIC AWARENESS PREREQUISITES

If this Handbook had been written just five years ago, one would have had to start from the beginning in a public awareness campaign: by explaining to people what is meant by recycling. But the recent "reawakening" of environmental awareness has swept across our nation and around the planet with meteoric speed. Today, anybody who reads a newspaper, thumbs through a magazine, listens to the radio, or watches TV already has a grasp of what recycling is all about.

This makes the job easier. Rather than starting at the beginning, a public awareness campaign can begin at the middle. The task now is to make the general environmental message specific: to bring recycling home to the community.

While instilling awareness, a program must also be sustaining. More than simply discussing the need to protect the environment, a community must be shown the steps they can take to help. People are ready to do more than talk. People are ready to act.

The real challenge in a public awareness campaign is to map out a systematic plan that involves all segments of the community. The goal is to have the people of the community assume ownership of their recycling program—to put their "stamp" on it. Not everybody can be involved in the marketing of operational aspects of the recycling program. But everyone—from seniors to preschoolers—can help communicate the recycling message. Like the conductor of a symphony, a recycling manager needs to direct and to inspire...and to bring every section of the orchestra in concert with the music.

Assessment of Community's Recycling Awareness

Research can be utilized to assess the level of community awareness and to find the starting point. A wide range of research methods are available, such as opinion surveys, statistics from secondary sources such as the U.S. Census, state statistical abstracts, convenience samples, and focus groups. Results from preresearch are used to establish a baseline of awareness. This becomes the starting point of planning measurable objectives.

It is important to assess the existing community's perception and knowledge. Communities planning to start backyard composting programs in Canada, California, Illinois, and New York have found that awareness levels can range from lack of "knowhow," a need to justify composting, and ecological concerns. Recycling planners needed to know if residents are aware of what backyard composting is and how to compost. There may be technical questions concerning the kind of materials composted and safety issues regarding pesticides and rodents. A California county hired an intern to raise awareness of backyard composting among residents before a pilot project began. A Canadian organization, City Farmer, uses media communication to gauge residents' perceptions about backyard composting. City Farmer spokesperson Michael L. Levenston wants to find out "if residents are willing to get involved with the program and follow directions."

Secondly, objectives should be compatible with operational requirements and identifiable with specific segments of the community. In the above example, City Farmer should measure the knowledge of composting and participation levels. This leads into another aspect of planning, which is to identify the audiences or public awareness segments.

Identifying Public Awareness Audience Segments

Mass Public Awareness versus Targeted Segments. The first public awareness approach includes directing efforts to everyone, whereas the second approach singles out groups based on the variables that define its average member and the recycling problem at hand. In the early 1900s, corporations boasted of having attained national recycling outlets without the aid of advertising. Stuart Ewen writes, "the trade journal *Printer's Ink* argued that these phantom national markets were actually inefficient, unpredictable, and scattered agglomerations of heterogeneous local markets."[2] Philip Kotler divides audiences by individuals, groups, and special publics.[3]

The purpose of identifying audience segments is to plan better recycling strategies with limited resources. Recycling actually may be segmented in an almost unlimited number of ways depending on budget resources. Normally, the recycling audience is divided into a small number of segments to keep data collection and analysis of the number of variables used to identify recycling segments manageable. Special public audiences, like the Audubon Society may be grouped for different reasons, such as winning support of citizen action publics.

Kotler lists four common segmentation variables: geographic, demographic, psychographic, and behavioristic.[3] Each is further broken down into a multitude of other variables, for example, region, age, social class, and attitude toward product. Recycling operation plans normally phase in collection systems one at a time for each part of a community. Segmentation would therefore logically be conditioned by each operational phase and the community to receive the service. For example, curbside (cb) collection is often initiated at single-family residential units. The recycling activity would be segmented into residential units to receive cb service and all other residential units (apartments, condominiums, trailer parks). Then, more research would be needed to learn how and if the segments are different.

Accurate identification of recycling segments, their subsegments, and the variables that they do or do not share will be used later in selecting public awareness strategies. It is the foundation of the communication strategy that is to come later. Determining how to choose a public awareness strategy for the new program is discussed in the next section.

Choosing Public Awareness Strategies

Every segment plays a role in reaching program goals. Managers must remember to choose strategies mindful of the ultimate goal, which is for every segment to participate and remove the greatest amount of material possible from the waste stream. Strategic action plans of successful public awareness recycling programs also act in harmony with program implementation schedules.

Managers may choose from among three strategies: undifferential, concentrated, and differentiated. An undifferentiated strategy aims to please the overall masses, reducing planning and research costs. A concentrated strategy, again, is a method used to save research and development cost because attention is focused on a large share of one or few audiences, whereas the differentiated approach is adopted when several segments are targeted and they are offered a separate service.[4]

Differentiated Public Awareness Strategy

Managers may choose the differentiated approach when there are separate collection systems targeted for segments, such as residential (single- and multifamily), commercial, and institutional. The differentiated method is appropriate if the services for the targeted segments differ, fees are scheduled accordingly, and educational materials are specific to each segment. Information describing the number and kind of containers, bins, buckets, or bags may vary, but the reasons for adopting the service are pretty much universal.

Because the ultimate goal is to achieve participation, more potential recyclers may be reached using a mixture of undifferentiated and differentiated approaches. As previously mentioned, the differentiated approach works best when specific offers of segmented collection systems (services) are paired with commercial and institutional and residential subsegments.

Undifferentiated Public Awareness Strategy

The undifferentiated approach can be useful in raising the baseline of awareness about disposal methods, biodegradability issues, waste reduction, and the recycling loop. In addition, it is a method to put generally misunderstood information about local solid waste problems in perspective by comparing local activities with state and national ones, thereby preparing public segments for future program actions.

In urban and rural communities with one collection system (service), an undifferentiated approach may be favored where services are less specialized for residential and commercial segments. Small rural communities, for example, may use drop-off containers or drop-off centers for recycling and refuse collection. Larger rural communities may have a two-tier collection system based on generator size or number of commercial units in a locale. Still, an undifferentiated method for even larger rural communities may be sufficient to satisfy program goals.

THE PLAN

The success of a recycling program rests as much with effective communications as it does with efficient operations. That is reason enough to take that first step in a public awareness campaign: drawing up a comprehensive plan. The following questions must be addressed:

- What are the goals for the recycling program?
- Who are the target audiences and how can they be reached?
- How much will it cost to involve each segment of the public?
- Who is going to help get the job done?

Defining the Timetable

Drawing up the timetable is not as overwhelming a job as it may seem. The key is to break down the whole into manageable parts. In industry, this is called short-interval scheduling. Set *general* goals for the next five years. From there, set *specific* goals for the next six months. Then do the same for the second six months, and so on. By the time this is finished, the timetable will be broken down into easily managed blocks.

A most valuable tool for establishing a timeline is a set of blank monthly calendars. Fill in target months and weeks, with an eye on a regular calendar. That way, certain segments of the recycling program can be timed to coincide with Earth Day, Arbor Day, Flag Day, and other observances.

Let's assume the recycling program is to begin with all single-family homes in a community. Families will recycle plastic beverage bottles, aluminum cans, newspapers, and clear glass containers. Here's how to start the "blocks" of the timeline.

Defining the Target Audience

Grouping audiences by *common interests* is one way to define them. All students, for example, have something in common: they attend school. All members of a

TABLE 9.1 Sample 5-Year Timeline Plan

General goals	
Year 5	30% recycling rate, all segments of the community.
Year 4	Phase in additional recyclables, all segments: cardboard, green and brown glass, mixed papers, other plastics.
Year 3	All businesses come on line.
Year 2	All multifamily homes come on line.
Year 1	Single-family homes participate at a 75% level.

Specific goals	
First 6 months	Begin collection.
	Initiate public education materials that reach every single-family household. Explain how, what, and when each household recycles.
	Make presentations to homeowner associations and other representative organizations for single-family homes.
	Start general-awareness campaign for community.
Second 6 months	Review any problem areas in collection.
	Do people need to know more about which plastics are acceptable and which are not?
	Plan a community recycling project as part of Earth Day celebration.

civic group share the common interest of their organization. Don't stop there, though. Look at audiences that are defined by *age group* as well.

- Where are the popular meeting places of teenagers?
- What's the best way to reach the seniors in the community?
- Find ways to cross-pollinate age groups.

One example would be a recycling project that joins eldercare centers with daycare centers for young children.

Finding Audience Targets. Look for a common link:

1. *Same interests:* schools, clubs, Chamber of Commerce
2. *Same age:* teenagers, seniors, preschoolers

When Should Audience Get Involved?

Remember that every segment of the community can help communicate the recycling message. The ultimate goal is to include everyone. In the plan, "block" those segments in the same way you did the timeline.

- What segments become involved immediately? One group might be elementary schools.

- Which segments are next or later? The various garden clubs, for example, might be a segment to involve later on in an Arbor Day activity.

BUDGETING

Starting Tips, Then Trimming

As was done with the timeline and the target audiences, block out the budget too. Establish a *separate budget* for each facet of your program. Isolate the costs of producing the educational literature for participants from the cost of holding a kickoff event. Itemize the cost of holding an Arbor Day celebration separately from the cost of running newspaper ads.

First break down the budget into activity segments. Then look for ways to trim. For example, free public service announcements (PSAs) on radio and TV might be as effective as paid advertising in the newspaper. A local community college might produce an information video, thus saving you production costs.

Preparing the Budget Plan

Budgets are formulated from information gathered during the public awareness planning stage. The budget reflects milestones of the operation schedule, as do the action strategies. The public awareness budget is a forecast of expenses to be incurred in the research, planning, coordination, and implementation of a recycling communication program.

The budget for programs should be roughed out for the program's duration, taking care to build in flexibility when forecasting for periods greater than one year. Actual budget dollar amounts for planning and implementation depend on the manager's creative use of available resources. Monthly evaluation reports will help managers adapt to the possible dynamic conditions brought about by changes in operation plans and market conditions. Generally, anticipated budget items are an administrator, other employees, research studies, communication costs, and internal departmental costs.

Programs must be continuously guided; therefore an administrator-manager controls budgeting activities. Managers wearing more than one hat can cost-allocate time to the respective departments, such as in smaller municipalities that direct the public information officer, public works director, or city manager to administer recycling programs. The costs of support services, research, and communication are an important part of the public awareness process. Estimating the costs for hiring a public research firm, graphics artists, printing, and radio sports, is done while future programming is being outlined.

If during the research phase a manager decides to hire a firm to survey audience segments for behavioristic characteristics, the survey may cost from $5000 to $50,000. Price ranges for research projects are a function of the research firm's size and the magnitude of these projects.[5] In-house research may cost the equivalent, if staff salary and overhead are cost-accounted to the project. Municipalities that bring staff in from other departments can count costs based on hourly or daily rate. Otherwise, it is hard to assess the real costs of the program. For instance, if the recycling manager conducts an in-house market survey to determine pre-startup awareness levels and utilizes in-house staff without assigning costs, then it is impossible to compare the costs of hiring an outside firm. It may not only be cheaper to hire a public research firm for research studies, but when specialized expertise is necessary, it may be more accurate.

A draft budget should be reviewed for unnecessary items and to double-check that the planning and the operations plan are synchronized. Research costs and other expenses related to objectives for each of the program elements can be forecasted for the program's duration.[5] After administrative expenses and direct implementation costs are prepared, the draft budget can be partitioned into sections according to each department's cost. Drafts should then be revised, if required, and finalized.

COMMUNICATIONS COMMUNITYWIDE

In a public awareness program, it is important to first reach the whole community with a "broadstroke" outlining the recycling plans in general terms. This may involve brainstorming ideas.

Brainstorming

Using the blank monthly calendar, begin the communications program with a blank sheet of paper. List every idea that comes to mind. Don't think about how much it will cost or how to implement it. That part comes later. For now, the important thing is to exercise those creative muscles. A few guidelines follow to keep brainstorming on course.

1. *Think grassroots:* The goal, remember, is to have the community take ownership of the recycling program. Aim for ways to reach the community that trigger their own grassroots momentum. Research to make sure of key elements in the community.

2. *Connect with your targets:* Get the most mileage from ideas. Match them with the appropriate segment. Creating artforms from recyclable materials, for example, is a better project for schoolchildren than for the Chamber of Commerce. "Link" the two by having the chamber display the creations.

3. *Cover all communications ground:* Explore every avenue of communications in the community, every outlet where people read, see or hear a message. Table 9.2 gives a starter list.

When a community recycles, everyone's a winner. The "prize" is being able to take pride in the community. The reward is knowing one is helping the environment. The recycling program is not a sweepstakes or a lottery or any other kind of contest. If promoted as such, sustained awareness and participation may be lost.

When prizes are gone, so is the interest in the program. Avoid the trap of prizes and contests. Experience has shown that they don't work. The true sales message revolves around intrinsic, rather than extrinsic, values. People recycle because it is the right thing to do.

Mobilizing

A surefire way to transfer ownership of the recycling program to members of the community is to enlist support in communicating the "good green news." Estab-

TABLE 9.2   Public Awareness Communication Checklist: Ways to Get a Message Across

1. Presentations to civic and environmental groups and to schools
2. Exhibits and displays—in malls, offices, museums, at community events
3. Ads—newspaper, television, radio
4. PSAs—newspaper, television, radio
5. Bus-stop advertising and billboards
6. Signage on bus and taxi exteriors
7. Recycling message tape when phone is "on hold"—your office and the Chamber of Commerce
8. Public libraries: community information brochures and fliers
9. Recycling messages printed on employees' pay stubs
10. Recycling messages on grocery store receipts
11. Newsletters: homeowner association, civic and environmental groups, in-house publications of local businesses
12. Decals on store cash registers: "Please help our community recycle"
13. Stickers on storefront and office windows: "We're a recycling community"
14. Recycling projects for scout groups, civic organizations, and schoolchildren. Example: design the community's recycling logo or develop a family of recycling characters
15. Newspaper, radio, television editorials
16. Street signs that announce, "You are in a recycling neighborhood"
17. Regular recycling column in the community newspaper
18. Incentives such as recycled notebooks, pencils, and rulers with an appropriate message

lish volunteer "banks" of individuals and groups that are willing to help convey the message. Target various audiences for source of volunteers. Some examples:

- The chairperson of a civic group
- The president of a corporation
- The environmental class of a local elementary school
- The president of a homeowners' association

Establish an informal, all-volunteer Citizens Advisory Council on Recycling. The council would report on a periodic basis. The council members would be composed of representative segments of the community—from businesses to environmental groups. They become part of the "frontline" communicators, disseminating the message through the ranks. This network will evolve into a speakers' bureau and the backbone of your campaign.

Identifying Communicators

Reliable communicators are the cornerstone of a good public awareness program. Municipal staff cannot do the job alone and informal communication networks will not let them. Increasing awareness to change habits takes more than a brochure in the mail or a television ad. It takes consistent information reinforced throughout structured and nonstructured networks.

Everyone hears information via nonstructured networks, at chance meetings with friends and neighbors and at charity events. A recycling manager should be concerned with the message that is transmitted informally. Informal network channels are influenced by "opinion leaders," people whose product opinions are sought by others. Boone and Kurtz (1986) contend that "opinion leaders are likely to purchase a new product before others do and to serve as information sources for others in a group."[1] Recycling can find readily identifiable opinion leaders in all segments of the population. They should know if the correct information about the recycling program is being transmitted.

Schools Help to Germinate Public Awareness

Schools and other institutions with opinion leaders are sources to disseminate recycling public awareness information. Realizing the importance of public education, state governments with mandated recycling programs have had solid waste curriculum developed to teach public school students about waste management alternatives. Schools can be great locations for releasing new information quickly. Information is disseminated to family members by the children who are being taught in school. Schools serve as a hot-house for continuously improving the community's knowledge level. Some schools start on-campus recycling programs after becoming aware of the environmental issues.

In time, each segment can be reached by informing opinion leaders, educators, community groups, and audience segments. Recycling managers should seek out communicators who are willing to participate on municipal recycling committees, speakers' bureaus, task forces, and advisory groups. Recycling professionals and consultants may be hired to plan and implement an awareness campaign for training communicators, organizing working committees, designing brochures, newsletters, etc.

Training the Trainers

The role of volunteers is to acquaint other members of the community with the recycling program. It is the recycling manager's role to train the volunteers and direct their efforts. It's worth taking (making) the time. A well-trained corps of volunteers can infuse your program with a high level of enthusiasm and energy. Also, these volunteers will assist in getting the message to everyone. Use their expertise on how best to involve people they are familiar with. They will open doors that would otherwise be locked shut.

Communicating with the Participants

Communicating occurs when information is transmitted from one individual to another. Communication is usually a function of public relations managers who play a prominent role in America's economy. Recycling managers need to become PR people and effectively employ public awareness communication tools to foster an understanding of the recycling program goals. Managers establish the means of communication, listen to participants, identify communicators, and time communications with the operational initiatives.

Media Outlets for Public Awareness. The means of communication can be elaborate television commercials, flyers, and mass media events. Financial accountability is extremely important, especially during recessions when revenues fall short of expected estimates and cutbacks are inevitable. "Trash for cash" campaigns used by private industry to collect aluminum and sometimes glass beverage containers taught the public what is now an outdated notion that recycling pays for itself. Expressions on this belief can become more prevalent when residents receive a bill for the collection of recyclables. As a result, managers must be prepared to justify program costs as a service fee to accentuate the positive benefits of recycling and the complexities of the recycling market.

A communications program for participants is one of the most critical elements of a public awareness campaign. It's those "fine lines"...with a very sharp point. One might have the best-designed truck, the most efficiently laid out collection route, and the most convenient-to-use containers available. But if the people who are to fill those containers don't clearly understand what to recycle, containers could come up empty on collection day.

Designing Educational Literature. In designing the educational literature for your participants, think like a reporter. Begin where all good journalists do, by answering the five W's and the H: who, what, when, where, why, and how. Figures 9.1 to 9.6 illustrate some examples of educational literature about recycling.

Once a week, everyday items like these need special treatment

Melbourne recycles

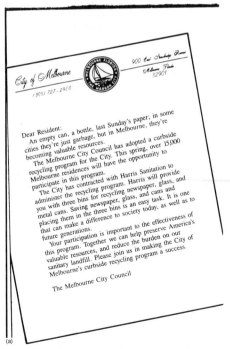

FIGURE 9.1 Total public awareness package, City of Melbourne, Florida. The comprehensive communications program featured: (*a*) A direct-mail announcement that included a letter from the Mayor. (*Courtesy of Waste Management of North America Inc., Southeast Region—Recycle America*)

Renewed savings for our future . . .
Melbourne recycles
Save this card for handy reference

Here's all you do

Separate your recyclable materials
into the three bins that Harris
Sanitation will deliver to your door
soon.

--- **Newspapers only**

--- **Glass bottles & jars**

--- **Beverage & food cans**

Convenient curbside collection
- Once-a-week pickup
- On your recycling day, set your filled bins at
the curb by **6:00 a.m.**

Questions? Call **984-8929**

Recycle America is a program of
Harris Sanitation

 A Waste Management Company in cooperation with City of Melbourne

(b)

Figure 9.1 (*Continued*) Total public awareness package,
City of Melbourne, Florida. The comprehensive communications program featured: (*b*) A doorhanger. (*Courtesy of Waste
Management of North America Inc., Southeast Region—Recycle America*)

Who. Basic as it may sound, are the participants identified? Needed is an accurate, current list of all street addresses in the targeted zones. Depending on the
complexity of the collection schedule, Zip Code sorting may be necessary.

What. Every piece of literature sent to participants should include the program's "vital statistics":

1. Specific materials to recycle (clear glass only? plastic beverage bottles only?)
2. Any preparations required (crush cans? remove caps from bottles?)
3. Location of recycling containers (take to the curb? to a centrally placed
   receptacle?)
4. When to recycle (weekly, biweekly, day of week, time of day?)

(c)

FIGURE 9-1 (*Continued*) Total public awareness package, City of Melbourne, Florida. The comprehensive communications program featured: (c) a pamphlet. (*Courtesy of Waste Management of North America Inc., Southeast Region—Recycle America*)

5. When to begin (date of first collection?)

When. Try to communicate with each household *at least twice; three times* if budget and time allow. *Stagger* your announcements. Example: Deliver the first communication four weeks before the start of collection, the second two weeks before, the third one week before.

Where. The best line of communication with your participants is a direct one: *direct mail and direct delivery.* Send announcements through the mail. Hang notices on doorknobs. Put reminders in bins (for curbside programs) or post them in common areas (for multifamily-home programs).

Renewed savings for our future . . . Melbourne recycles

Recycle America is a program of Harris Sanitation

A Waste Management Company in cooperation with City of Melbourne

(d)

(e)

FIGURE 9.1 (*Continued*) Total public awareness package, City of Melbourne, Florida. The comprehensive communications program featured: (*d*) a "how-to" guide. These last two were delivered with the recycling bins. (*e*) a self-adhesive sticker that residents placed on the bins. The sticker reminds them of their weekly recycling day. (*Courtesy of Waste Management of North America Inc., Southeast Region—Recycle America*)

FIGURE 9.2 "Leave-behind" card for items not picked up, City of Winter Park, Florida. This leave-behind card serves as an ongoing reminder to residents of what they can recycle. Collectors put the card in the recycling bin whenever they must leave behind unacceptable items. Note how the wording takes a negative situation and puts it in a positive tone. (*Courtesy of Waste Management of North America Inc., Southeast Region—Recycle America*)

Why. Evaluate every piece of literature delivered to participants. Can it be modified to save costs without diminishing the impact of the piece?

Example: In a direct-mail campaign, a self-mailer could be as effective as materials placed in an envelope; as effective—and cheaper.

Example: Is a plastic litterbag needed to hold the instructional materials delivered with the bins? The bins themselves are a handy holder.

How. Phrasing instructions is as important as what is said. Use *simple words and a positive tone.* Please don't write in negatives. Avoid saying "no" whenever possible. Include a "thank you" at the end of every message and be sure to include a phone number for participants to call if they have questions.

Incentives and Disincentives

There are dos and don'ts to follow when incorporating incentives into recycling programs. Since recycling is perceived as an environmental benefit, incentives should be tied to positive environmental topics to motivate participants. Environmentally related activities include: tree planting in parks on Arbor Day, giveaways manufactured with recycled material, recycled notebook paper, plastic park benches, and memberships in environmental organizations and local natural history and science museums. Publicize the tangible results of participation, such as the number of trees saved as bonus of newsprint recycling.

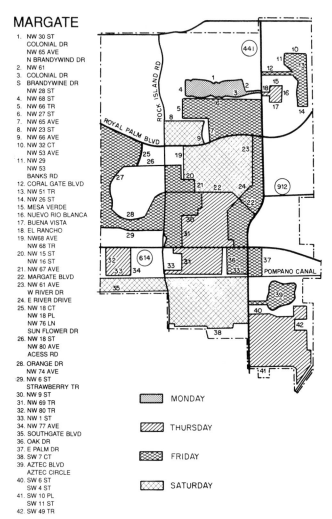

MARGATE

1. NW 30 ST
   COLONIAL DR
   NW 65 AVE
   N BRANDYWIND DR
2. NW 61
3. COLONIAL DR
   S BRANDYWINE DR
   NW 28 ST
4. NW 68 ST
5. NW 66 TR
6. NW 27 ST
7. NW 65 AVE
8. NW 23 ST
9. NW 66 AVE
10. NW 32 CT
    NW 53 AVE
11. NW 29
    NW 53
    BANKS RD
12. CORAL GATE BLVD
13. NW 51 TR
14. NW 26 ST
15. MESA VERDE
16. NUEVO RIO BLANCA
17. BUENA VISTA
18. EL RANCHO
19. NW68 AVE
    NW 68 TR
20. NW 15 ST
    NW 16 ST
21. NW 67 AVE
22. MARGATE BLVD
23. NW 61 AVE
    W RIVER DR
24. E RIVER DRIVE
25. NW 18 CT
    NW 18 PL
    NW 76 LN
    SUN FLOWER DR
26. NW 18 ST
    NW 80 AVE
    ACESS RD
28. ORANGE DR
    NW 74 AVE
29. NW 6 ST
    STRAWBERRY TR
30. NW 9 ST
31. NW 69 TR
32. NW 80 TR
33. NW 1 ST
34. NW 77 AVE
35. SOUTHGATE BLVD
36. OAK DR
37. E PALM DR
38. SW 7 CT
39. AZTEC BLVD
    AZTEC CIRCLE
40. SW 6 ST
    SW 4 ST
41. SW 10 PL
    SW 11 ST
42. SW 49 TR

MONDAY

THURSDAY

FRIDAY

SATURDAY

FIGURE 9.3   Recycling pickup days. Margate, Florida, residents received a newspaper with a city map showing pickup days of the week. (*Courtesy of Waste Management of North America Inc., Southeast Region—Recycle America*)

Disincentives can result if one community is confused with another. All communities are not alike. Incentives must be identifiable by the targeted segment. Volusia County, Florida, has a unique audience consisting of vacationers who visit for seasonal events, car and motorcycle races, and college beach weeks. The recycling messages match the segment. They are printed on useful promotional items—windshield screens, sunglass holders, and posters.

There may be large differences between rural and urban communities' perceptions about incentives. Aside from textbook reasons for creating incentives that are identifiable by the segment, costs must be justified. Publicly sponsored programs are

(a)

FIGURE 9.4 City of Cocoa Beach, Florida. With NASA and Cape Canaveral as their neighbor, residents of Cocoa Beach received communications that carried the community's special space program "stamp." The announcement piece was (a) a self-mailer. (*Courtesy of Waste Management of North America Inc., Southeast Region—Recycle America*)

scrutinized for spending funds on promotional items. Budget shortages and economic downturns are causing cutbacks in services and staff. Environmental goods donated to municipalities and donations in combination with municipal funds are acceptable. They convey a message of cooperation among constituents and can stress the practical relationship of government and business working together.

MONITORING PARTICIPATION

As soon as collection begins, establish a baseline for the program. It is vital to know how effective any part of the program is before continuing to the next phase.

- Draw up a *separate baseline* for each segment of the program: curbside, condo, and business.
- Include a *monthly and cumulative total for each segment* on amounts collected.
- Add one more column to this for a *grand total* of *all segments.*
- As much as possible, *isolate results by material*—papers, glass, metals, plastics.
- For curbside programs, monitor *monthly setout rates.* This is how to *estimate participation rates* (what every reporter will want to know).
- Calculate *landfill diversion rate.* Start with landfill tonnage and percentages prerecycling. Then compare with postrecycling figures.

Cocoa Beach has a great new mission

All systems 'go' for recycling
Convenient curbside service starts the week of October 30

- Check the sticker inside your bins for your weekly recycling day.
- Please set your filled bins at the curb by

7:00 a.m.

The right stuff
What to save in your recycling bins

- Glass bottles and jars (tops off, please)

Questions? Call

Harris Sanitation	or City of Cocoa Beach
Recycle America phone line	Public Information Officer
984-8929	**783-4911 (ext. 282)**

- Beverage cans (if you can, crush them first)

Recycle America is a service of Harris Sanitation

A Waste Management Company

in cooperation with the

City of Cocoa Beach

- Newspapers (no other paper, please)

Tip: It helps if you rinse all bottles first.

(b)

Please peel and place on front of Bottle bin

Tuesday
is your day to recycle
Please set your filled bins at the curb by **7 AM.**

The right stuff
- glass bottles
- beverage cans
- newspapers

Thank you!

Recycle America is a service of Harris Sanitation

A Waste Management Company

in cooperation with

City of Cocoa Beach

(c)

FIGURE 9.4 (*Continued*) City of Cocoa Beach, Florida. With NASA and Cape Canaveral as their neighbor, residents of Cocoa Beach received communications that carried the community's special space program "stamp." (*b*) A "how-to" card and (*c*) a sticker were delivered with the bins. (*Courtesy of Waste Management of North America Inc., Southeast Region—Recycle America*)

'Tree-mendous'

You've recycled
enough newspapers
to save 85,338 trees.

Recycling Tally

**Here's how many pounds
you've saved**

Aluminum	229,300
Steel	754,800
Plastic	810,000
Glass	4,478,800
Newspapers	10,039,800
Total	**16,312,700 pounds**
	- or 8,156 tons

*Figures are cumulative, from January 1990
through June 1991.*

Keep 'em coming!

- You can recycle all these:
aluminum and tin (steel) cans,
glass bottles and jars, plastic
beverage bottles (milk, juice,
water, soft drinks), and newspapers.
Place newspapers in a separate
paper bag.

**'Brown bag'
the extras**

- Have more recyclables than will
fit in the bin? Place your extras in
brown paper bags and set next to
your bin. (No plastic bags, please.)

How can we help?

If we can improve your garbage or recycling services, just let us know.
**Call the City's Solid Waste Division at 574-5250 or Recycling Office
at 574-5254. Or call Waste Management at 574-3000.**

FIGURE 9.5 Public awareness newsletter, City of Tallahassee, Florida. One method of on-going communications is the "Encore" newsletter. Mailed to all participating homes, the newsletter provides an outlet for reminding residents of the finer points of recycling—such as putting their newspapers only in paper bags and collection results. Note the "earth term" translation into number of trees saved under "Tree-mendous." (*Courtesy of Waste Management of North America Inc., Southeast Region—Recycle America*)

City of Hollywood
RECYCLING REPORTER
NEWSLETTER

April/May 1991

Update—Mini Drop Off Centers

During January, February and March, we have collected over 108 tons of glass bottles from our mini drop off centers. In these months, the City has saved $4100 in avoided tipping fees. We commend our Hollywood residents for their active support in making this new recycling program successful.

Many residents have suggested expanding the openings of the brown and green glass container to accept larger glass bottles. Our Central Sanitation Garage personnel are in the process of making this modification. The first has been completed and installed at Polk and 17th Avenue. Residents are advised that these containers are strictly for collecting aluminum containers and glass bottles. PLEASE! PLEASE! NO PLASTICS, NEWSPAPERS OR OTHER MATERIALS. Your neighbors are complaining about the unsightly conditions. Don't trash up your neighborhood.

Collection and Recycling Facility Expands Services

At the 56th Avenue Collection and Recycling Facility metals and white goods are being pulled from hardjunk. Also we welcome the participation of Goodwill who have located a new trailer on site to accept: used furniture in good condition, clothing and general equipment. We encourage Hollywood residents to take advantage of these new recycling services.

Score Card—Phone Book Recycling

During the last three weeks of March, Hollywood's Sanitation Division collected over 52 tons of phone books. At that rate, the Hollywood drive will exceed last year's score by 80%. To make this happen, we thank all the Hollywood residents, Hollywood Hills and South Broward High School students and Sanitation Division coordinating staff, Karen Kozakoff.

Stolen Wallet Recycled

During the phone book drive, Sanitation's phone book crew member, Charles Hudson, found a wallet in the collection bin located at Young Circle. It belonged to Paivi Saastamoinen and had been stolen the night before. Cash was gone but credit cards and driver's license were in the wallet. A grateful Paivi Saastamoinen has her wallet back and we thank Charles Hudson for his extra effort.

May is for Magazine Recycling

How many old magazines are laying around your house? Now you can get rid of them at the drop off bins we previously used for phone book collections. This will be a pilot program with bins marked "Magazine Recycling". They will be located at virtually all the same drop-off locations used during the phone book drive. See locations below.

1. Art & Culture Center—1301 S. Ocean Drive
2. Boat Ramp—South Northlake Drive
3. City Hall—2600 Hollywood Blvd.
4. Hardjunk Site—3400 N. 56th Avenue
5. Hardjunk Site—2400 Charleston Street
6. The Quest Center—6401 Charleston Street
7. David Park—Hollywood Blvd.
8. Dowdy Field—Johnson St./22nd Avenue
9. Boggs Field—Thomas/Sheridan and 22nd Avenue
10. Young Circle—Federal Hwy/Hollywood Blvd.
11. Water Plant—Back entrance from 35th Avenue
12. Seminole Park—64th Avenue, north of Charleston St.
13. Washington Park—Pembroke Road/52nd Avenue
14. City Parking—behind Pantry Pride—Van Buren/28th Avenue
15. Montella Park—Hayes/69th Way

Recycling Saving City $16,000/Month

With all our recycling activities (phone books, Christmas trees, glass bottles, aluminum, newspapers, metal & appliances), the City is avoiding approximately $16,000/month of solid waste disposal fees.

Plastics Recycling Planned for June

We have had numerous calls asking us to recycle plastics. Because of the high labor intensive collection operating costs, we have been reluctant to collect plastics. But now we have a plan to keep the operating costs low. Watch for announcements in the June/July Recycling Reporter and in your local newspaper.

PRINTED ON RECYCLED PAPER

FIGURE 9.6 Recycling newsletter insert into utility bill envelope, City of Hollywood, Florida. (*Courtesy of City of Hollywood, Florida.*)

Tracking Trends

A careful monitoring of a program will spot weak points and trends quickly. Establish a few months of activity before drawing any conclusions. For example, if a program that began in October experiences a sharp decline in collection amounts in December, wait to see what January brings. The December holiday season may have found many people away from home.

"Great Job!" The baseline also functions as a communications tool. This is the database for press releases or notices to participants, announcing what a great job people are doing. (Equate collection results to "Earth terms." Translate tons of newspaper collected into, for example, number of trees saved.) Psychologists call this positive reinforcement. We call it a good periodic pat on the back and thank you to participants. It can go a long way.

Case Study: The Frisbee. For a moment, think of a recycling program as a product. Most products follow a predictable life cycle: birth, peak, and, if not checked, decline. The Frisbee is one example. Its popularity crested the first few years on the market. Consumers were captivated by the sheer novelty of it. But as the new became the familiar and the familiar became old hat, the Frisbee's popularity started to wane. That's when Frisbee-throwing contests featuring animals as the catchers started to appear.

Reevaluation and Making a Change

Recycling programs follow a similar life cycle. An initial surge in the program may taper off once participants settle into a routine. That's fine, provided the setout rate and volumes are healthy and remain fairly constant. But if you see figures steadily dropping, that's when to take action. Here's the justification for the aggressive public awareness program.

- It may be that participants are confused over whether they can recycle certain materials. *The remedy:* more specific instructions.
- Perhaps they have forgotten all the materials they can save. *The remedy:* a reminder of everything they can recycle.
- Or it could be that a high turnover in occupancy, especially in apartment complexes, means you now have many "novice" recyclers. *The remedy:* another direct-mail or direct-delivery package.

One way to gauge why participation has declined is to conduct a short sampling survey of area residents by phone or mail. Present it as if it's a customer-service poll. "How can we help?" "What questions do you have?" And of course, include those two magic words: "Thank you."

Listening to Monitor Effectiveness

Managers must also listen. Listening is one of the least practiced skills. How, you might wonder, does a recycling program manager listen to the public? There are numerous ways to assess the public's responses toward a program. An excellent way to learn more about the audience's response is to monitor the products of the program and amounts of materials collected. Does the amount increase, decrease, or stay the same after public awareness activity. Observe the amount of material collected by type, i.e., more newspaper than aluminum. Is there a noticeable reduction in the MSW mainstream? Look at data before and after the public awareness communications.

Tracking telephone calls and letters is another means to learn response. Calls, letters, and drop-ins can be monitored. Monitor the number and reasons for calls received. Calls are "points of contact." When a citizen comes in contact with a government representative, an opinion is formed of the experience. Market researchers for the service industry are aware of this phenomenon. They have learned how to use points of contact by training every employee to be pleasant, helpful, and courteous toward customers. If, for example, a resident calls to complain that recycling is inconvenient, the recycling manager can view it as an opportunity to learn why someone may not participate. Others may respond the same. There may be reason to modify the program or to present a need for more explanation.

Increasing Participation

To increase participation one must build upon existing awareness levels. The goal is that eventually participants will perceive recycling programs as part of everyday living. At this point communication networks can be activated for special events like changes to a collection system, implementation of new technology, and shifting energy and resources to areas with low participation. Keeping the network of communicators together may require finding some creative incentives and some hard weeks to negotiate differences of opinion.

Participation is probably used as an indicator of a program's success above any other measure. However, the biggest cost may be measuring it. Furthermore, even quantitative methods have gray areas. Correlation versus causation determinations can be weak. Variables include seasonal variation—especially in resort locations. Reasons for participation may change over time, due to type of collection service or the fact that potential participants may not generate materials collected. The methods applied to measure these variables make it impossible to compare programs.

Before and after pictures of the tons of materials collected in a newly started recycling program can be compared with tons of material weights collected over time. Even though the amount of material collected fluctuates seasonally, particularly in communities with part-time residents, its reliability is greater than participation.

PROGRAM COST EFFICIENCY

One way to calculate the price of the program is to divide the cost of all communications materials by the number of participating households (or businesses). This produces the *cost,* but what is the full *value* of the program? In-kind services should be factored in as well.

In-kind Services

In-kind contributions will include any equipment, supplies, staff hours, or other services a company may contribute to your communications program. Ask the companies to provide "pro bono" invoices of their in-kind services. Include these costs in the per-household equation.

Measuring Benefits

Recycling program benefits are best measured over the long term. Three "yard-sticks" to use:

1. *Disposal avoidance cost:* Net savings in disposal fees realized by diverting materials from landfills or waste-to-energy plants.
2. *Revenue from sale of materials:* Whether guaranteed or market-based rates.
3. *Extension or useful life:* Diverting recyclable materials from a landfill, thus "buying time" for the facility by extending its useful life. In the long run, eliminating the need for a new or expanded landfill could save communities millions of dollars.

Costs and Evaluating Effectiveness

Recycling programs need community backing to survive competition with other mandated environmental initiatives that are competing with new services for water and sewer treatment and land use planning. In the November 1989 *Baltimore Magazine*, a former environmental aide to the city's mayor was quoted as saying "The City of Baltimore's duty is not to save the planet, but to save the city taxpayer." Four months later, the Baltimore City Council met to form a joint city and county task force to minimize waste and develop financing options for programs. Approximately one year later the city's first curbside collection began. Baltimore residents turned around their city council's decision not to spend revenues on curbside recycling. The turnaround happened because grassroots groups and individuals established the residents' demand for recycling. Funding for recycling programs can be publicly influenced, but is cost effectiveness an issue and how is it measured?

As a function of the level of educational activities and service, commonly measured recycling program variables are material tonnages collected, set-out rate, participation rates, type and frequency of service. Qualitative and quantitative methods, some experimental, have been applied to measure the effectiveness of recycling programs.

SUMMARY

Public awareness is a lot like recycling. It's dynamic, ever-changing, and constantly evolving. Already, we've come a long way from the days when the hottest thing to include with delivery of the recycling bins was a magnet. Not that magnets are a bad idea. But maybe there's a better way to use them now. They might be more effective, for example, in a follow-up campaign aimed at boosting low participation rates. That's the challenge, and the fun, of public awareness action. Putting a new beat to an old song. Finding a new, creative way to tell the same story.

It's easy to keep the communications program fresh. Just look at the kind of graphics used on television and in the newspapers, the ads that catch the eye in magazines. Then adapt and modify what works. Take a good idea and make it better. Take a proven method, like the wheel...and make it fly.

Aggressive public awareness programs are vital to kickoff recycling activities. When public interest slides, a new creative promotion must stimulate recycling action.

ACKNOWLEDGMENTS

The chapter authors acknowledge Mim Harrison, Consultant to the Regional Director, Corporate and Public Affairs, Waste Management of North America, Inc., and Bonnie Moore, Independent Consultant, Tampa, Florida, for their valuable assistance in the preparation of this chapter.

REFERENCES

1. Louis E. Boone and David L. Kurtz, *Contemporary Marketing*, 5th ed., The Dryden Press, 1986.

2. Stuart Ewen, *Captains of Consciousness: Adversity and the Social Roots of the Consumer Culture.* McGraw-Hill, New York, 1976.

3. Philip Kotler and Gary Armstrong, *Marketing: An Introduction,* Prentice-Hall, Englewood Cliffs, N.J., 1987.

4. Leonard L. Barry and James S. Hensel (eds.), *Marketing and the Social Environment: A readings text.*

5. Sidney C. Sufrin, *Ethnics, Markets and Policy: The Structure of Market Ethnics,* Chartwell-Brat Ltd., Bickley, Bromley, United Kingdom, 1988.

6. H. Frazier Moore and Bertrand R. Canfield, *Public Relations Principles, Cases, and Problems,* 7th ed., Richard D. Irwin, 1977.

7. Jeff Soloman-Hess, "Why Baltimore May Not Be the Last Place in American to Recycle," *Recycling Today,* Municipal Market Edition, Feb. 1991, pp. 50–54, 69.

8. Miriam Foshay and Anne Aithison, "Factors Affecting Yield and Participation in Curbside Recycling Collection Programs." *Resource Recycling,* March 1991, pp. 118–129.

9. Tom Polk, "Market Research for Market Development," *Resource Recycling,* Feb. 1991, pp. 68–71.

10. Lena Israel, "Reasoning Out Recycling Reluctance," *Waste Age,* March 1991, pp. 226–230.

11. Tom Watson, "Marketing Claims: The Wars Over Words," *Resource Recycling,* Feb. 1991, pp. 36–40.

CHAPTER 10
THE PSYCHOLOGY OF RECYCLING

Penny McCornack
President,
The EarthResource Company
Portland, Oregon

BACKGROUND OF RECYCLING BEHAVIOR

Speaking about a plan to reduce the amount of packaging going to landfills by 50 percent, William Rathje, head of the Garbage Project at the University of Arizona in Tucson, said, "I don't think it will happen. We're not dealing with garbage; we're dealing with lifestyle."[1]

Everywhere across the nation, solid waste officials and involved citizens are asking, "How can we increase recycling?" Are they not really asking, "How can we encourage Americans to change their behavior?"

The process of recycling necessarily begins with the individual. Therefore, the individual must have sufficient education and motivation to participate in solving America's waste disposal crisis. It sounds like a simple equation, yet the methods by which to modify attitudes to collectively achieve the desired result remain shrouded in the psychology of human behavior.

The roots of psychology are ancient, yet as a science, psychology emerged just over a century ago. It is generally recognized that psychology often lacks the accuracy and precision of other sciences such as chemistry, physics, or biology. Furthermore, the subject matter of psychology is variable. The behavior and mental processes of subjects change all the time. Available scientific research on the subject of recycling and conservation behavior is scant. Few theories have been comprehensively applied to this aspect of environmental involvement. However, it has been perceived by many that such research could potentially have a profound effect on what is statistically a crisis in the making. How the environment affects behavior has been the focus of most studies. The bulk of research within the emerging discipline of environmental psychology has failed to consider the reciprocal relationship between environment and behavior.

Not only do recycling rates suffer from the lack of useful research, the industry is plagued by underfunding, which in turn impedes technological progress. Increased rates require efficient and cost-effective technology balanced with the participation of household and commercial recyclers, to create a clean and well-sorted waste stream. As with other issues on the global priority list, there are no simple answers or large-scale proven applications that will move our nation forward at a pace of repair which exceeds our current rate of depletion. As with many social trends that emerge over time, it is likely that recycling will increase collectively as a result of community-based influence. Overall national policy and public opinion will be operative in establishing need, while local influence will induce citizens to act.

Although the 1960s inaugurated what is now thought of by many as the environmental movement, the 1970s and 1980s were decades in which vigorous efforts were made to create a more environmentally educated American public. Has this resulted in a significantly more informed and motivated public? An opinion poll published in the August 6, 1990, issue of *Chemical and Engineering News* and performed by Roper Organization of New York, found that the worst solid waste problem is perceived to be disposable diapers; however, these throw-aways account for less than 2 percent of the waste stream.[2] Apparently, the citizens who responded to this survey did not know that one of the most recycle-friendly materials, paper (including paperboard), comprises the largest portion of municipal solid waste at 41 percent, followed by yard wastes at 19.9 percent.[3]

In an interview with environmental specialist Jessica Tuchman Mathews, Ph.D., Bill Moyers spoke of polls which show that Americans do care deeply about the environment. Eighty-one percent are in favor of not allowing toxic waste to be dumped around the country; 74 percent strongly agree that government should be doing more to clean up the environment.[4] While statistics such as these are encouraging, Moyers shares the caution of many in expressing uncertainty about whether such optimism is justified.

Statistical widespread concern can be found in poll after poll, so why do Americans recycle at a rate of only 10 percent?[5] While the gross waste generated in the United States escalated from 88 million tons in 1960 to 158 million tons in 1986, representing a 57 percent increase, the percentage of resources recovered climbed only slightly, from 6.6 to 10.7 percent (Table 10.1).[6]

TABLE 10.1

	1960	1970	1980	1986
Gross waste generated, millions of tons	88	121	143	158
Resources recovered, percent of total	6.6	6.6	9.3	10.7

Psychological literature supports the outcome that what people say about their attitudes toward the environment is not consistent with their actions. One study that exemplifies this involves monitoring whether persons drop or retain a handbill given to them by an experimenter. Of those observed having littered, only 50 percent admitted to having dropped the handbill.[7] Another study involved the observation of college students walking past trash that had been intentionally put in their path. While 94 percent agreed that it should be everyone's responsibility to pick up litter, only 1.4 percent actually picked up the litter.[8]

Introducing the need for recycling and other conservation behaviors has not captured society's interest as did the introduction of advances such as the polio vaccine, the automobile, the television, or the flush toilet. These were perceived as enhancements to the American lifestyle. Although inherently vital to environmental safety and productivity, why are recycling, energy issues, and other conservation behaviors not also perceived as influential factors in augmenting the quality of life in the United States?

The adoption of new ideas in American society is mandatory for increasing recycling and other conservation behaviors. Recycling and solid waste management are relatively new public concerns. Historically, these have not been issues of widespread social importance. Even atrocities such as Hanford have only recently gained considerable attention. In the decades preceding the 1970s, the attention paid to the threats of environmental hazards was minimal. With regard to solid waste, the public simply had their garbage hauled away, burned it, or buried it. Recycling did not exist as a municipal philosophy or practice, and little public attention was paid to local waste management practices. For most, it was a simple matter to dispose of the garbage, utilize the plumbing, and leave anything extraneous to the soil.

Applying a framework for examining behavioral solutions to environmental problems, B. F. Skinner concluded that many environmental problems arise out of conflicts between the positive consequences of short-term behavior and the negative outcomes of long-term behavior.[9] An example of this is the well-known "tragedy of the commons" in which a grassy square was set aside for common use in the center of towns and hamlets, altering the private use of the land once available to inhabitants. Because this encouraged individuals to increase their herds, the cows eventually all died, having exhausted the grazing.[10] In the long run, this was collectively punitive, although the original intent was individually reinforcing.

Closer to home and current issues, one might view the outcome of the oil-dependent lifestyle of Americans as a prime example of conflict resulting from a lack of long-term objectives. Some environmental psychologists argue that without the guidance of a unified policy organized at a system level (e.g., federal and state programs), individuals will continue to practice ineffective conservation behaviors consistent with current policy.

Although the United States has no comprehensive federal-level recycling policy, the implementation of effective community programs is on the rise, and advances are being made at the state level. Chapter 2 in this Handbook speaks to these initiatives.

Globally, there is evidence that world leaders are uniting as a team to collectively address environmental issues that are no longer viewed as nationally segregated concerns. A new sense of shared destiny is emerging. The signing of the international treaty to protect the stratospheric ozone is an example of progressive effort to reduce worldwide environmental degradation.

At a 1988 meeting of the American Psychological Association, *New York Times* science news editor Daniel J. Goleman, Ph.D., presented a lecture entitled "The Psychology of Planetary Concern: Self-Deception and the World Crisis." In explaining why citizens do not alter their lifestyles to preserve rather than destroy their ecology, he cited denial, avoidance, and global indifference to the potential destruction of our planet as commonplace attitudes. At the end of the address, E. Scott Geller, Ph.D., professor of psychology at Virginia Polytechnic Institute and State University, asked Dr. Goleman "Whether it might be wise to define behaviors and contingencies that need to be changed in order to protect and preserve the environment and then set out to intervene for such a change,

instead of contemplating reasons for human denial of environmental problems."[11]

In agreement with Dr. Geller's call for action, this chapter is intended as
an investigation of various bodies of recycling and conservation research, to
explore possibilities that may enhance new approaches in the search to psy-
chologically motivate more people to recycle. If a common goal is assumed—
that recycling rates must increase and that we must first understand how to
contribute to this through greater motivation and commitment on behalf
of American citizens—then it is necessary to approach the psychology of
recycling.

MOTIVES FOR RECYCLING

A nationwide public opinion poll by Maritz AmeriPoll revealed why some people
do not participate in recycling:

- Thirty percent say it takes too much time.
- Nineteen percent ask, "Why should I?"
- Twelve percent say they don't know how to do it.
- Eight percent say it's too messy.
- Another 8 percent say they have no curbside collection provided.
- Twenty-three percent cite other reasons.[12]

A news brief in the November 15, 1990, issue of *Recycling Today* reports that,
"If curbside collection was easier, 91 percent of non-recyclers in Great Britain
would separate recyclables from their trash."

Such summaries are typical of the kind of information frequently printed in the
press and reported in recycling industry publications, yet in what way can this
information be translated to yield an effective result? What does this information
reveal? That recycling needs to be more convenient and cleaner? That curbside
needs to be easier and more widely available? That citizens need to be taught
how to recycle? The answer to these questions may be "yes"; however, a more
important question involves examining what might motivate the public to relin-
quish these considerations which are used as reasons for not recycling. Surveys
indicate that recyclers report experiencing the same inconveniences that
nonrecyclers view as deterrents, yet they recycle anyway.

Motivation, as it relates to recycling and conservation behavior, has been determined to be influenced by numerous components and combinations of components. The range is broad. Listed below are several factors that influence motivation, all of which have an effect on outcome:

- The credibility of a source of information or request
- The context in which information is delivered
- The frequency with which information is delivered
- The relativity of a request for action
- The degree to which an incentive is social or monetary in nature

• The extent to which an individual is already attitudinally disposed to a desired behavior.

Justification

A predominant theme in motivational behavior involves the role of justification. People are motivated to arrive at the conclusions they want to; however, doing so is constrained by their ability to construct seemingly reasonable justifications for their conclusions.[13] Much research in conservation behavior suggests that one of the most important factors underlying conservation behavior is an individual's ability to identify a reasonable justification for such behavior. This is certainly not unique to conservation behavior. The inclusion of justification is pervasive in nearly every act of human behavior; yet, despite the obvious nature of this fundamental supposition, it is often inadequately considered in approaches to influence recycling and conservation behavior.

Universality and Gratification

There is no evidence to indicate that recyclers represent a population segment with unique characteristics. A University of Michigan study which focused on conservation behavior and the structure of satisfaction themes conclude that conservation behavior is potentially satisfying to a broad cross section of a population[14] Although the study included a small number of participants, all of whom had a known interest in conservation, findings revealed universal themes which suggested that those who conserve do not have a special or unique outlook.

Research supports the notion that recyclers possess attitudes and motivations, which when combined with other "favorable conditions," create a difference in behavior. These other conditions include elements such as situational incentives, social norms, accessibility of attitude-appropriate behaviors, and other contingencies. Without these favorable conditions, even people with proconservation attitudes may not engage in conservation behavior.

This is encouraging, for it proposes numerous alternatives within varying clusters of individuals and lifestyles. With regard to approaches based on existing motivation, one cluster may be motivated to conserve resources to save money, while another cluster may be motivated by self-image and the desire to participate in reducing waste. With regard to approaches to modify behaviors, one cluster may be influenced by a particular persuasive communication, while another cluster may be influenced by a considerably altered message and method of delivery.

Consider the different messages that might be designed to encourage recycling for such diverse audiences as MTV viewers and members of a community senior citizen network. These audiences generally respond to significantly different approaches. A musical message delivered by fashionably dressed youth, or a musical icon of the time, encouraging recycling for environmental reasons may appeal to MTV viewers yet have little impact on senior citizens. An appeal to seniors, who often live on limited incomes, might include a message delivered by a senior who is known and respected in the community, encouraging recycling as a means to curb future waste disposal bills.

In his environmental broadcast production "After the Warming," writer and producer James Burke provides a frightening portrayal in a futuristically proposed commercial. Two parents wake their sleeping children, load them gently into a Mercedes, and drive down a dark street devastated with the scars of human disregard and destruction. They arrive at a steaming mountain of waste, a landfill. The children are led out of the car and left standing as the parents drive away. The tag reads, "Don't leave this to the children." While this evocative message would likely have an impact on viewers from a variety of social clusters, it might have the greatest effect on the segment of the population who are parents.

A 1983 study describing a postcampaign analysis of California's "War on Waste" indicates that there may be an advantage in presenting the benefits (of recycling) to the individual rather than emphasizing the benefits to society.[15] This is based on the premise that the extent to which one perceives gratification through a message, to justify time and effort, will determine how much attention is paid to the message.

A look at the $110 billion advertising industry supports this premise. Most ads are built around a conveyance designed to impart one primary perceived outcome: gratification. A car with a high miles-per-gallon (MPG) rating is not touted as contributing to the solution of the global energy crisis. It is advertised with the appeal of saving the consumer money.

Although messages that direct appeal toward the individual are commonly used, and may be thought to provide a more immediate and accessible link to justification, the preference of this notion is not consistently supported by conservation behavior research. Studies suggest that an individual's sense of community involvement can play an important role in motivation. Messages that depict a dual appeal may therefore be extremely effective.

Intrinsic and Extrinsic Motivation

The role of intrinsic and extrinsic motivation has been the basis of numerous environmental behavior studies. Intrinsic motivation might best be described as self-generated desire or reasoning based on any number of personally held justifications. An individual who is intrinsically motivated to recycle may partake in the activity for any number of reasons that do not involve specific external reward conditions such as receiving something tangible in exchange for recycling. Today, many people recycle because they consider it an environmental responsibility.

Extrinsic motivation involves externally induced incentives, such as monetary reward, prizes, "payoffs," and other rewards (which was once thought to have promising potential). The greatest criticism of the use of external incentives, as it relates specifically to recycling, is that once the external incentive is withdrawn, the desired behavior often diminishes significantly or ceases entirely. The use of extrinsic motivation to promote recycling is also not a cost-effective alternative in today's recycled commodities marketplace. If incentives that cost money are to be offered, it is expected that the funding should, at least eventually, be sustainable through the operation of the recycling program.

A 1979 paper recycling project at a Florida trailer park involved a newspaper recycling reward program whereby children delivering collected newspapers were awarded their choice of a toy within a particular price range, based on the amount of paper they gathered.[16] The average weight of newspaper collected per week increased dramatically; however, removal of the "prompt and prize" condition caused the recycling activity to return to previous levels.

A 1986 University of Michigan study investigated the role that intrinsic motivation and satisfaction play in the relatively ordinary conservation behaviors of household recycling and reusing.[17] The study suggests that a factor often overlooked in approaching environmental behavior studies involves satisfaction in terms of goals and rewards derived simply from participation in an ongoing activity.

Questionnaires were distributed that were designed to measure conservation behavior, satisfaction, and motivation. Of 959 surveys distributed, the study's data analysis was based on 263 responses. Findings support the notion that "involvement with a conservation activity can be seen as satisfying in its own right, suggesting that ecologically responsible behavior might be encouraged by helping people to discover that there are intrinsic payoffs (such as satisfactions derived from living by an ecological ethic, saving energy, having a chance to participate, being a member of an affluent society, etc.) associated with such activities. The satisfaction scales that emerged from the survey included frugality, participation, and prosperity. The motivation scales which were developed revealed that monetary reward was not a dominant motive for recycling.

A University of Colorado study points out that some applications of material incentives have been shown to evoke conservation actions that have no inherent relationship to an attitudinal disposition to favor such actions.[18] Energy tax credits demonstrate this point. There is no evidence that participation in such a program is motivated by the intent to make a contribution to resource conservation. It is expected that monetary incentive has been the basis for participation in energy tax credit programs. It is interesting to note here that access to energy-efficient systems does not necessarily result in energy savings. Lifestyle and motivation have been found to override the potential effectiveness of available energy-saving systems.

Seattle, Washington, enjoys a successful recycling program of national acclaim that involves 55 percent of the city's households. A rate incentive is the factor commonly attributed to the program's success. The city charges $18.55 per month for two cans of refuse and $13.55 if residents use only one can and separate their recyclables.[19] This incentive does not appear to represent substantial savings when considered in the context of an overall household budget. Does this savings alone constitute the reason for high motivation to recycle, or are other behavioral components contributing to the success of this program? Answers to these questions require further study.

Public Commitment

Public commitment has been found to be a promising behavioral change technique. This approach is based on the premise that when attitudes are publicly stated, they remain relatively stable and are likely to increase the performance of the behavior consistent with them. The use of public commitment techniques generally has included the employment of persuasive communication followed by a commitment request.

A 1984 study introduced an alternative social psychological approach derived from formulations of the minimal justification principle.[20] Under conditions of modest external pressure, three groups of a newspaper recycling study were

24. Jon Naar, *Design for a Livable Planet,* Harper & Row, New York, 1990, p. 17.
25. Geller, op. cit.
26. Cook and Berrenberg, op. cit.
27. Larson and Massetti-Miller, op. cit.
28. "Pollution: Puffery or Progress?" *Newsweek,* December 28, 1970, pp. 49–51.

CHAPTER 11
PAPERS

Byron L. Friar
Regional Director
Florida Business and Industry Recycling Programs (BIRP)
Lake Worth, Florida

Lisa Max
President, Betterworld, Inc.
Fort Lauderdale, Florida

Paper is approximately 40 percent of our nation's solid waste and 85 percent of postconsumer waste recovered for recycling. We now reclaim nearly 32 percent of the paper produced in the United States.* That recovery rate indicates the importance of recycled paper to the production of paper products in America.

Paper continues to increase in importance to the business and private lives of Americans. Between 1980 and 1990, the use of paper in the United States increased at twice the rate of the gross national product.† Because paper is our most prolific waste material, it presents a formidable solid waste management challenge. Many recycling opportunities are provided, however, by a strong, growing paper-recycling industry (Figs. 11.1 to 11.3).

NEWSPAPER

Newspaper is approximately 10 percent of our total waste stream. The average American home produces 28 lb of newspaper each month. Nationally, we are recovering 35 percent of it. The industry's goal is to reach 52 percent of recovery in 1995. The National Solid Waste Management Association, in its study, "The Future of Newspaper Recycling," projects a 65 percent recovery rate by the year 2000 and that the average American newspaper will have a 40 percent recycled content. The American Newspaper Publishers Association has made a commitment to double the present use of recycled newsprint by 1992. A survey by the equipment manufacturing firm of Black and Clawson revealed that more than half of the 36 North American newsprint producers will add new recycling equipment

---

*American Paper Institute and Franklin Associates, Ltd.
†New York Times News Service, July 13, 1990.

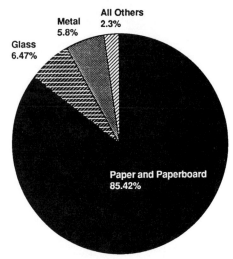

FIGURE 11.1 Paper leads recycling. Percentage (by weight) of postconsumer waste material recovered for recycling. (*Source: Franklin Associates, Ltd., 1986.*)

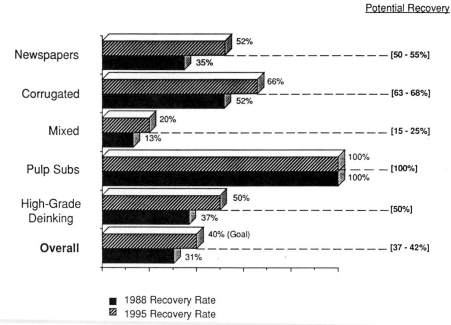

FIGURE 11.2 Potential waste paper recovery rates. (*Source: American Paper Institute and Franklin Associates, Ltd.*)

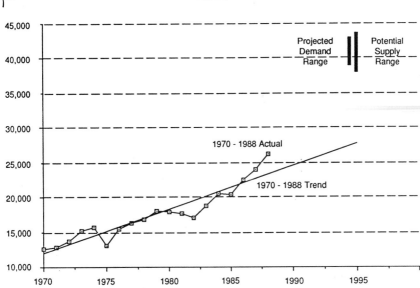

Recovery Trends For All Grades of Waste Paper - 1970 to 1995
(In Thousands of Short Tons)

FIGURE 11.3 Paper recycling: A 40 percent goal. (*Source: American Paper Institute and Franklin Associates, Ltd.*)

in the next three to five years. It is clear from all of this that the newspapers we read will soon have more than the present 14 percent recycled content. The following will explain uses for recovered newspaper other than the manufacture of recycled newsprint. All of these uses will be important in the effort to maximize the recovery of one of our most valuable secondary resources.

Specifications

The Paper Stock Institute's "Guidelines for Paper Stock: PS-90" (commonly shortened to PS-90) describes the four grades of recyclable newspaper. These standards were developed for professionals in the industry. The grades are based on quality and end use potential. The four grades, from lowest to highest quality, are

News (grade 6)

Special news (grade 7)

Special news deink quality (grade 8)

Overissue news (grade 9)

News (grade 6) may contain up to 5 percent of papers other than newspaper and may have prohibitive materials up to 0.5 percent and outthrows up to 2 percent.

Special news (grade 7) may not contain any paper other than newspaper and may not contain more than the normal percentage of rotogravure and colored sections. No prohibitive materials are permitted. As in grade 6, up to 2 percent outthrows are allowed.

Special news deink quality (grade 8) may not contain paper other than newspaper. No prohibitive materials are permitted. Outthrows are limited to 0.25 percent. Rotogravure and colored sections may not exceed the normal percentage.

Overissue news (grade 9) are unused overruns. The requirements are the same as for grade 8 except that no outthrows are permitted. Most often these are recycled by the publishing company, although satellite distribution centers distanced from the main plant might offer the material to local recyclers.

Grades 6 and 7 are used primarily for production of insulation and paperboard as well as in other applications where high quality (absence of contamination) is not of foremost importance.

Grade 8 is used to make newsprint again, as is grade 9. Quality is critical in all phases of the recycling process. This is the grade sellers find provides the most accessible market. This is the grade most new recyclers and nearly all local governments take to market.

PS-90 further requires that grades 7 and 8 be fresh, dry and not sunburned. PS-90 is intended to be a guide. Contract specifications should be negotiated between buyer and seller or they may jointly choose to adhere strictly to PS-90. In either case, it is important that the parties clearly understand what will be required and what penalty will apply if the specifications are not met. Quality control procedures should be implemented to assure adherence to the specifications.

Generation

The three primary means of generation of newspapers for recycling are

Overissue (overruns) at the publisher

County or municipal residential source separation

Commercial recovery

Recycling efforts often include any combination of these as well as individual initiatives.

Newspaper publishers usually recycle overissue paper and send it directly to deinking mills or insulation manufacturers. County and municipal governments generate old newspapers (ONP) for recycling by establishing residential curbside separation and collection programs as well as drop-off sites and occasionally buy-back centers.

Clearly the most popular and effective of these is the curbside program. Curbside recycling is convenient to residents. It gets entire neighborhoods and communities involved in achieving local recycling goals. It permits the recovery of relatively high-quality material because it is available immediately following the residents' use. Curbside recycling facilitates systems for the accurate tracking of effectiveness and participation in specific locations.

Drop-off sites are effective in residential areas predominated by multifamily dwellings. These sites are commonly located near the intersections of well-traveled streets or roads. They may also be placed at individual multifamily structures or complexes and at shopping centers. They are often placed at public works facilities.

Drop-off sites may be staffed or not. They usually consist of containers clearly marked to indicate which material is to be placed in each container. The containers might be barrels, front-end or rear-end load "dumpsters" with 2- to 10-yd^3 capacity or roll-off containers with up to 40-yd^3 capacity. These may be placed and serviced by local public works departments or by contractors.

The overwhelming majority of buy-back centers are private businesses. Some counties and municipalities have found, however, that establishing, sponsoring, and/or otherwise supporting buy-back centers helps to elevate the level of local participation in the overall recycling effort. It takes enthusiastic neighborhood and community support to sustain a public-sponsored buy-back center. The best motive for operating a business is for profit. Local government should not place itself in the position of competing with local business to market the same tons. Government's aim is to see that as much material is removed from the waste stream as possible. A successful government-sponsored buy-back center is one which receives material that would not otherwise have been removed from the waste stream.

For many years, commercial recovery of ONP has been the primary means of meeting newsprint end-user demand without placing unusual strains on deinking mills. These commercial enterprises include paper stock processors and waste disposal firms as well as recycling companies of varying sizes and types. They have been particularly successful in operations involving multifamily dwellings and church, charitable, and civic organizations. Newspaper deinking mills will occasionally operate collection systems, dealing directly with small generators close to the plant or satellite facility. This is done to provide the mill a degree of direct control of the source and flow of supply. In most cases, however, mills contract with the commercial recovery companies for significant tonnages of processed, baled ONP meeting high quality standards. As more state and local governments mandate diversion and recycling of newspaper as a means of solid waste management, commercial recovery companies are increasing their numbers of contracts with local governments to operate curbside and drop-off collection programs.

Although insulation firms and paperboard mills are additional substantial end users of ONP, they usually are not directly involved in promotion of ONP generation. Insulation manufacturers will, however, deal directly with generators.

Separation

To ensure quality and minimize handling and processing, ONP should be separated from all other wastes at or as close as possible to its source of generation. End users will reject entire shipments of ONP where there is any evidence the paper was, at any time, commingled with municipal solid waste. Quality, vector, and odor control measures would be too costly to permit acceptance of paper contaminated in this manner. Care must be taken to keep ONP separate from glass, metal, and plastic containers where multimaterial recycling programs are implemented. Contamination from food or beverage products can render the paper unusable.

Curbside programs allow for proper separation, provided residents have been fully instructed in the preparation of recyclables for setout. Instruction is equally important to maintaining quality in other recycling programs as well. Care must be taken additionally to prevent contamination of the paper during collection, loading, transporting, unloading, processing, and storing.

Collection

The most important goals in the collection process are cost-effectiveness and convenience to the participants. Curbside collection programs can be designed to use the existing refuse collection routes, days, and times. With modifications such as racks or trailers, it is possible to use the same equipment. Where refuse is collected more than one day each week, one of those days is usually designated for setout of recyclables. Curbside is generally the most convenient to residents because it requires the least change in habitual behavior (Fig. 11.4). The provision of curbside collection containers specifically for recyclables is helpful to residents and collection crews. Drop-off collection should be designed so that containers are emptied or exchanged when full but are not allowed to spill over. Adjustment flexibility to allow for seasonal and other volume variables can be built into the system.

FIGURE 11.4   Separate newspaper collection in special hopper on regular garbage truck.

Well-trained and prepared collection-crew members can provide valuable information regarding participation, setout rates, and quality of the materials being set out. Often they can make corrections at the curb, leaving unacceptable items in the container with a printed form which thanks the resident for participating and reminds the participant which items are acceptable.

Processing

The processing facility will provide feedback on quality in general as well as the level of specific contaminants. Most quality problems will involve telephone books, hard- and soft-bound books, magazines, and "junk" mail. The level of contamination will indicate how well the participants have been informed regarding what is acceptable and to what extent collection-crew members are successful in diverting contaminants and reinforcing quality requirements.

Quick vehicle turnaround time at the processing facility is important to the cost-effectiveness of the collection system. Under normal conditions, a processing facility should weigh in, dump, and weigh out any of the collection vehicles in common use today in no more than 15 to 20 minutes.

After the vehicle is weighed in, the paper is tipped onto the floor near the system which conveys it to the baler. Following inspection of the material, the grader will inform the driver of any quality concern. The paper will then be accepted and pushed by earth-moving machines onto the conveyor where sorting crews will remove contaminants as the paper moves toward the baler. The baled paper is warehoused until shipment to the mill.

Marketing

The market for ONP, as with any raw material, is directly related to the demand for the products to be made from it. These products include newsprint with recycled content, insulation materials, paperboard containers for a variety of consumer goods, and certain construction materials. If demand for these products is strong, so will be the demand for the raw material needed to manufacture them.

Recycling, to be successful, must be driven by markets. More precisely, recycling must be driven by demand for the end-use product. This has very important long-range and short-term implications for any entity planning to establish and sustain a recycling system or program. A thorough knowledge of how markets function and constant access to reliable current market information and informed projections are vital to the planning and development of any serious recycling effort. Encouraging and assisting the development of sustained demand for the end-use product should be the responsibility of everyone involved and should be an active part of every recycling agenda. Many state and local governments are introducing legislation and ordinances requiring that newspapers falling within their jurisdictions commit to increasing the use of recycled fiber in their publications. The percentages of increase and the time frames being required are very demanding. This is a direct result of the realization that the demand for recycled newsprint must be increased significantly and soon if ONP recycling is to succeed.

Also needed is expansion of present deinking mills and construction of new mills—new capacity to make the supply-and-demand formula work. All three—supply, demand, and capacity—must be in proper proportion to balance the equation. More capacity is currently under development. Construction of a deinking facility takes two to three years and an average investment of $60 million.

Several excellent trade publications available by subscription can provide education and updates on the markets for ONP. The most prominent of these are *Official Board Markets* or OBM (also called "Yellow Sheet"), *Fibre Market News, Mill Trade Journal, Waste Age/Recycling Times, Recycling Today,* and *Resource Recycling.*

A careful assessment of proximal and distant markets—local recycling companies to foreign mills—should be made prior to making the decision to promote generation of ONP for recycling. In areas where recycling is active and visible, the needed information might be readily available from a number of sources. In other areas, extensive research might be required. In either case, the information is vital to the decision-making process from the beginning. It is possible, at any given time, that market analysis will lead to a decision to limit or postpone a plan to generate ONP for recycling.

It is important to remember also that waste-paper markets are global and cyclical, responding to several economic and political factors. Market experts with decades of experience struggle to anticipate events which impact decisions in these dynamic arenas.

Steps to successful marketing of ONP include:

Acquiring knowledge of the ONP market in general

Researching each accessible individual market

Conducting informal talks with market representatives

Requesting formal proposals

Evaluating proposals

Entering into negotiations

Developing a legally binding agreement

Preparing for implementation

Implementing the provisions of the contract

Monitoring performance

Each step is vital to the process. Informal discussions will provide valuable current information. Formal proposals will normally allow for negotiation. Time is needed between the execution of the agreement and the implementation of its provisions for each party to prepare equipment, staff, and other resources.

It is essential that the parties clearly agree on performance, particularly regarding services to be provided and the required quality of the ONP. Monitoring will help to avoid or quickly resolve any potentially serious difficulty.

Present Newspaper Markets.   Major markets for ONP to be converted to newsprint are Jefferson-Smurfit, Garden State Paper, and Southeast Recycling Corporation, among others. Construction material manufacturers using significant quantities of ONP include U.S. Gypsum and Georgia-Pacific Corporation. The use of ONP in insulation production continues to grow. Paperboard manufacturers will use increasing amounts of ONP.

New Market Developments.   New uses for ONP are in the development stage. Stone Container is using the material on a limited scale as part of its feedstock in the manufacture of corrugated cartons. Experiments are under way which will determine how much ONP can be used for animal bedding, in composting operations, and for chemical reduction to ethanol, to name a few.

Costs and Avoided Costs

Recycling companies, large and small, will always operate with profit as the primary goal. Sound business planning and procedures will achieve that goal. Businesses considering recycling waste seek to offset the costs of recycling with waste-disposal savings and revenue, and, if possible, make a profit. Large businesses often add to bottom lines by recycling their waste. There is little opportunity to do so, however, if ONP is the product. There is simply too little margin for profit for small generators of ONP. Revenue can be derived by volunteer groups such as churches and civic groups where labor and other resources are donated.

Municipal and county governments are the least successful in generating revenue and savings sufficient to recover the costs of their ONP recycling programs. A cost-benefit analysis is a realistic means of evaluating the success of a local government effort. Startup and continuing costs will include

Market research

Promotional activities

Public education programs

Staffing

Equipment

Collection and transportation

Equipment maintenance and fuel

Printing and publishing

Avoided costs and other benefits will include:

Avoided tipping fees

Conserved landfill space

Reduced pollution control and repair costs

Conservation of energy, water, timber, and other resources

Recycling 1 ton of newspaper avoids the tipping fee for 1 ton of refuse and conserves 3.3 yd^3 of landfill space. Recycling 1 ton of paper reduces air pollution by 60 lb, a 74 percent reduction per ton, and reduces water pollution by 35 percent. Recycling 1 ton uses up to 70 percent less energy, 60 percent less water, and conserves 17 trees with an average weight of 500 lb.

Problems and Solutions

Most problems can be avoided by careful planning or minimized by diligent monitoring. Once a program has been implemented, the most common problems involve service by the contractor or municipal department collecting and quality of the material produced by the program. Other problems involve market changes, logistics, and legal or regulatory requirements.

It will take a reasonable amount of time for everyone to react appropriately to the new situation. Continuing education guided by feedback should be very helpful during that period. Following the period of adjustment, problems likely to persist without the introduction of corrective measures and the sources of these problems should become apparent.

Problem: Containers are overflowing before they can be serviced.

Solution: Provide additional containers.

Problem: Containers fill too slowly.

Solution: Reduce the number of containers or relocate them.

Problem: Telephone books and magazines are appearing in ONP loads.

Solution: Positively reinforce, through written and verbal communication to staff and participants, the need to keep these and other contaminants out of the ONP. At collection and delivery points, explain why the items present serious difficulties to newspaper recycling and suggest other means of recycling those items. Positive reinforcement is preferred to minimize alienation and loss of participants.

Problem: Participation is low.

Solution: Reward participation. Distribute numbered tickets. The participant with the lucky number wins a savings bond. Encourage competition between neighborhoods by publicly recognizing outstanding efforts. Award certificates, plaques, and trophies.

Problem: Staff performance does not meet expected standards.

Solution: Reward good performance. Use imagination.

Problem: The vehicles servicing the recycling program are fully loaded after completing half of the routes. Now they must unload at the processing center and return to finish the routes. Following a fire at the processing center during the night, the fire department temporarily closed the facility because of safety concerns. It will remain closed for at least one full day.

Possible solutions: (1) Locate another commercial facility where, at least, scale price is paid and get them to agree to accept deliveries until the processing center reopens. (2) Deliver to the closest facility which will accept the paper, negotiating the best price possible. (3) Deliver the material to a facility operated by a nonprofit group and declare it a contribution. (4) Deliver the paper to a materials recovery facility (MRF) operated by a local government or its contractor. If the facility is owned by the contractor and materials are purchased there, some payment might be expected.

Problem: Equipment available on the market is not suitable for a certain program design.

Solution: Design the equipment desired. Build it or buy available equipment and modify it to suit.

Legal and regulatory problems can be extremely difficult. At some point, statutes, codes, and ordinances must be searched to discover provisions likely to hinder recycling development. Efforts should be made to have the provisions altered or abolished.

Problem: A small municipality believes it will not produce quantities sufficient to attract a secure market.

Solution: Cooperative marketing, joining together with other municipalities or participating in a county program.

Problem: Multifamily involvement is developing too slowly. At the same time, there is a need to become aggressive in promotion of commercial recycling to begin to meet mandated goals.

Solution: Develop an MRF that will service municipalities and commercial recyclers.

CORRUGATED PAPER

Corrugated cardboard cartons, commonly known as "old corrugated containers" (OCC) in the industry, are the largest single source of waste paper for recycling and about 40 percent of all waste paper recycled in the United States (Fig. 11.5). Nationwide, we are recovering half of the cartons produced. Because commercial recovery of OCC is the most practical and productive approach to expanding OCC recycling, the following will focus on that sphere and how local governments can assist and benefit from commercial efforts.

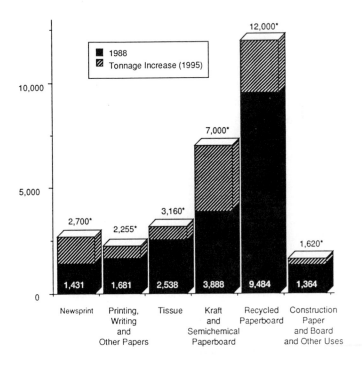

Total Domestic Waste Paper Consumption 1988........................20.4 million tons
Total Projected Domestic Waste Paper Consumption 1995. .....28.7 million tons

*Projected total tonnage figures for 1995

FIGURE 11.5 Domestic waste paper—consumption by end use, in thousands of short tons. (*Source: American Paper Institute and Franklin Associates, Ltd.*)

The future of OCC recycling appears to be very promising. Because of new and expanded uses and new capacity projects scheduled to come on line over the next few years, many industry experts predict a shortfall of the commodity in the marketplace as early as 1993. Efforts are already under way in response to projections. This is providing new awareness and opportunity for potential OCC recycling expansion.

Specifications

PS-90 describes grade (11) corrugated containers as consisting of baled corrugated containers having liners of either test liner, jute, or kraft and limits prohibitive materials to 1 percent and total outthrows to 5 percent.

As in the case of the ONP grades, individual markets develop more precise requirements. There are a number of contaminants which can limit the marketability of OCC. Purchasers will often list the contaminants in proposals as specifically prohibited. These include

Wax- or plastic-coated cartons

Any carton having contained produce, meat, or poultry

Any food, packaged or unpackaged

Any plastic or plastic foam (Styrofoam)

Bottles or bottle carriers

Promotional displays, signs, and advertising material

Dirt, floor sweepings, wood, metal, organic waste

Any kind of tape except kraft paper tape with water-soluble adhesive

Magazines, newspapers, paperbacks, carton paper, foil

Generation

The bulk of OCC readily available for recycling is generated at retail stores marketing groceries and other consumer goods and by the distribution systems supplying those outlets. The corrugated carton continues to be the most efficient container devised for the transportation of goods to market.

Separation

A system to separate corrugated carton waste from all other waste should be devised. Separation should take place where the cartons are unpacked. This will minimize handling and hidden contamination. Storage or staging areas should be designated. The OCC should be protected from contamination until final preparation for marketing.

Collection

Most markets will not collect loose OCC. They will, however, accept loose OCC if delivered. Many hauling firms and waste-disposal companies are beginning to experiment with collection routes for loose OCC. These commercial recyclers use front-end and rear-end load equipment similar to regular refuse collection equipment. The containers are painted in attractive colors and clearly marked

CORRUGATED CARTONS ONLY. This is an excellent option for relatively small generators, if it is available.

Commercial recyclers prefer to collect bales, particularly heavy, "mill-size" bales. Collection of bales is most efficient economically and logistically. A more suitable option, at times, is a compacting unit. Compactors can be placed and serviced from the outside of the building. The attached container, usually 40 yd^3 in capacity, is removed and replaced when full. Roll-off equipment is used. Equipment selection will be guided by market requirements and the needs and limitations of the business. Equipment may be purchased or leased independently or as part of the marketing contract.

Bales are collected locally from small generators. A tractor and flat-bed trailer with a lift truck are the vehicles normally used by the commercial recycling company. Large generators capable of storing truckload quantities of bales can arrange for mill-direct shipment. This allows the generator to shop the market for the best service and price available for individual truck loads.

Processing

Processing at the source of generation simply involves efficient handling and quality control systems. Processing at the market provides the generator with valuable feedback on quality. Information from the processing center or mill will suggest means of producing a product with higher quality, improving its market potential.

Marketing

The dynamics, concepts, and principles discussed in marketing ONP apply to OCC marketing also. OCC is used to manufacture construction material, particularly wallboard. OCC is also used to make the components of new corrugated cartons: linerboard and corrugated medium. Still another end-use product is recycled paperboard.

Turning OCC into new corrugated cartons will be the major areas of advancement in the near future and shows very promising potential for beyond. Until very recently, OCC was not widely used to make the linerboard component of the new carton. It was confined to the corrugated medium. Because the quality of the linerboard now produced from OCC has improved so greatly, its application in the manufacture of new cartons is rapidly expanding. This one application expansion is expected to result in a significant increase in demand for OCC.

Mills purchasing OCC include Union-Camp, Great Southern, Stone Container, and Macon Kraft.

Market conditions favorable to OCC recovery are projected to prevail over the next few years, at least. This will encourage more businesses to become involved. Many business managers are seeking means to reduce overhead. At the same time, they want to respond to increasing customer inquiries regarding environmental responsibility. Additionally, they want to keep pace with the environmental initiatives of competitors. OCC recycling presents an opportunity to address those desires. It is also an open door to local governments to provide encouragement and assistance to potential recyclers in their business communities.

An option that should be considered by counties and municipalities operating solid waste management facilities is front-end separation of OCC at the facility. This can work particularly well where relatively clean material from malls and shopping centers is being tipped by vehicles operated by or contracted to the same entity operating the facility. Separating OCC from regularly collected municipal solid waste requires more sorting and quality controls. Curbside collection of OCC, separated at the source, is another option.

Markets for OCC to be separated and recovered at transfer stations and landfills must be carefully selected prior to a decision to pursue such a program to ensure there will be a firm, long-term commitment to accept the material. These markets will require specific quality control standards. They will not hesitate to reject an entire load of OCC which does not meet contract specifications for quality. Many, if not most, of the end users of this material will be Asian or other foreign mills.

Costs and Avoided Costs

OCC recycling costs mainly involve equipment and transportation expenses. These include baler or compactor purchase or lease; installation of equipment including site preparation; lift truck purchase or lease; baling wire; equipment maintenance; training and employment of equipment operators; and freight charges and other shipping expenses.

Avoided costs and other benefits are generally the same as in ONP recovery. Prices for OCC are generally higher than those for ONP and for significant quantities of high-quality material, they can be considerably higher.

To project amounts of OCC production, consider that 50 to 70 percent of the total waste produced at a retail outlet will be OCC. Retail stores produce about 3 tons of OCC per every $100,000 in sales.

Problems and Solutions

The following may apply to the marketing of any recyclable materials:

Problem: A delivery or shipment has been rejected at the market as "failing to meet contract quality specifications rendering the material unusable for the purpose of the market."

Solution: Inform the market representative that you want to inspect the material. The seller should always inspect a rejected load to ensure it has been correctly identified and that there is sufficient justification for the rejection. Inspection is necessary also to understand precisely the reasons for rejection so that corrective measures can be taken. At the same time, any load being prepared for delivery or shipment should be inspected. Begin immediately retraining personnel to produce quality material. Inspection by the seller at the market also allows the consideration of options for disposition of the material to other markets without the incurring of return shipment costs.

Follow up on corrective measures. Rejections result in lost revenue and increased costs. Every effort necessary to avoid them should be made.

Problem: The market informs you that the carrier transporting a trailer load of material loaded and shipped by your personnel has been fined by the Department of Transportation because the trailer was over the legal weight limit. By contract, you will be back-charged for the fine.

Solution: Request a copy of the citation for your records. Retrain your employees and conduct follow-up inspections to be certain they are complying with instructions. If possible, have the trailers weighed on a public scale before they are released to the carrier.

Problem: Your baler is producing bales weighing 300 lb. Sixty days prior to the end of your contract, your market tells you it will not contract again for bales weighing less than 800 lb. The market will buy the smaller bales from you. It has, however, become too expensive to provide transportation for them.

Possible solutions: Deliver the bales; buy a baler that will produce 800-lb bales; find another market for the 300-lb bales.

OFFICE PAPER

Collection Systems and Marketing.

Office paper recycling programs are relatively simple to devise and operate. Many local governments offer instruction and assistance to businesses and other local governments including literature outlining entire sample programs and marketing advice. Some will provide supplies such as desktop containers, posters, and other promotional materials. Where local government assistance is not available, the same items are offered commercially and by nonprofit associations and industry representatives (Fig. 11.6).

Many recycling firms offer collection of office paper. Most, however, find it

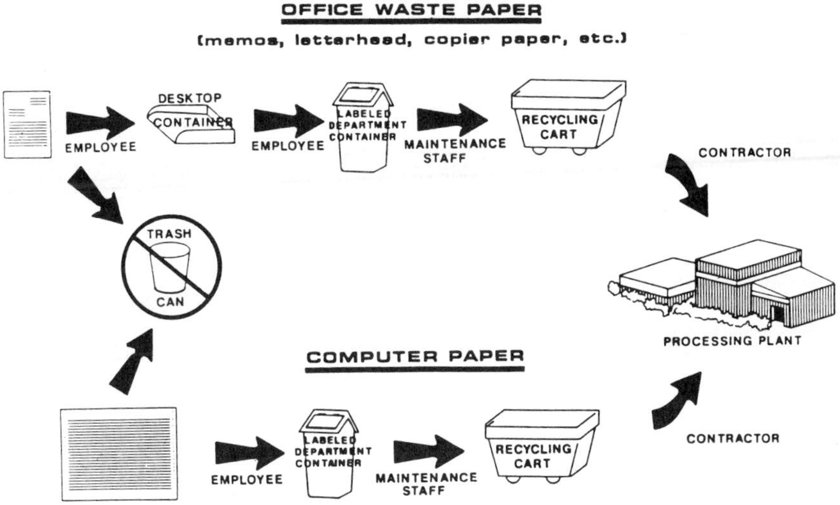

FIGURE 11.6 Office and computer paper recycling flow sheet. (*Source: Florida Business and Industry Recycling Program.*)

unprofitable to collect less than 2400 lb/week from any one account. Most will offer to evaluate office paper recovery potential at a particular business if a cursory examination indicates more than the minimum could be recovered (Fig. 11.7).

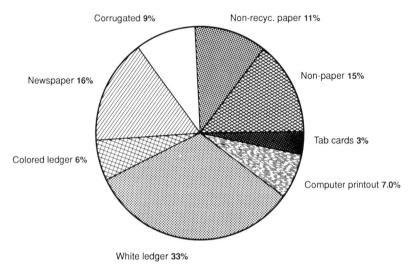

FIGURE 11.7   Composition of solid waste—general office. (*Source: SCS Engineers.*)

There are three basic types of office paper separation systems in wide use today. They are the desktop or deskside system with internal collection containers, the internal collection container system, and the external collection container system fed by internal containers.

The desktop or deskside system with internal collection containers is used most frequently where paper is generated primarily by desk-oriented employees and departments. A desktop tray or box is used to contain paper designated for recycling, while all other desk-generated waste goes into the usual waste receptacle. A box may be placed at the side of the desk instead of on top. Several central containers are placed in high-traffic areas and each is clearly marked to indicate which type of paper is to be placed in that container. The central containers are serviced by the recycling company. Employees are carefully trained to recognize the paper to be recycled and to separate it properly from all other desk waste. They are instructed to empty the desktop or deskside containers into the appropriate central containers as needed or when their duties will take them near the central containers.

The system using only central containers is implemented where paper generation is not desk-oriented, such as in print shops and data processing departments.

External containers fed by internal central containers are used where large volumes of one paper grade or mixed grades will be recovered.

With any of these systems continuing employee education must be a well-planned part of the program. The systems may be combined to meet the needs of very large generators and where paper generation is both desk-oriented and not desk-oriented.

Impact of Office Paper Recycling

The American Paper Institute estimates that as much as 85 percent of an office building's waste stream by weight is high-grade recyclable paper. This means, in essence, that we are throwing away tremendous savings and monies each year. Recovered office paper primarily feeds mills that manufacture tissue, paper towels, and toilet paper; however, the manufacture of recycled bond and printing paper is on the increase. Many domestic paper mills are under construction and/or retrofitting current equipment to handle the influx of secondary materials. In addition, much of the office paper recovered in this country is exported to nations that lack the resources required to make paper. Recovered secondary paper is the second largest item exported out of New York City harbor, and in many western ports ships loaded with waste paper can be found headed for Pacific Rim nations.

Step-by-Step Office Paper Recycling Program

Instituting an office paper recycling program can be a relatively simple task to undertake. The steps involved are easy and flexible enough to allow for many variations. Perhaps the most economical and least-complicated system is one where the materials being separated for recycling are done so at the source. This system is advocated primarily because it involves a change in habit and in mindset. By having to directly handle what we generate as discards, it makes us think. It is this thought process that is key to a successful recycling program. As behavioral changes occur, the spread of office paper recycling is quick and painless.

Step 1: Conduct Office Waste Audit. The first step initially involves conducting a waste audit to determine precisely what materials should be collected in the program (Table 11.1). Usually orchestrated by the chosen waste paper dealer or municipal recycling representative, it requires some degree of expertise. If the building being assessed is multitenant, then utilization of a questionnaire is oftentimes helpful. The information obtained from these tests assists in determining which recycling system is optimal.

Step 2: Create a Practical Collection System. The next step is to create a workable collection system. Since the success of any given office paper recycling program is dependent on employee participation, it is crucial to develop a convenient and simple program. While many people may be enthusiastic about implementing a recycling program at their place of work, this eagerness will soon dissipate if the system introduced is too complicated. Convenience is the lifeblood of a healthy office paper recycling program.

Step 3: Keeping Informed of Improvements. Keeping informed of updates and changes, particularly for the designated recycling coordinators, is equally important for the prosperity of a recycling program. Thus, attendance and participation in scheduled educational and informational seminars is critical. Taking the time

TABLE 11.1   Office Paper Audit

BUSINESS USAGE SURVEY

How much of the following is used in your company's office per month?

1. *White* paper (color of ink is not important), letter paper, envelopes, copy machine paper (No glossy finish)

   _____ pounds

2. Bond quality computer paper (Please attach a small sample of computer paper to this sheet.)

   _____ pounds

3. Computer print out cards

   _____ pounds

4. Brown or manila envelopes or folders

   _____ pounds

5. Newspaper (black & white only, no comics or advertising inserts)

   _____ pounds

6. Corrugated boxes

   _____ pounds

7. Other (Please list different kinds and amounts separately.)

   a. _____   _____ pounds

   b. _____   _____ pounds

   c. _____   _____ pounds

For any questions that you might have just call:
Florida Business and Industry Recycling Program
(407) 678-4200 or 1-800-FLA-BIRP

---

necessary to learn about the recycling program from the onset helps avoid potential problems and pitfalls later on.

Step 4: Management Support.   Soliciting upper management support for office paper recycling is required to properly implement any corporate program. This is particularly relevant when it comes to educating employees about recycling. Oftentimes overlooked, lack of proper training can kill an office paper recycling program later on. High levels of contamination along with a dropoff in enthusiasm results when training is ignored. Thus, be committed to properly educating participants about the when, where, why, and how of office paper recycling. Waste paper dealers and/or municipalities can often assist in this area. Obviously, the best way to encourage and inspire your staff to recycle is by setting a good example yourself. Show management support and provide detailed information on the advantages of recycling and the procedures of the collection method to ensure a successful program.

Step 5: Monitor and Maintain Interest. Finally, promote, monitor, and maintain the program on a constant basis. Be flexible enough to alter the program if necessary, and provide updates through newsletters, memos, meetings, and/or events. Promote and advertise the program's progress to motivate employees and reward those that excel.

Problems and Solutions

Problem: The annual disposal fee for a large 20-story office building in the heart of a bustling U.S. metropolis averages approximately $60,000. This fee is based on a 40-ton refuse container being pulled about two times a week, even with a compactor maximizing space. As a result of new disposal facilities recently incorporated into the region, tipping fees at the local landfill are rising more than 30 percent in the upcoming quarter. The building's management company has allowed for only the previous amount for waste services in its budgetary framework. Low occupancy rates combined with a recessionary economy prohibit an increase in expenditures across the board. Orders have come down from the top, reduce this potential expense or face a possible salary cut throughout your department to cover the additional costs.

Solution: Implementation of a buildingwide office paper recycling program would immediately reduce the amount entering the dumpster, thus necessitating fewer pulls, which translates into less monies required for disposal. Additionally, revenues would be generated from the sale of the recovered materials, which could offset the initial costs required to initiate the program and subsidize any future promotional campaigns. Ultimately, a smaller refuse container would be more than sufficient to handle the reduced solid waste stream, thus corporate objectives will have been achieved and even surpassed with the advent of a less costly method of handling the building's trash flow.

The above scenario depicts only one advantage of establishing an office paper recycling program. Environmental integrity is to many, the true motivation behind initiating office paper recycling; however, a multitude of other positive benefits can be derived.

Financial consequences are often a big impetus in establishing office paper recycling programs. The economics associated with the startup of a recycling program can be offset through savings from circumvention of escalating waste disposal costs and from the revenues from the sale of recycled materials. Most programs realize a complete recapture of startup costs within the first 6 to 12 months of operations.

Computer Printout

Computer printout is the most valuable of the high-grade office papers. It may have colored bars and may be impact or nonimpact (laser) type. Many markets prefer to purchase colored-bar paper. Usually it is green bar. Many markets prefer impact type or not to mix impact and laser. It is important in planning an office paper recycling program to determine precisely what the market requires.

Computer printout is generally considered too valuable to mix with other high-grade papers and should be kept separate and free from contamination. Some manifold white ledger paper may appear to be similar to computer printout. Where there is not absolute certainty, a market expert should be consulted.

White Ledger

White ledger should generally be considered any fine white writing, printing, typing, or copy paper containing no color other than black. The market must always be consulted for precise specifications. Certain qualities of book pages, completely separated from covers and bindings, might be allowed in this grade by certain markets.

Other Office Paper

Colored ledger should generally be considered any fine writing or printing paper containing any color other than black. The ledger grades exclude paper that is treated, coated, padded, or heavily printed.

In banks and insurance companies, computer printout and white ledger average about 30 percent each and colored ledger averages about 5 percent of the total waste (Fig. 11.8). In the general office, computer printout averages 7 percent; white ledger, 33 percent; and colored ledger, 6 percent of total waste. Seventeen percent of bank waste is tabulating cards.*

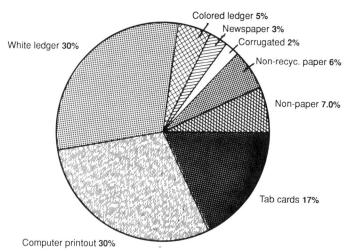

FIGURE 11.8   Composition of office solid waste—bank and insurance companies. (*Source: SCS Engineers.*)

---

*Source: SCS Engineers.

Computer printout, white ledger, and colored ledger are high-grade deinking papers which are used to make tissue and fine writing and printing papers. High-grade office paper is used to produce tissue, napkins, and paper towels more often than it is used to produce more office paper.

Other office grades that are recyclable, depending on market demand, are tabulating cards, file stock, and mixed grades. Banks and similar institutions produce significant quantities of tabulating cards, both manila and colored. File stock should be considered for recycling whenever files are purged. Mixed-grade recycling can be convenient for companies desiring not to incur sorting expense.

OTHER RECYCLABLE PAPER

Book Stock

Hard-bound books are occasionally sought by markets. Prices paid for book stock are relatively low because of the processing expense. Pages of hard-bound books are recovered as ledger, provided the pages meet the specifications for ledger. Soft-bound books may be recycled in certain low-grade mixes.

Telephone Directories

Telephone book marketing is beginning to develop. There are occasional foreign and domestic markets for preconsumer directories. These books are overruns. They have usually been sealed in plastic and palletized or palletized with shrink-wrap. The paper is very clean, just as freshly printed newspaper is. Some domestic insulation manufacturers find the books an acceptable raw material. Asian markets convert the books to paperboard and corrugated paperboard cartons. The limited product potential has been due to problems caused by the dyes and inks in the paper as well as the adhesives in the bindings and the coatings in the covers. Directory publishing companies are now producing what they claim is a "totally recyclable directory." Dyes, inks, adhesives, and coatings formerly used have been replaced by natural substances which are recycling-friendly and less harmful to the environment. It is hoped this will attract more markets for the directories.

Postconsumer directories have, on rare occasions, found markets. Modest programs, recovering 100 to 500 tons during a 2- to 3-month distribution window, have been supported by the publishers. These programs struggle to be cost-effective even with public and private financial assistance. Markets for preconsumer and postconsumer directories will not develop rapidly. There is, however, considerable public pressure to move forward and there is certainly ample potential. Some locations where test programs for postconsumer directories have been conducted include Phoenix, Arizona, and Seminole and Broward counties in Florida. The new materials and processes used in publishing the directories will help to speed the development of markets for both preconsumer and postconsumer generation.

When considering a directory recovery test program, it is important to estimate recovery potential before attempting to secure a market. The best test programs have recovered approximately 25 percent of the directories available in the target areas. Others have recovered about 10 percent. It is best to calculate high and low expectations in terms of tonnage. These are quoted to markets in the market search. The market must agree to accept any tonnages falling within that range. Once the market has been secured, planning for program activities may begin. Planning and development activities could take from 60 to 120 days, not including the distribution below.

Commercial and Industrial Scrap and Specialty Grades

At the same time large commercial and industrial production systems are reducing in-house waste through improvements in production technology, they are increasing their efforts to recycle to reduce costs associated with waste generation in their operations. The recycling industry works closely with these large companies to ensure significant sources of supply of high-quality, preconsumer waste paper. All the proper incentives are present in these relationships to support sustained efforts.

Local government can benefit by a knowledge of the nature and scope of local commercial and industrial recycling. A positive approach to local business and industry, expressing appreciation for waste reduction and recycling programs, and offering to publicly acknowledge them could provide information needed to demonstrate to state officials and the public that substantial waste-reduction programs are ongoing. This can also encourage others to become involved. In general, the most effective role that can be assumed by local government is one of support. At the state and local levels, incentives can be an effective means of promoting the development of new recycling programs as well as stimulating the expansion of existing recovery systems.

The greatest danger to the success of recycling is the inappropriate generation of raw materials. There must be, in place, sufficient end-use demand and conversion capacity to absorb the raw materials. To provide the proper basic incentives to invest tens of millions of dollars in one capacity project, there must be dependable sources of quality raw materials available in appropriate quantities at the same time end-use demand is sufficient to support conversion. The absence of this balance has limited the general availability of recycled paper and kept procurement costs high.

The success of recycling will depend primarily on market development, particularly on stimulating and sustaining growth in end-use demand. The market is made up of consumers. In our businesses and our homes, we are, all together, the market. Just as each of us has participated in creating the solid waste challenge, each of us must contribute to meeting that challenge. Individual purchasing decisions and aggressive procurement policies requiring recycled content in the products we buy will be the keys to successful paper recycling.

APPENDIX   PAPER GRADE DEFINITIONS*

The definitions which follow describe grades as they should be sorted and packed. *Consideration should be given to the fact that paper stock as such is a secondary material produced manually and may not be technically perfect.*

---

*Courtesy of Paper Stock Institute, Institute of Scrap Recycling Industries, Inc., "Guidelines for Paper Stock."

Outthrows

The term "Outthrows" as used throughout this section is defined as "all papers that are so manufactured or treated or are in such a form as to be unsuitable for consumption as the grade specified."

Prohibitive Materials

The term "Prohibitive Materials" as used throughout this section is defined as:

a. Any materials which by their presence in a packing of paper stock, in excess of the amount allowed, will make the packaging unusable as the grade specified.

b. Any materials that may be damaging to equipment.

Note: The maximum quantity of "Outthrows" indicated in connection with the following grade definitions is understood to be the *total* of "Outthrows" and "Prohibitive Materials." A material can be classified as an "Outthrow" in one grade and as a "Prohibitive Material" in another grade. Carbon paper, for instance, is "Unsuitable" in Mixed Paper and is, therefore, classified as an "Outthrow"; whereas it is "Unusable" in White Ledger and in this case classified as a "Prohibitive Material."

(1) Mixed Paper. Consists of a mixture of various qualities of paper not limited as to type of packing or fiber content.

Prohibitive materials may not exceed 2%

Total Outthrows may not exceed 10%

(2) (Grade not currently in use)

(3) Super Mixed Paper. Consists of a baled clean, sorted mixture of various qualities of papers containing less than 10% of groundwood stock, coated or uncoated.

Prohibitive materials may not exceed ½ of 1%

Total Outthrows may not exceed 3%

(4) Boxboard Cuttings. Consists of baled new cuttings of paperboard such as are used in the manufacture of folding paper cartons, set-up boxes and similar boxboard products.

Prohibitive materials may not exceed ½ of 1%

Total Outthrows may not exceed 1%

(5) Mill Wrappers. Consists of baled wrappers used as outside wrappers for rolls, bundles or skids of finished paper.

Prohibitive materials may not exceed ½ of 1%

Total Outthrows may not exceed 3%

(6) News. Consists of baled newspapers containing less than 5% of other papers.

Prohibitive materials may not exceed   ½ of 1%
Total Outthrows may not exceed   2%

(7) Special News. Consists of baled sorted, fresh dry newspapers, not sunburned, free from paper other than news, containing not more than the normal percentage of rotogravure and colored sections.

Prohibitive materials   None permitted
Total Outthrows may not exceed   2%

(8) Special News De-ink Quality. Consists of baled sorted, fresh dry newspapers, not sunburned, free from magazines, white blank, pressroom overissues, and paper other than news, containing not more than the normal percentage of rotogravure and colored sections. This packing must be free from tare.

Prohibitive materials   None permitted
Total Outthrows may not exceed   ¼ of 1%

(9) Over-Issue News. Consists of unused, overrun regular newspapers printed on newsprint, baled or securely tied in bundles, containing not more than the normal percentage of rotogravure and colored sections.

Prohibitive materials   None permitted
Total Outthrows   None permitted

(10) (Grade not currently in use—See Specialty Grade 29-S)

(11) Corrugated Containers. Consists of baled corrugated containers having liners of either test liner, jute or kraft.

Prohibitive materials may not exceed   1%
Total Outthrows may not exceed   5%

(12) (Grade not currently in use)

(13) New Double-Lined Kraft Corrugated Cuttings. Consists of baled corrugated cuttings having liners of either kraft, jute or test liner. Non-soluble adhesives, butt rolls, slabbed or hogged medium, and treated medium or liners are not acceptable in this grade.

Prohibitive materials   None permitted
Total Outthrows may not exceed   2%

(14) (Grade not currently in use)

(15) Used Brown Kraft. Consists of baled brown kraft bags free of objectionable liners or contents.

Prohibitive materials	None permitted
Total Outthrows may not exceed	½ of 1%

(16) Mixed Kraft Cuttings. Consists of baled new brown kraft cuttings, sheets and bag waste free of sewed and stitched paper.

Prohibitive materials	None permitted
Total Outthrows may not exceed	2%

(17) Carrier Stock. Consists of new unbleached kraft cuttings and sheets, wet strength treated, with printed or unprinted clay coating.

Prohibitive materials	None permitted
Total Outthrows may not exceed	2%

(18) New Colored Kraft. Consists of baled new colored kraft cuttings, sheets and bag waste, free of sewed or stitched papers.

Prohibitive materials	None permitted
Total Outthrows may not exceed	1%

(19) Grocery Bag Waste. Consists of baled, new brown kraft bag cuttings, sheets and misprinted bags.

Prohibitive materials	None permitted
Total Outthrows may not exceed	1%

(20) Kraft Multi-Wall Bag Waste. Consists of new brown kraft multi-wall bag waste and sheets, including misprint bags. Stitched or sewed papers are not acceptable in this grade.

Prohibitive materials	None permitted
Total Outthrows may not exceed	1%

(21) New Brown Kraft Envelope Cuttings. Consists of baled new unprinted brown kraft envelope cuttings or sheets.

Prohibitive materials	None permitted
Total Outthrows may not exceed	1%

(22) Mixed Groundwood Shavings. Consists of baled trim of magazines, catalogs and similar printed matter, not limited with respect to groundwood or coated stock, and may contain the bleed of cover and insert stock as well as beater-dyed papers and solid color printing.

Prohibitive materials	None permitted
Total Outthrows may not exceed	2%

(23) (Grade not currently in use)

(24) White Blank News. Consists of baled unprinted cuttings and sheets of white newsprint paper or other papers of white groundwood quality, free of coated stock.

Prohibitive materials   None permitted
Total Outthrows may not exceed   1%

(25) Groundwood Computer Printout. Consists of papers which are used in forms manufactured for use in data processing machines. This grade may contain a reasonable amount of treated papers.

Prohibitive materials   None permitted
Total Outthrows may not exceed   2%

(26) Publication Blanks. Consists of baled unprinted cuttings or sheets of white coated or filled white groundwood content paper.

Prohibitive materials   None permitted
Total Outthrows may not exceed   1%

(27) Flyleaf Shavings. Consists of baled trim of magazines, catalogs and similar printed matter. It may contain the bleed of cover and insert stock to a maximum of 10% of dark colors, and must be made from predominantly bleached chemical fiber. Beater-dyed papers may not exceed 2%. Shavings of novel news or newsprint grades may not be included in this packing.

Prohibitive materials   None permitted
Total Outthrows may not exceed   1%

(28) Coated Soft White Shavings. Consists of baled coated and uncoated shavings and sheets of all white sulphite and sulphate printing papers, free from printing. May contain a small percentage of groundwood.

Prohibitive materials   None permitted
Total Outthrows may not exceed   1%

(29) (Grade not currently in use)

(30) Hard White Shavings. Consists of baled shavings or sheets of all untreated white bond ledger of writing papers. Must be free from printing and groundwood.

Prohibitive materials   None permitted
Total Outthrows may not exceed   ½ of 1%

(31) Hard White Envelope Cuttings. Consists of baled envelope cuttings or sheets of untreated hard white papers free from printing and groundwood.

Prohibitive materials   None permitted
Total Outthrows may not exceed   ½ of 1%

(32) (Grade not currently in use)

(33) New Colored Envelope Cuttings. Consists of baled untreated colored envelope cuttings, shavings or sheets of bleached colored papers, predominantly sulphite or sulphate.

Prohibitive materials   None permitted
Total Outthrows may not exceed   2%

(34) (Grade not currently in use)

(35) Semi Bleached Cuttings. Consists of baled sheets and cuttings of untreated sulphite or sulphate papers such as file folder stock, manila tabulating card trim, untreated milk carton stock, manila tag; and should be free from any printing, wax, greaseproof lamination, adhesives or coatings that are non-soluble.

Prohibitive materials   None permitted
Total Outthrows may not exceed   2%

(36) Colored Tabulating Cards. Consists of printed colored or manila cards, predominantly sulphite or sulphate which have been manufactured for use in tabulating machines. Unbleached kraft cards are not acceptable.

Prohibitive materials   None permitted
Total Outthrows may not exceed   1%

(37) Manila Tabulating Cards. Consists of manila-colored cards, predominantly sulphite or sulphate, which have been manufactured for use in tabulating machines. This grade may contain manila-colored tabulating cards with tinted margins.

Prohibitive materials   None permitted
Total Outthrows may not exceed   1%

(38) Sorted Colored Ledger (postconsumer). Consists of printed or unprinted sheets, shavings, and cuttings of colored or white sulphite or sulphate ledger, bond, writing, and other papers which have a similar fiber and filler content. This grade must be free of treated, coated, padded or heavily printed stock.

Prohibitive materials   ½ of 1%
Total Outthrows may not exceed   2%

(39) Manifold Colored Ledger (preconsumer). Sheets and trim of new (unused by consumer) printed or unprinted colored or white sulphite or sulphate paper used in the manufacturing of manifold forms, continuous forms, data forms, and other printed pieces such as sales literature and catalogs. All stock must be uncoated and free of laser and office paper waste. A percentage of carbonless paper is allowable.

Prohibitive materials   ½ of 1%
Total Outthrows may not exceed   2%

(40) Sorted White Ledger (postconsumer). Consists of printed or unprinted sheets, shavings, guillotined books, quire waste, and cuttings of white sulphite or sulphate ledger bond, writing paper, and all other papers which have a similar fiber and filler content. This grade must be free of treated, coated, padded, or heavily printed stock.

Prohibitive materials	½ of 1%
Total Outthrows may not exceed	2%

(41) Manifold White Ledger (preconsumer). Sheets and trim of new (unused by consumer) printed or unprinted white sulphite or sulphate paper used in the manufacturing of manifold forms, continuous forms, data forms, and other printed pieces such as sales literature and catalogs. All stock must be uncoated and free of laser and office paper waste. A percentage of carbonless paper is allowable.

Prohibitive materials	½ of 1%
Total Outthrows may not exceed	2%

(42) Computer Printout. Consists of white sulphite or sulphate papers in forms manufactured for use in data processing machines. This grade may contain colored stripes and/or impact or non-impact (e.g., laser) computer printing and may contain not more than 5% of groundwood in the packing. All stock must be untreated and uncoated.

Prohibitive materials	None permitted
Total Outthrows may not exceed	2%

(43) Coated Book Stock. Consists of coated bleached sulphite or sulphate papers, printed or unprinted in sheets, shavings, guillotined books or quire waste. A reasonable percentage of papers containing fine groundwood may be included.

Prohibitive materials	None permitted
Total Outthrows may not exceed	2%

(44) Coated Groundwood Sections. Consists of new printed, coated groundwood papers in sheets, sections, shavings or guillotined books. This grade shall not include news quality groundwood papers.

Prohibitive materials	None permitted
Total Outthrows may not exceed	2%

(45) Printed Bleached Sulphate Coatings. Consists of printed bleached sulphate cuttings, free from misprint sheets, printed cartons, wax, greaseproof lamination, gilt, and inks, adhesives or coatings that are non-soluble.

Prohibitive materials	½ of 1%
Total Outthrows may not exceed	2%

(46) Misprint Bleached Sulphate. Consists of misprint sheets and printed cartons of bleached sulphate, free from wax, greaseproof lamination, gilt, and inks, adhesives or coatings that are non-soluble.

Prohibitive materials   1%
Total Outthrows may not exceed   2%

(47) Unprinted Bleached Sulphate. Consists of unprinted bleached sulphate cuttings, sheets or rolls, free from any printing, wax, greaseproof lamination or adhesives or coatings that are non-soluble.

Prohibitive materials   None permitted
Total Outthrows may not exceed   1%

(48) #1 Bleached Cup Stock. Consists of baled, untreated cup cuttings or sheets of coated or uncoated cup base stock. Cuttings with slight bleed may be included. Must be free of wax, poly, and other non-soluble coatings.

Prohibitive materials   None permitted
Total Outthrows may not exceed   ½ of 1%

(49) #2 Printed Bleached Cup Stock. Consists of baled printed formed cups, cup die cuts, and misprint sheets of untreated coated or uncoated cup base stock. Glues must be water soluble. Must be free of wax, poly, and other nonsoluble coatings.

Prohibitive materials   None permitted
Total Outthrows may not exceed   1%

(50) Unprinted Bleached Sulphate Plate Stock. Consists of baled bleached untreated and unprinted plate cuttings and sheets. May contain clay coated and uncoated bleached board.

Prohibitive materials   None permitted
Total Outthrows may not exceed   ½ of 1%

(51) Printed Bleached Sulphate Plate Stock. Consists of baled bleached untreated printed plates and sheets. May contain clay coated and uncoated bleached board. Must be free of nonsoluble ink or coatings.

Prohibitive materials   None permitted
Total Outthrows may not exceed   1%

CHAPTER 12
ALUMINUM CANS

Durene M. Buckholz
Solid Waste Administrator
Malcolm Pirnie, Inc.
White Plains, New York

GENERAL INTRODUCTION

Sources, Amounts, and Types of Aluminum Products

To determine the potential sources, amounts, and types of aluminum products, and to confirm that aluminum cans are one of the most feasible items to recover for recycling purposes, two factors must first be examined: aluminum consumption by market sector and product durability. Figure 12.1 shows consumption percentages for the major aluminum market sectors: cans and packaging, transportation, construction, exports, electrical, consumer durables, machinery and equipment, and other minor sectors. The packaging industry utilizes 27 percent of total aluminum production, making it the largest market for raw aluminum. The transportation industry follows with a consumption of 19 percent. The construction industry consumes 16 percent, 13 percent is exported, and 9 percent of total production is used for electrical purposes. Consumer durables utilize 7 per-

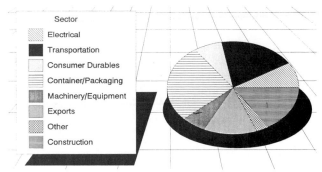

FIGURE 12.1 Aluminum market sector consumption. (*Source: U.S. Department of the Interior, Bureau of Mines, "Bauxite, Alumina, and Aluminum, 1989.*)

cent, machinery and equipment markets use 6 percent, and the remaining 3 percent is utilized by other minor markets.[1] The packaging, transportation, and construction sectors together account for a total of 62 percent of aluminum consumption.

Materials most suited for recycling are those intended for popular short-term consumer usage, which are discarded quickly, and which are present in large quantities in the solid waste stream. Aluminum products from the transportation and construction market sectors generally have long-term uses, measured in years, and are therefore less likely than packaging to be present in the municipal solid waste (MSW) stream in sufficient quantities for efficient recycling. Packaging materials, however, constitute approximately 28 percent of the waste found in landfills (Fig. 12.2) and have a consumer usage span of only a few days or months. Therefore, the majority of aluminum that can be efficiently recovered from the waste stream for recycling is considered to come from the packaging sector.

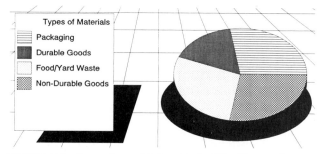

FIGURE 12.2   Types of materials found in landfills. (*Source: Congress of the United States, Office of Technology Assessment, "Facing America's Trash. What Next for Municipal Solid Waste?" October 1989.*)

Figure 12.3 indicates the major types of packaging materials found in landfills. Of the 28 percent of landfill space occupied by packaging materials, aluminum accounts for less than 1 percent by weight (Fig. 12.3), which does not appear large, unless volumetric comparisons are made. Approximately 80 percent of alu-

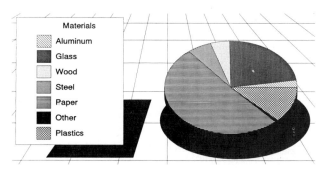

FIGURE 12.3   Packaging materials in landfills. (*Source: Congress of the United States, Office of Technology Assessment, "Facing America's Trash. What Next for Municipal Solid Waste?" October 1989.*)

minum in the municipal solid waste stream is from used beverage containers (UBCs).[1] The remaining 20 percent consists of items such as aluminum foil, flexible packaging, appliances, furniture, and so on. Because the majority of aluminum found in the municipal solid waste stream is in the form of UBCs, aluminum recycling efforts should focus on the recovery of this form of packaging.

Recycling of Aluminum Beverage Cans

Aluminum beverage cans are typically included in recycling programs. Increased concerns by the public regarding the environment, including growing concerns over decreasing landfill capacity, littering, and increasing energy prices, have prompted aluminum can recycling to steadily increase over the past two decades. As illustrated by Fig. 12.4, the number of aluminum cans collected through recycling programs has been steadily increasing on an annual basis since 1972. The aluminum industry has set a goal of recovering 75 percent of all aluminum beverage cans in 1991. Preliminary 1990 figures indicate an increase of approximately 14 percent over the 60.8 percent aluminum can recycling rate attained in 1989.

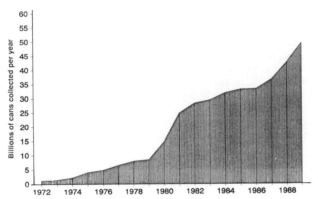

FIGURE 12.4 U.S. aluminum can collection. (*Source: Aluminum Association, "Aluminum Recycling. America's Success Story," 1989.*)

Aluminum cans are one of the most common items recovered through municipal and commercial recycling programs because they are easily identifiable by residents and employees. They also provide higher revenues than other recyclable materials. Also, as landfill space availability becomes scarce in many areas throughout the United States, the widespread use and recycling of aluminum cans will help to mitigate the depletion of remaining landfill capacity.

The beverage can is the most common product made of aluminum by the packaging industry. As previously stated, in 1989, recyclers recovered 60.8 percent of all used beverage containers, which was an increase of 6.2 percent of the volume collected during 1988.[2] The recycling of used beverage cans not only saves valuable landfill space, but also minimizes energy consumption during the manufacturing of aluminum products. Manufacturing new aluminum cans from UBCs uses 95 percent less energy than producing them from virgin materials,[2] an energy savings equivalent to tens of millions of barrels of oil each year.[3]

Manufacturing Aluminum from Used Beverage Containers

Manufacturing new aluminum products from used aluminum materials is referred to in the scrap industry as secondary aluminum production. In this process, aluminum, recovered through recycling programs, is melted in a furnace and mixed with other materials to produce an aluminum alloy that will meet industry specifications. Primary aluminum (virgin aluminum) is also added to ensure proper material specifications required for the final end-use product. After heating, the molten mixture is then cast into ingots, sheets, or aluminum products.

Approximately 95 percent of the UBCs collected nationwide are melted down and re-formed into aluminum sheets to be utilized in the manufacture of new aluminum cans. The remaining 5 percent is utilized by foundries in the production of ingot for other uses, and a small percentage is exported. The aluminum from used beverage cans will often be found in the form of new beverage containers on the supermarket shelf in as few as 90 days, thereby completing the recycling loop.[2]

Legislation

Existing or proposed legislative actions may guide the development of recycling programs. Comprehensive recycling laws and "bottle bill" legislation are both examples of laws that can impact aluminum can recycling activities. Bottle bill legislation typically mandates that a deposit, paid by the consumer, is placed on specific types of beverage containers. The deposit is refunded to the customer when the beverage container is returned to the point of purchase or to a redemption center. Beverage container deposits and comprehensive curbside recycling programs are two recycling collection approaches that compete for valuable recyclable beverage containers. Many states that initially adopted bottle bill legislation have also found it necessary to pass comprehensive recycling legislation in order to recover higher volumes of beverage containers. Conversely, those states that initially adopted comprehensive recycling plans have not found it necessary to adopt bottle bill legislation.[4]

Recovered used aluminum beverage containers demand a high price from the scrap market and consequently supply a critical portion of the revenues generated by municipal recycling programs and material recovery facilities (MRFs). For those MRFs located in nondeposit states, the operators rely on revenues from the sale of all beverage containers, including aluminum UBCs, to offset a portion of facility operating costs. For those publicly owned MRFs located in states with a deposit law (or bottle bill), more public funding is required to offset operating costs because fewer revenue-generating aluminum UBCs are delivered to the facility.

Mandatory source separation regulations, adopted by communities in which recycling programs are being developed, may also affect recycling efforts. Legislation can significantly impact program operation, especially if source separation and market preparation of recovered materials is mandated. For example, some counties have entered into intergovernmental agreements whereby member municipalities are required to bring their recyclables to a certain market, preprocessed per the market specifications. In this circumstance, participating communities benefit from economies of scale in marketing their recyclables since consistent, large quantities of materials generally demand a higher price from markets. In other locations municipalities are required to include aluminum cans in their recycling program, but are permitted to market the materials on their

FIGURE 12.5 Recycling laws and deposit legislation. (*Source: National Soft Drink Association, 1985. National Solid Wastes Management Association, "Special Report: Recycling in the United States, Update 1989."*)

own. By the end of 1989, the District of Columbia and 26 states had adopted comprehensive recycling laws (Fig. 12.5). Eight of these programs require mandatory source separation, and nine other states have adopted deposit legislation for the recovery of aluminum cans.[5] As shown in Fig. 12.5, eight states have enacted both mandatory recycling and deposit legislation. Delaware is the only state to have enacted only deposit legislation.

ALUMINUM CAN RECOVERY PROCESS

Implementing an Aluminum Can Recycling Program

As outlined by Fig. 12.6, a successful aluminum recycling program must have interaction between various entities including those involved with collection, sorting and processing, reclamation, and reuse. There are three generator sectors from which aluminum beverage containers can be recovered: residential households, commercial institutions, and manufacturing entities (other than those producing aluminum products). Collection practices in each of these sectors are outlined below.

Residential Collection. Communities have three basic options available for the collection of aluminum cans: drop-off (depot) centers, buy-back centers, and curbside collection programs. Depot centers and buy-back centers require that residents bring their aluminum cans and other source-separated materials to a specific location. Depending on the size of a particular community, multiple depot or buy-back sites may be necessary to make the collection of recyclables con-

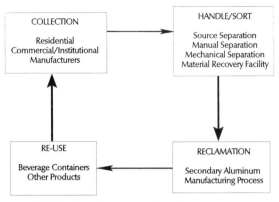

FIGURE 12.6   Recycling process flow diagram.

venient for all residents. Depot and buy-back centers differ only in that buy-back centers pay for the recyclables brought in by the residents. An evaluation of programs throughout the nation indicates that although effective in certain circumstances, these two types of collection programs are generally associated with overall low recovery rates.[6] Curbside collection programs, considered the most convenient collection method because the resident places recyclables at the curb, recapture relatively large quantities of recyclables. Aluminum UBCs can be separated as an individual commodity or commingled with other recyclables for collection as seen by the incidence of curbside collection programs implemented throughout the nation. For those communities providing curbside programs for recyclables separated by material type, collection is generally performed using compartmentalized vehicles. Recyclables are taken directly to processors or brought back to a central location for disposition into containers for transport to a processor. On the other hand, commingled recycling programs enable residents to mix various recyclable materials in one container. Compartmentalized vehicles are not needed in this scenario because the commingled material is typically brought to an MRF for separation and processing prior to sale to a secondary materials market. MRFs sort and densify (process) the individual components of a recyclable materials mix, such as aluminum cans, glass bottles and jars, and plastic beverage containers. In most cases, depot programs and buy-back centers do not offer commingling as an option and require residents to separate their recyclables by individual material type.

Reverse vending machines are also utilized to recover aluminum cans from residential sources and basically function as unstaffed buy-back centers. Rather than accepting coins and dispensing items for sale, reverse vending machines accept cans and return cash or an equivalent store credit coupon. Reverse vending machines are usually found in supermarkets and other retail trade establishments and may be utilized in conjunction with other recovery methods described in this section. Reverse vending machines are also widely used in bottle bill states.

Commercial-Institutional Collection.   The commercial sector can prove to be a large generator of recyclable materials, dependent on the number of commercial establishments within the program area and the types and volume of business conducted. In designing a commercial recycling program to recover aluminum cans, larger commercial establishments should consider designating a recycling program coordinator who would be responsible for program design, implementation, and oversight of operations. Determining what types of recyclable materials are generated by the business is the initial step in developing a program. The next step would be to determine the approximate amount of used aluminum beverage cans that are generated in order to ascertain the resulting volume or quantity of material. Markets should then be contacted to determine how the aluminum cans must be prepared. The market may provide a pickup service or processing equipment for the recovered aluminum cans. Market services should be evaluated early in the planning stages because they may affect municipal collection procedures currently in place for the commercial establishment. The marketing questions listed later in this chapter should be reviewed when selecting a market for the recovered aluminum cans. Based on the materials specification standards of the market, as well as the approximate volume of aluminum generated, and the procedure by which the material is going to be collected (i.e., in cafeterias, at central locations throughout the business, etc.), the type and number of collection containers needed can be determined. Furthermore, the type of processing equipment needed can be selected if required by the market and if volumes warrant. It is also important to determine storage space requirements, whether indoor or outdoor, to sufficiently and safely store the aluminum cans for the scheduled pickup. Resolution of transportation issues, such as whether delivery would be better handled by the market, a private hauler, the municipality, or by the business establishment itself, is critical. Under any scenario, records should be kept of the volume or quantity of aluminum cans collected through the program in order to facilitate accounting procedures and determine program success.

One major component of a successful aluminum can recycling program is the implementation of an effective publicity and education program for the employees. The program should be promoted periodically, utilizing initiatives that would provide maximum motivation.

Manufacturing Entities Collection. Manufacturing entities that have an "in-house" smelting process would most likely recover aluminum scrap or waste generated by their in-house manufacturing process. Scrap cast-offs or products not meeting specifications generated during the production of their specific commodity may in certain circumstances be returned directly to the manufacturing process and thus never enter the solid waste stream.

In general, a limited quantity of UBCs would be generated from this type of manufacturing process. Typical generation would be the result of an on-site food service, cafeteria, beverage vending machines, or brown-bag lunches. However, manufacturing entities collecting UBCs, regardless of their source, would generally collect the UBCs in a manner similar to the recovery process previously described for the commercial-institutional sectors.

Methods to Remove Aluminum from Other Recyclables

There are several methods for removing aluminum from other recyclables when collected in a commingled state. Manual separation is both the most common and labor-intensive option but is utilized in many MRFs. The method entails employees, located along conveyor belt picking lines, performing the physical separation of the commingled recyclable waste stream into its various components. Most mixed recyclable processing systems incorporate a magnetic separator within the processing line for the purpose of removing ferrous materials, thereby making it easier for employees to identify aluminum cans.

Manual separation of UBCs is normally deemed to be too labor-intensive for larger operations. In such cases, mechanical separation methods are often used. One mechanical separation system widely utilized as part of MRF processing systems is the nonferrous separator or eddy current magnet. The most common eddy current systems incorporate the use of opposing magnetic fields as a primary method to separate or divert aluminum from mixed plastic food and beverage containers. When the commingled recyclables traversing the conveyor belt reach the position of the magnetic field, the aluminum, due to its ability to hold an electric charge, is thrown into a catch hopper or conveyor by the magnetic field (see Fig. 12.7). The concept is similar to that of holding the positive and negative poles of two magnets within a short distance of each other, thereby creating a noticeable force as the magnets repel each other.

FIGURE 12.7   Eddy current technology. (*Source: Photo courtesy CRInc.*)

MARKETING

Market Specifications

When UBCs are manufactured into new products, the closed-loop recycling cycle can be considered complete. The most important component of an aluminum can recycling program is the identification, selection, and securing of markets for the recovered UBC material. The method of collection instituted for a recycling program and the form in which the material is sold will depend on market specifications. There are three major types of markets for aluminum cans: brokers, processors, and end users.

Aluminum scrap brokers are business entities that buy and sell recovered recyclable materials in processed or unprocessed form. In general, brokers do not process materials but merely serve as go-between for the generator and a processor or for the processor and an end user. Thus, brokers purchase, consolidate, and resell materials, providing a viable market outlet for many recycling programs.

Processors accept aluminum cans from municipal programs, postindustrial or postconsumer entities, and brokers. Aluminum is also accepted from some MRFs that separate, but do not bale or densify, the material. In the case of aluminum, the processor may buy loose aluminum cans from a municipality and bale them for sale to an end user.

End users are those manufacturers that clean and melt the aluminum into aluminum sheets, ingots, or blocks for reuse in the manufacturing of new cans or other items such as airplane or truck bodies. Many aluminum end users purchase processed and unprocessed materials directly from municipal programs in close proximity to their facilities.

Prices paid for recyclables can vary between markets, making it important to obtain as much information on markets as possible in order to secure the best deal for each individual recycling program. Other factors to take into consideration when selecting a market include material preparation requirements and market location. The quality of material being sold will be the most significant factor in determining the price paid by potential markets. Since recovered aluminum will become the raw material for the manufacture of new products, clean, uncontaminated material will be the most valuable.

Aluminum markets have material specifications that regulate the extent of contamination allowed in each delivery as well as the method by which materials will be prepared (Fig. 12.8). For example, some markets prohibit aluminum foil and pie pans from being commingled with aluminum cans. Also, where some markets require aluminum to be baled, others may accept flattened, loose material. Material specifications for the markets should be evaluated prior to initiating collection activities in order to ensure that the recycling program and operating scenario selected for implementation will prepare materials in a manner acceptable to the intended market. As previously mentioned, market location should also be taken into consideration when deciding which markets to utilize. A market that is in close proximity and requires minimal processing is usually of greatest interest to small-scale municipal programs. Costs usually associated with the marketing of aluminum cans include labor and energy for material preparation as well as vehicle operation and maintenance costs for material transportation.

Marketing services, offered by some aluminum end users, should also be considered and may include the provision of storage containers, processing equipment, and/or pickup services. A market may also be willing to assist in fostering an aluminum can recycling program by providing public relation services and assistance.

In many instances, municipalities have made arrangements with the aluminum recycling industry for the use of can flatteners and blowers to assist in reducing storage and shipping costs. Furthermore, some municipalities have established agreements whereby the market assumes responsibility for the transport of materials from the municipality to the processing location. A good marketing plan will include markets that require minimum transport and labor costs. However, a

LOOSE FLATTENED UBC*

UBC must be flattened using commercial flatteners and not compressed by other means.
Flatteners must be equiped with magnetic separators.

BALED UBC

12 to 17 lbs. per cu. foot for unflattened ubc scrap.
12 to 20 lbs. per cu. foot for flattened UBC scrap.
Bale must be dense enough to permit movement by fork lift.
Bales should be of uniform size
Bale Size:
 Minimum of 30 cu. ft. with minimum dimension of 24" in one direction and a maximum of 72" dimension in another.
 Preferred bale size is 3' x 4' x 5' or 60 cu. ft.
 Bales of two or more individual bales bonded together to meet preferred bale size specifications are not acceptable.
Banding:
 2.5 lbs. per bale deductor.
 Four to six 5/8" x .020 steel or aluminum bands.
 Six to fifteen #13 gauge steel or aluminum wired.
 Not Acceptable: bands or wire of other material; and use of support sheets of any material.

SPECIFICATIONS FOR LOOSE FLATTENED OR BALED UBC

Moisture not to exceed 1%.
Material to be stored indoors.
Any non-UBC material will be subject to deduction.
Shipment receieved meeting permissable moisture level and not otherwise contaminated, will be accepted.
Receiving facility has the option of accepting or rejecting a load.
If material does not meet the specifications as detailed above, the vendor will contact the deliverer prior to processing and
 review all deductions to be applied.
The prevailing weight is determined by the receiving facility.
Materials not covered in this specifications are subject to special arragements between the buyer and seller.

BRIQUETTES

Density: 35 to 45 lbs. per cu. foot.
Size:
 10 3/4" x 10 3/4" x 7 3/4"
 13 1/4" x 20 1/4" x 7"
 13 1/2" x 13 1/2" x 6 1/2"
 14" x 10 3/4" x 7"
Banding:
 7 lb. per bundle deductor will be taken for banding.
 Banding slots in both directions to facilitate bundle handling.
 5/8" x .020 steel straps minimum
 One band per row.
 Minimum two horizontal bands per bundle.
Bundle Specifications:
 All bisquettes comprising a bundle must be of uniform size.
 Bundle sizes: 41" to 44" x 51" to 54" x 54" to 56" (LxWxH).
Quality Specifications: See bale specifications.
General: Items not covered in this specification are subject to special arrangement between buyer and seller.

*Used beverage container.

FIGURE 12.8 Aluminum can market specifications. [*Source: Aluminum Recycling Market. 1990 Directory (References Manual).*]

higher market price may compensate for increased transport costs, especially when utilizing a regional marketing strategy.

The willingness of the market to provide a municipality with processing equipment, storage containers, and/or a pickup service will usually depend on the ability of the program to recover large quantities of clean, uncontaminated aluminum cans on a regular basis. A consistent supply of UBCs that continually meet market specifications will minimize marketing problems.

Potential revenue is understandably a major factor when selecting a market. Prices paid for UBCs vary depending on many of the previously mentioned factors. However, revenues generally increase in accordance with increased levels of material processing, returning to the concept of more money paid for a better product. Prices paid for aluminum cans are based upon preparation levels and can be quoted in a variety of ways. For example, UBCs may be whole and loose, flattened, densified, or shredded (uncommon).

When contacting markets, answers to the following questions should be obtained:

- What types of aluminum are currently purchased (e.g., UBCs, scrap aluminum siding, food trays, etc.)?
- How should the recovered aluminum cans be prepared for sale (material specifications)?
- What minimum (or maximum) quantities will the market accept?
- Is the market willing to provide storage containers, processing equipment, and/or a pickup service?
- What are the hours that the market site is open for delivery of materials?
- What is the current price being paid for each specified grade?
- How is payment made?
- Is a material purchase contract optional or required?

Material Preparation for Marketing

As previously mentioned, aluminum cans recovered through municipal recycling programs can be flattened and blown into a trailer or collected loose in bulk, and delivered to a processor. In turn, the processor will flatten and/or bale the aluminum cans for sale to an end user who smelts the material into aluminum sheet or ingot for use in the manufacturing of new aluminum cans or other aluminum products. Aluminum cans collected for recycling by commercial and industrial establishments are often delivered to processors in baled form. In some instances, processors and brokers provide storage containers and pick-up services to recover aluminum cans from the commercial sector. However, commercial programs are similar to residential programs in that if either service is provided by the processor, a minimum tonnage must generally be guaranteed by the commercial establishment in order for the processor to provide special services. Sample material specifications have been previously presented in Fig. 12.8.

End-Use Market

UBCs are commonly utilized by sheet manufacturers because the aluminum alloy used to make beverage cans is consistent among most can manufacturers and can be smelted into the proper concentration required for manufacturing new aluminum sheet. Approximately 95 percent of the UBCs recovered from the municipal solid waste stream are utilized directly by sheet manufacturers who produce new aluminum sheet for cans. A small amount of all UBCs are purchased by secondary smelters for the production of ingots. Secondary smelters sell the majority of their aluminum to foundries that can only tolerate a minimal amount of magne-

Commingled Collection Program

Borough of Park Ridge, New Jersey.   The borough of Park Ridge, New Jersey, has a resident population of approximately 8515 persons.[8] Park Ridge is composed of approximately 2500 single-family residences, approximately 300 condominium-apartment units, and approximately 75 commercial establishments within 2.6 mi[2].[7] During 1989, Park Ridge generated approximately 9990 tons of solid waste, including 37.5 tons of tree stumps and 438 tons of asphalt.[8] Of the total solid waste generated within the municipality, 68 percent (6786 tons) was attributed to the residential sector, and the remaining 32 percent (3201 tons) was generated by the commercial sector.[7] During the early 1980s, Park Ridge implemented a voluntary recycling program consisting of a depot. In 1988 the borough expanded its recycling efforts by implementing a mandatory recycling program requiring the recovery of paper, corrugated cardboard, leaves, Christmas trees, white goods, and commingled recyclables found in the solid waste stream. This program was implemented through a 1988 expansion of the depot center (Fig. 12.9), at which

FIGURE 12.9   Borough of Park Ridge, New Jersey: Depot Center.

corrugated cardboard, newspaper, commingled recyclables [plastic high-density polyethylene (HDPE) and polyethylene terephthalate (PET)] containers, glass, aluminum, tin, and bimetal cans), car batteries, waste oil, scrap metal, brush, and wood waste are collected. The depot program was expanded to include grass clippings in 1989.

To supplement the depot program, a mandatory curbside collection program was also instituted in 1988. The curbside program recovers mixed paper and commingled recyclables, corrugated cardboard, leaves, Christmas trees, and white goods from the residential sector as required by a municipal ordinance. In addition, the following materials are recycled voluntarily at the depot center: brush, grass clippings, car batteries, and motor oil. Collection of the commingled material (newspapers and commingled recyclables) from the residential sector is provided biweekly by the borough utilizing a 31-yd^3 packer truck operated by one full-time driver and two part-time laborers. Residents place paper curbside in bundled form adjacent to the commingled materials container. Within this program 2800 households are served, including four schools and the post office.[7]

Commercial and institutional establishments located within the borough (including schools) are required to recycle at least one of the following materials from their waste stream: corrugated cardboard, glass, food wastes, ferrous metals, high-grade office paper, and newspaper. A majority of the commercial establishments recover cardboard. Schools, however, have been recovering mixed paper, high-grade paper, aluminum and ferrous cans, glass, and corrugated cardboard. As such, Park Ridge's sources of aluminum include both the residential and institutional sectors. The aluminum cans, commingled with other recyclables, are taken to a local processor (approximately 15 mi from Park Ridge) where they are further prepared for sale to an end user.[8]

The borough does not receive any revenue for the material; however, the program can be considered profitable if the avoided tipping fees are taken into consideration. During 1989, the municipality recovered 327.8 tons of recyclables from residential and institutional establishments. Of these materials, approximately 3.06 percent, 10.03 tons, were aluminum cans. The cost for collection of the commingled recyclable materials for the town in 1989 was a total of $181,000. The operating and maintenance costs for the collection of commingled recyclables included collection ($110,000), processing ($58,000), administration ($10,000), and education-publicity ($3000). The avoided tipping fees, including all recyclable materials recovered within the borough, were determined by utilizing an avoided disposal fee of $98/ton. The total avoided cost for 1989 was $259,602, of which $138,474 was attributed to the residential recycling program.

The total UBC recycling program cost was estimated at $5537. This figure may appear high relative to other recycling programs due to the fact that the borough collected aluminum cans commingled with other recyclable materials and paid a tipping fee to a processor to separate the recyclable materials for sale to end users. The borough is paying to make the recycling program as convenient as possible for the residents of Park Ridge. As a result, the borough does not receive a revenue for the sale of the aluminum cans. However, the borough does benefit from a tipping fee savings which totaled $983 in 1989.

Mobile Buy-Back Center Program

City of Vallejo, California. California municipalities are required by state statute to have recycling depot centers within ½ mi of each grocery store exceeding a specified ceiling in total annual sales. To satisfy this requirement, the city of Vallejo (population of 104,000) developed a mobile recycling center program utilizing a Lodal 3000 vehicle (Fig. 12.10). This mobile buy-back system enabled the city to receive an exemption from the state of California, eliminating the need for the city to site and build multiple recycling facilities. The city's mobile buy-back center travels throughout the community, making scheduled stops at schools and various locations around the community to collect aluminum cans, glass containers, plastic PET containers, and newspaper. Materials are weighed at the time of delivery, and the residents receive the current redemption price for the aluminum, PET plastics, and glass containers delivered. Newspapers are accepted by the mobile unit; however, the residents do not receive any monies for the material. Every month, the mobile unit collects approximately 3 tons of aluminum cans. The total unit cost in 1989 for the city's new mobile recycling unit was $120,000. The initial capital cost of the mobile unit may appear high but could potentially be offset by the expenses incurred from operating multiple stationary recycling centers.

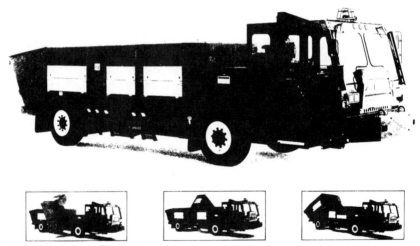

FIGURE 12.10   Lodal Eco 3000 recycling vehicle. (*Courtesy Lodal, Inc., Kingsford, Michigan.*)

Depot Collection Programs

Village of Ridgewood, New Jersey.   The village of Ridgewood, New Jersey (population 24,923), generated approximately 8500 tons of municipal solid waste during 1990. Of this amount, approximately 83 percent was generated in the residential sector and 17 percent in the commercial sector.[7] The village encompasses approximately 5.797 mi^2, with 8691 households and 307 commercial establishments.[7] The village's past recycling activities consisted of only a depot located in a convenient part of the municipality. The facility accepts aluminum, glass, plastic, tin cans, corrugated cardboard, high-grade paper, newspaper, textiles, used oil, and light iron, in multiple 12-ft-wide by 18-ft-high concrete areas at the depot. The total cost for the original five concrete bins was $12,000. An additional bin was added at a cost of $9000. The depot is open Monday, Wednesday, Friday, and Saturday from 8:00 A.M. to 3:00 P.M.; Tuesday and Thursday from 8:00 A.M. to 8:00 P.M.; and is closed Sundays and holidays. The recycling department consists of one recycling coordinator–enforcement officer and three laborers. The depot is staffed by at least one person at all times. Aluminum recovered through the depot is deposited in roll-off containers supplied by the vendor. The material is not processed in any way.

The village received approximately $0.35/lb for the nearly 40 tons of aluminum cans collected in 1989, generating approximately $26,859 in revenues. The price paid for the material varied slightly each month. The village saved approximately $3920 in tipping fees alone for the diverted aluminum, making the total cost savings of the aluminum segment of the recycling program approximately $30,620. The total cost of the program for 1990 was approximately $22,360. Fifty-five percent of the costs were attributed to salaries and 40 percent to the tip fee charged by paper recycling vendors. Operation and maintenance of the depot constituted approximately 5 percent of the total cost. The program recovered an approximate total of 16,527 tons of recyclables in 1989. Based on a $98/ton tipping fee at the county's transfer station, the total program avoided cost was $1,619,646.

The UBC program cost to the village during 1989 was approximately $40. The revenue generated through the sale of the UBCs and savings through the avoided tipping fee costs totaled $30,779.

On January 1, 1991, the village implemented a curbside recycling program to enhance its recycling efforts. The depot program will now be supplemented by the curbside collection of commingled aluminum, glass, plastics, and tin cans, along with separated corrugated cardboard, newspaper, junk mail and magazines, and light iron.

City of Hollywood, Florida. The city of Hollywood, Florida, is approximately 55 mi^2 and has a population of approximately 130,000 residents. The city has implemented a recycling program that enables residents to visit any of the 97 minidepot centers located throughout the community in order to deposit their glass and aluminum containers. These minidepot centers are made of four 0.37-yd^3 containers, each clearly marked to indicate the type of materials that should be deposited in the respective container (see Fig. 12.11). The depots, which were purchased through a state capital grant, cost approximately $1760 each. Each unit was placed on a concrete pad and bolted for security. The cost of each concrete pad was $240, bringing the total unit cost to $2000. The city utilizes a nonprofit organization for collecting the recyclables from the mini-drop-off centers. This nonprofit group, Faith Farm, provides the labor and vehicles for the collection and transportation of the recyclables at no cost to the city. Faith Farm also provides a security program to ensure that the minidepot centers are not tampered with. This program, which was initiated in December of 1990, collects approximately 5 tons of aluminum cans per month and approximately 45 to 50 tons/month of glass. The revenue generated through the sale of the recyclables is earmarked by Faith Farm for special programs to help rehabilitate troubled individuals.

Since Faith Farm provides collection and marketing of the UBCs at no cost to the city and the minidepot centers were purchased through a state grant, the city does not have any costs associated with the UBC segment of the recycling program. Additionally, because Faith Farm receives all revenues generated, the city does not receive any monies from the sale of the material. However, the city does benefit from avoided tipping fee costs. At the present disposal fee of $38/ton with an increase to $62.50/ton beginning June 1, 1991, and based on an estimated re-

FIGURE 12.11   City of Hollywood, Florida, minidepot center. (*Courtesy Haul-All Equipment Systems, Lethridge, Alberta, Canada.*)

covery goal of 5 tons/month, the city could potentially save $3138 through the recycling of aluminum cans in 1991.

Case Study Summary

This section provides a cost comparison of the various case study program scenarios described in the previous sections (Table 12.1). As previously stated, an annual UBC program cost is estimated. Annual costs were determined based on the total tons of recyclables collected and the total program budget for that year, resulting in an approximate cost per ton for all recyclables collected through the municipality's recycling program. The cost-per-ton figure was then applied to the total tons of UBCs collected to determine the estimated UBC recycling program cost.

When making program comparisons, please keep in mind the variables that affect program costs in each municipality. These variables include:

TABLE 12.1   Case Study Summary

	Project costs		
Municipality	Total program budget	Tons of UBC collected	Estimated total recycling program operating cost/ton
Garfield	$243,000	4.21	$172
Allendale	282,000	13.35	66
Park Ridge	181,000	10.03	552
Ridgewood	22,360	40.00	1
Hollywood	0	60.00	0
	Project savings and revenue		
Municipality	UBC avoided tipping fee savings	UBC material revenue	Total UBC program savings and revenue
Garfield	$552	$2,947	$3,499
Allendale	1,308	9,612	10,920
Park Ridge	983	0	983
Ridgewood	3,920	26,859	30,779
Hollywood	3,138	0	3,138

- Population of a given area
- Publicity and education efforts
- Program enforcement efforts
- Age of program and number of materials collected

  Market utilized (revenue)

  Availability of grants and loans

  Utilization of nonprofit groups for certain program tasks

TRENDS AND FORECASTS

Demand

The United States is the primary producer of aluminum and is also the world's largest market for aluminum products. The United States consumes approximately one-quarter of the world's primary aluminum alloy, with the aluminum can and packaging markets consuming the largest volume of aluminum production. The demand for aluminum has been increasing as new uses for the metal are developed. This trend is expected to continue.

It is anticipated, for example, that the automobile industry will expand its use of aluminum in the construction of body frames and engines to increase the fuel efficiency of vehicles. Because aluminum cans have become a popular packaging container, shipments of aluminum sheet from which cans are manufactured doubled in the 1980s.[1] It is also anticipated that the demand for aluminum beverage containers will remain strong because aluminum is viewed as a cost-effective packaging material. However, the use of plastic packaging materials may increase competition for the container market. The aluminum industry is also concerned with competition of expanding primary aluminum activities overseas. New primary aluminum production capacity is being developed in countries that possess lower electrical costs. As a result, it is expected that U.S. aluminum producers will be placing an increased emphasis on aluminum can recycling. This trend will continue to expand UBC recycling efforts, which have been on the rise since 1972 (Fig. 12.12).

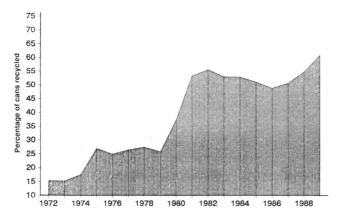

FIGURE 12.12   U.S. aluminum can recycling. (*Source: Aluminum Association "Aluminum Recycling. America's Success Story," 1989.*)

The aluminum industry's initiatives, however, do not end with recycling. The aluminum industry has also fostered source reduction activities to assist in minimizing the impact of UBCs on diminishing landfill space and to decrease manufacturing costs. As indicated in Fig. 12.13, the industry has developed methods to

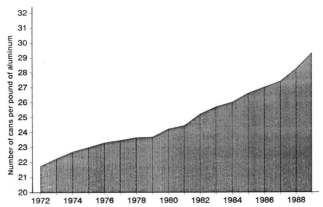

FIGURE 12.13   Aluminum can weight and source reduction. (*Source: Aluminum Association, "Aluminum Recycling. America's Success Story," 1989.*)

produce more cans per pound of aluminum. In 1989, aluminum manufacturers produced 28 cans per pound of aluminum as compared with 21.75 cans per pound in 1972.[2]

Price

As indicated by the trend for most recyclable materials in the late 1980s and early 1990s, the price paid for aluminum cans appears to be declining. The monthly average U.S. market price for primary aluminum ingot decreased during the past year as supply and demand balanced, and the same can be said for the price paid for UBCs.[9] The street price paid for aluminum cans dropped to approximately 29.3¢/lb in December 1990 to 30.7 to 35.8¢/lb during the previous year.[10] This has meant a price for the material to be paid by processors to be as low as 40¢/lb.[10] Although there has been a downward shift in the price paid for aluminum UBCs, resulting in less revenue generated by municipalities for the sale of recovered UBCs, it is still a high revenue-generating material when compared to other types of recyclables. Figure 12.14 graphically presents the average revenue generated by material type. In parts of the United States where solid waste disposal costs have skyrocketed, the avoided tipping fee costs for recovered recyclable materials have more of a financial impact on communities than does the revenue generated from the sale of recyclable materials. Therefore, a decrease in the price paid for UBCs in those areas would not affect recycling programs to the same degree as for communities where tipping fee costs are still minimal. Programs more apt to be affected by the decrease in price include not-for-profit organizations that provide recycling program services in exchange for the revenue generated from the sale of the recyclable materials, and those programs that donate material revenues to charity or nonprofit groups.

Although the supply and demand of primary aluminum experienced growth during the 1980s, the increased attention both domestically and abroad in the 1990s regarding waste disposal problems will provide an increase in activities for

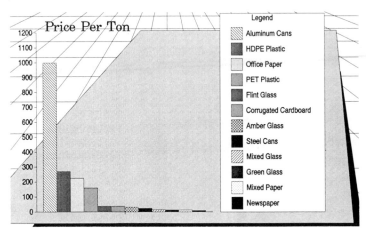

FIGURE 12.14 Average revenue generated per material. (*Source: Curbing Waste in a Throwaway World, July 1989.*[17])

the secondary aluminum industry as well. It is expected that this trend will again stabilize UBC prices.

CONCLUSION

As presented in this chapter, there are many advantages to recycling used aluminum beverage containers. These advantages include both financial and environmental benefits, as summarized below.

Avoided tipping fee: For every ton of aluminum recovered through municipal, commercial, institutional, or industrial recycling programs, the generator source or municipality will save or avoid the associated tipping fee costs charged at their local solid waste disposal facility.

Potential source of revenue: Revenue generated through the sale of aluminum cans will help to offset a portion of the costs associated with implementing and operating the recycling program.

Easily recovered: Because aluminum cans are easy to identify among other materials found in the municipal solid waste stream and since they are compatible with various types of recycling collection programs, they are easily recovered.

Increased demand: The demand for secondary aluminum has been on the rise for the last 10 years. Although aluminum beverage containers can be economically recycled back into their original form, other uses for recycled UBCs are constantly being developed.

Energy savings: An energy savings of 95 percent is associated with the production of new aluminum beverage containers from UBCs rather than from virgin materials. Thus, the recovery of UBCs makes economic sense for aluminum manufacturers because reducing energy consumption lowers operating costs and conserves petrochemical resources.

Public, private, or nonprofit organizations instituting a new recycling program should consider the recovery of aluminum cans. Aluminum has traditionally been one of the most stable materials to recycle in terms of markets, revenues, and program participation. The added advantages of energy savings and avoided disposal fees combine to make aluminum cans one of the most attractive components of any recycling program.

ADDITIONAL INFORMATION SOURCES

Alcan Rolled Products Company
Lake Road North
Oswego, NY 13126
(315) 349-0121

Aluminum Association
818 Connecticut Avenue
Washington, DC 20006
(202) 862-5163

Alcoa Recycling Company, Inc.
100 Clover Place
Edison, NJ 08818
(201) 225-9550

Anheuser-Busch Companies
One Busch Place
St. Louis, MO 63118
(314) 577-2000

Can Manufacturers Institute
1625 Massachusetts Avenue, NW
Suite 500
Washington, CD 20036
(202) 382-2090

Container Recovery Corporation
10733 Sunset Office Drive
Suite 400
Sunset Hills, MO 63127
(314) 957-9350

Council for Solid Waste Solutions
1275 K Street, NW Suite 400
Washington, DC 20005
(202) 371-5319

Institute of Scrap Recycling Industries
1627 K Street, NW Suite 700
Washington, DC 20006
(202) 466-4050

Keep America Beautiful, Inc.
9 West Broad Street
Stamford, CT 06902
(203) 323-8987

National Recycling Coalition, Inc.
1101 30th Street, NW Suite 305
Washington, DC 20007
(202) 625-6406

National Solid Waste Management
Association
10th Floor, 1730 Rhode Island, NW
Washington, DC 20036
(202) 659-4613

Reynolds Aluminum Recycling Co.
P.O. Box 27003
Richmond, VA 23261
(800) 228-2525

Solid Waste Association of North
America
P.O. Box 7219
Silver Spring, MD 20910
(800) 456-4723

United States Environmental
Protection Agency
Office of Solid Waste
401 M Street, SW
Washington, DC 20460
(800) 424-9346

ACKNOWLEDGMENTS

Assistance was provided by Stephen C. Schwarz, Robert J. Schneider, John R. Ettinghouse, Barbara A. Riley, Naomi Starobin, and Elizabeth Apgar of Malcolm Pirnie, Inc.; and John Dickinson of the Aluminum Association.

REFERENCES

1. *Facing America's Trash: What Next for Municipal Solid Waste?* Congress of the United States, Office of Technology Assessment, October 1989.

2. *Aluminum Recycling: America's Environmental Success Story,* Aluminum Association, 1989.

3. *Recycling: The State of the Art,* Malcolm Pirnie Technical Publication, 1988.

4. *Why Comprehensive Recycling Is More Effective Than Beverage Container Deposits,* Glass Packaging Institute.

5. *Forced Deposit Laws... There Are No Winners,* National Soft Drink Association, 1985.

6. *Beyond 25 Percent: Material Recovery Comes of Age,* Institute for Local Self-Reliance, April 1989.

7. *Recycling/Waste Composition Study (Bergen County, N.J.),* Malcolm Pirnie, Inc., August 1987.

8. *Beyond 40 Percent: Setting Recycling and Composting Programs,* Institute for Local Self-Reliance, August 1990.

9. *The Story and Uses of Aluminum,* Aluminum Association, 1989.

10. "Aluminum Price Drops Again," *Recycling Times,* December 18, 1990.

11. "The State of Garbage in America," *BioCycle Magazine,* April 1990.

12. *Starting at Home: Recycling to Protect Our Environment,* Anheuser-Busch Companies.

13. "Regulatory Economics Weigh Heavy on Nonferrous Scrap Consumers," *Phoenix,* Spring 1990.

14. "Aluminum Used Beverage Can Prices: National Averages 1990," *Recycling Times,* 1990.

15. "Recycled Aluminum Price Soars," *Castings,* July–August 1987.

16. *The Amazing All-Aluminum Can: Recycling Rate Still Setting Records,* Institute of Scrap Recycling Industries, 1987.

17. *Curbing Waste in a Throwaway World,* National Governor's Association, Washington, D.C., July 1989.

CHAPTER 13
GLASS BEVERAGE BOTTLES

Michael W. Gilmore
Solid Waste Planner
Camp Dresser and McKee Inc.
Melbourne, Florida

Tammy L. Hayes
Technical Writer for Solid Wastes
Camp Dresser and McKee Inc.
Tampa, Florida

INTRODUCTION

Less than a generation ago, jars and bottles were made only of glass. Over the last 20 years, high-density polyethylene (HDPE) and polyethylene terephthalate (PET) plastics have been used to make food and beverage containers. During the past 10 years, laminated paper materials and foil have also been combined to containerize foods and beverages. Still, the glass industry estimates that every person in the United States throws away approximately 85 lb of glass each year, and 7 billion glass containers are recovered and returned for remanufacture annually (Fig. 13.1).

Container glass is the glass that is used to make jars and bottles. It is the glass in soft drink bottles, beer bottles, mayonnaise and pickle jars, baby food jars, wine and liquor bottles, and many other containerized foods and beverages.

Container glass is the only glass that is being recycled in large quantities at the present time. Window panes, light bulbs, mirrors, ceramic dishes and pots, glassware, crystal, ovenware, and fiberglass are not recyclable with container glass and are considered contaminants in container glass recycling.

The common glass jar or bottle is unique in the recyclables manufacturing industry. One 12-ounce glass bottle, melted down and reformed, yields one 12-ounce bottle without any loss of quality. No waste or by-products are generated in the remanufacturing process, and the same glass can repeatedly make and remake one 12-ounce bottle. This trait makes glass one of the few manufactured goods that is 100 percent recyclable (Fig. 13.2).

Container glass is common in everyday use, yet it has unique properties that make it a special recyclable. For example, glass is made from common inert raw materials including white silica sand, soda ash, and limestone. Slag, salt cake, feldspar, aragonite, and cullet (crushed glass) are other ingredients typically used

FIGURE 13.1   Variety of food and beverage containers.

FIGURE 13.2   Remanufactured glass containers.

to manufacture glass containers. These raw and secondary materials are not in short supply; they are plentiful and easily obtainable.

The most unique or special consideration in marketing container glass is the need for color separation. Permanent dyes are used to make different-colored glass containers. The most common colorings are green, brown, and clear (or colorless). In the industry, green glass is called emerald, brown glass is amber, and clear glass is called flint. In order for bottles and jars to meet strict manufacturing specifications, only emerald or amber cullet can be used to make green and brown bottles, respectively.

Glass itself is not a threat to the environment because it is inert; it is not biodegradable. If exposed to weathering forces, glass breaks down into small particles of silica, basic beach sand, which is one of the most common elements on earth.

While only container glass is used to remake glass containers, glass cullet can be used in other manufacturing processes and industrial applications. For example, crushed and broken glass can be part of the aggregate used in bituminous road paving—we know this product as *Glasphalt.* Other uses of cullet as an aggregate substitute are discussed later in this chapter. Examples of glass reuse range from glass wool insulation and fiberglass to telephone poles and fence posts made from glass cullet and plastic polymer mixtures. These represent only a few of the newer markets that have been developed for cullet in recent years.

Using recycled container glass as cullet to make new glass container products conserves energy and reduces glass manufacturing costs. Energy is conserved because cullet melts down at a lower temperature than that required to combine the raw materials that go into making glass. This not only reduces energy costs, but increases furnace life as well. Depending on the amount of cullet being used, furnace life can be extended by as much as 15 to 20 percent. The conservation of energy, in turn, conserves natural resources such as our depleting supply of fossil fuels. For every 1 percent increase in the use of cullet, 0.25 percent of the energy needed is saved. In more practical terms, 9 gal of fuel oil is saved for each ton of glass that is recycled. Energy reduction and the extension of furnace life enable glass manufacturing plants to run more efficiently, thus reducing overall costs.

The recycling of glass containers has more impact on enhancing a solid waste recycling program than it does on reducing waste collection and disposal requirements. Glass containers represent approximately 2 percent of the solid waste volume. While every little bit counts, other wastes such as paper and yard waste comprise greater portions of the total waste volume. On the other hand, glass containers represent 7 to 8 percent of the weight of total solid wastes. Thus, the reduction of glass from the waste disposal system can be a significant contributor toward meeting recycling and landfill avoidance goals that are typically measured as a percentage of total weight.

Some communities use waste-to-energy or resource recovery facilities (plants that produce energy from the combustion of wastes) to reduce the volume of solid waste prior to its final disposal. The removal of glass from these waste streams is beneficial because plant maintenance is reduced, and the overall efficiency of the plant's operation is increased due to the removal of the noncombustible glass containers.

In general, glass recovery processes based on hand-picking or screening are effective in removing container glass from the disposable waste stream. Once recovered, glass containers are storable, transportable, and processible as a future feedstock to glass remanufacturing and other industrial processes.

It is estimated that all glass containers are manufactured using some amount of glass cullet. The percentage of cullet being used varies among manufacturers, but it is generally considered to be increasing. Overall industry averages indicate that approximately 25 to 35 percent of raw material needs are currently being supplied by cullet. The glass manufacturing industry expects to increase this cullet usage to 50 percent.

Most importantly, the continued recovery and recycling of glass containers is evidence of the stability of one industry to produce a desirable consumer product—the glass container—in a form that is totally recyclable as a remanufactured glass container. Thus, the glass container can be removed from the postconsumer waste stream and returned as usable feedstock to the glass remanufacturing process.

GLASS CONTAINER RECOVERY

For years, the glass container was a reusable product that was returned to the bottler or food packer for washing and refilling. Familiar examples of this recovery process are the returnable glass milk bottle, returnable soft drink and beer bottles, and prepared jars of food stuffs such as "canned" vegetables, fruits, and jams. Foods and beverages that were not packed in jars and bottles were packed in tin cans.

Traditionally, cullet was the glass recovered from breakage or rejects in the manufacturing process or in the washing and bottling processes. The age of "no deposit—no return" glass containers and other forms of "new and improved" food and beverage packing (e.g., aluminum and plastic containers) sent the majority of glass containers into the disposable waste stream.

Changes in postconsumer glass disposal have come about along with changes in solid waste collection practices. In general, glass containers that are recovered and returned for remanufacturing (Fig. 13.3) are the result of materials recovery practices that

- Recover glass containers in response to local bottle bills that prohibit landfill disposal and provide for the payment of container deposit money.
- Recover glass containers at decentralized collection depots for separated recyclables.
- Recover glass containers that have been separated from curbside refuse.
- Recover glass containers from commercial sources of food and beverage products (e.g., bars and restaurants).
- Recover glass containers from loads of mixed recyclables, typically including paper, glass, aluminum, and plastic materials.
- Recover glass containers from solid waste processing plants.
- Recover in-plant breakage and rejects in the glass container manufacturing process and in the food and beverage packaging industry.

Bottle Bill Glass Recovery

Beverage container deposit legislation, commonly referred to as a "bottle bill," is usually a state or local government law enacted to impose monetary deposits

FIGURE 13.3   Recovered green glass bottles.

on all beverage containers (not only the glass ones). The imposed deposits are refunded to persons returning beverage containers. Accompanying these laws are usually restrictions on the disposal of beverage containers. (More discussion about the ongoing bottle bill debate is provided later in this chapter.)

In most systems, beverage retailers are required to act as a container drop-off depot because a monetary fund is paid for each returned beverage container including glass, aluminum, bimetal, and plastic beverage containers. However, only beverage containers and not other food packages (e.g., glass jars, plastic jars, tin cans, etc.) are subject to the monetary deposit and refund.

Various systems exist to return the beverage containers to recycling markets such as the bottling industry, glass container manufacturers, and plastic bottle users and manufacturers. The local retailer or beverage wholesaler acts as the receiver of the postconsumer beverage containers and the refunder of the deposit money.

As discussed later in this chapter, bottle bill legislation has been in effect for more than 20 years (Oregon was the first state to enact a bottle bill in 1971). Currently, only nine states use bottle bill legislation to recover beverage containers.

Drop-off Centers

Glass containers are frequently recovered from drop-off centers that collect a variety of source-separated recyclables (e.g., paper, aluminum, plastic, and glass). Users of these facilities are mainly individuals participating in voluntary programs, but such facilities are incorporated into many types of voluntary and mandatory recycling programs. Glass containers either arrive already separated, or they are easily separated upon receipt. Glass containers are usually stored in bunkers according to color (green, brown, clear, and mixed). The glass may or may not be processed on-site for shipment to market outlets. When processing is involved, it typically consists of

- Volume reduction by breaking or crushing
- Cleaning by screening to remove metal neck rings, paper labels, and foreign debris
- Containerizing by color in gaylord boxes, drums, or truck beds for bulk delivery

The city of Hollywood, Florida, has a unique "no cost" mini neighborhood recycling drop-off centers program. The city purchased 128 custom-designed containers through a state grant. To avoid collection, handling, and transportation costs, the city works with Faith Farm, a nonprofit rehabilitation organization that helps the needy. Faith Farm collects the recyclables (aluminum cans and three colors of glass), polices the immediate area, and retains the revenue. In return, Faith Farm furnishes the city with tonnage reports required by the county and the state.

Curbside Separation and Collection

Glass containers are collected from the residential solid waste stream on a large-scale basis through curbside collection systems. Residents are typically asked to separate specific recyclables from the rest of the refuse set out. Thus, recyclables are typically segregated by type or in mixtures that can be further sorted at the curb by the collector or later at a separation and processing facility. These types of source-separation curbside collection systems appeal to citizenry due to their relative convenience. However, public education programs must be intensive and specific to encourage voluntary participation and to educate residents about cleaning and color-separation requirements prior to curbside setout.

After the curbside collection, the mixed or separated recyclables are stored for processing and bulk shipment to prearranged markets.

Recovery from Primary Commercial Sources and Multifamily Residences

Primary commercial sources of glass containers are restaurants, taverns, and other select public places (e.g., schools, recreation areas, and hotels) where considerable quantities of food and beverages are consumed, leaving empty glass containers for recycling or disposal. Experience shows that greater quantities of glass containers are recoverable from commercial sources than from the residential sector.

Since commercial sources were first approached as possible participants in large-scale recycling programs, various systems have been developed to increase the convenience, efficiency, and sanitation aspects of storing large quantities of empty, rinsed, or nonrinsed glass containers. For example, behind-the-bar glass bottle crushers have been installed to keep glass bottles separate from kitchen refuse. Services that provide daily or near-daily pickup of glass recyclables are the most effective in minimizing potential sanitation nuisances and reducing storage needs for empty containers.

Another segment of the commercial waste stream that produces glass containers is the multifamily dwelling (apartments and condominiums). While these are technically residential dwelling units, municipalities frequently defer refuse and recyclable collections to the commercial haulers.

Multistory apartment complexes having interior refuse chutes and low-rise complexes having parking lot refuse dumpsters require special collection considerations. In these areas, collection practices for recyclable materials have been developing much slower.

In communities where multifamily housing styles represent significant sources of recyclables, innovative concepts are beginning to be implemented to recover select recyclable materials. For example, user-based systems that rely on residents to containerize recyclables in special bags are being demonstrated. Bags of recyclables are deposited on each floor or gathered in the basements of each complex. These methods have been reported as cumbersome, inefficient, and resulting in low participation and recovery rates.

For collection systems using parking lot dumpsters, compartmentalized dumpsters have achieved some success in recovering recyclables. Like refuse collection, these systems require considerable equipment maintenance and supervisory control.

An example of a new equipment line has been implemented in Miami, Florida, to serve high-rise complexes using interior refuse chutes. The new equipment consists of an electric carousel bin arrangement located in the basement of each complex. On each floor, residents use a remote selection device to indicate which type of recyclable or refuse will be entering the chute. The rotary bin system responds to an electronic message and rotates the correct receiving bin into the proper position before signaling for the chute delivery. Staff labor services the collection bins.

Recovery from Mixed Recyclables

In response to user claims of inefficiency, inconvenience, and costliness, service vendors have begun to look at collection services for recyclables and refuse from commercial sources as a wet-dry issue. One result is a collection system that mixes dry recyclables (e.g., paper, aluminum cans, glass containers, and plastic) for collection and later separation. Regular "wet" refuse (e.g., food, soiled paper, diapers, fruit peelings, etc.) is collected in separate bags and handled as garbage.

Glass containers are usually recovered whole or slightly broken at the commercial collection facility. Hand-picking or screening is performed to recover glass from the mixed recyclables.

Recovery from Solid Waste Processing Systems

Solid waste processing systems have taken on several configurations since the early 1970s. Most often the glass component is handled according to its physical properties such as density and particle size. Glass usually becomes part of a "grit" fraction that is either marketed as an aggregate or disposed of in landfills. Processing systems that manufacture refuse-derived fuel (RDF) usually remove glass from the fuel product.

Newer solid waste processing systems are based on producing an organic product that can be marketed as commercial compost. In lieu of marketing arrangements, the compost product is often applied to marginal lands for land restoration. In these facilities, glass containers are broken or crushed in the separation and volume-reduction process and become part of the compost mixture. As a sand-size particle, glass is silica which is a useful component of compost posing no deleterious effects in the land restoration operation.

In solid waste processing systems, recyclables such as ferrous, aluminum, and plastic are removed prior to entering the process line. Recovery usually consists of hand-picking. If desirable, glass containers could be removed at the front end (the picking and separation stage) as whole containers for color sorting, processing, and marketing to glass container remanufacturers.

Recovery as In-Plant Cullet

The recovery of breakage and rejects in glass manufacturing plants and in bottling and packaging plants is still performed using traditional recovery methods. In a glass container manufacturing plant, a process line will result in a small percentage of breakage and imperfect containers. These are simply recovered as a by-product and reintroduced as cullet into the mixture at the appropriate time.

It is necessary to remember that glass container manufacturers are separate and distinct from bottlers and packagers of beverages and food products. In these plants, empty or partially filled containers that break or are rejected can be recovered, washed, and returned to the glass manufacturing process.

In summary, there are various methods of separating and recovering glass from the waste stream as there are for other recyclable materials. These methods are generally classified into two categories: source separation and processing. Source-separation methods include curbside collection, drop-off sites, and buy-back centers. Of these three, curbside seems to produce the best results, but this is highly dependent upon the characteristics of the community. It is one of the most convenient methods of residential recycling, and the generator performs the initial separation of materials. It also makes people think about what they're throwing away and where they're throwing it. However, curbside recycling programs can be expensive to set up and implement.

Overall, source separation is generally the preferred method of recycling by the industry and by the participants. It seems to achieve the highest participation and recovery rates and reduces contamination problems. However, because glass must be color-separated, three separate bins are necessary for storage purposes. This has sometimes been considered problematic due to space limitations. However, flexible bin arrangements, frequent shipments, and reliable market outlets can minimize these problems.

Usable container glass can also be recovered from commercial and industrial sources such as restaurants, bars, and glass manufacturers. Experience has shown that greater quantities of glass can be recovered from commercial sources than from the residential waste stream. Commercial glass recovery should be strongly considered as part of a community's initial and long-term glass recycling efforts for waste reduction purposes and to meet recycling goals.

PROCESSING GLASS CONTAINERS

Processing glass containers is directly related to the types of products that will be manufactured and the types of materials that will be replaced using postconsumer cullet. In the glass manufacturing industry, in-plant cullet has always been reintroduced into the production batch because it was a reliable, contaminant-free secondary material. However, the reuse of recovered postconsumer container glass took many years to become a bona fide segment of the recycling industry.

The basic requirement for using recycled glass containers to make new glass containers has not changed since in-plant cullet was first introduced as a secondary material ingredient. Glass must be clean, free of metal caps and neck rings, and most importantly, color-sorted. Due to these standard manufacturing criteria, glass processing has evolved over time to include a number of steps that assure a usable secondary material.

One of the most common elements of a grassroots volunteer recycling program was the time-consuming processing of glass containers. Countless hours were devoted by dedicated workers crushing green, brown, and clear bottles and jars. The most typical method involved a worker standing over a 55-gal metal drum using a hand-held tamper or mall to break a few bottles, and crush the glass pieces. The glass containers were usually cleaned before crushing and metal neck rings and caps could be removed first or screened out later. Paper labels were often removed before crushing. Crushing was usually required prior to marketing so that potential contaminants could be removed. Crushed glass was also more economical to ship because it had a higher density than whole bottles and jars.

The glass recovered and processed by small volunteer recycling centers was often an inconsistent material; therefore, other uses were gradually developed. For example, Glasphalt became a popular outlet for grit and glass that contained some foreign matter. However, the early uses of Glasphalt for road paving often resulted in substandard street surfaces. Bits of paper and metal were exposed to weathering, and wear was excessive. Consequently, glass processing had to be improved to produce a reliable, contaminant-free, and, when necessary, color-uniform material in order for recovered glass to be marketed in large quantities.

The basic container glass processing steps are:

1. Initial rinsing, cap, and lid removal
2. Color separation
3. Volume reduction by breaking or crushing
4. Packaging for market shipping
5. In-plant beneficiation

These steps are performed at various stages after postconsumer recovery and the intended marketing of the processed glass (Fig. 13.4).

Initial Cleaning and Color Separation

In residential recycling programs, the trend has been to require glass containers to be rinsed and have the caps and lids removed before placing them at the curb or taking them to a drop-off center. Some programs require color-sorting by the resident recycler, but curbside separating or hand-sorting at a recycling center is becoming more common. This tends to increase the convenience of setting out recyclables by the resident, and some amount of separation occurs at the collection or transfer center as a control measure anyway.

Recovery programs for mixed recyclables may be designed to include glass containers. When glass bottles and jars are recovered, it is usually by hand-

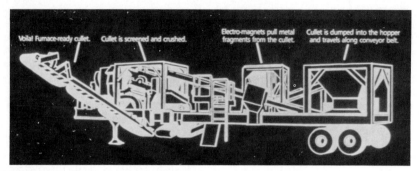

FIGURE 13.4   Glass processing equipment.

picking conveyor operations. Glass containers can be systematically sorted as they are picked from the process conveyor line. Some processing conveyors are designed so that hand-picking simply sorts the glass containers into individual conveyors that direct color-sorted containers to the breaking, screening, and bulk storage processes.

Glass Breaking and Crushing

Glass breaking is not desirable if it occurs before color separation. Broken glass is not readily separated from the mixed waste stream and becomes part of a mixed glass material that is of no real value to cullet users. In certain mixed-waste stream processing systems, the glass fraction of the waste stream simply becomes part of the grit residue which is landfilled or a component of a composted waste product. In compost, glass particles are beneficial because they have the same physical properties as sand.

If glass containers are to be recovered for marketing to glass container manufacturers or to other users of clean, contaminant-free glass cullet, then color-sorting needs to occur before breakage; metal neck rings, paper labels and food debris can be cleaned and screened from the glass after initial breakage and/or crushing; and storage of the processed cullet must assure that the bulk material is kept clean until it is packed for market (Fig. 13.5).

Packaging and Shipping

Container glass is a low-density material until it is broken and/or crushed. It then becomes a high-density material. Glass storage is usually required until enough of one color has been accumulated for cost-effective shipment to market. One example of the range between the amounts of the different glass colors is shown in the following breakdown from a recycling facility proposal made to Mercer County Improvement Authority, New Jersey, in 1988.

FIGURE 13.5 Storage of bulk cleaned, processed cullet.

Flint (clear)	38.5 percent
Amber (brown)	26.1 percent
Emerald (green)	15.4 percent
Mixed glass	20.0 percent

The above example ratio of colored- and mixed-glass cullet was an estimate for a proposed 180-ton/day processing facility of mixed recyclables.

Large amounts of glass cullet are frequently shipped as a bulk material in roll-off containers. Occasionally, gaylord boxes have been used to ship small amounts of exceptionally clean, uniformly colored glass to high-quality crushed glass users.

In-Plant Final Processing

Industry surveys indicate that the container glass used to make remanufactured glass bottles and jars is processed by intermediaries to meet the requirements of the manufacturer. In practice, color-sorted glass containers are shipped whole, broken, or crushed to the end users. Final cleaning is performed at the manufacturing plant by specialized beneficiation equipment to remove residual metals, plastics, and paper labels.

The cullet is then mixed with the raw materials used in the production of glass. After mixing, the batch is melted in a furnace at temperatures ranging from 2,600 to 2,800°F, depending on the percentage of cullet contained in the batch. The mix can burn at lower temperatures if more cullet is used. The melted glass is dropped into a forming machine where it is blown or pressed into shape. The newly

FIGURE 13.6 Glass melting furnace.

formed glass containers are slowly cooled in an annealing lehr. They are inspected for defects, packed, and shipped to the bottling company (Figs. 13.6 and 13.7).

In summary, the most important rule of thumb for recovering and marketing glass containers is to clean and color-sort them in order to produce a high-quality

FIGURE 13.7 Melted glass passes through forming machine for new glass shape.

recyclable product. It is not necessary to thoroughly wash glass containers in order to recycle them; a quick rinsing is usually sufficient, and paper labels do not need to be removed. Generally speaking, if the containers are clean enough to store in the home for a week, they are clean enough to be recycled. Many metals, stones, ceramics, and other foreign materials do not melt in the furnace with the materials that form glass and create stones or bubbles in the bottles. These bubbles or stones not only cause aesthetic problems, but weaken the bottle's wall as well. In the glass furnace, iron and lead contaminants settle to the bottom of the furnace tank and corrode its brick lining. Larger materials (e.g., steel lids and ceramics) often block feed lines from the furnace causing temporary production shutdowns. At the present time, there are no mechanical means of color sorting. Research and development in this area and in ceramic detection are promising; however, these functions are currently performed manually. Industry representatives indicate that meeting these quality requirements through consistent processing is the most difficult challenge in establishing and implementing successful glass recycling programs.

CONTAINER GLASS MARKETING

The successful recycling of recovered container glass depends on marketing a color-sorted and contaminant-free secondary material. Thus far, the biggest market has been the glass container manufacturing industry. When recovered glass does not meet manufacturing specifications, it can be used as an aggregate in Glasphalt or as a beneficial component of a soil conditioner product. These types of outlets usually depend on the local and/or regional availability of industries that would incorporate processed container glass into their manufacturing operations on a regular basis.

The primary end market for glass cullet is glass bottling manufacturing plants—there are currently over 80 of them throughout the United States. A vast majority of the glass recovered from the waste stream is used to make more glass containers (some studies cite up to 90 percent). These markets are generally available throughout the country. Glass manufacturing plants indicate a desire to increase their use of recovered glass. Bottle manufacturers are capable of using 80 to 90 percent cullet and most would like to use at least 50 to 60 percent. In fact, one Anchor Glass plant in Pennsylvania ran successfully on 100 percent used glass for seven weeks during the winter when frigid weather in Wyoming caused a disruption in the supply of soda ash to manufacturers around the country.

Markets for the three different colors of glass may vary by geographic location because some glass manufacturing plants only produce bottles of one or two colors. Large manufacturers may accept all three colors regardless of their production requirements and transport the color(s) they can't use to a "sister" plant in another location. However, hauling distances can affect the prices paid for different colors of cullet. As there is a greater demand for clear glass containers, prices are generally somewhat lower for brown and green cullet. If any gluts in the market do occur, it will be in the market for green glass because most of the green bottles used in this country are from imported beers, yet very few domestic products are contained in green bottles.

It is important to the glass container manufacturing process that the percentage of cullet used remain consistent over periods of time. It cannot vary on a daily basis. Therefore, glass manufacturers are usually conservative in determining the percentage of cullet used in the batch in order to ensure the availability of an adequate, steady supply.

Other markets for cullet have been identified through continuing research. Glass is or can be used in the manufacture of:

- Glasphalt, an asphalt made using a percentage of crushed glass for roadway applications
- Building and construction materials such as clay brick and tiles, masonry block, and Glascrete; as a lightweight aggregate in concrete and plastics; in glass polymer composites and extrusions; and FoamGlas for construction board and insulation
- Reflective paint for road signs (made from small glass beads)
- Glass wool insulation
- Telephone poles and fence posts (made by mixing cullet with plastic polymers)
- Agricultural soil conditioners to improve drainage and moisture distribution
- Artificial sand for beach restoration
- Fiberglass
- Abrasives
- Many other materials associated with the construction and textile industries

Most of these applications have been proven. A few are currently being used more frequently. The demand for glass by bottle manufacturers dropped in 1991 because of oversupplies from local recycling programs.

GLASS RECYCLING PROGRAM CONSIDERATIONS

In comprehensive solid waste management systems, recycling has become a typical program element along with refuse collection and waste disposal (Fig. 13.8). Many states mandate recycling goals in terms of waste disposal avoidance. Waste minimization programs are beginning to target the packaging industry as a primary place to reduce the generation of waste materials.

There are several issues that need to be addressed when considering glass recycling. In general, it is unlikely that glass containers would be the only targeted recyclable; it is typically one of the "big four" recyclable materials that also include aluminum, paper, and plastic.

First, it may be necessary to justify why glass recycling is important and if glass recycling can be cost-effective. After all, glass is made from relatively abundant and inexpensive virgin materials. Recycling glass does not save trees, for example, and therefore becomes a less emotional issue. However, the conservation of our energy supply (through the use of recycled glass cullet) is just as easily understood and accepted. Reducing the waste stream is also a major accomplishment when considering today's waste disposal problems. Although glass comprises a relatively small portion of the waste stream by volume (approximately 2 percent), glass recovery and recycling can have a significant impact on waste re-

FIGURE 13.8 Collecting separated glass in refuse truck.

duction by weight (7 to 8 percent in comparison) because glass is one of the heavier materials found in municipal solid waste.

In conjunction with other evaluation tasks, and as part of a comprehensive analysis of a community's solid waste generation characteristics, the amount of glass and sources of glass containers should be determined. The potential for marketing recovered glass to local and regional users of reclaimed glass should also be determined.

It is well known that glass containers are common in the residential waste stream. However, restaurants, taverns, recreational facilities, and institutions (e.g., schools) need to be considered as major generators of postconsumer glass as well. Restaurants and taverns in particular can derive many benefits from a glass recycling program. Although additional storage space is required, these businesses usually contract with private haulers for waste disposal on a per ton price basis and can therefore save a substantial amount of money on disposal costs due to the weight of glass. Many also generate a steady stream and large enough quantities of glass to negotiate good market prices. There are organizations throughout the country to assist businesses with setting up and implementing successful glass recycling programs. Some of these organizations are listed at the end of this chapter.

Other aspects of program implementation that need to be considered in the evaluation phase are legislative issues, cost factors, and program flexibility.

Legislative Issues

The Bottle Bill. The most infamous legislation affecting the use and recycling of glass beverage containers is known as *beverage container deposit legislation*

(BCDL). Commonly referred to as "bottle bills," these laws have been enacted to establish monetary deposits on beverage containers. Nine of the 50 states currently have bottle bills in effect: Connecticut, Delaware, Iowa, Maine, Massachusetts, Michigan, New York, Oregon, and Vermont. Legislation to enact bottle bills is pending in many other states as well, and efforts have been made to enact a national bottle bill on and off for almost 20 years (although they have not yet been successful). This has been very controversial among state governments, citizens, the recycling industry, and bottle manufacturers.

Bottle bill advocates believe that bottle bills provide a number of advantages:

- They reduce litter and litter-related costs such as pickup and disposal.
- They help to reduce the waste stream by diverting these materials from the landfill.
- They encourage reuse and recycling because of the economic incentives.
- They create markets to recycle the aluminum, glass, and plastic that is returned for deposit.
- They provide all of these benefits without cost to government.

Bottle bill advocates are also quick to point out that states with bottle bills are achieving higher recovery rates for beverage container materials than those without, and believe that industry is against such legislation in order to increase profits through the production or disposal of throwaways.

Those who oppose bottle bills include manufacturers and recyclers and their representative organizations. Their arguments against bottle bills include:

- They decrease the use of glass because retailers tend to shy away from selling glass containers due to the amount of space returned containers take up in the store, and consumers tend to use more aluminum and plastic containers because they are lightweight and easier to return.
- They force higher beverage prices.
- They are discriminatory because they only apply to beverage bottles and do not affect food containers and other packaging.
- The waste stream reduction achieved is much less than could be accomplished through successful recycling programs.
- They actually hurt existing recycling efforts by diverting the flow of beverage containers to retailers instead of recyclers.

An argument also exists between refillable versus nonrefillable glass. Nonrefillable bottles that are recovered from the waste stream are recycled, while refillable bottles are returned to the bottler to be used again. Both methods help to reduce the waste stream. However, fewer and fewer refillable bottles are being purchased and returned due to the inconvenience to the consumer. It is estimated that the average number of trips made by these bottles—as high as 50 in 1950—is now about 8.5.

Whatever one's standpoint on this issue, the effect and status of bottle bill legislation on the state and national levels should be considered when setting up a recycling program.

State Recycling Goals.   Other legislation related to glass-recycling programs includes state-regulated waste reduction goals and mandatory recycling programs.

Many states have adopted legislation that sets forth waste reduction goals by specified dates. Some of this legislation also mandates that a certain percentage of some materials be recycled. Glass is usually one of the "big four" materials specified in such legislation, along with aluminum, plastics, and newspaper. The status of state legislation should also be considered when setting up a recycling program. For example, if legislation in one's state mandates a 50 percent reduction in the amount of glass (and other specified materials) that is currently being disposed of to achieve say a 25 percent reduction in the overall waste stream, a local glass-recycling program will probably have to include the recovery of glass from commercial as well as residential sources in order to achieve the state-mandated waste reduction goals.

Mandatory Recycling Ordinances. Although most communities prefer to initiate recycling efforts through voluntary programs, many have already turned to mandatory programs in order to meet state or local recycling and waste reduction goals. Both voluntary and mandatory recycling programs can be effective. The success of voluntary programs depends largely on education, while mandatory programs rely on the various enforcement measures. This must also be considered when setting up specific program elements such as determining the amount of money necessary for public education programs versus the amount of money and effort required for enforcement.

Cost Factors

There are a number of cost factors that must be taken into account when setting up any recycling program. However, costs specific to glass recycling programs are mainly those associated with the color separation requirement. Additional containers are required for storage purposes, and additional labor costs are incurred because glass must be color-separated by hand.

Expenses associated with glass-recycling programs generally include:

- Collection costs
- Sorting costs (if collected mixed)
- Storage costs
- Transportation costs
- Other costs (e.g., public education and training and containers)

In order to determine these costs, several factors must be considered, such as the population served, characteristics of the geographical area (residential versus industrial, urban versus rural, etc.), the estimated weight of the glass expected to be recovered, the refuse collection service used (public or private), the method(s) of recovery (curbside collection, buy-back centers or drop-off sites), the type and location of the market(s), and the mode of transportation used to deliver the glass to the market(s).

Material sales revenues can be used to offset some of these program costs. A breakdown of material sales contributions and their associated values for typical programs are shown in Tables 13.1 and 13.2. Since less than half of the costs associated with typical multimaterial curbside programs are covered by sales revenues, remaining program costs must be met by other revenue sources (e.g., contract payments, grants, tax and surcharge revenues, and waste diversion credits).

TABLE 13.1 Sales Revenue Contribution by Material

Material	Percent of tonnage	Percent of revenue
Newspaper	56–70	57–65
Glass	15–22	10–20
Aluminum	1–2	15–20
Other	5–15	5–16

Source: "Comprehensive Curbside Recycling, Collection Costs and How to Control Them," Glass Packaging Institute, Washington, D.C., 1988.

TABLE 13.2 Materials Sales Values*

Materials	Value, $/ton
Newspaper	–40–15
Glass, clear (flint)	40–50
Glass, brown	30–50
Glass, green	15–40
Plastics, PET	150–210
Plastics, HDEP	160–200
Aluminum	700–800
Steel cans	40–80

*Prices effective August 1991 and based on clean, sorted materials delivered to end users. Low-range prices generally reflect prices in east and central United States. High-range prices generally reflect prices in western United States.

End-use markets currently pay $40 to $75/ton for uncontaminated color-separated glass. The prices paid by independent recyclers vary in accordance with the prices they receive from the end-use markets, transportation costs, the quantities of glass they receive and many other factors. There will be differences in the prices paid for recovered glass depending on whether it is sold to a recycling company or directly to a glass manufacturer. It is important to determine where the potential market is and what prices are being offered prior to implementing any glass-recycling program.

Avoided disposal costs should also be accounted for when determining the costs and revenues associated with glass recycling programs. For example, one Florida restaurant estimates that it saves approximately $28,000 in disposal costs by separating its glass for recycling. The restaurant does not receive any revenues for the glass but rather donates it to a Goodwill Industries recycling center because the avoided disposal costs alone are worth the effort. A New Jersey recycler estimates that the restaurants and bars involved in his program save $400 to $1200 monthly in refuse collection costs.

Program Flexibility

Flexibility is a key factor in any successful recycling program. Programs must be flexible enough to switch in and out of materials in order to accommodate changing market conditions. They must also be able to absorb fluctuating market prices. For glass, this can mean finding alternative markets for one or more colors and/or pursuing emerging markets for mixed cullet as the need arises.

Recycling programs should be assessed on a regular basis (at least annually) in order to determine what changes, if any, should be made to maximize participation, recovery rates, and sales revenues. These changes may be related to collection practices, education efforts, processing technologies, and/or materials marketing. Program flexibility will allow for such needed improvements without impacting other successful program elements.

SUMMARY

Potential Problems and Solutions

Representatives from various factions of the recycling industry cite contamination as the most common problem associated with glass recycling programs (mixed colors and/or foreign materials). Other problems include lack of communication, storage space, serviceability, and theft. Most of these problems are not specific to glass but also to other recyclable materials. Color contamination is specific to glass recycling, and storage space can be somewhat more of a problem for glass because of the color separation requirement.

The solution to most of these problems can be summed up in one word: *Education* (Table 13.3). The importance of early, continuous, long-lasting public education programs cannot be overemphasized in the field of recycling. In glass recycling, public education is needed for maintaining quality (i.e., eliminating contamination). Large producers of used glass can also overcome the storage problem by using a glass crusher. Just be sure that the potential market will accept the glass in crushed form. Many independent recyclers prefer to collect the glass whole to ensure that colors have not been mixed and that other contami-

FIGURE 13.9 Igloo containers from a drop-off center.

TABLE 13.3 Glass Recycling Made Easy

Glass Recycling Made Easy

Acceptable

Glass food and beverage containers can be easily recycled by glass container plants. Generally speaking, metal caps and lids should be removed but labels can remain.

Not Acceptable

The following materials are not recycled by glass container plants and should not be mixed in with container glass.

SODA BOTTLES

BEER BOTTLES

JUICE CONTAINERS

KETCHUP BOTTLES

WINE AND LIQUOR BOTTLES

FOOD CONTAINERS

MIRR

CE   C CUPS
A   ATES

FLOWER

RYSTAL

LIGHT BULBS

WINDOW GLASS

EAT RESISTANT
VENWARE

NKING
SSES

Source: Southeast Glass Recycling Program, Clearwater, Florida.

nants have been removed. However, glass manufacturing plants will generally accept recovered glass in either form.

Program Assistance

Due to the heightened public awareness of environmental issues in recent years and a strong commitment and effort by the glass industry in general, glass recycling has experienced the most rapid growth of any recyclable material. The industry itself has established ambitious goals and has assisted many communities in setting up successful glass-recycling programs. The following organizations have offered specific assistance in implementing glass-recycling programs.

- Glass Packaging Institute (202) 887-4850
- California Glass Recycling Corporation (916) 442-7002
- Carolinas Glass Recycling Program (North Carolina, South Carolina) (704) 525-8259
- Central States Glass Recycling Program (Illinois, Indiana, Wisconsin) (317) 872-4173
- Mid-America Glass Recycling Program (Louisiana, Missouri, New Mexico, Colorado, Oklahoma, Texas, Kansas, Arkansas) (501) 855-4703
- Mid-Atlantic Glass Recycling Program (Maryland, Virginia, District of Columbia) (703) 684-4421
- New Jersey Glass Recycling Association (201) 898-9123
- Pennsylvania Glass Recycling Corporation (717) 234-8091
- Southeast Glass Recycling Program (Florida, Georgia, Alabama, Mississippi) (813) 799-4917

REFERENCES

1. Alter, Harvey. 1988. The Greatly Growing Garbage Problem: A Guide to Municipal Solid Waste Management for Communities and Businesses. U.S. Chamber of Commerce Publication #0113. Washington, D.C.
2. Anchor Glass Container Corporation. 1990. Personal communication, Jacksonville, Fla.
3. Baker, V. David. 1990. Personal communication. Southeast Glass Recycling Program, Clearwater, Fla.
4. Barbero, Chris. 1990. Personal communication. Waste Management of North America, Inc., Philadelphia, Pa.
5. Bays, Benjamin J. 1990. Personal communication, The Owl Corporation, Baltimore, Md.
6. Bowlus, Dale R. 1990. Personal communication, Susquehannock Environmental Center, Inc., Bel Air, Md.
7. Citizens Against Throwaways. 1990. C.A.T. Tracks, March 1990, Florida Conservation Foundation, Inc., Winter Park, Fla.
8. Davol, Ben. 1990. Personal communication, Mid-Atlantic Glass Recycling Program, Alexandria, Va.

9. Gibboney, Douglas L. 1990. Personal communication, Pennsylvania Glass Recycling Corporation, Harrisburg, Pa.

10. Hintz, Mel. 1990. Personal communication, New Jersey Glass Recycling Association, Glen Ridge, N.J.

11. Malott, John P. 1990. Personal communication, Owens-Brockway Glass Containers, Lakeland, Fla.

12. Miller, Chas. 1990. Personal communication, Glass Packaging Institute, Washington,D.C.

13. National Soft Drink Association. 1990. Things You've Always Wanted to Know About Soft Drink Container Recycling, Washington, D.C.

14. New Jersey Glass Recycling Association. 1988. Highlights of New Jersey Glass Recycling Association's 1988 Fall Seminar, Morris Plains, N.J.

15. New Jersey Glass Recycling Association. 1989. Highlights of New Jersey Glass Recycling Association's 1989 Fall Seminars, Glen Ridge, N.J.

16. Resource Conservation Consultants. 1988. Comprehensive Curbside Recycling: Collection Costs and How to Control Them, Glass Packaging Institute, Washington, D.C.

17. Resource Recycling, Inc. 1990. *Bottle/Can Recycling Update,* May 1990, vol. 1, no. 4, Portland, Oreg.

18. Southeast Glass Recycling Program. 1989. *Southeast Glass Recycling,* Winter 1989, Clearwater, Fla.

CHAPTER 14
PLASTICS

Wayne Pearson

Executive Director
Plastics Recycling Foundation, Inc.
Washington, D.C.

INTRODUCTION

In 1989 about 58 billion lb of plastics was manufactured for sale and use in the United States, consisting of about 25 categories of materials. Of this, about half went into municipal solid waste (MSW) according to the EPA, who claim plastics make up about 8 percent by weight and 20 percent by volume of the roughly 180 million tons of annual MSW produced in this country (Fig. 14.1).

Roughly half or 15 billion lb of the plastics in the trash is packaging material and approximately 1 billion lb is postindustrial scrap (Fig. 14.2).

The plastics industry annually recycles several billion pounds of thermoplastic from trim and mold runners in their manufacture. This is called *regrind*. It is relatively clean and generally composed of a single polymer. The trim is gathered up, then densified or ground and blended with virgin resin at the front end of the process. The significance of this is that it demonstrates the reuseability of material that would otherwise by scrapped.

The primary focus of plastics recycling is on the thermoplastic component of the plastic garbage stream, which represents about 75 percent of all plastics manufactured. The entire spectrum of packaging is thermoplastic. This is fortunate because packaging, the element in the waste that is getting the most national attention and highest concern, represents about 30 percent of the total municipal solid waste. Packaging is dominated by paper and glass; plastics is 13 percent by weight.

Paper	48%
Glass	25%
Plastics	13%
Metal	9%

Nearly 80 percent of the major thermoplastic resins used in packaging in 1989 were polyolefin (LDPE, HDPE, and PP) as shown in Table 14.1.

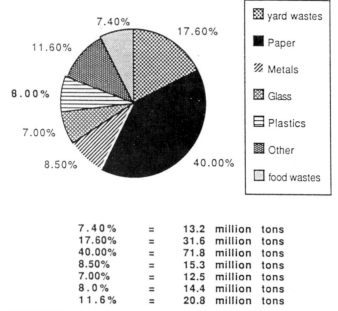

7.40%	=	13.2 million tons
17.60%	=	31.6 million tons
40.00%	=	71.8 million tons
8.50%	=	15.3 million tons
7.00%	=	12.5 million tons
8.0%	=	14.4 million tons
11.6%	=	20.8 million tons

FIGURE 14.1 Materials generated in MSW by weight.

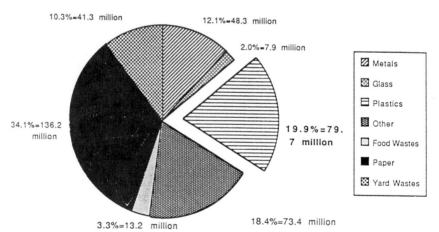

FIGURE 14.2 Landfill volume of discards in MSW.

On a volume basis, it is interesting to note that about 80 percent of the plastics packaging is in the form of rigid containers: beverage bottles, nonbeverage bottles, and other rigid containers. On a volume basis, film represents only about 20 percent. On a weight basis, however, rigid containers represent approximately half of plastics packaging that goes into the waste stream (Table 14.2).

TABLE 14.1 Plastics Used in Packaging, 1989

Polymer	Billion pounds	Major use
Low-density polyethylene (LDPE)	5.7	Shrink wrap
High-density polyethylene (HDPE)	4.4	Milk, water, juice, detergent bottles
Polypropylene (PP)	1.5	Snack food, film, ketchup bottle
Polystyrene (PS)	1.3	Pharmaceutical bottles, foam caps, etc.
Polyethylene terephthalate (PET)	1.0	Soft drink bottles
Polyvinyl chloride (PVC)	0.6	Water and salad oil bottles, household food wrap
Other	0.5	
Total	15.0	

TABLE 14.2 Plastics Packaging by Volume

Beverage bottles	25%
Nonbeverage bottles	25%
Other rigid containers	30%
Film	20%

Looking at the potential recyclables, we see the following items are reasonably viable in terms of technology and economics:

- Newspapers
- Aluminum and steel cans
- Glass bottles and jars
- Plastic beverage containers

It is interesting to note that on a volume basis the plastic beverage container is equal to about one-third of the volume of things that are recyclable today, namely, newspapers, nonplastic beverage containers, and plastic beverage containers. This is very significant, because it clearly shows that if plastic beverage containers were included along with traditional recyclables, namely newspapers and nonplastic beverage containers, the volume of material kept out of the landfill could be increased by 50 percent (Fig. 14.3).

In order for anything to be recycled from the garbage pile, it must be processed into a viable, clean raw material. That raw material must then be manufactured into a product. That product must then be marketed and distributed, and customers must be found and persuaded to buy and continue to buy this product made from material from the waste stream.

Thus, recycling requires four elements:

- Collection
- Sorting of raw materials
- Reclaiming the raw material to make a product
- Markets and paying customers for the product

The infrastructure for reclaiming, cleaning up, and producing products to sell is growing fast. There are a number of major companies involved in the business,

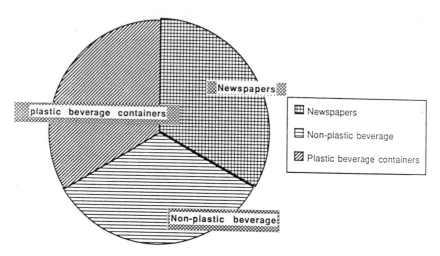

FIGURE 14.3   Volume of recyclables.

including Du Pont, Sonoco Graham, Wellman, wTe, Day Products United Resin Recovery, Quantum, Phillips, and Polysource, and the National Polystyrene Recycling Corporation. In addition, there is a growing number of manufacturers of plastics profiles using commingled plastic from the waste stream. This technology has been transferred to hundreds of communities who are examining how to collect and sort these materials and include them in their recycling programs, and it has been transferred to the industrial segment which takes the collected materials and cleans them up for subsequent use. End-use markets for the recovered generic polymers from beverage bottles are established and are larger than the amount of polymer that can be captured for recycling today.

Some driving forces are actually accelerating and expanding the demand for these recycled materials. These particularly include activities by packagers who wish to use a more environmentally attractive package by including recycled content. In addition, other forces are developing which will alter the economic incentives which would drive recycling. Examples of these are

1 . *Increased landfill charges:* Currently the *cost* for landfill in the United States is between $15 and $25 per ton and can be higher depending upon location. However, the *price* of landfilling is substantially higher, and rapidly increasing, and in some cases exceeds $150 per ton, because the supply of landfill has been severely reduced by legislation and by operation parameters set by the EPA making it very difficult to maintain present landfill capacity. This will be a powerful economic driving force to make recycling occur faster.

2. *Legislation that mandates products contain recycled material:* This legislation, seen most prominently in California and Connecticut for newsprint, will drive recycling. It is moving toward plastics. The way it works is that if a manufacturer of a product (i.e., newspapers) is forced by law to buy recycled material, that company will have to pay whatever price the market demands for

the recycled material. Consequently, recycled material could actually be priced higher than virgin material.

3. *Market demand for recycled content material:* As manufacturers of products decide that it could give them a competitive edge to use a package made with recycled-content material, they will design their package to include those materials, and will so advertise them. The package maker will then be forced to use recycled material in preference to virgin, just as though it were legislated. The price of recycled material could be equal to or higher than virgin. This will definitely drive people to want to recycle more waste material

4. *The price of oil:* If the price of oil were to increase substantially, either because of prices set by OPEC or a tax surcharge placed by the U.S. government, this would cause virgin material to cost more than recycled material and would be a powerful driving force.

The economics of plastics recycling can be attractive because it is not a capital-intensive operation and can be integrated easily with the manufacture of a plastic product. A company that manufactures a molded plastic product, or bottle or film, has the potential to process recycled material and use it as a part of the feedstock for the product they are manufacturing. The cost of raw material is low and can actually be below zero. An industry or community can, in some cases, afford to pay someone to take the raw material from the garbage pile, because paying for it to be taken away may be cheaper than paying for it to be incinerated or landfilled.

The same thing is true of materials that would be recovered from the waste stream that might be close to a generic material, such as solvent-separated polymers, or aqueous separation of polymers, where a clean 99.9 percent quality generic can be obtained or where mixed color is not a problem.

The quality of material processed from the waste stream has a major impact on the economics of recycling. For example, if one employs a mixture of several polymers from the postconsumer waste stream and has to put investment into cleaning and separating these polymers, such as aqueous sink float or solvent separation or simply not separating them and using them as a commingled mixture, the alternative of industrial scrap (available in excess of 1 billion pounds per year) will look very attractive to a processor. The industrial scrap generally has not been in the garbage pile and is reasonably uniform as to polymer type. Consequently, the work to process it into a useful raw material is less. This economic fact must be recognized and suggests that clean industrial scrap will be consumed first and preferentially to postconsumer.

The current trend is toward recycling, because we are deliberately shutting down alternative capacity to process garbage. It is reported that by 1995 only half of today's capacity for landfill will exist. The alternative is recycling. If the cost avoidance is included in the economics, it will make more components of the waste stream more attractive than virgin materials. Anticipating this, the plastics industry infrastructure is growing by leaps and bounds. About 5 years ago there were only about five plastic reclaimers in the United States using plastics from the postconsumer stream. In 1990 the number was close to 200 and growing.

It can be stated with a large degree of confidence that from a technical standpoint, the entire thermoplastic spectrum of the plastic component of the municipal solid waste can be processed into products that have utility. It also can be stated that the thermosetting components of the garbage pile can be processed by technologies which might include solvent separation, decoupling, or pyrolysis of the thermoset components. All of this technology has been demonstrated. Not all of it is economically viable given today's price of oil, or in other words, alternative feedstocks, but as the price of oil escalates with inflation and as the costs of alternative disposal methods rise, recycling of postconsumer plastics will become increasingly attractive. Given all the factors, plastics may be the most recyclable components in the trash.

The public's perception, however, is that there is something unnatural about plastics and since plastics dominate in terms of volume, the amount of packaging the consumer sees, and since the consumer visualizes that packaging as redundant excess and unnecessary, plastics is catching the major brunt of legislative constraint.

At this moment more than 24 states and the District of Columbia have enacted comprehensive recycling laws. These laws may include all or some of the following:

- Mandatory waste reduction goals
- Mandatory source separation
- Mandatory curbside or drop-off recycling

Thirty-seven states have passed plastic-container coding laws. These are laws which require coding of plastic bottles and/or rigid plastic containers as to resin type, and in the main the states are following the voluntary codes recommended by the Society of the Plastics Industry. Table 14.3 lists states that have passed plaster container coding laws.

The Plastic Bottle Institute of the Society of the Plastics Industry, Inc. (SPI) has developed a voluntary coding system for plastic containers which identifies bottles and other containers by material type, thus assisting recyclers in sorting plastic containers by resin composition.

The container coding system was created to provide a uniform national system for coding that meets the needs of the recycling industry, as defined by the recyclers and collectors themselves.

The code is a three-sided triangular arrow with a number in the center and letters underneath. The three-sided arrow was selected to isolate and distinguish the number code from other markings. The number inside and the letters indicate the resin from which the container is made; containers with labels or base cups of a different material may, if appropriate, be coded by their primary, basic material:

1 = PET (polyethylene terephthalate)
2 = HDPE (high-density polyethylene)
3 = V (vinyl)
4 = LDPE (low-density polyethylene)
5 = PP (polypropylene)
6 = PS (polystyrene)
7 = Other

TABLE 14.3 Plastic Container Coding Laws

Alaska	Michigan
Arizona	Minnesota—draft regulations on hold
Arkansas (enacted 1991)	Mississippi (enacted in 1991)
California	Missouri
Colorado	Nevada (enacted in 1991)
Connecticut—regulations approved	New Jersey
Delaware (enacted in 1991)	North Carolina
Florida—regulatory letter issued	North Dakota
Georgia	Ohio—draft regulations approved
Hawaii	Oklahoma
Illinois (amended to delay enactment date by one year to January 1, 1992)	Oregon (enacted in 1991)
	Rhode Island
Indiana	South Carolina (enacted in 1991)
Iowa	South Dakota (enacted in 1992)
Kentucky (enacted in 1991)	Tennessee
Louisiana	Texas
Maine—regulations approved	Virginia
Maryland (enacted in 1991)	Washington (enacted in 1991)
Massachusetts	Wisconsin—regulations approved

A number of communities and some states have elected to pass laws to ban certain specific packaging materials. Most notably are those states that are banning polystyrene foam containers, but a number of communities are going beyond that and are restricting plastics packaging to those very specific things which are, in fact, recycled.

There have been discussions of specific taxes on certain plastics packaging and the outright banning of some packaging concepts, such as the multilayer package, the aseptic package, and so forth. Dealing with this legislation is requiring a great deal of energy and financial resources from the plastics industry to create as near as possible a "level playing field" vis-à-vis nonplastic packaging materials.

Many of the governments are acting to ban or restrict plastics in order to get the attention of the plastics industry. This has resulted in action by the Council for Solid Waste Solutions (CSWS), the National Association for Plastic Container Recovery (NAPCOR), The Plastics Recycling Corporation of New Jersey (PRCNJ), and the Polystyrene Council.

COLLECTION AND SORTING SYSTEMS

The decision by governments to use recycling as a method for managing solid waste necessitates their finding a way to separate recyclable components from traditional trash. At this point all of the activity in this field falls under the jurisdiction and direction of the public sector and has been delegated by national, state, and county governments to the lowest possible level in the nation, namely, more than 8000 small townships and municipalities. Each of these governmental units has to figure out a method for gathering and separating the recyclables from the trash.

This is an enormous task for these people because we as a nation have perfected the management of trash and have achieved very low costs. In effect, trash disposal is a service industry where the trash is collected and hauled to a disposal site (either a landfill or incinerator), and the communities pay a fee for this service.

Under the new system of recovering recyclables and selling them to the private sector as raw materials to manufacture into products, the communities have to learn about private enterprise and the commodities market.

As a result of this background, we find every conceivable concept that can be imagined applied to this collection and marketing of recycled components. These range from drop-off and buy-back centers to collecting all of the recyclables at curbside in trucks and hauling them to a facility for sorting of major components (aluminum, steel, glass, paper, and plastics).

The design of trucks also runs the gamut depending on a variety of preconceived notions, most of which lead to higher labor and capital costs than the cost to collect trash. This in turn leads many in the public sector to believe that it is too costly to collect some items such as light-weight plastics and to turn to legislative bans to restructure the garbage pile to more easily collectible components.

The economic viability of recycling needs to be measured against the alternative strategies for dealing with solid waste. The cost of recycling contains these elements:

- The cost to collect
- The cost to sort
- Minus the cost of landfill avoided
- Minus the revenue from the recyclables sold by the material recovery facility

If the cost to collect and sort, minus the revenue, is calculated, it can be equated to the equivalent landfill cost avoided.

The net cost of recycling can be related to the cost of an alternate disposal, such as a landfill. The point at which they are equal is called the *break-even landfill cost*. Various parameters that affect the economics of recycling can be plotted against the break-even landfill cost. An analysis of recycling economics shows that the dominant variable is *capture rate* (the percent recovered from the homeowner) (Fig. 14.4).

As can be seen, the cost of a recycling program that captures 65 to 85 percent of the recyclables will be equivalent to landfill costs at $25 to $35 per ton. In other words, if costs to landfill MSW are equal to or higher than $25 to $35 per ton, a well-designed recycling program will be economically attractive.

From this study a capture rate of 65 percent or greater will produce an acceptable cost. The inclusion of plastics reduces that cost. However, if the capture rate falls substantially below 60 percent, the costs rise very rapidly due to the

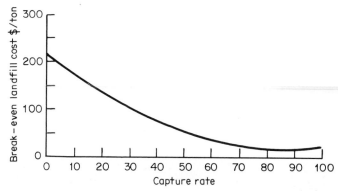

FIGURE 14.4   Break-even land cost vs. percent capture rate with plastics.

poor utilization of the capital and labor, both of which are intensive in the cost to collect and sort recyclables.

The research on the subject of collection of recyclables points to a very clear direction. Traditionally trash has been collected at the curbside of the homeowner. If the recyclables are separated by the homeowner and collected at that point, it is possible to capture 70 percent or more of the recyclables from the householder. By contrast, buy-back and drop-off approaches to gathering the recyclables from the homeowner will capture only 20 and 10 percent, respectively.

- Voluntary drop-off, 10 percent
- Buy-back centers, 15 to 20 percent
- Curbside collection, 70 to 90 percent

Research and commercial experience make it clear that the more complicated you make the job for the homeowner—that is, the larger number of individual sorts you ask the homeowner to make—the less you capture. Commingling the containers (glass, steel, aluminum, and plastics) is preferred (Fig. 14.5).

Implications from the research now being conducted in a number of places in the nation are that the project should be made extremely simple for the consumer and the collection truck should be a large-scale one, which will not "cube out" in a normal 8-h shift. A 30-yd^3 top-loaded truck such as Rhode Island and many other communities use has proven economical for collecting uncompacted newspapers, and glass, aluminum, steel, and plastic beverage containers (Fig. 14.6).

The cost of collecting and sorting recyclables represents about two-thirds of collection costs. For this reason an improperly designed system can generate high costs for the community. If a community has a poorly designed system, plastics, which have a high volume to weight ratio, will be blamed.

Since the capital cost for equipment to collect material at the curb, and the labor associated with getting the material into the truck, represents about 70 percent of total costs for collection, and therefore about 50 percent of total handling costs, it follows that collection systems should be designed to be highly efficient.

FIGURE 14.5   Curbside container for commingled plastics.

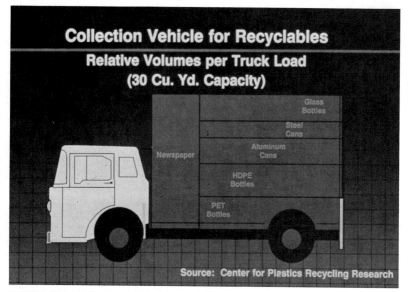

FIGURE 14.6   Collection vehicle for recyclables.

The larger the number of individual materials that must be picked up and placed in a particular spot in the truck, the more time it takes to fill the truck and the more hours the worker has to spend accomplishing this task. Consequently, the lowest cost of collection comes from large-scale, simplified processes that collect multimaterials in as large a container as is practicable. This can include a 13-gal plastic bag, lifted by a person, to a 90-gal bucket lifted by a robot arm.

Many studies have been undertaken to find ways to densify the plastic containers to recover their volume. The ideas range from asking householders to step on the plastic containers such as the program of NAPCOR (National Association of Plastic Container Recovery) to attempting to add densification equipment to collection trucks for recyclables. The problem with adding densification equipment is that it adds capital cost, increases labor cost, and reduces truck capacity, which merely adds to the collection cost.

Recent experimental data from the Center for Plastics Recycling Research (CPRR) show that compaction of recyclables in a traditional trash-hauling truck results in significant volume reduction, without increasing glass breakage. Moreover, if the recyclables are collected in plastic bags, the glass breakage can be reduced.

The results showed that the glass and steel do not compact, and therefore the glass does not break from compaction. Plastics and aluminum compact easily with a 90 percent volume reduction for them. The volume reduction with the mixed recyclables including glass, steel, aluminum, and plastics in the packer truck was a minimum of 35 percent and will be proportional to the amount of compactables (plastics and aluminum) in the recyclables mixture. The mixed recyclables in the plastics bag showed essentially the same volume reduction as the loose recyclables collected in bins.

Glass breakage did not occur due to compaction, but it does occur from loading, moving, and unloading the truck. Significantly, glass breakage was cut in half when the recyclables were in plastic bags. Corroborative evidence of the viability of this approach is being developed by a number of communities across the nation.

Once collected, the recyclables must be taken to a facility for processing them into a form suitable for sale as raw materials to those industries that can use the subsegments of the trash pile. For example, aluminum cans are separated and sold in a bale or blown loosely into a trailer for sale to the aluminum industry, which can melt the material down, reformulate the alloys, and use the recovered aluminum in a variety of ways, including new aluminum cans. In the case of glass, to be of value to the glass industry, the glass must be separated by color and must be absolutely free of any trash materials such as ceramics or metal. If the materials are sorted at the curb on a truck, they would come into a facility where the individual compartments of the truck would be unloaded into the appropriate place for subsequent packaging.

What is rapidly developing as the methodology for sorting is the material recovery facility, or MRF. A commingled mixture of recyclables is delivered to the facility, which is designed to separate these materials into their appropriate components either by hand or by a combination of automated and manual sorting. Steel and aluminum cans are easily separated from the glass and plastics by magnets and eddy currents, respectively. The glass and plastics can be separated from each other by mechanical means, and then they are separated into glass by color and plastic by polymer type, usually by hand (Fig. 14.8).

The technology for automating the separation of plastics is being developed in a pilot study at the Center for Plastics Recycling (CPRR) at Rutgers. It has been

FIGURE 14.7   Sorting at a materials recovery facility (MRF).

demonstrated that the beverage bottles can be separated into the following categories without a human hand touching them (Fig. 14.9):

PVC	Water bottles
Clear PET	Soft drink, wine, liquor
Green PET	Soft drink, wine, liquor
Translucent HDPE	Milk, water, juice
Pigmented	Detergent, pharmaceutical

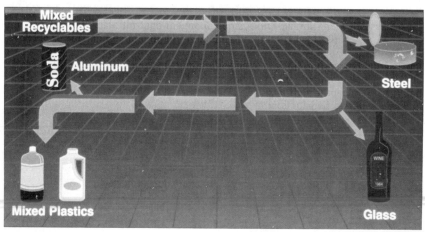

FIGURE 14.8   Sorting mixed recyclables.

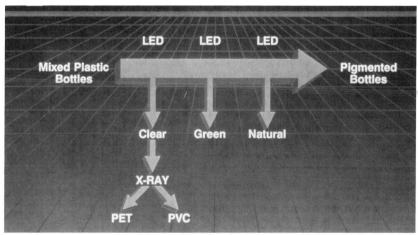

FIGURE 14.9 Separation of mixed plastic bottles.

This is accomplished by detecting the presence of the bottle on a conveyor belt using visible light rays for PET and HDPE and x-rays for PVC. Once detected, electronically activated devices eject the appropriate bottle from the conveyor belt (Fig. 14.10). The materials are then packaged for shipment after separation. A person assigned to the MRF negotiates prices for these commodities with a list of customers they have to purchase these materials.

FIGURE 14.10 Analysis testing of clear PET soft drink bottle.

terials in a family from each other becomes economically significant and important. For example, different molecular weights of high-density polyethylene have radically different properties and fit into significantly different market segments. The low-viscosity injection moldable base cup on the soft drink bottle is a significantly different material from the high-viscosity, high-molecular-weight material used in the milk bottle. There are literally hundreds of subsets of polymer types in each of the categories of resin types. As the needs of the marketplace develop, the technology exists to tap a variety of properties to achieve various levels of desired separation. One of the advantages of the molecular separation technology is that it permits the recovery of individual polymers from a multilayer package. Many modern packages will contain one or more polymers in combination to achieve properties such as an oxygen barrier and a moisture barrier. With this molecular separation technology, it has been demonstrated that these materials can be taken apart to recover the individual, original generic materials.

Another form of molecular sorting is to depolymerize the polymer to its original monomer. Some polymer esters such as polyethylene terephthalate (PET) and the methyl methyacrylates lend themselves to this approach.

Resin Reclamation

Once the materials have been captured and sorted, they represent a feedstock for a resin reclamation facility to clean up the polymer. A resin reclamation facility is capable of chopping up and washing the bottles and separating the materials into their components to produce a clean, generic polymer (Fig. 14.11). For example, clean PET can be produced at 99.9 percent purity. This is a high enough quality to compete with virgin PET. This process is capable of cleaning up PVC and

FIGURE 14.11   Plastic resin plant.

HDPE and has been used to clean up the polypropylene ketchup bottle and the ENVIROPET ketchup bottle.

The economics of reclamation are very favorable. A respectable, neighborhood-friendly PET reclamation plant of nominally 20 million lb per year can be built for approximately $2.5 million to produce a selling price of flake of about half that of virgin material, assuming that the raw material coming into the plant is baled PET bottles at 6 cents per pound (Table 14.5). This plant is designed to remove aluminum chips (from the cap). Packages that do not contain aluminum require less capital investment for cleaning.

TABLE 14.5   Economics of PET Reclamation

Capacity	20 million lb/year
Investment	$2.5 million
Purity	99.9% PET
Price	25 cents/lb F.O.B. plant (flake)
Revenue	$5 million/year
Profit	$1 million/year
Net return	20%

Source: Center for Plastics Recycling Research (1990).

Day Products of Bridgeport, New Jersey, the first licensee of the Center for Plastics Recycling Research at Rutgers University technology, has scaled up this technology tenfold to a 50 million pound per year plant. Another licensee, Handcor of Findlay, Ohio, is operating a plant to clean up polyethylene bottles. There are many commercial operations in the United States that employ their own proprietary technology to reclaim generic polymers from the trash. An additional 16 companies have licensed this technology from Rutgers.

It is possible to restore the properties of generic materials from the postconsumer stream that have been degraded due to the processing and/or use of the virgin material. In the case of PET the polymer can be "solid-stated" to restore molecular weight losses.

Based on preliminary findings from the research that is going on in this field, it appears that some properties can be restored by including additives, and properties can be substantially upgraded by including virgin material. The most likely case for the use of recycled material is to formulate it with virgin. The plastic industry traditionally blends almost every material, including virgin material, to achieve the properties specifically required by their customers. This technology is being employed today.

Another reclamation technology was alluded to in the discussion of molecular sorting. PET, for example, can be depolymerized through a methanolysis process, and the recovered monomer can be refined and used to derive a new polymer. The dissolution of polymers in an organic solvent system can recover a highly purified polymer molecule. The molecular purification technologies hold the potential for using recycled material in food contact packaging. Two issues need to be resolved, namely obtaining approval from the U.S. Food and Drug Administration (FDA) and a better understanding of the economics.

Trash Residues

Experience has shown that when householders are asked for beverage containers, they have a penchant for giving material not asked for. Initially this was thought to be indigenous to plastics, but it was subsequently learned that this happens in every category where the consumer delivers recyclables at the curb. Nominally, this amounts to 10 to 20 percent by weight:

- PET soft drink bottle, 50 to 60 percent
- HDPE milk jug, 30 to 40 percent
- Nonbeverage, 10 to 20 percent

The unrequested materials include nonbeverage containers, film, and even toys (Fig. 14.12).

It might be assumed that the consumer would have difficulty determining what plastics to deliver on the basis that there are so many different kinds of plastics, but in this case, we are asking the consumer to deliver only those containers from which he or she has drunk the contents. It is curious therefore that with this instruction, they would give a motor oil bottle.

When it is difficult or too expensive to separate generic materials, it is possible to deal with a commingled mixture of all of the polymers from the waste stream. Contrary to historical perception, those materials which are incompatible with each other can be processed in a variety of ways to overcome the negative properties derived from the incompatibility. A crude extruder such as the ET/1 can be used, but there are other variations on this equipment that can be employed (Fig. 14.13).

FIGURE 14.12   Various plastic containers.

FIGURE 14.13   Plastic extruding equipment.

The crudest application of this technology is in the form of commingled, extruded, or compression-molded profiles, which have found new market applications in landscape timbers, fence posts, marine applications, park benches, and so forth. Here a commingled mixture, uncleaned and containing scrap metal and paper, can be fabricated into useful products (Fig. 14.14).

This technology is moving toward the second generation, where the commingled mixture is "refined." That is, the metal and tramp paper are removed, whereupon the materials can be thoroughly mixed and melt-filtered. Compatibilizers can be introduced if necessary to achieve a variety of properties. These materials are then suitable for use in conventional molding and processing equipment, whereas the aforementioned crude profiles require very rugged extruders or compression molding equipment that can deal with the residual metal and/or other waste material.

Basically, then, there are two broad cuts that we seek in sorting the material. The first is to attain a high-quality generic material, similar in properties to the virgin counterpart that went into the waste stream in the first place, and second, when the economics prohibit recovering a generic material, the new emerging research information teaches us that these combinations of materials have potential large utility.

Currently, most of the technology for separating materials into their generic components is focused on materials used in rigid packaging. Very little effort has been applied as yet to the separation of polymers into their generic types from the flexible packaging arena. And virtually no work has been undertaken to separate polymers other than in a macroform from nonpackaging applications such as in the automotive, aerospace, and construction industries.

Cost Factors

It is technically feasible to recycle, recover, and reuse all of the discarded plastics packaging. However, with the exception of beverage bottles, economics limit

(a)

(b)

FIGURE 14.14 Useful products from recycled, uncleaned, commingled plastic mixture.

(c)

(d)

FIGURE 14.14 (*Continued*) Useful products from recycled, uncleaned, commingled plastic mixture.

cycled material, despite quality deficiencies, then the price of recycled material need not be discounted versus virgin. In fact, the price of recycled material could exceed the price of virgin. That would change economics substantially.

"Green" is a new marketing parameter. Heretofore, materials that are clearly inferior to virgin have commanded an inferior or discounted price. In fact, many of the nation's specifications, in addition to attempting to define properties, will contain the added phrase: "Must be virgin." This phrase has blocked the use of recycled material.

"Green" introduces the amazing notion that a material that is most likely inferior, in name, if not in specification, could command a premium price versus virgin. If this turns out to be the case, recycled resins will be able to tolerate higher costs for collecting-sorting-reclaiming, or will be more profitable. In any event, the green marketing parameter separates recycled from the virgin supply-demand curve and makes possible a wide range of strategies for marketing recycled materials.

The research sponsored by the plastics industry through the Plastics Recycling Foundation at the Center for Plastics Recycling Research is aimed at driving down the cost of collecting and sorting and upgrading the quality of the generics recovered through improved processing technologies so as to drive the value up. Industry and the recycling community are working on these same issues so that the number of plastic items in the trash pile that will become economically viable will increase with time.

In connection with minimizing the cost of collecting and sorting there are technologies that simplify collection, sorting, and cleaning.

- The molecular development of commingled plastics
- The development of new compounds and families of products based on refined commingled plastics

These technologies do not require plastics to be sorted, and they can simplify collection. Moreover, the range of plastics collected from the householder could be enlarged substantially. A wide range of unsorted baled or granulated postconsumer plastics would be shipped to a plant that could separate them into generic resins at the molecular level or could manufacture new compounds from the commingled unseparated materials. Both of these technologies will drive the cost of collecting and sorting down and at the same time will provide some reasonable level of value for the recovered generics and/or nongeneric (commingled) plastics.

MARKETING

Once the materials from the trash pile have been processed into their highest quality of generic form, they are suitable to compete in the huge markets that exist for these materials. Market research sponsored by the Plastics Recycling Foundation at the University of Toledo has developed the projected markets in Table 14.6, which illustrate the large potential for these materials. Today it is possible to recover PET, HDPE, and PVC from the postconsumer stream in very high quality suitable to penetrate and participate in the markets in competition with virgin.

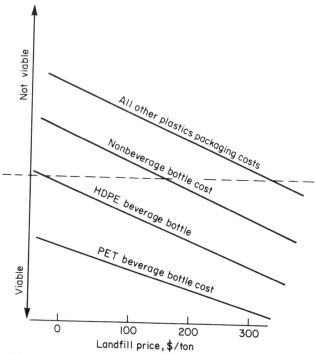

FIGURE 14.15 Graph—Variability of plastic packaging recycling vs. today's virgin prices based on oil at $30/barrel.

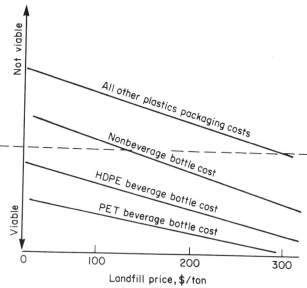

FIGURE 14.16 Graph—Variability of plastic packaging recycling vs. virgin prices based on oil at $35/barrel.

the degree of recycling at this time. Communities are not enthusiastic about collecting materials if their alternate methods of garbage disposal cost less. Therefore, it is necessary to consider the cost to the community as well as the cost to the reclaimer to determine the full cost of the recycled material. The fact that the recycled material must compete with virgin resin in quality and price must be taken into account when considering the markets.

The cost to the community includes the following:

- Cost to collect recyclables
- Cost to sort recyclables

From these two costs the community is entitled to subtract:

- The cost of collecting trash that is avoided (by diverting it to recyclables)
- The cost of disposal avoided (e.g., tipping fee at landfill)

The sum of these four items will be the net cost to the community. The community can recover some or all of that cost by selling the recovered recyclables. The price that they need to cover the cost would become the theoretical price the reclaimer should pay for a raw material.

The reclaimer will have the following costs:

- Raw material cost (equals community cost)
- Reclaiming cost (e.g., cost to convert the raw material to a product)
- Marketing expenses and overheads
- Profit and return on investment

The sum of all these items including the profit becomes the minimum price required to make an economically attractive venture for manufacturing a product derived from feedstock obtained from processing trash.

The next question becomes, Is the price higher or lower than the price of virgin material? The processing technologies today are good enough to manufacture a product essentially equal in quality to virgin. However, in a normal free market situation, a manufacturer will insist on receiving a discount to use what is deemed to be an inferior quality material.

If we take a look at the economic viability of plastics packaging recycling, considering the virgin prices based on oil at nominally $20 per barrel, we see clearly that beverage containers are economically viable with current costs to landfill, which are between $50 and $100 per ton. However, it is also clear that beyond beverage bottles, it is not economically attractive at today's price of oil even with significantly higher costs. for alternative disposal (Fig. 14.15).

If, however, the price of oil were to rise to $35 per barrel, then the cost associated with manufacturing virgin polymers would increase substantially. Therefore, even if recycled material were discounted, versus virgin prices, the price would be high enough to make it economical to collect, sort, and reclaim many plastic components from the waste stream (Fig. 14.16). This suggests that there is a future value to recycling that should be given consideration from the point of view of stockpiling material going into the trash stream to be utilized at a future time when the price of oil might be higher than $20 per barrel.

Another issue that surfaces here is that if the public decides to purchase re-

(c)

(d)

FIGURE 14.14 (*Continued*) Useful products from recycled, uncleaned, commingled plastic mixture.

TABLE 14.6 Projected Markets

Generic type	1995—Million pounds per year
PET	630
HDPE	530
PS	570
PVC	495
PP	900
Commingled (unrefined)	400

Quality is a problem that needs much additional work when we go beyond the beverage bottle. What is encountered immediately is color. Detergents, bleaches, pharmaceuticals, insecticides, and a wide range of tubs are packaged in a wide range of colored, or pigmented containers. It is very difficult to remove these pigments, and, moreover, it is very difficult to reuse the colors unless they can be matched up identically, like yellow with yellow and blue with blue. The show-through properties in multilayer utilization of these materials is still a problem to be solved.

All of this affects the price that one could receive and makes it more difficult to match up with the market subsets into which the material could go. It is no problem to take a mixture of colors if you could tolerate gray or black, and this is distinctly possible in soil, pipe, or products where color is not an issue.

Some of the technologies that have already been discussed in this chapter will have applicability to further refine the material. For example, molecular separation can remove the pigments. Other technologies are beginning to surface. Pigmentation that can be modified or destroyed through chemical reaction or processing parameters and substituting organic pigments for inorganic ones are processes under evaluation that have the potential for overcoming these barriers and opening up large markets and higher prices for recovered materials.

Of course, the recycled materials can be blended with virgin and other materials added for compatibility or to offset any deficiencies, and this too is already happening. Commercial products already exist which are derived from a combination of virgin and recycled material.

Another part of this equation of overcoming the quality is to create an entirely new product that is designed for use with virgin or in those new product arenas where the quality question can be side-stepped. Examples of this include park benches, picnic tables, and landscape timber from the unrefined, commingled material, and also new families of materials made from refined commingled products.

The plastics industry has in its grasp the technology to deal with these issues of quality, and probably they can overcome many of the economic deficiencies that exist as a result of the quality issue.

Currently two polymers, PET (polyethylene terephthalate) and HDPE (high-density polyethylene), from soft drink, milk, water, juice, liquor, and wine bottles can meet the criteria. These materials are being collected from the garbage pile and cleaned up to quality sufficient so that it is nearly impossible to tell the difference between the high-quality, cleaned-up, recycled material and the virgin material in a wide variety of existing uses ranging from fibers used in carpeting and insulation, to engineered plastics in automobiles, to packages.

These containers (Fig. 14.17) represent about 14 percent by weight and 25 percent by volume of the plastics packaging component of the waste stream. The nation is rapidly adopting the collection, sorting, and reclamation technologies for doing this and the infrastructure is growing rapidly. The markets for the generic materials are far greater than the capacity to collect these beverage bottles from the waste stream at this moment (Tables 14.7 and 14.8).

(a)

FIGURE 14.17   A sampling of new products from recyclable plastics.

(c)

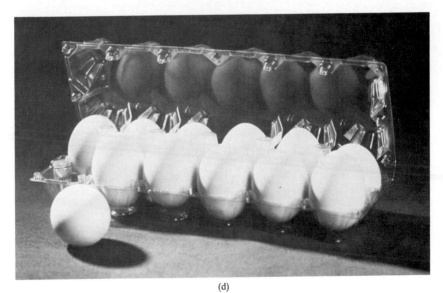

(d)

FIGURE 14.17 (*Continued*) A sampling of new products from recyclable plastics.

TABLE 14.7 Potential Demand for Recycled PET, Millions of Pounds

Fiber	420
Injection molding	100
Extrusion	90
Bottles (nonfood)	30
Building insulation	30
Exports	30
Total	700

Source: Center for Plastics Recycling Research.

TABLE 14.8 Potential Demand for Recycled HDPE, Millions of Pounds

Pipe	100
Pails	70
PET bottle bases	90
Crates and pallets	100
Bottles (nonfood)	130
Others	170
Total	660

Source: Center for Plastics Recycling Research.

FORECAST TRENDS AND NEEDED RESEARCH

The research is now focused on how to go beyond beverage bottles. The strategy is to develop the technology to reduce the cost of collecting, sorting, and reclaiming these materials, while at the same time increasing the value of the recycled materials so that they can gain a higher price in the market place. Research programs that are under way focus on collection, sorting-reclaiming, and end-use markets.

Collection

In collection the issues are

- Collection of all clean plastics
- Truck size and type
- Truck routing

The question is, What will the consumer give when asked to deliver all clean plastics? This includes all rigid containers (beverage bottles, detergent bottles, rigid tubs, and so forth) and nonrigid containers such as film. Trucks—size, type, and routing—are also key.

Sorting and Reclaiming

In the sorting and reclaiming of generics, the research is focused on three types of sorting. First is automated macrosorting, which is sorting a full container. Second is microsorting, which is sorting chips of containers after the containers have been shredded and chopped up. Molecular sorting examines dissolving polymers in an organic solvent; five or more polymers can be separated from each other in this system. While this technology may not be economically viable today, it will become more economically viable as the price of oil increases, and/or as we are able to drive the cost down for this methodology.

Clean or "refined" commingled plastics is a new field. These are materials that are chopped up and shredded and have been washed of major dirt and nonplastic material. A new family of compounds can be made for forming into either pellets or extruded profiles.

Uncleaned commingled plastic profiles (leaving metal, paper, and other contaminants) continue to be of interest.

End Use

End-use market research programs continue to focus on and expand the market opportunities for other polymers besides PET and HDPE, such as polyvinylchloride (PVC), polystyrene (PS), and polypropylene (PP). Market research is continuing on nongeneric uses including the previously mentioned new family of compounds and profiles.

FUTURE VALUE OF RECYCLING

Looking beyond plastic beverage containers, the technology is viable, but there is a lot of work to do to make it economically viable. The long-term benefit of recycling as a resource conservation and management strategy is obvious, and it is clearly a goal toward which we should work. However, the economic conditions needed to drive "total" recycling do not exist today.

Generally speaking, recycled plastic must compete with virgin material, in terms of both price and performance, although the issue of price versus (overall) cost should not be ignored. The big problem is that the current prices of most virgin materials are too low to drive recycling purely on the basis of price-driven economics. We are all aware that we cannot afford to dig up new oil or new coal in our country because the price of imported oil is so low. If the price of oil is strategically established by the Middle East countries to be just low enough to make it uneconomically sound for us to remove these virgin materials from our own country, how can plastics from the garbage pile compete?

Given the vagaries of the marketplace, the potential for recessions, and the uncertainty of the pricing of imported oil, the ability to "sell" recyclable components from the trash on a constant and ever-growing basis is problematic. In the absence of alternative trash disposal facilities (landfills and incinerators are being shut down and new ones not built), some form of storage for recyclables will be needed to provide capacitance for the system.

Finally, anything that is done to alter the basic economics to favor recycled material is going to have to have an inflationary effect. The question is, Is it better for the nation to rush toward reusing the garbage pile, despite the inflationary effect, or would it be wiser to selectively process the garbage pile now and store the valuable components in such a way that they could be recovered at some future date when the economics would be more favorable? The latter option seems worth evaluating.

A Proposed Solution: Store Recyclables

A strategy for managing our municipal solid waste while simultaneously conserving and managing our resources more effectively is to capitalize on the strengths that we have in our nation, especially including the eagerness of the consumer to participate in the managing of waste. We should encourage the building of the recycling infrastructure today. But in addition, we should also build *strategic storage facilities* (SSF) to stockpile multimaterial (plastic, metal, paper, and glass) recyclable sources for future reclamation and use.

The facilities for storing such materials could be as simple as abandoned quarries, salt mines, or any other large-volume container, where previously a virgin natural resource has been withdrawn, or a modern state-of-the-art landfill. With modern technology, limited resource recyclable materials could be stored in these SSF facilities in such a way as to prevent any harm for future recycling and reuse.

The knowledge we have already accumulated about what happens in landfills can be applicable here. For example, contrary to popular belief, wood fiber does not deteriorate severely in a landfill. What we are seeing is that without a sufficient quantity of water available, microorganisms cannot live and, therefore, paper fiber will not degrade. If steel rusts, it simply becomes iron oxide from whence the steel came originally; iron ore is iron oxide. Plastics can be stored. This carbonaceous material is simply the result of refining oil, gas, or coal and processing it into a plastic. We know that plastic is relatively easy to store because even moisture does not have a deleterious effect on it, practically nothing extracts from it, and microorganisms do not find nutritional value in it.

RESEARCH NEEDS

Storage Costs

The exact economies for storage are not presently known, but they should not be excessive. The cost to store our recyclables in units of homogeneous materials should not be significantly different from storing the material in a landfill in a heterogeneous mix as we do now, particularly with the help of the consumer in the segregation process. While the evidence for the storage of the material indicates that there is nothing environmentally to be concerned about, some research should be undertaken to assure ourselves that this is safe and environmentally sound. Research should be undertaken to determine the effect and cost of storing plastics and other valuable components of the trash.

Current Uses

The technology for the current utilization of the stored plastics would run the gamut from continuing to mine from the strategically stored materials those valuable components for which markets exist and/or are developing such as PET, HDPE, and PVC bottles. Material could be drawn from the SSFs to supply developing markets for commingled plastics as a feedstock to make a wide variety of products ranging from park benches to fences to marine boat docks, car stops, and traffic hardware.

Materials would be sold from these storage facilities to existing operations as they expand and have demand for raw materials. The plastics for which no markets exist today would be stored for its future value.

Future Uses

The technology exists for processing the stored plastic into their polymeric components by dissolving the polymers in solvents. The technology also exists for "cracking" the carbonaceous materials into monomers, which are the building blocks for the polymers. These existing fundamental technologies would, however, require only modification to make certain they are economically viable. In the process of recovering the organic material by these or alternative technologies, the inorganic components could be recovered as well. For example, if there were any cadmium and lead, glass, or any other valuable mineral in the plastic as a result of it being a pigment, a strengthener, or stabilizer, these components could be recovered. In our modern society, there is and will continue to be a need for metallic lead and metallic cadmium, for example, and other minerals such as glass. TiO_2 also has value.

Although we have indicated that much of the technology is at hand, there is a need for refinement and filling in the blanks. This is a logical place for research. The economics need to be developed based on the present price of oil and then extrapolated to that future price of oil where this strategic stockpile of raw material would have economic viability.

GLOSSARY OF PLASTICS TERMS

break-even landfill cost   This represents a net cost of recycling that can be related to the cost of an alternative disposal such as landfill. The point at which the cost of recycling is equal to the cost of the alternative disposal is called the break-even point.

capture rate   This represents the percent recovered from the homeowner versus the total amount of recyclables the homeowner possesses.

Coding System for Plastic Containers   Each plastic has been given a code number that can be molded into the bottom of a bottle. This coding system was developed by the Plastic Bottle Institute of the Society of the Plastics Industry (SPI) as a voluntary system for marking the containers to identify them by polymer type.

commingled plastics   A commingled plastic is a mixture of plastics that are normally incompatible but are mixed together by virtue of the way they are found in the trash.

macrosorting   This relates to the separation by manual or automated methodology of whole bottles or whole parts.

microsorting   This relates to the separation of different plastics when they are mixed in finely ground chips.

molecular sorting   The technology for sorting at the molecular level deals with dissolving the polymer in some suitable solvent such that the molecules of the polymer will dissolve in the solvent. It is possible to further refine-sort at the molecular level by depolymerizing the polymer back to its monomer. Examples of this would include the depolymerization of PET to DMT (dimethylene-terephthalate).

OPEC   The Organization of Petroleum Exporting Countries.

refined commingled plastics   Commingled plastics from the trash pile contain contaminants such as metal, paper, and dirt. These can be removed in a wash and grind process, thus producing a refined mixture. The mixture can be further refined by mixing these materials at the melt level and filtering at the melt level and further materials that have not been removed from the washing.

regrind   This is a relatively clean scrap usually trimmed from industrial manufacture. Because of its cleanliness and homogeneity, it can be densified and mixed with virgin material returned to the entrance of the machine and processed into the product.

thermoplastic   A thermoplastic polymer is one that can be deformed and reformed by heating and cooling.

CHAPTER 15
SCRAP METAL AND STEEL CANS

Richard R. Jordan
Divisional Vice President
Municipal Recycling Division
The David J. Joseph Company
Cincinnati, Ohio

Gregory L. Crawford
Director of Recycling
Steel Can Recycling Institute
Pittsburgh, Pennsylvania

SCRAP METAL*

History of Recycling Metal†

The history of recycling scrap metal dates back probably more than 5000 years—to the earliest days of iron making. Scrap use began in North America in 1642 when the first iron furnace was built in Massachusetts. During the American Revolution, iron kettles and pots were melted down for weapon making. During the Civil War, citizens were urged to donate old metal objects. War-time scrap drives continued through the Korean War.

Growth in demand for metal products during the Industrial Revolution greatly affected the scrap industry. Increased demand resulted in a higher value for scrap metals which stimulated an increase in the number of scrap collectors providing obsolete metal to mills and foundries. In addition, widespread distribution of manufactured items sharply increased the supply of scrap available. These developments led to increased numbers of scrap peddlers who collected scrap and delivered it to processors to earn a living.

Many of today's large scrap processors began as small collectors or peddlers back before today's modern processing equipment was developed. The scrap industry's development can be attributed to the large inflow of immigrants from

---

*Richard R. Jordan contributed this section to Chap. 15.
†Many of the historical facts presented are from information published by the Institute of Scrap Recycling Industries.

FIGURE 15.1   Scrap collectors sell metals of all types to processors.

other countries who—without any formal training and little or no money—learned the scrap business by spending years as collectors and peddlers. Indeed, it is sometimes said that the real essence of the industry's growth was the determination of people who made the transition from peddlers and collectors to become large processors (see Fig. 15.1).

Early scrap processors had little sophisticated processing equipment. Tools included chisels and sledgehammers to break apart large metal objects. The gas cutting torch was first used in 1910—and is still used today for large items. (The hydraulic shear, however, has replaced the torch as a means of cutting large volumes of scrap.) In the early 1940s, magnets began to be used to handle scrap. In the early 1960s, with growing numbers of abandoned automobiles left on the side of the road, the automobile shredder was introduced. The higher demand levels for scrap made the high capital outlays for processing equipment more worthwhile.

As the number of processors and dealers grew, consumers of scrap (mills and foundries) began buying from more than one source. This led to the need for standardization of descriptions for various scrap grades to facilitate communication between buyers and sellers.

In the late nineteenth century, the demand for scrap increased as the steelmakers began melting scrap in open hearth furnaces. Demand for scrap in steel production was further boosted in the 1900s as the electric furnace, which could use 100 percent scrap as its raw material, became popular in steelmaking.

Sources of Scrap Metal

Our attention in this chapter is directed toward ferrous scrap. Ferrous scrap can be divided into three major categories: home, prompt industrial, and obsolete—all of which are discards.

Home scrap and prompt industrial scrap are involuntary by-products of manufacturing processes. *Home scrap* originates in a steel mill; it is, for example, broken ingot molds and mill rolls, slab and billet crops, and scrap sheets from rolling mill cobbles. *Prompt industrial scrap* includes clippings from an automobile stamping plant or a card table manufacturer and turnings from a lathe at a machine tool shop. Prompt industrial scrap results from normal machining, stamping, and fabricating operations in the creation of products made from steel.

Obsolete scrap, the third major category, arises when a product made of iron or steel has served its useful life and is discarded. Railroads are important sources of obsolete scrap; nearly everything that a railroad owns is made of iron or steel and, when no longer usable, is discarded as scrap. Perhaps the largest single source of obsolete scrap is old automobiles. Over 10 million automobiles and small trucks are discarded in the United States each year, and approximately 1 ton of ferrous scrap can be recovered from each. Other examples of obsolete scrap are items that are discarded from demolition projects—manhole covers, old water pipes, kitchen sinks, etc.; as well as household discards such as toys, lawn mowers, lawn furniture, pots and pans, and steel cans (Fig. 15.2).

Obsolete scrap from construction and demolition debris is usually heavily contaminated with concrete, wood, and other nonmetallics. Once properly processed, this scrap is recyclable. Processing entails separating the metallic scrap from the nonmetallic waste, and then sizing the scrap metal to consumers' specifications. Mechanical as well as labor-intensive systems are available to provide such processing.

Cities must determine the economics of accumulating, sorting, separating, cutting, baling, or shredding scrap metals as well as the market and rejection risks they take by becoming processors. The alternative is to sell the scrap metals to established scrap processors who have already made capital investments in processing equipment and who possess the knowledge of an active participant in the metal recycling industry. Site-specific factors such as quantity of scrap metal available, nearness to end consuming markets, market risk tolerance, and envi-

FIGURE 15.2 Discarded obsolete steel products prior to processing.

ronmental issues must be examined before cities can make informed choices
as to the level of processing that will
yield them the most benefit.

Scrap metal should be included in
any recycling program. Ferrous metals
are magnetic and, therefore, easy to remove from the waste stream. Markets
exist that consume these metals.

The flowchart in Fig. 15.3 illustrates
the generation of home, prompt, and
obsolete scrap. Scrap generated in a
mill during the melting process is either
used again (as "home" scrap) or is
sold to a scrap processor or another
mill consumer. Industrial scrap is generated by steel fabricators and manufacturers of products containing steel.

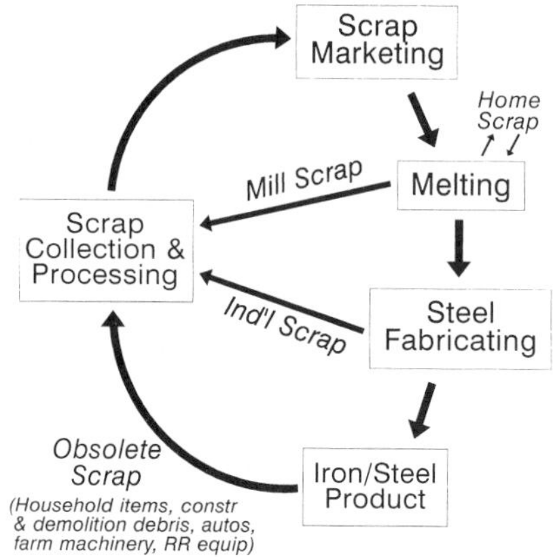

Once scrap is collected, it is then
processed into a form and size usable

FIGURE 15.3 Scrap metal recycling flowchart.

by a consuming mill or foundry in the melting process. Processing can involve
little more than sorting and reloading material for shipment or can be as involved
as cutting, shearing, baling, or shredding.

The scrap processor adds value to the scrap material collected—sorting it into
more similar grades and/or densifying or cutting it down into smaller pieces. For
example, shredding automobiles not only reduces the size of a car into pieces no
larger than a fist, but it also separates ferrous metals from nonferrous metals—
from all other materials (Fig. 15.4). As another example, loose clippings from an
industrial stamping process are made more usable (and valuable) to a steel mill if
they are densified into bundles.

Marketing

After collection and processing, the next step in the recycling chain is marketing
prepared scrap to steel mills and foundries. Although in many cases scrap is sold
directly to these markets by processors, a broker often plays a very important
role.

In the scrap industry, a broker is a person or company who buys and sells
scrap without physically handling the material. Brokers do not prepare or produce the scrap they sell and will not receive or use scrap they buy. Contrary to
the use of the word broker in many other places, it is of no significance in scrap
whether the brokers buy and sell for their own account or act as a paid agent for
someone else.

In scrap, the real distinction to be made is between a scrap broker and a scrap
dealer—simply on the basis of whether or not they physically handle scrap they
buy and sell. If they physically handle it, the function is as a dealer. If they do not
handle the scrap, the function is that of a broker.

This is not as simple as it may seem. Confusion will arise because in the scrap
industry there are few, perhaps no, firms that are 100 percent pure brokers or 100
percent pure dealers. In practice, firms are mixtures of both and perform functions as both brokers and dealers. Almost all brokerage firms have one or more

FIGURE 15.4 Shredded steel from junked autos and other steel products being loaded into railcars and ready for shipment.

scrap yards or storage and preparation facilities. Activities performed in these yards are not brokerage but dealer functions. And most dealers do some brokering—buying or selling scrap that they did not prepare and that they will not bring into their yards.

There is only one basic underlying function performed by a broker: to develop, analyze, and use information about the supply of, and demand for, various kinds of scrap. The function of a broker is to turn a widely scattered and unconnected multitude of scrap producers and scrap consumers into an orderly market where scrap can be bought and sold in almost any reasonable quantity and at almost any reasonable time.

The scrap brokers create this market by their knowledge of supply and demand and by their willingness to rely on this knowledge in making purchases and sales.

Transactions will go through brokers only if the producer and consumer are better off dealing with the broker rather than dealing direct. They will be better off if most of the time the broker has developed and analyzed better and more information than is available to either the dealer or consumer individually.

The broker is needed in the scrap industry because of its complexity. The marketplace for ferrous scrap is not national, rather it is composed of numerous marketing regions. Supply and demand imbalances exist within each of these regions. Surpluses may exist in areas where the production of prompt industrial scrap combined with the normal collection and processing of obsolete material exceeds the local demand. In a marketing region where the regular demand from consumers exceeds the collection and production of ferrous scrap, an apparent shortage exists. Such imbalances are brought to equilibrium primarily by interterritory shipments. A broker's knowledge of all these various marketing regions brings together buyers and sellers from "remote" regions.

Brokers perform two other functions within the scrap industry—they provide information and financing. In addition to market information, brokers frequently secure and pass on technical information as to equipment, government regulations, and general business news. A broker provides financing by paying a substantial percentage of the total value of a shipment (perhaps 50 percent or more) to the shipper immediately upon shipment, thus relieving the dealer of the necessity of waiting for the shipment to be received by the customer, weighed, inspected, unloaded, etc. On the other side of the transaction, the broker provides the consumer financing by granting terms of 20 days, 30 days, or more before the scrap must be paid for.

The broker also acts as an intermediary, or go-between, in representing the shippers and their problems to the consumers and vice versa. These include matters involving quality of scrap, grading, technical preparation, shipping time, nonshipments, rejections, hold-ups, etc.

The Scrap Metal Industry

For 1990, estimates of U.S. total ferrous scrap consumption were 71 million tons. Of this, 44 million tons represent purchases from outside sources (that which is not home scrap). Of the purchased scrap, 30 percent was bought by foundries, 70 percent by mills. Over the past 10 years (1981–1990), scrap purchases by mills and foundries have averaged about 41 million tons annually.

It is estimated that there are over 3000 scrap dealers (and thousands of industrial plants that generate ferrous scrap) in the continental United States and over 1200 scrap consumers—approximately 120 steel mills and 1100 ferrous foundries.

In addition to scrap demands within the United States, 10 to 13 million tons are exported each year (Fig. 15.5). Major markets include Canada, Mexico, South Korea, Turkey, Japan, India, and Taiwan—just to mention a few. The estimated 12.8 million tons of scrap exported from the United States in 1990 had an estimated value of $1.6 billion. The volume of exports represented 22 percent of total demand for U.S. scrap in 1990.

Scrap purchases are increasing in proportion to the amount of raw steel produced in the United States. In 1973, at the height of raw steel production, 151 million tons of steel were produced. During the past few years (1988–1990), the annual average has been 98 million tons. Domestic purchases of scrap, however, have grown slightly—from 45 million tons in 1973 to 47 million tons during the past few years.

The proportional increase in scrap usage is attributed to changes in technology. Increased use of electric furnaces (37 percent of raw steel production in 1990 compared to about 18 percent in 1973) has increased the demand for scrap since these furnaces can use a 100 percent scrap charge. Other technological changes in the steelmaking process have eliminated the amount of internal home scrap generation resulting in an increase in outside scrap purchases.

Scrap Metal Pricing

When talking about scrap prices, what we are really addressing is the structure of the scrap market, that is, how prices are established which permit the collection

FIGURE 15.5 Loading scrap into a vessel for export.

and processing of scrap in quantities necessary and sufficient to satisfy consumers' requirements. The first axiom of the ferrous scrap market is "Scrap is bought, not sold." Melting in a furnace is virtually the only use for ferrous scrap. Mills and foundries buy scrap *when they need it.* If mills and foundries do not need scrap to feed their furnaces, there is nothing the scrap dealer or broker can do to force a sale.

While the scrap market may be primarily demand-driven, it is occasionally supply-constrained. The market functions through the balancing of supply and demand. The prices of all grades of scrap, however, are not equally volatile nor is the supply of all grades equally elastic.

Prices of industrial scrap are volatile and responsive to changes in the steel industry's operating rate (i.e., scrap demand). Industrial plants must dispose of the scrap generated each month and therefore will accept the highest bid offered from interested buyers. Demand in the marketplace is a major determinant of the prices offered, and, during periods of low demand and operating rates, prices for industrial scrap fall sharply. Remember, there is no use for this scrap other than steelmaking.

Scrap dealers, on the other hand, do not need to sell scrap each month and can effectively resist or even refuse lower prices. A price "floor" may exist for obsolete dealer scrap but not for prompt industrial scrap. Industrial scrap supply is not price-elastic. Just as low prices offered do not limit tonnage produced, neither do higher prices expand supply. During periods of high steel mill operating rates when demand for industrial scrap is strong, buyers bid prices higher to draw the limited tonnage that is produced. Higher prices offered for dealer scrap, on the other hand, tend to stimulate the collection process and thereby expand supply—easing pressure on prices. Lower prices inhibit dealers' collection, supply contracts, and price erosion slows. Whether they are commercially motivated or public-service agencies, scrap recyclers must understand this price volatility and the fact that increasing the supply depresses prices—it does not stimulate demand.

Transportation to the Marketplace

As mentioned earlier, the marketplace for ferrous scrap is composed of numerous marketing regions. Scrap shortages in one region, for example, can be satisfied with purchases from another. The economic feasibility of moving scrap from one region to another depends on transportation costs.

Scrap moves in one of four ways: by railcar, truck, barge, or boat (export vessels). Since freight costs can make up as much as 25 percent or more of total scrap cost, transportation considerations are vital. Generally, scrap moved longer distances between origin and destination points with river access travels by barge, which usually offers the lowest per ton-mile cost. In general, shipments by land with shorter distances (less than 150 mi) are more efficiently moved by truck; longer land distances are more cost-competitive by railcar. There are, however, numerous exceptions to these generalizations.

Deregulation of the rail industry by the Staggers Act in 1980 created opportunities for negotiating special contract rates. Special freight rate advantages improve the competitiveness of remote scrap, which obviously increases the importance of transportation expertise in the scrap industry.

Reasons for Recycling Scrap Metal

Recycling of ferrous scrap in the United States will grow. Technological changes in the steelmaking process will likely continue to increase the amount of purchased scrap per ton of steel produced. Not only is producing new steel from scrap efficient, it obviously keeps obsolete iron and steel items from making their way into landfills, which alleviates an environmental problem.

Producing steel from scrap is also desirable in terms of energy conservation. It takes much less energy to make steel from scrap than from iron ore. Estimates are that it takes four times more energy to produce steel from iron ore than from scrap (Fig. 15.6). In the early 1970s an Environmental Protection Agency (EPA) study reported that producing 1 ton of steel from the scrap in an automobile vs.

FIGURE 15.6 Scrap being charged into a melting furnace.

from iron ore saves enough energy to supply the electrical needs of an average household in some areas of the country for an entire year.

In addition to energy savings, the EPA has identified other benefits of making new steel from scrap instead of iron ore and coal. These include a 90 percent savings in virgin materials use, an 86 percent reduction in air pollution, a 40 percent reduction in water use, a 76 percent reduction in water pollution, a 97 percent reduction in mining wastes, and a 105 percent reduction in consumer waste generated.

Conclusion

Each of the activities involved in the recycling process—discard, collection, processing, melting, fabrication, return to customer use, and eventual discard once again—is essential. If one of these key elements is missing, then recycling has not occurred. Opportunities for increased recycling are created by stimulating the flow of material through the cycle. Anything limiting or restricting the flow is a constraint, and encouraging an increase in just one of the cycle's activities without also stimulating the others will not expand recycling. The discard, collection, and processing activities collectively provide the supply of ferrous scrap. The melting, fabrication, and consumer reuse make up the demand part of the cycle.

Ferrous scrap is the most recycled commodity in the United States. Recycling ferrous scrap is certainly nothing new. In fact, the ferrous scrap dealer could be considered the elder statesperson in the recycling industry. Compared with recyclers of other items, the ferrous scrap dealer has the luxury of a long history and, with that, of well-established markets for the product.

FIGURE 15.7 Steel can products.

In the next section, one important metal product, the steel can, is presented starting with a history of its reuse.

STEEL CANS*

History of Steel Can Reuse

Steel cans may be one of the more recent scrap additions for the production of new steel, but they are by no means a new product themselves. Steel cans have been in use since the 1800s because of qualities such as simple production, safe and strong packaging, and stackability. In the early 1800s, Peter Durand, an English citizen, developed a process to preserve foods in metal "cannisters" that were produced from iron sheets coated with tin. Since then, steel cans have developed from heavy, cumbersome containers to the contemporary, lightweight versions that we see every day in grocery stores, in homes, and, now, in recycling programs.

What Is a Steel Can?

Steel cans are food, beverage, paint, aerosol, and other general-purpose containers whose base metal is steel (Fig. 15.7). In order to protect the contents from

---

*Gregory L. Crawford contributed this section to Chap. 15.

corrosion, steel cans usually have a very thin tin coating, about 30 millionths of an inch. Steel food cans, which make up more than 90 percent of all metal food containers, are often called "tin" cans because of this coating of tin. Some steel cans, such as tuna cans, are made with tin-free steel, while others have an aluminum lid and a steel body and are commonly called bimetal cans.

While the minor differences among tin plate steel, tin-free steel, and bimetal cans are interesting, no distinction is needed when recycling any of these steel cans. All empty steel cans are completely recyclable by the steel industry and should be included in any recycling program.

How Steel Cans Are Made. From the can production standpoint, there are two types of steel cans: three-piece cans and two-piece cans. The three-piece can typically contains a wide assortment of sizes and types of products. To produce these cans, the lids and bottoms of the cans are punched or cut out of rolls of tin plate that are gradually unwound. Once filled with holes, the tin plate is called a "skeleton" and sent back to a detinning company or steel mill as prompt scrap, to be used to produce new steel. Other rolls of tin plate are cut into the size of cans and rolled. The side seams are then welded at speeds higher than 500 can bodies per minute. The majority of welded cans have tin plate bodies, but have either tin plate or tin-free steel ends, which are mechanically crimped to the body.

The other type of steel can, the two-piece can, is usually referred to as draw-redraw (DRD) because of the production process. At present, about one-third of all steel cans are two-piece cans, which tend to be smaller cans, such as tuna and beverage cans. The major advantage to producing two-piece cans is that it eliminates both a side seam and a separate bottom end piece. The entire body and bottom is drawn from one piece of steel, so that the only seam is between the single-unit body and the lid. And this seam is simplified because there is no side seam overlap. More than 90 percent of all steel two-piece cans are made of tin-free steel. Tin plate may be used for the lids if a shiny appearance is desired, and for bodies that contain foods more likely to cause corrosion in the steel. Steel coils, coated on both sides, are usually the starting material for producing these cans, although flat sheet stock can also be used.

In the draw-redraw production process, a shallow cup is produced from a flat, circular blank that was punched or cut from the can sheet. The diameter of the cup is reduced as the can is deepened. The can-making presses usually allow for two or more cans to be formed with each press stroke (Fig. 15.8). Beading is performed to add strength to the can. Beads are grooves or ribs formed on the side of the container to stiffen the can body and to improve label retention. Lids are formed and crimped to the body as in the three-piece method.

Sources and Processing of Steel Cans

Steel cans are recycled through various collection programs, processing methods, transportation means, and end markets. Some of the collection methods include curbside collection, drop-off collection sites, multimaterial buy-back centers, resource recovery facilities, and waste processing facilities. Because steel cans are magnetic, they are typically separated from other recyclables or from

FIGURE 15.8   Production process of two-piece steel cans.

municipal solid waste through magnetic separation, making them the easiest recyclable to sort and handle in any recycling program (Fig. 15.9).

Curbside Recycling Programs.   Communities have several options to choose from
when implementing curbside collection programs. In the "commingled" curbside
collection system, residents separate recyclables from their household trash and
place them into one recycling box or bag that is later placed at the curb (Fig.
15.10). The recyclables often include steel and aluminum cans, glass jars and bottles, and plastic containers. Newspapers may be bundled for collection as well.
The steel can's magnetic property plays a valuable role in this recycling option
since magnetic separation is used in the material recovery facility (MRF) that receives, separates, and processes the recyclables to the specifications of the appropriate end markets for each material. In some communities, MRFs are referred to as intermediate processing centers (IPCs).

   In the case of a commingled curbside program, the collection vehicles enter the
MRF and tip their loads into a receiving pit or onto a tipping floor. The mixed

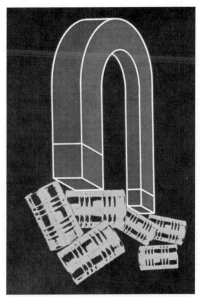

FIGURE 15.9 Magnetic property of steel cans.

recyclables are loaded onto a conveyor system from the pit or floor, and magnetic separation is used to remove steel cans. An overhead transverse magnetic separator conveyor is preferred over the slightly lower cost, end-pulley design because it sorts and handles higher volume easily.

Some of these MRFs are labor-intensive, with minimal equipment. In these facilities, after removal of steel, the other recyclables are sorted from a conveyor line by workers. Other MRFs are more capital intensive with less labor. Such systems are normally proprietary, so design equipment varies. As in any other system, magnetic separation for steel cans is the first and easiest part of the process.

A second form of curbside collection requires more participation from the residents but minimal sorting at the MRF. In this case, each type of recyclable material is source-separated in its individual box. Steel and aluminum cans may be placed in one bin, so an additional bin is not needed for the metals. The truck

FIGURE 15.10 Steel cans commingled with other materials in curbside bins.

used by the hauler has different storage compartments to keep the materials separate from one another. Steel cans are placed in the same compartment as aluminum cans because, later, the cans are magnetically separated at the MRF. Commingling the cans also means that no extra truck compartment is needed for the two metals. A variation of this type of curbside collection uses a single commingled box at the curb, but the hauler hand-sorts the materials into the different compartments on the truck when the material is picked up at the curb.

The MRF's processing for source-separated programs, such as those described above, differs somewhat from commingled programs. In this case, the processing requires relatively little equipment since metals, glass, and plastic have already been sorted, but careful inspection is necessary to avoid accidental mixing and contamination of these materials. Glass may need to be sorted by color and plastic by type depending on the details of the program. Magnetic separation allows steel and aluminum cans to be sorted easily. Each material is then processed for its respective end market.

Drop-Off Recycling Programs. A drop-off program enables the public to deliver their recyclables to a designated collection site, which may have collection boxes for commingled steel and aluminum cans as well as for other materials (Fig. 15.11). Drop-off collection sites provide a recycling option for communities where curbside programs are impractical because of low population density. Also, some communities develop drop-off collection sites as an interim program before beginning a curbside program.

Multimaterial Buy-Back Centers. Another option for communities is the multicommodity buy-back center. The aluminum industry can be credited with creating and developing buy-back centers across the country. Originally, these centers

FIGURE 15.11 Drop-off collection site.

purchased only aluminum beverage cans for recycling; however, the trend more recently has been toward centers that accept additional recyclable materials such as steel, glass, and plastic. Even though recycling centers were set up to handle beverage containers, some multicommodity centers now accept or buy clean steel food cans.

A different version of the buy-back center is the reverse vending machine, which collects beverage cans. Created primarily for the convenience of consumers, the machines pay one penny to the consumer for each steel beverage can that is inserted.

There are several types and sizes of reverse vending machines. The CoinBak is a small machine, about the size of a newspaper vending machine, in which the consumer turns a handle after inserting a can and is paid a penny. Other reverse vending machines are larger and more sophisticated with electromechanical capabilities to sort, weigh, flatten, and pay varied amounts of money. The machines that are about the size of soft drink vending machines accept single cans and are often used inside grocery stores. These machines may scan the can's price code bar graphic identification to determine who the originating distributor was. This facilitates accounting requirements in deposit states. Others are still larger, about the size of a turnpike tool booth, with the capability to accept batches of cans, and are used typically on the periphery of a shopping center parking lot. The medium and larger machines can be set up to handle both steel and aluminum beverage cans.

Commercial and Institutional Recycling. While initially restricted to residential programs, recycling has spread to the commercial area to include office buildings, businesses such as restaurants and hotels, and institutions such as hospitals, schools, and correctional facilities. The programs vary greatly depending on the nature of the establishment. Steel cans are found primarily in the food service operations where the large no. 10 steel food containers are used (Fig. 15.12).

FIGURE 15.12 Steel cans and closures.

The first step in commercial and institutional steel can recycling is to rinse the steel cans in order to remove most food particles. Rinsing is necessary for sanitation reasons; however, recyclers should avoid wasting water by rinsing the cans in leftover dish water or in empty spaces in an automatic dishwasher.

Once the cans are rinsed, they should be flattened in order to accommodate as many recyclables as possible. Flattening steel cans may be accomplished manually or mechanically. If the commercial establishment does not have a mechanical can flattener, recyclers should remove the bottom end of the can and step on the body of the open-ended can. The lid and bottom of the can should also be recycled.

The third step in commercial and institutional recycling is to remove the steel cans and other recyclables from the establishment. Often arrangements can be made with the waste hauler, who will provide for recycling steel cans and other materials. This normally means that the hauler provides and maintains a container for the recyclables. Another possibility for the business or institution is to work with a ferrous scrap processor or independent recycler. In this case, the steel cans will either be picked up by or delivered to the intermediate processor.

Steel cans are found in every commercial and institutional food service setting. The most common are the large, no. 10 cans. Additionally, many glass and plastic containers used in these kitchens have steel lids and closures, which should also be recycled.

Resource Recovery Facilities. Resource recovery plants require no separation of household or commercial-institutional trash. Instead, municipal trash is simply collected by garbage trucks and hauled to the plant. Waste-to-energy plants burn the trash directly to produce energy in the form of steam or electricity, while refuse-derived fuel plants process the trash to remove the unburnable components to produce organic combustible material for sale to other facilities for power generation in lieu of or as a supplement to coal, oil, or gas fuels. At many resource recovery plants, steel cans and other postconsumer steel products are magnetically separated from the solid waste stream, postburn or preburn, for recycling. The recovered steel normally consists of about 60 percent steel cans and 40 percent other postconsumer ferrous. Magnetic separation at these plants results in steel recycling rates of well over 90 percent. This is referred to as "automatic recycling." with about 125 resource recovery plants in operation across the country, at least 43 percent of them magnetically separate steel cans and other postconsumer steel products. The trend will continue toward full steel recovery from all of these facilities.

Waste Processing Facilities. A waste processing facility is somewhat like an MRF; however, all trash, rather than just the recyclables, is hauled to the facility for processing. Some communities may even refer to this facility as an MRF or resource recovery facility. After the trash stream is sized or shredded, perhaps with a flail mill, steel cans are magnetically separated from the municipal waste. Once separated, the recyclables are processed and shipped to end markets. The garbage is hauled to the local landfill.

Variations of waste processing facilities are now being seen at metro area transfer stations. These sites are used by public works or private haulers to empty their smaller, neighborhood trucks for loading and compacting into 40-ft trailers that will then be transported a longer distance to the landfill. During the emptying and transloading process, magnetic separation can be used to remove steel cans and other ferrous items for recycling as steel scrap.

In addition, some landfills have set up types of waste processing facilities at the landfill site itself in order to remove as much materials as possible and minimize landfill usage. As always, steel cans and other ferrous materials are magnetically separated.

Intermediate and End Markets

The locations and specifications of markets must be taken into account before beginning any recycling program. Collected steel cans are sold to a variety of intermediate processors and end markets. Intermediate processors, such as ferrous scrap dealers, provide a convenient service for smaller recyclers because they have the capacity to process truckload or railcar quantities of steel cans and ship them to the end market. Detinning companies, steel mills, and iron and steel foundries share the end-market role for recycling steel cans.

Steel Mills.   Steel mills, the major end market for most steel cans, purchase steel cans directly from larger recycling programs, intermediate processors, and detinners. The steelmaking process allows for a percentage of tin in the scrap material used for new steel production. With more than 120 operating steel mills in the United States, the steel industry has recycled more than 100 billion lb of used steel scrap of all types through remelting each year in the 1980s (Fig. 15.13).

Detinners.   As one of the major end markets for steel cans, detinning companies provide the steel industry with steel cans in the form of a no. 1 detinned bundle, a scrap grade. Through a chemical and electrolytic process, detinners remove the tin from tinned steel products. The detinned steel is then prepared to specification and sold to steel mills and foundries. The recovered tin, a valuable commodity, is sold to its commercial markets.

In the past, the primary function of detinning companies was to process in-

FIGURE 15.13   Scrap mix being added to basic oxygen furnace.

dustrial prompt scrap, the remnant scrap material that results from industrial fabricating processes such as can manufacturing. However, wholesale quantities of postconsumer steel cans from curbside programs and other sources have presented new opportunities for detinning companies.

In response, detinning companies have opened or planned new facilities in several parts of the country, including a number of satellite operations to collect and ship steel cans to its detinning plants.

Ferrous Scrap Dealers. Ferrous scrap dealers have always recycled a wide array of materials, including steel scrap (Fig. 15.14). Many scrap dealers are now handling retail and wholesale quantities of steel cans received from the public, curbside programs, voluntary drop-off programs, and resource recovery plants. The dealers prepare the steel cans according to end-market specifications and ship truckload or railcar quantities (Fig. 15.15).

Much as the detinning companies had formerly recycled only industrial prompt scrap, scrap dealers had formerly focused only on obsolete scrap, such as cars, white goods, and construction materials. Now, many scrap dealers are becoming involved in the business opportunities offered by processing large volumes of steel cans and other ferrous items recovered from municipal solid waste.

Iron and Steel Foundries. Iron and steel foundries are beginning to recognize their potential as end markets for steel cans. Several foundries are now using and further testing the use of steel cans to be used as a scrap resource for making ductile and gray iron products as well as cast steel. Foundries generally use a 30 to 40 percent purchased scrap mix, in addition to the same proportion of self-generated scrap, to achieve their final product. Even though the total capacity of the more than 2000 U.S. iron and steel foundries is less than the integrated and

FIGURE 15.14 Scrap yard accepts variety of postconsumer products.

FIGURE 15.15 Baled steel cans ready for rail shipment.

minimills, their geographic diversity will prove them to be as important as steel can scrap users.

The Steel Recycling Cycle

The steel industry currently recycles 66 percent of all steel produced including domestic and exported use of steel scrap. Cars, large appliances, machinery, and even the superstructure of demolished buildings continue to provide the steel scrap that is used to produce "new" steel.

Recycling of Steel Cans for Multiple Market Options. Steel food, beverage, and multipurpose cans are remarkable in many ways: they are magnetic, contain significant recycled material, and continue to be a solid, dependable package for a variety of products. But steel cans have yet another remarkable quality—they have many lives as many different steel products. All steel produced contains some amount of recycled steel, as explained above. But the different types of steel scrap are not limited to specific product types when they are remelted to make new steel. This means that the steel scrap used to produce a steel can could have consisted of other steel cans, an old car, a discarded refrigerator, and any other steel product. And that steel can, when it is recycled, will help to produce a new car, appliance, or even a new steel can. The diversity of steel scrap usage makes steel strong indeed as a material type.

Alternative End-Market Uses for Steel Cans.   One example of an alternative use for steel cans is in copper precipitation. Some detinning facilities detin steel cans and sell the steel cans to be used as precipitation iron for recovery of copper from low-grade ores. At the mines, the detinned steel product is placed in a solution of copper sulfate which causes a chemical reaction that, in turn, precipitates the copper from the solution for extraction. Steel cans are ideal for use as a raw material in the precipitation iron process because they are thin and dissolve quickly. This process helps to ensure that otherwise unrecoverable copper in low-grade ore, which has already been mined, can be used. The process aids the most efficient use of resources and helps to offset the need for increased mining activity.

Cost Analysis of Steel Can Recycling in Curbside Programs

Most curbside programs have a fundamental goal of conserving valuable landfill space by diverting recyclable materials from the municipal waste stream. Steel can recycling helps to achieve this goal by decreasing the amount of materials in the waste stream. However, before implementing a curbside program, other factors, such as collection, processing, and transportation to end market must be taken into account. Therefore, the revenue that can be generated through steel can recycling should be considered. The following paragraphs provide formulas for calculating total revenue for steel can recycling.

Economic Impact of Steel Can Recycling in Curbside Programs.   In most communities, steel cans are, by weight, 2 to 4 percent of the municipal solid waste. By diverting those materials from landfill, the community realizes a direct cost savings in its overall solid waste management costs. Using the estimate of .05 tons of steel cans a year per household, a community can calculate what tonnage it may expect by including steel cans in its curbside collection program:

0.05 tons/year × no. households × % participation

For example, a community of 200,000 households with a 75 percent participation rate would generate 7500 tons of steel cans per year.

The revenue available to a community from recycling steel cans can be estimated by using the following formula:

0.05 tons/year × no. households × % participation
        × $/ton purchase price − $/ton freight cost = steel can revenue

For example, the same hypothetical community, which sells its collected steel cans for $65 per ton to a detinner located within a $10 per ton freight cost, would receive

$$0.05 \times 200,000 \times 0.75 \times (\$65 - \$10) = \$412,500$$

If the same community had a landfill tipping fee of $41 per ton and transportation cost of $5 per ton to landfill for a total cost of $46 per ton, then the cost avoidance of the 7500 tons of steel cans would be

$$7500 \times \$46 = \$345,000$$

The addition of steel cans to the curbside recycling program of this community, assuming collection cost of recyclables or garbage are equivalent, would result in a total positive swing to the community's benefit of:

$$\$412,500 + \$345,000 \text{ or } \$757,500$$

Before examining the costs of steel can recycling, the overall curbside program costs should be clear. These costs vary from one program to another because of differences in operational methods and available assets of land, facilities, equipment, and labor. One community may have to purchase property and build an MRF. Another may have a site with a building that can be adapted for use as an MRF.

In a similar manner, some communities may be able to take existing trucks or trailers and adapt them for curbside collection use. Others may need to purchase new or used vehicles.

Finally, the processing equipment itself, including magnetic separation equipment, balers, crushers, flatteners, forklifts, and front-end loaders, can vary considerably according to the overall program design.

Typical Community Cost Analysis. A hypothetical example illustrates how the overall cost structure may look and how steel can recycling fits in. Assume a community has 50,000 households and that the program calls for a weekly curbside collection in all neighborhoods. With a 5-day collection week, the fleet of curbside collectors would serve 10,000 homes daily.

Fleet size depends on a number of variables. A collector could service 300 homes daily, for example, if each home set out its curbside box for pick-up. Some programs, however, may only see a weekly participation rate of 50 percent. One citizen with a full box will set it out on the appointed day, while a neighbor may not set his or hers out until the same collection day in the following week. Thus the truck may pass by 600 homes but only stop and service 300 homes. Assuming this to be the case, for a given week, and a given day, a fleet size of about 16 trucks would be needed with an additional 2 trucks for maintenance and scheduling flexibility. It is also assumed this community has an existing building that may be used without cost.

For this hypothetical community of 50,000 households, the estimated capital, operating, and overhead costs for the total recycling activity may be estimated as in Table 15.1.

Steel Cans' Impact on a Community's Program. Considering both the initial capital costs and the annual operating costs, the incremental costs for steel can recycling are hard to isolate at first glance. Looking closer, one will see that virtually no additional capital costs are needed for a program that includes steel cans. The baler is multipurpose handling paper, cardboard, aluminum cans, plastic, and

TABLE 15.1

Estimated capital costs	
Facility renovation, design, and improvements	$ 100,000
Fleet purchase (18 trucks at $50,000 each)	900,000
Baler purchase (automatic horizontal)	300,000
Conveyor sorting system	25,000
Magnetic overhead separator system	10,000
Household storage bins (55,000 at $5 each, includes 10% replacement supply)	275,000
Total capital costs	$1,610,000
Estimated annual operating costs	
Labor, collection (16 at $20,000/year)	$ 320,000
Labor, processing (6 at $14,000/year)	84,000
Electricity	10,000
Water	4,000
Fuel ($5,000 per truck)	80,000
Propane	2,000
Parts/maintenance	40,000
Lease forklift, front-end loader	8,000
Subtotal operating costs	$ 548,000
Estimated annual overhead	
Management	$ 30,000
Administration	20,000
Office equipment lease	2,000
Office supplies	1,000
Insurance	15,000
Promotion	25,000
Subtotal overhead	$ 93,000
Total operating costs	$ 641,000

steel cans. A magnetic separator is required in any event to assure that steel cans are not mixed with the aluminum cans.

The annual operating costs may be viewed as a constant, given a fixed crew size, regardless of the types of recyclables collected and processed. As a matter of accounting accuracy, however, the relative amount of time spent with each recyclable should be broken out from the total. Steel cans require no extra handling in the collection activity since they are mixed with the other recyclables.

Magnetic separation of steel cans during processing means that labor is not needed to pull them from the conveyor line. Labor becomes involved as the bins of separated steel cans are moved to the baler for infeed and as the bales are removed and stacked and subsequently outloaded for shipment to market. About 10 percent of the labor costs may be attributed to steel can processing incrementally, or using the above example, about $8400 annually. Other incidental costs may also be apportioned, if desired, to include electricity, water, propane, and fuel.

In this example, the incremental cost of adding steel cans to the curbside collection program could be analyzed as

Tons steel cans = 0.05 × 50,000 × 100% = 2500 tons steel cans/year

Revenue = 2500 × $55/ton = $137,500

Less operating costs = 8400 (labor) + 9600 (10% incidental) = $18,000

Steel can contribution to income and overhead = $119,500

Landfill avoided costs = 2500 tons/year × $46/ton = $115,000

Total steel can contribution to the community = $234,500

As this example illustrates, it can readily be seen that the inclusion of steel cans in the community curbside program would clearly benefit the community's bottom line.

Case Studies: Examples of the Various Types of Programs

A great variety of recycling programs are currently operating across the country. For this reason, this part of the chapter is devoted to discussing general principles of recycling programs and citing specific examples. The most common recycling program is curbside collection.

Example of a Curbside Recycling Program. Since July 1989, residents of Milwaukee, Wisconsin, have participated in a commingled curbside recycling program that includes the following recyclable materials: steel and aluminum cans, glass bottles and jars, newspaper, and PET and HDPE plastic. Other materials are currently being tested.

Once a week on a designated day, residents place their recyclables in a single bin at the curbside (Fig. 15.16). Newspapers are bagged or bundled separately. City employees collect and haul the recyclable materials to Recycle America's MRF, where the materials are processed. Recycle America, a subsidiary of Waste Management located in Milwaukee, sells the steel cans to local end markets.

In the first year of the program, more than 423,000 lb of steel cans were collected. In 1990, that amount increased to 505,082 lb of steel cans.

Now servicing 45,000 households, the program will expand to 60,000 households this summer. By the end of 1994, the entire city of 250,000 households will be part of the curbside program.

In addition, four grocery store drop-off locations serve residents who may not yet be serviced by the program, and a multimaterial drop-off container is periodically placed overnight at grade schools to encourage children to participate in recycling efforts.

FIGURE 15.16 Residents participating in curbside program.

Example of a Drop-Off Recycling Program. Conroe Recycling Company, located in Conroe, Texas, has provided drop-off recycling sites that accept steel cans for residents of Kingwood, the Woodlands, and Walden on Lake Conroe. The recyclables from these drop-off centers, including steel and aluminum cans, glass containers, cardboard, and high-grade paper, are processed at the Conroe Recycling Center, where this community's residents may also bring materials for recycling.

The company collects approximately 30,000 lb of steel cans per month, and with anticipated company expansion and greater consumer participation, the number of steel cans recycled will increase still more.

Example of a Multimaterial Buy-Back Center. The Adams/Brown Recycling Station, located in Georgetown, Ohio, is a multimaterial buy-back center that serves Adams and Brown County recyclers (Fig. 15.17). Opened in 1981, the center has grown from an aluminum, glass, and paper recycling center to one that accepts a large variety of materials, including aluminum cans and scrap, glass containers, various types of paper, steel food and beverage cans, plastic containers, used motor oil, car batteries, red metals, zinc, and lead.

In addition to accepting such a variety of materials, the Recycling Station has made recycling more convenient to consumers by providing a mobile buy-back center that operates in any one of five locations in Adams and Brown Counties. Officials from the Recycling Station recognize that convenience is a major concern to consumers. In fact, the organization's director suggested that eventually consumers will realize that making a trip to the recycling center is similar in concept to taking clothes to the dry cleaners. Both are necessary errands, and both can easily be incorporated into one's schedule.

As part of a community action program called Adams/Brown Counties Economic Opportunities, Inc., the Recycling Station receives funding from the Department of Natural Resources, Ohio's solid waste authorities, various private companies, and other sources.

Example of a Resource Recovery Facility. The Metro-Dade County Resources Recovery Fuel Facility (in Florida), one of the largest in the country, is also a leader

FIGURE 15.17 Trailer for transporting recyclables.

in front-end separation of postconsumer steel products (Fig. 15.18). Since 1981, when the plant opened, front-end magnetic separation has facilitated the recycling of postconsumer steel products. Now, the plant recovers over 700 tons of this mixed ferrous material per week. An estimated 60 percent of the ferrous ma-

FIGURE 15.18 Aerial view of Metro-Dade County (Florida) Resource Recovery Fuel Facility.

terial recovered from resource recovery facilities is steel cans. The magnetically separated materials are then sold to a metal processor for preparation and sale to end markets. In July 1991, the plant will begin processing the ferrous on a new shredding and cleaning system at the plant.

Ferrous materials are processed in two sections of the plant. Municipal waste is sized and crushed, and postconsumer steel cans, along with other small steel items, are magnetically separated with the use of belt magnets. Oversized household waste and bulky municipal trash are shredded in another area of the plant, and steel is separated through a system of drum magnets.

Currently processing 2500 tons of municipal solid waste per day, the plant processed 795,000 tons in 1990, generating 346,000 megawatthours (MWh) of electricity, and also recovering 34,900 tons of steel as well as 278 tons of aluminum. In the first quarter of 1991, 8673 tons of steel and 140 tons of aluminum were recovered.

Montenay Power Company operates Refuse-Derived Fuel plants and mass burn plants internationally. The company has operated the Metro-Dade facility since June 1985.

Example of a Waste Processing Facility.   Delta Waste Service, Inc., operates a waste processing facility at High Point, North Carolina. The facility recovers steel cans, cardboard, newspaper, computer paper, aluminum cans, all three colors of glass containers, HDPE and PET containers, metal scrap, and wood waste from the solid waste stream.

Refuse trucks deliver municipal waste to a conveyor belt, where a mechanical system breaks up the waste and 35 employees manually extract the recyclables. Magnetic separation is used to separate the steel cans and other postconsumer steel products from the waste stream.

Advantages of Steel Can Recycling

Communities implementing recycling programs are motivated by common concerns, principally saving landfill space and preserving precious domestic natural resources. Recycling programs are motivated by genuine concern for our environment, far more than the actual cost trade-offs of the program. Steel cans should be part of every community's recycling program because they are common household items that are easy to collect, are inexpensive to process, and have stable, well-established, long-term markets.

Landfill Savings.   It makes no sense to landfill materials that can be reused by domestic and foreign industries. The steel industry's goal is to recover and recycle 66 percent of all steel cans by the year 1995. It is estimated that about 100 million steel cans are used every day by American consumers. Diverting this quantity of material to reuse will conserve valuable landfill space. As landfill capacity declines and environmental protection measures increase, the cost of landfill operation is rapidly escalating, making such diversion even more critical.

Other Environmental Benefits.   But recycling steel cans does a great deal more than divert usable materials from landfill. Although steel cans are made with very common and inexpensive natural elements—iron ore, coal, and limestone—the reuse of steel cans in the manufacturing process preserves domestic natural resources for future generations. Every time a ton of steel cans, the average annual consumption of 20 households, is recycled, 2500 lb of iron ore, 1000 lb of coal, and 40 lb of limestone are preserved.

And steel can recycling saves energy. It is about 75 percent less energy intensive to make new steel from recycled steel than to start with iron ore. When 2 lb of steel cans are recycled (the average weekly consumption in a household), enough energy is saved to keep a 60-W light bulb burning for more than 2 days.

REFERENCES

1. American Iron and Steel Institute, Committee of Tin Mill Products Producers, *Steel Cans: No. 1 in Packaging Quality, Integrity; Where They Stand, Where They're Headed*, pp. 2–6.

2. Steel Can Recycling Institute, *Recyclable Steel Cans: An Integral Part of Your Curbside Recycling Program*, pp. 18–21.

3. Steel Can Recycling Institute, *Steel Cans and Recycling: Today's Environmental Partnership*.

CHAPTER 16
YARD WASTE

Ron Albrecht
Ron Albrecht Associates, Inc.
Annapolis, Maryland

INTRODUCTION

Yard waste is defined as the leaves or leaf fall, grass clippings or grass trimmings, and woody wastes—branches, trimmings, stalks, and roots—found in the municipal solid waste stream. The United States Environmental Protection Agency estimates that in 1988 yard waste constituted about 18 percent of the national municipal solid waste flow. Recovery of yard waste by processing into compost or mulch is an increasingly popular method of recycling solid waste. Further, yard waste recovery has the advantages of ease of separate collection since the materials are generated outside of the home, low costs of processing, and products familiar to many users.

States use different methods to encourage yard waste recovery. Some states, for example, Illinois, North Carolina, and Ohio, have legislation which bans landfilling of all yard wastes. Pennsylvania and New Jersey ban the landfilling of leaf waste. Florida bans the landfilling of yard waste in lined landfills and effectively requires recovery of yard waste by adopting a high recycling goal. Many state encourage market development by requiring or giving preferential status to the use of compost and mulch made from yard waste.

The expanding experience in yard waste programs has resulted in methods of estimating quantities of yard waste, efficiently collecting yard waste, processing the materials into marketable products, and distributing the products to constructive uses.

GENERATION OF YARD WASTE

The two major sources of yard waste found in the municipal solid waste stream are households and commercial activities. Household yard waste consists of the vegetative wastes resulting from the maintenance of lawns, trees, planting areas, and gardens by residents. Commercial activities of landscaping and grounds maintenance such as found at institutional establishments, golf courses, and cemeteries generate large quantities of yard waste. A difference between the two sources of waste is that residential yard wastes are generally collected with other wastes as part of municipal solid waste services, whereas commercial firms are responsible for transportation and disposal.

Although the EPA estimate of 18 percent can provide overall guidance for some situations, a better approach is to determine the amount of yard waste in a specific waste stream. It works best to conduct an intensive multiseasonal waste stream characterization or to estimate the yard waste content on the basis of data developed by a nearby similar community. Yard waste generation rates vary widely with locations, climate, and type of development, for example, suburban versus urban or rural, maturity of the area (whether newly built with small trees and immature lawns or large trees and established lawns), and local weather (whether a time of excess rainfall or drought). These all have definite impact on the waste stream. Examples of wide differences in yard waste production are Florida, where a long growing season and plentiful rainfall cause yard waste to exceed 30 percent of the total waste stream, and Pennsylvania where yard waste collected in rural counties is estimated as low as 5 percent because of other disposal options readily available to residents.

The blend of yard waste components, that is, the relative amounts of grass, leaves, and wood wastes, is variable. Relative amounts are specific to a particular study area. For purposes of preliminary planning the data given in Table 16.1 are accepted estimates.

TABLE 16.1 Types of Yard Waste as Percentage of Total Yard Waste (by Weight)*

Leaves	19–28%
Grass	54–64%
Woody waste	17–18%

*Based on Mid-Atlantic data.

Yearly generation patterns vary with the location, climate, and weather. A typical yearly pattern is shown in Fig. 16.1.

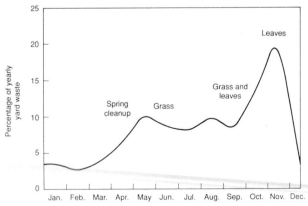

FIGURE 16.1 Seasonal distribution of yard waste.

Generation patterns in the temperate areas follow a seasonal pattern. January and February typically produce the minimum yard waste because growth is in the dormant stage. March and April's mild weather brings spring cleanup and grass starts to grow. Grass trimmings then become the major yard waste component until mid-October when leaf fall starts to dominate. A decrease in grass production because of drought conditions during July and August can be expected. Figure 16.1 does not show the decrease during these months and may illustrate the effects of local weather in a specific year.

The density of yard waste is an important factor in developing a management plan. Almost all solid waste management planning is done by mass, that is, on the basis of tonnage. Yard waste is frequently measured by volume because most yard waste sites do not have vehicle scales. Therefore an understanding of yard waste densities is important in keeping accurate records of yard waste activities. Table 16.2 presents a range of yard waste densities. It is advisable to randomly sample and weigh yard waste components to ensure the accuracy of records.

TABLE 16.2 Density of Yard Wastes

Material	Condition	Typical density, lb/yd^3
Leaves	Loose and dry	100–260
Leaves	Shredded and dry	250–350
Leaves	Compacted and moist	400–500
Green grass	Loose	300–400
Green grass	Compacted	500–800
Yard waste	As collected	350–930
Yard waste	Shredded	450–600
Brush and dry leaves	Loose and dry	100–300
Compost	Finished, screened	700–1200

Source: "Yard Waste Management—A Planning Guide for New York State."

The causes of wide density variations in yard waste components are the moisture content and method of collection and transportation. Wet leaves compacted in rear-end-loader compactor trucks are more dense than leaves collected by vacuum trucks, as shown in Fig. 16.2. Similarly wet grass is heavier than grass cut during dry weather.

Many communities have established programs to reduce yard waste generation by encouraging backyard composting, changes in landscape practices, and changes in turf management. Backyard composting programs encourage homeowners to compost yard waste on their properties. This encouragement ranges from the simple programs of giving out "how to" literature through the distribution of backyard composting units. Changes in landscape practices focus on the reduction of vegetative wastes by encouraging the use of mulches or decorative stone cover in place of turf. In some areas the concept of xeroscaping, creating a desertlike landscape with minimal water requirements and foliage production, is accepted. Changes in turf management involve leaving the grass trimmings on the lawn to recover the nitrogen content and reduce the quantity of waste. All of these practices can serve to reduce the amount of yard waste. Many of these pro-

FIGURE 16.2   Vacuum truck collecting leaves.

grams conflict with traditional landscape practices and are not well received by homeowners. Further, it is difficult to measure the effectiveness of these source-reduction programs. Exhibit 16.1 shows a sample pamphlet on home composting.

COLLECTION OF YARD WASTE

Yard wastes are generally collected by separate curbside collection or at drop-off sites. Curbside collection generally involves additional expenses because of the labor and equipment involved in additional pickup. Drop-off sites are generally voluntary and less expensive than separate collection, but are not as effective as curbside pickup because they are not as convenient to the residents. Collection strategies differ according to the type of yard waste.

Leaf collection is a seasonal operation beginning in October and usually ending in mid-December. Some communities limit the collection to street leaves while others allow residents to rake leaves to curbside for collection. The frequency of collection varies from once a year to weekly during periods of leaf fall. Leaves are collected in various ways, either loose or bagged, by different types of collection vehicles.

Bagged leaves can be collected in three types of containers: nondegradable plastic bags, biodegradable plastic bags, or biodegradable paper bags. Experience shows that the biodegradable paper bags simplify processing the leaves. However, biodegradable bags are more expensive than alternative plastic bags. Nondegradable plastic bags are the least expensive but do complicate processing

Steps For Making Compost:

1) Gather your materials and pile them at least 3 feet wide and 3 feet tall. Avoid packing leaves as this slows down decomposition. Your compost pile can be placed anywhere convenient in your yard.
2) Water as you combine all ingredients. The pile should be as moist as a squeezed out sponge.
3) Indent the top to collect rainwater.
4) Turn the pile monthly and water each time. Turning provides needed air and moisture. In winter it is best to leave it alone.

It can take several months or longer before your compost will be ready for use. How quickly your compost is ready depends on:

 • pile size,
 • aeration,
 • moisture, and
 • how often you turn the pile.

Benefits of Using Compost:

Well decomposed compost is perfect for most home gardening because it is usually near neutral pH (between 6.5-7.0).

Compost can be:

 • Tilled directly into your soil to improve water and fertilizer holding capacity.
 • Used as a mulch, 2 inches to 3 inches deep, to prevent water loss through evaporation.
 • Used in a soil mix for houseplants. Adding 1/4 compost to any soil mix adds organic matter and small amounts of nutrients.

Compost is not a fertilizer, but improves soil structure. Both sand and clay soils can be helped with the addition of compost.

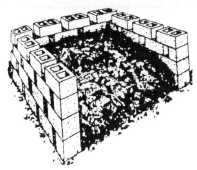

Concrete block can be built as single or multi-bin.

Recycled pallets make a great compost bin.

EXHIBIT 16.1 Pamphlet on home composting.

by littering the compost site and blinding the compost screens. In addition, pieces of the bags detract from the appearance of the compost. Some communities debag the leaves at time of collection or at the processing site. Debagging leaves involves a considerable amount of labor and is not considered cost-effective. The experience with biodegradable plastic bags is that the bags will deteriorate into plastic fragments which do not degrade during composting. Therefore the nondegraded plastic fragments interfere with processing and detract from final product quality, similar to the nondegradable plastic bags. Both types of plastic bags are available in several different colors. The problem of identifying yard waste set out for separate collection is simplified by requiring the use of a specific-color bag.

Biodegradable paper bags are expensive, $0.25 to $0.40 each, but have the advantage of degrading and disappearing into the compost. Many communities distribute preprinted paper bags through their government offices and supermarket chains. Residents are charged for each bag. The community then limits leaf collection to leaves bagged in the designated paper bags (Fig. 16.3).

A variety of methods are used to collect loose leaves. Residents are required to rake the leaves to curbside where different types of equipment are used to load the leaves onto collection vehicles. Vacuum trucks and hoses are used to suck the leaves into trucks (Fig. 16.4). Some vacuum collection systems are equipped with shredders to size reduce the leaves and increase their density. Front-end loaders are used to scrape the leaves from the roadway and load the leaves into dump trucks or rear-end-compactor trucks. Tractors with attachments and street sweepers are also used to collect leaves.

Brush and woody wastes are generated throughout the year. The spring and fall are the periods of greatest generation. Most communities require that woody wastes be restricted to items 2 in and under in diameter, cut to lengths no greater than 4 ft, and tied in bundles. The bundles facilitate loading and do not interfere with processing. Some communities offer special pickup of large quantities of brush. Collection vehicles include rear-end compactors, dump trucks with low sides, and scow trucks equipped with booms for pickup of large quantities.

The collection of grass clippings presents special problems in a yard waste system because the grass is readily degradable and can cause odors. If sealed bags are used, anaerobic conditions can develop in a very short period of time. In addition, bags of grass can be heavy because of the high moisture content. Perforated plastic or paper bags are made to try to control the development of anaerobic conditions. Plastic containers specially designed to promote the circulation of air are used by some communities for grass collection. The containers should be sized so that lifting them will not unnecessarily burden the collection crew.

Drop-off areas are inexpensive methods of collecting yard waste. The costs of labor and equipment needed to operate a a drop-off yard waste site are below the costs of curbside pickup. Many of the drop-off center programs issue identification and restrict deliveries to community residents. Since the program is voluntary and participation requires effort, the effectiveness of drop-off programs is well below the effectiveness of curbside collection programs. Drop-off centers can be complementary to developing curbside programs and can be used to offer services in outlying areas where curbside collection is not cost-effective (Fig. 16.5).

Appropriate locations for permanent drop-off centers include transfer stations, recycling centers, landfills, and other government-owned properties where space is available and the traffic will not create a public nuisance or hazard. Collection containers are often used as scheduled rotating drop-off points in areas convenient to residents. Most permanent drop-off centers have supervision in order to

FIGURE 16.3   Paper yard waste bag.

FIGURE 16.4   Rear-end loader discharging leaves. (*Courtesy of Brian Golob, DPRA, St. Paul, Minnesotta.*)

FIGURE 16.5   Citizen yard waste drop-off. (*Courtesy of Brian Golob, DPRA, St. Paul, Minnesotta.*)

prevent dumping of other trash and garbage. The collected yard waste should be promptly hauled to the designated processing site in order to prevent overloading the drop-off center and the possible development of odor and disease-vector problems.

Yard waste transfer stations are designed to receive materials from collection trucks. The primary purpose is to reduce the cost of hauling to processing sites;

however, they can be used to provide interim storage if the rate of collection exceeds processing capacity at citizen drop-off centers, and to receive yard waste from commercial generators. In addition, many yard waste transfer stations are constructed adjacent to municipal solid waste (MSW) transfer stations and can use the truck scales conventionally provided for MSW transfer. All yard waste transfer stations should be attended during the hours of operations. Records should be kept of the types and sources of the waste. Facilities should operate on a scheduled basis and be fenced to prevent vandalism and illegal dumping. Since yard waste processing facilities are generally located in remote areas, transfer stations can reduce the overall cost of the system.

PROCESSING TECHNOLOGIES AND SYSTEMS

Processing yard wastes into compost and mulch involves two different technologies. Both incorporate composting but differ enough to warrant separate explanations.

Composting can be defined as the biological decomposition of waste organic materials under aerobic conditions to a level of stability suitable for intended use or nuisance-free storage. Leaves and grass are readily compostable. Leaves are the primary feedstock for most yard waste composting. Leaves have a low nitrogen and moisture content and therefore require a long period of time to compost. Grass has a relatively high nitrogen and moisture content and as a result anaerobic conditions and bad odors can develop if the grass is not promptly and properly processed. Leaf composting has developed into three main processing techniques: low-level technology, intermediate-level technology, and high-level technology.

There is a minimal-level technology which involves stacking the leaves into 10- to 12-ft-high piles on remote sites. The piles are unattended for several years and natural decomposition processes changed the leaves into compost. Odor problems are avoided by the remoteness of the sites. Since the use of this technique is controlled by the availability of remote sites, the technology is limited to small rural communities. Further, the distinction between a minimal-technology site and a leaf dump is hazy. Many public health and environmental regulatory agencies will not permit minimal-technology yard waste composting facilities because of the resemblance to leaf dumps and the high risk of odor problems.

Low-level technology involves providing limited moisture and oxygen to the leaves (Fig. 16.6). Piles are constructed with incoming leaves to heights as high as 20 ft. After some volume reduction takes place due to decomposition and settlement, the piles are maintained at about a 6-ft height with a 14-ft base. The piles are turned once or twice a year with a front-end loader. Water is sometimes added at the time of turning. Using this system, compost can be made in about a year and a half.

Intermediate technology is the most frequently used method of leaf composting. Frequent turnings speed up the rate of decomposition and produce a finished product in less than a year. This allows reuse of the processing area for the next year's incoming leaves and conserves space. Many of the ideas used in intermediate-level processing were developed by cost-conscious private-site operators.

FIGURE 16.6 Low-level composting site in Massachusetts.

Although front-end loaders can be used to turn windrows, most intermediate sites use dedicated windrow turning machines (Fig. 16.7). Windrow turners provide more thorough aeration than is possible with a front-end loader. Further, turning with windrow turners is more efficient and economical than turning with front-end loaders.

FIGURE 16.7 Windrow turning machine.

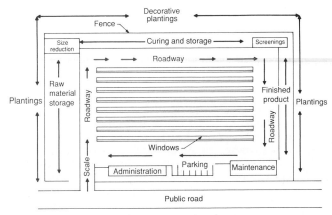

FIGURE 16.8 Typical yard waste processing site.

Windrows are turned several times a week. Water is added to maintain optimal biologic activity. In some instances nitrogen is added to the nutrient-deficient leaves. Using these methods, compost can be made in 6 months. A schematic layout for a intermediate-level processing site is shown in Fig. 16.8. The design incorporates areas for storage of incoming leaves, processing, screening, storage of finished product, and administration and maintenance. The site is fenced and buffered from neighbors by plantings and/or berms.

High-level composting technology involves the use of large aerated static piles on outdoor pads to accelerate the composting action. Water is added to bring the leaves to the optimal level for biologic growth. Similarly, nitrogen is added to adjust the carbon-to-nitrogen ratio to the desired level. No operating projects currently use high-tech procedures because the benefits do not justify the additional capital and operating costs.

The general parameters used to develop leaf composting windrow sites are given in Table 16.3.

TABLE 16.3 Windrow Composting of Yard Waste

	Low-tech	Intermediate-tech	High-tech
Loading rates, yd^3/acre	3000–3500	4000–5000	15,000–30,000
Windrow height, ft	6	6–8	8–10
Turn frequency	2 months	Monthly	Weekly
Processing time, months	18	10–12	4

Grass composting is complicated by the risk of odors. Because of the moisture and nitrogen content, grass is readily compostable and if not promptly and properly handled will putrefy and cause bad odors. In addition, grass's physical structure and tendency to mat together restrict the amount of void spaces available for air. Most professional yard waste composters reluctantly accept grass for composting. Because of the need to accept and process all yard wastes, two methods of processing have been developed.

A controlled amount of grass can be added to windrows of composting leaves. The amount of grass is between 25 and 30 percent by volume, that is, grass to leaves. The grass must be thoroughly mixed with the leaves and the windrows carefully monitored for aerobic conditions.

Another approach is to mix the grass with wood chips or wood mulch and windrow compost the mixture. The wood provides physical structure and voids for air. Since grass loses considerable volume (grass shrinks to 5 to 10 percent of its original volume when composted), the windrows can be reloaded with new grass. Theoretically this procedure can be repeated until the windrow becomes as dense as finished compost. Here again the importance of maintaining aerobic conditions cannot be overemphasized.

Woody yard wastes can be recycled into mulch, compost, or a combination of the two. Because of the high carbon content, woody wastes are slow to decompose. Generally this waste is not considered suitable for large-scale composting. However, small particle size, less than 0.5 in in diameter, pieces can be composted with other wastes.

Large branches are frequently chipped or shredded into wood chips or mulch. Woodchips can be used in municipal landscape projects, park pathways, and for all-weather roads or work surfaces. In order to meet commercial standards, mulch should have a longer particle than wood chips, be of uniform size, have a dark color, and be free of weed seeds. Some operators will cut large branches and trunks into stove length pieces and market firewood. Three types of equipment are most often used to size reduce wood waste: chippers, tub grinders, and heavy-duty hammer mills or shredders. Not included in this is the exceptionally heavy-duty equipment used to process land-clearing debris and stumps.

Chippers are an effective solution for small quantities of wood waste. Mobile tow-behind chippers (Fig. 16.9) are frequently used in maintaining road and utility rights of way. The equipment is limited in the size of material it can handle and has the disadvantages of low capacity and high labor requirements. However, chippers are readily available to most communities.

Tub grinders are named because of their tublike feeding chamber (Fig. 16.10). Material can be loaded into the tub using a front-end loader or knuckle boom

FIGURE 16.9   Tow-behind chipper.

FIGURE 16.10 Exterior of tub grinder.

grapple crane mounted on the equipment. Because of the size of the opening, a tub grinder can accept larger pieces than a chipper. The reduced-size material can be discharged onto a pile on the ground or loaded onto a receiving conveyor belt. A tub grinder costs between $60,000 and $140,000 depending on the capacity. Maintenance costs are high. Processing materials such as stumps and rocks will cause excessive wear and increase maintenance costs. Hammers must be rotated after 50 h of operation and must be replaced after 140 to 240 h of operation. Replacement hammers cost $900 to $2000 a set and take 3 h to replace. Figure 16.11 shows the interior of a tub grinder.

Heavy-duty hammer mills and shredders can be mobile or permanently mounted. This type of equipment can be fed directly by hand or with a conveyor belt. The advantages of this equipment are large-capacity throughput and ability to handle a variety of materials. Recently, several large yard waste sites have selected auger or screw shredders for size reduction. These devices were originally intended to reduce oversize bulky waste in the municipal solid waste stream and are rugged and reliable. The higher initial costs of auger shredders are offset by lower maintenance cost. Although the capital costs are high, probably $70,000 to $500,000, this type of equipment is capable of reducing any size waste that can be fed into the machine. A variety of sizes are available. A shredder in use at a yard waste processing site is shown in Fig. 16.12.

Both tub grinders and heavy-duty hammermills and shredders can be equipped with magnet separators to remove metal particles and screens to remove foreign particles and size the products. Decisions on the use of additional equipment to enhance product quality should be made on the basis of the quality of products needed for successful marketing.

Following size reduction, the wood fragments are screened to uniform sizes. The small-particle fraction generally contains a large amount of soil particles and is often marketed as top soil. The middle fraction, under 6 in and above 0.5 in, is further processed into mulch; the greater-than-6-in fraction is marketed as mulch for low grade uses such as barnyards or construction sites or as boiler fuel.

Processing the mid-size fraction into mulch involves building large piles with the mulch and allowing the piles to partially compost. As the piles are built, some

FIGURE 16.11 Interior of tub grinder showing hammers.

FIGURE 16.12 Intake hopper of screw auger shredder.

processors wet the mulch with water containing liquid nitrogen. This addition helps to control dust and the nitrogen accelerates the heat buildup in the piles. The limited composting destroys the weed seeds and insect larvae and darkens the color of the particles. The final mulch is weed-free and has a uniform color. Care must be exercised to prevent too much deterioration of the mulch, since this would shorten its effectiveness as a ground cover.

MARKETING

Marketing the final products is equally important as producing consistent high-quality compost and mulch. A yard waste program will not be successful unless the products are put to constructive uses. A marketing plan specific to the project and marketing area should be started early in project planning and frequently updated as marketing progresses. There are many successful marketing programs which can provide guidance on how to succeed. Examining operating marketing programs in similar nearby communities can prevent mistakes. A foundation of good marketing is to understand the products, uses of the products, and the methods of distribution.

Yard waste compost is a useful soil conditioner familiar to many potential users. Unlike compost produced from other wastes, for example, wastewater treatment plant sludge or municipal solid waste, this compost does not invoke concerns about reusing a waste material. Gaining user acceptance of yard waste compost is not as difficult as gaining confidence for these other composts.

The chemical macronutrient content of yard waste compost is low, well below accepted fertilizer standards. A typical chemical analysis is shown in Table 16.4. The nutrient content can be increased by adding other sources of nutrients to the compost. A careful study should be made of the costs and cost benefits and marketability of the fortified product before implementing this type of program.

TABLE 16.4 Nutrient Analysis of Yard Waste Compost

Nutrient	Range, %	Mean of leaf compost, %
Nitrogen (total)	0.3–2.0	0.6
Phosphorous	0.03–.5	0.1
Potassium	0.1–2.0	1.1

The compost should meet physical, biological, and chemical standards for soil amendments. The physical standards include a uniform dark brown color, have a uniform particle size, a pleasant earthlike odor, and be free of tramp trash such as bottle caps and paper, plastic, and glass fragments. These criteria can be met with conventional processing methods. The moisture content should be low enough, less than 45 percent, to allow spreading of the compost and prevent the development of anaerobic odor problems.

All users demand a weed-free and insect-free product. This can be achieved if the compost is properly processed. Concerns about chemical content are centered in two areas: heavy metal contaminants and pesticide and herbicide residuals. Numerous testings of yard waste compost show heavy metal content well below the standards for use on food-chain crops. A decade ago composts made from street leaves showed some lead content. The national change to lead-free gasoline has further reduced the lead concentration. Several municipalities have tested yard waste compost for herbicide and pesticide residuals. In every instance, the residuals are not detected or are below levels of concern. Pesticide and herbicide residuals tend to wash off foliage and are attracted to soil particles. Table 16.5 shows the chemical characteristics of yard debris compost.

TABLE 16.5 Chemical Characteristics of Yard Debris Compost

N	<1.0%
P	<2.0%
K	<0.4%
Mercury	0.06 ppm*
Arsenic	5.00 ppm
Cadmium	0.80 ppm
Chromium	23.00 ppm
Nickel	22.00 ppm
Lead	72.00 ppm
Zinc	160.00 ppm

*All units parts per million dry weight basis.

Compost is a soil conditioner or amendment. When mixed with natural soils, compost will increase moisture-holding capacity, retard erosion, and improve soil tilth. Compost is used to invigorate compacted or worn-out soils and increase productivity.

Mulch is used as groundcover around planting areas and trees and for decorative effect (Figure 16.13 shows mulching equipment.) A layer of mulch will conserve soil moisture and retard the growth of weeds. The specifications for mulch are similar to those for compost. The product should be free of weeds, insects, and chemical and biological contamination. The desirable physical standards include a uniform color and a particle size that allows the mulch to lock together when placed as a layer on the soil.

Products which compete with yard waste mulch include shredded bark, bark chips, pine chunks, and pine needles. Some users feel that yard waste mulch is inferior to other products because it contains a large amount of white fibers which deteriorate faster than rot-resistant bark and the color is lighter and less uniform than pure bark mulches. Figure 16.14 shows a mulch-coloring machine.

The users for both compost and mulch include home gardeners and landscapers, greenhouses, nurseries, topsoil suppliers, landscape contractors, professional groundskeepers, cemeteries, and golf courses. Many public agencies, including transportation departments, forest and park agencies, and public works, can use the products in the construction and maintenance of roadways, and parks and landscaping of building grounds and landfills. Markets for compost are seasonal. See Fig. 16.15. The largest amount of compost is used in the spring when soils are prepared for planting.

FIGURE 16.13 Yard waste mulching equipment. (*Courtesy N/R Associates, Boynton Beach, Florida.*)

FIGURE 16.14 Mulch-coloring machine. (*Courtesy N/R Associates, Boynton Beach, Florida.*)

Midsummer use is limited because plants are in the growth stage. In most marketing programs, shipments during the fall months are low. However, many marketing programs increase fall shipments through public education programs emphasizing the superior benefits obtained by using compost in the fall. A goal of the marketing program should be to ship compost to users on a year-round basis.

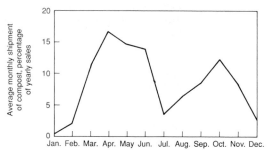

FIGURE 16.15 Average monthly shipments of compost.

This can be achieved by emphasizing sales to users such as topsoil blenders and contractors which can accept shipments and store the material pending use.

A variety of distribution methods are used to distribute yard waste products. Some small communities give compost and mulch to residents without charge at the production site. Others charge commercial users a minimum charge, perhaps one dollar per cubic yard. Many large systems operate marketing programs with professional sales people, advertising and offering hauling to the buyers.

Some communities do not have the ability or interest in managing a marketing program. Companies specializing in marketing soil products operate throughout the country. Many of these companies have proven records of successfully marketing compost and mulch. Some professional marketers guarantee the sale of the products and a net return to the producer. Evaluation of a professional marketing services should be included in the marketing study.

CHAPTER 17
WHITE GOODS

Richard R. Jordan
Vice President
Municipal Recycling Division
The David J. Joseph Company
Cincinnati, Ohio

DEFINITION

Generally, when reference is made to "white goods" in the scrap industry, one is talking about large appliances such as refrigerators, freezers, washers, dryers, stoves, furnaces, and water heaters. These items contain significant amounts of steel (mostly sheet). Many refrigerators, for example, contain at least 80 lb of steel, most of which is located in the doors and cabinets.

BACKGROUND

During the past decade (1980 to 1990), U.S. steel mills have shipped an annual average of about 3 billion lb of steel to appliance manufacturers. Shipments of major appliances from appliance manufacturers have averaged about 50 million units per year over the past 5 years—up from just over 35 million units per year during the previous 5 years.

According to published statistics, large appliances are replaced after about 15 years' use by the original buyer. An estimated 29 million units were replaced in 1991. Obviously not all of the units being replaced are ready for retirement. Other second-hand appliances are coming out of service at the same time. These figures, though, illustrate the huge quantity of discarded white goods showing up in scrap piles.

What does this mean for the environment? What happens to retired appliances if they are not recycled? Let us assume for a moment that all these large appliances were buried—with no processing. How much space would this take up? Using the appliance industry's estimates of expected replacements during 1991 and the approximate average size of these units, a pit 5 ft deep by 18 ft wide (the approximate width of a two-lane road) would be required to bury this scrap, which would stretch nearly 500 mi, or long enough to reach from Cleveland, Ohio, to New York City. That is just in 1 year!

The environmental contribution from recycling these products is indeed as great as the benefits of recovering the metals. Landfill space grows more precious yearly. Eight states already ban the disposal of large appliances in landfills: Florida, Louisiana, Massachusetts, Minnesota, Missouri, North Carolina, Vermont, and Wisconsin. As more states pass similar regulations, and as landfill disposal costs rise, the benefits for recycling will become more pronounced.

As growing concerns about the availability of landfill space reach the public's eye, more attention has been devoted to recycling. But recycling metals from appliances is certainly nothing new. The scrap industry has been doing it for over a century. Fortunately for municipalities—and anyone else interested in keeping appliances out of landfills—the demand for scrap metals over the years has supported the creation of a sophisticated recycling infrastructure. Development of markets for recycled metals is not something that suddenly needs to be encouraged just for appliances or to address concerns about landfill space.

Appliances are actually just one item in the recovery process of iron and steel from obsolete products. In most processing facilities, appliances are mixed with other items containing ferrous material—most notably automobiles. We can view recycling in basically three steps: recovery or collection, processing, and marketing.

RECOVERY (COLLECTION)

Impact of Demand

How do "retired' appliances make their way into the recycling stream? What incentives are there for recycling? The heating contractor who installs a replacement furnace, the plumber who installs a new hot water tank, and the appliance dealer who delivers a new washer and dryer—all generally take old *unusable* units with them. They can either drop these at a landfill site (if their state allows) or they can sell them to a scrap processor. What does the individual home owner do with appliances if a contractor or delivery service is not involved—take them to a dump site or scrap processor? Just abandon them in a field or alongside the road? The answer to each of these questions is based on economics.

There are labor and transportation costs associated with getting scrap to a processor. Whether obsolete appliances are collected or not is largely determined by whether the scrap processor is offering a price high enough to compensate these costs. If the price is not high enough to keep the home owner from dumping the old washer along the roadside, the price may be high enough to give a peddler incentive to pick it up and deliver it to the scrap yard. Also, it may depend on the weather. It takes more money to get someone out to collect scrap in the winter than it does in the spring. Obviously, it is an individual decision, but the point is that the higher the price offered by the processor, the more scrap will be delivered to the yard. And the more scrap the processor gets, the less he or she must pay for more. It is all simple supply and demand, and the market is quite elastic.

Economic Factors

The scrap processor, therefore, controls the flow of obsolete appliances and other scrap items into the yard by adjusting the price offered for material. To increase the flow, the processor must increase the price and vice versa. Factors that can affect the price include the proximity of populated areas (where scrap is generated) to the processor, ease of access to the yard (major highways, etc.), and even local restrictions on landfills. Also, the closer a processor is to another scrap buyer, the more he or she will have to compete for suppliers, and the more of a price increase it will take to attract additional supply.

Generally, scrap supplied in larger quantities will receive a higher price. The processor must compete more aggressively for a large scrap collector's business than for an appliance from an individual. The collector, whose livelihood is scrap, is willing to travel farther to collect and to deliver scrap in order to get the best price than is an individual carrying a single appliance. The scrap collector's time and transportation costs become proportionately less as the load size increases.

Appliances are delivered to scrap yards by all different types of haulers: installation contractors, scrap peddlers, individual home owners, and even municipal waste haulers. In a typical yard operation, the scale house (where scrap is weighed) is open to the public—anyone is free to bring in scrap, whether it is in a tractor-trailer, pickup truck, station wagon, or even a push cart (Fig. 17.1).

FIGURE 17.1   Peddler delivering appliances to a recycling scrap processor.

PROCESSING

Densification

What processing is performed on scrapped appliances depends on several factors such as volume, equipment costs, what final product local consumers want or need, and even space constraints. Processing options range from expensive shredding operations down to cutting sheet steel with a torch. Some processing may even be done by municipalities or scrap collectors before hauling the appliances to a processing yard. For example, to save transportation costs, a municipality may employ a baler or logger to densify or bundle appliances, which increases load weight per shipment and reduces per unit freight cost. This initial processing may also increase the scrap's value to the processing yard since densification increases handling efficiency. Once these bundles or logs reach the scrap yard, they may then be shredded. The two most common methods of processing appliances are baling and shredding.

Environmental Concerns: PCBs and CFCs

Before an appliance can be purchased by a scrap processor, certain environmental concerns must be addressed. Two harmful substances found in appliances are gaining more attention: polychlorinated biphenyls (PCBs) and chlorofluorocarbons (CFCs).

Removal and Disposal of PCBs and CFCs. PCBs are suspected carcinogens that do not break down. Since the substance may end up in rivers, it poses a threat to fish and other wildlife. PCBs may be found in capacitors manufactured before 1979 (federal law prohibited the use of PCBs in capacitor production beginning in 1979). Potential capacitor-containing equipment includes refrigerators, freezers, washing machines, microwave ovens, televisions, fluorescent light fixtures, heating and cooling equipment, and electronic equipment. Shredding of scrap products containing PCB capacitors and fluorescent light ballasts could produce PCB-contaminated waste by-products at a shredder.

The Toxic Substances Control Act (TSCA) addresses PCBs. Of particular concern are "running capacitors" (as opposed to starting capacitors), which are designed to increase a motor's efficiency. The capacitors are filled with oil—which may contain PCBs—to help dissipate heat. Running capacitors are often identified by their rectangular metal casings. Capacitors containing PCBs must be removed and disposed of properly prior to recycling; otherwise, most scrap processors will not accept the appliance.

Emissions of CFCs are linked to depletion of the earth's ozone layer. CFCs may be found in wall panel foam in refrigerators and freezers, and in refrigerants for refrigerators, freezers, and air conditioners.

Programs including recycling of CFC refrigerants should specify that reclamation of the refrigerant gas must take place prior to disposal and recycling of the unit in which the refrigerant is contained. Technology exists for recovering CFCs from refrigeration units. The cost ranges from approximately $1000 to $8000 per reclamation machine.

Processing White Goods

The flowcharts in Figs. 17.2 and 17.3 illustrate the movement of appliances through a processing facility. Figure 17.2 shows a typical baling operation, Fig. 17.3 a shredding facility. These charts depict the basic costs or value involved at each stage. The shredder operation is addressed in more detail.

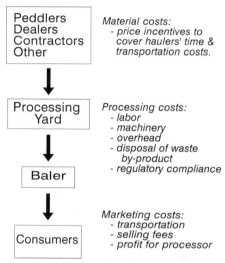

FIGURE 17.2   Baler flowchart.

Shredding

Appliances represent only part of shredder feed. Automobile shredders are expensive investments; machines can cost $3 million to $6 million per installation. A typical shredder can process 1 to 2 tons of appliances per minute, producing finished material averaging from as small as a fingernail to as large as a fist (Fig. 17.4). In an hour, a shredder can typically produce 65 to 100 tons of shredded steel.

The shredding process produces three output streams: shredded steel, nonferrous metals, and nonmetallics such as plastics, rubber, etc. (referred to as shredder residue). The ferrous and nonferrous metals are saleable. Shredder residue is landfilled.

MARKETING

Consumers of processed ferrous scrap include domestic steel mills and foundries, and export markets. A marketing infrastructure is well-established to handle

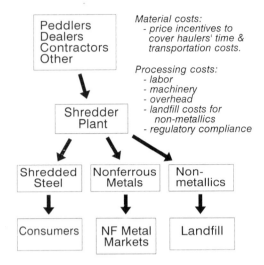

FIGURE 17.3   Shredder flowchart.

FIGURE 17.4   Shredded steel processed from appliances.

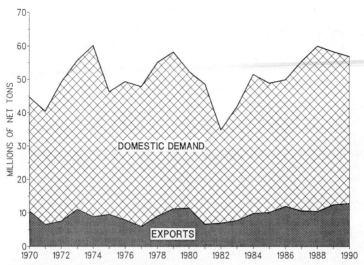

FIGURE 17.5 Demand for U.S. ferrous scrap.

prompt industrial and obsolete scrap generated in the United States. Old appliances fit neatly into this structure all across the country.

Over the past 10 years, the domestic market for ferrous scrap has been about 35 to 45 million net tons annually, exports have ranged from 7 to 13 million net tons annually. Even though U.S. steelmaking capacity has declined 34 percent since its peak in 1973, dependence on scrap as feedstock has grown due to technological changes in steelmaking, resulting in a proportional increase in scrap as a raw material. The graphs in Figs. 17.5 and 17.6 illustrate these concepts.

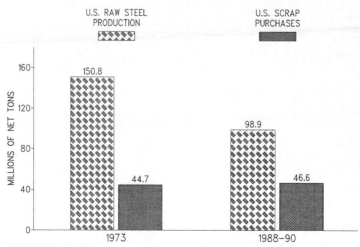

FIGURE 17.6 U.S. raw steel production and scrap purchases.

Fluctuations

Ferrous scrap prices rise and fall with the balancing of supply and demand. Although appliances are generally considered a "low-end" item in the scrap price spectrum, rare is the time when an obsolete appliance cannot be sold to a processor for some value. At times of higher scrap demand, prices paid for appliances rise with prices for other unprepared scrap.

Nonferrous Segments

Nonferrous scrap recovered by a shredding operation is generally sold to an intermediate processor that separates the various metals by type—aluminum, copper, zinc, and lead. Each of these metals is then marketed within its respective industries.

Closing the Loop

The mere collection of old white goods does not constitute recycling. To close the recycling loop, scrap from obsolete appliances resurfaces as metal in new appliances, automobiles, construction products, machinery, and other industrial and consumer goods (Fig. 17.7). Recycling of white goods (or anything else for that matter) does not occur until this reuse takes place.

FIGURE 17.7 Construction rebar produced from scrap that includes recycled appliances.

CHAPTER 18
TIRES

Michael H. Blumenthal
Executive Director
Scrap Tire Management Council
Washington, D.C.

OVERVIEW

Despite the fact that scrap tires represent slightly more than 1 percent (1.2 percent to be exact) of all solid waste, scrap tires present a special disposal and reuse challenge because of their size, shape, and physicochemical nature. Scrap tires are not generally collected with household waste by municipal authorities. Thus, scrap tires have traditionally been classified as a "special waste" or as a "durable product." This chapter will present information concerning the composition of a tire, the manner in which scrap tires are currently disposed, as well as some of the problems commonly associated with scrap tires. This section will also describe other uses and limitations for scrap tires. A section of case histories will further detail several of the current economically viable ways to use scrap tires. The final section presents a review of current state legislative activities relative to scrap tires.

Generation Rates

In 1990, there were some 278 million car and truck tires discarded in the United States. In 1984, the annual generation of scrap tires was approximately 1.05 tires per capita. The per capita generation rate has been steadily increasing. In 1987, the per capita generation rate was estimated at 1.15 scrap tires and for 1990, the scrap tire per capita generation rate is estimated to be 1.25.

At present, approximately 34.5 percent of the annually produced scraped tires are reused, recycled, or recovered. The remaining 65.5 percent, some 180 million scrap tires, are disposed of in landfills or added to the estimated 2 to 3 billion scrap tires already stockpiled.

Average Tire Composition and Characteristics

The average scrap automobile or light truck tire weighs approximately 20 lb. Heavy truck and industrial tires can weigh anywhere from 35 lb up to several hundred pounds. Since 1983 all new car and light truck tires, as well as virtually all replacement tires sold for passenger cars or light trucks, have been steel-belted radials. Steel-belted radial heavy truck tires are beginning to replace bias-ply heavy truck tires, which have been the norm in the trucking industry.

Tire industry sources estimated that 85 percent of all scrap tires are passenger car or light truck tires, 14 percent are heavy truck tires. The remaining 1 percent are specialty tires, ranging from motorcycle tires to aircraft tires to construction equipment and military tires.

To better understand the nature of a scrap tire, the composition of a typical tire casing is presented in Fig. 18.1a. Primary constituents of tires include polymers, carbon black, and softeners. The softeners are mainly composed of aromatic hydrocarbon oils, which in combination with the polymers give the tire a relatively high heating value (measured in British thermal units, or Btus). In order

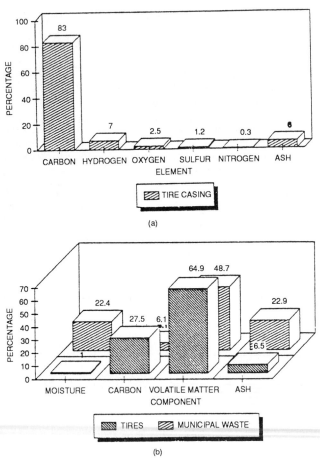

(a)

(b)

FIGURE 18.1 (a) Elemental composition of typical tire casing; (b) select components in tires and municipal solid waste.

to demonstrate this, the following comparisons between tires and municipal solid waste (MSW) are shown in Fig. 18.1*b*.

Percentage of Current Disposal Practices Nationwide

Nationally, recycling, reuse, and recovery practices for scrap tires currently consume about 34.5 percent of the tires discarded annually (see Fig. 18.2). The remaining 65.5 percent are landfilled or stockpiled. Those scrap tires not used as indicated above are generally disposed of in any of four manners. These disposal methods are

1. Scrap tires can be picked up by a commercial disposal service, which generally will bring them to an existing tire pile.
2. Scrap tires can be brought to a landfill, where they also tend to be placed in a pile.
3. Scrap tires can remain on the site of the waste tire generator.
4. Scrap tires can be indiscriminately dumped by the generator or transporter. This typically results in the dumping of scrap tires in an inappropriate manner.

Although none of these methods should be considered as proper disposal methods, the first three generally are the rule. Several states (e.g., Minnesota and Massachusetts) have banned the outdoor storage of large-scale tire piles (piles in excess of 50,000 waste tires). Yet, unmanaged or poorly managed, stockpiles of scrap tires are found in every state. The regulatory trend toward scrap tires is to ban them from landfills (see the section on legislation). Before such regulations become effective, however, improved disposal capacity has to be available, supplied either by the public or private sectors. The main factor contributing to large-scale piles or illegal dumping of scrap tires is typically the cost associated with their disposal. This is due in large part to the limited uses for scrap tires, and in part, to the relatively low cost to bring scrap tires to a disposal facility. While disposal costs can vary widely in different geographic areas of the United States,

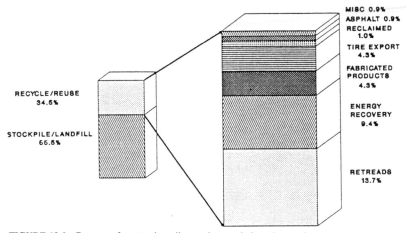

FIGURE 18.2   Percent of waste tires disposed, recycled, and reused.

scrap tire industry sources generally estimate the cost of adding one scrap tire to an existing pile at $0.25. This does not represent the entire cost of disposal. Typically, entrepreneurs, commonly referred to as "tire jockeys," collect scrap tires from the point of generation. Scrap tire generators are assessed a fee by the tire jockeys for removal of the scrap tire. This cost can range from $0.50 to $2.00 per tire. Collected tires are typically sorted to identify tires that can be retreaded, bias tires (which are sent to stamping plants) and tires which can be reused as is. The remainder are handled in a manner described earlier in this section.

ENVIRONMENTAL AND HEALTH ISSUES RELATED TO SCRAP TIRE DISPOSAL

Landfills

Landfills, traditionally the accepted method for disposing of scrap tires, are increasingly no longer accepting whole scrap tires for burial. The owners and operators of landfills cite two basic reasons for this restriction:

1. Due to their shape and composition, tires are not easily compacted nor do they decompose. Thus, scrap tires consume considerable amounts of landfill space. With diminishing capacity at most landfills, and the increasing cost associated with disposal of municipal solid waste, bulky materials are no longer accepted.
2. Due to the tire's hollow (doughnut) shape, air or other gases can be trapped, which makes tires buoyant. Whole tires that are placed into landfills over time "float" to the surface, breaking the landfill cover. This opening exposes the landfills to insects, rodents, and birds, and allows landfill gases to escape, all of which are undesirable. This also opens an avenue for precipitation to enter the landfill, creating an undesirable liquid (leachate).

Resource Recovery Facilities

Resource recovery facilities also generally reject scrap tires. Several reasons are cited for this. When incinerated in a resource recovery facility, scrap tires can create "hot spots" along the grate of the furnace, caused by the relatively high heating value (refer to Fig. 18.3). Tires also contain sulfur, zinc, and other trace metals. If a facility does not have the proper air emissions control equipment, or if this equipment is not functioning properly, the combustion of scrap tires could, possibly, cause a facility to exceed its air emissions permit levels. Additionally, if large quantities of scrap tires are introduced, and if there is insufficient resident time in the combustion chamber, the opacity, or color, of the exhaust emitted could be adversely affected. The rejected scrap tires are consequently piled and stored outdoors until they are removed from the premises.

Outdoor Storage

The problems generally associated with uncontrolled outdoor storage of scrap tires are threefold. First, scrap tires can catch fire. Once ignited, a tire fire is

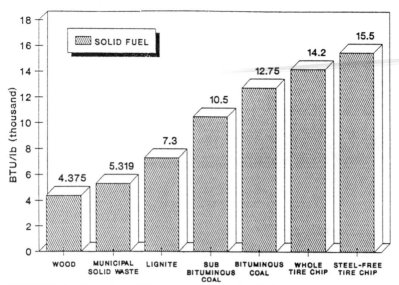

FIGURE 18.3 Comparison of Btus per pound of various fuels.

extremely difficult to extinguish. Uncontrolled combustion of tires at relatively low temperatures (less than 2000°F) tends to release significant amounts
of unburnt hydrocarbons (thick black smoke) and noxious emissions into the
atmosphere.

Second, the shape of a tire tends to catch, collect, and act as a reservoir for
rainwater. Furthermore, sunlight is absorbed by stockpiled scrap tires, creating a
warm and stable environment inside pile. The combination of water (which tends
to stagnate) with the warm conditions generally found in scrap tire piles creates
an ideal breeding ground for mosquitoes. There are no natural predators of mosquitoes in the piles, resulting in an unchecked population increase. These mosquitoes often are vectors for a variety of diseases. The third problem associated
with tire piles is that they serve as a nesting area for rodents, in particular the
Norwegian rat. While the tires themselves offer no natural attraction to rodents,
the conditions they create (presence of water, warmth, and the absence of light)
are as ideal living conditions for these creatures.

Proper storage techniques can minimize, if not eliminate, the potential environmental threats posed by scrap tire piles. Shredding the scrap tires and
placing them into blocks (or cells) not exceeding 100 ft (width) by 100 ft
(length) by 50 ft (height), reduces the dangers of uncontrollable fire and rodent
infestation. Shredding stockpiled scrap tires is also the most effective manner
in which to eliminate mosquito infestation, since water can no longer collect
and stagnate.

Since the vast majority of scrap tire fires have been caused by arson, adequate
fencing (10 ft high) and a secured gate can also significantly help reduce the
chances of fire. Spacing the cells at least 50 ft apart and at least 60 ft from any
buildings and the fence are additional safety considerations.

USES FOR SCRAP TIRES

Overview

The uses for scrap tires can be divided into two general categories: whole or processed. It should be noted that in this chapter uses for scrap tires exclude landfilling whole tires, since this disposal option is being rapidly phased out. Please note: the order in which the disposal options are listed does not denote any preference nor other ranking. General applications or disposal for scrap tires can be described as shown in Table 18.1.

TABLE 18.1 Applications and Disposal for Scrap Tires

Whole tire	Processed tire
Agriculture use	Cut or stamped dyed rubber
Artificial reef/breakwaters	Fuel
Crash barriers	Landfilling
Fuel	Pyrolysis
Soil erosion	Sludge composting
Retreads	Civil engineering

Processed Scrap Tire Options

The first step in processing a scrap tire is generally to reduce its size into pieces through the process of chopping, shredding, or grinding. This processing greatly enhances both the disposal options available as well as increasing the options available for finding second uses for the tire. The shredding of a whole tire reduces the tire into strips, ranging in size from 2 × 8 in to 2 × 2 in and reduces its volume by up to 75 percent.

Shredded tire handling can be facilitated through automation and shredded tires are typically cheaper to transport than whole tires. The costs associated to shred a scrap tire are approximately $0.50 to $0.90 per tire, depending on several factors. This cost, however, only represents the charge for size-reducing the scrap tire. Typically, there would be other costs to factor into the per tire cost of disposal, such as the cost of transportation, labor, and land. The following section expands the discussion of the applications for processed scrap tires.

Uses for Shredded Tires

Recycled Rubber Products. Scrap tires may be processed into various-sized particles which can be used to fabricate floormats, sandals, gaskets, or certain products otherwise manufactured from virgin rubber. Scrap tire rubber that has been size-reduced by a mechanical process is known as *ground rubber.* There are two general processing technologies available: ambient or cryogenic. Ambient grinding (at room temperature) produces rubber particles with a rough exterior surface. Cryogenic processing is performed at a temperature below the glass transition temperature. This is usually accomplished by subjecting scrap tire rubber to liquid nitrogen. Cryogenically produced ground rubber is typically smaller and finer than ambiently processed rubber. However, cryogenically produced ground rubber tends to be more expensive than ambiently produced ground rubber. In either process, steel and fabric can be separated from ground rubber by magnetic and gravity separators. Other uses for ground rubber are in athletic fields (running track or as part of a field support system), carpet underlay, parking curbs, railroad crossing beds, and as an asphalt additive (refer to Case Histories). Reidel Omni Products, Portland, Oregon, produces rubber railroad crossings using tire buffings. These tire buffings are procured from the retreading industry, where they are produced during the retreading operation. About 350 lb of buffings is used per track foot of the rubber railroad crossings. About 50,000 track feet of rubber railroad crossings were laid by Reidel in 1989. This represents about 10,000 tons of tire rubber buffings used in 1989. The service life of the rubber railroad crossing is projected to be about 15 years, as compared to about 4 years for asphalt railroad crossings. The major clients for the rubber railroad crossings are private railroads, with municipalities and cities being small-scale consumers.

Ground rubber has been used extensively in Japan in railway mats to suppress vibration and noise pollution. These pads are laid between the concrete and the ballast. About 70,000 tons of ground rubber was used to lay a stretch of 131 km of padded railroad tracks from 1975 to 1981. One of the largest commercial ground rubber plants, Tire Recycle Center, Osaka, Japan, has a capacity of 7000 tons per year. While recycling scrap tire rubber into new products may be the environmentally preferred manner in which to use scrap tires, there are physical limits to this application.

When rubber for tires is produced, adding sulfur to the rubber (vulcanization) strengthens it, allowing for longer product life. Scrap tire rubber can be "reclaimed" through a process of shredding, grinding, pulverization, and treatment with chemicals and plasticizers under pressure and heat (depolymerization). No technology at present can devulcanize rubber (breaking of the carbon-sulfur bond). Without devulcanization, use of reclaimed rubber is dependent on physical bonding, as opposed to chemical and physical-chemical bonding. A small fraction of reclaimed or recycled rubber may be used in manufacturing new tires, especially in the carcass and sidewall compounds. At present, recycled scrap tire rubber comprises approximately 0.5 to 1.0 percent, by weight, of new tires. The markets for reclaim rubber are, generally, as inks for copiers, sheeted rubber, and reclaimed butyl.

In the United States, approximately 3.4 million tires were used for reclaimed rubber in 1987, though the number of tires used for rubber reclamation has been decreasing. As of July 1991, only one tire-reclaiming facility in the United States is in operation, but is not supplying any reclaimed rubber to the tire manufacturing industry. The volume of tires used for reclaiming rubber has been decreasing due to

- Low incentive to reclaim rubber because of the availability of cheap synthetic rubber from petroleum
- Lower quality of the reclaimed rubber because of the loss of some of its elastic properties during processing.

Recent developments in the scrap tire recycling industry suggest that the potential for consuming significant quantities of scrap tires may be in reach. Several companies (Dodge-Regupol, Carlisle Rubber) are producing high-quality products, which have a combined potential to process over 10 million scrap tires annually. Research being conducted at Air Products, Inc., is testing ways in which finely processed ground rubber can be combined with polymers to produce new products. If this program is successful, Air Products, Inc., has indicated a potential need for a very significant quantity of scrap tires.

Tire Splitting. Tire splitting involves direct reuse of rubber strips obtained from tires in the manufacture of other rubber products. Fabric-reinforced rubber strips are obtained from tires by removing the bead and cutting away the tread from the tire. These strips are die-cast into different products such as dock bumpers, floor mats, conveyor belts, and blasting mats. Such use of tires represents a high-value use, as only minimal processing of the tire is required. The consumption of scrap tires by the splitting industry is minimal due to the low demand for its products.

Fuel Chips. Scrap tires can be shredded into 2-in-square chips or smaller and be sold or used as a source of fuel. Tires consist largely of carbon, some 83 percent by weight, which gives them a comparatively high heating value of approximately 15,000 Btus/lb. Tires also contain sulfur, zinc, steel, and trace elements which typically require the facility using this material as a source of fuel to have adequate emission control technology and the capacity to handle the postcombustion residues. Scrap tires as a fuel can typically be used in either a dedicated scrap-tire incineration facility, cement kiln, a pulp and paper mill, or a utility boiler. Kilns and mills usually limit tires as a supplemental fuel to approximately 2 to 20 percent of the fuel supply. Utility boilers, depending upon their configuration, can use up to 40 percent of the fuel in the chips.

Combustion technologies that lend themselves to use of scrap tires as a fuel are a wet-bottom boiler, a reciprocating stoker grade system (such as the Gummi Mayer tire facility in Germany, or the Oxford Energy scrap-tire-to-energy facility in Westley, California), a cyclone boiler, or the furnace of a pulp and paper mill.

Monofilling. Although landfill disposal is not an environmentally preferred alternative to scrap tire management, shredded tires may be disposed of in such facilities without difficulty. Several states currently allow shredded scrap tires to be disposed of with municipal wastes. This practice, over time, will be phased out. The practice of placing shredded or sliced scrap tires in a landfill dedicated to scrap tires (monofill or monocell) or in a similar facility (i.e., abandoned strip coal mines) to be used solely for scrap tires, is being considered, if not currently allowed (i.e., Ohio and North Carolina).

In general, monofilling can consume a significant quantity of scrap tires. Potential benefits that can be derived from this disposal method are that scrap tires would no longer pose environmental or health threats, would not be eyesores, and could help reclaim land with marginal utility. The major limitation to this disposal application would be the absence of marginal land and the costs involved to shred, transport, and handle the tires. While monofills do offer a disposal option for scrap tires, once placed into the ground it is unlikely that this material will be reclaimed for any future purpose. Furthermore, any other possible use of the scrap tire, such as a fuel, will probably be lost.

Pyrolysis. Pyrolysis is the process of breaking organic chemical bonds by heating. It is also known as destructive distillation. Pyrolysis, in the strictest sense, is combustion in the absence of oxygen. The technology is not new. Pyrolysis has been used in Europe since the late 1800s. Pyrolysis has been used to break down tires into several by-products (char, gas, oil, and steel). (Refer to Table 18.2.) The quantity produced of each is a function of the process used and temperature and

TABLE 18.2 Typical Yield per Tire and per Ton of Tires from Pyrolysis

Per tire	Per ton
2 gal oil	82–200 gal oil
7 lb char	500–800 lb char
3 lb gas (57 scf)	38–380 lb steel

can be as follows: Gas generation increases with increasing temperature; oil generation decreases with increasing temperature; char generation is dependent on process type rather than temperature. Pyrolysis temperatures vary between 500 and 1100°F.

Tire pyrolysis can be oxidative or reductive. In the oxidative process, oxygen or steam is injected and combustion of a portion of tire material takes place under substoichiometric conditions. The majority of pyrolysis processes are reductive. In reductive pyrolysis, hydrogen gas is added to produce a reducing atmosphere and to hydrogenize the tires. This results in the production of hydrogen sulfide gas and a reduction in the sulfur content of oil, char, and gas.

In the oxidative process the relative yield of gas is higher, but the heating value of that gas is lower than that produced in the reductive process. Gases from reductive processes have a high heating value, sometimes double that of natural gas. Gases typically contain paraffins and olefins. In oxidative processes gas also contains carbon monoxide, carbon dioxide, hydrogen gases, and nitrogen gases (if air is used). Typically, a portion of the gas is burned to heat the reactor.

U.S. Facilities. Only a few commercial pyrolysis units are operating in the country. Several experimental pyrolysis units have been tried, though none have demonstrated sustained commercial operation. Commercial facilities that have operated within the United States are

- J. M. Beers, Inc., Wind Gap, Pennsylvania

  A small pyrolysis plant

  Operating permit granted by Pennsylvania Department of Environmental Resources
- Conrad Industries, Centralia, Washington

  Demonstration unit with an operational capacity of 24 ton/day shredded tires; in existence since 1987

  Facility is operational on a part-time basis only

Sludge Composting. The same 2-in tire chips used as a source of fuel can be used as a bulking agent in a sludge composting facility. Shredded tires would be used as a replacement for or in addition to wood chips. Unlike wood, chipped tires would not decompose during the composting process. Although the tire chips could be removed and reused, their reuse requires the screening of the chips prior to the sludge's application. A commercial application for scrap tires in sludge composting uses the heat derived from scrap tire combustion to "melt" sewage sludge and helps to make a product that resembles shards of black glass. At present there is one commercial facility, located in New York, that has the capacity to use scrap tires in this manner.

Civil Engineering. For the past several years, scrap tires, both whole and processed, have been gaining acceptance in civil engineering applications. For example, whole scrap tires are being used in national parks as retaining structures. In this application, whole tires are bound into a geotextile retaining wall for steep-sided or exposed areas along roadways (Figs. 18.4 and 18.5). Scrap tires have proven to have several advantages in this application. They are typically less expensive than the conventional material they are substituting for, they are generally abundant, and be obtained quickly, while resolving a costly disposal problem.

In Florida, West Virginia, Ohio, and Pennsylvania, scrap tires are being used in landfills, either as a daily landfill cover or as part of the leachate collection system. In Florida, scrap tires substitute for the top 12 in of a 24-in protective soil layer, which was placed over a flexible geotextile membrane liner. The use of processed scrap tires provided a double cost saving, since their cost was less than the originally intended material and their use avoided the cost of disposal. Another point of consideration was that their use would also provide the desired level of protection that was sought.

In Minnesota, scrap tires have been used in a wide array of civil engineering applications. To date, scrap tires have been used to create new bicycle paths; as lightweight fill for roadbed construction; and as a replacement for sand and gravel, as a clean fill, in the parking ramp of the new Minneapolis Convention Center.

The use of scrap tires in civil engineering applications has raised one question: Does this use of scrap tires have any negative impacts? The main issue concerns leachate, a liquid that percolates over or through a solid, carrying with it some suspended particles. Tires are manufactured from a variety of materials; could any of these materials leach from the scrap tire? Studies by the states of Ver-

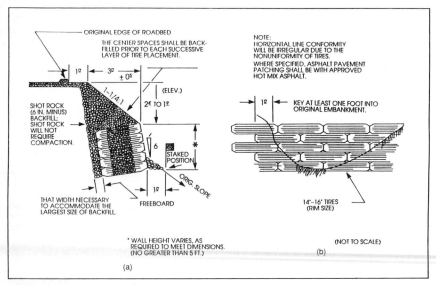

FIGURE 18.4 Typical used-tire retaining wall (wall shoulder construction). (*a*) Cross-section view; (*b*) fare view.

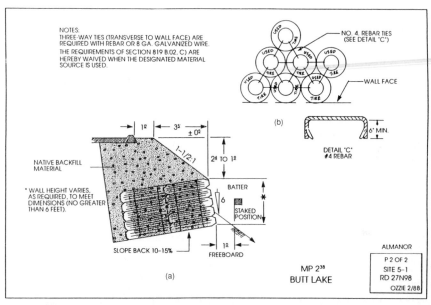

FIGURE 18.5 Typical used-tire retaining wall (construction detail). (*a*) Section; (*b*) Plan view (rebar tie plan). (*Source: Engineering Field Notes, Engineering Technical Information, vol. 22, 1990, United States Department of Agriculture.*)

mont, Connecticut, Illinois. Minnesota, and Pennsylvania have not demonstrated any adverse environmental effects from the use of processed scrap tires.

Whole Tire Applications

Whole scrap tire use is limited due to tires' size and properties, and the cost of transporting a bulky material. The following section describes most of the more common uses for whole scrap tires.

Artificial Reefs and Breakwaters. Artificial reefs are constructed by bundling scrap tires together then sinking and anchoring them in coastal waters. Under certain climatic conditions, these tires rapidly become encrusted with barnacles and other marine growths, creating an artificial reef attractive as a habitat to many kinds of fish. While this technique for tire disposal has been very successful along the Atlantic and Gulf coasts, similar work in fresh water has been tried but not yet proven.

Breakwaters can be constructed for placement offshore. Placement of these structures helps protect harbors and shorelines from tidal effects by adding stability to the beach and seafloor area. Research performed by the Goodyear Tire and Rubber Company has indicated that when scrap tires are properly constructed and installed, they can be successfully used as floating breakwater mats for protection of bays, harbors, and marinas. These mats can be easily installed and are readily adaptable as breakwater barriers. Whether scrap tires are used in this fashion is a function of cost relative to other breakwater devices. Other potential uses are as dune stabilization mats, marshland protection mats, river and stream bank erosion mats, and floating artificial reefs.

Crash Barriers. Stacks of tires laid horizontally (and usually encased in some sort of flexible container) have successfully been used as highway crash barriers at bridge piers, abutments, and other obstructions along highways. This option offers only a limited potential for significant consumption of scrap tires.

Fuel. As stated earlier, scrap tires are an excellent source of energy. Combustion facilities can be constructed or modified to burn whole tires as the only fuel source or to be able to burn whole tires along with other fuels and/or solid waste. Dedicated tire-only-fired incinerators and boilers necessarily require an adequate and continuous supply of scrapped tires. Successful operation of tire-only facilities is therefore cost-effective in geographic areas of high population and therefore high scrap tire density. Other geographic areas with lower scrap tire density could use incinerators or boilers which accept tires along with other fuels and/or solid waste. The energy released by combustion can be recovered in the form of electricity and/or steam—both salable products. This topic is further detailed in the case histories.

Agriculture Use. Scrap tires are a fairly common sight on most farms. Uses for scrap tires range from anchoring weights to secure tarmacs on feedstuffs to road boarder trim. Like other applications cited in this section, the number of scrap tires used in this manner is limited. The one major difference, however, is that agriculture typically uses scrap farm equipment tires, which are larger, heavier, and more difficult to process than passenger car or light truck tires. Therefore, this specialized use serves an important role to the overall scrap tire disposal and recycling situation.

Retreading. Since 1915, tire casings have gained an extended useful life by replacing the worn tread portion with new tread. The process is called *retreading,* sometimes *recapping.* There are two basic retreading systems: mold cure and precure. Regardless of which system is used, candidate casings are inspected upon arrival at the retreading facility for damage or stress wear that could adversely affect the casing. The general rule of thumb for the retread industry is that a worn casing is a sound casing, since if it were defective, the casing would have failed. Once the casing is determined acceptable, the remaining tread is buffed off and the casing is shaped to accept the new tread. During this process, the casing is inspected and tested again.

After the prepared casing is measured and repaired (if necessary), the new tread is applied. Advancements in the retread technology now allow for the replacement of portions of the metal beads and removal and replacement of the shoulder and sidewall portions of the casing. This advanced process is commonly referred to as remanufacturing. After the casing is cured, the retreaded tire is cleaned, inspected, painted, and marked with the appropriate identification. Figure 18.6 demonstrates the various parts of a tire.

It should be recognized that a retread is not a scrap tire. Conversely, scrap tires, by definition, are not suitable for retreading, since a "scrap" tire can no longer be used for its original purpose. At present, some 38 million tires are retreaded annually. The majority of retreads, some 95 percent, are truck tires. Virtually every truck tire casing that can be retreaded is retreaded. There are several reasons for this. First, retreaded truck tires enjoy a favorable price advantage

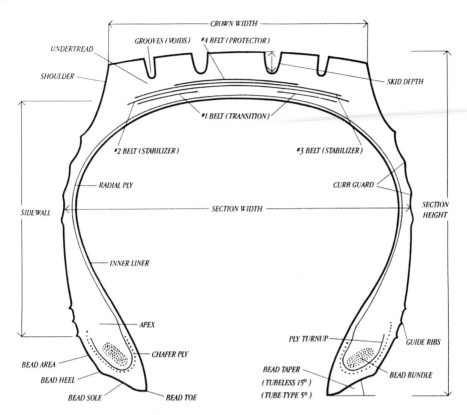

FIGURE 18.6 Tire cross section showing parts of a radial tire. (*Source: Truck Tire Retreading, Bandag, Inc., 1988.*)

over new truck tires; truck tire casings can now be retreaded several times, averaging three to five treads (lasting in total up to 500,000 miles); third, truck tire retreading has proven to produce a safe product, one which is widely accepted within the trucking industry.

Passenger car tire retreads do not enjoy a significant price advantage compared to new passenger car tires, especially the lower-priced imports. Also, the advent of the all-season radial tire has impacted this portion of the industry. Historically, a large portion of the retread market consisted of passenger car snow tires. Since all-season radials have replaced a significant portion of the snow tire market, it has also affected the retread portion of this market. New markets for passenger car retreads are emerging, particularly in the public sector, where federal, state, and local governments are beginning to have purchase preferences for retreaded passenger car tires.

CASE HISTORIES*

This section provides technology profiles for alternative reuse of scrap tires. The case studies herein provide a description of five technologies that can consume

---

*This section is based on *Scrap Tire Use/Disposal Study,* Scrap Tire Management Council, September 1990.

significant numbers of scrap tires annually (use as fuel in cement kilns, use as fuel in pulp and paper mills, use as fuel in utility boilers, use as fuel in dedicated tire-to-energy facilities, and reuse in asphalt). An explanation of the environmental, economic, and volume characteristics for each technology cited is provided.

Use as Fuel in Cement Kilns

Either whole tires or tire-derived fuel (TDF) can be used as supplemental fuel in cement kilns, depending on kiln size and technology. The technology is proven. At least seven U.S. kilns are currently burning tires or TDF on an operating basis, with at least five additional kilns burning whole tires or TDF on an experimental basis. Burning scrap tires or TDF in kilns does not adversely affect environmental performance or product quality.

Kilns currently burning TDF have volume capacities in the 0.5 to 3 million tires per year range. At an average burning rate of 1.5 million tires per year, we estimate that cement kilns could use approximately 60 million tires per year as auxiliary fuel by 1995. This assumes switchover of about 40 kilns with optimal scrap-tire-burning configurations (kilns with preheaters and precalciners), out of a total kiln population of about 240.

Principal barriers to further scrap tire use in this industry are

- Marginal cost advantage of TDF over typical kiln fuels (coal, petroleum coke); whole tires have a greater advantage, but can only be used in larger kilns with preheaters
- Air permit modification requirements for testing, and delays in issuing modifications
- Reliability of tire or TDF supply (risk to recovering capital investment)
- Certain kiln designs require costly feed system design modifications

Technology Description.   Cement is manufactured by controlled heating of a mixture of finely ground calcareous material (e.g., limestone), argillaceous material (e.g., clay or shale), and siliceous material (e.g., sand) to about 1500 to 1600°C in a rotary kiln. These materials provide the basic elements required in cement: calcium, silicon, aluminum, and iron. The high temperatures in the kiln cause decarbonation of lime and subsequent reaction with silica to form calcium silicates. The calcium silicate "clinker" is ground with gypsum to produce cement.

Rotary kilns are long, inclined, cylindrical furnaces through which the cement ingredients move in approximately 1 to 4 hours. Due to their unusually high operating temperature and long exhaust gas residence times in the burning zone, cement kilns have the capacity to use a wide variety of fuels safely, including tires or TDF. Tires or TDF are a good auxiliary fuel for coal- or oil-burning cement kilns because their:

- Btu value is comparable to or higher than typical coal used in making cement.
- Nitrogen, sulfur, and ash content is lower than typical values for coal.
- Steel content provides supplemental iron for the cement.

The high operating temperature in the kiln allows for complete combustion of tires and oxidation of steel beads or belts without adversely affecting kiln operation. Therefore, steel reinforcement does not need to be removed prior to using the tire as fuel. In fact, because iron is a basic ingredient in cement, and the temperature in cement kilns is high enough for complete combustion of steel to iron oxide, burning whole tires or TDF with steel content reduces raw material costs for supplemental iron for some kilns.

Cement manufacture is energy-intensive, requiring about 160 kWh of energy per ton of clinker produced. Typical energy costs are about $6.00 per ton of clinker. The form in which tires can be used as an auxiliary fuel, either whole or as TDF, is dependent upon the configuration of the kiln. Kilns with preheaters can utilize whole tires as fuel; kilns without preheaters can only use TDF, typically in 2-in by 2-in to 4-in by 4-in size. In either case, kilns must be equipped with separate fuel feed systems to utilize tires. Whole tires are fed to kilns using a mechanical feed system designed for tire charging. TDF may be fed using either mechanical or pneumatic systems. Mechanical feed systems have been successful in feeding TDF to cement kilns without any problems. Three of the cement kilns using TDF on an experimental basis used pneumatic blowers to feed TDF but experienced problems with feed line plugging caused by wire. Subsequently, one of these kilns has switched over to a mechanical feed system for TDF.

Typical feed rates in the cement kilns using TDF in the United States vary from 2 to 3 tons per hour, with about 10 to 25 percent of the Btu value of the fuel being provided by the tires. Average annual tire consumption at a typical facility is about 2 to 3 million tires.

Seven cement kilns in the United States use TDF as an auxiliary fuel, and another eight are using TDF on an experimental basis with intentions to install permanent systems. Tires have been widely used in Europe and Japan as an auxiliary fuel in cement kilns for several years. The U.S. facilities are listed below.

- Calaveras Cement, Reading, California

  Annual consumption: 2 million tires

  25 percent of Btu value of fuel is provided by tires

  Has used TDF as supplemental fuel for 5 years

- Arizona Portland Cement, Rillito, Arizona

  Approximate annual consumption: 3 million tires

  Uses 2-in by 2-in TDF at a rate of 2 tons per hour, expected to rise to 4 tons per hour

  About 10 percent of Btu value of the fuel is provided by tires

- Southwest Portland Cement Co., Fairborn, Ohio

  Approximate annual consumption: 1 million tires

  Whole tires used

  About 6 to 8 percent of Btu value provided by tires

  Modified air emissions permit

- Ashgrove Cement, Durkee, Oregon

  Has used TDF on an experimental basis for the last 2 years

  Expected approximate annual consumption: 0.4 million tires

  Completed trial burns for emissions testing for modified permit

  Public hearings for permit scheduled for October 1990

Pneumatic blower used to feed TDF
Uses 2-in relatively wire-free TDF

- Ideal Cement, Seattle, Washington

Has used TDF on an experimental basis for the last year
Expected approximate annual consumption: 1.4 million tires
Pneumatic blower used to feed TDF
20 percent of Btu value of fuel provided by tires
Uses 2-in relatively wire-free TDF

- Lafarge Cement, New Braunfels, Texas

Has used TDF on an experimental basis for 2 years
Expected approximate annual consumption: 1.3 million tires
Completed trial burns for emissions testing; permit issuance in process
Modified permit will place restraint only on percentage of tires allowed to be burnt (25 percent of the fuel)
9 to 10 percent of Btu value of fuel provided by tires
Auger feed system
Uses 2-in relatively wire-free TDF

- Gifford Hill Cement Co., Harleyville, South Carolina

Experimental use of whole tires
Test burn in May 1990
Expected approximate annual consumption: 1.2 to 1.5 million tires
20 percent of Btu value of fuel to be provided by tires
Joint venture with Oxford Energy and Radian Corporation

The foreign facilities using tires or TDF for fuel are

- Heidelberger Cement Plant, Germany

Total of 50,000 metric tons of tires burnt per year in six of its cement plants
Tires fed whole into the kilns
Percent of tires in the fuel feed varies from 10 to 20 percent

- Blue Circle Dry Process Cement Works, Hope, Sheffield, England

Annual consumption: 4700 tons (expected to increase to about 8000 tons)
Whole tires used
17 percent of fuel substituted by tires

- Sumitomo Cement Co., Japan
- Onada Cement Co., Japan
- Chichibu Cement Co., Japan
- Osaka Cement Co., Japan

Environmental, Economic, and Volume Characteristics

Environmental Characteristics. Use of tires as fuel in cement kilns typically reduces production of nitrogen oxides and does not adversely affect other components of kiln air emissions. This is due to the relative characteristics of waste tire materials compared to typical coals used in cement manufacture.

The average sulfur content of TDF is about 1.23 percent by weight, as compared to 1.59 percent for coal. The nitrogen content of TDF is also lower than that for coal, 0.24 percent by weight as compared to 1.76 percent. The ash content of TDF is about 4.7 percent by weight as compared to 6.23 percent by weight for coal. Sulfur in the TDF becomes incorporated into the calcining lime as calcium carbonate, which is a raw material in the manufacture of cement. All of the ash gets absorbed in the clinker, so there are no residues from the use of the TDF in cement kilns. No adverse effects on the quality of cement have been observed due to the use of TDF in cement kilns. The Bavarian State Institute for Environmental Protection (Germany) concluded that the best means of disposing of waste tires is to use them as a fuel in cement kilns.

Tests on kilns in the United States demonstrate that existing emission controls on kilns should be sufficient to enable them to use TDF as an auxiliary fuel, while meeting the emission standards as long as the percentage of TDF used is no more than 20 percent of the heat value of the total fuel used in the kilns.

Economic Characteristics

- Estimated break-even procurement cost = $30.00 to $45.00/ton
- Typical procurement fees:

  Calaveras Cement—$0.00/ton

  Arizona Portland Cement—charged only freight costs by city of Tucson for TDF, and $20 per ton including freight by Tucson Manufacturers, Phoenix, Arizona

  Lafarge Cement—$1 per million Btus (MMBtu) for TDF (compares to $1.60 per MMBtu for coal and $1 per MMBtu for petroleum coke)

  Southwest Portland Cement Co.—charges tipping fee to accept tires

- Capital cost for modification of the feed system

  Mechanical system: $250,000 to $500,000

  Pneumatic blower system: $60,000 to $100,000

- Typical cost of coal: $1.60 to $2.00 per MMBtu ($38 to $48 per ton)
- Typical cost of TDF: $1.10 to $1.80 per MMBtu ($30 to $50/ton)
- 50 percent reduction in iron ore consumption in the Calaveras Cement Plant from use of TDF

The major deciding factor for the use of scrap tires as a fuel is the procurement cost per ton of tires paid by the facility. Scrap tires compete with standard kiln fuels, coal, and petroleum coke. Typically, kilns are willing to pay for tires as fuel only at a discount to their normal fuel in order to recover the costs of the tire feed system and any test burns required for permitting. Given current coal costs, a procurement fee of as low as $0.35 per tire could make the use of tires economically attractive to cement kilns, depending upon their relative transportation costs for coal and tires.

For large kilns with preheaters capable of burning whole tires, the economics of using tires as fuel are good for both the kilns and for scrap tire suppliers. Kilns should be willing to pay about $0.75 to $1.00 per MMBtu for whole tires, or $21 to $28 per ton, depending on whether their usual fuel is coal or petroleum coke. This price provides a fee of $0.21 to $0.28 per tire to the tire supplier, and allows the kiln to make a profit on its investment in tire feed equipment. Mechanical feed equipment for whole tires is typically more expensive than equipment for TDF, running about $250,000 per plant for equipment capable of moving 1.5 million tires per year.

However, for kilns which must use TDF, the economics are more marginal. For TDF to be viable as an alternative fuel to coal, its cost needs to be less than coal, approximately $35 to $45 per ton. This cost is nearly equivalent to the shredding and transportation cost of the tires (approximate shredding costs for 2-in TDF is $20 per ton and $25 per ton for wire-free TDF). On the other hand, if the cement kilns charged a tipping fee to the tire disposers, as does Southwest Portland Cement in Ohio, the use of tires as an auxiliary fuel would be highly profitable.

There are about 240 cement kilns in the United States, of which about 40 to 50 are equipped with preheaters and precalciners required to utilize TDF efficiently. An unknown number of these plants may be capable of burning whole tires. About 20 percent of the cement kilns are located in areas where they can obtain petroleum coke at lower prices. Thus, it would be technically and economically feasible for a minimum of about 40 cement kilns to use TDF as an auxiliary fuel. If these kilns were to use TDF as an auxiliary fuel (at an average rate of 1.5 million tons of TDF per year), over 20 percent of the scrap tires generated annually in the United States could be consumed. This estimate does not include those kilns without preheaters that could utilize TDF.

Barriers to Further Implementation.   It has been demonstrated in previous burns that air emissions from kilns are not adversely affected by the use of TDF as an auxiliary fuel. However, most states require test burns of alternative fuels for cement kilns, including scrap tires. There are costs and disruptions associated with the test burns, and delays between submitting and receiving a permit modification to allow full-scale burning.

Kiln operators are concerned over availability of a continuous supply of TDF. In order to justify the capital expense of feed system modifications, kiln operators prefer having a long-term contract for tire supply that assures a return on their investment. Additionally, kiln operators are concerned about the potential fire hazards of maintaining a TDF inventory.

Use as Fuel in Pulp and Paper Mills

Dewired TDF can be used as supplemental fuel in pulp and paper mills; dewiring is required to avoid fuel-feeding problems. The technology is proven. About 12 U.S. pulp and paper mills are currently burning dewired TDF on an operating basis. Burning TDF in mill boilers does not adversely affect boiler operation, but has mixed effects on environmental performance (increases particulate diversity). These effects can be mitigated by limiting the percentage of TDF burned.

Pulp and paper mills currently burning TDF have volume capacities in the 0.5

to 3.5 million tire per year range. At an average burning rate of 1.5 million tires per year, we estimate that paper mills could use about 35 million tires per year as auxiliary fuel by 1995. This assumes switchover of about 25 percent of auxiliary fuel requirements to TDF.

Principal barriers to further use of TDF in this industry are

- Marginal cost advantage of TDF over typical mill fuels (coal, purchased hog fuel); dewiring increases TDF cost, decreasing its price advantage over coal (as compared to use in cement kilns)
- Air permit modification requirements for testing and delays in issuing modifications
- Remote location of many mills (higher transportation costs)
- Reliability of TDF supply (risk to recovering capital investment)

Technology Description. The manufacturing of pulp and paper requires substantial energy which is typically supplied through on-site boilers fueled with wood waste (hog fuel). Hog fuel typically varies substantially in Btu content and moisture. Therefore, pulp and paper mills often use high-heat-value fuels such as coal as supplements to hog fuel to give combination fuel boilers a more stable operation.

Since the mid-1970s, TDF has gained industry acceptance as an alternative to coal, gas, and fuel oil. The inherent high heat value and low moisture content makes TDF an ideal supplemental fuel. The price of TDF is usually below that of competing fuels and, because hog fuel boilers normally have a stoker grate feeding system designed to burn solid wood waste, TDF can often be burned with a minimum of capital investment.

TDF is normally mixed with the hog fuel in a conveyor feeding the furnace. The principal equipment modification necessary is the installation of a metering system capable of handling the high heat value of TDF. To minimize potential feeding complications (e.g., jamming) and ash contamination that may result due to steel wire tire beads and belts, pulp and paper mills often require that TDF be wire-free.

Mills that burn TDF in their boilers usually keep it below 10 percent of the total fuel loading on a Btu basis. Beyond this level, emission and feeding problems become more serious. Large mills can use as much as 100 tons of dewired TDF per day (about 3.5 million passenger car tire equivalents per year).

Currently, there are eight pulp and paper facilities in the United States using a total of about 11,000 tons of TDF per month. They are

- Fort Howard Paper, Green Bay, Wisconsin
- Great Southern paper, Cedar Springs, Georgia
- Inland-Rome Paper, Rome, Georgia
- Nekoosa Paper, Tomahawk, Wisconsin
- Willamette Industries, Albany, Oregon
- Jefferson Smurfit Paper, Newberg, Oregon
- Champion International, Bucksport, Maine
- Port Townsend Paper, Port Townsend, Washington

Environmental, Economic, and Volume Characteristics

Environmental Characteristics

- Emissions of polynuclear hydrocarbons are not significantly different when TDF is used as a supplemental fuel instead of coal or oil.
- Tests have shown particulate emissions to increase by between 38 and 93 percent when TDF was used as a supplemental fuel in a hog fuel boiler.
- Zinc emissions have been shown to increase by as much as 1,500 percent in similar tests, but concentrations remain within permit conditions.
- Emission levels of chromium, cadmium, and lead are lower for TDF than for oil.
- Sulfur dioxide (SO_2) and nitrogen oxides (NO_x) emissions are reduced when TDF is substituted for coal or oil.

Burning TDF in hog fuel boilers has mixed effects on environmental performance. However, SO_2 and NO_x emissions are reduced, as are emission levels for several heavy metals. In general, changes in the types of particulates can be kept within applicable emission limits by control of the percentage of TDF used as auxiliary fuel. The location of most paper mills in air pollution attainment areas simplifies the permitting process.

Similar to cement kilns, the attractiveness of TDF to a pulp and paper mill is highly dependent on the cost of competing fuels in the region, tipping fees available to local shredders, and resulting prices charged by shredders for TDF. Unlike cement kilns, pulp and paper mills must use dewired TDF, which has higher processing costs (about $27 to $37 per ton). Therefore, the economics are somewhat more marginal for paper mills than for cement kilns.

In general, TDF suppliers try to price their product between 15 and 25 percent less than coal. One mill in the southeast that burns 30 tons of dewired TDF per day and is paying $40 per ton ($1.42/MMBtu) considers TDF to be a "marginal" fuel. They plan to switch back to coal if the price of TDF goes over $45 per ton, but will make the necessary long-term capital investment to improve their feeding capability ($350,000) if they can secure a source of TDF for $25 per ton or less (note that this is less than the typical cost of dewired TDF production). A sample economic analysis from the perspective of this mill follows:

$$P = F + R - C - T - D$$

$P = ?$ = Profit per MMBtu burned in hog fuel boiler

$F = \$0.00$ = No tipping fee realized by mill

$R = \$0.47$ = Difference of cost between TDF and local coal prices per MMBtu

$C = \$0.00$ = No incremental difference in processing costs

$T = \$0.00$ = Prices are delivered product

$D = \$0.00$ = No incremental difference in disposal costs

$P = \$0.00 + \$0.47 - \$0.00 - \$0.00 - \$0.00$

$P = \$0.47$ per MMBtu burned

Since the facility burns about 280,000 MMBtu of supplemental fuel per year in its hog fuel boiler, the incremental profit is about $130,000 per year. For a capital investment of $350,000, the payback period is about 2.7 years.

The American Paper Institute reports that the 603 paper mills and 351 pulp mills in the United States consumed approximately 393,000 billion Btus in hog fuel boilers in 1989. If 25 percent of this capacity used 10 percent TDF on a Btu basis, the industry would consume about 35 million passenger tire equivalents per year; if 40 percent of capacity used 10 percent TDF, total consumption would be about 55 million passenger tire equivalents.

Barriers to Further Implementation. Barriers to further utilization of TDF at pulp and paper mills are similar to those to further use in cement kilns. However, because pulp and paper mills require dewired TDF, the economics of TDF use in pulp and paper mills are less attractive. Therefore, further use is primarily impeded by relative economics of dewired TDF production versus other fuels. The relatively marginal cost advantage of dewired TDF over competing fuels reduces pulp and paper mill incentives to invest in feed system and environmental permit modifications.

Many pulp and paper mills are located at or near raw material supplies, at substantial distances from population (and therefore tire generation) centers. Transportation costs provide an additional price disadvantage. Other barriers include the uncertainty of long-term supplies, which increases the risks associated with mill investment in permit and feed system modifications.

Use as Fuel in Utility Boilers

Either whole tires or TDF can be used as supplemental fuel in utility boilers, depending on boiler size and technology. The burning technology is being tested in wet-bottom boilers (whole tires) and cyclone boilers (dewired 1 × 1 in TDF) with promising results. At least three U.S. utility boiler facilities are currently burning or planning to burn tires or TDF on an experimental basis. Emission test results indicate that burning whole scrap tires or TDF in utility boilers does not adversely affect boiler operation, while offering improvements on environmental performance (reduced NO_x and SO_2 and particulates). Further, the economics of burning whole tires in wet-bottom boilers is approaching the favorable economics of cement kilns, particularly when a low tipping fee is charged, versus that of the typically higher tipping fees at landfills.

Utility boilers experimenting with TDF have volume capacities in the 0.5 to 3 million tire per year range. We estimate that utility boilers could use approximately 60 million tires per year as auxiliary fuel by 1995. This assumes that 25 percent of existing wet-bottom boilers will switch over to TDF for 10 percent of their fuel requirements. These boilers can accept whole tires or regular TDF. The estimate does not include boilers burning 1 by 1-in dewired TDF, because use of this fuel requires subsidies to offset high processing costs.

Principal barriers to further scrap tire use in this industry are:

* marginal cost advantage of scrap tires over coal; whole-tire burning requires separate, expensive equipment for fuel feeding, while dewired 1 by 1-in TDF suitable for feeding in coal systems could be more expensive than coal

* Air permit modification requirements for testing, and delays in issuing modifications

- Unproven reliability of whole-tire and TDF feed technology
- Reliability of TDF supply (risk to recovering capital investment)
- Extremely conservative and risk-averse nature of the utility industry

Technology Description.   Utility plants designed to burn coal can, depending on boiler type and ash-handling system, utilize whole tires or TDF as supplemental fuels. Boilers designed to burn coal with low-ash fusion temperatures (slagging type, or wet-bottom boilers) can burn whole tires or TDF because their ash-handling systems can accommodate slag formed by steel from tire beads and belts. Boilers designed to burn high-ash fusion temperature coal (dry-ash type) could only burn dewired TDF because their ash-handling systems are designed to remove dry material.

Conventional coal-feeding systems cannot be used to feed the supplemental tire fuel unless it has been very finely reduced and dewired. Typically, the size reduction required to feed TDF in conventional feed systems is uneconomical.

There are no major power-generating facilities known to be burning tires for fuel on an operating basis at the current time. However, a large midwestern utility is currently examining the possibility of burning whole tires in a wet-bottom boiler. This application would require construction of a secondary fuel feed system to charge whole tires to the boiler.

In a wet-bottom boiler, the furnace comprises a two-stage arrangement. In the lower part of the furnace, gas temperature is maintained high enough so that molten slag will drop onto the floor, where a pool of liquid slag is maintained and tapped into a slag tank containing water. In the upper part of the furnace, gases are cooled below the ash fusion point so that ash carried over into the convection banks is dry. This arrangement is particularly suited to the combustion of whole tires, since slag from steel in the tires can be managed by the slagged ash-handling system. Unfortunately, many wet-bottom boilers are older and may not have the air pollution control equipment necessary to contain the increase in particulate emissions expected when burning tires.

Several coal-fire-powered plants have been permitted to burn shredded tires (TDF). However, in all cases examined, the cost of shredding tires finely enough to work in most common furnace types has proven to be uneconomical without subsidies.

The State of Wisconsin recently established a 10-year subsidy program designed to encourage the use of scrap tires as an alternative energy source. The program is being financed by a $2 per tire tax on new tires sold in the state. Through the program, end users of TDF will be given a subsidy of $20 for each ton burned. In addition, the state is granting money to potential users to finance usage studies and capital investments. The state is also encouraging tire shredders to produce tire chips small enough to meet the requirements of cyclone boiler operators (1-in square or less). Currently, two industrial facilities and two utility power facilities have shown an interest in the program. The potential TDF consumption of these four facilities is between 3.5 and 4.5 million passenger tire equivalents per year (between 70 and 90 percent of the scrap tires disposed of in Wisconsin each year). Facilities using older cyclone boilers (pre-1975) are the most likely to utilize the program since these units are free from the more complex permitting requirements of newer units.

In response to the program, Wisconsin Power and Light Company has completed an initial test burn at its Rock River facility. Rock River consists of two older (mid-1950s) cyclone units with a combined capacity of 150 MW (megawatts,

10^6 W). Ground rubber was mixed with coal at levels of 5 and 10 percent on a Btu basis (approximately 1.5 and 3 ton/h). According to company sources, the results of the test were technically and economically promising. Both NO_x and SO_2 emissions declined while opacity increased only slightly. Other plant operating parameters were normal. The facility has now applied for a grant from the state to finance a testing program designed to examine the possibility of using a larger chip size (1-in square), explore possible ash contamination problems, and estimate the necessary capital requirements. In addition, the company is studying the possibility of integrating into the tire-shredding business.

Finally, boilers using fluidized-bed technology are suitable for burning a wide variety of fuels, potentially including whole tires and TDF. Fluidized-bed combustion has been proven feasible in plants of 300-MW capacity or less, and is viewed as a promising technology for "clean" coal applications because it can be used to reduce SO_2 and NO_x emissions during the combustion process. Therefore, it may see significant use in new coal-burning power plants. However, there are few, if any, fluidized-bed boilers in operation at utility plants at this time. Therefore, their potential contribution to scrap tire reuse within a five-year time period is negligible.

Environmental, Economic, and Volume Characteristics

Environmental Characteristics

- Because tires generally have less than 20 percent of the nitrogen content and 80 percent of the sulfur content of most coal, NO_x and SO_2 emissions have been shown to be reduced.
- Particulate emissions can be expected to increase when TDF is substituted for coal in pulp and paper mill boilers. be able to take the additional load.

Economic Characteristics

- Coal prices to utilities: $1 to $2 per MMBtu
- Tip fee earned by utility: $0.00 to $1.00 per tire
- Transportation cost: $0.10 per tire
- Capital investment: $1,000,000
- Incremental processing costs may increase slightly due to the difficulty in handling and storing tires

The following is a sample economic analysis for a wet-bottom boiler operated by a midwestern utility with a coal cost of $1.55/MMBtu and potential tipping fee revenue of $0.50/tire.

$$P = F + R - C - T - D$$

$P = ? =$ Profit per tire burned

$F = \$0.50 =$ Tipping fee per tire realized by utility

$R = \$0.47 =$ Coal savings per tire

$C = \$0.10 =$ Additional processing cost per tire

$$T = \$0.10 = \text{Transportation cost per tire}$$

$$D = \$0.00 = \text{No additional disposal cost}$$

$$P = \$0.50 + \$0.47 - \$0.10 - \$0.10 - \$0.00$$

$$P = \$0.77 \text{ per tire}$$

Since the facility is expected to burn 1.5 million tires per year, the incremental profit will be approximately $1.16 million. For a capital investment of $1 million, the payback period is less than one year.

Volume Capability. There are currently about 50 active wet-bottom boilers scattered around the country. Together these facilities generate approximately 2048 MW. Assuming a total thermal efficiency of about 30 percent, these facilities require about 740 million MMBtus per year in fuel input. If 25 percent of the wet-bottom boilers' generating capacity derives 10 percent of its energy input, the industry would consume about 62 million tire equivalents per year.

Barriers to Further Implementation. In general, utilities have relatively little incentive, under current conditions, to switch a relatively small percentage of their total fuel requirement to a fuel requiring air permit modifications and new feed systems. Because utilities' business is the reliable supply of electricity, and returns on investment are regulated by state public service commissions, utilities are generally very conservative in adopting new technologies that may have low reliability or otherwise affect their ability to consistently supply electricity.

However, pressures to reduce SO_2 emissions in pending acid rain legislation will lead coal-burning utilities to look for fuel-switching solutions that will reduce emissions without requiring flue gas desulfurization (FGD, or scrubbing). This should be particularly true for older plants where the capital costs for scrubbing may be prohibitive considering the remaining life of the unit, and for plants where space constraints prohibit construction of scrubber units. This in turn should lead to heightened interest by utilities in TDF as a supplement to high-priced low-sulfur coal, because of TDF's low sulfur content. However, the probable time frame for implementation of acid rain provisions (with the earliest limited-reduction requirements going into effect in 1995) indicates that these pressures are not likely to force significant use of TDF within a five-year time frame.

In addition to potential incentives to increase TDF use in existing units due to acid rain standards, there may be incentives to consider TDF as a supplemental fuel in new generating units as part of "clean coal" technologies. The Department of Energy estimates that utilities will need to add 110 GW (gigawatts, 10^9 W) of generating capacity by the year 2000 to meet rising demand. Currently, only 37.3 GW of new capacity is on the drawing board. Requirements for new generating capacity, and for cleaner-burning fuels or technology, may increase demand for fluidized-bed combustion units for coal burning in the late 1990s. However, this demand is not likely to significantly affect scrap tire utilization within a five-year period due to the long lead times required to design, site, and construct new power plants.

Potential Methods for Reducing Barriers

- Enhancement of the reliability of tire supply
- Development of additional research on operation of feed systems, effects on

boiler performance, and effects on air emissions and air pollution control equipment

- Dissemination of research results on whole tire and TDF use
- Increased marketing of TDF and whole tires to utilities
- Development of standardized approach and package of air permit modification for utility boilers
- Use of federal or state subsidies to encourage fuel utilization

The Wisconsin subsidy program has been successful in encouraging utilities to consider using TDF. The amount of the subsidy basically covers the increased cost of tire shredding to a 1-in^2 dewired particle size suitable for feeding into utility boilers through conventional feed systems. Thus, the subsidy, which is financed by a tax on tires, helps equalize the cost of highly processed TDF with coal.

Use as Fuel in Dedicated Tire-to-Energy Facilities

Either whole tires or TDF can be used as fuel in dedicated tire-to-energy facilities; existing and planned facilities are designed to burn whole tires to minimize fuel costs. The technology has been proven in the United States by Oxford Energy at its operating plant in Modesto, California, and West Germany by Gummi Meyer. Two additional plants are planned by Oxford to be in existence by 1995. The Modesto plant has had some operating difficulties due to tire handling, resulting in lower-than-projected utilization; however, Oxford states that these problems have been corrected. Environmental operation of the plant is satisfactory, although utilization has previously been temporarily reduced due to higher-than-expected NO_x emissions. Oxford states that these problems have also been corrected.

Oxford's existing and planned facilities have volume capacities of 4.5 to 10 million tires per year. If all four plants start up on schedule, they could use approximately 31 million tires per year as fuel by 1995.

Principal barriers to further scrap tire use in dedicated tire-to-energy facilities are

- High capital cost of facilities. Dedicated tire-to-energy plants cost between 2 and 7 times more to construct per megawatt than conventional coal power plants.
- Processing economics typically require some form of subsidy for costs to be favorable.
- Need to site new facilities. All planned tire-to-energy facilities are new plants which may encounter local opposition, delaying or foreclosing construction.
- Environmental permitting for new facilities.
- Reliability of fuel supply.

Technology Description.   Oxford Energy of Dearborn, Michigan, currently owns and operates the only power plants in the United States specifically designed to burn whole tires as its primary fuel source. The 14.5-MW facility, built adjacent to the nation's largest tire pile in Out, California (near Modesto), has been operating since 1987. The plant utilizes a technology successfully used at the Gummi Meyer tire facility in Landau, Germany, since 1973.

There are two tire incinerators in Germany operating at temperatures above 2000°F. During combustion, tires are supported on a reciprocating stoker grate. The grate configuration provides airflow above and below the tires, which aids combustion and helps keep the grate cool. The grate allows slag and ash to filter down to a conveyor system, which takes them to hoppers for sale off-site. Tires up to 4 ft in diameter and weighing 90 lb can be handled. A metal-detection system rejects tires with rims.

Each incinerator has its own boiler. The boilers produce 130,000 lb/h of 930 psig, 350°F steam, which combine to drive a single 15.4 (rated) General Electric steam turbine generator. The plant includes a full pollution control system, with fuel gas desulfurization, thermal de-NO_x, and a fabric filter baghouse. The three major by-products—metallic slag, gypsum, and high-zinc ash—are sold off-site.

According to company officials, as of April 1990, the facility was producing approximately 14.5 MW of electricity, burning 600 tires per hour, and remaining on-line close to 85 percent of the time. Operating problems experienced include

- A reduction in energy-recovery efficiency due to accumulated mud and water on tires from the tire pile. Company officials say this will not be a problem in future facilities since they will primarily burn tires coming directly off the road.
- During 1988, the facility was operating at only 12 MW due to NO_x emissions that were continuously close to the standards imposed by the State of California. The problem has since been corrected.
- Until recently, utilization rates were depressed due to various ancillary system problems.

The tire supply for the facility comes from both the adjacent tire pile and from a local tire collection service operated by Oxford. The tires collected by this service do not always go to the facility. Others are sold as used tires or retreadable castings, or shredded and sold as fuel to cement kilns and pulp and paper mills. Oxford pays the owner of the tire pile for each tire removed from the tire pile and charges a fee to collect tires in the surrounding community.

Oxford Energy currently has two additional whole tire-to-energy facilities in various stages of development. A 30-MW facility designed to consume 10 million tires per year is now operational in Sterling, Connecticut. Two additional 30-MW facilities located in Michgan, and Moapa, Nevada, are in preliminary or development stages. The following is a summary of those facilities in the U.S. and overseas:

- Oxford Energy, Out, California: 4.5 million tires per year
- Oxford Energy, Sterling, Connecticut (operational): 10 million tires per year
- Oxford Energy, Michigan (planned): 10 million tires per year
- Oxford Energy, Moapa, Nevada (planned): 9 million tires per year
- Gummi Meyer, Landau, Germany (two units): 3 million tires per year

Environmental, Economic, and Volume Characteristics

Environmental Characteristics

- High temperatures provide for complete combustion of tires while minimizing the emissions of dioxins and furans.
- For each tire consumed, the facility generates approximately 2.5 lb of metallic slag, 1.1 lb of gypsum, and 0.6 lb of high-zinc (45 percent) ash. Each of these by-products has been successfully marketed off-site.
- Facility was designed to use approximately 25 gal of process water for each tire consumed. All waste water is either evaporated or treated to meet California standards.
- Tires have a lower sulfur and nitrogen content than typical coal used in power plants. However, concentrations of zinc and chromium tend to be much higher, but remain within permit conditions.

Economic Characteristics

- Capital costs for new whole tire-to-energy power facilities are expected to exceed $3.5 million per megawatt of energy produced ($11 per tire per year capacity). The cost for a new coal-fired facility is usually in the range of $0.5 to $2 million per MW.
- Power generated at the Modesto facility is sold to Pacific Gas and Electric under a long-term contract. Currently, the buy-back rate is $0.083 per kilowatt hour. This is equivalent to approximately $1.84 per tire consumed.
- Oxford Energy currently pays Ed Philbin, the owner of the tire pile, a fee for each tire (fee is paid on a per pound basis) removed from the pile. In the third year of operation, this fee was $21 per ton ($0.21 per tire). The fee will increase to $24 per ton by the end of the sixth year.
- In 1989, Oxford Energy was charging $4 per truck tire for picking up at landfills in the local area.

The following is a sample economic analysis for the Oxford facility in Sterling, Connecticut:

$$P = F + R - C - T - D$$

$P = ?$

$F = \$0.50 =$ Estimate for tipping fee per tire

$R = \$1.41 =$ Revenue generated for each tire burned ($0.067/kwh)

$C = \$0.50 =$ Estimated processing cost per tire

$T = \$0.10 =$ Transportation cost for each tire delivered to plant

$D = \$0.00$
    $=$ Disposal costs per tire (facility is close to break even on by-product sales)

$P = \$0.50 + \$1.41 - \$0.50 - \$0.10 - \$0.00$

$P = \$1.31$ per tire burned

Since the facility is designed to consume about 10 million tires per year and capital costs are estimated at $100,000,000, the projected payback period is approximately 8.1 years. Some analysts have estimated the plant cost to be greater than $120,000,000, in which case the payback period increases to almost 10 years. Because of the extremely high capital requirements, whole tire-to-energy facilities will only be practical in those parts of the country with high electric rates and tipping fees.

Volume Capability.   The Department of Energy (DOE) estimates that utilities will need to add 110 GW of electricity-generating capacity by the year 2000, but only 37.3 GW is now on the drawing boards. Since the Oxford facility can generate 1 MW of every 300,000 units of annual tire consumption capacity, the annual U.S. dumping-stockpiling-landfilling of 180 million automobile tire equivalents could be used to supply the fuel needs of 0.830 GW of generating capacity or a little more than 1 percent of the capacity that the DOE estimates will be needed. However, the long lead times required to bring one of these facilities on-line make it highly unlikely that any plant other than those being proposed by Oxford will be operating before 1995.

Barriers to Further Implementation

- High capital costs for facility construction
- Low cost of alternative fuels such as coal, fuel oil, and gas
- Stringent environmental permitting requirements
- Public opposition to siting new power facilities
- Difficulty in securing a stable long-term supply

Potential Methods for Reducing Barriers

- Development of integrated tire collection and disposal systems (Oxford Energy has been successful at this) by plant owners
- Federal or state subsidies or tax credits to offset high capital expense

Reuse in Asphalt Paving

Scrap tire rubber can be used in asphalt paving either as part of the asphalt binding material or seal coat (both uses known loosely as asphalt rubber), or as aggregate (rubber-modified asphalt concrete, or RUMAC). Ground rubber is used in asphalt rubber; tire chips are used in RUMAC. Both technologies have been demonstrated commercially in small-scale applications in the United States and in Europe. However, there are some contradictions in the data available on the ease of use and performance of both asphalt rubber (particularly when used as a binding material) and RUMAC. Both are reported to approximately double the service life of pavings, although some results conflict with these findings. There are no recognized technical standards for either material in the United States.

Asphalt rubber seal coats use about 1600 tires per mile of two-lane road sealed. RUMAC uses between 8000 and 12,000 tires per mile of two-lane road repaved with a 3-in lift. The potential volume capability of reuse in asphalt paving exceeds the scrap tire supply; however, on a practical basis, we estimate that use within 5 years could equal or exceed 28 million tires per year.

Principal barriers to further scrap tire use in asphalt paving applications are

- High initial costs. Both asphalt rubber and RUMAC cost approximately twice as much as conventional asphalt.
- Marginal life-cycle economics. Service claims typically project doubling the life of conventional asphalt. However, doubling the life does not overcome the high initial costs when future costs are discounted.
- Lack of product specification by ASTM or other body.
- Concern over uniformity of scrap tire rubber.

Technology Description. Tires can be utilized in asphalt paving in two ways: asphalt rubber, which is typically used as a sealant or as a relatively thin interlayer between two paving layers; and in rubber-modified asphalt concrete (RUMAC), in which tire rubber chips replace part of the aggregate in the paving mix, which is then applied in the same manner as conventional asphalt.

Asphalt rubber is an asphalt cement that is produced by heating asphalt to about 400°F and adding presized ground rubber while blending constantly for about 45 min. Typically the ground rubber added is in the range of 15 to 25 percent of the total asphalt rubber cement. Asphalt rubber must be made immediately prior to use, because the material cannot be stored due to difficulties in maintaining rubber in suspension. Asphalt rubber mixing plants require little special equipment, as the asphalt rubber is premixed with the asphalt aggregate and is applied in the same manner as the standard asphalt cement.

To make asphalt rubber, tires must be ground to a maximum size of 16 to 25 mesh. If the scrap rubber is not ground finely enough, and the digestion (mixing and heating) conditions (temperature and time) are not severe enough, the resulting asphalt rubber cement is weakened and aggregate can break loose. Steel reinforcement and fabric must be removed from the scrap rubber for it to be used in asphalt rubber. Uses for asphalt rubber are

Pavement seal coats

Stress-absorbant pavement interlayers

Binders for surface courses

Subgrade seals

Lake and lagoon liners

Addition of scrap ground rubber to asphalt cement is reported to increase the ductility of the wearing surface, improve crack resistance, and reduce cold weather brittleness and hot weather bleeding.

RUMAC is asphalt pavement in which some of the aggregate in the asphalt mixture is displaced by ground or chipped tires. This method was invented in Sweden and is patented in the United States under the name Plus Ride by EnviroTire of Seattle, Washington. Plus Ride uses all the rubber in the used tires, including sidewalls, centerliner, and tread portions, recycling all but the steel and fabric. Plus Ride modified asphalt is a combination of asphalt cement, aggregate, and ground rubber from scrap tires. It has been used in highways, streets, bridges, and airports. Its advantages are increased flexibility and durability.

Both the Nordic Construction Co., Stockholm, Sweden, and the Swedish Road and Traffic Research Institute state that the performance of RUMAC is highly dependent on proper compaction of the pavement. The pavement has to be carefully laid, and extra care has to be taken in its compaction to prevent it from disintegrating.

Some U.S. facilities producing or using RUMAC are

- EnviroTire, Seattle, Washington, has patented RUMAC under the name Plus Ride. It has been successfully used in highways, streets, bridges, and airports. The patent expired in 1991.
- International Surfacing, Phoenix, Arizona.
- Cox Paving Co., Blanco, Texas.
- Eagle Crest Construction Co., Arlington, Washington.
- Manhole Adjusting Contractors, Monterey Park, California.
- Asphalt Rubber Systems, Riverside, Rhode Island.

Rubberized seal coats have been extensively tested in Phoenix, Arizona, where street resurfacing with rubberized seal coats began in 1966. Asphalt rubber has been successfully used in the southwest, California, and Texas.

The only foreign facility making and using RUMAC is Nordic Construction Co., Stockholm, Sweden. The Plus Ride process has been successfully used in limited applications for highway construction in Sweden for more than 20 years, where the process was originally developed. RUMAC has been used in repaving about 10 km per year of roads in Sweden, with the primary application being bridge paving. RUMAC pavement strips laid in Sweden have been short in length and, as a result, have not been evaluated for long-term performance. The longest single strip, a stretch 14 km long and 13 m wide, was laid in 1989 and is being evaluated for long-term performance.

In the next five years only about 100 km of RUMAC pavement is expected to be laid by the Nordic Construction Co. The Swedish Road and Traffic Research Institute confirmed superior performance such as good friction and abrasion and deicing characteristics of RUMAC pavement.

Environmental, Economic, and Volume Characteristics

Environmental Characteristics

- Some concern over constituents leaching from tire chips in road beds where bed is below the water table
- No other significant environmental concerns

Leach tests on tire chips used in roadbed materials show somewhat equivocal results for constituent leaching. However, leaching is only a potential concern where the roadbed is immersed in groundwater, which occurs only in relatively limited situations. Therefore, this environmental concern can be easily addressed through limitations on use.

Economic Characteristics

- Initial cost of RUMAC (Plus Ride) in the United States is about twice that of conventional asphalt.

- Cost of asphalt rubber is about 40 to 100 percent higher than the cost of standard asphalt.
- Cost of dense-graded asphalt concrete was approximately $3.04 per square yard compared to $6.13 per square yard (thickness not specified) for asphalt rubber in 1988 in California.
- Service life of asphalt rubber pavements is expected to be 20 years or more, compared to 10 to 12 years for asphalt pavements.
- Initial cost of RUMAC given to be 1.5 times that of conventional asphalt by Nordic Construction Co., Sweden and Swedish Road and Traffic Research Institute.
- Cost of RUMAC in Sweden given to be $2.50 per square meter per centimeter of thickness.
- Service life of RUMAC is about twice that of conventional asphalt concrete.

Asphalt rubber and RUMAC are both approximately twice the initial cost of the standard asphalt or aggregate they replace. Performance information on both asphalt rubber and RUMAC indicate that they both extend service life of pavements significantly when properly mixed and applied, between 80 and 100 percent. These data would tend to indicate that on a life-cycle basis, asphalt rubber and RUMAC are cost-competitive with standard asphalt and aggregate, but are somewhat more expensive due to the higher initial costs of these materials and discounting of future costs associated with more frequent repaving of standard asphalt pavings.

The higher initial costs of using rubber as an additive can be attributed to the cost of processing tire rubber, blending and mixing rubber with asphalt, added energy consumption and plant maintenance, and some modifications, such as need for more powerful pumps due to the higher viscosity of asphalt rubber and RUMAC.

Volume Capability

- 225 million tires per year, if 10 percent of the aggregate used annually in asphalt were replaced by rubber from tires
- 28 million tires per year if an asphalt rubber seal coat is used on only approximately 1 percent of the two-lane highways (approximately 17,500 m) replaced every year
- 8000 to 12,000 tires per mile for a two-lane highway overlaid with 3 in of RUMAC
- 1600 tires per mile for a two-lane highway for an asphalt rubber seal coat

There are about 3.5 million miles of paved road surfaces in the United States, a fraction of which are repaired or replaced every year. Total asphalt concrete laid each year in the United States is about 450 million tons. RUMAC uses about 60 lb of rubber per ton of mix, resulting in recycling of five tires per ton of RUMAC; each tire yields about 12 lb of rubber. Thus, about 12,000 tires can be recycled per mile of two-lane highway overlaid with 3 in of RUMAC pavement. Thus, RUMAC has the potential to use up all the scrap tires produced in the United States every year even if only one-eighth of the asphalt concrete laid each year were to be replaced by RUMAC. Asphalt rubber seals have the potential to use up about one-quarter of the nation's supply of scrap rubber every year.

Barriers to Further Implementation

- Use of worn tires as asphalt rubber additives is not accepted due to the uncertainty about durability, performance, and initial cost.
- Scrap polyethylene addition to asphalt provides an improvement of 20 percent and enhances both crack resistance at low temperatures and creep resistance at higher temperatures. Polyethylene will likely be the scrap raw material of choice, as it offers greater performance improvement over tires.
- High initial cost.
- Product specifications not laid out by ASTM.
- Lack of information on relative benefits and costs.
- Concern over availability of uniform-quality rubber from tires.
- Reluctance of highway administrators to take risks in using innovative material.
- Steel and fabric have to be separated from the tire, thus about 60 to 75 percent of tire is not used, and processing costs are high.

It is necessary to prove the effectiveness of asphalt rubber as an aggregate binder, as distinguished from the present membrane usage.

Potential Methods for Reducing Barriers

- Following up and documenting the performance, cost, and benefits from the use of rubber asphalt seal coats and RUMAC where used, as compared to asphalt
- Standardization of asphalt rubber additive product specifications by ASTM

The industry is wary of using asphalt rubber additives in laying pavement due to lack of information on the performance, relative benefits and costs, and also the lack of ASTM specifications for such products. Use of asphalt rubber seals and RUMAC has usually not been followed by cost-benefit economic and technical evaluations. Collection and dissemination of such information will go a long way in evaluating the possibility of RUMAC and asphalt rubber seals as a large-volume consumer of scrap tires.

Table 18.3 lists uses of scrap tires in fuel and in other technologies.

LEGISLATION RELATIVE TO TIRE DISPOSAL

A brief summary of state activities in scrap tire management is presented below. The summary is intended to present the reader with a brief overview of state efforts rather than a comprehensive document on all aspects of scrap tire management in each state. Sources of information include state regulations and legislation documents; *Scrap Tire News* (January 1991); and telephone interviews with contact person(s) listed for the state regulatory agency.

---

*Information has not been reviewed or approved by states' regulatory agency for the following states: Indiana, Maine, Montana, New Jersey, South Dakota, and Wyoming.

TABLE 18.3 Scrap Tire Use as Fuel and in Other Technologies

Technology	Environmental issues	Volume capability	Barriers
		Scrap tires as fuel	
Cement kilns	NO_x emissions reduced SO_2 particulate emissions not affected No waste residues No extra emission controls required	130 million tires if only 50 kilns used tires as auxiliary fuel	Test burns/review of air emission permits
Pulp and paper mills	SO_2, NO_x emissions reduced Zinc and particulate emissions not affected when using wire-free TDF, else increase dramatically	45–50 million tire equivalents by 1995 if 25% of mills used TDF	Environmental permitting Cost of competing fuels Industry inertia to use of alternative fuels
Utilities	SO_2 and NO_x emissions decrease Particulate emissions actually decrease	50–70 million tires per year if 25% of generative capacity of utilities equipped with wet-bottom boilers used tires as 10% of fuel	Restricted to three technologies: grate, cyclone, wet-bottom Feeding systems
Dedicated tire-to-energy facilities	Complete combustion of tires	30–50 million tires per year by 1995	Extremely high capital investment Continuous supply of tires Long permitting process
		Scrap tires used in other technologies	
Pyrolysis	Only 75–82% energy recovery No major emission problems	Unknown—though negligible at present	Inefficient energy recovery Variability in product quality Very low market potential for products No known commercial facilities Economically not feasible

Rubber recovery
  Crumb
  Reclaim
	Only part of tire processed—steel and fabric have to be removed
	No environmental problems
		Low—about 3–4 million tires annually	High capital outlays
			No ASTM product specifications

TABLE 18.3 Scrap Tire Use as Fuel and in Other Technologies (*Continued*)

Technology	Environmental issues	Volume capability	Barriers
Tire retreading	One of the best recovery methods environmentally Only 30% of energy required to produce a new tire used in retreading	38 million tires retreaded every year Volume capability has stabilized	Quality of retreaded tires is variable Availability of cheap new passenger car tires Consumer perception of retreaded tires as being of inferior quality
Splitting industry	No environmental effects or concerns	Minimal	Low demand for products Cheaper alternative products
Artificial reefs and barriers	No major environmental effects or concerns	Minimal	Cheaper alternative methods to build reefs Expensive tire disposal technology
Rubber in Asphalt	No adverse effect on environment Rubber-modified roads enhanced characteristics: Decreased road noise Increased resistance to ice formation Reduction of cracking Breaking time decreased on icy roads Totally resistant	65 million tires per year if asphalt rubber used on 1% of two-lane highways Eight times the annual supply of tires if RUMAC used for paving all roads resurfaced each year	No ASTM product specifications Inconsistent test results (uncertain durability and performance of pavement) Health and emission issues still need to be addressed Only 40–60% of the tire used—steel and fabric have to be removed Cost
Tire shredding (monofill or stockpiled)	No emissions Reduction of: Volume (up to ⅔) Fire hazard Mosquito infestation Rodent infestation	Unlimited	Availability of landfill capacity Permitting process Costs

Source: *Scrap Tire Use/Disposal Study,* Scrap Tire Management Council, September 1990.

Alabama

The 1990 legislature required and funded a Tire Recycling Study to determine the state's needs for scrap tire management. A tire recycling center was established at Gadsden State Community College to conduct the study mandated by legislature. The study was to be completed by July 1991 and to contain legislative recommendations.

State Solid Waste Act passed in May 1989 requires counties to develop a comprehensive solid waste management plan to include a recycling component to divert 25 percent of waste from land disposal. The plan to be completed by 1991 and include tire-recycling provisions. There is one monofill for shredded tires that is permitted and operating.

Permits required include

* A solid waste permit for facilities which dispose scrap tires
* Health permit for facilities which store and/or process tires

A manifest record showing origin of tires delivered to site and destination of tires leaving the site, stacking dimensions, separation distances, and size description is also required.

For further information on legislation, contact Jack Honeycutt, Department of Environmental Management, Solid Waste Branch, 1751 Congressman W.L. Dickerson Drive, Montgomery, Alabama 36130, telephone 205-271-7700.

For further information on recycling, contact Walter Nichols, Department of Environmental Management, Solid Waste Branch, 1751 Congressman W.L. Dickerson Drive, Montgomery, Alabama 36130, telephone 205-271-7700.

For further information on disposal, contact John Narramore, Department of Environmental Management, Solid Waste Branch, 1751 Congressman W.L. Dickerson Drive, Montgomery, Alabama 36130, telephone 205-271-7700.

Alaska

The state is in the process of developing a Solid Waste Management Plan that includes but does not deal specifically with scrap tires. Tires are generally landfilled and tire piles do not exceed 0.5 million tires. The Alaskan Department of Transportation was first in the United States to try rubberized asphalt.

For further information on rubberized asphalt contact Tim Moss, 5750 E. Tudor, Anchorage, Alaska 99507, telephone 907-338-4200.

For further information on state activities, contact Glenn Miller, Department of Environmental Conservation, Division of Environmental Quality, P.O. Box O, Juneau, Alaska 99811-1800, telephone 907-465-2671.

For further information on waste reduction and recycling, contact Marilyn Patterson, Governor's Waste Reduction and Recycling Task Force, P.O. Box A, Juneau, Alaska 99811, telephone 907-465-3500.

For other information, contact David Wigglesworth, ADEC Pollution Prevention Program, P.O. Box O, Juneau, Alaska 99811-1800, telephone 907-465-2671.

Arizona

The Waste Tire Disposal Statute A.R.S.44-1301 established a 2 percent tire fee on the retail sale of all new tires (the fee not to exceed $2.00 per tire). Major components of the law include

- Retail tire sellers are required to accept waste tires from customers at the point of transfer.
- Waste tire collection sites must register with the Department Environmental Quality.
- After January 1, 1992, no tires can be disposed at the landfills without first being shredded.
- Disposal of whole tires is banned.
- Acceptable methods of waste tire disposal are established, including retreading, chopping, or shredding, and hauling to out-of-state collection or processor sites.
- A waste tire grant fund is established using the funds collected from the tire fees.
- Grant funds will be used to provide monies to counties or private enterprise to construct and operate a waste tire processing facility and purchase equipment for that facility; to contract for a waste tire processing service; to remove or contract to remove waste tires from the county or other region; and to establish waste tire collection centers.
- Counties are eligible for *pro rata* share of the waste tire grant funds based on motor vehicle registration within that county.

The state distributes to interested parties a first draft of the Tire Grant Criteria. The final Tire Grant Criteria will be sent out at the time of call for proposals for the grant. The tire grant criteria will review proposals:

- That cover waste tire programs within small counties
- That provide for transportation to collection sites or processing facilities
- For operations that recycle the entire tire
- For operations that offer shredding or chopping of tires and transportation to collection sites or to processing facilities
- Containing other innovated methods of waste tire disposal

For further information contact Stephanie R. Wilson, Office of Waste Programs, Waste Assessment Section, Arizona Department of Environmental Quality, 2005 North Central Avenue, Phoenix, Arizona 85004, telephone 602-257-2318.

Arkansas

Three acts were passed during the 1991 legislative session that affect tires.

- Act 748 of 1991 provides for an income tax credit for equipment used exclusively to reduce, reuse, or recycle solid waste.
- Act 749 of 1991 is a comprehensive recycling measure. The act includes spe-

cific language regarding the hauling, storage, and disposal of tires and requires permits for these activities. Also, the act set a $1.50 per tire disposal fee on tires sold at retail. Monies derived are placed in a dedicated fund to provide grants for cleanup and establishment of waste tire collection centers.

• Act 752 of 1991 establishes regional solid waste management authorities and requires that regional authorities provide collection centers for tires.

Current regulations provide that tires that have been cut, sliced, or otherwise reduced from their whole form may be landfilled. Regulations for waste tires as provided by Act 749 are due to be promulgated by January 1, 1992.

For further information on tire recycling contact James Shirrell, Recycling Division Chief, Department of Pollution Control and Ecology, P.O. Box 8913, Little Rock, Arkansas 72201-8913, telephone 501-562-6533 extension 822.

For further information on waste tire disposal contact Tom Boston, Solid Waste Division Chief, Department of Pollution Control and Ecology, P.O. Box 8913, Little Rock, Arkansas 72219-8913, telephone 501-562-6533 extension 859.

California

Waste tire legislation AB 1843 passed in 1989. Effective July 1, 1991, collection of a $0.25 per tire disposal fee on all used tires left with a dealer or other seller. Fee expected to generate $2 to $3 million annually for the California Tire Recycling Management Fund.

The state's Integrated Waste Management Board will administer the fund. Effective July 1, 1991, the Integrated Waste Management Board is to begin a program in tire recycling, reuse, recovery, or reduction operations. Eventually, grants might go to facilities for tire shredding, crumb rubber production, the manufacture of products from used tires, or pyrolysis operations.

Effective July 1, 1991, the Integrated Waste Management Board will adopt emergency regulations for the permitting of major waste tire facilities (over 5000 tires). Permits from the Integrated Waste Management Board include fire prevention, security and vector control measures, tire pile size and height limits, closure, and pile reduction plans. Effective December 1, 1991, the Integrated Waste Management Board is to report on the feasibility of using tires as a fuel supplement for cement kilns, lumber operations, and other industrial processes.

AB 1843 also includes provisions for a statewide plan for establishing designated landfills that will accept and store shredded tires. There is a 0.5 percent purchase price preference for products made from materials derived from used tires.

AB 1322 also passed in 1989, allows the Department of General Services and Integrated Waste Management Board to promulgate regulations for the purchase of retread tires by the state and requires the use of retreads on state vehicles after July 1, 1991.

For further information on regulation and legislation, contact Tom Micka, Integrated Waste Management Board, 1020 Ninth Street, Suite 300, Sacramento, California 95814, telephone 916-327-9352.

For further information on grants, loans, and special projects, contact Ron McLaughlin, Integrated Waste Management Board, RCD-R&D Section, 1020 Ninth Street, Suite 300, Sacramento, California 95814, telephone 916-327-9361.

For further information on tire derived fuel, contact Martha Gildart, Inte-

The act provides that landfill operators have the right to refuse tires or require that they be shredded or chipped before being accepted for disposal. Tires may be considered as recyclable material and not regulated as solid waste under certain conditions. There are numerous unpermitted stockpiles of tires. The Environmental Protection Division is gathering information as to the locations and number of tires in these stockpiles.

There is a 15-member Recycling Market Development Council to determine what actions, if any, are needed to facilitate the development and expansion of markets for recovered materials, which might include recovered tires. The council is chaired by James Kundell, Carl Vinson Institute of Environment, University of Georgia, Tarrell Hall, Athens, Georgia, telephone 404-542-2736.

For further information contact Denni Jackson, Environmental Protection Division, 3420 Norman Berry Drive, Hapeville, Georgia 30354, telephone 404-656-2836.

Hawaii

A statewide Integrated Solid Waste Management Plan has been drafted for introduction to the state legislature. Tires are not specifically addressed. There is no direct information or state regulation regarding scrap tires except that tires are required on a county level to be shredded. There are no scrap tire piles on record.

A bill was introduced last year to address scrap tires. It was not passed as yet. The tires are shredded and landfilled. There is a waste-to-energy facility in Honolulu. Honolulu County is planning a scrap tire management program that would include provision for shredding tires to a TDF product for sale to Honolulu Power. Preliminary plans provide for an assessment on tire sales to fund the program.

For further information contact James Ikeda, Department of Health, Environmental Management Services Division, Five Waterfront Plaza, 500 Ala Moana Boulevard, Suite 250, Honolulu, Hawaii 96813, telephone 808-543-8226.

Idaho

HB 352 deals with fees from the sale of tires—acceptance of waste tires, collection sites, and disposal of waste tires. A retail seller of motor vehicle tires must collect a fee of $1 per tire for each tire sold. The fee will be paid to the Division of Environmental Quality for deposit on a quarterly basis in the waste tire grant account. By July 1, 1992, the Division of Environmental Quality will establish a program to make grants to counties or contracts with private entities to do any of the following, either individually or collectively,

- Contract for a waste tire processing facility service
- Remove or contract for the removal of waste tires from county landfills or removal of other existing unlawful tire piles in the state
- Establish waste tire collection centers at solid waste disposal facilities or waste tire processing facilities
- Each county will establish a program addressing waste tire disposal by October 1, 1992
- The Division of environmental Quality will provide an annual report to the leg-

islature on the grant program and include an examination of the adequacy of the funding.

An owner or operator of a waste tire collection site must register with the Division of Environmental Quality and provide information concerning the site's location and size and the approximate number of waste tires which are stored at the site. The permissible methods of waste tire disposal include

- Retreading
- Constructing collision barriers or using as playground equipment
- Controlling soil erosion or for flood control only if used in accordance with approved engineering practices
- Chopping or shredding
- Grinding for use in asphalt and as a raw material for other products
- Incinerating or using as a fuel or pyrolysis
- Hauling to out-of-state collection or processing sites

For further information contact Jerome Jankowski, Department of Health and Welfare, Division of Environmental Quality, Hazardous Materials Bureau, 1410 North Hilton Street, Boise, Idaho 83706, telephone 208-334-5879.

Illinois

HB 1085 (PA 86-452) enacted August 31, 1989, amends the Environmental Protection Act to create the Used Tire Management program which includes provisions for

- Cleanup of tire accumulations
- Development of markets for tire-based products
- Regulations to control mosquito infestations in tire accumulations
- Financial assistance to units of local government for these activities
- Establishes the Used Tire Management Fund effective January 1, 1990
- $0.50 of the revenue received per vehicle title will be deposited in the fund; approximately $1.7 million is expected to be generated annually

Final rules for licensing of waste tire transporters and waste tire storage requirements were finalized in 1990. The rules, which become effective in January 1992, apply to facilities storing more than 50 tires and include provisions limiting tire pile height and size, and assuring that tires are stored or processed in a manner that prevents water from accumulating in the tire. Site owners are also required to maintain daily records of tires received or processed, and submit annual reports. Sites with more than 5000 tires are required to have financial insurance to cover the cost of site cleanup.

Illinois Department of Energy and Natural Resources' Used Tire Recovery program awarded a low-interest loan to expand an existing used-tire processing facility in the state; is funding five TDF test burns in 1991; is making low interest loans available to fuel users to retrofit existing equipment or make improvements to facilitate the use of tire-derived fuel; and is conducting a test of passenger retread tire with the Illinois State Police. One study by the Department of Energy & Natural Resources is entitled *Illinois Scrap Tire Management Study.*

For further information contact Paul Purseglove, Illinois Environmental Protection Agency Division of Land Pollution Control, 2200 Churchill Road, P.O. Box 19276, Springfield, Illinois 62794-9276, telephone 217-782-6761 or Alan Justice, Illinois Department of Energy & Natural Resources, 325 W. Adams, Room 300, Springfield, Illinois 62704, telephone 217-524-5454.

Indiana

HB 1391 signed into law March 1990 establishes regulation on the disposal of lead acid batteries and scrap tires. The law

- Creates a scrap tire management fund, effective July 1991, to pay for cleaning up tire dumps when the responsible party is unknown or cannot afford cleanup; the scrap tire management fund is supported by permit fees from waste tire storage sites, appropriations, and other fees as established by the General Assembly.
- Creates permit requirements for scrap tire storage facilities to include at minimum: proof of financial responsibility, records to show quantity of tires handled, their source, the quality of material, i.e., shredded, cut or whole, shipped from the site and documentation showing its final destination; site closure plan; contingency plan for protecting public health and the environment.
- Requires Department of Environmental management to establish a Waste Tire Task Force to develop market plans for waste tires and further guidelines for waste tire storage.

HB 1391 also includes a 10 percent price preference for state purchase of supplies that meet recycled content requirement specified by the law.

For further information contact Joanne Joyce, Director Special Projects, Department of Environment Management, Office of Environmental Response, 5500 West Bradbury, Indianapolis, Indiana 46241, telephone 317-232-5964.

Iowa

House File 753, passed in 1989, bans whole tires from landfill disposal effective July 1, 1991. Iowa Department of Natural Resources submitted a scrap tire abatement report to the General Assembly as mandated in House File 753. The report recommends

- Scrap tire haulers be registered and bonded
- The use of TDF at the state's three public universities
- Local governments use tire chips as a leachate collection medium in landfills
- A financial mechanism to fund the program; the preferred method is a vehicle registration surcharge
- Modified bounty system for local governments only to receive rebates on pile cleanups

Iowa Department of Natural Resources drafted administrative rules for tire processing and storage facilities. Final rules define how tires must be processed for land disposal. Proposed rules include

- Permit requirements for facilities that store more than 500 tires
- Size limits on scrap tire piles; fire control requirements for storage sites
- Allowance for tire processing facilities to store a supply for processing

Department of Natural Resources prepared a study entitled *Waste Tire Abatement in Iowa: A Study to the General Assembly* that contains information on the number and geographic distribution of scrap tires, market development, method to establish reliable source of waste tires for users, and methods to clean up stockpiles.

For further information contact Teresa Hay, Iowa Department of Natural Resources, Wallace State Office Building, East 9th & Grand Avenue, Des Moines, Iowa 50319-0034, telephone 515-281-8975.

Kansas

The 1991 session of the Kansas Legislature amended certain provisions of a bill passed in 1990 which established a scrap tire program for the state. The bill bans the disposal of whole tires. The program, which will be placed by December 31, 1991, will include permitting of

- Scrap tire processing facilities and associated waste tire collection sites
- Scrap tire collection centers
- Scrap tire collectors
- Solid waste management facilities (to allow processing and monofill, daily cover or disposal in landfill of processed tires)

A grant program for

- Developing and implementing management plans for collection, abatement, recycling, and disposal of tires
- Encouraging recycling of tires
- Enforcing laws relating to collection and disposal of tires

Eligible grant recipients are cities, counties, and private companies, individually or jointly. The funding mechanism is

- $0.50 per tire excise tax on sale of new tires, including tires mounted on a vehicle sold at retail for the first time
- Estimated $1.3 million per year in tire fund revenues to be used for grants and program administration

For further information contact Kathleen Warren, Solid Waste Section, Bureau of Air and Waste Management, Department of Health and Environment, Forbes Field, Topeka, Kansas 66620-0001, telephone 913-296-1590.

Kentucky

HB 32, signed into law April 1990,

• Places a $1 per tire tax on retail sales of tires
• Establishes a scrap tire trust fund for cleanup of tire piles and to fund loan programs to develop uses for scrap tire material and for collection and storage programs
• Requires registration of piles with more than 100 scrap tires
• Requires that only tires rendered "suitable for disposal" be landfilled

For further information contact Linda Stacy, Department for Environmental Protection, Division of Waste Management, Frankfort Office Park, 18 Reilly Road, Frankfort, Kentucky 40601, telephone 502-564-6716.

Louisiana

A draft copy of regulation concerning scrap tire issues was published in the *State Register* on March 20, 1991. The regulations went through a complete rewrite that now exceeds federal regulations. Act 185, a solid waste recycling and reduction law passed in 1989, affects scrap tires in the following ways:

• Tires must go to permitted recycling or solid waste disposal or waste tire collection sites, effective January 1, 1990.
• Effective January 1, 1991, whole scrap tires will not be accepted at landfills for disposal; tires must be cut or shred prior to disposal.
• The Department of Environmental Quality has formulated draft regulations for used and scrap tire recycling in accordance with Act 185.

Draft regulations include

• Manifest and reporting requirements
• Site notification requirements; licensing requirements for transporters, scrap tire collection, storage, recycling and disposal sites
• Outdoor/indoor storage requirements
• Tire dealer responsibilities
• Provision for a $2 per tire tax on retail sale

For further information contact Barby Carroll, Department of Environmental Quality, Office of Solid and Hazardous Waste, P.O. Box 44307, Baton Rouge, Louisiana 70804-4307, telephone 504-765-0249.

Maine

LD 1431, passed in 1989, requires residents to pay $1 per tire advance disposal fee effective January 1, 1990, to fund pile cleanup and scrap tire recycling grants and loan programs. The legislation required the Department of Transportation to prepare a report on the use of ground tire rubber as an additive to asphalt concrete. The report was submitted to the legislature in March 1990. The legislature established a Department of Transportation recycling project including comprehensive review of feasible alternatives for using recyclable material in construction. Ground rubber from tires was one of several materials specifically identified for study. The report to legislature was due January 1, 1991.

Chapter 406 of the State Solid Waste Management Plan contains requirement for proper storage or disposal of scrap tires and the licensing of scrap tire storage and processing facilities. The rules which apply to tire storage facilities include provisions for surface water and groundwater protection. The Solid Waste Management and Recycling Plan, issued July 1990, estimates tires and rubber constitute 0.5 percent (11,300 tons) of the waste stream (based on 1988 figures). Under the state's proposed recycling goal of a 50 percent reduction by 1994, the state will need to recycle 7,500 tons of the estimated 11,061 tons of tires, the plan concludes.

For further information contact Terry McGovern, Department of Environmental Protection, Bureau of Solid Waste Management, State House Station 17, Augusta, Maine 04333, telephone 207-582-8740.

Maryland

Each year, Maryland discards about 4.3 million scrap tires. Abandoned tire piles are considered an eyesore and nuisance, providing breeding grounds for mosquitoes and other pests and creating potential fire hazards. To address the scrap tire disposal problem and to ensure proper storage and disposal, the Maryland Legislature passed a scrap tire management bill.

The bill establishes a tire recycling fee of up to $1, effective February 1, 1992, to be collected by retail tire dealers on the first sale of a new tire in the state, including new tires sold as part of a new or used vehicle. Dealers keep 1.2 percent of the gross amount of the fee collected and give the remainder to the Comptroller of the Treasury, which transfers these fees to the Used Tire Clean-Up and Recycling Fund. The funds may be used to clean up some tire pies or cover the costs related to the implementation of scrap tire recycling systems.

The bill requires that by July 1, 1992, all scrap tire haulers, collection facilities, and recyclers must be licensed by the department. The Maryland Environmental Service, a state agency of the Department of Natural Resources, and a nonprofit organization, is responsible for developing the statewide tire recycling system.

In 1989, the Scrap Tire Storage and Disposal Act was created. Under the law, which took effect immediately, tire dealers, recyclers, and other tire collectors may not store used tires unless they prove within 90 days that they have a market for the tires either by showing contracts for materials or otherwise documenting the firm's efforts to secure markets. If the above-mentioned persons do not satisfy the requirements for selling or disposing of the tires, they are required to use a state-approved disposal system. The law allows Maryland's Secretary of the Environment to take remedial action and/or removal of tires at any site if he or she determines disposal may be carried out improperly or in a way that threatens the environment.

For further information contact Muhammad Masood, Maryland Department of the Environment, Office of Waste Minimization and Recycling, 2500 Broening Highway, Baltimore, Maryland, telephone 301-631-3315.

Massachusetts

During last few years tire disposal was governed by policy defining tires as bulky waste, i.e., similar to disposal of solid waste. Stockpiles can be exempted for site assignment if there is a recycling operation at the tire dump. Tire dumps are subject to site design and operation standards. Two bills introduced in 1990 addressed scrap tires and both have been refiled in the 1991 legislature.

The bills act to protect the environment and public health by proper disposal of certain automotive wastes and encourage recycling. The bills

• Ban land disposal of whole tires effective December 1991 (regulation in effect)
• Allow the use of shredded scrap tire products as daily cover
• Provide for the abatement of scrap tire dumps
• Establish permit and registration rules for tire collectors and processors
• Encourage the establishment of scrap tire collection centers
• Establish an education program to encourage individuals to return scrap tires to collection centers
• Require the Department of Environmental Protection to initiate market development study for scrap-tire-derived materials
• Establish tire storage rules for tire collection sites
• Require tire retailers to use registered scrap tire haulers
• Set a $5 waste tire abatement fee charged on vehicle registrations and title transfers

Monies would be deposited in the Automotive Waste Reduction and Recycling Fund that

• Provides for abatement of scrap tire piles
• Provides grants to communities for pile cleanup and scrap tire programs
• Requires consumers to leave scrap tires with dealers
• Allows tire dealers to charge disposal fee

For further information contact John Pepi, Department of Environmental Protection, Western Region, 436 Dwight Street, 4th Floor, Springfield, Massachusetts 01103, telephone 413-784-1100.

Michigan

Two bills that affect tires were enacted into law in Michigan in 1990. HB 5339, an amendatory act to Michigan vehicle code, places a $0.50 tire disposal surcharge on each certificate of vehicle title. Monies from the surcharge will be deposited in the scrap tire regulatory fund. HB 4068, a scrap tire regulatory act, establishes the scrap tire regulatory fund to provide monies for scrap tire cleanups on public land and administrative costs of implementing and enforcing scrap tire regulations. HB 4068 regulates tire storage for uncovered tire collection sites with more than 500 and up to 2500 tires, with accumulations of 2500 to 100,000, and those with 100,000 tires and more. It also requires all scrap tire collection sites to register with the Department of Natural Resources (DNR) annually and pay a $200 per year registration fee. All scrap tire haulers must register with DNR and tire retailers must use registered scrap tire haulers for removal of their tires.

For further information contact Kyle Cruse, Department of Natural Resources, Waste Management Division, P.O. Box 30241, Lansing, Michigan 48909, telephone 517-335-4757.

Minnesota

The scrap tire law passed in 1985 requires a $4 tax on vehicle title transfers. This fee generates about $4 million per year in revenue to fund a well-defined stockpile cleanup program and grant and loan program for companies recycling, reusing, or processing tires. Aspects of Minnesota's Waste Tire management Program include

- Banning tires and tire-derived products from landfills
- Requiring tire dealers or businesses which sell tires to accept as many scrap tires from a customer as are sold to that customer
- Allowing tire retailers to charge a disposal fee
- Permitting transporters and storage facilities
- Conducting abatement of identified scrap tire stockpiles
- Conducting countywide amnesty day programs for abating household quantities of scrap tires

Minnesota reports the following progress in managing the state's scrap tires: New revisions to the Minnesota Pollution Control Agency waste tire grant and loan rules will allow companies that use tire-derived products, such as crumb rubber, to apply for grants and loans to help manufacture products incorporating scrap tire products. Transporter identification requirements and enforcement policies have been established and implemented. More than 50 percent of the state's 280 dump sites have been eliminated or are already in the process of being reduced.

For further information contact Andrew Ronchak, Project Manager, Waste Tire Management Unit, Minnesota Pollution Control Agency, Ground Water and Solid Waste Division, 520 Lafayette Road North, St. Paul, Minnesota 55155, telephone 612-296-7358.

Mississippi

Scrap tires come under the solid waste regulations. SB 2985, a disposal bill for batteries, tires, and household hazardous waste, has been adopted in the 1991 legislature. Proposed provisions include

- A $1 per tire fee on retail sale of tires
- A requirement that tires be shred prior to landfilling
- Registration permit requirements for tire haulers

A comprehensive waste minimization act was passed in 1990, to address methods of reducing waste generation in Mississippi by minimum of 25 percent by January 1, 1996.

For further information contact Billy Warden or Mark Williams, Department of Environmental Quality, Office of Pollution Control, Solid Waste Division, P.O. Box 10385, Jackson, Mississippi 39289, telephone 601-961-5171.

Missouri

Regulation is finalized and should be effective in July 1991. SB 530, an omnibus solid waste bill passed in 1990, includes provisions for regulating tires. It

- Places a $0.50 per tire tax on retail sales of most new tires
- Bans whole tires from disposal in a landfill, effective January 1, 1991
- Requires sites that store more than 500 tires for more than 30 days to obtain a permit from the Department of Natural Resources
- Requires a permit for hauling scrap tires obtained from the Department of Natural Resources

Sites that store fewer than 500 tires do not need a permit but must conform to storage requirements; waste tire haulers who carry more than 25 tires per load must obtain a Department of Natural Resources permit. Permit applications for existing sites or haulers must be submitted between January 1 and February 28, 1991. The law

- Requires tire dealers to use only permitted haulers and keep records of where their tires go
- Allows for tire tax funds to be spent for cleanup of tire dump sites and to provide grants to businesses that use scrap tires as a fuel or in a product
- Establishes an advisory council on scrap tires
- Requires the Department of Highway and Transportation to undertake demonstration projects using recovered rubber from scrap tires as surfacing material, structural material, subbase material, and fill consistent with standard engineering practices

HB 438 also establishes purchase preferences for products that use recovered material including retread tires.

For further information contact Becky Shannon, Department of Natural Resources, P.O. Box 176, Jefferson City, Missouri 65102, telephone 314-751-3176.

Montana

Regulation of tires comes under the Montana Solid Waste Act. Tires are currently accepted at landfills but are required to be separated and stockpiled or disposed in separate areas such as monofills. Scrap tire collection and storage facilities must be permitted in licensed as a landfill.

For further information contact Roger Thorvilson, Waste Management Section, Department of Health and Environmental Services, Solid and Hazardous

Waste Bureau, Cogswell Building, Helena, Montana 59620, telephone 406-444-1430.

North Carolina

SB 111, passed in 1989, levies a 1 percent sales tax on new tire sales and requires each county to provide a place to dispose of scrap tires. Tax became effective January 1990. Other provisions require that

- Counties provide a site for tire collection by March 1, 1990
- Scrap tire haulers register with the Solid Waste Branch to qualify for a merchant identification number
- Storers of more than 1000 scrap tires obtain a storage permit (exceptions for certain industries such as tire retailers)
- Counties be allowed to impose tipping fees for tires if sales tax fails to generate adequate funding
- Tire dealers, scrap tire processors, and solid waste disposal facilities be encouraged to set up scrap tire collection centers

Some tire sites are operated by counties and others are private. A list of registered haulers is available. Tires can be landfilled but must be shredded or sliced. There is no current funding at the state level. There are approximately 11 million tires and 1000 tire sites.

For further information contact Dee Eggers, Department of Environmental Health and Natural Resources, Division of Solid Waste Management, P.O. Box 27687, Raleigh, North Carolina 27611-7687, telephone 919-733-0692.

North Dakota

There are no laws, regulations, or legislation that are specific for scrap tires. Recycling of tires is encouraged by the North Dakota State Department of Health and Consolidated Laboratories. Some larger communities, chiefly in the eastern portion of the state, are actively transporting their tires for recycling, depending partially on the distance to markets. Tires are considered to be solid waste and when not recycled, they are allowed to be landfilled.

For further information contact Steven Tillotson, Department of Health, Division of Waste Management, 1200 Missouri Ave., Room 302, Box 5520, Bismarck, North Dakota 58502-5520, telephone 701-221-5200.

Nebraska

In Nebraska, there is no current legislation to regulate the disposal or recycling of scrap tires. The majority of Nebraska's used tires are either stockpiled or landfilled.

In July 1990, the Nebraska legislature passed Legislative Bill 163 providing for the Nebraska Department of Environmental Control to contract for the completion of a comprehensive solid waste management plan and also to give political subdivisions the opportunity to apply for grant funding for a wide-ranging solid waste management program, to include recycling and waste reduction programs, market development for recyclable materials, composting, technical assistance, household hazardous waste management programs, updating the disposal facilities, and other solid waste management activities.

Solid waste management grant funding will be made available to political subdivisions from a $1 fee assessment on each new tire sold in the state that could be used on any motor vehicle, motorcycle, trailer, semi-trailer or farm tractor; from an annual fee assessment of $25 on businesses in the state with retail sales of at least $30,000 and not more than $199,000; and from an annual fee assessment of $50 on businesses with sales of more than $199,000. The tire fee assessment began in October 1990; the retail business fee assessment began in July 1991.

For further information contact Danny Dearing, Environmental Program Specialist, Waste Reduction and Recycling Incentive Grants Program, Nebraska Department of Environmental Control, P.O. Box 98922, Lincoln, Nebraska 68509-8922, telephone 402-471-4210.

Nevada

A comprehensive solid waste management plan was before the legislature in 1991. The plan contains proposed requirements where counties establish plans for recycling of certain materials. There is no specific mention of scrap tires. There are over 1 million tires generate per year. There are stacks of scrap tires at many landfills. Any plan to dispose of commercial quantities of scrap tires would require review and approval by the designated solid waste management authority.

For further information contact John West, Solid Waste Section, Waste Management Bureau, Department of Conservation and Natural Resources, Capitol Complex, 123 W. Nye Lane, Carson City, Nevada 89710, telephone 702-687-5872.

New Hampshire

There are now regulations specific for scrap tires. HB 332-FN-A, Chapter 89-263, an automotive waste disposal law passed in 1989, provides for waste tires in the following ways:

- Authorizes towns to collect fees for collection and disposal of town motor vehicle wastes including tires, batteries, and used oil
- Provides for requests to the Office of State Planning to increase the town's fees if fees prove insufficient under existing legislation
- Requires the Office of State Planning to maintain and distribute to the state's towns a current list of approved contractors for collection and disposal of motor vehicle waste

The Solid Waste District Law (RSA 149-M:31) requires towns and districts to provide a site or access to a site for disposal of residents' tires. The state's 1988 Solid Waste Plan quantifies the state's annual scrap tire generation as 1 million tires and provides an inventory of solid waste facilities receiving scrap tires. Two pieces of legislation were passed in the 1991 legislature which address tires:

- A bill establishing a committee to study the development of a scrap tire management program
- A bill relative to the collection of automotive wastes

For further information contact Sharon Yergeau, Department of Environmental Services, Waste Management Division, 6 Hazen Drive, Concord, New Hampshire 03301-6509, telephone 603-271-2925.

New Jersey

Regulations specific for scrap tires are pending. Tires are considered as solid waste and tire piles are illegal. Engineers deal with scrap tires based on permits. There are no projects to deal with the waste tire problem, just a pending project to identify and clean up the most threatening tire piles. At this time, the project is in limbo; that is, there has been no action taken. There is a companion law to the tire reef program in the Office of Recycling that deals with scrap tires as a resource. The statewide mandatory recycling act passed in 1987 affects tires as follows:

- Tires qualify for municipal tonnage grant credits specified in the act
- Provision is made for industries purchasing new recycling equipment to receive a 50 percent tax credit against their state corporate business tax
- Department of Environmental Protection has a *Recycling Handbook for Selected Material* (batteries, waste paper, plastics, ferrous auto, and scrap tires) available
- State Department of Transportation is completing demonstration project for using tire-derived materials in road construction applications
- Department of Transportation is testing the use of retread passenger tires on fleet vehicles; a federal bill appropriating $1 million in funding to develop a model program to recycle tires specifies the facility to be located in New Jersey.

For further information contact John Schmitt, State of New Jersey, Dept. Environmental Protection, Division of Solid Waste Management, Bureau of Small Facility Review, CN 414 Trenton, New Jersey 08625-414, telephone 609-530-8885.

New Mexico

There are no regulations specific to scrap tires. There is legislation not yet introduced that encompasses a deposit on tires. Scrap tires are considered a problem waste. A waste tire bill has been drafted in the New Mexico Senate. Draft language includes an allowance for shredded tires to be used as landfill cover. The legislation would provide funds for counties to establish tire recycling programs and fund a state Department of Transportation study of road construction and highway maintenance projects incorporating waste tire rubber.

For further information contact George G. Beaumont, Solid Waste Bureau, Environmental Improvement Division, 1190 St. Francis Dr., Santa Fe, New

Mexico 87503, telephone 505-827-2959. For legislative update in New Mexico contact the Legislative Council Service at 505-984-9600.

New York

Scrap tires are a regulated solid waste and may require permits for transport. Most scrap tires now being generated in New York State are shredded and then stored or exported for fuel. A State Scrap Tire Utilization and Management Plan is contained in proposed 1991 legislation sponsored by some members of the New York State legislature. Proposed provisions of the draft measure are

• A funding mechanism to encompass new vehicle tire and replacement tire sales
• A requirement that the Department of Transportation use rubber-modified asphalt concrete (RUMAC) in 50 percent of the state's paving projects
• A requirement that the Department of Environmental Conservation (DEC) develop regulations for stockpile cleanup and management
• Encouragement for the Department of Economic Development to build a state recycling infrastructure for tires

An amendment to Chapter 226 (Section 27-0303) for the Environmental Conservation Law, passed by the New York State Legislature in 1990, designates commercial scrap tires as a regulated waste and requires transporters to obtain a permit from the DEC. Scrap tires are a regulated waste if they are transported for a fee for the purpose of reuse, recycling, or disposal. The law is designed to ensure that tires are transported to permitted tire recycling, processing, or storage sites. Scrap tire storage and processing facilities are regulated under terms of Part 360, "Solid Waste Management Facilities."

For further information on scrap tire management, contact Norman Nosenchuck, New York State Department of Environmental Conservation, Director, Division of Solid Waste, 50 Wolf Road, Albany, New York 12233-4010, telephone 518-457-6603 or Peter Pettit, New York State Department of Environmental Conservation, Division of Solid Waste, 50 Wolf Road, Albany, New York 12233-4010, telephone 518-457-8829.

For further information on scrap tire transport permitting, contact N. G. Kaul, New York State Department of Environmental Conservation, Director, Division of Hazardous Substances Regulation, 50 Wolf Road, Albany, New York 12233-7250, telephone 518-457-6934.

Ohio

House Bill 592, the State Solid Waste Law, effective in June 1988, defines scrap tires as a solid waste. This means that tires must be disposed only in a licensed and permitted sanitary landfill. The State Solid Waste Management Plan (adopted June 1989) requires

• Effective January 1, 1993, tires must be shredded or processed (cut, sliced, etc.) prior to disposal
• Effective January 1, 1995, neither whole nor shredded tires will be accepted for disposal at sanitary landfills

• Tires will only be accepted at tire monofills (shredded) or at legitimate recycling facilities

The Ohio Environmental Protection Agency (EPA) has drafted a rule for temporary storage of scrap tires. The draft rule has undergone a public comment period and has been refiled several times with the legislative board of review. It is expected to become final in early July 1991. The rule states

• The area of each tire pile is limited to 2500 ft^2.
• All piles must be covered except when working the pile.
• At least 50-ft fire lanes must be maintained around the perimeter of each pile.
• Open burning within 500 ft of a pile is prohibited.
• Vector control must be implemented, where appropriate.

Draft regulations for waste tire monofills were not completed in 1990. The Ohio EPA expects to prepare draft monofill regulations in late 1991.

Proposed waste tire legislation in 1990 was not enacted. New revised scrap tire legislation was redrafted and introduced in April 1991, and is being reviewed by Ohio EPA presently. The proposed bill would regulate scrap tire collection, storage, disposal, energy recovery and recycling facilities, require registration of scrap tire transporters and require shipping papers to track scrap tires from collection through final disposition.

For further information contact Natalie Farber, Ohio Environmental Protection Agency, Division of Solid & Hazardous Waste Management, 1800 Watermark Drive, P.O. Box 1049, Columbus, Ohio 43266-0149, telephone 614-644-3135.

Oklahoma

The Oklahoma Waste Tire Recycling Act, implemented July 1, 1989, charges a $1 per tire surcharge on new tire sales. Monies deposited in the Waste Tire Indemnity Fund are used as an incentive to help eliminate existing stockpiles of tires and to promote recycling of scrap tires by reimbursing facilities that process scrap tires.

The reimbursement program is broken into two distinct categories. The categories and the requirements to qualify for each of them are listed below.

• The Oklahoma State Department of Health (OSDH) permitted scrap tire processing facilities are eligible for reimbursement at a rate of $0.50 per tire, if they demonstrate that 25 percent of the tires their facility processes are from OSDH-designated illegal tire dumps.

• OSDH permitted scrap tire processing facilities are eligible for an additional $0.35 per tire reimbursement, if they demonstrate their facility is providing pickup and transportation of scrap tires from each and every county of the state on a regular basis.

Since July 1989, over $1,738,580.75 has been remitted to the two permitted tire-processing facilities in Oklahoma for the processing of 2,965,962 scrap tires. 63 OS §1-2324 states: "It shall be unlawful for any person to own or operate a site used for the storage, collection or disposal of more than fifty discarded vehicle tires under the thousand (10,000) pounds except at a site or facility permitted to accept discarded vehicle tires by the State Department of Health." The provisions of subsection A of this section shall not apply to: "Tire manufacturers, retailers, wholesalers and retreaders who store 2500 or fewer used tires at their place of business or designated off premise storage site."

The State Department of Health shall evaluate each scrap tire facility every three years. Upon completion of the evaluation, the department shall recertify for compensation only those scrap tire facilities which have acted to provide for recycling, reuse, or energy recovery from discarded vehicle tires.

For further information contact Glen Wheat, Department of Health, P.O. Box 53551, 1000 N.E. 10th Street, Oklahoma City, Oklahoma 73152, telephone 405-271-7160.

Oregon

Legislation was passed in 1987, under Oregon Administration Rules. The scrap tire law set up a self-funded comprehensive program for waste tires including:

* Regulation of storage and landfill of scrap tires
* Chipping requirement for landfilling tires effective July 1, 1989
* Regulation of transportation of scrap tires
* Disposal tax of $1 per tire on the sale of new tires to be used to clean up tire piles and to promote the use of scrap tires by subsidizing markets for scrap tires or chips

Implementation of Oregon's program began January 1988. As of May 1991 approximately 1.1 million tires have been cleaned up from 20 scrap tire piles. Department of Environmental Quality funded $1,107,100 of the cleanup costs. Further examples of implementation include the following:

* Five additional scrap tire pile cleanups are under way using public funds.
* One hundred and one scrap tire pile owners have voluntarily removed a total of 437,000 tires.
* Few regular storage sites have been permitted.
* Few landfills have modified their solid waste permits to add temporary storage of scrap tires.

In January 1990, the Department of Environmental Quality established a demonstration program allowing a higher subsidy ($0.01 per pound is the established subsidy) for uses of waste tires which do not yet have an established market in Oregon:

* Two rubber-modified paving projects were approved and completed in 1990.
* The Oregon State Highway Division conducted a project using tire chips as a light fill.
* The Department of Environmental Quality and the Metropolitan Service District will conduct demonstration projects to test rubber from scrap tires in paving projects using generic specifications for rubber-modified asphalt concrete suitable to Oregon's climate and paving practices.

- Two paper mills and one cement kiln are burning tire-derived fuel.
- Tire-derived fuel produced in Oregon is being used in three out-of-state cement kilns.

For further information contact Anne Cox, Department of Environmental Quality, Hazardous and Solid Waste Division, Solid Waste Section, 811 S.W. Sixth Ave., Portland, Oregon 97204-1334, telephone 503-229-6912.

Pennsylvania

HB 1059, a scrap tire bill was introduced in 1990, but died in the Senate at year's end. HB 2823, a bill which would have allowed monofilling as the only permissible method of waste tire storage and impose a 1 percent scrap tire tax on purchase of new vehicle tires, was introduced in 1990, referred to committee, but was not acted on. HB 297 containing a number of significant changes compared to HB 1059 has been introduced and referred to committee. There is an interim policy on tire storage.

For further information contact Jay Ort, Department of Environmental Resource, Bureau of Waste Management, P.O. Box 2063, Fulton Building, 200 North Third Street, Harrisonburg, Pennsylvania 17105-2063, telephone 717-787-7381.

Rhode Island

Tires are regulated by two laws passed in 1989. Chapter 514 of "Litter Control, Recycling and Hard-to-Dispose-of Materials" imposed a $0.50 per passenger tire tax on new tire sales effective January 1, 1990. Revenues from the tire tax will be deposited in the state hard-to-dispose fund along with monies generated from surcharges on other hard-to-dispose-of waste included in the bill. The state expects to generate $1.2 million per year from the fees to fund educational and technical assistance programs for collection, marketing, recycling, reuse, reduction, and safe disposal of hard-to-dispose-of materials and to establish a grant and research program.

P.I. 23-19 addresses tires in the following ways:

- It restricts disposal of waste tires by delivery to facilities operated by the state solid waste management corporation.
- It requires delivery to a licensed privately operated tire storage, recycling, or recovery facility, or delivery for transport to an out-of-state recycling facility.
- It bans the burning of scrap tires within the state as a source of fuel.
- It bans the export of tires for burning outside the state as a fuel source and within 30 mi of any reservoir watershed.
- It requires facilities storing more than 400 tires to obtain a license.
- It sets license requirements and fees for tire recycling and recovery businesses.
- It includes provisions for enforcement and for promulgating rules and regulations.

New state solid waste plan is expected to address scrap tires.

For further information regarding recycling and the hard-to-dispose-of fund, contact Victor Bell, Office of Environmental Coordination, 83 Park Street, Providence, Rhode Island 02903, telephone 401-277-3434. For information regarding licensing of tire facilities, contact Tom Getz, chief, DEM/Division of Air and Hazardous Materials, 291 Promenade Street, Providence, Rhode Island 02908, telephone 401-277-2808.

South Carolina

SB 388 (HB 3096), South Carolina's Solid Waste Policy and Management Act of 1991 contains scrap tire provisions similar to scrap tire language proposed in both 1989 and 1990 in the state. The proposed legislation contains the following provisions affecting scrap tires:

- Tax of $2 per tire on the sale of new tires.
- 3 percent ($0.06 per tire) of the fee would be retained by the dealers.
- $1.94 would revert to the state tax commission to be disbursed at the rate of $1.50 per tire to counties based on the number of vehicles registered in the county for establishing collection, recycling, and/or disposal systems for scrap tires.
- $0.44 would be deposited into a state scrap tire fund for research and development of alternatives to the land disposal of tires.

Tires are landfilled. Department of Health and Environmental Control currently has mandatory guidelines for the storage of tires.
For further information contact William Culler, Department of Health and Environmental Control, Bureau of Solid and Hazardous Waste Management, 2600 Bull Street, Columbia, South Carolina 29201, telephone 803-734-5200.

South Dakota

Revised solid waste regulations became effective July 1990.

- The regulations require general permits for solid waste facilities.
- Tire processing and storage facilities would be required to have general permits.
- The new rules also require tires to be cut into at least four pieces (tires are accepted in landfill if cut in half).
- Tires accumulated in separate areas must be removed annually.

Open burning of tires is prohibited except in areas with populations under 5000. Rules will be phased in between July 1990 and July 1992. Use of tire-derived fuel is limited because of the location of tire population and high transportation costs for remote areas.
For further information contact Dean Pease, Department of Water and Natural Resources, Division of Environmental Regulation, Joe Foss Building, 523 East Capitol, Pierre, South Dakota 57501, telephone 605-773-3151.

Tennessee

HB 1252 Solid Waste Management Act of 1991, states that effective January 1, 1995, no municipal solid waste disposal facility or incinerator shall accept for disposal any whole tires, except that certain incinerators may accept whole scrap tires (Section 33a). Effective January 1, 1995, each county shall provide, directly, by contract or through solid waste authority, at least one site to receive and store scrap tires if adequate sites are not otherwise available in the county for the use of the residents of the county (Section 33b). Landfill operators shall segregate whole, unshredded scrap tires at landfills and provide temporary storage for such tires until a mobile tire shredder shreds the scrap tires (Section 36b).

From monies available from the Solid Waste Management Fund, the Department of Health and Environment shall obtain six mobile tire shredders and operate them throughout the state as scrap tire disposal needs may require (Section 36c).

For further information contact Joseph House, Department of Health and Environment, Division of Solid Waste, Management Customs House, 4th Floor, 701 Broadway, Nashville, Tennessee 37247-3530, telephone 615-741-3424.

Texas

Texas law requires that

- All tires must be split, quartered, or shredded before disposal.
- If over 500 scrap tires are stored on public or private property, the site must be registered with the state.
- Tire haulers to be registered.
- A price preference of 15 percent be provided for use of rubber in asphalt paving projects.
- All used and scrap tire generators obtain an identification number.

Texas Department of Health expects to reintroduce a revenue bill to help fund scrap tire pile cleanup.

For further information contact Steve Reynolds, Department of Health, Bureau of Solid Waste Management, 1100 West 49th Street, Austin, Texas 78756-3199, telephone 512-458-7271.

Utah

Scrap tires are a solid waste, and disposal will require a solid waste permit. There is no special tire policy at the state level. Salt Lake County has a tire policy. SB 5 passed in May 1990, established a per tire graduated tax on all tire sales effective July 1, 1990, as follows:

- $1 per tire up to 14 in
- $1.50 per tire from 14 to 19 in
- $2 per tire from 19 to 26 in

Monies generated from the tax will be deposited in a recycling fund. End users can draw up to $20 per ton per use on products manufactured containing tire-derived material, including tire-derived fuel. The bill places a five-year sunset clause on the end-user incentive to be administered through local health departments. The law does not address regulations for the collection and storage of scrap tires. Salt Lake City regulates scrap tire collection through a manifest system.

For further information contact Ralph Bohn, Department of Environmental Quality, Bureau of Solid and Hazardous Waste, 288 North 1460 West, P.O. Box 16690, Salt Lake city, Utah 84116-0690, telephone 801-538-6170.

Vermont

H. 886, which became Act 286 after passage by the General Assembly in June 1990, prohibits the landfilling of tires after January 1, 1992; it authorizes a 5 percent price preference for products containing recycled materials and allows for an even higher price preference if the state and the user of the product agree on that amount.

The state Solid Waste Management Program, published in 1989, includes specific language addressing scrap tires in the state plan. It requires the state to develop and propose a disposal and deposit charge on tires at a rate high enough to encourage the return of tires to dealers and to fund scrap tire management programs (legislation requiring a $10 per tire deposit was introduced and defeated in 1990). The plan also recommends that the state investigate the feasibility of a mobile tire-shredding operation for the state and the potential for using rubber asphalt on state roads. Tires have been disposed in landfills, an act that became illegal on January 1, 1992. Landfills may continue to accept tires if they function as a tire-recycling facility of a transfer station. Several companies handle used tires in various ways, with many of them going out of state for varied use, including fuel. One operating company shreds tires for several uses, including subbase for drives and parking lots. This company is also using chips in place of crushed stone in drainage projects, septic systems, and leach fields.

There is a project in the town of Georgia that uses tire chips for subbase material in the constructions of a portion of a town road. The Agency of Transportation has used tire chips in one project for slope stabilization and has done some experimental work using asphalt rubber surface treatment. Tires have been allowed to be used for riverbank and slope stabilization work in several areas but only above low-water-level elevations and where environmental concerns are minimal. A study was commissioned entitled "A Report on the Use of Shredded Scrap Tires in On-site Sewage Disposal Systems." This was completed by Envirologic, Inc., 139 Main Street, Brattlebro, Vermont 05301. Based upon some surveys, up to 25 percent of the tires in the waste stream have actual road life remaining and/or are of a retreadable quality and should not be placed in the waste stream. Some work has been done in identifying tire storage facilities and storage piles.

For further information contact Eldon P. Morrison, Solid Waste Management Division, 103 South Main Street, Waterbury, Vermont 05676, telephone 802-244-7831.

Virginia

A scrap tire bill passed in 1989 imposes a tax of $0.50 on each new tire sold at retail effective January 1, 1990. The bill also establishes the Waste Tire Trust

Fund to receive net proceeds of the tax (retailers keep 5 percent for expenses), and it directs Department of Waste Management (DWM) to create a Scrap Tire Management Program. DWM has appointed a Used Tire Advisory Committee including a tire manufacturer, retailers, retreads, recyclers, and public interest groups to study and make recommendations for a management program.

Management program will include development and support of tire-derived fuel (TDF) including subsidies and assistance with permitting. Other disposal options will be supported when proven viable. DWM is establishing a statewide network of collection centers and plans no tipping fee for state tires. Most centers will be operated by prison inmates on state sites.

Virginia has performed rubberized asphalt trials and has an active research program. There is a small ongoing artificial reef program through Department of Corrections. DWM made a trial burn of TDF and coal, and is currently supporting trials of whole-tire burning in a cement kiln.

Current regulations limit accumulation at a recycling site to 1000 tires without a permit and prohibit burying whole tires. An expanded body of regulations is to be developed. With regard to tire piles, the state has only a partial inventory that identifies over 300 sites. They do not have much detail and the inventory is not in a form that can be easily reproduced. Cleanup of old tire piles is not going to be addressed until the current flow control program has been implemented.

For further information contact Bill Robinson, Department of Waste Management, 101 North 145th Street, 11th Floor, Richmond, Virginia 23219, telephone 804-786-8299.

Washington

HB 1671, the Waste Not Washington Act, passed a $1 per tire fee on retail sale of new tires for five years. Revenue projections for the assessment fee are $15 to $20 million over that time. For the 1989 to 1991 biennium, the Department of Ecology anticipates $2 million available for contracts. Authorized uses of the money are

- Grants to local governments for removal of tire piles and enforcement
- Information and education and marketing studies
- Contracts by the state

A Waste Tire Advisory Committee was formed to implement HB 1671 and to help formulate current policy.

The Department of Ecology is ranking the tire piles across the state based on environmental health and safety factors as well as developing a list of qualified contractors. The bill requires licensing rules for tire haulers. Tire haulers are required to pay $250 a year to obtain a carrier license. Haulers must document delivery of scrap tires under provisions of the current scrap tire law.

For further information contact Dale Clark, Tire Recycling Coordinator, Washington Department of Ecology, WRRLC, Mail Stop PV 11, Olympia, Washington 98504-8711, telephone 206-459-6258.

Wisconsin

AB 481 passed in 1987 established a $2 per tire fee on vehicle titles effective May 1, 1988. The fee generates approximately $3 million annually. Scrap tire abatement progress as of January 1991 shows

- Cleanup of the three largest stockpiles, completed in 1990
- Cleanup of four other sites with stockpiles of more than 1 million tires was initiated or is in progress
- Cleanup actions initiated at six scrap tire dumps containing less than 1 million tires
- Tires processed and removed from cleanup sites have been used for energy recovery at four facilities in the state and one energy user in South Dakota

A Waste Tire Management or Recovery Grant Program is intended to research new uses and expand existing uses, and funds projects using monies collected under provision of the scrap tire law:

- Air emission testing to evaluate emissions resulting from the combustion of waste tires with coal and wood waste
- Testing fly ash and bottom ash resulting from combustion of scrap tires and wood
- Environmental assessment of air emissions for the proposed scrap tire and medical waste incinerator
- Testing combustion technology
- Investigating fuel feed system designs to accommodate combustion of scrap tire material in fluidized-bed boilers
- Testing the development of various rubber products, e.g., bed liners for pickup trucks
- Testing leaching characteristics of shredded scrap tires

The Waste Tire Reimbursement Grant Program is designed to financially assist the cost of developing or operating certain types of scrap tire reuse, provides eligible companies a $20 per ton reimbursement for use of scrap tires or scrap tire material for energy recovery, construction, or in the manufacture of products.

Wisconsin's scrap tire law requires that scrap tire collectors, transporters, and storage and processing facilities be licensed. Act 355 enacted into law in 1990 requires all communities in the state to have mandatory recycling programs and bans numerous waste products, including scrap tires, from landfills starting in 1995.

For further information contact Paul Koziar, Department of Natural Resources, Bureau of Solid and Hazardous Waste Management, Box 7921, Madison, Wisconsin 53707, telephone 608-267-9388.

West Virginia

Tires are specifically regulated for storage and disposal. No more than 1000 tires can be stored unless permitted for storing a large number. Tires must be split, cut, or shredded prior to landfilling; shreds must then be dispersed in the workface of the fill with other wastes. Alternative burial plans for noncut or whole tires will be approved if the plan gives adequate assurance that tires will stay buried.

Mobile shredders are not required to have a permit. Stationary processing facilities must be permitted. The Division of Waste Management is conducting a feasibility study on the purchase of shredders for use in tire pile cleanup. Storage at processing facilities is limited to 2 piles of whole tires and no more than 18 piles of shredded tires. The allowed pile size is 200 ft × 50 ft × 15 ft.

For further information contact Paul Benedum, Department of Commerce, labor and Environmental Resources, Division of Natural Resources, Waste Management Section, 1356 Hansford Street, Charleston, West Virginia 25301, telephone 304-348-6350.

Wyoming

HB 213 was passed, amending the Solid Waste Management Act for solid waste storage and treatment facilities.

- Specific provisions for tires (defined as solid waste) were made to set reasonable amounts for storage of tires at retail stores, collection centers, landfills, etc.
- Bonding and location requirements were established and a permitting system for solid waste facilities was put in place.
- The accumulation of waste (including tires) prior to disposal was limited.

For further information contact Diane Hogle, Department of Environmental Quality, Division of Solid Waste, 122 West 25th Street, Cheyenne, Wyoming 82002, telephone 307-777-7752.

Tables 18.4 and 18.5 summarize, by state, the status of scrap tire legislation and the content of the laws, respectively.

TABLE 18.4   Status Report of Scrap Tire Legislation*

State	Draft*	Prop.	Regs.	Law	State	Draft	Prop.	Regs.	Law
Alabama	•				Montana				
Alaska					Nebraska				•
Arizona				•	Nevada				
Arkansas	•				New Hampshire			•	
California				•	New Jersey				
Colorado			•		New Mexico				•
Connecticut			•		New York		•	•	
Delaware					North Carolina				•
Florida				•	North Dakota				
Georgia					Ohio			•	
Hawaii					Oklahoma				•
Idaho					Oregon				•
Illinois				•	Pennsylvania			•	
Indiana				•	Rhode Island				•
Iowa				•	South Carolina		•		
Kansas				•	South Dakota			•	
Kentucky				•	Tennessee			•	
Louisiana				•	Texas			•	
Maine				•	Utah				•
Maryland				•	Vermont			•	
Massachusetts	•	•			Virginia				•
Michigan				•	Washington				•
Minnesota				•	Wisconsin				•
Mississippi	•				West Virginia			•	
Missouri				•	Wyoming			•	

*Draft: Draft being written/bill in discussion; Prop: Proposed/introduced in 1991 legislation; Regs: Regulated under specific provisions of solid waste or other laws (e.g., automotive wastes); Law: Scrap tire law passed.
Source: Scrap Tire News; January 1991.

TABLE 18.5 What the Laws Contain

State	Funding source	Storage regs.	Processor regs.	Hauler regs.	Landfill restrictions*	Market incentives
Arizona	2% sales tax on retail sale		✓		Bans whole tires	
California	$.25/tire disposal fee	✓	✓			Grants
Colorado		✓	✓			
Connecticut		✓				
Florida	$1/tire retail sales	✓	✓	✓	Tires must be cut	R&D grants
Illinois	$.50/vehicle title	✓	✓	✓		Grants/loans
Indiana	Permit fees/tire storage sites	✓			Tires must be cut	Grants
Iowa					Bans whole tires	
Kansas	$.50/tire retail sales	✓	✓	✓	Tires must be cut	Grants
Kentucky	$1/tire retail sales	✓			Tires must be cut	
Louisiana		✓			Tires must be cut	
Maine	$1/tire disposal fee	✓	✓	Draft		Grants/loans
Maryland	State budget appropriations	✓	✓	✓		
Michigan	$.50/vehicle title fee	✓	✓	✓		Grants
Minnesota	$4/vehicle title transfer	✓	✓	✓	Bans whole and cut tires	Grants
Missouri	$.50/tire retail sales	✓		✓	Bans whole tires	Funds/testing
Nebraska	$1/tire retail sales					Grants
New Hampshire	Town graduated vehicle registration fee	✓				

18.63

TABLE 18.5 What the Laws Contain (*Continued*)

State	Funding source	Storage regs.	Processor regs.	Hauler regs.	Landfill restrictions*	Market incentives
North Carolina	1% sales tax on new tires	✓	✓	✓	Tires must be cut	Funds county tire collection
Ohio					Tires must be cut	
Oklahoma	$1/tire surcharge new tire sales	✓	✓		Tires must be cut	Grants
Oregon	$1/tire disposal tax on new tire sales	✓	✓	✓	Tires must be cut	$.01/lb.
Pennsylvania		✓				R&D grants
Rhode Island	$.50/tire tax on new tire sales	✓	✓			
South Dakota		✓	✓		Tires must be cut	
Tennessee					Bans whole tires	
Texas		✓			Bans whole tires	
Utah	Graduated tax per tire size					$20/ton
Vermont					Tires must be cut	
Virginia	$.50/tire disposal fee on new tire sales					Funds/testing
Washington	$1/vehicle registration	✓	✓	✓		Grants
Wisconsin	$2/tire per vehicle title fee	✓	✓	✓	Tires must be cut	$20/ton

*Majority of states have imposed regulations that require tires to be cut, sliced, or shredded prior to landfilling. Some allow for above-ground storage of shreds at landfills. Ohio, North Carolina, and Colorado are considering or allowing monofills for tire shreds. Whole tires are discouraged from landfills in most cases by law or by high disposal fees.

Source: *Scrap Tire News,* January 1991.

CHAPTER 19
BATTERIES

Ann Patchak Adams
Project Leader
Roy F. Weston, Inc.
Detroit, Michigan

C. Kenna Amos, Jr., P.E.*
Former Technical Director
Roy F. Weston, Inc.
Detroit, Michigan

INTRODUCTION

The disposal of batteries has become an ever-increasing topic of discussion in the last few years due to the presence of heavy metals such as mercury, lead, and cadmium in those batteries. In response to these concerns, there has been an increase in battery collection programs and legislation controlling the production and disposal of batteries. This brings forward some key questions, What is a battery and why has its disposal become such an issue? What is the impact of the disposal of batteries on the environment? What are the mechanisms for removing batteries from municipal solid waste (MSW), and what do we do with the batteries once they have been removed?

To answer these questions it is best to distinguish between lead-acid automotive-type batteries and typical household-type batteries that are used in consumer items such as flashlights, radios, and watches, because the means by which these two types of batteries are handled and disposed of are quite different. This chapter attempts to answer these questions and, in turn, discuss the major issues concerning the collection of batteries.

DEFINITION AND COMPONENTS OF BATTERIES

A battery is an electrochemical device that has the ability to convert chemical energy to electrical energy. The basic battery consists of an anode (negative electrode), a cathode (positive electrode), and an electrolyte (a liquid solution through which an electric current can travel) (Fig. 19.1). The potentially hazard-

---

*Currently with ENSR Consulting and Engineering, Fort Collins, Colorado.

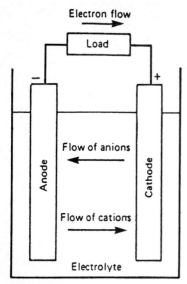

FIGURE 19.1 Electrochemical operation of a battery cell. (*Linden, 1984*)

ous components of batteries include mercury, lead, copper, zinc, cadmium, manganese, nickel, and lithium. These components serve various functions; mercury, for example, is most commonly used to coat the zinc electrodes to reduce corrosion and thereby enhance battery performance.[34]

Lead-Acid Batteries

The lead-acid battery, also known as a wet battery, is typically used in automobiles and other motor vehicles. Most automotive lead-acid batteries contain sulfuric acid and approximately 18 lb of lead.[34] The smaller lead-acid batteries are used in items such as video camcorders and power tools.

Household-Type Batteries

The household battery industry is estimated to be a $2.5 billion industry[27] with annual sales of nearly 3 billion batteries.[10] These batteries, also known as dry cells, are used in over 900 million battery-operated devices. The average family owns about 10 such devices and purchases approximately 32 batteries per year.[27] There are two basic types of household batteries: single-use primary cells and rechargeable secondary cells.[27]

There are five common primary-cell batteries: alkaline-manganese, carbon-zinc, mercuric-oxide, zinc-air, and silver-oxide (Fig. 19.2 and Table 19.1). The alkaline-manganese battery (Fig. 19.3) is the most common and is used in items such as flashlights, toys, radios, cameras, and some appliances. Typically these batteries come in sizes AAA, AA, C, D, and 9-V. Until 1989, the typical alkaline

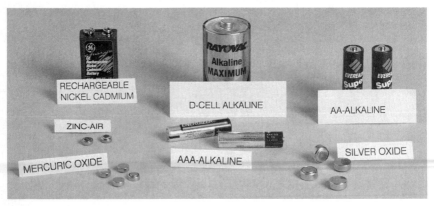

FIGURE 19.2 Typical household batteries.

TABLE 19.1 Common Household Batteries: Types, Components, Sizes, and Uses

Popular types and sizes	Cathode (negative electrode)	Anode (positive electrode)	Electrolyte	Common uses
Alkaline: 9-V, D, C, AA, AAA, button	Manganese dioxide	Zinc	Alkaline solution	Cassettes, radio, etc.
Carbon-zinc: 9-V, D, C, AA, AAA; Heavy-duty carbon-zinc: 9-V, D, C, AA, AAA	Manganese dioxide	Zinc	Ammonium and/or chloride; Zinc chloride	Flashlights, toys, etc.
Lithium: 9-V, C, AA, coin and button	Various metal oxides	Lithium	Organic solvent or salt solution	Cameras, calculators, watches
Mercury: D, C, AA, AAA, button, some cylindrical	Mercuric-oxide	Zinc	Alkaline solution	Hearing aids, pacemakers, photography
Nickel-cadmium: 9-V, D, C, AA, AAA	Nickel-oxide	Cadmium	Alkaline solution	Photography, power tools
Silver: button	Silver-oxide	Zinc	Alkaline solution	Hearing aids, watches, photography
Zinc: button	Oxygen	Zinc	Alkaline solution	Hearing aids, pagers

Source: Information reprinted from Minnesota Pollution Control Agency, "Household Batteries in Minnesota: Interim Report of the Household Battery Recycling and Disposal Study." March 1989, reprinted from Linden, 1984.

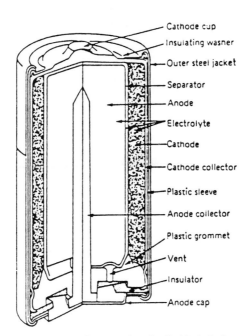

FIGURE 19.3 Cross section of cylindrical alkaline–manganese dioxide cell. (*Figure reprinted from MPCA, 1990, who reprinted the figure originally with courtesy of Duracell, Inc.*)

19.3

battery contained up to 1 percent mercury, by weight of each battery. During 1990, at least three large domestic battery manufacturers began manufacturing and marketing alkaline batteries with less than 0.025 percent mercury, by weight of each battery.[22] These newly marketed alkaline batteries contain approximately one-tenth of the amount of mercury contained in the typical alkaline batteries.[8] The National Electrical Manufacturers Association (NEMA) estimates that 4.25 alkaline-manganese batteries are sold per capita per year.[22]

The carbon-zinc battery (Fig. 19.4), similar to the alkaline battery, is available in the same sizes as the alkaline-manganese battery. These batteries contain up to 0.01 percent mercury, by weight of each battery.[8] NEMA estimates that 3.25 carbon-zinc batteries are sold per capita per year.[22]

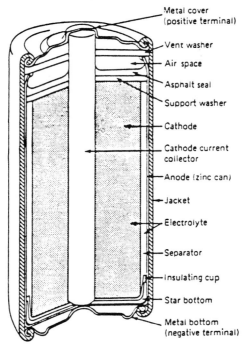

FIGURE 19.4   Cross section of a carbon-zinc cell. (*Linden, 1984*)

The mercuric-oxide battery (Fig. 19.5) is most typically marketed in a small button shape and is used in hearing aids, medical devices, calculators, wrist watches, and cameras. This battery has a positive electrode material, which is mercuric oxide, and contains 35 to 50 percent mercury, by weight of each battery.[24]

The zinc-air battery (Fig. 19.5) was developed to replace the mercuric-oxide battery used in hearing-aid devices. The positive electrode for these batteries is oxygen taken from the air. The mercury content has been significantly reduced from that of the mercuric-oxide battery to approximately 2 percent, by weight of each battery.[8]

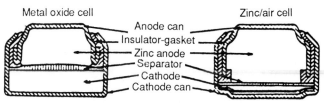

FIGURE 19.5   Cross section of metal-oxide and zinc-air button cells.
(*Linden, 1984*)

The silver-oxide battery (Fig. 19.5) is used most commonly in calculators,
watches, and cameras. Its positive electrode material is silver oxide. This type of
battery contains less than 1 percent mercury, by weight of each battery.[8]

The lithium battery comes in many shapes and sizes but most are marketed in
a small button or cylindrical shape (Fig. 19.6) and are used most commonly in
cameras, watches, memory back-up systems, and in many industrial and military
applications. The positive electrode is lithium and a variety of materials are used
for the negative electrode: sulfur dioxide, manganese dioxide, and carbon
monofluoride to name a few.[15] The manganese dioxide is the most common type
of consumer battery. Lithium batteries are known for their long shelf life, which
is up to 10 years. Two issues currently limit the increased marketing of lithium
batteries. First is the development of a cost-effective consumer battery that could
compete with alkaline batteries. Second is the fact that lithium is a combustible
material in water, which raises concerns about consumer safety.

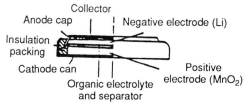

FIGURE 19.6   Cross section of lithium manganese dioxide flat cell. (*MPCA, 1990, who printed drawing with
courtesy of Duracell, Inc.*)

The most common secondary-cell or rechargeable battery is the nickel-
cadmium battery (Fig. 19.7 and Table 19.1), which is commonly found in rechargeable appliances. The negative and positive electrodes are cadmium and
nickel-oxide, respectively. These batteries are 17 percent cadmium, by weight of
each battery.[22]

BATTERIES AND HEAVY METALS IN THE ENVIRONMENT

In a report prepared for the U.S. Environmental Protection Agency (EPA),
Franklin Associates[10] estimated that in 1986, approximately 941,000 tons of lead

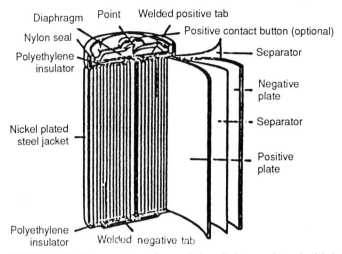

FIGURE 19.7 Cross section of a sealed, coiled-type, sintered nickel-cadmium cell. (*Reprinted from Mercury Refining Company, Inc., "Household Battery Information Package," 1989*)

were used in the production of batteries. It is also estimated that 78 percent of the 941,000 tons (700,000 tons) of lead, from approximately 78 million batteries, was discarded. Of the total amount of lead discarded, 562,000 tons were reclaimed and 138,000 tons from approximately 15 million batteries were discarded in the MSW stream (Tables 19.2 and Fig. 19.8). The disposal of lead-acid batteries produces approximately 65 percent of the lead in the MSW stream.

TABLE 19.2   Lead and Cadmium Discarded in MSW 1970 to 2000

	Year		
	1970	1986	2000
Lead from lead-acid batteries, in short tons	83,825	138,043	181,546
Percent of total lead discards	50.9	64.6	64.4
Cadmium from household batteries, in short tons	53	930	2,035
Percent of total cadmium discard	4.4	52	75.8

Source: Franklin, 1989.

The amount of lead consumed in the production of batteries is expected to increase through the year 2000,[10] by approximately 28 percent over 1986 production levels, to 1.2 million tons in the year 2000 (Fig. 19.8 and Table 19.3).

In 1986, the U.S. consumption of cadmium was 4800 tons.[10] Of the cadmium consumed in 1986, 26 percent of the 4800 tons (1268 tons) of cadmium was used in the production of batteries. It is also estimated that 73 percent of the 1268 tons (930 tons) of cadmium entered the MSW stream (Tables 19.2 and Fig. 19.9). The

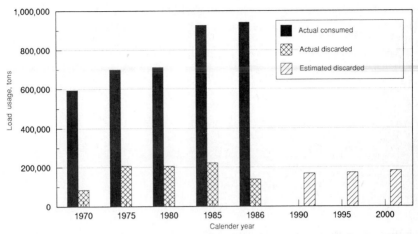

FIGURE 19.8 Lead usage in the United States for consumer battery production. (*From "Characterization of Products Containing Lead and Cadmium in Municipal Solid Waste," Franklin Associates, 1989*)

TABLE 19.3 Lead, Cadmium, and Mercury Consumed in the Production of Batteries (in short tons)

	Year		
	1970	1986	2000
Lead used in lead-acid batteries*	593,453	941,155	1,240,000†
Cadmium used in nickel-cadmium batteries*	167	1268	2285
Mercury used in batteries‡	753§	695	62¶

*Information provided from "Characterization of Products Containing Lead and Cadmium in Municipal Solid Waste in the United States, 1970–2000," Franklin Associates, Ltd., January 1989.
†Data extrapolated from 1986 data. ‡Information provided by the National Electrical Manufacturing Association (NEMA). §1983 data used; 1970 data not available. ¶1990 data used; 2000 data not available.

disposal of nickel-cadmium batteries into the MSW stream accounts for 52 percent of total cadmium entering the MSW stream each year.[10]

The amount of cadmium consumed in the production of batteries is also expected to increase through the year 2000[10] by approximately 80 percent over 1986 production levels, to 2285 tons in year 2000 (Figs. 19.8 and 19.9).

In 1988, the U.S. consumption of mercury was 1755 tons. Of the mercury consumed in 1988, 13 percent of the 1755 tons (225 tons) was used in the production of batteries. Of that 225 tons, approximately 73 percent (173 tons) is estimated to have been used in the production of mercuric-oxide batteries. Of the 173 tons used in mercuric-oxide batteries, approximately 126 tons were used in nonconsumer batteries (i.e., medical, military, and other industrial applications). Therefore, at least 56 percent of the mercury used in the production of batteries is used in nonhousehold-type batteries. One would assume that essentially all of

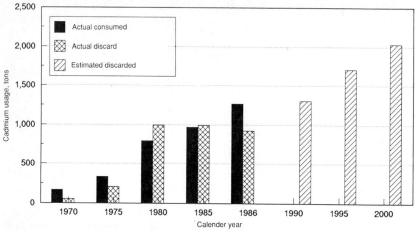

FIGURE 19.9   Cadmium usage in the United States for consumer battery production. (*From "Characterization of Products Containing Lead and Cadmium in Municipal Solid Waste, Franklin Associates, 1989*)

the mercury from household batteries enters the MSW stream, and an unknown amount of mercury from nonconsumer batteries enters the MSW stream.

Unlike lead and cadmium, the amount of mercury consumed in the production of batteries is expected to continue to decrease. In 1983, the mercury consumed in the production of batteries was 753 tons; in 1988 mercury consumption decreased to 225 tons and is estimated to decrease to 62 tons in 1990 (Table 19.3 and Fig. 19.10).[22] No further projections on future mercury consumption are available. However, Franklin Associates, Ltd., is preparing a report for the EPA

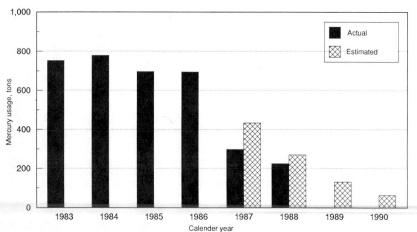

FIGURE 19.10   Mercury usage in the United States for consumer battery production. (*From the National Electrical Manufacturing Association (NEMA) 1987 and 1988 surveys*)

which will characterize mercury-containing products in MSW. This report is expected to be released in 1991.

Most household batteries are disposed of in MSW and are sent to either a sanitary type II landfill or to a municipal waste combustion (MWC) facility.[26] A smaller number of batteries are sent to a composting facility. The metals' contribution to the environment from the incineration, landfilling, or composting of household batteries will pose different concerns, depending upon the method of disposal.

Understanding the environmental fate of metals contributed by batteries in a landfill is a function of the conditions of the batteries when landfilled and the conditions of the landfill itself. The casings of household batteries are most commonly made of paper, plastic, or metal. The various conditions that can develop in a landfill affect the rate at which the casings will degrade or decompose. A 1978 study conducted in England[14] indicated that the following conditions affect the rate of degradation: the nature of the casing; the degree of electrical charge left in the battery; the extent of exposure to landfill leachate; and the oxygen content of the landfill.[18] The mobility of the metals in a landfill and the potential for groundwater contamination are also controlled by numerous conditions. These conditions include the design, construction, operation, and maintenance of the landfill (e.g., the liner, soil characteristics, leachate collection-and-detection systems, daily cover, final cover, etc.).

The release of metals from a battery in a landfill may not however, in and of itself, be problematic. The principal issue is the potential for those metals to contaminate groundwater, which is a function of the landfill's construction, its soil characteristics, and its proximity to groundwater.

The incineration of batteries also poses two major potential environmental concerns. The first is the release of metals into the ambient air, and the second is the concentration of metals in the ash that must be landfilled. Generally, mercury is more likely to be emitted in the stack gas and cadmium and lead will concentrate in the ash.[18] The fate of metals released from batteries during incineration is mainly a function of the boiler combustion temperature, the metals' volatilization temperature, and the presence of other nonmetallic compounds.[18]

The fate of metals in the ash, once landfilled, will be the same as those previously stated for landfills. However, the ash from many incinerators is disposed of in monocells (also known as monofills or landfills that accept only MWC ash). According to an EPA study, it appears that leachate from these facilities and even from codisposal facilities (i.e., where MSW and ash are landfilled together) is nonhazardous and predominantly less potentially harmful than the MSW-only landfill leachate.

Composting is the process of changing MSW into a humuslike (i.e., soil-like) product. Of the three disposal methods, composting is the least used method of disposal, although its use is increasing. The environmental concerns associated with composting are the quality of the humuslike product and the limitation on the uses of the humus. Also, potentially objectionable odors are produced. According to the Minnesota Pollution Control Agency (MPCA) report, *Household Batteries in Minnesota,*[18] most composting facilities sort the MSW prior to composting to minimize the amount of metals in the compost. The MPCA noted that batteries do not appear to pose a composting problem for facilities that manually and mechanically sort the MSW. However, for those facilities which only manually sort the MSW, there is a higher probability that because of their size, the small button batteries will not be removed from the compost material. The

MPCA estimated that two mercury button batteries in a kilogram of compost contain enough mercury to limit the end use of the humus.

One difficulty in determining the impact of the metals contained in the batteries on the environment is that the requirements for pollution control at landfills and MWCs are becoming increasingly more stringent. Also, pollutant measurement and risk assessment analyses are being refined. Consequently, landfill leachate data may be from landfills that were constructed years earlier and, therefore, may not reflect the more recent stringent design-and-construction regulations now imposed upon the owners and/or operators of landfills. In addition, it is often difficult to establish that the leachate was contaminated with heavy metals specifically from batteries. Similarly, air emissions data from MWCs may not necessarily reflect either the state-of-the-art air pollution control technologies that are still being researched or completely accurate and precise emissions data.

LEAD-ACID BATTERIES

Attitudes toward recycling batteries vary significantly among the participants. The consensus among interested parties, industry, legislators, municipalities, independent researchers, consultants, and nonprofit organizations, seems to be that it is beneficial to reclaim lead-acid batteries. The Battery Council International (BCI) has developed model legislation to be used by states in developing a lead-battery collection program (see Appendix A). NEMA and the Battery Products Alliance (BPA) have also developed model legislation to assist individual states in their recycling efforts for small, nonvehicular lead-acid and nickel-cadmium batteries.[17]

The main provisions of the BCI model legislation are as follows: (1) Any person is prohibited from disposing of a lead-acid battery into mixed MSW. (2) Each battery improperly disposed of constitutes a violation subject to a fine. (3) And there is also a take-back provision, stipulating that any person selling lead-acid batteries must accept used lead-acid batteries and post written notices indicating that batteries can be returned.

As of June 1990, in the United States, 28 states have enacted disposal prohibitions for lead-acid batteries (Fig. 19.11) and 25 states have mandatory take-back provisions for lead-acid batteries (Fig. 19.12).

Various states have enacted legislation controlling the disposal of lead-acid batteries. In March 1990, the state of Michigan enacted Public Act Number 20, to govern the disposal of lead-acid batteries and to establish a legislative committee to review the effectiveness of the lead-acid battery regulations. The main provisions of Michigan Act Number 20 pertaining to the disposal of lead-acid batteries are the following:

1. A person shall dispose of a lead-acid battery only at a retailer, distributor, manufacturer, or collection center.
2. Retailers of lead-acid batteries must post a written notice indicating that spent batteries are accepted for recycling.
3. Beginning January 1, 1993, a purchaser of a lead-acid battery must exchange a used lead-acid battery for the battery purchased or pay the retailer a $6.00 deposit.

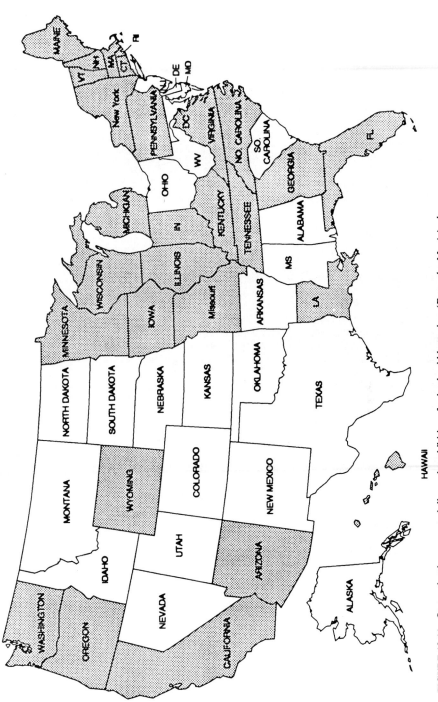

FIGURE 19.11 States that have enacted disposal prohibitions for lead-acid batteries. (*From the Municipal Solid Waste Program, OSWER, EPA, 1990*)

19.11

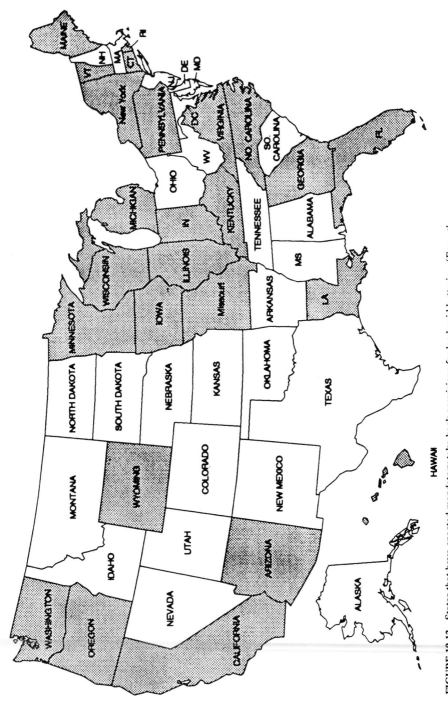

FIGURE 19.12 States that have enacted mandatory take-back provisions for lead-acid batteries. (*From the Municipal Solid Waste Program OSWER, EPA, 1990*)

19.12

The legislative committee submitted a report in December 1990, evaluating the lead-acid battery disposal programs and concluded that no changes are currently necessary to the existing management of lead-acid batteries and that the effectiveness of this program should be reviewed again before December 3, 1993.

Most lead-acid batteries are collected at local automotive service or repair garages. Some of these batteries are collected through local household hazardous-waste collection programs operated by local governments. Overall, the collection and recycling efforts for lead-acid batteries appear to have been successful.[25] The lead-acid battery collection and recycling programs tend to be successful because the automotive garages and repair centers serve as centralized collection points. Additionally, there is no or very little inconvenience caused to the consumer. Ultimately, the primary motivation for the recovery of automobile batteries is profit from the sale of lead.[34]

According to EPA estimates, approximately 80 percent of lead-acid batteries are being reclaimed. The batteries are collected by battery distributors and are then transported to reclamation centers where lead and polypropylene are recovered, generating a toxic residue that requires special disposal. Recycling technologies are developing in which the lead, polypropylene, and sulfuric acid will be recovered with a resulting nontoxic residue.

There currently are no formal domestic programs for collecting small lead-acid batteries. Consequently, it is difficult to determine the number of these batteries that are being recycled and their contribution of lead to the environment. It is reasonable to assume that the disposal and recycling rates for small lead-acid batteries purchased for home use parallels the disposal and recycling patterns of other household batteries.

HOUSEHOLD BATTERIES

Attitudes Toward Recycling Household Batteries

A consensus on the collection of household batteries has not developed as quickly as for lead-acid batteries. Attitudes toward recycling household batteries vary from no recycling to recycling a limited number of batteries (specifically mercuric-oxide and nickel-cadmium) to recycling all types of household batteries.

For years, the battery industry has maintained that consumer disposal of batteries into municipal landfills and MWCs does not pose a hazard to human health or the environment. Regardless of the battery industry's position, the industry has responded to public concerns regarding the disposal of batteries. Low-level mercury-alkaline batteries and hearing-aid (zinc-air) batteries have been developed. Additionally, NEMA and BPA are developing model legislation which would require that nickel-cadmium batteries be removed from appliances and that these batteries then be collected.[1] The battery industry's response to concerns regarding the disposal of batteries eventually will redefine the issues associated with battery collection programs.

Program managers for the Hennepin County, Minnesota, Battery Collection-and-Recycling Program and New Hampshire/Vermont Solid Waste Project have outlined an approach that reflects the NEMA-proposed legislation and the policies being adopted in Europe by the European Economic Community (EEC).[13]

They concluded that, instead of collecting all types of household batteries, mercury and cadmium can be more effectively removed from the MSW stream through the following:

1. Legislation that would limit the amount of mercury in alkaline batteries to 0.025 percent, by weight of each battery.
2. Efforts focused on recycling button batteries and larger mercuric-oxide batteries, rather than all household batteries.
3. Legislation which would require that rechargeable batteries be removed from appliances.

The EEC-NEMA approach indicates that battery collection programs will need to be established to collect the nickel-cadmium and button-size batteries. Concern has been expressed that the button batteries are not well labeled. Consequently, programs that target button batteries will have difficulty separating reclaimable mercury-oxide and silver-oxide batteries from lithium and other batteries that cannot be reclaimed.

Most battery programs in the United States, however, are designed to collect all types of batteries (Table 19.4). Switzerland similarly has recently developed legislation that requires the separate collection and recycling of all household batteries regardless of the toxicity. Sumitomo, a Japanese company that has developed a pilot facility for reclaiming metals from all household batteries, has recently been awarded a contract to develop a 2000-ton/day recycling facility in Switzerland.[32]

Another prevalent attitude is that more effort should be placed on and directed toward collecting batteries utilized by industry, hospitals, the utilities, the military, and the communications market. Examples of these types of batteries include power supplies for mainframe computers, emergency lighting, battery-operated medical tools, medical monitoring devices such as the Holter heart monitor, back-up battery systems for radio and television broadcasts, and police radios. Under the federal Resource Conservation and Recovery Act (RCRA) batteries collected from these sources would be classified as a hazardous waste and, consequently, are subject to transport, storage, and disposal requirements (Subtitle C requirements). Consequently, few household battery collection programs have targeted these batteries. The contribution of heavy metals to the environment from these sectors is unknown.

As an alternative to voluntary battery collection programs, advocates of battery recycling have suggested placing a refundable deposit on batteries, similar to that required for aluminum and glass beverage containers. Requiring a refundable deposit appears to be becoming a common practice for lead-acid batteries and is being reflected in much of the recently drafted and enacted legislation. A refundable deposit on household batteries, however, is more complex than a deposit on lead-acid batteries. A deposit on household batteries requires that the following questions be addressed:

1. Who will pay for collection containers, collection, and disposal of the batteries?
2. At which point, if any, in the collection process will the batteries become classified as a hazardous waste?
3. What types of precautions, if any, will the collectors (i.e., retail stores) have to consider to accommodate the volume of returned batteries?

TABLE 19.4 1990 Household Battery Collection Programs

Battery collection program	Contact	Type of collection program	Type of batteries collected	Management of batteries
AL-Huntsville	Karen Schoening 205-880-6054	Curbside, with recyclables	All types	Will be landfilled in a HW landfill
FL-Gainesville	James Abbott 904-495-9215	Drop off rural SW collection centers and at HHW collection days	All types	Seal in concrete and store up to one year in 55 gallon drums before sending to municipal solid waste landfill
KS-Overland Park	Ron Tubb 913-381-5252	Drop off at 6 retail stores	Button batteries	MERECO
KY-Louisville	Ray Hilbrand 502-625-2788	Pilot drop off at recycling center	All types	Sent by Waste Management of Kentucky to a HW incinerator
MI-Detroit	Phil Brown 313-876-0449	Drop off at recycling centers and neighborhood City Halls	All types	Combination of landfilling and reclamation
MI-SOCRRA	Tom Waffen 313-288-5150	Libraries, school recycling centers and curbside pickup	All types	Combination of landfilling and reclamation
MN-Minneapolis	Mark Oyaas 612-348-6157	Curbside with recyclables, and drop off at retail stores	All types	Sorted by type, placed in 55 gallon containers, then hauled to HW landfill
MO-23 counties	Marie Steinwachs 417-836-5777	Drop off at retail stores	Button batteries	MERECO
NH/VT-28 towns	Carl Hirth 603-543-1201	Drop off at transfer stations, municipal offices and retail stores	All types	Sent to HW landfill in South Carolina
NJ-Warren County	Mary Briggs 201-453-2174	Drop off at municipal offices, recycling centers in 14 communities, curbside in 9 communities	All types	Buttons, lithium, and nicads go to MERECO and all others go HW landfill
NJ-Somerset County	Mike Elka 201-231-7031	Curbside with recyclables—4 times per year	All types	Batteries are stored in plastic lined barrels for 90 days then sent by HW contractor to HW landfill

Legislation Affecting the Collection of Household Batteries

Currently, there are no federal regulations governing the collection, recycling, or disposal of household batteries. However, a few states have adopted legislation controlling the disposal of batteries.

In April 1990, the Minnesota State Legislature enacted a law (Minnesota Stat-

19.15

TABLE 19.4   1990 Household Battery Collection Programs (*Continued*)

Battery collection program	Contact	Type of collection program	Type of batteries collected	Management of batteries
NY-Little Valley	Richard Preston 716-938-9121	Drop off at transfer stations, curbside, looking to expand stores	All types	MERECO
NY-New York City	Sean Hecht 212-677-1601	Drop off at retail stores	Buttons and Nicads	Only storing until check on MERECO's status
NY-Poestenkill	Lois Fisher 518-283-5100	Drop off at landfill/recycling center	All types	MERECO
NY-Rochester	Alice Young 716-244-5824	Drop off in municipal buildings and retail stores	Button batteries	MERECO
NY-Rye	Frank Culross 914-967-7604	Drop off at DPW recycling center	All types	MERECO
NY-Scarsdale	Jim Rice 914-723-3300	Drop off at recycling center and incinerator	All types	MERECO
NY-Slingerlands	Mike Hotaling 518-765-2681	Drop off at highway garage	All types	MERECO
NY-Southold	Jim Bunchuck 516-734-7685	Drop off at retail stores	All types	MERECO
NY-Woodstock	Bill Reich 914-679-6570	Drop off at recycling center and retail stores	All types	MERECO
PA-Pottstown	Jim Crater 215-323-8545	Drop off at community recycling center	Button and Alkaline	MERECO
VA-Chesapeake	Jennifer Ladd 804-420-4700	Curbside	All types	Tidewater Fiber is storing, plan to send to MERECO
WA-Bellingham	Lisa Schnebele 206-384-1057	Drop off at recycling center and retail stores	All types	Alkaline and carbon-zinc sent to hazardous waste landfill in Oregon, all others to MERECO

Source: Dana Duxbury & Associates, November 1990.

ute 115 A.9155) regulating used dry-cell batteries (see Appendix B). The provisions of the law include the following:

1. Individuals are prohibited from placing into the MSW stream mercuric-oxide, silver-oxide, nickel-cadmium, or sealed lead-acid batteries purchased for use by a government agency, or an industrial, communications, or medical facility.

2. The manufacturer of a button-cell battery has to ensure that each battery is clearly identifiable as to the type of electrode (i.e., mercuric-oxide, zinc-oxide, or silver-oxide) used in the battery.

3. After February 1, 1992, alkaline batteries with a mercury concentration greater than 0.025 percent, by weight of battery, cannot be sold.

4. After January 1, 1992, button-cell batteries with a mercury concentration greater than 25 mg cannot be sold.

5. After July 1, 1993, a manufacturer (excluding exemptions) may not sell, distribute, or offer for sale a rechargeable consumer product unless the battery can be removed.

The state of Michigan through Public Act Number 20, in addition to the lead-acid requirements, required the joint legislative committee to study safe use and disposal of nickel-cadmium and mercury batteries. In a December 1990 report, the legislative committee developed some recommendations that paralleled the requirements of the Minnesota legislation, namely:

1. All batteries must be removable from the products or devices in which they are used.

2. As of January 1, 1992, the mercury content of alkaline and carbon zinc household batteries must be less than 0.025 percent, by weight of each battery.

Through the EEC, some states in Europe have issued a proposal that is expected to become law in January 1992, to control the manufacturing and disposal of household batteries. Some of the key provisions include a ban on batteries containing more than 30 percent mercury, by weight of each battery, and a ban on alkaline batteries containing more than 0.025 percent mercury, by weight of each battery. The EEC proposal would also require that batteries be removed from products and that EEC states establish separate collection, disposal, and recycling programs.

It is reasonable to assume that as more states and countries adopt legislation requiring batteries with lower levels of mercury and easy removal of rechargeable batteries, that lower-level mercury batteries and removable nickel-cadmium batteries will become the most widely available, if not the only, household batteries available on the market.

Establishing a Battery Recycling Program

Although the removal of batteries from the MSW stream prior to disposal by landfilling or incineration may be desirable, there are many issues to consider:

1. Do all batteries need to be removed? If not, which ones?

2. Who should remove the batteries?

3. What is the best approach for removing the batteries?

4. Who should pay for the battery removal program?

5. What is the most cost-effective means for removing the batteries from the MSW stream?

6. What should be done with the batteries?

7. Will the ultimate disposal of the batteries be environmentally sound?

These questions must be answered prior to establishing a successful battery collection program.

The recycling efforts for household batteries are not as well developed as those for lead-acid batteries. The following discussion describes approaches to establishing a household-type battery collection program.

Prior to developing a recycling program, the first step is to determine the types of batteries to be collected. The types of batteries collected will affect public relations strategies, locations of collection centers, types of collection containers, and final disposal. Three of the more common collection strategies include (1) only button batteries; (2) button batteries and nickel-cadmium batteries; and (3) mixed batteries (i.e., button, nickel-cadmium, carbon-zinc, and alkaline batteries). Another fundamental step in developing a recycling program is thorough knowledge of local, state, and federal regulations for collection, transport, storage, and disposal of batteries. This preliminary research must precede the design of the battery collection program. These regulations are often different in each state and can be ambiguous; however, at the federal level, it is clear that wastes generated in a household are nonhazardous (i.e., Subtitle D wastes) and/or exempt from RCRA regulations for transport, storage, and disposal (i.e., the Subtitle C requirements).

Prior to starting a battery collection program, it is essential to know the state regulations controlling the collection of batteries. In the state of Michigan, household batteries are classified as nonhazardous from collection to disposal. However, in the state of Minnesota, batteries are regulated as a hazardous waste, at the last point of consolidation prior to disposal.[30] Classification of household batteries as a hazardous waste will control the manner in which the batteries are transported, stored, and disposed.

After completing the preliminary research, the next step in developing a battery collection program is to develop a public relations program for education and awareness. The following is a list of potential promotion strategies:

1. Develop a theme and logo.
2. Establish frequency of promotions.
3. Develop newsletters, posters, and notices.
4. Utilize public service announcements (PSAs), TV, radio, print, school-education programs, retail advertisements, and community groups.

The third step is to establish battery collection centers, which could occur simultaneously with the development of the public awareness program. The various options that exist appear to be a function of the type of batteries to be collected. The New Hampshire/Vermont Solid Waste Project, which is responsible for a rural area of 38 towns, with a total population of 75,000, targets all types of batteries. As collection centers, this program uses retail stores that sell dry-cell batteries, town offices, and transfer station–recycling drop-off centers. The city of Detroit, Michigan, program, which also targets all types of batteries, uses 12 neighborhood city halls, fire stations, police stations, schools, and neighborhood recycling centers. The Hennepin County, Minnesota, pilot program uses both curbside pick-up and retail stores as collection centers for all types of discarded, spent batteries. The Environmental Action Coalition (EAC) program in New York City focuses on button batteries and uses physicians' offices, hearing-aid centers, and retail stores selling watches and cameras as the collection centers. The EAC program has recently been expanded to include nickel-cadmium batteries and uses retail stores as collection centers. Experience gained in the Hennepin County program indicated that curbside recycling was six times more successful for total number of batteries collected than the retail store drop-off method. Conversely, in the collection of button batteries, EAC indicates that retail stores and physicians' offices appear to have been more successful as collection centers.[7]

Determining who will collect the batteries is often a function of the types of collection centers used. For example, those programs which use retail stores as collection centers have often utilized volunteer groups, neighborhood block clubs, League of Women Voters, senior citizens, Boy Scouts, Girl Scouts, etc., to collect and sort batteries. The city of Detroit has used the city mail trucks to perform two services: deliver-collect mail and pick up batteries. In Hennepin County, officials negotiated with the organization collecting the other curbside recyclables to also collect the batteries. EAC tried two different approaches: retail stores were provided with mail-back containers that could be mailed to EAC when filled; or EAC staff or volunteers collected the batteries. EAC indicated that there was more response when EAC collected the batteries because less effort was required by the retail stores.

There are various containers that are acceptable for the collection of batteries. For individuals to use at home for storage of spent batteries, most programs have small plastic bags printed with a recycling logo, mailed to households. The bags are also placed on display at local drop-off centers. Curbside collection programs use a similar type of resealable plastic bag. Retail store collection centers have also been provided with different sized buckets to store the spent batteries; 2-gal plastic minnow buckets appear to have been particularly successful because they are not too heavy to lift when filled and they have a spring-loaded lid which ensures that the batteries are stored securely (Fig. 19.13). The New Hampshire/ Vermont program uses 5-qt silver-colored buckets. The EAC program uses small cardboard boxes (provided by the Mercury Refining Company in Latham, New York), which have an opening in the lid for disposal of button batteries and a second opening that can accept up to D cell batteries. Citizens are asked to dispose of only rechargeable batteries in this part of the box.

In the development of any recycling program, the frequency and timing of collection must be established and well publicized. The collection schedule may differ at each collection point, and is a function of the type of collection center used and the type of batteries being collected. For programs that utilize retail stores and collect all types of batteries, determining pick-up frequency will require experimentation because some stores will collect more batteries more quickly than others. For programs that utilize retail stores, but collect only button and/or nickel-cadmium batteries, the pickup frequency may be less. In the event more frequent

FIGURE 19.13 Typical battery collection container.

pickups are necessary, all of the collection centers should have a contact with a telephone number who can be called for pick-ups. Pickup in curbside programs will most likely coincide with the collection schedule for other recyclables.

It must be determined how the batteries, once collected, will be stored until a sufficient number of batteries have been collected for economical and efficient disposal. Depending on whether it classifies household batteries as a hazardous or nonhazardous waste, each state will indicate how batteries should or must be stored. For states that classify the batteries as a hazardous waste, the collected batteries may have to be stored in polyethylene 55-gal plastic drums that are corrosion-resistant. A full 55-gal drum can weigh up to 800 lb. In states in which batteries are classified as nonhazardous, although a polypropylene plastic drum may be prudent, the use of any type of container is permitted. The more frequently a collection program disposes of its batteries, the less concern there is over the type of container. Regardless of how batteries are classified, all collected batteries should be stored in an adequately ventilated area with appropriate safety and fire-prevention measures.

When a sufficient number of batteries have been collected, they may be disposed of or recycled. Those batteries being sent for recycling or disposal (i.e., to a landfill) must be transported with U.S. Department of Transportation (DOT) shipping papers. A hazardous waste manifest is required in those states which classify batteries as hazardous waste. As mentioned earlier, each state determines how collected batteries must be handled. Also, note that regardless of how a specific state may classify batteries (i.e., hazardous or nonhazardous waste), the disposal or recycling facility (particularly if it is located in another state) may require the batteries to be packaged and manifested as though they were a hazardous waste.

Disposal and recycling opportunities should be located and contractually established in the initial stages of developing a recycling program. Battery recycling programs are frequently misnamed in that few batteries are actually recycled. At present, the only household batteries that can be recycled (i.e., actually reclaimed or remanufactured) in the United States are silver-oxide, mercuric-oxide, and nickel-cadmium batteries (Table 19.5). Most U.S. companies that accept nickel-cadmium batteries send the batteries to France or Sweden for reclamation. However, one company, Inmetco, located in Ellwood City, Pennsylvania, accepts nickel-cadmium batteries. They extract the nickel and the cadmium is sent to Zinc Corporation of America in Palmerton, Pennsylvania, who manufactures a zinc-cadmium alloy. Currently, there are no companies in the United States that can reclaim the components of alkaline or carbon-zinc batteries. Consequently, most collected batteries currently are deposited in a hazardous waste landfill. Interestingly, batteries in the typical MSW stream are deposited in type II sanitary landfills. The regulatory compliance status of all of the companies listed in Table 19.5 should be investigated prior to use as a disposal facility, in order to ensure that there are no restrictions or environmental problems that could prevent batteries from being sent to these facilities.

The final step in any battery recycling effort is to develop an evaluation program. This evaluation program should include a comparative statistical analysis to other battery collection programs, assessment of the number of households served, percentage of public participation, percentage of types of batteries collected, and strategies to maximize participation. The development of a recycling program can take up to 3 months, and such programs may change frequently based upon periodic evaluation. A timeline of typical activities is shown in Fig. 19.14.

TABLE 19.5   Firms that Accept Waste Batteries for Disposal or Reclamation

Mercury Refining Co., Inc.
(MERECO)
790 Watervliet-Shaker Road
Latham, NY 12110518) 785-1703, (800) 833-3505

Accepts all household batteries. Will pay for mercury-silver. Nickel-cadmium batteries accepted for free. Charge for alkaline and lithium batteries. Mercury and silver-oxide batteries refined on-site, other cells marketed for disposal or reclamation.

Quicksilver Products, Inc.
200 Valley Drive, Suite 1
Brisbane, CA 94005
(415) 468-2000

Accepts mercury batteries. Charge for batteries, depending upon type and volume. Require specific packaging. Currently accept only commercial and industrial batteries. Anticipate accepting household batteries in 1992.

Environmental Pacific Corp.
PO Box 2116
Lake Oswego, OR 97055
(503) 226-7331

Accepts all batteries.

Inmetco
PO Box 720, Rt. 488
Ellwood City, PA 16117
(412) 758-5515

Accepts nickel-cadmium batteries only. Charge for batteries. Extract nickel and send cadmium to Zinc Corporation of America.

Bethlehem Apparatus Co.
890 Front Street, PO Box Y
Hellertown, PA 18055
(215) 838-7034

Accepts mercury batteries.

NIFE
Industrial Boulevard
PO Box 7366
Greenville, NC 27835
(919) 830-1600

Accepts nickel-cadmium batteries only. Charge 0.70¢ per pound. Will accept batteries from household hazardous waste programs as long as there is a guarantee that the batteries are nickel-cadmium. Generator receives certificate of disposal. Batteries are broken up on-site and sent to a plant in Sweden for reclamation of cadmium.

Universal Metals and Ores
Mt. Vernon, NY
(914) 664-0200

Accepts nickel-cadmium batteries only. Pays 0.15¢ per pound for loads over 2000 pounds. Will accept batteries from household hazardous waste programs as long as there is a guarantee that the batteries are nickel-cadmium. Batteries are exported to Asia or Europe for reclamation as long as batteries are dry cells. Batteries can be shipped as a nonhazardous material.

F.W. Hempel & Co., Inc.
1370 Avenue of the Americas
New York, NY 10019
(212) 586-8055

Accepts nickel-cadmium batteries only. Charge for batteries. Will accept batteries from household hazardous waste programs as long as there is a guarantee that the batteries are nickel-cadmium. No processing performed on-site. Batteries are sent to France for processing.

Kinsbursky Brother Supply
1314 N. Lemon Street
Anaheim, CA 92801
(714) 738-8516

Accepts lead-acid and nickel-cadmium batteries. Charge 0.40¢ per pound for nickel-cadmium batteries. Pay for lead-acid batteries depending upon type and quantity of batteries. Will accept batteries from household hazardous waste programs as long as there is a guarantee that the batteries are nickel-cadmium. Lead plate and nickel sent to smelter. Cadmium sent to France. Batteries must be received as a hazardous waste.

BDT
4255 Research Parkway
Clarence, NY 14031
(716) 634-6794

Accepts alkaline and lithium batteries. Charge per pound. Crush, neutralize, and dispose of as hazardous waste.

Source: Information provided by the Environmental Action Coalition, and personal communication with company representatives.

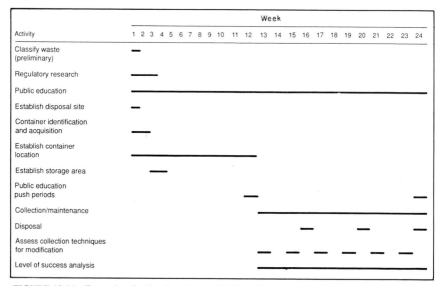

FIGURE 19.14   Example of a timeline for establishing a battery collection program.

The cost for developing a household battery collection program varies significantly based upon the types of batteries collected, the method of collection, and whether the batteries are classified as a hazardous or nonhazardous waste. It may be difficult for municipalities to utilize volunteer labor or to rely upon volunteers for a long-term program, and, consequently, most battery collection programs will have to incur the cost of a program coordinator and staff. Most nonprofit groups, however, cannot afford the costly land disposal fees for mixed batteries and, consequently, may limit their collection to specific types of batteries (e.g., EAC, which collects only button and nickel-cadmium batteries). The most significant expenses will be for transportation, disposal, and salaries. Printing, advertisements, collection containers, storage containers, and storage are often only a small portion of the total cost. The Southeastern Oakland County Resource Recovery Authority (SOCRRA) in Michigan has established a battery collection program.[29] Table 19.6 shows the breakdown of costs for the SOCRRA battery collection program. Because batteries in Michigan are classified as nonhazardous, operating a collection program is less expensive than if the batteries were classified as hazardous. Table 19.7 shows the cost of operating the same program assuming the batteries are classified as a hazardous waste. A reasonable current assumption for the transportation fees for hazardous

TABLE 19.6   Estimated Annual Cost of Battery Collection Program in States That Classify Batteries as Nonhazardous*

Buckets and decals	$600
Flyers	910
Plastic bags	2000
Disposal	2030
Labor	3500
Miscellaneous	675
Total	$9715

*Program for 6000 lb/month servicing area population of 325,000.
Source: Information provided by Tom Waffen, general manager of Southeastern Oakland County Resources Recovery Authority, 1991.

TABLE 19.7 Estimated Annual Cost of Battery Collection
Program in States that Classify Batteries as Hazardous

Buckets and decals	$600
Fliers	910
Plastic bags	2000
Labor	3500
Miscellaneous	675
90 polyethylene drums	5400
Transportation (assume 50 mi @ $4.00/loaded mile)	800
Disposal	2030
Total	$15,915

waste is approximately $4 per loaded mile. Hazardous waste and land-disposal fees for the New Hampshire/Vermont Solid Waste Project are approximately $300 per drum. This rate will likely vary between disposal facilities and from region to region. As can be noted from Tables 19.6 and 19.7, the operation of a battery collection program where the batteries are classified as a hazardous waste is approximately 39 percent more expensive than a collection program where the batteries are classified as a nonhazardous waste.

Household Battery Collection Program Effectiveness

The collection of household batteries requires that the consumer play an active role in the process. The success of any battery collection program will depend, in large part, upon the ability of the public to change its MSW disposal habits, and change is dependent upon education (i.e., public awareness programs). The collection of household batteries has not been successful because of the large volume of batteries used, the lack of public education, the lack of centralized collection centers, and the inability to remove most rechargeable batteries from the appliances in which they are used. The access to rechargeable batteries is a significant issue, because approximately 80 percent of the nickel-cadmium batteries are permanently affixed to an appliance for consumer safety and cannot be removed.[13]

The New Hampshire/Vermont Solid Waste Project began collecting batteries in May 1987. Between May 1987 and October 1990, the New Hampshire/Vermont Solid Waste Project collected more than 13 tons of household batteries.[23] The capture rate of total battery volumes for the project area is estimated to be 18 percent. In May 1990, the Greater Detroit, Michigan, Resource Recovery Authority initiated a battery collection program. From May to November 1990, approximately 10 tons of batteries were collected.[11] The SOCRRA program collects approximately 3 tons a month.[29]

Various countries have been collecting batteries for a number of years. At least 11 European countries, including Sweden and Austria, have initiated battery collection programs. Japan, which has an established recycling program to collect alkaline and carbon-zinc batteries, has experienced less than a 10 percent recovery rate for cylinder-shaped batteries and 27 percent of button-shaped batteries.[34]

Trends in Household Battery Production and Reclamation

Carbon-zinc and alkaline-manganese primary-cell batteries have the largest share of the market. A Duracell study indicated that 75 percent of all the batteries purchased in the United States by 1990 will be alkaline. The sales of carbon-zinc batteries are approximately 20 percent that of alkaline batteries and are declining.[18] The sale of alkaline batteries is expected to continue to grow.

According to the Office of Technology Assessment of the U.S. Congress, the market share for mercuric-oxide batteries between 1981 and 1987 decreased from 72 to 68 percent, while the demand for zinc-air batteries increased from 14 to 40 percent. The sales of silver-oxide batteries have increased slightly. The sales of nickel-cadmium batteries are expected to significantly increase through the year 2000.[10]

There are alternatives to recycling, other than incineration and landfilling. These alternatives include finding substitute materials to replace the heavy metals currently used in batteries. Three domestic battery companies have recently begun marketing low-mercury-level batteries in the United States, as have already been marketed in Europe. Other battery manufacturers will likely develop and market similar batteries. There also is ongoing research by the battery industry to replace lead, mercury, and cadmium in batteries with nickel hydride, rechargeable lithium, and lower amounts of mercury.

As the battery industry seeks substitute materials for the hazardous constituents currently used, there is research by at least two foreign companies (i.e., Sumitomo in Japan, and Recytech, S.A., in Switzerland) to develop recycling technologies for all types of primary-cell household batteries.[9] A configuration of a treatment process is shown in Fig. 19.15. Currently, however, the technology to recycle all types of household batteries has not been developed or used in the United States. As landfill costs continue to increase and additional environmental regulations are enacted, the economic incentives to reclaim battery components are likely to increase.

SUMMARY AND CONCLUSIONS

1. According to EPA studies, approximately 80 percent of the discarded lead-acid batteries are being collected and recycled.

2. The unreclaimed 20 percent of lead-automotive batteries is estimated to contribute approximately 65 percent of the lead found in MSW. Consequently, the federal government and many state governments, with support from the battery industry and trade associations, have proposed legislation mandating the recycling of lead-acid batteries and requiring that the retailers of these batteries collect used batteries.

3. Through enactment of new legislation to ensure that an even higher percentage of lead-acid batteries will be recycled and removed from the MSW stream, the amount of lead found in MSW will decrease, thus decreasing the amount of lead released to the environment.

4. Although most participants in the legislative process agree that the components of lead-acid batteries should be reclaimed, controversy remains about the reclamation of the components of household-type batteries.

5. While the battery industry is researching alternative components to the heavy metals currently used in batteries, the date is unknown as to when these alternative components will be used. Low-level mercuric batteries are already being marketed in the United States.

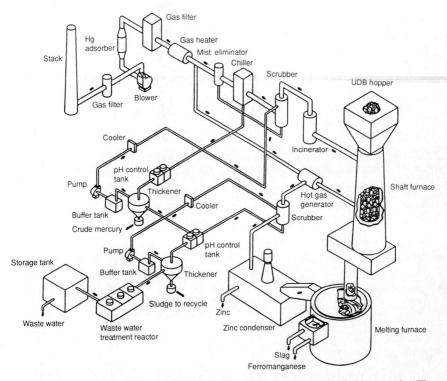

FIGURE 19.15 Configuration of the Sumitomo Treatment Process. (*Fiala-Goldiger et al., "The Status of Battery Recycling in Switzerland," Presented to the Second International Seminar on Battery Waste Management, 1990*)

6. Currently, most batteries collected through household battery collection programs are disposed of in hazardous waste landfills.

7. Currently, there are no recycling facilities in the Unites States that can practically and cost-effectively reclaim all types of household batteries, although domestic facilities that can reclaim button batteries do exist; most nickel-cadmium batteries are being reclaimed in Europe.

8. Although some battery collection programs are directed toward the collection of button, nickel-cadmium, and nonconsumer batteries, most programs collect all consumer batteries and no nonconsumer batteries.

9. There are insufficient incentives to encourage extensive recycling of household batteries.

10. It is likely that batteries which contain less mercury or other non-hazardous substitute materials will become widely marketed in the United States before large-scale reclamation of all types of batteries occurs in the United States.

ACRONYMS

BCI   Battery Council International
BPA   Battery Products Alliance
EAC   Environmental Action Coalition
EEC   European Economic Community
EPA   Environmental Protection Agency
GDRRA   Greater Detroit Resource Recovery Authority
MDNR   Michigan Department of Natural Resources
MPCA   Minnesota Pollution Control Agency
MSW   Municipal solid waste
MWC   Municipal waste combustor; also known as a solid waste incinerator.
NEMA   National Electrical Manufacturing Association
RCRA   Resource Conservation and Recovery Act
SOCRRA   Southeastern Oakland County Resource Recovery Authority

APPENDIX A. LEAD-ACID BATTERY RECYCLING LEGISLATION

Model Legislation*

Be it enacted by the legislature of the State of _____

Section 1. Lead Acid Batteries; Land Disposal Prohibited

a. No person may place a used lead acid battery in mixed municipal solid waste, discard or otherwise dispose of a lead acid battery except by delivery to an automotive battery retailer or wholesaler, to a collection or recycling facility authorized under the law of (state), or to a secondary lead smelter permitted by the Environmental Protection Agency.
b. No automotive battery retailer shall dispose of a used lead acid battery except by delivery to the agent of a battery wholesaler, to a battery manufacturer for delivery to a secondary lead smelter permitted by the Environmental Protection Agency, or to a collection or recycling facility authorized under the law of (state), or to a secondary lead smelter permitted by the Environmental Protection Agency.
c. Each battery improperly disposed of shall constitute a separate violation.
d. For each violation of this section a violator shall be subject to a fine not to exceed $ _____ and/or a prison term not to exceed _____ days (as appropriate under state code).

Section 2. Lead Acid Batteries; Collection for Recycling

a. A person selling lead acid batteries at retail or offering lead acid batteries for retail sale in the state shall:

---

*Courtesy of Battery Council International, Washington, D.C.

(1) accept, at the point of transfer, in a quantity at least equal to the number of new batteries purchased, used lead acid batteries from customers, if offered by customers; and

(2) post written notice which must be at least 8-½ inches by 11 inches in size and must contain the universal recycling symbol and the following language:

    (i) "It is illegal to discard a motor vehicle battery or other lead acid battery."

    (ii) "Recycle your used batteries."; and

    (iii) "State law requires us to accept used motor vehicle batteries or other lead acid batteries for recycling, in exchange for new batteries purchased."

Section 3. Inspection of Automotive Battery Retailers. The (appropriate state agency) shall produce, print, and distribute the notices required by Section 2 to all places where lead acid batteries are offered for sale at retail. In performing its duties under this section the division may inspect any place, building, or premise governed by Section 2. Authorized employees of the agency may issue warnings and citations to persons who fail to comply with the requirement of those sections. Failure to post the required notice following warning shall subject the establishment to a fine of $ _____ per day (as appropriate under state code).

Section 4. Lead Acid Battery Wholesalers. Any person selling new lead acid batteries at wholesale shall accept, at the point of transfer, in a quantity at least equal to the number of new batteries purchased, used lead acid batteries from customers, if offered by customers. A person accepting batteries in transfer from an automotive battery retailer shall be allowed a period not to exceed 90 days to remove batteries from the retail point of collection.

Section 5. Enforcement. The (appropriate state agency) shall enforce Sections 2 and 4. Violations shall be a misdemeanor under (applicable state code).

Section 6. Severability. If any clause, sentence, paragraph, or part of this chapter or the application thereof to any person or circumstance shall, for any reason, be adjudged by a court of competent jurisdiction to be invalid, such judgment shall not affect, impair, or invalidate the remainder of this chapter or its application to other persons or circumstances.

Analysis of Proposed Lead-Acid Battery Recycling Model Legislation*

Section 1. Lead Acid Batteries; Land Disposal Prohibited

a. The legislation would prohibit individuals from disposing of used lead acid batteries except by delivery to the following:

- Battery retailers or wholesalers
- State-authorized collection or recycling facilities, or
- A secondary lead smelter permitted by the US Environmental Protection Agency

---

*Courtesy of Battery Council International, Washington, D.C.

b. Battery retailers would be required to deliver used batteries to:

- The agent of a battery wholesaler
- A battery manufacturer for delivery to a secondary lead smelter permitted by EPA
- A state-authorized collection or recycling facility, or
- An EPA-permitted secondary lead smelter

c. Each battery improperly disposed of would constitute a separate violation, with such violation subject to the penalties deemed appropriate by each state.

Section 2. Lead Acid Batteries; Collection for Recycling

a. Battery retailers would be required to:

- Accept at least as many used batteries (if offered by customers) as new batteries purchased
- Post a written notice of the size and with the content required by the statute

Section 3. Inspection of Automotive Battery Retailers.   The model legislation would direct the appropriate state agency to distribute the notices required by Section 2 to all battery retailers, and would grant that agency the authority to enter for inspection any covered place, building or premise. Failure to comply with Section 2 may result in warnings or citations as well as monetary penalties.

Section 4. Lead Acid Battery Wholesalers.   Battery wholesalers must accept at least as many used batteries (if offered by customers) as new batteries purchased. Wholesalers accepting used batteries from retailers must remove the batteries from the retail point of collection within 90 days.

Section 5. Enforcement.   Violations of Sections 2 and 4 would be a misdemeanor under the model legislation.

Section 6. Severability.   This section contains standard severability language.

APPENDIX B. STATE OF MINNESOTA DRY-CELL BATTERY LEGISLATION*

[An Act] relating to waste; prohibiting the placement of certain dry cell batteries in mixed municipal solid waste; requiring labeling of certain batteries by electrode content; establishing maximum content levels of mercury in batteries; requiring that batteries in certain consumer products be easily removable; providing penalties; proposing coding for new law in Minnesota Statutes, chapters 115A and 325E.
Be it enacted by the legislature of the state of Minnesota:

Section 1. [115A.9155] [Disposal of Certain Dry Cell Batteries.]

Subdivision 1. [Prohibition.]   A person may not place in mixed municipal solid waste a dry cell battery containing mercuric oxide electrode, silver oxide elec-

---

*Chapter No. 409, H.F. No. 1921.

trode, nickel-cadmium, or sealed lead-acid that was purchased for use or used by a government agency, or an industrial, communications, or medical facility.

Subd. 2. [Manufacturer Responsibility.]

(a). A manufacturer of batteries subject to subdivision 1 shall:

(1). Ensure that a system for the proper collection, transportation, and processing of waste batteries exists for purchasers in Minnesota; and

(2). Clearly inform each purchaser of the prohibition on disposal of waste batteries and of the system or systems for proper collection, transportation, and processing of waste batteries available to the purchaser.

(b). To ensure that a system for the proper collection, transportation, and processing of waste batteries exists, a manufacturer shall:

(1). Identify collectors, transporters, and processors for the waste batteries and contract or otherwise expressly agree with a person or persons for the proper collection, transportation, and processing of the waste batteries; or

(2). Accept waste batteries returned to its manufacturing facility.

(c). A manufacturer shall ensure that the cost of proper collection, transportation, and processing of the waste batteries is included in the sales transaction or agreement between the manufacturer and any purchaser.

(d). A manufacturer that has complied with this subdivision is not liable under subdivision 1 for improper disposal by a person other than the manufacturer of waste batteries.

Sec. 2. [325E.125] [General and Special Purpose Battery Requirements.]

Subdivision 1. [Identification.] The manufacturer of a button cell battery that is to be sold in this state shall ensure that each battery is clearly identifiable as to the type of electrode used in the battery.

Subd. 2. [Mercury Content.]

(a). A manufacturer may not sell, distribute, or offer for sale in this state an alkaline manganese battery that contains more than .30 percent mercury by weight, or after February 1, 1992, 0.025 percent mercury by weight.

(b). On application by a manufacturer, the commissioner of the pollution control agency may exempt a specific type of battery from the requirements of paragraph (a) if there is no battery meeting the requirements that can be reasonably substituted for the battery for which the exemption is sought. The manufacturer of a battery exempted by the commissioner under this paragraph is subject to the requirements of section 1, subdivision 2.

(c). Notwithstanding paragraph (a), a manufacturer may not sell, distribute, or offer for sale in this state after January 1, 1992, a button cell alkaline manganese battery that contains more than 25 milligrams of mercury.

Subd. 3. [Rechargeable Tools and Appliances.]

(a). A manufacturer may not sell, distribute, or offer for sale in this state a rechargeable consumer product unless:

(1). The battery can be easily removed by the consumer or is contained in a battery pack that is separate from the product and can be easily removed; and

(2). The product and the battery are both labeled in a manner that is clearly visible to the consumer indicating that the battery must be recycled or disposed of properly and the battery must be clearly identifiable as to the type of electrode used in the battery.

(*b*). "Rechargeable consumer product" as used in this subdivision means any product that contains a rechargeable battery and is primarily used or purchased to be used for personal, family, or household purposes.

(*c*). On application by a manufacturer, the commissioner of the pollution control agency may exempt a rechargeable consumer product from the requirements of paragraph (a) if:

(1). The product cannot be reasonably redesigned and manufactured to comply with the requirements prior to the effective date of this section;

(2). The redesign of the product to comply with the requirements would result in significant danger to public health and safety; or

(3). The type of electrode used in the battery poses no unreasonable hazards when placed in and processed or disposed of as part of mixed municipal solid waste.

(*d*). An exemption granted by the commissioner of the pollution control agency under paragraph (c), clause (1), must be limited to a maximum of two years and may be renewed.

Sec. 3. [325E.1251] [Penalty.]   Violation of sections 1 and 2 is a misdemeanor. A manufacturer who violates section 1 or 2 is also subject to a minimum fine of $100 per violation.

Sec. 4. [Application; Effective Dates.]   Section 1 is effective August 1, 1990. Section 2, subdivisions 1 and 2, are effective January 1, 1991, and apply to batteries manufactured on or after that date. Section 2, subdivision 3, is effective July 1, 1993, and applies to rechargeable consumer products manufactured on or after that date. Notwithstanding section 2, a retailer may sell alkaline manganese batteries from the retailer's stock existing on the effective dates for the two levels of mercury in section 2, subdivision 2, and rechargeable consumer products from the retailer's stock existing on the effective date of section 2, subdivision 3.

REFERENCES

1. Baum, Barry G., "Model Legislation for Nickel Cadmium and Small Lead Battery Recycling," presented at the Second International Seminar on Battery Waste Management, November 5–7, 1990.
2. Bureau of Mines, Minerals Yearbook, "Mercury," 1987.
3. Bureau of Mines, Minerals Yearbook, "Lead," 1988.
4. Bureau of Mines, Minerals Yearbook, "Cadmium," 1988.
5. Council of the European Communities, Draft Common Position on Batteries and Accumulators Containing Certain Dangerous Substances, September 1990.
6. Dickinson, Paul, Ultra Technologies of Kodak, Personal communication, March 1991.

7. Environmental Action Coalition, Personal communication with Mr. Sean Hecht, program coordinator, November 1990 to January 1991.

8. Eveready. Personal communication with Mr. Dave Dibell, product quality manager, November 1989.

9. Fiala-Goldiger, J., and M. A. Rollor, "The Status of Battery Recycling in Switzerland," presented at the Second International Seminar on Battery Waste Management, November 5–9, 1990.

10. Franklin Associates, Ltd., *Characterization of Products Containing Lead and Cadmium in Municipal Solid Waste in the United States, 1970 to 2000,* U.S. EPA, January 1989.

11. Greater Detroit Resource Recovery Authority, Personal communication with Mr. Phil Brown, program coordinator, November 1990 to January 1991.

12. Hinchey, Maurice D., "Household Batteries, Management or Neglect?" A Staff Report to the chairman, New York State Legislative Commission on Solid Waste Management, 1988.

13. Johnson, R., and C. Hirth, "Collecting Household Batteries," *Waste Age,* pp. 48–52, 1990.

14. Jones, C. J., P. J. McGugam, and P. F. Lawrence, "An Investigation of the Degradation of Some Dry Cell Batteries," *Journal of Hazardous Materials,* vol. 2, pp. 259–289, 1978.

15. Kodak Ultra Technologies, personal communication with Mr. Paul Dickinson, March 1991.

16. Linden, D. (ed.), *Handbook of Batteries and Fuel Cells,* McGraw-Hill, New York, 1984.

17. Michigan Legislative, "Report of the Joint Legislative Committee on Batteries," State of Michigan, December 1990.

18. Minnesota Pollution Control Agency, *Household Batteries in Minnesota: Interim Report of the Household Battery Recycling and Disposal Study,* March 1990.

19. National Electrical Manufacturers Association, "Written Statement of the NEMA and the Battery Products Alliance Concerning Household Battery Disposal," 1989.

20. National Electrical Manufacturers Association, personal communication with Mr. Fred Nicholson, section staff executive, November 1989.

21. National Electrical Manufacturers Association, "Mercury Usage in the U.S. Consumer Battery Production," from the NEMA public information document, 1990.

22. National Electrical Manufacturers Association, personal communication with Mr. Fred Nicholson, section staff executive, February 1991.

23. New Hampshire/Vermont Solid Waste Project, personal communication with Mr. Carl Hirth, program coordinator, December 1990.

24. New York State Legislative Commission on Solid Waste Management, September 1988.

25. Pillsbury, Hope, "Battery Recycling and Disposal in the United States: A Federal Perspective," presented at the Second International Seminar on Battery Waste Management. November 5–7, 1990.

26. Roos, C. E., J. Kearley, R. Quarles, and E. J. Summer, Jr., "Reducing Incineration Ash Toxicity due to Cadmium and Lead in Batteries," presented at the Second International Seminar on Battery Waste Management, November 5–7, 1990.

27. Seeberger, Donald, "A Study of Two Collection Methods for Removing Household Dry Cell Batteries from a Residential Waste Stream," Division of Environment and Energy, Hennepin County, Minnesota, 1989.

28. Serracane, Claudio, Electrolytic Process for the Recovery of Lead from Spent Storage

Batteries," presented at the Second International Seminar on Battery Waste Management, November 5–7, 1990.

29. Southeastern Oakland County Resource Recovery Authority, personal communication with Mr. Tom Waffen, general manager, March 1991.

30. State of Minnesota, personal communication with Ms. Karen Arnold, February through March 1991.

31. Taylor, Kevin, David J. Hurd, and Brian Rohan, "Recycling in the 1980s: Batteries Not Included," *Resource Recycling,* May/June 1988, pp. 26–59.

32. Toshio, Matsuoka, "Sumitomo Used Dry Battery Recycling Process," presented at the Second International Seminar on Battery Waste Management, November 5–9, 1990.

33. U.S. Environmental Protection Agency, "Characterization of MWC Ashes and Leachates from MSW Landfills, Monofills, and Co-disposal Sites," Office of Solid Waste and Emergency Response, Washington, D.C., EPA 530-SW-87-008A, vol. 1, October 1987.

34. U.S. Congress Office of Technology Assessment, "Facing America's Trash: What's Next for Municipal Solid Waste," OTA-O-424, U.S. Government Printing Office, Washington, D.C., October 1989.

35. Wallis, George, and S. P. Wolsky, "Options for Household Battery Waste Management," presented at the Second International Seminar on Battery Waste Management, November 5–7, 1990.

CHAPTER 20
CONSTRUCTION AND DEMOLITION DEBRIS

Edward L. von Stein
Manager
CalRecovery, Inc.
New Haven, Connecticut

INTRODUCTION

Historical Perspective

In Europe and the United States, construction and demolition debris, generally defined as waste or remaining building materials, was typically disposed with other solid wastes through the early to mid-twentieth century. Recycling of construction and demolition debris was first conceived as a response to the scarcity of building materials and the expense of disposal. In Europe, particularly Germany, after the widespread destruction brought about by World War II, millions of tons of building rubble remained to be handled. Since rebuilding the transportation infrastructure was a priority, Germany developed an early lead in the recycling of rubble into new highway construction products. For example, by 1987, some 100 million tons of rubble had been processed into aggregate and other products in Berlin alone.[1] In the United States, however, it was not until the introduction of incineration in the early 1900s, and later of resource recovery in the 1970s, that the separate disposal of largely incombustible rubble justified the added expense. In these systems, high maintenance cost and excessive machine wear brought about by heterogeneous waste streams favored the adoption of local solid waste disposal ordinances that required separation of the largely incombustible construction and demolition debris fraction.

Since the 1980s in the United States, separate disposal has usually meant separate landfills. In addition to separate construction and demolition (C&D) or bulky waste landfills, stump dumps to receive tree stumps resulting from land clearing, and pits to receive the residue from asphalt paving became common in larger municipalities.

As interest in recycling as a means of controlling the burgeoning municipal solid waste stream grew in Europe and the United States during the 1970s and 1980s, attention was focused on separately collected waste, including C&D de-

important ways. Current regulations generally require that such landfills include leachate collection, storage or treatment, and monitoring systems; periodic cover; and other elements familiar to MSW landfill operators. Concern with the migration of landfill gas may not directly parallel the MSW landfill, unless there is concern over organic contamination of the incoming C&D.

In many states, the construction of landfills designed for C&D disposal may be about as costly as MSW landfills on a per acre basis. Landfill liners, leachate collection systems, and gas control facilities may be required. Since, however, local regulations may not require the application of daily cover, operating costs can be limited and 5 to 10 percent of the volume reserved for cover can provide usable disposal volume.

Other methods of disposal of C&D wastes (i.e., the production of wood chips from wood wastes) are common in the northeastern United States. Woodchips from C&D are often used as a boiler fuel in the large-scale generation of industrial power.

CONSTRUCTION SITE SOURCE SEPARATION

At the construction site, laborers are typically assigned to clean up the site at the end of each workday. Workers dump materials into 20- to 50-yd^3 open-top roll-off containers leased from disposal firms. The items listed in Table 20.6 can be segregated for reuse or resale.

TABLE 20.6 Typical Construction Site Materials Targeted for Reuse or Resale

Material	Raw material
Construction-grade lumber	Wood
Ornamental trim	Wood
Metals	Steel, nonferrous
Tiles	Clay
Bricks	Clay
Electrical hardware and wire	Copper, aluminum
Plumbing hardware and copper pipe	Copper, bronze, brass

These materials may be destined for incorporation into new work at the same construction site, if allowed by contract, or for use on another project. Alternatively, resourceful contractors may have ready external markets for materials.

Larger demolition projects may warrant a separate roll-off box for set-aside materials. Projects involving construction several stories above grade may include job-site fabricated plywood chutes to drop materials directly to roll-off boxes at grade, or wheelbarrows may be wheeled to elevators for the trip to street level.

Little is known of the actual economics of source separation at construction sites, although the advantages to a contractor include the ability to contain some of his or her material and operating costs, as well as the ability to offer C&D recycling as an add-on to the basic construction service for those clients that might be attracted to recycling.

MARKETS AND MARKETING

On-Site Uses

By far the most accessible market for source-separated demolition debris is the construction project under way at the site itself. Minimal or no marketing overhead is related to such use, and transportation, processing, and storage costs are minimized. While some contracts may allow or stipulate reuse (i.e., historic renovation), the use of any but virgin materials in the final product may be prohibited in other cases (i.e., governmental contracts). Only recently has the routine practice of biasing publicly funded construction specifications toward the use of only new products made from virgin materials come under scrutiny. By early 1991, states such as New York, California, Minnesota, and Wisconsin had revised their purchase specifications to permit the use of recycled products. Typical products that may be reused on site are listed in Table 20.7.

TABLE 20.7   Target Construction Site Recyclables

Material	On-site uses
Wall studs, other construction-grade lumber and timber	Temporary or permanent framing and general construction
Plywood	Concrete forms, floor protection, or as replacement for new plywood
Used brick & tile	Decorative facades
Electrical hardware	Electrical hardware

Homeowners' residential do-it-yourself projects typically absorb a portion of the wood and plywood recovered from renovations under way at the same property. Thus, waste lumber from one demolished room of a home may become the structural framing of an added or renovated space.

Markets

Table 20.8 lists typical markets for C&D materials. Historically, reuse in place of new wood and use as fuel have been important outlets for wood waste. Other materials do not have long market histories.

In third world countries, wood scavenged from demolition sites may be sold for use in home heating. Treated wood, including railroad ties, telephone poles, and pilings, is unsuitable for use as fuel, however. When not used as an organic energy source, wood waste may be sold to wood mills as a composition board component, or chipped for use as groundcover. Demolition wood may be contaminated with metals (e.g., fasteners) or paints, but may still be salable.

In the highway industry, pavement recycling is becoming widely accepted. Recycled asphalt pavement competes not only with the application of new bituminous pavement, but also with glasphalt that contains crushed recycled glass as a portion of its aggregate, and with asphaltic material with recycled rubber tire content. Interestingly, then, the asphalt pavement industry is a preferred market

TABLE 20.8 Typical Markets for Recyclables from C&D

Material	Typical markets
Wood waste	Fuel wood
	New construction
	Remodeling
	Mulch, landscaping material
	Animal bedding
	Particle board
	Construction forms
Asphalt pavement	Asphalt pavement
Concrete	Foundation stone
	Road construction
Masonry	Foundation stone
	Road construction
Brick	Decorative facades
Structural steel	Reinforcing steel
	Structural steel
	Other steel
Aluminum	Aluminum fabrications

for at least three competing recycled materials and one or more products from virgin materials.

Crushed concrete from which reinforcing steel has been separated can be used as a replacement for natural aggregate in foundation subgrades for construction, road construction, or other applications. Coastal areas have used concrete rubble to construct artificial reefs. Pinellas County, Florida, operates one of the largest such programs in the United States.[11]

Scrap metal, including ferrous and nonferrous metals such as aluminum (from window wall demolition), brass and copper (from old roofs, roof flashing, electrical and plumbing fixtures, and decorative uses), and others, often find ready markets in urban areas. Scrap yards act as market intermediaries between contractors, who separate the materials, or waste disposal firms that provide the on-site waste container, and the end users such as wire mills and aluminum extruders.

Waste Exchanges

Regional governments have established waste exchanges as an approach to assisting industry with waste disposal. The waste exchange concept provides for the creation of an information clearinghouse that publishes periodic, anonymous listings of available industrial waste materials and of raw material needs.

Of the seventeen waste exchanges operating in North America in 1990, most are able to deal with C&D. Exchanges have been created nationwide, including

Seattle Exchange, King County, Washington

Renew Exchange, Texas Water Commission

Northeast Industrial Exchange, New York

International Marketing and C&D Recycling Overseas

International markets have historically developed at a faster rate than domestic markets. In Germany, for example, reserves of naturally occurring construction materials such as gavel have already been depleted in the vicinity of Berlin and in north Germany, and are projected to be exhausted by the year 2000 near Hanover.[12] Recognizing this situation, in 1980 in then West Germany, some 47 percent of excavated material, building rubble, and road debris (140,000,000 tonnes) was reused as fill or was processed into new raw material.

CONSTRUCTION DEBRIS RECYCLING METHODS

Table 20.9 summarizes C&D recycling methods. These practices are discussed in detail in this section.

TABLE 20.9 C&D Recycling Methods

Material	Practice	Equipment
Concrete	Manual separation	Hand tools only
	Crushing	Bulldozer
		Rock crusher
Structural steel	Manual separation	Hand tools only
Wood waste	Manual separation	Hand tools only
	Shredding	Wood hog
	Chipping	chipper
Nonferrous metals	Manual separation	Hand tools only
Roofing material	Manual separation	Hand tools only
Steel	Magnetic separation	Magnetic separator
	Manual separation	Hand tools only

Structural Steel

Contractors or other project participants may occasionally be responsible for disposition of excess structural steel upon termination or completion of a building project. Such steel can be sold "as is" through advertisements in public or trade media, or can be collected at the site or by market intermediaries. Quantities economical for shipping are returned to the production mill for credit. Alternatively, it may be sold to local scrap dealers. It may ultimately be remanufactured or made into reinforcing steel or other shapes.

Contaminants may include field welds, surface finishes such as mill primer, or rust. Such contaminants may be acceptable if the steel is to be reused as is for other construction, or they may need to be removed prior to remanufacture. Processing is usually limited to manual separation with or without mechanical assistance from mobile equipment at the site.

Wood Waste

Extra construction-grade lumber or timber, plywood, and the like are often collected by the contractor and incorporated into additional construction at the site or elsewhere. Contaminants typically include nails, water or insect damage, or rot. Construction workers typically cut away visible contamination prior to incorporation into new work, since contamination could render the construction unacceptable to the building owners, municipal or architectural inspectors, or lead to a structural failure.

Aluminum

Unused but unneeded extruded aluminum shapes are typically sold to an aluminum ingot producer, a fabricator, or a metals broker. Aluminum scrap from fabricators has historically been acceptable for reuse internally at the fabricator's shop, or as raw material for another industry member. It is economical to extrude new aluminum shapes from a mixture containing as much as 40 percent aluminum scrap.

Contaminants include surface finishes and corrosion products. Typical problems caused by surface finishes are exemplified by the experiments of aluminum extruders who tried to use postconsumer beer cans in production runs, but found that the lacquer surface finishes cause problems in the furnaces. Aluminum alloyed with other products likewise can cause an entire batch of material to exceed specified tolerances.

Processes for separating aluminum from other metals are limited to manual separation.

Other Nonferrous Metals

Extruded, rolled, forged, or manufactured shapes, drawn copper wire, and other types of nonferrous metals are recovered manually at the construction site. Typical contaminants include plastic, such as wire coatings or faucet handle inserts; fibers or rubber, such as faucet washers or fiber wire insulation; metallic sheathing of electrical conduit; and cross contamination of metals.

The processes available to recover these nonferrous metals are visual inspection and manual separation.

Demolition Debris Recycling Practices

Building Demolition Practices

General.   Recycling practices in building demolition projects are similar to those of the construction industry. The principal difference is the increased homogeneity of the target materials. Practices vary with the size of the building, conditions of the demolition permit, preferences of and equipment available to the demolition contractor, and the economics of locally available disposal alternatives.

Concrete.   Concrete requiring disposal results from demolishing building foundations, floors, and occasionally, roofs and structural elements. Removing or repairing sidewalks, storm or sanitary sewer appurtenances, and the like also generate waste concrete. Markets for concrete were already discussed.

Contaminants include reinforcing steel, either bar shapes or wire mesh; fasteners, adherent surface finishes, including ceramic, asphaltic, or other tiles; and adherent bricks. Mortar may be considered a contaminant if strength requirements are strict in the reuse application.

Crushing concrete is often performed by running a tracked bulldozer over the material several times, although this practice may generate disagreeable noise and dust. Other processing includes manual sorting, the use of mobile jaw crushers, and magnetic separation.

Roofing Materials. Table 20.2 provided an estimate of the composition of roofing material. Laboratory test results by Paulsen et al. indicate that "acceptable paving mixtures that include roofing waste can be made."[6] The paving industry, however, has not widely adopted the practice of incorporating such material. This condition may be due in part to the relative difficulty of securing adequate quantities of source-separated roofing waste. Equally important may be the costs of disposing of unused portions of the old roofing.

Contaminants may include the original roofing substrate, which may be wood or metal.

Steel and Nonferrous Metals. Contaminants found in white goods may include capacitors, plastics in the form of wire sheaths and controls, insulation (such as fiberglass batts in refrigerators or dishwashers), and off-spec metals. Electrical equipment may generate electric motor "fluff," plastics, and paper.

Plumbing systems may include off-spec metals such as tin-lead solder used in joints of copper pipes, paint, insulation, and components of valves such as rubber washers, stem packings, and petroleum-based lubricants.

Wood. Contaminants may include surface treatments, as discussed under "Wood Waste" above, gypsum or other wallboard, plaster, lathe, electrical components, floor or wall covering, fasteners, and plumbing pieces.

Manual separation and shredding are the most common wood-waste processing methods.

Restoration and Reuse

The simplest C&D recycling strategy is often to renovate all or part of a structure and rededicate it to a new use. This alternative should always be considered as part of the demolition planning process. Successful examples abound in most cities, including reuse of factory space as offices, reuse of schools as public structures including governmental offices and senior centers, and the reuse of railroad stations as commercial space. Typical planning concerns include those listed in Table 20.10.

Technology

General. The earliest C&D recycling projects in (West) Germany were designed to produce material that could compete with virgin supplies. This approach proved to be too costly. Second-generation projects employed simpler technology (i.e., jaw crushers alone or in conjunction with impact crushers and magnetic separators) to process material.[12] The most prevalent approach to recycling demolition debris at present involves visual inspection and manual separation.

Heavy-duty, preengineered, or custom-designed equipment is available in several configurations to facilitate these processes. Systems include mobile, semimobile, and fixed arrangements. Mobile plants use a flatbed trailer as a plat-

TABLE 20.10   Typical Concerns in Planning for Reuse of a Structure

Adaptability to future use
Life-cycle cost of renovations
Remaining useful life of structure
Environmental and public health liability
Structural integrity
Local zoning and land use requirements and preferences
Cost of demolition

form for prescreening, crushing, magnetic separation, and final screening equipment, together with conveyors, chutes, and controls. Systems can typically be set up in less than a day by deploying hydraulically jacked legs and raising and aligning the equipment for proper materials flow. Semimobile plants, although also delivered to a site by truck, are larger than mobile units and may require up to three days to make ready for operation at a site.

In Europe, fixed or portable plants have been used to process excavation or building rubble into fresh raw materials. Fixed plants which can process in the range of 300 to 400 ton per hour of infeed (12,000 × 1000 mm, or 4 ft × 3 ft) typically involve the following processes:

* Infeed
* Screening system, either single- or multiple-stage
* Crushing system, usually two-stage
* Magnetic belt separator

Mobile plants can operate up to 100 ton per hour, assuming feed material of the same size and using magnetic separation and a screening system. One class of mobile plants, mobile sorting systems, provides stations for laborers, a sorting conveyor belt, and often a magnet to ease the removal of ferrous material. Belts are typically mounted at waist height for the most safe and efficient picking.

The sorting receptacle is typically at either side of the sorter. Up to six stations can be accommodated on a trailer that contains an infeed hopper and an inclined belt section as well as a horizontal picking section.

To provide an overview of the range of equipment available from just five of the manufacturers producing equipment to serve this field, Table 20.11 lists selected equipment and manufacturers. Detailed information can be obtained from local manufacturers' representatives.

Fixed plants are permanently mounted and provide the greatest range of capacity. Equipment in fixed plants is simple and generally includes tracked bulldozers and hydraulically operated mobile jaw crushers.

Ravensburg, Germany, C&D Recycling Facility.   An example of a large fixed, highly mechanized C&D recycling facility at Ravensburg, Germany, has been processing C&D, "trade" or commercial waste, and bulky items into ferrous, wood, cardboard, and aggregate fractions since it began operating in November 1988. This plant was originally built with a partial construction grant from the German federal government to develop two pieces of equipment. Site specifica-

TABLE 20.11 Selected Equipment Manufacturers

Equipment	Manufacturer
Knuckleboom crane/grapple	Ramey
Oscillating screens	West Salem Machinery Co.
	Maschinenfabrik Bezner
Wood hogs (chippers, shredders)	West Salem Machinery Co.
	Maschinenfabrik Bezner
Tub grinders	Haybuster Manufacturing Inc.
	Norcia
Screening drums	Lindemann Maschinenfabrik GmbH
Magnetic separators	Eriez Magnetics
	Dings Magnets
Vibrating process equipment	General Kinematics Corp.
Picking systems	Mayfran International
	Maschinenfabrik Bezner

TABLE 20.12 Site Description: Ravensburg, Germany, C&D Recycling Facility

Design Parameter	Value
Area of site	12,000 m^2
Area of building	950 m^2
Design capacity, C&D	80 m^3h
	40 ton/h
Trade & bulky	150 m^3/h
Installed power	155 kW
Screening machines	2 (Type BSM)
Inclined sorting machines	2 (Type SSM)
Pneumosifter (air classifier)	1
Magnetic separators	2
Compactor	28 m^3
Air pollution control	34,000 m^3/h
	38.5 kW
	4 intakes

Source: Ref. 14.

tions are as summarized in Table 20.12, and a block flow diagram is presented in Fig. 20.1.

Material arriving at the facility is weighed and dumped in a tipping hall. Unacceptable material and homogeneous loads are diverted into containers without processing. Material to be processed is visually inspected and elevated from an infeed pit to a bucket screen which diverts larger pieces such as pallets, milled lumber,...furniture and gutters through an enclosed manual picking room of trade waste and bulky materials for cardboard wood and ferrous metals prior to loadout as reject.

The small fraction from the bucket screen (up to about 1 ft) is screened, sifted, and mechanically sorted into 3 debris fractions, 2 ferrous metal fractions, and 1

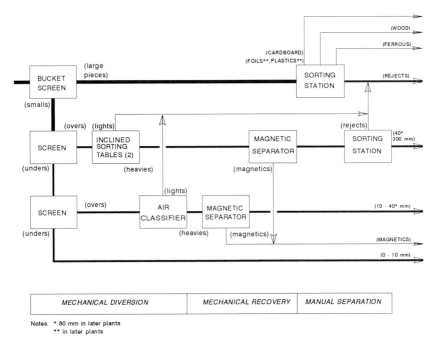

FIGURE 20.1 Flow diagram of Ravensburg, Germany, C&D recycling facility.

miscellaneous portion. The two smaller debris fractions are used as fill. The finest material is screened into three fractions, with the larger two streams being delivered to inclined sorting machines for separation by density into usable debris and miscellaneous fractions. The debris fraction is conveyed past a magnetic separation stage and through a manual picking station while the miscellaneous fraction is treated as a reject stream.

The finest fraction (0 to 40 mm) is screened into two fractions. The larger of these fractions (10 to 40 mm) is air-classified to remove light waste, while the smaller fraction (0 to 10 mm) is conveyed directly to a bunker. The larger fraction is subjected to magnetic separation prior to being stored in a bunker.

Modern Mechanized Plants. The Ravensburg facility is one of several plants operating in Europe that recover products from C&D. Selected additional domestic and European plants are identified in Table 20.13, and a block flow diagram of the Basel, Switzerland, plant is provided in Fig. 20.2. The Basel, Switzerland, facility is also illustrated in Fig 20.3. This list is not meant to be a census, but rather merely identifies several representative projects.

Pavement Recycling
Jones presented a summary of the status of in-situ pavement recycling practice in the United States.[16] The process is reportedly appropriate in resurfacing pavements in

TABLE 20.13 Selected European C&D Facilities

Location	Status	Capacity
Ravensburg, Germany	Operating	600 yd³/shift
Bad Reuzen	Operating	100 tons/h
Basel, Switzerland	Operating	1000 yd³/shift
Zurich, Switzerland	Operating	1000 yd³/shift
New York, N.Y.	Operating	1800 yd³/shift
Boston, Mass.	Planned	1000 yd³/shift

Source: Refs. 14 and 15.

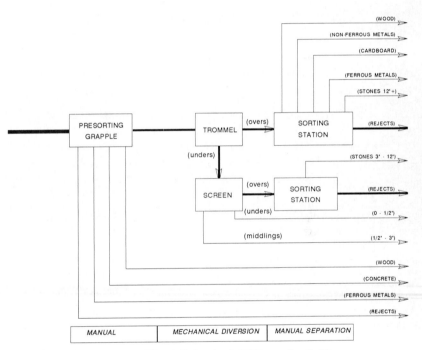

FIGURE 20.2 Flow diagram of Basel, Switzerland, C&D recycling facility.

which hardening has occurred in the uppermost ¾ in of pavement surface, which results in surface failures, including cracks. Decreasing availability of new raw materials and consequent increases in cost have fostered interest in the process. Steps in recycling generally include pavement removal, pavement crushing and heating, adding aggregate and asphalt, and/or an asphaltic modifier. Recycling in place involves heater scarifying, adding a modifier, screeding, and rolling.

To facilitate procurement and control of pavement recycling projects, standard specifications have been established by a trade association, the Asphalt Recycling and Reclaiming Association.[16]

FIGURE 20.3 C&D processing facility—Basel, Switzerland. (*Photograph courtesy of Lindemann Recycling Equipment, Inc.*)

ISSUES

Radon

The health effects of exposure to radon have long been known; recently, however, it has become apparent that sources of radon production may include typical construction substances such as bricks, concrete, foundation stone, and other building materials. Therefore, the reuse of these materials is increasingly reconsidered in light of their potential adverse health impacts.

Research by Lettner and Steinhausler indicates that the release of radon ^{222}Rn from gypsum products may be related to and may increase with the moisture content of the material.[17] Experiments indicated that increasing moisture content of concrete, soil, and shale caused an increase in the release of ^{222}Rn compared to dry materials. Also, some gypsum products may release higher levels of radon than most other common construction materials.[17]

Asbestos

Building demolition debris from older structures typically contains some quantity of asbestos, which is specifically regulated by federal and state agencies. Because of the costs involved in separating asbestos contamination, which must often be performed by specialized firms, the presence of asbestos many render such C&D uneconomical to recycle.

Other Contaminants

Wood waste contamination may include lead-based paint or preservatives such as creosote, pentachlorophenol, any of several water-borne preservatives and fire retardants. Arsenic may also be present.

REGULATORY AND LEGAL

Federal Regulations

In the United States, national solid waste disposal legislation is contained in the Resource Conservation and Recovery Act (RCRA) of 1976, as amended. Congress has directed the Administrator of the Environmental Protection Agency to establish regulations and guidelines for waste disposal in a range of areas. However, no federal-level national recycling legislation mandates the recycling of C&D.

State Requirements

Many states in the United States have enacted recycling requirements—targets and goals—and some states, including Connecticut, mention specific materials in their legislation. Current legislation does not mandate the recycling of C&D in any state, however. Since states are establishing high recycling diversion targets, however, the consideration of the inclusion of C&D in local programs is often necessary to meet goals.

State Permits

The Connecticut statutes discuss solid waste management in Chapter 446d, Sections 22a-207 through 22a-255. A C&D recycling facility with a throughput capacity greater than 200 lb/h (8 tons per day) and that may include named equipment such as pulverizers, compactors, shredders, and balers must operate under permits. The Commissioner of the Connecticut Department of Environmental Protection (CDEP) is authorized to issue construction and operation permits once the need for the facility has been demonstrated. Key provisions of the regulations are as follows:

1. Recyclable materials may be removed from the waste stream at the point of generation, or before disposal, and may be transported to a facility for recycling.
2. The CDEP may use a revolving fund for financial, legal, and technical planning by municipalities.
3. The commissioner may designate recyclable materials, and those items are prohibited from disposal within the waste stream.
4. Construction materials may be regulated as litter if disposed outside a permitted site; a fine of up to $10,000 per day may be levied.

Application requirements for a permit to construct a C&D recycling facility include the preparation of an engineering description of the site and the facility, investigation of site hydrology and geology, preparation of operating plans and manuals, site life, closure, and postclosure. Specific technical requirements include that incoming material storage capacity equal to 24 h if facility capacity is greater than 100 tons per day, but operation such that incoming material is not stored on site for more than 48 h.

ECONOMICS

Little information is available on the economics of recycling C&D. This situation arises in part because of the relatively short track record of the practice. Projects such as the Ravensburg, Germany, plant may reflect higher-than-expected operating costs if the throughput of C&D has not reached design capacity. Further, many recycling projects have been undertaken by the private sector; commercial recyclers consider their particular economics to be part of their competitive advantage and are unwilling to reveal details. Equipment vendors report, however, that operating costs for centralized facilities may be as low as $11 to $15 per ton, although these estimates are unconfirmed.

Table 20.14 provides a list of selected equipment costs, based on second-quarter 1991 information. Table 20.15 provides the cost categories for an estimate of capital costs for a centralized C&D recycling facility and may be used as a basic checklist. Table 20.16 lists the operating cost categories for a centralized facility.

TABLE 20.14 Capital Costs of Selected C&D Recycling Equipment

Equipment name	Cost range
Tub grinder, mobile	
With Knuckleboom	$200,000
Without Knuckleboom	$100,000
Pedestal crane systems	$35,000–$150,000

TABLE 20.15 Capital Cost Categories for a Centralized C&D Recycling Facility

Site costs (minimum 3.0-acre site)
   Acquisition
   Permitting
   Developing
Buildings (typically, enclosed process building, administrative space, and scalehouse)
   Design
   Construction
   Fixed process equipment (typically, sorting, conveying, baling, and densifying)
   Mobile equipment (Typically, front-end loader, high lift, and yard tractor)

Equipment vendors report that construction of a 35,000- to 40,000-ft^2 building to enclose a sorting system may be completed for $2,000,000, and sorting equipment may cost $1,500,000. After the inclusion of all project costs, however, and assuming that the site can be developed and a building can be built for the relatively low figure of $50.00 per square foot, it is probable that at least $5,000,000 will be required for construction.

REFERENCES

1. Heckoetter, Dr.-Ing. Ch., *Recycling of Building Rubble, Aufbereitungs Technik,* nr. 8, 1987, p. 443.

TABLE 20.16 Categories of Annual Operating and
Maintenance Costs for a Centralized C&D Facility

Operation
  Labor
    General manager
    Weighmaster
    Shift supervisor
    Mobile equipment operator
    Sorters
    Fixed-equipment operators
    Maintenance
    Laborers
  Utilities
  Consumables
    Fuel
    Spares and lubricants
    Baling wire and other supplies
  Administration and overhead
    (Varies with each installation)
  Residual disposal
    Tip fee times tons tipped
    Transportation of residuals

---

2. Section 22a-209 of the *General Statutes of the State of Connecticut,* Regulations of the Department of Environmental Protection, Concerning Standards for Solid Waste Landfill.

3. 6NYCRR Part 360, *Solid Waste Management Facilities,* Effective December 31, 1988, NYS DEC, Division of Solid Waste, Albany, N.Y.

4. 25PaCode Ch 271, *Municipal Waste Management, General Provisions,* effective April 9, 1988, EQB, Harrisburg, Pa.

5. Davidson, Thomas A., and David Gordon Wilson, "U.S. Building-Demolition Wastes: Quantities and Potential for Resource Recovery," *Conservation and Recycling,* vol. 5, no. 2/3, pp. 113–132, 1982.

6. Paulsen, Greg, Mary Stroup-Gardiner, and Jon Epps, "Recycling Waste Roofing Material in Asphalt Paving Mixtures," *Transportation Research Record* 1115.

7. City of New Haven, *A Request for Qualifications for a Front End Solid Waste System,* December 20, 1990.

8. Town of North Hempstead, Nassau County, New York, *Final Request for Proposals— Recycling System Design, Equipment installation and Operations,* March 13, 1987.

9. Monroe County Solid Waste Management Plan/Draft Generic Environmental Impact Statement.

10. Baumeister, Theodore, ed., *Standard Handbook for Mechanical Engineers,* 7th ed., McGraw-Hill, New York, 1967.

11. Brochure, *Pinellas County Artificial Reefs,* Pinellas County Department of Solid Waste Management, undated.

12. Oldengott, Dr.-Ing. M., "Recycling of Building Rubble - Importance and New Crusher Technology," *Aufbereitungs-Technik,* nr. 6/1985.

13. Stein, Volker, "Recycling of Demolition Waste and Its Influence on the Market of Natural Mineral Building Materials," *Conservation and Recycling,* vol. 10, no. 2/3, pp. 53–57, 1987.

14. *Sorting Construction-Demolition Waste Ravensburg Project,* Maschinenfabrik Bezner GmbH & Co. KG, undated.

15. *Processing of Construction and interior Demolition Waste,* Lindemann Recycling Equipment, Inc., New York, undated.

16. Jones, George M., P.E., *In Situ Recycling of Bituminous Pavements.*

17. Lettner, H., and F. Steinhauser, "Radon Exhalation of Waste Gypsum Recycled as Building Material," *Radiation Protection Dosimetry,* vol. 24, no. 1/4, pp. 415–417, 1988.

18. Wilson, David Gordon, P. Foley, R. Weisman, S. Frondistou-Yannas, "Demolition Debris: Quantities, Composition and Possibilities for Recycling," a paper in the *Proceedings of the Fifth Mineral Waste Utilization Symposium,* Chicago, Ill., April 13–14, 1976.

CHAPTER 21
HOUSEHOLD HAZARDOUS WASTES

John C. Glaub, Ph.D., P.E.

INTRODUCTION

Household hazardous waste (HHW) arose as an issue in waste management in the 1980s. During that decade, various communities across the United States addressed the issue by developing plans, programs, and facilities to keep HHW out of the solid waste stream and to provide options for properly managing these wastes. In a relatively short period of time, alternative HHW programs have become a mainstream waste management practice.

Concern over HHW arose as the presence of hazardous waste in the municipal solid waste (MSW) stream became a well-recognized matter. Recognition of the matter has been brought about by a variety of factors, including (1) the results of environmental monitoring at solid waste landfills (some of which did not receive commercial or industrial wastes), (2) the continued lowering of detection limits of laboratory instrumentation, (3) the results of solid waste characterization studies, (4) observations made in load-checking programs at solid waste landfills and transfer stations, and (5) hazardous incidents involving refuse collection workers and equipment. The increased sorting and handling of wastes in the growing number of recycling operations is further placing the MSW stream under observation.

Without HHW management alternatives, most HHW is improperly disposed of in the refuse, down the drain, or in the soil. Furthermore, many HHWs are simply stored for long periods of time. These storage and disposal practices can result in various health, safety, environmental, and legal problems. This chapter discusses HHW issues and programs for properly managing HHW.

HAZARDOUS WASTE IN MUNICIPAL SOLID WASTE

Definition of Household Hazardous Waste

Hazardous wastes are defined under federal law as discarded materials that are not specifically excluded from regulation as a hazardous waste and that either (1) exhibit the characteristics of ignitability, corrosivity, reactivity, or toxicity or (2) are specifically listed as hazardous wastes. [Details of the federal definition are given in the Code of Federal Regulations (CFR), Title 40, Part 261.[1]] Of particular note here is that household wastes are one category of materials that is specifically excluded from regulation as hazardous waste under federal law, i.e., the Resource Conservation and Recovery Act (RCRA).

States also establish their own definition of hazardous wastes; state regulations can be no less stringent than federal regulations. Some states follow federal regulations exactly, while others typically follow federal regulations closely in organization and content with some additional restrictions (e.g., additional listed wastes, more rigorous extraction procedures for determining toxicity, reduced exclusions from regulation as a hazardous waste).

HHWs are discarded materials from residences that meet the criteria of hazardous waste. Although exempted from regulation by federal law and most state laws, HHWs contain the same chemicals as may be found in industrial hazardous wastes. This regulatory ambiguity has led to much of the confusion and inaction in managing HHW. However, there is widespread agreement in the waste management field that HHW should be kept out of the solid waste stream even where legally it is not a hazardous waste. It should also be noted that some states do not exempt HHW from regulation as hazardous waste.

Typical Wastes

Examples of HHW are given in Table 21.1. The table is organized alphabetically according to common material name and gives the typical hazard class of the material. In some cases, more than one common name for the same material is listed to aid in using the table.

It should be noted that product constituents may vary among manufacturers of similar products. For example, some drain cleaners are bases, some are acids, and some are noncorrosive, chlorinated solvents. Product constituents may also vary with time for the same manufacturer. Some pesticides have changed ingredients several times while retaining the same product name. Therefore, a qualified chemist should be responsible for actual determination of a material's hazard class.

Examples of hazardous materials in commercial products are given in Table 21.2. In some cases, a chemical is present as an ingredient in the product; that is, the chemical is intentionally used in the product for specific purposes. In other cases, the chemical may be present as a "contaminant" because it is used as a precursor in the synthesis of another chemical in the product or because it may be a by-product in the synthesis of another chemical in the product. It is often very difficult to obtain a pure chemical compound because of the reaction kinetics in its formation.

For example, methylene chloride is commonly used as a key ingredient in paint removers, whereas benzene may be present in trace amounts (above the detection limit of laboratory instrumentation) because of the reaction kinetics in the formation of another product ingredient such as toluene.

Some chemicals are now under various degrees of restricted use in commercial products, for example, benzene and trichloroethylene. However, it is very common for some household products to be stored in garages and basements for over 20 years. Such storage practices have been repeatedly observed in HHW

TABLE 21.1 Common Household Hazardous Wastes

Material	Typical hazard class*	Material	Typical hazard class
Acetone	Flammable liquid	Methyl ethyl ketone	Flammable liquid
Aerosols	Flammable gas, nonflammable gas	Mineral spirits	Flammable liquid
Alcohols	Flammable liquid	Moth balls	ORM-A
Ammonia (NH4OH; 12% < NH4 < 44%)	Corrosive (base)	Muriatic acid (hydrochloric acid)	Corrosive (acid)
Ammonia (NH4OH; NH4 < 12%)	ORM-A	Nail polish	Flammable liquid
Ammunition (small arms)	Explosive C	Nail polish remover	Flammable liquid
Antifreeze	Poison B†	Naphtha	Flammable liquid
Batteries—automotive	Corrosive (acid)	Naphthalene	ORM-A
Bleach (sodium hypochlorite: Cl < 7%)	ORM-B	Naval jelly	Corrosive (acid)
Bleach (sodium hypochlorite: Cl > 7%)	Corrosive (acid)	Nitric acid (<40%)	Corrosive (acid)
Brake fluid	Flammable liquid	Nitric acid (>40%)	Oxidizer, corrosive (acid)
Butane	Flammable gas	Oil—lubricating	Combustible liquid
Camphor oil	Combustible liquid	Oil—motor	Combustible liquid
Carbon tetrachloride	ORM-A	Oven cleaner	Corrosive (base)
Chlorine (pool)	Oxidizer	Paint—oil-based	Flammable liquid
Chloroform	ORM-A	Paint—water-based	‡
Contact cement	Flammable liquid	Paint remover	ORM-A
Degreasers	ORM-A	Paint thinner	Flammable liquid
Diesel fuel	Combustible liquid	Pesticide	Poison B, flam. liquid
Drain cleaner	Corrosive (base) Corrosive (acid) ORM-A	Phosphoric acid	Corrosive (acid)
		Polyurethane coatings	Flammable liquid
		Pool acid	Corrosive (acid)
Fireworks	Explosive C	Propane	Flammable gas
Flare	Explosive C	Rubber cement	Flammable liquid
Floor polish	Flammable liquid	Rug cleaner	ORM-A
Fuel oil	Combustible liquid	Shellac	Flammable liquid
Fungicides	Poison B	Shoe wax	Flammable solid
Furniture polish	Flammable liquid	Silver nitrate	Oxidizer
Gasoline	Flammable liquid	Spot remover	ORM-A
Glue—epoxy	Flammable liquid	Sterno	Flammable solid
Glue—model airplane	Flammable liquid	Strychnine	Poison B
Hydrochloric acid	Corrosive (acid)	Sulfuric acid	Corrosive (acid)
Hydrogen peroxide	Oxidizer	Toilet bowl cleaner	Corrosive (acid)
Ink	Flammable liquid	Transmission fluid	Flammable liquid
Insecticides	Poison B, flammable liquid	TSP (trisodium phosphate)	Corrosive (base)
Kerosene	Flammable liquid	Turpentine	Flammable liquid
Lacquer	Flammable liquid	Upholstery cleaner	ORM-A
Lighter fluid (charcoal lighter)	Flammable liquid	Varnish	Flammable liquid
Lime (calcium hydroxide)	ORM-B	Warfarin	Poison B
Linseed oil	Flammable liquid	Weed killer	Poison B, flam. liquid
Lye (sodium hydroxide)	Corrosive (base)	White gas	Flammable liquid
Mercury (metallic)	ORM-B	Wood preservative	Poison B
Methylene chloride	ORM-A	Wood stain	Flammable liquid

*Typical hazard class is given; however, product constituents may vary. Hazard class for a particular material should be determined by a qualified chemist. In some cases, more than one hazard class may apply.

†Not a hazardous waste under federal law; however, some states regulate as a hazardous waste.

‡Water-based paint disposal regulations vary by state. Water-based paints are generally nonhazardous. However, water-based paints may be hazardous if they contain elevated concentrations of heavy metals, particularly mercury.

TABLE 21.2 Hazardous Materials in Commercial Products

Chemical	Potential products containing chemical	Chemical	Potential products Containing chemical
Benzene	Dry cleaning fluids, fumigants, gasoline, insecticides, motor oil, paint brush cleaner, paint remover, rubber cement, solvents (various), spot remover	Tetrachloroethylene	Degreasers, dry cleaning fluids,drying agents, heat transfer medium, paint remover, spot removers, vermifuges
Carbon Tetrachloride	Degreasers, dry cleaning fluids, drying agents, fire extinguishers, fumigants, laquers, propellants, refrigerants, solvents (various)	Toluene	Adhesives, dry cleaning fluids, dyes, gasoline, motor oil, paint, paint remover, perfumes, pharmaceuticals, solvents (various), spot removers, wood putty
Chloroform	Anaesthetics, fluorocarbon regfrigerants, fumigants, insecticides, laquers, pharmaceuticals, solvents(various)	1,1,1-Trichloroethane	Aerosol propellant, degreasers, drain opener, furniture polish, oven cleaner, paint remover, pesticides, rug cleaner, septic tank cleaner, shoe dye, shoe polish, solvents (various), spot removers, upholstery cleaner
1,2-Dichloroethane	Degreasers, finish removers, fumigants, gasoline, paint remover, penetrating agents, scouring compounds, soaps, solvents (various), wetting agents	Trichloroethylene	Adhesives, degreasers, dry cleaning fluids, dyes, fumigants, fur cleaner, paint, pharmaceuticals, shoe cleaner, shoe polish, solvents (various)
Ethylene Dibromide	Fire extinguishers, fumigants, gasoline, solvents (various), waterproofing preparations	Vinyl Chloride	Adhesives for plastics, intermediate in polymer production
Methylene Chloride	Aerosol propellant, degreasers, dewaxers, fumigants, furniture refinishers, hair spray, oven cleaner, paint, paint brush cleaner, paint remover, septic tank cleaner, shoe cleaner, shoe polish, solvents (various), spot removers, wood putty	Xylene	Caulking compounds, dyes, gasoline, insecticides, motor oil, paint, paint remover, rubber cement, shoe dye, solvents (various)

collection programs. Therefore, materials entering the waste stream may contain chemical constituents that were in use 20 or more years ago.

Quantities in the Waste Stream

A number of waste characterization studies have provided estimates of the quantity of hazardous waste in MSW. Table 21.3 summarizes the results of various

TABLE 21.3 Quantity of Hazardous Waste in Municipal Solid Waste*

Location	Date	Residential	Com./ind.†	Self-haul	Total	Reference
Mission Canyon Landfill (Los Angeles County, Calif.)	1979	—	—	—	0.13	2
Puente Hills Landfill (Los Angeles County, Calif.)	1981	0.0045	0.24	—	0.15	2
Marin County, Calif.	1986	0.40	—	—	—	3
San Mateo County, Calif.	1987	0.29	—	0.59	—	4
Portland, Oreg.	1987	0.01	0.21	0.05	0.09	5
Santa Cruz, Calif.	1988	—	—	0.39	0.36	6
Berkeley, Calif.	1988–89	0.20	0.60	—	0.40	7
Sacramento County, Calif.	1989	0.27	0.20	0.29	0.25	8
San Antonio, Tex.	1989–90	0.40	0.50	0.30	0.34	9
Burbank, Calif.	1990	0.40	1.09	—	—	10
Sunnyvale, Calif.	1990	0.09	0.45	3.09	0.83	11
Palo Alto, Calif.	1990–91	0.37	0.08	—	—	12
Tulare County, Calif.	1991	0.47	0.83	0.04	0.38	13
Del Norte County, Calif.	1991	0.83	0.09	—	—	14
Stockton, Calif.	1991	0.28	0.01	1.22	0.30	15

*Disposed waste stream.
†Commercial/industrial.

studies. The table shows a breakdown according to source (i.e., residential collection vehicles, commercial collection vehicles, and self-haul) as well as for the total waste stream.

The results vary considerably. Measurements of the amount of hazardous waste in the residential waste stream range from 0.0045 to about 1 percent. Estimates for hazardous waste in the total waste stream range from approximately 0.1 to 1 percent.

Composition of HHW

A breakdown of the composition of HHW is presented in Table 21.4. The table is based on operating experience at periodic collection programs and permanent collection facilities. Unfortunately, different operators report such data using different component categories. An effort was made to standardize the categories as much as possible in the table. By far the most common category of wastes is paint.

PROBLEMS ENCOUNTERED

Worker Injuries

Improper management of HHW can result in injuries to workers in waste management operations. Such workers include refuse collectors, material recovery facility sorters, and equipment operators at material recovery facilities, transfer stations, waste-to-energy facilities, and landfills. As recycling operations expand

TABLE 21.4 Composition of Household Hazardous Waste[16–20]

Component	Alameda County, Calif. (1987)	San Francisco, Calif. (1988–89)	Ontario, Canada (1989)	Milpitas, Calif. (1990)	Palm Beach County, Fla. (1990–91)
Latex paint	30.8	8.4	30.0	12.9	18.5
Oil-based paint	32.8	25.0	26.0	17.0	24.2
Waste oils	12.3	26.6	10.0	20.2	22.7
Misc. flammables*	3.1	20.9	14.0	10.8	14.4
Poisons	5.0	4.2	7.0	3.1	2.9
Corrosives	3.3	7.2	10.0	4.2	3.4
Oxidizers	0.5	1.3	1.0	0.3	0.3
Aerosols	2.3	3.4	1.0	2.7	1.4
Batteries	0.0	1.0	0.0	11.6	9.6
Other†	9.9	2.0	1.0	17.2	2.6
Total	100.0	100.0	100.0	100.0	100.0

*Includes miscellaneous flammable liquids and solids.
†Reported material categories vary among programs.

in solid waste management, there will be increased sorting and handling of waste materials; correspondingly, workers will have increased exposure to hazardous wastes if present in the waste stream.

The National Solid Waste Management Association has documented a variety of worker injuries due to disposal of hazardous waste in the solid waste stream.[21] Exposure to hazardous waste has resulted from spills, spraying (e.g., from packer trucks during compaction), touching, fumes, fires, and explosions. Injuries have included burns (acid, caustic, and thermal), blinding, eye irritation, respiratory problems, rashes, nausea, and unknown chronic problems.

Equipment and Property Damage

Hazardous wastes disposed of in refuse also can cause equipment and property damage. The most common incidents involve fires in refuse collection trucks or transfer trailers. Virtually every company or municipal agency that collects refuse has experienced a vehicle fire due to improperly disposed hazardous wastes. Fires are typically the consequence of either flammables coming into contact with an ignition source or incompatible materials mixing and reacting. Sometimes the materials come from different sources (e.g., brake fluid from one home and pool chlorine from another). Compaction vehicles tend to liberate materials from containers, thereby contributing to hazardous incidents, but hazardous incidents also occur in loose loads. In addition, landfill equipment such as dozers and compactors have been damaged as the result of improperly disposed hazardous wastes.

Waste processing facilities have also experienced damage due to hazardous wastes disposed of in the waste stream. The most serious incidents reported have been shredder explosions. Most of the problems to date have occurred in refuse-derived fuel (RDF) processing plants, but the same hazard exists for wood and yard waste processing operations and MSW composting operations.

Environmental Contamination

The potential impacts of hazardous wastes in MSW landfills can be evaluated by examining the leachate and landfill gas generated at these sites. For purposes of comparison, 10 organic constituents are examined here: (1) benzene, (2) carbon tetrachloride, (3) chloroform, (4) 1,2-dichloroethane, (5) ethylene dibromide, (6) methylene chloride, (7) tetrachloroethylene, (8) 1,1,1-trichloroethane, (9) trichloroethylene, and (10) vinyl chloride. The 10 compounds were selected because of the extensive data available on them. Each of these compounds is also examined in Table 21.2.

The U.S. Environmental Protection Agency (EPA) has correlated leachate data from 53 landfills.[22] The concentrations of various hazardous constituents are shown in Table 21.5. All 10 chemicals were detected in MSW leachate. Methylene chloride was found at the highest concentrations (220,000 parts per billion) and at the greatest number of sites (60 percent).

TABLE 21.5 Concentrations of Organic Constituents in Leachate from MSW Landfills[22]

Chemical	Concentration range, ppb	Percent of sites where detected
Benzene	4–1,080	34
Carbon tetrachloride	6–398	4
Chloroform	27–31	15
1,2-Dichloroethane	1–11,000	11
Ethylene dibromide	5–5	2
Methylene chloride	2–220,000	60
Tetrachloroethylene	2–620	21
1,1,1-Trichloroethane	1–13,000	25
Trichloroethylene	1–1,300	32
Vinyl chloride	8–61	11

Analysis of landfill gas also provides an indication of constituents in landfills. The results of extensive testing of landfill gas by the California Air Resources Board are presented in Table 21.6.[23] The table summarizes results from 288 sites—271 nonhazardous waste sites and 17 hazardous waste sites. The terms "hazardous" and "nonhazardous" were used in the study to distinguish between sites that are known to have accepted hazardous waste and sites that are not known to have accepted hazardous waste.

The analyses were conducted on samples drawn from wells within the landfill. All of the 10 specified chemicals were detected in landfill gas. The lowest value observed is approximately equal to the detection limit for that compound. Benzene, methylene chloride, tetrachloroethylene, and trichloroethylene were found in more than half of the nonhazardous waste landfills; 1,1,1-trichloroethane and vinyl chloride were found in just under half of the nonhazardous waste sites.

Some interesting comparisons may be noted between the leachate and landfill gas analyses. Methylene chloride was found at the highest concentrations in leachate as well as in landfill gas at nonhazardous waste sites. Ethylene

TABLE 21.6 Concentrations of Organic Constituents in Gas from MSW Landfills[23]

Chemical	Nonhazardous waste sites*		Hazardous waste sites†	
	Concentration range, ppbv‡	Percent of sites where detected	Concentration range, ppbv	Percent of sites where detected
Benzene	500–29,000	51	500–791,000	82
Carbon tetrachloride	5–2,100	8	< 5	0
Chloroform	2–171,000	27	2–200	29
1,2-Dichloroethane	20–34,100	18	20–12,000	24
Ethylene dibromide	1–2,000	7	1–55	12
Methylene chloride	60–260,000	56	60–42,000	59
Tetrachloroethylene	10–62,000	72	10–10,000	88
1,1,1-Trichloroethane	10–21,000	49	10–14,000	59
Trichloroethylene	10–20,000	68	10–5,700	82
Vinyl chloride	500–120,000	47	500–60,000	53

*271 sites.
†17 sites.
‡ppbv = parts per billion by volume

dibromide and carbon tetrachloride were found at the lowest percentages of sites in both the leachate and landfill gas analyses.

The California Air Resources Board concluded that the "overall composition of landfill gases from hazardous and nonhazardous sites appear to be similar, with no major distinguishing characteristics which would indicate from what type of landfill the sample was obtained." The Board goes on to state, "The data show that, based on landfill gas testing, there is hazardous waste in 86 percent of the landfills tested, regardless of what type of waste the site is known to have accepted. The landfill gas testing results show that nonhazardous landfills may contain concentrations of toxic gases equal to or exceeding those of hazardous landfills."

HHW MANAGEMENT PRACTICES

Source Control

The most important aspect of HHW management is source control. The objectives of source control are to reduce the amount of HHW generated and to prevent improper disposal of those wastes that are generated. Source control is thus aimed at preventing problems before they happen. Two key elements of source control are public education and prohibited waste control programs at waste management facilities (i.e., transfer stations, material recovery facilities, waste-to-energy facilities, landfills).

Public education is vital in providing the community with information about HHW management alternatives. The public must be informed about what types of household materials are hazardous, why they are hazardous, how to use nonhazardous materials in place of products that are hazardous, and how to properly dispose of hazardous wastes that are generated. A public education flier is illustrated in Fig. 21.1. As the public becomes more aware of HHW issues, progress can be expected in reducing the generation of these wastes. Public education is discussed further later in this chapter.

Prohibited waste control programs are aimed at preventing prohibited wastes, such as hazardous and other specific prohibited wastes, from entering a waste management facility. Other prohibited wastes depend on facility permit restrictions and may include latex paint, liquid wastes, sludges, ash, asbestos, dead animals, infectious wastes, and various additional materials. Prohibited waste control programs are sometimes referred to as load-checking programs or as hazardous waste exclusion programs, although they usually include control of certain nonhazardous wastes as well.

Prohibited waste control programs have been instrumental in forcing the issue of providing disposal options for HHWs. These programs result in the rejection of HHW at waste management facilities and also at the curb. At the same time, they educate residents about the hazardous nature of certain wastes they produce.

There are six major components of prohibited waste control programs:

- Customer notification
- Personnel training
- Waste characterization
- Waste inspection
- Record keeping
- Management of wastes identified

Customer notification consists of (1) informing refuse haulers, residents, businesses, and local agencies that the facility does not accept the prohibited wastes specified and that a load-checking program is in place at the facility (e.g., periodic mailed notices); (2) posting signs at prominent locations around the facility, including the site entrance, gate-house, and tipping areas (Fig. 21.2); (3) placing decals on waste containers; (4) responding to customer inquiries concerning waste acceptance policies; and (5) providing public education about proper waste management alternatives for the prohibited wastes.

The effectiveness of the prohibited waste control program depends in large part on the capabilities of the facility staff. Therefore, it is very important to thoroughly train facility personnel, including management, gate-house attendants, equipment operators, traffic coordinators (spotters), recycling sorters, and load-checking staff. In addition, refuse collection workers play an important role in identifying and preventing problems at the source of waste generation. Many refuse collection companies instruct workers to remove HHW from garbage cans and leave it at the residence or to simply leave the entire can as is. Personnel should be trained in (1) identifying prohibited wastes, (2) understanding the effects of these wastes on human health and the environment, and (3) proper handling and response procedures for their job category.

To judge whether a waste can be accepted at the facility, procedures must be established for characterizing the waste. The first level of information is often provided by the customers themselves; they generally know what their wastes consist of or at least what they were used for. The next level involves physical assessment by facility personnel, e.g., examination of product labels, detection of odors, and observation of unusual materials or containers. If the waste cannot be

Learn to Use These Safe Substitutes as Alternatives to Toxic Household Products

Product	Alternatives and preventative methods

HOUSEHOLD CLEANERS

Product	Alternatives and preventative methods
AEROSOL SPRAYS	Choose non-aerosol containers, such as pump-spray, roll-on, or squeeze types.
ALL-PURPOSE CLEANERS	Mix 1 quart warm water with 1 tsp. borax, TSP, or liquid soap. Add squeeze of lemon or splash of vinegar. Never mix ammonia with chlorine bleach.
AIR FRESHENERS	Open windows and doors and use fans to ventilate. Place box of baking soda in closets and refrigerator. Simmer cloves and cinnamon in boiling water. Houseplants help clean the air and herb sachets provide a pleasant smell.
CHLORINE BLEACH	Use borax or baking soda to whiten. Borax is a good grease-cutter and disinfectant. If you use bleach, choose the non-chlorine, dry bleach. Never mix chlorine bleach with ammonia or acid-type cleaners.
DEODORIZERS	For carpets, mix 1 part borax to 2 parts cornmeal, sprinkle on liberally, and vacuum up after 1 hour. For kitty litter, sprinkle baking soda in bottom of box before adding litter.
DISINFECTANTS	Use 1/2 cup borax in 1 gallon of hot water. To inhibit mold or mildew, do not rinse off the borax solution.
DRAIN OPENER	To prevent clogging, use drain strainer on every drain. Pour boiling water down the drain once a week. To unclog, use rubber plunger or metal snake.
FLOOR CLEANER	For vinyl floors, mix 1/2 cup white vinegar or 1/4 cup TSP with 1 gallon of warm water. Polish with club soda. For wood floors, mix 1/4 cup oil soap with 1 gallon of warm water.
FURNITURE POLISH	Dissolve 1 tsp. lemon oil in 2 pints mineral oil. Or use oil soap to clean and a soft cloth to polish. Rub toothpaste on wood furniture to remove water stains.
GLASS CLEANER	Mix 1/4 cup white vinegar in 1 quart warm water, apply to glass, and rub dry with newspaper.
MILDEW CLEANER	Scrub mildew spots with baking soda or sponge with white vinegar. For shower curtain, wash with 1/2 cup soap and 1/2 cup baking soda, adding 1 cup white vinegar to rinse cycle.
OVEN CLEANER	Mix 3 tbsp. of washing soda with one quart warm water. Spray on, wait 20 minutes, then clean. For tough stains, scrub with very fine steel wool pads (0000) and baking soda.
RUG AND UPHOLSTERY CLEANER	Use non-aerosol, soap-based cleaner.
SCOURING POWDER	Use brand which does not contain chlorine or better yet, use baking soda.
SPOT REMOVER	Dissolve 1/4 cup borax in 3 cups of cold water. Sponge it on and let dry, or soak fabric in the solution prior to washing it in soap and cold water. Use professional dry cleaner for stubborn stains.
TUB AND TILE CLEANER	Use scouring powder or baking soda.

PAINT PRODUCTS

Product	Alternatives and preventative methods
PAINT AND STAINS	Latex or other water-based paints are the best choice. Enamel paint, stain and varnish are available in a water-base. Clean-up does not require paint thinner.
PAINTS FOR ARTISTS	Use with good ventilation. Never put brush in mouth. Powdered paint is hazardous if inhaled, so wear protective gear or use pre-mixed paints.
PAINT REMOVER	Use heat gun and scraper to remove paint, wearing proper protective gear. Strong alkali-type paint removers are available. A strong TSP solution (1 pound to 1 gallon hot water) may do the job. Brush on, wait 30 minutes, then scrape off.
PAINT THINNER AND SOLVENTS	Hold brush cleaner in closed jar until paint particles settle to bottom. Pour off clear liquid and reuse. Save paint sludge for collection.
WOOD FINISHES	Shellac, tung oil and linseed oil are finishes derived from natural sources. Shellac is diluted with an alcohol solvent, while the oils are diluted with turpentine for better application. Use with proper protection and ventilation.
WOOD PRESERVATIVES	Avoid using ones which contain pentachlorophenol, creosote or arsenic. When possible, use decay-resistant wood, e.g. cedar or redwood.

PESTICIDES & FERTILIZERS	
CHEMICAL FERTILIZERS	Compost, which can be made in your own backyard from grass clippings, food scraps and manure, is the best soil amendment. Other organic soil amendments include manure, seaweed, peat moss, and blood, fish and bone meal.
FUNGICIDES	Remove dead or diseased leaves and branches. Sulfur dust, sulfur spray and dormant oil spray (which does not contain copper) are the least-toxic products to treat plant diseases.
HERBICIDES (weedkillers)	Pull or hoe weeds prior to weeds going to seed. Use mulching (alfalfa hay is a good mulch) to keep weeds down in garden area.
INSECTICIDES (indoor)	Good sanitation in food prep and eating areas will prevent pests, while weather-stripping and caulking will seal them out. For crawling insects, use boric acid or silica aerogel in cracks and crevices. To keep out flies, keep door and window screens in good repair. Use fly swatter and sticky flypaper.
INSECTICIDES (garden)	Hose off plants with water using a jet spray nozzle. Use beneficial insects, e.g. lady beetle and praying mantis. When only a few bugs are found, spot treat with rubbing alcohol. A bacteria, B.T., is effective against caterpillars. Less-toxic sprays include insecticidal soap, pyrethrum or a homemade garlic/red pepper spray.
INSECTICIDES (pets)	Vacuum frequently and dispose of bag afterwards. Use good flea comb and flick fleas into soapy water. Dietary supplements may be helpful, e.g. brewer's yeast. Use herbal or d-limonene shampoos or dips.
MOTHBALLS	Place cedar chips, dried lavendar or herb sachets in drawers or closets to discourage moths.
SNAIL AND SLUG KILLERS	Fill shallow pan with stale beer and position at ground level. Or, to capture snails during the day, overturn clay pots leaving enough room for snails to crawl underneath. Snails also like to attach to boards. Collect and destroy.

AUTOMOTIVE PRODUCTS	
ANTIFREEZE	Small amounts may be diluted and put down a drain connected to the sewer system (not a septic tank).
BATTERIES	Old auto batteries can be exchanged when purchasing new battery or recycled at battery recyclers.
GASOLINE	For cleaning off grease, use non-toxic degreasers
MOTOR OIL	Synthetic motor oil lasts longer than regular motor oil, thus reducing amount of oil used. Motor oil can be recycled at participating service stations.
TRANSMISSION FLUID AND BRAKE FLUID	May be mixed with waste oil and recycled at participating service stations.

FIGURE 21.1 Public education flier. *(Courtesy of San Diego Environmental Health Coalition.)*

21.11

FIGURE 21.2 Prohibited waste control signs.

identified by the above procedures, field chemistry methods may be employed, e.g., pH measurement or flammability tests. In some cases, additional assessment may be needed, such as laboratory analysis.

The key component of prohibited waste control programs is often a random load-checking program. The load-checking program serves to detect and deter the disposal of prohibited wastes at the facility. A typical load-checking program consists of randomly diverting a specified number of loads per week for detailed inspection. The loads are spread and an inspector carefully examines the contents for prohibited wastes. Residential self-haul loads are a common source of HHWs. In addition to the load-checking inspections, all site personnel have the responsibility in the conduct of their work for observing prohibited wastes delivered to the facility.

Record keeping provides documentation of the prohibited waste control program. Records should be maintained for (1) load-checking reports, (2) event reports (i.e., emergencies, injuries, or special incidents), (3) training records, and (4) wastes shipped from the site.

If prohibited wastes are identified, they must be properly handled, stored, and disposed of. If the source of the waste is known, the waste may be returned to the source or shipped to a hazardous waste treatment, storage, or disposal facility (TSDF) at the source's expense. If the source is not known, the facility must have established procedures for disposing of the waste and for assumption of generator liabilities. It is common for cities or counties to assume generator liabilities in the case of HHWs from unknown generators.

While source control measures help reduce the amount of HHW generated and prevent its improper disposal, the public must also be provided with options for taking HHWs that are generated. The following sections discuss these types of HHW management programs.

One-Day Collection Programs

The most common type of HHW management program to date has been the 1-day collection program. Such programs have been referred to by a variety of names in different communities, including Toxic Away Days, Toxic Disposal Days, Amnesty Days, and Toxic Round-Ups. In these programs, HHWs are brought to a specified site on a specified day. The wastes are then taken from the public, usually free of charge, and properly packaged for recycling, treatment, or disposal. Participation rates in 1-day collection programs have typically been in the range of 1 to 3 percent of households in the community.

A typical layout for a 1-day collection program is illustrated in Fig. 21.3. The major functional areas of a one-day collection program are

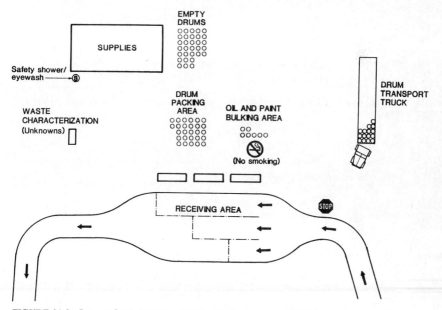

FIGURE 21.3   Layout for 1-day household hazardous waste collection program.

• Entrance area
• Receiving area
• Sorting area
• Packing area
• Storage area
• Loading area

Signs at the site entrance as well as along roads in the site vicinity direct traffic to the program. Upon arrival at the program, the public is typically given questionnaires and fliers regarding the program. A sample questionnaire is shown in Fig. 21.4. An example of a flier is given in Fig. 21.1. The questionnaires collect data

---

QUESTIONNAIRE FOR SALINAS TOXIC DISPOSAL DAY

1. How did you hear about Toxic Disposal Day?
   ___ (a) flyer at work   ___ (d) TV/radio announcement
   ___ (b) direct mail piece   ___ (e) word of mouth
   ___ (c) newspaper ad/article

2. Where do you live?
   ___ (a) City of Salinas
   ___ (b) North County
   ___ (c) other (specify) _____.

3. How many households are represented by your delivery of hazardous household waste materials?
   ___ (a) one   ___ (c) three
   ___ (b) two   ___ (d) more than three _____.

4. Did you know about toxic household materials previously?
   ___ yes   ___ no

5. How have you disposed of toxic household waste in the past?
   ___ (a) garbage   ___ (c) dump on ground
   ___ (b) sewer   ___ (d) other _____.

6. Did you know before this project that it was not safe to dispose of toxic waste in the garbage?
   ___ yes   ___ no

7. Do you feel this is a worthwhile service for the community?
   ___ yes   ___ no

   Why? _____.

8. How often do you think this service should be available?
   ___ (a) weekly   ___ (c) twice a year
   ___ (b) monthly   ___ (d) once a year

9. Would you be willing to pay a fee (50 cents or $1) for this service?
   ___ yes   ___ no

10. Comments:
    _____
    _____
    _____
    _____

FIGURE 21.4 Questionnaire for household hazardous waste collection program.

about the program users, wastes delivered to the site, previous disposal practices, and program needs of the community. The fliers provide public information about proper household hazardous waste management, including source reduction. The questionnaires are either collected just before entering the receiving area or at the receiving area itself.

The receiving area is preferably divided into multiple lanes to facilitate traffic flow and waste removal. Traffic cones and signs are used to divide the lanes. At the receiving area, people in the vehicles are met by site personnel. Only qualified site personnel should be allowed to handle the hazardous waste once vehicles reach the site. The site personnel inspect the wastes delivered and ask the users about the contents of any wastes that are not in their original containers or are not readily identifiable. (If the resident does not know what the substance is, they may at least know what it was used for, e.g., to kill weeds.) This information is conveyed to the sorting personnel to assist in minimizing the amount of unidentified wastes received. The site personnel then remove the wastes from the vehicles and take them to the sorting area. Rollable carts are helpful for moving the wastes around the site. After the wastes are removed from the vehicles, the vehicles exit by the designated route. Special parking areas should be available for vehicles requiring extra attention (e.g., nonhousehold wastes, unidentified wastes, spills).

At the sorting area, trained personnel sort the wastes according to Department of Transportation (DOT) hazard class (and specific disposal site categories if necessary). The sorted wastes are either lab-packed or bulked into drums for transporting to recycling, treatment, or disposal facilities. The drums are appropriately labeled and manifested.

The drums are then loaded onto a hazardous waste transport truck and removed from the site within a relatively short period of time—ranging from one to several days in accordance with prevailing regulations.

In some communities, 1-day collection programs have evolved into periodic collection programs, in which the procedures described above are repeated on a regular basis one or more times per year. Some of the shortcomings encountered in 1-day collection programs include (1) long lines and waiting times for users of the program, (2) lack of scheduling convenience, (3) high costs per day of operation, and (4) limited recycling of wastes. However, these programs have been very successful in diverting hazardous wastes from the solid waste stream and in educating the public. One-day programs allow communities to offer an HHW management program without large capital investments, while retaining the flexibility to develop a more comprehensive program in the future.

Permanent Facilities

In efforts to develop long-term solutions to the management of HHW, some communities have developed permanent HHW facilities. Such facilities typically consist of a building constructed for the processing and storage of HHWs delivered to the site by residents. Wastes are shipped from the facility to recycling, treatment, or disposal facilities when full truck loads are accumulated or when storage time limitations are reached. The facility essentially functions as a hazardous waste transfer station (restricted to HHW unless otherwise permitted).

Permanent facilities offer residents the convenience of year-round disposal services. Residents do not have to store up wastes for the next 1-day collection event or sit in long lines to deliver their wastes. One of the most common occasions for HHW disposal is upon moving, and seldom does a resident's move coincide with a 1-day collection event. From the operator's perspective, the distributed waste flow (as compared to 1-day programs) results in a more controlled and manageable operation.

Another major benefit of permanent HHW facilities is increased recycling and treatment of hazardous wastes with a corresponding decrease in land disposal. Some permanent facilities report less than 10 percent of wastes being sent for landfilling. In contrast, 1-day collection programs often involve lab-packing the majority of wastes received and sending such wastes to landfills. In comparison to 1-day programs, recycling is enhanced at permanent facilities as a result of (1) facility features for bulking and treating wastes, (2) protection provided by the building against weather, (3) more evenly distributed waste flow rates, (4) increased processing time available, and (5) increased testing capabilities to verify a waste container's constituents.

A layout for a permanent HHW facility is presented in Fig. 21.5. The major functional areas of permanent HHW facilities are

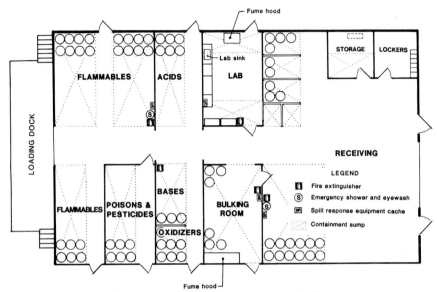

FIGURE 21.5 Layout for permanent household hazardous waste facility.

- Entrance area
- Receiving area
- Sorting area
- Waste characterization area (laboratory)
- Treatment and/or bulking area
- Packing area
- Waste storage area
- Supplies storage area
- Loading area

The flow of vehicles and wastes at a permanent facility generally follow that described for the 1-day collection programs. The major differences include lower daily traffic and waste volumes, increased waste characterization prior to packing, and additional bulking and treatment operations.

The design and construction of hazardous waste storage facilities is governed by a set of overlapping regulations, including building codes, fire codes, Subtitle C of RCRA, state hazardous waste regulations, and local ordinances on the storage of hazardous materials. Some of the key building requirements pertain to secondary containment, separation of incompatible materials, fire suppression, ventilation, electrical systems, and building materials. These requirements result in the costs of HHW facility design and construction being relatively high.

A permanent HHW facility can function in an HHW management system in a variety of roles, including (1) a single facility serving the community, (2) a core facility with satellite stations located around the community to provide greater service and convenience, and (3) a core facility for a mobile collection program. HHW facilities can also provide storage for hazardous wastes found in load-checking programs at solid waste management facilities. In addition, HHW facilities play a valuable role in educating the public about proper HHW management.

Portable Facilities

A lower capital-cost alternative to a permanent HHW facility is a portable storage facility. Portable storage facilities usually consist of one or more prefabricated storage units. An example of a portable storage facility is given in Fig. 21.6. These units are available with a variety of options. The base units typically include secondary containment sumps, chemical-resistant coatings, passive ventilation, static grounding connections, and locking doors. Options include fire suppression systems (water, dry chemical, or halon), explosion-proof lighting and electrical systems, heating and/or air conditioning, forced-ventilation, explosion-relief panels, floor grates, customized interiors (walls, shelving, cylinder racks), and alarm systems.

FIGURE 21.6 Portable hazardous waste storage facility.

The storage capacity of the largest units typically does not exceed forty 55-gal drums. The smallest units may have capacities of less than 10 drums. In general, portable storage facilities have less storage capacity than permanent facilities; however, the modular nature of the storage units could allow siting multiple units to expand overall capacity.

The units can usually be moved with a forklift. Some are designed to be moved by a roll-off truck or trailer. This mobility offers advantages for certain applications. For example, portable storage facilities can serve as satellite stations for a permanent facility or for storage of hazardous wastes found in load-checking programs at solid waste management facilities.

Portable storage facilities offer flexibility in implementing an HHW management system. Portable facilities can be installed during an interim period with a permanent facility implemented at a later date. The portable storage facility can then still be used in conjunction with the permanent facility in one of the various roles discussed above.

Limitations of portable facilities include restricted bulking capabilities and storage space. Restricted bulking capabilities reduce the amount of wastes that can be recycled. The importance of these limitations depends upon the size and characteristics of the community.

Mobile Programs

Mobile HHW collection programs have been developed to provide more convenient service to residents. Mobile programs can be broken down into two categories: (1) door-to-door collection programs and (2) mobile collection facilities.

Door-to-door collection programs involve picking up HHWs at individual homes. The wastes must be categorized and secured for transport to a hazardous waste facility, e.g., a hazardous waste transfer station (fully permitted TSDF or HHW facility). Hazardous waste hauling permits are thus required for operation of door-to-door collection programs. These programs are typically run on an appointment basis. Such programs are not widespread at this time but can be offered as an extension of the services provided by a core HHW facility.

Mobile collection facilities combine some features of 1-day collection programs and some features of portable storage facilities. A layout for a mobile collection facility is shown in Fig. 21.7. Collection sites are set up at different locations throughout the year. The collection site may be open at a given location for a period ranging from several days to several weeks. The collection sites may make use of a portable storage facility, or wastes may be hauled to a storage facility elsewhere in the area.

TECHNICAL REQUIREMENTS FOR MANAGING HHW

Personnel Training

Well-trained personnel are crucial to the success of an HHW program. Personnel training requirements will depend on the type of HHW program implemented and on the job category of each employee—operational personnel may vary from

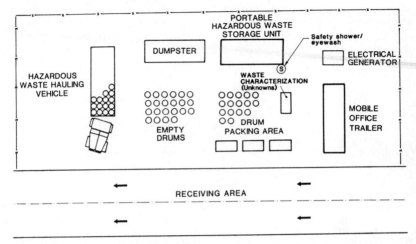

FIGURE 21.7 Layout for mobile household hazardous waste collection program.

technicians to chemists. Examples of topics to be addressed in training programs are given in Table 21.7. The operation's safety officer has ultimate responsibility for determining the specific training needs of each individual. All applicable OSHA requirements must be complied with.

All employees should receive initial as well as refresher training. Much of the training required involves information that is not taught in academic programs, but rather is learned "on the job." Furthermore, regulations change frequently, thereby necessitating training updates.

Records should be maintained for all employee training. These records provide a good check on training needs and also document training for review by regulatory agencies.

Equipment and Materials

A list of typical equipment and materials used in HHW operations is presented in Table 21.8. The list is presented as a guideline. Specific requirements for equipment and materials should be determined for each program.

Safety

Intrinsic to the definition of hazardous wastes is the potentially harmful nature of the materials so classified. Therefore, safety is of paramount importance in the management of these materials. To help ensure a safe operation, workers should be properly trained, wear protective equipment, and follow carefully established operating procedures.

During routine operations, workers should wear protective clothing, protective gloves, safety eyewear, and footwear appropriate to the task being performed. Table 21.8 lists various types of safety equipment. The different materials used in protective clothing and gloves exhibit different chemical

TABLE 21.7 Sample Training Program Topics

Topic	Items covered
Health and safety	Toxicology; health effects of hazardous materials; first aid, CPR; accident prevention–safety procedures; medical surveillance program
Use of protective equipment	Levels of protection; use of respirators (air-purifying, supplied-air, SCBA); glove alternatives and compatibilities; coverall alternatives and compatibilities
Hazardous waste regulations	40 CFR (federal hazardous waste regulations); 49 CFR (federal transportation regulations); state regulations; local regulations
Chemistry of hazardous materials	Overview of chemistry basics; incompatibilities of chemicals; uses of hazardous materials in consumer products; hazardous material classification (e.g., DOT)
Waste identification procedures	Product labels; customer information; physical assessment; field chemistry
Facility operation and maintenance procedures	Waste receiving; waste sorting; waste packing (lab-packing, bulking, manifesting, labeling); vehicle operation; routine clean-up procedures; routine inspection procedures (daily, weekly, monthly); site security
Emergency response	Personnel responsibilities; spill containment; fire control; emergency support services; evacuation procedures; decontamination; notification requirements
Record-keeping procedures	DOT manifest; drum inventories; incident logs; facility inspection records; training records; medical records; internal reports (monthly, annual); reports to regulatory agencies

compatibilities. The program's safety officer is responsible for making determinations of proper safety equipment.

Emergency Response

An emergency response plan should be developed for every HHW program. Periodic drills should be conducted at permanent HHW facilities. The emergency response plan should identify the responsible roles of site personnel (including designation of an emergency coordinator), describe response procedures for different types of emergencies, and identify emergency services to be called if necessary. Emergency telephone numbers should also be listed at the site, including fire, police, ambulance, hospitals, spill reporting agencies, and CHEMTREC (emergency information service of the chemical industry).

The emergency coordinator is responsible for evaluating the emergency situation and for directing the response or seeking assistance from emergency services. Following are general procedures for qualified personnel to respond to emergencies.

TABLE 21.8 Equipment and Materials used in HHW Operations

Category	Items
Safety equipment	Protective clothing (e.g., Tyvek, saran-coated Tyvek, polycoated splash suits) Protective gloves (e.g., neoprene, nitrile, viton, latex, polyethylene) Safety eyewear (glasses, goggles, face shields) Dust masks Boots Hard hats
Emergency response equipment	Fire extinguishers (ABC-rated) Air-purifying respirators (half- or full-facepiece) Respirator cartridges (organic vapor–acid gas cartridges, pesticide prefilters) Supplied air emergency masks (5- to 30-min) Self-contained breathing apparatus (SCBA) First aid and burn kits Emergency blankets Emergency shower and eyewash units Hose (connected to running water) Spill containment and cleanup kits (e.g., spill pillows, dikes) Noncombustible absorbent material (including dry sand) Decontamination solutions Plastic buckets Hazardous material recovery containers with lids Overpack drums Barricade tape Plastic tarps Brooms Dust pans (nonsparking) Shovels (nonsparking)
Packing materials	Drums Spare drum lids and rings Absorbent Funnel Drum liners Drum pump Drum wrenches (drum bolt, bung) DOT labels
Material handling equipment	Hand trucks Rollable carts Plastic tubs
Communication equipment	Telephone Two-way radios Alarm system
General supplies	Tables Markers, pencils, clipboards Record-keeping forms (including manifests, drum inventory forms) Reference documents Field chemistry kit Tool box Signs Traffic cones
Mobile equipment	Fork lift (with drum grabbers) Emergency response van Hazardous waste transport truck (provided by hauler)

The area of the spill, fire, or explosion should be cleared of all persons not wearing protective equipment or not trained in emergency response techniques. Except for minor spills, all waste receiving should be halted and the general public kept a safe distance upwind. Emergency response personnel should don protective equipment appropriate to the incident, with the nearest qualified personnel to the incident responding first. Other site personnel should provide support from a safe distance as needed, e.g., assist in communications, deliver supplies, and monitor the situation.

In the event of a hazardous liquid spill, clean-up operations begin with spreading a noncombustible absorbent material around the perimeter of the spill. The absorbent material is then carefully placed on the liquid until absorption is complete. The materials are cleaned up by sweeping into an appropriate container.

In the event of a hazardous solid spill, the material is cleaned up by directly sweeping it into an appropriate container.

In the event of a fire or explosion, the responsibility of site personnel is that of fire control (if safe) rather than fire extinguishing, unless the incident is minor. The fire department should be notified immediately, and only trained site personnel should assist in fire control efforts while awaiting the fire department's arrival. Dry chemical fire extinguishers and/or inert materials (e.g., dry sand) may be useful in fire control. To the extent possible, other potential ignition sources should be removed from the area.

After mitigation of the emergency incident, it may be necessary to decontaminate equipment and surfaces that came into contact with the hazardous materials, depending on the material. The waste generated by the decontamination process and the protective clothing worn by emergency response personnel should be disposed of as a hazardous waste.

Finally, appropriate agencies should be notified of the emergency incident and applicable recordkeeping should be completed.

Characterization of Unknowns

One of the greatest operational difficulties in HHW programs is dealing with unknowns. At a minimum, the hazard class of each material must be determined to allow for safe and legal storage, transport, and disposal. The amount of unknowns can be reduced by collecting information about any wastes received that are not in their original containers or are not readily identifiable as described in "One-Day Collection Programs," earlier in this chapter. However, some capabilities for identifying unknowns are still required.

Field chemistry techniques, similar to those used in spill response, are well suited to characterizing unknown HHWs. An example of this approach is the HazCat method developed by the California Department of Industrial Relations. Field chemistry utilizes tests such as pH, flammability, solubility, oxidation, and reactivity to categorize unknowns into DOT hazard classes. Field chemistry kits are assembled to provide the supplies necessary to conduct the categorization tests.

Storage Requirements

Storage of hazardous wastes is subject to a variety of requirements, including

- Secondary containment
- Separation of incompatibles

- Distance to property line
- Distance to structures on site (depending on fire-wall ratings)
- Fire suppression
- Ventilation
- Electrical systems
- Building materials

Hazardous material storage criteria are established in building codes, fire codes, RCRA Subtitle C, state hazardous waste regulations, and local ordinances. Specific requirements are determined by the local building official and fire marshall; the requirements will depend upon the occupancy classification given and other discretionary rulings. The storage of flammables usually invokes the most stringent requirements with regard to HHWs.

Record Keeping

Some record keeping is regulatory mandated, while other record keeping is motivated by good operational control. An example of required records are hazardous waste manifests, which must be completed for all hazardous wastes shipped from a site. Manifest records must be maintained for 3 years. Many disposal sites also require waste profiles and drum inventories for all lab-packed wastes (i.e., an itemization of each container in the lab pack with a description of its contents). Permit conditions may also stipulate certain record-keeping and reporting requirements.

Record-keeping needs are greater for storage facilities than for 1-day collection programs. Examples of records and reports to be maintained for an HHW operation include

- Hazardous waste manifests
- Drum inventories
- Employee training records
- Employee medical records
- Permits
- Operation plan
- Facility inspection records
- Incident log
- Internal reports
- Reports to regulatory agencies

RECYCLING AND TREATMENT ALTERNATIVES

Paint

As the largest component of most household hazardous waste streams, paint is a major target for recycling and/or treatment. Potential benefits include cost savings, material recovery, and diversion from land disposal. Paint is classified into two basic categories: (1) latex (water-based) and (2) oil-based. Recycling and treatment alternatives for these categories of paint vary accordingly.

Latex paint recycling is a fairly common practice. There are various types of paint recycling programs, including waste exchange, low-grade recycling, and high-grade recycling. Paint exchange typically involves either giving away the paint in its original container (i.e., paint in good condition and in full or nearly-full containers) or bulking (consolidating) the paint into drums for giving away or sale at a relatively low price. Low-grade recycling generally consists of bulking the paint into 55-gal drums, reprocessing the paint by a paint manufacturer into a low-grade paint, and returning the paint to the program for a fee. Because the recycled product is a low-grade paint, it is typically given away to community groups or local agencies; uses of the paint include graffiti control and general painting where specific requirements are not important. Outside use is often recommended. High-grade recycling involves bulking the paint for reprocessing by a paint manufacturer into a salable product.

Some latex paint is not recyclable because either it is in poor condition or it contains hazardous constituents. Potential hazardous constituents include mercury, lead, and other heavy metals. Mercury has been used as a biocide in paint. It was banned from interior latex paint in 1990 but is still allowed for exterior latex paint. Lead was used as a pigment in paint until it was banned in 1973. HHW programs still receive paint containing lead and can expect to receive paint containing mercury for many years. Paint containing high levels of heavy metals could be screened out of the recycling program by means of checking container labels and testing suspect containers when labeling information is not available.

Recycling oil-based paint is not commonly practiced; however, some programs (particularly permanent facilities) bulk oil-based paint for use as a supplementary fuel. Waste exchange programs serve to reclaim additional oil-based paint. Recycling oil-based paint has been demonstrated to be technically feasible and may provide greater alternatives in the future.

Oil

Recycling used motor oil is probably the oldest and most common HHW recycling practice. The rates of oil recycling have varied over the years as a result of several factors, including oil prices, oil purchasing patterns, and regulatory controls on used oil. Ambiguities over the designation of used oil as a hazardous waste resulted in a reduction in oil recycling in the 1980s. The importance of used oil collection and recycling is increasingly recognized at federal, state, and local levels.

In addition to HHW programs, used oil is collected at automotive service stations, recycling centers, transfer stations, and landfills. Oil is also collected in some curbside recycling programs. The EPA estimates that less than half of the oil from do-it-yourselfers who change their own oil is collected; the remainder is put in the garbage, poured on the ground, poured down sewers, etc.[24] So more complete collection of used oil is still a big challenge for communities.

Used oil collected in HHW programs can be readily recycled. The oil should be bulked into either an oil storage tank or 55-gal drums. Used oil will normally contain some contaminants from its use in an engine (e.g., water, gasoline, sediments, and heavy metals), but it is important to guard against unusual contaminants in the oil received, particularly PCBs and chlorinated solvents. The presence of such major contaminants will likely result in the load being rejected by

21. National Solid Waste Management Association (NSWMA), "Examples of Small Quantities of Hazardous Waste in Trash," NSWMA, Washington, D.C., 1984.
22. United States Environmental Protection Agency, *Report to Congress on Solid Waste Disposal in the United States,* EPA/530-SW-88-011B, Washington, D.C., October 1988.
23. State of California Air Resources Board, *The Landfill Gas Testing Program: A Second Report to the California Legislature,* Sacramento, California, June 1989.
24. United States Environmental Protection Agency, *How to Set Up a Local Program to Recycle Used Oil,* EPA/530-SW-89-039A, Washington, D.C., May 1989.

CHAPTER 22
DROP-OFF STATIONS AND BUY-BACK CENTERS

Liane R. Levetan
Chief Executive Officer
De Kalb (Atlanta) County, Georgia

To be of lasting benefit, recycling must remain economically feasible along with its appeal to citizens' stewardship of the environment and the world's resources.

With this in mind, one cannot predict a single recycling method, but many to accommodate varied local resources, markets and the degree of citizen participation. *Drop-off stations* and *buy-back centers* for recyclable goods offer highly practical means for citizen and small business participation in the waste reduction effort. They function well alone or as adjuncts to curbside recycling.

Few communities have mandatory recycling, although some states and localities are setting guidelines and goals to reduce their waste volume through recycling. In Georgia, for instance, a state law establishes a goal of reducing waste volume received by all landfills by 25 percent per capita within five years.

This chapter deals with drop-off stations and buy-back centers (Fig. 22.1), and some factors to consider before establishing either one as a method of collecting recyclable materials. Local conditions may warrant both types of collection, even

FIGURE 22.1 Typical buy-back center–recycling market.

in conjunction with curbside pickup, but it will be wise to evaluate anticipated volumes of each material to be collected as well as how it will be delivered to a recycling processor.

THE DROP-OFF STATION

By definition, a drop-off station is a bin or series of bins (usually untended) where depositors simply leave recyclable materials such as newsprint, aluminum cans, glass, or other materials for pickup by a recycling processor or an intermediary agent. Ideally, depositors would sort recyclable materials correctly, pick up their spills, and close bin hatches where necessary to protect their contents from the weather. This often proves not to be the case, however. Ultimate responsibility for proper sorting and maintenance of the drop-off station, therefore, rests with the collector and should be incorporated in an operational plan.

Depositors receive no pay for bringing their recyclable materials to a drop-off station. They do, however, have the satisfaction of knowing that their contribution will help preserve natural resources, save energy that would be needed to process raw materials, and reduce the amount of waste that must be buried or incinerated.

An exception regarding pay is where the drop-off station is sponsored by a school or civic group which receives compensation from the processor based on weight for allowing bins to be placed on its grounds. In most cases, such pay is directed to educational or charitable projects from which the whole community benefits.

With a drop-off station, the private enterprise recycling processor or collector usually bears the cost of the container and transporting its contents when full. Municipal recycling programs may place collection bins on public land where available. Otherwise, sites for bins are generally donated or leased. Some states have environmental grant programs which may help a local government purchase containers and sites for recycling.

Since depositors at a drop-off station receive no pay, far fewer citizens normally participate than would at a buy-back center. Because no one is present to monitor a drop-off station, vandalism and contamination are more prevalent.

Proper separation of materials is essential for a successful recycling project. At a drop-off station, a careless depositor who mixes colored glass with clear or magazines with newsprint could be responsible for the entire load ending up in a landfill. Glass manufacturers lack the technology to remove color from the molten batch; any amount of mismatched glass contaminates the batch. Separation of newsprint that has been contaminated with magazine stock—or garbage—is generally too labor-intensive for the collector to justify. As a result, all the contaminated load goes to the landfill.

Community Drop-Off Program

An example of typical problems with a drop-off station was seen at a major Atlanta market where the management placed containers for customers to deposit aluminum, three colors of glass, and plastic drink bottles. This was a very high traffic location visited by homemakers and, late in the day, by many office workers.

The collection firm provided posters and bin labels with very specific instructions on proper depositing. They emphasized separation of glass by color and removal of paper or plastic bags before dropping materials into the bins. This recycling program was reluctantly abandoned after one year. While a quantity of materials was being reclaimed for recycling as intended, contamination in the glass bins due to careless sorting and the inclusion of garbage in all the bins were persistent. Processors reject loads mixed with garbage because they cannot justify the cost of pulling out garbage. The recycling firm was having to pay to dispose of contaminated loads at a landfill.

In this case, what started as a good civic project by a recycling company and a local merchant became merely a garbage collection process, and a costly one at that. It would likely have been successful if the merchant could have monitored depositors enough to discourage abusers.

In another metro-Atlanta suburb an enthusiastic Clean and Beautiful Committee proved for itself the value of monitoring. The organization initiated a drop-off program for glass and aluminum recycling at six locations. Besides the parking area at their own headquarters, they designated five neighborhood shopping strips as their sites and obtained the cooperation of merchants and their landlords. Only one drop-off site consistently accumulated uncontaminated material, the one monitored frequently at the Clean and Beautiful education headquarters. All containers were clearly marked and instructions were posted; however, many contributors at the shopping strips ignored them. Where monitoring was frequent and visible to depositors, few tried to drop off their garbage, and glass was well sorted.

To divert more hazardous material from the landfill, some localities set aside "Amnesty Day" once a year for citizens to bring hazardous waste items from their homes, such things as old paint, used motor oil, insecticides, and antifreeze. These are collected in safe containers for transportation to a proper hazardous waste disposal site.

Volunteer Group Support

A promising approach with drop-off stations is to link them with a specific group of users: members of a church, school students, workers at a large industry, or an office building occupied by a single company. Such groups can be educated about the importance of separating recyclable materials, and to an extent members of the group monitor each other.

To be successful in such a setting, the recycling program needs three elements: *M-E-M*. This acronym stands for *motivation, education,* and constant *monitoring.* Of the three, education of the people who will participate in recycling is the easiest to effect. Community Clean and Beautiful projects have plenty of informative materials, as do environmental groups and trade associations within the waste management field. Part of a good education effort on recycling will be a discussion of cost avoidance through a reduction of the waste-stream volume. County and municipal officials can tell you how much it costs per ton to dispose of solid waste. Every ton that is recycled means that the citizens of a community avoid that cost in taxes or in the fees they pay for garbage collection.

Public Awareness and Motivation

Monitoring an in-house recycling program at a church or factory must be an exercise in persuasion rather than coercion. Obviously, people who don't want to take the time to separate materials properly will simply refrain from participating. A responsible volunteer (or team of volunteers if it's a big operation) can be appointed to call the recycling firm for pickup when containers are full and to see that signs are in place. The same persons might advertise and advance the program by reporting how many pounds have been collected or how many dollars earned.

Motivation is much easier among members of an organization or workforce than among the general public. The sponsoring group will have designated a use for anticipated earnings at the start of the recycling program, and if it is a popular cause, motivation follows naturally. A church might decide to earmark earnings for youth projects, the homeless, or programs for the elderly. Office building tenants might set the money aside for an annual party, employee recreation facilities, or a charitable cause. Aside from the monetary motivation, members of the group will be encouraged to learn periodically what their combined action has accomplished for the environment.

In-House Corporate Program

A drop-off recycling program at corporate headquarters of The Coca-Cola Company in Atlanta employs the methods described above and has become so successful that it could serve as a model for other in-house efforts. Coca-Cola's main office complex occupied by about 3000 employees recycling 1.2 million pounds of material in two years, earned over $50,000 cash for local charities, and made significant savings in its own waste disposal costs.

Recycling starts with desktop folders for office white paper, a relatively high-priced commodity. These are collected daily by the cleaning crew. Snack areas have containers for collecting glass and aluminum. Participation from top management down contributes to motivation. Indeed, employees have conditioned themselves to think, "Is this recyclable?," when they are ready to discard almost anything.

The office recycling habit carries over into their homes with the support of the company. Containers for glass, paper, aluminum, and plastic are placed in a covered parking area employees can reach easily to deposit recyclables from home (Figs. 22.2 and 22.3).

Where the sponsoring group is small and their accumulation of recyclable goods doesn't warrant frequent pickup by the buyer, it may be more practical to establish a schedule of "recycling days." As with the time-honored school paper sale, members of the organization can be told that recycling containers will be on location certain days of the month only. This will assure them that they will have a convenient place to take their materials and that they needn't store them indefinitely. The collector, on the other hand, will find it economically feasible to bring containers to a location that can fill them once a month, but would not have enough volume to justify leaving containers on site full time.

COMPARING COSTS

In comparing the two types of recycling collection points, it is obvious that a drop-off station takes less capitalization. It may consist of as little as a roll-away

FIGURE 22.2   Recycling bins in Coca-Cola Atlanta headquarters.

(a)

FIGURE 22.3   (*a*) Coca-Cola employee transports material from parked car to collection bin.

bin or a large hamper than can be emptied by the processor's collection truck (Fig. 22.4).

Several metal fabricators offer for sale sturdy roll-off truck bodies that are compartmentalized to receive a variety of materials through small hatches placed at about eye level for depositors. Collector trucks with tilt-beds and winches deliver empty containers to a drop-off station and pick up the filled ones.

Table 22.1 indicates prices of two types of bins, those placed and emptied by a front-loader truck and those designed to roll off and on a tilt-bed truck. As one

(b)

FIGURE 22.3 (*Continued*) (*b*) Employee deposits recyclables into corporate operated drop-off station.

(a)

FIGURE 22.4 (*a*) Truck unloads roll-off recycling container.

can see, containers can be custom-made with openings, capacity, and signage to suit the type of items to be collected.

Amortization of container cost is difficult to pinpoint due to variable market prices for recyclables. Bin costs may look like a better bargain, however, when you consider the escalation of tipping fees that has occurred due to more stringent environmental requirements for siting and building landfills.

(b)

FIGURE 22.4 (*Continued*) (*b*) Roll-off waste containers were fitted with ports for deposit of recyclable materials. Compartments inside are hinged to open in sequence for unloading at recycling center by tilt-bed trucks.

TABLE 22.1 Typical Containers and Costs for Drop-Off Stations

Type	Size/specifications	Price*
Roll-off bin	15 ft, 26 yd^3, 3 ports per side, no compartments	$2500
Roll-off bin	20 ft, 35 yd^3, 4 ports per side, no compartments	2900
Roll-off bin	15 ft, 26 yd^3, 3 ports per side, 3 compartments	3100
Roll-off bin	20 ft, 35 yd^3, 4 ports per side, 4 compartments	3800
Front-load container	4 yd^3, painted and lettered	410
Front-load container	6 yd^3, painted and lettered	530
Front-load container	8 yd^3, painted and lettered	590

*Prices effective July 1991.

Drop-off station bins can be designed to make it difficult for people who might pilfer their contents and sell them to a buy-back center. At an untended location, a pilferproof container might be worthwhile (Fig. 22.5). Another defense would be to locate drop-off stations where there is ample light at night and people on the premises at all times, for instance, at a fire station or a heavily traveled area.

Since depositors receive no pay for their donations to a drop-off station, they can't be expected to go much out of their way. To be effective, drop-off stations need to be located on citizens' ordinary routes of travel and be easily accessible. Among the types of locations that have been successful for drop-off stations are

School grounds	Sports arenas
Fire stations	Stadiums
Public parks	Theater parking lots
Shopping malls	Local government centers

FIGURE 22.5   Mini drop-off station in town house development. (*Courtesy Municipal Sales and Services, Lakeland, Florida.*)

The donor of a site for a drop-off station deserves—and will probably insist on—consideration of sanitation, safety, and aesthetics around the station. Not all depositors may be neat; some arrangement needs to be made to keep the area around collection bins clean and free of debris. Bins themselves (Fig. 22.6) need to look clean and freshly painted or depositors won't want to touch hatch lids or risk getting clothing smudged by rust and grime. An agreement between the collector and the site donor or lessor should include arrangements for maintenance of the area, bins, and signs.

On the safety side, the recycling collector should check often for jagged metal or loose bolts on collection devices that might injure a user.

Placement of a collection bin is also a safety consideration. While it needs to be easy to find, neighbors may complain if it seems too obtrusive or incompatible with other land use in the area. Traffic must have a safe approach, meaning adequate space for exit and entry back into traffic and no sight obstructions that might put pedestrians at risk. In any event, a collection bin needs to be accessible to depositors in their personal autos and to the truck that will empty it or haul it off. If on a paved drive, for instance, will the pavement support the weight of the truck that will service the bin?

Part of the locational decision, therefore, should be based on the cost of preparing and maintaining the collection bin site relative to the volume of materials to be deposited there. It may prove more cost effective to pay to lease a site at a shopping mall parking lot than to prepare a less suitable one that is donated. Figure 22.7 shows a collection bin site.

(a)

(b)

FIGURE 22.6 (a) Standard commercial waste bins converted with opening for recycling. (b) Drop-off station containers with hydraulic dumps. (*Courtesy Haul-All Equipment, Ltd., Lethbridge, Alberta, Canada.*)

THE BUY-BACK CENTER

In contrast to the "donation" nature of the drop-off station, a buy-back center pays the depositors directly for their recycling efforts. A buy-back center customer simply earns cash along with the satisfaction of practicing good environmental stewardship.

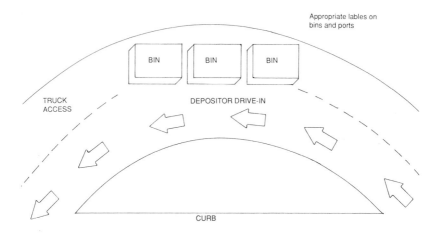

FIGURE 22.7   Drop-off station layout.

Typically, a buy-back center (Fig. 22.8) will handle a greater volume of materials than a drop-off station. A community might support one buy-back center better than it would a score of drop-off stations.

The buy-back center will be staffed, have a permanent location, and will be operated as a small business subject to zoning restrictions and all other local regulation. Its total appearance from the identifying sign throughout its grounds must emphasize that this is *not* a "junkyard." Orderliness and good sanitation are essential whether the center is operated by a local government agency or by private enterprise.

Nothing is more important to citizen participation in a buy-back center than *location*. Depositors' convenience must be the first consideration.

At the start of the 1990s, comparatively few buy-back centers occupied new buildings specifically designed for that purpose. Most have converted existing buildings in well-established commercial districts. They may be located along with other service establishments and neighborhood retail stores in areas with light commercial to light industrial zoning. It is not unusual

FIGURE 22.8   Buy-back center.

to find a buy-back center in a former service station. These have several readymade characteristics for a successful recycling location: paved drive-in area, level lot, good street access, and bays at ground level for receiving materials. Leasing and renovating an existing building, of course, would mean lower upfront cost of opening a buy-back center than building from the ground up.

Location Checklist

A checklist for determining the suitability of a potential buy-back location would include the following:

1. High visibility and convenience for depositors
2. At a minimum, a nearly level full acre with space for depositors' autos to drive through
3. Adequate space for loading accumulated materials into trucks bound for material processors
4. Fully enclosed secure building for receiving recyclable materials and sheltering equipment
5. Fenced lot if zoning permits outside storage
6. Compatibility with neighbors

Operation Factors

A buy-back center that accepts only aluminum cans and newsprint can start operations with a minimum of equipment. The more varieties of material that will be accepted, the more equipment will be needed (Fig. 22.9). One general rule, however, is that the more appropriate equipment available for handling recyclable materials, the less personnel required.

At a minimum, a buy-back center accepting aluminum cans and newsprint will need a floor scale with digital readout and a can-sorting machine. A digital scale is best because there's nothing arbitrary about reading the weight, and the depositor should be invited to see what the scale registers. Floor scales suitable for a buy-back center are in the $3000 cost range.

Not all drink cans are made of aluminum, and while the steel ones are marketable, they cannot be mixed with the aluminum ones. The can-sorting machine removes steel cans magnetically.

Balers and a can sorter with flattener are optional for centers that deal only in newsprint and aluminum. Newsprint is often taken from the floor scale directly to a trailer where center employees stack it compactly for shipment to the pulp mill.

One of the most efficient ways of handling aluminum cans for recycling is to drop them into a sorting machine from which an air blower propels them directly into a trailer often supplied by the aluminum company that will remanufacture them.

Some buy-back centers use combination crusher/separators for aluminum cans (Fig. 22.10). With such equipment, a depositor may weigh cans and then drop them into the hopper of a crusher/separator. A few noisy seconds later, the flattened cans are blown from a pipe at the opposite end of the machine into a trailer for shipment. A typical crusher/separator costs about $1800 and requires approximately 3 × 14 ft of floor space. Prices and designs vary considerably,

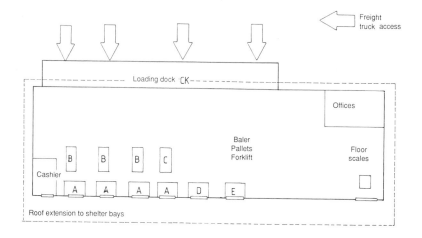

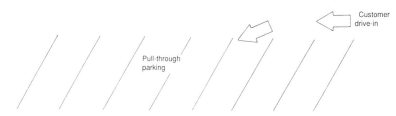

FIGURE 22.9   Buy-back center layout.

FIGURE 22.10   Buy-back center's baler for aluminum cans.

however. For a new installation, check the market for the most up-to-date equipment and competitive pricing.

Adding Materials Requires More Equipment

Buy-back centers across the nation are also finding markets to recycle glass, corrugated board, office paper, plastic drink bottles, copper, and other metals. They may not find markets for all these materials in all locations, but where markets exist, domestic sources will collect and sell them.

Different materials require different equipment in the buy-back center. Glass must be segregated by color: clear, green, and brown. For densifying purposes, glass can be crushed on site. This process requires a glass crusher.

Corrugated board has to be flattened and strapped into bundles or baled in a press for transport to a paper mill. While strapping is inexpensive, it does require considerable labor. Balers may be of simple downstroke design, or may incorporate large conveyor systems onto which employees feed boxes and box board. Most balers, it should be noted, can handle a variety of materials.

When corrugated board, newsprint, office paper, plastic bottles, or aluminum cans are baled, the center will need either a forklift or pallet jacks to load materials. A loading dock facilitates efficient handling.

DESIGN AND OPERATION

With both types of recycling collection systems, drop-off stations and buy-back centers, design and operation are inseparably linked. Design of facilities will dictate the way the whole system works. In either case, the person who lays out a location should keep in mind a *flowthrough* pattern for safety and efficiency.

With the drop-off station, clearly stated instructions should guide a depositor to the off-loading point, then tell him or her what to deposit where. An exit marker would do well to include a short, positive message about environmental awareness.

The only other flowthrough consideration for a drop-off station is access for the service truck that will haul away the materials. It needs room to maneuver without endangering adjacent buildings or parked cars. And don't forget that a truck needs more overhead clearance than cars.

The buy-back center, of necessity, has a more complex function. Essentially its operations involve *receiving, handling, storing,* and *shipping* with *accounting* at both ends of the process and *cashiering* near the start. These activities suggest a layout which provides drives and parking space for depositing customers on one side of a building and bulk shipping of the accumulated materials on the other. For safety, pull-through and diagonal parking on the customer side would eliminate backing up and would accommodate cars with trailers better than slot parking would. Figure 22.11 shows a buy-back center exterior layout.

The customer side of the building needs access to the floor scales first, since all materials must be weighed and receipted by a center employee. Upon leaving the scales, customers could be directed to the proper bay or hopper for depositing each type of material. When completed, they take their receipts to the cashier for payment.

One proven design for a center is to have a series of small bays or windows in a line down the customer side of the building. Each would be clearly marked

FIGURE 22.11 Exterior view of buy-back center.

"aluminum cans," "brown glass," "green glass," "clear glass," "newspapers," "plastic bottles," "copper," "brass," etc.

A depositor would park and unload all the materials into a rolling canvas hamper or a cart provided by the center. The first stop would be the floor scales where a center employee weighs each type of material separately and records it on a receipt. The depositor, with receipt in hand, would then proceed to the proper windows or bays to drop the recyclable goods into waiting hoppers. The window arrangement speeds sorting and keeps customers safely away from the crushers, balers, forklifts, and other machinery being used by center employees.

If space doesn't allow a lineal arrangement of bays for each type of material, customers might drop their goods through a single hatch onto a conveyor. Inside, employees would push the materials off the conveyor into appropriate bins for loading on trucks bound for processors. To reduce the labor requirement for sorting goods inside the center, depositors could be instructed to use boxes provided by the recycling center for each type of material they place on the conveyor. Inside, employees would empty the boxes into appropriate bulk containers and return empty boxes to where other depositors may use them over and over.

Direction and Instruction Signage

Good signage can save a depositor from frustration and encourage his or her return. A good sign, by the way, is one that can be read instantaneously. Keep the messages short and clear. Their purpose is to guide depositors, not scold them.

A simple START HERE sign over the floor scale should suffice, then arrows painted on the walls or floor could guide a depositor to the proper clearly labeled window for each type of material. A depositor's last stop would be the cashier's window, and that is also the best location for handing out educational flyers, price lists, and notices of the center's business hours.

Personnel to operate a buy-back center can be the biggest ongoing expense. It is important to match labor to the volume of material being received, of course, and that is difficult until the center has experience on which to draw. Records of depositor visits will reveal a pattern, in time, that should enable a manager to predict how many employees will be needed on certain days of the week and months of the year. A center that averages 100 depositors on a weekday may find that 300 on Saturday is common.

Buy-back centers sponsored by local government agencies may be able to draw on a contingent of volunteers, but it takes a long roster to cover six days of operation each week. Also, someone has to manage the center's money, negotiate sales to processors, and direct the volunteer labor day to day. It is unlikely that a reliable volunteer will perform such a task long-term. Some paid staff positions should be anticipated.

In some communities, the law allows nonviolent offenders to be sentenced to "community service" in lieu of jail terms and as a condition of probation. If local authorities and sentencing judges agree, community service detainees can augment the staff of a publicly operated recycling center.

Privatization

With the current trend toward privatization, however, city and county governments are increasingly reluctant to take on new service responsibilities. Where the volume of recyclable materials can support a private, commercial venture, local governments will most often choose not to use taxpayers' money to compete.

A privately owned buy-back center will need a large enough drawing area to furnish a profitable volume of materials. Those materials won't be profitable to handle unless there are industrial processors within reasonable distance to buy them. For that reason, most will be located in metro areas and population centers of 90,000 or more.

While surveys do indicate certain per capita figures on how much recyclable glass, aluminum, etc., an average household will produce, no one can predict the level of local participation until recycling is tried. A good education program by the private company combined with local government support will go a long way toward assuring participation in programs that are emerging all over the country.

In Gwinnett County, Georgia, the Clean and Beautiful Program opened a buy-back center with an initial land donation from the county. Within three years it was self-supporting, and the volume of goods recycled continues to increase annually.

Another private enterprise recycling firm recently introduced an innovation with strong appeal to environmentally conscious citizens. In conjunction with its conventional buy-back center, Mindis Recycling opened its first "Mindis Mart" (Fig. 22.12) in 1991 combining a state-of-the-art recycling operation with an educational center and a store specializing in environmentally friendly items. These include categories of merchandise such as household goods, recycled office products, containers and recycling bins for the home, environmental products, gifts, stationery, and other merchandise made from recycled materials and renewable resources. The store draws attention to nature with bird houses, lawn accessories, and tee-shirts imprinted with environmental messages.

The center offers educational programs to groups interested in waste management and recycling. By arrangement, they may tour the part of the center where materials are prepared for shipment to processors and may see the equipment in

FIGURE 22.12   Recycling mart combines collection with environmental education.

operation. Community groups and schools have made use of the store to reinforce the recycling concept.

INVOLVING THE PUBLIC

With both drop-off stations and buy-back centers it's a good idea to start with a
bang. Local broadcast media will often use spot public service announcements to
promote a recycling program. Offer them interviews in which a spokesperson for
your organization explains how much energy recycling saves. (Reusing aluminum
cans collected in 1988 alone saved energy equivalent to the electric power the
City of Boston uses round the clock for one year.) Or tell how many trees can be
saved by recycling a ton of newsprint.

For a successful recycling program, it is imperative to involve as much of the
community as possible. Public officials may be willing to cut a ribbon at a buy-
back center or to have themselves filmed dropping their own household's collection into a drop-off station. Local businesses, especially large employers, may
help introduce your recycling campaign with ads in the local paper and notices
distributed to employees and customers. They know it's good business to be
identified with a positive environmental effort.

Chambers of commerce, civic clubs, schools, churches, scouts, and others
may solicit commitments to recycle from their members. Another way to enlist
citizen support for more recycling is to ask people to help identify major generators of recyclable goods. Hotels, bars, and restaurants typically throw away
large quantities of glass and plastic. Office buildings and government agencies

generate tons of waste paper that can be sold for reprocessing, not to mention the aluminum cans that accumulate daily from their cold-drink machines.

Waste products and scrap from manufacturing are probably being recycled by the factories that generate them, but management could help the recycling effort by encouraging employees to bring cans, glass, and other materials from their homes to recycling drop-off containers in the company parking lot (Fig. 22.13).

FIGURE 22.13   Roll-off recycling container in company parking lot.

COMMERCIAL AND CIVIC PARTNERS

Astute business people realize that anything so universally good for America can be good for business, too. Recycling programs can get more mileage, so to speak, by encouraging tie-in promotions with local businesses.

Another way to encourage recycling at a buy-back center is to maintain accounts for churches and charities. Depositors may credit those accounts instead of taking cash for their recyclable goods. One center in metro-Atlanta has over 400 such accounts. Funds are distributed to the designated charities monthly.

Most customers of buy-back centers, however, will take cash for their materials. Many homemakers make regular trips to the centers either weekly or monthly. Often it is extra earnings for children who are collecting recyclable goods to earn money for a special purchase. Other regular depositors, many of them elderly, are very serious about supplementing their incomes at the buy-back center.

Another item on the positive side is cost avoidance for the community that collects for recycling. Every bottle and can picked up from the roadside means less tax-paid labor to clean up litter. Every ton of material processed into a new use means a ton less garbage to be transported and buried in costly landfill space.

CHAPTER 23
TRANSFER STATIONS

L. T. Schaper
Partner, Black & Veatch
Kansas City, Missouri

R. C. Brockway
Project Engineer, Black & Veatch
Kansas City, Missouri

INTRODUCTION

Historically, solid waste was collected in "packer" type collection vehicles (Fig. 23.1) which delivered the waste directly to landfills. As landfills closed, haul distances became greater, giving rise to the use of transfer stations where the waste is transferred to large-capacity transfer trailers. The trailers are then hauled to the

FIGURE 23.1 Packer-type collection vehicle. (*Photo courtesy of Leach Company.*)

landfill. Transfer stations currently being designed are typically enclosed in a building to reduce problems associated with noise, odor, and blowing litter and to provide an aesthetically pleasing facility. Advantages associated with transfer stations have resulted in a rapid growth in the number constructed in the past three decades. The principal benefits derived from a transfer station are summarized as follows:[1]

1. *Economy of haul:* Transfer truck legal payloads of 18 to 25 tons can be obtained as compared to the 4- to 10-ton legal payload of most collection trucks. This results in fewer trips to the disposal site, allowing the collection fleet more time on the route to perform collection service. An overall reduction in capital and operating cost for the collection fleet can result.

2. *Labor savings:* Many route trucks operate with two- or three-person crews. The additional travel time of the truck to the disposal site keeps these workers from their refuse collection duties. Since transfer trucks require only a one-person crew, a reduction in nonproductive time can be achieved.

3. *Energy savings:* Over-the-road fuel use of collection equipment and transfer tractors are similar. Significant fuel savings will be experienced as a result of the fewer trips required to the disposal site.

4. *Reduced wear and tear:* A total mileage savings will result from the fewer trips. However, just as important is the reduction in the number of flat tires and damage to power trains and suspension systems that results from operation on muddy and irregular landfill surfaces.

5. *Versatility:* The flexibility of a transfer system allows the solid waste manager the freedom to shift the waste destination with minimal impact on collection operations.

6. *Reduction of landfill face:* Since the length of the landfill dumping face is generally determined by the number and type of vehicles using the site, a reduction in the number of vehicles will result in a smaller working area, less daily cover requirements, and safer conditions at the landfill due to reduced traffic. A landfill which receives only waste hauled in transfer trailers may require a working face which is less than half that required for a landfill receiving a similar quantity of waste hauled in packer-type vehicles.

The concept of multiple transfer stations serving a disposal site is common today. Historically, several disposal sites served a large city or metropolitan area. As land use becomes more urbanized, public resistance to new disposal sites increases. The current trend is to use a network of transfer stations from which waste is transported to a remote sanitary landfill or energy-recovery facility. Transfer stations can be located on relatively small parcels of land and are perceived by the public as more compatible with urban development than sanitary landfills.

The remainder of this chapter deals with various aspects of transfer stations including site considerations, station types, transfer trailers, transfer economics, and other considerations.

STATION TYPES

Transfer station types include

• Direct dump—no floor storage

- Direct dump—floor storage
- Compactor
- Pit
- Combination

All types are well established and many successful examples of each type of transfer station are in operation. There are a large number of compactor stations, in part because this concept has been promoted by sales representatives of equipment manufacturers. The pit concept has traditionally been popular on the west coast. The direct-dump concept has gained popularity as improved self-unloading, open-top trailers have been developed.

Direct Dump—No Floor Storage

The direct-dump station is a two-level facility in which collection vehicles on the upper floor discharge through hoppers directly into open-top transfer trailers on the lower floor. A typical direct-dump transfer station is shown in Figs. 23.2 and 23.3. The concept is inherently efficient because equipment and labor necessary to load the trailers are minimized. A significant feature of this concept is that the trailer-loading operation must be capable of handling wastes as they are received.

FIGURE 23.2 Typical direct-dump transfer station.

The concept dates back at least to the 1950s, when it was used by the Los Angeles County Sanitation District.[2] It is appropriate for small or large stations with the size determined by the number of direct-dump hoppers. Several variables control the capacity of a hopper, including the payload of collection vehi-

FIGURE 23.3 Trailer receiving waste from above.

cles, average unloading time, number unloading simultaneously at a hopper, and capacity of the transfer trailer. Representative values for these variables are

Average collection vehicle payload	6⅔ tons
Average unloading time per truck	6 min
Collection trucks unloading simultaneously in each hopper	2
Capacity of the transfer trailer	20 tons
Time to level load and change transfer trailers	7 min

Based on these conditions, the 20-ton transfer trailer would be loaded in 12 min and 7 min would be required to level the load, move it out, and replace it with an empty trailer. Three transfer trailers would be loaded each hour, providing a peak capacity of 60 tons per hopper per hour. Achieving this loading rate depends on collection trucks being available to unload and empty transfer trailers also being available. This situation only occurs a few hours per day, so that a single hopper with peak collection vehicle deliveries during 4 h of the day and no deliveries at other times would have a capacity of approximately 240 tons per day.

Because transfer trailers usually can be loaded at a faster rate than the round-trip time to the disposal site, extra transfer trailers are needed to store the waste during peak hours. Peak storage for this type of station is in transfer trailers rather than in a pit or on the receiving floor. Although it is possible to provide receiving-floor space for storage, the simplicity and efficiency of the direct-dump concept is negated. The extra trailers used for peak storage are temporarily stored on the transfer station site until tractors are available for the trip to the disposal site. A yard tractor is used to move the loaded trailers from the transfer station to the yard storage area and to move empty trailers to the transfer station.

Direct-dump transfer stations typically use a stationary clamshell device as shown in Fig. 23.4 to distribute the solid waste in the transfer trailer. The clamshell will also provide a degree of compaction of the solid waste in the trailer. The clamshells are typically provided with a specially designed grapple as shown in Fig. 23.5. The grapple can be opened and closed to move solid waste around in the trailer and it can be closed to allow it to be used in compacting the solid waste. A disadvantage of this type of station is lowered efficiency if the clamshell is out-of-service for maintenance. It cannot be replaced with another unit. Some stations keep backhoes available for temporary use when this happens.

FIGURE 23.4 Stationary clamshell distributes solid waste into trailer.

FIGURE 23.5 Specially designed grapple for clamshell. (*Photo courtesy of Crane Equipment Corp.*)

Rubber-tired mobile excavators as shown in Fig. 23.6 can be used as an alternative to the stationary units. In general, these units are two to three times as expensive ($100,000 to $150,000 each) as stationary units. However, they can provide more flexibility than stationary units. One mobile unit can serve several hoppers that are not continuously being loaded. If a mobile clamshell requires servicing, it can be removed from the area and another unit can take its place.

Direct Dump—Tipping-Floor Storage

Many stations which have the capability for direct dumping of waste from the collection vehicles to the transfer trailer also utilize floor storage to increase station capacity during peak hours. A station with floor storage is shown in Fig. 23.7. This concept results in substantial changes to both station construction and operation.

The station construction cost is significantly increased due to the larger tipping floor area required to accommodate the stored waste. This larger tipping floor area results in the need for larger building space and therefore significantly increases cost.

Operation methods and costs are also increased. Storage of wastes on the tipping floor result in the need for a large wheel loader (Fig. 23.8) to load waste into

FIGURE 23.6 Mobile excavator.

FIGURE 23.7 Transfer station floor storage (tipping floor).

the open-top trailer. There are equipment and labor costs associated with the wheel loader. The wear of the wheel loader's bucket on the tipping floor also increases maintenance cost. Stations of this type typically utilize hardened concrete toppings to protect the underlying structural concrete. Iron aggregate toppings are the most common type used to protect the concrete surfaces. These

FIGURE 23.8 Large-wheel loader operates on tipping floor.

toppings are typically 1 to 1½ in in thickness and cost from $10 to $15 per square foot installed. Many operators of transfer stations consider the high cost of toppings to be worthwhile compared to the cost and problems associated with having the station out of service for long periods while concrete repairs are made. It should be noted that while the hardened concrete toppings will wear better than ordinary concrete, they too will eventually wear away and need to be replaced.

The advantage of this concept is that during peak periods, the station capacity is not limited by the rate at which transfer trailers can be loaded. There are economic trade-offs between station costs and transfer trailer costs which must be evaluated by the design engineer.

The direct-dump type of facility with tipping-floor storage is also more suitable for a combined transfer station and materials-recovery facility. The tipping-floor storage provides the ability to separate materials which can be recycled.

Compactor

Many compactor transfer stations have been constructed in the United States in the past few decades. Typically they are a two-level operation with collection vehicles unloading onto a receiving floor or into a hopper at the upper level. The solid wastes are then moved into the compactor and compacted into a transfer trailer at the lower level. Figure 23.9 shows a typical compactor.

When compactor stations use the receiving floor as a waste storage area, a wheel loader is used to pick up the waste and load it into the hopper. Depending on the loader equipment capability and the operators' skill, it may be practical for one operator to load more than one compaction hopper.

Another compactor station concept is to provide a large hopper to receive wastes directly from the collection vehicle. The receiving hopper is at a right angle to the compaction hopper and the transfer trailer. The waste is pushed by a large hydraulically operated blade from the receiving hopper into the compaction hopper and then compacted into the transfer trailer. The transfer trailers are

FIGURE 23.9   Compactor at transfer station. (*Photo courtesy of J. V. Manufacturing Inc.*)

closed-top mechanical or hydraulic system types sized to handle the maximum legal payload. The concept has proven successful and generally has high reliability. The hydraulically operated equipment requires reasonable maintenance.

Historically, compactors have compacted the waste within the trailer. This requires the use of heavy-duty trailers. Within the last few years, compactors that compact the waste within their own chamber (see Fig. 23.10) and then discharge (or push) the waste into the transfer trailer have become widely used. Compactors such as this allow the use of lighter-weight trailers since no compaction takes place within the trailer.

Pit

The pit concept has been in use for many years in some of the country's largest transfer stations. The principal advantage is the large storage capacity. It provides storage for peak deliveries and allows transfer haul to be operated on as much as a 24-h basis, if desired. The pit concept is shown in Fig. 23.11.

Whether waste is stored overnight in the pit depends on regulatory requirements and operator preference. It is common to leave some waste in the bottom of the pit to reduce damage to the pit floor from the track-type dozer equipment used to crush and handle the waste. This equipment damages the floor at a rapid rate unless some protection is provided.

Pit stations have proven to be capable of handling bulky waste. Equipment working in the pit can crush and break up the bulky waste in preparation for loading it into transfer trailers.

TABLE 23.1   Transfer Station Design Alternatives (*Continued*)

System description	Advantages	Disadvantages
Compaction—direct dump to push pit feeding stationary compactor		
Collection vehicles dump directly into a push pit. Hydraulic push blade moves waste into compactor chamber. The stationary compactor pushes and compacts the waste into the trailer. A self-contained hydraulic ram ejects the load from the compactor.	See advantages of the "direct dump to stationary compactor" concept. Push pit provides some storage for peak waste loading.	See first three disadvantages of "direct dump to stationary compactor" concept. Construction of push pit and purchase of hydraulic ram results in capital expense.
Direct dump to area pit		
All vehicles dump into large central pit. Bulldozer in pit breaks up and compacts bulky waste. Bulldozer pushes waste to load open-top trailers. Moving bottom trailer arrangement available for unloading at landfill.	Utilizes a convenient and efficient storage area that does not clutter unloading area. With material crushed and compacted in the pit by the bulldozer, maximum loads are attainable without further processing. Peak loads may be handled easily with many incoming vehicles capable of being unloaded at the same time. Drive-through arrangements for loading transfer vehicles can be easily worked into the facility plan.	Construction of receiving pit and purchase of the bulldozer require considerable capital investment. Time is required to place and remove canvas or metal tops to prevent littering during transport. Unloading into the pit and then loading the transfer trailers is less efficient than direct dump to trailers.

Site Layout

The layout of buildings and roadways on a site is one of the most important factors in designing a successful transfer station. A typical site layout of a transfer station is shown in Fig. 23.13. A counterclockwise flow of traffic will result in fewer crossing traffic patterns. Left turns are also easier to make since the driver is on the left side of the vehicle and has a better view. The scale house should be located where suitable queuing distance can be provided such that vehicles will not back up onto access roads.

Public users of the facility should be kept separate, if possible, from the private haulers and transfer trailers. This is true not only within the transfer building itself, but also on the site roadways.

Ramps are required for most transfer stations. There will be either a ramp up to the tipping floor, a ramp down to the transfer level, or a combination of the two. The height difference between the tipping floor and the trailer loading level is usually around 18 ft. Splitting the difference between elevating the tipping floor above grade and lowering the trailer loading level below grade will minimize the slope and length of the ramps. Locating the trailer level below grade may not be practical due to fac-

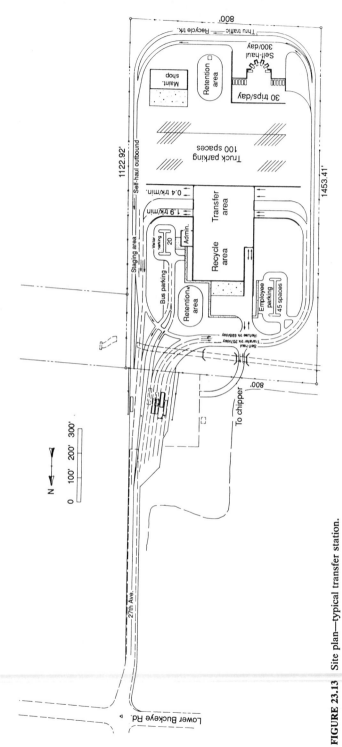

FIGURE 23.13 Site plan—typical transfer station.

23.14

tors such as groundwater and potential flooding. Locating the tipping floor at grade will lower the overall height of the transfer station. The height of a station can be of great concern to local residents. However, locating the tipping floor at grade will result in more cost for the transfer level due to its greater depth below grade.

Adequate area should be provided for trailer storage, employee parking, and visitor parking. Employees and visitors should not be required to walk across lanes of traffic unless absolutely necessary. Maintenance, wash, and fuel facilities should be located such that they do not interfere with the flow of traffic around the station site.

Sites should be selected and laid out to allow room for future expansion of the transfer station. Additional processing such as a material recovery facility, wood processing, and waste-to-energy should be considered in the layout, providing sufficient room is available at the site.

Adequate signs should be provided along the access roads to the site, at the site entrance, and along the roadways on the transfer station site. It is especially important that sufficient signs be provided for the general public that use the facility. These people will not use the site often and should be carefully directed to the appropriate locations around the site. Figure 23.14 shows some of the signs used at the Montgomery County Transfer Station.

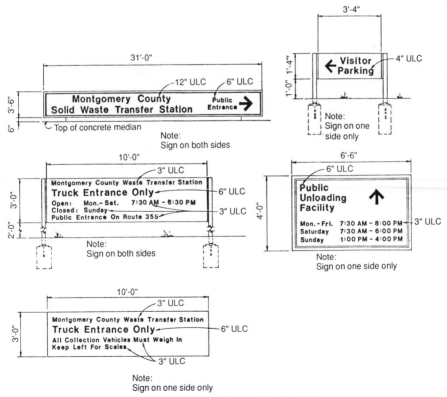

FIGURE 23.14 Direction signs—Montgomery County Transfer Station.

Access and Traffic Impact

Transfer stations are best served by major traffic arteries. Two chief advantages are easier access and reduced impact on adjacent development. Easy access can reduce travel time and result in low collection and transfer haul costs.

To reduce impact on existing traffic, improvements to service roads may be needed to accommodate transfer station traffic. Consideration should be given to the need for signals, turnoff lanes, and additional traffic lanes.

Location

Station location is important to secure the best system economy. Transporting solid waste in collection vehicles is expensive, especially if a large collection crew travels with the vehicle. To minimize collection costs, the transfer station should be located within the area of the collection routes served. The site having the lowest hauling cost is typically located between the centroid of the collection routes served and the disposal site.

Zoning

Local laws and ordinances determine zoning requirements for a transfer station. Land for a transfer station usually must be zoned to be commercial or industrial and often a special use permit is required. Obtaining a change in zoning can require extensive effort. Zoning hearings require expertise from engineers, environmentalists, and lawyers. Personal contacts with the public perceived to be affected by the proposed facility are essential to success and effective visual aids to communicate the concept to the public and to zoning officials will be needed.

Figure 23.15 lists zoning requirements and recommendations for a transfer station located in a rapidly developing area of southern Florida. Requirements such as these can significantly increase the costs of developing a transfer station.

Public Acceptance

Obtaining a transfer station site can be a major challenge due to public reluctance to accept a solid waste facility. Public acceptance is enhanced if the factors discussed above are properly handled. For example, the site should be properly zoned, large enough to provide screening, and served by an adequate road system.

It will probably be important to involve citizens and community leaders in the transfer station site selection. This can be accomplished by forming a task force to assist with siting and design of the transfer station. If representatives of community organizations are convinced the site is reasonable, organized public opposition can be minimized.

Public acceptance can sometimes be more easily obtained by locating a transfer station on public land. It may be practical to locate the station at a site previously used for solid waste disposal. If this is possible, precedence has been established for similar land use and opposition may be less.

Architectural treatment and landscaping are tools the designers can use to en-

ZONING PETITION

STAFF RECOMMENDATIONS
The staff recommends approval of this petition, subject to the following conditions:

1. All areas of internal circulation within the site shall be posted with signage restricting speeds to fifteen (15) miles per hour or less. In addition, signage shall be posted within the site directing all drivers to avoid excessive acceleration within the site and on the access road.

2. The petitioner shall retain the stormwater runoff in accordance with all applicable agency requirements in effect at the time of permit application. However, at a minimum, this development shall retain onsite 100% of the stormwater runoff generated by a three (3) year-one (1) hour storm as required by the Permit Section, Land Development Section. If the drainage system is not adequately maintained as determined by the County Engineer, this matter will be referred to the Code Enforcement Board for enforcement.

3. Prior to the issuance of a building permit, the petitioner shall convey to the public an 80 foot right-of-way for the northerly access road between Military Trail and Central Boulevard.

4. The petitioner shall construct concurrent with the four-laning of Military Trail a left turn lane, south approach, and a right turn lane, north approach.

5. The petitioner shall construct Military Trail as a four-lane median divided section from its northern terminus north of Donald Ross Road north to the project's entrance, plus the appropriate paved tapers. This construction shall be completed within 18 months of the approval for the Special Exception.

6. Surety required for the offsite road improvements as outlined in the above two conditions shall be posted by the petitioner with the Office of the County Engineer not later than fourteen (14) months from the date of approval of the Special Exception.

7. The proposed site is located within the Zone 3 area designated on the Zones of Influence Maps incorporated as a part of the County Wellfield Protection Ordinance. The petitioner shall comply with the following conditions:

    a. The lake area (0.7 acre) located in the center of the site shall be developed as a dry stormwater retention area.

    b. Stormwater drainage on the site will be routed to maximize natural filtration.

    c. Only periodic routine inspections and maintenance of vehicles and equipment will be performed at this site. The southern

FIGURE 23.15 Zoning requirements and recommendation of transfer station.

portion of the transfer facility, approximately 45 feet by 58 feet, will be developed with a concrete barrier to contain any possible spillage or leakage during routine maintenance.

d. The petitioner will comply with all conditions for a facility located within Zone 3 as specified in Section 5.03 of the Ordinance. In addition, the petitioner will also comply with the restrictions for Zone 2, as specified in Section 5.02 (a), (b), (c), (d), (e), (f), (i), and (j).

8. The petitioner shall prepare an "Alternative Landscape Betterment Plan", which exceeds the requirements of the County Landscape Code, in the following manner:

   a. The petitioner shall plant thirty-five (35) trees within the ten (10) foot landscape strip along the western property boundary, which exceeds the number of required perimeter trees (19) in this area by eighty-four percent (84%).

   b. The petitioner shall plant a minimum of seventy-five percent (75%) native tree species for all trees required by this petition.

   c. All trees planted by the petitioner, as a requirement of this petition, shall be at a minimum height of ten (10) feet to twelve (12) feet upon planting.

   d. A hedge, a minimum thirty-six (36) inches in height at time of planting, shall be installed within the ten (10) foot landscape strip along the west property boundary. Said hedge shall consist of all native plant material as defined in Section 500.35 of the County Landscape Code.

   e. Landscaping shall be preserved and/or installed as appropriate per Section 500.35 of the County Landscape Code and Section 500.36 (Vegetation Removal) of the County Landscape Code, as shown on the site plan presented at the public hearing. The petitioner shall preserve existing significant vegetation along all perimeters of the site to effectively screen the proposed development. In addition, all significant existing landscaping shall be preserved within the open space areas, not disturbed by structure, parking, change in grade elevations, or access road. Appropriate measures shall be taken to protect these preservation areas during site clearing and construction.

   Acceptance of this plan will be filed with official records of the Planning, Zoning, and Building Department.

9. Failure to comply with the conditions herein may result in the denial or revocation of a building permit; the issuance of a stop work order; the denial of a Certificate of Occupancy on any building or structure; or the denial or revocation of any permit or approval for any developer-owner, commercial-owner, lessee, or user of the subject property. Appeals from such action may be taken to the County Board of Adjustment or as otherwise provided in the County Zoning Code. Violations of the conditions herein shall constitute violation of the County Zoning Code.

FIGURE 23.15 (*Continued*) Zoning requirements and recommendation of transfer station.

hance the acceptability of a transfer station. The architectural treatment of the station should be compatible with adjacent development. If there are commercial buildings nearby, the transfer station can be designed to have the appearance of a commercial structure similar to that shown on Fig. 23.16. Exterior treatment of transfer stations can include metal siding, tilt-up concrete panels, and precast concrete panels. Preengineered metal buildings placed on a concrete foundation are often used for transfer stations. Figure 23.17 shows a transfer station using a combination of metal siding and precast concrete panels for architectural treatment.

FIGURE 23.16   Exterior design of transfer station.

Landscaping and screening should be used where appropriate to reduce visual and noise impacts of the transfer operation and associated traffic. Screening can be provided with trees, shrubs, fencing, or walls. Earth berms can minimize visual impact and reduce noise levels.

The impact of a transfer station on its surroundings is due to several factors. Even though the installation is attractive, landscaped, and screened, it must be operated conscientiously to be a good neighbor. A common complaint is trash along roads near the station. Consistent policing of roads near the site is essential to maintain a reputation as a good neighbor.

Land Cost

Land is one of several items making up the total cost. It is usually a relatively small part of the total capital and operating cost. Land cost would typically be a very few percent of the station construction cost. It may be wise to pay the amount necessary for a site which best meets other criteria. If a higher land price

FIGURE 23.17   Exterior of transfer station—use of precast concrete panels and metal siding.

also means reduced public opposition or savings in site development or access road costs, it can be a good investment. Transfer station costs including land costs are covered later in this chapter.

TRANSFER TRAILERS AND UNLOADING EQUIPMENT

Transfer trailers are an integral part of the transfer system and the type required is directly related to the station type. For example, a direct-dump or pit transfer station requires an open-top trailer, as shown in Fig. 23.18, while a compactor-type station requires an enclosed trailer with a push-out blade as shown on Fig. 23.19.

FIGURE 23.18   Open-top trailer. (*Photo courtesy of Brothers Industries, Inc.*)

FIGURE 23.19 Enclosed trailer with push-out blade. (*Photo courtesy of Thiele, Inc.*)

Open-Top Trailer—Push-Out Blade

Hydraulically operated push-out blades can be used to unload open-top trailers. The trailer must be constructed to withstand forces from the push-out blade without cross-bracing to interfere with top loading. Such a trailer is heavier than other open-top trailers and therefore, due to highway weight limits, provides a smaller legal payload.

Open-Top Trailer—Chain and Moving Floor

Originally, open-top trailers were unloaded with a rope net placed in the front of the trailer. Cables attached to the net were hooked to a tractor at the landfill and the tractor pulled the net with the solid waste out of the trailer. The need for landfill equipment to assist unloading was a significant disadvantage. A drag chain trailer bottom with flights was developed to provide for self-unloading open-top trailers. The moving floor system provides the same self-unloading ability. The moving floor concept comprises a series of undulating floor slats, which move the wastes out of the trailer. Figure 23.20 shows a moving floor bottom. The moving floor systems, such as those made by Keith Manufacturing Co., are made of aluminum or steel floor slats that extend the full length of the floor bed. The slats are hydraulically powered and move in a four-step process, as follows, for unloading the trailer:

1. Every third slat moves forward 6 to 10 in, sliding under the load. The load does not move since the majority of the load is supported on the two-thirds of the slats that do not move.

2. A second group of one-third of the slats moves forward underneath the load. Again the load does not move since two-thirds of the slats remain stationary.

3. The third group of slats moves under the load as described in steps 1 and 2. Again the load does not move.

FIGURE 23.20   Trailer with moving floor. (*Photo courtesy of Keith Mfg. Co.*)

4. All floor slats move together (6 to 10 in), in one motion, toward the rear of the trailer. Since all slats are moving at the same time, the entire load moves toward the rear of the trailer.

The open-top trailers vary in capacity with 105-yd^3 capacity being quite common.

Open-Top Trailer—Landfill Tipper

A landfill tipper as shown in Fig. 23.21 may be used to unload open-top trailers at a disposal site. It is a semistationary piece of equipment that is periodically moved to unload the solid waste reasonably near the working face. A principal advantage of such equip-

FIGURE 23.21   Trailer at landfill tipper unit. (*Photo courtesy of Columbia Trailer Co.*)

ment is that it requires no unloading mechanism built into the trailer so that payloads are greater and maintenance is less. A disadvantage is that the unloading point is not always at the working face of the landfill, making it necessary to move the solid waste from the unloading point to the active face. This may increase the exposure of the trash to wind and birds. The concept has been used at major sites for several years and has proven successful.

Enclosed Trailer with Push-Out Blade

The enclosed compactor-compatible transfer trailer with push-out blade is a reliable and proven design. The higher compaction achieved in this trailer results in a legal payload in a smaller volume. Usually a legal payload can be achieved with a trailer volume in the range of 65 to 75 yd^3. This compares with 100 to 110 yd^3 for open-top noncompaction trailers. Maintenance requirements are difficult to document, but the sturdier construction inherent in these trailers tends to reduce maintenance.

TRANSFER ECONOMICS

Anticipated lower system costs are generally a factor in the decision to construct a transfer station. A cost model can be used to predict transfer haul costs. While the input to the model is unique to each locality, the approach is generally applicable. A transfer haul model includes the following elements:

- Transfer station capital cost
- Transfer station operating cost
- Transfer haul equipment capital cost
- Transfer haul equipment operating cost

The total transfer haul cost is the sum of the four elements. Costs are expressed in terms of dollars per ton of waste handled.

Station Capital Cost

Station capital cost is influenced by a number of variables including station capacity, land area and cost, site drainage requirements, subsurface conditions, screening and landscaping, utility needs, type of architecture, extent of building enclosure, and auxiliary facilities, such as employee amenities, maintenance facilities, and scales. A conceptual plan is needed as a basis for estimates of capital costs. Since many of the costs are site-specific, it is desirable to develop a site plan for the cost estimate.

Engineering economics are used to determine an annual cost premised on an estimated useful life, salvage value, and interest rate. The annual cost can be converted to a per ton cost by dividing the total annual cost by the annual tonnage.

Station Operating Cost

Elements of operating cost include labor, utilities, supplies, and maintenance. Labor, utilities, and supplies are relatively easy to estimate. Labor cost should include any extra cost for overtime or staff for extra shifts as well as all applicable overhead and fringe benefit costs. Maintenance costs can be estimated by using a small percentage of the construction cost.

Operating costs should be calculated on an annual basis and converted to dollars per ton by dividing by the tons to be handled per year.

Transfer Equipment Capital Cost

Transfer haul equipment includes the tractors and trailers for over-the-road hauling as well as yard tractors for maneuvering trailers at the transfer station. The capital cost must also include extra equipment needed to handle peak quantities and spare equipment to replace tractors and trailers out of service for maintenance. The amount of equipment needed for peaks varies with the type of station. For example, the direct-dump station with no floor storage requires trailers for storage of waste received during peak periods.

Spare equipment needed for service during repair of regular equipment depends on original quality, age, condition, and operator care. An allowance of 10 percent is considered adequate by many operating agencies. Transfer equipment costs should be amortized over the anticipated useful life to obtain an annual cost. The annual equipment cost can be converted to dollars per ton by dividing by the tons to be handled each year.

Transfer Equipment Operating Cost

Two categories of transfer haul operating costs are as follows:

• Variable costs, which are directly related to the miles driven
• Fixed costs, which are a function of time rather than miles

Variable costs include items such as repairs, tires, fuel, and lubrication. These costs can be calculated as the product of cost per mile times the miles per round trip, divided by the average number of tons per load.

Fixed costs include labor, insurance, and taxes. Overtime, fringe benefits, and applicable overhead costs should be included.

The total transfer equipment operating cost is the sum of the fixed and variable costs. As before, these costs should be expressed in terms of dollars per ton of waste transferred.

Transfer System Cost

The transfer system cost is the sum of the four components. This total transfer haul cost may then be compared with the cost of direct haul in collection vehicles. An example of an economical analysis of transfer versus direct haul costs follows.

Detailed Economic Analysis

Making a cost comparison of direct haul in a packer-type vehicle versus transfer haul requires analyses of three components. These components are direct haul cost, transfer haul cost, and transfer station cost. The development of examples of these costs is based on a government-owned and -operated system. Therefore, no costs are included for either taxes or profit. To utilize the cost model for private operations, allowances for these costs should be included.

Direct-Haul Cost. The costs for direct haul in a 25-yd^3 rear-loading type vehicle are developed in Tables 23.2 through 23.4. Equipment costs used in the tables were obtained from equipment manufacturers. Table 23.2 shows the data on which the cost model is based. Table 23.3 develops the fixed costs, which are not closely related to mileage driven. The fixed cost shown in Table 23.4 equals the round trip travel time plus the unloading time multiplied by the fixed cost per hour (Table 23.3) and divided by the average payload in tons. Table 23.4 also develops the variable costs, which are dependent on miles driven. The variable-haul cost equals the variable cost per mile shown in Table 23.2 multiplied by the round-trip mileage and divided by the tons hauled. Table 23.4 shows the total direct haul cost expressed as both cost per ton and cost per ton-mile. Costs are developed for both a two- and three-person crew. The model shows that direct haul in a 25-yd^3 collection vehicle with a two-person crew costs at least $0.42 per ton-mile.

TABLE 23.2 Direct-Haul Cost Data for a 25-yd^3 Rear-Loading Packer*

Annual fixed costs	
Truck	
Capital investment, $/unit	70,000
Estimated service life, years	5
Salvage value	13,000
Cost of debt, %	9.0
Body	
Capital investment, $/unit	30,000
Estimated service life, years	10
Salvage value, $	1,400
Cost of debt, %	9.0
Truck and Body	
Licenses, personal property tax, and	11,000
insurance	
Spare equipment for downtime, %	10.0
Labor cost including supervision:	
2-person crew	32,000
3-person crew	44,500
Overhead, %	15.0
Average Payload, tons/load	8
Average Speed of Truck, mph	40
Variable costs per mile	
Fuel: 4 mpg	$0.24
Oil, lube, service, etc.	$0.01
Tires: 20,000 mi/set	$0.09
Truck repairs	$0.10
Subtotal	$0.44
Overhead	$0.07
Variable cost per mile	$0.51

*Representative travel variables: Miles per trip (one way): 10, 20, 30, 40, 50. Average unloading time: 15 min.

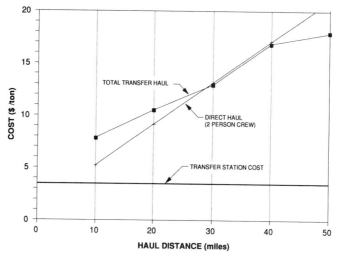

FIGURE 23.22   Direct haul vs. transfer cost graph.

trailers. For shorter distances, direct haul is more economical. For greater distances, transfer haul is more economical. Figure 23.22 illustrates that transfer haul would be more cost effective than direct haul in a 25-yd^3 packer vehicle with two-person crew if the distance to the landfill is more than approximately 30 mi. The break-even point for transfer haul and a packer truck with a three-person crew is shown by the cost model to be about 20 mi.

OTHER CONSIDERATIONS

Transfer stations can be adapted to the unique needs of the system. Auxiliary facilities may include office space, restrooms, scales and scale house, employee showers and dressing room, lunch room, maintenance facilities, fuel storage and dispensing area, and truck storage area. These facilities can have a substantial impact on site and structure requirements. Their availability may complement the basic station and enhance its usefulness.

Resource Recovery and Recycling Compatibility

Resource-recovery considerations have become an important element in the overall transfer station plan. Almost all new transfer stations being designed allow for some type of resource recovery. Many existing transfer stations are being retrofitted to handle resource-recovery operations. These operations may include separation and handling of materials for recycling or processing of waste into fuel for energy-recovery facilities. New transfer stations can be designed to initially include material-recovery facilities (MRFs) or can be designed to add an MRF at a later date. The MRF and transfer station can be housed in the same building or the MRF can be in a separate building. Provisions should be made for rejects (unrecoverable materials) to be conveyed from the MRF to the transfer station for disposal.

Recycling. Materials recovery at transfer stations can include manual separation of materials on the tipping floor or along processing lines, mechanical methods of separating materials, or a combination of both. Many transfer stations (see Fig. 23.23) provide roll-off containers for individuals to drop off recyclables. Floor separation of materials most often includes the recovery of corrugated and wood materials. Commercial collection vehicles often contain loads with a high percentage of these materials, making them economical to recover. Conveyors with manual picking stations can also be used to recover materials from the waste stream.

FIGURE 23.23   Roll-off containers at transfer station.

Separation and handling equipment such as magnetic separators, air classifiers, trommel screens, disk screens, glass crushers, and balers can be added to increase capacity and efficiency of the recycling operations. Figure 23.24 shows a plan view of a combination transfer and recycling facility.

These material recovery operations can use considerable floor space in an existing transfer station. It is important to evaluate the space requirements carefully to make certain that there is enough room for both material recovery and transfer operations in the same building.

Energy Recovery. Transfer stations have been used as processing facilities for refuse-derived fuel. Transfer stations can also be planned to service a future energy-recovery facility. The waste receiving area can serve as a receiving area for an energy-recovery plant. Stations can be constructed with a removable wall to allow a future energy-recovery facility to be constructed adjacent to the transfer station.

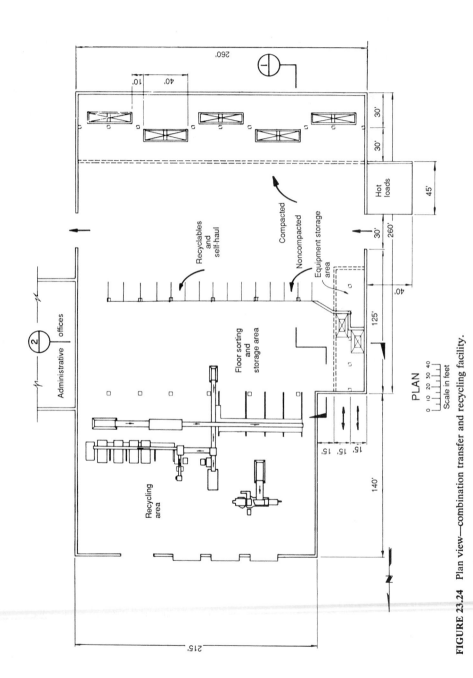

FIGURE 23.24 Plan view—combination transfer and recycling facility.

REFERENCES

1. Mosley, R. W., "The Transfer Station—Benefits and Design," Unpublished paper by Engineer with Department of Street and Sanitation Services, City of Dallas, Texas.
2. Bowerman, F. R., "Municipal Refuse Transfer Stations," *American Public Works Association Yearbook,* pp. 191–194, 1962.

CHAPTER 24
MATERIALS RECOVERY FACILITIES

Keith R. Connor
Project Manager, Black & Veatch
Kansas City, Missouri

David A. Dorau
Project Manager, Black & Veatch
Kansas City, Missouri

INTRODUCTION

History

The evolution and history of recycling is discussed in the first part of this Handbook, and the history of processing facilities is discussed specifically in Chap. 6. The reasons for the development and evolution of processing facilities are discussed briefly below, to put this chapter into perspective.

Processing facilities initially developed in response to the need to handle the growing quantities of recyclables. They have now become a "self-fulfilling prophecy"—their success has increased the popularity of recycling, requiring the construction of still more processing capacity.

Refuse and recyclables came from numerous uncontrolled sources and their quality varied. Processing facilities served as central collection points and locations where materials were processed to market specifications. As a result, many processing facilities became known as *intermediate processing facilities* (IPFs).

Processing facilities serve the function of a broker, collecting from several haulers and distributing to several markets. Alone, small haulers could not meet market specifications or profitably deal with buyers for a wide range of materials. Through the processing facility, materials from several sources, collected through several haulers, can be matched with several markets.

Another trend in waste management is the combination of transfer and processing facilities. This is a logical combination, because both have similar site requirements (access to transportation routes, industrial zoning, and a central location) and both use similar facilities (tipping floor for receiving and processing material and for shipping). Also, some materials initially directed to a transfer facility, such as commercially generated old corrugated cardboard (OCC), are often taken to a processing facility instead. Combining the two facilities in one location eliminates one transfer operation.

Definitions

Several types of processing facilities have evolved to accommodate the variety of recycling systems. Unfortunately, the recycling community has not established a consistent set of labels for these various facilities. Several facilities are defined below in order of increasing complexity of processing. These definitions will be used throughout this chapter; however, they are not universally accepted by the industry.

Some facilities operate as receiving and shipping centers. They simply accept various materials, ensure that materials are separated correctly, and ship them to other processing or manufacturing facilities. Such centers, called *drop-off facilities*, include no processing equipment. If a drop-off facility pays patrons for recyclables, it is called a *buy-back center.* Depending on their locations, drop-off and buy-back operations may be enclosed, but they are different from the facilities discussed in this chapter, because drop-off and buy-back centers deal directly with the public. Also, these facilities do not typically contain any equipment.

If recyclables are source-separated, the facility does not need any sorting equipment. Source-separated recyclables that are collected through a curbside program are taken to one or more places for storage and subsequent shipment. The facility need consist only of hoppers for receiving and storage of the materials until they are shipped. The receiving hoppers may be located outdoors if they are protected from pilferage and vandalism. Such a facility may include provisions for the removal of contaminants, but generally, all materials received are already separated. Such a facility could be called a "load-out" facility because it serves as a central receiving and shipping center but does not process any materials.

Although no equipment is needed for separation at a load-out facility, equipment may be added for processing to increase the value of the recyclables. Processing is usually limited to preparing the material for markets by baling, crushing, flattening, etc. If the facility contains such equipment, it is justifiably called an *intermediate processing center* (IPC). However, because these facilities do not require any equipment for separation, they differ from the processing facilities described below.

Recycling programs that collect various recyclables together produce a stream of intermixed, or commingled, recyclables. If a facility receives commingled recyclables, separation equipment is necessary as well as equipment for preparing the materials for market. Such a facility is commonly called a *materials recovery facility* (MRF). This term has been used to describe virtually every type of facility, from drop-off center to mixed waste processing facility. In this chapter, *MRF* means a facility that receives commingled recyclables. The term "commingled recyclables" has different meaning in different parts of the country. Most commingled processing systems separate, or demingle, only the containers—glass, plastic, and aluminum—and do not attempt to separate fibers, either from the containers or from other types of fiber. In this chapter, *commingled* means containers only, unless otherwise noted.

The type of recycling facility with the most complex processing system is one that receives unprocessed refuse, that is, refuse that has not been separated in any way that would concentrate the amount of recyclables. Unprocessed waste is also called raw garbage or mixed waste. A facility that receives unprocessed refuse is called a mixed waste processing facility or simply a *waste processing facility* (WPF). WPFs generally recover less than 20 percent of the waste stream they receive. The remainder is primarily organic material that can be composted or processed into refuse-derived fuel (RDF) for waste-to-energy facilities. The type of processing equipment used at these facilities differs depending on whether the final product is compost or RDF.

An attempt to establish categories of systems is usually confounded by overlapping categories. An example is a type of collection-recycling system that combines source separation with mixed waste processing. In this approach, recyclables are bagged separately from the mixed waste, often in blue bags, but collected in the same vehicles as the mixed waste. This approach is called cocollection or "blue bag" collection. At the processing facility, the bags of recyclables are removed from the other waste and processes as commingled recyclables. The remaining waste may be processed as mixed waste or simply landfilled.

Another new type of facility defies classification into a single category, because it accepts both mixed waste and commingled recyclables. Such facilities process both waste streams efficiently because they are designed to process mixed waste, but they allow source-separated recyclables to be introduced at a later stage in the processing line. In this way, commingled recyclables, which have already been separated to a significant degree, can bypass some stages of separation in the process line.

SYSTEM ECONOMICS

The cost-effectiveness of a processing facility is not simply a function of the facility costs. The costs of developing, implementing, and operating a processing facility must include all the elements of the processing system, including collection, transportation, processing, and shipping. For example, an IPC will have a lower initial cost than a WPF because the WPF has much more processing equipment. However, the collection costs for the IPC system, which requires separate collection of source-separated recyclables, will be much greater than the collection costs for the WPF. During the planning and evaluation of alternative collection and processing systems, the system must be evaluated as a whole. It is misleading to consider the costs of only the physical facilities.

Collection costs are a significant portion of the total cost of any recycling system, and collection systems for source-separation programs are more complex than those for simple trash collection. Commingled and source-separated systems typically require the collection route to be covered twice—once for trash and once for recyclables. Commingled recyclables can be collected with existing collection vehicles, but source-separated recyclables require special compartmentalized recycling vehicles, an addition cost. The compaction feature of existing packer collection vehicles, however, may not be usable on commingled recyclables collection because it may cause excessive breakage depending on the recyclables collection. Only cocollected, or "blue bag," waste systems offer separation at the source without additional collection vehicles.

Separation involves a cost, whether it is done within the facility or at the source. Recyclables that are source-separated by the generators mean an additional cost of time and inconvenience to the generators. Commingled recyclables that are sorted as they are emptied into the collection vehicle require additional time during collection, although the need for additional separation at the facility is eliminated. The system should be considered as a whole so that the full cost of separation is included, regardless of where it is incurred.

The choice of system also influences the degree of participation, which determines the cost-effectiveness of the recycling program. Mixed waste processing does not require any additional effort on the part of the generators and, therefore, has 100 percent participation. Source-separated systems require more work on the part of the generators and thus have lower participation.

The cost of containers for collection also influences the cost of the program. Commingled, source-separated, and cocollected recyclables all require buckets, bins, or bags. Mixed waste recycling does not require any additional containers. Some containers, however, also offer a method of distributing the costs of the collection system to the users. For example, approved bags that must be purchased by generators establish a "pay by the bag" system.

CONCEPTUAL DESIGN

Objectives

A well-conceived design should optimize the many variables to produce an efficient facility. Among the variables to be considered are the following:

- Collection cost
- Shipping cost of the processed material
- Capital cost
- Operating and maintenance cost (processing)
- Sufficient material storage space
- Public and employee safety
- Public education
- Product quality

Some of these variables may compete with each other. The optimum solution varies from site to site, depending upon local and regional characteristics and priorities. As a result, identifying an optimum concept may become analogous to the question posed by the great thinkers in the Middle Ages, "How many angels fit on the head of a pin?" It is an interesting exercise of questionable merit. With these objectives in mind this section will lay out some of the design considerations the owner of a facility or his or her consultant should be aware of when developing a concept for an MRF.

Market Specifications

The designer must know the market the system will be supplying and understand its specifications to the degree possible. This is said with the understanding that material markets, particularly intermediate ones, are dynamic. Specifications change with supply and demand. For example, if a supply of color-separated high-density polyethylene (HDPE) appears, a prior specification calling for clean mixed plastics may become obsolete. The ways the supply and demand for various materials may affect the facility design are discussed below.

1. *Paper:* The paper market is perhaps the most dynamic of all recyclables markets. Privately operated paper sorting lines are continually adjusted to optimize the mix of sorting labor to meet various market specifications. When foreign markets are available, paper that undergoes little sorting can have a strong market. The low cost of labor overseas (the Pacific Rim and Mexico) makes this a strong option. Specifications normally deal with the quality of the product and the form in which it is shipped. Haul distances to recycled paper plants usually make baling advantageous. Specifications for paper typically list a baled density, a maximum moisture content, and the maximum percentage of contamination by nonspecified paper.

2. *Glass:* A glass market requires that glass be separated by color, and it may or may not call for delivery of cullet. Some processors claim that crushed glass is easier to handle. The end market probably has a glass crusher, so crushing is done to facilitate transportation and handling. Bottle caps and other contaminants may be expressed at a maximum allowable limit. Color separation is essential. Manufacturers of glass containers accept flint (clear) glass in batches of amber or green glass, but green and amber glass are considered contaminants in batches of any color but their own. Plate glass is also considered a contaminant in container glass because it has a lower melting temperature.

3. *Plastics:* HDPE is generally the most readily marketable plastic. Polyethylene terephthalate (PET) markets are less predictable but appear to be growing. Color separation of PET enhances its marketability. Clear or natural-colored PET is more marketable than green; consequently, if bales are not color-separated, there may be an upper limit on the allowable percentage of green PET. Since bottle caps are a contaminant to both HDPE and PET, they may be limited in the specifications.

4. *Metals:* Specifications for aluminum cans usually call for densification. A smaller brick of cans can bring a small premium over larger, less dense bales on the market. Because the detinning process to which tin cans are subjected involves dipping in chemical baths, the specification for their delivery may limit the density of the bales. Bimetal cans—cans with tin sides and aluminum ends—are not acceptable to either aluminum or tin processors.

Sizing

MRFs can be classified into two types: municipal MRFs and merchant MRFs. This classification has to do with the relationship between the facility and its supply of recyclables. Municipal MRFs are guaranteed a flow of recyclables from a community. Merchant MRFs, on the other hand, must compete in the market for their supply. Municipal MRFs may be operated by local government or, more often, by a partnership between the public and a private enterprise. Such an arrangement allows the project to have the public's access to capital markets for the construction of the facility. It also allows for the operational flexibility that an entrepreneur with performance-based incentives brings to the facility.

Currently the need for processing centers far exceeds the numbers of such facilities, so the need for flow control ordinances between a community and its

MRF has not been critical. In this environment of excess demand, merchant MRFs have proliferated. Such facilities offer their services in a competitive environment and are often privately owned and operated. Mandatory recycling in east coast communities has fostered many merchant MRFs.

Sizing is critical to MRFs, whether municipal or private, but it may be approached differently. The waste stream to a municipal MRF is a function of the following:

- Households in service area
- Sign-up rate
- Capture rate
- Level of setout

A merchant MRF would be subject to these variables as well as the fluctuations in material deliveries caused by competition and markets. This chapter will focus primarily on the sizing requirements of a municipal MRF because they are more basic.

Before embarking on design of a large MRF it is advisable to run a pilot project in neighborhoods which typify the entire community. If a pilot program is not practical, the characteristics of neighboring or similar communities could be substituted.

Large service areas result in economies of scale, but smaller service areas have lower collection costs. In practice, the size of the service area is often set by geopolitical boundaries.

In a voluntary program, only 40 to 60 percent of those who signed up can be expected to actually participate. In communities with effective public education programs or where landfilling of recyclables is banned, the sign-up rate can approach 100 percent. Signing up should not be mistaken for participation in either voluntary or mandatory recycling. The argument has been advanced that capture rates are higher for programs requiring less effort on the part of the participant. Recent findings, however, indicate that capture rates may depend more on public education efforts than on the type of program.

The magnitude of setout is dependent upon the materials covered by the program. Programs that include the collection of plastics, aluminum, glass, and tin cans can anticipate monthly contributions of 20 to 30 lb per household. If newspapers are included, this weight can double.

Using these general guidelines we would estimate the daily throughput for an MRF processing commingled recyclables for a community of 100,000 households as follows. Assumptions:

100,000 households

70 percent sign-up

– 50 percent capture

– 20 lb per month of recyclables

Calculation:

$$100{,}000 \text{ households} \times \frac{70}{100} \text{ sign-up} \times \frac{50}{100} \text{ capture}$$

$$\times 20 \text{ lb/mo-household} = 700{,}000 \text{ lb/mo}$$

Assuming the collection is distributed evenly over 22 working days, daily tonnage received at the MRF from this community of 100,000 households will be

$$700{,}000 \text{ lb/mo} \times \text{mo/22 days} \times \text{ton/2000 lb} = 15.9 \text{ tons/day}$$

Before proceeding with sizing the facility, the operating assumptions of the MRF must be well defined. Questions relating to operation to be addressed are as follows:

- What are the normal operating hours?
- Can hours be expanded on an as-needed basis?
- Is operating double shifts an option?
- How much system redundancy must be provided?

After answering these questions, the designer can begin to develop a concept based on vendor systems with known throughput capacities, or to conceptualize a new system. Figure 24.1 shows a material flow diagram for an MRF processing primarily industrial waste.

A material balance flowchart such as Fig. 24.1 is a useful tool for developing an understanding of the system processing requirements. Throughput tonnage should be separated into constituent materials. The flow of material should be expressed in both weight and volume, because both are used in material handling analysis.

Site Layout

An important consideration in the site layout for an MRF is a sound traffic plan prepared by a competent traffic engineer. Factors that the traffic engineer should consider include the following:

Incoming materials (number and type of collection vehicles)

Outgoing materials (number and type of vehicles)

Material weighing requirements

Estimated peak hour traffic

Public access

Auxiliary functions (transfer station, public drop-off, HHW drop-off)

This information on traffic will be incorporated into a site plan that should minimize the number of traffic intersections, lane changes, and merges. In particular the public's opportunities to interface with other traffic will be minimized.

Because of the many steps involved in the normal use of the facility, it is important to have a basic understanding of queuing theory for the site and facility layout.

MRFs are labor-intensive, and whenever the personnel in either the MRF or the collection vehicles are idle, the efficiency of the operation is reduced. Ideally, material would arrive and be processed at the uniform rate throughout the facility's working hours, and all facilities would be sized accordingly.

Determining the number of scales at a scale house is an example of how a facility should be sized, taking into account the results of queuing analysis. Con-

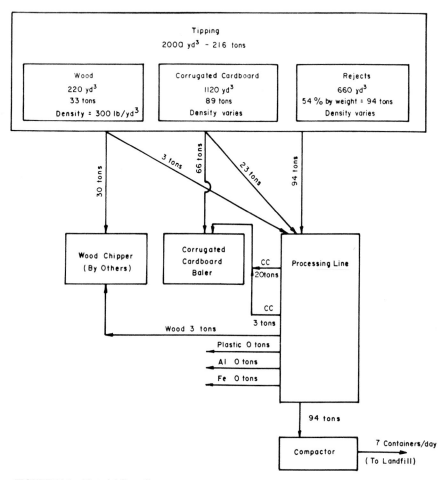

FIGURE 24.1   Material flow diagram.

sider that the scale house receives an average of 20 vehicles each hour, and the average duration of each transaction is 2 min.

Determine the average length of stay in the line as follows:

$$\lambda = \frac{\text{vehicles}}{\text{hour}} = 20$$

$$\mu = \frac{\text{weighings}}{\text{hour}} = 30$$

$$\omega = \frac{\rho}{\mu(1 - \rho)} \qquad \text{where } \rho = \frac{\lambda}{\mu} = \frac{20}{30} = 0.66$$

$$\omega = \frac{0.66}{30(1 - 0.66)} = \frac{0.66}{10} = 0.06 \text{ h} \times 60 \text{ min/h}$$

$$= 3.96 \text{ min in the line}$$

These calculations assume that the arrival times and service time distributions are exponentially distributed over the time period under analysis.*

Economics must be applied to the problem at this point to help decide if a 4-min wait by each of the 20 vehicles arriving each hour is acceptable. Economically, the question is whether the shorter waiting time achieved by adding a second scale would be justified.

The average wait with two scales operating would be calculated as follows:

$$\lambda = \frac{20}{h}$$

$$\mu = \frac{60}{2}(2) = 60$$

$$\rho = \frac{\lambda}{\mu} = \frac{20}{60} = 0.33$$

$$\omega = \frac{0.33}{60(1 - 0.33)} = 0.008 \text{ h} \times 60 \text{ min/h} = 0.48 \text{ min}$$

In actuality, even less time would be required with two scales if switching lines between the scales is allowable.

In this example the time lost by not using a second scale is

$$20 \times 8(3.96 - 0.48) = 556.8 \text{ min/day}$$

Assuming this situation prevails 250 days per year, the annual cost of employees' time at $10/h spent waiting in line is

$$556 \text{ min/day} \times \text{h/60 min} \times 250 \text{ day/year} \times \$10/\text{h} = \$23,200/\text{year}$$

This annual cost must be compared against the annual capital and operating and maintenance costs of a second scale to determine whether the layout of the MRF should incorporate a second scale.

This method of analysis can be applied to other situations where waiting and interference with the batch flow of materials through the process is involved. Other areas at the MRF that may benefit from such analysis are

- Drop-off of recyclables into designated slots
- Loading recyclables onto conveyors
- Loading balers

---

*Waiting line models, Ernesto Ruiz-Pala, Carlos Avila Beloso.

Facility Layout

The principal guideline in the layout of a recycling system is to minimize handling of materials while still meeting the market specifications. Most existing systems require a high degree of manual handling in order to meet the needs of the material markets. Any effort to minimize this handling must begin with the layout of the processing lines.

One example of how to minimize multiple handling of materials is to arrange hoppers and containers so that the system delivers directly to the container or vehicle in which the material will exit the facility. Another equally important design concept is to arrange the sorting lines so that "negative sorts" of the material with the largest volume will occur. Material that is negatively sorted in contrast with "positively sorted" is not physically removed from the material flow, it simply falls off the end of the belt. On each sort line the product that goes off the end of the line (and there should always be such a material even if it is rejects) should also be the material with the largest volume, because this material is not handled by the sorters. The process must be designed so that negatively sorted material meets market specifications.

Adequate storage area must be provided in the layout. Discussions with operators of existing facilities reveal that few facilities have floor space that is underutilized. Storage is required for incoming material and for material awaiting shipment to market.

Space should be provided for at least 1 day's delivery of recyclables. In this way, if the processing equipment is not functioning for one shift, the facility can still accept and store recyclables for processing during an emergency second shift. Additional storage may be required if the normal operating hours of the facility exceed the period during which collection is carried out. For example, a facility that operates two 8-h shifts daily, while collection is done during only one shift, will need storage for 8 h worth of material as standard operating practice. If the system is to be designed to allow for occasional down time, additional space may be required.

Turning radii and operating heights of collection vehicles should be taken into consideration when laying out a new facility. Most new MRFs should be designed with maximum clear spans and operating heights of 25 to 30 ft in areas where mobile equipment will be operating. MRFs are noisy and busy. Therefore, the designer must be aware of layout considerations that might affect worker safety and comfort. Washing facilities should be located away from heavy traffic lanes. Handling of large quantities of glass can be particularly noisy. For this reason in some MRFs, glass bunkers are located outside of the processing building.

PROCESSING SYSTEMS

Single Vendor Systems

Some processing systems are preengineered to serve a wide variety of applications. The systems often include proprietary equipment and configurations. Such systems are commercially available from companies that will design, construct, operate, and provide financing for the facility. Preengineering is no guarantee that the components or the system will work well, but some of the uncertainty can be eliminated by evaluating the system's performance in existing applications.

Figure 24.2 shows a preengineered system. This system is designed to process unsorted, mixed municipal solid waste. It has a capacity of up to 200 tons per day, according to the manufacturer. This system can handle higher capacities by adding processing lines.

FIGURE 24.2   Buhler/Reuter mixed waste processing system, Eden Prairie, Minnesota. (*Courtesy of Buhler/Reuter.*)

Component Systems

A preengineered system may not be appropriate if the processing needs are non-standard. The dynamic status of current recyclables markets combined with the many different collection methods in use has not allowed for the development of a generic processing system that functions in multiple locations. If a preengineered solution is not appropriate, the alternative is to design a processing system to meet the site-specific requirements. Such a system may include customized equipment, but more often, such recycling systems consist of standard components (screens, conveyors, etc.). The challenge in designing a processing system for a particular application is to select the correct equipment, size it appropriately and cost-effectively, and arrange it efficiently. Thus the major difference between systems is the arrangement and combination of the components. The standard equipment used in most systems is discussed in the following section.

Types of Systems

The configurations of both vendor systems and custom systems depend upon the type of waste to be processed. Systems can be designed to process any of the following materials:

- Presorted streams of a single recyclable material
- Presorted streams of mixed recyclables
- Mixed streams that are high in recyclables, for example, commercial waste high in corrugated cardboard

Processing the first type of stream is simple, consisting of size reduction (shredding or baling) and screening. Processing the second type of stream is frequently the goal of a processing facility. Figure 24.3 shows a layout for one such facility. This layout for commingled recyclables also provides locations where materials can be introduced into the line midway to bypass unnecessary processing steps.

A system for processing the mixed waste stream is shown in Figure 24.4. This system also provides for removal of some hazardous and nonprocessible materials, such as lead-acid batteries and automobile tires. It does not allow glass recovery because glass is broken in the trommel.

PROCESSING EQUIPMENT

Preparation

Some processing lines reduce the size of the material for ease in further processing and conveyance. A hammer mill is commonly used for reducing the size of solid waste. It consists of one or more spinning shafts to which hammers are attached. The hammers may swing freely or be rigidly attached; the swing hammer is most commonly used in solid waste processing. Hammers may be sharp for chopping or blunt for beating. The tearing and beating motion of the hammer makes the hammer mill particularly effective on paper fiber and brittle material such as glass. The particle sizes of the solid waste are reduced through impact with the hammers and the grate across the output opening. Output particle size is controlled primarily by the size of the grate openings.

Size reduction equipment for municipal solid waste requires a motor in the range of 200 to 1500 hp. A minimum of 10 hp is required for each ton per hour of capacity. Power requirements increase exponentially as particle size decreases.

Shredders have exploded while shredding municipal solid waste. For this reason, they are often housed in an explosion-protected enclosure and their use is preceded by visual inspection. Because they homogenize the waste, they are seldom used at the front of the processing line if significant materials recovery is planned. Ferrous metal is an exception, because it is easily recovered from shredded waste. More commonly, shredding is used after initial screening, if at all. Shredding is also used at the end of the process to prepare materials for markets or to process the "rejects" for beneficial use as RDF or compost.

Separation

The essence of processing is separation of materials. Several methods have been developed, each with its strengths and preferred applications. Some combination of methods is usually required to process a mixed waste stream.

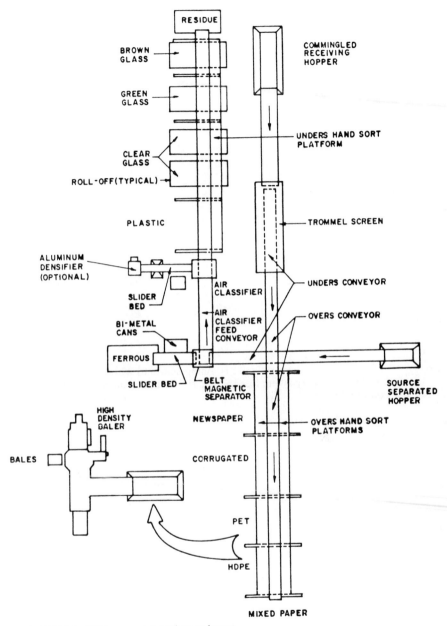

FIGURE 24.3 MRF processing equipment layout.

Hand Sorting. Hand sorting is a part of most processing systems. Hand sorting may take place on the tipping floor, on a sorting line, or both. Large materials such as corrugated cardboard, hazardous materials, and materials that could damage the processing equipment are removed by hand on the tipping floor. On a sorting line, a belt conveyor moves the stream past workers, each of whom is

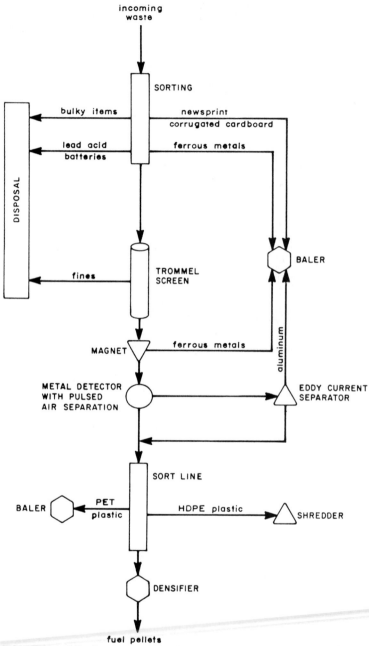

FIGURE 24.4 Mixed waste processing flow diagram.

FIGURE 24.5 Sorting lines.

responsible for removing one or more types of material. Figure 24.5 shows a sorting line.

Sorting conveyors must be designed around productivity levels of workers. They are often designed to travel at variable speeds for optimum performance and flexibility under various loadings. Belt speeds vary between 10 and 60 ft/min.

Screens. The purpose of the screen is to separate items according to particle size. Several different types of screens are typically installed in a processing line.

Trommel Screens. A trommel screen is a cylindrical, horizontal, rotating screen that sorts material by size. Figure 24.6 shows a trommel screen. The trommel is set at a slight angle, and the refuse tumbles through the cylinder as it rotates. Oversized objects (overs), such as plastic bottles, move through the cylinder while undersized objects (unders), such as cans, bottles, and other small items, fall through holes in the cylinder.

The trommel may also be designed to open bags of waste and reduce the size of breakable items, especially glass. Spikes or knives fastened to the inside of the cylinder can help rip bags open. Trommels are designed with paddles, called lifters, fastened to the inside of the rotating trommel, which lift and drop the waste. The impact helps to open the bags and to break glass. Trommels can be designed to minimize glass breakage by controlling their rotational speed and by designing the paddles to keep material in the lower portion of the trommel. Spikes and lifters can be bolted, rather than welded, to the trommel to facilitate replacement.

Trommel screens have been used for decades to sort industrial and manufacturing materials and, more recently, to sort solid waste. The lifting, dropping, and

FIGURE 24.6   Trommel screen. (*Courtesy of Triple/S Dynamics, Inc.*)

tumbling in the trommels also serve to untangle and separate materials; this is important for effective screening.

Trommel sizes range from approximately 5 to 12 ft in diameter and from 20 to 70 ft in length. Trommels larger than this cannot be shipped because of the size and weight limits for most trucks and even for rail hauling. Large trommels can be shipped in segments and erected in the field, but field construction may not be as good as shop fabrication. Trommels may be enclosed in shrouds for dust control.

Screens may be bolted or welded to the frame. Bolting is preferred so that the screen can be removed for maintenance or to change the size of openings.

A series of trommels with different-sized openings can be used to sort materials into several size categories. Alternatively, a single trommel can sort for multiple categories by varying the size of openings between different sections of the trommel. For example, the first half of the trommel might contain 2-in openings and the last half 6-in openings. This will result in sorting the waste stream into three groups—less than 2 in, 2 to 6 in, and larger than 6 in.

Two types of drive systems are used for trommels—chain and trunnion. With the chain drive, the trommel is connected to a motor by a chain. With the trunnion system, the trommel cylinder is supported at several points by drive wheels. The wheels drive the trommel through friction, which results in less direct transfer of power than with a chain drive. This can create drive problems, especially if the trommel must be started under load.

Table 24.1 shows the characteristics of some standard-sized trommels. Many trommels, however, are designed for site-specific requirements. The costs of trommels range from approximately $50,000 to $400,000, excluding structural support, shipping, and erection. The costs vary depending on sizes, dust enclosures, bolted vs. welded screens, and similar options.

TABLE 24.1 Trommel Screen Characteristics

Dimensions			Length of screen, ft	Screen characteristics	r/min	Weight, lb†	Angle, °
Length, ft	Nominal diameter, ft	Rated capacity, tons/h*					
40	8.5	55	30	As required	Varies	40,000	5, others available
50	10.5	75	40	5-in-diameter holes, 55% open area, other sizes available	13	80,000	5, others available
60	12.5	120	48	5-in-diameter holes, 53% open area, other sizes available	11–12	120,000	3–8, adjustable

*Based on density of 15 lb/ft³ for unprocessed refuse.
†Including trommel, hopper, dust cover, and bases, excluding concrete piers.
Source: Based on standard trommel designs offered by the Heil Company.

Disk Screens. The disk screen consists of successive rows of vertical rotating disks. The tops of the rotating disks form a moving surface that tumbles and conveys the solid waste, and smaller material falls through the openings between the disks (Fig. 24.7). Disk screens occupy less space than trommels, have lower capital cost, produce less dust, and require less operating power. However, disk screens may not separate materials as well as trommels because they do not agitate the waste as vigorously. For example, a heavy, wet load of waste may travel over the disks as a solid mass.

The opening size on disk screens can be varied by changing the size and spacing of the disks. Disk screens are most effective when they are sized so that the majority of the material falls through the disks.

Screens separate by size only, so it is possible that light and dense materials such as paper and metals will be sorted out together, if they have the same size. Therefore, screening is often followed by air classification.

Air Classification. Air classifiers sort by density and aerodynamic properties of the materials. The materials to be separated are introduced into an air stream. Based on size, shape, and density, some materials are entrained in the air stream and carried off while others drop out. Unfortunately, air classifiers may treat particles of the same material differently, depending upon their size and shape. For example, an uncrushed aluminum can or a flat piece of foil may be sorted with the light fraction, whereas a crushed can or a balled piece of foil may be sorted with the heavy fraction.

The air supply to an air classifier should be adjustable to accommodate local conditions and changes in the composition and moisture content of the waste.

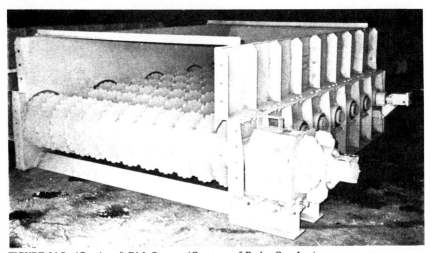

FIGURE 24.7 (*Continued*) Disk Screen. (*Courtesy of Rader Co., Inc.*)

Most air classifiers are followed by a cyclone separator that removes the lightest materials, including dust, before the air is exhausted, through a filter, to the atmosphere.

The two major categories of air classifiers used in solid waste processing are vertical classifiers and air knives.

Vertical Air Classifiers. In vertical air classifiers, the material is introduced from the top and air is introduced from the bottom (Fig. 24.8). Several variations of the design have been produced by incorporating zigzags, baffles, and other ob-

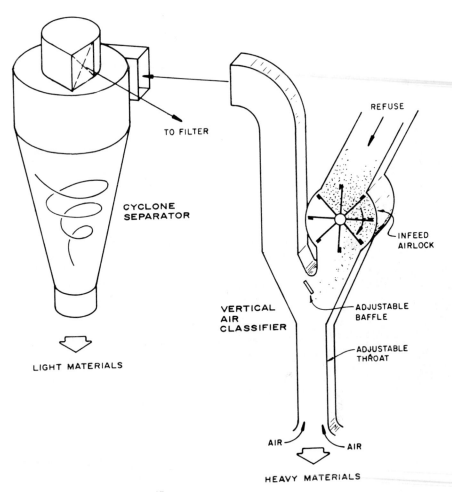

FIGURE 24.8 Vertical air classifier.

stacles that increase turbulence. The added turbulence and longer residence time help break up aggregated particles for better sorting. A feature common to many vertical air classifier designs is a sharp bend in the path of the air stream. Presumably, heavier waste particles with higher inertia will not be able to make the bend and will thus be sorted into the heavy fraction.

Air Knives. The air knife does not attempt to entrain light materials. Rather, it introduces a sharp curtain of air, through which the material passes. Light materials are propelled out of the flow and sorted with the light fraction (Fig. 24.9).

The air knives have capacities as high as 125 tons per hour and require 40- to 50-hp motors. They are designed for a finer separation of materials of different densities. For this reason, air knives may be used to clean up mixed nonferrous metals, such as those generated by eddy current processing. The cleaning con-

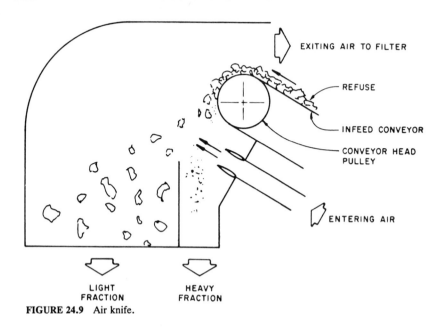

FIGURE 24.9   Air knife.

sists of separating the heavy fraction such as castings, forgings, and rolled stock from the light fraction such as cans and other light-gauge metals.

Eddy Currents.   Nonferrous metals can be removed from waste streams by inducing repulsive magnetic fields that propel the nonmagnetic materials out of the stream. The repulsive forces are the result of eddy currents developed by alternating magnetic fields. This process is known as eddy current separation.

Eddy current separation is most often used to remove aluminum after initial screening. It can remove up to 98 percent of nonferrous metals with a similar level of product purity. Its energy consumption is low compared to other separation methods.

Magnetics.   Ferrous metals have a property that allows them to be separated from other materials—magnetism. Although magnetic separation cannot separate tangled ferrous and nonferrous materials, it can often produce a marketable steel product for a relatively small investment. In addition, the removal of ferrous metals enhances the processes that follow. In all types of magnetic separation, the materials to be separated pass near a magnet that removes the ferrous materials, transports or deflects them, and deposits them into a bin or onto another conveyor.

Magnets are either permanent or electromagnets. The three major types of equipment used for magnetic separation are the head pulley, the suspended drum, and the suspended belt magnet.

1. Figure 24.10 shows a magnetic head pulley. The forward pulley in the conveyor is a magnet. Nonmagnetic materials, unaffected by the magnet, fall onto the next conveying device. Magnetic materials travel through the free-fall zone and are dropped on the other side of the splitter. The conveyor belt must be

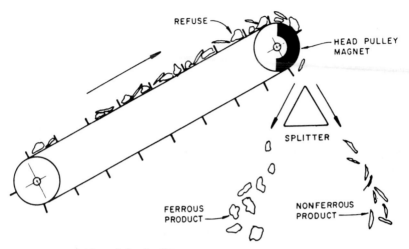

FIGURE 24.10 Magnetic head pulley.

cleated to ensure positive discharge of the ferrous materials. Some nonmagnetic materials such as paper, plastics, and textiles may be trapped with the magnetic material, so an additional cleaning step may be necessary.

2. A suspended drum magnet consists of a stationary magnet inside a rotating drum. Ferrous metals are pulled to the face of the drum, held against the drum as it travels, and then discharged free of the nonmagnetic materials. Figure 24.11 shows an arrangement of two drum magnets. The first is installed for underfeed, and the second for overfeed. By reducing the size of the magnet or increasing the distance to the magnet, the magnets can be made to discriminate between large

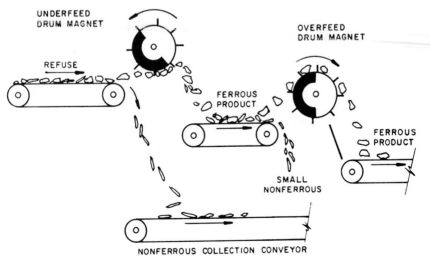

FIGURE 24.11 Magnetic drum arrangement.

and small ferrous particles. This results in cleaner separations and separation even among ferrous materials of different sizes.

3. The belt magnet consists of a fixed magnet located between the pulleys of a conveyor. The magnetic conveyor is suspended above the flow of materials, either in line (parallel) or transverse to the flow (Fig. 24.12). The in-line arrangement is preferred by some for cleaner separation and more efficient operation. Unlike the head pulley and drum magnet, the belt magnet has belts that are subject to wear. The belts may be protected by installing stainless steel wear plates on the belts. Suspended drum and belt magnets are less likely than head pulley magnets to entrap nonmagnetic materials because these materials are released as the magnetic materials travel through the air. Some carryover can be expected, nonetheless.

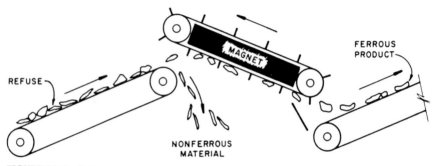

FIGURE 24.12   Belt magnet.

Multiple magnets may be used in belt magnets as shown in Fig. 24.13. The pickup magnet must be the strongest to draw ferrous materials from greater distance. Transfer magnets need not be as large; this results in some cost savings.

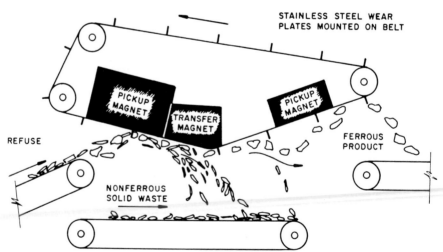

FIGURE 24.13   Multiple belt magnet arrangement.

An additional cleaning step can be incorporated into the belt magnet by placing a second pickup magnet following a discharge point, as shown on Fig. 24.13. This allows entrapped materials to be released.

Conveyors

From the time materials arrive at the processing facility until they leave, they must be conveyed through the various processing points. Several means of conveyance are used. On the tipping floor, materials that are not suited for processing, and large recyclable items may be conveyed manually or with mechanical equipment. The remaining materials are likely to be conveyed (pushed) by a loader to a receiving pit. Conveyors are often used to move the materials horizontally and vertically. Materials may also be conveyed by gravity down chutes and slides, and light materials may be conveyed through ductwork by air.

Rubber belt is the most popular type of conveyor. They are relatively low in cost, are quiet, and do not interfere with magnetic separation. However, the rubber belts are susceptible to damage from sharp, heavy, or hot materials.

There are two major drive systems for belt conveyors. The belt may be attached to a chain drive system, in which case it is not part of the drive system, but merely "goes along for the ride."

Alternatively, the belt may be driven by motors attached to its pulleys. Although these belts do not last as long as chain-driven belts, they may cost only half as much.

Where conveyors are subjected to heavy, damaging loads, such as sharp, heavy objects or great dropping heights, a metal pan design is recommended. These conveyors consist of hinged metal plates, usually with metal sidewalls, which are resistant to damage. Metal pan conveyors, however, are expensive, noisy, and require more maintenance than belt conveyors.

The horizontal auger, or screw conveyor, has found limited use in solid waste handling. One of its advantages is that it opens bags as it conveys the materials.

An advantage of chain-driven conveyors is that they can change gradient. For example, a single chain-driven conveyor can travel horizontally for a given distance, then incline upward, and finally travel on a level plane. A system of conventional belt-driven conveyors would require three separate belts to achieve this same effect.

Inclined conveyors usually have risers or paddles attached to the belt for positive lifting. Conveyors can incline up to approximately 30°, and up to 45° if the height of the risers is increased.

The depth of the material on the conveyor, the conveyor width, and its travel speed determine the flow rate of the material. The depth of material can be increased or decreased by transferring the material to a slower- or faster-moving conveyor. Waste streams can also be divided into or combined from several belts. The proper flow rates of the various conveyors are critical to synchronizing the elements of the processing system. The speed of individual conveyors or of the entire system may be controlled automatically for improved efficiency. For example, the speed of the conveyor feeding a shredder may be controlled by the loading on the shredder so that the feed rate will drop when more difficult material is processed. Conveyors and other parts of the processing system can usually be shut down by tripping an emergency shutoff switch.

Densifying

Materials are prepared for transport to markets by decreasing their volume and increasing their density by using compactors, balers, densifiers, and glass crushers. The decision whether to densify material before shipping should be based primarily on market specifications and transportation costs.

Operators must determine the form in which material is delivered to the markets for further processing. In most cases, densification of recyclables is preferred. Table 24.2 presents material density estimates that can be used in evaluating transportation costs.

TABLE 24.2 Relative Densities, lb/yd^3

	Loose*	Compacted	Baled*	Crushed 1/2 in	1/4 in
Newsprint	600		900		
OCC	150	300	1100		
PET	30		750		
HDPE	25		750		
Aluminum cans	50		650		
Steel	150		—		
Solid waste	400		1200		
Mixed paper	600		900		
Glass	600		—	1800	2700

*New York State Department of Environmental Conservation, *A Planning Guide for Communities,* January 1990.

Recycled fiber mills are equipped to handle standard-sized bales. Baled material generally brings a higher price. A compactor costs less than a baler but cannot consolidate the material to the same density as a baler. Compactors can be used where an intermediate market is involved, because the intermediate market will rebale the material to meet the mill's specifications.

Since most markets are equipped to receive baled materials, selecting a compactor over a baler could limit the markets available to the MRF operator. This factor must be evaluated against the lower capital costs and higher transportation costs of a compactor.

The network for plastics recycling is not as well established at this time, but baling is the preferred method of material handling.

Aluminum is typically baled or "briquetted" in smaller densifiers. The selection of densifying equipment for aluminum should focus on the appropriate size of equipment for the throughput quantity.

Improvements and advancements in baling equipment are forthcoming as the equipment manufacturers recognize the specific needs of the MRF industry. Newer balers come equipped with sophisticated controls that allow a single baler to bale multiple products, each to specified dimensions and weights. Some balers allow for unattended baler stations.

Some materials are difficult to bale because they have a memory for their original shape. Such materials can be handled more easily if a fluffer is installed above the baler charge hopper.

The decision to include a glass crusher in a system depends upon the intended means of transportation. Glass plants are invariably equipped with their own glass crushers capable of converting whole bottles into ¼-in, furnace-ready cullet, or intermediate cullet. Because of its high density, the amount of crushed glass transported by highway is often limited by weight restrictions.

Processing

After materials are shipped from the MRF or WPF, they are further processed and purified before use as feedstock in manufacturing new products. Such processing may include washing, rinsing, drying, and further size reduction or separation and removal of contaminants. Although these processes and the related equipment are integral to recycling, they are not discussed here because they do not take place in the MRF or the WPF. Nonetheless, these processes and the associated equipment could be incorporated into the design of a recycling facility to increase the value of the recyclables.

FINAL DESIGN

Architectural Considerations

The architectural design of an MRF depends largely on its location. MRFs have been successfully installed in existing buildings or warehouses. In such retrofit installations the modifications to the building were not of an aesthetic nature. Rather the structure was modified to accommodate the processing equipment.

At the other end of the spectrum is an attractive building designed to be accepted by the surrounding immediate community as part of a larger solid waste transfer operation. The architectural efforts to make a larger transfer or MRF operation acceptable by its community can be significant. Such a facility can be designed to resemble a commercial office building, to make it compatible with surrounding structures. Another architectural approach is to make the facility visible in an attractive manner, to draw the community's attention to the efforts required to manage solid waste effectively. It is the design architect's responsibility to recognize the aims and needs of the owner and to utilize his or her professional skills in designing an attractive facility that offers a safe and pleasant working environment.

Mechanical Considerations

Design considerations for different sorting technologies were discussed earlier in this chapter. Designing a conveying system to link the various of the facility elements is critical to an effective system. Layout and design of conveyor systems requires a thorough knowledge of mechanical engineering principles and extensive operating experience. Some of the guidelines to consider in laying out a system are as follows:

- Minimize changes in direction.
- Allow 2-ft drops between conveyors.

- Use metal conveyors whenever heavy impacts are anticipated.
- Generally increase the speed of travel as material progresses through the system.

The first step in designing a conveyor system is to select the dimensions of the belts. The following equations can be used to select the width and the travel speed for a flat belt:

$$C = V \times A_n$$

$$A_n = \text{nominal cross-sectional area (ft}^2) = \frac{h_n \times (b - 2s)}{144}$$

where C = belt capacity
V = belt speed, ft/min
h_n = nominal material heights, in
b = belt width, in
s = standard edge distance = $0.055 \times b + 0.9$, in

A reasonable belt speed for a conveyor charging the system is 10 to 20 ft/min. Hand sorting can be efficiently done with belt speeds around 50 ft/min. In the layout of such hand-sorting operations, it is important to consider when selecting the belt width the reaching and twisting motions by the pickers when belt height should also be comfortable for the pickers.

Drive requirements are calculated from the following formula:

$$P = \frac{T_e \times V}{33,000 \times E}$$

where P = power, hp
T_e = effective tension, lb
V = belt speed, ft/min
K = motor efficiency

T_e is the effective tension required to drive the belt at the drive pulley. The main forces to be overcome are as follows:

- Gravitational load to lift material
- Frictional forces at design speed
- Force to accelerate the material as it is fed onto the conveyor

Calculating the effective tension of the conveyor by identifying these forces requires an understanding of the conveyor equipment proposed.

The Conveyor Equipment Manufacturers' (CEMA) handbook presents the formula for calculating effective tension for rubber belts as

$$T_e = LK_t (K_x + K_yW_b + 0.015W_b) + W_m(LK_y \pm V) + T_{am} + T_{ac}$$

where L = length of conveyor, ft
K_t = ambient temperature correction factor
K_x = friction factor of idlers
W_b = weight of belt, lb/ft

W_m = weight of material, lb/ft
V = vertical distance, ft
T_p = tension resulting from pulleys
T_{am} = tension resulting from force to accelerate
T_{ac} = tension from accessories (skidboards, plows, etc.)

Many of the values of these coefficients and associated forces can be determined from CEMA. The CEMA handbook also provides guidelines for graphically estimating power requirements for rubber belt conveyors. However, because solid waste and recyclables are generally at the lighter end of the material spectrum, graphic solution with a high degree of accuracy is not possible, and analytical solutions are preferable after initial estimates by graphic solutions.

An adaptation of the formula for effective tension for metal belt conveyors is as follows:

$$T_e - (W_b + W_m)(H_f + V) + W_b(H_f - V)(1 + C_1 + C_2) + D$$

Where the second component $(H_f - V)$ is considered only if it is additive, and

where H = horizontal distance, ft
f = friction factor from manufacturer
C_1, C_2 = curve friction factors from manufacturer (where applicable)
D = $0.41h^2B$, skirt friction
h = exposed skirt height
B = length of skirt

Example. Size the motor for the following 500-in, straight, elevating, steel-belted conveyor. Conveyor specifications:

$$H = 400 \text{ in}$$

$$V = 300 \text{ in}$$

$$W_b = 15 \text{ lb/ft}$$

$$f = 0.05$$

$$h = 42 \text{ in}$$

$$W = \text{belt width} = 72 \text{ in}$$

$$\gamma = \text{material density} = 15 \text{ lb/ft}^3$$

$$d = \text{average depth of material} = 2 \text{ ft}$$

Solution

$$W_m = \frac{W(d)\gamma}{12} = \frac{72(2)15}{12} = 180 \text{ lb/ft}$$

$$H_f = \frac{400}{12} \times 0.05 = 1.7 =$$

$$D = 0.04112(42)^2 \frac{500}{12} = 3013 \text{ lb}$$

$$T_e = (15 + 190)\left(1.7 + \frac{300}{12}\right) + W_b(H_f - V) + 3013 \text{ lb}$$

$$= 5206 \text{ lb} + 3013 \text{ lb}$$

$$= 8219 \text{ lb}$$

After determining the required tension, one must verify that the selected belt is designed for this loading. Horsepower is calculated from the effective tension of the belt moving at 20 ft/min using the horsepower equations as follows:

$$\text{hp} = \frac{8219 \times 20}{33,000 \times 0.80} = 7.45, \quad \text{use 10-hp motor}$$

Considerations to keep in mind for designing recyclables conveying systems, some of which are reflected in the above equations are as follows:

• Frictional load is significantly increased by the inclusion of plows.
• Plowing of nonhomogeneous material is difficult.
• Belt skirts significantly affect frictional load to the point that wider belts may be more economical than belt skirts.

Electrical Considerations

Allowances for additional floor storage will enable the facility to continue receiving material in the event of a power outage. Power outages are normally considerably shorter than the full day of storage recommended for these facilities, so with flexible operating conditions, the inconvenience resulting from power outages will be relatively insignificant and provisions for backup power need not be made.

The control system for an MRF may provide for the following:

• Sequenced startup of conveyors and other equipment
• Local control of conveyor belt speed
• Remote control of system (optional)
• Local emergency shutdown controls

Manufacturing of accurate records of total plant input and output is the most important part of system monitoring and can be accomplished without sophisticated instrumentation. An example of additional instrumentation is equipment for monitoring the nominal height of material on the infeed belt conveyor material. This measurement allows control of the conveyor's belt speed so that a constant feed rate is maintained.

OPERATIONS

Personnel

As mentioned previously, flexibility is crucial to the success of an MRF. After equipment is selected and installed, the adaptability of the MRF to changing market demands is largely dependent upon the flexibility of its management and operation.

Many private MRFs are constantly adjusting their systems to optimize their output. Their managers utilize techniques that reward the line workers for surpassing established goals. Another common practice is to rotate personnel through the plant so that their tasks are varied.

Several municipally owned MRFs, on the other hand, have shown initiative by employing lower-cost work forces such as institutionalized laborers. The decision to reduce operating costs in a labor-intensive facility in this manner should be evaluated in light of the reduced efficiency or lack of flexibility that may be associated with such a labor force.

Equipment

Regularly scheduled maintenance of the equipment as suggested by suppliers is essential. If equipment failures result in frequent downtime, not only do operations become more difficult but the facility may also lose the all-important public confidence. The redirecting of recyclables as a result of extended downtime in the MRF could be fatal to public interest in recycling.

Several high-volume facilities (over 100 tons per day) schedule a shift each day for maintenance to clean conveyor belts and other equipment. The abrasion caused by glass can be particularly damaging to the system unless regular cleaning is performed. Other maintenance tasks, such as lubricating idlers, can be performed less frequently at intervals recommended by the supplier.

In general, an MRF is not as maintenance intensive as other solid waste handling systems such as RDFs or composting facilities. The waste stream received at the MRF is more homogeneous and therefore less abrasive to the equipment. In addition, the processing equipment is intended to separate the stream of recyclables into its constituents, not to pulverize the waste.

COST

Capital Cost

It should now be apparent that processing facilities labeled MRFs come in a variety of types and sizes. Recycling is an emerging market, and the materials handling equipment manufacturers as well as specialty equipment manufacturers are only beginning to gain experience in the area. Processing capacities and materials recovered vary from one system to the next, so it is difficult to develop a basis of comparison of costs. For planning purposes, however, capital costs for an MRF can be assumed to range from $5 to $18 per ton of material recovered. Costs per ton are at the higher end of the range when only containers are recovered and when more mechanized systems are used. When fibers are included, the unit costs are lower, even though the total capital outlay may be considerably higher.

Operating and Maintenance Costs

Equipment operating and maintenance costs vary with the equipment selected. For estimating purposes, annual equipment maintenance costs are 5 percent of equipment capital costs and site maintenance costs are 1 percent of civil site cost.

Manual labor often constitutes a large portion of the operating costs. In determining the number of manual pickers needed, the following average picking rates can be applied to the projected throughput stream that is to be hand-sorted:

Glass sorter: 800 lb/h

Plastic sorter: 500 lb/h

Corrugated and other paper sorter: 800 lb/h

In addition, personnel will be needed to operate rolling stock and to operate and maintain other major pieces of equipment. These personnel can add costs of $10 to $20 per ton recovered. Obviously, systems with higher capital costs should have a trade-off in lower operating and maintenance (O&M) costs as a result of reduced staffing requirements. It is important to develop a conceptual design and to estimate the associated staffing requirements for a proposed MRF. Because there are many concepts for MRFs, only after developing cash flow projections and income statements for specific facilities can their capital and O&M costs be estimated with any level of accuracy.

Additional Guidelines

Experience has shown that under today's markets conditions, MRFs that recover material at a total system cost less than the revenues they receive for their recyclables are rare. The cost to process material received at the MRF is about equal to the revenues from the processed materials. This does not take into account the additional costs assignable to an MRF outside of processing costs such as the collection cost and the disposal cost of rejects.

In addition to these financial costs which are assignable to a proposed MRF, a developer or municipality should consider the frequently significant economic system costs. Avoided costs for collection and disposal must be considered by the investor in order to make informed decisions.

CHAPTER 25
INTEGRATING RECYCLING WITH LANDFILLS AND INCINERATORS

John C. Glaub, Ph.D., P.E.

INTRODUCTION

Integrated waste management includes landfilling and incineration (waste-to-energy) as components of the total integrated system. The basic role of landfills and incinerators in an integrated system is to manage nonrecyclable wastes; accordingly, they are at the bottom of the integrated waste management hierarchy. Landfills and incinerators can further contribute to integrated waste management by serving as sites for recycling operations.

Recycling operations at landfills and incinerators can be instrumental in helping communities meet their recycling goals. As national, state, and local recycling percentages are adopted, increasing attention will be placed on the role that landfills and incinerators can play. This chapter examines the types of material recovery operations in practice at landfills and incinerators and discuses key issues associated with such operations.

ADVANTAGES TO IMPLEMENTING RECYCLING AT LANDFILLS AND INCINERATORS

Siting Advantages

Landfills and incinerators are generally well-suited places to conduct recycling operations. They are the sites in our communities to which wastes are delivered and accordingly provide access to the materials in the waste stream. They are permitted waste management facilities, and the public is usually accepting of these locations being used for waste management operations (albeit a resigned acceptance in many cases). Therefore, the difficulties involved in siting and permitting a new solid waste facility can often be avoided by locating recycling operations at existing landfills and incinerators.

Some recycling operations require a large area, and some are most economically conducted outdoors. Appropriate sites may therefore be difficult to locate in urban areas. Landfills often provide good sites for these operations. Many incinerators also have substantial areas available around them, although others are more tightly constrained.

Operational Advantages

Landfills and incinerators also offer operational advantages for many types of recycling activities. Site features that offer operational advantages to recycling at landfills and incineration facilities are compared in Table 25.1.

TABLE 25.1 Comparison of Site Features at Landfills and Incinerators with Respect to Recycling Operations

Facility	Typical site feature	Advantage to recycling
Landfill	Large land area	Composting
		Stockpiling for periodic processing
	Isolated	Less impact of operations on surrounding land uses
	Use of materials on site	Creates internal market for compost, soil, concrete, asphalt
Incinerator	Covered building	Protection from weather
		Paper recovery
	Concrete floor	Better working conditions for employees
		Cleaner materials for recovery
		Structural support for processing equipment
	Paved roads	Facilitates use by public for drop-off and buy-back centers

Landfills typically have large areas of land available, which offer advantages for composting and stockpiling for periodic processing (e.g., concrete and asphalt recycling). The relative isolation of most landfills results in less impact of the recycling operations on surrounding land uses. Also, landfills are in some ways an ongoing construction project that uses materials. This creates an internal market for compost, soil, concrete, asphalt, etc.

Waste-to-energy facilities can often provide a covered building for material recovery operations, which offers protection from weather and correspondingly enhances paper recovery. Concrete floors in these facilities provide better working conditions for employees than dirt or mud (i.e., in comparison to landfills), cleaner materials for recovery, and structural support for processing equipment. Waste-to-energy facilities are also more developed sites, providing paved roads, parking, etc., thereby facilitating use by the public for drop-off centers, buy-back centers, and household hazardous waste collection facilities.

The operational links between recycling and landfilling-incineration also offer a variety of advantages as discussed later in this chapter. These include shared equipment and back-up capacity. In addition, the close proximity between the recycling and landfilling-incineration operations results in efficient and inexpensive hauling of residues.

Recycling, in turn, offers many advantages to landfilling and incineration operations. To landfilling, recycling offers saved air space—an ever more valuable asset to landfills. Saved air space translates to longer site life and greater total revenue flows to the landfill. Recycling can be beneficial to incineration operations by improving fuel properties, reducing ash disposal costs, downsizing boiler requirements, and removing large items that can cause material handling problems. Impacts on fuel properties are discussed in the next section and impacts of specific material recovery operations are discussed in the section on Problems Encountered.

Regulatory Advantages

The growing volume of recycling regulations and policies makes it advantageous to landfill and incinerator operators to conduct their own recycling operations. Such regulatory and policy issues include percent diversion requirements or goals, taxes on landfilled quantities, and permit conditions requiring recycling. Running their own programs gives landfill and incinerator operators internal control that recycling goals are being met. It also provides for optimizing the integrated waste management system by linking the components together. Finally, where tipping fee taxes are imposed on disposed quantities, it gives the operators the opportunity to avoid the tax on materials they divert from disposal.

OPERATIONAL LINKS BETWEEN RECYCLING AND LANDFILLING-INCINERATION

Traffic

When recycling operations are integrated with landfilling or incineration operations, traffic coordination is extremely important. This applies to (1) vehicles using recycling vs. disposal areas, (2) vehicles carrying processible vs. non-processible wastes, (3) public vs. commercial collection vehicles, and (4) vehicles delivering wastes to the site vs. site vehicles. These various categories of vehicles should be kept separate to the extent possible. In addition, cross-traffic (i.e., vehicles crossing in front of other vehicles) should be minimized.

A well-planned entrance facility can serve a valuable role in traffic coordination. Some recycling operations (e.g., drop-off and buy-back centers) are best located as part of the entrance facility. There are trade-offs between locating them before or after the gatehouse as discussed in a later section. In either case, traffic flow should be carefully considered. The smooth flow of traffic leaving the gatehouse for various tipping areas should also be incorporated into the site design. Figure 25.1 illustrates different approaches to locating recycling operations at entrance facilities.

Traffic coordination can be achieved by good facility design, signage, use of traffic coordinators (also referred to as spotters), and directions from the gatehouse attendant.

Materials Flow

Efficient materials flow is also important when integrating recycling with landfilling or incineration operations. Processible materials should be kept separate from nonprocessible materials; clean loads should be kept separate from mixed loads. The flow of materials toward recovered products vs. toward landfilling-incineration should be distinct and efficient. Residue from recovery operations should end up in a location convenient for handling in the landfilling or incineration operation. Finally, the capability to readily load out recovered materials to markets should also be provided. A materials flow diagram for an integrated waste management facility is shown in Fig. 25.2.

Material Properties

By removing materials in recycling operations, the material properties of the waste stream entering the landfilling or incineration operations are changed. These changes include both physical and chemical properties. The resulting impacts on incineration operations offer many benefits. Recycling can reduce ash content, lower the toxicity of the ash, raise the ash fusion temperature, provide a more consistent heating value, raise the heating value (in many cases), reduce air emissions, and reduce chloride content. As a consequence, ash disposal costs are reduced, and boiler efficiency is increased. Slagging is reduced due to the increase in ash fusion temperature. Decreased chloride content reduces boiler wall and tube corrosion.

Other material properties affected include bulk density and moisture content. These properties may either increase or decrease in value, depending on the recycling operation.

Equipment Requirements

Equipment can often be shared between recycling and landfilling operations or between recycling and waste-to-energy operations. Potentially shared equipment includes wheel loaders, dozers, and roll-off trucks. Although this equipment is used for other operations at the facilities, it often is not being used full-time. By coordination and scheduling, this equipment can serve the needs of the recycling operations, especially for small-scale operations. Large-scale operations require backup equipment, which can be used in the recycling operation rather than sitting idle. Substantial recycling operations will clearly require dedicated equipment, but again there is a potential for shared backup equipment rather than separate backup equipment for each operation. Shared equipment thus results in improved overall economic efficiency of the recycling-landfilling operations or the recycling-incineration operations.

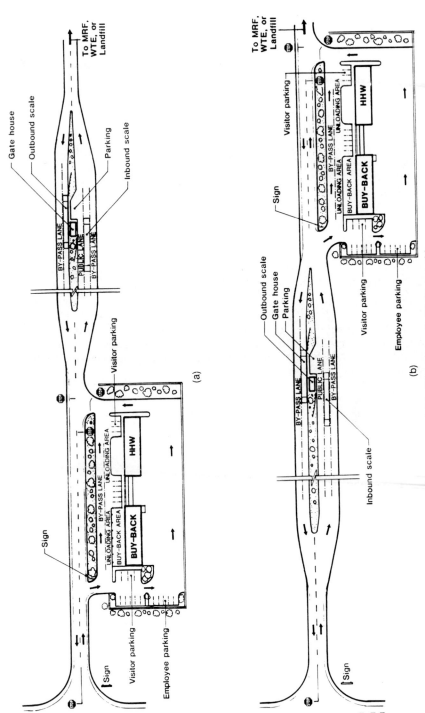

FIGURE 25.1 (*a*) Entrance facility layout with recycling before gatehouse; (*b*) entrance facility layout with recycling after gatehouse.

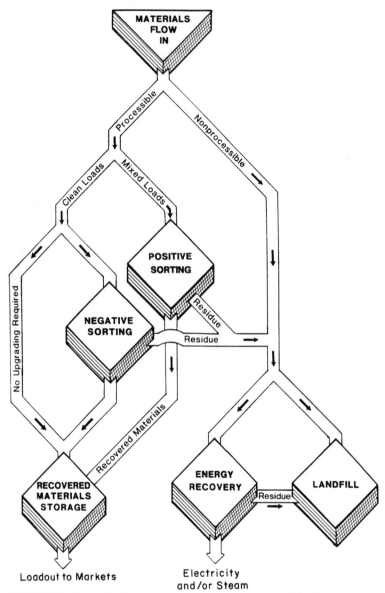

Loadout to Markets   Electricity
and/or Steam

FIGURE 25.2   Materials flow at an integrated waste management facility.

Backup Capacity

Landfilling and incineration operations offer an on-site backup to recycling operations if the recycling operations incur downtime or if peak waste flows exceed the throughput capacity of the recycling operation. These periods should be minimal in a well-run operation; nevertheless, backup capacity is another functional link between recycling and landfilling-incineration operations.

TARGET MATERIALS

Materials

Materials commonly targeted for recovery in recycling operations at landfills and incinerators are shown in Fig. 25.3. The figure indicates the type of vehicle in which these materials are typically delivered to the facility and the relative recoverability of the materials from the various sources. The ratings shown on the table may vary by community and can be refined from this general rating to a more site-specific analysis and/or to include subcategories of materials. Figure 25.3 is intended to present a guide to targeting materials in the waste stream for recovery.

MAJOR CATEGORY	RECOVERABILITY BY VEHICLE TYPE				
	RESIDENTIAL PACKER TRUCKS	COMMERCIAL PACKER TRUCKS	LOOSE ROLL-OFFS	COMPACTED ROLL-OFFS	SELF-HAUL
Asphalt	○□	○□	●■	○□	●■
Concrete	○□	○□	●■	○□	●■
Glass	◐▨	◐▨	◐▨	◐▨	○▨
Metals	◐▨	◐▨	●■	○▨	◐■
Paper	◐▨	●■	●■	●■	◐▨
Plastic	◐▨	●■	●■	●■	◐▨
Soil	○□	○□	●■	○□	●■
Tires	○▨	○▨	◐▨	○▨	●▨
Wood Waste	◐▨	◐▨	●■	◐▨	●■
Yard Waste	●□	○□	◐▨	○□	●■

KEY: SOURCE RATING ● Major   RECOVERABILITY RATING ■ High
     ◐ Moderate   ▨ Moderate
     ○ Minor   □ Low

FIGURE 25.3 Recoverability of target materials.

The materials targeted in various recycling operations differ as a function of waste stream characteristics, the distribution of waste-generating sources (i.e., residential, commercial, and industrial), site constraints, local climate, and local market conditions.

Various reusable goods are also often recovered at landfills and incinerators. Such goods include appliances, automotive parts, bicycles, electric motors, flower pots, furniture, lawn mowers, and mattresses. In some cases, repairs are required, but in other cases, the goods are in suitable working condition. Salvaged goods are either sold directly to the public or to another business that will reuse or resell them.

Sources

The key to recovery is economically segregating the materials relatively free of contamination from other types of materials, for example, recovering corrugated paper free of other paper grades, plastic, glass, metals, etc. The degree of difficulty in doing this depends on the condition of the materials delivered to the facility.

Source-separated materials are, of course, the easiest to recover. The next easiest are high-concentration loads (i.e., loads consisting primarily of one material). Typical high-concentration loads include corrugated paper, office paper, yard waste, wood waste, concrete, asphalt, and soil. Mixed waste loads are the most difficult to process and consequently influence the operator's selection of target materials. Nevertheless, a variety of materials are successfully being recovered from mixed waste loads at landfills and incinerators. Commercial, industrial, and self-haul loads are generally more recoverable than residential packer truck loads.

MATERIAL RECOVERY OPERATIONS

The various types of material recovery operations in practice at landfills and incinerators are shown in Table 25.2 The operations are broken down according to their function in waste receiving or waste processing. These operations are discussed in greater detail in other chapters of the handbook. Each operation is summarized in the following section with particular consideration given to its integration with landfilling and incineration facilities.

TABLE 25.2   Material Recovery Operations at Landfills and Incinerators

Function	Operation
Receiving	Drop-off center
	Buy-back center
	Diversion of high-concentration loads
Processing	Dump-and-pick (salvaging)
	Mixed waste processing lines
	Composting
	Wood waste processing
	Concrete and asphalt recycling
	Soil recovery
	Tire processing
	Curbside recycling processing
	Postincineration recycling
	Household hazardous waste facilities

Drop-off Centers

Drop-off centers are the simplest means to receive source-separated materials from the public. Such facilities are also the most common recycling facilities at landfills and incinerators. Drop-off centers can be implemented with relatively minor capital expenditures, although site development, paving, and retaining wall costs at the better-constructed facilities can run several hundred thousand dollars. Operational costs are low; the required staffing may be either one person or unattended. (Site supervision is recommended to control the types of wastes left at the facility.) Since the materials are received free and facility costs are low, the net revenues to the facility operator are about the same as or close to the gross revenues received from the sale of materials.

Drop-off centers can be located either before or after the gatehouse at the landfill or incineration facility; each location has its advantages and disadvantages (see Fig. 25.1). Drop-off centers are often located before the gatehouse to provide an incentive to recycling before entering the disposal site. Materials left at the recycling facility are not charged for at the gate. In addition, residents may readily use the drop-off center even if they do not have any refuse to discard at the landfill or incinerator. Locating the drop-off center after the gatehouse provides for better site surveillance and security. It is still possible to not charge users for recyclables if the drop-off center is after the gatehouse,but it may be operationally awkward.

Buy-Back Centers

Buy-back centers typically achieve greater recovery rates than drop-off centers. They can be readily located at either landfills or incinerators. Capital costs are only slightly greater than for drop-off centers, with additional costs typically required for scales and a minor amount of equipment (e.g., conveyors, magnetic separator). Operating costs are slightly higher due to the equipment and staffing. Because operators control the price differential between that paid by the brokers or mills and that paid to the public, buy-back facilities are usually profitable undertakings for operators. Difficulties can occur at times of depressed market prices, particularly in communities with multiple buy-back centers.

Buy-back centers are usually located before the gatehouse at landfills and incinerators. In addition to serving residents, many buy-back centers do substantial business with small commercial customers who make a living collecting recyclable materials for sale.

Diversion of High-Concentration Loads

Many loads arriving at landfills and incinerators contain high concentrations of a single material. As noted earlier, common types of high-concentration loads include corrugated paper, office paper, yard waste, and wood waste. In communities experiencing a high level of construction activity, high-concentration loads of soil, concrete, and asphalt are also received. Diversion of high-concentration loads can be coupled with most of the processing operations listed in Table 25.2 (as appropriate to the specific material) and correspondingly contribute to increased material recovery rates. At landfills, high-concentration loads can be diverted to designated processing or storage areas. At incinerators, high-concentration loads can be diverted either to a separate tipping area within the building or to an outside tipping area (e.g., for asphalt, concrete, wood waste, yard waste).

Dump and Pick or Salvaging

Salvaging from mixed waste piles, often referred to as "dump and pick," is the simplest method for recovering materials from a mixed waste stream. It is a very old practice that is receiving renewed use at both landfills and incinerators around the country. Some dump-and-pick operations at disposal sites have been ongoing for decades.

At certain facilities, dump and pick is practiced only on high-concentration loads, whereas at others it is practiced on the entire waste stream (i.e., whatever loads are available at the site). Because dump-and-pick operations at landfills are strongly affected by weather, their focus is often limited to metals and reusable goods. In addition to these materials, dump-and-pick operations in covered buildings (such as at incinerators), may target paper, particularly corrugated cardboard. Dump-and-pick operations are best suited for low- to medium-volume landfills or incinerators.

Mixed Waste Processing Lines

Some of the more aggressive material recovery operations at landfills and waste-to-energy facilities use mixed waste processing lines consisting of mechanical and/or manual separation processes. Indeed, the refuse-derived fuel (RDF) approach to waste to energy is based on processing the waste prior to combustion and separating a fuel fraction from the noncombustible fraction(s), often including recovery of materials, such as ferrous, aluminum, and glass. The use of mixed waste processing lines is growing at landfills in efforts to increase material recovery rates. Some landfills utilize portable conveyor systems unprotected from weather; other landfills have constructed enclosed processing buildings (i.e., MRFs) as part of the entrance facility to the landfill.

Operations focused on material recovery generally place a greater reliance on manual separation, whereas operations focused on energy recovery (e.g., RDF facilities) use mechanical separation to a greater degree. Manual separation is often required to meet the demanding specifications of secondary materials markets; contamination levels must be much lower than are typically allowed in fuel markets. Most of the mechanical waste processing experience in the United States to date is based on RDF processing, dating back to the St. Louis resource recovery plant in 1972. However, mechanical waste processing technology is being increasingly applied to material recovery operations.

Unit processes commonly employed in mechanical processing include screening, air classification, magnetic separation, eddy current separation, ballistic separation, flotation, and shredding. Manual separation equipment consists of conveyors and sorting platforms. A sorting platform provides a comfortable working environment for the sorters and helps achieve a productive and efficient recovery operation (e.g., as compared to a dump-and-pick operation). Manual separation can be conducted either in (1) a positive sort mode, where target recoverable materials are removed from the mixed waste stream, or (2) a negative sort mode, where contaminants are removed and the remaining material becomes the recovered product.

At landfills using mixed waste processing lines, it is common to process only specific types of loads and to divert others directly to the landfill face. A similar approach can be employed at waste-to-energy facilities. As illustrated in Fig. 25.3, highly recoverable loads include commercial packer trucks, roll-offs, and self-haul wastes.

Composting

Composting continues to grow as a solid waste management practice at landfills and incinerators. The most common material composted is yard waste. Much attention has been turned to yard waste, because it typically constitutes 20 to 30 percent of the residential waste stream; composting programs can therefore contribute substantially to meeting a community's percentage recovery goals. (The amount of yard waste may be higher or lower for a given community depending on geography, season, and landscaping characteristics.) Yard waste composting results in a high-quality product. Additional materials being composted include food-processing wastes and sewage sludge. Composting raw municipal solid waste (MSW) or a processed MSW fraction (e.g., an unders fraction from a trommel screen) is also receiving increased attention.

It is usually advantageous to keep yard waste out of waste-to-energy facilities because its high moisture content tends to reduce the heating value of the fuel and its high nitrogen content can contribute to elevated NO_x concentrations.

Landfills generally have more available space than incinerators; however, successful composting operations are in place at several incinerators. The turned windrow system is by far the most commonly used composting technique at landfills. In-vessel systems are, however, being used increasingly for composting yard waste or other solid waste materials. In-vessel systems offer advantages for incinerators and other solid waste facilities with space constraints.

Wood Waste Processing

Where markets are available, wood wastes are being diverted from the waste stream and processed for recovery. Such operations process either only wood wastes (e.g., lumber, pallets) or combined wood wastes and yard wastes. Wood waste processing operations are in place at many landfills.

Wood waste processing can also provide several benefits to incineration operations. Large wood items, such as logs and thick lumber, typically do not undergo complete combustion (particularly in mass-burn facilities). In RDF facilities, much wood and yard waste ends up in reject streams (e.g., air classifier heavies fraction, trommel screen unders). Lumber and tree trunks and limbs can also present material handling problems in waste-to-energy facilities, such as bridging in feed hoppers in mass-burn plants or in mechanical processing equipment before the primary shredder in an RDF plant. Finally, as mentioned in the previous section, yard waste tends to adversely affect fuel properties.

The major markets for recovered wood waste materials are for wood chip fuel and soil amendment. Some wood chips are being sold for ornamental landscaping and some for use in sewage sludge composting operations. Another potential use is in particleboard manufacturing.

Typical equipment used in wood waste processing comprises a grinder, a screen, and related conveyors. A variety of grinders are in use, including tub grinders, hammer mills, and shear shredders. Likewise, several different types of screens are in use, including trommels, disk screens, and flatbed screens. The wood waste is first ground, then screened, with the oversized material being sold as wood chips and the undersized material (often referred to as "fines") as soil amendment. The fines may be composted or sold directly to buyers (such as wholesale soil dealers) who blend them with other soil materials.

A less capital-intensive alternative employed at some landfills involves simply diverting, crushing, and hauling the wood wastes to another wood waste processing site. In this type of operation, a track-mounted dozer or loader is typically used to crush the waste.

Moisture content is an important parameter affecting the marketability and market price of wood chip fuel. Wood chip fuel is often purchased on a dry ton basis. Furthermore, the dry ton price itself may vary with different moisture content ranges. For example, the dry ton price for a load of wood chips with a moisture content between 30 to 40 percent may be lower than for a load with a moisture content between 20 and 30 percent. Drying yard wastes before they are processed for wood chip fuel is therefore beneficial.

Landfills typically have an advantage over incinerators for drying yard waste, because of the greater land area available. The material is stockpiled after it enters the site and the oldest material is processed first.

Concrete and Asphalt Processing

In terms of tonnage or recovery rate percentage, concrete and asphalt recycling can offer one of the greatest reductions in the amount of waste entering disposal sites. Obviously, concrete and asphalt are also good materials to keep out of an incinerator. The two general approaches to concrete and asphalt recycling are (1) establishing a processing facility at a site and (2) stockpiling materials for periodic processing by mobile equipment brought to the site. Concrete and asphalt processing equipment is expensive, and therefore substantial quantities of wastes are required to economically justify the equipment. Accordingly, concrete and asphalt recycling is usually best practiced on a regional basis using one of the two approaches described above.

Processing equipment consists of screens, crushers, magnetic separators, and conveyors. Size reduction typically is achieved using a multistage approach (i.e., multiple crushers), with each unit designed for a specific range of size reduction. Crushing equipment used includes hammer mills and jaw crushers. Grizzly screens are often used in the early stages of processing, and single-deck or multideck flatbed vibratory screens are commonly used for grading the final products. The products are sold as a variety of construction materials, such as road base and aggregate.

Area requirements are large, in the range of 5 to 10 acres. The large area is consumed by stockpiles of the incoming waste materials, the processing system, and stockpiles of the product materials. Again, landfills tend to be better suited than incinerators for this type of an operation, although some incinerators do have sufficient surrounding area.

Also worth noting is that recovered concrete and asphalt materials are commonly used at landfills in place of construction materials (e.g., rock and gravel) for road base, winter tipping pads, drainage construction, erosion control, ditch lining, and leachate collection systems. In these applications, the materials are often first worked over by dozers to break them up. The benefits of using the concrete and asphalt materials are thus twofold: (1) substituting for natural construction materials and (2) saving landfill space by not being disposed of in the landfill burial cell.

Soil Recovery

Loads of clean or relatively clean soil are sometimes delivered to disposal sites. The sources of such loads include construction projects, utility companies, road maintenance crews, and, occasionally, home owners. Most landfills make good use of these materials for cover and on-site construction, and some have even resold them for off-site use. Soil recovery is more readily carried out at landfills than at incinerators.

Tire Processing

Tire processing can provide a variety of benefits for landfills and incinerators. The problem of tires rising to the surface of landfills is well known. Tire processing prevents this problem as well as saves landfill space. Since whole tires often do not combust completely in MSW incinerators, tire processing can be helpful by recycling the tires or at least shredding them. Tire shredding results in more complete combustion of tires in MSW incinerators.

Shear shredders are the most common type of processing equipment used. However, shredding is not always necessary for tire recovery to off-site markets. Tires are often shredded for efficient storage and transportation and for mitigation of vector problems, especially mosquito breeding.

Curbside Recycling Processing

As residential curbside recycling programs are implemented in more and more communities, facilities for processing the collected materials are often located at landfills or incinerators because of the ease of siting. Materials from both commingled and multicontainer recycling programs are being processed at landfill and incineration facilities. The processing operations may be enclosed, partially enclosed, or open. The approach taken is usually driven by climate.

Processing equipment requirements for multicontainer systems are, of course, less than those of commingled systems. Equipment used includes conveyors, magnetic separators, can flatteners, glass crushers, balers, and scales. Equipment varies among facilities and depends upon market requirements, available funding for the facility, and the size of the operation.

Curbside recycling programs help keep glass and metals out of incineration facilities. As a consequence, heating value is increased and ash content is decreased.

Postincineration Recycling

The most common type of postincineration recycling is recovery of ferrous metals from the ash by means of magnetic separation. Screens (e.g., trommels) are often used to process the ash prior to magnetic separation. Some facilities also recover nonferrous metals from ash. In addition, ash can be processed for other uses, including aggregate, road base, and concrete construction blocks.

Concern over heavy metals concentrated in the ash has limited ash recovery. The application of solidification processes on incinerator ash and the implementation of alternative recycling programs for such materials as batteries can mitigate the heavy metal problem and allow more beneficial uses of the ash. Ash from tire incineration facilities is sometimes processed for zinc recovery.

Household Hazardous Waste Facilities

Household hazardous waste facilities also can be integrated into landfill and incinerator operations. These facilities serve several roles in an integrated system, including (1) preventing the improper disposal of hazardous wastes in solid waste facilities, (2) providing proper handling and storage of hazardous wastes identified in other operations (e.g., recycling, transfer), and (3) recycling of various hazardous materials (e.g., paints, solvents, batteries). Household hazardous waste facilities are discussed in greater detail in Chap. 21.

Household hazardous waste facilities can be very beneficial to an incineration facility by reducing heavy metals in the ash and flue gas. Collection of such items as batteries can help the incinerator meet emission limits and potentially decrease the cost of ash disposal.

The entrance facility to the landfill or incinerator is a good location for the household hazardous waste facility—either before or after the gatehouse, depending on available space, traffic flow, and security considerations. Locating the hazardous waste facility before the gatehouse generally provides for easiest use by the public, but there may be overriding considerations or simply operator preferences that lead to its placement after the gatehouse.

Integration of Components

The alternative material recovery operations can be combined with landfilling and incineration operations in a variety of ways as is best suited to a particular community's waste stream and site conditions. An example of integrating material recovery operations at a landfill is presented in Fig. 25.4. A similar example for integrating material recovery operations at an incineration facility is shown in Fig. 25.5.

PROBLEMS ENCOUNTERED AND PROBLEM AVOIDANCE

Proper planning, design, and equipment selection are important in achieving successful recycling operations at landfills and incineration facilities. Implementing recycling at a new landfill or incinerator is, of course, much easier than retrofitting operations at an existing facility. The following sections discuss some of the problems encountered in implementing recycling at landfills and incinerators with guidelines for avoiding such problems.

Space Constraints

Lack of space can severely restrict the types of recycling operations that can be implemented. Space constraints can also affect the working conditions, appearance, and recovery rates of recycling operations. Many existing landfills and incineration facilities were not designed with recycling in mind. In designing new facilities, ample space should be provided in the entrance facility to the site as well as for any other major recycling operations elsewhere on the site (see Figs. 25.1, 25.4, and 25.5). In older facilities, available space should be optimized by

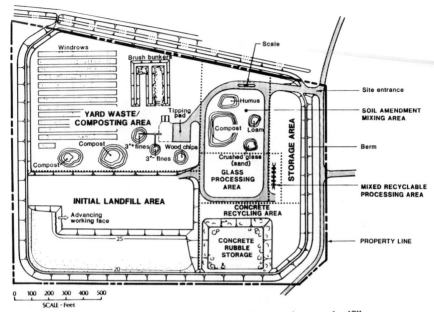

FIGURE 25.4 Layout for integrated waste management operations at a landfill.

analyzing potential recycling operations with respect to the characteristics of the waste stream entering the facility, the space requirements of the alternative operations, and the potential recovery rate for each alternative.

Design Incompatibilities

Design incompatibilities between recycling operations and landfills or between recycling operations and incineration facilities often preclude certain types of recycling. For example, if vehicles discharge into a deep pit at an incineration facility, access to the material for recovery is lost or at least hampered. Highconcentration loads, such as paper, yard waste, and wood waste, are mixed with other materials and contaminated. This type of a problem can be mostly avoided by use of a tipping floor instead of a pit. Certain design incompatibilities may be inherent in the facility's functional requirements. Although landfills may appear to have a lot of area (e.g., for composting), they are usually configured to have a topography that sheds water. Consequently, very little flat area is available on completed portions of the fill. To avoid this problem, either (1) sufficient native land should be set aside from the beginning for the recycling operation, or (2) recycling operations requiring a large, flat area can be relocated throughout the phased development of the fill.

Undercapitalization

Undercapitalization is often a major problem in recycling operations. This problem may be the result of poor planning, lack of commitment to recycling, or sim-

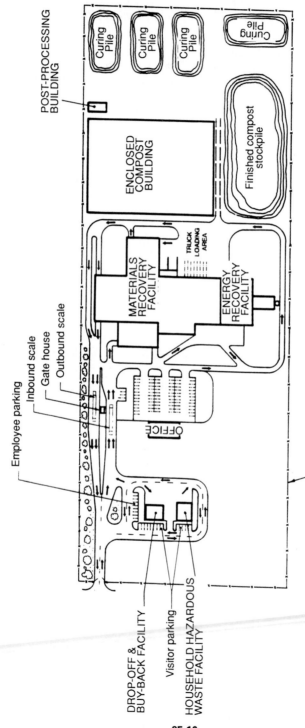

FIGURE 25.5 Layout for integrated waste management operations at an incineration facility.

ply the harsh reality of limited available funds. An example of undercapitalization is the misapplication of a down-stroke baler. Undercapitalization can lead to discouraging performance, low recovery rates, and messy operations. The solution is to provide adequate funding through tipping fees at the landfill or incineration facility (or other funding means). Obtaining the support of the public and of local government officials for including recycling in the community's integrated waste management system is also important.

Safety

Greater attention is being paid to safety issues as recycling becomes a mainstream waste management practice. There are many safety hazards in material recovery operations at landfills and incineration facilities. These include (1) working around heavy moving equipment, such as loaders and dozers; (2) picking and handling of waste materials with the associated risk of injury from such items as sharp-edged metals, hypodermic needles, and broken glass; and (3) exposure to hazardous wastes. To protect workers, a safety program for the facility should be developed, including safety training and protective clothing standards for all employees. A program to detect and deter hazardous wastes from entering the site is also a valuable tool in protecting site workers (see Chap. 21). Finally, good facility design is essential in providing safe working conditions.

Weather

Weather has a big impact on outdoor recycling operations, which are typical of landfill recycling operations. Working conditions are difficult in rain, snow, or mud. Wind and wetness make paper recovery difficult. The extent of weather problems depends on geographic location. The solution to such problems is to provide shelter from the elements in an enclosed or partially enclosed structure.

Markets

For any recycling operation to be successful, it must have stable markets for its recovered materials. This is true for recycling operations at landfills and incineration facilities as well as at any other locations. Markets have been addressed in detail in other sections of the handbook. The key point noted here is that in planning recycling operations at landfills or incineration facilities, a thorough market analysis should be undertaken.

Permitting

Permit conditions can actually restrict recycling operations at some landfills and incineration facilities. This often comes as a surprise to facility operators when trying to implement a program. Restrictions commonly arise in land use permit conditions. The problem is becoming worse as other land uses surround waste management facilities, particularly in urban areas. Another type of problem occurs when established landfill end-use plans (i.e., after the landfill closes) conflict with new plans for ongoing recycling activities at the site. This occurs, for example, if the site is designated to become a park. The best approach to avoid permitting restrictions is to include recycling operations in the facility's permits as early as possible.

ECONOMICS

Economic Incentives

There are a variety of economic incentives for recycling at landfills and incineration facilities. These are broken down according to facility operators and users in Table 25.3.

TABLE 25.3 Economic Incentives for Recycling at Landfills and Incineration Facilities

Party	Economic incentive
Landfill operator	Saved air space
	Revenues from sales of materials
	Tax on landfilled quantities
Incineration facility operator	Reduced ash disposal costs
	Revenues from sales of materials
	Reduced incinerator capital costs
	Reduced incinerator O&M costs
Facility user	Free drop-off of recyclables
	Buy-back of recyclables
	Preferential tipping fee for recyclable loads
	Reduced base tipping fee resulting from recycling savings

More and more landfill operators are recognizing the value of saving airspace for the economic potential it represents. For every cubic yard of material recycled, the landfill operator can resell that airspace. Recycling also brings revenues to the landfill operator from the sale of recovered materials. Another economic incentive is the cost avoided from taxes on landfilled quantities; such taxes are not assessed on recycled quantities.

A major economic incentive for incineration facility operators to implement recycling is to reduce ash disposal costs. They also receive revenues from the sale of recovered materials. Because recycling results in a lower throughput capacity for the incinerator, it can be downsized and thereby reduce capital costs of the facility. Additional savings may be realized from lower incinerator operation and maintenance costs.

Facility users are very important in helping make recycling work. Various economic incentives can be given to users to encourage their participation and assistance in achieving good recovery rates in the different recycling operations. It is common to offer free drop-off of recyclable materials at landfills and incineration facilities; therefore, facility users are only charged for wastes disposed of.

Buy-back centers offer further economic incentives by paying for the recyclable materials. To encourage users to deliver loads in a manner that facilitates recycling, a preferential tipping fee may be set for relatively clean, high-concentration loads. Finally, users may benefit (at least in the long term) from a reduced base tipping fee that results from including recycling in an integrated waste management system.

Capital and Operating Costs

The capital and operating costs of the alternative recycling operations are presented in other sections of the handbook. The reader is referred to the corresponding sections for details. The focus of the discussion on costs of recycling at landfills and incineration facilities is on cost avoidance, as described in the following section.

Cost Avoidance

When looking at the big picture of integrating recycling with landfill and incineration operations, one of the key economic issues that arises is cost avoidance. This section presents a methodology to account for cost avoidance in analyzing the economics of a recycling operation at a landfill or incineration facility. Cost avoidance can be realized as the result of various factors, including avoided disposal costs, avoided hauling costs, avoided taxes, reduced operation and maintenance costs, and saved air space (at a landfill).

To be economically profitable, tipping fees must cover the total costs incurred in running an operation (i.e., O&M costs plus amortized capital costs), offset by revenues from the sale of recovered materials and avoided costs. At break-even,

$$T_0 = C - R - A \tag{25.1}$$

where T_0 = break-even tipping fees
C = total costs (O&M plus amortized capital costs)
R = revenues from sale of materials
A = avoided costs

It is important that these parameters are all expressed on the same basis. The analysis presented here is based on unit costs of dollars per gate ton, where gate ton refers to tons entering the facility. Some cost parameters may need to be converted from dollars per recovered ton to dollars per gate ton. For example, unit revenues from the sale of materials are typically given in terms of the weighted average market price (i.e., dollars per ton sold). Unit conversion is given by

$$(\$/\text{gate ton}) = (\$/\text{recovered ton}) \times (\text{recovery rate}) \tag{25.2}$$

If the weighted average market price for materials recovered is $100 per ton and the recovery rate for the operation is 75 percent, then this is equivalent to $75 per ton of material in the gate (i.e., $75 per gate ton).

Figure 25.6 illustrates the use of the recycling cost analysis methodology with accounting for avoided disposal costs. The figure depicts the break-even cost of a

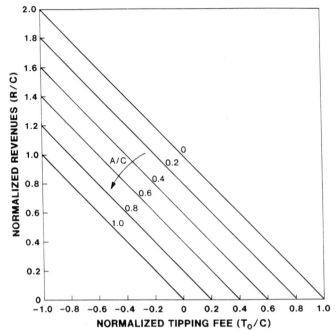

FIGURE 25.6   Break-even cost analysis of recycling operations.

recycling operation as a function of tipping fees, revenues from the sale of recovered materials, and avoided costs. To serve as a general cost analysis tool, the cost and revenue terms have been normalized by the total unit cost of the operation. Tipping fees are given on the horizontal scale. Positive values represent a fee charged for accepting the materials at the facility; negative values represent a price paid for the materials. The vertical scale indicates revenues from the sale of recovered materials. The band of lines cutting across the figure account for avoided costs. Several examples of using the figure follow.

Assume the total unit cost to run a recycling operation is $30 per ton, the operation achieves a 60 percent recovery rate, the market price for recovered materials is $40 per ton, and there are no avoided costs. The normalized revenues would then be equal to 0.8 (i.e., 0.6 × $40/$30). Moving across the figure to the zero avoided cost line and vertically down to the tipping fee axis yields a normalized tipping fee of 0.2, which is equivalent to $6 per ton (i.e., 0.2 × $30).

If the above example were a landfill operation subject to a $6 per ton tax on landfilled quantities (A/C = $6/$30 = 0.2), then the break-even tipping fee would be $0 per ton.

Assume another operation for target materials with a relatively high market price of $120 per ton, a 75 percent recovery rate, and a total unit cost of $50 per ton to run the operation. Even with no avoided costs, the break-even tipping fee would be a minus $40 per ton. In other words, the facility operator could pay $40 per ton for this material and still break even.

The figure can also be used in a variety of other recycling cost analyses, such as determining the market price needed to break even for operations with no tipping fees, or determining tipping fees if recovered materials had to be given away while still accounting for avoided costs.

Privately run facilities usually would like to make a profit on their operations (although a particular break-even operation within the overall facility operations may be suitable to a private operator in certain cases). The cost analysis methodology presented here still applies, with the following adjustment:

$$T_p = T_0 + PC \tag{25.3}$$

where T_p = tipping fee with profit
P = profit margin

If in the first example above, which yielded a break-even tipping fee of $6 per ton, a profit margin of 15 percent was applied, then the tipping fee including profit would be $10.50 per ton (i.e., $6 + 0.15 × $30).

CHAPTER 26
PROCESSING YARD WASTES

Richard J. Hlavka
Recycling Specialist
SCS Engineers
Seattle, Washington

INTRODUCTION

There is a wide range of possible processing methods and systems for yard wastes. These can be grouped into two broad categories:

- Processing at the *site* of generation
- Processing at a *central facility*

This chapter provides background information on yard waste composting, discusses processing equipment that can be used, and describes processing systems.

BACKGROUND

Yard waste is generally defined as grass clippings, leaves, and small branches. The degree to which branches can be processed depends upon the available equipment and the approach to composting that is employed. Successful composting of woody materials such as branches, within a typical time frame of 18 months or less, generally requires that this material be chipped or shredded to provide greater surface area for microbial action.

Wood waste, such as large branches, logs, and other wastes generated from land-clearing activities, log yards (timber storage), and similar activities, can also be processed to produce landscape mulch or a fuel. The ability to process wood waste allows facilities to handle mixed loads instead of accepting only source-separated materials. Other types of waste, such as construction and demolition debris, may also be processed at these facilities with the use of some additional equipment.

Composting is accomplished by microorganisms that use the organic materials in yard waste as a food source. For composting, the most important microorganisms are bacteria and fungi. The specific microorganisms that are active in a compost pile depend on the temperature, the raw materials placed in the compost pile, and the stage of the composting process. Oxygen is required by many of the types of bacteria and by most fungi. These type of bacteria and fungi are classified as aerobic microorganisms.

When oxygen is depleted, as can occur in the interior of piles, the composting process becomes anaerobic ("without oxygen"). Under anaerobic conditions, microorganisms cannot break down organic materials as quickly or as completely. This causes the composting process to slow down and causes odors due to the formation of partially oxidized compounds. The partially oxidized compounds generated by anaerobic microorganisms can also be toxic to plants.

Yard waste is typically placed into windrows (long piles) for composting (see Fig. 26.1). Windrows provide beneficial composting conditions, make efficient use of space, and allow access for turning and watering. The shape of windrows in cross section (height and width) can be triangular or trapezoidal, with the length varied as desired. The trapezoidal shape can be used to increase absorption of precipitation. The triangular shape sheds water and loses heat more effectively.

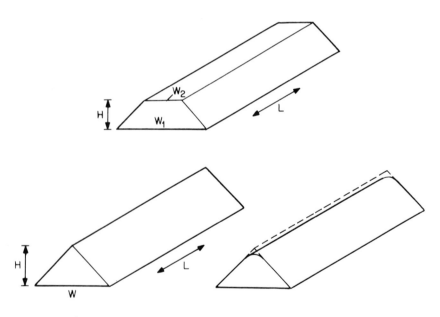

H = height, W = width, L = length

FIGURE 26.1 Compost windrows (h = height, w = width, l = length).

Windrow size can also be used to control temperatures and moisture levels. For instance, the larger the cross section of the pile, the greater the internal temperature achieved. Smaller piles lose water more rapidly through evaporation. Thus, pile size and shape can be used to regulate temperature and moisture content. The dimensions and shape of the pile should be adapted to local conditions and needs.

As the composting process proceeds, compost piles must be "turned" occasionally. Turning includes in-place mixing, rolling the piles over, and mixing as the pile is moved over. Turning of compost piles provides a number of benefits, including

- Mixing to produce a more uniform end product
- Aerating to provide oxygen and remove carbon dioxide
- Breaking up clumps of materials that may be present to provide mixing and better composting
- Moving materials on the outside of the pile to the interior of the pile to expose them to more ideal composting conditions, thus speeding up the composting process
- Moving materials on the outside of the pile to the interior of the pile and exposing them to higher temperatures to destroy pathogens and weed seeds

A typical compost pile, made from readily degradable materials such as grass clippings, will warm up very quickly from heat released by biological activity of the microorganisms. Often within days, temperatures of 150°F, or about 66°C, will be achieved (see Fig. 26.2a). At this temperature, only thermophilic (heat-loving) microorganisms will survive and continue to break down the organic material. As oxygen is consumed and the readily degradable materials (simple sugars and proteins) are broken down into humus, carbon dioxide, and water, the biological activity slows down. If compost piles are left undisturbed, the temperatures will eventually drop, and mesophilic (medium-temperature) microorganisms will take over at temperatures below about 110°F (45°C).

Frequent turning of the piles or forced aeration will sustain pile temperatures until the raw materials are broken down into the finished compost (see Fig. 26.2b). Less-frequent turning will achieve the same result but more slowly, as biological activity is alternately slowed by the lack of oxygen and then increased by turning and aeration (see Fig. 26.2c). In either case, pile temperatures will eventually cool, signaling that the composting process is nearing completion. At this point, the original organic material has not been completely broken down but has been degraded to a point where it is relatively stable and continued degradation will only occur very slowly.

The carbon-nitrogen (C/N) ratio has a significant impact on the ability of microorganisms to break down waste materials. To be efficiently composted, a raw material must provide these elements in the proportions required for the respiration and reproduction of the microorganisms. The C/N ratios of many common materials can be found in resource books or can be determined by testing. The C/N ratio of mixtures can also be calculated through the use of a weighted average of the C/N ratios for each component of the mixture. A C/N ratio in the range of 20 to 35 is best.

The C/N ratio for grass clippings is about 20, which places it at the low end of the acceptable range (i.e., too much nitrogen). More importantly, however, the grass clippings have a tendency to become too compact and proper aeration is difficult to maintain. With excess nitrogen and poor aeration, some of the nitrogen will be converted to ammonia and subsequently lost through volatilization and leaching. These factors are the primary cause of the odors for which grass clippings are notorious.

The C/N ratio for leaves is too high (too much carbon), which causes the composting process to proceed more slowly. The actual C/N ratio for leaves var-

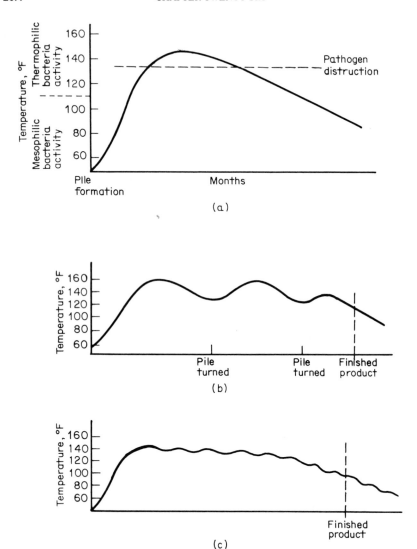

FIGURE 26.2 (*a*) Compost pile temperature vs. time from initial pile construction, with no turning of the pile; (*b*) compost pile temperature with frequent turning; (*c*) compost pile temperature with occasional turning.

ies depending upon the type of tree. To the extent that grass clippings and leaves can be mixed, near-ideal composting conditions can be created. The strategy employed for central processing sites in some locales is to mix leaves from the previous fall with grass clippings generated in the spring and summer.

The biological activity that takes place in a compost pile causes substantial reductions of volume. With or without shredding, composting results in smaller particle sizes and increased densities. Changes in density from 50 to 100 lb/yd^3

for incoming materials to 1500 to 1800 lb/yd^3 for finished compost are typical. The volume of the finished compost is often only 25 percent of the volume of incoming materials. As the volume of materials is reduced, windrows may have to be combined or shortened to maintain adequate pile (cross section) size. The volume reduction is partially caused by a reduction in mass. The microbial respiration that takes place in the composting process causes up to one-half of the mass to be lost as carbon dioxide and water.

OVERVIEW OF THE PROCESSING METHOD

The choice of yard waste processing method will depend on many factors, including

- The types of yard waste to be composted. For instance, if brush and other wood materials are to be composted, shredding or chipping prior to composting or extremely long composting periods will be necessary. If the incoming material is bagged, one or more steps in the process will have to be directed at removing the bags.
- The markets that are available for the finished products and the quality demanded by those markets. If a large market exists for low-quality material, then processing can be minimal.
- The budget that is available for purchase, operation, and maintenance of the site and equipment.
- Site conditions, especially if an existing site is being used or if land use is a constraint in the area.
- Desired turn-around time to produce a final product from the composting process.
- Local and state regulations, which may affect the need for runoff controls and other operational parameters.
- The volumes to be processed.
- The choice of collection method, which will affect the quality and condition of the incoming material.
- Existing equipment that may be available.

PROCESSING EQUIPMENT

A variety of different types of equipment are employed in the composting process, although composting can also be achieved with a minimum of equipment. These types of equipment are described below.

Shredding-Grinding-Chipping Equipment

Shredding equipment is often used at yard waste processing sites to reduce the size of incoming materials. Especially for woody materials, biodegradable bags, and bulky items, shredding will substantially improve the results of the composting process. Contaminant removal should be done prior to shredding, however, because any contamination present in the incoming materials will be reduced in size and spread throughout the materials by shredding. Contaminant removal should also be done prior to shredding to avoid equipment damage caused by metals and other foreign objects that may be in the yard wastes.

The wood chips resulting from a shredding operation can be mixed with yard waste for composting or sold as a mulch or a fuel ("hog fuel"). If the chips are to be composted, they must be reduced in size to 2 in or less.

Shredders can be stationary or they can be combined with trailers to be used as mobile units. A shredder can be combined with a crane to allow it to be self-feeding.

Screens can be attached to most types of shredders to allow the product to be sized accurately, but matching the proper screen to a shredder can be difficult and has caused serious start-up problems for some facilities. Screening after grinding is often a better approach.

A variety of shredders for yard wastes are available, including hammer mills, tub grinders, screw-type grinders, and chippers. These are described in further detail below.

Hammer mills, also called "hogs," break up materials through the pounding action of "hammers." Hammer mills can be vertically or horizontally fed. Vertical hammer mills may be gravity-fed from conveyors (see Fig. 26.3). Horizontal models employ feed conveyors and may have power-feeding elements. For instance, one horizontal hog on the market employs a spiked roll to feed the material into the hammers. Power feed mechanisms such as this can also be de-

FIGURE 26.3   Vertical hammer mill. (*Photo courtesy of Cedar Grove Compost Co., Seattle, Wash.*)

signed to control the amount of material that is fed into the hammers to avoid overloading the grinder. Throughputs up to several hundred tons per hour are available. The cost of this equipment ranges from $25,000 to $300,000.

Tub grinders can handle a wide variety of material, including leaves, brush, logs up to 1 ft in diameter, construction and demolition wood waste, and other materials (see Fig. 26.4). Throughputs as high as 50 tons per hour are possible. The cost of this equipment ranges from $70,000 to $300,000.

FIGURE 26.4 Tub grinder. (*Photo courtesy of Cedar Grove Compost Co., Seattle, Wash.*)

Screw-type grinders have performed well for wood waste. This type of shredder consists of a set of slowly rotating (10 to 30 r/min) screws moving in opposite directions. Material falls between the threads and is slowly crushed and sheared by the threads. This type of grinder is typically gravity-fed. The design of this type of shredder allows it to be self-feeding because material is pulled in as it is caught by the screws, and an excess of material cannot be forced through the screws. The angle of the screw threads, the depth of the threads, and their rotational speed can be varied to accommodate different materials. Throughputs as high as 100 tons per hour are possible.

Chippers employ a rotating disk with blades on the surface to cut up the material. The wood is fed against the face of the disk, and the blades chip off pieces of the wood. Chippers are rated by the size (diameter) of material that they can accommodate. Chippers are available in sizes sufficient to handle trees up to 20 in in diameter. The size of the chipper should match the size of the material to be processed. The larger models may have difficulty handling smaller branches and brush effectively, and it would be expensive to operate them for this purpose. Chippers may produce stringy material when used on green brush, especially for equipment with low horsepower and/or dull blades. To avoid this problem, it is necessary to maintain the chipper in good condition and/or allow the brush to dry before chipping. Processing rates up to 40 tons per hour are possible. The cost of this equipment ranges from $10,000 to $75,000.

Windrow Turners

Windrow turners provide effective mixing and turning of the windrows. Some success has been reported with the use of windrow turners for bag ripping and removal, but it is generally more effective to remove the bags before composting or through a later screening step. Windrow turners are not essential to the operation of a composting site. For small sites, a dedicated piece of equipment such as a windrow turner would not be cost-effective. General equipment such as front-end loaders, which may already be available and used for other activities at the site, can be used for most small sites. For medium to large sites, and where high quality is necessary for the finished product, windrow turners can be used.

A variety of windrow turners are available. Models are available that can handle windrows up to 22 ft wide (in two passes) and 11 ft high. The operation of the windrow turners vary, with some models turning and mixing the compost piles in place (see Fig. 26.5) and some models mixing as they pick up and move the compost piles over. Either method has its advantages depending on the site and mode of operation. Windrow turners are available as self-propelled units or as attachments to tractors and loaders. Turning rates as high as 4000 tons per hour can be achieved. The cost of this equipment ranges from $20,000 (for tractor attachments) to $300,000.

FIGURE 26.5   Windrow turner. (*Photo courtesy of Cedar Grove Compost Co., Seattle, Wash.*)

Screening Equipment

Screening is an essential step for producing high-quality compost. A variety of different types of screens have proved useful in processing yard waste, including trommel screens, disk screens, and vibrating screens. When screening is done prior to composting, it removes some contaminants, diverts larger materials (that need to be shredded), breaks up clumps, and mixes materials which helps the composting process. When done after composting, screening removes noncomposted materials (contaminants and raw materials that need further composting) and produces a fine-grained material that has a much higher level of acceptance by potential consumers. Plastic bags are a problem for screens, although some types of screens have been used with limited success to remove plastic bags. For most screens, the presence of bags will cause a substantial reduction in the throughput of the screen.

Disk screens are often used to screen incoming yard waste to separate woody and bagged materials from the grass clippings, leaves, and other small materials (see Fig. 26.6). A disk screen consists of several rotating shafts with disks on each shaft which are spaced to allow only a specific size of material to fall between the disks. The small-sized material is sent directly to the composting area, while the oversized material is sent to a shredder. With disk screens, screening rates as high as several hundred tons per hour can be achieved. The cost of this equipment ranges from $5000 to $50,000.

FIGURE 26.6 Disk screen. (*Photo courtesy of Cedar Grove Compost Co., Seattle, Wash.*)

Trommel screens have been used for many years to screen soils and peat moss. This screen consists of a rotating drum with holes in the surface of the drum. The drum is set with a declining angle so that material which is fed into the high end will move to the other end for removal. Trommel screens are relatively versatile and resistant to clogging, if operated correctly. To prevent clogging of the screen, rotating brushes are often placed outside of the trommel (see Fig. 26.7). Trommel screens can be designed with more than one size of opening along the length of the screen so that the material can be separated into several different fractions. This design is generally not necessary for yard waste or compost.

Trommel screens are generally best used to screen the finished compost or as a secondary screening step. With trommel screens, screening rates as high as 150 tons per hour can be achieved. The cost of this equipment ranges from $15,000 to $500,000.

FIGURE 26.7   Trommel screen. (*Photo courtesy of Pacific Topsoils, Inc., Seattle, Wash.*)

Vibrating or shaking screens are simply screens that shake. These screens are set at a slight angle, with the incoming material fed in at the upper end and the oversized material removed from the lower end. Material that goes through the screen is collected below. With vibrating screens, screening rates as high as 300 tons per hour can be achieved. The cost of this equipment ranges from $10,000 to $100,000.

Miscellaneous Other Equipment

Different types of nonspecialized heavy equipment can be used in the composting process. Front-end loaders are a key piece of equipment for moving material around on-site, pushing it into piles for storage or forming windrows. Watering trucks are useful in dry climates, or during dry periods, so that water can be applied to maintain adequate moisture levels for composting. Watering trucks can also be used to control dust at sites if this is a problem. A variety of other trucks are also useful, especially dump trucks, which are used to transport compost to markets or, at some sites, to move material around the site.

The use of aeration equipment is an option that can speed up the composting process while also allowing for more controlled conditions. This equipment typically consists of tubing with numerous holes which is laid beneath the compost windrows. Air is blown or sucked through the tubing. This system can have high maintenance costs, however, and short-circuiting of the airflow can greatly reduce its effectiveness. In general, aeration is not cost-effective where only yard wastes are being composted.

It is also generally not cost-effective to use enclosed systems, such as composting vessels or troughs, if only yard wastes are being composted. However, composting operations can be covered with a simple pole barn or similar structure in rainy climates to reduce runoff.

PROCESSING SYSTEMS

The two basic approaches to processing discussed in this chapter are

- Processing at the site of generation
- Processing at a central facility

The first case is relatively simple and consists of either backyard composting or mobile shredders. For the second case, there are a wide range of possible facilities and combinations of equipment that can be used. To simplify the discussion, two model approaches are presented for processing at central sites.

PROCESSING AT THE SITE OF GENERATION

Processing at the site of generation is typically accomplished by

- Backyard composting, which is generally performed by a residential generator using little or no processing equipment
- The use of mobile equipment, such as the mobile shredders that are used by commercial generators (landscapers, tree cutters, and others) and public sector agencies (public works and parks departments)

Backyard Composting of Yard Wastes

Composting materials generated on site at residential properties is called "backyard composting" because it is often performed in the backyard. However, this term has come to encompass a broader variety of activities, including composting on site by businesses, institutions, and apartment buildings. There are many possible approaches to backyard composting, including the emerging use of "worm bins" for handling food wastes. This chapter only attempts to summarize the most important points for backyard composting.

Backyard composting has a number of advantages, including

- *Cost:* Backyard composting can be done with little or no direct expenditures by the generator or others.
- *Efficiency:* The raw materials and the finished product do not have to leave the site of generation.
- *Benefits:* The finished product (compost) is very beneficial to almost any type of soil as a soil amendment or a mulch.

Some potential problems with backyard composting are

- *Aesthetics:* Aesthetic concerns include visual and olfactory factors. The pile may look messy unless an investment is made in some type of enclosure. Odors may be a problem if the pile is placed close to a neighbor's home or patio, or if large quantities of grass clippings or animal manures have been added.
- *Vermin:* Experience has shown that only the most poorly managed compost piles will provide food or habitat for rodents and other pests. In some urban

areas, however, this possibility has caused a great deal of concern and ordinances have been enacted regulating the materials that can be composted or requiring rodentproof enclosures.

Management of backyard composting piles consists of layering raw materials and occasional turning to provide aeration and mixing. If a variety of raw materials are available at the same time, such as leaves and grass clippings, these should be added to the piles in layers. If only one material is being added, as is often the case, this material should be layered with finished or partially finished compost, or with small amounts of soil.

The length of time until a finished product is ready depends upon the raw materials and the intensity of management. The following practices will decrease the amount of time required to produce a finished compost:

- The compost pile must be large enough to retain heat and moisture, but not so large as to prevent adequate aeration of interior portions of the pile. Ideal dimensions will vary depending upon the climate and the season, but for freestanding piles this generally translates to a pile 4 to 5 ft high and 5 to 6 ft at the base. For smaller enclosed systems, such as a bin or drum, sunlight can help bring the pile up to temperature.
- Frequent turning will promote aeration and provide mixing.
- In drier climates (or for piles in sunny locations), watering will be necessary to keep the pile moist, but not too wet. Watering should be sufficient to make the pile damp throughout, but not so moist that more than a few drops of water can be squeezed from a handful of coarse material such as leaves.
- In very wet climates, covering the pile (but not so tightly as to prevent aeration) will prevent it from becoming too wet.
- For leaves, corn stalks, and other high-carbon materials, the addition of nitrogen fertilizer will speed the composting process.
- For grass clippings and other materials that have a tendency to compact, premixing or layering with a coarser material, or with partially finished compost, will help provide aeration.
- For coarse or woody materials, shredding to a size less than 2 in is necessary.

Backyard composting can be accomplished using

- Free-standing piles, which are the least expensive method that can be used (see Fig. 26.8).
- Bins made from wood, concrete blocks, or other materials (see Fig. 26.9).
- Pits or depressions, which may be useful in dry climates to avoid moisture losses.
- Barrels or drums, which are set up so that they can be rotated frequently to promote mixing; these have been used successfully by many people.
- Wire fencing, which can be used to provide a temporary or adjustable enclosure.
- Plastic bags (anaerobically) to contain the compost with the addition of water (for dry materials), nitrogen (for materials with high C/N ratios), and lime (to offset the greater amount of organic acids produced by the anaerobic process).

FIGURE 26.8 Backyard compost pile.

FIGURE 26.9 Backyard compost bin from King County, Washington, distribution program.

Backyard composting can be accomplished using no equipment beyond lawn mowers and rakes, but recently there are an increasing number of equipment manufacturers catering to the residential market. Besides the variety of enclosures that are now sold for backyard composting, there are now available a number of chippers and shredders that are specifically designed for residential use. Chippers and shredders can be used on leaves, brush, and other materials to speed up the composting process. Brush can be difficult for the homeowner to handle, but if chipped or shredded, it can be used as a mulch or added to the compost pile.

Shredding equipment designed for household use varies from 1.2 to 16 hp may be driven by gasoline or electric motors, and can handle brush up to 3 in in diameter. Some of this equipment can be used to produce a mulch (wood chips) or compostable material (smaller particle sizes) with the use of removable screens that control the size of the finished material. The cost of these units ranges from $250 to $1650.

The Use of Mobile Equipment for Processing Yard Wastes

The use of mobile equipment includes

- Portable shredders for wood wastes that are used by private companies and public agencies for brush generated by tree-cutting operations
- Larger shredders brought to central facilities to handle stumps and bulky wood waste that has been collected or stockpiled over a period of time
- Shredders set up temporarily at work sites to handle land-clearing waste

The use of shredders to process branches and other wood waste from tree and brush removal is widely practiced as a method of waste reduction. Unfortunately, the resultant chips are too often disposed of as a solid waste instead of being put to a beneficial use. These chips can be mixed with yard waste for composting or used as a coarse mulch. As a mulch, the chips can be applied around trees in parks and along streets, used on trails, offered to home owners, or left on site.

Some facilities have found it more economical to hire a shredder to come to their site to eliminate a backlog of stumps or logs, rather than for the facility to purchase the shredding equipment required for this job. These facilities include landfills that encourage separation of yard material and bulk topsoil dealers that accept yard waste and land clearing debris. Such facilities typically already have the equipment to handle other yard wastes and may not be able to justify the large capital expense for a shredder to handle a small quantity of stumps.

Chippers and shredders have also been set up temporarily at sites where land is being cleared for development or, less frequently, where timber is being harvested.

PROCESSING AT CENTRAL SITES

To divert substantial amounts of yard waste from the municipal solid waste stream, many areas choose a combination of waste reduction methods (backyard composting and mulching of grass clippings) and the use of central processing facilities. The central facilities are designed to handle the yard waste that home owners and commercial generators (lawn services, landscapers) are unable, or unwilling, to handle on their own property. The design of the central facilities ranges from very simple sites to sites requiring the use of many pieces of specialized equipment.

The costs and benefits of different approaches vary depending on the area and the needs. For areas with plenty of available land and low quantities of yard wastes, a "low-tech" approach using very little special equipment is probably best. The low-tech approach requires longer composting periods to produce a lower-quality material, requires more acreage per annual ton of material, and is dependent upon easy markets for the finished product.

For areas where large quantities of yard wastes provide economies of scale, and/or land is very expensive, a "high-tech" approach using specialized equipment such as screens and windrow turners may be the best. Although this approach requires more space for associated operations (shredding, screening, runoff ponds, etc.), a high-tech site can handle more tons per acre due to a quicker throughput rate. The high-tech approach also produces a higher-quality compost that is more easily marketed.

Another consideration for low-tech sites is that they can be decentralized. In other words, a system of many such sites can be set up to serve a given area. The larger capital investment required for a high-tech site requires the construction of regional facilities serving a large area or handling larger quantities of material.

The choice of approach may be dictated in part by the presence of state or local regulations. Some states require permits and additional controls for sites that exceed a given size (in tons per year). Regulations in some states also address capacity (cubic yards per acre), windrow size, buffer distances, distance to groundwater, environmental controls, and other site and operational parameters.

Siting requirements for low-tech sites are made easier by the fact that they are typically smaller and so require fewer environmental controls (i.e., runoff collection and treatment) in addition to requiring less land.

Siting considerations for most central sites include

Housing: Proximity to housing can be a problem due to the potential for the generation of odors and other impacts. Even small sites using the low-tech approach present the potential for odors because the piles are turned infrequently and will probably become anaerobic between turnings. The high-tech sites will create more noise and dust due to the increased level of activity and equipment operations. Buffer zones of 50 to 500 ft are required by some states.

Traffic: The ability of access roads to handle truck traffic must be considered. The sites may have truck traffic bringing raw material in and/or removing finished compost. Nonresidential streets are preferable in most cases. Also, the sites must be easily accessible to the general public if a drop-off program is to be successful.

Surface water: Sites should not be located immediately adjacent to surface water, such as lakes and streams, to avoid water quality impacts. Flood zones are also to be avoided. Separation distances up to 1000 ft between composting operations and surface water are required in some states.

Groundwater: Processing sites should not be placed in areas upgradient from shallow wells that are used for drinking water. There is a possibility that nitrates and other compounds may leach from the composting materials and cause health problems. In general, infiltration of water from the composting operation should be avoided by composting on impermeable soils or composting "pads." In some states, compost sites are required to maintain a separation distance, typically 5 ft, to groundwater.

Utilities: Low-tech sites can usually do without utilities, such as electricity and water, but high-tech sites have a greater need for these services.

Colocation: Locating compost sites near solid waste or public works facilities is also a consideration. For instance, colocation with landfills provides some economies for equipment usage; poor-quality compost can be used to provide cover material; wood chips can be used for temporary roads; and siting can often be accomplished without a problem. However, some areas recommend against colocation with landfills due to the potential for either operation to aggravate the problems of the other. Compost operations can aggravate odor, litter, and runoff control problems at landfills. Other colocation possibilities include mining operations, topsoil companies, public works or parks departments facilities, and other locations where heavy equipment may already be in use or where similar operations are being conducted.

Permits and ordinances: Siting may be affected by various permit requirements, local ordinances, zoning codes, land use regulations, and solid waste management plans for states, counties, and other levels of government. All of these may affect the location of compost sites, buffer zones, and operational parameters such as the need for runoff control methods.

For any type of site, there are similarities in the requirements for the condition of the incoming material. To be composted, materials must be unbagged. There are pilot efforts that have been conducted in the use of biodegradable bags, composting in the bag, and mechanical debaggers, but the results of these efforts have been less than encouraging. Improvements have been made in the use of biodegradable bags, but most efforts to date have discovered that the bags take much longer to break down than the yard wastes. The delay in bag decomposition interferes with the composting process and hinders the marketability of the end product.

The problem with composting in the bags is that the bags must be removed later. The use of mechanical debaggers to remove plastic bags, whether before or after composting, has been only partially successful. There are new mechanical debaggers on the market that are still undergoing field-testing. Windrow turners and screens have also been used to remove bags with partial success, but many facilities still depend on manual methods.

For dry materials, it is important that sufficient water be added initially. Once moist, the materials should not need additional water, although the low-tech processing approach with the longer composting period will benefit from the absorption of precipitation.

Possible processing alternatives include

No processing: An option used by some companies and agencies involves the use of "static piles," where the yard waste is simply placed in one large pile of no particular shape and allowed to sit undisturbed until composting is finished. This approach is clearly the least expensive but requires additional time (3 to 4 years) and space. This approach generates an end product of fairly low quality, due to the dependence on anaerobic decomposition methods, the lack of screening, and other factors.

A low-tech processing method: This method employs windrows that are turned occasionally using front-end loaders. Very little other equipment is needed for this approach, and it generates a low-quality end product (but better quality than the static pile approach described above) at a low cost. This approach is appropriate for areas with lower quantities of yard waste to be composted and where land is available at low cost. The low-tech processing method is described in greater detail in the discussion following this section.

A high-tech processing method: This method also employs windrows, but these are turned frequently. Additional processing at the beginning and finish produces a high-quality compost. The cost of this approach is moderate as long as large quantities are being processed. This approach also makes it possible to handle a wider variety of materials, such as brush and other wood wastes. The high-tech processing method is described in greater detail in the discussion following this section.

Aerated static piles: With this method, piles are constructed over perforated tubing and left undisturbed during the composting period. Air is forced through the tubing to provide aeration. Although some areas have reported success with this approach, it is not widely used. This approach requires the purchase of new, dedicated equipment such as blowers and tubing. Problems with the aerated static pile approach include the nondegradation of materials on the exterior of the pile, uneven moisture conditions, lack of mixing, and the need to operate and maintain the aeration equipment.

Forced aeration: Aeration is used more effectively at facilities that also provide some mixing. Mixing at some facilities that use forced aeration is done as frequently as daily. The aeration can be automatically or manually controlled to provide temperature control for the piles. Subsurface trenches are sometimes used with this approach. As with static piles, there are generally better, more cost-effective approaches for yard wastes, but this method may be employed where very quick turnaround times are desired; in highly urban areas where total containment of the composting process is necessary; or where sewage sludge and/or solid wastes are included in the incoming materials.

Enclosed vessels: Examples of enclosed vessels include large horizontal cylinders that rotate or stationary circular tanks with mixers. As with forced aeration, above, this option is generally not cost-effective for yard wastes alone. Such systems are typically only necessary if there is a significant need to decrease the composting period or control odors because of site conditions or location. If other wastes are being added which present a risk of odors or pathogens, such as sewage sludge or municipal solid wastes, the additional control provided by enclosed systems may be necessary.

Two of these approaches are discussed in greater detail below: the low-tech processing method and the high-tech processing method. Both of these methods employ windrows for the active composting period. The low-tech operation employs no specialized equipment. The high-tech operation requires more equipment and personnel, including equipment that is very specialized. The capital and operating costs of the high-tech option is much greater than the low-tech operation, but the quality of the end product and the potential throughput for a given site size is also much higher with the high-tech approach.

The Low-Tech Approach to Composting Yard Wastes

The low-tech approach to composting involves piling yard waste into windrows and occasionally turning these windrows to provide mixing and aeration. This type of composting typically requires 1 to 2 years. A longer period may be required if woody material is included or if the markets demand a highly finished and stabilized product.

This approach demands more space per ton of capacity than more high-tech processing methods due to the lengthy residence time of the yard wastes. Since incoming materials do not leave the site for 1 to 2 years, and there may be a lag time in marketing the finished product, the site must be sufficiently large to contain the amount of yard waste generated in about 2 years, plus buffer areas and access roads.

Yard waste can be dropped off at the site by the public and/or brought in by larger generators (lawn services, landscapers, separate collections by waste haulers). Yard waste is generally brought to the site in bulk (i.e., no bags) or debagged by the generator as it is dropped off. The low-tech approach assumes no screening equipment is available. The site should be staffed to ensure that contaminants are kept to a minimum, or the contaminants will have to be removed manually. Manual removal can be expensive and ineffective for many types of contaminants. The site monitor can also help to promote the program by assisting people who are dropping off yard waste or picking up compost, answering questions on the use of compost, and providing information on related topics.

The yard waste is typically deposited initially in a specific receiving area. As space is needed in the receiving area, the yard waste is pushed into a windrow for composting. This windrow can be moved away from the receiving side as it is turned during the next 12 to 18 months. The other side of the site can be used for removal of the finished product. Other modes of operation are also possible and should be selected based on site conditions.

The approximate dimensions of the windrows should be 6 to 12 ft high, 12 to 30 ft wide at the base, up to 6 ft wide at the top, and as long as necessary (or as long as the site will allow). A flat top will allow rainfall and other precipitation to be captured by the windrow more effectively, which may be necessary to maintain moist conditions in the pile for the long composting period required by this approach.

If the incoming materials are sufficiently moist, as is typically the case with grass clippings, a triangular shape (for the cross section of the pile) can be used to shed water more effectively. If the incoming materials are dry, watering should be done to provide sufficient moisture initially and then is optional in all but the driest of climates.

The composting process will cause the height of the windrow to diminish rapidly over the first few months, and the pile should be turned and reshaped as necessary to maintain a minimum height of 5 to 6 ft. During cold weather, piles with smaller dimensions will cool off and the composting process will slow down or stop. Larger pile sizes are often used in very cold climates for the initial pile construction of fall leaves to allow the composting process to proceed over the winter months. In warm weather, piles can be lower in height to maintain better aeration without losing excess heat. Smaller pile sizes should also be used for potentially odorous materials such as grass clippings to prevent increased odors from anaerobic conditions.

This option requires the least investment in new equipment. The operation of a low-tech site generally requires only a front-end loader. Other pieces of nonspecialized equipment may be necessary for site preparation (graders and other road-building equipment) and maintenance.

Preparation of a site for low-tech composting includes clearing trees and brush (some should be left in the buffer zones for screening) and grading to provide a slope of 1 to 3 percent. The slope is to provide adequate drainage of the site. Care must be taken to avoid directing the runoff where it will impact surface water bodies or other sensitive areas. Grading should be done to allow runoff water to move between the piles.

The site should be prepared with clay or other impermcable material where the composting will take place, all-weather access roads, and access control using gates and fences. Depending upon the location, the entire site may not need to be fenced. The roads can be surfaced in some areas using gravel or wood chips, but mixing these materials with the yard waste should be avoided.

The quality of the final product will be relatively low. The presence of sticks and the small amounts of contaminants (bottles, cans, small scraps of plastic) that inevitably show up will detract from the marketability of the compost. With the publicity and education of potential users, however, most programs using this approach have not had any difficulty in marketing the compost if it is offered free or at a low cost. Primary markets have included home owners, public works and parks departments, and landscapers.

A possible layout is shown in Fig. 26.10. This layout shows the receiving area close to the main entrance because of the greater amount of incoming vs. outgoing traffic. If for no other reason, there will be a greater number of vehicles bringing in materials than picking up finished compost since there are significant volume reductions during the composting process. Three windrows are also shown. Windrow 1 has been formed from incoming material. Windrow 2 is material that has been at the site for about 1 year. Windrow 3 is finished material that is available for pick up by the general public and small contractors. This arrangement allows yard waste to be moved from one side of the site to the other as the compost piles are turned.

The cost of developing and operating a typical site is shown in Table 26.1. This

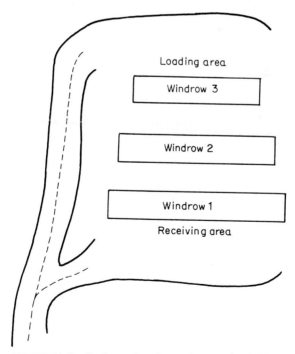

FIGURE 26.10 Site layout for a low-tech processing facility.

TABLE 26.1 Cost Estimate for a Typical Low-Tech Processing Site

Item	Estimated cost or amount*
Assumptions:	
Annual capacity	500 TPY†
Open hours	32 h/week‡
Site development and other capital costs:	
Land	5 acres
Site preparation (clearing, grading), $3000/acre	$15,000
Surface preparation (impermeable base for compost piles and all-weather surface for main roads)	$5000–$25,000
Signs	$100–$300
Fencing and gates	$1000–$60,000
Siting and permitting	NA§
Site improvements (landscaping, utilities)	NA
Runoff controls	NA
Equipment	NA
Buildings	NA
Miscellaneous equipment and supplies	$500–$3000
Operations and maintenance:	
Annual salaries (one part-time site monitor)	$12,000–$20,000
Front-end loader rental, $600/day	$6000
Watering	NA
Screening and shredding	NA
Other equipment O&M	NA
Insurance	$200–$1000
Public education and promotion	0–$2000
Testing	0–$500
Revenues:	
Compost revenues	0
Avoided costs	Variable

*All costs shown are 1990 costs.
†500 tons per year (TPY) = 750 – 1000 tons of on-site capacity.
‡Hours of operation assumes 40 h per week during the busy season(s) and fewer hours during the slow season(s).
§NA = not applicable; item is not a typical expense for this type of site.

cost estimate assumes a site capable of accepting 500 tons per year. This translates to 1000 tons of on-site capacity to allow for a composting period of 18 months and short-term storage of the finished product. Some of the costs are shown as ranges because the actual expense will vary widely in different areas. Ideally, a municipality would be able to use land and equipment currently owned and would not incur any additional capital cost for these items. Colocation of the compost site with another facility will also reduce expenses by allowing shared use of water and toilet facilities.

The High-Tech Approach to Composting Yard Wastes

The high-tech approach is more involved, but it allows the handling of a greater variety of materials and produces a higher quality end product. The increased amount of processing at this type of site allows a greater variety of material to be accepted while at the same time producing a higher quality of compost. Wood waste can be accepted and shredded to produce chips that can be sold as a mulch material or added to the compost pile. This type of site may be open to the public but primarily receives materials from yard waste collections, transfer vehicles, and private companies (landscapers, land developers, etc.).

This approach can result in finished compost after 90 days or less. To accomplish this requires maintaining control over the temperature, moisture, and oxygen content of the windrow, as well as controlling the size of the incoming material and the dimensions of the windrow. It is also necessary to turn and mix the piles frequently with one or two screening steps at the end of the process. In addition to the use of general equipment such as front-end loaders, this approach requires specialized equipment for chipping, grinding or shredding, turning windrows, and screening.

The use of specialized equipment such as windrow turners is generally cost-effective for larger volumes of material, typically for amounts in excess of 10,000 tons per year. At this level, windrow turners provide quicker and more efficient turning of compost piles. The turners are more efficient at mixing the materials in the windrows, breaking up clumps, mixing wet and dry materials, and can be used to assist with removal of contaminants such as plastic bags.

The moisture content of the incoming materials is more critical for the high-tech processing method if the quick turnaround time is to be achieved. Water should be added (or allowed to drain and evaporate for materials that are too wet) to achieve a moisture content of 40 to 60 percent by weight. Once this has been accomplished, the piles will generally not need any additional water during the composting period.

The land requirement per ton of annual capacity is less than the low-tech approach due to the shorter composting time, even though additional space is needed for related functions. Additional space is needed for offices and garages, processing of incoming materials, a stabilization pile, screening and storage of finished materials, and runoff retention ponds.

Figure 26.11 shows a typical site layout for a high-tech processing site. Figure 26.12 shows the flow of materials through this type of site. As shown, the process begins with a coarse screening to separate finer materials such as grass clippings and leaves from the larger material such as brush. The brush is diverted to a shredding operation prior to being mixed with the finer fraction for composting. After mixing, the materials are placed in a windrow and turned frequently, often about once per week[1], until the composting process is nearly complete. The compost is then placed in a much larger pile and allowed to stabilize for about 1 month. The compost from this pile is screened to remove contaminants and materials that have not broken down completely. The screened compost can be marketed as is or mixed with other materials to produce topsoil or special blends.

This type of site typically has greater control of surface water runoff, due in part to the large size of this type of operation. Runoff can be diverted to holding or treatment ponds. The runoff may also be recirculated to the composting operation if watering is necessary. Grading of the site should provide a slight slope (1 to 3 percent). Windrows should be placed running uphill or downhill to allow runoff to move between the piles to the ponding area. Testing at one site has shown that the runoff is fairly clean, containing only high BOD and suspended soils.[1]

The initial cost of this type of facility is substantially greater than the low-tech approach due to the increased capital expenditures for equipment and site preparation. Due to increased volumes, however, the cost per ton may not be signif-

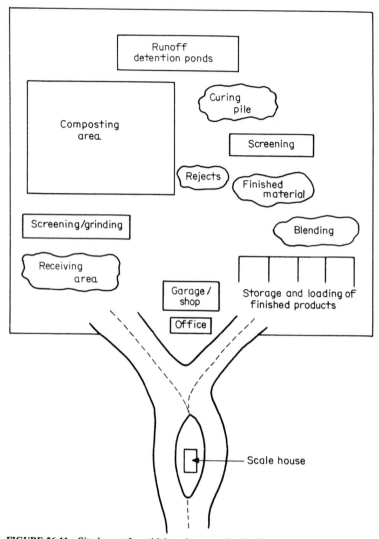

FIGURE 26.11   Site layout for a high-tech processing facility.

icantly greater than the low-tech processing method. The higher quality of compost produced by the high-tech approach should generate significant market
revenues, which will help offset the increased capital and operating costs.

Table 26.2 shows typical costs for a composting site that employs the high-
tech processing approach. This table assumes a site capable of handling about
50,000 tons of yard and wood waste per year. The hours that this site is open
reflect extended hours to accept deliveries, but only one operating shift is assumed. As with the costs for the low-tech site, some of these costs are difficult to
accurately project due to the impact of local conditions and so are simply shown

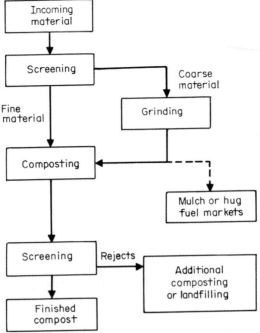

FIGURE 26.12 Flowchart for processing materials at a high-tech compost facility.

as "variable." This is especially the case for land costs, siting and permitting, runoff controls, and salaries. In Table 26.2, site preparation expenses includes clearing, grading, installing an impermeable composting pad, and paving the main access roads on the facility grounds. The expense for buildings assumes a very simple structure for a maintenance shop and a trailer for the office space.

ISSUES AND ANSWERS

This section addresses select issues that have a bearing on most or all of the processing systems that could be used.

Biodegradable Bags

Most attempts to incorporate biodegradable bags into the composting process have reported poor results. Many have concluded that the bags may be degradable but do not break down as quickly as the yard waste does and so detract from the appearance of the finished compost. Paper bags have broken down more completely than degradable plastic bags in some cases, and the paper can always be screened out and returned to composting piles to finish composting. Some pilot efforts have observed that composting is initially retarded by either type of

TABLE 26.2 Cost Estimate for a Typical High-Tech Processing Site

Item	Estimated cost or amount*
Assumptions:	
Annual capacity	50,000 TPY†
Open hours	10 h/day, 6 days/week
Site development and other capital costs:	
Land	45 acres‡
Site preparation, $3000/acre	$135,000
Surface preparation (compacted compost pads, paving)	$100,000–$150,000
Signs	$500–$5000
Fencing and gates, $10/ft	$20,000–$60,000
Siting and permitting	Variable
Shredders (hammer mill and tub grinder)	$350,000
Windrow turner	$150,000
Screens (trommel and disk screen)	$180,000
Front-end loader	$100,000
Trucks (2)	$150,000
Conveyors	$32,000
Buildings	$150,000
Site improvements (landscaping, utilities)	Variable
Runoff controls	Variable
Engineering	Variable
Miscellaneous equipment and supplies	$500–$7000
Operations and maintenance:	
Salaries (15–22 full-time employees)	Variable
Equipment O&M, incl. fuel	$50,000–$100,000
Testing	$500–$5000
Insurance	$1000–$50,000
Public education and promotion	$1000–$50,000
Disposal of rejects from screening	$1500–$3000 TPY
Revenues:	
Compost revenues	$4–$10/ton§
Avoided costs	Variable

*All costs shown are 1990 costs.
†TPY = tons per year.
‡Site size provides sufficient space for peak flow and possible future expansions.
§Usually sold by the cubic yard.

bag, which do not allow mixing, aeration, or wetting of their contents until they begin to break down.

Improvements have been made recently in the formulation of plastic degradable bags, but the results of pilot efforts to compost these are not fully available. Agencies or companies interested in using biodegradable bags of any sort should conduct pilot efforts first to test the performance of the bags in their system.

Compost Maturity vs. Nitrogen Availability

In the composting process, bacteria that are instrumental in breaking down the organic compounds may temporarily tie up all of the available nitrogen in their cell structure. As the composting process nears completion, there is a die-off of the bacteria, which then release the nitrogen so that it is available to plants again. With any compost, however, there is the risk of a surge in bacterial activity when the compost is mixed into garden soil or blended with other materials to produce a topsoil or other product. This surge can tie up available nitrogen temporarily and hinder plant growth.

To avoid nitrogen availability problems, compost should be mixed into gardens every 2 to 4 weeks. If this is not possible or if the compost is of questionable quality, nitrogen fertilizers should be added with the compost. Mixtures of compost and other materials should be monitored for 1 to 2 weeks after blending to check for the generation of heat as an indication of bacterial activity. If heat is detected, it would be best to hold the mixture for a short time before distribution to avoid consumer problems with plant stunting.

Additives to Assist the Composting Process

A number of materials can be used to enhance the composting process, although some of these additives are of questionable value. Potential additives include

Fertilizers: To compost high-carbon materials (materials with high C/N ratios), it is beneficial to add a fertilizer that contains nitrogen or to add another raw material that is high in nitrogen. Rarely are other nutrients present in such low quantities that they limit the growth of microorganisms. For those who wish to improve the nutrient content of the finished product, it is better to wait until the compost is finished and then blend in additional materials as desired.

Lime: Lime is considered by some to cause an increase in the rate of decomposition and a reduction of odors. An increase in decomposition rate is suggested because the lime may offset organic acids produced in the early stages of decomposition. These acids may decrease the pH of the compost pile to a point where microbial activity is hindered. Although lime has been shown to increase the rate of decomposition in this manner, the lime may also convert ammonium-nitrogen to ammonia.[2] The subsequent off-gassing of the ammonia will cause nitrogen loss and increased odors. Unless raw materials other than yard wastes are being composted and these materials are inherently very acidic, the addition of lime is generally not necessary or advisable.

Bacterial inoculants and enzymes: Some products are being sold on the basis that they will improve composting rates and results. These products contain inoculants ("starter" bacteria) and/or enzymes that are supposed to help break down yard wastes. Unfortunately, no independent research is readily available which demonstrates the ability of these products to improve the results of backyard or large-scale composting. Further, it is generally agreed that such products are not vital to the composting process. For instance, no evidence is available which suggests that a shortage of bacteria exists in compost piles which would be cured by the addition of an inoculant.

Measuring Amounts of Yard Wastes Composted

Measuring the amount of yard waste that is being composted will be necessary in most cases. It will be necessary not only in areas that will be striving to meet established recycling and composting goals, but as a public information tool to encourage participation. Installation of truck scales at all composting facilities would allow for easy measurement of incoming quantities, but this cost cannot be justified for smaller compost sites. Simply weighing the finished product would not resolve the problem due to the significant losses of weight (up to 50 percent) that occur as a result of the composting process. Surveys can be used by occasionally weighing individual deliveries by different types of vehicles to derive an average figure for the weight of a load by type of vehicle. By then counting the total number of the different types of vehicles, the total weight of material can be estimated.

In the absence of other methods, the weight of material received at a site can be estimated based on volume and density measurements. This should be done a few weeks after formation of the windrows. This amount of time will avoid substantial losses caused by biological activity, but will allow time for the piles to settle and moisture to even out. The volume of a windrow can be determined by first deciding if the shape of a cross section is closest to a trapezoid or triangle, then taking measurements and making calculations using formulas appropriate to the shape.

If the windrow is closest to a triangular shape, the volume can be determined by

$$\tfrac{1}{2}WHL$$

where W = average width at bottom
H = average height of pile
L = length of windrow

For a trapezoidal shape, volume is determined by

$$\tfrac{1}{2}(W_1 + W_2)HL$$

where W_1 = average width at bottom
W_2 = average width at top
H, L = defined as above

In either case, the density is determined by extracting a sample of the pile sufficient to fill a container of known volume and then weighing it. This must be done with care so as to avoid fluffing or compacting the sample. For a given windrow, this procedure must be repeated a number of times from a number of locations, and the results averaged to yield a figure that can be applied to the entire pile. A minimum of four to six measurements should be taken, depending on the size of the pile and the variance encountered with the results of the first few samples.

Marketing Information

Markets are briefly discussed here because they have a strong influence on the choice of processing systems. A number of materials can be produced from yard waste, wood wastes, and other compostable wastes, and the end products can be used by a variety of groups. Generally, the more intensive processing methods will yield higher-quality composts that can compete for a greater variety of markets.

To some extent, the end product is predetermined by the type of waste material. For example, it is difficult to produce a mulch material from yard wastes such as grass clippings. However, there is also some flexibility to the end product. Wood wastes and brush, for instance, can be chipped and added to a composting system, sold as mulch, or sold as hog fuel. Yard waste can be directly land applied, sold as a soil amendment, or mixed with soils to produce a topsoil mixture. End products should be designed based on the capacity of available markets and the specifications of those markets.

The following products can be derived from yard and wood wastes:

Compost: Composted yard wastes of high and medium quality can be sold in bulk or bagged as a soil amendment. Compost of medium quality could be used by orchards and others. Low-quality compost cannot usually be sold but can be given away for use in gardens and for agricultural purposes, erosion control, and applications where aesthetics are not a major concern. Compost of high quality could be bagged, but low-quality compost should be directed to bulk uses such as agricultural applications. Bagging operations require special expertise and equipment. It is generally best to subcontract the bagging of compost so that the market for this material can be tested before making a substantial investment in the equipment and training necessary for bagging.[1]

Mulch material: Various grades of wood chips may be marketed as a mulch material in bulk quantities or bagged for retail sales. These chips can replace bark traditionally used for landscaping and other uses. Other uses include application to park trails, temporary roads, farm yards, and other areas where stabilization of the surface soil is desired.

Topsoil mixtures: Blending compost with soil to produce topsoil (bulk) or potting soil (bagged) can be done. For markets that intend to use topsoil mixtures or compost for growing plants, the compost must be highly stabilized before use or a nitrogen-containing fertilizer must be added in sufficient quantities to ensure that some free nitrogen is available for plant growth. Also, mixtures should be monitored for 1 to 2 weeks after blending to check for the generation of heat as an indication of bacterial activity.

Hog fuel: Wood wastes and other woody materials from land clearing debris can be ground or shredded to produce hog fuel. This requires the removal of all soil and the production of large chips that can be burned for heat in industrial boilers.

Specialty products: Specialty products include animal bedding, coarse mulch for erosion control, landfill cover, organic material for remedial action at contaminated sites, and soil amendment for land reclamation sites. These markets may require significant efforts to absorb substantial quantities of material unless there is an existing demand for the product.

The following groups may act as markets:

Public agencies and government contractors: Procurement policies and practices for public agencies and their contractors could be revised to encourage the use of compost and related products. In doing this, as with other market development efforts, it is important to avoid displacing products that are currently in use and that are derived from waste materials.

Nurseries, orchards: High-quality compost would be required by nurseries and landscapers for some applications, such as top dressings to conserve moisture and reduce weeds, and as part of a mix to be used for potting trees and plants.

Garden centers: Garden centers and related retail outlets (grocery and hardware stores) can sell bulk and bagged wood chips, compost, and topsoil mixtures. These outlets typically serve the general public and so demand high-quality products.

Soil dealers, distributors: Soil (and bark) dealers and distributors can handle a variety of products. As dealers of bulk materials, they may be able to handle low-grade products if they have customers that will use this type of material.

Farmers: Farmers can use low-quality composts to improve their soil, but this group will object to the presence of contaminants such as plastics.

National parks and forests: Forested areas and national parks can act as markets for compost where soil preparation or top dressing is needed. National parks and other recreational settings can also use wood chips as a substitute for bark on trails or as a mulch.

County residents: County residents will pick up compost and wood chips if free or at a low cost.

Landscapers: Landscapers can use products similar to residential users but may be able and willing to use a wider variety of materials because they are aware of the possible applications for different grades of products. For instance, landscapers are more likely to use large quantities of material for things such as the application of topsoil and building of berms at sites of new construction, or for renovations at existing sites.

Industry: Industrial markets include the use of wood chips as hog fuel and some of the specialty applications mentioned above, in addition to being a consumer of compost and mulch materials for use on the company's property.

GLOSSARY

aerobe A microorganism that employs oxygen in the process of breaking down organic material.

aerobic With oxygen, typically used in reference to a biological decomposition process that occurs in the presence of and through the use of oxygen.

anaerobe A microorganism that does not employ oxygen to break down organic material. Most anaerobes can function only in the absence of oxygen, although some microorganisms are "facultative" and can act as aerobes or anaerobes.

anaerobic Without oxygen, typically used in reference to a biological decomposition process that cannot occur in the presence of oxygen.

C/N ratio The ratio of carbon to nitrogen in the raw materials or the finished product.

compost The relatively stable end product of a process employing biological decomposition.

composting Biological degradation of an organic material.

hog fuel Chipped or shredded wood wastes (including bark) that are used as a fuel, typically in industrial boilers.

humus An organic material consisting of a mixture of organic compounds such as humic acid, fulvic acid, and humin; "humus" is often used interchangeably with "compost."

inoculant A source of microorganisms useful in the composting process.

maturity The degree to which the compost is stable, or the process of rapid degradation is finished.

microorganisms Includes bacteria, fungi, and other microscopic plants and animals.

mulch A material that is applied to the surface of soil to reduce weed growth, conserve moisture, protect dormant plants from freezing, and/or enrich the soil.

soil amendment A material, such as compost, that is mixed into soil to improve beneficial properties such as the ability to retain water and nutrients.

source-separated materials Materials that are kept separate from other wastes at the source.

windrows Long piles typically used for composting yard wastes.

yard wastes Generally defined as grass clippings, leaves, small branches, garden wastes, and related materials. In some areas, wood wastes such as larger branches and stumps may be included.

REFERENCES

1. J. Allen, 1991. Personal interview, February 28, 1991, J. Allen, P.E., Cedar Grove Compost Co., Seattle, Wash., a large-scale commercial yard waste composter.
2. C. Rosen et al., 1988. *Composting and Mulching: A Guide to Managing Organic Yard Waste,* AG-FO-3296. Revised 1988, by Carl Rosen, Nancy Schumacher, Robert Magaas, and Suzanne Proudfoot. Minnesota Extension Service, Department of Soil Science, Univ. of Minnesota.

CHAPTER 27
COLLECTION EQUIPMENT AND VEHICLES

Bob Graham, P.E.
Director Engineering, RIS Ltd.
Toronto, Canada

INTRODUCTION

The concept of source separation of recyclable materials from trash is not new; however, a new breed of collection vehicles and associated equipment has been developed in the past 10 years to meet the exploding needs of municipalities across North America that are implementing collection of source-separated recyclables.

Early attempts at collecting these materials usually focused on recovering one material only, such as newspaper, using a pickup truck or van. This type of collection from residential units was not complicated, but even then, operators recognized the limitations of using a small-capacity vehicle that was not specifically designed to provide efficient, safe collection of curbside material. As the number of materials added to a program grew, these problems became more apparent.

About 1980, when it became clear that more and more municipalities were becoming serious about implementing multimaterial curbside collection programs, truck manufacturers responded to the potential market opportunity by designing collection vehicles that were meant to be used specifically for collection of these materials. New markets also evolved for a variety of associated collection equipment such as household recycling containers, roll-out carts, and a host of other containers to service the commercial, industrial, and institutional sectors.

This chapter explores the factors that should be considered in selecting a particular vehicle, container, bin, or collection system for recyclables collection programs and reviews the types of equipment available for curbside, drop-off, commercial, business, and multifamily applications. For use in the future, we will show how recycling collection equipment is changing to adapt to the need to collect more and more recyclables efficiently, as legislation or waste management practices call for higher and higher solid waste recovery goals.

CURBSIDE COLLECTION

Program Design

Curbside collection programs, by their nature, are best suited to single-family residential dwellings or those multifamily or townhouse units that have convenient ground floor access to the curb. The selection of collection equipment for a multimaterial curbside program is contingent not only on the details of the equipment itself, but on numerous other program design considerations related to the separation and storage activities at the household, curbside setout and collection details, and the proposed processing and marketing arrangements. It is important to understand how these factors interact and how they impact the selection of collection equipment.

The fundamental concept behind a multimaterial curbside collection program is to rely on the householder to properly separate recyclable materials from what is normally thrown out in the trash and to routinely place these materials at the curb for collection in a manner prescribed by the program designer. Some of the major issues that must be resolved in the collection program design include:

- What materials should be included in the program?
- What preparation steps will the householder be requested to perform (e.g., rinse jars, remove labels, flatten cans)?
- Should a household container (or containers) be used, and if so, what type and size?
- What will be the collection frequency?
- How will materials be set out at the curb—what degree of material commingling will be allowed?
- What will be the role of collection personnel at the curb: sort materials into separate compartments, remove nonrecyclables, etc.?
- How will materials collected be processed?

Obviously, many of these issues are interrelated and will have a direct bearing on the type of collection vehicle required. For instance, the materials to be included in the program are usually governed by market availability and conditions; the frequency of collection and the number of items to be included will affect the size and perhaps the type of container to be used, and the degree of mixing materials together (commingling) will impact the efficiency of the collection operation and the complexity of the processing operation.

The variety of system components related to the operations that occur in the household, at the collection point, and at the processing facility are shown schematically in Fig. 27.1. The program designer's role is to select the components that are most appropriate for the jurisdiction in question and to make sure that they are properly integrated to ensure an efficient, cost-effective program with maximum recovery of recyclables.

Materials. The majority of curbside programs collect a core group of materials that typically consist of newspaper, glass jars and bottles, ferrous and nonferrous beverage and food cans, and high-density and PET (polyethylene terephthalate) plastic beverage containers. Depending on local market conditions, some of these materials may not be included in a given program, or conversely, the list may be broadened to include more materials. With the current push to maximize diversion from conventional disposal alternatives such as incineration and landfill, the list of curbside materials collected is growing. Programs now often include such items as magazines, telephone books, household corrugated, boxboard, mixed paper, textiles, sheet plastics, and a full range of other plastic containers.

The materials selected for program implementation as well as the materials

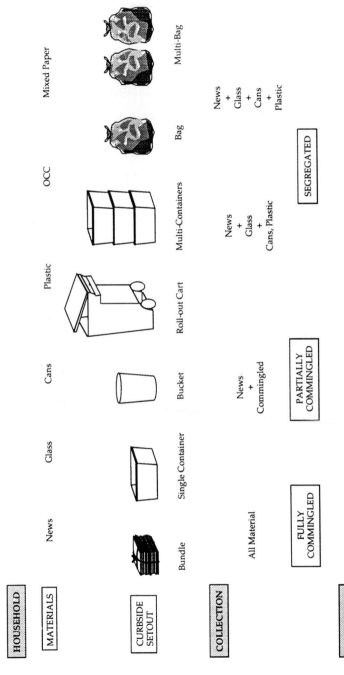

FIGURE 27.1 Curbside collection of recyclables integration of system decisions.

that might be considered at some future date for incorporation into the program will obviously impact the choice of collection equipment. The household recovery rates of each material and the associated volumes are important considerations in choosing the type of household container that might be used as well as the type and design of collection vehicle. It is important that when selecting this equipment, as much consideration as possible be given to the flexibility of the system to accommodate either new materials that might be added to the program and/or increases in the recovery levels of each material.

Convenience. Experience has shown that for a multimaterial curbside collection program, material recovery is maximized when the program is made convenient for the householder. The program designer will likely require the householder to separate recyclables from the trash, prepare the recyclables, store them until collection day, and carry them out and set them at the curb in a specific manner. Each of these steps poses a certain level of inconvenience to the householder. By complicating or adding to any of these steps, convenience drops, and some participants may decide that they are no longer willing to take that additional step. As a result, program participation falls, as does material recovery.

Household Containers. The use of a household container has been shown to dramatically increase material recovery rates for curbside collection programs and illustrates the importance of convenience to the resident. The container, whether a box, a bucket, a cart, a bag, or combinations of these, assists the resident both with storage of recyclables and in transporting these materials to the curb for collection. The container also serves to assist collection personnel to distinguish recyclables from trash that may be set out at the same time and also has value as a visual promotional tool to remind the public about recycling. There are generally four basic types of household containers in use today: rectangular boxes, cylindrical buckets, roll-out carts, and bags.

The most popular household container for the majority of North American curbside programs is the single, rectangular container (commonly known as the "blue box"). The box may be used inside or outside the house (wherever conveniently accessible) to store recyclables. When the container is nearly full, residents place it at the curb on the designated collection day. In most programs that use a single container, the resident places all loose containers in the box and sets bundled or bagged newspaper on top of or beside the box at setout.

Convenience plays an important part in container selection, since the number of containers and their size may have an impact on program participation. The container should be of sufficient capacity to hold the anticipated volume of recyclables between scheduled collections and yet not so large that the weight of a full container poses a problem for setout. Multiple containers for designated recyclables have been used successfully in many curbside programs, although these require more space in or at the household, are more inconvenient to carry to the curb, and are more costly than a single container. They may also adversely impact the collection productivity, as discussed in the following section.

Buckets are used in the same manner as rectangular containers but have several different features. They are typically more universally available and often cheaper per unit than a box, are not as convenient as a box if the collector is required to sort material at the curb, and are more prone to blow away when empty on a windy day.

Roll-out carts that are conventionally used for automated collection of trash and yard waste are now being used in some curbside programs that collect a broader range of recyclables. These carts typically range in size from 30 to 90 gal, are convenient to roll to the curb, and are normally lifted and unloaded by means of an hydraulic mechanism on the collection vehicle. Cart storage may pose a problem at the house if space is limited or if multiple carts are required. In addition, the carts are relatively expensive and by their nature dictate that virtually no further sorting will be done at the curbside.

A growing number of communities are testing bag systems for the collection of recyclables. Individual kraft and plastic grocery bags are used in some programs as an inexpensive means of having the householder segregate and set out recyclables at curbside. Demonstration programs are now testing larger, color-coded polypropylene, polyethylene, or burlap bags for recyclables. The primary advantage of bag systems is that the bags can be collected using the same truck as trash, often at the same time, potentially reducing system collection costs. Disadvantages include the problems associated with bags ripping, the need and extra cost of removing the bag from the recyclables, and perhaps the most critical, finding an efficient, cost-effective, sustainable, and convenient means of bag distribution for the householder.

Curbside Collection Operations. Once recyclables are set out at the curb, there are several tasks that the collector typically may be required to perform. These include

- Sorting recyclables into individual bins or compartments of the truck
- Segregating nonrecyclables or contaminants from the materials loaded
- Returning empty containers or carts to the curb after loading

Whether to collect recyclable materials commingled or segregated is a key issue because of its implications to overall program design and especially collection efficiency. Selection of one or the other mode of setout and collection influences materials targeted, truck type, and the design of the processing facility.

The degree to which recyclables are mixed in the collection vehicle can be defined by three main options: full commingling of all materials, partial commingling of container materials, or complete material segregation.

- *Full commingling:* Recyclables are set out together and loaded into the collection vehicle unsorted (fiber and container materials together).
- *Partial commingling:* At a minimum, the collection vehicle is divided into at least two compartments, usually to separate fiber materials from the remaining container materials. A truck with more than two compartments may have further segregation of materials (e.g., plastics combined with glass, or cans combined with plastics).
- *Segregation:* All materials are placed in their own compartment in the collection vehicle. All plastics or all colors of glass may be commingled but different materials are not mixed together.

Partial commingling or full segregation of materials typically results in slower collection times per stop than commingled collection. Obviously, the more sorting done at the truck, the more time spent per stop. Therefore, as a collection crew sorts recyclables into more and more categories, the number of stops achieved per hour should decline. In addition, a program which involves multiple curbside sorts will find it increasingly difficult to add new materials. This will be discussed in more detail in the next section.

The point of curbside collection is the second opportunity in the program to initiate segregation of recyclable materials—the first is having the householder set out materials already segregated into the recyclable streams corresponding to how they will be collected in the collection vehicle. Even if the recyclables are all set out in one container, or recyclable streams are mixed in multiple containers, the collector may be required to segregate the recyclables in the collection vehicles to integrate with the processing facility. As already mentioned, the opportunity for segregating recyclables from roll-out carts or bags is limited.

The second task of collection personnel might be to sort out items placed at the curb that are not part of the recycling program. In most jurisdictions, these are left behind in the household container (sometimes with an accompanying note to the householder) so that the householder becomes educated as to the materials that are and are not acceptable. In programs where recyclables are set out using kraft or plastic bags and segregation of recyclables is required, there is an operational issue of what to do with the bag after the contents are loaded into the vehicle. Assuming that the bag cannot be left at the curb, an additional compartment may be necessary in the truck to store these materials. Again, for commingled collection programs that utilize large bags or roll-out carts, sorting of contaminants and nonrecyclables is not practical. The final step for the operator is usually to return the household container(s) or roll-out cart to the curb when empty.

Selection of Curbside Collection Vehicles

The foregoing illustrates how many of the program design details dictate some of the features necessary in the collection vehicle. Other key criteria to be considered in selecting the appropriate collection vehicle are

- Capacity
- Vehicle dimensions
- Flexibility
- Design features
- Cost

Capacity. The desired capacity of a vehicle is a function of the quantity and volume of materials to be collected in a given period and size or weight regulations that exist in a given state or local municipality. Most dedicated recycling collection vehicles vary in theoretical capacity from 15 to 31 yd^3; however, actual capacity will usually be somewhat less.

Vehicle Dimensions. The physical shape of the vehicle, its length, width, and height, may be important in some jurisdictions. Narrow streets or lanes, limited clearance at underpasses or bridges, headroom restrictions at processing facilities, turning radii in cul-de-sacs, etc., may influence selection decisions.

Flexibility. One aspect that is often overlooked is how flexible the collection vehicle is to adapt to changes in material types collected or variations in material volumes brought about by seasonal fluctuations during the course of the curbside program. One sure fact is that things change. More and more programs are looking to increase diversion of materials from traditional disposal options such a landfills by adding more materials to the curbside program. The addition of these materials and/or the program design changes that the operator would like to put in place as a result of these additions is often hindered by the limitations of vehicles already in place.

The vehicle that was originally purchased to serve a specific program design may now not have the flexibility to accommodate changes in the program. For instance, is the current collection vehicle suitable if adding one more materials to the collection program required that this material be segregated in another separate compartment of the truck? Can one more compartment be added? Does this necessitate commingling other materials, and what is the associated impact on the processing operation? Many curbside operators are now dealing with these and similar questions.

Design Features.   The primary consideration in selecting a collection vehicle for use in a multimaterial curbside collection program should be collection efficiency. While this is a function of many of the program design elements previously discussed, the truck design itself greatly impacts the collection efficiency. It is therefore important to understand what comprises the daily collection tasks.

The normal workday for a curbside collection crew will involve a certain portion of nonproductive or noncollection time. This is the amount of time during a workday that is devoted to startup, vehicle safety checks, travel time to the collection route, travel time to the MRF to unload, unloading time, lunch and breaks, etc., that is, all of the time in a normal workday except the time spent actually collecting recyclables.

The actual time on the route comprises two parts: picking up material at each stop and driving time between stops. The driving time between stops is not influenced by the type of collection vehicle. It is a function of a number of factors, including the setout rate (the number of households on a route that have recyclables at the curb for pickup), the density of the households on the route, and the amount of traffic delays encountered (stop signs, traffic lights, congestion). The minimum travel time on a given route would be the time for the truck to travel the route under these conditions without making any stops.

The type of truck utilized directly impacts the time spent loading material, the collection efficiency, and ultimately the cost of the collection operation. Vehicles designed specifically for curbside collection are more efficient than regular trucks (like cube vans or pickup trucks). Some of the specific factors that affect collection efficiency are itemized below:

1. *Right-hand drive, stepout cab:* If the driver also loads material, a right-hand drive cab with a low-profile curbside stepout design minimizes the time it takes for the driver to exit and enter the vehicle during the collection. This design also minimizes the amount of wear and tear on the driver, a factor that reduces driver efficiency as the day progresses.

2. *Length of vehicle:* Loading a longer vehicle, such as a trailer, will take more time than a regular-length truck.

3. *Loading height:* Vehicles with a low loading height are more efficient to load. Loading heights range from 40 to 100 in, with most vehicles exhibiting a loading height of about 45 in. Some manual-loading vehicles require the operator to insert removable panels along the side of the truck to contain recyclables as the truck fills. Therefore, as the truck fills along the collection route, the loading height increases, making the loading operation more difficult and less efficient.

4. *Vehicle capacity:* Capacity indirectly impacts collection efficiency, in that fewer trips are required to unload material and thus less "nonproductive" time is spent in the entire collection operation. Generally, the larger the capacity, the more efficient the collection.

5. *Degree of sorting:* As mentioned earlier, stop time per household increases with each additional material sort that the driver does at the truck. Commingled collection is faster than segregated collection using the same vehicle. Depending on the physical features of the truck and the type of household container(s) used, each additional sort at the curb can add a minimum of 5 seconds to the stop time.

Furthermore, the more sorts that are required, the more chance that any one compartment or bin will fill up or "cube out" before another. Once one of the compartments fills, the truck must return to the MRF to unload, even if the other compartments are not full. This is inefficient use of truck capacity.

With segregated collection, as more and more materials are added to the sorting requirement, the more the likelihood that one of the compartments will "cube out" earlier than the others.

6. *Hydraulic loading:* Many collection vehicles now have hydraulic lifting devices on the side, front, or rear to assist in loading recyclables into the truck. Low-level hoppers are used on some vehicles to store the recyclables (segregated or commingled). This provides easy, accessible loading of recyclables into the hopper, and when the hopper fills, the operator engages the lifting mechanism to empty the recyclables into the truck. The lifting mechanisms are usually also equipped to handle one or more roll-out carts at a time.

In many collection operations, hydraulic loading mechanisms have increased collection efficiency by 15 percent.

7. *Unloading:* Some vehicles are easier to unload than others. Again, the more time spent off-loading recyclables, the less time available in a given day to spend on the collection route.

Costs. Consideration should be given to both the capital and operating cost of a collection vehicle. Dedicated collection vehicles generally range in price from about $40,000 to $100,000, depending on the generic type of vehicle and its design features. While capital cost of the vehicle is perhaps the most obvious cost that will be considered in selecting a truck, annual operating cost is a larger portion of the annual collection cost and should be carefully examined. At least 50 percent of the annual operating cost of a one-person-operated vehicle is typically made up of salary and benefits. Obviously, as the crew size increases, this percentage grows. This is why much of the focus of recycling vehicle designers has been on trying to provide efficient material collection utilizing only a single driver and loader.

Many of the design features previously reviewed impact not only the capital cost of the vehicle but also the operating cost. While the capital cost of incorporating right-hand-drive capabilities with convenient stepout to the curb may be high, the reduction in operating cost resulting from the increase in operator efficiency will more than offset this. Similarly, other physical features that impact the collection efficiency, such as loading height and the cycle time of hydraulic mechanisms, will also directly impact collection efficiency and thus operating costs.

Other obvious contributors to operating cost are fuel economy, maintenance and repair costs, insurance, and license fees. When all other considerations are equal, some operators may select collection vehicles based on the availability of a distributor to supply parts, the maintenance and repair record of a given vehicle model, or the individual preference of the vehicle operator or mechanic.

COLLECTION VEHICLE TYPES

In general, there are three generic types of dedicated collection vehicles for curbside collection of multimaterial recyclables: trailers, open-bin trucks, and closed-body trucks. Almost any other type of truck can be used in curbside programs, but these three types of vehicles have proven to be the most popular.

A summary of the characteristics of these three generic types of collection vehicles follows. Advantages and disadvantages of each vehicle type are highlighted in Figs. 27.2 to 27.9. No attempt has been made here to document details of all of the manufacturers and models of curbside collection vehicles currently available in North America. This list is constantly changing and expanding. The reader is referred to several recycling trade journals that periodically publish this information.

Trailers

Many curbside programs, especially at the demonstration stage, start by using a trailer for material collection. The major advantage of a trailer over a truck is its relatively low cost. Trailers typically range in price from $11,000 to $20,000 and can be pulled by a pickup or flat-bed truck that is usually standard issue for a municipality. Primary disadvantages of trailers are lack of maneuverability and capacity. Many different trailer designs can be found, including compartmentalized units that end-dump, side-dump, or carry removable bins that are hydraulically lowered for off-loading materials (Fig. 27.2).

Advantages	Disadvantages
• low cost	• difficult to maneuver
• hydraulic unloading	• two-person operation
• separate compartments	• low weight and volume capacity
• hitch to existing pick-up or behind side-loading garbage truck	• tarps required
• flexible – use as drop-off or for other duties	

FIGURE 27.2   Recycling trailer, advantages and disadvantages.

Bin Trucks

These are trucks that have between two and four individual bins (open or enclosed) for recyclables that are typically manually loaded from the side or the top. The operator has some flexibility in determining the individual bin sizes, and the bins have hydraulic hoists that allow the bins to dump to either side or the rear. These vehicles range in capacity from 11 to 28 yd^3 and range in price from about \$35,000 to \$60,000 (Fig. 27.3).

Advantages	Disadvantages
• dual drive	• requires tarp for rainfall or litter control
• one-person operation	• limited flexibility of compartments — fixed number and size
• hydraulic unloading	
• low loading height	• 16 -30yd^3 capacity
• easy entry/exit	• high capital cost
• side or rear unloading	• lower cargo weight
• distinct, specialized truck contributes to promotion effect	• more glass breakage

FIGURE 27.3 Open-body recycling truck, advantages and disadvantages.

Closed-Body Trucks

The manual-loading version of this vehicle consists of an enclosed, compartmentalized body that is typically loaded from the side(s) and unloaded from the rear. Movable, lockable, top-hinged interior dividers create compartments for segregated materials. By unlocking successive dividers and tipping the body, segmented materials are unloaded. The maximum capacity of the truck is 31 yd^3 and capital costs range between \$50,000 to \$65,000 (Figs. 27.4 and 27.5).

Many manufacturers now offer a closed-body truck that hydraulically loads recyclables through the use of a side trough or divided container at the front of the vehicle. When sufficient recyclables accumulate, they are lifted and loaded into the top of the vehicle. While these trucks are similar in rated capacity to the manual versions, they have greater usable capacity because they are top-loaded. Prices range from \$60,000 to \$85,000 (Fig. 27.6).

Others

While the foregoing are the most popular and widely used vehicles for the collection of recyclables at curbside, there is a wide variety of other types of vehi-

Advantages	Disadvantages
• one-person operation	• high capital cost
• dual drive	• no auto loading capability for 90 gallon carts
• easy exit and entry	
• low loading height	• not useful for O.C.C. collection
• compartment flexibility	
• hydraulic unloading	
• larger operational capacity than standard closed body truck	
• folding, hinged side panels	

FIGURE 27.4 Low-profile closed-body truck, advantages and disadvantages.

Advantages	Disadvantages
• one-person operation	• high loading height as compartments fill up — maximum volume is not achieved
• dual drive	
• easy exit and entry	• high capital cost
• compartment flexibility to handle changing material mix	• not useful for O.C.C. collection
• hydraulic unloading	
• adaptable to multi-family with auto-loading feature	
• distinct, specialized recycling truck contributes to promotion effect	

FIGURE 27.5 Closed-body recycling trucks, advantages and disadvantages.

Advantages	Disadvantages
• one-person operation	• high capital cost
• dual drive	• not useful for O.C.C. collection
• easy exit and entry	
• compartment flexibility to handle changing material mix	• roof height when loading (some models)
• hydraulic unloading	
• distinct, specialized recycling truck contributes to promotion effect	
• hydraulic side buckets result in constant low loading height for curbside collection	
• capable of automatically servicing 75 gallon collection carts from apartments and commercial establishments	
• full volume capacity can be utilized (31 cu. yds.)	

FIGURE 27.6 Hydraulic side-loading trucks, advantages and disadvantages.

cles that should be noted here. These include conventional flat-bed trucks, step and curb vans, and refuse packer trucks. While these vehicles were not designed specifically for curbside collection and generally are not well suited for the task, they are used in many smaller municipalities primarily because of their availability. Comparative characteristics of these vehicles are presented in Figs. 27.7 to 27.9.

Advantages	Disadvantages
• flexibility for other uses	• two- or three-person operation
• low capital cost	• high loading height
• availability — can be replaced during breakdown	• usually requires forklift for unloading
• used equipment available	• limited capacity
• ship direct to market	• poor entry/exit
	• limited promotion

FIGURE 27.7 Flat-bed trucks, advantages and disadvantages.

Advantages	Disadvantages
• low capital cost, low maintenance	• left hand drive only
	• manually unloaded
• widely available, rentals widely available	• two-person operation
• easy replacement in emergencies	• limited storage capacity and cargo weight
• flexible for other uses	• tend to be overloaded, leading to higher maintenance, and shorter life
• generally economical to operate	
• excellent maneuverability	• difficult to sort materials
• no special driver licencing	
• low loading height	
• quick delivery	

FIGURE 27.8 Step vans and cube vans, advantages and disadvantages.

Advantages	Disadvantages
• available and familiar in most communities	• difficult to adapt to multi-material collection
• well suited for garbage collection — may integrate recycling with garbage collection	• normally two- or three-person operation
	• high capital and operating cost related to hydraulic system
• easy to load and unload	• only one compartment available for one material
• high cargo weight	
• suitable for collection of O.C.C.	• contamination problems when also used for garbage collection, could render collected material useless
• low loading height	
• loader can ride on back	
• if clean, suitable for "news only" collection	• confusion with regular garbage collection is disincentive for residents (not if good signage)

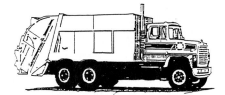

FIGURE 27.9 Packer trucks, advantages and disadvantages.

MULTIFAMILY COLLECTION

In many respects, designing collection systems to service the wide variety of multifamily housing types is more difficult than for single-family residences, especially if an attempt is made to integrate collection equipment for both services. Recycling system options within existing multifamily buildings are typically governed by design, space, and operational constraints, making it difficult to plan and implement effective recycling systems. Very often, space is limited to even handle the garbage generated within these structures, let alone adding a new requirement to provide a separate system for recyclables. When residents are required to carry recyclables to the ground floor or to the basement, they are often supplied a recycling bag to make this effort more convenient.

Many townhouse and apartment complexes utilize various sizes of roll-out carts, igloos, or front-end containers to store source-segregated recyclables. In many cases, the system to be used parallels the system used for garbage collection. Roll-out carts can be collected with conventional compartmentalized curbside collection vehicles that are equipped with hydraulic lifting mechanisms, or alternatively, a packer truck with a similar lifting device can be used if the recyclables are commingled. These carts can be located either inside or outside of the building, depending on available space, and when full, can be wheeled to the curb or to some convenient location on the property for collection.

Igloos—bell-shaped containers that are lifted using a crane truck—are attractive, distinctive containers that have become popular in many noncurbside recycling applications. These containers are usually lifted over a compartmentalized open-top truck and the contents unloaded through the bottom of the igloo into the respective compartment. Crane trucks are relatively expensive and are limited both in total capacity and in the number of compartments that can be used (Fig. 27.10).

Advantages	Disadvantages
• one person operation	• requires a minimum number of depot locations to be economical
• 'igloo' shape recognized internationally	
	• high capital cost
• materials separated by participants	• not suitable for curbside collection
• number of depot containers at any site can be varied according to demand	• depots not integrated with curbside collection

FIGURE 27.10   Crane trucks, advantages and disadvantages.

Dumpster containers are also used at multifamily dwellings, although their use normally requires residents to bring recyclables to the container and because of their long standing association with trash collection, their use may not be perceived by the residents as a serious attempt to institute a good recycling program. These containers are collected and hauled individually by roll-off trucks (Figs. 27.11 and 27.12), or by standard front-end refuse-collection vehicles that are normally used for garbage collection.

Advantages	Disadvantages
• available on a contract basis	• not suitable for curbside collection
• handles a variety of container sizes	• not all boxes are compatible with all trucks
• divided roll off boxes can be used as depots	• few municipalities handle enough containers to justify owning a truck

FIGURE 27.11   Roll-off trucks, advantages and disadvantages.

Advantages	Disadvantages
• large variety of containers available	• left hand drive
• costs can be shared with non-recycling operations	• requires a minimum level of containers to be worthwhile
• some containers stack for storage	• depots and curbside operations must be handled independently

FIGURE 27.12   Hook lift truck, advantages and disadvantages.

More consideration is now being given to incorporating recycling into the design of multifamily structures rather than trying to add the system after the facilities are designed and constructed. These include multichute systems, carousel units at the bottom of a single dedicated recycling chute, stacked containers on rolling carts located in enlarged garbage/recycling rooms on each floor, and the provision of dedicated storage space in each residential unit for segregated recyclables.

When it is not physically possible to incorporate recycling services at each multifamily facility, or when economics dictate a less expensive (and less effective) collection alternative, depots or drop-off sites can be used to service these residents. These are typically sited at locations within the community that are convenient to residents, such as shopping centers, libraries, and town halls. There is an infinite variety of customized designs of drop-off (depot) or buy-back facilities, but most utilize igloos or compartmentalized roll-off containers to receive and store recyclables.

INDUSTRIAL, COMMERCIAL, INSTITUTIONAL (ICI) SYSTEMS

There are many point sources of recyclables within a municipality that provide significant quantities of recyclables. These include such facilities as commercial office buildings, hotels, hospitals, schools and universities, bars, and restaurants. As for multifamily dwellings, the design of recycling systems to service these facilities, in most cases, is specific to each location.

Once the internal system is designed to assist in the segregation and storage of recyclables, most of these facilities will utilize rolling carts or front-end containers for the collection of these materials. The type, size, and number of containers to be used will depend on the number of materials segregated, the recovery rates, the collection vehicle to be used, and the capability of the processing facility or end market to accept commingled or segregated recyclables.

MULTIUSE CO-COLLECTION VEHICLES

More and more municipalities throughout North America are now legislating targets for waste diversion from landfills. These ambitious targets are requiring a thorough evaluation and implementation of alternative waste management strategies, including the collection of more residential material streams, such as organics, household hazardous wastes, and garbage at the same time as more traditional recyclables. As the challenge has been met to develop a dedicated vehicle to collect curbside recyclables in recent years, the future challenge is to design a collection methodology to efficiently and cost-effectively collect all of the other material streams that are likely to evolve.

Several earlier attempts were made in North America in the 1970s to develop a collection vehicle that collected two material streams at once. The concept never did catch on, but has now resurfaced as a result of the waste-reduction pressures on municipalities and the success of these dual-purpose trucks in Europe. Several truck manufacturers are now developing prototype multimaterial collection vehicles to meet this need.

Much of the European work has been focused on how to collect a "wet" or primarily organics stream and a "dry" residential stream comprised primarily of recyclables from the regular residential garbage. Many pilot programs are now under way to test the two-stream (clean wet and other, or clean dry and other) system or the three-stream system (clean wet, clean dry, and garbage). The goal of these programs is to find a system that accomplishes the recovery and quality objectives of each stream, while maximizing collection deficiencies and minimizing collection costs.

Recent truck designs have evolved with a two-compartment collection vehicle, split either horizontally or vertically. Trucks that are vertically split, at this time, would appear to have more design and operational difficulties to overcome than vehicles that are split horizontally. For instance, these trucks must be designed to accommodate the potential of differential weight distribution caused by density differences of the collected material fractions and the weight of compaction equipment. These problems are minimized with the horizontal split configuration.

A more recent concept in the use of dual-compartment collection vehicles involves the use of split household containers. Each household has two containers (typically roll-out carts) that are divided vertically. Using these compartments, the resident can effect a four-stream material split; for instance, organics and recyclables that are divided into fibers and sheet plastics and container materials (glass, cans, plastic bottles, etc.), and the fourth stream, which is the remaining garbage. Each container would be collected on an alternating schedule, perhaps weekly, using the dual-compartment truck. The hydraulic lifting mechanism on the truck is positioned such that as the container is lifted and dumped, each of the two materials streams empties into their respective compartment of the truck (Fig. 27.13).

Advantages	Disadvantages
• integrates garbage, recycling and composting collections	• high capital cost
• automated cart lifters reduce worker fatigue and injury	• two or three person operation
• compaction of individual compartments available, if desired	• roof height may be a problem
• handles a wide range of collection container sizes	• compartments may fill at different rates
• hydraulic unloading	• requires use of collection carts

FIGURE 27.13   Dual-compartment collection truck, advantages and disadvantages.

In this manner, four material streams can be collected using the same vehicle, effectively eliminating many of the potential material quality concerns and the need for more than one type of collection vehicle. Within some limitations, the capacity and compaction functions of the two compartments can be selected to suit the material mix. Again, the horizontal split would seem to offer an operational advantage, in that two roll-out containers could be loaded at once, resulting in increased collection efficiency. Clearly, the current task at hand is to minimize collection system efficiencies and costs while increasing the materials to be recovered from the waste stream.

CHAPTER 28

PROCESSING EQUIPMENT

Kenneth Ely Jr.
President, Ely Enterprises Inc.
Cleveland, Ohio

INTRODUCTION

Today's recycling equipment serves diverse situations: factories and distribution centers compress and bundle wastepapers; shopping malls have aluminum collection sites; automobile manufacturers incorporate their own recycling centers. Also, more and more recycling facilities group together various types of equipment. These centers process varieties of materials at once.

Over the years, technical innovations have enhanced processing equipment with higher accuracy, better safety features, a more economical use of energy, and greater speed. This has led to the development of peripheral types of equipment. Shredders shred and pretreat materials prior to baling or compacting. Conveyor systems transport material quickly through all aspects of the recycling process.

In addition, more specific types of technology have developed in response to various material markets. For example, can flatteners evolved because of the need to compress beverage cans for transportation. Also, glass crushers are popular because they produce a form of glass called *cullet,* which resemble small glass pebbles. (Cullet is the preferred form of glass with glass manufacturers.)

Most recently, recyclers have seen very sophisticated processes developed due to the growth of the recycling industry as a whole. These processes further improve accuracy and speed, especially in the areas of sorting. Eddy current separators pull nonferrous metals from a conveyor line. Similarly, optical glass separation systems sort glass according to color. Optical plastic separation systems also sort plastic according to type. These techniques have come a long way from recycling's humble beginning.

In the twenties and thirties, recycling machinery was very labor-intensive. Balers were often hand-cranked, and it wasn't until the thirties that electrical baling units outsold hand-operated machines. Crude by today's standards, these machines relied on a series of ratchets and chains to bale materials.

Throughout the thirties, forties, and fifties, electromechanical machines were produced that were large and durable. As a testament to this durability, some of these machines are still operating today. At that time, recycling came under the auspices of junk and scrap metal dealers.

Of course, during the sixties, a growing awareness of the need to recycle, coupled with technological advances, produced an array of safer, faster, and more powerful equipment. The advent of hydraulics meant that material could be easily compressed and reshaped. Today we see the results of these developments in powerful balers, compactors, and densifiers.

In the nineties, recycling equipment is catching up with the computer chip. Manufacturers are producing more and more machinery with programmable intelligence. Such technology yields in-depth information concerning throughput, production time, density, etc. Most types of equipment are available with computerized options. Larger pieces of machinery can even connect to a modem for on-line adjustments by the manufacturer.

Despite this technology, an important concern for potential buyers of recycling equipment is flexibility; are a certain technology and its by-products limited to one specialty market? One should be aware of how widely marketable a certain recycled material will be after processing. Such an awareness can aid a customer in avoiding equipment that will be obsolete a few years after its purchase.

Of course, the truly conscientious customer will make the most successful purchases. Customers should buy from the manufacturers and dealers with the best reputations. Recycling is a field where slipshod equipment and service quickly come to light. The technology is too advanced and the processes too demanding for it to be otherwise.

With today's emphasis on recycling, the multitude of different types of processing equipment is truly vast. This includes convenient appliances such as "reverse" vending machines and under-the-counter can flatteners. For our purposes, however, we will focus on the more commonly used equipment.

BALERS

Since the advent of large-scale recycling in the 1950s and 1960s, the baler has played an increasingly important role in recycling. The reason why is simple: as more varieties of waste products are handled in larger amounts, efficient storage and handling methods become essential. The baler is simply a bundling system, fulfilling a modern, economical need—packaging uniformity. In this case, the "packaging" encompasses recyclable products made from plastics, papers, or metals. The final product is a densely packed cube of sorted or mixed waste products that has been tied with plastic or wire. These waste bales are easily stacked for shipping or storage.

Depending on need, balers are available in a variety of sizes and configurations. These sizes range from smaller, easily transported vertical balers, to larger horizontal balers. All types of balers have similar elements which include: a "feedhopper" area, into which the recyclables are fed; one or more "rams," the flat surfaces which compress the material; and the "baling chamber" or "compression chamber," where bale compression takes place.

Vertical Balers

Vertical balers are the most popular baling units in the marketplace today. Typically, a vertical baler has a ram that moves from an upright position, down through a hopper area, into the baling chamber. This ram is driven from above by a hydraulic cylinder, although some units incorporate two cylinders, which pull the ram down into the compression chamber (Fig. 28.1).

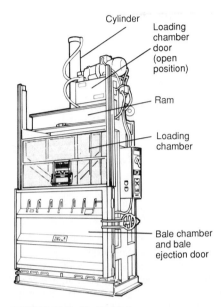

Cylinder

Loading chamber door (open position)

Ram

Loading chamber

Bale chamber and bale ejection door

FIGURE 28.1 Vertical baler.

The operator feeds materials into the hopper area through a safety window. This safety window prevents the machine from operating while it is open. Once the hopper is full, the operator simply closes the safety window and pushes a button to begin the compression cycle. Following compression, the ram moves upward again, opening the safety window to accept another charge of materials. This process continues until a bale of a certain density has been formed. Some units today determine density automatically, through use of a pressure relay. Other baling units rely on a visual sighting by the operator to determine the complete formation of a bale.

When a sufficiently dense bale has been formed, the entire mass is bound with wire strapping or plastic. This is accomplished manually, by opening a door to the baling chamber and running precut lengths of wire, or similar material, through a manual tying arrangement. A recycler will typically use 12- to 14-gauge wire, depending on the material being recycled.

Today's vertical balers can produce bales ranging in length from 18 to 72 in. The most common bale today measures 30 by 48 by 60 in, a standard, acceptable mill size for most recycled materials.

After the bale has been tied, it is ejected from the chamber by means of either a "kick-plate," which ejects the bale from below, or a series of chains connected to the ram which tighten as the ram is raised. Tying time takes between 5 and 10 min, while the overall baling time varies from as little as a half bale an hour to two or three bales an hour. Of course, the type of material being baled determines the bale time.

Vertical balers are very versatile. Recyclers can use the machines to process nearly all grades of waste paper, corrugated cardboard, foam scraps, ferrous and nonferrous metals, steel scrap (provided it is a light gauge), used beverage containers, and plastic bottles. A vertical baler has even been used to compress peppers at a spice plant in Texas for easier transportation across country. There are some technical concerns with certain materials, however. For instance, because newspaper is not very compressible, it requires an even distribution throughout the feed hopper. If this step is not followed properly, bale quality will suffer, and the bale might not hold together. Also, plastic bottles should have all caps removed to ensure that no air is trapped within the bale.

Vertical balers are electrically operated, with motor size ranging from 1 to 30 hp. The power comes from hydraulics, where the motor turns a pump which directs the flow of oil to a hydraulic cylinder. Due to their low horsepower, these machines are very economical to run. Cylinder sizes vary from 2 to 10 in. A typical 60-in baler would incorporate a 6-in cylinder and a 10-hp motor. An important consideration when comparing balers is hydraulic system pressure and cylinder size. Occasionally, a manufacturer will downsize a unit's cylinder size while operating at a higher system pressure. Although this practice keeps the equipment's purchase cost down, it ultimately leads to premature system breakdowns. One would do better to invest in a baler with a large cylinder and a system pressure in the 1800- to 2200-lb/in^2 range.

Vertical balers are usually self-contained and easily transported. Machines are transported on their sides, and after being placed on end and having power connected, they are set to operate. Once installed, a single-cylinder downstroke baler requires about 13 ft of vertical clearance space.

Vertical balers range in price from $4000 to $30,000. Some of the factors determining price are unit size, motor horsepower, and the size of the hydraulic cylinder. A typical example of a more expensive baler would be a 30-hp unit with a 10-in cylinder for high-density baling. While vertical balers are convenient due to size, one should keep in mind that they are almost exclusively hand-fed and cannot be automated. Of course, because of this, vertical balers have the lowest output of all balers.

Upstroke Balers

Another type of baler, similar to the vertical baler, is the upstroke baler. The most striking characteristic of an upstroke baler is its underground charging chamber (Fig. 28.2). Installation of an upstroke unit requires a foundation and a

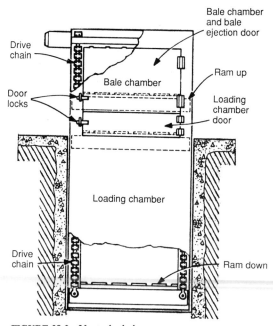

FIGURE 28.2   Upstroke baler.

pit constructed below ground level. The material to be recycled is pushed across the floor and into the baling chamber, which is usually 12 to 18 ft deep. After the baler's doors are closed, the ram moves upward, above the floor line, and into the baler's compression section. The process is repeated until a sufficiently dense bale has been produced, whereupon the doors to the baling chamber are opened and the bale is tied off.

Upstroke balers, like vertical balers, come in different sizes, producing from a 54-in-long bale to a 72-in-long bale. Also, motor sizes vary from 10 to 25 hp. Upstroke balers in the 25-hp range are often called "high-density" balers, because they can produce bales of extra-high density. Unlike the hydraulic rams found in vertical balers, most upstroke baler rams are electromechanical; that is, they are gear-driven and rely on a series of chains to pull the ram up into the baling chamber. There are some hydraulic ram upstroke units on the market, however.

Upstroke balers were in widespread use throughout the fifties and sixties, but have since drastically lost popularity. Nevertheless, some upstroke units are still produced in very small numbers. One can also purchase used units.

The main reason for the upstroke baler's decline is the inherent construction costs. These costs, which include digging a pit, setting a foundation, and installing the unit, are very high. A recycler who installs the unit on leased property faces the prospect of a future change of location. Needless to say, you can't take the foundation and pit with you.

Likewise, resale is difficult, as the new owner must dig out the old unit, transport it to the new location, and then dig a new pit at a new location. Potential customers should beware that spare parts are difficult to find and very expensive. The units themselves are probably already well used. Additionally, the units from the fifties and sixties do not have today's safety features.

All this would lead us to ask why anyone would buy such a unit today. The most obvious reason, besides a possible bargain price, is high-density baling. Accordingly, the majority of upstroke balers sold today are high-density units.

Horizontal Balers

As the name implies, horizontal balers compress materials in a horizontal manner. These balers can process the same materials as vertical balers, although the potential throughput of a horizontal configuration is far greater. Horizontal balers are available with motor sizes ranging from 5 to 150 hp. All horizontal units feature hydraulically driven rams. Higher-end large-volume units also offer such optional features as continuous feed and automatic-tying mechanisms. Of course, these diverse sizes and features also add up to a large spectrum of horizontal unit prices, ranging from $7000 to $500,000.

Closed-Door Manual-Tie Horizontal Balers. The most basic type of horizontal baler is the closed-door manual-tie horizontal baler, which operates in a fashion similar to vertical balers (Fig. 28.3). The closed-door baler features a hopper area that accepts either conveyor-fed, hand-fed, or cart-dumped material. These units incorporate a photoelectric relay within the hopper area. When enough material has filled the hopper to block this relay, the ram cycles forward, compressing the material from the hopper into the baling area. Because this is a horizontal system, it will accept new charges into its hopper area while the ram is cycling forward. The excess material simply accumulates above the ram and then tumbles into the baling chamber as the ram retracts from the baling chamber.

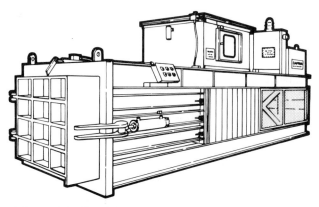

FIGURE 28.3   Closed-door horizontal baler.

Like vertical balers, these units compress material in a series of laminations. At a certain point, a pressure setting indicates that enough material has accumulated to form a bale and alerts the machine's operator via a horn or buzzer. The operator must then switch the system from an automatic mode to a manual mode. The ram moves forward one final time to hold the bale in place. The bale is then tied manually.

Although closed-door balers process a wide variety of materials, large-scale baling of certain materials may necessitate the addition of accessory equipment, such as a shredder or a conditioner. These devices prepare material for baling by decreasing its infeed density per cubic foot. This accessory equipment is necessary to avoid jamming or stalling while processing large amounts of wastepaper. Because the unit's photoelectric eye may not recognize the high density of these papers, too much material may tumble into the hopper area for the ram to compress at one time.

Closed-door horizontal balers are available in different sizes, producing bales ranging from 42 to 72 in in length, with cross sections ranging from 24 × 24 in to 48 × 48 in. Often, the desired throughput as well as the material to be processed help determine a particular baler's size and features. For example, a machine with a large feed opening would lend itself more to baling bulky cardboard than to baling paper trim.

New closed-door horizontal balers start in price at about $12,000 and can cost as much as $60,000, depending on motor and cylinder size. Motor size varies from 5 to 50 hp, while the cylinder size runs from 4 to 10 in. As with vertical balers, cylinder size and system pressure determine ram pressure, while motor size and pump assembly dictate the cycle time.

Closed-door unit maintenance is relatively easy and inexpensive. Nevertheless, proper use of the machine is essential. Because of the amount of force produced by the machine, misuse will result in substantial damage and very heavy repair costs. Note: operators should pay extra attention to the status of the "wear plates," which are attached to the bottom of the ram and the floor. Since the horizontal ram moves across the floor of the machine, this series of wear plates periodically wear out and must be replaced.

Open-End Automatic-Tie Horizontal Balers.   The open-end automatic-tie horizontal baler is similar to the closed-door manual-tie baler, but on a larger scale

(Fig. 28.4). The open-end baler operates in the same way as the closed-door baler in regards to infeed and cycling. Instead of compressing the bale against a fixed baling chamber with a door, however, the open-end baler continuously extrudes the material. The open-end baling chamber incorporates tension cylinders, which apply varying degrees of pressure against the baling chamber walls. These tension cylinders are extended during bale compression until the correct bale density is determined by the unit's pressure setting. At this point, the tension cylinders ease their pressure, allowing the compressed formation to escape. To maintain a continuous process, an automatic tying mechanism wraps and ties wire around the emerging bale. Like the closed-door balers, the open-ended versions produce their bales through a series of laminations which push more material into the bale with each ram stroke.

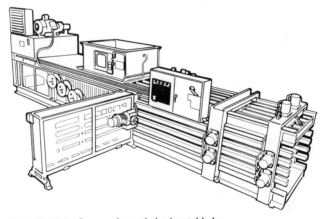

FIGURE 28.4 Open-end autotie horizontal baler.

Open-end balers excel in continuous, large-scale applications, such as box plants or large wastepaper plants. Like closed-door balers, open-end balers are often accessorized with shredders or conditioners to prepare material for baling.

Open-end units feature motors ranging in size from 20 to up to 150 hp. Cylinder sizes commonly range from 6 to 12 in, while smaller sizes are rare. Open-end unit feed openings differ according to need, from 30 × 30 in to 48 × 72 in. Likewise, baling sizes vary. Of course, since the final bale is extruded continuously, the machine's operator determines the bale length.

Due to larger motor sizes, the operational costs of these machines is somewhat higher than the previously mentioned balers. Also, these units' maintenance procedures and costs reflect their more sophisticated technology (automatic tying system, tension cylinders). Labor costs and processing times are lower, however, due to the automatic tying system.

Two-Ram Horizontal Balers.   Two-ram horizontal balers were designed in the late sixties for very large-scale baling without any preparation via a shredder or conditioner. As the name implies, this type of baler incorporates two rams: one to compress the material from the feed opening into the compression chamber in a series of laminations and a second side ram to laterally eject the bale (Fig. 28.5).

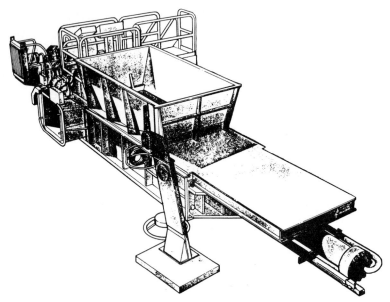

FIGURE 28.5   Two-ram horizontal baler.

In addition, these machines feature a shear-knife assembly where the ram and baling chamber are fitted with large blades. Thus, the movement of the ram creates a scissorslike action, which slices excess material protruding from the hopper area into clean, even bales. As with the open-end balers, the bale is then neatly wire-tied via an automatic tying system.

Two-ram balers are ideal for large-scale waste operations, where a wide variety of materials are processed. They will easily bale aluminum cans, cardboard, wastepaper, plastic, and steel scrap.

As with other types of balers, two-ram balers are available in different sizes and with different features. Motor sizes range from 50 to as high as 300 hp. Main ram cylinder sizes typically run from 10 to 18 in, while the ejector ram cylinders are usually between 8 and 14 in in diameter. Feed openings are large, normally 5 ft wide by 5 to 10 ft long. Depending on the unit, two-ram balers cost between $120,000 and $500,000.

Two-ram balers are versatile machines. Due to their large feed openings and motor sizes, they can handle a formidable variety of recyclables, provided there is an abundant supply of material to be processed. It is possible for a two-ram baler to actually process materials faster than an operator can feed it. For this reason, an infeed conveyor is often necessary.

Compared to other balers, two-ram units are expensive to run and maintain. Higher horsepower means higher energy cost. Nevertheless, throughput capacity is also greater. Thus, a two-ram unit's operating cost per ton of material is usually more economical.

Also, these machines are susceptible to a high degree of wear and tear when processing materials on a large-scale. This is illustrated by the periodic replacement of the metal wear plates lining the hopper area, baling chamber, and the ram faces. These metal plates eventually wear down, and new plates must be welded or bolted onto the surfaces.

CONVEYORS

Conveyors set the pace, so to speak, at most processing centers. They move recyclables from one point to another, facilitating the flow of unloading, sorting, processing, bundling, and finally, transportation or storage. Conveyors ensure that this flow is constant.

Different types of conveyors serve many different industries, but for recycling purposes only two types are prominent—the slider-bed conveyor and the direct-drive conveyor. Slider-bed conveyors are usually smaller and less powerful than direct-drive conveyors. Both types have their advantages and disadvantages, and it's important that the right conveyor be used for the right situation.

Slider-Bed Conveyors

A slider-bed conveyor is basically a belt that runs a certain length between two or more pulleys—from a few feet to hundreds of feet (Fig. 28.6). The recyclable material sits on the belt, which moves along as the pulleys turn. A motor turns the pulley via a reducer unit, which is a geared mechanism that applies torque to the pulleys. A frame system holds the motor, reducer, belt, and pulleys secure.

FIGURE 28.6   Slider-bed conveyor.

The slider-bed conveyor incorporates a rubber or synthetic belt, stretched taut, running the length of the conveyor. These conveyors rely on friction between the head pulley or driveshaft and the belt to provide movement for the conveyor.

Drive units are located either near the discharge end or in the middle of the conveyor belt. The discharge or "head-shaft" unit, consisting of a motor and reducer unit, powers the conveyor from the point where it expels its material. Thus, the motorized unit pulls the belt upward. The middle location or "center-drive" unit drives the conveyor from beneath the middle of the conveyor's length.

One of the advantages of the center-drive system is that it keeps the drive unit away from contaminates on the surface of the belt. In a recycling operation, materials such as broken glass or liquid can quickly end up in the drive unit. With a drive unit near the conveyor's discharge area, that is more likely to occur. Unfortunately, there isn't always enough room to accommodate a center drive on the underside of a conveyor. Also, a center-drive unit is usually more expensive than a head-shaft unit.

Slider-bed-type conveyors will feed both small and large processing applications, but they are better suited for the smaller. For instance, a slider-bed conveyor with a 12-in-wide belt is ideal for feeding a glass crusher or can flattener. On a larger scale, however, such as a 48-in-wide belt feeding up and into a baler, heavy loads might present difficulties because the system relies on tension to keep the belts moving forward. A heavy load of waste materials might cause too much friction, causing belt slippage or even nonmovement.

An important consideration with slider-belt conveyors is the type of belt and belt thickness being used in the system. For some materials, cleated belting may be necessary. Cleats are the upraised backstops on a belt surface that keep material from sliding backward.

Belts should be of a sufficient thickness, especially when processing commingled materials. As with the drive unit, broken glass will get under the belt and slowly wear it down, as well as the steel bed that the belt slides across.

The amount of materials that are allowed to creep under the belt can be greatly diminished by means of "troughing" the conveyor bed. With troughing, the sides of the steel bedframe, and thus the belt running over it, are turned upward, so that the material being transported tumbles toward the center of the belt. This cuts down on the amount of belt surface area that transports material, however. Some units feature side skirting, where the conveyor frame sidewalls overlap the belt, holding it in place and keeping material from getting under the belt. Other units feature corrugated belt sidewalls. Thus, any residue, such as broken glass, is kept from getting under the belt and is expelled with the rest of the material.

Slider-belt conveyors are generally less expensive than direct-drive conveyors. Prices are from $1000 or more, depending on length, motor size, reducer size, and belt width. Nevertheless, a slider-belt conveyor is maintenance-intensive and incurs a lot of wear and tear.

Aside from periodically lubricating the bearings and shaft assemblies, the majority of maintenance involves the belt, which inevitably stretches. Once the belt has stretched, the operator must adjust its tension via the shaft assemblies. This stretching often leads to belt "walking," or shifting heavily to one side or the other. A walking belt quickly results in frayed edges or a torn belt, as the side of the belt rubs against the metal frame. Some innovative features are available which diminish the effects of stretching. One method is the "crowned pulley," where the pulley turning the conveyor belt is tapered slightly lower on its ends than in its center. This serves to add tension to the belt center, so that it doesn't shift easily to either side. Another means of avoiding belt shifting is a guide tab in the bottom of the belt that fits into a notch running the length of the frame bed.

Direct-Drive Conveyors

Direct-drive conveyors excel at moving heavy loads in large quantities; slider-bed conveyors move hundreds of pounds of material an hour, but direct-drive units move thousands of pounds (Fig. 28.7). These qualities are ideal for large recycling facilities and transfer stations, especially for transporting material up and into large compactors and balers. Normally, a direct-drive conveyor will cost more than a similar-sized slider-bed conveyor, and they are often custom built. Usually, a direct-drive unit will be built recessed into the ground, with a long, flat loading section between 10 and 100 ft long. Material is pushed across the floor and onto the belt. The conveyor then carries the material up an incline and toward wherever it is feeding.

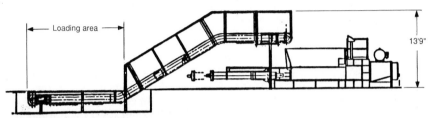

FIGURE 28.7   Direct-drive conveyor.

These conveyors feature a chain and sprocket system to drive the conveyor. This alleviates the slippage that slider-bed conveyors experience under heavy loads, as neither friction nor belt tautness are involved.

The belts are usually composed of steel segments, connected together in an interlocking "piano hinge" fashion. Variations on the steel belt usually involve rubber, with a steel subframe beneath for support. Steel belts are preferable for more abrasive applications, such as commingled materials, wastepaper, metals, and solid wastes. Both types incorporate chains on both sides of the belt, which mesh with drive and tail sprockets.

The most important belt and chain maintenance concerns are cleaning and lubrication. Chain lubrication and cleaning should take place at least once a week, if not more often. Nowadays, most conveyors can be outfitted with an automatic lubrication system. These systems feature an oil reservoir that lubricates the chain via brushes or valves when the conveyor moves.

Chain design is an important aspect of the conveyor system. Some chain systems incorporate a roller assembly, so that the belt and chain move easily over the frame bed without dragging. Other chain systems do not incorporate rollers, however, and rely on the motor's horsepower to drag the belt over a high-density plastic-lined frame bed. Although chains without rollers are less expensive, they are not conducive to heavy load factors. In a heavy load situation, such as a commingled recycling plant, a chain-driven conveyor system is subject to high wear and tear. In one case at a transfer station, a conveyor's frame bed had to be replaced after only 18 months, because it was not equipped with rollers. As is so often the case with recycling machinery, a bit more money in the initial investment far outweighs potential future repair expenses due to inadequate equipment.

Depending on the application, direct-drive conveyors vary in width from 24 in to 10 ft. In addition, one can choose between different chain types, chain sizes, motor sizes, and reducer sizes, according to the desired carrying capacity. Carrying capacity is an important consideration. At any given time, with the belt loaded with material from base to discharge point, the conveyor should be able to transport its load, starting from a stationary position.

Conveyor purchasers should make sure that a system's frame will adequately support the belt when it is fully loaded. A smart option is a series of "load bars" or "impact bars." These bars run the length of a conveyor and provide support beneath the belt. Load bars keep a belt from deflecting downward while under a heavy load. Usually the underside of the steel belt is outfitted with a small piece of metal called a "wear shoe" so that the belt is not riding directly on the load bar.

Prices for direct-drive conveyors run from $15,000 and up, depending on the conveyor length, width, motor size, and accessory features as described above.

SHREDDERS

Shredders, as their name implies, digest a vast array of objects into much smaller pieces. These objects include scrap metal, plastic, aluminum, and wood. The shredder's versatile "diet" has led to its use in other areas besides recycling. For example, they now serve in construction and demolition for breaking down building materials. On a small scale, this often involves confidential papers or store coupons. On a larger scale, shredders destroy damaged or used products that could be redistributed under a warranty claim. Shredders come in a variety of shapes and sizes, from portable paper shredders to huge shredders that devour flattened automobiles at the rate of one per minute. One of the advantages of shredders is that their by-products fill other needs, such as shredded newspaper for animal bedding or wood chips for a garden or compost.

All the different shredders in use today can be classified into two different categories: high-speed, low-torque versions and low-speed, high-torque versions.

High-Speed, Low-Torque Shredders

The first category, high-speed, low-torque, incorporates a single shaft with either fixed knives or swinging knives and hammers rotating at very high speeds (Fig. 28.8). These speeds vary between 1000 and 3500 r/min, although the latter is somewhat extreme. These knives or hammers work against either a grate through which shredded materials pass or a stationary bedknife assembly. Shredded materials include aluminum cans, used beverage containers, paper scrap, and, as previously mentioned, automobiles.

A high-speed shredder pulverizes whatever it is fed. It relies on brute force and is very noisy. High-horsepower motors are essential, meaning 50 hp and up. Accordingly, electrical costs can be astronomical, and customers are well advised to analyze potential operating costs.

There are possible hazards with high-speed shredders. First of all, because materials are so heavily pulverized, a high-speed unit can produce a lot of dust. This creates a potential fire hazard. Should a knife or hammer hit a metal object, such as a nail, and produce a spark, the dust in the air could ignite immediately. Also, jam-ups could spell disaster. Should a high-speed shredder encounter an object that it cannot cut through, there is no reverse or overload setting. Some-

FIGURE 28.8   High-speed, low-torque shredder: (*a*) with grate; (*b*) without grate.

thing has to give way, either the material or the revolving shaft. Preferably, the machine will simply jam up, although shafts have been known to break. Should this occur, one must open the machine and remove the object. Although repair may not be necessary, this removal step consumes time.

Of course, both high- and low-speed shredders are maintenance-intensive due to their violent type of work. With a high-speed shredder, maintenance involves periodically turning the hammers or knives. Usually, knives are double-sided. Once both sides are worn down, however, one must either replace them or resurface them. Resurfacing entails rewelding a work surface on the knives, followed by resharpening to a cutting edge.

Low-Speed, High-Torque Shredders

Low-speed, high-torque machines utilize two or more shafts with protruding teeth (Fig. 28.9). The shafts rotate counter to each other. These machines require lower horsepower to shred because they apply higher torque, via gear reduction, to the shafts. One could say that high-torque shredders are more subtle than their high-speed counterparts, methodically puncturing and ripping rather than blindly slashing and pulverizing. This sort of design is perfect for shredding tires, due to the tires' high resiliency.

Of course, low-speed shredders require less horsepower than high-speed units. Motor sizes are usually below 100 hp and sometimes even below 50 hp. Additionally, low-speed machines can respond to jam situations. Should someone overload the unit, the motor has the ability to sense, through an overload relay, that it is drawing too much amperage. The unit then reverses itself to clear the jam and again reverses itself in an attempt to recut the material. Should a series of reversals fail to process the overload, the machine will shut itself off and indicate an overload situation.

Another advantage to low-speed shredders is less noise. The machines will run at under 80 db, usually below the industry levels that require earphones. High torque and lower speeds also eliminate huge amounts of dust, greatly reducing the fear of spontaneous combustion.

The spectrum of shredder sizes and prices in the market is very broad, ranging from $2500 paper shredders to huge $500,000 scrap metal units. For

FIGURE 28.9   Low-speed, high-torque shredder.

general recycling facilities, however, a good guideline would be: low-speed shredders cost between $25,000 and $250,000 and high-speed units between $50,000 and $500,000. The main thing is to realize one's precise needs. Needs mean size, type, and amount of material to shred; operating speed; and particle size after shredding. Sometimes this requires a combination of shredders rather than just one unit, where the operator shreds the material and then reshreds the output. The more specific the need, the easier it is to determine the type of shredder. For example, those who are planning on shredding tires should ask questions such as, "Auto or truck tires?" And even then: "Will these be regular or radial tires," and "What is the desired throughput and particle size?"

This is not to say that one shredder cannot process a multitude of different materials. But, it's more prudent to determine as specifically as possible the main use of a shredder. Also, it would be a wise move to study that shredded material's market before making a substantial investment.

COMPACTORS

Compactors became popular in the 1960s, as a reaction to increased hauling and disposal rates. At that time, businesses began searching for a more effective way to dispose of their wastes. The answer was the compactor.

Stationary and Self-Contained Compactors

The first stationary compactors compressed material into roll-off boxes, large metal structures usually measuring 8 × 8 × 22 ft (Fig. 28.10). When enough material was accumulated that no more could be added, a hauler detached the box and hauled it away to a landfill.

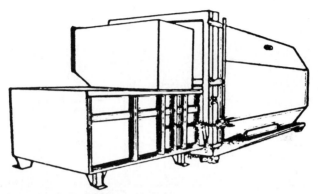

FIGURE 28.10 Stationary compactor.

This system was ideal for dry wastes. Some industries, such as restaurants and hospitals, disposed of partial liquid wastes, however. This presented problems. Because the compactor was separate from the container, liquid waste resulted in spills and residue. This residue left an odor and often attracted animals and insects. Consequently, the self-contained compactor was introduced (Fig. 28.11).

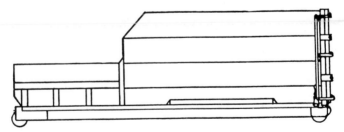

FIGURE 28.11 Self-contained compactor.

Self-contained compactors were simply a compactor and a roll-off box housed together on the same platform. For hauling, the electrical power unit was separated from the assembly. These self-contained units included a liquid retention area underneath the compactor to prevent spillage.

Vertical Compactors

Within the last decade, the market has seen the introduction of a third type of compactor, the vertical compactor (Fig. 28.12). This type of compactor is ideal for low-volume applications, and where space is limited.

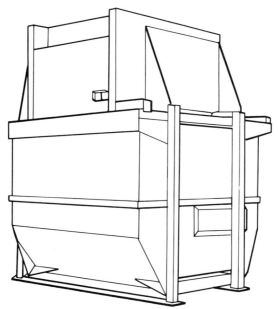

FIGURE 28.12   Vertical compactor.

Today, all three types of compactors offer a wide range of choices for individual recycling and disposal programs. But, as with all recycling machinery, customers should precisely identify their needs before purchasing a compactor. All too often, customers buy the wrong unit for their situations. Usually, these choices result from hasty decisions based on misleading advice. There are four basic criteria that one should address before purchasing a compactor: the desired compaction force; the density of the final product; the feed opening size; and the amount of necessary receiving and container storage space.

The first two criteria are synonymous with the terms "compression ratio" and "capacity." Compression ratio measures the before and after effects of a compactor on its material. Thus, a compactor with a 4-to-1 compression ratio will produce material that is four times more compressed than before it was processed. Generally, stationary compactors have a compression ratio of 4 to 1, self-contained units ratios are 3 or 4 to 1, while vertical compactors' ratios are only 2 or 3 to 1. Of course, these are only guidelines. Actual results will depend on the type of material being compacted.

A compactor manufacturer measures its machines' processing capacity in cubic yards. This yardage does not indicate the amount of material processed into the receiving container. Rather, yardage refers to the amount of material that a compactor can receive and process in one stroke. This measurement is not precise, however. For instance, a 2-yd^3 compactor may only actually process 1½ yd^3 of material. That is because this capacity represents an approximation established by the manufacturer. Because manufacturers' ratings are so inconsistent, the National Solid Waste Management Association (NSWMA) established compactor rating guidelines. Therefore, when comparing compactor processing capacities, one should always consider the NSWMA ratings.

Receiving container space is rated by the amount of cubic yards it can contain. One can find nearly any size container for a given situation. One size compactor can be coupled with several different-sized containers, depending on the amount of material to be processed and the anticipated hauling frequency.

One might feel that the easiest decision is to choose the largest container possible and haul as little as possible. Unfortunately, with applications such as restaurants, nursing homes, and hospitals, this would contribute to odors and pest problems.

The compactor uses hydraulics in a manner similar to the baler. The size of the cylinder and system pressure determine the compression level. Also, as with balers, the market offers a large variety of motor and hydraulic cylinder sizes. The amount and type of material to be processed should determine the correct horsepower and cylinder size.

Stationary compactors range in capacity from a ½ yd^3 to 12 yd^3. The smaller-capacity compactors are ideal for apartment buildings and hospitals, where they are chute-fed. Often, such units are housed in old incinerator rooms and incorporate a photoelectric relay to start compaction when enough material has accumulated. The receiving container may only hold 2 yd^3 of material and require daily hauling.

Another common compactor is the 2-yd^3 compactor, which is usually coupled with a 40-ft receiving container. One typically finds these units behind large department stores, mall areas, and medium-sized businesses.

Compactors of 6- to 12-yd^3 capacity are designed for very large applications, such as transfer stations. In these applications, a fleet of collection trucks deposits waste in a tipping area. The material is pushed across a floor with a front-end loader into the compactor. From there the material makes its way to landfills in large transfer trailers. Stationary compactors cost between $5000 and $25,000, although large transfer units can cost over $100,000.

Self-contained compactors generally have smaller feed openings and thus smaller capacities. This is the result of both compactor and receiver being contained in one unit. Feed opening sizes are limited to 2-yd^3 and under, while overall unit length doesn't exceed 24 ft. These units' receiving container capacities are usually 36 yd^3. Self-contained units list for between $10,000 and $20,000, depending on size and optional features.

Vertical units feature similar-capacity compactors as self-contained units. Their receiving containers are smaller, from 3 to 8 yd^3. Of course, one doesn't purchase a vertical compactor for its capacity, but rather, for its size.

Vertical compactors are markedly less effective than other compactors. As mentioned earlier, compression ratios do not exceed 2 or 3 to 1. This is because vertical compactors exchange smaller motor and hydraulic features for size convenience. Prices for these units are in the $6000 to $9000 range.

All compactors require a firm concrete foundation. Softer foundations, such as asphalt, are simply incompatible. The weight and motion of the compactor will cause the unit to literally sink into the asphalt.

The uses of compactors need not be limited to traditional waste hauling. The machines often prove ideal in recycling facilities for processing commingled residue. After sorting, each material can be loaded into its respective compactor for storage while awaiting processing, or for transportation to another site.

Because compactors are so diverse, they are also ideal for industrial-plant recycling programs. A plant can often substitute a compactor for a baling system. Some large car plants and distribution centers have incorporated two compactors: one to process industrial residues and one to prepare cardboard for recycling. In this situation, the key is to identify a nearby papermill or wastepaper dealer who will accept the compressed cardboard in receiving containers.

GLASS CRUSHERS

Glass crushers pulverize all types of glass, usually containers, into the gravel-size pieces called *cullet*. Cullet is a preferable form of glass for recyclers because it is denser. This fluid form simplifies transportation and is furnace-ready. Thus, glass companies more readily accept cullet because it is one step further along in the meltdown process.

There are several different types of glass crushers on the market today. These vary in complexity from a simple sledgehammer and 55-gal drum device to sophisticated conveyor-fed units. The latter types incorporate conveyors which drop material onto either a set of rotating blades, a rotating hexagonal drum, or a series of rotating chains. There are several brands of conveyor-fed glass crushers offered on the market today, and prices range from $2500 to $5000 (Fig. 28.13).

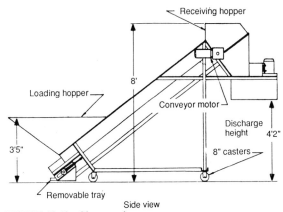

FIGURE 28.13 Glass crusher.

Conveyor-fed glass-crushing units are electrical. The motors are small, usually under 4 hp. Because glass is such an abrasive material, these machines require periodic crushing mechanism replacements. As with shredders, part replacement and careful maintenance come with the territory.

CAN FLATTENERS AND BLOWERS

Can flatteners are a means of flattening beverage cans for ease of handling and transportation (Fig. 28.14). Most machines are geared toward aluminum can flat-

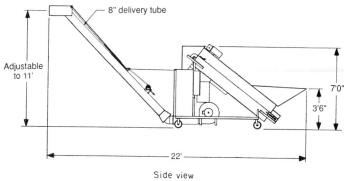

Side view

FIGURE 28.14 Can flattener.

tening because aluminum has a higher value. Can flatteners are coveyor-fed and they use a magnetic charge to separate aluminum cans from steel and bimetal cans. The magnet is contained in the head pulley of the conveyor. As the materials pass around the head pulley, ferrous containers remain on the belt. Aluminum containers, which aren't magnetically attracted, simply fall into the flattening device. After the other cans pass around the head pulley, they fall into a reject chute underneath the conveyor.

Once in the flattening area, the aluminum cans are crushed either by a wheel rolling against a stationary plate or two wheels counterrotating against each other. Following this operation, the flattened cans are simply expelled into a blowing tube. This tube transports the cans up into a storage bin via a strong current of air.

As with glass crushers, there are several manufacturers of can flatteners in the market today. The market prices for a can flattener with blower range between $5000 and $10,000. Most brands feature motor sizes under 10 hp. Since the process is abrasive, identifying which units are most durable is an important concern. Maintenance for these units consists mainly of lubrication. While the machine may not be as maintenance-intensive as a shredder, for example, one should routinely inspect the unit's condition.

Most can flatteners today are manufactured to process aluminum but not steel, because the head roller is magnetic and difficult to change. Even without the magnet, one encounters difficulties with oversized institutional cans. The problem is that the can will not fit into the crushing mechanisms and will simply bounce around above them as they turn. Fortunately, some manufacturers are creating units specifically for steel cans.

CAN DENSIFIERS

For large-scale recycling operations, a more practical method of processing steel and aluminum cans is the can densifier (Fig. 28.15). The can densifier forms the cans into a brick that weighs about 18 lb and measures a cubic foot (14 × 12 × 8 in) in dimension. These bricks are stacked on a skid for transportation to an aluminum smelter or metals-processing facility.

At one time, metal companies paid a premium for the more densely packed material, because it was furnace-ready. Correspondingly, densifiers grew in pop-

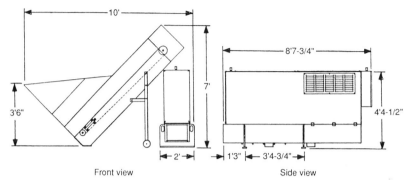

FIGURE 28.15 Can densifier.

ularity. Today, the premium is no longer the rule but the exception. The metal companies began to find impurities in the blocks of material. Also, there were sometimes high moisture contents in the materials, due to the cans' previous contents. Flattened cans usually have lower moisture content after being transported through an air blower and stored in trailers. If the materials have too high a moisture content, aluminum companies will deduct a percentage for moisture. Since the metal companies could not perfectly ensure quality control, the companies discontinued their premiums.

Can densifiers are similar to horizontal balers. Their large cylinders apply tremendous pressure to the cans. The ram faces are specially configured to indent each cube. These indents allow a steel banding to be wrapped around a skid full of cubes. Thus, cubes are uniformly banded and easily stacked.

Another consideration with densifiers is the high volume of cans that are required to form a dense cube. This means that shipments may be somewhat sporadic, affecting an operation's cash flow.

Densifier maintenance is very similar to that of a horizontal baler. Older densifiers have a lot of moving parts and hoppers which require a good deal of maintenance. Today's units, however, are generally very efficient and easy to operate and maintain.

ALLIGATOR SHEARS

An alligator shear is a large machine for cutting metal (Fig. 28.16). A hydraulic cylinder moves the shears up and down when an operator pushes down on a foot pedal. The shear is used to cut and prepare miscellaneous pieces of metal, such as plumbing valves or aluminum siding, for further processing. Most commonly, scrap metal yards rely on these machines for preparing large amounts of material.

Formerly, alligator shears operated continuously through a fly-wheel assembly. Materials were fed through the rapidly moving blades. Unfortunately, the machines had no safety features, and losses of limbs and lives occurred. Today, these shears incorporate a foot pedal and hydraulics in order to ensure safety. These features have also led to higher prices, and today alligator shears start at $9000 and go up to $30,000 or more, depending on size.

FIGURE 28.16   Alligator shear.

Both blade and cylinder sizes are variable. Blades lengths start at 4 in for small valve-processing applications, and continue on up to 36 in.

HIGH-TECH MACHINERY

The term "high tech" here describes those "cutting-edge" processes that are past the development stage and yet aren't in widespread use. One of the most promising recycling developments today involves the automatic separation of aluminum, plastics, and glass.

Eddy Current Separator

An eddy current separator is a device that applies an eddy current, or magnetic field, to commingled recyclables on a conveyor line (Fig. 28.17). This current repels aluminum the way two magnets repel each other. When applied to mixed material, the eddy current separator will quickly and efficiently remove all aluminum from the other materials more efficiently, perhaps, than humans. In the sort term, however, the cost of the eddy current system is considerably higher than labor costs: between $80,000 and $150,000.

On the other hand, potential buyers will need to weigh the economical aspects. Sorting commingled material is an unskilled, low-paying occupation with a high turnover rate. Eddy current separators do not quit their jobs or fail to show up for work. Nor do they file workers' compensation claims or require heavy insurance. And, as this technology progresses, less and less expensive versions of the system should appear on the market.

Eddy current systems will probably play a large role in commingled separa-

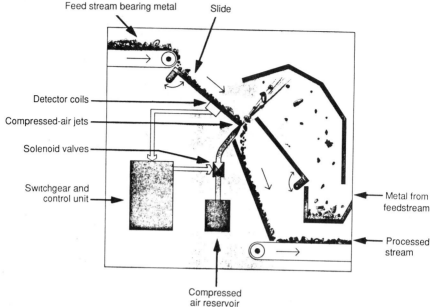

FIGURE 28.17   Eddy current separator.

tion, but the verdict is still out, as the machines haven't existed long enough to precisely establish operating costs or production rates.

Optical Color Screening

Another recently developed recycling technology is the sorting of plastics and glass based on optical screening. In the case of glass, the sorting is by color—green, brown, and clear. Traditionally, this job was carried out by workers on an assemblylike conveyor line. Needless to say, this type of work is also tedious. Reliable workers generally don't stick around a long time. Once again, it's too early to tell if the system will justify its costs. The technology is considered in its prototype stages. A good estimate of future prices for such a system would be in the $250,000 to $300,000 range.

Some potential drawbacks exist with optical glass sorting. First, if glass is dirty or stained, the optical sorter may provide a false reading. A clear glass container might be sorted in with the brown glass. Second, these glass objects must pass by the sorter in a single-file configuration. This proves tricky and time consuming when dealing with huge quantities of containers in different sizes and shapes.

A similar system for sorting plastic containers is being developed. Plastics are sorted by chemical composition: PET, HDPE, and PVC. As with glass, the optical sorting system will determine the makeup of a container and sort accordingly. At this stage, the system is in the prototype phase. Future price estimates are similar to those of glass-sorting systems. It is estimated that only large-scale operations (10 tons per hour or more) could justify such costly high-tech expenditures.

Mini MRF

The mini MRF (materials recovery facility) system is a recent development geared toward lower-volume facilities. The system processes commingled materials with a minimum of labor. This process incorporates product size separation, magnetic separation of aluminum and steel, and air separation of plastics from heavier glass. Still, the final sorting relies on visual inspection.

Currently, these small systems are available and being heavily advertised in trade publications. They cost between $75,000 and $300,000, depending on size and options.

The market for high-tech recycling equipment is still very young. In order for it to "mature," purchasers must possess precise, accurate figures, such as cost and output of the new equipment versus its labor, insurance, and compensation costs. Only then can a buyer justify purchasing such technology.

A final word that cannot be stressed enough: before buying a piece of equipment, know the reputation of its manufacturer and distributor. Resources are available to buyers. Customers should ask questions such as "Does the manufacturer conform to standards set by the American National Standards Institute, for balers and compactors? Is the manufacturer's equipment approved by Underwriter's Laboratory? Does the manufacturer carry product liability insurance? And, what is the company's history and financial status?"

Because recycling is the upcoming growth industry for the nineties, we are witnessing exciting innovations in processes and technology.

CHAPTER 29
RECYCLING PROGRAM PLANNING AND IMPLEMENTATION

Thomas A. Jones, Jr.
Waste Recovery and Recycling Specialist
R. W. Beck and Associates
Waltham, Massachusetts

The planning and implementation of a recycling program, like the proverbial team of blindpersons describing an elephant, can be a complex and frustrating endeavor. Complex because most recycling programs have many parts; frustrating because often the parts do not appear related to one another. Composting yard waste is at least as different from marketing glass as a pachyderm's ear is from its trunk.

Planning and implementation call for expertise in commodity markets, engineering, public finance, environmental law, and many other areas. This chapter focuses on three areas which will be important to a potential recycling program developer: (1) program planning and development, (2) staffing, and (3) financing. Because most multimaterial recycling programs are developed by the public sector, the chapter assumes this perspective.

PROGRAM PLANNING AND DEVELOPMENT

Too often planning seems to be the refuge of bureaucrats and consultants. Acres of forests have been leveled to provide paper for "planning documents" that are now gathering dust in municipal closets. The first point to be made is that the purpose of planning is not to produce a written document. The effort made to plan must be appropriate to the activity. A walk on the beach does not require a feasibility report. On the other hand, building a material recovery facility requires more than some back-of-the-envelope calculations. Properly done, planning should make an activity easier, more efficient, and even more enjoyable.

One purpose of this section of the chapter is to describe the planning process for a municipal recycling program. It is intended to take the reader from that heady conceptual stage, when the ideas for program activities are developed on paper, through the development of a comprehensive recycling program. It also includes some discussion about how programs are updated over time. Since recycling programs come in all shapes and sizes, the section highlights four critical steps which are common to all programs. A separate subsection is devoted to each step.

The first subsection describes the "idea" stage, where the goals and broad concepts of program options are developed. A community that is contemplating the development of a recycling program faces a wide variety of options, in terms of program components and operations. Although recycling is an ancient and well-established activity, large-scale municipal programs are a relatively recent phenomenon. The chapter outlines the elements which many existing municipal programs now include.

The second subsection focuses on evaluating program options. The Seattle Recycling Potential Assessment (RPA) model, a sophisticated computer model, is used to provide a concrete example of a planning methodology. At this stage of program planning ideas are weighed against each other and the conceptual begins to become real. The third subsection, still using Seattle's RPA model, discusses the overall plan, that is, the choice of options based on overall program goals and available resources. It is here that the dynamic nature of program planning is critical.

The fourth and final subsection describes the development of a schedule. That is, the logically ordered work tasks must be assigned a duration, and be allocated resources. There are a range of approaches to this function, from a loose, plan-as-you-go approach to a more rigorous quantitative approach, such as the Critical Path Method (CPM) or Performance Evaluation and Review Technique (PERT). The rigor a municipality applies to its planning effort will be determined by a number of factors which are also discussed in this final section.

The product of this planning effort should be a program set within the constraints of time and available resources. The plan should provide guidance to the staff, the community leaders, and the citizens.

The first part of the chapter is a general introduction to the planning process and deals broadly with important planning issues. However, it may not provide the necessary amount of detail for a particular community. For this reason, references to specific programs and other sources of information are included throughout the chapter.

Mandatory versus Voluntary Recycling

The question of whether a community should require recycling or not is rapidly being answered by state legislation. As of January 1, 1991, 28 states had mandated recycling, and municipalities in these states must enact programs to meet state guidelines. By the end of 1991, several more states will be added to this list. A few states, such as Massachusetts, cannot mandate recycling, but have enacted waste bans which prohibit certain materials, such as yard waste, cardboard, and newspaper, from landfills and combustion facilities by specified dates. Municipalities in these states must develop recycling programs or face penalties for violating the waste bans.

For communities not affected by state-mandated recycling legislation or waste bans, the issue of whether the recycling program will be mandatory or voluntary should be addressed early in the planning process. Successful programs of either type will have strong public education and promotion. They will also be convenient, offering residents and businesses a relatively easy way to place materials out for collection. No community can expect mandated recycling to replace convenience or public education. They must go hand in hand. The components of a convenient collection program and an effective public education program are described below.

Given a convenient, well-publicized program, voluntary recycling has achieved very high participation rates. Typical mandatory programs may be slightly more successful, but they also incur the cost of enforcement, in the form of recycling inspectors who check to see that trash does not contain recyclable material and lawyers who defend court challenges. Penalties may range from the town's refusal to pick up trash which contains recyclables to a system of graduated fines.

In some instances, communities have passed mandatory recycling legislation but have chosen not to enforce it. This allows the town to show they are serious about recycling without immediately incurring the cost of enforcement. If participation is disappointing in spite of a vigorous public education program, the town always has the option of developing an enforcement mechanism.

As recycling has become institutionalized across the country, the debate over mandatory versus voluntary recycling has quieted. It is no longer a question of whether people should recycle, but how they will recycle.

Program Components

In order to provide some substance to the discussion which follows, the chapter begins with a discussion of some examples of program elements. No effort has been made to present the program of a specific community, or to suggest that the configuration of components presented here is the "best" one. Indeed, if the experience of communities developing recycling programs up to now shows anything, it is that recycling programs are quite site-specific. Factors, including the composition of the waste stream, the availability of secondary material markets, the economy of the region, and the political climate of the community, will influence the final shape of the program.

The discussion of the program components below is not intended to be comprehensive. These components are presented elsewhere in the Handbook in far greater detail. However, a general understanding of these components will be the foundation of the later discussion of activities and sequencing. In some cases, the options available within a component are presented, but in all cases, a general approach is recommended as a part of this typical program.

Recycling is a closed-loop process in which products which are purchased and used are then collected and reused, avoiding the cost and environmental damage associated with waste disposal. This reuse may include the reuse of the product itself, such as a book in a used book exchange, or it may include the reuse of the product material. The making of new glass from recycled cullet is an example of this.

The components of a recycling program should be viewed as links in a chain of activities which make recycling a reality for the community. Each of the links must have its own integrity, but each must also be connected to the other components of the program. The program described below contains five links: *education, collection, processing, marketing,* and *procurement.*

Education and Promotion.   The first link in this chain is an educational program. The success of a recycling program will depend to a large degree on the knowledge and enthusiasm of the residents and businesses who are participating in it. From implementation of a new program to the maintenance and development of an ongoing program, an effective program of education and promotion is critical. The program must be well-organized and accurately target its intended audience. For example, programs in Miami, Florida; New York City; and Los Angeles; as well as other large metropolitan areas, translate their written materials and spoken public services announcements into Spanish for Hispanic residents.

For our purposes, the education and promotion can be divided into five elements. First, the citizens and businesses in the service area should be given a general education in recycling. This will not only help any specific program to get under way, but it will prepare the way for additions to the program weeks or months later. Second, the specific program which has been developed must be promoted. People have to know the details. What materials will be recycled? How are the materials to be prepared? How will they be collected? Participants need to know the answer to these questions, among others. Third, there must be a means of keeping people informed about the progress of the program as it develops. Fourth, an ongoing effort at source reduction, eliminating waste altogether, should be a part of the educational component. Finally, school projects should be developed to prepare the next generation of recyclers, and to help reinforce the existing program. Together, these five facets can provide a comprehensive and effective education and promotional program.

General Public Education.   For a recycling program to work, the public must grasp a few simple principles about recycling. These principles include an understanding of the "recycling loop," the increased value of materials which have been separated and cleaned, and the importance of markets. The principles can be applied to curbside collection programs, yard waste composting programs, or tire recycling programs.

This kind of education can be accomplished through public service announcements (PSAs) on local radio and television stations, newspaper articles, speakers at service organizations, and promotional activities at community fairs. It is usually helpful if this kind of general education precedes a specific collection program. It can stimulate interest, build enthusiasm, and generate commitment.

The thrust of a general education program should come before specific programs are implemented, but there should be an ongoing effort to educate new residents and reinforce the lessons to long-time citizens.

Our typical program assumes an active general education component, particularly in the early stages of the recycling program.

Program Promotion.   Once the policy decisions have been made, the community will be ready to implement a specific recycling program. It may be a curbside collection program; it may be the opening of a drop-off facility; or it may be a multifaceted program reaching a number of different generator types. However, all programs will have certain characteristics which must be communicated to the potential participants.

It will operate within certain geographic boundaries, it will target certain materials for collection, it will require some degree of separation and preparation of materials, it will have some type of schedule, and there may be other aspects to it. For example, if it is a mandatory program, the consequences of nonparticipation should be made clear.

The most effective way of getting the specific details of the program to the potential participants is to contact them directly. This may be done through a mailing which goes to residents along with utility bills, for example, or it can be hand-delivered to homes or apartments. It is also helpful to have a "hotline" to inform residents.

Promotional material should arrive just before the implementation of the program. If it is sent out too far ahead of program implementation, people will forget, lose the information, and grow impatient. If it is sent out after the program has started, people will become confused and frustrated. The timing of this facet of the program is critical.

Progress Reports.   Once the program has begun, it is a good idea to keep citizens informed about the progress of the program. How much material has been collected? What have the revenues been? How much has been saved through avoided cost? A regular quarterly, semiannual, or annual report is a good way to provide this type of information. It should be set up on a regular schedule and use a format which is easy to understand.

Source Reduction Education.   Source reduction refers to programs which reduce the amount of waste which is created at the source which normally generates it. That is, by each individual resident or generator. The idea is to cut the amount of waste which is generated, not just recycle the waste which is produced.

Most of the efforts at source reduction are educational, and they aim at helping waste generators understand how they can reduce their waste. Commercial waste audits are conducted to show how businesses can reduce waste. Environmental shopper programs are developed to show consumers how to cut waste through more intelligent buying habits. Regional waste exchanges can assist industries in finding companies that might be interested in using certain materials that are now being thrown away.

School Programs.   The educational programs discussed above focus on the potential participants of a recycling program—residents and businesses. But there are several reasons to incorporate an educational program for children as a part of the overall program. Children are an unusually effective way to reach their parents and other relatives. A child who has been taught the importance of recycling will often convince parents who have otherwise ignored it. In addition, the continuing success of recycling will depend on an educated citizenry and teaching the next generation of citizens the importance of recycling is an excellent investment.

School programs should be an ongoing and regular part of the school's curriculum and can be integrated into a number of different disciplines, such as math, social studies, and economics.

Collection.   The second link in the recycling chain is the collection of materials. This can mean collecting the recyclable materials from residents or businesses at the curb, or having the generators drop off the materials at collection centers. Curbside collection can be accomplished in several different ways and a municipality may wish to explore a number of different options simultaneously before settling on one.

This is what Denver, Colorado, is doing. The City of Denver is running three pilot collection programs at the same time. For six months, the City of Denver is offering a three-bin curbside collection program to some residents. In this program residents separate their recyclables into three categories, usually paper, glass, and metal. These recyclables are collected in a special compartmentalized truck. The second collection program is a one-bag commingled program where all recyclables are placed in a specially marked bag which is collected with the rest of the garbage in a rear-loading packer truck. It is then taken to a central facility where it is sorted and prepared for market. The third program involves the sorting of all garbage at a mixed waste processing facility. At the end of six months, each program will be evaluated.

However, most municipalities decide on a preferred system before implementing an actual program.

Curbside Collection.   For most densely populated towns and cities, the collection of recyclables at the curb is most common. Like the collection of mixed solid waste (MSW) at the curb, the collection of recyclables may be the direct responsibility of the community's public works department, or it may be carried out by private haulers, through contracts, or through an "open market." It is important to remember that the collection of recyclables requires far more continuity than the collection of MSW. First, a specific set of materials is collected (newspaper, clear glass, aluminum cans, etc.). While all families may not place out all these materials, the collection system must be prepared to accept the targeted materials. Second, the materials must be handled in a prescribed way. They may have to be sorted at the curb by the driver, for example. Tops may have to be removed from glass bottles. Each collection vehicle must adhere to the prescribed procedure. Once the materials have been collected, they must be driven to a processing center to be prepared for market.

If the community is collecting recyclables through the department of public works or other municipal agency, it must begin planning well before the public places material on the curb. If the program is to have the materials separated at the curb, either by the resident or the driver, special recycling trucks must be evaluated and selected for purchase. Collection routes must be designed and integrated with the existing MSW collection routes. Drivers must be trained to handle the new equipment and become familiar with the new procedures.

If the collection is to be carried out by a private hauler through a contract, the type of program must be developed, competitive bids solicited and evaluated, a bidder chosen, and a contract negotiated. This process may take a year or more to complete.

Curbside programs are designed for single-family homes, or multifamily homes of three or four. For apartment complexes, another approach must be used. Most apartment recycling takes place at a central facility where residents bring their recyclables. Because the turnover of tenants is usually higher in apartment buildings than in single-family homes, public education programs are particularly important for apartment tenants.

Drop-off Centers.   In many small rural communities, recyclables may be collected at a drop-off center. Here again, a certain collection protocol must be observed. Only the targeted materials will be accepted at the drop-off center and they must be prepared and sorted in a specific way. For this type of program, the drop-off center becomes the focus of the program. It must be designed and built to accommodate not only the current needs of the community, but to handle the anticipated growth of the program. This may mean more people using the facility, or more materials accepted at some future date. Once the facility is built, it must be staffed and maintained. Records should be kept of materials collected so that progress can be monitored. Some communities, such as Buffalo, New York, offer residents a choice of either curbside collection or drop-off. This, of course, complicates the job of the planning entity in implementing the program.

Self-haul facilities may also include an area to put yard waste for composting and a "dump-and-pick" operation where recyclables are separated from other disposed trash.

The program outlined here includes both curbside collection and drop-off centers. The two programs need to be coordinated. The drop-off centers must be created and publicized, and a pilot program conducted.

Well-run drop-off programs need not be located in rural areas. One of the oldest and most successful drop-off programs in the country operates in Wellesley, Massachusetts, a suburb about 30 mi from Boston.

Processing.   Once the materials have been collected, they must be prepared for market. This is the third link in the chain. Preparation will depend on the type of material collected, the volume of material collected, the demands of the market for each material, and the arrangements for transportation between the processing center and the market. Table 29.1 shows the processing options for several sample materials.

TABLE 29.1   Material Processing Options

Material	Processing options
Newspaper	Baled or loose
Corrugated cardboard	Baled or loose
Metal cans	Crushed, baled, or loose
Glass	Crushed or loose
Plastic containers	Baled, granulated, pelletized
Tires	Shredded or whole

The processing of these materials usually takes place at a dedicated building called a materials recovery facility (MRF) or intermediate processing center (IPC). These types of facilities receive collected materials, sort them, densify them, and ship them to end-use markets.

While there are a variety of possible ownership and operating configurations, the facilities are often owned by the city and operated by a private vendor. Sometimes the city will operate the facility itself, or the facilities can be "merchant" facilities which are owned and operated by a private firm.

The processing facility is a key element of the recycling program. If the facility is to involve a private vendor, the procurement procedure must be set in motion so that the facility is ready once the materials are ready to be collected.

The coordination of the collection system and the processing facility cannot be stressed too much. The facility's receiving area must be compatible with the types of vehicles used for collection. For example, doors must be large enough to accommodate the vehicles. The degree of sorting at the curb must be assumed in the processing facility.

The materials must be prepared to meet the quality standards demanded by the end markets. This means that those standards must be well understood and agreed upon, preferably through contracts, before the facility is designed so that the processed materials will be acceptable to the end markets. If they fail to meet those standards, the entire recycling system will break down and the material will have to be landfilled.

Marketing.   The fourth link in the recycling chain is marketing. This is the selling of processed materials to an end-use market. Each targeted material will have a separate market with its own price, quality standards, and characteristic fluctuations. For example, newsprint will be sold to a newspaper broker or directly to a mill. The buyer will demand that the paper be relatively free of contaminants and other types of paper when it is delivered. The price will fluctuate depending on a number of factors, including export demand, current supply, and the general strength of the domestic economy.

Every material which the city plans to collect must have a market. In most cases, it will be possible to obtain contracts for the material, although in some areas where markets are soft, strong contracts for some materials will not be available. In these cases, the city must decide whether or not it wishes to accept the risk of collecting and processing these materials in hopes of selling them without a contract.

Procurement.   The final link in the recycling chain, and one which is often overlooked, is procurement. The willingness of end-use markets to take material is directly tied to demand for products made from recycled materials. If no one demands newsprint made from recycled fiber, the newsprint mills have little incentive to produce it. On the other hand, if there is a substantial demand, the mills will be actively looking for sources of recycled fiber.

Procurement policies can be developed for two kinds of products. For products which are directly consumed by the city, such as office paper, the city can develop purchasing guidelines which specify that these products must contain a certain amount of recycled material. For example, the city can require that office paper must contain a certain percentage of postconsumer office waste.

The city may develop a closed-loop recycling program where it consumes products it creates. For example, it may use a tub grinder to process construction and demolition debris and then use the resulting aggregate in its own paving and building projects.

The city may also encourage businesses within its jurisdiction to "buy recycled," thereby building up the demand for recycled products. Local newspapers can be urged to use recycled newsprint and plastic fabricators can be urged to use recycled plastic scrap.

Evaluating Program Options: Seattle's Planning Model

It has already been pointed out that the rigor and formality of the planning process varies widely. In Canada's Province of Ontario, the planning process is becoming more rigorous through the efforts of the provincial government, which has been moving to formalize the planning process since the enactment of the Environmental Assessment Act in 1975. It is likely that a number of planning guidelines will be passed down from the province to individual municipalities.

Formalized planning is often found in metropolitan areas such as Seattle, Washington, and San Jose, California, which have large complex programs. Small cities typically use a less formal approach. For example, Loveland, Colorado, a city of 40,000 people north of Denver, has created it program by listening carefully to its own citizens, surveying programs in other parts of the country to see what is working, and "using common sense."

Planning for recycling must involve an examination of all components of the solid waste management system, as well as consideration of broader public-sector issues. Recycling cannot be considered in isolation. Although the way in which such an examination is structured may differ from location to location, the components are quite widely accepted. In general, they include the jurisdiction's waste stream, recycling program options, the effect of recycling programs on disposal, and the solid waste management system costs. The number of ways this information can be arranged is manifold.

One of the most sophisticated planning models now in use is Seattle's Recycling Potential Assessment Model (RPA model). The RPA is a computer model which was developed in 1988 by the Seattle Solid Waste Utility (the "Utility") to "evaluate the feasibility and cost-effectiveness of many recycling options open to the City." It was part of a broad planning process which Seattle began when it faced the loss of its landfill. The RPA model contains four modules with input sections which provide the model with a set of common variables. The modules are solved simultaneously. The following discussion uses the Seattle RPA model as one example of how to evaluate program options.

Waste Stream Forecast. The recycling program should be built on assumptions about the quantity and composition of the waste being generated. Information on the waste stream will be used to size facilities and programs, estimate revenues from secondary material markets, and gauge the success of program goals.

A comprehensive waste stream forecast will provide the answers to three broad questions.

1. *What is the current composition of the waste stream? That is, what materials are available for recycling?*For the sake of program development, the question must be applied to various generator categories—residential, commercial, institutional, and industrial. These categories may be subdivided even further. Residential into single-family and multifamily households; commercial into offices, large retail stores, restaurants, hotels, and so on. These estimates of current waste composition may be based on four-season waste sampling programs which provide a statistically accurate estimate of the composition, or on national estimates which are applied locally. Figure 29.1 shows the estimate of the waste developed by Seattle for its RPA model in 1988. This was one of the crucial inputs to their planning process.

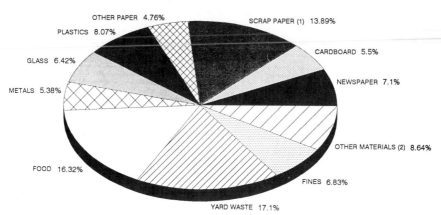

FIGURE 29.1 Seattle residential waste composition. (1) "Scrap paper" includes office and computer paper; (2) "Other materials" includes rubber, wood, diapers, textiles, leather, ash, ceramics, rocks, drywall, fiberglass, debris, and hazardous materials. (*Source: Seattle Solid Waste Utility.*)

2. How much waste is currently generated? The answer to this question is not the total number of tons delivered to the local landfill. Rather, it is total amount of waste generated, the "gross generation," which includes waste diverted from disposal through private recycling. That is, rather than discarding corrugated cardboard, some supermarkets may be collecting and baling cardboard on their own, long before a municipal recycling program has begun. The cardboard is waste, part of the gross generation of waste, but the amount of solid waste the supermarket actually sends to the landfill is its "net generation." The City of Seattle, with a strong environmental ethic, estimated that voluntary and private recycling was achieving about a 24 percent recovery rate from all waste. Knowing how much waste is generated means having an estimate of both gross and net generation. Again, knowing this for various classes of generators will help in targeting recycling programs.

3. What is going to happen in the future to the quantity and composition of the waste; that is, what social, demographic, and economic forces will affect the generation of waste and will each individual citizen become more or less wasteful? Over the past 20 years the average amount of waste generated by each American has increased. Will efforts at source reduction curb this trend? Will the population of the area increase, thereby increasing the total amount of waste to be disposed? Will the number of households and the size of households increase? Will the economic climate stimulate new businesses which will generate waste, or will it force bankruptcies and inhibit consumption, thereby decreasing the amount of waste generated? As difficult as these questions may be to answer, some estimate of future generation is necessary. Figure 29.2 shows the projections for waste generation used by Seattle in 1988 as an input for its RPA model.

The RPA model allows for different generation forecasts to be applied to different generator categories, including a forecast of private recycling. The infor-

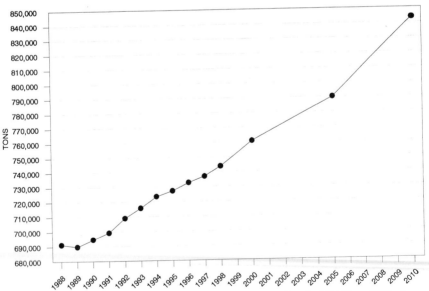

FIGURE 29.2   Seattle waste generation, 1988 to 2010. (*Source: Seattle Solid Waste Utility.*)

mation in the waste stream module is then used to evaluate the effects of various recycling programs.

Recycling Program Options.   Program options integrate elements into generator-specific and material-specific approaches. Examples would be backyard composting, curbside yard waste collection, apartment recycling, and drop-off centers. For each option, the RPA model takes participation (how many households actually use the program) and efficiency (how much material is actually diverted) as inputs.

Program costs are also inputs to this module. Costs which are not dependent on program size are fixed costs; those costs which vary with the number of participants or the number of tons collected are variable costs. These costs are developed for each program. Variable costs can be recalculated each time participation or efficiency rates are changed. To show another effect of each program on the solid waste management system, the RPA also calculates the avoided cost for each program. That is, the RPA calculates the cost of disposing of each ton diverted. This is termed the "benefits per ton." Figure 29.3 compares the benefits per ton with costs per ton for the backyard composting program.

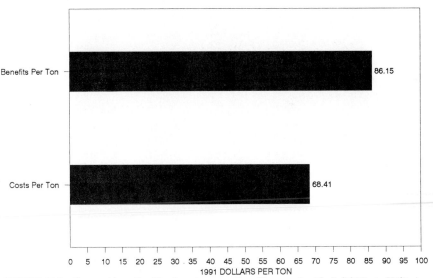

FIGURE 29.3   Cost and benefit of backyard composting. (*Source: Seattle Solid Waste Utility.*)

The RPA model can combine different sets of programs to form different recycling scenarios. For example, Scenario 1 for RPA includes the following eight programs:

1. Waste reduction
2. Backyard composting
3. Curbside yard waste
4. Self-haul yard waste

5. Curbside recycling
6. Apartment diversion
7. Business and industrial recycling
8. Drop-off recycling

Scenario 2 is the same, except two new programs, apartment recycling and a self-haul dump-and-pick operation, are added. Scenarios can be compared on the basis of costs, benefits per ton, and total tons recycled. Each scenario can also be compared to the city's recycling goal. Because the waste composition estimates, participation and efficiency rates, and costs are projected into the future, the effect of these programs over time can be projected.

The Total System. The RPA model passes the individual program costs onto the system cost module, which aggregates the information about recycling rates and costs from all programs. These aggregated costs are then combined with the costs for disposal of the solid wastes not reduced or recycled. This provides the total system cost for the program. Figure 29.4 projects the percentage of total number of tons recycled for the period from 1988 to 2000 compared to the estimated total waste generated.

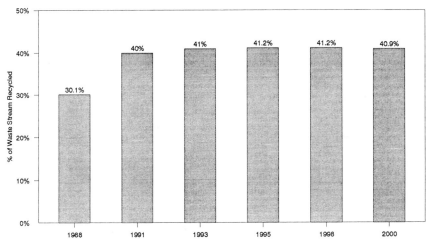

FIGURE 29.4   Seattle waste recycling rate. (*Source: Seattle Solid Waste Utility.*)

Average Rates. Once the total system costs have been calculated in the system cost module, the RPA will calculate the rates needed to recover the revenues needed to operate the programs. These rates are sector-specific; that is, the costs associated with commercial-sector programs are allocated to the commercial revenue requirements. The same process is used for residential programs. The total revenue required for each sector is divided by the number of tons disposed by each sector to determine the average rate.

Because a change in rates may affect the behavior of participants, the RPA model includes a loop which feeds the new rate back into the generation model. If generation and disposal change as a result of the new rates, the program and system costs are recalculated and new revenue requirements and new rates are determined. This iterative process continues until the system is in balance.

Revising the Model. In 1988, the City of Seattle set a recycling goal of 40 percent by 1990 and the Solid Waste Utility developed its plan with this goal firmly in mind. The recycling plan developed by the Seattle Solid Waste Utility in 1988 was implemented and tracked. Over the next several years, new information on waste composition and generation, private recycling, participation rates, program efficiencies, and costs became available. This new information was used to update the RPA model in 1991.

According to the RPA model, the city had moved from 30 percent recycling in 1988 to 40 percent recycling in 1991. However, more aggressive goals for recycling in future years had been set. The city wished to reach 60 percent recycling by 1998 through cost-effective programs and the Utility needed to design a set of program options that would achieve this goal. This meant that the RPA model had to be updated, a new set of program options developed, and the model rerun.

Updating the model began with revisiting the waste stream assumptions. The composition of the waste disposed had changed since 1988 as a result of the on-going recycling programs, as well as economic and social factors. A comparison of the composition of the residential waste in 1988 and 1990 is shown in Fig. 29.5.

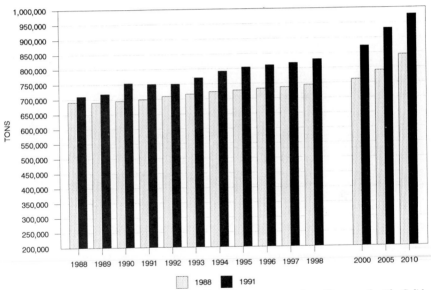

FIGURE 29.5 Comparison of Seattle's residential waste generation. (*Source: Seattle Solid Waste Utility.*)

In addition to changes in the assumptions about waste composition, two other factors were found to alter the projected amount of recycling in Seattle. First, the method of calculating the overlap between private sector recycling and the Utility-sponsored recycling changed. Second, the three years of operating experience provided more realistic assumptions. These factors resulted in changes which are shown in Fig. 29.6.

Two new and more aggressive recycling scenarios were developed to achieve the 1998 goal of 60 percent recycling. The new scenarios are outlined in Table 29.2.

The recycling rates of the new scenarios were compared with the city's goals and, as Fig. 29.7 shows, none of the three scenarios met the 1998 goal of 60 per-

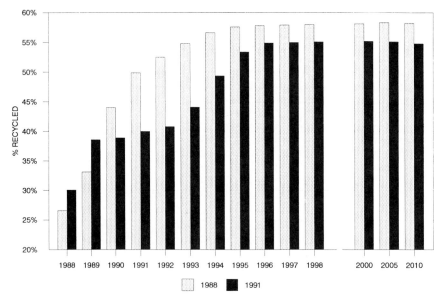

FIGURE 29.6 Comparison of recycling rates. (Includes new factors: three years of operating experience and changed calculation method.) (*Source: Seattle Solid Waste Utility.*)

TABLE 29.2 Recycling Scenarios for Seattle Model

	Existing programs	Scenario 1	Scenario 2
Waste reduction	x	x	x
Backyard composting	x	x	x
Curbside yard waste	x	x	x
Self-haul yard waste	x	x	x
Curbside recycling	x	x	x
Apartment diversion	x	x	x
Business/industry recycling	x	x	x
Drop-off program	x	x	x
Apartment recycling		x	x
Self-haul dump and pick		x	x
Mandatory commercial paper			x

cent. The benefits and costs of the programs were also calculated. Figure 29.8 shows the costs and benefits for Scenario 2, as well as the number of tons recycled by each program in 1998.

Seattle's RPA model allows the Utility to update the model as new information becomes available, revise the programs as goals or other circumstances change, and check to see that the whole system is in balance. These are the goals of any planning system, whether the system is a complex computer model like Seattle's or a regular discussion of a rural town's drop-off program.

To move from program design to implementation requires two further steps: definition of the work to be done and scheduling.

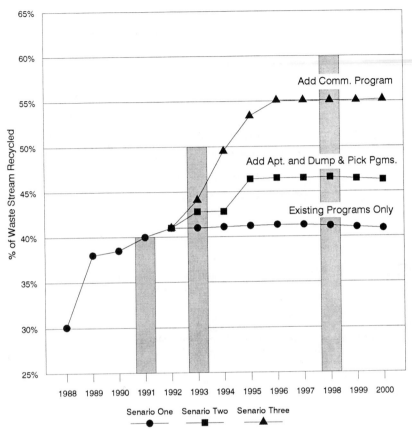

FIGURE 29.7   Recycling rates and Seattle's recycling goals. (*Source: Seattle Solid Waste Utility.*)

Defining the Work

No matter how complex, or simple, the recycling program is, it can be put into action more easily if the activities involved are clearly defined. In practice, the work should be broken down into discreet elements which can be carried out, managed, and monitored with the resources of the organization.

The planner who is defining activities must strike a balance between two extremes. The first is offering very broad rather vague guidelines for staff members. The second is providing meticulously detailed instructions describing every step of every activity. The former leaves staff members wondering what is needed and the latter leaves no room for individual initiative. The best way to strike this balance is to involve those who will be responsible for carrying out the work in defining it.

For example, there is little doubt that developing a school recycling curriculum with the teachers who will be using it in the classroom will result in a better curriculum. The same thing is true for outlining the steps which will need to be taken to develop a recycling curriculum. The people who do the work are the experts and can help define the jobs which must be done. Furthermore, involving

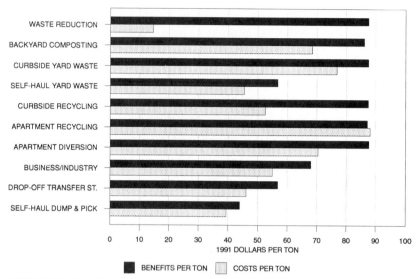

FIGURE 29.8   Benefits and costs of programs in Senario 2. (Added elements: Self-haul dumps and pick, and apartment recycling.) (*Source: Seattle Solid Waste Utility.*).

those responsible will generate a sense of commitment which will be essential once the work is started.

But there are other hazards in defining work tasks, even with the help of those doing the work. First, external conditions change over time. Shifts in the economy, movements in the secondary material markets, the promulgation of new solid waste management regulations, and the evolution of processing technologies, for example, often undermine even the most carefully developed instructions. Recycling is a particularly dramatic example of this because it has evolved so rapidly during the past five years. The planner of a recycling program will have to be especially nimble to keep up with the changes in the business. In this sense, a sound plan must be dynamic, adjusting to the shifts in external conditions.

Programs must also be dynamic in terms of growing to meet local demands. That is, recycling programs evolve in scope and sophistication. Almost as soon as a program is defined, there are pressures to enlarge it. For example, Seattle set more aggressive recycling goals even before the previous ones were accomplished. Markets for new materials, such as plastics, may develop. Technology becomes available to process more cost effectively. Residents and businesses want to recycle more kinds of materials. Programs want to keep up with these kinds of demands.

Developing a Work Breakdown Structure (WBDS).   One formal approach to defining the work to be done is called, logically enough, the work breakdown structure (WBDS) of the program. As an example of what a WBDS looks like, consider the school recycling curriculum which a city wishes to develop as a part of its public education program. Shown below is a simple WBDS for setting up a recycling curriculum in a school.

Task 1   Meet with teachers and school officials to discuss and develop the goals of the program.

Task 2   Develop recycling curriculum materials.

Task 3   Conduct workshops to introduce recycling resource materials to teachers.

Task 4   Monitor program with teachers.

In many cases, like this one, the order of the tasks is self-evident. In other, more complicated situations, the most efficient order of the tasks is not clear. In either case, the "logic" of the order will determine the overall program goals, the task definitions, and the availability of resources.

Defining Program Goals.   It is illogical to discuss program goals after the components of the program have been determined and the tasks defined, but this highlights a common problem with many recycling programs. While efforts to develop the program move rapidly ahead, the reasons for the program are never clearly articulated. This is a considerable handicap to planning, because it is the program's goals which help set priorities and against which progress is measured.

Although there are a number of different goals which communities cite in justifying their recycling programs, the goals generally fall into one of two broad areas. Although both types of goals generally play a part in most programs, it is instructive, for our purposes, to draw a distinction.

The first type of goal is economic. In areas where tipping fees are high and landfill capacity is limited (or nonexistent), recycling can offer a cost-effective means of managing a significant fraction of the waste stream. Bound by high costs, diminishing disposal capacity, and an ever stricter regulatory environment, a community in such an area will develop a source-reduction and recycling program to shrink its flow of solid waste, thereby cutting the cost of solid waste disposal. Many communities in the northeastern United States find themselves in this situation.

On the other hand, there are successful recycling programs in communities where the tipping fee is less than $20 per ton and the landfill has a life of 30 years. Many of these communities see recycling as a means of saving energy and natural resources. For example, Boulder, Colorado's, recycling program is not the result of outrageous tipping fees and closing landfills. It is part of a broad range of environmental programs carried out by concerned citizens.

This is not to say that these same environmental concerns are not shared by communities with high tipping fees, or that cost-effective recycling programs are not the goal of communities with low tipping fees. However, it is instructive to note the way in which priorities are ordered by the two types of communities.

A program driven primarily by economics will be evaluated accordingly. Program costs will be developed, evaluated, and justified in terms of the high tipping fees. A recycling program which costs more than the avoided cost of disposal will not be well-received. Financial analysis will play an important role in determining program priorities. In a community without the pressure of high tipping fees, program priorities may be determined by less quantifiable benchmarks, such as minimizing environmental damage or conserving resources.

The point is that a clear articulation of the goals of the program will inform all the decisions that follow. Without such an articulation, confusion, frustration, and wasted resources can result.

Establishing Program Sequence and Timing. The WBDS outlined above presents the work necessary to develop a school recycling curriculum. It should be emphasized again that each individual program will contain different elements and approach the tasks in different ways. Nevertheless, the activities within any program must be carried out in a particular sequence. The timing of tasks and subtasks will be a critical element in the success of the program. Certain tasks must precede others. For example, residents must be given information about the curbside collection of recyclables before the collection trucks arrive so that the targeted materials can be properly prepared. On the other hand, disseminating information too far ahead will raise expectations and enthusiasm prematurely.

It should be noted that the timing of a program can be influenced by many outside factors. For example, as a result of a long period of negative publicity about the closing of the landfill and a period of rapid rate increases, Seattle's Solid Waste Utility felt compelled "do something" positive and do it quickly. The utility implemented a curbside recycling program, although it was not clear how this program would fit with the other recycling programs. Rarely does a city have the luxury of taking as much time to plan as it would like.

The sequencing of activities will be particularly difficult and important at the beginning of the program when many tasks will begin at about the same time. Certain tasks, where the planner has some control, should be given ample time. The time necessary to evaluate proposals, for example, will vary depending on how many proposals are received. Contract negotiations are another area where it is difficult to know ahead of time how much time will be needed. It is wise to allot more than enough time for these types of activities.

A second issue underlying planning efforts of this kind will be scarcity of resources. Only rarely will a planner have all the resources available to carry out the "ideal" program. In fact, it is likely that the expectations for the program will be very high and the resources available to carry out the program will be very modest. Therefore, priorities must be determined. This brings us back to program goals which, if clearly stated, should help set the task-ordering priorities. All program elements are not equal and a good planner will recognize this early in the planning process.

Sequence Planning with a Gantt Chart. One simple way to present and manipulate the sequence of program activities is with a Gantt chart. This is simply a visual means of showing a number of tasks over a specified period of time. The activities are arranged in sequence and given a visual "weight" according to their duration. Figure 29.9 below shows one type of a Gantt chart for the tasks under "School Programs."

Note that each activity is assigned a certain period. It is estimated that the activity can be carried out during this period. The chart indicates the task order, the length of time allotted for each task, and the length of time allotted for the entire group of tasks. Sometimes it is useful to identify milestone events or documents which mark the end of a particular task. This kind of signal is useful to all participants, for it indicates concrete progress toward the overall program goals. For example, the completed curriculum (B) might be a milestone document in the school recycling program activities (Fig. 29.10).

The Gantt chart is particularly useful with a relatively small program. It becomes a less useful tool as the size and complexity of the program grows. It also does not reflect the priorities among many tasks taking place simultaneously. Nevertheless, the exercise of assigning a time period to each task is a very useful

LIST OF TASKS:
   TASK 1 MEET WITH TEACHERS AND SCHOOL OFFICIALS TO
           DISCUSS AND DEVELOP THE GOALS OF THE PROGRAM

   TASK 2 DEVELOP RECYCLING CURRICULAR MATERIALS

   TASK 3 CONDUCT WORKSHOPS TO INTRIDUCE RECYCLING
           RESOURCE MATERIALS TO TEACHERS

   TASK 4 MONITOR PROGRAM WITH TEACHERS

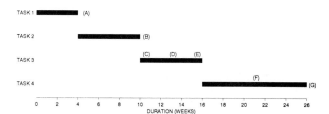

(A) PUBLISH STATEMENT OF GOALS
(B) PUBLISH CURRICULAR MATERIALS
(C) (D) & (E) TEACHER WORKSHOPS
(F) INTERIM PROGRESS REPORT
(G) EVALUATION OF PROGRAM

FIGURE 29.9   Gantt chart for developing recycling curriculum with milestones.

LIST OF TASKS:
   TASK 1 MEET WITH TEACHERS AND SCHOOL OFFICIALS TO
           DISCUSS AND DEVELOP THE GOALS OF THE PROGRAM

   TASK 2 DEVELOP RECYCLING CURRICULAR MATERIALS

   TASK 3 CONDUCT WORKSHOPS TO INTRIDUCE RECYCLING
           RESOURCE MATERIALS TO TEACHERS

   TASK 4 MONITOR PROGRAM WITH TEACHERS

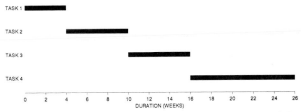

FIGURE 29.10   Gantt chart for developing recycling curriculum for a small program.

exercise for the planner. It is a necessary first step in developing a program schedule.

Program Scheduling

It was pointed out above that recycling programs may be developed for different reasons, have different goals, and go about accomplishing their goals in different ways. The differences among programs will also be manifest in the approaches to planning. Some programs evolve with little or no planning in the formal sense. Ideas are put forth and argued over, funds sought and won, and programs implemented. The participants understand intuitively what needs to be done and when. Other, larger programs may be more formal, using something akin to a Gantt chart to schedule activities. Programs that are relatively small or which are in the early stages of evolution are often carried out with very little formal planning and this is perfectly appropriate.

However, as programs become larger and sophisticated, the need for more rigorous, formal planning increases. Intuition and simple Gantt charts cannot handle the complexities of the program. For those interested in this more rigorous approach to planning, this section of the chapter concludes with a discussion of program scheduling models.

Program Scheduling Models.   The science, and art, of project scheduling has grown rapidly over the past several decades, driven primarily by large contracts for the federal government involving hundreds of tasks, and thousands of people, and millions of dollars. Building hydroelectric dams, Stealth bombers, or space satellites are examples of such projects. These huge projects could not be conducted without some way of ordering the tasks, assigning responsibility, and monitoring progress.

Two examples of scheduling models which are often used for large, multitask programs are the Critical Path method (CPM) and the Program Evaluation and Review Technique (PERT). Both models seek to identify the sequence of tasks and activities which will take the most time. Both models require the construction of a network which articulates the logic of the overall program. Although similar in approach, PERT differs from CPM in terminology and in its ability to incorporate probability into its time estimates. This makes PERT particularly useful in scheduling activities characterized by uncertainty. The PERT model has been used in the example below, although some comments about the CPM model are also provided.

The PERT model will first be considered in terms of time, as a limiting factor, and will then be considered in terms of time, cost, and resources, as limiting factors.

Network Construction—Time Models.   Once the separate tasks for the program have been defined, the proper sequence of tasks must be determined. This has already been discussed above. Using this information, a network is built of the tasks. The logic of the network is shown through a series of notations which indicate activities and events. Activities take time and resources; events mark the beginning or completion of activities. For example, negotiating a contract would be an activity. An executed contract is an event. Figure 29.11 shows the notation commonly used to indicate activities and events in the PERT and CPM scheduling models.

FIGURE 29.11   Notation for PERT and CPM models.

The arrows denote activities and the circles or nodes denote events. In developing the network, the precedence relationship of events can be shown by placing the nodes in logical order. The PERT model, and the CPM model, can show a variety of types of precedence relationships, as Fig. 29.12 shows.

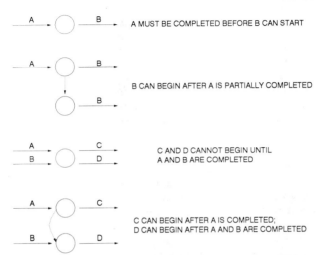

FIGURE 29.12   Notation for precedence relationships in PERT and CPM models.

After the activities have been defined and the logic of their precedence relationships has been established, the next step is to determine the time estimates for each activity. For CPM, which is the simpler of the two models, a single time estimate based on current conditions is required. Remember that since the activities themselves may change during the course of the project, the time estimate can only be a best guess. The most accurate estimate is likely to come from the individuals responsible for the work. Again, a critical planning element requires consultation with the staff.

The PERT model requires a more rigorous approach to estimating the time for projects. It asks for three estimates:

- An optimistic time, which would be the minimum reasonable period of time required to complete an activity. In terms of probability, there would be probability of 1 percent or less that the activity would take less time than this.
- A most likely time, which would be the estimate which would be used in the CPM network.
- A pessimistic time, which would be the maximum reasonable period required to complete an activity. In terms of probability, there would be a probability of 1 percent or less that the activity would take more time than this.

This statistical basis of these estimates will be used to calculate the expected times and the variance of the activity times. Again, whether the CPM model or the PERT model is used, the time estimates should be gathered from those who will be performing the activity.

The PERT model estimates activity times using the three estimates. Consider the tasks identified to develop the collection of recyclables at a drop-off center.

Task 1:   Determine location of drop-off centers.

Task 2:   Integrate drop-off program with curbside program.

Task 3:   Purchase drop-off containers.

Task 4:   Arrange for pickup of materials and delivery to processing facility.

Task 5:   Develop promotional materials and signage.

Task 6:   Publicize drop-off program.

Task 7:   Conduct pilot program.

First, we must designate the precedence relationship among these seven tasks. Using the model notation, we begin the two independent activities (Fig. 29.13a).

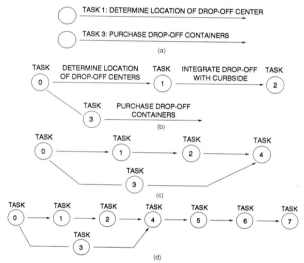

FIGURE 29.13 (a) PERT notation for developing drop-off centers—Tasks 1 and 3. (b) PERT notation for developing drop-off centers—Tasks 1, 2, and 3. (c) PERT notation for developing drop-off centers, Tasks 1 to 4. (d) PERT notation for developing drop-off centers, Tasks 1 to 7.

As the diagram indicates, there are two independent activities in this program, that is, two activities which do not require a preceding activity. The two activities are selecting the drop-off sites and procuring the drop-off containers. It is assumed that the selection of materials to be collected and their preparation has been determined earlier.

Only after the drop-off sites have been selected can the drop-off program and the curbside program be integrated and this is noted as in Fig. 29.13b. The arrangements for collecting the materials can only be made when the sites have been selected and the containers procured, which is noted as in Fig. 29.13c.

With the information about drop-off sites and collection schedules available, the promotional materials can be developed, the program publicized, and the pilot program begun. Figure 29.13*d* is the notation for the tasks defined under drop-off centers.

Next the estimated time (ET) for each task should be determined. To accomplish the first task, locating the drop-off centers, data on the service area must be gathered and evaluated. Information on population density, traffic patterns, the planned routes for curbside service, and available sites must be assembled. Then a group of potential sites may be chosen and visited to determine a ranking. Finally, the proposed locations should be reviewed by an independent group for reasonableness. The optimistic time (denoted as *a*) for this task is reported to be 4 weeks by the team who will be responsible for carrying it out. This assumes that all the data are readily available, there will be numerous available sites from which to choose, and the team will work smoothly together.

The most likely time (denoted as *b*) is 7 weeks. This assumes the data can be obtained after some searching, that sites can be found after some searching, and that the team works together reasonably well. The pessimistic time (denoted as *c*) is 12 weeks. This assumes that much of the data are not available and must be developed, that the few available sites must be researched carefully, and that there is some friction among team members.

The ET for this task is calculated by using the following formula:

$$ET = \frac{a + 4b + c}{6} = \frac{4 + 28 + 12}{6} = 7.33 \text{ weeks}$$

This formula is based on a beta distribution which gives the "most likely" time four times the weight of the optimistic and pessimistic distribution.

Next, the variance for each activity is calculated with the formula:

$$\text{Variance} = \left(\frac{b - a}{6}\right)^2 = \left(\frac{12 - 4}{6}\right)^2 = \left(\frac{8}{6}\right)^2 = 1.77$$

The greater the difference between the optimistic time and the pessimistic time, the greater the variance. Table 29.3 shows the optimistic, pessimistic, and most likely times for each of the seven tasks, as well as the ET and the variance for each one. The figures used below are hypothetical.

The purpose of all these calculations is to determine the critical path. The path

TABLE 29.3 Expected Times (Weeks) and Variance for Each Task

Task	Optimistic time	Most likely time	Pessimistic time	Expected time	Variance
1	4	7	12	7.33	1.77
2	3	6	10	6.17	1.36
3	6	10	15	10.17	2.25
4	2	3	4	3	0.11
5	4	6	12	6.67	1.78
6	2	3	4	3	0.11
7	6	10	20	11	5.44

is laid out along the sequence of tasks which must be followed to complete the activity most efficiently. In a program with tens or hundreds of tasks, this is valuable information for the planner. The key to locating the critical path is finding "slack" time. If an activity has slack time, it is not on the critical path. There is no slack for tasks on the critical path. To calculate slack time in the PERT model, we place the ET and variance for each task in the program notation, as shown in Fig. 29.14.

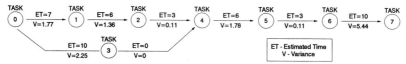

FIGURE 29.14 Notation with estimated time and variance.

Below the notation, two times are shown for each task. The T(E) of each task is the earliest expected completion time and is calculated by summing all ET's of each task from point zero forward to the given task. Therefore, the T(E) of Task 1 is 7; the T(E) of Task 2 is 7 + 6 or 13; the T(E) for Task 3 is 7 + 6 + 10 or 23, and the T(E) of Task 4 is 7 + 6 + 4 or 17 and so forth. The total T(E) for all seven tasks is 38 weeks.

The T(L) is the latest expected completion time for a task and is found by setting T(L) equal to the T(E) total of 38, and moving backward through the network. Therefore, Task 7 has a T(L) of 38; Task 6 has a T(L) of 27; and so forth. Note that Task 3 has a T(E) of 10 and a T(L) of 13. The difference of 3 weeks between these two is slack time. That is, Task 3 could be started at week 7 immediately upon completion of task 1, or it could be started at week 12 and completed at week 16 simultaneous with task 2. The 5 weeks of slack time is between week 7 and week 12. Because Task 3 has slack time, it is not on the critical path. None of the other tasks has slack time. Therefore, the critical path goes through the following tasks – 1,2,4,5,6,7, as shown in Fig. 29.15.

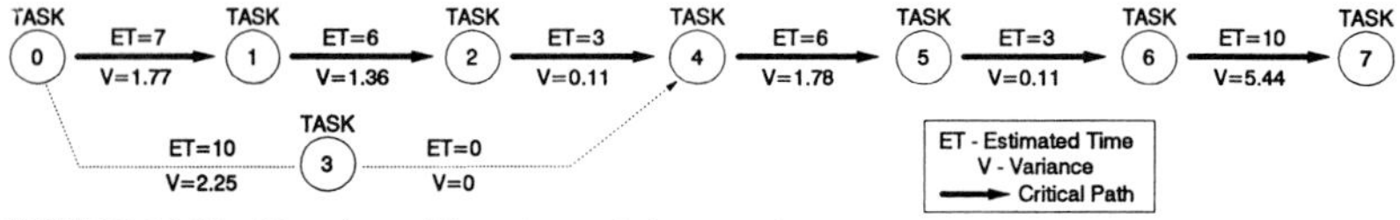

FIGURE 29.15 Notation with estimated time, variance, critical path.

It has been pointed out before that the kind of information provided by this model will be useful for programs with many components and tasks, with limited resources, and significant investments in staff and other resources. For small programs, it is probably not worth the time and effort to develop this type of network and a simple Gantt chart may be the only scheduling tool necessary.

The PERT model can also determine the probability of completing the project on a given date. For example, let us assume that the City Council has requested that the pilot program for the drop-off centers be completed 38 weeks from today. The PERT model will show the probability of meeting this deadline using the formula:

$$Z = \frac{\text{due date} - \text{earliest ET for last activity}}{\sqrt{\text{sum of variances on the critical path}}}$$

For the drop-off center activities, the values would be

$$Z = \frac{38 \text{ weeks} - 42 \text{ weeks}}{\sqrt{9.61}} = \frac{-4}{3.1} = -1.29$$

Because the PERT model uses a beta distribution, the Z value of 1.29 must be looked up on a table of areas of cumulative standard normal distribution. A value of -1.29 shows a value of 9 percent. In other words, there is a 9 percent chance of completing the pilot program within 38 weeks.

The PERT and CPM models can also be used to develop the minimum cost schedules using inputs about the expected cost of activities, given certain time constraints. Often these models require an iterative process which can be accomplished most efficiently with a computer. There is software available for constructing these models.

Once a schedule has been developed, whether it is a Gantt chart for a modest program or a sophisticated computer model capable of spinning out probable completion times, work can begin. The plan should provide direction, set priorities, and indicate activity times. The plan should be revisited regularly to confirm its relevance in the face of changing conditions. It should be a critical tool in building an effective recycling program.

STAFFING

A recycling program can have no greater asset than a first-rate staff. People make programs go. Unfortunately, there is no magic formula for locating and retaining effective staff members. Of course, salaried staff members are only one group of people who can make recycling programs successful. Other groups may include volunteer workers, employees of private sector firms, and consultants.

Recycling is a multidisciplinary activity. A recent survey of recycling experts was conducted by Rob Grogan, a doctoral student at the Harvard School of Education, to ascertain the skills and knowledge which a recycling coordinator might require. The most important skills identified were, first, managing information and recycling records and, second, understanding the economics of recycling. Other skill areas, in descending order of importance, were publicity and promotion, budgeting, secondary material marketing, local government, vehicle routing and specifications, disposal options: costs and technologies. This is an imposing list.

The first two subsections focus on professional staff members—where to find them and how to recruit and retain them. The third subsection considers the most effective way to supplement the efforts of these recycling professionals.

Locating Potential Staff Members

Recycling, in terms of large public-sector programs, has been going on for less than a decade. It is still a young industry without an established cadre of trained workers. In some regions, the demand for trained recyclers has outstripped the supply. However, there is a growing network of experienced recyclers. The word "experienced," as used here, refers to anyone with more than a few years of work in the field.

Many of the traditional sources of trained professionals are still developing. A few colleges and universities have developed, or are developing, specific degree programs in recycling. Many others offer recycling as a part of waste management curriculum which may be part Engineering Department or the Environmental Studies or Natural Sciences Department. The University of Maine, Michigan State University, and the University of Wisconsin have all developed programs in waste management which include recycling. Many graduate schools in public policy use recycling case studies to examine waste management issues. Also, many of the best recruits from colleges are those students who helped to develop or run the college's own recycling program. One clue as to where to find well-trained recyclers is to look for those schools with the best recycling programs.

Often the needs of the program will point toward specialized skills. That is, a program seeking help in secondary markets might look to paper companies or glass manufacturers for candidates. A person who has conducted promotional campaigns for the local public interest research group or environmental organization might be ideally suited to designing a recycling promotional campaign. Other kinds of specialists such as chemists (for insights into plastics recycling), mechanics (for collection vehicle evaluation), or bankers (for help in financing) may also prove valuable. Providing training in recycling to a skilled professional is often the best strategy.

Finally, because recycling is still in a formative phase, many highly motivated individuals have been drawn to it. Placing an ad in one of the trade journals can result in responses from people with a broad range of backgrounds. The next step is to convince them to join your staff.

Recruiting and Retaining Staff Members

Often, the private sector has an advantage over the public sector in recruiting and retaining skilled workers. Private firms can usually offer higher salaries, better benefits, and superior working conditions. In fact, some firms look to the public sector for recruits because of the valuable experience a municipal recycling program can provide. Facing this kind of competition, what can the public sector offer?

First, it can appeal to a recruit's sense of social altruism. Public service still attracts many of the country's most able workers, and this is particularly true of those in recycling. There seems to be a strong sense of idealism among those entering the recycling field. Helping to solve a community's waste management problems offers powerful outlet for this idealism.

Second, the job is invariably challenging. The problems are enormous; the resources are limited; and the solutions require a combination of enlightened public policy, appropriate technology, and a balancing of market forces. The attraction of a challenging position which improves community life can be very powerful to a hard-working idealist.

Retaining effective staff members is probably a greater challenge than getting them in the first place. Here, the conditions which keep staff members are no different than those which keep any other kind of worker. Staff members need recognition and positive reinforcement. They should be rewarded for good work with greater responsibility and, hopefully, better pay and benefits. Although a positive working environment—open, collaborative, and responsive—is critical to keeping a talented staff, there are limits to its effectiveness in the face of shrinking real wages and benefits.

Supplementing the Staff

Even the most talented staff may not provide all the expertise and help necessary to run an effective recycling program. There are times when outside help is necessary and it is important to recognize these times and respond appropriately. There are, at lest, two groups of "outsiders" that may effectively supplement the work of the professional staff—volunteers and consultants.

Many recycling staffs use volunteers to provide site-specific assistance in particular programs. For example, curbside collection of recyclables is often supported by volunteer block leader programs. In this type of program, a local resident takes responsibility for encouraging neighbors to recycle. This responsibility can include providing promotional material produced by the city, monitoring the success of recycling in the neighborhood, and meeting with new families to inform them about the program. A similar kind of program is often used in multifamily dwellings. An apartment resident will take charge of the recycling area of the building and encourage new tenants to participate in recycling.

Although volunteer help is not paid, neither is it "free." To be effective, volunteers need to be recruited, kept up-to-date, and thanked (often) for their efforts. This all will take time from the professional staff. Volunteers who are recruited and abandoned will soon disappear. On the other hand, the local assistance that these volunteers provide is almost impossible to duplicate, even if additional staff members could be paid. Volunteers are most valuable in making local contact and providing on-site assistance. They are less valuable as temporary workers in the office, carrying out functions which a paid staff member could just as easily be doing.

Many recycling programs, particularly in small towns or neighborhoods, have begun as volunteer programs. The all-volunteer staff finds a site, arranges for the collection of recyclables, publicizes the program, and markets the material. Countless recycling programs have been started this way. Community leaders too often view these programs as a "free" recycling program which can go on forever. Unfortunately, these volunteer programs seldom become permanent. After a while, sometimes a long while, the volunteers burn out and the recycling program wilts away. Communities with all-volunteer recycling programs should decide if the program is worthwhile. If it is, it deserves public support in the form of professional leadership. Volunteers can still help, but recycling should become a city service with a budget and paid staff. If the program does not warrant this kind of support, the community should not be astonished when it dies a quiet death.

Nonprofit organizations are another kind of volunteer help that can often supplement the work of a professional staff. Environmental groups, such as the Sierra Club and the Audubon Society, often publish helpful technical reports or can be consulted on topics of interest to the program. Legal issues and new solid waste regulations are usually reviewed by organizations such as the Environmental Defense Fund and the Environmental Law Foundation. A familiarity with the work of local and national nonprofit groups can often be useful to a municipal recycling program.

Professional consultants can also supplement the work of a professional staff, if they are used judiciously and well. Consultants can provide a range of services, from very specialized expertise to broad program support. A good consultant should offer the benefits of experience with recycling programs in other areas, specific technical skills, and a high degree of objectivity. Their work usually covers a specified, and limited, period of time. Unfortunately, they are usually quite expensive. However, for a limited project, it may cost less to hire a consultant than to hire a permanent staff member whose salary and benefits must continue after the project is completed.

Consultants are best used when the following three conditions are met. First, the work which the consultant will do is clearly defined and limited. It makes no sense to hire a consultant until the scope of work is clear. Second, the work of the consultant will not duplicate or usurp the work of a staff member. This is not only wasteful of program resources but it can be very dispiriting to the staff member who may feel "replaced" by the consultant. Third, there are adequate resources to monitor the work of the consultant during the project. Turning a consultant loose on a project without adequate monitoring is unfair to the program and the consultant. The costs of hiring a consultant include not only the consultant's fee but the staff time required to work with the consultant during the project. Working together, the staff member and the consultant should develop a product that will serve the program.

FINANCING A RECYCLING PROGRAM

The final section of this chapter addresses the financing of recycling programs. This is a complex and highly technical topic, which is introduced here to provide an overview of financing options. No attempt is made to describe all of the many approaches which specific communities have employed. Rather, this is a menu of potential sources of funds which can be investigated as the program moves toward implementation. All of these sources may not be available to all programs, but at least some of them will be and will deserve a closer look.

In developing a plan to pay for recycling, it is instructive to look at the way in which other large solid waste projects, such as landfills and waste-to-energy facilities, have been financed. Recently there has been a call, particularly by the Environmental Defense Fund, to "level the playing field" for waste management projects. If the recycling program will be responsible for diverting solid waste from disposal, it should be given equal footing with other technologies.

State Grants

In order to encourage recycling, particularly in the light of rapidly diminishing landfill capacity, many states have created grant programs which offer direct funding for the planning and implementation of recycling programs. Northeastern states such as Pennsylvania, New York, Vermont, and Rhode Island have spent millions of dollars to develop recycling programs. State grants may support the writing of feasibility studies for recycling, the implementation of pilot recycling programs, research of secondary materials markets, the purchase of collection vehicles, and many other kinds of programs.

Both Rhode Island and Massachusetts have used state funds to construct material recovery facilities (MRF) and purchase collection vehicles. The MRFs in Johnstown, R.I., and Springfield, Mass., are now being used to process recyclables collected from communities in those states. Unfortunately, as state budgets have begun to show significant deficits, these planning grants and state-supported programs are disappearing. This source of funds will depend, among other things, on the fiscal health of the state.

Revenue from Material Sales

Recycling has the potential to generate revenue through the sale of recycled materials. This potential is limited by the type, volume, and quality of the materials collected, as well as the health of the secondary materials markets. There are two kinds of market risk which have plagued programs recently.

First, the price levels of certain materials have fallen dramatically during the past several years. Communities which had counted on material sales for a significant percentage of their budgets have been dismayed to see the markets slump. For example, a few years ago, many communities were selling old newspapers to brokers for $25 per ton or more. Now they must pay $25 per ton to have the newspaper taken away. While this is less than the tipping fee for disposal, this $25 cost has had an obvious impact on programs that had counted on the revenue from the sale of newspaper to support their program.

The second risk in relying on revenue from the sale of materials has been the risk of having loads rejected. As more material has entered the market, the level of contamination in some loads has risen, according to the end markets. This, in turn, has led to a tightening of quality standards demanded by the markets. For example, in the past year, some recycling programs have had loads of glass and aluminum rejected because the loads contained too many contaminants. Metal caps and neck rings in the glass, and lead, sand, and water in aluminum cans, led end users to refuse to accept loads. Not only do rejected loads mean a loss of revenue, but they also mean that the cost of collecting and processing the materials has been wasted. Furthermore, the rejected loads must either be landfilled, or reprocessed, incurring additional expenses.

Given these market risks, most programs which look to material sales as a source of funds use very conservative estimates.

Taxes

Many programs seek at least some of their funding through municipal taxes. This is particularly true where recycling is regarded as part of the solid waste management program. That is, the collection and disposal of waste, including recycling, is supported through taxes.

While this would appear to be a ready source of funds, there is fierce competition for tax dollars from other municipal services, such as fire, police, and education. In addition, there are limits to the amount a community can tax its residents and businesses. Raising taxes is generally accompanied by intense public scrutiny, and often by public debate, outcry, and anger. As a result, recycling programs are generally looking for other sources of funds to replace, or at least, supplement, tax revenues.

Tipping Fee Surcharges

Another source of funds for a recycling program is a surcharge. These are the fees charged at landfills and incinerators for disposing or processing of waste, in addition to the regular tipping fee. In many cases, a supplemental amount, as low as $1 or $2, is added to the tipping fee to pay for recycling programs. This has the advantage of assessing those who are generating the waste. One interesting twist to this source of funds is that, as the recycling program becomes more successful, less waste is disposed and the revenue from the tipping fees decreases. When this happens, the answer is to increase the supplement.

User Fees

Many communities have developed municipal services that are supported by the citizens that use the service, rather than by the entire community through the tax base. The "enterprise fund" does not rely on taxes. They have their own set of fees which generate revenues and are budgeted separately.

There is a large and growing variety of user fees for solid waste. The simplest of these is a flat rate for all residents receiving garbage collection service. Another popular option is the "variable can rate" which provide different levels of service for different rates. The city of Renton, Washington, for example, offers two levels of weekly collection, a 30-gal or 15-gal container for a monthly fee. These fees include the cost of collection and disposal of garbage, and the collection, processing, and marketing of recyclables. The variable can rates also provide an economic incentive for recycling and source reduction.

Bonds

Bonds are another source of public sector funds for recycling. Bonds are a common way of raising money for capital-intensive projects such as incinerators and MRFs. Most cities have the ability to incur debt through the issuance of bonds. There are two types of bonds generally used.

General obligation ("GO") bonds are backed by the financial strength of the city or state. However, there are limits on the amount of debt a city or state can incur. If this limit has been reached through the use of GO bonds for other kinds of projects, this option will not be available. This is one limitation in issuing GO bonds. Repayment schedules for GO bonds often require large amounts of money in the first years of operation, which may increase the cost of recycling in the early years when the program is just getting started. Conversely, earlier amortization of the debt will result in lower total interest cost, reducing the cost of recycling during the repayment period of the bonds. It is generally better to have the repayment schedule and the facility revenues closely matched in order to stabilize recycling fees.

The second type of bond is a revenue bond. Unlike GO bonds, which are backed by the financial resources of the city, revenue bonds are backed by revenue generated by the project. The repayment schedule and the revenues can be closely matched. In addition, revenue bonds have the advantage of not affecting the city's debt limit.

However, since the investor is relying solely on the economic strength of the project, the project has to be able to generate adequate revenues to pay the bondholders and maintain adequate coverage levels. Revenues may be generated by the sale of recyclable materials and by user fees at the facility. The market risk involved in the sale of recyclable materials has already been discussed. For a bondholder, repayment cannot be based on material sales because the market risk is too great.

Charging a fee at the gate of the facility will generate revenue, but could lead to a reduction in recycling. There must be some compelling reason to expect that this fee will be collected. The reason may be in the form of flow control, an ordinance which requires that all recyclables in the service area be delivered to the facility. Without flow control, there is a risk that the recyclables could go to another facility, resulting in a loss of fees and lost revenues.

Bonding is a common source of funds. GO bonds will be attractive as long as the city has not reached its debt limit and does not have competing needs for these bonds. If they do, revenue bonds can be used as long as the revenues from the project are certain and will cover the payments to the bondholders.

Private Financing

In cases where public-sector funds are not available to support an entire recycling program, help from the private sector may be sought. Generally, a private firm will risk its own resources, if it believes it has a reasonable opportunity to make a profit.

The collection of recyclables, for example, is often carried out by a private firm. The collection services may be offered through competitive bid by the city which will guarantee the hauler of all the customers in the service area. The City of Seattle has two contract haulers, Waste Management, Inc., and Rabanco, which collect and process recyclables for city residents. If an equitable contract can be worked out, this arrangement has advantages for both the city and the hauler. The hauler is assured of a large group of customers without any competition, and the city receives collection services at a known cost.

A private firm may also build and operate an MRF. Like revenue bondholders, a private firm which puts its capital at risk will want some kind of assurance that all recyclables in the are will be delivered to its facility. A flow-control ordinance or a belief that there will be little or no competition from other facilities can provide this assurance.

A city which relies on a privately owned and operated facility must also realize that it is exposed to risk of abandonment. If the owner of the facility decides to close the doors—because the facility is not making a profit or because a better opportunity has opened up somewhere else—the city will have no recourse but to develop another facility or curtail its recycling program. For this reason, many MRFs are publicly owned, but privately operated.

There are many other financing arrangements such as leasebacks and combinations of the options discussed above. These options offer great flexibility, but they also require careful study. The financing of a recycling program should reflect the local economic and political conditions, as well as maturity of the recycling program and availability of strong secondary material markets, and the number of households and businesses to be served.

CHAPTER 30
PUBLIC AWARENESS PROGRAMS

Peter L. Wolfe
Public Affairs Manager
Malcolm Pirnie, Inc.
White Plains, New York

INTRODUCTION

Public Policy and Recycling

Often a last-minute consideration by municipal decision makers implementing solid waste recycling projects, public information programming remains fundamental to recycling's success beyond the short term. Indeed, failure to consider public education as a technical component, similar to equipment purchases and market identification, may doom the most organized municipal recycling efforts.

Of course, the need to "sell" recycling to the public is not at issue. The public's embrace of the recycling ethic is fairly widespread, due in large measure to the "greening" of our culture. On the other hand, turning this philosophy into action requires an understanding of the diversity present in most communities and the reasons why individuals *choose* to participate or not. (See Chap. 10, The Psychology of Recycling.) Although there are still those who are more often motivated by the stick rather than the carrot, given the appropriate incentives and ease of implementation, the vast majority of Americans will participate in a recycling program. Indeed, between March 1989 and February 1990, the number of Americans that regularly sorted their trash rose from 14 percent to 24 percent, according to an S. C. Johnson and Son and Roper Organization poll (*American Demographics,* February 1991, p. 28). This is far short of the 50 percent recycling mandates passed by many state legislatures, but is steady growth nonetheless and may be indicative of more and more programs coming on line.

Public education programs also vary in style and content as much as the recycling projects they promote. Although many similar elements will make up a particular program, the degree to which they are used is often predicated by local conditions. In this sense, no two educational campaigns are alike nor are there necessarily any standard guidelines to be followed during implementation.

This is not to suggest that the forms of communication used to promote participation are simply a matter of random selection. (It should be noted here, the

30.1

terms *public education, public relations,* and *communications* are interchanged frequently but will generally refer to the promotional aspects of a recycling program.) The packaging of an education program requires careful consideration of each communication process based on frequency, cost, retention, and audience response. Choosing the proper mix of each and acquiring the approval of decision makers who may lack public affairs experience is the major challenge facing most practitioners.

Where then to begin? Subsequent sections will examine many of the methods and types of communication used to educate the public on recycling. However, it is worthwhile to develop an understanding of the political, economic, and environmental realities that have pushed recycling into the mainstream (once again).

The American Experience

There is no doubt that recycling has been a part of American culture for some time. Scrap operations have been around for years, reaching their peaks during the world war periods. Educational efforts of that time called for the support of "our boys overseas" by recycling our scrap into the mechanisms of war. The call to recycling is no less important at the end of this century and mirrors the crisis themes of earlier years. Indeed, the public's collective consciousness is well-versed on the need for and reasons behind recycling as one element of an expanding global environmental perspective. Recycling has been "hip" for some time.

For this reason, the battle for heightened public awareness is already won. The war still rages, however, as well-intentioned public policy can fail to consider its own impact on local communities. As an example, legislation mandating recycling percentages may fail to consider market-driven forces that can impede success in the short term. This, coupled with the strain new laws place on limited municipal resources, puts many recycling programs (which must rely on public support) at a disadvantage.

Communicating

This would suggest that the difficulties with recycling startup (available markets, ownership of recyclables, equipment procurement, union requirements, etc.) would need to be worked out in advance of local program implementation and any education component. On the other hand, experience shows that many of these details can remain unresolved yet startup may be less than a few weeks away. From a public education posture, this can be disastrous as communicating the specifics of a recycling program may be rushed or haphazardly accomplished.

Flexibility, therefore, is a common feature of the most successful education programs. This is particularly critical to recycling pilot efforts, where full-scale or multimaterial programs may take several years to implement. Clearly, informing the public in an ever-evolving program creates significant communication challenges. Challenges which, if not properly responded to, can severely impact participation rates.

Understanding the communication process, therefore, becomes central to the success of public education programming. The formulation of messages, their delivery using various media, and the follow-up necessary to ensure consistency, requires communications savvy, an element often lost among the more administrative concerns of recycling implementation. Knowing the local community, particularly across socioeconomic lines, is also invaluable to program planning and fundamental to establishing dialogue between local government and the constituencies they will rely on for recycling's success.

The various phases and components used to implement successful public education programs will be examined. Approaches to program management as well as "shopping lists" of activities will be explored. Key to any effort, however, is credibility, both in the messages communicated and, more importantly, in the commitment to the education process. Inasmuch as the public has demanded recycling, municipal officials, business leaders, and the public must be supportive of the recycling education function and recognize its primary role to recycling's success.

STARTING A PUBLIC AWARENESS PROGRAM

"The first steps are often the most difficult." This is certainly a recycling truism. Indeed, gaining cooperation of a varied constituency and building the momentum necessary to move the program through its many cycles can be as important (and risky) as a child's first walk. As with any event, however, planning is fundamental to success and the first step to getting started.

Research

Before any communication can be effective, some level of understanding must be gained regarding the audience to be communicated with, particularly if the communication is attempting to change behavior. This not only requires awareness of various demographic influences, but will rely on the proper interpretation of local attitudes. Research can accomplish this goal, and can be used in many forms. Furthermore, it provides an opportunity to evaluate and project community trends, and ensures that promotional programming remains current and appealing. Research will also determine which resources work best for a particular program, and what funding and media outlets are available. The goal here is to *tailor* a communications effort to reach a variety of subgroups, with messages that will persuade *most* citizens in the community to recycle.

Audience Identification

There are several means toward gathering audience information, but none are more beneficial than direct interviews with potentially affected constituents. This will require sufficient staff capability, but at a minimum, may involve a recycling coordinator "making the rounds" in an effort to create reliable audience profiles. Door-to-door or telephone surveys, attendance at community meetings, and participation with school and civic events are several ways in which to gather useful information.

In a more formalized method, focus groups can be conducted where community representatives are brought together in a round-table forum to discuss the pros and cons of varying promotional ideas. Local universities may even provide the resources for conducting this type of survey as part of a business class project (e.g., speak with the head of the business department). Additionally, "behind-the-scenes" demographic investigations (reviews of tax roles, school populations, business, etc.) can further refine audience profiles and may uncover additional resources for program implementation (e.g., the city clerk's office can provide direction for acquiring this type of information).

In whatever form, initial research efforts should attempt to answer the following:

- What socioeconomic groups make up the community?
- How aware are citizens of recycling? (What experience have they had?)
- What is the educational level of most constituents?
- Where do the citizens get their information? Radio and TV news programs? Newspapers? Talk shows? Posters at local stores?

As program planning advances, it may be worthwhile to pretest logos or promotional graphics, determining what will serve as the most attractive vehicles for a message. Such pretesting will gather feedback on communication materials before they are printed, recorded, or produced, thereby saving costs. In some programs, public contests are conducted to acquire logos and themes. This public involvement provides excellent publicity to the impending recycling program and is successful at starting up the public education process. Questionnaires can also provide a vehicle for the public to comment and feel as if they are contributing to the program. The level of response to any of these activities also acts as a bellwether for anticipating public participation concerning the recycling issue in their community. Finally, failure to conduct research can be very costly in terms of time and money. Materials that have no audience appeal, are confusing, or at worst, offend, can severely impact recycling participation over the long term.

Identifying Resources

The number of recycling programs that can devote significant resources to the public education function are among the minority. Most recycling programs have spent available capital funds on the more operational requirements of their program (curbside bins, vehicles, salaries). Conversely, more care will need to be given to the education effort, so as to maximize the effectiveness of any resources that *are* available.

As noted above, all opportunities to involve the community in the planning process as early as possible should be taken advantage of. Citizens groups and local organizations can provide valuable input and assistance in developing a public education plan, as well as the labor for implementation, often on a volunteer basis. As an example, Boy Scouts can assist in the distribution of recycling bins, generating publicity for their local troop and the recycling program as well.

Community Groups and Neighborhood Councils. As a resource, a recycling awareness message can often "piggyback" other communication efforts. For example, the City of San Diego's recycling program spread its message with the help of the *I Love A Clean San Diego* special interest group. Seattle, Washington's, program was assisted by the *Friends of Recycling.* In many instances, "block leader" programs can be initiated where a local resident acts as a resource for a neighborhood's recycling implementation. These individuals can be recruited to communicate face-to-face with resistant residents, or to make initial contact by hand-delivering materials (door to door).

Media. The use of news publications and other forms of the media are a common and economical publicity resource. Media coverage in the form of feature articles and advertisements run in local newspapers, public service announcements issued to local radio and television, as well as community access programming on cable television stations are low-cost ways to reach thousands of community members. Speaking directly with editors to determine how best to use these resources is beneficial in the short term but also goes a long way toward establishing press contacts for longer-term publicity. Steps for properly using the media are outlined in subsequent sections.

The Public School System. Information and recycling materials distributed during school presentations and assemblies do reach children's homes. Teachers and administrators usually welcome the opportunity to host an environmental speaker as well. Many school systems are now developing solid waste curricula in response to the growing public concern (see Fig. 30.1). It is also important to remember that in many households, it is the children who are responsible for taking the trash out. They'll also be given the job to recycle.

Often, solid waste organizations can act as a resource for the public schools to develop a waste management and recycling curriculum. The Rhode Island Solid Waste Management Corporation, for instance, provides educational materials to the public school system for use in recycling experiments and demonstrations. The agency also works closely with a number of schools and universities to promote new environmental policies and programs. The state legislature of Minnesota has gone even further and established the Minnesota Waste Education Program in 1987, in order to develop a unified approach to waste education in schools and communities throughout the state. Among the program's objectives are the development of school programs and curricula on waste topics for grades K to 12, and to advocate and help implement their usage in the public schools.

Utilities. Utilities can often assist with a recycling program, by allowing public education materials to be mailed along with bills and notices as extra inserts. This idea has similar applications for large "in-town" businesses that can distribute information to employees via paychecks, bulletins, and cafeteria displays. Municipal mailings can also incorporate logos and phrases on mailing envelopes to increase awareness (see Fig. 30.2). The use of recycled paper is also helpful.

State and Federal Agencies. Many state departments of environmental protection have created handbooks, promotional materials, and programs for use by local recycling programs. These materials usually have a minimal cost and agency personnel can provide guidance on their use. The U.S. Environmental Protection Agency's Office of Solid Waste in Washington, D.C., can provide resource materials as well (Fig. 30.3).

Environmental and Trade Organizations. There is no shortage in the number of organizations available to provide information on recycling issues from a local, national, and international perspective. The American Paper Institute in New York; the National Resource Recovery Association; U.S. Conference of Mayors in Washington, D.C.; Inform, Inc., New York; and the World Watch Institute in

Check all the non-paper items thrown away in your classroom and add your own:

1.	Rubber Bands _____	11.	_____
2.	Paper Clips _____	12.	_____
3.	Aluminum Foil _____	13.	_____
4.	Plastic _____	14.	_____
5.	Styrofoam _____	15.	_____
6.	Soda Cans _____	16.	_____
7.	Glass Jars or Bottles _____	17.	_____
8.	_____	18.	_____
9.	_____	19.	_____
10.	_____	20.	_____

Which items could have been reused at least once?

1.	_____	6.	_____
2.	_____	7.	_____
3.	_____	8.	_____
4.	_____	9.	_____
5.	_____	10.	_____

How about several times?

1.	_____	6.	_____
2.	_____	7.	_____
3.	_____	8.	_____
4.	_____	9.	_____
5.	_____	10.	_____

FIGURE 30.1 (a) Recycling classroom assignments.

Washington, D.C., are but a handful of groups that can provide literature, database information, legal assistance, and public education expertise for a recycling program. Many organizations like the Audubon Society or Nature Conservancy will operate on a local chapter level, providing resources and sometimes staff for even the smallest of programs. As non- or not-for-profit organizations, their as-

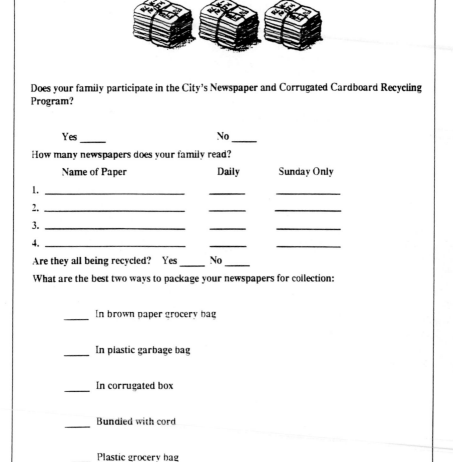

FIGURE 30.1 (*Continued*) (*b*) Home assignments. (*Courtesy of Waterbury Regional Resource Recovery Authority.*)

sistance can be limited and small expenses may be incurred for materials. On the whole, however, these organizations can provide valuable counsel for instituting a public education campaign and supporting it through its various stages.

Community Events. Recycling representatives often get excellent visibility at community fairs and other events, especially when distributing free items such as key chains and buttons. Such events provide another opportunity for face-to-face contact and question answering. As an example, the City of San Diego sent mem-

FIGURE 30.2   San Diego curbside recycling logo.

FIGURE 30.3   Learning about Municipal Solid Wastes. (*Courtesy of GRCDA, Silver Spring, Md.*)

bers of its Community Outreach Team to cover a dozen fairs and parties, often accompanied by their recycling mascot, Rascal the Cat (Fig. 30.4). Bloomington, Minn., took advantage of a 1989 city hall rally to kick off curbside pickup, followed by a series of community events.

FIGURE 30.4 Rascal, the Trash Cat.

Creative Design. For writing and designing public education materials, local art or advertising classes may welcome internship programs that provide "real-life" experience. Working with a marketing consultant or firm, perhaps at discounted or pro-bono rates, can also ensure a professional approach to materials creation.

Planning

Planning a public awareness campaign must take into account many factors, including budgetary constraints, the time available until startup, targeted audience, and type of program (i.e., curbside pickup versus drop-off center; single versus multimaterials). Although few recycling efforts will have the time to develop a formalized plan, goals and objectives should be agreed to prior to initiating education efforts so as to minimize confusion during startup. The plan will undoubtedly change as research reveals new information, trouble spots are identified, and the recycling program progresses; however, an initial plan should outline the following.

Audience Identification. As noted above, this is a critical first step that must be planned for appropriately.

Goals. What is to be gained from the education process? To simply state public participation as the campaign goal may be too broad. Certainly, one's aim is to bring the recycling message to individual publics that make up the community. However, very *specific* goals must be set in order to reach the various community segments. Goal setting here refers to determining, planning, and implementing communication strategies and events to penetrate the school system, ethnically diverse areas, low-income neighborhoods, etc. Examples of such goals are "conducting recycling education presentations at all grade schools in the community," "producing and distributing a bi-lingual recycling flyer," and "organizing a series of recycling fairs in low-income apartment complexes."

Public education goals are distinct from collection and capture rate goals, though the two will reflect one another. Several individual education goals successfully met will inevitably increase capture rates.

Available Resources. This includes identifying available money, staff, publicity vehicles, and media outlets. It is important to anticipate how each resource will relate to particular promotional components so as to maximize those resources.

Schedule. Coordinating the public education campaign with the program implementation deadline is critical to campaign success. Heavy publicity too far in advance can become stale, losing audience interest. Too late, and word may not have enough time to get out. Although there are no fast rules for scheduling, several guidelines are offered below. It is also important to take into account local and seasonal community events, which can impact program startup. For example, campaigns that are initiated in early September may have to compete with many "back-to-school" activities and promotions.

Staffing. For many current programs, an official recycling coordinator is not only assigned to conduct the recycling program but must implement the public education component as well. Sometimes an assistant or two, perhaps help from the solid waste management technical staff, can be relied on. It is rare that any given recycling program, regardless of the municipality's size, will have more than a few individuals whose time is purely devoted to the public education function. Often volunteers will play a key role in the communication process, sometimes actually directing the publicity program.

Program staffing decisions depend almost entirely upon the allocated budget, but the norm is for staff members to wear several hats due to limited funds. This may require the public education function to be located in the public works department, mayor's office, or another appropriate area. Access by interested parties, not to mention a "manned" phone are key concerns. (The City of Hollywood, Florida, has a catchy, easy-to-remember hot-line number—96-CYCLE.) As a rule of thumb, the more help available, the better chances are for getting out timely messages. For programs that are well-funded, outside public relations consultants and artists or a full-time public relations director can be hired.

However, since funding dictates that staffing traditionally is limited, interagency *resource sharing* is critical to program development. For example, a recycling coordinator can work with the Department of Transportation to create signs for recycling depots. Statistical information and/or accounting services can be provided by city finance departments. Creative services can be tapped, too. Lacking funds to hire an outside graphic artist, the City of San Diego's recycling program, for example, used the services of the City's own graphic arts department to prepare brochures, flyers, and promotional item artwork.

In all cases, implementing a recycling public education program requires the commitment and cooperation of the *entire* municipal structure. A meeting with department heads early in program development can help identify contacts and resources available to you within the municipal system.

Recycling Message and Media Strategies

Message and media strategies are planned according to the specific audiences being targeted, and also within budget limitations. Media selected and the messages formulated often need to account for adult and student audiences, low-income areas, and multilingual groups. Due to the higher costs associated with electronic promotional methods, most educational campaigns will rely on printed promotional pieces. Attractive direct mail brochures and flyers are an efficient means of reaching the entire community. They can be mass-mailed to entire Zip Code regions, and at bulk-mail rates if time is not a concern. These pieces are easily saved and displayed for reference in a household, and their design and production can be tailored to the available budget.

Posters, stickers, and cards can provide "point-of-contact" promotions, particularly where recycling activities can most logically take place. For example, a poster placed in an employee lounge adjacent to vending machines can encourage recycling, particularly if receptacles are made available. Similarly, a magnetized stick-on for the family refrigerator acts as a constant reminder in the home.

Bumper stickers, buttons, and other premium items, whether they promote a local politician or global cause, are guaranteed visibility. There is an up-front cost for these items (ranging from a few cents to a dollar or two a piece), and they can be given away or sold for a minimum amount to offset costs. Audience research is critical, because some communities may not be as likely to use a particular type of promotion.

Newspaper advertisements are an excellent means of reaching a large number of households, as a local newspaper is widely read as an information source. Since newspapers are usually among the first materials to be recycled, providing direction on how to recycle "this" paper is an effective promotion. Often these announcements, including pickup schedules, are free of cost as a public service on a space-available basis. Even paid newspaper advertisements can be fairly reasonable, depending on day of publication and frequency of inserts.

Television promotion is far-reaching, and a feature spot will do much to encourage participation and enhance enthusiasm. Of course, paid television advertising is prohibitively expensive and may be too broad for specific audiences being targeted. Television does offer a news vehicle, however, and press releases announcing the startup, outstanding results, or other milestones of a recycling program should be sent in on the chance they might be picked up for local news interest. Visible events (fairs, seminars, contests, fund-raising events, etc.) are also more likely to receive coverage, particularly as many news broadcasts will have "fill time" built into their broadcasts.

By far, the most successful public awareness strategies are those that incorporate as many points of contact with the community as possible. Recycling awareness is accomplished more thoroughly when mailers, newspaper advertisements, public service announcements, buttons, key chains, customized grocery bags, mugs, tee shirts, and special events are used together to penetrate a community, than when only one or two of these are used (Fig. 30.5).

Scheduling

While programs vary, there seems to be a common timetable for scheduling initial public awareness efforts. In scheduling, it is important to keep in mind that if the program's startup is advertised too far in advance, community members may forget about it altogether by the time the date arrives. The most effective startup campaigns usually stagger announcements and information about the campaign, with promotions becoming more frequent as the startup date approaches. A typical schedule is outlined below.

Publicity for a recycling program ideally begins at least several months in advance, beginning with some general recycling articles in local newspapers. Announcements at regularly scheduled meetings of the agency or authority responsible for recycling implementation are most common. Top municipal officials are

Coming soon ...
To a curb near you ...

Curbside Recycling!

The City of San Diego, Waste Management Department will be delivering recycling bins to your neighborhood **this Saturday.**

You will receive three bins: **white** for mixed household paper; **orange** for newspaper; and **blue** for plastic bottles, glass and cans.

The recycling bins will be delivered to your front door, along with an information packet on what materials can be recycled.

Additionally, Waste Management Department employees and volunteers from "I Love a Clean San Diego" will be going door-to-door to answer questions about the Curbside Recycling program.

If you have any questions, please call the City's **Recycling Hotline, 533-5353,** 7 a.m. to 5 p.m., weekdays.

City of San Diego
Waste Management Department

(a)

FIGURE 30.5 Curbside recycling doorknob poster.

often the initial spokespersons, with detailed communications being handled by a program coordinator.

Flyers or brochures, on average, are first distributed to recycling program households one month before the program actually begins—at minimum a few weeks ahead of implementation time, announcing what recyclables will be collected and how residents should comply. Often, these promotional materials may be distributed along with curbside bins for programs using this method. Subsequent newspaper advertisements can be run one week before startup. Promotion of the program will generally taper off as recycling is integrated into community life. Many communities have run weekly ads for their program during the first

(b)

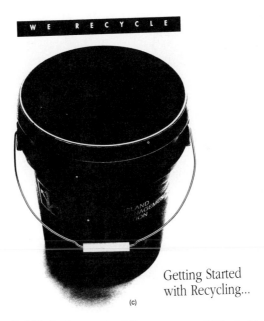

WE RECYCLE

Getting Started
with Recycling...

(c)

FIGURE 30.5 *(Continued)* *(b)*Curbside recycling follow-up poster; *(c)*Rhode Island Poster—
"What Should I Do First?"

three months, then reduced to monthly ads, using only occasional spots to advertise special events and new recycling tips once the program has taken off or new phases are added to the program.

Public service announcements, poster displays, and special events should attempt to "saturate" targeted audiences during the startup period, hopefully creating a groundswell of interest that will carry the program several weeks into its development. It is not uncommon for participation to taper off, however, as the

Glass Recycling Made Easy

Acceptable

Glass food and beverage containers can be easily recycled by glass container plants. Generally speaking, metal caps and lids should be removed but labels can remain.

Not Acceptable

The following materials are not recycled by glass container plants and should not be mixed in with container glass.

SODA BOTTLES

BEER BOTTLES

JUICE CONTAINERS

KETCHUP BOTTLES

WINE AND LIQUOR BOTTLES

FOOD CONTAINERS

MIRR

CE   C CUPS
A   ATES

FLOWER

YSTAL

LIGHT BULBS

WINDOW GLASS

EAT RESISTANT
ENWARE

NKING
SSES

"Printed on recycled paper."

(d)

Bloomington Residents Recycle!

How Much Will I Pay Per Month?

Single Family Homes and Duplexes . . . $1.00

Multiple Family Dwellings, including
Apartments, Town Houses, Condos
and Mobile Homes . . . . $0.87 per unit

Exemptions:

If you leave for part of the year and shut off your water, you may ask to have the recycling charge discontinued for that period. There is a reconnection charge.

There will not be an exemption for persons who do not choose to use curbside collection service. If you have extraordinary circumstances which you believe exempt you from this charge, you may file a formal appeal within 30 days of the mailing of your bill. Appeal applications may be picked up at the Public Works Building, 9930 Logan Avenue South.

**Do You Have
Any Recycling Questions?**

Call the
B.R.R. Hotline
887-9685
TTD: 887-9677

This is
printed
on
recycled
paper.

B.R.R.

(e)

FIGURE 30.5   (d)Glass recycling made easy; (e)Bloomington Residents Recycle (B.R.R.).

novelty of the program wears thin. (This may also be due to the up-front collection of recyclables stored in anticipation of program startup and a subsequent drop off due to fewer available recyclables.)

Table 30.1 lists a typical order of events in planning your recycling public awareness program. It is important to remember that flexibility is critical to the scheduling process. Last-minute program changes, unforeseen difficulties, and even a bout of bad weather can impact the best made plans for any recycling education program. Prudent planners will build options into their educational efforts so that if a particular event fails to materialize, program communications will continue. Of course, this is most important for kickoff events designed to "springboard" a program into the community's mainstream. Having a backup plan not only acts as an insurance policy but may even get implemented, thereby expanding program education efforts.

TABLE 30.1 Planning and Timing Recycling Events

Appropriate time frame	Public education element
1 year to 6 months before startup	Initial plan formulation; research (ongoing)
6 months; ongoing	Goal setting and strategies; phase-in of program
2–3 months before startup	General recycling articles in newspaper
1–2 months before startup	Mailer; backup support of TV and radio public service announcements; general news articles about recycling, condition of landfill, etc.
3–4 weeks before startup	Major newspaper articles and advertisements describing the details of the program
The week of startup	Kickoff event (citywide rally, special day, etc.)
2 weeks to 1 month after startup; ongoing	Evaluation; subsequent reminders as needed

EFFECTIVE COMMUNICATION STRATEGIES

When designing a recycling public education campaign, practitioners tend to focus initial energies on the creation of tangible promotional items (fact sheets, mailers, etc.). This is usually in response to scheduling pressures that leave little time for planning and preparation. The result is that the public is often besieged with messages on the "whys" of recycling, as these are easier to prepare, rather than the "how to" of a particular program. Often, program specifics are left to a news item in the local paper or a handout placed in a recycling container a week or so in advance. Because of this, key information may not reach an audience and subtle differences in those audiences may not be accounted for, causing low participation rates over the long term.

To avoid this, sufficient audience research should be undertaken as a means toward "packaging" a proper balance of generic and specific communication elements. Although there may be little time for this type of research, this step can be fundamental to program development. Methods for gaining valuable demographic information using limited resources are highlighted in earlier chapters. As a basis for understanding, however, it is necessary to consider the dynamics involved with the communication process and their influence on the messages created for any program.

Persuasion almost always consists of convincing an individual that their participation is beneficial—to them. Whether buying a car, selecting an entree, or exercising the right to vote, one's decision to do this or that is largely predicated by some influence. The advertising industry makes its living in this way, creating favorable product images, enticing some kind of consumer reaction, hopefully a positive one. This axiom has a divisive side when taken in the form of a threat, real or perceived, so that participation is coerced. (Often, recycling programs that "mandate" compliance attempt to use this type of strong-arm persuasion.)

Barriers

From any perspective, however, persuasion will require overcoming some barriers. For recycling programs, this usually means recognizing the inconvenience separating materials in the home can cause (and yes, recycling is an inconvenience) and finding an easy, simply communicated means to solve this. Public reaction has generally included complaints that recycling takes too much time in an already time-constrained world; is a dirty process requiring on-going cleaning and storage; or is difficult to comply with, particularly if recyclables must be brought to another location. This perception may be based on personal experience, presuppositions, or collective word of mouth, but is rooted in the nation's "throwaway" disposal habits of years prior, which are not easy to change.

Being Audience-Specific

For these reasons, program messages must attempt to minimize the apparent inconvenience of recycling by appealing to the positive benefits of participation. Socioeconomic factors can often influence these perceptions and be a key to a communication's success. Whereas white-collar, upscale areas may respond to messages promoting the environment and resource savings, urban areas may tend to focus on the economic payback recyclables offer. Benefits therefore should be audience-specific while delivering clearly defined instructions on how the individual is to participate. This can be a tricky process, particularly when limited resources may restrict the frequency of communications developed.

Message Design

Every attempt must be made to avoid complicated, fragmented, or infrequent communications. Inasmuch as the recycling program should be designed to minimize inconvenience, so too, the program's communications must be readily understood and acted upon. Information that is simply stated, upbeat, and repeated often has the greatest chance at success. Step-by-step identification of the who, what, when, and how is imperative. Messages should also be presented through attractive, visually appealing means.

What rules can be applied to the creative development of a recycling communications program? As a first step, program identity should be consistently conveyed and legitimized. Usually this is initiated with the establishment of a program logo and theme. This is important because it will separate the program's messages from the thousands of others that will impact on identified audiences. "Name-brand" recognition, so to speak, is crucial to program participation because once credibility has been established, communications incorporating program logos and themes will have a greater recognition. Similarly, slogans, jingles, or cartoon characters can provide instant recognition so that messages are easily attributed to the program. As examples, Keep America Beautiful, Inc.'s Indian representative remains an instantly recognizable figure for antilitter campaigns, even though this image is over a decade old. Similarly, Timex's "It Takes a Licking and Keeps on Ticking" has been assimilated into American language as a colloquium for many years now. Closer to the recycling message, San Diego's mascot, Rascal the Cat, and their "We're Not Trash" logo and Rhode Island's Oscar, a seagull-like cartoon mascot of the *Ocean State Cleanup and Recycling* division of the Department of Environmental Management are assisting each of these diverse recycling programs with their recognition campaigns (see Fig. 30.6).

It is also imperative that messages convey simple ideas. Lengthy descriptions of environmental benefits and "saving the ecosystem" may be interesting, but do little for participation. Participants wish to devote minimal time to recycling. Similarly, the information needed to participate must be easily learned, easily applied, and require little time to assimilate into the daily routine.

This is where proper audience research can be most beneficial. By tailoring messages to identified groups, communications can push the most positive aspects of participation with a given audience. If "saving the environment" is a primary concern among residents in a particular neighborhood, promotional efforts should play to this collective mindset by stressing the benefits recycling will have on the local ecosystem. Correlations between the amount of newspaper recycled versus the use of virgin trees is an example of this type of promotion. Where economics is an issue, campaigns that stress the savings associated with offsetting landfill disposal costs may be more affective.

Although few programs can afford the slick, first-rate production quality of commercial advertising and promotions, a professional approach to the design of graphics, text, and all promotional materials should be strived for. Inasmuch as tangible communications pieces must deliver information, they also act to represent the organization that has put them out. The goal there is to acquire the highest professional quality so as to improve audience recognition and credibility with the program. Achieving successful results with your printed materials is possible without the use of a professional public relations or graphic design agency, if a few simple guidelines are followed.

Materials should be readable, uncluttered, and simple, with a mixture of text and illustrations that will make the reader want to read the piece. The text should be large enough to read easily, and printed in a standard type style (nothing so fancy or calligraphic that it is pretty but hard to read). Allow for some white space—wide margins, space around pictures, and enough interline spacing on the text will make the piece more attractive and less tedious for the reader (see Fig. 30.7).

The copy should be lively, and be aimed at the average reading level (at approximately the eighth grade level). Try to avoid using technical terms that might be misunderstood or that may "turn off" an audience.

Clean line-art drawings carefully placed on a page can be very effective, so

(a)

(b)

FIGURE 30.6 (*a*) "Poster—"Hey! We're Not Trash." (*b*) Ocean
state cleanup and recycle poster.

Fall Leaves Are Not Garbage This Year!

This Fall the leaves you rake from your yard will not be added to the piles of garbage accumulating in the City's landfill, the North End Disposal Area. Instead, they will be piled at John Coe Park where they will be turned into "black gold", or leaf compost, for use in landscaping and gardening. This is just part of the City's new approach to waste management, and keeps the City ahead of State mandates.

The City encourages residents to compost their leaves on their own property as much as possible. Information on home composting is available from the Recycling Office. However, residents who do not wish to compost their own leaves and want them removed must now put the leaves out for collection in special biodegradable paper bags. The bags will be available to the public in major grocery stores. When full, residents can roll the tops shut on the bags or simply leave them open and standing at the curb. It will be unlawful to dispose of any material other than leaves in these bags, and leaves will not be collected unless they are in the special composting bags.

Collection of the bagged leaves will take place on the last four Wednesdays in November.

However, residents and private haulers can bring leaves (only) directly to the composting site, John Coe Park, starting October 10, 1989. See the back of this page for details and directions to the site, and information regarding City collection.

The composting of Waterbury's leaves is a good idea for many reasons. Most importantly, it saves valuable landfill space for material that cannot be disposed of in other ways. The valuable and useful product which results from this process helps the City save money and resources, and is an excellent example of how a waste material, when looked at in a different way, can be seen as a resource.

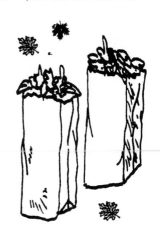

FIGURE 30.7 (a) "Fall Leaves Are Not Garbage This Year."

there is no real need for more elaborate drawings and pictures if a budget does not allow them. The lack of real drawing ability can be overcome by using "clip art" packages (inexpensive books of graphics specifically for this purpose), or by tracing and slightly modifying existing images. Many solid waste and recycling symbols are universal and can be used without restrictions.

Let The City Collect Your Leaves, Or......

If you find that your leaves are piling up before the scheduled leaf collection for your neighborhood and want to get rid of them, residents of Waterbury and Wolcott can bring their leaves directly to the composting site at John Coe Park until Saturday, December 16, 1989, loose or in the special bags. Any other containers used to transport the leaves to the site must be taken home after emptying. The site will be open to accept leaves Monday through Saturday, 7:00am to 3:00pm. There will be no charge to bring leaves to the site, however residents should bring proof of residency, such as a driver's license.

John Coe Park is located in northwest Waterbury off of Brookside Road. Please refer to the map at the right for directions.

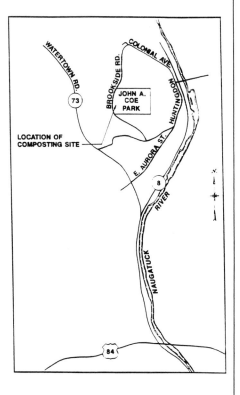

Municipal Leaf Collection Schedule

You'll have two opportunities this November if you want the City to pick up your leaves. These will be the **second** and **fourth** Wednesdays (the 8th and 22nd) for residents with regular municipal waste collection on Mondays and Thursdays, and the **third** and **fifth** Wednesday (the 15th and 29th) for those with regular waste collection on Tuesdays and Fridays.

Information for residents interested in the finished compost will be available from the Refuse Department at 574-6857, or the Recycling Office in the Spring of 1990.

Waterbury Regional Resource Recovery Authority

FIGURE 30.7 (*Continued*) (*b*) "Let the City Collect Your Leaves Or—."

The use of color(s) in your pieces is advisable, and will make any material more eyecatching and pleasant to look at. However, the cost of production will rise with each additional color used. In selecting one or two colors to use, coordinate with the city or town's colors, or establish colors that will exclusively identify the recycling program consistently throughout all your printed material.

Colors can be selected from a standard color chart obtained from a printer, or incorporate process colors—basic colors that are not custom-mixed.

Make every effort to print materials on recycled materials, indicating this somewhere on the piece with the recycling symbol. It is important that the sponsoring organization practice what it preaches.

RECYCLING PRESS COVERAGE

Media coverage, such as newspaper articles, radio announcements and interviews, and even television spots can be low-cost ways to communicate with hundreds to thousands of community members about a recycling program. By using the media, it is possible to provide the "how to" of participation while at the same time promoting the credibility of the program by way of third-party reference. In order to gain media coverage, it helps to approach the various media proactively, rather than waiting for their call.

Print Media

Local daily and weekly papers are often quite willing to write a feature story regarding a recycling program, just as long as the story has an angle that makes it newsworthy. The kickoff of the program will certainly be news, as might participation rates, outstanding individual or community participants in the program, special collection days, or a program milestone (a goal achieved, the program's anniversary, etc.). Interviews with community recycling leaders or the recycling coordinator also make interesting feature articles.

Press releases sent to the attention of the special features editor, environmental editor, or the general news editor of the newspapers, will help announce events, but a followup phone contact is always helpful to better chances of coverage. Press releases, typed double-spaced on the recycling organization's or municipality's letterhead, should be written in standard press release format: FOR IMMEDIATE RELEASE, or FOR RELEASE ON (date) should be written as the first line. A headline should appear next. The first paragraph begins with a dateline, which includes the date and place of release. Press releases are written in inverted pyramid style, with the most important, newsworthy information at the top, followed by paragraphs of supporting information in order of decreasing importance. A contact person and phone number should appear either at the top or the bottom of the release (see Fig. 30.8).

If a good photo is available, send a black-and-white print along with the release. If the release does not interest the editor, sometimes a captivating photograph and caption will be printed instead. Although a release must compete with many others that often sit piled on a busy editor's desk, one carefully crafted release may be all that's needed to develop a permanent press contact. Of course, when a reporter calls, relevant information should be handy—names, dates, collection figures. If a photograph was not sent with the release, offer to send one or to be available for a photojournalist.

Press Conferences

Press conferences should be used only when there is *timely, critical, and highly newsworthy* information to convey. Program startups, market identifications, or

James G. Martin, Governor James T. Broyhill, Secretary

North Carolina
Department of Economic and Community Development

| Release: | Immediate | Date: | October 18, 1989 |
| Contact: | Al Ebron (919) 733-2230 | | |

STATE-WIDE SERIES OF SOLID WASTE MANAGEMENT SEMINARS SCHEDULED

RALEIGH, NC - The Energy Division, North Carolina Department of Economic and Community Development, is sponsoring the 1989 Seminar on Solid Waste Management in North Carolina, from November 7-16, at six locations throughout the state. Featuring recognized experts in the fields of waste-to-energy, recycling and environmental protection, these full-day seminars are designed to educate public officials, public employees and decision-makers on national, regional and local perspectives of solid waste disposal.

The dates and locations of each seminar include: **Raleigh, NC** (McKimmon Center- NC State University), Tues., November 7; **Washington, NC** (Civic Center), Wed., November 8; **Fayetteville, NC** (Cumberland County Library), Thurs., November 9; **Salisbury, NC** (Holiday Inn), Tues., November 14; **Lenoir, NC** (Holiday Inn), Wed., November 15; **Asheville, NC** (Quality Inn - Biltmore), Thurs., November 16. Further information and a free brochure are available from Mr. Al Ebron at the Energy Division of the NC Department of Economic and Community Development (919-733-2230).

Each seminar will look at solid waste issues from North Carolina's regional perspectives. Issues to be discussed are landfilling, recycling, implementation strategies, economics and ways to integrate methods of reducing and managing waste. Case studies will also be presented.

The State's Regional Councils of Governments and Commissions are contributing professional support to the 1989 seminar series. Speakers include representatives from the North Carolina Recycling Association, Sun Shares, Madison Environmental Alliance, and State and Local Agencies.

FIGURE 30.8   North Carolina Press Release—Seminar.

crisis situations will usually require a formalized meeting between program managers and the press. As an event, press conferences can make or break a recycling program as it attempts to stand up to a naturally critical review by the press.

Like all events, planning is essential. When applicable, a notice sent in advance of the conference is helpful to announce the who, what, when, and where. Although details should be left for the conference, the press will need some indication on what the conference is about prior to devoting a reporter to cover it.

Materials, including a formal press release, should be duplicated for distribution. "Backgrounders," fact sheets that provide information on how the program arrived at this stage in its development, as well as photos, a conference agenda, and names and titles of conference speakers should be available. Much of these materials can be contained in a press kit, a folder in which each of these items can be collected. When budgets allow, these folders can be printed with program logos and designs.

Recognizing that reporters from a variety of media may attend, efforts should be made to accommodate their needs. A conference late in the day may be suitable for TV, but would leave most papers to cover the event in the next day's news. Graphics in a handout may be suitable for reproduction in a newspaper, but TV may respond better to visual displays used during the conference.

For the sake of the program's integrity as well as credibility among the press, it is imperative that conference presenters rehearse statements in preparation. This usually goes without saying. Yet, a harried official, who receives a written statement just prior to walking in front of the lights, is not uncommon. Every effort must be made to prepare spokespersons so as to maintain professionalism and credibility. For those who have never spoken with the press but are required to, it is best to acquire some counsel from a local speaker's group, university, or professional trainer. An early investment in this area can do wonders for a program's communication efforts.

Radio

Radio can be approached in much the same way as print media, but is more selective in audience contact. In addition to on-the-hour news and specials, talk programs may run on a weekly basis providing opportunities for in-depth interviews. Another form of promotion with radio (and TV) is the use of public service announcements (PSAs). PSAs are brief announcements that a radio station will pay or read, free of charge, as a public service. The broadcast of a PSA can reach thousands of people. The only drawback with the PSA is that radio stations tend to play them as "fillers" as time permits, and unlike paid advertising spots, a PSA may not be delivered on a regular schedule or during a prime listening time.

Public Service Announcements

PSAs are usually 15-, 30-, 45-, or 60-second timed spots prerecorded or read live. (Sometimes a local or official or celebrity can be used as the narrator for greater impact.) The shorter the PSA, the more likely it will be played. A 30-second PSA can be fit into many more time slots than a 60-second PSA.

Written PSAs will be read out loud or prerecorded. Language, therefore, should be kept simple, direct, and captivating, with the sentences relatively short, and incorporating action words to avoid creating a boring, stagnant spot (see Fig. 30.9). Repeat important information often (at least twice for phone numbers and pickup days). Most people listen to a radio as they are actively engaged with some other activity. Rarely is a pencil handy, so repetition is necessary. Before submitting a PSA to the radio station, it should be read out loud to detect any trouble spots (tongue twisters, difficult sentences, etc.).

PSAs can be typewritten, double-spaced, with wide margins on letterhead. The timed reading length should be indicated on top. A contact name and phone number are also necessary. The radio station will need time to review any PSA,

"Waterbury Recycles"

Public Service Announcement (PSA)

(15 seconds)

Our garbage is the number one environmental problem facing this City. Unless we find new ways to dispose of our trash, we'll soon have no place to put it—what then?

We know that one part of the solution is recycling, that is, the separation of those materials in our garbage that once again can be put to good use.

Starting _____ , all single-family and some multi-family homes, on city-collected routes only, will be required to separate newspapers from their trash.

Details on how to save your newspapers for special pick-up, at no cost to you, is being sent to you. Please read this material carefully. We need your help so that "Waterbury Recycles!"

FIGURE 30.9 Sample radio public service announcement.

edit, if necessary, and put it through internal production channels. If a PSA is timely, the radio station should be given ample notice to prepare it.

Television

A television features editor can be approached the same as a newspaper features editor—by press release and/or phone call. Television editors work on very tight deadlines and short notice, so in order to have a chance at a television spot, a recycling story must be timely and exceptionally interesting. It also must lend itself to a *visual display.* A story covering a program kickoff will have more visual appeal if, for instance, a colorful mascot is parading around shaking people's hands, or if children are participating in a can-crushing contest.

Opportunities for getting time on television are greater with local, smaller TV stations or cable channels than with larger, national network affiliates, simply because recycling programs are generally locally oriented news and do not lend themselves to standard national broadcasts.

Crisis Communications

When approached by the media regarding a negative aspect of the recycling program (record low participation rates, complaints of missed pickups, program controversy, etc.), it is imperative to maintain openness of communication and a level of cooperation. Never attempt to avoid the media. Better to answer questions directly, while citing past achievements, recognizing current problems, assuring remedial action is under way. Subsequent stories that, at a minimum, provide an official comment will offset criticism that may come from many quarters. Something positive may also be picked up and elaborated on by a third party.

Paid Use of the Media

If budgets allow, paid advertising as a media outlet can be useful. Though relatively expensive, a well-designed, carefully placed advertisement in a newspaper or magazine can provide high visibility. Similarly, a professionally recorded ratio announcement played in the right time slots can be very effective. The frequency of placements will also determine the number of discounts given. Shopping around is always cost-effective, assuming there are several media outlets to choose among. Most TV and radio station and newspaper account managers are also helpful in determining the best use of the advertising dollars and can provide creative assistance with the design of the advertising piece.

Follow-up

Never assume that a reporter's story or even a paid advertisement will get it right. Mistakes can happen, particularly if scheduling is tight. Published articles or news features must be reviewed immediately. If confusion or incorrect information has been propagated by the piece, odds are the phones will soon ring with a confused constituency on the other end. If the wrong date is published in an ad, recyclables could end up on the curb weeks in advance of pickup, immediately throwing a well-planned program into chaos.

When errors are made, the quicker and more comprehensive the response the better. To begin, mistakes should be brought to the attention of the reporter, senior editor, publisher, or owner as the case may warrant. Although a correction would normally be made in follow-up editions or broadcasts, the potential impact of the error may warrant more than a short, easily glanced-over correction notice. Work with editors to approach the issue at the same level of news importance as the original story—not as simply a clerical mistake requiring a quick fix. Also, be cooperative rather than combative, as this will yield beneficial results, particularly if suggestions can be discussed to remedy the situation.

In most cases, however, the information reported will be correct (although not always at the level of importance desired) and useful to the receiving audience. Timing other promotional items (delivery or newsletters, bins, etc.) with an ad or news report helps to create the repetition suggested earlier. Copies of printed articles or ads can also have a second life as reprints for media kits, or handouts to small groups. Be sure to thank editors and reporters as well. They will be needed again as the recycling program develops.

COMMUNITY INVOLVEMENT PROGRAMS

Regardless of the funds available for creating promotional materials, all recycling programs can take advantage of community outreach as the most effective means for generating participation among a desired constituency.

Outreach

Outreach methods used in the public information segments of a recycling campaign most often use group interaction for disseminating specialized information and answering public concerns. Usually aimed at specific target groups, outreach operations, while labor-intensive, are especially useful in harnessing the organized participation of vested interest groups. As a result, these programs require individuals who act in key educational leadership roles. These roles may take the form of speaking to schools and business and citizen groups; directing neighborhood councils that encourage local support of the recycling program; acting as liaisons with teachers and student groups; operating information booths at regional events; leading commercial and residential workshops; or directing or implementing demographic surveys to judge the effectiveness of the program's proposed or actual informational and educational methods. To some extent, specialized recycling guides and monetary incentives such as variable trash rates may also be viewed as part of an outreach effort.

Staff Education

Although each of these outreach programs have singular advantages and disadvantages, individuals must be knowledgeable about the recycling program to be able to communicate effectively on a group or one-on-one basis. Program workers, particularly volunteers, should undergo some type of training regarding the specifics of the recycling program, the concerns of the groups with whom they will be interacting, as well as the municipality where the program will be implemented. To some extent, well-produced videos can also be used effectively in conjunction with trained speakers to supplement presentations.

Programming

One of the more labor-intensive outreach tools, the municipal hot line, is designed to answer public concerns and questions on an individual and immediate basis. The ideal, a 24-hour line, usually supplements telephone workers with an answering machine during off-hours. In addition to directly communicating specific information on an as-needed basis, this tool also has the advantage of using only superficially trained workers, since most questions tend to be general in nature, regarding scheduling, material separation, packaging, etc. Of course, a fact sheet with easily referenced answers to commonly asked questions is helpful and will help maintain consistency of the information relayed.

School programming is an essential method of public education in the truest sense of that term, because practical as well as theoretical recycling information is brought into the learning process. This will not only benefit programs where particular student body may reside, but also fosters life-long habits that will prove beneficial on a global scale. Also, lessons learned are generally incorporated into the home, particularly if they are presented as a family-oriented activity.

In addition to the more typical presentations by a recycling program coordinator, field trips to recycling separation centers or recycling plants answer the question of what happens to the materials after collected. In this way, natural curiosity is replaced with a fundamental understanding of the recycling process, often to level far greater than the parents, who will ultimately have the day's events repeated at the dinner table.

Contests where students create new things out of recyclable materials can be both educational and fun. In the mind of a fourth-grader, a discarded (but clean) plastic milk container takes on many possibilities, particularly if he or she is free to decorate, add to, and generally let his or her imagination produce some tangible new toy or device. This type of program is a favorite with science and art teachers alike, combining resources within a given school. Awards for the top creations can be as simple as the presentation of a certificate by a local official or program mascot. This will increase the publicity capabilities of the event as well. Other contests have included citywide participation in logo creations, slogans, and mascot designs. These events must be coordinated effectively so as not to become overburdened or poorly managed.

Fairs or block parties provide an ideal time to promote a program in particular neighborhoods. A booth, operated by local volunteers, can distribute information and answer questions. Can-crushing contests, guessing the number of recyclables in a container, or art contests are ways to drum up interest and media coverage. Local businesses, including local scrap dealers and paper companies, may, depending on the size of the event, donate materials, food, and beverages (bins for recyclables a must!). Local officials would do well to make an appearance in support of the event.

Cleanup events at local parks and public areas provide an ideal connection with the recycling message. Often, cleanup programs are supported by the local Chamber of Commerce or some other entity that will welcome the support of the recycling program. The twentieth anniversary of Earth Day in 1990 led to many new promotional events and can provide an opportunity for communicating the recycling message.

The establishment of a speakers bureau (or the inclusion of a recycling staff person on an existing bureau) increases the opportunity for communicating with targeted groups. Presentations to civic groups, seniors, or any interested party require little setup and are welcomed by these organizations. Handout materials and the use of a slide or video show will break up the presentation, maintaining interest while saving the energies of a staff person who may have several presentations in a week.

Each of these events can be modified to specific need and according to available resources. It is important, however, to infuse the highest level of quality into all programming that is undertaken. Poorly managed events can result in negative public response. Better to do a few things well then many more which may be poorly received.

MEASURING PROGRAM EFFECTIVENESS

Perhaps the easiest and most common way to assess the effectiveness of a recycling public education program is to simply look at the quantity of recyclables collected and extrapolate a percentage based on prior knowledge of the waste stream. This will certainly provide some concrete indication on whether or not the populace is recycling. By looking at collection data from specific geographical areas or programs, it is also possible to pinpoint how successful individual neighborhoods are. Of course, this does nothing to answer the question "why," and, unless investigated according to other criteria, is of little use as a measurement of promotional efforts for recycling program managers.

Earlier chapters discussed the need to establish public education goals that relate to the communication processes being undertaken for the public education program, as opposed to the quantity of materials collected. This same thinking should apply when judging the effectiveness of an education campaign. Goals judged according to communication principles will yield a beneficial understanding of what is successful and what is not.

Assessments

This will require an organized followup program, incorporating many of the same components used during the initial research phase of the education program. In many respects, many of the interviews and surveys conducted at that time are worth repeating. Questions to be answered can include

- Are audiences clearly defined?
- Do target audiences receive appropriate messages?
- Have communications been frequent enough?
- Can new socioeconomic considerations be identified?
- Are there competing or similar messages?
- Has the proper medium been used for a message?
- What works? What doesn't?

Answers to these questions can be acquired by speaking with many of the individuals and groups originally canvassed during the research phase of the program. It is also helpful to conduct random, spot surveys of residents in neighborhoods where participation is both good and poor. In addition to asking questions on the effectiveness of the communications program, another opportunity has been created to gather information on participant habits, prejudices, and ideas. This "new" information can be valuable for introducing new recyclables into the program or for followup promotional activities. In effect, audience profiles can be refined for further focusing the public education campaign.

Changes

In the event there is a problem, often slight modifications are all that may be necessary to improve a particular form of communication or element of the program. Simply jazzing up promotional items or increasing distribution frequency may have marked results. However, when an action is shown to have minimal or disastrous results, it should be replaced with another, regardless of resources already expended, so as to maintain the integrity of other education elements that are successful.

Measurements

Several quantitative measurements can be borrowed from the marketing and advertising fields, however, to help assess a particular education element. When us-

7. ing a direct-mail piece, for instance, a retention/response rate of only 2 to 5 percent is considered good. Of course for industries who may be mailing to hundreds of thousands of potential customers (as with mail-order firms), the significance of this percentage can be translated in very strong sales figures. When applied to a recycling program, however, a compliance rate of at least 10 to 15 percent should be strived for at the start, gradually increasing based on the extent of followup activities and troubleshooting that is undertaken. For one material (e.g., newspapers), a collection rate over 50 percent is not uncommon at the outset of the program.

8. The amount of returned mail will also give a fairly good indication of the validity of the program mailing list.

For a telephone hot line, several calls an hour just prior to the startup of a program can be encouraging, particularly if the number was publicized through some other mechanism (e.g., brochure mailer, advertisement). Of course, a truer judgment of the overall communications effort can be made based on the type of calls coming in and the degree of confusion being relayed.

9. Collection personnel can be a leading indicator of the communications success, particularly for residential pickup programs. The condition of recyclables when collected (e.g., washed, bundled, or separated appropriately) or the number of households actually participating on a given street can yield a valuable profile of the community's response. Collection personnel may also have important technical suggestions once a program is under way that could impact future program communications. Many recycling coordinators will also follow collection vehicles during the first weeks of a program to see for themselves the success or pitfalls of program startup.

10. For drop-off centers, periodic visitations are a must, particularly during various hours of operation. In some cases, poorly marked access or directions will turn potential recyclers away simply due to the frustration of locating the center. Centers should also be maintained for cleanliness and security. Residents who don't feel comfortable when dropping off materials will not participate over the long term.

Summary

Public education programming remains an essential component to recycling's success. Not only does the public education function ensure participation, but it can be instrumental in maintaining program integrity over the long term. Flexible in their application, public education programs can be simply designed or full-scale, multifaceted productions requiring any range of costs.

Staffing needs can vary to include one identified recycling professional or a handful of volunteers combining talents to get the job done. Regardless of resources, however, advance planning is critical, particularly for large-scale, multimaterial programs. This includes the proper research of audiences to be communicated with and the identification of available resources for getting the message out. These messages should incorporate lively text and graphics and can be produced professionally or with nonprofit assistance. Program assessments, based on communications criteria, offer a means to identify needed changes and program successes.

Acknowledgments to Evelyn Snitofsky and Madeline Aron for their assistance in preparing this chapter.

End Markets

- Knowledge of international, national, state, and local market opportunities
- Knowledge of other marketing opportunities such as market cooperatives and market development options
- Knowledge of market specifications (contaminants, shipping requirements, bale specifications, etc.)
- Knowledge of longer-term trends

Recycling Program Management

- Skill in program management such as managing budgets, managing people, and managing equipment (maintenance, proper operation, safety)
- Knowledge of and skill in managing an efficient processing and collection (e.g., routing efficiency and production efficiency) and in communicating with the public and public officials
- Knowledge of full range of equipment options for collection and processing including recently developed or state-of-the-art technologies or approaches including drop-off collection, curbside (dedicated vehicles), curbside (co-collection approaches), multimaterial processing, approaches for integrating organics collection and composting, and opportunities for corresponding savings in garbage collection
- Knowledge and skill in selection of and management of contractors

Promotion

- Knowledge of and ability to coordinate promotion based on the fundamental principles of promotion (consistency, targeting of message, etc.)
- Knowledge of promotion ideas for recycling
- Skill in utilizing community as a resource
- Skill in developing and maintaining strong support of council
- Skill in public and one-on-one presentations
- Skill in dealing with the media

Local Government

- The skill of being able to continually foster local government support (recycling program managers)
- Knowledge of relevant state and local laws

Other Important Topics

- Monitoring

- Design and implementation of recycling programs for multifamily and institutional/commercial and industrial (ICI) sectors
- Composting

In this chapter, an exploration of how training can be used to develop the capability of recycling program staff members and managers will be covered. In the first half of this chapter the principles behind how to define training needs and what the typical training needs in the recycling profession are will be addressed. In the second half of this chapter the considerations necessary in designing a training plan for the recycling program manager and the recycling program staff members and utilizing training practices that accomplish *true* learning—not just the "hear and forget" variety will be addressed.

DEFINING TRAINING NEEDS

Whatever business or profession a program manager is in, and particularly in the recycling field, difficulties arise when trying to squeeze in training opportunities. Generally speaking, it takes time, money, and most importantly, is difficult to find the exact program to meet the needs of each staff member. Frequently, recycling program staff members and managers find themselves wasting time sitting in sessions that are only vaguely useful with their attention slipping back and forth from the session to other concerns at home or at the office. This situation is all too common and truly unfortunate, because it is only by addressing an *individual's own learning needs* that training can be worthwhile and productive.

Learning Needs for Recycling Manager and Staff

When starting to think about potential training initiatives for a recycling manager or for the recycling staff, there can be no better starting point than defining the training need. In other words, what is the outcome in *performance* terms that the job type requires? Improvement in performance or capability is the bottom line of training and may be accomplished using the following procedures:

1. *Define the full list of performance requirements for the job function* (otherwise known as competencies). For example, two performance requirements for the position of a commercial recycling program coordinator may include:
   a. Ability to understand and apply applicable rules, regulations, policies, and procedures relating to the commercial-sector recycling program.
   b. Ability to communicate effectively both orally and in writing with area business and community leaders and the general public.
2. Evaluate the list generated above and *note whether the competency requires information or knowledge of a particular subject, or whether it requires a proficiency in a certain skill.* For example, the first competency noted above requires broad *knowledge* of the recycling program, whereas the second competency refers to a specific *skill* in being able to deal with the media. See Table 31.1 for examples of required skill competencies and knowledge competencies for various recycling program positions.
3. *Describe the gap between the current and ideal level of proficiency in each competency area for the recycling program manager and for the recycling*

TABLE 31.1 Recycling Job Performance and Competency Requirements

Position	Performance requirement (examples)	Competency requirement	
		Knowledge	Skill
Administrative Recycling Manager	Develop countywide recycling plan consistent with state mandates. Coordinate public and private entities.	Regulations, policies, and procedures relating to the recycling program.	Writing technical reports, implementing programs, communications, and public relations.
Multifamily Recycling Specialist II and Commercial Program Development	Act as a consultant on multifamily dwellings and private haulers. Negotiate contracts.	Rules, policies, and procedures relating to multifamily recycling program.	Writing and public speaking. Effective public relations abilities.
Recycling Specialist I—Single Family. Institutional Special Wastes	Coordinate the development and maintenance of single-family, institutional, and special waste recycling.	Residential and institutional programs. Resolving hard-to-handle complaints for single-family homes.	Knowledge of word processing and spreadsheet development, typing, and communications skills—oral and written.
Public Information Specialist	Researches and writes publications for the Solid Waste Authority. Prepares annual reports. Develops press kits.	Journalistic principles and practices. Marketing and research techniques. Public relations, typography, and graphic design.	Assemble and write a wide variety of interesting publications. Oral and written communications skills.
Operational Recycling Manager	Responsible for all aspects of the recycling center. Coordinate activities between pilot and contract collection programs and the materials recovery facility.	Principles and practices of recycling programs. Materials, equipment and supplies used in implementing recycling programs.	Oral and written communications skills. Working relationship skills Plan and coordinate projects.
Recycler I	Maintenance of facility. Receiving, processing, and packaging recyclables.	Operate mobile and stationary equipment, i.e., trucks, balers, forklift, crushers, and loaders.	Sufficient physical strength to perform manual work. understand and follow oral and written instructions.
Recycling Collection Supervisor	Supervise and coordinate activities or workers engaged in the curbside collection process.	Of practices, methods, tools, equipment, and materials of the curbside collection program.	Supervise semiskilled workers, operate equipment, public relations, and maintenance of daily logs.
Contract Manager (Recycling)	Management of collection contracts and interlocal agreements with municipal governments.	Contract management techniques and tools. Managerial, accounting, and budget practices of the recycling program.	Computer skills in word processing, spreadsheet, and database. Present clear and concise reports. Establish procedure and contract requirements.

Source: Solid Waste Authority of Palm Beach County, Florida.

staff. For example, using the same example as above, the commercial recycling program coordinator may have an excellent understanding of the planned commercial-sector recycling program, but has limited knowledge of the relationships between various policy-making entities that may impact the successful implementation of the program. Similarly, this person may have an excellent ability to prepare for talks and presentations, but his or her actual delivery and presentation style is weak.

This type of analysis results in a very specific description of training needs for the commercial recycling program coordinator that allows the recycling program manager to focus on improving the required performance. The training plan that would be established for this person would *not* need to address general-level information on recycling program operation, nor provide general training on presentations. Rather, the training plan would be quite specific and would provide:

1. *Training on policy development by entity, responsibility, and contact person:* For example, how are state rules implemented through state regulatory agencies or how do flow-control policies of recovered materials at the state level affect the successful implementation of a commercial-sector recycling program? As much as possible, the trainee would not only observe the process but also communicate directly with decision-making entity's staff persons. Flowcharts and diagrams of the rules, regulations, and the entities developing and implementing them as such may also prove to be useful.

2. *Training and practice on how to deliver presentations:* Several practice sessions could be arranged for the trainee to practice the delivery of presentations. Practice presentations could be made to more experienced colleagues who could offer practical advice and tips. Alternatively, practice sessions could be taped and then self-analyzed. Ideally, mock situations should be created for the trainee to become more comfortable with a range of challenging situations (such as answering difficult questions, dealing with hecklers, etc.). Finally, the trainee could attend any one of the many presentation training seminars that are offered by private training companies.

The example outlined above illustrates the importance of being specific about training needs so that the subsequent training can focus exactly on the performance improvement that is required. By thinking through the training needs of the recycling program manager and the recycling staff in this manner, the first step in ensuring that training efforts are effective both in terms of cost effectiveness and improvements in capability will be achieved.

An inventory of potential competencies is provided for several typical recycling positions in Table 31.1. Every job is different; therefore the inventory will probably require modifications or additions. Use Table 31.1 as a shopping list or prompt to complete a training needs inventory.

ADDRESSING TRAINING NEEDS

Once *what* the training needs of the recycling program manager and the recycling staff are defined, the next step is to determine *how* best to address these needs. Not all learning environments that we encounter as adults are ideal. A lot of the learning environments, in fact, are not time efficient and do not allow actual learning to occur. In other words, maybe a recycling staff had fun, or met interesting people, but did they learn? Whether the trainee decides to simply enroll in an existing training course or program or the department decides to offer on-the-job or more formal training, to meet the training needs, it is important to know the ways in which adult learning can be enhanced and ensured.

The Learning Process for Recyclers

Typically at recycling conferences and seminars, attendees are asked to sit back and listen to presentations and watch slides. Then, when coffee time comes, the real learning begins when all of the recyclers form impromptu groups and start sharing recycling success or horror stories and new market contacts and promotion ideas. What we know about how we learn is exemplified by the above description. Recyclers learn when they are actively involved, applying new information to their own situations and drawing upon and using their own experiences or those of their colleagues.

Some general rules of thumb for effective training include

- As much as possible, ensure that the information or skill being addressed in the training is *relevant and practical.* Especially with recyclers, the more practical the better. *On-the-job training is absolutely the best form of training possible.*
- Allow for *practice and application of the new information or skill.* This ensures that the new material will actually be remembered.
- Provide opportunities for participants to *draw upon their own experiences* and to share them and analyze them with others.
- *Treat your trainees with respect and acknowledge that they come into the training with well-developed problem-solving abilities and with experiences that are already relevant to the training.* Trainees are not empty vessels waiting to be filled—they have lived, learned, and have experiences already that you are simply adding to.
- Remember that most people have limited capacity for lecture. After one-half hour, most people begin to lose attention.
- Use a variety of training techniques whenever possible.

Designing a Training Plan

A training plan outlines how training needs will be addressed. Some training needs may be simply met by enrolling in a seminar offered by existing training or recycling organizations. Other learning needs may be met in a more tailored manner such as specially designed in-house training sessions for groups of staff or a mentoring buddy system for a new staff member. In general, a 6-month training plan should be developed (and followed up and revised) for all staff members. Training plans should spell out how each of the training needs that have been identified for each staff member can be met and should draw upon a full variety of training options such as occasional seminars, reading assignments, on-the-job opportunities, and attendance at professional association meetings.

In addition to attending existing training courses, there are a host of possible training techniques or training options that can be used to meet remaining learning needs. Each type of training option is best suited to meet a particular kind of

TABLE 31.2 Training Activities and Accomplishments

Training options	Can be used to accomplish:
Individual readings or individual readings with an associated work assignment	General introduction/awareness or preparation for more detailed skill development to follow.
Lecture presentations	Same as above. Use to introduce material that the participant will then be called upon to utilize or apply in some fashion. Keep lecture segments to 1/2 hour and break up the lecture segments with a variety of learning techniques.
Discussions, sharing of experiences, e.g., within staff, or other program operations.	Good way to help broaden participants' exposure to different approaches and programs.
Discussion of issues (e.g., the role of mandatory versus voluntary enforcement of recycling) (within staff, or with others)	When issues are discussed (rather than presented) then a better understanding and empathy for the issue may result. Discussions are a good way to sensitize the participants to key issues or the main themes of the subject matter, before they are covered in more detail.
Role playing and practicing	Most useful for skill development (e.g., developing management skills, communication skills, etc.). Basic principles/characteristics or techniques of the skill should be introduced or the participant should be allowed to "discover" these things as part of the training (e.g., one of the keys to dealing with aggressive journalists is not to be intimidated). Then the training should provide ample opportunity for practicing and in many situations as possible. Trainees should be able to learn a lot from self-criticism, but criticism from peers can also be constructive if done in a nonthreatening manner.
On-the-job training	There is truly no better training opportunity than learning on the job. However, sometimes we neglect these training opportunities. For example, take your new public relations and promotions coordinator to your next public meeting or council meeting, rather than go alone. It is likely to be a terrific training opportunity.

learning need whether it is simple awareness building or skill development. Examples of training options with related accomplishments are shown in Table 31.2.

Several states have developed and delivered special training programs to complement state funding programs or to support the accomplishment of legislated recycling targets or goals. Florida, Maryland, Michigan, Rhode Island, North

TABLE 31.3 Training Plan for a Commercial Recycling Program Coordinator

Performance requirement	Competency requirement		Training option
	Knowledge	Skill	
Supervise the development of commercial/industrial and institutional recycling programs. Interacts with commercial businesses and material markets.	Ability to understand and apply applicable rules, regulations, policies, and procedures relating to the commercial sector recycling program. Degree in public or business administration.	Ability to establish and maintain a credible and effective working relationship with the public, administrative, and governmental officials, news media, and co-workers.	Attendance at state and local government workshops and forums; practice sessions with recycling program manager for public presentations; review of professional market journals; regularly scheduled discussions with market representatives to discuss international, national, state, and local market opportunities.
Integration of these individual projects into the countywide recycling program that includes operation, design, development, and implementation. Ongoing project evaluation and modification.	Two years' experience in business management, program development, or waste management/ recycling. Ability to develop and implement commercial programs as directed by the countywide recycling plan.	Ability to understand and prepare technical reports related to commercial recycling.	Technical writing courses; review of existing commercial recycling reports; attendance at trade shows.
Assist with all activities related to multifamily programs.		Ability to communicate effectively both orally and in writing to community leaders and general public.	Practice sessions with colleagues; attendance at training seminars offered by private sector.
Assist the executive director, operations director, and recycling coordinator in development of project procedures, reporting and tracking material recovery, and participation in education programs and fiscal programs.		Ability to speak, understand, and write the English language sufficiently to converse with the general public, peers, and subordinates; respond to inquiries and to make entries on reports and records.	Computer software training (word processing, database management); attendance at state-sponsored recycling coordinator's training course; review and analysis of existing similar programs.
Directs subordinate personnel and perform related work.		Ability to supervise a small group of professional subordinates personally.	Attendance at program management/ supervisory training workshops.

Source: Solid Waste Authority of Palm Beach County, Florida.

Carolina, and Ontario, Canada, have or are planning such programs sponsored through their relevant State Department of Environmental Regulations or Department of Natural Resources. Short courses are now offered by several universities (e.g., University of Wisconsin, Rutgers University in New Jersey, Clemson University), trade associations [e.g., Solid Waste Association of North America (SWANA)], and trade journals (e.g., *Waste Age Magazine*).

Managing and Delivering Training

With demanding day-to-day recycling activities and problems, training can get pushed to the back burner. There are three ways to prevent this from happening.

1. Set objectives (in the training plan) and track accomplishment of each objective. A good way to improve the likelihood that the training plan is acted upon is to establish joint accountability between the staff member and manager for the accomplishment of the training objectives.

2. Build training opportunities into the day-to-day job as much as possible. Every day can be a learning experience. Even "disaster days" present learning opportunities, in fact, sometimes the most effective learning occurs when mistakes are made!

3. Use other resources as much as possible. For example, if the recycling program is having problems with contaminants (either in collection or processing operation), bring in representatives from markets to talk about the importance of avoiding contaminants or a tour of one of the mills (e.g., a glass plant) to demonstrate the problem with contaminants.

Example Training Plan

An example training plan is provided for a commercial recycling program coordinator in Table 31.3. Again, every job is different and will require: (1) *defining program needs*; (2) *defining job classification* to achieve the program needs; (3) *defining training needs* for the individual selected to fulfill the job; and (4) *designing the training plan* to achieve the training needs objectives.

CHAPTER 32

RECYCLING PROGRAM FACTORS AND DECISIONS*

Barbara J. Stevens
President, Ecodata, Inc.
Westport, Connecticut

INTRODUCTION

This chapter presents various factors for a community to evaluate before deciding on a recycling program. The options range from complete reliance upon municipal or public sector workers and equipment to a complete reliance upon the private sector, with various gradations in between.

Wherever possible, information is presented in a manner that should be helpful to a recycling planner trying to initiate a program. The information should provide useful insights into the planning process to other interested individuals and organizations, including advocacy groups, recycling and other solid waste professionals, and interested citizens. The descriptions of the options and the decisions that must be made should help interested parties participate in the process of option formulation, influence the outcome of the policy selection process, and affect the manner of program implementation (Table 32.1).

The next section defines the terms that will be used throughout the chapter. These definitions may not be used identically in all literature, but they will be used consistently throughout the remainder of this chapter. This section also contains some examples of communities that employ the various organizational arrangements for their recycling programs. The section "Decision Matrix" highlights the factors that a decision maker might wish to consider in narrowing the list of options for organizational arrangements for recycling services. Major factors are considered first, such as the degree of recycling which must, by law, be achieved. Recycling services, it is stressed, consist of several program elements, and it is not necessary that each element be provided in the same manner. For example, recycling collection could be handled by a private firm under contract to the community, while processing and marketing could be handled by a regional

*Support for the preparation of this chapter furnished by the National Solid Waste Management Association (NSWMA), Washington, D.C.

TABLE 32.1   Factors to Remember

Residential sector
  • Programs only affect about half the waste stream
  • To recycle 25 + % of waste stream, usually need to consider
    nonresidential waste stream as well
Nonresidential sector
  • Government policy can encourage recycling
  • May require different programs than residential sector
  • Private sector most often acts as collector/processor in this sector
  • Programs affect about half the waste stream

public sector entity. The section "Pursuing Each Option" contains specific suggestions on how to implement the various options for recycling programs. In each section, information is provided for the community wishing to use that option as the means of handling all elements or just one element of the recycling program.

OPTIONS—ORGANIZATIONAL ARRANGEMENTS FOR RECYCLING PROGRAMS

Main Organizational Alternatives

There are four main organizational alternatives for establishing a recycling program or some of the elements of a recycling program. These main organizational alternatives, arranged in order of the least to the most government involvement, are *private, franchise, contract,* and *municipal* (Fig. 32.1). Each is discussed below.

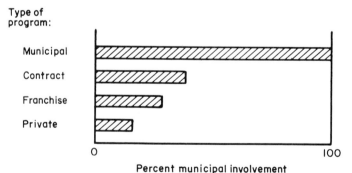

FIGURE 32.1   Types of recycling programs by extent of municipal involvement.

Private is the name given here to the arrangement that involves government the least. Basically, in this arrangement, firms are allowed to provide the services without interference or intervention by the local government. Market forces determine the extent to which the local private sector would initiate a recycling program, the materials which would be recycled, the customers which would be included in the program, and the percentage of the waste stream which would be diverted from the landfill.

It is possible to have a private sector recycling program with or without government incentives. Private sector recycling with no government incentives generally occurs in areas where economic conditions make such a program profitable. Typically, this condition prevails in areas where there are large generators of high-value recyclable products (such as office buildings generating high-value paper scrap or stores with large corrugated cardboard generation), and/or a high disposal fee. Such conditions typically prevail in the older, large urban centers of the northeastern part of the United States. For example, private sector recycling is common in such cities as New York City, Boston, and Philadelphia, to name a few.

Government incentives can be used to encourage private sector recycling in communities where the prevailing economics alone do not justify establishing such a program. Such incentives can be based on microeconomic theory or on a quota system. For example, if the local disposal site is owned by the city, the city could increase the tip fee as a means of encouraging recycling, or the city could pass a regulation that in order to qualify for a license, a waste hauler would have to demonstrate that at least a minimum percentage of materials collected was actually recycled.

The private arrangement is consistent with government licensing of firms involved in the hauling, processing, marketing, and publicizing of recycling programs. Except in the case of a government program requiring haulers to meet a recycling quota, there is usually little enforcement necessary in such a system. However, unless prevailing disposal fees are very high, or unless all waste generators in a community are high-volume generators of high-value recyclables, private sector recycling alone is not likely to serve a majority of waste generators in a community or to result in the highest potential diversion of waste from the disposal site.

The *franchise* arrangement is defined as one in which the local jurisdiction authorizes one firm to provide a given service to a given category of customers in a specified area. The franchise may be exclusive, in which only one firm is allowed to provide the specified services in the specified area, or nonexclusive, in which more than one firm is allowed to offer services in the specified area. The holder of the franchise bills its customers directly, and the firm may be required to pay a franchise fee to the community in return for granting the franchise. In solid waste collection, franchise fees are often revenue producers for local governments, with fees often set in the 5 to 10 percent of gross revenues range. For recycling, the franchise fee may be negative, providing a subsidy just sufficient to induce the private sector to provide the services.

The *contract* arrangement is very similar to the exclusive franchise arrangement. In this arrangement, a single firm has the government-granted right to provide specific services to a specified category of customers in a specified area. However, unlike the exclusive franchise system, whereby the firm receives its revenues via billing customers individually, in the contract arrangement, the firm is paid in one check by the local jurisdiction itself. If there is any billing of the individual customers, it is done by the local government or its agents, but not by the contractor.

Municipal service occurs when employees of the local jurisdiction perform the tasks required to delver the service, and the equipment required to perform the services is similarly owned or leased by the local jurisdiction. In a municipal arrangement, public sector workers drive the collection vehicles, sort the recyclables, market the commodities derived from the raw recyclables, and enforce participation and containerization requirements. Customers may be billed directly for the services provided, or the services may be financed from general property tax (or other) revenues.

Considerations Regarding the Options

The scale of operations can affect the costs of service to a community. Previous studies have shown that there are significant economies of scale in refuse collection, with per ton or per household costs decreasing by about 20 percent as the scale of operations increases to about five collection vehicles per day. No further economies of scale are available after this point. There is no reason to assume that these results do not pertain to recycling collection as well as refuse collection, as the nature of the routing and collecting operations are very similar. Thus, communities considering more than one arrangement, for example, one area of a city with municipal collection and one area with contract collection, should understand that they may pay extra for diversity, so long as each area is not large enough to require at least five vehicles each day.

Many communities select different recyclables collection methods for different sectors. For example, one arrangement may be used for recyclables service from single and small multifamily buildings, while another arrangement entirely is used for recyclables collection from commercial and large apartment buildings.

Often, communities choose a recycling arrangement to coordinate with the refuse collection alternative which prevails in their community. For much of the country, commercial refuse collection is handled with the private system, and communities with this type of refuse collection are often unwilling to use arrangements for recycling services which will cause local refuse haulers to go out of business. Thus, government incentives in the private system are a popular method of initiating commercial recycling programs in such communities. Often, the residential and small business sectors are combined and have a refuse collection system which differs from that of the large-scale commercial sector. In such communities, the recycling arrangement for the small residential sector will typically also differ from that of the large commercial sector.

Examples of Use

The *private* arrangement is often used for the commercial sector, particularly in areas where high disposal fees favor recycling for economic reasons. Examples of cities where there is a well-developed private sector recycling program include many of the large older urbanized areas, including New York City, Newark (New Jersey), Philadelphia, Boston, Seattle, Los Angeles, and Portland (Oregon). Some smaller communities, where the arrangement for refuse collection is the private system, have elected to use the private arrangement for recycling service as well. An example of the latter is Westport, Connecticut, which implemented private recycling when mandated by Connecticut law in 1991.

Private recycling systems can also be implemented with incentives from, or ordinances passed by, the government. For example, an ordinance could be passed requiring any franchised hauler to offer recycling services (for a fee, where the economics of recycling do not justify the service at no fee) to all customers. Such restrictions are being considered by many cities, including, for example, Philadelphia, Pennsylvania. Alternatively, the government could offer an incentive, such as setting a lower franchise fee for materials delivered to recycling centers than for materials delivered to disposal sites. Such programs are being considered by other cities, including, for example, San Jose, California.

The *franchise* arrangement for recycling is probably most common in communities granting an exclusive franchise for both refuse collection and recyclables services. In this way, a single fee to the customer can include the refuse and recycling services. It is not common for communities to franchise recycling contractors and to then expect customers to pay the full costs of the service. Seattle, Washington, for example, subsidizes the costs of recycling services provided to multifamily dwellings, paying a per ton fee to recyclers selected as the exclusive franchisees. The difference between the recyclers' costs and the fees charged to customers is covered by the subsidy paid by the city—an amount determined in the process of competitive procurement. In Illinois, the villages of Schaumburg and Streamwood jointly procured the services of refuse collection and recyclables services, awarding the contract in the manner of an exclusive franchise, whereby the selected firm must bill customers for the joint services of refuse and recyclables collection and dispersion (see Table 32.2 for the outline of the specifications in the franchise agreement for these communities).

In most areas of the country, the prevailing prices for refuse disposal and recycled commodities do not on their own justify initiation of recycling programs from small generators. Such small generators would include residences and small commercial establishments. For recycling to occur from such establishments, it is typically necessary for the local jurisdiction to subsidize the program in some manner. This is easily accomplished when the organizational arrangement selected for the recycling program is that of *contract*. Contracts for recycling services are found in many communities, including Seattle, Washington, San Jose, California, the state of Rhode Island, Cape May County, New Jersey, and Philadelphia, Pennsylvania. The contractor can be paid a fixed amount per unit serviced or processed or a varying amount per unit serviced or processed, with the fee changing according to the actual or expected change in revenues from sale of commodities.

Cities with their own municipal refuse collection systems very often initiate a municipal recycling program—serving the same establishments serviced by the refuse collection system. New York City, Philadelphia, Pennsylvania, and Chicago, Illinois, are examples of cities which fit this organizational description. In each case, the municipal recycling crews service the residential establishments from which municipal crews collect refuse.

DECISION MATRIX

The Need for More Than One Decision Process

A community deciding on the organizational arrangement for recycling services may wish to subdivide the service into two or more groups, perhaps using a different organizational arrangement for the different components. Recycling services, in their entirety, are multifaceted. At a minimum, they include a publicity or education component, an enforcement component, a collection component, a processing component, and a marketing component. The first two components typically involve less monies than the latter three. They are typically handled by

TABLE 32.2 List of Franchise Recycling Specifications
Agreement of villages of Schaumburg and Streamwood, Illinois

1.00	Definitions
2.00	Service required
	2.01 Residential service
	2.02 Service exclusions
	2.03 Service for certain condominium projects
3.00	Term of contract
	3.01 Initial term
	3.02 Automatic renewal
	3.03 Exclusive contract
	3.04 Renegotiation
4.00	Contractor qualifications
	4.01 Minimum experience
	4.02 Access to landfill
	4.03 Access to materials processing facility
	4.04 Adequate finances
	4.05 Adequate rolling stock
	4.06 Recycle logo
5.00	Contract provisions*
	5.01 Weekly service
	5.02 Resident notification
	5.03 Receptacle location
	5.04 Refuse receptacles
	5.05 Recyclable material receptacles
	5.06 Unlimited number of receptacles
	5.07 Noncontainerized materials
	5.08 Office paper program
	5.09 Additional services
	5.10 Hours of operation
	5.11 Holidays
	5.12 Nonresidential services
	5.13 Septemberfest packer truck
	5.14 Workmanlike performance
	5.15 Emergency provisions
	5.16 Refuse collection vehicles
	5.17 Recyclable material collection vehicles
	5.18 Refuse disposition

specialized departments or private firms, and they are not typically handled by the solid waste professionals which might otherwise collect refuse or collect, process, and market recyclables. Processing and marketing are often treated as a unit, but there is no reason why this must be so. Some firms are able to collect the refuse, but they are unable to process and market the collected materials. A decision maker, then, should apply the decision matrix considerations to each of the components of the recycling service, in the process of deciding how recycling services should be provided in any given community. Table 32.3 shows the options for each program element.

Certain basic considerations affect the level of government involvement which can be expected to be required. For example, in states where recycling goals are mandated by law, the government can expect to be involved in ensuring that the stated goals are actually met. The higher the level of recycling mandated, as a

TABLE 32.2 List of Franchise Recycling Specifications (*Continued*)
Agreement of villages of Schaumburg and Streamwood, Illinois

	5.19 Recyclable material disposition
	5.20 Right of inspection
	5.21 Monthly report
	5.22 Complaint response
6.00	Compensation
	6.01 Charges for single-family residential service
	6.02 Charges for multifamily residential service
	6.03 Charges for service to the village
	6.04 Collection of charges
	6.05 Recyclable material sales revenue
7.00	insurance, bond, and performance provisions
	7.01 Automobile liability insurance
	7.02 Liability insurance
	7.03 Worker's compensation insurance
	7.04 No limit on insurance amounts
	7.05 Village culpability
	7.06 Performance bond
	7.07 Failure to perform
	7.08 Adherence to all appropriate legislation

*Although the specifications refer to this as a contract, the selected contractor is not paid by the local governments, but rather "shall look solely to the customer for the payment of the monthly charge." When the firm bills customers directly, the agreement is a franchise, in our terminology.

TABLE 32.3 Program Element Options

Recycling program element	Who does the work?
Publicity	Public or private
Enforcement	Public or private
Collection	Public or private
Processing	Public or private
Marketing	Public or private

Note: Each program element can be considered separately in deciding on the organizational arrangement for a recycling program.

percentage of the waste stream, the more the community is likely to need to make use of programs in addition to market forces to achieve goals. The government involvement would typically occur when programs are mandatory, and the government would take responsibility for enforcing compliance. Although the government would have to pass the legislation in these cases, the actual day-to-day operations of the various program elements could be conducted according to any of the organizational arrangements listed above.

Factors to Consider in the Decision-Making Process

Because there are several individual components to the recycling program, it is usually necessary to consider each one separately in the decision process. Then, if the decision is to handle two or more program components with the same organizational arrangement, it may be possible to link the components with the activities of a single governmental entity or private sector procurement. The decision process regarding the best arrangement for each of the various components of the recycling program can be reduced to a consideration of the elements discussed below and listed in Table 32.4.

TABLE 32.4   Organization Factors Checklist

Choosing an organizational arrangement checklist of factors to consider for each program element

Factors	MUN	CON	FRAN	PRI*
1. Costs				
2. Administrative burden				
3. Experience in recycling				
4. Legal constraints				
5. Customer satisfaction				
6. Source of funds				
7. Community satisfaction				
8. Market risk				
9. Financial risks				
10. Flexibility				
11. Integration with systems				

*MUN—Municipal, CON—Contractor, FRAN—Franchise, PRI—Private.

Costs. Cost of the component under the various arrangements is an important input to the decision-making process. Costs can be divided into start-up and ongoing categories. Expenses included in the start-up category are the expenses of personnel recruitment, training, and system planning. Included in system planning, especially for the municipal arrangement, are the costs of specifying and procuring capital equipment or facilities. For the contract or franchise options, the start-up costs include the costs of preparing the specifications for the procurement and the actual expenses associated with soliciting and reviewing responses, overseeing the selected firm during the start-up period, and planning for ongoing administrative oversight of the contractor.

Estimating ongoing costs varies somewhat for the various arrangements. The different cases are considered below.

Municipal. In order to estimate start-up and ongoing costs, it is necessary to have an estimate of the type and number of personnel and pieces of equipment which will be needed to perform the work. For any of the components, it is necessary to have competent, trained personnel in charge of the work. An important consideration is the quantity of work which will be required. For example, with publicity, if only a part-time level of effort will be required, a community might not wish to hire and train a municipal worker but might prefer to use the services of a professional advertising agency. However, if the city already has a graphics department, which could supply the services using existing personnel, such an alternative might be attractive.

For the components of the service which are ongoing, including the collection and the processing and marketing of the commodities, the community needs to ask how many people will be required, with what skills, and whether the community has experience in implementing and supervising programs using workers with these skills and responsibilities. Where experienced supervisors are already on board, they can provide estimates of the numbers of individuals needed; consultants may be necessary to form estimates of needs in areas where the community does not have in-house experience.

Similarly, the number and type of pieces of equipment which will be required can be estimated by supervisors already working for the community, or by planners or consultants using information from comparable communities. For processing and collection components, it is necessary to decide how the materials will be sorted by the generators, and how (if at all) the materials will be sorted by the collectors. These decisions affect the costs of the collection vehicles, the work rates of the collectors (and, consequently, the number of collection crews which will be required), and the nature and types of processing lines necessary.

Estimates of the ongoing costs should include some amortization of capital equipment, even though the budgetary process of the community might not include such items in the operating budget. The reason to include amortization of capital equipment in the estimate of the cost of municipal service is to facilitate comparison of the costs of municipal service to the cost of service provided by a private firm. Whereas the city might buy the capital equipment from one budget and cover the costs of personnel from another, the private firm would include the amortized costs of capital equipment and the costs of ongoing personnel in the single price charged to the community. To compare the cost of municipal service to the cost of service from the private sector, the city must follow a similar procedure of aggregating all its costs, to be covered from whatever budget, into a single, comprehensive figure.

Other ongoing costs which should be considered are the costs of insurance or self-insurance to cover accidents to personnel and property, in the case of jurisdictions which are self-insured. Costs of replacing equipment or containers for recycling need to be included, as do costs of supervision, vehicle repair and maintenance, fuel, other fluids, and the costs of personnel to handle inquiries and complaints.

All of these costs can be aggregated to equal an annual estimate of the costs of providing the service. Table 32.5 provides a checklist of the cost components for municipal service. This estimate can then be divided by the number of service units (households or stops or tons, depending on how the community thinks of its service requirements) to obtain an estimate of the unit cost of municipal service.

TABLE 32.5 Municipal Cost Checklist

- Direct labor costs
- Fringes—even if included in the budget of another department
- Capital expenditures—include the amortized costs of these cost components
- Customer inquiry service—labor, fringes, utilities, etc.
- "Hidden" expenses—allowance for self-insurance losses, or worker's compensation claims, when self-insured, etc.
- Supervisory or management costs
- Equipment operation and maintenance costs—even if from another department or no additional workers expected to be hired (if workers have extra time to work on this program, the extra time could also be allotted to another program)
- Facility costs (rent or operation) for dispatch, repair, and management facilities

Contract and Franchise Service. The cost of contract and franchise service can be estimated by using data from nearby communities, if nearby communities employ contractors in a similar manner. Alternatively, the relative expected work rates from contractor or franchise crews can be estimated by using ratios observed from refuse collection activities in communities nearby. Finally, a solicitation of proposals or bids could be used to determine what the private sector would change to provide the components or components under consideration (Table 32.6).

TABLE 32.6 Sample Price Proposal Sheet from Recycling Procurement

Refuse and Recyclables Contract—1990/Bid Form

Collection of Refuse and Recyclables
in the Borough of Wind Gap
Northampton County, Pennsylvania

SUBMITTED BY: _____
                          (Name of Contractor)

_____
              (Address)

	1st year	2nd year	3rd year	Total
3-yr. contract:				
2-yr. contract:				
1-yr. contract:				
Price per unit for additional residences:				

_____
              Company

By: _____

Title: _____

Note: This request for bids asks the bidder to quote a fixed price for a given number of households, with a per household fee for additional residences. Other procurements ask for bids on a per ton collected basis, or on a lump sum basis.

To the prices quoted by the private sector contractors, the community must add the expected ongoing costs of contract administration in order to obtain the overall expected cost of this alternative. Typically, such costs do not exceed 4 percent of the total price charged by the contractor. For the contract arrangement, if there is to be billing of individual customers by the government rather than by the private firm, the jurisdiction needs to add the expected cost of such billing to obtain the total costs of the system.

Private Service. For service provided under the private alternative, the major start-up cost would be incurred by the private sector firms. Additionally, regulations might be required to provide incentives or requirements to the private sector firms to set up recycling programs. Ongoing costs here are included in the prices charged to customers by the private firms involved in providing the service component(s). A rough estimate of the cost of this alternative can be obtained by considering the prices of contractor service, where similar services are provided pursuant to a government contract, and adding a percentage to reflect the uncertainties of a free market environment as compared to an exclusive territory or market. Alternatively, prices in other communities can be adjusted by relative wage rates prevailing in the areas to get an estimate of costs in a particular jurisdiction.

All of these cost estimates should be considered in light of cost to the local government, cost to the customers, and overall program cost. Table 32.7 provides a format for this comparison. In a municipal program, the government pays all the program costs, and it may or may not charge customers a user fee which covers these costs. Here, there is the possibility of structuring fees so that the public perceives the program's costs as less than they actually are. Similar observations apply to the contract system, where the government pays the private firm the costs for the services it provides and user fees may or may not be charged which equal total program costs.

TABLE 32.7 Comparing Public and Private Sector Costs

Arrangement	Cost for city work	Fees to contractor	Overall costs
Municipal—total cost per Table 32.6			
Contract or franchise:			
• Payment to firm			
• Cost of procurement and supervision			
• Billing expenses			
• Enforcement costs			
Private:			
• Prices charged customers			
• Publicity costs			
• Enforcement costs			

The private arrangement, by contrast, is by definition funded by a user fee. The local government, here, generally pays for just a small portion of the service costs under this arrangement, and user fees cover the majority of program costs. Thus, in the private arrangement, customers pay full program costs, and they therefore may perceive this service to be more costly than a municipal or contract service where no user fees are charged or where user fees are set at a level well below that required for cost recovery. The selection of an arrangement can affect a community's ability to influence public perception of program costs; choosing an arrangement which requires that customers pay the full cost of recycling may be politically unpopular in some communities. However, this might not be a drawback in areas where use of the facility or service is voluntary.

Administrative Burden. The various arrangements require different administrative burdens upon the local jurisdiction. In general, the private arrangement requires the least administrative commitment from the local jurisdiction, while the municipal arrangement requires the greatest. In between, in terms of commitment, are the contract and the franchise arrangements. The contract and franchise arrangements require administration, and the contract system requires the community to conduct any individual billing of customers. Often, in recycling, such billing is not an additional cost, as the fee for refuse collection is adjusted to cover the desired portion of the expenses of recycling as well as the costs of refuse collection. In general, the public does not seem ready to accept that fees increase when recycling begins, so there is a desire on the part of many communities not to initiate a separate fee for recycling *per se.*

Experience in Providing Recycling Service.   The extent to which the local jurisdiction's employees are experienced in providing recycling services, or in providing services similar to those required for recycling, is an important determinant of the decision on whether to create a municipal or other type of service or service component. Many municipalities have experience in collection but do not have experience in the processing or marketing of the commodities collected. Lack of in-house experience would tend to mitigate against selecting the municipal arrangement, especially for communities located near large urban areas where experienced private sector firms are already established and capable of providing the services.

Legal Issues.   Local ordinances may limit a community's ability to establish certain arrangements. For example, local ordinances may limit the length of time for a contract, or the extent to which a franchise arrangement (which generates funds to the community) may be allowed. Of course, the law can always be changed, or the system modified to conform with the law. For example, San Diego's People's Law of 1919 specifies that there will be no fee charged residents for solid waste services, a provision which appears to eliminate the franchise or private arrangement for residential recycling services, absent a referendum repeal of the law.

Customer Satisfaction.   An important issue to local officials is the extent to which citizens approve of services provided by the government. When service is provided by municipal employees, local officials sometimes feel that they have greater control over the quality of service provided than when service is provided by a private firm. However, with properly structured contractual agreements, the private firm can be fully as motivated as an elected official to provide high-quality service. Contracts or franchises can require that firms go back promptly to collect any "misses" and they can even allow for misses which are probably the fault of the resident rather than the fault of the contractor. Similarly, service parameters such as the placement of containers after emptying, the extent of noise, the placement of covers, and the hours of collection and processing can be specifically stated in contracts, sometimes allowing even more control over performance than when a municipal work force performs the service. There is no evidence that, on average, customer satisfaction differs significantly when service is provided by a public sector entity as compared to private sector firms.

Sources of Funds.   In an economically self-supporting program, funds to provide recycling services come from the generators of the recyclable commodities, the markets buying the processed commodities and the avoided disposal costs (i.e., the money the community or business saves by not having to pay disposal fees for recycled materials). For large commercial establishments, market forces alone often justify recycling, at least in some areas of the country. For the small commercial and residential sectors, market forces alone do not generally justify setting up curbside (or sometimes even other less expensive types such as drop-off) recycling programs, so some new source of funds, in addition to those listed above, is generally required. For the small customer, these additional sources are usually general tax revenues or a subsidy from user fees for refuse collection.

In all cases, capital expenditures are usually required before service can begin. With a municipal service, funds are required not only for ongoing program support but also for start-up capital expenditures, for example, to purchase the recycling vehicles and containers and to construct a material processing facility. Such funds can come from bond revenues, or through lease purchase of equipment. With bond issue, the alternatives include general obligation bonds and special purpose bonds, where the repayment would be secured by the value of the assets purchased with the monies or by a dedicated user fee (e.g., a tip fee at a materials processing facility) revenue source. In the case where borrowed monies are secured by a dedicated revenue stream, it is necessary to be able to guarantee that the materials will flow to the facility charging the fee; for recycling facilities, this means that a commitment to deliver recyclables to a processing facility would have to be obtained, ideally, with the length of the commitment matching the term of the bond issue.

For some communities, limits on the quantity of debt which can be issued have been reached, and alternative sources must be found for capital. The need for capital commitment can be reduced via lease of vehicles and reliance on the private sector to provide processing and marketing of recyclables. Contracting or franchising, or relying on the private arrangement, of course, reduces the need for capital expenditures by the local government. The contract arrangement requires the community to pay the contractor's ongoing expenses; included in these charges is amortization of the capital investments which have been made by the contractor. The contract or franchise alternative allows the community to shift the burden of raising capital from the community to the private sector; the community then guarantees to use the facility for a specified term, paying the contractor's fees from user fees or general tax revenues.

In some areas, user fees for refuse collection are set high enough to pay for recycling services as well. Where significant numbers of recyclables are collected, and where the user charge system is volume- or quantity-based (thereby allowing generators who recycle an opportunity to save money on refuse collection and disposal), such systems can be expected to be very successful in encouraging participation in recycling. This is the model which was used by Seattle; when the quantity-based fees were implemented along with a recycling program (which included yard waste collection) participation increased by over 25 percent and quantity of waste sent to the disposal site decreased by 40,000 tons per year, from 188,800 to 143,087 tons, a 24.2 percent decrease.

Community Satisfaction, Benefits, and Costs.   The very existence of a recycling program provides the opportunity for positive feelings on the part of citizens. Helping to save scarce resources by avoiding disposal and reusing products is basically a desirable environmental objective. Many of the satisfactions of the program cannot be measured economically. Volunteers are often willing to operate such programs, just for the satisfaction of helping to improve the environment. Whatever organizational arrangement is selected for a full-scale program, usually communities try not to displace those volunteer and private sector organizations which previously conducted recycling programs in the community. Often, the less structured the program, the easier it is to allow the volunteers and private sector recyclers to continue to operate. Overall community satisfaction will undoubtedly be increased if no one is unwillingly put out of business as a consequence of implementing a communitywide recycling program (Fig. 32.2).

Communities arranging for local services are often concerned with the possibility of service interruption. For some services, such as refuse collection, interruption in service can have health consequences in addition to nuisance value. Recyclables which are separately collected from refuse pose less of a health hazard if not regularly collected than does regular municipal solid waste. Most of the problems associated with service interruption here fall into the category of nuisance rather than health hazard.

Each component of the recycling service can be interrupted. Collection, processing, and marketing can each be halted by a labor dispute. If the component is provided by a contract or franchise, the agreement with the city can exact financial penalties for such service disruptions, and most private firms will obtain other workers to continue to provide service even when faced with a labor action. With municipal or private service, a labor dispute may well result in an interruption of the affected component.

Technical difficulties in equipment deployment or maintenance can also affect service reliability. With experienced providers, however, this is unlikely to occur. Again, contracts can exact financial penalties for failure to process or market commodities in a timely manner. To the author's knowledge, there is no evidence that service disruption is more or less likely to occur with contract or franchise service than with municipal service; instances of such events have not recently occurred. Recent instances of service disruption or threatened service disruption have occurred in areas where a unionized work force provides private refuse collection services to communities (New York and New Jersey areas).

FIGURE 32.2   Another issue—risk of service interruption.

Market Risk.   In establishing a recycling program, there is the inherent risk of a change in the prevailing prices for processed commodities. To the extent that prices increase, the overall profitability of the program should increase (provided, of course, that materials are not diverted to other programs, such as buyback centers); however, when prices decrease there is the risk of reduced revenue or loss. As more and more communities begin recycling programs, and as the supply of recovered commodities increases, prices might be expected to drop, at least in the short run until demand adjusts and prices seek new equilibria. One advantage of the arrangements which include the private sector is that the community has a chance to share this market risk with another entity—the involved private firms. With a municipal arrangement, the community alone must bear all the market risk. Figure 32.3 describes how two communities handled the recent collapse in the newspaper market.

Financial Risks.   When any new program is established, estimates must be made concerning the expected costs and revenues. For a recycling program, these estimates are especially volatile, as behavior changes can occur rapidly or slowly, depending upon motivation and other factors. The unit costs and net costs of providing the service depend greatly on the level of participation and the extent to which participants prepare recyclables as directed. Again, the arrangements which involve a private firm provide the opportunity to share these risks with another party, as compared to the municipal delivery option. Some communities

What happens when the market for recyclables collapses? In 1989–90, the market for newspaper in the East collapsed—with prices dropping from $35 a ton to negative figures.

Communities with long-established relations with markets may be able to continue to receive a positive price for the commodity, even with excess supply. Example: Howard County, Maryland, with a long-standing newspaper recycling program—since 1982—was able to continue to receive $20 a ton even when other communities' newsprint was being turned away from the plant.

Communities with new programs will usually suffer the most from drops in market prices. Example: The Town of Babylon, New York, with a newspaper collection program established in 1987 and without a long-term contract, suffered from market fluctuations. In January 1988, they received $20 per ton for newsprint; in August 1989, $10 per ton; in October 1989, $5 per ton; in January 1990, they paid $30 per ton to the market; in April 1990, they received $5 per ton for the material. Since this experience, the Town has formed a marketing cooperative with other local governments, to enhance their negotiating power with markets.

FIGURE 32.3 Financial risks.

feel that they will pay more when there is uncertainty regarding these factors, such as participation rate and diversion quantities, which affect program economics; these communities prefer to shoulder the risk of the program start up so that they may later provide reliable data on which to solicit a contract. These uncertainties can also be addressed in an initial solicitation with appropriately structured clauses.

Flexibility. Many communities perceive (probably correctly) that the recycling industry is in a state of rapid technological and institutional change. These communities believe that markets will develop soon for materials which are presently considered nonrecyclable, and that some markets presently available may not continue to prevail. If these beliefs are correct, then it will be desirable to have the type of recycling program which can be easily modified to react to changes in market conditions (Table 32.8).

The municipal arrangement allows easy change in collection, processing, and marketing procedures, without the intervening step of contract renegotiation

TABLE 32.8 Building in Program Flexibility

For truckside sorting programs:
- Use equipment with variable numbers of compartments and variable compartment sizes

For processing:
- Specify equipment with multiple uses—e.g., loaders, conveyor belts, roll-off containers, balers, etc.
- Aim for modular design to allow expansion without extensive redesign

For marketing:
- Prespecified repayment for additional materials—consider a published price base or indexed value
- Incentive payments for innovative market development

which might be required were a contract or franchise system selected. Conversely, the private arrangement is driven primarily by market forces, and this arrangement would be expected to react to changing conditions, probably even more swiftly than the municipal system might. Again, it is possible to address some of the flexibility issues through proper structuring of contracts and franchises; perhaps the greatest defense against being "locked out" of a market opportunity due to a restrictive contract or franchise is to avoid unnecessarily long terms for these agreements. In a recycling contract, the term might be considered unnecessarily long if it exceeded the expected useful life of the majority of the capital equipment. As most processing equipment has a shorter life than does a building, even for materials processing facilities, some communities are separating the ownership of the building from the ownership and operation of the facility. The former element of the program might have a term of up to 20 years; the latter would be on the order of about half that, based on expected equipment operating lives.

Whatever the nature of the arrangement, it is important to remember that for program flexibility, it is necessary to involve not only the collector, the processor, and the marketer, but also the generator. For residents and small commercial establishments, initiation of a recycling program often means a change in behavior. Many communities would be loathe to ask residents to stop recycling a commodity which they had previously been recycling—many community programs are implemented with the specific proviso that residents are free to continue using buy-back centers and other recycling methods to recycle if they so wish. For source-separated programs, whether it be a drop-off center or a curbside program, communities are probably more willing to add a commodity to the list of recyclables than they are to drop a material from the list of acceptable recyclables. So, while flexibility is an important consideration, the interface with the public sector may mean that (for source-separated programs) practically speaking, it is not feasible to drop a commodity, but only to add one. Therefore, it may be more important to allow for adding commodities to contracts than for subtracting them.

Integration with Existing Systems. Recycling services are different from refuse collection services, yet each addresses components of the discard stream emanating from residential and commercial establishments in a community. In a new program, particularly, the percentage of the discard stream which will be diverted from the refuse can to the recycling container is unknown. What is known, at least to some degree of accuracy, is the size of the total discard stream. The refuse collection entity, faced with a reduction of unknown magnitude in quantity of waste it must collect is probably unwilling to commit itself in advance to any rerouting or reduction in work force. The entity charged with setting up the recycling program is also uncertain of the quantities of materials which must be collected (Fig. 32.4).

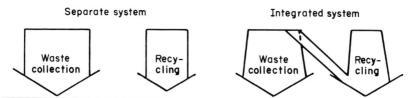

FIGURE 32.4   Integrated waste and recycling programs save dollars. Usually, integrating the waste collection service with the recycling service allows some savings in waste collection costs. These released resources (personnel, for example) are available for the recycling program.

In this situation, often a merging of the two entities can result in greatest efficiencies and risk reductions. In the short run, assuming no changes in consumption and discard behavior, every ton of material diverted from the refuse stream is a ton of material diverted to the recycling stream. If the same firm or agency collects both the refuse and the recyclables, at least they know the aggregate tonnage that needs to be collected, and any tons lost on the refuse side will be reclaimed on the recycling side. Any workers which can be freed up on the refuse side as a consequence of reduction in waste quantities can be used in the recycling workforce (Table 32.9). Generally, a reduction in tonnages can be expected to reduce the costs of refuse collection, but a community will not see this reduction in costs in most refuse contracts or in most franchises as prices are typically quoted in dollars per household, and the actual number of tons of waste will be known with uncertainty except in cases where recycling programs are fully mature. However, if the two services are contracted for together, the aggregate price tends to be lower than when the services are contracted for separately, as the aggregate quantity to collect per household is then a known, whatever the success of the recycling program.

TABLE 32.9   Cities with Integrated Systems

These cities have reduced the number of refuse collection crews as their recycling program has expanded: Newark, New Jersey   Norwalk, Connecticut   New Haven, Connecticut   Hollywood, Florida

Another advantage to arranging for refuse and recycling collection to take place in the same manner is that this facilitates coordination of schedules. Most communities have observed that recycling participation increases when recyclables and refuse are collected on the same day. If one private firm is collecting refuse and another private firm is collecting recyclables, arranging for this same day service is somewhat harder than when the same entity, be it a private firm or a public sector agency, is responsible for both collections.

After considering all the above factors, for each of the components of a recycling program, a community will hopefully be able to determine which organizational arrangement is optimal for its own situation. The decision may be to use one organizational arrangement for one component, and another for the other components of the system. This is a common result of the decision-making process. For example, the community could decide to use a regional processing facility (as, for example, is required of communities in New Jersey counties), and to use a municipal work force for residential recyclables collection and to use the private arrangement for commercial recyclables collection. This is the decision adopted by Montclair, New Jersey. San Francisco, California, contracts with a private firm for collection, processing, and marketing of residential recyclables. The decisions of the two communities are consistent with prevailing arrangements for refuse collection; in Montclair, residential refuse collection is via municipal work force, whereas commercial refuse is collected pursuant to the private arrangement; in San Francisco, all refuse is collected by one of two firms with exclusive franchise arrangements.

PURSUING EACH OPTION

Each of the major arrangements is considered below. For each, the roles of the local government are identified and the steps necessary to achieve program implementation are discussed. Throughout, the emphasis is on the steps required of the local government, rather than, say, the steps required of the contractor which might be selected by the local government.

The Private Arrangement

The government interested in encouraging private sector recycling can promote companies which are presently recycling. The government might also deliver recyclables from government buildings to these recyclers. Announcements, education programs, and awards are the major types of government involvement short of providing a direct subsidy or legislating recycling activities.

The government may act directly to effect recycling by modifying local ordinances. For example, the community may require licenses of vehicles used to collect and transport waste materials. The licenses could be granted only to firms which can demonstrate that they actively participate in recycling programs. Perhaps even more strongly, a condition of the license could be demonstrated recycling activities. The demonstration required might be a monthly or annual report indicating the quantity of waste materials collected in the aggregate, and verifiable records, such as weight tickets, indicating that a prespecified level of recycling actually occurred. Such ordinance changes are commonly considered by communities in states, such as Connecticut, Pennsylvania, and California, which have adopted legislation requiring all local jurisdictions to achieve significant levels of recycling of the entire municipal waste stream by specific dates.

It is also possible for the government to subsidize one or more of the elements of a recycling program, to encourage private sector recycling via the marketplace. Local tax credits could be offered to businesses which source-separate recyclables or to firms which collect and/or process recyclables. The local government could guarantee to purchase products made of recyclables, thus encouraging entrepreneurs to set up manufacturing facilities. For example, plastics recycling can often be instigated if a secure market for finished products is available. The government could also assist in siting and permitting facilities involved in recycling.

Many jurisdictions undertaking such activities, particularly in states which mandate specified levels of recycling, will wish to know how effective their programs actually are. Instituting some type of reporting system will enhance a community's ability to measure program effectiveness. One difficulty in setting up such a program is the likelihood that private arrangement recycling activities will pertain to the discard stream of more than one community. For example, recycling collectors may route their trucks into more than one community, on a daily or weekly basis. Processors may accept wastes from more than one community. Thus, knowing how many tons of recyclables are processed by firms located in a community is not the same as knowing how much private sector recycling is taking place, as a percentage of the community's discard stream. In obtaining data from private firms operating in this arrangement, it is important to phrase questions exactly to elicit the desired information. If the community wishes to know quantities of materials *generated within its boundaries* which have been recycled, then data are probably most successfully obtained from collectors or generators; this information can be supplemented by information from processors, so long as the geographic issue is carefully delineated.

The Franchise Arrangement

This arrangement applies both to exclusive and nonexclusive arrangements. Each is considered below.

Nonexclusive Franchises.   Nonexclusive franchises are very similar to the private arrangement discussed above. The main difference between the private and the nonexclusive franchise arrangement is that in the latter arrangement the community can assess a franchise fee (positive or negative) on the private firm. Typically franchise fees take the form of a percentage of revenue. Some communities have ordinance provisions requiring that no profits be made from franchise fees. In these communities, the ordinance could be changed, or the fee could be set just to cover the administrative costs of record keeping and franchise monitoring. With the specific reporting requirements of laws such as California's AB 939 and Pennsylvania's Act 101, the record keeping and monitoring functions will not be without significant cost, especially for arrangements, such as the private and nonexclusive franchise, where more than one firm is involved.

To implement this system, the community must draft the franchise agreements and establish the criteria by which firms will be awarded the franchise. With the nonexclusive system, typically the franchise is awarded to any firm meeting some basic eligibility criteria. Compliance with reporting requirements is a good criterion to include as a condition for continued award of the franchise, as it makes the jurisdiction's reporting job easier.

The franchise agreement can also specify the quality of services which must be performed, and it can specify remedies for failure to achieve specified quality levels. These quality levels could relate to the percentage of materials which are to be recycled, types of materials which will be handled, and the types of collection equipment which might be required. It is possible to have various levels of franchise fees, with lower fees for firms recycling higher percentages of the discard stream. It might also be possible to structure the franchise payment so that the basic fee would be credited for each ton of materials recycled—up to a total or even a negative overall franchise fee payment due.

In the nonexclusive franchise arrangement, as firms are competing with one another, it is typically not necessary to set rates. In this arrangement, competition among service providers can be relied upon to regulate rates.

It can be difficult to specify exactly which types of services will be provided under this arrangement, however. As the franchise firms bill the customers directly and pay fees to the local government, the local government does not have the enforcement power of the purse in this arrangement (as it does in the contract arrangement, for example, where the local government pays the private firm). The easiest penalty to enforce—removal of the franchise authorization—may be too harsh for minor service infractions. Less severe penalties, however, may be difficult to enforce. The community could specify in the agreement, for example, that penalty payments would be made by the firm to the city for each occurrence of a specific type of infraction, for example, if a collector loaded source-separated recyclables into a mixed refuse load, for example, the penalty might be $X extra payable to the city.

Exclusive Franchises.   The exclusive franchise is the same as a contract, except that billing of customers is done by the firm, so payment is direct from customer to firm instead of from city to firm. The exclusive franchisee is selected in the same way that a contractor is selected—either by competitive procurement or by negotiation.

Because of the exclusive nature of the agreement, it is important that the franchise agreement require the franchisee to provide the specified type of service to the specified category of customer. For recycling services, this means that service must be provided, even if the quantity of recyclables is smaller than the firm might wish. Without competition among service providers, rates are generally established in the franchise agreement. The rates can be set in the procurement itself, with a bidding or price proposing process. In some franchises, the community adopts rate-based regulation, auditing the expenses of the firm and setting rates to cover approved expenditures and allow a reasonable rate of return. This method of regulation is common in the Bay Area around San Francisco and is practiced by communities including San Francisco, Oakland, Hayward, and Fremont. To the extent that the firm providing the services operates in jurisdictions other than the local community, and to the extent that services other than that covered by the franchise are provided, the rate-based rate regulation system presents thorny problems associated with evaluating how to allocate overhead items, how to assess charges by parent and other related companies, and how to evaluate relative efficiency. In most cases, determining the price via a competitive procurement process, with subsequent price adjustments based on predetermined indices over the term of the agreement, is easier and requires less governmental expenditure than does the rate-based rate of return methodology.

The term of the franchise agreement is an important policy variable. Typically, the lowest prices are obtained when the term matches the expected useful life of the major capital equipment to be used in delivering the service. For collection, the major capital is the vehicles and recyclables containers, with expected lives in the order of 5 to 7 years; this would be a technologically optimal length of time for the collection agreement. For processing, major equipment can be expected to last from 10 to 15 years, with the building itself having an even longer expected lifetime. Technology here would argue for a long-term contract—on the order of 15 to 20 years. However, communities must consider the desire to remain flexible as another determinant of the agreement's term. Desire for flexibility might argue for shorter terms.

Performance guarantees with franchise systems can take the form of a performance bond or irrevocable letter of credit (Fig. 32.5). Such an instrument may be called in the instance when the franchisee is determined not to be performing the work. When more minor service difficulties arise, it is desirable to have less dramatic means of exacting desired levels of service. Financial penalties may be difficult to exact, as the flow of funds is from the private firm to the jurisdiction, rather than the other way around. One way around this difficulty might be to require an escrow account to be established, from which the city might retain the right to withdraw penalty amounts, as per relevant performance provisions of the agreement between the franchisee and the community. Another alternative would be to retain an independent firm to receive the monies (billed by the franchisee) and remit predetermined percentages to the city and the contractor, subject to the city's direction. This alternative, of course, tends to give the franchise the same characteristics as the contract, in terms of performance guarantees; the franchisee, however, would retain the responsibility of billing customers, a key characteristic of the franchise system.

CHUBB GROUP OF INSURANCE COMPANIES

CHUBB   15 Mountain View Road. P.O. Box 1615. Warren. NJ 07061-1615

August 8, 1988   FEDERAL INSURANCE COMPANY

CITY OF OKLAHOMA CITY
200 North Walker
Oklahoma City, Oklahoma 73102

                     WASTE MANAGEMENT OF OKLAHOMA CITY, A DIVISION OF
RE: Principal: WASTE MANAGEMENT OF OKLAHOMA, INC.
     Bid Date: August 10, 1988
     Project: Commercial and residential collection - Northeast

Gentlemen:

We, the FEDERAL INSURANCE COMPANY, hereby agree that in the
                        WASTE MANAGEMENT OF OKLAHOMA CITY, A DIVISION OF
event an award is made to WASTE MANAGEMENT OF OKLAHOMA, INC.

on the project as captioned, and a mutually acceptable contract

is signed, we will execute or arrange for the execution of the

necessary final bonds.

This commitment will remain in full force and effect until

        October 8, 1988   , unless extended in writing by the

undersigned.

Very truly yours,

FEDERAL INSURANCE COMPANY

BY: _Karin E. Bogard_

     Karen E. Bogard, Attorney-in-Fact

FIGURE 32.5   Consent of surety for performance bond.

In procuring the franchise services, it is wise to require respondents to provide
only the information which is to be directly useful in evaluating capability and
proposed services. If the franchisee is to be allowed to charge the proposed price
schedule, and if this is to be determined via a competitive bid process, then it is
not necessary to ask the private sector to provide a pro forma worksheet
whereby they estimated their expenses and profits in order to arrive at a bid
price. Requiring such information (interesting but not necessary to the process)
may deter firms from responding and make the procurement less competitive
than it otherwise might have been. In general, the simpler the requirements of the
respondent, and the more complete the information provided in the procurement

(ideally, including the draft contract agreement between the jurisdiction and the to-be-selected firm), the better the outcome, in terms of lower prices and enhanced competition.

Typically, the franchise is awarded to the financially and technically competent firm who offers to perform the service at the lowest fee to the customers. In some procurements, the jurisdiction may wish to pay a small premium above the lowest price offered in order to award the work to a more experienced or reliable firm. To avoid legal difficulties concerning the evaluation of proposals, it is wise to specify in advance what minimum experience qualifications are required (Table 32.10). For collection of recyclables, there is little justification regarding one type of equipment over another (assuming one is discussing the same level of service—the same type of containers, frequency, etc.). For processing and marketing, some firms may be able to guarantee markets more reliably than others or may have a more flexible processing system. Such factors can justify the decision to award the processing component to a firm who might not be the absolute low price proposer.

TABLE 32.10 Minimum Experience Guidelines

- Experience identical to or related to that required under this procurement.
- Experience in which the proposer has used the organizational approach proposed here.
- Experience with the type of equipment to be used in San Jose.
- Experience in providing the type of service to be provided in San Jose.
- Experience in transition and implementation of services identical to or similar to services required under this procurement.
- Experience in curbside collection of recyclables into a compartmentalized vehicle.
- Experience in processing and marketing the quantities of recyclables expected to be collected pursuant to this procurement.
- Documented ability to provide necessary equipment as evidenced by vendors' commitments to produce and deliver proposer's selected equipment on proposer's schedule.
- Demonstrated ability to locate, prepare, and start the necessary support services for this project.
- Demonstrated ability to meet all financial obligations, to perform services even in adverse circumstances, and to obtain necessary financing for performance of the scope of services.

The Contract Arrangement

The contract arrangement, which gives the local jurisdiction control over the specification of the services to be provided, as does the exclusive franchise arrangement, also allows the local jurisdiction to control the flow of funds to the firm performing the work. This added feature enhances the community's ability to enforce desired work standards; a community concerned with assuring the quality of work might find a contract arrangement more satisfactory than an exclusive franchise arrangement for this reason.

A contract is typically let pursuant to a private firm's response to a community's issue of a *request for proposals or bids* (RFP/B). In general, a community must make basic programmatic decisions before the RFP/B can even be issued. These issues are addressed below.

Basic Decisions. The most basic decision which any community initiating a recycling program via contract with the private sector must make is the scope of services to be performed by the contractor. A recycling program typically has three main components for each category of generator: collection of recyclable materials; processing of collected recyclable materials (which may include manual and/or mechanical sorting, size reduction, baling, etc.); and marketing of processed recyclable materials. Table 32.11 displays the headings of the RFP issued by the city of Seattle for curbside recycling services.

TABLE 32.11 Recycling Request for Proposals (RFP) Table of Contents, Seattle, Washington

Introduction

Section A. General Program Description

  1. Background
  2. Program goals and objectives
  3. Solicitation purpose
  4. Program description summary
  5. Nature of request for proposals

Section B. Scope of Work

Section C. Proposal Requirements

  1. General
  2. Bond
  3. Forfeiture of bond
  4. Qualifications of contractor
  5. Disqualification of contractors
  6. Design proposal
  7. Marketing proposal
  8. Management proposal
  9. Publicity and education proposal
 10. Economics proposal
 11. Equal employment opportunity
 12. WMBE
 13. Impacts on private recyclers

Section D. Evaluation Process

  1. Evaluation
  2. Negotiations
  3. Interviews
  4. Rights and option of the city

Section E. System Description and Performance Requirements

  1. Technical performance requirements
    1.1 Geographic alternates
    1.2 Collection requirements
    1.3 Processing requirements
    1.4 Transportation and marketing responsibilities
    1.5 Publicity and education requirements
    1.6 Permits and licenses
    1.7 Guaranteed collection and processing
    1.8 Reporting requirements

TABLE 32.11 Recycling Request for Proposals (RFP) Table of Contents, Seattle, Washington (*Continued*)

2. Management performance specifications

    2.1 Responsibilities of participants
    2.2 Schedule
    2.3 Contract term
    2.4 Performance bond
    2.5 Management control
    2.6 Audit
    2.7 Personnel practices
    2.8 Compliance with WMBE
    2.9 OSHA/WISHA
    2.10 Contract approval
    2.11 Other considerations

3. Economics and financing

    3.1 Fees and payments
    3.2 Insurance
    3.3 Indemnity
    3.4 Wage increases for employees and other costs
    3.5 Assignment or pledge of monies by the contractor
    3.6 Assignment; subcontracting; delegation of duties
    3.7 Liquidated damages
    3.8 Payment for labor and materials
    3.9 Deduction from payments because of contractor's failure to make collections

4. Taxes

    4.1 Sales taxes
    4.2 City business tax
    4.3 Other taxes

Appendices

A. Women and minority business requirements
B. Affirmative action bid specifications
C. Program budget forms
D. Collection sector map
E. Noncollusion affidavit
F. Bond sheet
G. Seattle area recycling resources
H. Seattle municipal code chapter 20.46
I. Proposer's checklist

A community must decide whether it wishes to contract with a single firm for all three components of the recycling program (a "full-service" contract), for just two (typically, collection and processing), or for just collection. If a community decides to contract for anything other than full-service recycling, then the community must make additional arrangements for the components of the recycling program not procured under the RFP/B.

Contracting for collection only of recyclable materials is attractive for communities desiring to establish their own municipal processing and marketing program or for communities which are allowed to use a nearby processing plant developed by another community or by the private sector. For example, in New Jersey and Connecticut, communities frequently have access to regional or county processing and marketing plants. Use of such a multicommunity facility is desirable when a community is too small to capture economies of scale in developing its own processing plant, and when the collection method is such that processing is necessary.

Another reason why communities might decide to procure collection services only may be based on the nature of the collection firms in the local market. A community located in a market where major national solid waste management firms operate might reasonably expect a response to a bid requesting any combination of services, ranging from collection only to full service. However, if only small local firms provide refuse collection service in a particular area, or if only one major national firm is present, then the community might wonder how many bids or proposals it might receive in response to a request for full-service recycling. Here, the fear is that the local firms, familiar only with collection, might not respond to a full-service RFP/B, leaving the community to receive but one response.

This factor is relevant mainly for small communities, those too small to attract entry by major national firms in response to their RFP/B. The conditions necessary for a national firm, for example, to enter a new market vary from market to market, but new entry may not occur if the number of persons being serviced is less than 50,000. Communities concerned about the number of responses likely to their RFP/Bs should conduct preliminary discussions with potential contractors, those both presently in the market and those who might potentially enter via a response to the RFP/B, to determine levels of interest and configurations of services likely to elicit a response.

Still another reason why communities might decide to procure collection services only is that recycling services are being procured simultaneously with refuse collection services. In this case, limiting the procurement to collection is often felt to maximize the competition for the contract. Indeed, it is even possible and often desirable to procure recycling services conditionally, at the same time that refuse collection services are being procured. For example, in a 1988 procurement of refuse collection services, Oklahoma City included the provision that the city would have the right to require the contractor to initiate once-a-week curbside collection of up to three source-separated recyclable materials for a fee not to exceed 21 percent of the then-prevailing per household fee for refuse collection. This conditional procurement provides the city with an advantageous price for recycling collection, allowing the city to plan for processing and marketing of recyclables, knowing exactly what collection will cost. Also, the conditional procurement allows for coordinating refuse collection and recyclables collection contracts, even though recyclables collection may not begin concurrently with the start of a refuse collection contract.

In sum, to decide the basic structure of the recycling procurement, a city must consider its individual preferences regarding involvement in processing and marketing, and whether processing and marketing alternatives exist and are available to the community. The city must also consider the capability of likely bidders to provide services other than collection, and the city must weigh any expected decrease in numbers of bidders if services other than collection are procured along with collection. The larger the city and the greater the number of large firms operating in the city's local market, the less relevant is this consideration.

Recycling Collection Issues. In preparing a contractual document for recycling collection services (whether a community contracts for full-service recycling or for just recycling collection services alone, these comments will be applicable) a community is wise to specify clearly the services required. A well-written procurement and contract document will specify exactly what is desired, and the document will also allow for future modifications to service specifications. Some of the most important issues to cover in the procurement document and contractual arrangement include the following.

What. The community must specify what materials it wishes the recycling contractor to collect. For curbside programs, these materials are usually those for which there are nearby markets or brokers. If the exact names of the materials cannot be specified, then the number of separate materials should be specified, and limits placed on the relative volume or weight of each of the materials to be collected. This latter comment is most relevant for procurements conducted in advance, such as that of Oklahoma City referred to above. It is always desirable to provide for a future change in the list of commodities to be collected by the recycling collection contractor. For example, a clause in the contract could state that up to two additional commodities would be collected with no additional segregation of commodities, for a percentage increase in the then prevailing fee equal to 25 percent of the increase in volume of recyclables attributable to the additional commodities. Such language was included in the 1988 garbage–yard waste procurement in Seattle, for example.

Who. The request for bids or proposals must specify exactly which households or businesses in the community are to receive the recyclables collection service. Often, it is easiest to specify that the same establishments which receive regular refuse collection service also receive recycling service.

However, letting a contract for recycling collection service is a good opportunity to examine the definition of establishments under existing refuse collection arrangements. Many communities providing residential service define residential units as those with fewer than, alternatively, four, three, or two dwelling units per building. Often, when it is time to let a contract, the community finds that there is no ongoing data collection procedure in the jurisdiction which determines exactly how many housing units fit into the specified category. The number of housing units in the specified category is important to the contractor, especially if the contractor is reimbursed on a per household served basis. Thus, to avoid onerous and time-consuming surveys of each building in a community to determine the number of dwelling units, it is advisable to establish rules for reimbursement of contractors which are related to regularly collected data in the jurisdiction. The contractor may be required to collect recyclables from all establishments meeting certain criteria; it is not necessary that the contractor's payment be linked to the same definition. For fair treatment of contractors and a minimization of their risk (which can be expected to be translated into a reduced price to the locality), it is desirable if the basis of payment is closely linked to the requirements of service delivery.

When. Here, the community needs to specify how often the recyclable materials will be collected. It has been quite clearly indicated, in cities which have experimented with recyclables collection on the same day as refuse collection (as compared to on a different day), that same-day collection increases participation. This effect may be due to the difficulty of learning new behaviors, peer pressure, or other unknown causes. However, a community which desires to capitalize on this factor must specify not only that recyclable materials will be collected X times per month, but also that the day of collection will coincide with the scheduled refuse collection for each household serviced. Also, the prospective contractor is able to submit a more competitive price if she or he knows in advance whether recycling activities will be mandatory or voluntary.

Why. In order to maximize public participation in recycling programs, it is usually necessary to initiate an education program. (Chapters 9 and 30 contain more information about this important topic.) This may take many forms, but the direct contact between the collector of recyclable materials and the generator of these materials is usually a key component of any effective program. Local jurisdictions contracting with private firms for collection of recyclables may still want to retain control over the content of the communication between the collector and the customer. This can be accomplished by specifying in the request for proposals that the locality will retain the right to approve materials to be delivered to customers, including door hangers, leaflets, flyers, included in bills, if relevant, etc.; the contract must also specify the conditions (e.g., improper segregation or preparation of recyclable materials) under which the collector must deliver one of the items to the household. Table 32.12 highlights some reasons for tagging customers' recyclable set-outs. Most localities find that it is wise to require an initial delivery of an informational pamphlet, as well as reinforcing reminders to those households participating incorrectly or not at all.

TABLE 32.12 Reasons for Tagging Recyclables

- Too much contamination (e.g., aluminum foil contaminated with food
- Nonrecyclables (e.g., porcelain or china mixed with glass jars and bottles)
- Wrong materials (e.g., magazines bundled with newsprint)
- Wrong containerization (e.g., newsprint not properly bundled or tied)

How. It is important for the community to know how the generator must prepare recyclable materials prior to collection, and in how many compartments it wishes the collector to haul these materials. Clearly, it makes no sense to require more elaborate sorting on the part of the household than on the part of the collector. Imagine the disillusionment of generators who carefully set out separated cans and bottles who observe a collector loading them willy-nilly into the same compartment. It is possible, however, to require generators to place all recyclables in one container and to require the collector to sort into separate bins in the recycling vehicle prior to delivery to the processing plant. More common is the requirement that the collector's vehicles contain the same number of compartments as the categories into which generators are required to sort their recyclables materials. Here, it is wise to consider the future and evaluate whether the community is likely to add additional materials to the list of recyclables during the term of the contract. It is usually easier to negotiate or implement a clause in the contract which allows addition of another recyclable material if the additional material does not require segregation in collection. For example, consider the following collection methods:

1. Collection of commingled cans and glass and separate collection of newspapers
2. Collection of commingled cans, glass, and plastic, and separate collection of newspapers commingled with corrugated

3. Collection of commingled cans and glass, separate collection of newspapers, and collection of plastics and corrugated segregated from the other recyclable materials.

A community requiring collection method (1) would be able to negotiate a more favorable price for future collection method (2) than for future collection method (3).

Where. For residential recycling, materials are picked up either at central drop-off areas or at individual residences. In the latter case, recyclable collection is usually at the curb. Curbside collection of any material is less costly than backyard or frontyard collection of that material, as curbside collection minimizes walking time to and from the collection vehicle. Curbside collection also allows generators to set their recycling containers out in a visible location, thereby validating their support for recycling. The peer pressure to participate generated by such a process can be important in encouraging households to recycle. A community needs to specify where recyclable materials will be located for pickup. It is also desirable to indicate in the request for bids what containerization requirements will be enforced by the locality.

Specification Preparation. These are several general observations concerning the writing of the specifications for work. In addition to specifying what must be done, it is important to think ahead to the end of the term, to allow for easy transition, and to ensure that no one firm will have an unfair advantage when it becomes time to relet the contract. Important issues in this regard include

- *Equipment Ownership:* Recycling containers frequently last beyond the initial term of the contract. If the community does not want to give an advantage to the incumbent contractor, it would be wise to specify that containers distributed by the incumbent contractor as a part of establishing the service become the property of the community upon the termination of the contract. Then, the next contractor selected will not have to pay to distribute containers again (this itself is a costly procedure), and the incumbent will not have the competitive advantage of being the only contractor who would not have to do such distribution.

- *Multiple Service Providers:* Many communities, particularly large communities, are concerned that viable competitors will no longer be in business, able to compete, when the term of the first contract is over. To alleviate this worry somewhat, large communities often use a district plan, granting contracts to more than one competitor; sometimes the competitors include municipal agencies as well as private firms. Cities using this model include Seattle, Washington; Boston, Massachusetts; Oklahoma City, Oklahoma; Phoenix, Arizona; Dallas, Texas; Fort Worth, Texas; and Newark, New Jersey.

- *Future Bidding Specifications:* It is wise to include clauses in the agreement which would require the contractor to provide information which would assist the city in procuring competitive bids in the future. In franchise agreements, billing files should be turned over from one contractor to another, so that the customer file need not be re-created each time a new agreement is initiated (and so that the incumbent will not have a unique competitive advantage). In contract agreements, it would be helpful to know the quantities of recyclables, ideally by route, and the seasonal patterns, if any, again by route. In St. Louis Park, Minnesota, the recycling contractor collects participation information using handheld computers, for input into the city-operated billing system.

Cities need also to consider the "what if" aspects of a contract procurement. Specifying exactly what work is required is important. It is also important to specify what will occur if the required work is not performed as delineated in the contractual documents. The most successful agreements cover the eventualities of a total failure to perform the work as well as less major service irregularities.

Major failures to perform are typically covered by *force majeure* clauses, in which causes are deemed not to be the responsibility of the contractor. Typically, no human-caused events other than war are included in this list, thus not including strikes as an incident of *force majeure*. The jurisdiction is protected against failures caused by the contractor by, typically, a performance bond, which is frequently in the amount of 6 months' payments to the contractor, and in clauses which allow the community to use the contractor's equipment on an as-necessary basis to provide the service.

Minor failures to deliver service can range from a missed collection (perhaps the responsibility of the generator, who may have placed the container at the curb after the contractor's collection vehicle passed by) to failure to collect on an entire day, to rudeness, failure to monitor recyclables for proper preparation (and appropriate tagging of rejected containers to help educate the public), failure to maintain vehicles properly, failure to provide proper insurance to the jurisdiction, etc. Often, to the extent that these occurrences can be envisioned in advance, they are listed in the contract, and a dollar penalty is associated with each such occurrence. The penalty is set high enough to make it well worth the contractor's management efforts to try to avoid such occurrences, while not so high as to be unreasonable.

Recycling, Processing, and Marketing Issues.   The issues which arise in establishing contract parameters for processing are generally similar to those which arise in collection. In processing and marketing, however, there are additional issues relating to the sharing of risk of market price changes for commodities, interaction between the collection contractor and the processing contractor, and control over the processing decisions, regarding which commodities will actually be produced.

The basic issues of delineating what is to be performed, when, where, how, and why apply to processing as to collection. The commodities which are to be received and processed can probably be specified in advance, at least for the start of the contract, but the community may wish to retain some flexibility to change components in midterm in response to changes in market conditions.

Often, processing contracts require the processor to market commodities at the best available prices. Enforcement of such a clause can be difficult, as it requires the jurisdiction to be as aware of market opportunities for recycled commodities as the contractor responsible for marketing. Sharing the profits from successful marketing is one way to make such clauses "self-enforcing." For example, communities such as San Jose, California, have recycling contracts which require the contractor to share a percentage of revenues from marketing commodities whenever monthly gross revenues exceed a prespecified limit. Even such a clause as this, which motivates the contractor to seek the best available prices, as the contractor is allowed to keep a majority of such revenues, requires some enforcement on the part of the jurisdiction—including, at the minimum, a periodic auditing of the records of the contractor.

To avoid issues of auditing and enforcement, some processing and marketing contracts do not include a provision for sharing revenues. In these contracts, either the entire risk of change in market prices is borne by the contractor or the risk is shared in a formula tied to published prices, rather than to revenues received. When the entire risk of processing and marketing is borne by the contractor, the jurisdiction typically pays the contractor a set amount per household or per ton handled. The contractor is then free to keep the profits (if any) from the sale of commodities. This is the model adopted by Seattle in its recycling program for source-separated household recyclables and for yard waste. Alternatively, the jurisdiction can pay a fee to the contractor, with the magnitude of the fee determined by changes in the market prices for commodities. The city of Philadelphia uses this approach, relying on market prices as published in the *Recycling Times* to compute an index number, which is then applied quarterly to establish the tipping fee for recyclables delivered to the contractor's processing facility.

Another issue arises in setting performance standards for the processor. Typically, communities are interested in recycling as much as possible of the materials delivered to the processor—they would like a minimum of bypass waste sent to ultimate disposal. The processor can guarantee to meet bypass guarantees only if the purity of the incoming feedstock stream can be assured or if the contract allows for loads containing unacceptably high levels of contamination to be rejected. The contract with the collector must be coordinated with that of the processor, to allocate responsibility for rejecting inappropriately prepared materials prior to collection and for rejecting loads which mistakenly included such materials. Collection methods alone can also affect the processing efficiency. For example, breakage of glass in collection reduces the ability to color-sort this commodity; in areas of the country without markets for mixed glass, breakage in collection may foreclose the possibility of recycling.

Jurisdictions may also wish to assert control over the manner in which commodities are marketed. For example, when yard wastes are composted, the community may wish to develop a brand name and identity, with an ongoing history of product performance. If this is the case, then the contract must provide for community ownership of the brand, at the termination of the processing contract.

Processing facilities can require extensive capital investment. This long-lived investment might justify a term of up to 20 years. Many communities balk at establishing such a long term for processing, as they feel that recycling technologies and markets are too volatile to justify such a commitment. As an alternative to the long-term contract, some communities, such as Cape May, New Jersey, have procured a processing facility from the private sector, with a private firm selected to design and build the facility. The private firm is also awarded an operating contract for a term much less than the expected useful life of the facility—say 5 years. It is expected that, barring unsatisfactory performance or drastic shifts in market conditions, that the operating contract will be renewed for successive periods.

The Municipal Arrangement. To establish an in-house recycling program, all the planning necessary to set up a contract or franchise arrangement must take place, and more. The jurisdiction must be clear on what materials will be collected, when, from whom, in what types of containers, and delivered to which processing location. Additionally, the jurisdiction must attempt to predict participation and diversion rates, so that volumes and weights of materials to collect can be estimated. The volume and weight estimates affect the selection of recyclables containers for use by households and the specification of recycling vehicles. While general predictions of volumes of materials will assist in sizing the compartments in the collection vehicles, ideally specified so that all compartments fill up at approximately the same time, it is not necessary to attempt perfection in this specification, as waste stream composition, participation, and, even, materials eligible for collection can all be expected to change over the useful life of the vehicles.

With work rates and vehicle needs comes the determination of the number of collectors that will be required. In the municipal arrangement, some of these workers may be freed up from refuse collection routes, which can typically be extended as recycling is implemented. The number of workers required is a function of crew size, work rate, distance to the processing facility, type of collection, and personnel practices regarding such matters as vacations, holidays, and length of the work week. When personnel have been recruited, they must be trained in collection methodology, vehicle operation, safety, and routes. Planners and supervisors are typically also required to initiate a municipal program.

Processing facilities require careful specification of equipment components and the physical layout of the equipment and the flow of commodities in the plant. Consideration needs to be given to the type of collection vehicles and the interface between these vehicles and the processing plant. With a well-configured system, it is possible to avoid dumping on a floor, with subsequent loading of recyclables onto conveyors with a bucket or scoop, and instead deposit recyclables directly onto the conveyors, without requiring the additional handling and loading step.

The municipal arrangement theoretically allows the jurisdiction complete flexibility to change systems as desired, but these opportunities must be balanced against the need to change behavior on the part of the public each time such a change is implemented. In addition, once municipal workers whether unionized or not, become permanently employed in the recycling program, it may be difficult in practice to disrupt established staffing patterns. Thus, even if a new technology becomes available to allow collection or processing with fewer workers, implementation may be resisted by interest groups fearing loss of employment.

The public sector service also leaves the jurisdiction with no private sector partner with whom to share the risk of liability—personal or property, or the risks of changes in the markets for recyclables. An additional risk which the municipality shoulders alone is the risk of capital obsolescence. If the jurisdiction finances its own program, then its expenditures on capital are a sunken cost, which may not be fully recoverable if technology changes during the expected useful lifetime of the equipment or plant.

Other liability risks which the community bears alone are potential liability for the quality of materials delivered to processors. For example, if contaminated materials are delivered to markets, the impact of these materials may not be observed until after they have been combined with other materials and processed. At this time, it may be discovered that the glass is not the proper color or that the paper has been discolored by laser paper contained in the feedstock or that the cardboard is rendered useless due to odor from a pesticide once contained in the recycled materials. In any of these cases, the typical risk is that the newly produced material cannot be used for its intended purpose—and the community delivering the contaminated material may be liable for the loss on the production load, if it can be proved that contamination originated in the materials delivered by the community. Until legislation is passed which exempts public entities from liability arising from the sale of recycled goods, after the community collects them, this potential exposure will remain. Public entities, with their "deep pocket" resource of taxation, would be especially attractive targets for financial restitution. This exposure, pending legislation, can be lessened through careful disclaimer clauses in purchase and sale contracts.

While there have been no comparative studies of the costs of recycling services provided by the public sector as compared to the private sector, there is no reason to believe that, at least for collection, general results differ from those which have been found for refuse collection. In that area, municipal agencies in large cities, with populations over 50,000, deliver service at an average cost significantly in excess of the price similar sized cities pay to private contractors; there are, however, individual cities which achieve results opposite to this general conclusion. For example, Phoenix, Arizona, has a municipal agency which competes against the private sector in that city's procurements of refuse collection services, and the public agency has recently been selected as the low price proposer for all the refuse collection districts in that city. Thus, cities considering municipal service need to evaluate whether their costs will significantly exceed those of the contract or franchise arrangement.

In any arrangement, there are considerations which affect overall program efficiency and effectiveness. These include allowing adequate time for program initiation, planning for flexibility, changing elements as appropriate in response to changes in the external and the internal environment, and measuring the success of the program on an ongoing basis. These elements are discussed below.

PROGRAM EVALUATION AND CORRECTIVE ACTION

Typical Planning Requirements

A longer time period than might be expected is typically required to implement a recycling program. Consideration of the alternatives and a decision regarding the type of program and the preferred organizational arrangement can occupy periods of several years, especially in large cities with numerous interest groups and affected parties. Even in small communities, it is not unusual for a planning group to spend at least a year deciding upon the basic form of the recycling program.

Once the basic decisions regarding the program have been made, the action steps for implementation must occur. For the private arrangement, necessary legislative changes can sometimes be accomplished quickly, and sometimes they can take years. Franchise and contract arrangements each require somewhat the same procedures: (1) preparation and issue of procurement documents, (2) receipt of and evaluation of proposals or bids, (3) selection and signing of agreement, (4) interval between selection and beginning of work, and (5) beginning of program. Procuring services of the private sector without an adequate time interval for each of these procurement milestones tends to reduce competition among private firms, to decrease their efficiency in preparing the proposal and gearing up for contract initiation, and, consequently, to result in higher prices to the community.

Of particular importance is to allow for the appropriate time interval between award of the contract and beginning of the work. Particularly for a processing facility, where construction and permitting may be required, an interval of between 1 and 2 years will probably not be too long, depending upon the local difficulties involved in siting and permitting, and construction. Even for programs where the contractor need not site and permit a new facility, such as collection-only contracts, capital equipment must often be procured, and this can take up to 6 months, in some cases.

In sum, once the planning has been completed, for a contract or a franchise arrangement, it typically require at least a year to procure and achieve start-up of collection services and perhaps another year to procure and achieve start-up of a recyclables processing facility. A similar time frame applies to the municipal arrangement. Whereas in this arrangement it is not necessary to prepare the request for proposals or bids or to evaluate the responses from the private sector, it is necessary to prepare procurement documents for capital equipment, and to comply with governmental requirements for personnel recruitment and training. Typically, with the municipal arrangement, it is also necessary to coordinate the start of the program with the annual budget cycle, especially when new capital equipment is required.

Program Flexibility

Flexibility to add new materials to the list of recyclables or to alter the collection and processing technology in response to new developments is a primary concern of officials of most jurisdictions. Perhaps the primary step a community can take to preserve this option is to enter into contracts and franchises that are not overly long, say about 5 years. Changing the technology of collection or processing is costly when initiated prior to the normal time for equipment replacement. However, there may be instances when such replacement is required, if, for example, technology changed so that there was no market or only a very undesirable market for materials prepared the "old" way. It is certainly possible and probably desirable to include a "contract opener" clause which would allow renegotiation of any or all elements of the contract in the event of major technology change or market shift. The jurisdiction can probably protect itself more easily against market shift which causes the contractor to be unable to market the recyclables by citing such a failure as a cause for contract termination.

Allowing for too much change in the terms of a contract can increase, probably unnecessarily, the price which the community must pay. For example, if the contract allows the community to change the commodities to be collected, to change the quantities which must be processed, to change the number of separate commodities which are collected, etc., then the flexibility to the community increases the risks of cost-increasing change to the contractor, and the community can expect to pay more for the flexibility. Ideally, a community interested in a competitive price and flexibility should insert flexibility clauses which do not place all the risk on the contractor and which do not cause the community to pay more for an option which is extremely unlikely to occur. For example, it is unlikely that a new collection technology will be developed and implemented within the next few years which would justify changing the collection methods in a contract with just a few years until the expiration of the term.

Program Modification

Communities continue to modify their programs to enhance effectiveness and to reach a wider population. For example, a community might expand a residential recycling program to include small commercial establishments generally located along the regular residential routes. With a private arrangement or a municipal arrangement, these establishments can be incorporated by the existing recycling vehicles, perhaps with some rerouting, depending upon how many such establishments there are. With a contract or franchise arrangement, careful structuring of the procurement and contract documents can also make this type of modification easy. For example, the contract might say that, with 6 months' notice, the city would have the right to require the contractor to collect recyclables from up to X additional residential or commercial establishments, all to be located within the contract or franchise area, for a unit fee equal to the per unit fee then prevailing in the contract. Planning ahead for increased service can make implementation in the future easier and less costly. In this example, planning to require the regular recycling contractor to include new categories of generators in the service is more efficient than contracting with a second firm whose collection vehicles would cover the same areas of the community as do those of the regular recycling contractor.

One area which should be highlighted is the relationship between regular refuse collection and recyclables collection. Where the two services are performed by the same firm and covered by the same contract, integration is probably already achieved, so long as the services are provided with a single fee. However, when the community pays one fee for refuse service and another fee for recyclables services, and when each fee is expressed per household terms, then better integration can be achieved. When the refuse collection contract comes due, the specification should be changed so that the community gets a rebate, at least equal to the disposal fee per ton times the number of tons of recyclables collected, from the households covered by the contract. When contracts come due at different times, it may be necessary to live with a few years of nonintegration, but the disposal savings from diverting recyclables from the refuse stream is clearly available to the community by simply respecifying the collection contract.

Enforcing Programs Requirements

Mandatory recycling programs typically involve monitoring for participation. Participation can be enforced by inspection of the residual refuse, to check for the presence of materials which should be in the recycling rather than the refuse container. This method is practiced by several of the communities in New Jersey, including Jersey City and Newark, where mandatory recycling programs have the longest track record. The sanitation inspectors generally warn and instruct first-time offenders in proper recycling behavior. Second- and third-time offenders are often fined, and in some communities a court appearance for repeated offenses is a possibility.

Recycling programs can also be enforced by checking on participation in the recycling program itself. Various communities require their collectors to determine participation, often using automatic counters to indicate the number of setouts on a route. There is just a small leap from this approach to determining which generators on a particular route actually set out recyclables, of which kind, and in what quantities. Peninsula Sanitation in California uses handheld computers operated by the drivers of a multifamily recycling route to record the number of containers, by type of material, collected from each stop on the route. Such a system is probably easiest to implement on a containerized route, as the driver already typically has a printout indicating the stops to service, in order, each day. For can or residential collection, routes typically do not list the establishments to service each day, and generating such a list could be time-consuming and expensive. Some communities are issuing scannable labels to establishments on curbside recycling routes, and these labels are scanned in the process of each collection to determine participation, and, in some cases, to generate a recycling credit on the solid waste bill. Figure 32.6 shows collectors using handheld computers to scan customer-identifying labels on recycling bins. The presently used scanning procedures increase collection time per stop by 10 to 20 percent. St. Louis Park, Minnesota, and Clinton County, Pennsylvania, use such systems, and other communities, such as Charlotte, North Carolina, are considering their implementation. The system has the advantage of providing accurate information regarding participation while allowing for innovative billing systems, which can result in reduced sanitation fees for establishments which participate in recycling programs.

FIGURE 32.6 Handheld computer scanning customer code to monitor recycling participation. Monitoring system can serve as a billing system component; households typically receive reduced bills or credits against flat fees for participation in the recycling program. This system has been reported to increase participation rates in voluntary programs 10 to 20 percent.

Voluntary programs, of course, do not enforce participation among customers. However, such programs may employ inspectors to enforce compliance with program regulations and to encourage participation. The electronic monitoring of participation, coupled with a billing system which credits customers for participating in recycling, has allowed Munster, Indiana, to achieve a 97 percent participation rate in a voluntary curbside recycling program.

At present, either approach for enforcing recycling—observation of materials in the refuse or tabulation of participation in the recycling program—is not costless. If tabulation of recycling participation increases collection costs by 5 to 10 percent, inspection of refuse manually is likely to increase the costs even more. The main benefit of such programs is an increase in the volume of materials recycled, and consequent increases in the revenues from sale of product and avoided disposal costs. Better management information systems can also be provided in the course of enforcement of mandatory recycling statutes.

Measuring Performance

No program can be implemented and maintained at peak efficiency and effectiveness without constant evaluation. For program evaluation, it is necessary to know what is being done, by whom, at what costs. In a recycling program, desired information includes the following:

- *Quantities of recyclable materials collected, by category of generator, by type of material:* For example, to know the pounds of newspapers, commingled glass and cans, and yard waste collected from single-family homes.
- *Percentage diversion of the waste stream, by category of generator:* For single-family homes, the aggregate of the refuse collected plus the recyclables collected is the denominator of this percentage, with the quantity of recyclables collected as the numerator. Of course, it is also desirable to compute the overall diversion of the waste stream, using aggregate community waste generation (from all sources) as the denominator.
- *Cost of the recycling program:* For private sector arrangements, the prices charged by the private firms providing the service may be used as indicative of the cost to the community. For municipal arrangements, it is important to include all the program costs, even those which may not be included in the operating budget, such as amortization of capital equipment, vehicle repair and maintenance, etc.
- *Participation and satisfaction with the system:* The participation rate can be difficult to measure, because some generators may place recyclables for collection less often than the service is offered. A telephone survey to inquire as to satisfaction can be helpful, and the indicated participation from such a survey typically gives an upper limit to actual participation levels. Address-specific recording of containers placed for collection is necessary to compute a totally accurate participation rate. Unless a community has a program whereby user fees are tied to participation in the recycling program, it is probably wiser to spend scarce resources to determine the diversion rate rather than the participation rate.
- *Sales of materials and prices at which the materials are sold:* It is desirable to obtain this information, even if the payments to the private contractor are not tied to these variables. The information helps the community to develop its economic picture of the recycling program, and the data will be useful in aggregate form for developing additional recycling programs.

While there is no national data base regarding recycling rates and costs, the programs presently being established by the various states are in effect creating the basis for such a system. It is probable that standards for cost accounting and measuring diversion and participation rates will be established in the not-too-distant future. Any community with a well-thought-out measurement system will be well positioned to adapt to any future record-keeping requirements. The next chapter, "Data Collection and Cost Control," addresses these very important topics in greater detail.

CHAPTER 33
DATA COLLECTION AND COST CONTROL

Daniel E. Strobridge
Associate Solid Waste Planner
Camp, Dresser & McKee, Inc.
Tampa, Florida

Frank G. Gerlock
Senior Solid Waste Planner
Camp, Dresser & McKee, Inc.
Tampa, Florida

INTRODUCTION

Recycling is an essential component of an integrated waste management system. The success of a recycling program can be measured not only by its ability to reduce the quantity of solid waste being landfilled or incinerated, but also by the costs incurred to operate the program. Economic evaluations are performed to determine which methods of recycling make the most sense economically. For example, is it more cost-effective to operate two-person curbside pickup crews or one-person crews? The collection and analysis of data can help show which are the least-cost methods for program operation.

The capital and operating costs of a comprehensive multimaterial recycling program are significant expenses which will not necessarily be met by material sales revenues. The magnitude of these expenses requires that the system be managed as efficiently as any other public works service. To do this, system data must be collected periodically for a broad number of program parameters. Cost analyses and management decisions can then be based on this information.

In addition to aiding management decisions, the collection of certain data is required by various state and federal regulations. The solid waste regulations in a number of states require documentation of recycling efforts and material quantities recycled. Federal lawmakers are preparing to revise the Resource Conservation and Recovery Act and may include national goals for recycling.

This chapter addresses methods of data collection, suggests which data should be collected to facilitate efficient program management, gives examples of data collection forms and procedures used by existing programs, demonstrates methods of data analysis, and describes techniques for controlling recycling program costs.

DATA COLLECTION

Planning and managing a recycling program requires the collection and analysis of several types of data. A good data collection and management system (DCMS) is a valuable tool that should be used to evaluate the efficiency of a recycling program and to plan program improvements and expansions.

Types of Data

The data needed to plan and manage a recycling program are essentially the same, regardless if the system is operated by a municipality or a private contractor. However, the information required to support a municipally operated program may need to be more comprehensive to ensure proper governmental accountability.

Before data are collected and analyzed, it is important to determine the objectives for use of the data. When these objectives are identified, the DCMS can be designed. For example, data may be used to show:

- Volume of material diverted from the waste stream
- Number of households serviced
- Source of waste (i.e., commercial, residential, multifamily)
- Number of setouts serviced per day
- Participation rate per month
- Participation rate for each material type
- Frequency of participation per month
- Route size
- Time to complete route
- Number of containers per truckload

Data Collection Methods

Information may be collected manually or by electronic automated methods. The choice of which method to use must consider factors such as:

- Available resources (e.g., budget, staff, available technical expertise)
- System size
- Available time
- Data requirements

Until recently, automated systems were principally used for data input, manipulation, and presentation of data; manual methods were used primarily for data collection. However, with the increased development and use of high-technology devices like optical laser disks, geographic information systems, and hand-held computers, it is not possible to implement a completely automated DCMS.

Before data are collected, by manual or automated means, the manner in which they will be analyzed should be determined. Data must be input in a format that will achieve the desired results. Questions to be answered include

- What types of data are being collected?
- What quantity of data is being collected?
- How many runs of data will there be?
- How will the data be organized?

Quantities of Recyclable Materials. Since the major benefits of a recycling program are directly related to the quantities of materials collected, the first task in data collection should be to estimate the amount of material that can be recovered. This can be calculated easily by multiplying the total solid waste generation quantity times the percentage of selected recyclable material in the waste stream times the estimated participation rate. Table 33.1 shows an example of this formula, excluding estimates of participation rates. This initial calculation is extremely helpful in assessing the future accomplishments of a recycling program.

TABLE 33.1 Indiana Jones County, Estimated Quantities and Composition of Recyclable Materials in the County's Solid Waste Stream (tons per year, rounded)

		1990	1991	1992	1993	1994	1995	2000
Estimated total solid waste generation		150,123	156,127	162,373	168,868	175,623	181,857	218,228

Selected recyclable material	Estimated percent of waste stream*	Recyclable quantities						
		1990	1991	1992	1993	1994	1995	2000
Newspaper	12.0	18,015	18,735	19,485	20,264	21,075	21,823	26,187
Corrugated cardboard	10.0	15,012	15,613	16,237	16,887	17,562	18,186	21,823
Office paper	2.5	3,753	3,903	4,059	4,222	4,391	4,546	5,456
Aluminum	1.5	2,252	2,342	2,436	2,533	2,634	2,728	3,273
Plastic (containers)	0.5	751	781	812	844	878	909	1,091
Glass containers	6.0	9,007	9,368	9,742	10,132	10,537	10,911	13,094
Yard waste	15.0	22,519	23,419	24,356	25,330	26,344	27,279	32,734
Bimetallic cans	2.5	3,753	3,903	4,059	4,222	4,391	4,546	5,456
Totals	50.0	75,062	78,064	81,186	84,434	87,812	90,928	109,114

*From national and state waste composition data.

Next, a sensitivity analysis should be performed to determine the yearly tonnages of selected recyclable materials that could be recovered at various recovery rates. This is done by multiplying the selected recyclable material component total annual tonnage by the estimated rate of recovery. Tables 33.2 through 33.5 show the results for rates of recovery at 5, 15, 30, and 50 percent, respectively. This example indicates that a recovery rate of 50 percent of all recyclable materials would be necessary to achieve a 25 percent reduction in the total waste stream. Of course, the actual waste stream composition and recovery rate for each material will vary.

Materials Market Survey. After recyclable materials have been identified, potential markets must be investigated. A telephone survey will indicate which mar-

TABLE 33.2 Indiana Jones County Estimated Recyclable Material Quantities at 5 Percent Recovery Rate* (tons/year)

Recyclable material†	Total solid waste generated					
	1990	1991	1992	1993	1994	1995
	150,123	156,127	162,373	168,868	175,623	181,857
Newspaper	901	937	974	1,103	1,054	1,091
Corrugated cardboard	751	781	812	844	878	909
Office paper	188	195	203	211	220	227
Aluminum	113	117	122	127	132	136
Plastic (containers)	38	39	41	42	44	45
Glass	450	468	487	507	527	546
Yard waste	1,126	1,171	1,218	1,267	1,317	1,364
Bimetallic cans	188	195	203	211	220	227
Totals	3,753	3,903	4,059	4,222	4,391	4,546

*Yields a 2.5 percent waste stream reduction. That is, if 5 percent of the total recyclable materials shown in this table were recovered, it would reduce the total solid waste generated in the county by 2.5 percent.

†Recyclable materials shown represent the percentage of the total waste stream composition developed in Table 33.1.

TABLE 33.3 Indiana Jones County Estimated Recyclable Material Quantities at 15 Percent Recovery Rate* (tons/year)

Recyclable material†	Total solid waste generated					
	1990	1991	1992	1993	1994	1995
	150,123	156,127	162,373	168,868	175,623	181,857
Newspaper	2,702	2,810	2,923	3,040	3,161	3,273
Corrugated cardboard	2,252	2,342	2,436	2,533	2,634	2,728
Office paper	563	586	609	633	659	682
Aluminum	338	351	365	380	395	409
Plastic (containers)	113	117	122	127	132	136
Glass	1,351	1,405	1,461	1,520	1,581	1,637
Yard waste	3,378	3,513	3,653	3,800	3,952	4,092
Bimetallic cans	563	586	609	633	659	682
Totals	11,259	11,710	12,178	12,665	13,172	13,639

*Yields a 7.5 percent waste stream reduction. That is, if 15 percent of the total recyclable materials shown in this table were recovered, it would reduce the total solid waste generated in the county by 7.5 percent.

†Recyclable materials shown represent the percentage of the total waste stream composition developed in Table 33.1.

kets purchase or use the materials targeted for recovery, current market prices and specifications, and willingness of potential markets to execute purchase contracts. Figure 33.1 is a sample questionnaire that may be used for telephone interviews. Table 33.6 shows how the data collected from interviews might be summarized.

The amount of revenue that can be expected from the sale of materials can be

TABLE 33.4 Indiana Jones County Estimated Recyclable Material Quantities at 30 Percent Recovery Rate* (tons/year)

Recyclable material†	Total solid waste generated					
	1990	1991	1992	1993	1994	1995
	150,123	156,127	162,373	168,868	175,623	181,857
Newspaper	5,404	5,621	5,845	6,079	6,322	6,547
Corrugated cardboard	4,504	4,684	4,871	5,066	5,269	5,456
Office paper	1,126	1,171	1,218	1,267	1,317	1,364
Aluminum	676	703	731	760	790	818
Plastic (containers)	225	234	244	253	263	273
Glass	2,702	2,810	2,923	3,040	3,161	3,273
Yard waste	6,756	7,026	7,307	7,599	7,903	8,184
Bimetallic cans	1,126	1,171	1,218	1,267	1,317	1,364
Totals	22,518	23,421	24,356	25,330	26,343	27,279

*Yields a 15 percent waste stream reduction. That is, if 30 percent of the total recyclable materials shown in this table were recovered, it would reduce the total solid waste generated in the county by 15 percent.
†Recyclable materials shown represent the percentage of the total waste stream composition developed in Table 33.1.

TABLE 33.5 Indiana Jones County Estimated Recyclable Material Quantities at 50 Percent Recovery Rate* (tons/year)

Recyclable material†	Total solid waste generated					
	1990	1991	1992	1993	1994	1995
	150,123	156,127	162,373	168,868	175,623	181,857
Newspaper	9,007	9,368	9,742	10,132	10,537	10,911
Corrugated cardboard	7,506	7,807	8,119	8,443	8,781	9,093
Office paper	1,877	1,952	2,030	2,111	2,195	2,273
Aluminum	1,126	1,171	1,218	1,267	1,317	1,364
Plastic (containers)	375	390	406	422	439	455
Glass	4,504	4,684	4,871	5,066	5,269	5,456
Yard waste	11,259	11,710	12,178	12,665	13,172	13,639
Bimetallic cans	1,877	1,952	2,030	2,111	2,195	2,273
Totals	37,531	39,034	40,593	42,217	43,906	45,464

*Yields a 25 percent waste stream reduction. That is, if 50 percent of the total recyclable materials shown in this table were recovered, it would reduce the total solid waste generated in the county by 25 percent.
†Recyclable materials shown represent the percentage of the total waste stream composition developed in Table 33.1.

estimated using the data collected in the two previous steps. Multiply the estimated quantity of each material by the estimated sale price of that material. Table 33.7 shows a graphic display of projected revenues.

As much information as possible should be gathered on a monthly basis from the materials market contractor. Important considerations are (text continues on page 33.11)

INDIANA JONES COUNTY
MATERIALS MARKET SURVEY QUESTIONNAIRE

COMPANY NAME: _____

ADDRESS: _____

CONTACT PERSON: _____

PHONE NO.: _____

Listed below are materials being considered for recovery from the study
area's solid waste.

1. Please check the materials your company purchases, and indicate any
    minimum or maximum quantity you typically purchase and the quantity,
    if any, you are currently receiving from within Indiana Jones County.

		Minimum Quantity	Maximum Quantity	Quantity from Indiana Jones
____	Newspaper	_____	_____	_____
____	Corrugated Cardboard	_____	_____	_____
____	Other Grades of Paper	_____	_____	_____
____	Light Gauge Ferrous Metals (tin and bi-metal cans)	_____	_____	_____
____	Heavy Gauge Ferrous Metals (appliances and misc.)	_____	_____	_____
____	Other Metals	_____	_____	_____
____	Aluminum Cans	_____	_____	_____
____	Glass	_____	_____	_____
____	Plastic	_____	_____	_____

MCGH0T.1/9   Page 1

FIGURE 33.1 Materials market survey questionnaire.

INDIANA JONES COUNTY
MATERIALS MARKET SURVEY QUESTIONNAIRE

	Minimum Quantity	Maximum Quantity	Quantity from Indiana Jones
____ Yard Trash	_____	_____	_____
____ Wood Waste	_____	_____	_____
____ Composted Materials	_____	_____	_____
____ Resource Recovery Residue	_____	_____	_____

2. What are your company's specifications (or specific requirements) for the materials you purchase?

_____

_____

_____

_____

3. For each material checked in Question No. 1, please indicate the unit price you are presently paying for the material and the basis for your price offering.

Material	Current Unit Purchase Price	Pricing Basis
_____	_____	_____
_____	_____	_____
_____	_____	_____
_____	_____	_____
_____	_____	_____
_____	_____	_____

MCGHOT.1/9   Page 2

INDIANA JONES COUNTY
MATERIALS MARKET SURVEY QUESTIONNAIRE

4. Would you be willing to purchase all the material checked in Question No. 1 from the study area?

_____ Yes   _____ No

If no, please list the materials you would be interested in purchasing.

_____

_____

5. Would your company be willing to enter into an intermediate or long-term purchase agreement for materials recovered from the study area's solid waste?

_____ Yes   _____ No   _____ Maybe

6. Would your company be willing to offer a floor price (a minimum purchase price regardless of market conditions) for the purchase of these materials?

_____ Yes   _____ No   _____ Maybe

7. Would your company be willing to provide containers, processing equipment, or transportation for recyclable materials?

_____ Yes, Please indicate which _____

_____

_____ No

8. Please provide any other information about your company or recycling programs which might be helpful to our project.

_____

_____

_____

_____

_____

_____

TABLE 33.6 Indiana Jones County Materials Market Survey

Company & address	Materials purchased	Specifications	Current purchase price	Willing to contract	Offer floor price	Provisions
Tin-Can Man 3021 SW 1st Terr No Name, OK	Aluminum cans	Aluminum only	$0.50–0.70/lb	Yes	Yes	Containers and transportation are highly possible if built into the negotiations.
	Corrugated cardboard	Separate from other materials	$25–40/ton	Yes	Yes	
Contact: Jim McCann 555-555-5555	All other grades of paper, except newsprint		Competitive	Yes	Yes	
Can Reclaim Recovery Corp. Fairview, AL	Aluminum cans	Aluminum only, no impurities (e.g., steel, dirt, plastic)	$0.45–0.47/lb	Yes	Possible	Containers and transportation would be provided.
Contact: Rick Dees 555-555-5555	Glass	Separated by color, no caps or metal rings, labels OK	$50/ton minus delivery and handling costs	Yes	Possible	
	Newspaper	Newspaper only	$20/ton	Yes	Possible	
	Aluminum scrap		Competitive	Yes	Possible	
	Radiators		Competitive	Yes	Possible	
	#1 & #2 copper		Competitive	Yes	Possible	
	Brass		Competitive	Yes	Possible	

33.9

TABLE 33.7 Projected Revenue from Sale of Recyclable Material, Indiana Jones County

Material	15%				30%				50%			
	Volume, tons		Revenue/yr, $		Volume, tons		Revenue/yr, $		Volume, tons		Revenue/yr, $	
	1990	1995	1990	1995	1990	1995	1990	1995	1990	1995	1990	1995
Newspaper	2,2702	3,273	81,060	98,190	5,404	5,547	162,120	196,540	9,007	10,911	270,210	327,330
Corrugated cardboard	2,252	2,728	112,600	136,400	4,504	5,456	225,200	272,800	7,506	9,093	375,300	454,650
Bottle plastic	113	136	113,000	136,000	225	273	225,000	273,000	375	455	375,000	455,000
Aluminum cans	378	409	371,800	449,900	676	818	743,600	899,800	1,126	1,364	1,238,600	1,500,400
Glass	1,351	1,637	54,040	65,480	2,702	3,273	108,080	130,920	4,504	5,456	180,160	218,240
Ferrous metals	563	682	16,890	20,460	1,126	1,364	33,780	40,920	1,877	2,273	56,310	68,190
Totals	7,319	8,865	749,390	906,430	14,637	17,731	1,447,780	1,808,850	24,395	29,552	2,495,580	3,023,810
Waste stream reduction	4.9%				9.8%				16.4%			

*The prices used are for demonstration purposes only. Actual revenue may vary: newspaper, $30/ton; corrugated cardboard, $50/ton; aluminum, $1000/ton; glass, $40/ton; ferrous metals, $30/ton; PET bottles, $100/ton.

33.10

- How will diverting the recyclable material contribute to the established recycling goal?
- Does current market value justify the cost of recycling the selected material?
- Do avoided disposal costs make the project cost-effective?

When materials are selected for a recycling program, there are no firm rules that apply universally to all communities. However, diversion goals and marketability typically are the most significant factors.

Route Data.   After a recycling program is established, data must be collected and analyzed to determine:

- Level of participation
- Volume of material being collected
- Operational efficiency

More specifically,

- Participation rates for specified time periods
- Participation rates by material type
- Route productivity
- Crew hours worked
- Overall collection rate
- Crew productivity

Data that must be collected include

- Collection route identification
- Crew identification
- Total number of service addresses
- Total number of setouts
- Total number of truckloads
- Truckload weight
- Time on route
- Time between stops
- Time to pick up each setout
- Demographs/density
- Miles on route
- Type of service location (single-family, multifamily, commercial)
- Type of materials set out
- Tonnage of materials set out
- Geography
- Weather

The frequency of data collection will vary with the type of data collected. Data such as number of service addresses, demographics, geography, type of service location, and miles enroute will be collected only once (unless the route changes).

Information that should be collected monthly would include time between stops and time required to pick up each setout. Data that should be collected daily include collection route and crew identification, number of setouts, number of truckloads, truckload weight, time on route, and type and volume of materials set out.

Route Data Collection Protocol.   A sample data collection form is shown in Fig. 33.2. Data collection forms should be simple and easy to complete, with no enroute calculations required. The steps for route data collection should be thoroughly rehearsed, with "hands-on" practice by the people who will collect the information. Sample forms should be developed with examples of correct data input, and potential problems should be discussed.

If there are sufficient workers, it is recommended that a trained data collector accompany each driver on the first run. The driver may watch as the data are collected, and questions can be raised and answered. On the second run, the driver should record the data, and the trained data collector should observe and answer questions.

Initially, data logs should be checked daily to ensure that they are completed correctly and generating the appropriate types of information. If adjustments are necessary, it is much easier to make them early in the program.

DATA ANALYSIS

Data analysis must be accurate and timely. The value of careful data analysis cannot be overstated, for it is the analysis that will determine the direction the program should take to assure its continued success.

Methods of Analysis

The data that have been collected must be organized into a format that is convenient for use. Data may be organized manually or with an automated system. If an automated system is used, the data use objectives should be considered when a software package is selected. Some elements to consider are

- The data input screen should imitate the data collection form.
- The data verification process should be incorporated in the program.
- Accounting requirements should be satisfied.
- The system should be flexible enough to allow for change.

When data summaries are required, reports can be generated by Lotus 1-2-3 or dBase III Plus. Reports can be designed to show information and relationships regarding participation, frequency, cost, and many other facets of a recycling program. The following example describes how data may be used

```
DATE: _____          No. of Households
                                Served on Route:    _____

VEHICLE I.D.: _____  No. of Set-outs:    _____

ROUTE I.D.:   _____

OPERATOR:     _____

WEATHER:      _____

Location:                       Time            Mileage

Beginning                       _____        _____

Leaving Lot:                    _____        _____

Beginning on Route:             _____        _____

Leave for Disposal Site:        _____        _____

Arrival at Disposal Site:       _____        _____

Leave from Disposal Site:       _____        _____

Arrival Back on Route:          _____        _____

Leave for Disposal Site:        _____        _____

Arrival at Disposal Site:       _____        _____

Leave from Disposal Site:       _____        _____

Ending on Lot:                  _____        _____


                                Type of
Disposal Activity               Material        Weight

Load #1     Aluminum, Cans                      _____

            Newspaper                           _____

            Glass                               _____

            Plastic                             _____

            Yard Waste                          _____

                    Prepared By:

                    _____    _____
                    Operator                    Date
```

FIGURE 33.2 Recycling route information.

Data	Use
Tonnage/time period lbs/setout/load	Project total tonnage for collection, transport, processing, and marketing
	Determine type of pickup and containers

	New equipment	Used equipment
Horizontal baler	$44,000–270,000	$20,000–100,000
Vertical baler	6,000–14,000	2,000–8,000
Glass crusher	2,000–6,000	1,000–4,000
Can separator	2,000–5,000	1,000–2,000
Can flattener	3,000–8,000	1,000–4,000
Can densifier	13,000–28,000	8,000–16,000

Of course, additional processing costs should not exceed additional revenues generated by processed waste.

Public Education Costs

Without public education and promotion of a recycling program, there will be no materials to collect. The cost of public education typically ranges from 1 to 10 percent of the operating budget. Although public education is not a major expense, careful assessment of program operations can ensure that the expenditures are used in the most effective manner.

Marketing, Administration, and Overhead Costs

Marketing costs usually include the costs of locating buyers for the materials and arranging delivery. The labor cost for marketing is generally included under administrative cost. Administration and overhead costs can include items such as

* Program management
* Utilities
* Site lease
* Supplies
* Telephone
* Insurance
* Taxes and permits
* Accounting
* Conferences and training

Cost savings can be realized if in-kind services are used. For example,

* Using existing staff for vehicle maintenance
* Using existing staff for program administration
* Using existing facilities such as offices, phones, and computers

When in-kind services are used, it is difficult to assign an accurate cost-saving value.

SUMMARY

Cost control is an ongoing, dynamic endeavor performed by management. The data collection techniques, as previously outlined, can assist in preparing information for the decision-making process. Current thinking tends to consider recycling an integral part of a comprehensive solid waste system. The costs for a recycling program may range from $30 to $60 per ton of recyclable material collected and transported to market. However, despite the fact that recycling may have a higher cost per ton than another alternative, it is presently at the forefront of public interest. The application of cost control methods will allow a recycling program to be implemented as efficiently as possible.

CHAPTER 34
QUALITY CONTROL MONITORING FOR RECYCLABLE MATERIALS

Stephen A. Katz
Vice President, New England CRINC
North Billerica, Massachusetts

Scott W. Spring
Business Development, New England CRINC
North Billerica, Massachusetts

INTRODUCTION

A recycling program's success is largely dependent upon its ability to consistently produce high-quality, marketable end products. Recycling programs must have stable markets for processed materials in order to assure a program's sustainability and cost-effectiveness. Educational, design, and operational measures at all stages of the recycling process—source separation, collection, delivery, presort inspection, and outload—can assure the production of high-quality, salable products and hence program success.

IMPORTANCE OF QUALITY CONTROL

The importance of producing quality recyclable materials is clear: recyclables are commodities and are treated as such by the end markets. The supply and demand for recycled products is constantly in flux, and so are the prices paid to recyclers. In order to reap the highest possible price, recyclers must demonstrate to the end markets that processed material conforms to specifications and is consistently available in sufficient quantities.

Revenues from the sale of recyclables serve to offset the other costs of implementing and sustaining a recycling program. Costs can include

- Feasibility studies, waste audits
- Solid waste management consulting

- Recyclables collection and transfer
- Recycling containers
- Educational materials and publicity
- Recycling facility site and structure
- Processing equipment (conveyors, magnets, crushers, screens)
- Processing costs (labor, supplies, utilities)
- Materials marketing management

Recycling is overwhelmingly a *cost-avoidance measure* for communities and industry. The frequently encountered "cash for trash" mentality ignores the economic realities of establishing a comprehensive municipal or commercial recycling program. While materials do have a certain value in the marketplace, very rarely do the revenues from the sale of recycled materials offset all costs of collecting, processing, and transporting the recyclables. As disposal costs at landfills and incinerators continue to rise, recycling has increasingly become a more attractive waste management tool and cost-avoidance measure.

The importance of processed material quality and high revenue generation for a materials recycling facility is shown in the equation below:

$$\text{Cap costs} + \text{O\&M costs} + \text{Trans. costs} - \text{revs} = \text{net processing cost}$$

where Cap costs = Capital costs
    O&M costs = Operations and maintenance costs
    Trans costs = Processed materials transportation costs
    Revs = Material revenues

The importance of producing high-quality end products is clear. End markets recognize high-quality material and will compensate those recyclers who consistently produce contaminant-free products.

QUALITY CONTROL PROBLEMS

In addition to recyclable materials, processors often receive significant amounts of *rejects*. Rejects may consist of

- Recyclable items not currently accepted (potential recyclables)
- Nonrecyclables
- Hazardous wastes
- Cross-contaminants

A "potential recyclable" might be a piece of scrap metal found in a curbside collection container. Although the recycling program might accept tin cans and other postconsumer metals, there is no guarantee that absolutely all scrap metals are accepted for recycling. "Nonrecyclable" refers to an item typically found in municipal solid waste, such as a coffee filter, mistakenly placed in a recycling container. "Hazardous wastes" includes household hazardous wastes such as paint and automotive products. These potentially harmful wastes often require special handling. Finally, "cross-contamination" can be a problem in multibin systems which require residents to separate various types of recyclables into product-specific bins.

It is ironic that the overzealous recycler is often responsible for rejects in the material stream. Although scrap metal and plastic toys may be *technically* recyclable, they are not always *logistically* recyclable. In order for a municipal or commercial recycling program to succeed, generators need to recycle only designated materials. A high-quality recycling program has the means to detect and remove reject materials.

LINES OF DEFENSE

From the generator to the end market, the recyclables typically pass through many stages. It is possible to monitor materials for quality control throughout the recycling process. An aggressive educational campaign serves to reduce the percentage of contaminants in the material stream. Other lines of defense include the detection and removal of rejects at specific junctures of the recycling process. The multiple lines of defense at a large-scale materials recycling facility (MRF) are described below.

Educating the Generator

Perhaps the single most important and effective quality control measure recyclers can take is the implementation of comprehensive educational campaigns geared toward creating positive recycling habits. Clear and concise educational materials which inform participants about the "dos" and "don'ts" of recycling can have a tremendous impact on the quality of materials received. Explaining the importance of recycling to a specific community or business is also an effective way of raising participation rates and improving material quality.

Educational brochures and newsletters should clearly specify which recyclables are included in the program and what preparation (if any) is required. Graphics can be used effectively to show generators what materials are accepted (see Fig. 34.1). Recyclers should also explicitly list unacceptable (reject) items.

Common reject items in curbside collection programs include the following:

- Ceramics
- Window glass
- Scrap metal
- Scrap plastics
- Junk mail

Each of these degrade processed material quality and can lower revenues. Some, such as ceramics, can be very damaging to an end-markets' manufacturing equipment. These and other rejects should be explicitly listed as "nonrecyclable."

Information should be distributed at the start of the recycling program, and monthly or quarterly reminders serve to solidify good recycling habits. Educational materials should be tailored to the specific audience that the recycler is trying to reach. Brochures designed for a wealthy, educated community may look very different than those geared toward an inner-city community. Some cities have found it necessary to produce recycling literature in several languages.

RECYCLE	WE DO ACCEPT	WE DON'T ACCEPT
Glass Jars & Bottles 	All food and beverage glass jars and bottles • all jars and bottles must be completely empty and rinsed • discard caps and lids	• caps or bottle tops • window glass, dishes, or drinking glasses • ceramics, light bulbs etc. • glass vases or pottery
Newspaper and Corrugated Cardboard 	Newspapers and corrugated cardboard • both should be clean and dry • bundle or bag your newspaper (paper bags only!) • corrugated cardboard boxes must be cut into individual sheets no larger than 2 1/2 by 3 feet	• newspaper inserts • magazines or phone books • junk mail • cereal, rice or cookie boxes • detergent cartons
Plastic Bottles 	Plastic soda bottles, milk, water and juice jugs and laundry detergent bottles • all bottles must be completely empty and rinsed • all beverage bottles (soda, milk etc.) must be flattened • discard caps and lids	• cottage cheese or margarine tubs • plastic film or wraps, no plastic bags • styrofoam containers • plastic flower pots • caps or bottle tops
Metal Cans 	All beverage and food cans made of metal (aluminum and tin cans) • CANS only • all cans must be completely empty • please rinse your cans	• aerosol cans • aluminum foil or pans • aluminum siding or other scrap metal • pie pans or frying pans

FIGURE 34.1 Educational brochure for households.

Educating the Hauler

Haulers that transport recyclables from curbside collection programs can play an important role in monitoring and improving material quality. Haulers, in addition to homeowners, need to be educated about the importance of keeping rejects out of the process flow. Training programs for drivers and incentive programs have been successfully used by municipalities across North America.

Drivers in curbside collection bin programs have the opportunity to inspect commingled materials before they are loaded into the truck. Materials that do not meet delivery standards should be left at the curb so that residents realize what is not acceptable. Some hauling firms have designed special stickers which allow drivers to specify the reason that a material does not meet specifications (Fig. 34.2). This prevents rejects from entering the process flow and simultaneously serves to educate homeowners.

Haulers involved in other types of recycling programs such as drop-offs have fewer opportunities to monitor material quality. Still, procedures may be put in place which hold generators and haulers accountable for the quality of recyclable material.

MATERIALS RECYCLING FACILITIES

Central sorting and processing facilities for postconsumer recyclables are commonly used to consolidate recyclables from a region and prepare them for ship-

WASTE SYSTEMS, INC.

UNACCEPTABLE
FOR RECYCLING DUE TO:

BOTTLES / CANS NOT RINSED CLEAN

METAL / PLASTIC RING NOT REMOVED

CLEAR PLASTIC BOTTLE AND JAR /
CAPS NOT REMOVED

LABELS NOT REMOVED FROM CANS

PLASTIC — NOT LABELED 1 or 2

ITEM NOT INCLUDED
IN COLLECTION PROGRAM

FIGURE 34.2   Sticker list of unacceptable materials.

ment to market. These facilities are known as materials recycling (or recovery) facilities—MRFs.

Residents separate recyclable materials into one bin and place nonrecyclable refuse in another. The commingled recyclables are delivered to an MRF where they are mechanically sorted into their respective fractions. Recyclable materials in MRF programs typically include the following:

PET plastic containers	Newspaper
HDPE plastic containers	Corrugated cardboard
Aluminum food and beverage containers	Magazines
Aluminum foil and pie tins	High-grade office paper
Tin-coated steel containers	Kraft bags
Glass food and beverage containers	

Highly mechanized MRFs allow municipalities to recover 20 to 30 percent of their waste for reuse. Combined with effective composting programs, recovery rates of over 50 percent are possible. With landfill and incineration costs rising exponentially, communities worldwide are turning to recycling as a cost-effective waste management tool.

A well-designed MRF has three main areas of activity:

- Tipping area (recyclables unloading)
- Processing area (sorting, removal of contaminants, baling)
- Shipping area (loading docks, transfer equipment)

Quality control monitoring can take place in all three areas (Fig. 34.3).

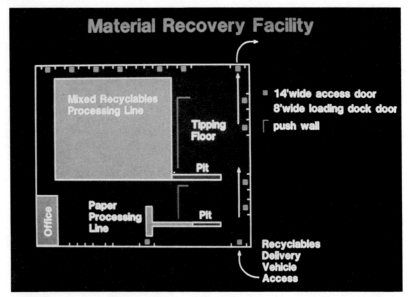

FIGURE 34.3   MRF areas for quality control monitoring.

Tipping Area Monitoring

Most recycling facilities reserve the right to reject loads which contain over a certain percentage of reject materials. In this way, haulers have an incentive not to deliver nonrecyclables to the MRF. Warnings and fines can prevent haulers from repeating mistakes. Personnel on the tipping floor visually inspect loads of recyclables for large volumes of mistakenly delivered municipal solid waste, yard waste, and household hazardous waste. Often, MRF personnel are equipped with a camera to record the condition of incoming loads. Tipping floor inspections are especially crucial during the recycling facility startup so that both residents and haulers are informed early on about what is not accepted at the MRF.

Processing Area Monitoring

Regardless of the quality and intensity of education programs, reject materials will continue to arrive at the MRF. Rejects vary in volume depending upon the materials collected and the collection method. In successful, large-scale curbside collection programs, rejects typically equal 3 to 5 percent of the total incoming tonnage.

An inspection, or "presort," station should be a part of every recycling facility design. This is a dedicated station for the removal of nonrecyclable materials and any objects which could injure or damage workers or equipment. In mechanized MRFs, the material is conveyed past the station and rejects are deposited into a chute and onto another conveyor. Reject conveyors from throughout the processing system move material to a central rejects container.

Workers at the presort station are equipped with protective Kevlar gloves and sleeves which eliminate the risk of cuts and scrapes. A thin flow of material at this stage in the processing system is crucial to allow workers to remove reject materials effectively. Well-educated sorters can remove the vast majority of rejects at the inspection station.

Materials Screening

Often reject materials are too small to remove by hand, and hence screening machines are used to remove all small contaminants and fines. Shaker screens remove all materials of less than a certain diameter, usually about 1 in. Automated screens are a cost-effective way of ensuring high-material quality (Fig. 34.4).

FIGURE 34.4 Automated screens ensure high material quality.

Avoiding Cross-Contamination

High-throughput automated facilities must be designed for a specific stream of recyclables in order to avoid cross-contamination. Metals in the plastics stream or glass in the plastics stream are classified by end markets as contaminants. Gravity-based separation of glass and plastics, for example, produces noticeably less cross-contamination than the traditional air classification method. Air classifiers rely on bursts of air to separate lighter materials from heavier glass. However, this system is difficult to regulate and does not handle crushed plastics and aluminum well.

Inclined sorting machines rely on gravity to separate glass from lighter materials. Glass rolls down the belt while lighter-weight plastic and aluminum are carried to the side by rotating chains (Fig. 34.5).

FIGURE 34.5   Inclined sorting machine separates glass from lighter materials by gravity.

Electromagnets which remove all ferrous containers must be carefully placed in the system to remove only ferrous cans. Glass, paper, and other contaminants may be caught by the moving ferrous containers if the magnet is not at the correct height and orientation (Fig. 34.6).

FIGURE 34.6   Electromagnets remove ferrous containers.

TABLE 34.1 Material Specifications

Material	Baling and sorting requirements	Nonconforming materials	
Aluminum	Aluminum containers will be baled to industry standards (approximately 52" × 30" × 40"—16–20 lb/ft^3). Aluminum will be baled and shipped in trailer loads. Maximum contaminants:	Iron—up to 1.0% per bale Lead—up to 1.0% per bale Moisture—up to 4% per bale	
Tin cans	Tin will be baled in approximately 52" × 30" × 40" sized bales weighing 33–40 lb/ft^3, with minimal quantities of food products, labels, etc. remaining. Tin cans will be baled and shipped in trailer loads. Maximum contaminants:	Aluminum—up to 5% per bale Labels remaining—up to 10% per bale Moisture—up to 5% per bale	
PET plastic	PET soda bottles are baled in approximately 52" × 30" × 40" sized bales weighing 650–750 lb. PET plastic will be shipped in trailer loads. Color separation is not required.	Total nonconforming materials may not exceed 4% per bale.	
HDPE plastic	HDPE plastics bottles will be baled in approximately 52" × 30" × 40" sized bales weighing 650–750 lb. HDPE plastic must be processed so as to be capable of being shipped in trailer loads.	HDPE—not less than 95% per bale Miscellaneous plastic—up to 4% per bale	
Glass	Glass will be sorted by color into amber, flint and green subfractions prior to being crushed. Major contaminants are refractory materials, metals, non-container glass and plastics. Paper labels are tolerated. Cullet size will be approximately 1/2" to 2."	Flint cullet: Amber cullet: Green cullet:	not less than 95% flint, up to 2.5% green, up to 2.5% amber not less than 90% amber, up to 10% flint, up to 10% green not less than 85% green, up to 15% flint, up to 10% amber
Newspaper	Newspaper is baled to a 45" × 45" × 50" sized bale weighing approximately 1175 lb. Material shall consist of sorted fresh newspaper, not sunburned, free from papers other than news, with not more than the normal percentage of rotogravure and colored sections.	Prohibitive materials: None permitted Total nonconforming materials will not exceed 2% per bale	
Corrugated	Corrugated containers are baled to 45" × 45" × 50" bales weighing approximately 980 lb. Material shall consist of corrugated containers having liners of test liner, jut or kraft.	Prohibitive materials may not exceed 1% per bale Total nonconforming materials may not exceed 5% per bale	

QUALITY CONTROL CHECK

Once the commingled recyclables have been separated at the MRF, a final quality control check can be performed to verify that all contaminants have been removed. End markets for glass are particularly sensitive to contamination by ceramics, lead glass, light bulbs, etc. In order to maintain glass quality, facility staff can review the crushed or semicrushed glass during loadout. End markets are very stringent about material conforming to specifications. Higher prices are paid for high-grade materials that meet all requirements.

See Table 34.1 for a list of typical end-market specifications. Final specifications are determined by the individual end users and change as technology advances.

EDUCATION, DESIGN, OPERATIONS

Thorough educational programs, experienced system design, and a well-managed operation are the keys to producing high-quality recyclable materials. Recycling programs that aim to educate participants about the requirements and goals of recycling are more likely to be free of reject materials. Reaching the generator and spreading the word about what rejects are and why they are harmful is the starting point of a successful program.

A carefully engineered processing system improves the detection and recovery of rejects. Cross-contamination will not be a problem if the system and system components are designed specifically for the volume and mix of incoming recyclables.

Recycling facility operations, regardless of size or sophistication, which budget adequate equipment, labor, and resources will be the most effective in minimizing rejects and maximizing material revenues.

CHAPTER 35
CASE HISTORIES

Lisa Wagner Haley
Environmental Scientist
Haley Environmental Consulting and Engineering
Kirkland, Washington

Kevin McCarthy
Recycling Specialist, CH₂M Hill
Sacramento, California

David C. Sturtevant
Solid Waste Project Manager, CH₂M Hill
Bellevue, Washington

Reuter Recycling of Florida, Inc.
Pembroke Pines, Florida

A SMALL RURAL COMMUNITY: THE ARCATA COMMUNITY RECYCLING CENTER'S PROGRAM*

Program Overview

An excellent example of a comprehensive, well-established recycling system is that managed by the Arcata Community Recycling Center (Fig. 1). This private nonprofit recycling center, located in northern California, has been in operation for 20 years. Unlike many programs which have been established in response to recent attention to the solid waste crisis, this program was borne out of a general concern for the environment, particularly for resource conservation. The program truly is comprehensive—incorporating education on conservation and waste minimization with a system for exchange of reusable items with the collection, processing, and marketing of many different recyclable materials.

---

*Case history prepared by Lisa Wagner Haley with the support of Kate Krebs, Executive Director, Arcata Community Recycling Center, Inc.

FIGURE 1

Demographics

The center is located in Arcata, California (population 15,300 in 1990 up from 12,340 in 1980), on the northern California coast in Humboldt County. The town is approximately 300 miles north of San Francisco and 95 miles south of the Oregon border. The county is rural in nature in terms of population densities, distance from metropolitan areas, and its resource-based economy. Several small communities are located within the 3600-mi^2 area of the county. Many are isolated by narrow roads and rugged terrain. Arcata itself is a typical small university town, located in an area of higher population density.

Most of the economy historically has been based on natural resource industries. Within the town is Humboldt State University, which is also a major employer of local residents. In recent years, the area has become increasingly popular to tourists. Many residents, therefore, are employed in the retail or service sector.

Solid Waste Collection Services

Arcata's residential and commercial waste is handled by a private hauler. The city council, which reserves the city's right to approve the rates, holds a franchise agreement with the private company. Solid waste is collected on a weekly basis. Customers pay a flat fee for one-can service and additional charges are added if the household places more than one 30-gal can at the curb. Commercial establishments arrange billing based on the frequency and volume of service. The waste is taken to a transfer station in a neighboring city, where it is compacted and hauled to the nearby landfill. The site owner estimates the site has at least 10 more years of operating capacity.

Program History

The original recycling operations began in 1971, as a project of Northcoast Environmental Center (NEC), a nonprofit consortium of environmental groups from the Arcata area. A recycling drop-off site was established, which was staffed completely by volunteers. The majority of organization of the program was carried out by three people, who researched the feasibility of the project, identified markets for materials collected, and rallied volunteers to staff the site and donate the use of trucks for transporting collected materials to market. The drop-off site was established on a vacant lot in Arcata and was open to the public on Saturdays. Volunteers received, sorted, and processed the materials donated. Materials accepted included newspaper, aluminum, and glass. A local scrap dealer accepted the aluminum, and the other materials were shipped by rail to markets in central California. One hundred tons of recyclables were collected the first year.

The program soon came to be known as the Arcata Community Recycling Center, and its operations continued to be cosponsored by the NEC. The program received funds from the county's federal revenue share in 1973, which were used to purchase the program's first collection vehicle. This also allowed them to move their operations to the present site at 9th and N Streets. Here, they increased the hours they remained open to the public and increased business collection service. In 1975, they received additional funds to purchase a baler, forklift, and a 2-ton truck. The county also provided assistance by providing labor through the VISTA, CETA, JIPTA, and other job-training programs. In the seventies, programs such as these were viewed as part of environmental and resource conservation, not as a part of solid waste management, and this was the motivation behind the county support.

Financial assistance from the center's founding organization, the NEC, provided a means for hiring a project director. Wesley Chesbro was hired to fill this role. He now serves as a Humboldt County Commissioner.

In 1975, the ACRC negotiated an agreement with the Arcata Garbage Company to collect recyclable materials from their residential and commercial customers. The city of Arcata allocated $600 to expand these collection services. High-grade paper and cardboard were collected from area businesses and newspaper, glass, and aluminum were collected from the residences. Also in 1975, the ACRC set up multimaterial drop-off sites in five of the area's outlying towns. The center began to buy back newspaper from community groups who collected them as a fund-raising activity.

In 1979, the ACRC incorporated separately as a nonprofit organization from the Northcoast Environmental Center. The recycling center received a $62,500 grant from the California Waste Management Board to design and construct a mobile collection vehicle to be used for commercial collection routes.

In 1981, the center designed and implemented "Project Recycle" at Humboldt State University, the city of Arcata and Humboldt County offices to collect high-grade ledger paper.

In 1980 to 1982, when the secondary markets' crash devastated many recycling programs, the center survived by laying off staff and cutting back services. This included ceasing pickup of materials from outlying rural towns. Luckily, though, community groups continued the pickups. Other local recycling programs closed.

Understanding the importance of regional communication and cooperative efforts, the center obtained funding from Apple computers to establish the Western Rural Microcomputer Network. The network linked five rural collection centers (Bend, Oregon; Grants Pass, Oregon; Arcata, California; Chico and Visalia, California) to allow them to share information on markets and transportation.

ACRC encouraged community groups to establish recycling as part of their fund-raising activities by designing a "community buyback service" in 1983. In 1985, the program was awarded the "Best Recycling Center in California" award by the California Resource Recovery Association.

From 1985 to 1986, a capital fund drive was conducted to raise $46,000 of the necessary $90,000 to purchase a processing and warehouse site. A pilot program was implemented in 1985 called the Neighborhood Recycling Network. Sets of three canisters for glass, aluminum cans, and newspaper were placed in the two trial neighborhoods, and block leaders were recruited to help spread the word about the program. This project was jointly funded by the Department of Conservation, Division of Recycling, city of Arcata, and Humboldt Area Foundation. The total cost of the pilot project was $12,500.

ACRC was selected as one of seven models used by the Ford Foundation–funded report "Case Studies in Rural Solid Waste Recycling" in 1987. This program was the only one west of the Mississippi chosen for study.

In 1989, the program received the "Best Integrated into the Community Recycling Center" from the California Integrated Waste Management Board and the "Special Achievement in California Recycling" award from the California Resource Recovery Association.

In order to conduct research on the feasibility of developing local markets for secondary materials, funding was obtained in 1988–1989 from the state Rural Renaissance and the Ford, Shalan, and Irving foundations. The research findings were disseminated locally, statewide, and nationally.

In 1990, the Environmental Protection Agency Region IX awarded a contract to ACRC to develop a small-scale secondary glass remanufacturing facility on the north coast. By 1990, the commercial collection pickup had become more sophisticated. The truck used for collection had been equipped with a mobile cardboard baler to allow for baling the cardboard while in route. Cardboard and office paper are currently collected from approximately 250 establishments and comprises almost 35 percent of all materials collected by the ACRC. Some businesses have agreed to pay the ACRC an amount equal to their monthly garbage bill savings for this service.

In 1991, a Rural Recycling Network was designed for collection service based on the Neighborhood Recycling Network model developed earlier for two outlying communities. A Raise the Roof fund drive collected over $30,000 from 1990 to 1991 to pay for construction of a roof over the buy-back receiving yard. The level of materials processed rose from 100 tons in the first year of operation to over 500 tons in 1986.

The administrators of this program have obviously made significant efforts to obtain funding from private foundations and government agencies. These sources have proven critical for many aspects of operations. However, the sale of recyclables provided the majority and the most consistent portion of ACRC revenues.

Funding sources from 1971 to 1991 area as follows:

Private foundations and corporate donors

Humboldt Area Foundation

Shalan Foundation

James Irvine Foundation

Tides Foundation

Apple Computers

Owens Illinois Brockway

Alcoa Recycling

Northwest Paper Fibres

Weyerhauser West Coast

Simpson Paper Company

Government agencies

California Waste Management Board

California Department of Conservation, Division of Recycling

U.S. Environmental Protection Agency, Region IX

Office of Appropriate Technology

County of Humboldt, Private Industry Council

County of Humboldt, Redwood Region Economic Development

County of Humboldt, Youth Employment Training

City of Arcata

The ACRC Program Today

The Arcata Community Recycling Center manages a complete program which includes a donation drop-off and buy-back site, a community buy-back program, commercial collection, Humboldt State University campus collection, a self-service oil change station, a reusables depot, a neighborhood recycling network, a community recycling education program, and more.

Current operations for the ACRC have been in the same location since 1974. The recycling center accepts aluminum cans, newspaper, glass bottles and jars (clear, green, and brown), plastic PET bottles, office paper (sorted white paper, colored paper, computer printout paper), cardboard and brown paper bags. Over 50 percent of these materials are received as drop-off donations from area residents. Operations at the facility are managed by five core staff, including a full-time executive director, three part-time operations staff, and a part-time reusables depot manager. The center relies on about five part-time individuals from county work programs for materials processing.

Permanent staff and labor from the county's general relief program are responsible for processing the materials to prepare them for market. They mechanically flatten and blow the cans into an Alcoa semi-truck; sort and pack unbroken wine bottles by size and shape, and crush the glass by color; bale the cardboard; and accumulate newspaper and high-grade paper in gaylords. Materials are stored in and around the ACRC building until marketed.

The ACRC currently has two flat-bed trucks (1½- and 2½-ton capacities) for collection of recyclables. Other equipment includes two magnetic metal separators; platform scale; large and small baler; four bottle crushers; forklift; pallet jack; bins, barrels, and gaylords for storage; metal container bins for recycling drop-off; aluminum can flattener and blower; banding gun; hand tools; and a small paper shredder.

Public education efforts include fall ads in the local papers, door hangers, and brochures. Presentations are given to community groups; "block captains" and other volunteers spread the word. The ACRC keeps funding low and time as a higher priority in advertising the program. Surveys are conducted to gauge the success of these efforts. A 1984 survey revealed that 75 percent of Arcata's residents knew about the program and 60 percent made use of it at least once a month.

The center is open Wednesday through Saturday from 9:00 A.M. to 5:00 P.M.; 24-hour recycling bins are located at the back gate of the center. Earnings from recyclables can be donated to one of over 300 groups on a posted Community Buyback Program list, or donated to the center.

In addition to accepting donations, California Redemption Value carbonated beverage containers can be redeemed for marked prices. These containers must be kept separate from other containers. Scrap value is offered for aluminum cans, glass bottles and jars, and newspapers.

The center is organized into stations which are clearly marked with instructions on how the materials are to be accepted. (See Fig. 2.)

Commercial Collection Routes

In Arcata and neighboring communities, the ACRC offers a free collection service for pickup of office paper and cardboard boxes. Participants in this program include approximately 250 schools, offices, and businesses, both large and small. A copy of the "Office Paper Recycling Guide" is displayed in Fig. 3.

Neighborhood Recycling Network

As many program managers are learning, an effective way of advertising a recycling program is by making use of community resources. The ACRC has established a neighborhood recycling network, where trained volunteer block leaders distribute pamphlets and information on details of the ACRC recycling program. Displayed in Fig. 4 is an example of a flyer which briefly discusses the "ethic" of recycling and provides instructions for preparing materials.

Community Recycling Education

To educate the community about recycling, speakers have been trained, slide shows have been developed, and tours have been established to promote awareness and participation of the community. Area schools can participate in recycling projects, receive in-class presentations, and learn why recycling is so important for our future.

Humboldt State University Recycling Program

In cooperation with the Arcata Community Recycling Center, recycling containers are located throughout the Humboldt State University campus. The HSU Associated Students office provides information for students interested in participating in the program.

Self-Service Oil Change Station

A garage is maintained for those interested in a do-it-yourself oil change. The garage is kept clean and dry and tools are available for loan. Citizens can change their own motor oil, leave it in the ACRC tank, and it will be recycled. A $1.00 donation is requested for this service.

HOW TO RECYCLE

IT'S EASY!

Separate and sort your recyclable materials at home immediately after you have used them. Call us for tips on how to set up a recycling area in your home or office.

Arcata Community Recycling Center

OPEN FOR BUYBACK & DONATIONS

Corner of 9th and N Streets
Arcata

HOURS:
Wednesday through Saturday,
9 a.m. to 5 p.m.

ALUMINUM CANS

- emptied & rinsed
- flattening not required
- New: all aluminum cat food cans
- CA REDEMPTION VALUE*
- NO "tin" cans (soup, beans, etc.)

NEWSPAPERS

- bundled in paper bags or with twine
- folded flat and stacked (must be dry)
- NO magazines, office paper or envelopes, phone books, or junk mail

GLASS BOTTLES & JARS

- emptied & rinsed
- lids & labels are O.K.
- sort by color: clear, green, brown
- CA REDEMPTION VALUE*
- NO mirrors, ceramics or windows

PLASTIC P.E.T. BOTTLES

- remove caps
- CA REDEMPTION VALUE*
- NO milk jugs or juice containers

OFFICE PAPER

- sort white paper, colored paper, computer print-out paper (xerox copies are O.K.)
- NO envelopes
- commercial collection available— see SERVICES

CARDBOARD & BROWN PAPER BAGS

- flatten boxes and fold bags (must be dry)
- brown corrugated cardboard only
- NO six-pack cartons or waxed boxes
- commercial collection available— see SERVICES

FIGURE 2

OFFICE PAPER RECYCLING GUIDE

COMPUTER PAPER
Continuous computer paper with perforated strips may be recycled as is. Here are the two recyclable types:
- white with green stripes computer paper
- white with blue stripes computer paper

Plain white computer paper may be put in the white paper recycling bin.

WHITE PAPER
It's a high grade of paper, and therefore valuable. White paper consists of the following:
- white letterhead stationery
- plain white bond copying paper (NO off-white or natural)
- white typing and writing paper
- white forms
- white carbonless forms
- white manila tab cards (index cards)
- white cover stock
- adding machine tape
- white lined composition paper
- other dull-finish white paper

COLORED PAPER
Keep colored paper separate from white and computer paper. Colored paper consists of the following:
- colored letterhead stationery
- colored bond copying paper, including off-white and natural (NO goldenrod or florescents)
- colored typing and writing paper
- colored forms
- colored carbonless forms
- colored manila tab cards (index cards)
- colored cover stock
- other dull-finish colored papers

Printed on Recycled Paper, Of Course!

FIGURE 3

Reusables Depot

Donations are accepted of clothing, books, and household items that are in good, reusable condition. On approval, they also accept furniture, building materials, reusable packaging materials, and other items for resale. Typical items available for purchase include canning jars, homebrew bottles, and gallon jugs as well as kitchen goods. Items can be purchased at bargain prices or buy-back earnings can be swapped for depot items.

UNACCEPTABLE MATERIALS

Be careful not to "contaminate" your paper recycling containers with unacceptable materials. If you're recycling an old report, for example, you will have to take it apart and separate into white paper, colored paper, and throw away plastic covers or other binding. If you're recycling a white paper form, be sure to throw away the carbon. **WHEN IT COMES TO OFFICE PAPER RECYCLING, IF IN DOUBT, THROW IT OUT!** Here's a handy list of what NOT to put in your office paper recycling containers:

- magazines and catalogs
- junk mail
- ENVELOPES
- tissue paper
- FAX paper
- coated (glossy) paper
- goldenrod or florescent copy papers
- ditto masters
- blueprint papers
- photographs
- phone books (no part may be recycled)
- carbon paper
- adhesive stickers, labels or tape
- waxed paper
- waxed paper delivery boxes
- waxed 6-pack cartons
- paper plates, cups, food wrappers or containers
- styrofoam
- plastic
- vellum sheet protectors
- rubber bands
- paper clips
- metal fasteners (STAPLES ARE O.K.)
- bindings
- construction paper or art paper (NO crayon, oil or acrylic paint)
- cellophane
- garbage

NOTE: NEWSPAPERS, CARDBOARD AND BROWN PAPER BAGS are recyclable! Keep them separate from office paper, but do recycle them. **MANILA FILE FOLDERS** may be reused or brought to the recycling center to be reused. Bring in your **LASER-PRINTER PAPER** to have it tested for recyclability.

ARCATA COMMUNITY RECYCLING CENTER is open for office paper recycling Wednesday through Saturday, 9 a.m. to 5 p.m. at the corner of 9th and N Streets. Drop off your office paper in the warehouse in the clearly marked recycling boxes. Call 822-4542 if you have any questions...and thanks for recycling!

FIGURE 3

Other Services

Reusable Styrofoam peanuts can be donated or taken out.

Reusable paper egg cartons can be brought in or taken out.

Bimetal California Redemption Value beverage cans are accepted for donation or buy-back.

Aluminum scrap items such as foil, TV dinner trays, and pie plates are accepted for donation only.

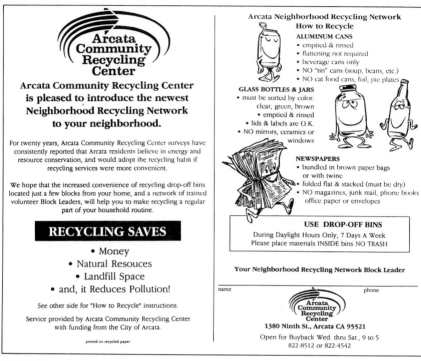

FIGURE 4

Future Plans

With 20 years in operation, the ACRC recycling program is well established. Its program managers hope to continue to add materials for recycling as markets improve. Operations are constantly being evaluated and improvements made for more efficient operations. In Arcata, taking out the recyclables is just a part of the daily routine.

*A MEDIUM SUBURBAN COMMUNITY: MADISON, WISCONSIN**

Program History

Madison, a university city with a population of 190,000, has long been a pioneer in the field of recycling. In 1968, Madison developed and implemented the first curbside collection program for newspapers. Curbside collection programs have also been developed for brush, large metal items, yard wastes, and household recyclables. Many of these programs have evolved from voluntary efforts to

---

*Case history prepared by Kevin McCarthy and David C. Sturtevant.

mandatory programs as the city has faced rising costs of disposal, enhanced public support and awareness of resource conservation, and more stringent state mandates (e.g., banning a wide range of recyclables from landfills).

Program Description

From 1968 through 1991, Madison has been actively establishing, implementing, and fine-tuning a number of recycling programs targeting the following materials:

- Newspapers
- Brush, tree trimmings, and logs
- Large metal items (i.e., white goods)
- Yard wastes (i.e., leaves, grass clippings, and garden wastes)
- Waste oil
- Office paper
- Scrap metals
- Asphalt and concrete
- Lead acid batteries
- Paint products
- Telephone books

The programs described below, will achieve an estimated 1991 recycling rate of 41.5 percent.

Madison's curbside collection of newspaper was begun in 1968 as a voluntary, pilot program and later expanded citywide in 1970. On the same day as their refuse collection, residents place bundled newspapers curbside, and the material is collected and loaded into special racks attached to refuse packer trucks (Fig. 1). The collected material is ultimately transferred to semi-trailers and shipped to market in Alsip, Illinois. In 1990, a total of 3,420 tons of newspaper were collected for recycling.

Beginning in 1972 for tree cuttings (i.e., logs) from city forestry operations and 1976 for residential brush and tree trimmings, Madison has chipped these materials and transferred the chips to local composting facilities. Chips are also made available to the general public. Residents are offered the following services:

- Separate monthly curbside collection of brush and tree trimmings from April through October on a scheduled basis.
- Separate curbside collection of Christmas trees in January.

The collected materials are chipped at the curb or at a centralized processing facility. A total of 16,269 tons of brush and tree trimmings were collected in 1990.

Since 1976, Madison has offered separate weekly curbside collection of white goods (i.e., stoves, refrigerators, water heaters, downspouts, gutters, and miscellaneous recreational equipment). When providing residents with large or bulky item collection, city crews set aside metal items for separate collection. These items are later collected with a dump truck, transferred for storage in 30-yd^3 roll-off bins, and the bins are serviced by a local scrap dealer. In 1990, 1,053 tons were recovered for recycling.

In 1978, the city initiated a waste oil recycling program by establishing three

FIGURE 1   Special rack for newspapers attached to refuse packer.

drop-off sites. Two additional sites were added in 1979. Each site consists of a 275-gal tank mounted on a 3 ft × 5 ft × 6-in concrete pad. Each tank is equipped with a special pouring spout. Metal containers are also available at each site so residents can discard containers used to transport the oil. A total of 42,866 gal of waste oil was reclaimed in 1990.

Madison began recycling leaves in 1980. Nine years later, mandatory recycling of all yard wastes was implemented. The city provides separate scheduled curbside collection of yard wastes with two collections in April and three in the fall. Residents place the materials in loose piles at the curb and city crews use a "dust pan" approach to collect; rear-loader packer trucks are equipped with a dust pan attachment into which city crews sweep the material (Fig. 2). The collected material is transported to area farms for direct soil applications or to compost facilities operated by Dane County. From May through September, Madison does not offer curbside collection services for yard waste but operates three drop-off centers for these materials. In addition, the city encourages residents to reduce their yard waste generation by leaving grass clippings on lawns and/or practicing backyard composting. A total of 16,269 tons of yard wastes were collected for recycling in 1990.

Madison's interest in household recyclables dates back to the 1987 startup of two drop-off centers for glass containers. In 1989, this program was expanded to 13 drop-off centers, all of which accept glass, aluminum cans, tin cans, and PET and HDPE plastic containers. Over 720 tons of these materials were collected for recycling in 1990.

Curbside recycling of household recyclables was initiated in 1989 through the efforts of four neighborhood groups conducting biweekly curbside collection of

FIGURE 2 Dust pan attachment to sweep yard waste into rear-end refuse truck.

commingled bagged recyclables. With the February 11, 1991, kickoff of the city's mandatory weekly curbside collection of household recyclables, including cardboard, these groups discontinued their efforts. The city's program serves approximately 58,000 residential housing units and consists of residents purchasing specially marked clear plastic bags from locally designated retail outlets, placing bottles and cans into the bags, and setting the bags curbside on their regular refuse collection day. Residents are also asked to flatten and bundle cardboard containers for curbside placement alongside the bagged recyclables. City crews pick up the recyclables using a recycling collection truck and transport the material to a MRF. The MRF is responsible for processing and marketing the collected recyclables.

The city's park division has also developed a program for collecting recyclable containers. Recycling containers are strategically located throughout city parks and are also provided for special events such as summer concerts.

As for other city department recycling efforts, since 1975 the city has required all employees to recycle office paper. In 1990, this resulted in the recovery of 199 tons of paper. The city's public works department is separating out and recovering scrap metals. In addition, Madison has been recycling both asphalt from city streets and concrete from sidewalks since 1975. Asphalt is either reprocessed by city crews or sold to an asphalt manufacturer. Concrete is crushed into aggregate by a sand and gravel operation. A total of 19,634 tons of asphalt and 3,000 tons of concrete were recycled in 1990.

Within the past two years, Madison has implemented recovery programs for paint products and telephone books. Telephone books can be placed curbside and picked up by city crews. Telephone books can also be returned to drop-off sites provided by a local department store chain. As for paint products, Madison and Dane counties offer a program whereby residents may drop off selected items, which are later reused, recycled, or disposed at a hazardous material facility.

Finally, the remaining materials in Madison's waste stream are sent to a "reduction plant" which processes combustible materials into refuse-derived fuel (RDF). The RDF is shipped to a local utility where the material is burned to generate steam and electrical power. Noncombustible materials, except ferrous metals, are separated and transferred for disposal at a landfill. Ferrous metals are magnetically separated out from the noncombustible materials and recycled. RDF accounts for 21.9 percent of Madison's waste stream and landfilling is used for 36.3 percent.

Public Education and Information

Madison's significant educational activities have focused on the implementation of yard waste recycling in 1989 and the recently implemented curbside recycling program for household recyclables. The city's most comprehensive efforts to date have focused on the curbside recycling program. The city, with the assistance of a public relations firm, has been conducting a multifaceted outreach program consisting of

- Neighborhood and community group outreach through meetings and a newsletter
- Use of direct mail for a brochure entitled the "Recyclopedia"

- Development and distribution of posters
- Development and distribution of TV, radio, and transit PSAs using local and national celebrities
- Press conferences and other media events
- Special mailings to businesses and landlords

Program Funding

Currently, Madison's recycling programs are financed primarily through property taxes and with revenue from the sale of recyclables. However, based on the provisions of a recently adopted statewide recycling law, the state will be reimbursing some portion of the city's net recycling program costs. The city is also considering moving away from a property tax–based funding system to a volume-based refuse pricing system for its residential customers. See the 1990 Summary Sheet (Table 1).

TABLE 1 Summary Sheet for City of Madison, Wisconsin, Solid Waste Collection and Disposal Costs

Total annual costs	$7,567,210
Revenues	203,458
Net annual costs	$7,363,752
Total tonnage	182,280
Net cost per ton	$ 40.39
Net annual cost per capita (Population, 191,262)	$ 38.50
	($3.21/mo.)
Net annual cost per residential unit (Residential units, 52,985)	$138.98
	($11.58/mo.)
1990 Curbside recycling start-up costs	
Labor	$ 12,592.30
Benefits	3,833.29
Mileage	1,064.48
Special services	1,844.15
Special supplies	100.00
Office equipment	222.85
Advertising	88,600.00
	$108,257.07

Future Program Activities

Madison has a busy agenda for future program activities, such as

- Expanding curbside collection to include magazines, polystyrene, and other plastic containers specified by the state
- Providing assistance to businesses and institutions in setting up office paper recycling programs
- Developing recycling opportunities for bulk wood wastes

- Expanding existing household hazardous waste recycling programs
- Integrating existing and new curbside collection systems so as to minimize costs and lessen energy impacts
- Encouraging source-reduction efforts

Lessons for Other Programs

With its experience in implementing a diverse set of recycling programs, Madison has learned some important lessons including

- Focusing program education from the perspective of letting customers know "why, how, when, where, and what to recycle;" this will reduce possibilities for consumer confusion.
- Recognizing some of the hidden costs (e.g., site maintenance, disposal of materials not accepted, etc.) associated with properly running drop-off centers.
- Developing contingency plans for a program starting off too successfully (e.g., higher recovery of materials than expected).
- Planning any program changes far in advance.

A MEDIUM URBAN COMMUNITY: SANTA FE, NEW MEXICO*

Program History

Given several inherent obstacles to recycling in New Mexico, including low waste disposal fees and limited proximity to recycling markets, recycling in New Mexico made great strides with the kickoff of Santa Fe's curbside recycling program on July 2, 1990; New Mexico's first curbside collection program. The City of Santa Fe (population 60,000) and the local Keep America Beautiful affiliate, Santa Fe Beautiful, have implemented other programs including

- Telephone book recycling
- Christmas tree recycling

Program Description

Santa Fe's voluntary curbside recycling program provides 19,000 residences (i.e., housing units in 16 plexes or below) with weekly curbside collection of commingled glass bottles and jars, aluminum cans, tin cans, PET soda bottles, clear HDPE milk jugs, and newspapers. Residents place commingled recyclables into an 18-gal container and set the container out curbside the same day as their refuse collection. Materials are collected and sorted into bins on a recycling collection truck operated by a private company under contract to the city. The materials are later processed and sold to markets in the southwest and midwest. The city's pro-

---

*Case study prepared by Kevin McCarthy and David C. Sturtevant.

gram has proven popular with citizens as reflected in a monthly participation rate of 80 percent. In 1990, the curbside program diverted 1,012 tons of glass, 270 tons of metals, 44 tons of plastic, and 1,126 tons of newspapers.

As for telephone book recycling, in cooperation with a local telephone book distributor, drop-off sites have been established. In addition, Santa Fe Beautiful has worked with the local telephone company to promote their collection efforts. Collected telephone books are marketed to a firm which shreds the books for use as insulation material.

Christmas tree recycling has been a regular event during the holiday season for the past six to seven years. Christmas trees are collected curbside and chipped and used for mulch. The city also chips tree trimmings and shrubbery found on street medians.

While encouraging Christmas tree recycling, Santa Fe Beautiful promotes the purchase of living trees instead of cut trees through a "Giving Tree Project." Local nurseries reported a tripling of living tree sales in 1990.

Public Education and Information

Santa Fe has carried out a variety of community education efforts. For its curbside recycling program, an extensive campaign was launched complete with "Carlos Coyote," the program mascot, brochures printed in English and Spanish, public service announcements (PSAs), media events, and a personal letter from the mayor to all curbside recipients. Ongoing public education includes weekly Carlos Coyote cartoons in the Sunday newspaper, attendance by Carlos Coyote at parades and other local events, PSAs, and a volunteer block leader program (Figs. 1–5). Other recycling educational activities include an annual school awareness program for K–6 grades, bumper sticker giveaways, distribution of brochures, public presentations, and Santa Fe Beautiful Litter Lympics events.

Program Funding

So far, the city's recycling activities have been funded through surplus capital improvement funds and the general fund. In 1990, the city's curbside recycling program was financed through $350,000 from a surplus capital improvement fund. Revenues from the sale of recyclables are returned to the city's general fund to help offset program costs. This year, the city allocated $425,000 from the general fund to pay for the program. These funds are paid out to a private contractor which provides the collection, processing, and marketing services for the program under a four-year contract with the city.

Educational programs sponsored by Santa Fe Beautiful are funded through a combination of city monies, grants, in-kind services and donations, and membership dues.

Future Program Activities

With recent passage of a comprehensive recycling law in New Mexico, Santa Fe and other cities will be under increasing pressure to expand existing programs

FIGURE 1

and start up new recycling efforts. Currently, Santa Fe is focusing its efforts on initiating commercial sector recycling activities.

Lessons for Other Programs

The early success of Santa Fe's recycling efforts is attributed to a multisector participatory approach coupled with strong support from elected officials. In ad-

FIGURE 2

FIGURE 3

FIGURE 4

FIGURE 5

dition, a particularly effective approach has been to stress the win-win community benefits of recycling. Finally, since the city relies on general fund revenues to finance their programs, a strong focus should be receiving a stable revenue stream from recycled materials sales by developing long-range pricing arrangements.

A LARGE URBAN COMMUNITY: THE AUSTIN, TEXAS, RECYCLING PROGRAM*

Program Overview

Recycling Week, "Cash for Trash," and a fleet of Recycling Block Leaders are the components of success for the City of Austin's recycling program (Fig. 1). Voluntary curbside pickup is offered to households for commingled recyclables in 5-gal plastic buckets or 14-gal recycling containers. The program began with a pilot project in 1982 and completed its expansion phase in 1989, bringing weekly collection to 110,000 households. Commercial collection of office paper is offered to public schools and businesses.

FIGURE 1

---

*Case study prepared by Lisa Wagner Haley with the support of the Austin Recycling Program staff.

Demographics

Austin, the capital of Texas, is populated by 481,000 people and is growing at a rate just under 1 percent per annum. The city limits encompass 185 mi^2 with a population density of four persons per acre (Fig. 2).

FIGURE 2

Per capita income is \$15,711, according to the U.S. Department of Commerce figures for 1987. Presently, unemployment is 4.4 percent and is gradually decreasing. Major public-sector employers include the University of Texas, Bergstrom Air Force Base, and various agencies of federal, state, and local government. High-technology systems and services dominate Austin's corporate employment market.

Solid Waste System

Refuse is accepted at three different landfills, two private and one public (operated by the city of Austin). The city landfill tracks municipal collections, which include 110,000 single-family residential accounts that produce approximately 160,000 tons of solid waste per year. Using data obtained from the City Planning Department and the Department of Health, the average statewide per capita generation rate of solid waste is calculated to be 5 lb per person per day.

Presently, Texas has one-sixth of the nation's operating landfills, and tipping fees average approximately \$10 per ton. Therefore, Austin has been able to implement waste-reduction programs as a preventive measure, rather than a reaction to a disposal crisis. They are making the fullest use of existing resources and carefully weighing future benefits against immediate program costs.

The city provides solid waste collection service to the area's single-family dwellings, while private haulers collect from multifamily dwellings and businesses.

Program History

During the 1970s, a growing number of citizens began recycling residential waste materials at drop-off centers established and maintained by Ecology Action (EA), a nonprofit volunteer organization. By 1980, EA was operating nine multimaterial centers, servicing newspaper recycling bins on the University of Texas campus, and initiating an office paper recycling program.

In 1981, when the market for old newspaper crashed, the organization was forced to cut back on the scale of its operations. Citizen recyclers appealed to the city council for a municipal curbside program. A citizens' task force was appointed and a consultant was commissioned to develop a solid waste study and a 20-year plan.

In 1981, the city adopted the Solid Waste Management Plan, which called for an integrated program, including a pilot curbside recycling program, technical assistance for backyard or other decentralized composting, a waste-to-energy facility, transfer stations, and permitting of a new landfill.

In 1982, a pilot curbside recycling program was established in two neighborhoods to service 3000 homes. In 1983, the service area was expanded to include 12,000 homes. By 1989, the final expansion phase of the program was completed, bringing weekly curbside collection to 110,000 households. In 1983, the city abandoned its attempt to permit a new landfill in the face of organized opposition on the part of neighboring residents.

To promote and advertise the recycling program, block leaders were recruited in 1983. Five-gal buckets were made available from the local fire stations (Fig. 3).

BLOCK LEADERS NEEDED!

We're looking for ~~a few~~ lots of good people!

FIGURE 3

In 1984, a referendum was approved to construct a 600-ton/day waste-to-energy plant. In 1984, the project was canceled due to revised economic projections, persistent environmental concerns, and the ubiquitous NIMBY (not-in-my-backyard) syndrome.

In 1988, the week of September 11 to 17 was designated "Recycling Week." During this week, new developments in the program are publicized, new block leaders are actively recruited, and businesses, schools, and citizens groups are recognized for their achievements and participation in the recycling and waste-reduction program. Also in 1988, a privately sponsored program was implemented, called "Cash for Trash"; $100 in cash prizes are offered to randomly selected curbside recyclers.

In September 1989, city staff conducted an informal survey of local recycling businesses, government agencies, and nonprofit groups to arrive at an educated estimate of the total amount of recycling activity in Austin. All contacts were asked to estimate the volume of materials received from outside Austin and deduct them from their totals. The figures in Table 1 are based on responses to this survey, with the exception of City of Austin figures, which are based on recovery rates.

Figures were also calculated for items such as auto bodies, car batteries, clothing, household items, small appliances, books, waste oil, and paint. These items were calculated separately because they are not normally found in the

TABLE 1   Amount of Material Recycled in Austin Survey

Materials	City of Austin, tons	Commercial, tons	Nonprofit, tons
Metal	500	65,060	62
Glass	2,800	2,750	300
Paper	6,700	35,000	1,780
Yard waste	2,790	4,800	5,628
Subtotals	12,790	107,610	7,770

Total: 128,170 tons/year = approximately 23.5% recycling rate

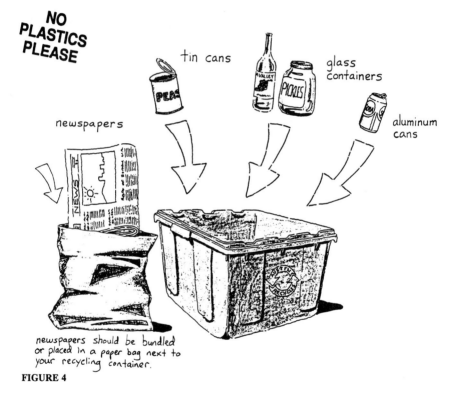

NO PLASTICS PLEASE

tin cans

glass containers

newspapers

aluminum cans

newspapers should be bundled or placed in a paper bag next to your recycling container.

FIGURE 4

waste stream, are only temporarily kept out of the waste stream by repair and/or reuse, or because they are not considered solid waste (Fig. 4).

Program Description

The program is a voluntary system offering weekly curbside collection of materials. Newspapers, corrugated boxboard, and kraft paper grocery bags are collected together; glass containers and cans (both steel and aluminum) may be commingled and set out in a separate container. In approximately 40 percent of the service area, a single 14-gal container is used for all materials (this was started in August 1990).

Block Leaders.   To promote the program, Austin has enlisted over 1,050 block leaders. The block leaders make home visits to their neighbors, distributing pamphlets (Fig. 5) on recycling and composting, yard signs, and bumper stick-

HOW TO RECYCLE WITH THE CITY OF AUSTIN RECYCLING PROGRAM

Recycling Hotline
479-6753

Environmental and
Conservation Services

* Place the materials listed below at the curb (separate from garbage) in containers by <u>8:00 a.m.</u> on your recycling day (see map).

GLASS BOTTLES & JARS, ALUMINUM & STEEL FOOD CANS & FOIL

* Remove food residue; lids
  & labels may be left on

* Place together in a paper grocery
  bag, box, or any open container
  (no plastic bags, please)

* Please <u>NO</u> aerosol cans, window
  glass, Pyrex, or ceramics

NO PLASTICS PLEASE

NEWSPAPERS

* Remove advertising inserts

* Stack in a paper grocery bag,
  or bundle with string

* Please <u>NO</u> telephone books,
  mail, or magazines

CORRUGATED BOXES

* Flatten to less than 3 feet on any side
* Bag/bundle with newspapers or separately

Printed on Recycled Paper

FIGURE 5

ers. They provide explanations of how materials should be prepared for collection.

Recycling Week.   Recycling Week was implemented to increase awareness of the city's recycling program by highlighting events and new developments in the program. Local newspapers, radio stations, and television networks contribute to the effort by covering the events and circulating press releases prepared by the city's public information office.

Tonnage of materials collected, calls to the recycling hot line and the number of volunteer block leaders recruited all increase by significant amounts during and after this public awareness and education activity.

Keep Austin Beautiful (a local chapter of the association Keep America Beautiful) promotes their commercial recycling programs during Recycling Week. The program promotes recycling in public schools and honors the school with the highest per capita recycling totals at the end of the school year. The Keep America Beautiful Clean Recycler Program promotes recycling and responsible waste management practices in Austin businesses.

Drop-off Recycling.   In addition to curbside collection, drop-off boxes are located around the city. Residents who do not have curbside pickup use these boxes to deposit their newspaper, and at some locations, their glass and metal as well. The sites are managed by private recyclers.

The city contracts with a private recycler for the operation of a recycling station at the landfill. The station receives 400 to 500 tons of material each year, primarily large appliances and bulky scrap metal. Landfill customers are assessed a $10 surcharge for the disposal of major appliances, which provides an incentive for them to return them to the drop-off station instead.

Several buy-back operations also exist in the area. These businesses buy newspapers, cardboard, glass, aluminum cans, and bulky metals. Some also accept used clothes, appliances, furniture, and building materials, which are often repaired and resold.

Yard Waste Recycling.   A pilot leaf collection program diverted more than 1300 tons of yard waste during the peak leaf-fall periods in late autumn and early spring of 1989/90, utilizing regular garbage collection vehicles and crews (Fig. 6). Collection personnel identify and pick up leaves as they are normally set out, so that no special procedures are required by residents. The leaves are taken to a wastewater treatment facility, where inmates of a local correctional complex remove plastic bags and other extraneous materials. The leaves are then mixed into windrows of treated sewage sludge along with wood chips provided by the city's tree service contractor. The composting process, which takes 10 to 12 weeks to complete, yields a finished product which is marketed commercially through local garden shops and landscape businesses. Forty-five percent of Austin's sewage sludge is treated in this manner. The remainder of the treated sludge is applied to agricultural land leased by the city and an area farmer, with profits from the annual hay crop shared by both parties.

In 1990, the city council appropriated funds to purchase a brush shredder for the diversion of wood waste at the landfill. The material generated by this operation will be used in the composting operation described above, made available for on-site composting, sold as a mulch, an industrial fuel supplement, or used as cover material for the landfill.

COMPOSTING

A Guide To
Organic Recycling

City of Austin

Environmental and Conservation
Service Department

FIGURE 6

Christmas Tree Recycling.   For the past six years, the Austin Parks and Recreation Department has collected Christmas trees for recycling on the two weekends following Christmas. In 1990 to 1991, over 45,000 trees were collected by over 200 volunteers at 13 drop-off locations, with roll-off containers provided by local waste haulers. Tree donors receive pine seedlings in return for their participation in the event. The trees are shredded with chippers donated by local tree service companies and applied as mulch to city park lands.

Home Chemical Collection.   In the spring, the annual Home Chemical Collection Day provides city residents the opportunity to safely dispose of hazardous material which would otherwise go to the landfill. In 1989, 3400 gal of used motor oil and 398 auto batteries were recycled as part of the event; 1200 gal of usable paint was reclaimed for use in local housing rehabilitation projects.

Procurement Policies

In an effort to set an example of waste reduction and recycling in municipal facilities, the city council established a purchasing policy in October 1988, which created a 10 percent price preference for the purchase of recycled paper products by city agencies. Prior to the city council's Comprehensive Recycling Resolution of January 1990, which redefined recycled paper to conform with the latest EPA procurement guidelines, the city's purchasing department experienced some difficulty in receiving bids for fine paper with a certified percentage of postconsumer fiber. There has been no such problem with coarse paper products.

Markets

Periodically, recycling brokers are invited to bid on all curbside materials, and given the opportunity, through their bids, to suggest additional recyclables which could be collected by the city (Fig. 7). Local delivery is specified, forcing out-of-town businesses to work with local brokers or establish a local recycling operation. In the most recent bid invitation (December 1988), bidders were allowed to bid on both separated and commingled materials. Both a floor price (not to be lowered during the term of the contract) and an escalator price (started as a percentage of a particular market quotation) was solicited for each material.

FIGURE 7

A three-year contract for all materials was awarded to ACCO Waste Paper, allowing the city the economies of commingled collections and a single point of delivery. To process commingled containers, ACCO has established a separate mechanical and manual sorting line, employing 14 mentally retarded adults through a local social service agency to staff the new facility.

The final market for Austin's newspaper is a deinking mill in Mexico City which produces recycled newsprint. Glass container cullet is sold to the Owens-Brockway plant in Waco, Texas, where it is recycled into new containers. Aluminum cans are sent to Alcoa plants in Arkansas and Tennessee, and tin cans are processed into structural reinforcing rods at the Structural Metals minimill in Seguin, Texas.

Although marketing materials locally through commercial brokers has the advantages of stimulating the local economy and utilizing private-sector expertise, it cannot fully protect a community from the vicissitudes of the market. Over the past three years, Austin has seen revenues from the sale of recyclables shrink as total recycling tonnages collected have grown. As local, state, and national recycling activities escalate, markets tend to decline or become saturated, increasing the need to develop new markets, identify alternate markets for as many materials as possible, and to gain access to those markets. This is an area which is yet to be explored by the City of Austin.

Results

With 10 years of projected capacity in the municipal landfill and a disposal cost of $10 per ton, there is no immediate garbage crisis in Austin. In the absence of any hard economic pressures to recycle, city programs, with the exception of in-house efforts, have remained strictly voluntary. Although a grant program for recycling activities has been established on the state level, recycling on the part of waste generators is encouraged largely through educational and promotional campaigns.

Participation in the curbside recycling program currently stands at 65 percent, with monthly collections averaging 1000 tons, or approximately 7.5 percent of single-family residential waste. This volume breaks down as follows:

News/corrugated   67%

Glass   28%

Tin/steel cans   3.5%

Aluminum cans   1.5%

Yard waste efforts account for an additional 1 percent.

Future Plans

The Solid Waste Advisory Commission (SWAC), appointed in 1988 to study Austin's solid waste management situation and make recommendations for its future, is considering options which reduce the convenience of waste production, such as volume-based garbage fees and the rescheduling of solid waste collections. Residents currently receive twice-weekly garbage and once-weekly recycling pickup. An alternative under consideration is to offer one garbage, one recycling, and one yard waste collection each week.

The city council has called for the city staff and SWAC to develop a mandatory recycling plan if the recovery of recyclables from the residential waste stream has not reached a 20 percent rate following the citywide distribution of curbside containers and the implementation of a volume-based garbage fees.

While there has developed an almost universal understanding of the long-term benefits of recycling, present-day costs remain a constant concern. As the curbside recycling workload has increased, so has the need to improve the program's operational efficiency. This issue is being addressed through the development of flexible collection routes to equalize the workload among crews and minimize overtime. In order to avoid the inefficiency inherent in crews consisting of a driver and a loader, all new vehicles purchased for the program will be designed for single-person operation. As weekly setout rates increase, routes will also be designed for right-side service only, to minimize operator motion outside the vehicle.

Experience has proven that convenience is essential to voluntary participation, and the combination of household containers and commingled curbside collection appears to be the ultimate in recycling convenience. The city staff hopes that the single-container system for recycling collection and disincentives for generation of waste will result in maximum levels of recycling in Austin.

A LARGE URBAN COMMUNITY: SAN FRANCISCO, CALIFORNIA*

Program History

After creation of the San Francisco Solid Waste Management Program in 1978, the city initiated an integrated management approach to addressing its solid waste needs. This integrated approach relies on waste reduction, waste reuse, recycling, hazardous waste management, and landfilling. In 1980 the city formally began a recycling program that has grown from a fiscal year 1980–1981 budget of $100,000 to over $900,000 in fiscal year 1990–1991. The city's successful recycling efforts resulted in the National Recycling Coalition naming San Francisco the Best Urban Recycling Program in 1990.

Program Description

San Francisco (population 724,000) has implemented a series of successful recycling programs that have yielded at least a 25 percent recycling rate, not including any diversion from scrap metals, asphalt, and curbside recycling efforts. Programs have been developed and implemented for the following targeted waste streams:

- Single-family and multifamily residences
- Government offices
- Commercial businesses

On April 3, 1989, the city kicked off its voluntary curbside recycling program which will ultimately serve about 170,000 households and small buildings with up to five units. Residents commingle glass bottles and jars, aluminum cans, tin cans, and plastic soda bottles in 14-gal plastic bins provided to them by a private refuse hauler under contract to the city. Residents place recyclable papers including newspaper, junk mail, cardboard, and magazines into a separate paper bag. On the morning of their collection day, residents place the bin and bag curbside and recycling collection trucks come by and pick up the material. The collected materials are transferred to a material recovery facility (MRF) where they are separated and marketed for sale.

This program has proven highly successful with over 18,000 tons of materials recycled in the first 18 months including 15 million glass and plastic bottles and 8

*Case history prepared by Kevin McCarthy and David C. Sturtevant.

FIGURE 1 Material recovery facility in San Francisco.

million aluminum and tin cans (Fig. 1). With its current average monthly participation rate of 80 percent, this program is expected to divert 7 percent of the total
waste stream by 1992; this will give the city an overall recycling rate of 32 percent
by 1992 (Fig. 2).

A similar program has been implemented for large apartment buildings with
six units or more with the only difference being that materials are collected in
centrally located 60- and 90-gal containers. The same materials collected in the
curbside program are collected in this program. When completed, the apartment
recycling program will serve 3,500 buildings totaling about 70,000 units.

The city offers other recycling opportunities for residents such as Christmas
tree recycling, home composting, and phone book recycling. Since 1987, the
city's "Treecycling" program has recovered Christmas trees from residents with
last year's efforts reaching a 50 percent recycling rate. Collected Christmas trees
are chipped for mulch or fuel. Under contract with the San Francisco League of
Urban Gardeners (SLUG), the city offers home composting workshops in a demonstration garden site for the general public and schools. So far ten workshops

FIGURE 2   Conveyor moves recyclables in a MRF.

have been held with 300 participants and other workshops have drawn 45 elementary and high school teachers (Fig. 3).

As for commercial businesses, the city has developed several programs including recycling and waste-reduction technical assistance, a "buy-recycled" program, and telephone book recycling. The city provides businesses with an office paper recycling guide, desktop sorters, and waste reduction tips. In addition, city staff conduct "how-to" seminars and provide other waste audit services for businesses. In 1990, over 50,000 private-sector employees were offered recycling opportunities through new office recycling programs. To complete the recycling loop, the city is also producing a purchasing guide so businesses can implement "buy-recycled" programs. Finally, for the past five years, the city has been working with the telephone company to encourage recycling of old phone books. This program has consisted of a recycling message on the bags used to distribute phone book sets, a four-page section in the yellow pages on recycling, and a letter sent to businesses urging them to recycle and giving them instructions on how to recycle their old phone books.

FIGURE 3 Meeting of San Francisco's League of Urban Gardeners conducting a recycling study.

Besides the city-operated and/or -funded programs, there are over 30 privately operated buy-back and drop-off centers throughout the city (Fig. 4). All total, recyclable materials collected include high-grade paper, newspaper, mixed paper, magazines, phone books, cardboard, glass bottles and jars, whole wine bottles, aluminum cans, tin and bimetal cans, Christmas trees, PET plastics, HDPE plastics, paint, Styrofoam packing peanuts, used motor oil, and car batteries.

Public Education and Information

While far reaching, the city's recycling programs have been accompanied by a diverse array of public education and information activities targeting curbside recipients, consumers, the general public, school-age children, and businesses. Notable public education and information activities have included (Fig. 5):

- A citywide "It's Easier Than You Think" advertising campaign focusing on the ease of recycling.
- An environmental shopping campaign developed and promoted in cooperation with a major grocery chain. The campaign included the distribution of over 50,000 environmental shopping guides.
- Development and distribution of a "Holiday Waste Reduction Guide" offering tips on environmentally sensitive gifts, decorations, packaging, and entertainment.
- A home composting campaign that included the development and distribution of a series of home composting brochures.
- A "Thanks Tons" campaign designed to congratulate and encourage residents' and business' recycling efforts.
- A school education program consisting of a K–5 curriculum ("the 4th R"), pre-

FIGURE 4 Typical drop-off center.

FIGURE 5 Bus billboard advertisement for a recycling slogan.

sentations to individual classes on recycling, and field trips to a recycling center and transfer station.

Ongoing educational activities focus on using public service advertising on radio and television, busses, transit shelters and stations, billboards, billing inserts, voter pamphlets, exhibits at neighborhood fairs, columns and ads in neighborhood papers, a trilingual hot line, and other means to cost effectively reach as many residents as possible (Fig. 6).

Program Funding

The city's solid waste program, including the recycling program, is funded through fees on garbage rates (i.e., rates charged residents and businesses). Currently, homeowners pay variable rates based on the number of cans they put out for collection; $8.49 per month is charged for one 32-gal can and $3.86 per month for each additional 32-gal can. In the near future, the rate structure will include a 20-gal can option so residents will have an even greater incentive to generate less waste.

Future Program Activities

Planned future recycling activities include:

- Expanding existing programs
- Residential and institutional organic waste composting
- Waste exchange program
- Donation and repair centers directory
- Amending the city building code to require space for recycling in all buildings
- Conducting market research
- Development of an automated multichoice, multilingual hot line recycling information hot line
- Translation of all informational materials into Spanish and Chinese
- Six- to twelve-grade recycling curriculum
- Community college recycling curriculum

Recommendations for Other Programs

The strength and ultimate success of the city's recycling program has been its diversity in recycling opportunities offered to residents and businesses. These opportunities have been designed to reflect the city's characteristics such as the existing waste management systems, waste stream composition, and cultural diversity. Programs in other communities should be similarly tailored to fit the characteristics unique to the community.

Relatedly, programs should build upon local and existing resources so appropriate needs are addressed. In addition, this will allow for positive and cooperative interaction between the public, private, and nonprofit sectors.

FIGURE 6

Finally, when educating residents and businesses, recycling message(s) should be conveyed from different angles so the target audience is given a diversity of options for acting on the message.

A MAJOR URBAN COMMUNITY: LOS ANGELES, CALIFORNIA*

Program History

Moving beyond a divisive battle over development of a waste-to-energy project, the Los Angeles City Council in May 1987 called for a mandatory, citywide recycling program. In June 1988, Mayor Tom Bradley established a goal of reducing and recycling 50 percent of the waste stream collected by the city; the city's Bureau of Sanitation collects trash from all single-family residential units and small apartment buildings (i.e., four units or less). A year later, the city issued a Recycling Implementation Plan (RIP) which outlined a series of recommendations for a comprehensive recycling program. During the summer of 1989, the city moved forward with the RIP and created a new Recycling and Waste Reduction Division (RWRD) within the Bureau of Sanitation to implement residential recycling programs and citywide education and information activities. To address the remaining and largest portion of the waste stream, the city created an Integrated Solid Waste Management Office (ISWMO) directly under the Board of Public Works to help foster, initiate, and plan for commercial-sector recycling.

---

*Case history prepared by Kevin McCarthy and David C. Sturtevant.

Program Description

The City of Los Angeles has begun to aggressively implement an integrated set of recycling programs addressing both residential and commercial waste generators. In September 1990, the city started the first phase of its mandatory curbside recycling program with subsequent and final rollout over a three-year period for collection of household recyclables and a five-year period for yard debris. The program phase-in is necessary due to the large number of residential units to be served [i.e., nearly 800,000 homes, concurrent phase-in of automated waste collection, and need for sufficient lead time for development of material recovery facilities (MRFs)] and a yard-waste composting facility. The city is in the process of developing mandatory enforcement procedures and an antiscavenging ordinance.

The actual program consists of weekly curbside collection, on the same day as refuse collection, of commingled glass bottles and jars, aluminum cans, tin cans, PET soda bottles, and clear HDPE containers placed by residents in 14-gal plastic bins (Fig. 1) and also bagged or bundled newspapers placed on top of the bins. Recycling collection trucks transfer the material to a MRF and the material is separated and marketed for sale. In addition, an automated refuse collection truck picks up yard debris placed curbside in 60-gal containers (Fig. 2). The collected yard debris is transferred to a yard debris processing facility. Since 1989, the city has conducted a Christmas tree recycling program. Beginning this year, the program will consist of pilot curbside collection and seven drop-off centers. Residents bringing their tree to a drop-off center will be offered free compost.

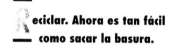

Reciclar. Ahora es tan fácil como sacar la basura.

Recycling. Now it's as easy as taking out the trash.

FIGURE 1   Multilanguage recycling posters.

They're bigger. They're better.
—— They're new and they're free.

Son más grandes. Son mejores.
—— Son nuevos y son gratis.

FIGURE 2   Multilanguage recycling posters.

As for commercial-sector recycling, the ISWMO has initiated a generator-based approach which focuses on identifying and targeting those sectors generating the most waste. ISWMO is currently developing a waste characterization database for targeted generators and later will develop specific waste reduction and recycling strategies for these generators.

In the interim, ISWMO has focused its energies on the following activities:

- Creating trade association (e.g., grocers, restaurants, hospitals, and landscapers) recycling task forces
- Developing and sponsoring a series of workshops (e.g., office recycling, hospital recycling, hotel recycling, and composting) outlining successful programs, marketing/procurement issues, and waste audit procedures
- Making available videotapes on workshops held to date
- Developing recycling resource guides (e.g., on recycled paper, recycled paint, thrift shop directory, recycled toner cartridges, and "grasscycling")
- Producing a newsletter highlighting ISWMO activities and noteworthy recycling efforts in the community

On the waste reduction front, the city is implementing several programs including:

- A "junk-mail" campaign
- Pilot backyard composting program servicing approximately 30,000 participants

- A "Don't-Bag-It" outreach effort encouraging residents to leave grass clippings on their lawns

Public Education and Information

In the spring of 1991, the city hired three public relations contractors to assist with public education and information activities in three areas: curbside recycling program, citywide recycling awareness, and school-age recycling curriculum. Curbside recycling education is under way in the city and consists of an overall multilingual (i.e., English, Spanish, Korean, Mandarin, and Cantonese) campaign of community meetings, door-to-door canvassing, door hangars, and display booths exhibited throughout the city (Figs. 3 and 4). Citywide recycling awareness will be kicked off this fall with an ad campaign for television and radio, newspapers, and billboards. Finally, a school-age curriculum was begun citywide in September.

Program Funding

All of the city's recycling programs are financed using general fund revenues. This is accomplished through two departments: (1) the ISWMO with a 1991 budget of $4 million to plan and facilitate recycling in the private commercial sector, and (2) the Bureau of Sanitation, Division of Recycling, for the operation of municipal residential recycling activities. The city is considering funding future commercial recycling efforts through business license fees.

Future Program Activities

The city will continue to roll out its curbside recycling program to all city residents over the next three to five years. Additionally, the city recently completed a 12-week pilot program for collection of mixed paper and will be determining when to add this material to its curbside program. Other materials under consideration include corrugated containers, colored HDPE containers, and mixed plastics.

As noted above, the ISWMO will be developing generator-specific waste reduction and recycling strategies for those generators producing the greatest amount of trash in the city. Such a focus on these generators will give the city the best return on its investment in term of monies spent to increase the recovery of recyclables. In addition, the city will then be able to identify other generators which will need more technical and/or financial assistance to reduce or recover material from their waste streams.

Lessons for Other Programs

The unique challenges facing the city's recycling efforts are primarily a result of its enormous and culturally diverse population, currently at nearly 3.5 million residents. Particular challenges include program funding and education. With the predominant use of general fund revenues to fund a city's program, as with the City of Los Angeles, strong emphasis should be given to including avoided disposal cost savings as well as material sales revenues in the program balance sheet; this allows for a more accurate assessment of program costs and benefits.

FIGURE 3 Spanish language recycling poster.

While seemingly obvious, this is especially important given the fiscal constraints and realities facing most local governments.

As for recycling education, the city emphasizes citizen involvement through providing them with opportunities to participate and incentives to do so. These messages must be tailored to the particular audience. However, given the recent deluge of "green marketing" messages (e.g., diapers are compostable or polystyrene is recyclable), it is particularly crucial that citizens clearly understand the recycling opportunities (e.g., types and ways to recycle materials in their area) offered to them.

"LOS PERIODICOS DE AYER SE HACEN LOS PROBLEMAS DE MAÑANA."

— EL MAESTRO "GURU"

En Los Angeles se tiran más de 1,000 toneladas de periódicos al día, suficiente para que extiendan casi 6 millas y media de altura.

Estos periódicos desechados no sólo obstruyen los basureros, sino que también contribuyen a la contaminación ambiental y al derroche de nuestros preciados recursos naturales.

La alternativa es muy clara. Si simplemente reciclamos todos los periódicos que ahora tiramos, estaremos ahorrando un espacio significante en nuestros basureros además de más de 7 millones de galones de agua y aproximadamente 17,000 árboles al día.

Reciclando periódicos viejos no es la única manera en la que podemos ayudar a prevenir una crisis de basura en Los Angeles.

A continuación hay varios métodos convenientes y efectivos para reducir, reusar y reciclar para poder alcanzar niveles de basura aceptables. ¿Por qué no los recorta y los pega a su refrigerador para referirse a ellos fácilmente? Si cada uno de nosotros hacemos el mejor esfuerzo para reducir la cantidad de basura que producimos, nuestro esfuerzo colectivo resultará en una dramática reducción en los desperdicios de Los Angeles.

☞ Cuando aregle el jardín, deje el pasto recortado sobre el césped en vez de echarlo en una bolsa para el camión de la basura. El hacerlo puede ahorrar un espacio considerable no sólo en los basureros municipales sino en sus botes de basura. ☞ Convierta en abono los desechos del jardín. ☞ Compre enseres y herramientas recargables. ☞ Use pilas recargables. Cada año se botan millones de pilas desechables que contienen carcinógenos y otros tóxicos. ☞ Arregle las cosas en vez de tirarlas y comprar artículos nuevos. ☞ Lleve las sobras de pintura, del aceite del motor, y productos que son peligrosos en el hogar (Household Hazardous Waste Roundups). ☞ No use bolsas de basura en los recipientes de la ciudad; éstas sólo ocupan espacio y no son reciclables. ☞ Cuando llegue a su vecindario el programa de reciclamiento de la ciudad, participe juntando y poniendo los periódicos viejos al lado de su recipiente amarillo el día de la recogida. Para aún más información sobre como puede reducir diariamente la acumulación de basura, llame gratis al 1-800-773-CITY (1-800-773-2489).

NO HAGAMOS DE LOS ANGELES UN BASURERO.

UN MENSAJE DEL MAESTRO "GURU"
Y LA CIUDAD DE LOS ANGELES

(RECORTE Y GUARDE—EL MAESTRO "GURU")

FIGURE 4 Spanish language recycling poster.

A SMALL RURAL COUNTY: AUBURN, WASHINGTON'S, RECYCLING PROGRAM*

Program Overview

The City of Auburn is located in King County, Washington, approximately 20 miles from the city of Seattle (Fig. 1). The county's comprehensive solid waste management plan includes an aggressive recycling goal which requires that communities reduce their waste by 50 percent by the year 1995 and 65 percent by the year 2000. In order to meet this goal, the City of Auburn has implemented a voluntary waste reduction and recycling program. Residents take their recyclables to multimaterial drop sites and have the option of signing up for the curbside collection of yard waste.

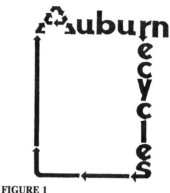

FIGURE 1

Demographics

The City of Auburn is a 20.7-mi^2 incorporated municipality located in the Green River Valley of King County Washington, positioned between Seattle and Tacoma. It is estimated that the 1990 population included 34,150 citizens. (Fig. 2).

The city's origin is that of an agricultural community, and now lures individuals from many different backgrounds. The areas largest employer is nearby Boeing, Inc. The largest sector of employment within the city is in manufacturing, second is in trade.

FIGURE 2

The city boasts easy access to state highways and close proximity to both the port of Seattle (the closest deep-water port to the far east) and the port of Tacoma.

Program Description

The program for waste reduction and recycling consists of several components, integrating technical assistance, increased public educational campaigns, and increased level of services.

The waste reduction element includes

*Case history prepared by Lisa Wagner Haley. The City of Auburn, Solid Waste Division is acknowledged for their support for the preparation of this case history.

- A school education program
- The King County Master Composter program
- Promoting reuse through an annual swap meet, a newspaper column, and dissemination of informational material
- Source reduction and procurement workshops for business and industry

The residential recycling element includes

- An expanded drop-off program of 20 to 30 multimaterial sites for collecting materials from single- and multifamily residents
- Promotion through mailers, instructional brochures, and a media campaign through the local news

The commercial/industrial sector element includes

- A technical assistance program designed to help businesses identify waste reduction opportunities and set up their own recycling systems
- Collection services offered by private contractors
- A privately owned commercial buy-back center
- Promotional and informational materials including a sign-up card, a self-audit form, fact sheets, a cost/savings worksheet, and a news media campaign

The yard waste management element includes

- An education campaign for home composting, including a demonstration site and volunteer outreach
- Curbside yard waste collection
- Program promotion through a mailer and instructional brochure

The rates incentive program element is structured to encourage

- Reduction
- Participation in the recycling program

The legislative element of the program

- Encourages allocating space for recycling through land-use codes
- Discourages scavenging and theft through ordinances
- Establishes a procurement policy that reduces waste and mandates the purchase of products made from recycled materials

The monitoring component of the program will track

- Residential and commercial solid waste tonnage
- Recycling rates: participation and material amounts by program

After only two months of implementation of these new program components, the tonnages of materials collected in some instances more than doubled! (Fig. 3).

FIGURE 3   Recycling poster, King County, Washington.

The program, which is offered to citizens, consists of conveniently located multimaterial drop sites and optional curbside collection of yard waste. The rate incentive structure was implemented so that the more residents recycle and reduce waste, the less they pay for garbage service.

The reason for using a drop-off system instead of implementing curbside pickup is that a private contractor has already been capturing an estimated 3.3 percent of the total waste stream through a program consisting of 75 drop boxes and because the service can be provided to residents at no cost to them, where a curbside program costs an additional $2 to $5 per month. The contractor is willing to expand this system by establishing new drop-off sites and adding to the types of materials accepted for recycling.

Currently, the only method of disposal available to Auburn is to take solid waste to King County's Cedar Hills landfill. At the county's rate of disposal, the landfill will reach capacity in 20 years. By reducing the volume of waste in King County going to the landfill, the county hopes to add an additional 20 years to the life of the facility. The tipping fee at the county landfill will increase from $47 to $66 per ton in 1992.

The current rate structure for collection of solid waste, including taxes, is as shown in the table at the top of page 35.47.

Residents have the option of signing up for the service level they feel would best suit their needs. These program changes were implemented May 1, 1991. Customers of the garbage service were all provided a "Residential Recycling Guide," which describes the entire program, discusses incentives for recycling

Garbage service	Rate	90-gal yard waste toter
10-gal can*	$ 3.00	$4.50
20-gal can	6.00	4.50
1 can†	7.00†	4.50
2 cans‡	14.50	4.50
60-gal toter	14.50	4.50
90-gal toter	22.00	4.50

*To qualify for the 10- or 20-gal service, customers must sign up for the yard waste toter or show proof that they are composting.
†Can is a standard 30-gal size.
‡Each additional can is $7.50 per can.

(not only the reduction of disposal costs, but saving landfill space, conserving energy, reducing reliance on natural resources, and keeping the city clean) (Fig. 4). They are provided the choice of phoning in their service level or returning a mail-in card printed in the handbook. If they do not change their service level by the start of their billing date, they are automatically billed at the one-can rate. They are reminded that they will be charged at the additional can rate for each extra can they set out.

The instructions in the handbook are simple and basic, as is the program. Instructions are provided on how to set up a home recycling center, using cardboard boxes and paper bags as receptacles for the materials. Materials collected include newspaper, mixed paper, corrugated, three colors of separated glass, aluminum, two types of plastics, and tin. An estimate is given on the space required for accumulating a month's worth of material as 3 ft by 3 ft. Drop boxes are situated in convenient locations, such as school, church and store parking lots. We all accept that you leave the store carrying bags of groceries. This method promotes the idea that you also arrive with bags of recyclables and leave them in the bin before you do your shopping. Some neighborhoods pool their recyclables and take turns taking them to a drop site.

A key factor pointed out in the booklet is to find a method that is convenient and stick with it. Several places in the book list the city Recycling Coordinators telephone number, which can be called for assistance.

Specific instructions for material preparation are shown in the pamphlet reprinted in Fig. 5. The pamphlet concludes with a listing of all area drop-off centers, categorized by the material each accepts. It also provides a listing of resources, sign-up instructions, and a mail-in card.

Future Plans

Since mailing of the booklets, plastics (PET and HDPE) were added to the materials accepted at the drop sites.

The city's contractor plans to construct a materials processing facility in the near future. This will allow for the collection of even more types of materials and will also allow the residents one more choice in how they like to recycle.

The city staff is investigating the feasibility of a used-oil collection program.

Auburn
Residential
Recycling
Guide

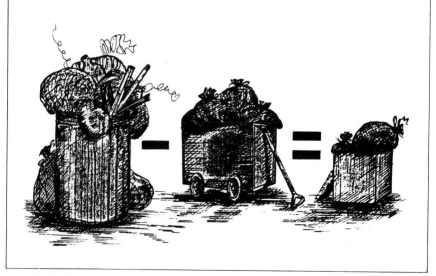

FIGURE 4   King County, Washington, recycling guide.

PAPER

Paper is classified into various grades; NEWSPRINT, CARDBOARD (known as "corrugated"), HIGH-GRADE or LEDGER PAPER, and MIXED PAPER (advertising mail, magazines, and non-corrugated cardboard).

All of these paper materials are accepted at Auburn's drop sites.

Collect clean, dry paper material in a box at home and then empty into the appropriate bin at the drop site.

Please do not recycle paper towels, disposable diapers, paper plates, tissues, greasy, waxy or plastic coated paper or candy wrappers.

When paper is recycled, it is made into all kinds of things like cereal boxes, new paper and even building materials.

Remember, for every ton of newspaper recycled, 17 trees are saved.

GLASS

There are many ways to re-use your glass jars. Fill them with nuts and bolts, use them for canning, storing dry goods, or use them to make terrariums and other crafts.

Even if you re-use your glass bottles and jars, you will still have a lot left over.

RECYCLE THEM! Wash them and remove the lids and rings. Be careful not to break them. Take all of your glass bottles and jars to a conveniently located drop site. The bins are marked "Brown", "Green", and "Clear", so you can separate by color.

The glass you recycle will be melted down and re-made into new glass containers.

Drinking glasses, window glass, light bulbs or mirrors are not acceptable at this time.

FIGURE 5   Recycling instructions—King County, Washington.

HOUSEHOLD METALS

If you look around your house and garage, you will find many recyclable metal items. While all of the ones listed may not be collected at the drop sites, they all can be recycled or re-used. For ideas of where to take those odd metals, call 1-800-RECYCLE or Auburn's Recycling Coordinator at 931-3047.

Some examples of metals you may find around the home:
*ALUMINUM FOIL, PIE PLATES, TV DINNER TRAYS
*LAWN MOWERS
*BATTERIES AND OTHER CAR PARTS
*ALUMINUM LAWN CHAIRS, LADDERS, SCREEN DOORS
*COPPER WIRE AND PIPE
*SHEET METAL, APPLIANCES

You may take Aluminum Cans, Foil, Pie Plates and TV Dinner Trays to the drop sites. Be sure to rinse off all food material.

Tin Cans are also acceptable at the drop site. To prepare the cans for recycling, wash them, remove the labels, remove both ends and flatten.

Aluminum and Tin are processed and recycled differently so you need to collect them separately. If you have trouble telling them apart, tin cans have a side seam and are attracted by magnets.

"Americans throw away enough aluminum every three months to rebuild our entire commercial air fleet."

FIGURE 5   (*Continued*)

YARD WASTE

In Auburn, yard waste is 17% of the total waste stream. That means you can drastically reduce your waste and the amount of waste going to the landfill by either composting your yard trimmings at home, or by participating in the curbside collection of yard waste.

When you sign up for this service, the contracted hauler will supply you with a 90 gallon wheeled toter. In this toter you may put lawn trimmings, weeds, and twigs up to 3" in diameter. Yard waste in plastic bags will not be accepted.

Animal and Food Waste is not acceptable in your yard waste container.

Your yard trimmings will then be taken to a composting facility where it will be composted into a nutrient rich soil conditioner. Many of the composting facilities bag and re-sell this compost in local stores.

If you would like more information on home composting, you may call Auburn's Recycling Coordinator at 931-3047, or you may call King County Composting Information at 296-4466.

FIGURE 5   (*Continued*)

A MEDIUM SUBURBAN COUNTY: CHAMPAIGN COUNTY, ILLINOIS*

Program History

Founded in 1978, the Community Recycling Center (CRC) is a not-for-profit multimaterial processing center with a goal of maximizing recovery of recyclables from the Champaign County, Illinois, waste stream (population 120,000). Over the past 10 years, CRC has been actively involved with implementing and carrying out a variety of recycling activities, including

- Curbside recycling
- Used motor oil collections
- Household hazardous waste collection events
- Buy-back and drop-off centers
- Multimaterial commercial collection programs
- University recycling programs
- Cooperative purchasing of recycled paper
- Community outreach and recycling education

Because of the success of many of these programs, CRC was selected "The Best Recycling Center in the Country" in 1990 by the National Recycling Coalition.

Program Description

Currently, CRC is providing the collection, processing, and marketing of recyclables from the following sources:

- A buy-back center and drop-off center located at its processing facility in Champaign
- Nine rural village drop-off sites throughout Champaign County
- 300 Champaign-Urbana businesses (e.g., bars, restaurants, offices, and schools)
- Administrative and academic buildings at the University of Illinois and Parkland College

CRC's buy-back center and drop-off center accept materials 5 days a week. The materials taken include glass bottles and jars, aluminum cans, tin cans, bimetal cans, PET soda bottles, clear HDPE milk jugs, newspaper, magazines, cardboard, and high-grade paper. In 1990, 1000 tons of materials were collected and CRC paid out over $241,000 to recyclers using the buy-back center.

The nine rural village drop-off centers make up what is known as the Hometown Recycling Program. Established in 1988, this was Illinois's first countywide rural recycling program and is operated by CRC under a full-service contract with Champaign County (Fig. 1). Drop-off sites are available 24 hours a day and accept glass bottles and jars, aluminum cans, tin cans, bimetal cans, clear HDPE milk jugs, and newspapers. In 1990, 558 tons of material were collected.

---

*Case history prepared by Ken McCarthy and David C. Sturtevant.

FIGURE 1 Rural village drop-off center, Champaign County, Illinois.

CRC also operates a multimaterial commercial collection program in the cities of Champaign and Urbana. CRC provides businesses with 55-gal drums for the collection of some or all of the following materials: glass bottles and jars, aluminum cans, tin cans, bimetal cans, newspaper, cardboard, and high-grade paper (Fig. 2). CRC empties the bins and spots new bins for each business participating in the program. In addition, CRC can also provide businesses with in-house collection containers. CRC charges $6 per pickup for the collection service. Approximately 1500 tons were collected in 1990.

Initiated in 1981, CRC handles the collection, processing, and marketing of glass bottles and jars, aluminum cans, tin cans, bimetal cans, clear HDPE containers, cardboard, and high-grade paper from administrative and academic buildings on the University of Illinois and Parkland College campuses.

FIGURE 2 Removing drop-off center section, Champaign County.

From the fall of 1986 until July 1991, CRC handled all facets of the curbside recycling programs for the cities of Champaign and Urbana. However, due to an inability of CRC and the cities to reach agreement on a new service contract, another contractor was selected to run the programs. CRC continues to collect materials from a curbside recycling program serving county residents. In addition, negotiations are under way regarding CRC providing education and outreach for Champaign, Urbana, and the county's curbside recycling programs.

Along with CRC's recycling efforts in Champaign County, other efforts are spearheaded by the Intergovernmental Solid Waste Disposal Association (ISWDA). This agency was formed in July 1986 by the cities of Champaign and Urbana and Champaign County. ISWDA has been involved with preparing a solid waste management plan for the county, sponsoring household hazardous waste collection events, and development of a material recovery facility (MRF)/ transfer facility. Most noteworthy, ISWDA has pursued development of a MRF and selected a vendor to design, build, and operate the facility. As currently envisioned, the MRF will serve dual functions of processing mixed residential and commercial, construction and demolition waste, and source-separated recyclables. Given the source-separation approach of past and existing programs implemented by CRC, the relative priority and sizing of the facility to meet these dual functions has raised considerable debate in the Champaign County area.

Public Education and Information

With its comprehensive and diverse recycling programs in place, CRC has long focused on public education and information. In 1980, CRC started the first "Recycling Week" in Illinois, and in 1983 was the first recycling center to hire an education coordinator. Educational activities have included producing numerous booklets, flyers, and fact packs covering composting, sources of environmentally friendly home products, sources of commercial collection containers, recycling facts, and other areas. Videos and books are also available at a CRC library. CRC has conducted active community outreach with direct educational services provided to over 4000 schoolchildren and adults in 1990.

Program Funding

CRC's operating budget of $1.1 million in 1991 was derived primarily from the sale of recyclable materials and from service contracts with Champaign County, commercial collection accounts, and other programs. A small portion of the budget also comes from individual and corporate donations, memberships, and state grants.

Future Program Activities

Building on its existing programs, CRC plans the following initiatives:

- Find private sponsors for drop-off centers in Champaign and Urbana.
- Establish recycling programs for areas not currently served within Champaign and Urbana.
- Establish recycling programs in large apartment buildings (i.e., five or more units).

- Expand commercial-sector recycling.
- Market products made from recycled materials.
- Expand recycling education programs.

Regarding the first initiative, CRC previously operated eight drop-off centers in the Champaign and Urbana area, but discontinued operations due to financial difficulties. Thus, they are seeking to reestablish drop-off centers with private-sector assistance (e.g., from grocery stores).

Lessons for Other Programs

Given the not-for-profit status of CRC, strong consideration must be given to how such a status or role integrates with the efforts of local governments. In the case of CRC and ISWDA, while pursuing seemingly complementary courses, disagreements have arisen over their respective approaches to recovering recyclables from the waste stream. A current dispute over the relative merits of and/or levels of source separation versus mixed-waste processing will be a reoccurring debate across the country as the public, elected officials, private industry, and environmentalists grapple with how best to maximize recycling.

A LARGE URBAN COUNTY: MECKLENBURG COUNTY'S RECYCLING PROGRAM*

Program Overview

Mecklenburg County's recycling program has three objectives: to meet the 1993 state recycling goal of 25 percent; to economically produce high-quality recyclables; and to encourage within the community and region recycling and conservation (Fig. 1). To meet these goals, the county has implemented a multi-faceted recycling program, with three distinct areas of concentration: residential, industrial/commercial, and wood and yard waste composting.

FIGURE 1

Charlotte, the county's principal city, boasts one of the largest publicly run curbside recycling programs in the country. The program began with pilot curbside collection, which provided the county the necessary data for sizing the now operational materials recovery facility and allowed program managers to evaluate options for the permanent collection program.

Other components of the program include a series of drop-off recycling centers (including one at the landfill), yard waste collection, and an aggressive business recycling program.

---

*Case history prepared by Lisa Wagner Haley with the support of the Mecklenburg County Solid Waste staff.

Demographics

Recent population estimates show Mecklenburg County has approximately 511,433 citizens. The county's principal city is Charlotte. The area is referred to as the "trucking capital of the United States" and many feel it is becoming the financial capital of the southeast. Major employers in the area include IBM, Duke Power Company, First Union Bank, and NCNB (Fig. 2).

CHARLOTTE ℠

FIGURE 2

Solid Waste Management

Solid waste from Mecklenburg County is currently accepted at three facilities (Fig. 3). The county's Harrisburg Road landfill, which opened in 1974, has almost reached the end of its 17-year life. Waste is also taken to a private landfill in an adjacent county, and to the 85,000 ton/year capacity mass burn waste to energy plant. The location of a new county landfill is pending site approval from the state.

FIGURE 3

Program History

In 1975, the first request was made by Mecklenburg County citizens that they be provided drop-off centers to bring in materials for recycling. In 1982, funds were first appropriated to begin a promotional strategy under the guidance of a public relations and marketing firm, to inform the public about the concept and need for recycling.

Beginning in 1983, voters began showing their support for making waste to energy a part of their waste disposal by voting to set aside general obligation bonds approved to fund the construction of the facility. Also in 1983, the county started its wood waste recycling program with the purchase of a tub grinder which was used to shred wood scraps, pallets, and tree limbs.

In 1984, the Mecklenburg County Board of Commissioners began developing a comprehensive plan for waste disposal. Phase I of the voluntary pilot curbside recyclables collection program was implemented in February 1987. The program expanded to include 16,000 homes by August 1989.

During the pilot stage of the curbside collection program, three types of round and square containers were tested. Participating residents were polled and it was found that the 14-gal square container was the favorite. The color "warm red" was chosen to symbolize the urgency of the need to recycle. In 1986, a temporary materials processing facility was purchased.

In June 1988, the North Mecklenburg Household Waste and Recyclables center opened in the northern part of the county. Prior to this, north county residents who did not receive garbage and curbside recycling collection services had no choice but to travel over 30 mi to the county-operated landfill. A pilot yard waste mulch program was established in 1988, which produced 3500 tons of mulch in its first year of operation.

A pilot program was initiated in 1987. Recyclables were taken to a temporary 12-ton/day materials recovery facility where materials were prepared for market. Plastic bottles were granulated and stored in large gaylord boxes awaiting shipment to Southeast Container in Ashville, N.C. A manual sorting line was used where employees separated cans from bottles, and glass was separated by color. A magnetic separator was added later as a more efficient method of separating cans. Aluminum was purchased by Republic Alloys Inc. and glass was purchased by Owens Brockway.

In searching for a location to site a new materials recovery processing facility in 1988, the county encountered large-scale public opposition, similar to that experienced by those opposing the siting of landfills and incinerators. A neighborhood group even sued the county for fear that the facility would bring noise, odor, and unwanted traffic to their neighborhood.

In August 1989, the county selected Fairfield County Redemption (FCR) of Stratford, Connecticut, to locate, construct, and operate its material recovery facility. They flew citizens to their Connecticut facility to show them first hand how little the recycling center impacted the surrounding community.

FCR secured a five-year contract with the county to operate the new facility. For the first year, 75 percent of profits exceeding $41,000 were shared with the county. The contract has since been renegotiated. FCR is responsible for marketing the materials.

In January 1990 the FCR materials recovery facility opened. Unique features of the building include a gift shop where visitors can purchase goods made of recyclable material, an exhibit area where larger items can be displayed, and a conference area where lectures can be presented.

Program Description

Currently, 109,000, or 85 percent of the 121,000 single-family homes in Mecklenburg County, are served by curbside recycling. A single 14-gal container is provided to residents in which plastic (HDPE and PET), glass, steel, bimetal, and aluminum beverage and food containers are commingled along with newspaper, which is stacked on top or underneath the container (Fig. 4).The theme RECYCLE NOW and the warm red color of the boxes were chosen to emphasize the urgent need to recycle.

Collection of recyclables occurs weekly on the same day as curbside trash collection. Recycling trucks with a single operator/collector transport the commingled materials (paper separated) to the material recovery facility. Participation rates for curbside collection exceed 80 percent on a monthly basis, i.e., 80 percent of the homes which have a red box fill it with recyclables and place it at the curb at least once a month. On an average, each home that recycles is contributing 425 lb of recyclables a year to the program and collectively diverting 19,500 tons of resources from burial in the local landfills.

FIGURE 4

The percentage of materials collected each week by weight are

Newspaper, 73 percent

Glass, 16 percent

Plastics, 4 percent

Aluminum, 1.5 percent

Residue, 5.5 percent

The residential recycling program also includes a network of drop centers for recyclables not included in the curbside recycling program. There are 14 drop centers with 8 more in the planning stage. In addition to the same materials collected at curbside, some of the drop centers accept corrugated containers, used motor oil, and lead-acid batteries (Fig. 5).

The North Mecklenburg Household Waste and Recyclables Drop Center, which opened in June 1988, provides residents in the northern part of the county with a conveniently located facility to drop household waste and recyclables. To deposit household waste at the center, residents must bring in the following amounts of recyclables: passenger car, 3 bags; single-axle trailer, 6 bags; van or pickup truck, 6 bags. The center is staffed by one person and is opened three days a week. Approximately 135 tons of recyclables were received at the center during its first year of operation.

The most extensive material recovery effort is located at the Harrisburg Road Landfill Recycling Drop Center, where in addition to the materials mentioned, a wide variety of scrap metals are accepted from incoming loads of waste.

In 1990, residential recycling provided 77 tons per day of highly marketable materials to the county's privately owned material recovery facility. In the first five months of 1991, this figure increased to 82 tons/day. The facility was de-

Questions or Concerns
About Drop Center Recycling?
Call 704-336-6087
Monday-Friday 9 a.m.-5 p.m.

FIGURE 5

signed to handle 65 to 70 tons/day, with the flexibility for expansion. The facility employs a unique system, combining the processing center with an amphitheater, a specially designed observation gallery, computers which allow users to interactively learn about recycling, and finally, exhibits and a gift shop featuring products made with recycled materials.

In the beginning, a tipping fee of $7.50 per ton was paid to FCR by the county for every ton of recyclables delivered to the material recovery facility through municipally operated collection programs. The county operated the 14 drop-off centers and encouraged home owners who are not part of the curbside collection program to bring their recyclables, free of charge, to any of the drop-off centers (Fig. 6).

FIGURE 6

During the first six months of operation, January to June 1990, the facility processed 7,975 tons of newspaper, glass jars and bottles, PET and HDPE plastic containers, and aluminum and steel cans. Revenues of $315,912 were generated from the sale of materials. From July 1990 to June 1991, 19,955.2 tons of newspaper, glass, plastic, steel and aluminum were delivered to the MRF (Fig. 7).

The estimated recovery rate of recyclables from the solid waste stream is 25 percent. On an average week, Charlotte residents recycle 384 tons of material.

Commercial and industrial sector recycling activities are maintained through a Business Waste Recycling program. An easy-to-follow guide is provided to interested businesses (Fig. 8). It explains the possibilities, practicalities, and benefits of starting a recycling program at the workplace. Examples are provided of typical large-quantity items found at restaurants and bars, grocery stores, manufacturing firms, and offices. The guide covers all aspects of a program—from designating a recycling coordinator to designing the program, securing markets and monitoring success.

A special program was created by

FIGURE 7

FIGURE 8   Business Waste Recycling Guide, Mecklenburg County, N.C.

Recycle Your Office Paper!

FIGURE 9

the county staff called the PAPER CHASE which focuses on recovery of high-grade (white ledger and computer) paper in office buildings. PAPER CHASE has been implemented in most county and municipal buildings and is recovering 70 tons per year of office paper (Fig. 9).

Yard waste is not accepted at the drop centers, but it is collected at curbside on a weekly basis. Residents are encouraged to place the yard waste in 40-gal fiber drums or trash containers for curbside pickup in order to prevent unnecessary operational problems due to plastic bags.

In 1991, a new compost processing facility was to begin operations. The 15-acre site will target 30,000 tons of material per year.

Currently, yard waste is processed at an 8-acre mulch/compost facility, located in the northern part of the county. The site adjoins the North Mecklenburg Household Waste and Recyclables Drop Center. Local county residents may bring their clean yard waste free of charge to the facility from 8:00 A.M. to 3:30 P.M., Monday through Saturday.

The yard waste is debagged and processed through a slow-speed shredder and a tub grinder for initial processing before being placed into windrows for biological treatment. Detailed testing and cultivation, in addition to proper windrow turning, ensure desired characteristics. The final process involves separating the product into two different sizes. The product larger than ⅜ in is sold as mulch, and the particles smaller than ⅜ in are sold as compost. Mulch and compost are purchased from the facility Monday through Saturday, 8:00 A.M. to 3:30 P.M.

The program managers have found that to ensure high-quality, contaminant-free materials for all aspects of the program, they need to devote a heavy emphasis to promotion, education, and convenience for the recycler (Fig. 10).

FIGURE 10

A public relations and marketing firm was hired to assist in promoting the Mecklenburg County program. Numerous press releases were issued to television and radio stations, periodic media briefings were conducted, and special news opportunities were created. In addition to news coverage, most of the local newspapers and several of the local television and radio stations ran public service announcements and editorials supporting recycling. Additionally, the community-owned public television station produced two 30-min documentaries on the solid waste crisis and the steps Mecklenburg County was taking to address the problem.

The county sponsored recycling conferences, which were designed to attract business people and news coverage. Annually, the county presents awards to outstanding recyclers, both individuals and organizations. Specially designed materials are sent to targeted audiences, such as those living in curbside collection areas, selected businesses, and potential conference attendees.

Future Plans

The program recently added collection of household hazardous wastes. The first one-day event will be sponsored in 1992. The materials collected will be recycled when feasible and otherwise properly disposed of by a private vendor. Recommendations for an ongoing program are being developed.

The next goal targeted by the Mecklenburg County program is to increase the level of recycling in the commercial sector. To facilitate processing of these materials and increase market value, the county hopes to begin operations at a material recovery facility for commercial-sector recyclables by 1993. In addition to targeted collection programs, they will implement front-end separation of recyclable materials at the 600 ton/day incinerator which is due to begin operations in 1996 (Fig. 11).

FIGURE 11

FIGURE 12

MULTIPLE CITIES: SOLID WASTE COMPOSTING FACILITY*

Background

The Florida cities of Dania, Hallendale, Pembroke Pines, and Pompano Beach selected Reuter Recycling of Florida, Inc., to assume responsibility for providing a system to manage the solid wastes created within their cities. The facility is one of the largest and most technologically advanced solid waste composting operations in the United States.

Reuter, Inc., of Minnesota managed the project and teamed up with Buehler, Inc., for equipment design and manufacturing. Process design was accomplished as part of the joint effort. Reuter, Inc., is responsible for construction detail as well as being the owner and operator of the facility.

Process Description

The process description details the overall flow scheme and identifies the basic elements of the material recovery and composting system. (See Figs. 1 to 3 for aerial view and coarse and fine treatment flow diagrams.)

The main processes of the system are:

1. Coarse treatment
   a. Receiving
   b. Coarse screening
   c. Handpicking
   d. Shredding
   e. Magnetic separation
2. Composting

---

*Case history prepared by Reuter Recycling of Florida, Inc.

FIGURE 1   Aerial view. (*Smith Aerial Photography, Inc.*)

    a. Mixing, homogenizing, screening
    b. Aerobic decomposition
3. Fine treatment
    a. Secondary shredding
    b. Secondary screening
    c. Ballistic separation
4. Compost storage

This operation produces, from the processible waste stream, a humuslike sub-stance which can be used as a soil amendment. Also aluminum, plastics, corru-gated paper, and ferrous metals can be separated and recycled. Figures 2 and 3 graphically depict the overall process flow and equipment configurations.

Identical parallel-processing equipment lines are installed, each sized to han-dle one half of the total plant input. The facility is built to accommodate 660 tons/ day of refuse with space available to process an additional 330 tons/day. Con-struction and equipment costs were $48.5 million.

Receiving

Receiving activities begin at the truck scales, where all incoming and outgoing vehicles (whether delivering refuse or collecting finished compost) metals, re-jects, etc., are weighed. One scale is used for arriving vehicles while the other scale is used for vehicles leaving the facility. Road access is designed so if one scale is out of service, vehicles entering and leaving the facility can be routed to the second scale.

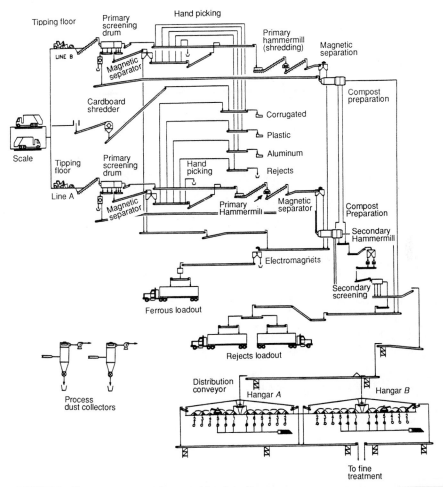

FIGURE 2 Coarse treatment and compositing flow diagram.

Arriving refuse vehicles, after weighing in, are directed to the receiving area of the plant. The receiving area consists of an enclosed concrete pad, also referred to as a tipping floor, on which the refuse vehicles will directly discharge their loads. Nonprocessible materials such as white goods, rolled carpets, and hazardous wastes, are manually removed from the waste stream at this point and set aside for separate pickup. The remaining waste is pushed by a front-end loader onto the receiving conveyors, which feed the processing systems.

The receiving conveyor transfers the waste from the tipping floor to the inlet of the primary screening drum. Processing input capacity can be controlled by varying the speed of the receiving conveyor and also by an adjustable metering gate which acts as a strike-off for materials being transferred.

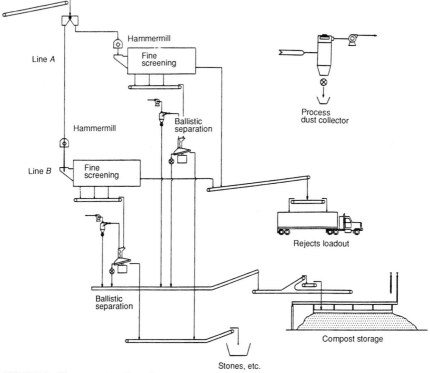

FIGURE 3   Fine treatment flow diagram.

Coarse Screening

Raw wastes transferred from the tipping floor by the receiving conveyor are delivered to one end of a rotary trommel or drum screen. The drum screen consists
of a cylindrical screen rotating inside of an enclosed housing, which is aspirated
and kept under a slight negative pressure for dust and odor control. The screen
has a series of internal baffles which rip open bags and empty their contents. The
waste is tumbled inside the drum and passed over varying hole sizes for separating the waste stream into fine, medium, and coarse fractions.

The fine fraction, consisting of mostly food and yard waste, is transported
from the drum to a magnet for ferrous removal and transferred by a series of conveyors to the mixing drum. The medium fraction is transferred by conveyors to
the handpicking area for material recovery. The oversize fraction is conveyed to
the handpicking area on a separate conveyor for material recovery.

Handpicking

The medium and coarse fractions of the waste stream are transferred through the
handpicking area by a flat belt conveyor where manual sorting is performed. Depending on markets, handpicked products could include plastics, corrugated,

newsprint, and aluminum. Recovered products are dropped through chutes onto cross conveyors which carry the sorted materials to balers. The handpicking conveyors are equipped with variable-speed drive to optimize recycled product recovery rates. The handpicking conveyors also allow the opportunity for additional removal of nonprocessible or hazardous wastes from the material stream.

Shredding

From the handpicking area, the medium and coarse fractions of the waste stream are transferred via conveyors to the primary shredder. The shredder reduces the waste to a size desirable for further treatment.

Magnetic Separation

After shredding, the medium and coarse fraction passes by electromagnets for ferrous metal removal. The recycled ferrous metal is transferred by conveyors to the ferrous load-out, and deposited to bins or trucks for shipment. The remaining waste stream is fed to the mixing drum for further processing.

Mixing, Homogenizing, Screening

The coarse and medium fraction is joined with the fine fraction and both are fed into the mixing and screening drum. The purpose of the mixing and screening drum is to mix the refuse with water to adjust its moisture level, to add nutrients to adjust critical chemical parameters, and to homogenize the individual waste components within the drum through an intensive mixing action.

At the end of the mixing section, the processed waste is screened into a fine fraction which is transported directly to the compost hangers, a medium fraction which goes through further processing, and an oversize fraction, consisting mostly of nonbiodegradable material, which is transferred to the rejects load-out.

The medium fraction is fed into a hammermill to further reduce particle size and then passed through a small screening drum to separate more compostable material. This small fraction is transferred to the compost hangers while the oversize fraction joins the reject stream from the mixing drum.

Aerobic Decomposition

In the compost area, conditions are created in the refuse mixture with respect to moisture, oxygen, and temperature, which are favorable for rapid, massive development of microorganisms on an industrial scale.

The decomposition process takes place in a covered hanger. The prepared raw compost arrives from the coarse treatment area where two primary windrows are created in the middle of the compost hanger. This method of windrow formation provides a high degree of homogeneity within the mixture.

After one primary windrow has been formed, a special windrow-turning machine moves through the pile, repositions it into the second row, and from there to the third row, and so on. The windrow-turning machine reclaims and builds up a windrow at the same time. This process gives assistance to the aeration and homogenization of the compost. It takes place five times during approximately six weeks of retention time in the compost hanger.

To compensate for the loss of moisture by evaporation during decomposition, water can be added automatically by a special device mounted on the windrow-turning machine. Through the high temperatures (exceeding 140°F) an aerobic, exothermic decomposition process takes place and persists for a considerable period of time. This process, plus the vigorous activity of the microorganisms, produces a compost material which is rendered thoroughly hygienic.

A windrow aeration system provides the necessary amount of oxygen during the entire decomposition phase. This controlled aerobic decomposition, along with adequate amounts of oxygen in the compost pile, results in a minimum amount of odor emission from the process. Air drawn through the windrows is passed through a biological (earth) filter for further odor control.

After a retention time in the compost area of approximately six weeks, the compost is ready to be transferred to the fine treatment area, at the appropriate moisture content.

Fine Treatment

The compost from the last windrow is transferred to the fine treatment area by the windrow turner and a series of conveyors. At the entrance to the fine treatment building, the compost stream is split and fed into two parallel fine treatment lines. In the initial step, the coarse compost runs through a hammermill for particle size reduction. After this step, the compost is transported via conveyors to the opposite end of the screening drum where a fine compost is removed. The oversize material becomes a reject fraction.

The fine compost is passed through a destoner/ballistic separator to remove stones, glass, and other "foreign matter." The foreign matter removed in this process is discarded as rejects.

Storage

Finished compost is transferred to a load-out and storage hanger where it is stacked under a roof, ready for shipment.

APPENDIX A

RECYCLING INFORMATION AND SOURCES

Lori Swain
Project Manager, SWICH
The Solid Waste Association of North America
Silver Spring, Maryland

Mary Aldridge
Intern, SWICH
The Solid Waste Association of North America
Silver Spring, Maryland

Herbert F. Lund, P.E.
Editor-in-Chief and Recycling Consultant
Pompano Beach, Florida

FEDERAL AGENCIES IN THE UNITED STATES

EPA Administrator
U.S. Environmental Protection Agency
401 M Street, SW (A-100)
Washington, D.C. 20460
(202) 260-4700

Office of Solid Waste
U.S. Environmental Protection Agency
401 M Street, SW (OS-300)
Washington, D.C. 20460
(202) 260-1099

EPA Regional Office Hotlines

Region 1 (Connecticut, Massachusetts, Maine, Vermont, New Hampshire, Rhode Island).
General Number - 617-565-3715
Hazardous Waste Ombudsman - 617-223-1461

Region 2 (New Jersey, New York, Puerto Rico, Virgin Islands).
General Number - 212-264-2515
Superfund Hot line - (NY) 800-722-1223, (NJ) 800-346-5009
RCRA Hot line - 800-732-1223

Region 3 (Delaware, Maryland, Pennsylvania, Virginia, West Virginia, District of Columbia).
General Number - 800-438-2474
Waste Minimization Hot line - 800-334-2467 (Pa.)/ 800-826-5320.

Region 4 (Alabama, Florida, Georgia, Kentucky, Mississippi, North Carolina, South Carolina, Tennessee).
General Number - 800-282-0239 (Ga.)/ 800-241-1754 other states
Hazardous Waste Ombudsman - 404-347-7109

Region 5 (Illinois, Indiana, Michigan, Minnesota, Ohio, Wisconsin)
General Number - 800-572-2515 (Ill.)/ 800-621-8431 other states
Hazardous Waste Ombudsman - 312-353-5821

Region 6 (Arkansas, Louisiana, New Mexico, Oklahoma, Texas)
General Number - 214-655-2200
Hazardous Waste Ombudsman - 214-655-6765

Region 7 (Iowa, Kansas, Missouri, Nebraska).
General Number - 913-236-2803
Hazardous Waste Ombudsman - 913-236-2800

Region 8 (Colorado, Montana, N. Dakota, S. Dakota, Utah, Wyoming).
General number - 800-759-4372
Hazardous Waste Ombudsman - 303-294-7036

Region 9 (Arizona, California, Hawaii, Nevada, American Samoa, Guam, Commonwealth of the Northern Mariana Islands, Republic of Palau, Federated States of Micronesia, The Republic of the Marshall Islands).
General Number 415-744-1500

Region 10 (Alaska, Idaho, Oregon, Washington).
General Number - 206-422-5810
Hazardous Waste Ombudsman - 206-442-4280

STATE AGENCIES

Alabama
Chief, Land Division
Department of Environmental Management
1751 Congressman W. L. Dickinson Drive
Montgomery, Alabama 36130
(205) 271-7730

Alaska
Chief, Solid and Hazardous Waste Management Section
Division of Environmental Quality
Department of Environmental Conservation
3200 Hospital Drive
Juneau, Alaska 99811-1800
(907) 465-2671

Arizona
Assistant Director, Office of Waste Programs
Arizona Department of Environmental Quality
2005 North Central Avenue, Room 202-A
Phoenix, Arizona 85004
(602) 257-2318

Arkansas
Chief, Solid Waste Division
Department of Pollution Control and Ecology
8001 National Drive
PO Box 8913
Little Rock, Arkansas 72219
(501) 562-7444

California
Chief Executive Officer
Integrated Waste Management Board
1020 Ninth Street, Suite 300
Sacramento, California 95814
(916) 322-3330

Colorado
Director, Hazardous Materials and Waste Management Division
Department of Health
4210 East 11th Avenue - Room 351
Denver, Colorado 80220
(303) 331-4830

Delaware
Director, Division of Air and Waste
  Management
Department of Natural Resources and
  Environmental Control
89 Kings Highway
Dover, Delaware 19901
(302) 739-4764

District of Columbia
Department of Public Works
Office of the Director
65 K St. N.E., Lower Level
Washington, D.C. 20002
(202) 939-7192

Florida
Director, Division of Waste
  Management
Department of Environmental
  Regulation
2600 Blair Stone Road
Tallahassee, Florida 32399-2400
(904) 488-0190

Georgia
Chief, Environmental Protection
  Division
Georgia Department of Natural
  Resources
205 Butler Street, S.E., Room 1154
Atlanta, Georgia 30334
(404) 656-2833

Hawaii
Chief, Solid and Hazardous Waste
  Branch
Department of Health
Environmental Management Division
Five Waterfront Plaza
500 Ala Moana Boulevard, Suite 250
Honolulu, Hawaii 96813
(808) 543-8255

Idaho
Department of Health and Welfare
Division of Environmental Quality
Hazardous Materials Bureau
1410 North Hilton Street
Boise, Idaho 83706
(208) 334-5879

Illinois
Chief, Illinois Environmental
  Protection Agency
2200 Churchill Road
Springfield, Illinois 62794-9276
(217) 782-6760

Indiana
Branch Chief, Solid Waste
Department of Environmental
  Management
Office of Solid and Hazardous Waste
  Management
105 South Meridian Street
Indianapolis, Indiana 46225
(317) 232-3501

Iowa
Chief, Air Quality and SW Protection
  Bureau
Department of Natural Resources
900 East Grand Avenue
Henry A. Wallace Building
Des Moines, Iowa 50319-0034
(515) 281-8852

Kansas
Division Director
Department of Health and
  Environment
Division of Environment
Forbes Field
Building 740
Topeka, Kansas 66620
(913) 296-1535

Kentucky
Manager, Solid Waste Branch
Department for Environmental
  Protection
Division of Waste Management
Frankfort Office Park
18 Reilly Road
Frankfort, Kentucky 40601
(502) 564-6716

Louisiana
Administrator, Solid Waste Division
Department of Environmental Quality
Office of Solid and Hazardous Waste
PO Box 44307
Baton Rouge, Louisiana 70804-4307
(504) 342-1216

Maine
Bureau Director
Department of Environmental
  Protection
Bureau of Solid Waste Management
State House Station 17
Augusta, Maine 04333
(207) 582-8740

Maryland
Department of the Environment
Hazardous and Solid Waste
  Management Administration
2500 C Highway
Baltimore, Maryland 21224
(301) 631-3386

Massachusetts
Director, Division of Solid Waste
Department of Environmental
  Protection
One Winter Street, 4th Floor
Boston, Massachusetts 02108
(617) 292-5961

Michigan
Chief, Waste Management Division
Department of Natural Resources
PO Box 30241
Lansing, Michigan 48909
(517) 373-2730

Minnesota
Director, Groundwater and Solid
  Waste Division
Minnesota Pollution Control Agency
520 Lafayette Road, North
St. Paul, Minnesota 55155
(612) 296-7777

Mississippi
Department of Natural Resources
Bureau of Pollution Control
2380 Highway 80 West
Jackson, Mississippi 39289
(601) 961-5171

Missouri
Chief, Solid Waste Section
Department of Natural Resources
Environmental Quality Division
Waste Management Program
205 Jefferson Street
Jefferson City, Missouri 65102
(314) 751-3176

Montana
Manager, Solid Waste Program
Department of Health and
  Environmental Sciences
Solid and Waste Bureau
Cogswell Building
Helena, Montana 59620
(406) 444-1430

Nebraska
Chief, Department of Environmental
  Control
Land Quality Division
301 Centennial Mall South
Lincoln, Nebraska 68509-8922
(402) 471-4210

Nevada
Division of Environmental Protection
Bureau of Waste Management
123 West Nye Lane
Room 120
Carson City, Nevada 89710
(702) 687-5872

New Hampshire
Department of Environmental
  Services
Waste Management Division
6 Hazen Drive
Concord, New Hampshire 03301-6509
(603) 271-2905

New Jersey
Division of Solid Waste Management
Department of Environmental
  Protection
840 Bear Tavern Road
CN 414
Trenton, New Jersey 08625
(609) 530-8591

New Mexico
Chief, Special Waste Bureau
Environmental Improvement Division
Health and Environment Department
Harold Runnels Building
1190 St. Francis Drive
Santa Fe, New Mexico 87503
(505) 827-2775

New York
Director, Division of Solid Waste
Department of Environmental
  Conservation
50 Wolf Road
Albany, New York 12233-4010
(518) 457-6603

North Carolina
Director, Division of Solid Waste
  Management
NC Department of Environment,
  Health & Natural Resources
401 Oberlin Road
Raleigh, North Carolina 27611-7687
(919) 733-4996

North Dakota
Coordinator, Solid Waste Program
Department of Health
Division of Waste Management
1200 Missouri Avenue, Room 302
Box 5520
Bismarck, North Dakota 58502-5520
(701) 221-5200

Ohio
Chief, Division of Solid and
  Hazardous Waste Management
Ohio Environmental Protection
  Agency
1800 WaterMark Drive
Columbus, Ohio 43266-0149
(614) 644-2956

Oklahoma
Waste Management Service
Oklahoma State Department of Health
1000 N.E. 10th Street
Oklahoma City, Oklahoma 73152
(405) 271-7047

Oregon
Administrator, Hazardous and Solid
  Waste Division
Department of Environmental Quality
811 S.W. Sixth Avenue
Portland, Oregon 97204-1390
(503) 229-5356

Pennsylvania
Director, Bureau of Waste
  Management
Department of Environmental
  Resources
200 North Third Street, Fulton
  Building
Harrisburg, Pennsylvania 17120
(717) 787-9870

Rhode Island
Division Chief, Waste Management
  Branch
Department of Environmental
  Management
Division of Air and Hazardous
  Materials
291 Promenade Street
Providence, Rhode Island 02908
(401) 277-2797

South Carolina
Chief, Bureau of Solid and Hazardous
  Waste Management
Department of Health and
  Environmental Control
2600 Bull Street
Columbia, South Carolina 29201
(803) 734-5200

South Dakota
Division Director
Department of Water and Natural
  Resources
Division of Environmental Regulation
Foss Building
523 East Capitol
Pierre, South Dakota 57501
(605) 773-3153

Tennessee
Chief Solid Waste Management Unit
Department of Health and
  Environment
Division of Solid Waste Management
Customs House, 4th Floor
701 Broadway
Nashville, Tennessee 37247-3530
(615) 741-3424

Texas
Director Plans & Programs
Division of Solid Waste Management
Department of Health
1100 West 49th Street
Austin, Texas 78756-3199
(512) 458-7271

Utah
Executive Director, Bureau of Solid
  and Hazardous Waste
Division of Environmental Health
288 North 1460 West
Salt Lake City, Utah 84116-0690
(801) 538-6170

Vermont
Solid Waste Management Division
103 South Main Street
Waterbury, Vermont 05676
(802) 244-7831

Virginia
Executive Director, Department of
  Waste Management
101 North 14th Street
James Monroe Building, 11th Floor
Richmond, Virginia 23219
(804) 225-2667

Washington
Assistant Director, Solid and
  Hazardous Waste Management
  Program
Department of Ecology
Mail Stop PV-11
Olympia, Washington 98504-8711
(206) 459-6029

West Virginia
Assistant Chief, Solid Waste
Department of Commerce, Labor and
  Environmental Resources
Division of Natural Resources
Waste Management Section
1356 Hansford Street
Charleston, West Virginia 25301
(304) 348-5929

Wisconsin
Chief, Solid Waste Management
  Section
Department of Natural Resources
Division of Environmental Quality
Bureau of Solid and Hazardous Waste
  Management
Madison, Wisconsin 53707
(608) 266-0520

Wyoming
Manager, Solid Waste Program
Department of Environmental Quality
Division of Solid Waste
122 West 25th Street
Cheyenne, Wyoming 82002
(307) 777-7752

SOLID WASTE INFORMATION SOURCES SPONSORED BY THE FEDERAL GOVERNMENT

Center for Environmental Research Information: Central point of distribution for EPA research results and reports; (513) 569-7562

Asbestos Ombudsman: Responds to questions and concerns about asbestos in schools issues; (800) 368-5888; (202) 557-1938

Emergency Planning and Community Right-to-Know Information Hot Line: Provides communities and individuals with help in preparing for accidental releases of toxic chemicals. This hot line, which complements the RCRA/ Superfund Hot line, is maintained as an information resource rather than an emergency number; (800) 535-0202; (202) 479-2449

National Appropriate Technology Assistance Service: Provides information on waste and materials management in reference to energy issues. Operated by the U.S. Department of Energy; (800) 428-2525

National Pesticides Telecommunications Network Hot Line: Provides information on pesticide-related health, toxicity, and minor cleanup to physicians, veterinarians, fire departments, government agencies, and the general public. Also provides impartial information on pesticide products, basic safety practices, health and environmental effects, and cleanup and disposal procedures; (800) 858-7378; (806) 743-3091 (in Texas)

New England Solid Waste Research Library: Research library for 650 subject headings (updated quarterly). Most information focuses on New England, although information is available on other U.S. regions and Europe; (617) 573-9687

RCRA/CERCLA Superfund Hot Line: Responds to questions from the public and regulated community on the Resource Conservation and Recovery Act, and the Comprehensive Environmental Response, Compensation and Liability Act (Superfund). Responds for requests for RCRA and Superfund documents; (800) 424-9346; (202) 382-3000

Rural Information Center: Library of information pertaining to rural issues sponsored by the U.S. Department of Agriculture; (301) 344-2547

SWICH (Solid Waste Information Clearinghouse): USEPA/Solid Waste Association of North America–sponsored national information center on solid waste information. Information is available on-line as a bulletin board and a 6200-volume library and through fax and mail requests; modem: (301) 585-0204; Fax: (301) 585-0297

Toxic Substances Control Act (TSCA) Assistance Information Service: Provides information and publications about toxic substances, including asbestos; (202) 554-1404

USEPA Procurement Hot Line: Distribute copies of various federal procurement guidelines and provides lists of manufacturers and distributors of products meeting these guidelines. (703) 941-4452

ASSOCIATION RESOURCES

Aluminum Association
900 19th St. NW
Washington, DC 20006
(202) 862-5100

American Paper Institute
260 Madison Ave.
New York, NY 10016
(800) 878-8878

Aseptic Packaging Council
1000 Potomac St. NW
Suite 401
Washington, DC 20007-8565
(800) 277-8088

Association of State and Territorial
  Solid Waste Management Officials
444 North Capitol St. NW
Suite 388
Washington, DC 20001
(202) 624-5828

Coalition of Northeastern Governors
400 North Capitol St. NW
Washington, DC 20001
(202) 624-8450

Compost Council
114 South Pitt St.
Alexandria, VA 22314
(703) 739-2401

Council on Plastic Packaging and the Environment
1001 Connecticut Ave. NW
Suite 401
Washington, DC 20036
(202) 331-0099

Environmental Defense Fund
257 Park Ave. South
New York, NY 10010
(212) 505-2100

Foodservice and Packaging Institute
1901 N. Moore St.
Suite 1111
Arlington, VA 22209
(703) 527-7505

Glass Packaging Institute
1801 K St. NW
Suite 1105-L
Washington, DC 20006
(202) 887-4850

Institute for Local Self Reliance
2425 18th St. NW
Washington, DC 20009
(202) 232-4180

Institute for Scrap Recycling
  Industries
1325 G St. NW
Suite 1000
Washington, DC 20005
(202) 466-4050

Keep America Beautiful
Mill River Plaza
9 West Broad St.
Stamford, CT 06902
(203) 323-8987

Local Government Commission
909 12th St.
Suite 205
Sacramento, CA 95814
(916) 448-1198

National Association for Plastic
  Container Recovery
4828 Parkway Plaza Blvd. Suite 260
Charlotte, NC 28217
(704) 357-3250

National Association of Counties
440 First St. NW
Washington, DC 20001
(202) 393-6226

National Association of Towns and
  Townships
1522 K St. NW
Suite 600
Washington, DC 20005
(202) 737-5200

National League of Cities
1301 Pennsylvania Ave. NW
Washington, DC 20004
(202) 626-3000

National Oil Recyclers Association
c/o Thelen, Marrin, Johnson and
  Bridges
1101 Pennsylvania Ave.
Suite 800
Washington, DC 20036
(202) 822-6424

National Recycling Coalition
1101 30th St. NW
Suite 305
Washington, DC 20005

National Resource Recovery
  Association
The U.S. Conference of Mayors
1620 Eye Street, NW
Washington, DC 20006
(202) 293-7330

National Soft Drink Association
Solid Waste Management Department
1101 16th St. NW
Washington, DC 20036
(202) 463-6700

National Solid Waste Institute
10928 North 56th St.
Tampa, FL 33617
(813) 985-3208

National Solid Waste Management
  Association
1730 Rhode Island Ave. NW
Suite 1000
Washington, DC 20036
(202) 659-4613

Partnership for Plastics Progress
(formerly: Council for Solid Waste
Solutions)
1275 K St. NW
Suite 400
Washington, DC 20005
(800) 243-5790

National Tire Dealers and Retreaders
Association
1250 I St. NW
Suite 400
Washington, DC 20005
(202) 789-2300

Plastics Recycling Foundation
1275 K St. NW
Washington, DC 20005
(202) 371-5200
Executive Director
PO Box 189
Kennett Square, PA 19348
(215) 444-0659

Polystyrene Packaging Council Inc.
1025 Connecticut Ave. NW
Suite 515
Washington, DC 20036
(202) 822-6424

Scrap Tire Management Council
1400 K St. NW
Washington, DC 20005
(202) 408-7781

Solid Waste Association of North
America (SWANA)
PO Box 7219
Silver Spring, MD 20910
(301) 595-2898

Steel Can Recycling Institute
Foster Plaza 10
680 Anderson Drive
Pittsburgh, PA 15220
(800) 876-7274

U.S. Conference of Mayors
1620 I St. NW, 4th Floor
Washington, DC 20006
(202) 293-7330
(National Resource Recovery
Association)

Vinyl Environmental Resource Center
1 Cascade Plaza, 19th Floor
Akron, OH 44308
(800) 969-8469

WASTE EXCHANGES

Alberta Waste Materials Exchange
William Kay
Industrial Development Department
Alberta Research Council
PO Box 8330, Postal Station F
Edmonton, Alberta
Canada T6H 5X2
(403) 450-5408

California Waste Exchange
Toxic Substances Control Division
400 P Street
Sacramento, CA 65814
(916) 322-0476

Canadian Waste Materials Exchange
Dr. Robert Laughlin
Ortech International
Sheridan Park Research Community
Mississauga, Ontario
Canada L5K 1B3

Industrial Material Exchange Service
Diane Shockey
PO Box 19276
2200 Churchill Rd., #31
Springfield, IL 62794-9276
(217) 782-0450

Montana Industrial Waste Exchange
Sharon Miller
PO Box 1730
Helena, MT 59624
(406) 442-2405

Northeast Industrial Waste Exchange
Lewis Cutler
90 Presidential Plaza, Suite 122
Syracuse, NY 13202
(315) 422-6572

Texas Water Commission
Hope Castillo
PO Box 13087
Austin, TX 78711-3087
(512) 463-7773

Pacific Materials Exchange
Bob Smee
South 3707 Godfrey Blvd.
Spokane, WA 99204
(509) 623-4244

Resource Exchange & News
Kay Ostorwski
400 Ann Street, NW
Suite 301A
Grand Rapids, MI 49505
(616) 363-3262

Southeast Waste Exchange
Mary MacDaniel
Urban Institute, UNCC Station
Charlotte, NC 28223
(704) 547-2307

Southern Waste Information
  Exchange
Eugene Jones
PO Box 960
Tallahassee, FL 32302
(800) 441-SWIX

RECYCLING PERIODICALS

American City & County
Communication Channel, Inc.
255 Barfield Road
Atlanta, GA 30328

Biocycle
American Bio Tech, Inc.
JG Press
419 State Ave.
Emmaus, PA 18049
(215) 967-4135

Recycling Today
GIE, Inc.
4012 Bridge Ave.
Cleveland, OH 44113-3320
(800) 456-0707
(216) 961-4130

Resource Recycling
Resource Recycling, Inc.
1206 NW 21st Ave.
Portland, OR 97210
(800) 227-1424
(503) 227-1319

Scrap Processing & Recycling
Institute of Scrap Recycling Industries
1325 G St., NW
Suite 1000
Washington, DC 20005

The Recycling Magnet
Steel Can Recycling Institute
Foster Plaza 10
680 Andersen Drive
Pittsburgh, PA 15220
(800) 876-SCRI

Resource Recovery FOCUS
National Solid Wastes Management
  Association
1730 Rhode Island Ave., NW
Suite 1000
Washington, DC 20036

Resource Recovery Report
Resource Recovery Report
5313 38th Street, NW
Washington, DC 20015
(202) 362-6034

The Paper Stock Report
The weekly update on the paper
  recycling market
13727 Holland Road
Cleveland, OH 44142-3920
(216) 362-7979

Environment Week
King Communication Group, Inc.
627 National Press Building
Washington, DC 20045
(202) 638-4260

Greenwire
The Daily Executive Briefing on the
  Environment
282 N. Washington Street
Falls Church, VA 22046
(703) 237-5130

Integrated Waste Management
McGraw-Hill, Inc.
1221 Avenue of the Americas
New York, NY 10020
(800) 223-6180

Solid Waste Report
Business Publishers, Inc.
951 Pershing Drive
Silver Spring, MD 20910-4464
(301) 587-6300

The NRC Connection
National Recycling Coalition, Inc.
1101 30th Street, NW
Suite 305
Washington, DC 20007
(202) 625-6406

COPPE Quarterly
Council on Plastics and Packaging in
  the Environment
1275 K Street, NW
Washington, DC 20005

Scrap Tire News
Recycling Research, Inc.
Suffield, CT 06078
(203) 668-5422

ISWA Times
International Solid Waste Association
ISWA General Secretariat
Vester Farminagsgade 29
DK-1780 Copenhagen V
Phone: +45 33 15 65 65
North American Office: (301)
  585-5105

MSW Management
Forester Communications
1640 Fifth Street
Suite 108
Santa Monica, CA 90401
(310) 576-6180

Reusable News
United States Environmental
  Protection Agency
Solid Waste and Emergency Response
401 M Street, SW
Washington, DC 20460

Recycling Manager
Capital Cities/ABC, Inc.
Diversified Publishing Group
825 Seventh Ave.
New York, NY 10019
(212) 887-8528

The Soft Drink Recycler
National Soft Drink Association
1101 16th Street, NW
Washington, DC 20036
(202) 463-6700

Pollution Prevention News
United States Environmental
  Protection Agency
Office of Pollution Prevention
401 M Street, SW (PM-222B)
Washington, DC 20460

Recycling Times
Waste Age Magazine
5616 W. Cermk Rd.
Cierco, IL 60650
(202) 861-0708

RCRA Review
4444 W. Alexis Road
Toledo, OH 43623

Environmental Protection
Stevens Publishing Corporation
225 N. New Road
Waco, TX 76710
(817) 776-9000

Resources
The Environmental Resources
 Management, Inc.
855 Springdale Drive
Exton, PA 19341
(800) 544-3117

Waste Tech News
1311 Madison St.
Denver, CO 80206
(303) 394-2905

Waste Age
1730 Rhode Island Ave., NW
Suite 1000
Washington, DC 20036
(202) 861-0708

CHECKLIST: EVALUATING RECYCLING COMPANY SERVICES

After determining what materials are available for recycling, the coordinator should contact reliable recycling companies that can provide full service to your business. The coordinator will benefit from using the services of the recycling company, especially from sharing ideas on the best type of recycling program for your individual company.

When interviewing recycling companies ask the following questions:

1. Will the recycling company help you organize and promote your program?

2. Has the recycling company done this type of business program in the past? Will they give references?

3. Is the recycling company willing to sign a long-term contract?

4. Will the recycling company provide only "scheduled" or "on call" pickups? How much notice is required?

5. Can the recycling company provide the equipment you need to ensure the success of your program? Your needs may include baling equipment, containers for workstation separation, central collection and dock containers, or a storage trailer.

6. Will the recycling company assure payment for your recyclables? What are the terms?

7. Will the recycling company pick up your paper in the event that the value of your recyclables decline?

8. Will the recycling company mandate a minimum pickup weight requirement? Is there a pickup charge?

9. Will the recycling company also shred your confidential documents? Will they securely store them until their destruction date?

TABLE A.1 Conversion Figures

	Weight, lb
Glass (average weights per unit)	
10-oz single-serving juice container	0.19
12-oz container	0.23
20-oz container	0.38
75-gal caddy gilled with glass (uncrushed)	174
46-gal bin filled with glass (uncrushed)	107
40-yd roll-off filled with glass	24,000
1 yd^3 glass	600
Aluminum (average weights per unit)	
10-oz single-serving container	0.06
90-gal caddy filled with aluminum cans	23
46-gal bin filled with aluminum cans	12
40-yd roll-off filled with steel cans	8,000
1 yd^3 aluminum	60
Tinplate steel (average weights per unit)	
10-oz food or beverage can	0.20
12-oz food or beverage can	0.07
18-oz food or beverage can	0.11
75-gal caddy filled with steel cans	54
46-gal caddy filled with steel cans	33
40-yd roll-off filled with steel cans	8,000
1 yd^3 tinplate steel	200
Fine paper, newspaper, old corrugated (OCC) (average weights per unit)	
75-gal caddy filled with fine paper or newspaper	212
1 school newspaper	0.05
1 daily newspaper	0.7
1 yd^3 fine paper	500
40-yd container filled with flattened OCC	6,000
1 yd^3 flattened OCC	150
1 yd^3 newspaper	500

TABLE A.2 Conversion Factors for Recyclables

Material	Volume	Weight, lb
Newsprint, loose	1 yd^3	360–800
Newsprint, compacted	1 yd^3	720–1000
Newsprint	12-in stack	35
Corrugated cardboard, loose	1 yd^3	300
Corrugated cardboard, baled	1 yd^3	1000–1200
Glass, whole bottles	1 yd^3	600–1000
Glass, semi crushed	1 yd^3	1000–1800
Glass, crushed (mechanically)	1 yd^3	800–2700
Glass, whole bottles	One full grocery bag	16
Glass, uncrushed to manually broken	55-gal drum	125–500
PET soda bottles, whole, loose	1 yd^3	30–40
PET soda bottles, whole, loose	Gaylord*	40–53
PET soda bottles, baled	30" × 48" × 60"	500
PET soda bottles, granulated	Gaylord*	700–750
PET soda bottles, granulated	Semi-load	30,000
Film, baled	30" × 42" × 48"	1100
Film, baled	Semi-load	44,000
HPDE (dairy only), whole, loose	1 yd^3	24
HPDE (dairy only), baled	30" × 48" × 60"	500–800
HPDE (mixed), baled	30" × 48" × 60"	600–900
HPDE (mixed), granulated	Gaylord*	800–1000
HPDE (mixed), granulated	Semi-load	42,000
Mixed PET & dairy, whole, loose	1 yd^3	Average 32
Mixed PET, dairy and other rigid, whole, loose	1 yd^3	Average 38
Mixed rigid, no film or dairy, whole, loose	1 yd^3	Average 49
Mixed rigid, no film, granulated	Gaylord*	500–1000
Mixed rigid & film, densified by mixed plastic mold technology	1 yd^3	Average 60
Aluminum cans, whole	1 yd^3	50–74
Aluminum cans, whole	1 full kraft paper grocery bag	Average 1.5
Aluminum cans	55-gal plastic bag	13–20
Ferrous cans, whole	1 yd^3	150
Ferrous cans, flattened	1 yd^3	850
Leaves, uncompacted[8]	1 yd^3	250–500
Leaves, compacted	1 yd^3	320–450
Leaves, vacuumed	1 yd^3	350
Wood chips	1 yd^3	500
Mulch	1 yd^3	200–300
Grass clippings	1 yd^3	400–1500
Used motor oil	1 gal	7
Tire, passenger car	1	12
Tire, truck	1	60
Food waste, solid and liquid fats	55-gal drum	412

*Gaylord size most commonly used 40" × 48" × 36"
Source: National Recycling Coalition, Washington, D.C.

TABLE A.3   Recycling Audit Worksheet

All waste bins inside and outside the building should be checked and the relevant data and comments recorded in the space provided below.

Bin #	Composition by material, %	Is it a typical composition? (Y/N)	Contamination* H,M,L† source	Collection frequency	Appearance or size constraints for additional bins	Comments
	Glass ⎯⎯ Metal ⎯⎯ Organics ⎯⎯ Fine paper ⎯⎯ OCC ⎯⎯ Plastics ⎯⎯ Other ⎯⎯					
	Glass ⎯⎯ Metal ⎯⎯ Organics ⎯⎯ Fine paper ⎯⎯ OCC ⎯⎯ Plastics ⎯⎯ Other ⎯⎯					
	Glass ⎯⎯ Metal ⎯⎯ Organics ⎯⎯ Fine paper ⎯⎯ OCC ⎯⎯ Plastics ⎯⎯ Other ⎯⎯					

*Contamination refers to the contamination of potential recyclables with other wastes that deem the product unmarketable, e.g., food grease on OCC.

†H = High; M = Medium; L = Low.

TABLE A.4 Recovery Estimates Worksheet

Company/Institution: _____

Contact: _____ Phone: _____

Address: _____

Target material: _____

Recovery estimates can be obtained by using consumption data or waste generation data. The actual recovery will be below calculated consumption and generation levels. Losses of material due to contamination, discarding of recyclable materials off-site, etc., must be incorporated into the final recovery estimate.

Consumption Data

Amount consumed (provided by contact): _____ lb/wk.

If units come in a variety of sizes, calculate the *average size* before using conversion

figures._____

_____

If the data available are units/wk.; convert to lb/wk.

_____ units/wk. × _____ lb/unit* = _____ lb/wk.

Use Conversion Figures Sheet, Table A.1.

Estimated Recovery:

consumption (lb/wk) − _____ material loss recovery (lb/wk.) due to off-site disposal, staff participation level, contamination, etc. = _____ potential recovery (lb/wk.)

Generation Data

Information gathered in waste audit can be used to calculate generation rates:

_____ refuse container volume in yd^3 × _____ % target material in container

_____ # of full containers/wk. = _____ yd^3 generated/wk.

Estimated Recovery:

_____ consumption (lb/wk) − _____ material loss recovery (lb/wk.) due to off-site disposal, staff participation level, contamination, etc. = _____ potential recovery (lb/wk.)

CONVERSIONS (lb to yd^3)

Volume estimates may be required to help determine how quickly your truck will fill and what volume of storage containers the site will need.

Use Table A.1.

_____ estimated recovery (lb/wk.)/weight of 1 yd^3 of material (lb) = _____ estimated recovery (yd^3/wk.)

TABLE A.5 Storage Container Data and Evaluation

Container type	Volume capacity, yd³	Material capacity, lb		Cans				Advantage/disadvantage
		News	Glass	Steel	Alum.	PET	Commingled	

32-gal garbage can
Standard can, available from hardware stores
Suitable for any manual collection system
	0.18	N/A	108	29	11	5.4	49	A Easy to get
								  Inexpensive
								D Must be manually unloaded
								  Holds small amount

55-gal drum
Used drums
Suitable for any manual collection system
	0.3	N/A	180	48	18	9	82	A Low or no cost
								  Can be located inside or outside
								D Not mobile
								  Must be manually unloaded

Semi-automated collection cart
90-gal wheeled plastic carts
Serviced by rear-loading packer or recycling truck fitted wit hydraulic lift
	0.5	250	300	80	30	15	138	A Holds large volume yet has narrow design to fit inside buildings
								  Highly mobile
								  Can be mechanically loaded
								D Somewhat expensive

Bulk lift container (steel)
2 or 3 yd³ on casters
Modify lids to only accept recyclables
Serviced by front- or rear-end loader or Esy Mobile Container System
	2	1,000	1,200	320	120	60	552	A Large capacity
								  Portable
								  Can be mechanically serviced
								D Somewhat expensive
								  Must usually be located outside building

Igloo (fiberglass)
1.5 to 4 yd³
Serviced by roll-off truck with compartments, fitted with hydraulic crane
	1.5–4	1.5 yd³ = 750
		4 yd³ = 2000
			1.5 yd³ = 900
			4 yd³ = 2,400
				1.5 yd³ = 240
				4 yd³ = 640
					1.5 yd³ = 90
					4 yd³ = 240
						1.5 yd³ = 45
						4 yd³ = 120
							414
							1,104
								A Attractive
								  Can be mechanically serviced
								D Expensive
								  Small openings
								  Locate outside, 36 ft² per igloo

Roll-off container
Can divide into sections
Need to cover open tops
	10–60
	common size is 40 yd³
		40 yd³ = 20,000	40 yd³ = 24.000	40 yd³ = 6,400	40 yd³ = 2,400	40 yd³ = 1,200	11,040	A Very large capacity
								  Use for storage and transport
								D Expensive
								  Locate outside, about 100 ft.²

TABLE A.6 Monthly Total Weight of Glass Recyclables Worksheet

	Package size	Single container weight, oz	Number of cases per month		Average case weight, lb		Weight
Beer							
Beer	12 oz	7	×		10.5	=	
Heavy bottle	12 oz	11	×		17.1	=	
							Subtotal
Liquor	1.75	34	×		12.75	=	
Liter	18		×		13.5	=	
	750 ml	15.5	×		11.6	=	
							Subtotal
House wine	4 liter	41	×		10.25	=	
	3 liter	36	×		9.0	=	
	1.5 liter	28	×		10.5	=	
							Subtotal
Varietal wine	1.5 liter	28	×		10.5	=	
	750 ml	15.5	×		11.6	=	
	375 ml	13	×		19.5	=	
	187 ml	7.5	×		11.25	=	
							Subtotal
Champagne	1.5 liter	40	×		15	=	
	1.0 liter	32	×		24	=	
	750 ml	23	×		17.25	=	
	187 ml	13	×		19.5	=	
							Subtotal
Other							
Wine cooler	12 oz	7	×		10.5	=	
Bar mixes	10 oz	5.6	×		8.4	=	
Mineral water	11 oz	9	×		13.5	=	
Perrier water	6.5 oz	5.3	×		7.9	=	
							Subtotal
Total weight of monthly glass containers used							Total

TABLE A.7 Weekly Waste Generation by Occupied Square Foot

Generator segment	Waste production, lb per occupied ft^2 per week	lb/year
Office	0.05	2.6
Industrial	0.06	3.12
Transportation, communication, and utilities	0.10	5.2
Retail	0.22	11.44
Wholesale/warehouse and distribution (WWA)	0.06	3.12
Public and institutional (Public)	0.04	2.08

Source: Westchester County's Solid Waste Management Plan, Malcolm Pirnie, Inc., White Plains, N.Y.

TABLE A.8 Commercial Waste Quantity and Composition

Generator	Paper	Cardboard	Plastic	Metals	Other
Office	65%	15%	6%	2%	12%
Industrial	35%	20%	25%	6%	14%
Retail	35%	40%	8%	1%	16%
Transportation, communication, utilities	20%	15%	15%	5%	45%
Wholesale/warehouse and distribution	25%	32%	25%	7%	11%
Public	45%	10%	5%	6%	34%

Source: Westchester County's Solid Waste Management Plan, Malcolm Pirnie, Inc., White Plains, N.Y.

APPENDIX B
GLOSSARY

Herbert F. Lund
Belle Lund
Pompano Beach, Florida

A

abatement   The reduction in landfill pollution by source reduction and waste recycling.

acid gas scrubber   A device that removes particulate and gaseous impurities from a gas stream. This generally involves the spraying of an alkaline solid or liquid, and sometimes the use of condensation or absorbent particles.

acrylonitrile butadiene styrene   A high-durability plastic-rubber blend. The acronym ABS is commonly used.

acute exposure   Receipt of a large dose of a hazardous substance over a short period of time.

ADF   Advanced disposal fee; a fee for disposing of a product which is included in the product's price.

aeration   The process of exposing bulk material, such as compost, to air. *Forced aeration* refers to the use of blowers in compost piles.

aerobic   A biochemical process or condition occurring in the presence of oxygen.

aerobic digestion   The utilization of organic waste as a substrate for the growth of bacteria which function in the presence of oxygen to stabilize the waste and reduce its volume. The products of this decomposition are carbon dioxide, water, and a remainder consisting of inorganic compounds, undigested organic material, and water.

agricultural wastes   Solid wastes of plant and animal origin, which result from the production and processing of farm or agricultural products, including manures, orchard and vineyard prunings, and crop residues, which are removed from the site of generation for solid waste management. Agricultural refers to SIC Codes 011 through 0291.

air emissions   Solid particulates (such as unburned carbon) and gaseous pollutants (such as oxides of nitrogen or sulfur) or odors. These can result from a broad variety of activities including exhaust from vehicles, combustion devices, land-fills, compost piles, street sweepings, excavation, demolition, etc.

air knife A blower device that employs an airstream to push selected material(s) off a conveyor.

air pollution The presence of unwanted material in the air in excess of standards. The term "unwanted material" here refers to material in sufficient concentrations, present for a sufficient time and under circumstances to interfere significantly with health, comfort, or welfare of persons, or with the full use and enjoyment of property.

air classification A process in which a stream of air is used to separate mixed material according to the size, density, and aerodynamic drag of the pieces.

algal bloom Population explosion of algae (simple one-celled or many-celled, usually aquatic, plants) in surface waters. Algal blooms are associated with nutrient-rich runoff from composting facilities or landfills.

aluminum can or container Any food or beverage container that is composed of at least 94 percent aluminum.

alternatives Other possible ways of dealing with, treating, or disposing of wastes.

amber cullet Broken brown glass containers.

anaerobic A biochemical process or condition occurring in the absence of oxygen.

anaerobic digestion The utilization of organic waste as a substrate for the growth of bacteria which function in the absence of oxygen to reduce the volume of waste. The bacteria consume the carbon in the waste as their energy source and convert it to gaseous products. Properly controlled, anaerobic digestion will produce a mixture of methane and carbon dioxide, with a sludge remainder consisting of inorganic compounds, undigested organic material and water.

animal bedding An agricultural product, occasionally made from waste paper, for use in livestock quarters.

animal and food processing wastes Waste materials generated in canneries, slaughterhouses, packing plants, or similar industries.

antiscavenge ordinance A governmental regulation prohibiting the unauthorized collection of secondary materials set out for pickup by a designated collector.

aquifer A geologic formation, group of formations, or part of a formation capable of yielding a significant amount of groundwater to wells, springs, or surface water.

asbestos Fibrous forms of various hydrated minerals, including chrysotile (fibrous serpentine), crocidolite (fibrous reinbecktite), amosite (fibrous cumingtonite-grunerite), fibrous tremolite, fibrous actinolite, and fibrous anthophyllite.

ash The residue that remains after a fuel or solid waste has been burned, consisting primarily of noncombustible materials. (See also *bottom ash* and *fly ash*.)

ash pit   A pit or hopper located below or near a furnace where residue is accumulated and from which it is removed.

ASTM   American Society for Testing and Materials.

avoided costs   Solid waste management cost savings resulting from a recycling program. One cost saving can be avoided disposal fees. Another avoided cost can be the saving in garbage collection costs through rerouting and extended truck life.

auto-tie   A mechanical device that automatically wraps a bale with wire.

"away"   An unknown place where people "throw" things and expect never to deal with them again; in reality there is no such place.

B

back-end materials recovery   Secondary materials recovery from incinerated municipal solid waste.

backyard composting   The controlled biodegradation of leaves, grass clippings, and/or other yard wastes on the site where they were generated.

baghouse   A municipal waste combustion facility air emission control device consisting of a series of fabric filters through which MWC (municipal waste combustion) flue gases are passed to remove particulates prior to atmospheric dispersion.

bale   A densified and bound cube of recyclable material, such as waste paper, scrap metal, or rags.

baler   A machine used to compress recyclables into bundles to reduce volume. Balers are often used on newspaper, plastics, and corrugated cardboard.

ballistic separator   A device used in some composting operations that separates inorganic materials from organic matter.

base load   A continuous stream or electrical output over a given period of time at design conditions.

baseline recycling systems   Systems that identify whether a new recycling collection program is diverting material that otherwise would have been disposed or whether that material is being diverted from another recycling collection system. Example: Municipal source separation and curbside collection programs are to be introduced in an area with active private sector recycling.

beneficiation   In recycling, the mechanical process of removing contaminants and cleaning scrap glass containers. Originally a mining industry term for the treatment of a material to improve its form or properties, such as the crushing of ore to remove impurities.

beverage industry recycling program   A state coalition of beverage producers, packagers, wholesalers, and retailers that undertake activities in support of recycling, particularly buy-back centers.

biodegradable   A substance or material which can be broken down into simpler compounds by microorganisms and other decomposers such as fungi.

biodegradable material Waste material which is capable of being broken down by microorganisms into simple, stable compounds such as carbon dioxide and water. Most organic wastes, such as food wastes and paper, are biodegradable.

block-leader promotion The use of volunteers to promote recycling collection service in a specific block or neighborhood.

bimetal can or container Any metal container composed of at least two different types of metals, such as a steel container with an aluminum top.

bogus corrugating medium The fluted middle of corrugated containers made entirely from waste paper.

biomass Any organic (wood, agricultural, or vegetative) matter; key components are carbon and oxygen.

bottle bank A mobile, divided bin used for receiving, storing, and transporting glass containers for recycling.

bottle bill Legislation requiring deposits on beverage containers; appropriately called Beverage Container Deposit Law (BCDL).

bottom ash The nonairborne combustion residue from burning fuel in a boiler. The material falls to the bottom of the boiler and is removed mechanically. Bottom ash constitutes the major portion (about 90 percent) of the total ash created by the combustion of solid waste.

broker An individual or group of individuals that act as an agent or intermediary between the sellers and buyers of recyclable materials.

Btu (British thermal unit) Unit of measure for the amount of energy a given material contains (e.g., energy released as heat during combustion is measured in Btus). Technically, 1 Btu is the quantity of heat required to raise the temperature of one pound of water one degree Fahrenheit.

buffer zone Neutral area which acts as a protective barrier separating two conflicting forces. An area which acts to minimize the impact of pollutants on the environment or public welfare. For example, a buffer zone is established between a composting facility and neighboring residents to minimize odor problems.

bulk-cullet box A pallet-sized reusable corrugated container used to ship cullet. See also *gaylord container.*

bulking agent A material used to add volume to another material to make it more porous to airflow. For example, municipal solid waste may act as a bulking agent when mixed with water treatment sludge.

bulky waste Large items of refuse including, but not limited to, appliances, furniture, large auto parts, nonhazardous construction and demolition materials, trees, branches,and stumps which cannot be handled by normal solid waste processing, collection, and disposal methods.

buy-back recycling center A facility which pays a fee for the delivery and transfer of ownership to the facility of source-separated materials for the purpose of recycling or composting.

bypass waste Solid waste which has been contractually committed to a facility, but which is diverted when the facility is unavailable or is not able to process due to size, etc.

C

capital costs Those direct costs incurred in order to acquire real property assets such as land, buildings, and building additions; site improvements; machinery; and equipment.

capture rate A standard reporting practice of all materials collected or captured as related to the total available designated materials. The rate should include collected deposit containers if part of the recycling program. Capture rate equals designated materials recovered divided by the total designated materials available.

carcass The foundation structure of a tire, including sidewalls, bead, and cord.

CERCLA Comprehensive Environmental Response, Compensation, and Liability Act (Superfund Act), 1980. This act provides funds for emergency cleanup of spills and cleanup of abandoned or inactive hazardous waste sites.

centralized yard waste composting System utilizing a central facility within a politically defined area with the purpose of composting yard wastes.

chain-flail crusher A simple, low-volume glass container crusher using a motor-driven chain.

charcoal A dark or black porous carbon prepared from vegetable or animal substances (as from wood by charring in a kiln from which air is excluded).

chronic exposure Receipt of a small dose of a hazardous substance over a long period of time.

claw truck A specially designed attachment to a front-end loader used to pick up loose yard waste at the curb.

Clean Air Act Act passed by Congress to have the air "safe enough to protect the publics health" by May 31, 1975. Required the setting of National Ambient Air Quality Standards (NAAQS) for major primary air pollutants.

Clean Water Act Act passed by Congress to protect the nation's water resources. Requires EPA to establish a system of national effluent standards for major water pollutants, requires all municipalities to use secondary sewage treatment by 1988, sets interim goals of making all U.S. waters safe for fishing and swimming, allows point-source discharges of pollutants into waterways only with a permit from EPA, requires all industries to use the best practicable technology (BPT) for control of conventional and nonconventional pollutants and to use the best available technology (BAT) that is reasonable or affordable.

co-collection The collection of ordinary household garbage in combination with special bags of source-separated recyclables.

co-composting Simultaneous composting of two or more diverse waste streams.

coding In the context of solid waste, coding refers to a system to identify recyclable materials. The coding system for plastic packaging utilizes a three-sided arrow with a number in the center and letters underneath. The number and letters indicate the resin from which each container is made: 1 = PETE (polyethylene terephthalate), 2 = HDPE (high density polyethylene), 3 = V (vinyl), 4 = LDPE (low-density polyethylene), 5 = PP (polypropylene), 6 = PS (polystyrene), and 7 = other/mixed plastics. Noncoded containers are recycled through mixed plastics processes. To help recycling sorters, the code is molded into the bottom of bottles with a capacity of 16 oz or more and other containers with a capacity of 8 oz or more.

codisposal   Burning of municipal solid waste with other material, particularly dewatered sewage sludge.

cofiring/burning   Municipal solid waste in a combustion unit along with other fuel, especially coal.

cogeneration   Production of two forms of energy from one source.

collection   The act of picking up and moving solid waste from its location of generation to a disposal area, such as a transfer station, resource recovery facility, or landfill.

combustible   Various materials in the waste stream which are burnable, such as paper, plastic, law clippings, leaves, and other organic materials.

commercial sector   One of the four sectors of the community that generates garbage. Designed for profit.

commercial solid waste   Solid waste originating from stores; business offices; commercial warehouses; hospitals, educational, health care, military, and correctional institutions, nonprofit research organizations; and government offices. Commercial solid waste refers to SIC Codes 401 through 4939, 4961, and 4971 (transportation, communications, and *certain* utilities), 501 through 5999 (wholesale and retail trade), 601 through 6799 (finance, insurance, and real estate), 701 through 8748 (public and private service industries such as hospitals and hotels), and 911 through 9721 (public administration). *Commercial solid wastes do not include construction and demolition waste.*

commercial unit   A site zoned for a commercial business and which generates commercial solid wastes.

commercial waste   Waste materials originating in wholesale, retail, institutional, or service establishments such as office buildings, stores, markets, theaters, hotels, and warehouses.

commingled recyclables   A mixture of several recyclable materials into one container.

compacting drop box   A roll-off box attached to a compacting device for receiving and compressing a secondary material, such as old corrugated containers.

compactor   Power-driven device used to compress materials to a smaller volume.

composite liner   A liner composed of both a plastic and soil component.

composition   A set of identified solid waste materials, categorized into waste categories and waste types.

compost A humuslike relatively stable material resulting from the biological decomposition or breakdown of organic materials.

compost substrate Organic biodegradable material that can be used as a feedstock for a composting process.

composting The controlled biological decomposition of organic solid waste under aerobic conditions. Organic waste materials are transformed into soil amendments such as humus or mulch.

composting facility A permitted solid waste facility at which composting is conducted and which produces a product meeting the definition of "compost."

concentration The amount of one substance contained in a unit of another substance.

conservation The planned management of a natural resource to prevent exploitation, destruction, or neglect.

construction and demolition (C&D) waste Solid wastes, such as building materials and packaging and rubble resulting from construction, remodeling, repair, and demolition operations on pavements, houses, commercial buildings, and other structures. Construction refers to SIC Codes 152 through 1794, 1796, and 1799. Demolition refers to SIC Code 1795.

consumption The amount of any resource (material or energy) used in a given time.

container A receptacle or a flexible covering for the shipment of goods.

container cullet Broken scrap glass bottles and jars. See also *cullet.*

container deposit legislation Laws that require monetary deposits to be levied on beverage containers. The money is returned to the consumer when the containers are returned to the retailer. Also called "bottle bills."

contaminant A material that is harmful to the recycling process when included with a recyclable material. Called "contraries" in some countries.

corrosive Defined for regulatory purposes as a substance having a pH level below 2 or above 12.5, or a substance capable of dissolving or breaking down other substances, particularly metals, or causing skin burns.

corrugated container According to SIC Code 2653, a paperboard container fabricated from two layers of kraft linerboard sandwiched around a corrugating medium. Kraft linerboard means paperboard made from wood pulp produced by a modified sulfate pulping process, with basis weight ranging from 18 to 200 lb, manufactured for use as facing material for corrugated or solid fiber containers. Linerboard also may mean that material which is made from reclaimed paper stock.

corrugating medium Fluted paperboard used in making corrugated boxes. Paperboard made from chemical or semichemical wood pulps, straw, or reclaimed paper stock, and folded to form permanent corrugations.

corrugated paper Paper or cardboard manufactured in a series of wrinkles or folds, or into alternating ridges and grooves.

cost-effective A measurement of cost compared to an unvalued output (e.g., the cost per ton of solid waste collected) such that the lower the cost, the more cost-effective the action.

counts   Population and household see *population and household counts.*

crusher   A mechanical device used to break secondary materials such as glass bottles into smaller pieces.

cryogenic processing   The freezing and cracking of secondary materials to assist in separation.

cullet   Broken or waste glass used in the manufacture of new glass.

cultivation   In composting, accelerating the decomposition of biodegradable wastes by turning, watering, aerating, loosening, and/or inoculating the waste with microorganisms or fertilizer to lower the carbon/nitrogen ratio.

curbside collection   Collection of recyclable materials at the curb, often from special containers, to be brought to various processing facilities.

curbside recycling program   Refers to a program that sponsors scheduled pickup of recyclable items from household curbs.

cycle   A periodically repeated sequence of events.

curbside-separate   To separate commingled recyclables prior to placement in individual compartments in a truck providing curbside collection service; this task is performed by the collector.

D

decompose   To separate into constituent parts or elements or into simpler compounds; to undergo chemical breakdown; to decay or rot as a result of microbial and fungal action.

decomposition   The act of undergoing breakdown into constituent parts. Breaking down into component parts or basic elements.

degradable   Capable of being broken down into smaller components by chemical, physical, or biological means.

degradability   Ability of materials to break down, by bacterial (biodegradable) or ultraviolet (photodegradable) action.

degradable plastics   Plastics specifically developed for special products that are formulated to break down after exposure to sunlight or microbes. By law, six-pack rings are degradable; however, they gradually degrade, causing litter and posing a hazard to birds and marine animals.

degradation   (Also biodegradation) A natural process that involves assimilation or consumption of a material by living organisms.

deink   The removal of ink, filler, and other nonfibrous material from printed waste paper.

delacquer   Process used to remove lacquer from scrap metals, such as aluminum cans.

demurrage (1) The detention of a truck or railroad car for the loading or unloading of secondary materials. (2) The compensation paid to the shipper for detaining the truck or railroad car.

densified refuse-derived fuel (d-RDF) Refuse-derived fuel which has been compressed or compacted through such processes as pelletizing, briquetting or extruding, causing improvements in certain handling or burning characteristics.

densifier A machine developed in the 1980s to compress used aluminum cans into a small, dense brick.

Department of Environmental Regulation (DER) In some states DER is the agency charged with the enforcement of environmental and recycling laws.

deposit Matter deposited by a natural process; a natural accumulation of iron ore, coal; money paid as security.

designated materials Each material designated for collection and described in the same manner that the materials are specified for separation. For example, when citing glass, specify whether it is color-separated or mixed; for plastics, whether soda bottles, or PET, or whether yard wastes are collected separately.

detinner A company that buys steel cans and each tin mill products, and removes the tin through any of several processes, selling the detinned steel to steel mills and foundries, and the recovered tin to its appropriate markets.

detinning Removing tin from "tin" cans by a chemical process to make both the tin and steel more easily recycled.

devulcanization The processing of scrap tires by use of a thermochemical reaction.

dioxin The generic name for a group of organic chemical compounds formally known as polychlorinated dibenzo-*p*-dioxins. Heterocyclic hydrocarbons that occur as toxic impurities, especially in herbicides.

direct energy Vigorous exertion of power from the source without interruption.

"dirty" MRF See **full MRF, waste recovery facility (WRF), mixed-waste processing facility.**

disposable Something that is designed to be used once and then thrown away.

disposable The process of solid waste management through landfilling or transformation at permitted solid waste facilities, or other repository intended for permanent containment of waste.

disposal capacity The capacity, expressed in either weight in tons or its volumetric equivalent in cubic yards, which is either currently available at a permitted solid waste landfill or will be needed for the disposal of solid waste generated within the jurisdiction over a specified period of time.

disposal cost savings Savings of reduced waste-hauling requirements, avoided tipping fees, and other operational cost savings related to waste disposal because of the operation of a recycling program.

disposal facility A collection of equipment and associated land area which serves to receive waste and dispose of it. The facility may incorporate one or more disposal methods.

disposal index   Materials disposed per capita at time of measurement divided by materials disposed per capita at reference time. A per capita disposal index measures the difference in quantities of materials disposed with reference to a base period.

disposal obligation   The obligation of the county to provide for the disposal of all solid waste generated in each contract community and in the unincorporated county and delivered to a resource recovery system disposal facility or transfer station designated pursuant to the plan of operations.

disposal surcharge   A special fee levied against waste disposal volumes.

diversion alternative   Any activity, existing or occurring in the future, which has been, is, or will be implemented by a jurisdiction which could result in or promote the diversion of solid waste through source reduction, recycling, or composting, from solid waste landfills and transformation facilities.

diversion rate   The amount of material recovered divided by the amount of material recovered and material disposed. A measure of the amount of waste material being diverted for recycling compared with the total amount that was previously thrown away. It describes quantities diverted from land filling, incineration, or by exporting to another disposal site.

door hanger   A printed card, distributed to households and hung on a door, promoting a recycling service.

DOT   Department of Transportation.

Downstroke baler   A baling device in which the compression ram and platten move down vertically in the chamber.

drained whole batteries   A scrap metal grade consisting of lead-acid batteries free of liquid and extraneous materials.

drop-off center   A method of collecting recyclable or compostable materials in which the materials are taken by individuals to collection sites, or centers, and deposited into designated containers.

dump   A site where mixed wastes are indiscriminately deposited without controls or regard to the protection of the environment: now illegal.

durability   The ability of a product to be used without significant deterioration for its intended purpose for a period greater than the mean useful product lifespan of similar products.

E

ecosystem   A system made up of a community of living things and the physical and chemical environment with which they interact.

eddy-current separation   An electromagnetic technique for separating aluminum from a mixture of materials.

effluent   The liquid leaving wastewater treatment systems.

embedded energy   The sum of all the energy involved in product development, transportation, use, and disposal.

electrostatic precipitator (ESP)   A gas-cleaning device that collects entrained particulates by placing an electrical charge on them and attracting them onto opposite-charged collecting electrodes. They are installed in the back end of the incineration process to reduce air emissions.

emission   Discharge of a gas into atmospheric circulation.

emission standard   A rule or measurement established to regulate or control the amount of a given pollutant that may be discharged into the atmosphere.

emissions   The solid, liquid, and gaseous substances exhausted to the environment.

endanger   To expose to danger or put in a position of peril.

end market or end use   The use or uses of a diverted material or product which has been returned to the economic mainstream, whether or not this return is through sale of the material or product. The material or product can have a value which is less than the solid waste disposal cost.

energy   Ability to do work by moving matter or by causing a transfer of heat between two objects at different temperatures.

energy recovery   The conversion of solid waste into energy or a marketable fuel. A form of resource recovery in which the organic fraction of waste is converted to some form of usable energy, such as burning processed or raw refuse, to produce steam.

enterprise fund   A fund for a specific purpose that is self-supporting from the revenue it generates.

entanglement   Process whereby animals get caught and die in nets or other materials that have been discarded.

environment   The external conditions of an organism or population; the term "the environment" generally refers to the sum total of conditions—physical and biological—in which organisms live.

environmental impact statement (EIS)   A document prepared by EPA or under EPA guidance (generally a consultant hired by the applicant and supervised by EPA) which identifies and analyzes in detail the environmental impacts of a proposed action. Individual states also may prepare and issue an EIS as regulated by state law. Such state documents may be called environmental impact reports (EIR).

environmental quality   The overall health of an environment determined by comparison to a set of standards.

enviroshopping   The act of purchasing merchandise with consideration for the environment. An awareness of how products impact the Earth's environment and natural resources and how it changes a consumer's choice in purchasing.

EPA   U.S. Environmental Protection Agency; the federal agency charged with the enforcement of all federal regulations having to do with air and water pollution, radiation and pesticide hazard, ecological research, and solid waste disposal.

export density The preferred density of a processed secondary material destined for shipment to another country.

external costs Of, relating to, or connected with outside expenses.

fee Dollar amount charged by a community to pay for services; see **tipping fee.**

F

facility operator Full-service contractors or other operators of a part of a resource recovery system.

feasible A specified program, method, or other activity can, on the basis of cost, technical requirements and time frame for accomplishment, be undertaken to achieve the objectives and tasks identified by a jurisdiction in a countywide integrated waste management plan.

feasibility analysis A detailed investigation and report to determine whether a particular project is suitable, reasonable to pursue, and capable of being successfully completed.

ferrous Pertaining to, or derived from, iron. (In resource recovery, often used to refer to materials that can be removed from the waste stream by magnetic separation.)

ferrous metals Any iron or steel scrap which has an iron content sufficient for magnetic separation.

ferrous scrap dealer A business that acquires used commercial and consumer steel products and processes them to be recycled in steel mills.

fine A penalty in a dollar amount finite having limits or being limited; not endless in quantity or duration.

flint glass Clear or uncolored glass.

fluffer A device used to fluff waste paper in order to improve baling effectiveness.

fly ash All solids including ash, charred papers, cinders, dusty soot, or other matter that rise with the hot gases from combustion rather than falling with the bottom ash. Fly ash is a minor portion (about 10 percent) of the total ash produced from combustion of solid waste, is suspended in the flue gas after combustion, and is removed by pollution control equipment.

flow control A legal or economic means by which waste is directed to particular destinations. For example, an ordinance requiring that certain wastes be sent to a combustion facility is waste flow control.

food waste All animal and vegetable solid wastes generated by food facilities, as defined in California Health and Safety Code section 27521, or from residences, that result from the storage, preparation, cooking, or handling of food.

forced deposits   A term for container deposit legislation used by opponents of such measures. See *container deposit legislations*.

foreign cullet   A glass industry term for cullet supplied to a glass producer from an outside source.

front-end loader   (1) A solid waste collection truck which has a power-driven loading mechanism at the front; (2) a vehicle with a power-driven scoop or bucket at the front, used to load secondary materials into processing equipment or shipping containers.

front-end recovery   The salvage of reusable materials, most often the inorganic fraction of solid waste, prior to the processing or combusting of the organic fraction. Some processes for front-end recovery are grinding, shredding, magnetic separation, screening, and hand sorting.

full material recovery facility (MRF)   A process for removing recyclables and creating a compostlike product from the total of full mixed municipal solid waste (MSW) stream. Differs from a "clean" MRF which processes only commingled recyclables (see *WRF*, *"dirty" MRF*).

furnace   An enclosed refractory or waterwall structure where the preheating, drying, igniting, and burning take place.

G

garbage   Solid waste consisting of putrescible animal and vegetable waste materials resulting from the handling, preparation, cooking, and consumption of food, including waste materials from markets, storage facilities, handling and sale of produce, and other food products. Generally defined as wet food waste but not synonymous with "trash," "refuse," "rubbish," or solid waste.

gas control system   A system at a landfill designed to prevent explosion and fires due to the accumulation of methane concentrations and damage to vegetation on final cover of closed portions of a landfill or vegetation beyond the perimeter of the property on which the landfill is located and to prevent objectionable odors off-site.

gaseous emissions   Waste gases released into the atmosphere as a by-product of combustion.

gas scrubber   A device where a caustic solution is contacted with exhaust gases to neutralize certain combustion products, primarily sulfur oxides (SO_x) and secondary chlorine (Cl).

gaylord container   A large reusable corrugated container used for shipping materials (dimensions approximately 40 by 48 by 37 in).

generation rate   Total tons diverted, recovered, and disposed within reference time divided by the population. The annual per capita generation rate is the total tons generated in 1 year divided by the population of residents.

generator   Any person, by site or location, whose act or process produces a solid waste; the initial discarder of a material.

glass   An inorganic substance consisting of a mixture of silicates.

glassmaking   The process of making glass from raw materials (lime, sand, soda, and cullet).

Government Refuse Collection and Disposal Association   A Silver Spring, Maryland, organization representing municipalities that collect and/or dispose of solid waste. Also known as GRCDA. (Name changed to SWANA)

government sector   One of the four sectors of the community that generates garbage. The administration of the public policy and affairs of an area.

grab sample   A single sample of a secondary material taken at no set time for evaluation or testing.

grains per cubic foot   A measure of airborne particulates or dust expressed in weight (grains) per unit of gas (1 ft^3). One pound equals 7000 grains.

granulator   A mechanical device that produces small plastic particles.

grapple   A type of crane bucket having more than two teeth.

grate   A device used to support the solid fuel or solid waste in a furnace during drying, ignition, or combustion. Openings are provided for passage of combustion air.

gravel   Loose rounded fragments of rock.

gravity separation   The separation of mixed materials based on the differences of material size and specific gravity.

green waste   Usually refers to a combination of large brush, stumps, and yard waste; in some cases, may include some food waste.

gross national product (GNP)   The total market value of all the goods and services produced by a nation during a specified time period.

groundcover   Material used to cover the soil surface to control erosion and leaching, shade the ground, and offer protection from excessive heaving and freezing. Some ground covers are produced from yard waste compost.

groundwater   Water beneath the earth's surface that fills underground pockets (known as aquifers) and moves between soil particles and rock, supplying wells and springs.

growth rate   Estimation of progressive development; the rate at which a population or anything else grows.

H

habitat   Place or type of place where an organism or community of organisms lives and thrives; contains food, water, shelter, and space.

hammermill shredder   A broad group of machines that crush, chip, or grind materials. Hammermill shredders typically employ high-speed rotating equipment with fixed or pivoting hammers on a horizontal or vertical shaft.

hammermill   A type of crusher used to break up waste materials into smaller pieces or particles, which operates by using rotating and flailing heavy hammers.

haul distance   The distance a collection vehicle travels from its last pickup stop to the solid waste transfer station, processing facility, or sanitary landfill.

haulers   Those persons, firms, or corporations or governmental agencies responsible (under either oral or written contract, or otherwise) for the collection of solid waste within the geographic boundaries of the contract community(ies) or the unincorporated county and the transportation and delivery of such solid waste to the resource recovery system as directed in the plan of operations.

hazard   Having one or more of the characteristics that cause a substance or combination of substances to qualify as a hazardous material, as defined by section 66084 of Title 22 of the California Code of Regulations.

hazardous material   Chemical or product that poses a significant threat to human health and/or the environment while being transported.

hazardous substance   Chemical that is dangerous to human health and/or the environment while being stored or used.

hazardous waste   Waste which because of its quantity, concentration, or physical, chemical, or infectious characteristics may pose a substantial present or potential hazard to human health or the environment when improperly treated, stored, transported, disposed of, or otherwise managed.

HDPE (high-density polyethylene)   A recyclable plastic, used for items such as milk containers, detergent containers, and base cups of plastic soft drink bottles.

heavy-media separation   The use of a fluid medium to separate materials. The fluid's density lies between the heavy and light fractions being separated.

heavy metals   Hazardous elements including cadmium, mercury, and lead which may be found in the waste stream as part of discarded items such as batteries, lighting fixtures, colorants, and inks.

high-grade paper   Relatively valuable types of paper such as computer printout, white ledger, and tab cards. Also used to refer to industrial trimmings at paper mills that are recycled.

high-grade waste paper   Waste paper with the most value, consisting of the pulp substitute and deinking high-grade categories.

home sector   One of the four sectors of the community that generates garbage. As it refers to environment; a place of origin.

horizontal baler   A baling device in which the ram and platten move horizontally in the chamber.

household hazardous waste   Those wastes resulting from products purchased by the general public for household use which, because of their quantity, concentration, or physical, chemical, or infectious characteristics, may pose a substantial known or potential hazard to human health or the environment when improperly treated, disposed, or otherwise managed. (See Chapter 21.)

household hazardous waste collection   A program activity in which household hazardous wastes are brought to a designated collection point where the household hazardous wastes are separated for temporary storage and ultimate recycling, treatment, or disposal.

humus The organic portion of soil providing nutrition for plant life: a dark substance resulting from the partial decay of plant and/or animal matter.

Hydrapulper Trade name for a pulp mill machine that uses a rotor and blades to mix dry fibers, such as waste paper, and water to produce a pulp slurry.

hydrogeology The study of surface and subsurface water.

I

igloo A half-sphere container used at drop-off centers for the receipt and storage of residential recyclable materials, such as glass and metal containers.

ignitable A substance that is capable of burning rapidly and has a flash point less than 140°F.

illegal dumping Disposing of waste in an improper manner and/or location and in violation of waste disposal laws.

impact An effect on the environment or on living things.

impermeable Restricts the movement of products through the surface.

implementation The accomplishment of the program tasks as identified in each component.

incidental catch Accidental capture and drowning of nontarget animals, such as porpoises, in fishing nets.

incineration An engineered process involving burning or combustion to thermally degrade waste materials. Incinerators must meet clean air standards. This process is used particularly for organic wastes. The wastes are reduced by oxidation and will normally sustain combustion without the use of additional fuel.

incinerator A facility designed for the controlled burning of waste; reduces waste volume by converting waste into gases and relatively small amounts of ash; may offer potential for energy recovery.

incinerator ash The remnants of solid waste after combustion, including noncombustibles (e.g., metals) and soot.

industrial solid waste Solid waste originating from mechanized manufacturing facilities, factories, refineries, construction and demolition projects, and publicly operated treatment works, and/or solid wastes placed in debris boxes.

industrial unit A site zoned for an industrial business and which generates industrial solid wastes.

industrial waste Materials discarded from industrial operations or derived from industrial operations or manufacturing processes, all nonhazardous solid wastes other than residential, commercial, and institutional. May also include small quantities of waste generated from cafeterias, offices, or retail sales departments on same premises. Industrial waste includes all wastes generated by activities such as demolition and construction, manufacturing, agricultural operations, wholesale trade, and mining.

inert solids or inert waste A nonliquid solid waste including, but not limited to, soil and concrete, that does not contain hazardous waste or soluble pollutants at concentrations in excess of water-quality objectives established by a regional water board pursuant to Division 7 (commencing with section 13000) of the California Water Code and does not contain significant quantities of decomposable solid waste.

infectious waste Waste containing pathogens or biologically active material which because of its type, concentration, or quantity is capable of transmitting disease to persons exposed to the waste.

informed decision A conclusion or course of action based on facts.

infrastructure A substructure or underlying foundation: those facilities upon which a system or society depends; for example: roads, schools, power plants, communication networks, and transportation systems.

ingestion Eating; swallowing.

inorganic Not composed of once-living material (e.g., minerals); generally, composed of chemical compounds not principally based on the element carbon.

inorganic refuse Noncombustible waste material made from substances composed of matter other than plant, animal, or certain chemical compounds of carbon. Examples are metals and glass.

inorganic waste Waste composed of matter other than plant or animal (i.e., contains no carbon).

in-plant waste Waste generated in manufacturing processes. Such might be recovered through internal recycling, energy recovery, and/or through a salvage dealer. Also referred to as preconsumer waste.

institutional waste Waste materials originating in schools, jails, hospitals, nursing homes, research institutions, and public buildings. The materials include packaging materials, food wastes, and disposable products.

integrated solid waste management A practice of using several alternative waste management techniques to manage and dispose of specific components of the municipal solid waste stream. Waste management alternatives include source reduction, recycling, composting, energy recovery, and landfilling.

integrated waste management A solid waste management strategy that ranks the preferred alternatives in the following order: source reduction and reuse, recycling, resource recovery, and landfill disposal.

intensive recycling A concept promoted by opponents of waste-to-energy systems, whereby municipal recycling efforts target all recyclables in the waste stream.

intermediate processing center (IPC) Usually refers to a facility that processes residentially collected mixed recyclables into new products for market; often used interchangeably with **materials recovery facility (MRF)**. A facility where recyclables which have been separated from the rest of the waste are brought to be separated and prepared for market (crushed, baled, etc.). An IPC can be designed to handle commingled or separated recyclables or both.

intermodal shipping   The linking of two forms of transportation, such as trucks and railroads, to ship materials. For example, one might use intermodal shipping by loading secondary materials in a truck trailer, having it trucked to a railroad yard, putting the trailer on a railcar, moving the trailer by rail and unloading it for truck delivery to the receiving mill.

internal costs   Expenses of, relating to, or occurring within the confines of an organized structure.

in-vessel composting   A composting method in which the compost is continuously and mechanically mixed and aerated in a large, contained area.

investment tax credit   A reduction in taxes permitted for the purchase and installation of specific types of equipment and other investments.

J

jurisdiction   The city or county responsible for preparing any one or all of the following: the countywide integrated waste management plan, or the countywide siting element.

L

landfill   A large, outdoor area for waste disposal; in sanitary landfills, waste is layered and covered with soil.

landfill by-products   Chemicals and gases that result from the biodegration of waste in a landfill or interaction with rain and environmental conditions. Two by-products that must be monitored are leachates and methane gas.

landfill liner   Impermeable layers of heavy plastic, clay, and gravel that protect against groundwater contamination. Most sanitary landfills have at least two plastic liners or layers of plastic and clay.

large-quantity generator   Sources such as industries and agriculture that generate more than 1000 kg of hazardous waste per month.

leachate   Liquid that has percolated through solid waste or another medium and has extracted, dissolved, or suspended materials from it, which may include potentially harmful materials. Leachate collection and treatment is of primary concern at municipal waste landfills.

limited   Restricted in number or supply, such as limited natural resources.

limited supply   Restricted amount of a product or resource available at a given time.

liner   A continuous layer of low-permeability natural or synthetic materials beneath or on the sides of a landfill or landfill trench which controls the downward or lateral escape of leachate.

liner   A layer of natural clay or manufactured material (various plastics) which serves as a barrier to prevent leachate from reaching or mixing with groundwater in landfills, lagoons, etc.

litter   Highly visible solid waste discarded outside the established collection disposal system. (Solid waste properly placed in containers is often referred to as trash and garbage; uncontainerized, it is referred to as litter.) Litter accounts for about 2 percent of municipal solid waste.

logger   A mechanical device used to flatten scrap metal such as white goods. Many loggers are mobile and are taken periodically to disposal sites to process collected scrap metal.

long-term impact   Future effect of an action, such as an oil spill.

low-grade paper   Less valuable types of paper such as mixed office paper, corrugated paperboard, and newspaper.

LULU   Locally unwanted land use: for example, jails, airports, and landfills.

M

magnet   A body having the property of attracting iron and producing a magnetic field external to itself.

magnetic separator   Equipment usually consisting of a belt, drum, or pulley with a permanent or electromagnet and used to attract and remove magnetic materials from other materials.

magnet separation   A system to remove ferrous metals from other materials in a mixed municipal waste stream. Magnets are used to attract the ferrous metals.

mandatory recycling   Programs which by law require consumers to separate trash so that some or all recyclable materials are not burned or dumped in landfills.

manmade   Made by people rather than that which occurs naturally.

manual separation   The separation of recyclable or compostible materials from waste by hand sorting.

manufactured (materials)   Substances no longer in their natural or original state; products of a manufacturing process.

manufacturing sector   One of the four sectors of the community that generates garbage. Responsible for making, developing consumer goods.

marine wastes   Solid wastes generated from marine vessels and ocean work platforms, solid wastes washed onto ocean beaches, and litter discarded on ocean beaches.

market development   A method of increasing the demand for recovered materials so that end markets for the materials are established, improved, or stabilized and thereby become more reliable.

MARPOL Annex V   An international agreement which bans the dumping of plastic trash at sea.

mass-burn facility   A type of incinerator that burns solid waste without any attempt to separate recyclables or process waste before burning.

mass combustion   The burning of as-received, unprocessed refuse in furnaces designed exclusively for solid waste disposal/energy recovery.

mass burn   A municipal waste combustion technology in which solid waste is burned in a controlled system without prior sorting or processing.

materials market   The combined commercial interests that buy recyclable materials and process them for reuse. The demand for goods made of recycled materials determines the economic feasibility of recycling.

materials recovery   Extraction of materials from the waste stream for reuse or recycling. Examples include source separation, front-end recovery, in-plant recycling, postcombustion recovery, leaf composting, etc.

materials recovery facility (MRF)   A permitted solid waste facility where solid wastes or *recyclable* materials are sorted or separated, by hand or by use of machinery, for the purposes of recycling or compacting. Same as an IPC. Sometimes, the term "MRF" is used to refer to a mixed-waste processing facility; in which case, it is sometimes called a "dirty" or "full MRF." (Also see *WRF, Waste Recovery Facility*) When MRF is used synonymously with IPC, it is sometimes called a "clean MRF."

mechanical pulp   Pulp produced by grinding wood into fibers.

mechanical separation   The separation of waste into various components using mechanical means, such as cyclones, trommels, and screens.

medium-term planning period   A period beginning in the year 1996 and ending in the year 2000.

metal   A mineral source that is a good conductor of electricity and heat, and yield basic oxides and hydroxides. One of the hidden treasures in garbage.

methane   An odorless, colorless, flammable, and explosive gas produced by municipal solid waste undergoing anaerobic decomposition. Methane is emitted from municipal solid waste landfills, can be used as fuel.

microorganisms   Microscopically small living organisms that digest decomposable materials through metabolic activity. Microorganisms are active in the composting process.

midnight dumper   An idiomatic term for an individual or business that disposes of waste in an illegal, stealthy manner.

mineral   A naturally occurring substance of inorganic origin and internal crystalline structure; for example, metals are obtained from mineral resources.

mixed paper   A waste type which is a mixture, unsegregated by color or quality, of at least two of the following paper wastes: newspaper, corrugated cardboard, office paper, computer paper, white paper, coated paper stock, or other paper wastes.

mixed refuse   Garbage or refuse that is in a fully commingled state at the point of generation.

mixed-waste processing facility A facility which processes mixed refuse to remove recyclables and, sometimes, refuse-derived fuel and/or a compost substrate.

model Graphic, mathematical, verbal, or physical representation of a process or phenomenon.

modular combustion unit A self-contained, typically shop-assembled, incinerator designed to handle small quantities of solid waste. Several "modules" or units may be combined in a plant, as needed, depending on the quantity of waste to be processed.

modular incinerator Smaller-scale waste combustion units prefabricated at a manufacturing facility and transported to the MWC facility site.

monitoring well A well created to check the quality of the substance within, usually water.

mulch Ground or mixed yard wastes placed around plants to prevent evaporation of moisture and freezing of roots and to nourish the soil.

mulch mowing The practice of leaving grass clippings on the lawn after mowing rather than bagging them for curbside collection or using them as compost or for mulch.

multi-material A collection or processing system handling more than one secondary material. For example, a drop-off center accepting newspaper and aluminum cans is considered a multimaterial operation.

municipal solid waste (MSW) Includes nonhazardous waste generated in households and commercial and business establishments and institutions; excludes industrial process wastes, demolition wastes, agricultural wastes, mining wastes, abandoned automobiles, ashes, street sweepings, and sewage sludge.

municipal solid waste composting The controlled degradation of municipal solid waste including after some form of preprocessing to remove noncompostible inorganic materials.

municipal wastewater The combined residential, commercial, institutional, and industrial wastewater generated in a given municipal area.

N

National Ambient Air Quality Standards Federal standards which limit the concentration of particulates, sulfur dixide, nitrogen dioxide, ozone, carbon monoxide, and lead in the atmosphere.

natural Determined by nature, occurring in conformity with the ordinary course of nature; a state of nature untouched by civilization.

natural resource Material or energy obtained from the environment that is used to meet human needs; material or energy resources not made by humans.

net diversion rate The fraction of total refuse not disposed as a result of recycling.

NIMBY (not in my back yard) Refers to the fact that people want the convenience of products and proper disposal of the waste generated by their use of products, provided the disposal area is not located near them.

nitrogen   A tasteless, odorless gas that constitutes 78 percent of the atmosphere by volume. One of the essential ingredients of composting.

nonbiodegradable   A substance that will not decompose under normal atmospheric conditions.

nonferrous metals   Any metal scraps that have value and that are derived from metals other than iron and its alloys in steel, such as aluminum, copper, brass, bronze, lead, zinc, and other metals, and to which a magnet will not adhere.

nonpoint source   Undefined wastewater discharges such as runoff from urban, agricultural, or strip-mined areas which do not originate from a specific point.

nonrecyclable   Not capable of being recycled or used again.

nonrecyclable paper   Discarded paper which has no market value because of its physical or chemical or biological characteristics or properties.

nonrenewable (resource)   Not capable of being naturally restored or replenished; resources available in a fixed amount (stock) in the earth's crust; they can be exhausted either because they are not replaced by natural processes (copper) or because they are replaced more slowly than they are used (oil and coal).

normally disposed of   Those waste categories and waste types which (1) have been demonstrated by the Solid Waste Generation Study to be in a solid waste stream attributed to the jurisdiction as of January 1, 1990; (2) which are deposited at permitted solid waste landfills or transformation facilities subsequent to any recycling or composting activities at those solid waste facilities; and (3) which are allowed to be considered in the establishment of the base amount of solid waste from which source reduction, recycling, and composting levels shall be calculated.

O

old corrugated containers   As a paper-stock grade, baled corrugated containers having liners of test liner, jute, or kraft. The boxes are generated in retail stores, factories, and homes when merchandise is removed from them. A common acronym is OCC.

old newspaper (ONP)   Any newsprint which is separated from other types of solid waste or collected separately from other types of solid waste and made available for reuse and which may be used as a raw material in the manufacture of a new paper product.

open dump   A site where solid waste is illegally discarded in an uncontrolled area.

operational costs   Those direct costs incurred in maintaining the ongoing operation of a program or facility. Operational costs do not include capital costs.

organic   Composed of living or once-living matter; more broadly, composed of chemical compounds principally based on the element carbon, excluding carbon dioxide.

organic waste Solid wastes originated from living organisms and their metabolic waste products, *and from petroleum,* which contain naturally produced organic compounds, and which are biologically decomposable by microbial and fungal action into the constituent compounds of water, carbon dioxide, and other simpler organic compounds.

other plastics All waste plastics except polyethylene terephthalate (PET) containers, film plastics, and high-density polyethylene (HDPE) containers.

outthrow Waste paper so manufactured or treated or in such a form as to be unsuitable at another grade. For instance, old newspapers are an outthrow when selling old corrugated containers but not an outthrow of mixed waste paper.

overissue newspaper Printed newspapers that were not circulated and are available for recycling.

over-the-scale trade The volume of business at a dealer or processor generated from purchasing materials delivered by independent scavengers, peddlers, individuals, and others. Also called **door trade.**

P

packaging Any of a variety of plastics, papers, cardboard, metals, ceramics, glass, wood, and paperboard used to make containers for foods, household and industrial products.

packer (1) A processing operation where waste paper is converted into paper stock and baled for shipment to consumers. (2) A solid waste collection vehicle employing a compaction mechanism.

paper Made from the pulp of trees. Paper is digested in a sulfurous solution, bleached and rolled into long sheets. Acid rain and dioxin are standard byproducts in this manufacturing process.

paperboard A type of matted or sheeted fibrous product. In common terms, paperboard is distinguished from paper by being heavier, thicker, and more rigid. See also specialty products.

partially allocated costs The costs of adding a recycling program to an existing operation such as a waste hauling company or public works department. Also known as incremental costs.

participant Any household that contributes any materials at least once during a specified tracking period.

participation rate A measure of the number of people participating in a recycling program compared to the total number that could be participating. Participation rate is calculated by dividing the number of households source-separating by the total number of households served. In a setting where there are single-family detached homes, it is possible to calculate the participation rate by keeping a setout log, by address, for each and every household. Twelve weeks is a reasonable tracking period. In assessing true participation some households may separate materials for recycling, but sell or donate them elsewhere, rather than set them out for pickup.

participation/setout ratio A multiplier used to estimate participation where setouts are easily counted but it is not possible to conduct a full participation survey. As a short cut, the participation rate can be extrapolated from the setout rate and the participation rate obtained from a sample area.

$$\text{Participation/setout ratio} = \frac{\text{participation rate}}{\text{setout rate}}$$

As a hypothetical example, a participation/setout ratio of 2.5 might be derived from a program with a 30 percent weekly setout rate and 75 percent participation rate that was documented from a representative portion of the route:

$$\frac{75 \text{ percent participation rate}}{30 \text{ percent setout rate}} = 2.5$$

If another similar weekly program were found to have a 25 percent setout rate, the 2.5 participation/setout ratio could be applied to estimate the participation rate:

25.0	setout rate
× 2.5	participation/setout ratio
62.5	participation

The multipliers found to be accurate and useful are 2 to 2.5 for weekly programs, 1.5 for biweekly programs, and 1 for monthly programs. An interesting and potentially useful finding would be the point in a program's history that participation rates begin to "decay," and require a renewed educational and publicity efforts. One reason that participation drops is that one in five households changes its address each year. Thus approximately 20 percent of households would require more than an annual educational message.

personification Attribution of personal qualities; representation of a thing or abstraction as a person or by the human form.

PET (polyethylene terephthalate) A plastic resin used to make packaging, particularly soft drink bottles.

petroleum A mineral resource that is a complex mixture of hydrocarbons, an oily, flammable bituminous liquid, occurring in many places in the upper strata of the earth.

photodegradable Refers to plastics which will decompose if left exposed to light.

plan of operations The plan for the operation of a resource recovery system.

planned obsolescence The practice of producing goods that have a very short life so that more goods will have to be produced.

plastic resins Chemical components of plastics.

plastics Synthetic materials consisting of large molecules called polymers derived from petrochemicals (compared to natural polymers such as cellulose, starch, and natural rubbers).

particulate matter (PM)   Tiny pieces of matter resulting from the combustion process that can have harmful health effects on those who breathe them. Pollution control at MWC facilities is designed to limit particulate emissions.

particulates   Suspended small particles of ash, charred paper, dust, soot, or other partially incinerated matter carried in the flue gas.

passbys   The total number of potential participants on a residential recycling collection route.

pathogen   An organism capable of causing disease.

pelletizer   A machine that produces chips or granules. Pelletizers are commonly used in plastics processing.

percolate   To ooze or trickle through a permeable substance. Groundwater may percolate into the bottom of an unlined landfill.

permeable   Having pores or openings that permit liquids or gases to pass through.

permits   The official approval and permission to proceed with an activity controlled by the permitting authority. Several permits from different authorities may be required for a single operation.

permitted capacity   That volume in cubic yards or weight in tons which a solid waste facility is allowed to receive, on a periodic basis, under the terms and conditions of that solid waste facility's current Solid Waste Facilities Permit issued by the local enforcement agency.

permitted landfill   A solid waste landfill for which there exists a current Solid Waste Facilities Permit issued by the local enforcement agency.

permitted solid waste facility   A solid waste facility for which there exists a Solid Waste Facilities Permit issued by the local enforcement agency.

platten   The rectangular face of a baling ram. The platten pushes or compresses the secondary material into the baling chamber.

point of generation   The physical location where the generator discards material (mixed refuse and/or separated recyclables).

point source   Specific, identifiable end-of-pipe discharges of wastes into receiving bodies of water; for example, municipal sewage treatment plants, industrial wastewater treatment systems, and animal feedlots.

pollutants   Any solid, liquid, or gaseous matter which is in excess of natural levels or established standards.

pollute   To contaminate; to make impure.

pollution   Harmful substances deposited in the environment by the discharge of waste, leading to the contamination of soil, water, or the atmosphere.

polyethylenes   A group of resins created by polymerizing ethylene gas. The two major categories are high-density polyethylene and low-density polyethylene.

polyethylene terephthalate   A lightweight, transparent, rigid polymer resistant to chemical and moisture, and with good insulating properties.

polymer   A large molecule containing a chain of chemically linked subunits (monomers).

polyolefins   A plastics subgroup including polyethylene and polypropylene.

polystyrene   A hard, dimensionally stable thermoplastic that is easily molded. PS is a common acronym.

polyvinyl chloride   A plastic made by polymerization of vinyl chloride with peroxide catalysts. A common acronym is PVC.

population and household counts   Include a count or an estimate of the number of persons the household serves and the housing densities within the program area. Because many resort communities experience seasonal fluctuations in population figures should indicate whether it is based on year-round residents, peak population, or a calculated average.

population, housing, and land use descriptions   These descriptions should include median age, income levels, and education, type of housing, density of development, and proportions of single- or multifamily homes: Inclusion of a description of housing density is a good indicator of urbanization and thus good background information for comparison of programs. Type and extent of commercial development. Gross leasable area (GLA) can serve as a rough indicator; it can be derived from a census of retail trade and may be available from county economic development offices. Mention should be made of any unusual factors that would cause the waste stream to differ from the community it is being compared to or from national averages. These factors would include climate, generation of special industrial or vegetative wastes, unusually large business concerns, government agencies or institutions, transient resort populations, large retirement population, a large student population associated with colleges and universities, or vacation area.

postconsumer recycling   The reuse of materials generated from residential and commercial waste, excluding recycling of material from industrial processes that has not reached the consumer, such as glass broken in the manufacturing process.

precycling   Activities such as source and size reduction, material selection when shopping, and reducing toxicity of products in manufacturing prior to recycling which helps reduce the amounts of municipal solid wastes generated. A term coined in Berkeley, California, which involves a commitment to improve the environment through conscious decision making when shopping; for example, replacing plastic coffee cups with porcelain mugs or cardboard egg crates replacing plastic containers.

private collection   The collecting of solid wastes for which citizens or firms, individually or in limited groups, pay collectors or private operating agencies. Also known as private disposal.

privatization   The assumption of responsibility for a public service by the private sector, under contract to local government or directly to the receivers of the service.

processable waste   That portion of the solid waste stream which is capable of being processed in a mass burn resource recovery facility, including all forms of household and other garbage, trash, rubbish, refuse, combustible agricultural, commercial and light industrial waste, commercial waste, leaves and brush, paper and cardboard, plastics, wood and lumber, rags, carpeting, occasional tires, wood furniture, mattresses, stumps, wood pallets, timber, tree limbs, ties, and logs, not separated and recycled at the source of generation, but excluding unacceptable waste and unprocessable waste.

processed   Treated, or made by a special process or treatment, especially when involving synthesis or artificial modification.

processing   The procedures used to prepare, refine, preserve, or otherwise change the initial form of materials or products.

product   An outcome or an object; the amount, quantity, or total produced.

program   The full range of source reduction, recycling, composting, special waste, or household hazardous waste activities undertaken by or in the jurisdiction or relating to management of the jurisdiction's waste stream to achieve the objectives identified in the source reduction, recycling, composting, special waste, and household hazardous waste components, respectively.

pulp   A moist mixture of fibers from which paper is made.

pulp substitutes   Unprinted, clean waste paper that can be used directly in papermaking.

purchase preference   A preference provided to a wholesale or retail commodity dealer which is based upon the percentage amount that the costs of products made from recycled materials may exceed that of similar nonrecycled products and still be deemed the lowest bid.

PURPA   The Public Utilities Regulatory Policies Act of 1978. A federal law whose key provision mandates private utilities to buy power commissions and equal to the "avoided cost" of power production to the utility. The act is intended to guarantee a market for small producers of electricity at rates equal or close to the utilities' marginal production costs.

putrescible waste   Solid wastes which are capable of being decomposed by microorganisms with sufficient rapidity to cause nuisances from odors or gases and capable of providing food for, or attracting, birds and disease vectors.

PVC plastic (polyvinyl chloride)   A typically insoluble plastic used in packaging, pipes, detergent bottles, wraps, etc.

pyrolysis   The process of chemically decomposing an organic substance by heating it in an oxygen-deficient atmosphere. High temperatures and closed chambers are used. The major products from pyrolysis of solid waste are water, carbon monoxide, and hydrogen. Some processes produce an oillike liquid of undetermined chemical composition. The gas may contain hydrocarbons, and frequently there is process residue of ash and a carbon char.

R

rack collection   The collection of old newspapers at the same time as residential waste collection. The waste paper is placed in a side or front rack attached to the waste collection truck.

radioactive   A substance capable of giving off high-energy particles or rays as a result of spontaneous disintegration of atomic nuclei.

RAO   Responsibility assumption overload; a phenomenon whereby individuals feel powerless regarding a problem.

rate structure   That set of prices established by a jurisdiction, special district (as defined in Government Code section 56036), or other rate-setting authority to compensate the jurisdiction, special district, or rate-setting authority for the partial or full costs of the collection, processing, recycling, composting, and/or transformation or landfill disposal of solid wastes.

raw materials   Substances still in their natural or original state, before processing or manufacturing; or the starting materials for a manufacturing process.

RCRA   Resource Conservation and Recovery Act of 1976; requires states to develop solid waste management plans and prohibits open dumps; identifies lists of hazardous wastes and sets the standards for their disposal.

reactive   For regulatory purposes, defined as a substance which tends to react spontaneously with air or water, to explode when dropped, or to give off toxic gases.

recover   To reclaim a resource embedded in waste.

recovered materials   Those materials which have known recycling potential, can be feasibly recycled, and have been diverted or removed from the solid waste stream for sale.

recovered material   Material which has been retrieved or diverted from disposal or transformation for the purpose of recycling, reuse, or composting; does not include those materials generated from and reused on site for manufacturing purposes.

recovery rate   All discarded materials that have been recovered through various recovery strategies including yard waste, composting, and reuse. Designatet materials recovered plus returned via deposit divided by the total designated materials available.

recyclables   Materials that still have useful physical or chemical properties after serving their original purpose and that can, therefore, be reused or remanufactured into additional products. Waste materials that are collected, separated, and used as raw material.

recycle   To separate a given material from waste and process it so that it can be used again in a form similar to its original use; for example, newspapers recycled into newspapers or cardboard.

recycled   Composed of materials that have been processed and used again.

recycling   The act of extracting materials from the waste stream and reusing them. Recycling generally includes collection, separation, processing, marketing, and the creation of a new product or material from used products or materials. In general usage, recycling refers to the separation of recyclable materials such as newspaper, aluminum, other metals or glass from the waste. This includes recycling of materials from municipal waste, often done through separation by individuals or specially designed materials recovery facilities; industrial in-plant recycling; and recycling by commercial establishments.

a. Recycling, *primary* is remaking the recyclable material into the same material in a process that can be separated a number of times (e.g., newspapers into newspapers, glass containers into glass containers)

b. Recycling, *secondary* is remaking the recyclable material into a material which has the potential to be recycled again (e.g., newspaper into recycled paperboard)

c. Recycling, *tertiary* is remaking the recyclable material into a product that is unlikely to be recycled again (e.g., glass into asphalt, paper into tissue paper)

recycling bin   A container in which to place recyclables.

recycling center   A place where recyclable items are taken for processing.

recycling loop   A process through which materials that might otherwise be wasted are collected and processed for conversion into new products that otherwise would have been discarded.

recycling processor   A generic term for businesses and operations that prepare secondary materials for sale to end users. Waste paper dealers, scrap metal yards, drop-off centers, and buy-back centers are examples of recycling processors.

recycling program   Should include the following: types of collection equipment used, collection schedule, route configuration, frequency of collection per household, whether curbside setout containers are provided by the program, publicity and educational activities and budget, financial evaluation (costs, revenues, and savings), processing and handling procedures, market prices, ordinances and enforcement activities.

recycling rate   A percentage ratio of the weight of solid waste collected for recycling to the total solid waste weight collected for disposal in landfills and waste incinerators. In several areas the recycling rate may include waste materials such as scrap metal from cars and salvaged steel from old ships and other materials collected by private buy-back centers. A true recycling rate should be based on tonnages of municipal and commercial solid waste normally disposed of in landfills. Scrap metals from private buy-back centers never enter landfills. The basic purpose of determining the recycling rate is monitoring recycling progress for diverting solid wastes from the landfills.

reference waste   Varies by different classification schemes to describe waste types. For example, when a community reports on its "waste," it may refer to all of the wastes delivered to a disposal site, all of the wastes collected by the public works department, or all of the wastes generated by residences, which may or may not include multifamily residences. Wastes are defined by management strategy, collection sector, and type of generator, respectively.

reference waste classification   Uses two major categories: municipal solid waste (MSW) and industrial waste. MSW further consists of four subdivisions: residential single-family, residential multifamily, institutional, and commercial.

refractory   A material that can withstand dramatic heat variations. Used to construct conventional combustion chambers in incinerators. Currently, waterwall systems are becoming more common.

refuse-derived fuel (RDF)   A solid fuel obtained from municipal solid waste as a result of mechanical process or sequence of operations, which improves the physical, mechanical, or combustion characteristics compared to the original unsegregated feed product or unprocessed solid waste. Usually, noncombustibles and recyclable materials are removed. The fuel may be sized for the specific requirements of the furnace where it will be burned, producing a "fluff" or shredded RDF. In some processes, RDF may be compressed into pellets or cubes, producing a densified RDF (d-RDF).

refuse-derived fuel facility   A type of incinerator that separates recyclables from solid waste before it is burned.

region   The combined geographic area of two or more incorporated areas; two or more unincorporated areas; or any combination of incorporated and unincorporated areas.

regrind   Ground-up recyclable plastics.

reject   One of the 4 R's of solid waste management and part of the precycling process, whereby a person consciously chooses *not* to purchase or consume an item or energy source.

rejects   Material rejected at the beginning of processing.

renewable (resource)   Capable of being naturally restored or replenished; a resource capable of being replaced by natural ecological cycles or sound management practices.

renewable resources   A naturally occurring raw material or form of energy, such as the sun, wind, falling water, biofuels, fish, and trees, derived from an endless or cyclical source, where, through management of natural means, replacement roughly equals consumption ("sustained yield").

request for bid   A mechanism for seeking bidders to supply recycling goods and services or to purchase secondary materials. An acronym is RFB.

request for proposal   A mechanism for seeking qualified firms or individuals to supply recycling goods or services. A common acronym is RFP.

request for qualifications   A mechanism for determining the experience, skills, financial resources, or expertise of a potential bidder or proposer. Commonly abbreviated as RFQ.

repairability   The ability of a product or package to be restored to a working or usable state at a cost which is less than the replacement cost of the product or package.

re-refining   The use of petroleum-refining techniques on used motor oil to produce lubrication stocks.

residential solid waste   Solid waste originating from private single-family or multiple-family dwellings.

residential unit   A site occupied by a building which is zoned for residential occupation and whose occupants generate residential solid wastes.

residential waste   Waste materials generated in houses and apartments. The materials include paper, cardboard beverage and food cans, plastics, food wastes, glass containers, old clothes, garden wastes, etc.

residue　Materials remaining after processing, incineration, composting, or recycling have been completed. Residues are usually disposed of in landfills.

resource　A natural or synthetic material that can be used to make something else; for example, wood resources are made into paper and old bottles can be made into new ones.

Resource Conservation and Recovery Act of 1976 (RCRA)　This law amends the Solid Waste Disposal Act of 1965 and expands on the Resource Recovery Act of 1970 to provide a program to regulate hazardous waste; to eliminate open dumping; to promote solid waste management programs through financial and technical assistance; to further solid waste management options in rural communities through government grants; and to conduct research, development and demonstrate programs for the betterment of solid waste management, resource conservation and recovery practices.

resource recovery　A term describing the extraction and utilization of materials and energy from the waste stream. Materials recovered, for example, would include paper, metals, and glass which can be used as "raw materials" in the manufacture of new products. Energy is recovered by utilizing components of waste as a fuel or feedstock for chemical or biological conversion to some form of fuel or steam. An integrated resource recovery program may include recycling, waste-to-energy, composting, and/or other components, with a landfill for residue disposal.

retention basin　An area designed to retain runoff and prevent erosion and pollution.

returnable　Can be returned for deposit and/or reuse.

reusability　The ability of a product or package to be used more than once in its same form.

reuse　The use of a product more than once in its same form for the same purpose; e.g., a soft-drink bottle is reused when it is refined to the bottling company for refilling; finding new functions for objects and materials which have outgrown their original use; to use again.

reverse vending machine　A machine which accepts empty beverage containers (or other items) and rewards the donor with a cash refund.

roll-off container　A large waste container that fits onto a tractor trailer that can be dropped off and picked up hydraulically.

rotary kiln　An enclosed waterwall, cylindrical barrel-shaped device which is utilized for the combustion of materials at high temperatures. Agitation of the material is accomplished through slow rotation of the barrel.

rubber　An amorphous polymer of isoprene derived from natural latex of certain tropical plants or from petroleum.

rubber-asphalt　A product that combines ground-up scrap tires and asphalt. It is primarily used in highway, runway, and street projects as a stress-absorbing membrane interlayer.

rubbish Nonputrescible solid waste (excluding ashes), consisting of both combustible and noncombustible waste materials.

runoff Water (originating as precipitation) that flows across the surface of the ground—rather than soaking into it—eventually entering bodies of water; may pick up and carry with it a variety of suspended or dissolved substances. In many cases, the runoff is a leachate composed of toxic compounds.

S

sanitary landfill A method of disposing of refuse on land without creating nuisances or hazards to public health or safety. Careful preparation of the fill area and control of water drainage are required to assure proper landfilling. To confine the refuse to the smallest practical area and reduce it to the smallest practical volume, heavy tractor-like equipment is used to spread, compact, and usually cover the waste daily with at least six inches of compacted soil. Modern, properly engineered sanitary landfills are lined with compacted clay or an artificial (plastic) liner; have leachate collection systems to remove the leachate for treatment and disposal; and have systems to collect and remove methane gas generated in the landfill.

salvage The controlled removal of solid waste materials at a permitted solid waste facility for recycling, reuse, composting, or transformation.

scavenger One who illegally removes materials at any point in the solid waste management system.

scavenging The uncontrolled and unauthorized removal of materials at any point in the solid waste management system.

scrap Products that have completed their useful life, such as appliances, cars, construction materials, ships, and postconsumer steel cans; also includes new scrap materials that result as by-products when metals are processed and products are manufactured. Steel scrap is recycled in steel mills to make new steel products.

scrubber A device for removing unwanted dust particles, liquids, or gaseous substances from an airstream by spraying the airstream with a liquid (usually water or a caustic solution) or forcing the air through a series of baths; common antipollution device that uses a liquid or slurry spray to remove acid gases and particulates from municipal waste combustion facility flue gases.

seasonal Those periods of time during the calendar year which are identifiable by distinct cyclical patterns of local climate, demography, trade, or commerce.

secondary ingestion Process whereby plastics or other materials eaten by animals at low levels of the food chain show up in animals at higher levels of the food chain.

secondary material A material that is used in place of a primary or raw material in manufacturing a product.

secure landfill A landfill designed to prevent the entry of water and the escape of leachate by the use of impermeable liners.

separate collection A system in which specific portions of the waste stream are collected separately from the rest to facilitate recycling or otherwise improve solid waste management.

setout A quantity of material placed for collection. Usually a setout denotes one household's entire collection of recyclable materials, but in urban areas, where housing density makes it difficult to identify ownership of materials, each separate container or bundle is counted as a setout. A single household, for example, may have three setouts: commingled glass, metals, and newspapers.

setout rate An empirical measure obtained by counting the number of households that set out materials on their assigned collection day and the number of households in the service area. The setout rate is not a measurement of true participation, as participants may choose to set out materials less frequently than the service is provided. Whenever a setout rate is cited, it is desirable to also provide information about the geographic boundaries, population, and type of households served (single-family, or mixed), the period of time when counts are made, and whether it is per route or all routes together. The time of day that observations are made is important to note, if not done simultaneously with pickup. An accurate setout count could only be made at the actual time of collection.

$$\text{Setout rate} = \frac{\text{number of individual setouts on collection day}}{\text{total number of households served}}$$

short-term impact Immediate effect of an action, such as an oil spill.

short-term planning period A period beginning in the year 1991 and ending in the year 1995.

shredder A mechanical device used to break up waste materials into smaller pieces by tearing, shearing, cutting, and impact action.

shrinkage The difference in the purchase weight of a secondary material and the actual weight of the material when consumed.

SIC code The standards published in the U.S. Standard Industrial Classification Manual (1987).

sludge Solid matter that settles to the bottom of septic tanks or wastewater treatment plant sedimentation tanks; must be processed by bacterial digestion or other methods, or pumped out for land disposal, incineration, or composting.

small-quantity generator Sources such as small businesses and institutions that generate less than 1000 kg of hazardous waste per month.

soil The loose top layer of the earth's surface in which plant life can grow.

soil amendment Any material, such as yard waste compost, added to the soil to improve soil chemistry.

soil conditioner Any material, such as yard waste compost, added to the soil to improve the physical soil structure.

soil liner Landfill liner composed of compacted soil used for the containment of leachate.

solid waste Garbage, refuse, sludges, and other discarded solid materials, including those from industrial, commercial, and agricultural operations, and from community activities; does not include solids or dissolved materials in domestic sewage or other significant pollutants in water resources, such as silt, dissolved or suspended solids in industrial waste water effluents, dissolved materials in irrigation return flow or other common pollutants; any nonliquid, nongaseous waste.

solid waste disposal facility   Any solid waste management facility which is the final resting place for solid waste, including landfills and incineration facilities that produce ash from the process of incinerating municipal solid waste.

solid waste generation study   The study undertaken by a jurisdiction to characterize its solid waste stream.

solid waste management   The systematic administration of activities which provide for the collection, source separation, storage, transportation, transfer, processing, treatment, and disposal of solid waste.

sort   The process of separating materials into specific categories.

source reduction   The design, manufacture, acquisition, and reuse of materials so as to minimize the quantity and/or toxicity of waste produced. Source reduction prevents waste either by redesigning products or by otherwise changing societal patterns of consumption, use, and waste generation. Any action that avoids the creation of waste by reducing waste at the source including redesigning products or packaging so that less material is used.

sorted color ledger   As a paper stock grade, consists of printed or unprinted sheets, shavings and cuttings of colored or white ledger, bond, writing and other papers. This grade must be free of treated, coated, padded, or heavily printed stock.

sorted white ledger   As a paper stock grade, consists of printed or unprinted sheets, shavings, books and cuttings of white ledger, bond, writing and other papers. This grade must be free of treated, coated, padded, or heavily printed stock.

source reduction   An action that reduces the generation of waste at the source.

source separation   The segregation of various specific materials from the waste stream at the point of generation. For example, households separating paper, metals, and glass from the rest of their wastes. Source separation makes recycling simpler and easier. Residences source-separate recyclables as part of a curbside recycling program.

source separation legislation   Legislation that is intended to facilitate collection of designated materials for recycling, composting, or reuse by specifying how such materials are to be segregated and set out for collection. It usually prohibits mixing of such designated materials with wastes that are to be disposed. This is often referred to as *mandatory recycling legislation,* and discourages disposal and encourages recycling of selected items within municipally collected waste stream.

special news deink quality   As a paper stock grade, consists of baled, sorted, fresh dry newspapers, free from magazines and containing no more than the normal percentage of colored sections.

special wastes   Refers to items that require special, separate handling, such as furniture, mattresses, tree trunks, white goods, concrete, and asphalt, tires, hazardous wastes, bulky wastes, and used oil.

specialty products   A category of fiber products including insulation board, roofing felt, cellulose insulation, animal bedding, hydromulch, and molded pulp. The other two principal forms of fiber products are paper and paperboard.

spreader stoker   A horizontal moving grate, perforated to permit feeding underfire air for combustion, typically used in waterwall furnaces designed to burn refuse-derived fuel. Fuel is introduced by pneumatic or mechanical means over the grate in a manner which spreads the fuel over the stoker (grate); 30 to 50 percent burns in suspension, with the remainder burning on the grate.

stack (chimney, flue)   A vertical passage for conducting products of combustion to the atmosphere.

stack emissions   Air emissions from combustion facility stacks.

static pile system   A composting method in which air ducts are generally installed under or in the base of compost piles, or windrows, so that air can be circulated through the pile.

statistically representative   Those representative and random samples of units that are taken from a population sample. For the purpose of this definition, population sample includes, but is not limited to, a sample from a population of solid waste generation sites, solid waste facilities and recycling facilities, or a population of items of materials and solid wastes in a refuse load of solid waste.

steel   A malleable alloy of iron and carbon, which is 100 percent recyclable, and also has recycled content. Steel is used to make a variety of products, such as cans, car parts, appliances, construction materials, tools, toys, and hundreds of other products for consumer and commercial use.

steel can   A rigid container made exclusively or primarily of steel. Used to store food, beverages, paint, and a variety of other household and consumer products, all of which are 100 percent recyclable.

stewardship   Taking responsibility; caring for and protecting an entity such as resources and the planet.

stoichiometric air   The amount of air theoretically required to provide the exact amount of oxygen for total combustion of a fuel. Municipal solid waste incineration technologies make use of both sub-stoichiometric and excess air processes.

styrofoam   Also known as polystyrene, a synthetic material consisting of large molecules called polymers derived from petrochemicals. Experts agree that styrofoam will never decompose.

substitute   To put or use in the place of another.

Subtitle C   The hazardous waste section of the Resource Conservation and Recovery Act (RCRA).

Subtitle D   The solid, nonhazardous waste section of the Resource Conservation and Recovery Act (RCRA).

Subtitle F   Section of the Resource Conservation and Recovery Act (RCRA) requiring the federal government to actively participate in procurement programs fostering the recovery and use of recycled materials and energy.

sulfate pulp   Kraft pulp produced by chemical methods using an alkaline solution of caustic soda and sodium sulfite. Sulfate pulp is used primarily in paperboard and coarse paper grades.

sulfite pulp   Acid pulp produced by chemically cooking wood using sulfurous acid. Sulfite pulp is used for most printing and tissue grades of paper.

Superfund   Common name for the Comprehensive Environmental Response, Compensation and Liability Act (CERCLA) to clean up abandoned or inactive hazardous waste dump sites.

surface water management system   Systems designed, constructed, operated, and maintained to prevent surface water flow onto waste-filled areas.

sustainable   The ability to support, endure, or keep up.

SWMA   The 1988 Florida Solid Waste Management Act.

T

tare   The weight of extraneous material, such as pallets, strapping, bulkhead, and sideboards, that is deducted from the gross weight of a secondary material shipment to obtain net weight.

thermomechanical pulp   Pulp produced by heating wood, then subjecting it to repeated compressions and stress relaxations between opposite bars and grooves to break the wood into fibers.

thermoplastics   Plastic material that can be melted to a liquid or semifluid state, which then rehardens when cooled.

thermosets   Plastic material set to permanent shapes when heat and pressure are applied during forming and which cannot be softened again when reheated.

throwaway lifestyle   A way of living characterized by a high level of product consumption and discarding, especially if the products are meant for one-time usage.

throwaway society   A society characterized by a throwaway lifestyle (see above).

time period   As a specific time period and a particular start date for a recycling program measurement.

tin   A natural element used as a coating on steel cans to stabilize the flavors of the contents. The use of tin as a coating material goes back in history to about 300 B.C.

tin can   A term sometimes used to describe a steel food can—foods were first canned in the early 1800s. Technological developments have allowed for the tin coating on a can to become progressively thinner, to the point that tin now represents less than one-third of 1 percent of the weight of a steel can.

tire-derived fuel (TDF)   A form of fuel consisting of scrap tires shredded into chips (TDF).

top dressing   A covering material, such as yard waste compost, spread on soil without being plowed under.

tipping fee   A fee, usually dollars per ton, for the unloading or dumping of waste at a landfill, transfer station, recycling center, or waste-to-energy facility, usually stated in dollars per ton; also called a disposal or service fee.

tipping floor   Unloading area for vehicles that are delivering municipal solid waste to a transfer station or municipal waste combustion facility.

ton   A unit of weight in the U.S. Customary System of Measurement, an avoirdupois unit equal to 2000 pounds. Also called short ton or net ton; equals 0.907 metric tons.

toxic   Defined for regulatory purposes as a substance containing poison and posing a substantial threat to human health and/or the environment.

trade waste   A European term for recyclable materials such as envelope cuttings and boxboard cuttings generated by manufacturers.

transfer station   A place or facility where waste materials are taken from smaller collection vehicles (e.g., compactor trucks) and placed in larger transportation units (e.g., over-the-road tractor trailers or barges) for movement to disposal areas, usually landfills. In some transfer operations, compaction or separation may be done at the station.

transformation facility   A facility whose principal function is to convert, combust, or otherwise process solid waste by incineration, pyrolysis, destructive distillation, or gasification, or to chemically or biologically process solid wastes, for the purpose of volume reduction, synthetic fuel production, or energy recovery. Transformation facility does not include a composting facility.

trash   A term used for wastes that usually do not include food wastes and ashes but may include other organic materials, such as plant trimmings, or material considered worthless, unnecessary, or offensive that is usually thrown away. Generally defined as dry waste material, but in common usage it is a synonym for rubbish or refuse.

trommel   A perforated, rotating, slightly declined cylinder which may be used in resource recovery facilities to break open trash bags, remove glass in large enough pieces for recovery and remove small abrasive items such as stones and dirt. Trommels have been used to remove steel cans from incinerator residue.

tub grinder   Machine to grind or chip wood wastes for mulching, composting, or size reduction.

turbidity   Cloudiness of a liquid.

U

unacceptable waste   Motor vehicles, trailers, comparable bulky items of machinery or equipment, highly inflammable substances, hazardous waste, sludges, pathological and biological wastes, liquid wastes, sewage, manure, explosives and ordinance materials, and radioactive materials. Also includes any other material not permitted by law or regulation to be disposed of at a landfill unless such landfill is specifically designed, constructed, and licensed or permitted to receive such material. None of such material shall constitute either processable waste or unprocessable waste.

unprocessable waste   That portion of the solid waste stream that is predominantly noncombustible and therefore should not be processed in a mass burn resource recovery system; includes, but is not limited to, metal furniture and appliances; concrete rubble; mixed roofing materials; noncombustible building debris; rock, gravel, and other earthen materials; equipment; wire and cable; and any item of solid waste exceeding 6 feet in any one of its dimensions or being in whole or in part of a solid mass, the solid mass portion of which has dimensions such that a sphere with a diameter of 8 inches could be contained within such solid mass portion, and processable waste (to the extent that it is contained in the normal unprocessable waste stream); excludes unacceptable waste.

upstroke baler   A baling device in which the compression ram and platten move upward into the chamber. Pit balers are a type of upstroke baler.

U.S. Environmental Protection Agency (EPA)   The federal agency created in 1970 and charged with the enforcement of all federal regulations having to do with environmental pollutants.

used beverage cans   Cans generated from the consumption of beer, soft drinks, juice, and other beverages. The reference is typically to used aluminum cans. Also known as UBC.

used brown kraft   As a paper stock grade, consists of baled brown kraft bags free of objectionable contents.

used oil   Oil that has been utilized for a purpose and is ready to be discarded or recycled.

V

variable container rate   A charge for solid waste services based on the volume of waste generated measured by the number of containers set out for collection.

variable can rate   A charge for solid waste services based on the volume of waste generated, measured by the number of containers set out for collection.

vector   An agent, such as an insect, snake, rodent, or animal capable of mechanically or biologically transferring a pathogen from one organism to another.

vegetative waste   Waste materials from farms, plant nurseries, and greenhouses that are produced from the raising of plants. This waste includes such residues as plant stalks, hulls, leaves, and tree wastes processed through a wood chipper.

vermicomposting   The use of worms to digest raw or stabilized organic waste.

vertical baler   Downstroke or upstroke baler.

vibrating screen   A mechanical device which sorts material according to size.

vinyl   A polymer of a vinyl compound, derived from ethylene.

virgin (materials)   Term describing raw materials as yet unused; for example, virgin aluminum has not yet been fabricated into cans; compare recycled aluminum.

volume   A three-dimensional measurement of the capacity of a region of space or a container. Volume is commonly expressed in terms of cubic yards or cubic meters. Volume is not expressed in terms of mass or weight.

volume-based rates   A system of charging for garbage pickup that charges the waste generator rates based on the volume of waste collected, so that the greater the volume of waste collected, the higher the charge. "Pay-by-the-bag" systems and variable can rates are types of volume-based rates.

volume reduction   The processing of waste materials so as to decrease the amount of space the materials occupy. Reduction is presently accomplished by three major processes: (1) mechanical, which uses compaction techniques (baling, sanitary landfills, etc.) and shredding; (2) thermal, which is achieved by heat (incineration) and can reduce volume by 80 to 90 percent; and (3) biological, in which the organic waste fraction is degraded by bacterial action (composting, etc.).

volumetric net diversion rate   Same as net diversion rate, except the fraction is measured as a volume instead of a weight.

voluntary separation   The participation in waste recycling willingly, as opposed to mandatory recycling.

W

waste   Anything that is discarded, useless, or unwanted; opposite of conserve, as in "to waste."

waste categories   The grouping of solid wastes with similar properties into major solid waste classes, such as grouping together office, corrugated, and newspaper as a paper waste category, as identified by a solid waste classification system, except where a component-specific requirement provides alternative means of classification.

waste composition   The relative amount of various types of materials in a specific waste stream.

waste diversion   To divert solid waste, in accordance with all applicable federal, state, and local requirements, from disposal at solid waste landfills or transformation facilities through source reduction, recycling, or composting.

waste diversion credit   A financial incentive provided to municipalities or private recycling operations based on the tonnage diverted from the waste stream.

waste exchange   A system which allows the waste from one activity to be used as a resource in another activity.

waste exchange   A computer and catalog network that redirects waste materials back into the manufacturing or reuse process by matching companies generating specific wastes with companies that use those wastes as manufacturing inputs.

waste generator   Any person whose act or process produces solid waste, or whose act first causes solid waste to become subject to regulation.

waste management   (Also integrated solid waste management) A practice of using alternative techniques to manage and dispose of specific components of the municipal solid waste stream. Waste management alternatives include source reduction, recycling, composting, energy recovery, and landfilling.

waste minimization   An action leading to the reduction of waste generation, particularly by industrial firms.

waste paper   Recyclable paper and paperboard.

waste paper hydromulch   A growing medium produced from waste paper.

waste recovery facility (WRF)   A process for separation of recyclables and creating a compostlike material from the total of full mixed municipal solid waste stream. Differs from a "clean" MRF which processes only commingled recyclables (See *"full"* or *"Dirty" MRFs*).

waste reduction   Reducing the amount or type of waste generated. Sometimes used synonymously with source reduction, decreasing the quality of materials and/or products that must be disposed. Simple volume reduction as crushing, baling, yard waste chipping.

waste stream   A term describing the total flow of solid waste from homes, businesses, institutions, and manufacturing plants that must be recycled, burned, or disposed of in landfills; or any segment thereof, such as the "residential waste stream" or the "recyclable waste stream." The total waste produced by a community or society, as it moves from origin to disposal.

waste type   Identified wastes having the characteristics of a group or class of wastes which are distinguishable from any other waste type, except where a component-specific requirement provides alternative means of classification.

water table   Level below the earth's surface at which the ground becomes saturated with water. Landfills and composting facilities facilities are designed with respect to the water table in order to minimize potential contamination.

water treatment plant   A facility designed to improve water quality; removes impurities from drinking water or cleans sewage prior to final discharge.

waterwall furnace   Furnace constructed with walls of welded steel tubes through water is circulated to absorb the heat of combustion. These furnaces can be used as incinerators. The steam or hot water thus generated may be put to a useful purpose or simply used to carry the heat away to the outside environment.

waterwall incinerator   Waste combustion facility utilizing lined steel tubes filled with circulating water to cool the combustion chamber. Heat from the combustion gases is transferred to the water. The resultant steam is sold or used to generate electricity.

weight-based rates   A system of charging for garbage pickup that charges based on the weight of garbage collected, so that the greater the weight collected, the higher the charge. The logistics of implementing this system are currently being experimented with.

wetland Area that is regularly wet or flooded and has a water table that stands at or above the land surface for at least part of the year. Coastal wetlands extend back from estuaries and include salt marshes, tidal basins, marshes, and mangrove swamps. Inland freshwater wetlands consist of swamps, marshes, and bogs. Federal regulations apply to landfills sited at or near wetlands.

wet scrubber Antipollution device in which a lime slurry (dry lime mixed with water) is injected into the flue gas stream to remove acid gases and particulates.

white goods A term used to describe large appliances such as refrigerators, washers, and dryers. The terminology was derived from the standard white color of these appliances that existed until recent years.

windrow A large, elongated pile of composting material.

windrow system A composting system in which waste is placed in windrows to compost and either aerated (in static pile system) or turned periodically.

windrowing The placement and management of compostable material in piled rows, where microorganisms break down organic material into a finished compost product.

wood waste Solid waste consisting of wood pieces or particles which are generated from the manufacturing or product of wood products, harvesting, processing, or storage of raw wood materials, or construction and demolition activities.

Y

yard trash Vegetative matter resulting from landscaping maintenance or land clearing operations and includes materials such as tree and shrub trimmings, grass clippings, palm fronds, trees, and tree stumps.

yard waste Leaves, grass clippings, prunings, and other natural organic matter discarded from yards and gardens. Yard wastes may also include stumps and brush, but these materials are not normally handled at composting facilities.

REFERENCES

1. National Resource Recovery Association, The United States Conference of Mayors, "A Solid Waste Management Glossary," Washington, D.C.
2. Florida Department of Education, Tallahassee, Florida.
3. Steel Can Recycling Institute, Pittsburgh, Pennsylvania.
4. The National Recycling Coalition," Measurement Standards and Reporting Guidelines." Washington, D.C.
5. California Integrated Waste Management Board—Title 14, Chapter 9, Article 3—Definitions.
6. Resource Recycling, Inc., "Glossary of Recycling Terms and Acronyms."

APPENDIX C
ABBREVIATIONS

ADF   Advanced disposal fee

ANSI   American National Standards Institute

APWA   American Public Works Association

BAN   Bond anticipation note

Btu   British thermal unit

C&D   Construction and Demolition materials

CERCLA   Comprehensive Environmental Response, Compensation and Liability Act

CHEMTREC   Emergency Information Service of the Chemical Industry

CPRR   Center for Plastic Recycling Research

CSS   Curbside sort

CSWS   Council for Solid Waste Solution

CSWMP   County Solid Waste Management Plan

DEP   Department of Environmental Protection

DER   Department of Environmental Regulation

DOT   Department of Transportation

EIS   Environmental impact statement

EPA   Environmental Protection Agency

EPtox   Extraction procedure toxicity test

ESP   Electrostatic precipitator

FCM   Fully commingled

GO bond   General obligation bond

HDPE   High-density polyethylene

HHW   Household hazardous waste

HSWA   Hazardous and Solid Waste Act of 1984

IPC   Intermediate processing center

IRB Industrial revenue bonds

kw Kilowatt

LAER Lowest achievable emission rate

LDPE Low-density polyethylene

MR Mixed degradables

MRF Materials recovery facility

MSW Municipal solid waste

MSW-RDF Municipal solid waste and refuse-derived fuel processing facility

MWC Municipal waste combustor

MW Megawatt

NAAQS National Ambient Air Quality Standards

NAPCOR National Association of Plastic Container Recovery

NESHAP National Emission Standards for Hazardous Air Pollutants

NIMBY Not in my backyard

NIOSH National Institute for Occupational Safety and Health

NPDES National Pollutant Discharge Elimination System

NSPS New Source Performance Standards

NSWMA National Solid Wastes Management Association

OCC Old corrugated cardboard

ONP Old newspaper

OSHA Occupational Safety and Health Act

PCB Polychlorinated biphenyl

PCDD Polychlorinated dibenzodioxin

PCDF Polychlorinated dibenzofuran

PCRB Pollution Control Review Board

PET Polyethylene terephthalate

PP Polypropylene

PPB Parts per billion

PPM Parts per million

PRCNJ Plastic Recycling Corporation of New Jersey

PSA Public service announcement

PSD Prevention of significant deterioration

PVC Polyvinyl Chloride

RAN Revenue anticipation note

RCRA Resource Conservation and Recovery Act

RDF   Refuse-derived fuel

RFQ   Request for qualifications

RFP   Request for proposals

SARA   Superfund Amendment and Recovery Act

SIP   State implementation plan

SQG   Small-quantity generator

SWANA   Solid Waste Association of North America

SWDA   Solid Waste Disposal Act

TAN   Tax anticipation note

TCDD   Tetrachloro-p-dibenzodioxin

TPD   Tons per day

TSS   Truckside sort

UBC   Used beverage containers

US EPA   United States Environmental Protection Agency

VOC   Volatile organic compound

WCS   Waste characterization study

WPF   Waste processing facility

WRF   Waste recovery facility

REFERENCES

1. The Solid Waste Association of North America (SWANA), Silver Spring, Maryland.
2. National Recycling Coalition Measurement Standards and Reporting Guidelines, Washington, D.C.
3. Westchester County, New York Solid Waste Management Plan.

INDEX

The editor acknowledges Belle and Holly Lund and Fran and Sam Silverman for their assistance in the preparation of this index.

---

*Page numbers have bold chapter prefixes; figure and table numbers are in parentheses after their page numbers.